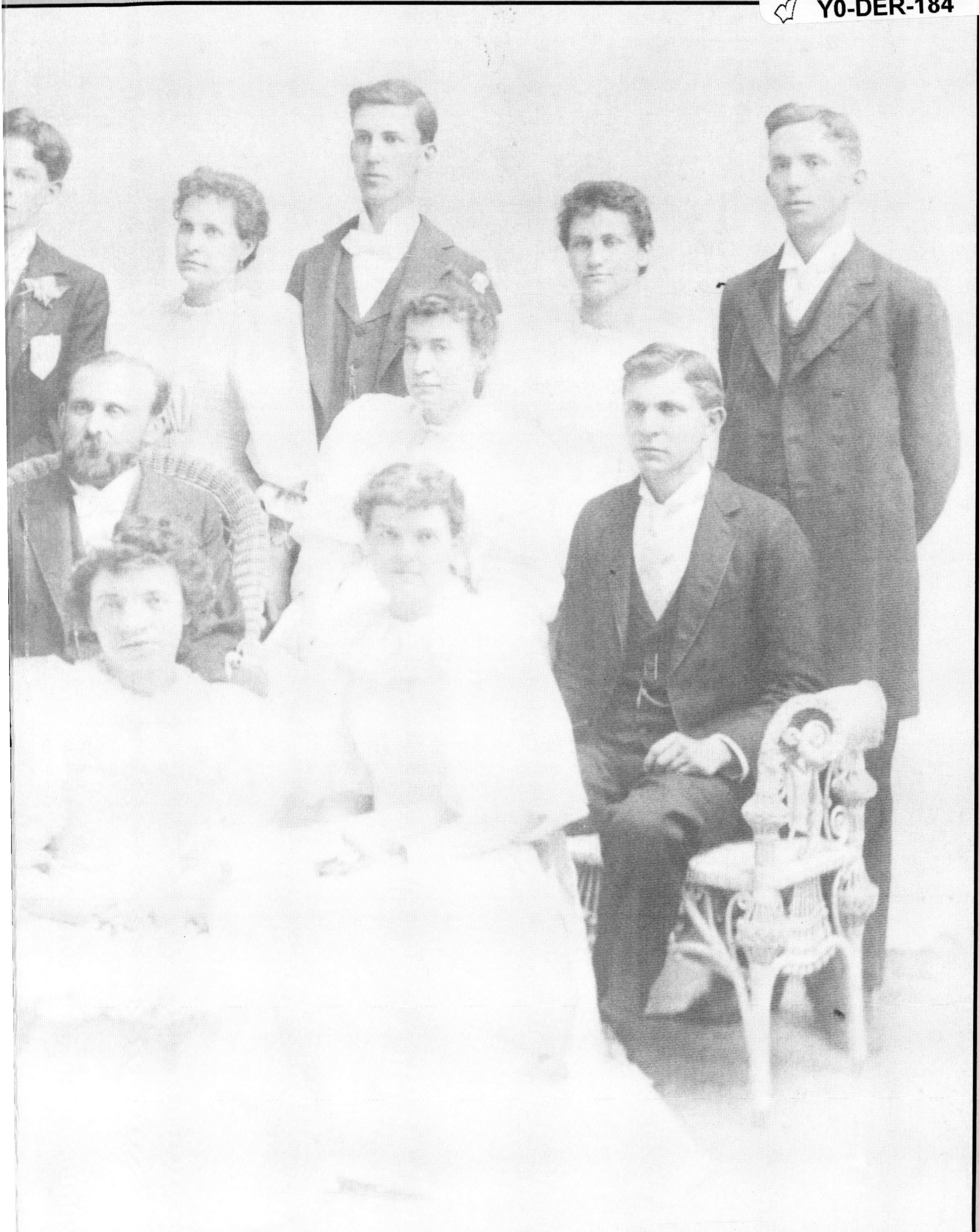

Compiled by the
Howard County Genealogical Society

Turner Publishing Company
Publishers of America's History
P.O. Box 3101
Paducah, Kentucky 42002-3101

Co-published by Turner Publishing Company and Mark A. Thompson, Associate Publisher

Copyright © 1995
Howard County Genealogical Society

This book or any part thereof may not be reproduced without the written consent of Turner Publishing Company.

The materials were compiled and produced using available information; Turner Publishing Company, Mark A. Thompson and the Howard County Genealogical Society regret they cannot assume liability for errors or omissions.

Designer: Elizabeth Dennis

Library of Congress Catalog
Card No. : 93-61220

ISBN: 1-56311-119-5

Printed in the United States of America

Limited Edition of 1100 copies of which this book is number: __610__

CONTENTS

Acknowledgments	**6**
Townships	**7**
Center	8
Clay	13
Ervin	15
Harrison	18
Honey Creek	20
Howard	27
Jackson	35
Liberty	39
Monroe	44
Taylor	48
Union	51
Churches	**57**
Schools	**97**
Clubs & Memorials	**105**
Businesses	**111**
Families	**137**
Index	**344**

Front endsheet photo – The Kokomo High School Class of 1894 taken June 8, 1894.

Back endsheet photos – **Top:** Wayman A.M.F. Anna C. Clayborne Mission Society in the early 1900s. (l. to r.) Mamie Jackson, unknown, Cora Ramey, Nettie Perkins, Illene Yarbor, Elsie Bassett, ? Duggard, Laura Barber, Cordelia Walden, Hazel Dunnigar, Ida Tanner, Mrs. Patterson, Elizabeth Winburn, Lola Morgan, Anna Vaughn, Mamie Carlilse, Blanche Jackson, Georgia Waldon, Edna Black, Julia Fouts, Clara Hall, unknown, Mrs. Turner, Sudie Walters, and Mamie Griffin. **Bottom left:** 1925 Kokomo High School One Mile Relay Team. (l. to r.) Arol "Brownie" Hall, Murl Abbott, ? Bell, and Harry Murphy. **Bottom right:** The 1937 Globe Trotters of Globe American Corporation. (l. to r.) Back row: Harry Huston, scorekeeper; Howard Sullivan, 1B; Mac Young, RF; Ross Currend, 3B; Garland Huston, CF; and Russell Schmidt, RF. Center row: Richard Critchley, 1B; Franklin McKee, SS; Don Smith, LF; George Eckert, C; Ed Snodgrass, P; and Chester Alexander, 2B. Front row: John Platt, Manager; Wilbur Schmidt, RSS; George Schmidt, Jr., bat boy; Harland Huston, P; and Arol "Brownie" Hall, Coach.

HOWARD COUNTY GENEALOGICAL SOCIETY

The Howard County Genealogical Society began at an organizational meeting on Monday, Oct. 2, 1972. The following people were present: Mr. and Mrs. Owen Freeland, Mrs. Elmer Stetler, Judge Lester Winslow, Mrs. Gary Springer, Mr. and Mrs. Howard Pyle, Mr. and Mrs. Charles Lacy, Mr. Fred Wright and Margaret Tolan Cardwell. The group decided to call themselves the Genealogy and Local History Club of Howard County. Prior to the meeting the Library had felt a need for the aid of an informed and enthusiastic group to be helpful in the choice of materials for the genealogical collection which it desired to build. With this in mind the Library had offered to sponsor the club and provide a meeting place for it. The second meeting brought many new people and a set of temporary officers. From 1972 through 1975, the group was headed by a chairperson: after 1975, the designation was president. The following persons served in the position:

Judge Lester Winslow	1972-1973
Jane Pyle	1974-1975
Gerald Cheek	1976-1977
Patricia Rabbe	1978-
Howard Pyle	1979-1980
Lee Bromley	1981-
Miriam Hackenbracht	1982-
Rachel Jenkins	1983-1984
William Barker	1985-
Carolyn Wheeler	1986-1987
Hertha White	1988-1990
Candy Jones	1991-to date

Over time the Society has been given information in many areas and explored many different resources. It has also provided the Library with materials to support the genealogical collection and with books donated in memory of deceased members. With a variety of speakers it has gained new insights and found additional ways to pursue its elusive ancestors. The Society has sponsored workshops which brought more information and resources. The Society has also made field trips to the library at Fort Wayne and to the Church of Latter Day Saints branch library. It has taken its members to programs and workshops throughout our area. It has honored three of its members with life memberships:

Margaret Cardwell	March 2, 1987
Delores Spicer	March 7, 1988
Barbara McIntosh	June 3, 1991

The Society has also had several names; as noted at first it was the Genealogy and Local History Club of Howard County; then it was the Howard County Family History Society. Finally, it became known as the Howard County Genealogical Society.

Members of the Society have spent many hours of volunteer time in the genealogy and local history department. At one point in time, the department was not open if there were not any volunteers available. They have indexed, copied, tracked down and preserved countless records of Howard County. They have made Howard County come alive in the history of its people.

Memorial to the Deceased Members of the Howard County Genealogical Society

William Barker

Lee Bromley

Virginia Bromley

Charles William Franklin

Owen Freeland

Ruth Freeman

Miriam Hackenbracht

Bette Hughes

Charles Lacy

Don Martin

Anita Merrell

Patricia Rabbe

Ferol Stahl

Ethel Stetler

Judge Lester Winslow

These members contributed much to preserving the genealogy and history of Howard County.

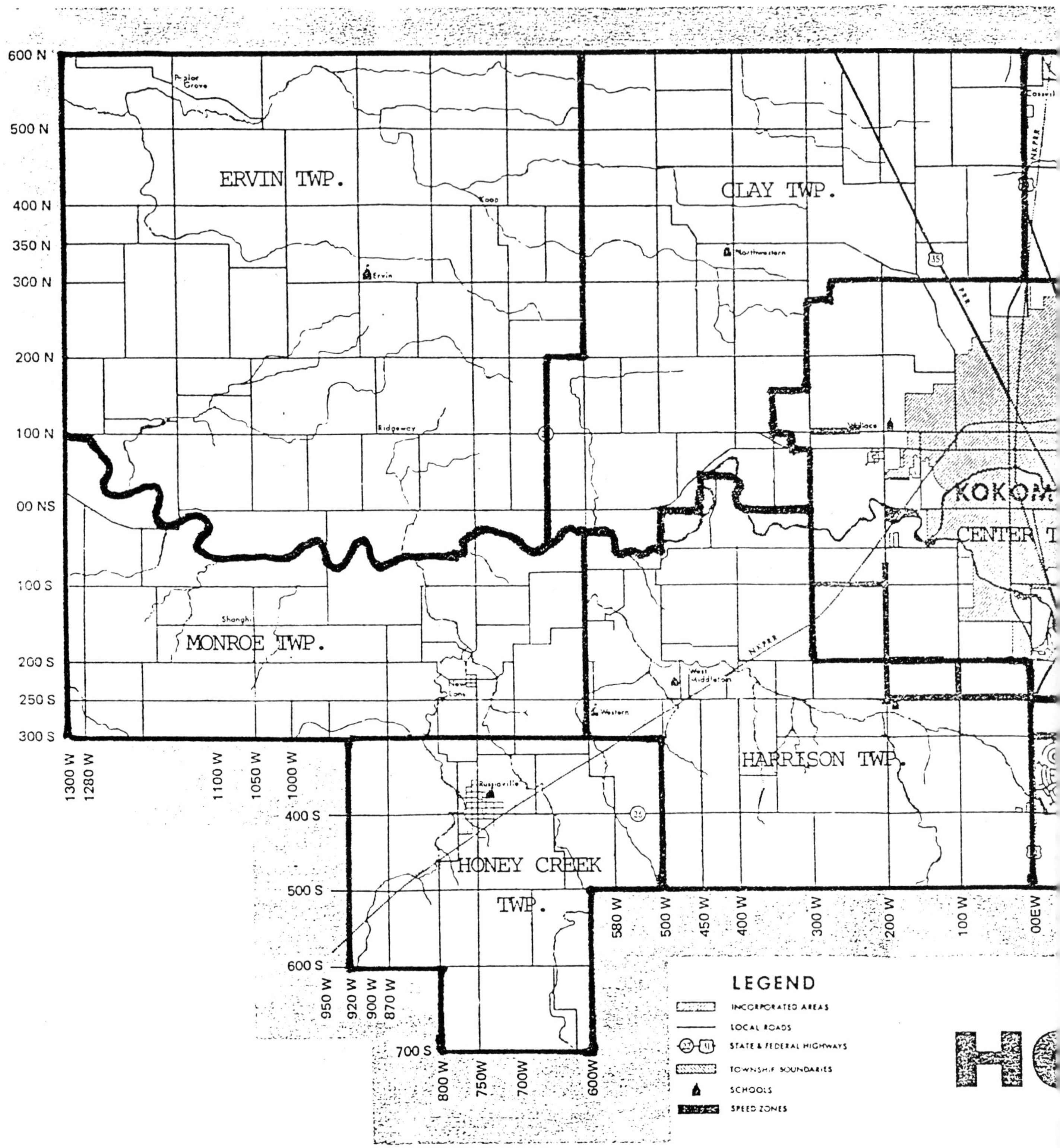
600 N
500 N
400 N
350 N
300 N
200 N
100 N
00 NS
100 S
200 S
250 S
300 S
400 S
500 S
600 S
700 S
1300 W
1280 W
1100 W
1050 W
1000 W
950 W
920 W
900 W
870 W
800 W
750W
700W
600W
580 W
500 W
450 W
400 W
300 W
200 W
100 W
00EW
ERVIN TWP.
CLAY TWP.
MONROE TWP.
HARRISON TWP.
HONEY CREEK
TWP.
KOKOM
CENTER T
Ervin
Ridgeway
Northwestern
Shanghai
Western
West Middleton
Russiaville
LEGEND
INCORPORATED AREAS
LOCAL ROADS
STATE & FEDERAL HIGHWAYS
TOWNSHIP BOUNDARIES
SCHOOLS
SPEED ZONES
HO

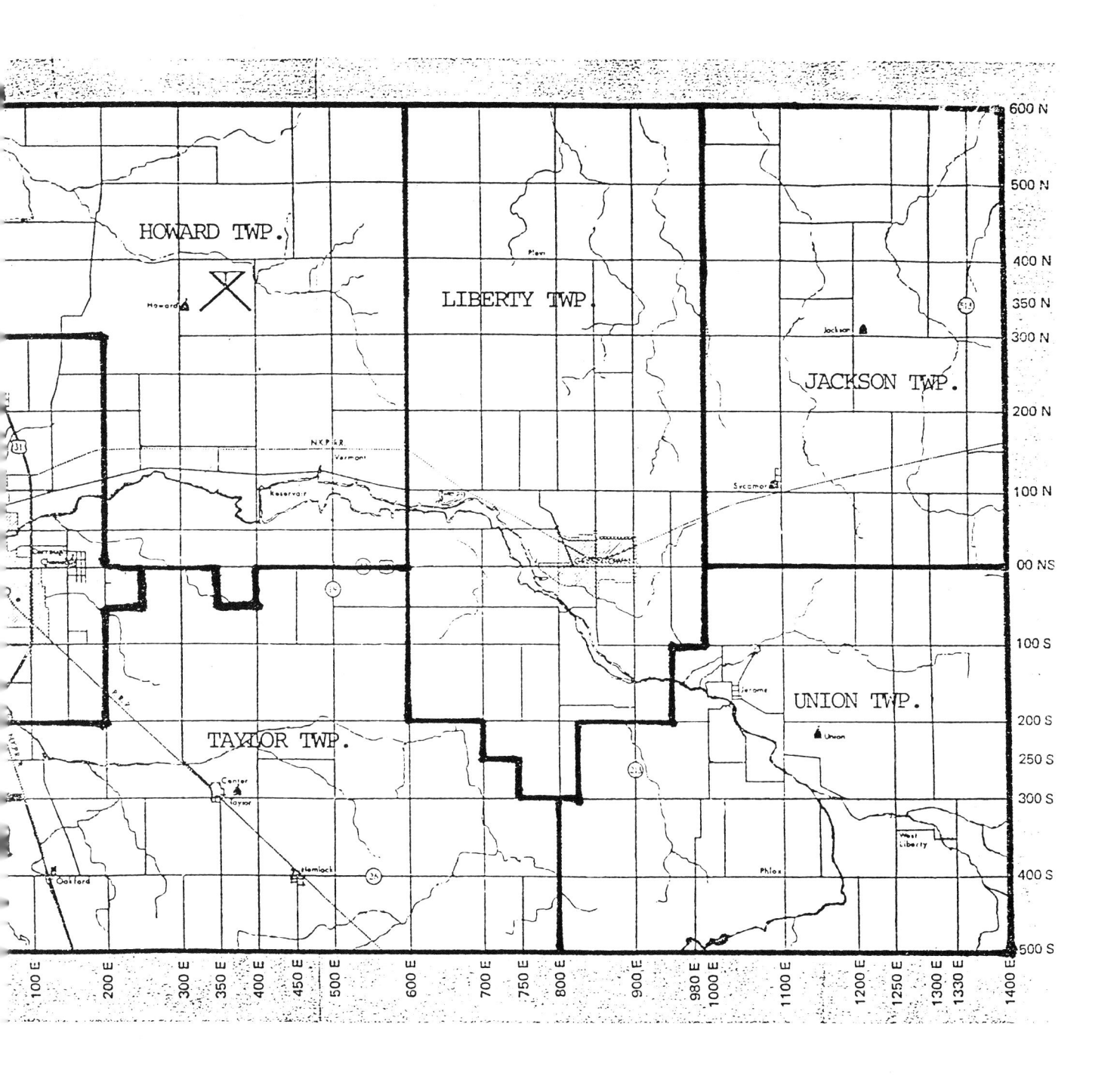

HOWARD COUNTY

- HOWARD TWP.
- LIBERTY TWP.
- JACKSON TWP.
- TAYLOR TWP.
- UNION TWP.

Book Committee (l. to r.) Front row: Delores Frazier, Hertha White, Candy Jones, Carol Graf, Dallas Lunsford, Vivian White. Second row: Rusty Frazier, Ron Tetrick, Margaret Cardwell, Arletta Williams, Jacqueline Taylor, Joyce Sparks, Sue Sheagley, Carolyn Wheeler, Mary Blangy, Janice Blanchard. Back row: Ed Riley, Robert White, and Mark A. Thompson, Co-publisher with Turner Publishing Company. (Missing from photograph are Karen Sosbe and Madeleine Holt)

Acknowledgments

The Howard County Genealogical Society appreciates the support and help of the Kokomo Howard County Public Library in making the Howard County Family history book a success.

Our gratitude to Rick Gonzalez who designed the seal for the cover.

We also want to thank all who have helped to make this book possible. It is not plausible to list all who have helped by answering numerous questions, researching family and public records, allowing use of information, furnishing photographs, proofreading, and helping with publicity for the project. We also are indebted to those who have purchased books. Our gratitude goes to each one who has helped to preserve and record the history of Howard County, Indiana, and its people.

TOWNSHIPS

John L. Johnson (1882-1945) ready to go on the rural route in Liberty Township in 1923. The building on the left is the old Greentown State Bank, the little one on the right is Don's Barber Shop. The picture is looking north on South Meridian Street.

CENTER TOWNSHIP

When David Foster came to Ervin Township in 1840 he little realized the changes that were going to take place. When he bought land in 1842 from a Fort Wayne banker and Indian trader, he had no thoughts of a town called Kokomo, even though part of his land was to be the site of the town. Howard Co. was in those days called Richardville after a Miami Chief. David Foster gave land which at that time was considered worthless and named the town after another Indian. He called it the "ornriest town after the ornriest Indian he knew." Kokomo's namesake was never proven to be a Chief of the Miami Indians. He lived in the area of Peru but the tribe ran him off. He was said to be lazy and shiftless, and he was whipped in his only known fight.

Probably one of the most important days in the history of Kokomo came on October 6, 1886. In a cornfield near what is now Park Avenue and Armstrong Street, the drill had reached a depth of more than 920 feet when it happened. Natural gas came to the surface in a great rush, and the city went wild with excitement. Almost overnight Kokomo was transferred from a rural trading center into an industrial hub. The offer of free gas, free land and a bonus brought hundreds of new people and many new factories to Kokomo. At least 25 businesses came as the result of such inducements.

The 20th century came to Kokomo with a promise of great industrial and commercial growth. A slight setback was realized during the panic of 1907, but the recovery was quick. The population doubled in the first 15 years of the new century.

Some of the early businesses established in Center Township were Kokomo Steel and Wire-1901; D.C. Jenkins Glass Co.; Byrne, Kingston and Co.-1903 (became Kingston Products); Superior Machine Tool Co.-1906; Globe Stove and Range Co.; Haynes Stellite Co.-1912; Kokomo Sanitary Pottery-1910; Hoosier Iron Works-1917; Turner Mfg. Co.-1920; and Kokomo Malleable Iron Works-1922.

Dirigold, later called Dirilyte, brought by Carl Molin, a Swede, took over the south end of the old Haynes Complex in 1926. Dirilyte was used mostly for silverware. Wolf Mfg. Co.-1917-began production of radio and phonograph cabinets in the Apperson Building on North Washington St. Sterling Div. of Reliance Mfg. Co. replaced Wolf Mfg. Co. in 1933 and began making cotton dresses and field jackets for the Army during WWII with employment of 1200. Crosley Radio moved from Cincinnati in 1935 to the former Haynes Body Plant on Home Ave. A few months later it was sold to General Motors.

May 1, 1936, a purchase agreement was signed and in the Crosley facilities, the new Delco Radio Division of General Motors began one of the great success stories within the framework of General Motors.

Delco's 1936 operations began with only 428 employees and a single building. Construction on Plant 2 began in October 1937 to the south of Plant 1 and, within its 36,000 square

John Bryant's Livery Stable 1903-1919.

Brothers Thomas B. Jay (left) and Joseph P. Jay (right) at the Jay Bros. Drug Store on the NE corner of Main and Mulberry about 1908.

Kokomo Red Sox dugout in 1911. The Treasurer of the team, James Troyers, is seated in suit and hat.

South Main Street looking north during the great flood of 1913.

Clyde Parker

The Courtland Hotel and First Christian Church on North Main ca. 1920s.

feet, began producing carburetors for General Motors in 1938. In November, 1940, Delco produced its one-millionth car radio.

By the end of the war, Delco had added two White Stars to its Army-Navy "E" Award and had been recognized as one of GM's top safety achievers during the course of the conflict.

As 1942 closed, Delco began dismantling the abandoned Malleable Iron Works on South Berkley Road for materials to build Plant 3.

War's end brought other changes as Delco returned to civilian needs. Plant 6, a 100,000 square-foot structure south and east of the Home Avenue complex was built in 1948 to handle assembly and engineering offices.

From that point with only a slight hesitation for the Korean and Vietnam Wars, Delco's growth was continuous.

Some of the highlights are: 1956-the high power transistor was introduced; 1961-the semiconductor manufacturing plant and the engineering building were located at U.S. 31 and Lincoln Road; 1962-Delco Park was established on East Sycamore Road; 1964-250,000 square feet manufacturing facility (Plant 9) was built at U.S. 31 and Boulevard; and the 40th million auto radio was produced. The 50th million auto radio was produced in 1968 and the 200th million speaker was made in 1981.

In 1983 a $204 million capital improvements and expansion project was announced. Fab III, the Corporate Technology Center, and the Engineering Research Center are the latest expansion buildings. Delco Electronics, as it is now called, is the world leader in automotive electronics.

Chrysler came to Kokomo in 1937 and located at the old Haynes Automobile Plant on Home Avenue. A friendly, Christian climate; honest city and state government; trainable people; good labor climate; and available utilities and transportation were incentives for location. The citizens were eager for industry and donated funds in order to bring Kokomo from the economic slump after the Depression. Operations began in 1937 with four to six hundred employees.

At the beginning of World War II, the plant reverted immediately to the production of antiaircraft guns and tank parts which had originally been made in Sweden. This war effort brought many women into the plants to do the assembling of the parts.

In 1955 the present facility was begun. This was to be for the manufacture of automatic transmissions. Ten engineering units were produced in the new plant November 1955. By March 1956, the plant was in full operation with 1600 employees. The Home Avenue plant was converted to one of the world's largest aluminum die casting facilities. Since the transmission plant opened, many million transmissions have been built. In addition, eighty percent of all the mechanical tappets used by Chrysler-built engines have been produced here.

The high quality standards maintained here at Chrysler have earned for the employees of the Kokomo Transmission Plant recognition as "The Master Craftsmen of the Transmission Industry." In 1964 the plant built 1,000,000 transmissions which were shipped in 457 railroad carloads and 3,276 truckloads.

Irma Stores Ball Club in 1936.

An area of approximately 20 acres is utilized by the Chrysler Plant. Chrysler suffered extensive damage during the 1965 Palm Sunday tornado, but removal of debris, cleanup, repair and return to operation was accomplished extremely quickly and smoothly. A total of 8,716 transmissions were built the week following the tornado. Splendid cooperation by employees and businessmen in the Kokomo area brought this about.

In 1890 Elwood Haynes moved from Portland, IN to Greentown, IN where he became superintendent for the Indiana Gas and Oil Co., which was about to begin the construction of a pipe line from the Indiana Gas Field to Chicago. He had a great deal of driving to do and it occurred to him that some method of locomotion over the highways other than his horse and buggy might be procured.

He considered three different types of engines: steam, electric, and gasoline. He ordered a one-horsepower marine upright, two-cycle, gasoline engine from the Sintz Gas Engine Co. of Grand Rapids, MI. He began to work on his "horseless carriage."

After formulating his plans, he took them to Elmer and Edgar Apperson's Riverside Machine Shop (founded 1888) where they repaired and built both machines and bicycles. They charged Haynes 40 cents an hour. The car was ready for a trial run July 4, 1894. The "horseless carriage" was driven from 100S, 150E one and one-half miles into the country, was turned around, and was driven into the city at an average of eight miles per hour.

In 1898, Haynes decided to produce cars on a mass basis. He entered into partnership with Elmer and Edgar Apperson May 24, 1898, creating the Haynes-Apperson Company. The capital stock was $25,000, and directors included Elwood Haynes, Elmer Apperson, G.W. Charles, J.W. Polley, and W.H. Reed. In 1895 a double cylinder engine was used.

In 1899, Dr. Ashley Webber realized the automobile would be of tremendous aid in his profession. He asked that Haynes deliver it personally to prove its stability. Dr. Webber lived in Brooklyn, NY. The trip was 1050 miles and was completed with an average speed of fourteen miles per hour. This gave Haynes nation-wide publicity and impetus to his work.

In 1901, the Appersons formed their own company - Apperson Brothers Automobile Company. Elmer became president and general manager. Edgar was the secretary, treasurer, and experimental engineer. In 1902, their first car was produced and the price was $3,500. Elmer died March 20, 1920, and is buried in Crown Point Cemetery. October 22, 1955, the city of Kokomo named a thoroughfare-Apperson Way- after the famous brothers. Edgar attended these ceremonies. On May 12, 1959, he passed away.

Elwood Haynes wrote a creed for his employees: "To build well; to build faithfully; to create intelligently; to hold character above every other consideration; these are the ideals expressed in the Haynes. And of them and upon them we achieve the four essential factors of car character: beauty, strength, power, and comfort."

Kokomo did not become the automotive center because of two reasons. The cost of steel and coal transportation was great. Also, people wanted varied styles and other companies were thus organized and provided competition.

A marker showing where Haynes began the first car ride was dedicated July 4, 1922. His daughter and son-in-law, Mr. and Mrs. Glen Hillis, purchased the home Haynes built in 1914-15 and where he lived until his death. Elwood Haynes became ill (flu) in 1925 and never recovered. He died April 13, 1925. Mr. and Mrs. Hillis deeded the home to the city to be used as a museum.

Since Edison's Magniscope was demonstrated in the old Opera Hall, the cinematic industry has made significant progress. The first movie house in Center Township was the Crystal which was located at 210 North Main St. in 1905. The following year, the Theatorium opened at Main and Superior. In 1907, the Airdrome, which was probably an open air theatre, was on the corner of Union and Walnut. At the rear of 314 North Main was the People's Theater. The Acme and Summer Theaters also were opened in the same time period. The Ideal was opened in 1909 in what had been a shoe store on the east side of the square. It was later called the Cort, and the building was razed in 1917. The Gem was at the SE corner of Webster and North Streets.

In 1915, the Paramount, which was later called the Fox, was opened at 110 West Mulberry Street and was closed in the 1940's. At about the same time, the Grand was located on North Main Street. The Victory, later known as the Indiana, was on the corner of Main and Taylor, the current site of First National Bank. It was razed in the 1960's.

Downtown Kokomo had several other theaters: the Star, the Sipe, Pictureland, the Isis, the Colonial and the Wood.

The last of Kokomo's old theaters was the Palace which opened in 1936 on the south side of Markland near Main. It closed in 1944.

Today the downtown theaters are but memories, gone the way of a large part of the businesses. The two local malls house a total of 11 theaters.

Center Township had a significant part in each of the Great Wars, WWI and WWII. Kokomo had a very active part in the supply of munitions during WWI. Mr. Charles Muckerhern was permanently stationed in Washington, D.C., as a representative of the local manufacturers. With his help, and the efforts of the local Chamber of Congress and many others, Kokomo manufacturers were able to obtain war contracts and renew them when necessary. These manufacturers provided excellent workmanship and met their delivery requirements. At least 14 firms were involved in this war effort, making the city second in Indiana in the number of firms involved.

The Globe Stove and Range Co. had a prime contract with the U.S. Army Ordnance to make four inch mortar shells. The Liberty Pressed Metal Co. made incendiary aerial bombs. These were the first aerial bombs with fins. A unit is on display at the Haynes Museum in Kokomo. This company became, after the conflict, the Conron-McNeal Co. which made roller skates.

The Superior Machine Tool Co. made various types of artillery shells under a prime contract with the War Department. This company made the first American howitzer shell.

The declaration of war with the Axis countries brought many changes to Kokomo and Center Township. Many of us can remember the draft, rationing, scrap drives, and women replacing men in the factories. Many factories that had converted to war-time production, or were created for that purpose during WWI, had changed back to peacetime products. Once again changes had to be made to war-time products, and Kokomo manufacturers were no different.

Globe Stove and Range Co., which was now Globe American Co., made what was another of Kokomo's "firsts." Two types of metal lifeboats were made for cargo and troop ships which included the "Elwood Haynes" Liberty Ship, and the "Kokomo Victory."

Banking in Center Township during the early part of the 20th Century reached its peak during the period from 1912 to 1927. There were seven open at the same time.

During the great stock market crash, all the banks in Kokomo were closed. With no banks available for funds, many of the local employers paid their employees in scrip. Two institutions which came from the ruins of the Great Depression are currently serving the public in Center Township. These are the Union Bank (later the Ameritrust and currently the Society,) and the First National Bank. At the current time there are 11 banks serving Center Township and its environs.

Schools in Center Township have come a long way from the log school house on the corner of Washington and Walnut which was the first school and the first free school. This school was built in 1845. The first high school was built in the 1870's on the corner of Taylor and Washington.

By 1902, two additional schools had been erected, including Central Junior High School on the high school lot. A new high school was planned in 1914 on the location of the current high school. On March 25 of that year, the old high school burned down.

Kokomo had been blessed with many great educators. One of the greatest was C.V. Haworth who was named Superintendent of Schools in 1913. For the next 33 years he directed the operation of the school system. In addition to making education an important commodity in the community, he oversaw the building of McKinley, Jefferson, Riley, Roosevelt, Wallace, Willard, and Douglas schools as well as additions to the high school and the donation of the stadium. A gymnasium which bore his name was opened in 1925. It burned in 1944. Memorial Gymnasium replaced it in 1949.

In 1946, O.M. Swihart established a $1.00 tax rate for a cumulative building fund. Over the next 25 years several new schools were built including Bon Air, Elwood Haynes, Lafayette Park, Maple Crest, Pettit Park, Sycamore, Boulevard and Haworth High School.

In 1953 the Center Township and the Kokomo School Systems combined to form the present district. The new Darrough Chapel School was built in 1964. The old building which was erected in 1901 with additions made in 1918 and 1938 was then razed.

The enrollment in Kokomo-Center Township Schools reached an all time high in 1968 with 13,230 students. That year the local high school was split with the addition of Haworth High School. The two schools merged again in 1984 with both the downtown and the south facilities being used.

Kokomo has always been a sports-minded community. Many people's lives were affected by a man who is remembered as "Circus John." John Wesley Byers, or Circus John, or Chiro, was one of the most legendary individuals to live in Kokomo. Until sidelined by his physical and mental infirmities, his daily routine was one spectacular appearance after another. His penchant for flamboyant exhibitionism evidently stemmed from roustabout, to featured rider and roper in "Wild West" shows.

The legend he wrote in Kokomo was baseball. He played, he coached, he cajoled financial support, and he never was remiss in "hamming it up" or staging sensational play on the diamond. Spring training always started for Circus just after Christmas and he customarily appeared in the downtown streets in baseball uniform with snow and ice still on the ground, but with ever high hopes for a triumphant diamond season just ahead.

No one ever knew how old Circus was, but he was well over 90 at death, and he was still playing baseball when past 80. During his long periods of residence in Kokomo, Circus vented most of his interests to teaching youngsters the game he loved so well. He played with adult teams, but most of his time was spent with "his kids" at Foster Park.

His influence upon them extended beyond the game—he mixed a lot of "character building" with it. For one thing, he would brook no profanity from his boys and his favorite punishment was making them wash their mouths out with soap after an outburst of what he called "nasty words." One local businessman, when informed of Circ's death, recalled the "washing out" process and remembered that it "tasted like h ——."

As an example of his flamboyant life style, one game scheduled in old Highland Park, when Circus was approximately 63 years old, opened with the siren on Sam Moore's ambulance blasting away at the gate in center field. The ambulance careened across the field and halted in a cloud of dust near home plate. Attendants carefully lifted out a stretcher upon which was a form wrapped in a coonskin coat. The old man laboriously arose from the stretcher, pulled off the coonskin, another overcoat or two, a half dozen suit coats and vests, and finally, when he got down to the baseball uniform, let out a war whoop, jumped about four feet in the air and started a razz-ma-tazz pepper ball game that had the fans screaming with delight.

He played Negro professional ball in several cities, including Lexington, KY, Cleveland, Buffalo, and Utica, NY.

He first migrated to Kokomo from Peru (then the Circus center of the U.S.) in the off season, and worked in the Jewell Laundry. He left here for several years while playing professional ball and came back in the mid twenties and devoted the rest of his active years to the game he loved while maintaining himself by doing odd jobs which, of course, never interfered with his activities. His only survivors were his sister, Mrs. Mary L. McClain, and his nephews, Clarence Edmondson and Bobby Warren McClain.

Globe American Corporation in Kokomo at a production milestone ca. 1951.

What may be offered as a truly unique baseball game was played in August 1919. The St. Andrew Episcopal Church team played the team from the United Brethren Church. The game went 12 innings, and the St. Andrews team won by a score of 12 to 11. What was unique about it was that the St. Andrews team was, all nine of them, brothers. The Critchley brothers were sons of James and Ellen Critchley, who lived at that time at 1300 Vaile Avenue.

George, the youngest at 11, made the first hit and scored two runs. The line-up was as follows: Robert-3rd base, James-shortstop, John-1st base, Edward-center field, Albert-left field, and George-right field. Thomas, the 10th brother, was utility.

There have been many great basketball teams and individual players over the years. The high school boys have one state championship in 1961 and the girls have state championships from 1992 and 1993 with a runner-up spot in 1994. There have been great football, track, golf and swimming teams and individuals in reach of these sports.

Kokomo, at one time, had a professional baseball team. There were Class "D" teams of both the Red Sox and the Dodgers playing at the field in Highland Park. Orlando Cepeda was one of the noted players who played in Kokomo. The American Legion Post 6 has for a number of years had a baseball team which has made its mark on many fields. The American Legion World Series was held in Kokomo in 1985.

The first mail in or out of the frontier village of Kokomo was moved on horseback and by ox-cart from a log cabin trading post in the middle of what is now Main Street just south of Superior Street.

In 1845 Austin North, Kokomo's first postmaster, was commissioned to open a post office in his general store at the SE corner of Main and Superior Streets.

11

Later the Post Office was located in the Spraker block just east of the Francis Hotel on West Mulberry St. In 1902 the Post Office was moved to the Stewart block on East Walnut St. where it remained until the Federal Building was completed in 1912 at 120 East Mulberry St.

From 1912 until 1978, the main Kokomo Post Office and other federal offices were located in what is now the Howard Co. Government Office Building.

During a period of remodeling in the early 1930's the Post Office was located in the Dispatch Building at Buckeye and Mulberry Streets. For a few years a branch office was located on S. Lafountain Street.

For the past 16 years Kokomo's Main Post Office Building has been the long modern one-floor structure at 2719 S. Webster Street. This building has more than 70,000 square feet with the work area having more than 50,000 square feet.

Now a Sectional Center, the post office has employees working each day in shifts around the clock.

The Post Office recently became a processing center for Marion, Logansport, and Peru. Mail is also sorted to the carrier level for 67 associate cities. With its new multiposition letter sorting machine, 44,000 letters an hour can be handled. There are 12 consoles. Manually, 77 designations could be sorted, but the machine can sort 277 designations.

Kokomo had the first woman to manage a sectional center. Celestine Green was Kokomo Postmaster from January 4, 1956, until the summer of 1987 when she became Postmaster at Gary.

From 1840 to 1865, Kokomo area law enforcement was a service provided by the Howard Co. Sheriff. In 1865 Kokomo held its first town election which served officially to inaugurate the town government. John Williams was elected "town marshal" and he in turn appointed John Patterson his deputy. The marshal's office system remained in effect until April 1901 when the law enforcement arm of Kokomo's government system was formally changed to a Metropolitan Police Department. The department was then headed by a Superintendent of Police, who was Ross Taylor, the last town marshal. Taylor's first metropolitan force consisted of six men whose equipment was limited to side arms and uniforms. Around 1915, the department purchased a Haynes chassis with a rear compartment for the first police patrol wagon and purchased a Harley Davidson motorcycle to complement a fleet of four bicycles. Through its history, the department has evolved through many changes from using horses or traditional walking beats to using bicycles and the trolley cars, followed by the use of the automobile.

Kokomo's present day police force has an authorized personnel staff of sworn officers, both men and women, and a complementary staff of dedicated civilian support personnel.

Over the years many changes have occurred relative to the continuing operation of the Kokomo Police Department. When the department was formally re-organized in 1901, its government system was changed to that of a Board of Public Works and the Mayor. Modern and more complex service needs have resulted in greater specialization within the department in areas such as uniform patrol, criminal and special professional standards, victim's services, planning and research, crime prevention and inspection. There have been many continuing changes such as the installation of modern radio communications, the specialization of department functions, the 911 System and a continuing quest for professionalization.

The current Police Department is made up of 100 sworn personnel, 48 non-sworn, 13 permanent and one PAL. They have 25 marked cars, 23 non-descript, a 1968 Harley Davidson three-wheeler, one Cushman three-wheeler, one Dodge Van Crime Machine, one Blue/Silver Hazardous Device Unit, and three white patrol bicycles.

In February 1868, a successful effort was made to organize the Kokomo Fire Department. The leading spirits of this move were D.F. Davis, D.O. Freeman and M.S. Sellers. The original equipment of a few buckets, ladders and a brake pump engine, built by William Moore of the city, cost a total of $400.00. They had no uniforms, owing to internal difficulty with the hook and ladder company and brake pump being divided and separate organizations. Each was recognized by the City Council. The department numbered about 50 men.

A reorganization occurred in 1872 under the order of the City Council. The Bucket Co. disbanded and the Kokomo Hook and Ladder Co. No. 1 took its place. The engine and hose cart and ladder wagons were drawn by hand.

As the department grew, horses became a mainstay by pulling the wagons, the engines and the hose carts. The horses were replaced in 1915 and 1916 when the department went to full motorization.

In 1894 the new City Building, located at 112 North Washington, included the Fire and Police Departments. As the city grew, the department added Station No. 2 at Home Avenue and Harrison Street and No. 3 at 311 W. North Street. No. 2 remained in service until being relocated in 1979 with No. 1 Station. The No. 3 Station was relocated in 1961. The No. 5 Station was built at 2400 W. Sycamore. In 1963 No. 6 Station was built at 1716 E. Boulevard.

In 1974 the Department reached its peak of 128 men who worked 56 hours per week. The addition of women to the department came in 1991 under the present fire chief, Joseph Zuppardo.

Center Township, under the direction of Jean Lushin, township trustee, maintains one piece of equipment which is used for those fire calls in Center Township outside the city of Kokomo.

The Kokomo-Center Township Fire Department is currently made up of 120 personnel, two of which are women. There are six stations located throughout the city. The equipment consists of six fire engines, one township engine, two ladder/rescue trucks, one aerial truck, one snorkel, one ambulance, one backup engine, one hazardous material truck, and one chief's car.

The history of Kokomo and Center Township was affected very notably by a great number of businesses and individuals. A few have been mentioned here. The contributions of all the others is in no way negated by the fact that they were not mentioned here. *Submitted by Richard L. Frazier*

Vermont Bridge at Highland Park

Monument for the pioneers of Kokomo.

The new fire truck delivered to Center Township in August 1990.

Kokomo's Orphan Train

The orphan trains moved 150,000 children across the Midwest from 1854 to 1929. Kokomo's orphan train arrived in October of 1889 with 24 children on board. Both the *Kokomo Dispatch* and the *Kokomo Gazette Tribune* published articles about the proceedings.

The following children were placed in families as listed: Mary G. Ring with James Courtland and Mrs. Blacklidge; Jennie C. Steele with H.H. and Mrs. Stewart; Arthur Steele with Miles R. and Mrs. McBeth; Charles J. Steele with John and Mrs. Nesbit; Marion E. Steele with J.G. and Mrs. Hockett; Ida M. Smith with Thomas and Mrs. Huston; Elizabeth B. and Delbert H. Smith with Dr. J. McLean and Lucy Moulder; Ira G. Clark with Henry and Linnie T. Edwards; George A. Whitman with William A. and Mrs. Stanley; William H. Burding/Burdine with W.P. and Jane Sellers; Lena Pope with Mrs. Kate F. Martin; Nina Fairbanks with Eli and Alice D. Quaintance; Charles A. Patterson with George and Mrs. McGowan; Harold Ralph with G.E. and Mrs. Meck; George Shultz with Daniel Tyson and Mrs. Reiff; Christie Shultz with B.F. and Mrs. Redmond; James McDonald with George W. and Mrs. Landon; Charles Metchear with B.F. and Mrs. Harness; Rachel Morrison with Mrs. Mary Close; Margaret Morrison with Miss Katie Kellar; Henry Keenan with Jesse Ault; Willard Stoddard with J.M. and Mrs. Darnell; and Walter Gould with A.K. and Mrs. McElwee. Walter Gould had a sister and brother in Denver, Miami County, IN. Herbert Stygles and Willie Stoddard were brought here from Peru, Miami County, IN. for placement. Herbert Stygles was taken to Russiaville, IN.

Some of our orphans were adopted; some of them married and became part of the community; and some went back to the Boston, MA area which had been home. There is no doubt that these children and their descendants contributed greatly to the fabric of Kokomo and Howard County's society.

CLAY TOWNSHIP

All of the land in Howard County was once a part of the Great Miami Indian Reserve. The Miamis first sold the "Seven Mile Strip" to the government for canal purposes in 1838. The government then sold the land along the proposed canal to settlers. On November 28, 1840, the Miamis gave up the Great Miami Reserve, and with it, sold their last remaining lands in Indiana. Thus, Howard County was one of the last counties to be organized in the state.

Joseph Taylor is believed to be the first non-Indian resident of the present Clay Township. He took a claim in the southwest corner of the township in the fall of 1838. When he found out that his claim was in the Miami Indian Reserve and not in the "Seven Mile Strip," he abandoned the land. An Indian (name unknown) took over the land. He hired a man named Heart to make some improvements to the land. When the Indian could not pay for those improvements, Heart took possession of the land. In 1840 Heart sold the land to Thomas A. Long of Marion County. Long employed a man named "Chris" Comer to plant a small patch of corn which is believed to be the first corn planted in Clay Township.

After Taylor left his claim, McHagey McHone became the first permanent resident, when he took up residence near the McHone Prairie in the north central area of the township in June 1840.

Originally, Clay Township, along with Harrison, Howard, Taylor, and Center Townships were called Kokomo Township. The Acts of the Legislature in 1851 and 1852 allowed division into the present units. Clay Township was named for Henry Clay, prominent Kentucky statesman. It consists of approximately 27 sections of land which is primarily black loam soil but does have some clay soil, particularly in the southern half of the township.

The first schools were subscription schools in which parents banded together to contract with a teacher to teach their children, usually for a set time and a set amount of money. Starting about 1845, construction started on one-room schoolhouses in the eleven school districts in the township. The first, No. 1, was built on the Simmons farm southwest of Shiloh with Charles Price being the first teacher in Clay Township. Others and their approximate locations were: No. 2 Fairview, 360W on Pete's Run Pike (now Ind. #22); No. 3 name unknown, 530 W 100N.; also No. 3 North Star, 80 W 360 N; (there was a duplication for No. 3 for some unknown reason); No. 4 Clay Center, 350 W 350 N; No. 5 Paddy, 520 W 500 N; No. 6. Rickard, 100 W 550 N; No. 7 Jewell, 175 W 450 N; No. 8 Macedonia, 300 W 500 N; No. 9 name unknown, 500 W 375 N; No. 10 Woodland, 500 W 220 N; and No. 11 name unknown, 350 W 200 S. Also Colored School No. 2 was located about 475 North 600 W. These schools were made of hewn logs, and were twenty feet square, with a shingle roof. They also had only one window for light, and oiled paper was used to let the light through and keep the cold out. The patrons were allowed to help with construction of these schools in lieu of paying taxes to construct them. The log schoolhouses were replaced by frame buildings as time went on. Then, in the 1880's the frame

The students of Fairview School in Clay Township on September 21, 1915. The teacher is DeLos Spraker.

structures were replaced by double layer of brick buildings with slate roofs. The brick buildings were used until the high school was built, and two of them are still standing (Clay Center and Macedonia).

These one-room schools were used to educate the residents' children through the eighth grade. Education beyond the eighth grade required the student to go to Kokomo, Galveston, or New London where they had high schools. Not many students went on to high school because of transportation required to get there and the limited need for a high school education.

In the spring of 1920, petitions for a high school were circulated, and construction was started in the summer of 1921. When completed, Clay Township High School cost approximately $75,000. Teachers for the 1921-1922 school year were: Charles Mills, Macedonia; Carl Williams, Clay Center; Mary Poore, Paddy; Marie Bolinger, Fairview; and Stacy Davis, Jewell. Then on September 4, 1922, Clay Township was certified a grade school and high school. There were three years of high school offered the first year. The staff included: L.M. Keisling, principal, Harry Gray, Ernestine Unversaw, Esther Redding, and Mrs. W.J. Wakefield, teachers in the high school; and Charles Mills, Carl Williams, Mary Donahue, and Marie Bolinger teaching in the grade school.

Other teachers from 1899 to 1915 were: Grace Rofelty, A.W. Hunt, Mabel Garr, Luella Chambers, Sena (Stewart) Matlock, Leora Spraker, Charles Laird, Bettie (Stewart) Miller, William Miller, Frank Hartman, John Rayl, Harry Miller, DeLos Spraker, Dalton Turley, Frank W. Smith, Anna Price, Maud Shaddock, Florence G. Whitman, Bertha Wilson, May Somsel, Ethel Johnson, D.V. Seaver, A.C. Campbell, Wesley Ball, Levina French, William Hobson, Russell McCaughan, Essie McClelland, Garnet Spencer, J.P. Costlow, Carrie Kenworthy, Buell Shrader, Myron Gates, R.R. Hamilton, Maurice Ashley, Lydia Crandall, Charles Graham, Hilda Zell, Richard Lee, Frank Devore, Mildred Talbert, P.B. Shinn, Rola Mygrant, and Verna (Smith) Spraker. These names were taken from the graduation programs of this period.

The Clay Township High School was commissioned in 1923, and the first class of 12 was graduated April 22, 1924. The school continued through 25 years until it was consolidated into Northwestern High School with the fall term of 1948.

The Clay Township high school building was located very near the center of the new Northwestern School Corporation, and it was selected for the new high school. The elementary students were assigned to either Ervin or Howard Township School with those living west of Melfalfa Road going to Ervin and those living east of Melfalfa Road going to Howard. The division line changed with the addition of the Northwestern Elementary School in the early 1970's and the later closing of Ervin. Howard Township School is still in use for grades one through six. Also, additions to the Clay building started in 1956, and the present Northwestern High School dwarfs the original building which is still standing.

Early churches in Clay Township conducted services in the residents' homes, and, later, divine services were held in some of the schools. The first church, a log structure, was built by the Methodists on Spice Run in the southeast corner of the township. It was later replaced by a church built at Shiloh in 1874. There was also a church at Jewell and an African Methodist Church near the Colored School No. 2 in the northwest corner of the township.

There was a post office at Shiloh, another at Jewell and possibly a third at Foster's Trading Post near Wildcat Creek in southwestern Clay Township. Also, George W. Smith operated a post office from his home on the east side of Bell Prairie about 80 rods from the Cass County line, because the mail route from Kokomo to Logansport went past his house.

There may have been Indian burial grounds, a cemetery near Wildcat Creek, and another near the African Methodist Church, but the only present day cemetery in Clay Township is at Shiloh.

Jewell was an unincorporated village that consisted of a general store, church, school, blacksmith shop, and holding pens for livestock. A railroad and an interurban ran through Jewell, and it was a depot for both passengers and livestock. There is no evidence of Jewell today, and the interurban tracks were removed and replaced by a highway built in 1941.

In the early days there were several sawmills and blacksmith shops, but the main business of the township was and is farming. At one time Frank Haynes operated a cheese factory, and there were three dairies delivering milk into Kokomo which were operated by Ralph Deardorff, William Cameron and Ward Haynes, but there is no visible evidence of them today. Horace and Lula McKinney operated a gasoline station, grocery, and used car lot at the junction of 150 W 300 N for many years; Walter Seitz later bought the business and substituted a small foundry for the used cars. The Meyers brothers ran a pattern shop at 300 N and Apperson Way North. Also Pete Robertson ran a grocery store at about 320 W 200 N. The Ropes Corporation was a wholesaler of underground water handling equipment on U.S. #31 north of 450 N for many years. The Bolingers (Sherman, his wife Fern, and sister Viola) operated a restaurant across the road from the high school where they sold large hamburgers for a dime and soup for a nickel. Also, there have been many roadside stands where residents have sold fruits and vegetables in Clay Township.

Most of the activities in Clay Township have been and are related to the school or agriculture. One of the highlights of the school year occurred in January with the Farmers Institute. Many farmers participated in the all day meeting which included a pot luck lunch. They discussed farm problems, national problems, politics, etc., and it was a good time to renew friendships. It was a fun day for students because it was almost like a day out of school. The lack of a dynamic leader led to the demise of the Farmers Institute. Similar fates have engulfed other farm organizations such as the National Grange, Farm Bureau Cooperative Association, and others. Thus, the Northwestern High School remains as the focus of activities in Clay Township as well as in Howard and Ervin Townships.

Present day businesses include: Ortman's Well Drilling, Jefferson House of Flowers, Richard Smith's Garage, Mitchell's Garden Tractors, Bolingers Welding Shop, and H&H Plastering Company. These firms supplement the agricultural pursuits of Clay Township today.
Submitted by John E. Haynes

The Shiloh Methodist Church built in 1874.

The remodeled Shiloh Methodist after the addition of the education unit in 1908.

ERVIN TOWNSHIP

Ervin is the largest township in Howard County and was named for Associate Justice Robert Ervin (1844-1850). It lies one mile east of Michigan Road (St. Rd. 29) between the Wildcat Creek on the south and Little Deer Creek on the north with Clay Township to the east. The area is mostly plains today, but at one time there were lots of woods and swamps. It consists of 40 sq. miles. The "Seven Mile Strip" was part of this township. Boundaries were set when the county commissioners met in 1846. It is just about the same today. Originally Ervin was part of Monroe Township in 1844 until the county name was changed to Howard County from Richardville County.

Miami Indians in 1838 lived along the Wildcat and other creeks in the area. The Indians sold this ground to the U.S. Government for $1.90 an acre and the government turned it over to the State of Indiana. At this time the land went up for sale from the state for $3.00 to $5.00 an acre. The first tax rate was twenty-five cents and today (1994) it is $7.35.

Early Settlers

Most of the early pioneers came from Ohio and Pennsylvania. They were of English, German and Scotch descent. Others came from Cass, Carroll and Clinton Counties. They brought most of their personal things. However, those from states south of the Ohio Valley could not bring much. The majority of the people were farmers, but there were also stone-masons, plasterers, carpenters, millwrights and blacksmiths. Also, there were trappers and hunters. Robert Walker, from Peru, started the changing times by urging his neighbors Isaac Price, Joseph Taylor and his son George to come with him in the fall of 1838. They built two cabins. The Walkers and Prices moved with their families in February of 1839. Isaac Price and his wife, Mary Catherine, had the first white child born in Ervin Township. Mary Catherine Price was born August 15, 1839. November 10, 1839, Mrs. Price died, which was the first death in Ervin Township and second in the county, the first being Thomas Landrum.

More pioneers, George W. Brown and his father, came in 1838. 1839 brought Capt. John Harrison, soon after this Joshua Barnett; and in 1841 Jacob Price, the father of Isaac Price; 1842-1843 Alexander Forgy and James McCool came. Jefferson and Elizabeth White with their eight children came in 1844 from Johnson County, Indiana; in 1845 William Malaby, Luther and Alvin McDowell and Ambrose Wilson arrived. About the same time, Hile Hamilton and his wife and five children came from Union County, Indiana; in 1846 George Salmons and his wife arrived. Harrison Gillam, Joseph Polk, and Peter Rice also came along with their families. Others were Joseph Early, Sr. and John B. Early; Abraham Brubaker, John Bluford Hawkins, Jacob Lawrence, Levi Beckner, Abram Brubaker, Joel Brower, Jackson McDowell, James Ridgeway and Ephrum Woods, J.L.D. Hanna, Amos Bates, Samuel Bortsfield, Ralph French, Francis M. Power, Silas Baldwin, and Robert Coate, who was the first school teacher at Olinger School. Also coming were Benjamin Tucker, John Rider, Henry Gillam, Abram Flores, Burrell Bell and Joseph Bright. In 1849 Dr. I.W. Martin arrived. Robert and Lucretia Ritchey from Johnson County came in 1850. About the same time Jacob and Rebecca Mason, along with their children, came to Ervin Township. Jeremiah and Elizabeth Harrell, the parents of Lucretia Ritchey, came with the balance of their family. In 1854 William and Saloma Butcher arrived with their son John B. Butcher, age eleven.

There were two colored settlements - Rush located at 450 N. - 600 W. and Bassett at 400 N. - 950 W.

The early settlers of the Bassett community were free slaves from Parke County, Indiana. The first minister of the Free Union Baptist Church was Zachariah Bassett, the father of Richard Bassett. Some of the other black families in the Bassett community were William Ellis, Thomas Artis, Reuben Griggs, Nancy Mosley, Thomas Hall, Gertrude Vaughn and Samantha McDaniels. The Rush settlement families were: William Hardemon, Charles Harmon, Adaline Locust, Daniel Rush, Henderson West, Richard Barrington and Doc Harvey.

James and Jesse Barnett, along with Robert Walker, laid out the town of Caroline, probably with the intention of checking the growth of Kokomo on the southeastern part of section thirty-six and the northeast part of section one. The lots were large, five by ten rods. A record was made of this plot in Deed Record A on pages 12-13 on January 14, 1845. On this town site stood a log church erected and occupied by the Baptists. A new place of worship was finally built on the present site of the Judson Baptist Church. When that old log structure disappeared, nothing was left of the town of Caroline.

Ervin Township Notables

Richard Bassett–1893 State Legislature, **R. Alan Brubaker**–Judge of Howard County Circuit Court, **Burchard Davidson**–Judge of Superior Court I, **Howard Gilbert**–Kokomo Police Captain, **Raymond Gilbert** – 1952-1960 Kokomo Mayor, **Luther McDowell**–1890-1891 State Legislature, **Glen Ritchey**–1955-1957 County Commissioner, **Dr. Harold Ritchey** – Helped develop Solid - Propellant Rocketry and served on Purdue University Board of Trustees, and **Guy Wilson**–Purdue University Board of Trustees.

The children of Jesse Jr. and Mary A. (Batey) Nash have their photo taken in front of the largest sycamore stump in the world. Seated: Ellis Nash, May Nash, and Ernest Nash. Standing: Charlie Nash and Fred Nash.

Sycamore Stump

The large sycamore stump that is housed in a building at Kokomo Highland Park came from Ervin Township. It grew at the edge of the Wildcat Creek on the Capt. John Harrison farm which was owned by Tighlman A. Harrell. It is said the tree could be seen from the bridge on 750 W (Newcom Bridge).

Ervin Township Firsts

Known as Cromwell's Mill - Joshua Barnett — Store and Mill
David Bates — Blacksmith
Poplar Grove — Post Office
Friends at Poplar Grove, est. 1842 — Church
Poplar Grove — School House
Robert Coate — Teacher
David Cline, Esq. — Justice of Peace
Daniel Flora, David Smith, William King — Trustees
Jesse C. Barnett — First appointed Sheriff
John Harrison — First Elected Sheriff
William Riffe/Riffle - d. Nov. 11, 1861 13th W.Va. Reg. — First death of a Civil War Soldier

Reference Materials

Howard County Atlas - 1877
History of Howard and Tipton Counties - 1883 - Blanchard
History of Ervin Township - 1971 - Owen Freeland
History of Ervin Township - D.W. Tucker
Private Collections of Mary Blangy and Hertha White

Ervin Township Cemeteries

Name (also known as)	Location
Barnett (Ehrman)	00 NS - 700 W
Bassett Cemetery – Colored	400 N - 950 W
Bell Mound (Mound)	350 N - 1175 W
Brown (Oak Mound, Old Butler)	550 N - 1200 W
Indian Cemetery – 6 Indian Graves	100 N - 1225 W
Michael Price Farm – Small Cemetery	125 N - 1250 W
North Union (Salmons, Boswell, Union, Bethel)	450 N - 800 W
Pete's Run	125N - 1175W
Poplar Grove Friends (Pickett)	550 N - 1120 W
Price (Hauck, Newcom)	00 NS - 720 W
Rush Cemetery – Colored	450 N - 600 W
South Union Cemetery (Straughn, Union, Wilson)	00 NS - 1050W

Ervin Townships Churches

Name	Location
* **Baldwin United Brethren**	400 N - 800 W
* **Bassett Baptist** – colored	400 N - 950 W
* **Bethel Friends** •	400 N - 710 W
Community Bible Ministries Sept. 1993	150 N - 1150 W
Hillside Missionary Baptist Church	100 N - 1220 W
Judson Baptist Church •	200 N - 750 W
* **Old German Baptist Brethren Church** 1882 - 1944	100 N - 1075 W
* **Old German Baptist Church of the Brethren** June 5, 1993 •	150 N - 1150 W
* **Poplar Grove Friends**	575 N - 1125 W
Poplar Grove United Methodist •	500 N - 1150 W
* **Rush Baptist** – colored	450 N - 600 W
* **Zion Christian** – Wildcat Zion Church	00 NS - 900 W
* **Zion Lutheran Church**	400 N - 675 W

* Non-Existent
• See History in Church Section

Ervin Towship Schools

No.	Name	Yrs. Oper.	Location
	Olinger	1846 (1st School)	500 N - 1150 W
	Zion Lutheran	1871 - 1920	400 N - 675 W
1	Garbert Fire	1916 - 1917	500 N - 700 W
2	Heinmiller	1893 - 1927	500 N - 1000 W
3	Butcher	1893 - 1927	500 N - 1150 W
4	Nogo	1888 - 1927	350 N - 1150 W
5	Center	1883 - 1927	250 N - 900 W
6	Hite	1891 - 1918-19	300 N - 700 W
7	Endicote	1885 - 1927	100 N - 825 W
8	Mason	1885 - 1927	00 NS - 820 W
9	Early	1903 - 1927	100 N - 1050 W
10	Hawkins	1885 - 1927	200 N - 1175 W
11	Kappa	1889 - 1927	400 N - 800 W
	Ervin Twp. School	1927 - 1948	300 N - 900 W
12	Burchfield		200 N - 825 W
1	Bassett (colored)		400 N - 950 W
2	Rush (colored)		450 N - 600 W

Schools numbered one through twelve were all frame school buildings in the beginning. All except number one were changed to brick construction at the dates listed. Number one stayed frame. The only central school building for the whole township was Ervin Township School. The 1948 graduating class was the last senior class. The decision was made to consolidate the three townships of Ervin, Clay and Howard in 1948.

Ervin Township Post Offices

Bassett
July 9, 1886 - December 20, 1894
First Postmaster - Henry P. Bassett

Cornstalk
July 2, 1875 - August 14, 1877
First Postmaster - Simon P. Woods

Crittenden
June 24, 1851 - July 21, 1854
First Postmaster - Isaac Haworth

Ervin
February 6, 1863 - April 15, 1897
First Postmaster - Dr. I.W. Martin

Kappa
June 9, 1886 - June 14, 1917
First Postmaster - James Lane

Nogo
June 21, 1880 - January 28, 1886
First Postmaster - James Gray

Poplar Grove
August 8, 1855 - July 29, 1896
First Postmaster - Benjamin D. Pickett

Ridgeway
April 7, 1879 - August 30, 1902
First Postmaster - John E. Nice*

* Township History states First Post Office 1862 and First Postmaster - Daniel Booerholser

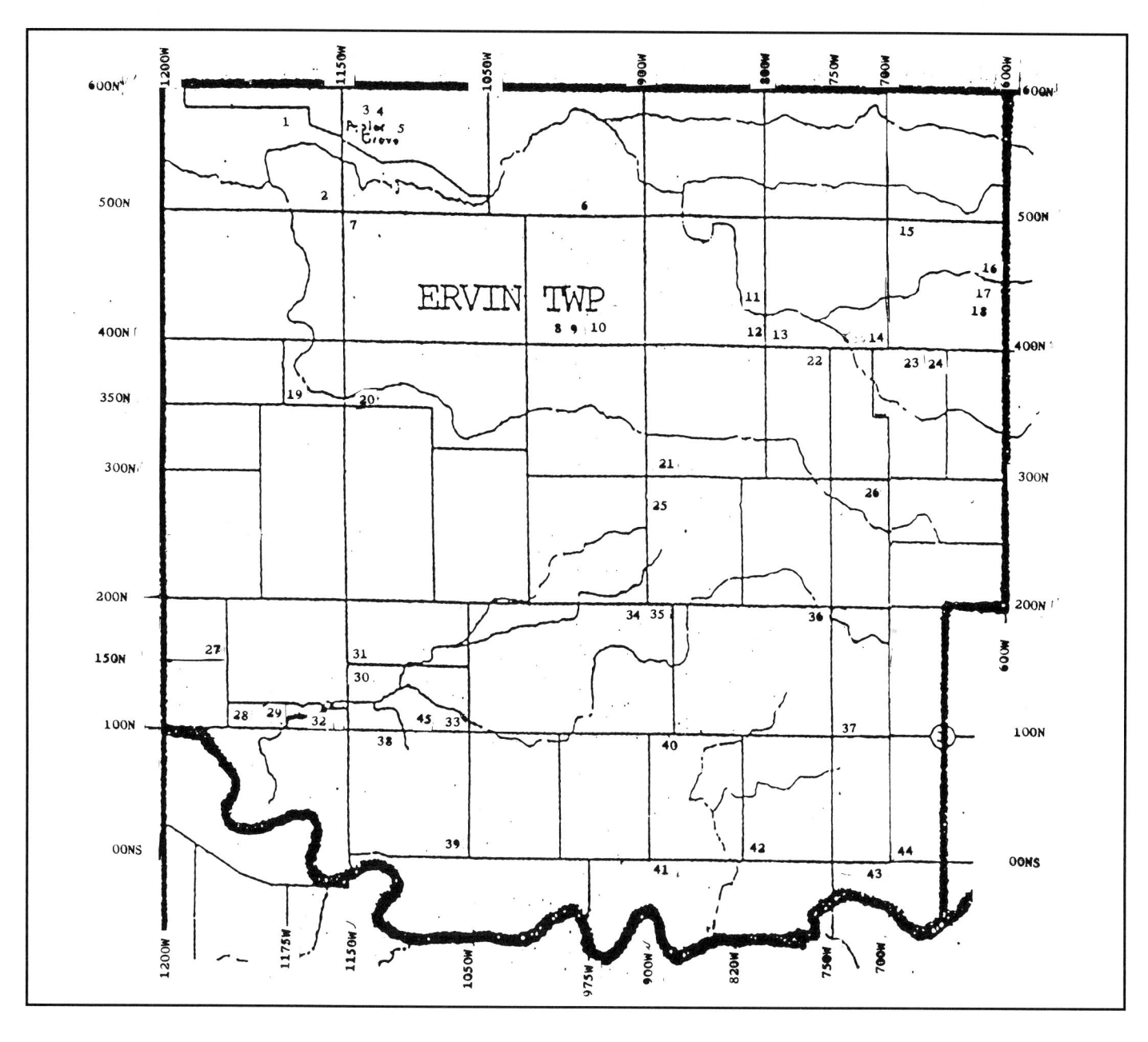

Key to Map of Ervin Township

1 Brown, Oak Mound Cem.
2 #3 Butcher School
3 Friends Church
4 Friends Cem.
5 1st School - Olinger
6 #2 Heinmiller School
7 Poplar Grove Church
8 Bassett Baptist Church, Colored
9 #1 Bassett School, Colored
10 Bassett Cemetery, Colored
11 North Union Cem.
12 Baldwin Church
13 #11 Kappa School
14 Bethel Friends Church
15 #1 Garbert School
16 Rush Cemetery, Colored
17 Rush Church, Colored
18 #2 Rush School, Colored
19 Bell Mound Cemetery
20 #4 Nogo School
21 Ervin Twp. School
22 Kappa Post Office
23 Zion Lutheran School
24 Zion Lutheran Church
25 #5 Center School
26 #8 Mason School
27 #10 Hawkins School
28 Burial ground on Michael Price Farm
29 Pete Run Cem.
30 Indian Cem.
31 Church of Brethren/now Community Bible Ministries
32 Hillside Missionary Baptist Church
33 #9 Early School
34 Ervin Post Office
35 #12 Burchfield School
36 Judson Baptist Church
37 #7 Endicott School
38 Cornstalk Post Office
39 South Union Cemetery
40 Ridgeway Post Office
41 Wildcat Zion Christian Church
42 #8 Mason School
43 Price Cemetery
44 Barnet Cemetery
45 Old Order Brethren Church

Information taken from Postal History of Indiana by J. David Baker

HARRISON TOWNSHIP

Harrison Township is located in the southwestern part of Howard County and contains nearly twenty-one and a half sections of land. The eastern part of Harrison borders on U.S. 31; the southern part borders Tipton County; the western part borders Honey Creek and Monroe Townships and the northern part borders Clay and Center Townships, part of which lies within the city of Kokomo.

Origin of the name and the first settlers was learned from Judge T.A. Long. When the township was laid out, it was named in honor of John Harrison, at whose house the first election in the county was held, although James Brooks, one of the pioneer hunters and trappers, came to the reserve in 1838. The first man that we have any knowledge of settling in this township was Martin Crist who, in company with Judge Long, came in the fall before the land was for sale. Mr. Crist took a claim on the north half of Section Seven.

Later in the season of 1840 Joseph W. Heaton, Thaddeus Baxter and Thomas McClure came from Kirklin, in Clinton County, and took up claims. During the season of 1841 David Bates, James Hamilton and Charles Harmon arrived and following them in rapid succession came Bernhart Learner, William Coats, Philip Ramseyer, James Scott, Nathan Comer, Clinton Gray and Bland Jones.

There are two villages in Harrison Township, Alto and West Middleton. Stephen Brooks had Alto surveyed and recorded in the Land Office Reports, in April 1848. Alto is at the corner of Alto and Dixon Roads, the main roads in the township. Before the year had closed in 1848, there was a store, a cabinet shop, a blacksmith shop and a boot and shoe shop. In the first years of its existence, there was as much trade there as in Kokomo.

The first physician was Dr. J.H. Kern; the first merchant and postmaster was R. Cobb; the cabinetmaker was W.B. Judkin.

There was Heltzel's Grocery and Meat Market on the corner of Alto and Dixon Road. They sold the family business to Woody's which is in Alto yet today. There is also Mike's Pizza, Speedway Service Station, Blue Moon Diner and the Howard County Children's Center. Harrison Township Fire Station is the only fire station within the township and is manned by volunteers.

If you want to read more about the history of this township, see the *Howard & Tipton County History,* by Charles Blanchard, in the Kokomo/Howard County Public Library.

West Middleton is located about four and a half miles west of the present U.S. 31 on County Road 250 S. It was laid out by Mr. William Middleton in the year that the Frankfort and Kokomo Railroad was built. Road 250 S (Alto Road), was originally known as the New London-Kokomo Gravel Road, the first of its kind in the county. It was built in the years 1869 to 1871 at a cost of $27,000. The road was sponsored by a number of citizens of the community, including Captain B. Busby, Dr. W.W. Hinton, Isaac Ramsey, Josiah Beeson, Shadrach Stringer, Samuel Stratton, C.S. Wilson, Joseph Stratton, Hiram Newlin and Richard Terrell.

Middleton and Torrence families at the home of Wm. and Jane Middleton in West Middleton. (l. to r.) Back: Wm. Middleton, Pearl Leach, May Middleton, Sarah Torrence, Jane Middleton (seated in rocker), and Etta. Middle: John Middleton, Ross Torrence, Charles Middleton, Anna Middleton, and Ruth Torrence. Front: Florence (Middleton) Hamilton and Geneva (Torrence) Beck.

West Middleton High School

West Middleton United Methodist Church in 1984.

The Kokomo-Frankfort Railroad was built in 1873-74, and the village was established at the intersection of the railroad and the New London Gravel Road.

A store building was erected in 1873, and the post office was established on November 23, 1874. The post office started as a fourth class office and was changed to a third class in 1954 by then Postmaster Opal Edwards. It has been housed in five different buildings, all within one hundred feet of each other. The present building was erected in early 1950 by Forrest and Opal Edwards. In the years gone by there were rural routes. Mail has been delivered to the post office by train, interurban and truck. This post office celebrated its one-hundredth anniversary on November 23, 1974.

Schools were an important part of the community, the first being taught by Thomas Stubbs. Later a school was erected about one-half mile east of the present community. In 1881 a brick school was built in the village and in 1909 a consolidated school building was erected for the township to include a high school. The first high school class to graduate was in 1910 with three members: June Alley, Hazel Stratton and Florence Stratton. B. Frank Shadel was the first principal. Marion Coe was trustee and C.E. Stratton, Elmer Bowen, and William Sellars were the Advisory Board members. The largest graduating class was in 1937 with twenty-two members. There were about 425 graduates of West Middleton High School; 81 people served as high school teachers; there were sixteen principals with Richard Rea perhaps serving the most years, and 33 grade school teachers.

The Board of Trustees of Monroe, Harrison and Honey Creek Townships met on August 12, 1948 and approved the consolidation of the three schools. The name chosen was Western School Corporation. This now is the only school within Harrison Township. In 1961 the West Middleton High School building was condemned and torn down.

Three churches were built in the 1880's. The first was the Christian Church built on lots purchased from William Middleton. Charter members were George and Francis Newkirk; Fannie and Cornelius Heaton; G.W. and Jane Amons, Jr.; Ira Hickman; Elizabeth and Matilda Kenworthy; Armanda Randall; Lavinna Brooks; and Nancy Veach.

The Society of Friends services were held above the store in 1876. In 1885 a lot was bought and the church was completed and dedicated in August of 1886 at a cost of $1200. Allen Kenworthy was the first pastor. Charter members were Jesse & Elizabeth Ratcliffe; Alpheus & Martha E. White; William & Jane Middleton; Susan Griffith; John & Rachel Ratcliffe; William & Hannah Smith; Robert & Sarah Torrence; Jeremiah & Lydia Cox; A.C. & Martha Ratcliffe; and I.F. & Marietta Street.

The third church to be built in West Middleton was the Methodist Episcopal Church. The earliest recorded Sunday School was here in December 1886. In the fall of 1887 a lot was purchased and a church constructed. The trustees were Charles S. Wilson, John Wilson, J.T. Hopper, S.N. Bowen and Charles Stratton. It is located at 2428 S 480 W.

Postmasters of Harrison Township

Name	Date Of Appointment
David Dillman	November 23, 1874
Ansel R. Wiltsin	March 29, 1875
Thomas I. Wilson	October 30, 1876
James Quick	August 19, 1878
Thomas J. Thorne	May 31, 1881
Amos C. Ratcliffe	December 14, 1831
James Parson	December 7, 1882
Charles E. Middleton	August 4, 1884
William H. Orr	May 25, 1885
Henry A. Sinks	December 7, 1885
Silas D. Ramseyer	December 20, 1887
Samuel N. Bowen	March 21, 1888
Jacob Komitt	December 10, 1889
Charles W. Long	September 18, 1891
Allen Kenworthy	August 15, 1892
Jesse D. Garr	September 18, 1891
John R. Grubbs	August 10, 1897 (17 yrs)
Guy W. Bowen	July 31, 1914 (35 yrs)
Faye Ferguson	August 1, 1949
Carmon Long	Acting Postmaster April 1, 1950
	Received Commission July 1, 1950
Opal Edwards	Acting Postmaster August 16, 1951
	Received Commission May 9, 1952
	Retired June 1, 1973 (21 yrs)
Ruth Newby	Acting Postmaster June 2, 1973
	Received Commission September 15, 1973
Barbara Rayl	OIC August 18, 1979
Janice Varney	Acting Postmaster December 15, 1979
	Received Commission January 26, 1980
	Retired November 20, 1992
Bonnie Rice	OIC November 21, 1992 to July 1, 1993
Margarette Rose	OIC July 1, 1993 to present
Rose McLay	Postmaster

Horace Proyer, Paul Etherington and County Extension Agent Everett Johnson.

Harrison Township Cemeteries

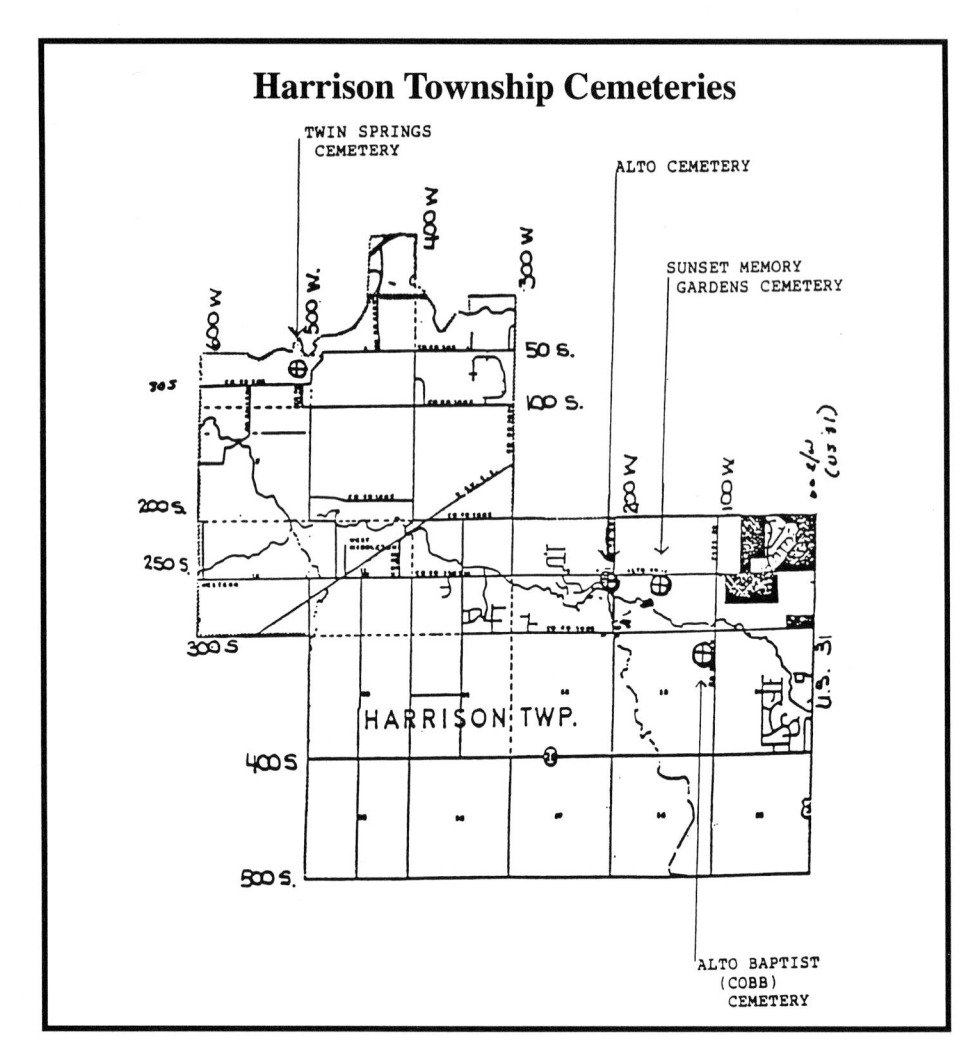

(Map showing Harrison Twp. with labeled cemeteries: Twin Springs Cemetery, Alto Cemetery, Sunset Memory Gardens Cemetery, Alto Baptist (Cobb) Cemetery)

The other churches in the township are Chapel Hill at 2600 W Alto Road; Alto United Methodist, 2102 W. Alto Road; First Friends Meeting, 1801 Zartman Road; Jesus Christ of Latter Day Saints, 332 W 300 S; Lutheran Holy Cross at 3401 S. Dixon Road; Westside Baptist SBC, at 100 S 300 W and Southdowns Wesleyan at 175 W 400 S. West Middleton Friends Church is located in the village of West Middleton.

There are at least four cemeteries in the township. Twin Springs is located at 520 W 80 S; Alto Baptist (Cobb) Cemetery at 300 S (Center Road) 100 W (Park Road). Henry Cobb donated two acres of land to the Alto Baptist Church to be used as a cemetery on March 1, 1850. Alto Cemetery is in Alto just south of the intersection of Alto Road and Dixon Road. Sunset Memory Gardens Cemetery is privately owned at 2101 Alto Road West.

The information about West Middleton was found in the book at the Kokomo/Howard County Library, *West Middleton Out of the Past*, by Ruth Newby, Helen Ferguson and Betty Robbins, copyrighted in 1976.

The only airport in the township today is Glendale located at 3460 S 400 W. The name came from the father, Glen Etherington, and his son, Dale. In 1966 they built the first hangar, and three more were built in the three succeeding years. They can house twenty aircraft at the present time. In June 1961, Dale, the son, traded a car for one-half interest in a Stenson 180-2 and started to get his private ticket. He soloed in 1948 at the old Ruzicka Airport on South Lafountain Street where Super Test Filling Station is now located (1994). Ruzicka Airport was later moved to Center Road east of Glendale Airport in the 1960's.

The township has enough businesses to be a town in its own right. There are White's Meat Market and several small businesses in Southdowns Addition facing Highway 26, just west of U.S. 31. Chippendale Golf Course is located at 500 S and Park Road (100 W). A residential area, The Moors of Chippendale, has been added to the west of the golf course. Several other residential areas are being developed or planned to the north along Highway 26. There are a number of businesses on the west side of U.S. 31, between 200 and 300 S, the oldest probably being Cordova's Fine Candies. The United Presidential Life Insurance Company has built a new facility south of Alto at Center Road and Dixon.

West Middleton has Don's Country Inn and Pizza; one of the original stores, built in 1873, houses the Earthware Shop, owned by Dave Bledsoe; local artist, Mike Sears, owns Country Originals. There is an Indian Trading Post and Drago Amusements, along with several other small businesses at the present time (1994).

HONEY CREEK TOWNSHIP

Honey Creek Township is located in the southwestern section of Howard County within the boundaries of county roads 300S-700S and 500W-920W. It was originally a part of the Seven Mile Strip of the Miami Indian Reserve and was first organized in 1842 as a part of Clinton County. The people in the northwestern portion of the township were closer to the county seat of Howard County and wished to be added to that county. A bill was passed enabling the citizens of the bordering townships to detach themselves from the county. It took three petitions before the majority of the twenty-three voters were granted their wish at the March term of the Commissioner's Court of Clinton County in 1859.

The first settlers that came in 1838 must have had a lonely existence as the nearest trading post was in Burlington, ten miles away, and had to be reached by horseback or foot. They were forced to travel six miles to Middlefork to send or receive mail as that was the nearest post office. In 1847 a private service was installed to carry mail from Burlington to New London, Indiana.

Henry Stuart opened the first store located near Russiaville in 1842 with goods being transported by wagon from Cincinnati, Chicago, and Lafayette. Wild game, honey, roots, herbs, and furbearing animal skins were used in exchange for supplies.

The town of Russiaville was founded by Martin Burton, of Indianapolis, in 1844. Mr. Burton and Edom Garner owned the land and were the original town builders. The first store in the town of Russiaville was built on the corner of Main and Liberty Streets. A grist mill was erected near Squirrel Creek and served until a flouring mill was built in 1852. The mill was destroyed by fire in 1870. The citizens realized the need for this commercial enterprise and assisted in the rebuilding of the mill.

BELGIAN SOUND PURE BRED STALLION
Enrollment No. 20405A

Monitor's King
No. 16743

Owned by
GEORGE ETHERINGTON and JOHN GORDON

Transportation

The town grew slowly until the railroad line between Frankfort and Kokomo, known as the F. & K. line, was built in 1873-74. By 1880 Russiaville had every type of retail business known in larger cities as the Clover Leaf line gave markets to the West as well as the Eastern seaboard. The interurban line from Frankfort to Kokomo was opened in September 1912, and at one time made ten round trips daily. Cooper Rollins and Walter Mendenhall were station attendants. This line closed down in 1932 due to a financial collapse as well as the transportation by automobile. Hines Bus Lines provided bus service between Frankfort and Kokomo in June 1932, the day after the interurban line was discontinued. The last day of operation for this run from Kokomo to Frankfort was July 13, 1953. Three Russiaville residents, Junie Hendrickson, Ora Butler and Dick Burgett, were on board the bus.

Education

One of the first schools in Howard County was taught in a log cabin in 1842. By 1876 there were five school districts with an enrollment of 150 students. There were two one-room schools and one four-room building used for a high school. A new school was built in 1894 in Russiaville and had the first graduating class in 1898. This building was replaced in 1904 with a two story brick building to accommodate grades one through twelve. The first basketball team was organized in 1906 by T.A. Hanson. The team was called the Russiaville Cossacks, and the school colors were red and white. The team played on the back lot of the school yard. Later they played in the assembly hall, moving the desks out of the center of the floor. Several years later, a gymnasium was built behind the school and named Lindley Hall in honor of W.W. Lindley who had taught school and been principal of Russiaville, before becoming County School Superintendent on June 5, 1937. Others who served as principal were Lozell Johnson, Lloyd Powell, Norvel Lindley and Chester Ellis. Long term elementary teachers were Florence Wright, Cora Kessler and Georgia Hart. Other teachers from the Russiaville area were Jeanette Carter, Helen Carter, Lenora Cline, Edna Mae Chandler, George McCoy, Harry Oilar, Hope McCain, Mary Padgett, Dorothy Carter, Pauline Conway, Mildred Talbert, Lucille Oilar, Edith DeWeese, Omar Unrue and Elmer Stewart.

Russiaville High School had its last graduating class in 1949 with 18 graduates. Due to the consolidation of Honey Creek, Monroe and Harrison township schools, the Russiaville High School building became Western High School in 1950 with 44 graduates. A new high school was built in Harrison Township in 1955 with the Russiaville building being used for elementary grades until the tornado destroyed it and the gym on April 11, 1965. Today a playground, pavilion and water tower replace the old school and gym.

Mrs. Robert (Roberta) Lineback took over the kindergarten in 1961 from Don and Lois Williams. The school was moved from the

Lelah Burgett can be seen in the third row, fifth child from left in this Russiaville School picture.

Russiaville Cossacks 1923-1924 Standing: George McCoy, Tom Gifford, Chester Graham, Bill Lewis, Bernal Mills, and Arthur Miller. Seated: Pat Taylor, Coach Tresler, and Clarol Dick.

Russiaville High School 1904-1965

Oldest church in Honey Creek Township

Baptist Church before the tornado in 1965.

Baptist Church after the tornado of 1965.

United Methodist Church in 1994

First Baptist Church in 1994

Friends Church

Christian Church and Fellowship Hall

Honey Creek Missionary Baptist Church

Russiaville Baptist Church to a building downtown where the tornado tore off the roof, leaving the desks in neat little rows. The class was moved to the New London Friends Church until remodeling was completed at the Lineback residence 1 mile west and 1/2 mile north of Russiaville. The last graduating class was in May 1971. In the fall of that year, Western began offering kindergarten classes at which time Mrs. Lineback became a member of the Western faculty. The Norfolk & Western Railroad donated the Clover Leaf depot dated 1894, to be used for a branch library. On April 9, 1986, it took Helvie Movers of Flora about two hours to move it to the town hall site. The cost was $3000 which was paid by the town board, fund-raisers and private donations. Volunteers did most of the work in the renovation. The Kokomo-Howard County Public Library donated shelves, books and furniture. The new Russiaville Branch of the Library opened its doors on June 5, 1989, with an Open House. The committee members for this project were the first to see their dream materialize. They were Sandy Smith, chairman; Lois Johnson, Jeannie Spangler, Maggie Hanson, Linda Vary Downey and Jacque Williams.

Churches

Lynn Friends Church is located two and one half miles east of Russiaville on State Road 26 where it originated in 1852. An article written by Madeline Wilcox was published in the December 7, 1972 edition of the Kokomo Tribune, giving a detailed history of this church. At the present time they meet on Sunday mornings with Glenn Fisher, Clerk of Monthly Meeting, with 15-20 members in attendance. Larry Talbert is Sunday School Superintendent.

The Christian Church has 325 active members with a Sunday school and worship service on Sunday morning with a youth program meeting in the evening. Bible studies are held midweek. Mark Matthews is the minister and Craig Taylor is the associate minister. Former residents, Rick and Kathy Walden, serve as missionaries in Thailand. The church was destroyed in the tornado of 1965. The dedication service of the new church was held on November 6, 1966. The Fellowship Hall was dedicated September 28, 1975, and is used for social functions by the congregation and the community. Former pastors were Fenton Messenger, Gene Dye, John Jeffries, David Woods, Ron Wagoner, James Coffman and Walter Kelly.

The United Methodist Church has 60-70 in attendance for Sunday school and the morning worship service each week. David Mullens is the pastor of this congregation. A Kids Club for junior age children and a youth group meet regularly. Bible studies are held throughout the week, meeting in homes and at the church. Methodist Women's meetings are held the 1st Tuesday of each month. The present church was damaged by the tornado but is now in good repair. The former church was destroyed by fire in 1942, and the congregation met in the Burris home until the new building was completed. Some former ministers were Earl Clayton, Dawson Liggett, Roy Helms, Dale Milner, Wayne Baxter and Armour Keller.

First Baptist Church of Russiaville is led by Pastor Ronald DeGraaff. 80 active members meet each Sunday for Sunday school and worship services which are held in the morning and evening. A mid-week prayer meeting, a children's ministry, as well as a Ladies Missionary Fellowship, are other ministries of the congregation. The former church was totally demolished in the tornado. A new church and parsonage were constructed on the same location in 1966. The dedication was held on August 28, 1966, with Dr. Paul Jackson, National Representative of General Association of Regular Baptist Churches, as guest speaker. Former pastors were Richard Curtis, Roy Clark, Raymond Riley, Edwin Cockrell, Don Williams, Milton Barkley, Daniel P. Douglass, Fredrick Buntz, James Storey and Steve Agal.

Honey Creek Missionary Baptist Church is the newest church in the township, located at the south edge of Russiaville. It was organized in 1961 with 14 charter members under the leadership of Rev. Dallas Hensler. A house was purchased and renovated to hold services where 25 people attended the first meeting in February 1962. Plans were made for the construction of a church which was begun in September 1969; the first service held in the completed basement was on December 31, 1969. The upper portion was completed July 18, 1971. A fellowship building was erected in 1972. All properties are debt free. There are 350 members with 85-120 attending Sunday school. The church holds morning and evening services on Sunday, prayer meeting mid-week, weekly youth meetings and Ladies Club once a month. The current pastor, Melvin Eller, and his wife live in the new parsonage which was built in 1992. Other pastors were Otheniel Finlay, Conrad Lindsay, Kermit Goins and Luke Freels. The Kokomo Tribune published an article written by Madeline Wilcox in the May 1, 1976 edition with a detailed history of this church.

Russiaville Friends has 120 members under the leadership of Pastor Brooks Martin. They meet for Sunday school and worship services on Sunday mornings. They have a Young Friends Youth program and two Women's Circles, one meeting in the evening and one during the day once a month. A complete history can be found in the Church History Section of this book.

Organizations

The Russiaville Lodge No. 82 Free and Accepted Masons meet on the 2nd Monday of each month except in July and August, at 140 N. Union St. They have 220 members. The officers are: Worshipful Master, James Kuhns; Senior Warden, Clifford Phipps; Junior Warden, Billy Bradley; Secretary, David Pottenger; Treasurer, Joe Greer; Senior Deacon, Jeff Hendershot; Junior Deacon, Jim Watkins; Senior Steward, Jeff McClurg; Junior Steward, Richard Kingery; Tyler, Max Randall.

Russiaville Order of Eastern Star No. 130 meet on the 1st Thursday of the month except in June and July and on the first and third Thursdays in February. Those serving as officers are: Worthy Matron, Linda Singer; Worthy Patron, Dwight Singer; Associate Matron, Beverly Shepherd; Associate Patron, Richard Shepherd; Secretary, Diane Godfrey; Treasurer, Donna Kenworthy. The Rainbow Girls stopped meeting in 1992.

Floyd Marshall Post 412 of the American Legion was organized in 1946 with 22 charter members. At the present time there are 110 members. They meet on the 1st Tuesday of each month at the Legion Hall, on Main St., which was built after the tornado. The Officers are: Commander, Ralph Pinkerton; Vice Commander, Paul Rollins; Adjutant, Ken Toney; Finance Officer, Sterling Johnson; Sergeant At Arms, Dick Whitehouse. Honey Creek has served our country well by providing it young men for the Armed Forces. Many have made the supreme sacrifice for our freedom.

The American Legion Auxiliary Unit 412 was organized in 1948 under the direction of Mary Padgett serving as the first president. There are 82 members, and meetings are held on the 1st Monday of each month at the Legion Hall. Officers at present are: President, Melinda Simmons; 1st Vice President, Donna Schaeffer; 2nd Vice President, Mary Beth Cox; Secretary, Kathy Parker; Treasurer, Esther Parker; Chaplain, Marianna Taylor; Historian, Mickey Kanable. Charter members who still hold membership are: Phoebe Goodnight, Dottie Ingels, Mary Juanita Sheffer, Marianna Taylor, Betty Waddell, Gertrude Younkin, Almina Townsend and Margaret Pingleton.

The Russiaville Lions Club was organized in 1945 with O.G. (Pud) Marshall as President. Harry Huttinger, Gene Redding, Darrell Milburn and Kennard Stout also held offices. There were 41 charter members. Current membership is 56. Meetings are held on the 1st and 3rd Mondays of the month at the Lions Club building. Present officers are: President, Max Randall; 1st Vice President, Mark Lyons; 2nd Vice President, Lin Ortman; 3rd Vice President, Dave Cameron; Secretary, Jeff Young; Treasurer, Don Riebe; Lion Tamer, Charles Catron; Tail Twister, Walter Korba; Director, Jeff Stout. The only active charter members are William Martin Sr. and Kennard Stout.

Russiaville Little League was actually started in Forest, Indiana, in 1966. They moved to Russiaville on property owned by the Lions Club and began clearing the field for a ball

Russiaville Lions Club

Town Hall and Masonic Lodge

American Legion Hall

Grocery Depot

Fire Department and Stout's Home Furnishings

Coach's Corner Auto Sales

Russiaville Auto Techs

Shopping Plaza

The Bottle Shop and Mr. J's Pizza

Cakes by Denzel and Western Tax

Sewage Treatment Plant

Hollingsworth Saw Mill – Darin, Cale and Joel Hollingsworth

A & J Farm Supply

Bill Martin Jr., Bill Sr., Ed Martin, Max Martin, & Carl Wisehart.

Branch Library

diamond. Some of the men helping with this project were: David Reser, Hugh Stewart, Dick Chaplin, Bob Kirkendall, Jack Waddell, Cleo Hale, Lowell Warden, Don Chasteen, Albert Hill and Max Snodgrass. Officers who also helped were: President, Charles Rollins; Vice President, Robert Robey; Secretary-Treasurer, Robert Waddell. There were four teams for boys ages 9-12. In 1987, the Little League switched to the Bambino League for boys ages 8-12. Current officers are: President, Roger Ryan; Vice President, Steve Dungan; Player Agent, Jeff Davidson; Secretary, Steve Chaffee; Treasurer, Jerry Maden and Equipment Manager, Brent Milburn. The Minor League Vice President is J.R. Sutherlin.

The Russiaville Girls Softball League had its origin in 1979. The Pixie League is for girls 8-12 years of age. They have nine teams. The High School League consists of four teams for girls ages 13-18. Current officers: President, Vacant; Vice President, Ted Kenworthy; Secretary, Rita Buchanan; Treasurer, Jerry Maden; and Umpire in Chief, Mark Gifford.

Medical

Physicians treating the ills of the community were Dr. A.H. Miller, Dr. Robert M. Evans, Dr. Orville Fosgate, Dr. Russell Fosgate and Dr. John Ware. Dental needs were met by Dr. Glenn Bollinger and Dr. Joseph Lantz. Pharmacists were Clarence Kemp, Jean Swayzee, Harry Huttinger and Mark Reed. For many years, Dr. J.H. Mills was the only veterinarian until Dr. W.J. Means came to Russiaville.

Commerce

Bank Officers: Leon Vandivier, Elmer Watson and Don Smith. Insurance Agents: Howard Brubaker, Howard Greenlee and Lowell Johnson.

Business

In 1890, the first furniture store was started by Albert Stout who added the funeral parlor two years later. Upon Albert's death, his son Wallace took over. Then later Wallace's two sons, Burrell and Kennard, followed in the business. Jeff Stout, Kennard's grandson, carries on the family tradition. Dry Goods stores were operated by O.G. (Pud) Marshall; and Logan and Anna Harding. Hardware dealers were Jake Padgett; Charlie Lewis and son Gilbert; and Robert Kanable. Max Martin is the only hardware proprietor at the present time. Grocers have been numerous: John Kanable; Tom Brant; Clifford Chew; Charles Chew; Fern Orem; Russell Cook; Earl Waddell and Eugene Waddell. Today, Randy Waddell has the only grocery in town. Having owned some type of restaurant, the following have literally served others: Anna and Logan Harding; Nellie Orem; Lelah Cook; Russell Durr, Hope McCain; Nora and Byron Earlywine; Dick and Kay Jarrett; Floyd and Jerry Hamilton; Claude Stanley; Zena Kelly; Buck Carter; Virgil Townsend; Oren McQuinn and Randy Waddell. The only restaurant now open is owned by Robert Rosenbaum. Automotive services were provided by the following: Russell Rinehart; Kenneth and Lincoln Goodnight; Bill and Ray Chandler; Gene Fillenwarth; Ira Taylor Jr.; Reese Fisher; Bill Copeland; Ray Sample; and Jim Lipinski. The barbers were: Sylvester Hamilton; Harley Uitts; Wayne Billiter; Jack Talbert; and Carl Wisehart, who is the only barber in business today. Beauticians operating shops in their homes were Mary Inez Goodnight, Nora Earlywine and Harriet Selph. Ruth's Beauty Shop, owned by Ruth Pickering, is the oldest hairdressing salon in town. Other beauticians are Phyllis McQuinn, Marsha Talbert, Myrna Waddell, Jean Van Horn, Pam Gullion, and Saralyn Martin, owner of the Wooden Nickel, and her daughter Lisa Finch.

Fuel oil distributors were Robert "Choppy" Kirkendall and Chet and Bob Waddell. Leland "Cinco" Wright offered pick up and delivery service for dry cleaning. Leslie and Opal Randall had the first greenhouse and florist shop in town. Hugh Strauss operated a sign company. Marion Duncan had a trucking business. Walter Dowden owned a paint and wallpaper shop. Ora Butler was proprietor of the pool hall before selling it to Carl "Buck" Heaton. Other recreations were the skating rink or free movies each week shown behind Chandler's Garage. Raymond Rodgers Lumber Co. also made brooms. The Russiaville Lumber Co. sold out to Functional Devices. Grain companies were owned by Luther Talbert and Max Sellers. John Lipinski delivered coal for the Sellers Coal Co. Joel Hollingsworth and sons, Darin and Cale, continue at the saw mill which was started by Joel's father, Nelson Hollingsworth. Snyder Heating and Plumbing was begun by Henry Snyder, father of David Snyder, who is the present owner. Garnet Heaton was in the poultry business and bought and sold furs. A convenience store with a filling station is operated and owned by Brian Adams. The Bottle Shop and Mr. J's Pizza are in the building owned by Durfee McKoon. The MiniMall owner is Gayle McMinn. Martin's Appliance Store is still family-owned and operated by Bill Martin Sr., Bill Jr. and Janet Miller. Martin Refrigeration Service is owned by Ed Martin, the oldest of "Red" Martin's sons. Ralph Sipes' son, Gary, carries on the Electrical Contracting business. Decorated cakes and cookies are homemade at Cakes by Denzel Hanson. Stitches by Doramae Hargrave is a clothing alteration shop. Western Tax is owned by Dale Brenton. Coach's Corner is a used auto dealership owned by Bob Jarrett. A. & J. Farm Supply is operated by Ted Salsbery. Petrolene Gas Service keeps propane gas supplied to residential and commercial customers. B.J.'s Specialty Shop is a gift shop for one of a kind gifts owned by Jeanette Ryan. Brad Newton is proprietor of the car wash. Jack Waddell has been in the TV repair business for many years.

Robert Waddell Memorial Little League Park

Delta Commons Apartments

Mobile Home Park

Journalism

George Woody, Joe Maloney, Harry Fawcett and Deke Noble have all been publishers and owners of The Russiaville Observer. George L. Woody compiled and published a book about the years from 1904-1917. "The Story of Russiaville and Honey Creek Township, Howard County, Indiana" can be found in the Kokomo-Howard County Public Library in the Genealogy Room.

Housing

Steven Johnson of Kokomo is the present owner of the Mobile Home Park which has 39 lots. He purchased it in 1977 from Forrest Edwards who owned it at its beginning in 1972. Delta Commons was built in 1985 on part of what used to be the Oakley Carter farm. There are 20 apartments with a Club House and laundry facilities.

Charles Wayne Orem and Gene Waddell in 1939.

Agriculture

Howard County Extension Director, Robert McCormack, reports the farmers in Howard County are excellent producers of pork, corn and soybeans. Their yields are in the top ten in the State of Indiana in corn and soybean production. They are in the top third of all counties in the state in total agricultural receipts, while being 82nd out of 92 counties in land area.

Politics

The citizens of Honey Creek Township have politically remained predominantly Republican. Precinct One voted 108 Republican and 61 Democrat while Precinct Two, which is the town of Russiaville, voted 133 Republican and 97 Democrat in the May 3, 1994 Primary. Voters Registration provided these figures.

Government

The Post Office in Russiaville was opened in 1848 or 1849, establishing it as the authorized post office. Today approximately 1600 families including four rural routes are provided mail service. Sue Herr is the current Postmaster; Pat Sipes, Clerk; Mail Carriers are Marji Bailey, Opal Wyrick, Gary Grice and Lewis Taylor. Others who have been Postmaster are: Bill Lewis, Dale Watson, Glen Newby and Sam Talbert.

Incorporation was the main concern of everyone as it was needed for federal aid in rebuilding properties and public facilities destroyed in the Palm Sunday tornado on April 11, 1965. Bill Martin, Eugene Waddell, Darrell Milburn, Glenn Bollinger and Milton Barkley formed a committee called Rebuilding of Russiaville, Inc. These men served as ex officio governors until the town was incorporated and town officials were elected. A petition for incorporation was filed with the Howard County Board of Commissioners on May 18, 1965. Russiaville became an incorporated town on Tuesday, July 20th, 1965. The town board election was held in August and those elected were: Ray Chandler, Jack Talbert, Robert Kirkendall, Lynvall Thomas, Mabel Hughes, Clerk; and Virgil Chandler, Town Judge. Services offered to residents were sanitary sewers, fire protection, street construction, maintenance and lighting, water works, stream pollution control, storm sewers, planning, zoning and subdivision. The town was divided into five wards and provided for a corporation limit of 275 acres. The budget was around $18,500, with a tax rate of $2.02 per $100 assessed evaluation. Attorney Robert J. Kinsey provided legal counsel for the rebuilding of Russiaville. Joseph J. Phillips wrote an article about the incorporation of Russiaville in the May 20, 1965 edition of the Kokomo Morning Times.

The current town officials are composed of a town council made up of five members: President, Leonard Pavey; Vice President, Sterling Johnson; Jack Waddell; Michael Deardorff and Donald Parvin. Clerk-Treasurer, Linda Downey; Executive Secretary of Planning Commission, Lee Eckert; Town Marshall, Roger Waddell; Deputy, Jon Zeck; Fire Chief, Isaac Hollingsworth; Volunteer Ambulance Service, Michael Reser. Robert Oilar is township trustee. There are 987 inhabitants within the town limits of Russiaville.

Disasters

Fires have taken their toll on the citizens of Honey Creek Township. In 1870, the flour mill burned and it was rebuilt by the citizens. A complete block of the business district was destroyed by fire in 1937, which merchants rebuilt. In 1942, the Methodist church was the next major fire. A beautiful new church was built on the same location. The Sign Co. located in the old skating rink burned in 1953, but the worst disaster of all was the Palm Sunday Tornado on April 11, 1965. At 7:35 p.m., three tornadoes ripped through the main business district leaving it in piles of rubble. Many homes were literally blown away while others were leveled to heaps of debris; few escaped the ravages of this storm. Three people were killed and many hospitalized, some in critical condition. Security measures were quickly enforced by local volunteers, State Police, Civil Defense, National Guard, State Highway Department and Air Police from Bunker Hill. American Red Cross volunteers and local citizens formed search parties to account for every person known to be a resident. The Lions Club community building was used to set up cots for those who had no place to go. The Salvation Army set up the kitchen, and Med-O-Bloom Dairy provided drinking water in sealed cartons and dry ice to preserve frozen foods. Indiana Bell set up a mobile communication system for local people to make and receive calls. Public Service had electric power reconnected in certain districts within hours. The community building located at the north edge of town was "The Business District." Russiaville's Postmaster, Glen Newby, continued postal service with townspeople picking up their mail and rural patrols having mail delivered. Government loan officers and insurance adjusters shared the space with the local business people: Howard Greenlee's Insurance, Jerry Hamilton's restaurant and Waddell's Grocery with Fay Myers as cashier. This was the rehabilitation center where residents were striving to recover from the shock of seeing nearly everything familiar destroyed in such a short time. Russiaville has since rebuilt its business

Water Tower

U.S. Post Office

district on Main and Union Streets. It is quite different from the old town but the spirit of the citizens remains as strong as their pioneer ancestors who didn't give up in hardship or adversity. Although dwellings and churches have been rebuilt, some lives have physical and emotional scars remaining. It has been twenty-nine years since that terrifying storm and for some families, lives were changed forever.

Earlier histories about Honey Creek township are in the History of Howard County by Jackson Morrow published in 1909 and Charles Blanchard's 1883 publication of Counties of Howard and Tipton, Indiana.

Jacqueline Taylor-Chasteen compiled this information from the sources already mentioned and numerous Russiaville and Honey Creek township residents. A special thank you to those who so graciously gave of their time in contributing to this project.

HOWARD TOWNSHIP

Howard Township is located in the north central part of Howard County. It is about six miles square with a notch in the southwest corner. It is bounded by Liberty Township on the east, Center and Taylor townships on the south, and Center and Clay townships on the west. Miami County lies along its northern edge.

Howard Township was originally part of Kokomo Township when the county was first organized as Richardville County in 1844. In 1846 Howard Township was created. Like the county, it was named in honor of Tilghman A. Howard, a distinguished lawyer, soldier, and politician from Tennessee. He had been the leader of the Indiana Democrats at the time of his death Aug. 16, 1844.

At the time of settlement most of Howard Township was covered with a dense hardwood forest. The pioneer farmers struggled to clear the trees and convert the forest to farmland. One story is told of how some early settlers kept a fire going for two years as they burned the logs they cut while clearing their land. By 1870 more than half the land had been cleared. Today the largest wooded area left in the county is the 100 acre Miller Woods located in Section 26, northwest of Vermont.

The north fork of Wildcat Creek provides the major drainage for the southern part of Howard Township just as it does for most of Howard County. In the mid-1950's the Wildcat Creek Reservoir was created with the construction of the dam along 400 East. This flooded parts of Sections 25, 26, 35, and 36 in southern Howard Township. The major part of the reservoir lies between 400 and 600 East and is encompassed by the Wildcat Creek Reservoir Park. The northern part of Howard Township is drained by the south fork of Deer Creek. This stream also drains much of Clay and Ervin Townships as it flows northwest toward the Wabash River.

The land in Howard Township is mostly level, but there are some parts that are gently rolling. Most of the soil is classified as the Crosby-Brookston type, except for the northeastern corner which is the Blount-Pewamo class. (Over fifty percent of the county's soil is in these two classifications.) There is a peat bog that lies in the south-central part of the township in sections 21, 22, and 23 that the early settlers called the "five mile slough" or the "prairie". This area was a wetland until the early settlers dug ditches to drain it. During a dry time in 1894-1895, this bog caught on fire and burned for 20 months. It burned from three to five feet deep and covered an area up to a quarter of a mile wide, and two miles long. This fire killed many of the area's remaining rattlesnakes.

A giant rock is located in the southwest quarter of Section 3 on what was once the Grinslade farm, now the Nancy Riley farm. This megalith stands about five feet tall, is eight feet across and twelve feet long. No one knows how much of it is buried in the earth, and it is presumed that it was deposited there centuries ago by the Wisconsin Glacier during the Ice Age. It has always been a curiosity, and early settlers reported that it was the site for Native American ceremonies. During the early part of this century, enough material was removed from the stone to construct foundations for two area barns. In the 1920s students from Howard School made trips to see the rock.

When the earliest settlers arrived in the 1840s, there were apparently only a few Native Americans living in Howard Township. They were mainly Miamis who lived in villages near Cassville and Vermont. The village at Cassville is reported to have been the largest native settlement in the county. A chief named Shap-pau-do-sho lived there, and another chief named Nip-po-wah headed the village near Vermont.

When the Miamis gave up the Miami Reserve to the U.S. Government under the Treaty at the Forks of the Wabash in 1840, they kept several small personal reservations. One of these was given to Chief Jean Baptiste Richardville, the successor to Little Turtle as head chief of the Miamis. It was referred to as "Float Section #7" and was located where the Wildcat Creek Reservoir is on both sides of 500 E. Chief Richardville died in 1841, and his heirs sold the reservation.

There were only about 200 Miamis left in Howard County when they were removed to Miami County, KS in the summer of 1848. The Native Americans who lived in Howard Township were a part of this migration. Benjamin Franklin Learner, an early resident, recalled that Chief Nip-po-wah and his followers visited the Learner home just prior to their removal to Kansas. Those who left the village near Cassville included a white female captive similar to Frances Slocum, who had lived with the Miamis for many years. In 1867 the 69 surviving Miamis were forced to move again to the Indian Territory, now Ottawa County, OK. Today their descendants are organized as the Miami Tribe of Oklahoma.

According to the county histories, the earliest known settler in Howard Township was a man named Kimball. He arrived with other settlers, (names unknown), in 1840 and lived with the Native Americans at Cassville for two years before moving on.

Others early settlers were:

1841: Jacob Good (See related information in the Family History Section.)

1842: Abner Garringer, Alexander Garringer, David Garringer, Isaac Garringer, Martin Smith, George Spitzenberger.

1843: Ephraim Bates, David Fawcett, Christian Loffer, Daniel Loffer, Simon L. Loffer, David Tyler, Frank Tyler, James Tyler, Joseph Tyler, Nathaniel Tyler.

1844: Wilson Brewer, ____ Dix, Bernhart Learner, John W. Lewis, Henry Loop, Martin V. Smith.

1845: James Bell, John G. Goyer, John Haas, William Stanley, Edmund Wright.

1846: Andrew Caldwell, James Caldwell, William Hutson, Thomas Ralston, Thompson Simmons, James Stevens, Rev. Jacob Stover.

1847: Carey Brown, Noah Carter, Smith Chambers, David Davis, Mahale Dorman, John Evans, Vespasian Goyer, Mrs. Kiser, Phineas W. Johnson, Samuel Lewis, John D. Lockridge, Larkin Meyers, George Stewart, Jacob G. Templin, Timothy Templin, David Truax, John Wright.

1848: Jacob Albright, Harrison Archer, Zephaniah W. Baker, James Bell, William Bradbury, Andrew Bray, W.J. Brewer, S.A.J. Brisey, William Brookbank, Michael Branson, John W. Clements, Samuel Coffman, Patrick Costlow, James Davidson, Charles Elliott, Alfred Farlow, Washington Garrell, Henry G. Hemper, Thomas Hill, John W. Jackson, Charles V. Justice, John Kane, Samuel King, O. Kiser, Caleb Lane, Newton Mills, William McCormick, Lewis Odom, Robert D. Palmer, Clerwell Pickett, George Rarey, John F. Russell, Peter Shook, Jesse Slider, William M. Stark, John Swift, John F. Tate, John Terrell, G. Tirey, Charles Thomas, W.W. Thompson, John Tribbett, Dennis Truax, Thomas Watkins, William Webb, Brinton Webster, W.B. Wilt.

1849: Jacob Brunk, William Lemaster, Jacob Shrock.

1850: See the listing at the end of this section for other heads of families in Howard Township who were enumerated in the 1850 Census.

The first election in Howard Township was held in 1848 at the residence of Carey Brown near 300 N and 300 E. The following officers were elected: Daniel Martin, Salathiel Good, and Timothy Templin, trustees; James Pollock, clerk; Whalen Todhunter, treasurer; Andrew Caldwell and Wesley Jackson, Justices of the Peace.

The first white child born within the present limits of Howard Township was John and Grace Kane's daughter, who was born in the spring of 1848.

Rev. Skillman performed the first marriage in 1847 uniting Larker North and Martha Dix.

David S. Farley built the first brick house in Howard Township in 1862. It is located at 3436 E. 100 N. Later it belonged to the Hunter and Obermeyer families. Keith and Judy Lausch are the current owners.

Salem Cemetery was the first burial ground in Howard Township. It is located on 350 E. north of 100 N. and is maintained by the township trustee. It was laid out by Bernhart Learner in 1848 and is named for the Salem United

Brethren Church, which stood across the road west of the cemetery from 1873 to 1963. The first burial was Catherine Bates in 1848. One hundred fifty-four names were recorded when the stones were read in 1968. The following surnames represent the majority of the burials: Bates, Bone, Crabtree, Fye, Goodwine, Goyer, Learner, Miller, Rarey, and West.

The Hopewell Cemetery is located near the spillway of the reservoir dam on 400 E. north of 50 N. It was named for the Hopewell Methodist Episcopal Church which stood nearby. (See the related article on the Hopewell Church.) Colescott, Lenington, Smith, Springer, Templin, and Trees are the major surnames represented. It is maintained by the township trustee.

Zion Cemetery is located at 400 N. and 500 E. next to Kokomo Zion United Methodist Church. The original cemetery lot was donated by Andrew J. Troyer, and it has been enlarged with subsequent additions. It is an active cemetery maintained by the church. Three hundred forty-seven names were recorded when the stones were read in the 1960s, and there have been additional burials since then. The following surnames represent a majority of the burials: Grau, Hochstedler/Hochstetler, Kennedy, Klingman, Kring, Lantz, Metz, Schafer, Shrock, and Troyer.

The Hutson Cemetery is located on the north side of 450 N. about one-tenth of a mile west of 200 E. It lies on what was the William Hutson farm in the 1870s. Thirty-six names were recorded when the stones were read in 1968. Many of the surnames were Caldwell, Evans, Hutson, and Townsend. The cemetery is maintained by the township trustee.

Although it lies on the north side of 600 N. at U.S. 31 in Miami County, the Cassville Cemetery belongs with Howard Township. Its two hundred seventy-four recorded burials are a roll call of the early inhabitants of the Cassville neighborhood. Some of the more numerous surnames are Caster, Cotterman, Cunningham, Davis, Grinslade, House, Lemaster, Moore, Richey, Russell, Smith, Snider/Snyder, Waisner, Weaver, and Winterrowd.

There are several other small cemeteries or burial sites in Howard Township. One lies on the north side of 400 N. across from the Kokomo Municipal Airport. It is north of Deer Creek and west of the David Schafer residence. When Mr. and Mrs. James Gorman recorded the cemetery in the 1960s, the stones had been broken and scattered about the pasture. The Gormans were able to identify the following names: Emily Batson, Jane Batson, ___ Batson, John Caldwell, Harriet Jackson, Anna Laboyteaux, Hannah Martin, ___ Martin, Alsa Watkins and Thomas W. Watkins.

Barbara, Salome, and Sidney F. Lantz are buried on the Samuel and Leah Miller farm on the south side of 400 N. at about 580 E. Access is through the farm lanes behind the Miller home and Variety Store.

Salome and Jacob Burkholder and a third person are buried on the Orem Hochstedler farm south of 600 N. at about 575 E. Access is from 600 N. south across a field.

Four members of the Martin family, early settlers in the Vermont neighborhood, were buried west of the present Hillsdale United Methodist Church parsonage at 4893 E. 100 N. Their unmarked graves lie in the parking area for the Wildcat Reservoir Park.

The Hopewell Methodist Episcopal Church (1845-1915) was located at 50 N. and 400 E. (See the related article in the Church Section.) Three-tenths of a mile west of this intersection lies the grave of Howard Township's famous Civil War horse. (See related article about Old Bob.)

The Hopewell neighborhood was the site of an early murder in Howard County. It was the result of a lovers' triangle involving James Brewer, Elijah Tyre, and a Miss Garringer. It seems that Brewer had courted Miss Garringer and promised to marry her when he returned from an extended trip. While he was away for a few months, Elijah Tyre convinced Miss Garringer to marry him instead. When Brewer returned, he and the new Mrs. Tyre resumed their previous relationship.

One night in 1849, while the couple was at David Garringer's cabin, Tyre and a group of his friends broke in and dragged Brewer outside. They took him a short distance east near the Hopewell Church and tied him to a tree. They beat him with switches until he was bloody. Although his assailants had blackened their faces for a disguise, Brewer still recognized them. He cursed them and vowed to kill all of them. In a fit of rage, Tyre suddenly took out his knife and stabbed Brewer in the heart, killing him. The others were horrified. They never intended to kill Brewer, only teach him a lesson.

The following day the bloody switches were found, but Brewer's body was gone. A search party was organized, but found nothing. The Justice of the Peace issued arrest warrants for various suspects, but they were not prosecuted due to lack of evidence. Most of the suspects left the area.

The case was never solved, although residents of the Hopewell community had their theories about what had happened. Many years later on his deathbed, Elijah Tyre confessed that Brewer had been put to death, but denied that he had killed him. Later on, shortly before his death, Daniel Rarey, a respected citizen of Howard Township, identified Tyre as the murderer. Rarey had been a suspect in the case, but had refused to participate in the attack. Brewer's remains were never found.

The Vermont Methodist Episcopal Church (1875-1900) was located on the present site of Hillsdale United Methodist Church at 4893 E. 100 N. This congregation was organized in 1875, because it was difficult to cross Wildcat Creek to get to the Hopewell Church during flood times. James Miller and Jacob Brunk donated the land for the brick church which was built for about $2,500. In 1877, there were about 30 members. This congregation died out after 1900, and the building was used as a school after the Vermont School burned.

Salem United Brethren Church began in 1848 when Rev. Jacob Stover organized six neighborhood couples as Salem Class. For two years they met at Stover's cabin. In 1850, the group moved to the Loffer School which was located just west of 3634 E. 100 N. The class met there for eight years and moved again in 1858 to the Loop School south of the bridge on 300 E.

After meeting in schools for 25 years, the congregation built a brick church north of 100 N. on 350 E. west of Salem Cemetery at a cost of $2,500. It was dedicated on Oct. 26, 1873 at Salem Church, United Brethren in Christ. The building was used for worship until the Salem and Bethany Churches merged to form Hillsdale in 1918. It stood for 90 years until it burned in 1963.

An interesting event took place at Salem Church in about 1880 when the annual meeting of the White River Conference of the United Brethren Church was held there. Bishop Milton Wright of Dayton, OH, attended the conference and brought along his teenage sons, Wilbur and Orville. While they were waiting for dinner to be served, the Wright brothers entertained themselves "flying" grasshoppers. They would catch the insects, hold them with two fingers, give them a flip, and watch them sail through the air. It was lots of fun, and the races were even interesting to the adults.

Years later, M.L. Garrigus, who had witnessed the grasshopper episode, wrote Wilbur Wright to inquire if he remembered the grasshoppers, and if the event had any bearing on their development of the first airplane. Wright replied that he did remember it, and that it gave him an idea.

Bethany United Brethren Church (1872-1918) was built on the David E. Smith farm on the northwest corner of 200 N. and 600 E. It was a small frame building set on piers. In 1898, the members of Bethany Church agreed to build a new frame church 32 ft. by 44 ft. with a 14 ft. ceiling. It would be adjacent to the old building and have a solid foundation. It was constructed between Sept. 12 and Nov. 15, 1898, at a cost of $982.04 and was dedicated debt-free on Dec. 18, 1898. The old church was sold for $65 and moved to become part of the residence at 6274 E. 100 N.

In 1919, after the Bethany and Salem congregations merged, the Bethany Church was torn down, and the materials were used to construct the present parsonage at Hillsdale.

Rich Valley Christian Church (1885-1962) was located at 500 N. and 300 E. where Rich Valley Mennonite Church is now. (See related article in the Church Section.)

The Cassville Christian Church had its beginning in 1845 when Laomi Ashley held a meeting at the Thomas Martindale cabin near Cassville and organized a society of the Christian or "New Light" Church. The group was reorganized in 1853 and met at the Martindale School until 1860 when they purchased a building site in Cassville. They constructed a frame building about 40 by 55 ft. at the cost of $1,500. This building was used for worship until 1866 when it was sold to the township for use as a school. A new 40 by 60 ft. frame church was built in about 1870. It is not known when this church ceased.

Cassville United Methodist Church was organized in 1849 as the Cassville Methodist Episcopal Church. Their first house of worship was constructed in 1856, and the present church dates from 1873. The present minister is Michael West and the membership is 66.

Kokomo Zion United Methodist Church is located at 400 N. and 500 E. It was organized in

1865 at the "Effengeleiche Geiminschaft" or Evangelical Church by the German-speaking residents of northeastern Howard Township. Part of the present house of worship dates from 1866, although the building has been remodeled several times. The most recent addition was completed in 1968.

The first parsonage was constructed in 1919 with bricks from the Holler School. It was razed in 1994 when a new parsonage was built. The present minister is Paul Wohlford, and the membership is 158.

Hillsdale United Methodist Church is located at 4893 E. 100 N. near 500 E. It began in 1918 when Salem and Bethany United Brethren Churches merged to form Hillsdale Chapel United Brethren Church. Subsequent mergers made it a part of the Evangelical United Brethren denomination in 1946 and the United Methodist Church in 1968. The present building dates from 1929 with an addition in 1965. The parsonage was built in 1919 with materials salvaged from the Bethany Church. The present minister is Jeff Newton, and the membership is 145.

The First General Baptist Church is located at 3017 E. 100 N. near 300 E. This congregation was organized in Kokomo in 1955, and they built their present building in 1967. Brad Swain is the current pastor, and there are 70 members.

Rich Valley Mennonite Church is located at 500 N. and 300 E. in the former Rich Valley Christian house of worship that dates from 1896. The Mennonites purchased it in 1962 when the Christian Church disbanded and have made two additions to the original structure. The founding group were members from the Howard-Miami Mennonite Church and a mission church in Kokomo. They are affiliated with the Sharing Concern Bible Conference. The present leadership includes Emanuel Hochstedler, bishop; Joel Stoll, deacon, and Marlin Beachy, minister. The membership is 40.

Bethany Fellowship Church is located at 500 N. and 500 E. on the site of the Holler School. The congregation organized in 1964, and they built their present house of worship in 1965. They are affiliated with the Beachy group of Amish-Mennonites. The church membership is 85, and the ministers are Ernest Graber, Ronald Graber, Marvin Beachy, and Enos Miller. The church operates Bethany Fellowship School at 5169 N. 600 E. for grades 1 to 12 with an enrollment of about 50. They celebrated the 25th anniversary of the school in 1994.

During the late 1840's and early 1850's there was a substantial migration of Amish from Holmes and Tuscarawas Counties, OH, to northeastern Howard County and southern Miami County. In about 1860 there was a division in this group with the progressives forming the Howard-Miami Mennonite Church and the conservatives maintaining the Old Order Amish. Also, several Amish joined the Zion Evangelical Church. Today there are many descendants of this group who still live in the area. Some of the more common surnames are Beachy, Bontrager, Gingerich, Herschberger, Hochstedler/Hochstetler, Mast, Miller, Troyer, and Yoder.

The Old Order Amish are divided into two church districts with the division at the Howard and Miami County line. Each district holds weekly meetings at a member's home and have preaching on alternate Sundays. Services are conducted in German. There are approximately 50 members in the south or Howard district. Marvin Otto is the bishop; Elmer Otto and Freeman Otto are ministers; and Lester Hochstedler is a deacon. In 1946 three Amish families totaling over 20 members left the Howard district and moved to Buchanan County in northeastern Iowa.

The village of Cassville is located on Deer Creek in the northwest corner of Howard Township in Section 6. It was laid out in 1848 by William and Nathan Stanley and first named Pleasant Springs. In 1854 it was changed to Cassville in honor of Lewis Cass, a U.S. Senator from Michigan for whom Cass County was named. Cassville quickly became a shipping point on the newly-built Indianapolis, Peru, and Chicago Railroad. By 1860 it had two churches, I.O.O.F. lodge, two general stores, grocery, flour mill, two saw mills, hotel, tannery, and varied trades and professions. The population was 125.

By 1883 Cassville had declined to a dozen houses, two churches, and a school. Its population was 90. The businesses had all disappeared possibly due to the proximity of Kokomo, Miami, and Bunker Hill. Twenty-two postmasters served Cassville from 1848 until the post office closed in 1906.

Today Cassville continues to be a small residential community with only two businesses, the Cassville Market, Inc., located at 5582 N. 00 EW. and the County Line Restaurant.

Vermont was laid out in 1849 by Milton Hadley. It was located in Section 25 on the north side of Wildcat Creek near the intersection of 100 N. and 500 E. Charley Ellison, an early resident, operated a grocery and saloon. The saloon attracted the rough characters from the surrounding area, and Vermont developed a bad reputation. Benjamin Jackson, John Colescott, Charles Lindley, and James Miller were subsequent store owners prior to 1900. Joshua Galloway operated a blacksmith shop and tannery. Some thought Vermont had a chance of becoming the county seat, but this was not to be.

When the Toledo, Delphos, and St. Louis Narrow Gauge Railroad was completed in 1880, the original site of Vermont was abandoned in favor of the new rail station a short distance north. Vermont had a post office from 1849 to 1856 and again from 1882 to 1904. Roy Gates ran the post office and store for many years. In 1883 there was a grain business operated by Russell, Dolman and Company of Kokomo. Later there was a farmers' co-op. This operation was replaced in about 1925 by Charles Kurtz's Vermont Coal and Feed Store. He sold coal, feed, tools and seeds. He also bought and sold cattle and hogs. He operated the business until the 1940s when he sold it to Gerald Shirar. Today Vermont consists of one house and the Vermont Feed and Grain Company.

The Vermont covered bridge was located where the present bridge spans the Wildcat Creek Reservoir on 500 E. The Smith Bridge Company of Toledo, OH, contracted for the bridge in 1874 and constructed it in

Katie Lee Collier, Scott Hutchison, and Marilyn G. Holt walking through the Vermont Covered Bridge in 1950.

1875. Residents of the Vermont community built the stone abutments and hauled all the materials from Kokomo to the site. The 95 foot span was guaranteed to sustain a rolling weight of 5,600 pounds per linear foot. Its total cost was $991.62.

In 1957, when the reservoir was under construction, the Howard County Historical Society and the Kokomo Lions Club led the fight to save this last covered bridge in the county. Many individuals and groups donated to a special fund to pay the costs of moving it to Highland Park in Kokomo where it now spans Kokomo Creek.

For more than 20 years after Howard Township was organized, there were no gravel or hard-surfaced roads. Dirt roads were kept up by a road supervisor who was paid $1.50 a day for 45 days during the year. Howard Township was divided into road districts, and all able-bodied men between 21 and 50 years were required to work on the roads from two to four days every year. Their major activities were filling mud holes and repairing bridges.

The need for better roads resulted in the construction of several gravel toll roads beginning in the 1860s. Two of these roads crossed the southern part of Howard Township. The first was the Kokomo, Greentown, and Jerome Gravel Road or Pike which followed the present route of 100 N. (Sycamore Road) east from Kokomo to Greentown and then angled to Jerome. This 12 mile road was begun in 1869 and was finished in 1871, at a cost of $38,000.

The second toll road was the Kokomo and Greentown Gravel Road or Pike which began at a toll gate at Union Street and Vaile Avenue in Kokomo and followed the present route of 50 N. (Waterworks Road). This road ran eight and two-thirds mile east and joined the Kokomo, Greentown, and Jerome Gravel Road at the west edge of Greentown. It was completed in 1874 at a cost of $23,218.

These toll roads were built by private companies with investors' capital. The leading promoters of these roads were the people who lived near them, the ones who would benefit most from their improvements. By 1900, the toll roads were taken over and maintained by the county, toll-free.

The Strawtown Pike crossed the eastern portion of Howard Township on its way from Strawtown on the White River to Peru on the Wabash River. This was a main north-south road that crossed Wildcat Creek at the Vermont Bridge on 500 E.

The Peter Touby Pike, which snakes its way across Howard Township from southwest to northeast, was constructed in 1882 at a cost of $28,860. It was an eight mile gravel road engineered by Michael McGlynn, a pioneer road builder. He came to the U.S. in 1848 from Ireland and eventually brought his construction skills to Kokomo in 1861.

Howard Township's dirt roads were improved beginning in 1907 when the state legislature passed the three mile gravel road law. Under this act any road under three miles in length could be improved by a petition of fifty freeholders. Much of the gravel for such improvements came from Lantz's Pit located at 3527 N. 500 E. It is now known as Arrowhead Springs Water and Recreation Park, operated by Steve and Lynn Lantz.

Prairie School which was closed in 1916 was located at 300 E & 300 N.

Rich Valley School which was closed in 1916 was located at 300 E & 500 N.

In the early 1900's a half mile of concrete roadway was built on 400 E. north of Wildcat Creek Bridge. Prior to this time the road washed out each time the creek flooded. A similar road was constructed at Jerome.

Two major highways form the western and southern borders of Howard Township. U.S. 31, once known as the Range Line Road, follows the western boundary of the township. It was paved between 1920 and 1929. U.S. 35/Indiana 22 follows the southern boundary and was also constructed during the 1920's.

The Indiana Railway and Light Company built an interurban line along the south side of U.S. 35/Indiana 22 from Kokomo to Marion. The line was opened to Greentown in 1903, and extended to Marion in 1905. The Indiana Union Traction Company operated another interurban north from Kokomo through Cassville. The last cars ran from Kokomo in 1938.

The first railroad in Howard County was the Indianapolis, Peru, and Chicago line that reached Kokomo in 1853. It was extended along the western border of Howard Township to Peru in 1854, passing through Cassville. This village soon became a key center where farmers shipped their grain and livestock to Indianapolis or Chicago.

At its peak there were four passenger trains a day each way, but the development of the interurbans and automobiles caused the railroads to decline. Through the years this line has been a part of the Wabash, Lake Erie and Western, New York Central, Nickel Plate, Norfolk and Western, and Norfolk and Southern systems.

A second railroad crossed the southern part of Howard Township east-to-west. It was constructed in 1880-1881 as the Toledo, Delphos & St. Louis Railroad. It was a narrow gauge track that joined with the Frankfort & Kokomo Railroad to connect St. Louis and Toledo. One Sunday in 1887, the entire 400 miles of rails were shifted to make it standard gauge. This line was subsequently known as the Cloverleaf, Nickel Plate, Norfolk & Western, and Norfolk & Southern Railroad.

For about 30 years around the turn of the century, Vermont was a station on this line with passenger, freight, and mail service. By 1941 the Nickel Plate Railroad discontinued its passenger trains and stopped carrying Kokomo's mail. Today it still carries grain shipments from Vermont Feed and Grain Company.

The Kokomo Municipal Airport occupies most of Section 15 east of Howard School. It got its start in 1941 when the U.S. Government was looking for sites on which to build auxiliary flying fields. Air-minded Kokomo civic leaders obtained the Shockley farm and adjacent land totaling 360 acres and offered it to the city and U.S. Government for an airfield.

With the establishment of the Bunker Hill Naval Air Training Station, now Grissom Air Force Base, the Municipal Airport was taken over by the Navy as an auxiliary field. After World War II, it was returned to the city of Kokomo.

In 1974 the airport was expanded to 427 acres, and the runways were lengthened. They were resurfaced in 1977.

Various airlines have provided Kokomo with passenger, freight, and mail service through the years. Among them are Turner, Delta, North Central, Lake Central, Allegheny, Air Wisconsin, Sky Stream, and Direct Air, Inc. There has been no air service since 1988. Ron Gilbert has been the airport manager since 1981.

Just north of the airport lies what was known as the Ko-San Farm. In 1933 Carl Broo and Max Gerber, president of Kokomo Sanitary Pottery, began raising and training standardbred harness racing stock there. They started with one horse and gradually increased their herd to 18 by 1950. They raced the county fair circuit for several years. One of their best known horses was Ko-San-P.

The first school in Howard Township was taught by Salathiel Good during 1845-1846 in a cabin on the northeast corner of Bernhart Learner's farm. This was a subscription school for three months with about 15 students.

A second log school was built in about 1848 on Christian Loffer's farm in Section 27. Among the early teachers there were Salathiel Good, Anna Gordon, and Harriet Smith.

In 1850 a school was built on David Smith's farm where the Wildcat Creek Reservoir is now located. About the same time Isaiah Roberts taught school in Section 16 south of Cassville.

The first public school was built in 1854 on Timothy Templin's farm in Section 35. Salathiel Good was the first teacher, followed by C. Pettijohn, Thomas Armstrong, and Richard Templin. Other early teachers were David Evans, Daniel Martin, Warren Truax, Isaac Whittaker, Joseph Dixon, and William Styer.

In 1885 the old school districts were abandoned and Howard Township was divided into eight districts. Eight new brick one-room schools replaced the old log schools. Later one district was eliminated, and its students were transported to the Cassville School by a school hack. The other district schools included Rich Valley located on the northwest corner of 500 N. and 300 E. across the road from the Rich Valley Church; Prairie School located where the Lloyd Bontrager residence now stands at 2969 N. 300 E.; Brown School located on the southwest corner of 300 N. and 500 E. near the Dan Taflinger residence; Holler School located on the southeast corner of 500 N. and 500 E. where the Bethany Fellowship Church is located; Vermont School located on the west side of 500 E. south of 100 N. near the reservoir; and the Loop School located on the west side of 300 E. south of Wildcat Creek. All of these schools have been torn down.

In 1912 a movement was started to centralize the schools into one graded and high school, but the plan was temporarily defeated in the courts. At that time there was no high school in the township. If students wanted to continue their education beyond 8th grade, they had to go to Kokomo High School or somewhere else.

Howard Township finally did agree to consolidate its one-room schools into a central building for grades one to twelve. The new school was built in 1916-1917 at a cost of $40,000. It was dedicated on Oct. 18, 1917. (See related information in the School Section.)

According to the 1850 census, Howard Township had 636 inhabitants in 114 dwellings on 79 farms. By 1990 it had grown to a population of 2,694. The 1994 plat of the township lists approximately 240 landowners who own 10 or more acres.

For over 100 years, Howard Township remained agricultural, but during the last 30 years, there has been much residential growth. This is probably due to its nearness to Kokomo and highways 22, 31, and 35. Several subdivi-

Howard Township School about 1920.

Howard Township Basketball Team in 1924. (l. to r.) Back: Claude Byrd, Noel Underwood, Franklin Van Sickle, John Troyer, and Coach Cecil Webb. Front: Paul Mast, John Rinehart, Albert Sommers, and Edwin Riley.

sions have been added or are currently being developed. The two largests additions are Hillsdale and Hillcrest, located on 100 N. in sections 27 and 28. Other subdivisions include Lone Star at 00 NS and 400 E; Sonesta Shores on 50 N. between 500 and 600 E; Ruhl Gardens on 400 E. south of 00 NS; Brookhaven on 100 N. across from Hillsdale; Ceramic south of Cassville; Harper at 600 E. and 00 NS; Abston Acres on 400 E. between 50 N. and 100 N; Eastgate on 50 N. west of 300 E; Hopewell east of 400 E. on 50 N; and Rangeline at U.S. 31 and 35 at 400 N.

Early Homes of Howard Township

A measure of prosperity and the necessity for more living space for growing families created something of a building boom as landowners began to replace their original log cabins with larger, more comfortable dwellings. Brick making industries in the area made this building material available, along with the abundance of native hardwoods.

Several of these sturdy historic homes are located in Howard Township and are lovingly cared for by their present owners. Located on East Sycamore Road (100 N) as it winds its way along the Kokomo Reservoir where the Wildcat Creek once meandered along its course are some of the finest old homes in Howard County.

Built of brick made on the farm, the 1862 home of David S. Farley was the first brick house in the township. Located at 3524 E. 100 N, it is now owned by Keith and Judy Lausch. There have been several modifications made throughout the years.

The James Miller house, also thought to have been built about 1862, is located at 4758 E. 100 N. It is believed that Mr. Miller, farmer and tile factory proprietor, made the bricks for several of the large brick homes in this area. Now owned and carefully maintained by Gordon and Dianna Dell, this lovely old home stands like a sentinel among others as much as 100 years younger. Its original shutters and the scrolled canopy above the entrance are still in place. The surrounding walkway includes many "Kokomo" brick.

Across from the entrance to Wildcat Creek Reservoir Park on what was once known as the "Float Section" is the original home of David Smith. It was at this location that the Vermont Covered Bridge spanned the Wildcat Creek. The 1877 atlas records that the first crop of corn in the township was grown on this farm by Jacob Good in about 1842. The home is now owned by John Christenson. The portico and shutters have been removed from the square brick structure, otherwise it looks essentially as it did many years ago.

The original Jacob Brunk home, later acquired by the James Miller family, and for many years known as the Miller home, is located at 5130 E. 100 N. It is now owned by Bob and Betty Mickelson who have restored it with true sensitivity. The date is uncertain, but it too was probably built in the 1860s. It was first a frame house with the brick being added later. The spacious L-shaped porch was added sometime after the house was built. Recent modernization includes an attached garage at the rear of the house. The grounds are beautifully landscaped. Passers-by cannot help but notice the Mail Pouch Tobacco advertising sign authentically copied on the barn, certainly reminiscent of by-gone days.

The Willits-Kurtz home at 5859 E. 100 N. was built in 1865 for the C.C. Willits family. The farmland, part of which was deeded to Chief Richardville of the Miami Indians, was bought in 1853. Designated a "Hoosier Homestead" by the State of Indiana, it has been kept in the family for well over 100 years. The large square frame dwelling with back extension features an interesting two-door front entrance. There is no central hall; each door opens into separate rooms at the front of the house. Lester T. Kurtz, great-grandson of C.C. Willits, is the present owner of the house and the farmland situated on the south side of the road. Michael Jackson, great-great grandson of C.C. Willits, owns the farmland lying on the north side of the road.

The Markland-Hullinger home, built in 1880, is located at 5532 E. 200 N. The square brick structure features a back extension with side door entrance. The front door opens directly into the living room. The exterior of the house is essentially unchanged from its original appearance except for a sunroom which was recently added on the east side. The home and grounds are beautifully cared for by Ned and Joan Hullinger who bought the farm from the Marklands in 1970, after having lived there and farmed the ground since 1943.

Early settlers in the northern section of Howard Township soon recognized the need for a main route into Kokomo. Thus they banded together in the construction of what became known as the Touby Pike, taking its name from pioneer Peter Touby who was instrumental in its building. Its many twists and turns reflected the necessity to follow the higher ground in what was in those days a very swampy area.

One of the outstanding homes along this route was that of James Caldwell. Constructed of double and triple thick red brick walls, it certainly speaks of strength and stability. In 1912 Thomas W. Underwood purchased the farm and made several changes and additions to the house before his family moved there in about 1915. Other modernizations followed through the years. The home is now owned by the Underwoods' grandson, Ronald Schafer. Recent exterior decorating has given much of the home a warm Victorian charm.

As the Touby Pike reaches 400 N., it turns more directly eastward. At 250 E. at the site of the old flowing well, the Yager-Smith family home can be seen back the lane. An interesting feature of this house is the central hall with its curving stairway. The house is now owned by Barry Kratzer.

North of the Touby Pike at 2315 E. 500 N. stands the large frame dwelling built by Albert C. Touby. Built in 1898 of lumber from the farm, it is finished with beautiful golden oak interior woodwork. For many years it was the home of the Emmett P. Touby family. In 1976 the farm was sold to the Stites family, and it is now the residence of Ronald and Mary Stites. Some modifications were made; however, it still retains a quiet dignity.

At 300 E., 400 N. the Touby Pike straightens its course past the Kokomo Airport. Across the road and back the lane on the north is the David Schafer residence at 3644 E. The ownership of this farm has changed several times, having for a time been held by Kokomo industrialist Max Gerber who made some changes and additions to the house.

Turning north at 450 E., the road borders farms still kept in the families of early pioneers Troyer and Metz. The Metz-Schafer house at 4141 E. 500 N. was built in 1894, replacing a log cabin. It is now the home of Orval and Sharon Schafer-Gingerich.

Just beyond 500 N. on 450 E. is the large brick Yoder-Helmuth home. Acquired by Joseph J. Helmuth in 1906, it has been beautifully maintained through the years. Farmed by J.J. Helmuth's son Dewey for many years, it is now the home of Dewey and Mildred Helmuth's daughter, Mary Lou and her husband, Ronald Rich.

There are, of course, other historic homes in the area. Many turn-of-the century farm homes were built, replacing original log structures. Several of these would have historic interest, although many have been extensively remodeled and updated to make them more functional for the owners' lifestyles. All homes speak of their own time and place in the history and development of the area. Submitted by Virginia Coan

Union School #4 (1883-1906) located in Howard Township at SE corner of Section 7 on county roads 400 N - 100 E. Elias Locke was the landowner since the early 1870s and the house has remained in the family. Union School No. 4 was remodeled into a home soon after its closing. Great-great-great-grandson, Clay R. Silence, now resides there. The building as a school can be seen in the photo on the left around 1903. The right photo shows the building as a house in 1994.

Businesses and Organizations located in Howard Township

ADI Screen Printing
4758 E. 00 NS

Arrowhead Springs Water & Recreation Park
3527 N. 500 E.

Bill's Flea Market
00 NS near 200 E.

Bontrager Excavating
2229 E. 250 N.

Carter Lumber Company
4292 N. 00 EW

Carter Plumbing, Electric & Heating
4316 N. 00 EW

Cassville Market
5582 N. 00 EW

County Line Restaurant
00 EW near 600 N.

Hazzitall Quilts
3557 E. 00 NS

H & H Plastering and Supplies, Inc.
3301 Apperson Way N.

Howell Motors, Inc.
5084 E. 00 NS

J&J Signs
904 E. Smith Rd.

Kocolene Oil Corp. Service Station
4204 N. 00 EW

Kokomo Municipal Airport
3637 E. 400 N.

Kokomo Quarter Midget Club
350 E. & 150 N.

Kokomo Shrine Club, Inc.
5518 E. Markland Ave.

Koko Motel
4112 N. 00 EW

Lilly Building Supply
4562 E. 00 NS

Miller's Variety Store
400 N. near 600 E.

Panda Vans, Inc.
St. Rd 19 at Highway 22/35

Price Auto Sales
2016 E. 00 NS

Schlabach Construction Co.
5337 E. 250 N.

Tate Model and Engineering
300 N. at Apperson Way North

Vermont Feed and Grain, Inc.
1471 N. 500 E.

Wagler Corporation
2660 N. 300 E.

Wickes Lumber
U.S. 31 Bypass North

1850 Howard Township Census

(Heads of families and names of persons with different surnames residing in the household)

Antrim, William
Archer, Washington
Baker, Zephaniah W.
Bates, Ephriam
Bates, John
Batson, Nathaniel
Batson, Thomas
Bell, James
Belt, Joshua
Bickle, Aaron
Bogue, Samuel
Bradbury, William
Branson, Joseph
Branson, Michael
Brewer, Henry
Brewer, Lorenzo
Brewer, Wilson
Brown, Carey
Brunson, Sylvester
Burns, Hugh
Caldwell, Andrew P.
Caldwell, James
Calvin, Hiram
Carter, Adam
Carter, Noah
Davidson, James
Edmonds, Clarrissa
Elliott, James P.
Evans, David
Evans, John
Farlow, Alfred
Faulkinraugh, George
Garinger, Absolum
Garinger, Alexander
Garinger, David
Garinger, Elizabeth
Garinger, Isaac
Garinger, John
Good, Jacob
Good, Salathiel
Gosnol (Garrell), Washington
Haas, David
Haas, John
Hadley, Milton
Harley, Angelina
Harley, Joshua
Hemper, Henry
Henderson, William
Holler, Daniel
Huffman, Nancy J.
Jackson, Benjamin
Jackson, Harriet
Jackson, Jane
Jackson, John W.
James, David
Jaons, Milton
Jewell, Milley
Justice, William
Kain, John
Kenner, Regina
Lemasters, Isaac
Lane, Caleb
Laughlin, Daniel
Layton, Sarah
Learner, Barnhart
Lellington, John
Lewis, George
Lewis, Samuel
Liepler, Nancy
Lindley, Charles
Lockridge, Andrew
Lockridge, John D.
Loffer, Christian
Loffer, Simon
Luckey, James
Mallet, Martha
Mallet, Westley
Martin, Daniel
Martin, John
Martin, Shepherd
Martin, William
Martindale, Samuel
Mash, James
Miller, Absolem
Miller, John J.
Moon, James
Moon, Jesse
Moon, Solomon
McCormick, William
Oakley, John
Odim, David
Odim, John
Odim, W.G.
Palmer, Robert
Poisel, Abner
Polock, James
Polock, James
Rani, Daniel
Ring, Samuel
Rizer, Okey
Roberts, Josiah M.
Rolston, Thomas
Simmons, Thompson
Smith, Reuben
Snider, Barbara
Spear, Robert
Spunce, Enoch
Stafford, Charles
Stanley, Nathan
Stanley, William
Starks, William
Stephens, James
Steward, Henry
Stover, Jacob
Tate, John
Templin, Timothy
Terral, John
Tharp, Esaes
Thrailkill, Dorsin
Thrailkill, Mary
Tierce, Christian
Truax, David
Truax, James M.
Tyler, Nathaniel
Tyre, John
Walter, Ambrose
Watkins, Amanda
Watkins, Thomas
Webb, James
Wibel, Elizabeth
Wibel, Levi
Williams, Ansen J.
Williams, Arthur
Winterode, J.D.
Wood, William
Wordyke, John
Wright, Edward
Wright, Josiah
Wright, William

The 1850 Howard Township Census lists 635 total inhabitants living in 114 dwellings on 79 farms.

Howard Township Landowners in 1877

Landowners and section locations as shown on the map on page 57 of the Kingman Brothers Atlas of Howard County, IN.

Adair & Butler, 18
Alexander, J.C., 4
Babylon, E., 15
Bacon, William (estate), 34
Barnes, William W., 14, 15, 22
Beck, W.E., 17
Belt, J., 9, 10
Brimey, J., 6
Brown, A.W., 23
Brown, O.H., 15
Brown, W.M., 17
Brunk, Jacob, 25, 36
Brunomiller, B., 25
Burkholder, J., 1
Burton, W.R., 28
Butler & Adair, 18
Caldwell, A., 3
Caldwell, J.S., 17, 18
Carter, J. (estate), 36
Carter, L., 36
Carter, Noah, 36
Carter, N.U., 2
Caster, L., 6
Cemer, A., 25
Champ, E., 11
Christner, P., 2
Clark, J.S., 23
Colscott, W., 28
Conkle, G.S., 10
Cook, H.C., 25
Cooper, W.B., 35
Costlow, P., 33
Crabtree, E., 16
Crilley, M., 33
Crousore, J., 33
Crumley, J.C., 10, 15, 16
Cunningham, J., (estate), 5
Curlee, J.R., 28
Davis, A., 18
Davis, B., 17
Davis, H.C., 17
Davis, H.H., 16
Davis, L., 18
Dehaven, J.W., 24
Dorman, L.V., 28
Dorman, M. (estate), 28
Dorsey, J., 23
Dotter, J. (estate), 2, 10
Drinkwater, W.W., 22
Elliott, A.M., 15
Ellis, R.B., 21
Endrues, W., 3
Fahl, J., 10
Farley, D.S., 17
Fawcett, D., 28
Fisher, L., 11
Forsythe, L., 17
Frakes, T., 27
Frazee, W.S., 24, 22
Frazier, J., 15, 22
Funk, W., 28
Gallison, J., 24
Garber, J., 2

Garringer, J., 22
Glidden, J.W., 22
Goodwin, J., 28
Goodwine, C.P., 22
Goyer, C., 33
Goyer, J.G., 22
Goyer, V., 33
Grau, J.A., 14
Grinslade, T., 3
Hardin, E.A., 5
Hardin, T., 5
Headley, E., 18
Headley, W.B., 18
Heagy, H., 9
Hempster, H.G., 22, 27
Henderson, W., 7
Henderson, W.N., 6
Hill, J.L., 17
Hochstedler, Zach, 2
Hocker, G.W., 9, 10
Hullinger, L., 14
Hutson, W., 3, 7, 8, 17
Jackson, C.A., 36
Jackson, C.S., 3
Jackson, E., 3, 36
Johnson & Murphy, 21
Johnson, I.C., 6
Johnson, P., 13
Jones, W.S., 10
Karr, K.A., 28
Keyton, G., 34
Kritzer, L., 2, 3
Kuhns, D., 3
Lamb, H., 24
Learner, B., 26, 35
Learner, J.W., 26
Lemaster, William, 6
Lenington, J.T., 24
Lindley, J., 25, 36
Locke, E., 28
Maher, T., 23
Markland, D., 24
Marquis, J.G., et al, 17
Marshall, E., 15
Marshall, J., 13
Martin, D., 27
Martin, M., 21
Martindale, D., 6
Martindale, J.L., 6
McClelland, W., 25
McGraw, J.H., 7
Medlan, J., 22
Medlin, N.A., 13
Mence, S.W., 8
Metz, H., 2, 11
Miller, J., 26
Miller, J.M., 13
Mishler, B., 1, 12
Moore, J.C., 7
Murphy & Johnson, 21
Murray, J.A., 33
Myers, M., 9
Neall, F.C., 6

Nevergall, H., 24
Nixon, R., 25
Norton, C.B., 4
Oakley, J.M. estate, 23
Odon, L. et al, 15
Odon, L.W., 12
Owings, N.J., 27, 34
Pursley, J. estate, 3
Pyke, J.W., 15, 22
Ramey, R., 21
Randall, D., 27
Rankin & Weaver, 4, 5
Rarey, D., 23
Reeder, J.M., 7
Reem, J., 13
Rhoda, G., 3
Rhodes, J., 21
Ricketts, F., 28
Ricketts, M., 23, 24
Riggs, W., 35
Riley, W.H., 3, 4
Roberts, H.C., 21
Ross, C., 35
Roth, J., 15
Sale, W.S., 35
Sceary, E., 28
Shirk, E.H., 21
Shockley, E., 16
Shrader, S., 28
Shrock, E., 12
Shrock, J., 14
Shumacker, J., (estate), 1, 12
Sipee, A., 11
Smith, D., 24, 26, 35, 36
Smith, F.M., 25
Smith, M., (estate), 6
Smith, W.E., 27
Stevens, S., 36
Stewart, G., 13
Stewart, J.C., 7
Studabaker, W., 1

Swartz, S., 5
Tate, George D., 33
Teagardin, A., 34
Templin, J.G., 35
Templin, T., 35
Trick, J.C., 18
Troyer, A., 13
Troyer, A.B., 10, 11
Troyer, A.E., 12
Troyer, E.R., 11
Troyer, J.E., 14
Troyer, N., 2
Touby, A.C., 9
Touby, P., 8, 9, 16, 17
Truax, David, 6
Truax, E., 6
Tyler, D.A., 27
Tyler, J.W., 22, 25
Tyler, S.W., 28
Tyre, O., 13, 22, 24
Vanlue, W., 23
Waddle, M., 28
Waisner, S., 5
Waldrick, F., 28
Weakley, M.F., 17
Weaver, Daniel, 11
Weaver & Rankin, 4, 5
Weisenberger, G., 12
Welsh, Erastus, 33
White, J.W. (estate), 15
Wible, L., 1
Wilkinson, B.F., 24
Willits, C.C., 25, 36
Winterrowd, J.D., 8
Winterrowd, M.C., 7
Wise, S.P., 24
Wise, W.A., 23
Wright, E., 9
Yeager, J.C., 9, 16
Yoder, C.C., 2, 3
Young, A., 18

History of Howard Township submitted by Ed Riley.

JACKSON TOWNSHIP

Jackson Township, when first formed in December 1846, extended from range line No. 4 east to Grant County on the east, and from Miami County on the north to the township line No. 23, eight miles long by six miles wide. In the original division into townships, June 17, 1844, it formed a part of Green Township, in Richardville County. At the December term 1846, of Commissioner's Court, Green Township was divided east and west, making the Congressional Township Line between Townships 23 and 24 north. At the March 1853 meeting of the Board of Commissioners of Howard County, upon the petition of citizens of Green and Jackson Townships, the townships were divided as at present, so as to make three townships. These were named respectively Liberty, Union and Jackson and so they still remain. Jackson Township thus contains 24 squares, six miles north and south by four miles east and west.

The soil is a deep, black loam, very fertile and well adapted for general farming purposes, producing in abundance all the grain and fruit indigenous to northern Indiana. There are two main waterways in the township, Deer Creek and Pipe Creek. Deer Creek is also called Honey Creek and Sugar Creek in the 1986 Platbook of Jackson Township. Jackson Township is noted for its vast forests of good timber: walnut, poplar, ash, linden, oak, hickory, elm, maple, sugar and beech. Much of it was destroyed in clearing, and many millions of feet of lumber have been shipped away.

The township was settled from the north side and the south, in two separate settlements, which were separated by the very wet land in the center. Jackson was settled much later than any other township. Among the early settlers, in the northeastern part, were William Ebright, William Taylor, W.W. Braden, Ezra Reynolds, Samuel Darby, Joseph Hockett, Ziba Marine, David Stanfield, R. Shinn, Stephen Peters, Frank Shinn, Hugh Means, Abram Wrightsman, Turner Sullivan, William Braden, William Detamore, Asa Marine, Thomas Kirker, Solomon Burris, Henry Parker, Graner Bryant, Samuel H. Riggs, Thomas Addington, Thomas Darby, Ham Miller, Calvin Miller, Meredith Maple, John Sullivan, Lemuel Powell, John Powell, John Clellan, James Hollingshead, John Cook, Caleb and George Linsicum.

In the south side of the township, the early settlers were John S. Garrigus, William Hatfield, Jonathan Wright, William Golding, R. Turner, Painter S. Maxwell, John McCormick, Abraham Davis, John McCormack, Daniel Cate, William B. Morris, Jonathan Reeder, Smith, Todd, Isaac & Thomas Jesiop, Casky, Brunk, Fleek, James Hogland, Andrew Hart, Andrew Bates, William Miller, Valentine Somers, Joseph Bates, Eugene Brown, Asa Gossett, Alexander Rhea, Horace Somers, George Cruthird, Squire Clevenger and P.W. Gossett.

Jackson Twp. had Indian villages on both Little Pipe Creek and Honey Creek. Members of the Miami tribe lingered in the township several years after the whites established homes here.

Looking ready for action, the Sycamore Athletics of 1910, a professional baseball team, paused to pose for photographer. (l. to r.) Front: Curt Scherer, Ray Moss, unidentified and Ray Bond. Second row: Arthur Cranor, George Ball and Guy Pickett. Standing: Glen Harper, Tolly Spurgeon, Howard Harper, "Pop" Jones, Clarence Kessner.

Sycamore School

Jackson Township in 1850 had 584 inhabitants. The high point in population was reached in 1894 when the census showed 1,387. The 1920 census gave the township's population as 771.

The earliest death in the township of which there is any record was that of the wife of Stokes Maxwell, which occurred in 1850. It is thought that the first birth also occurred in this family; Riley Maxwell was born in 1848, a few months after his parents settled in the township.

The township was named in honor of Andrew Jackson. He was the first President to be elected from what was then considered the western part of the United States.

Sycamore

The little town of Sycamore is the only town in Jackson Twp. It was founded in the year 1881 by O.P. Hollingsworth. It was called Sycamore because a two-trunk sycamore tree stood in the center of the two main streets. The first post office was established May 23, 1881 with Frank T. Hoover as postmaster. The office was discontinued on Oct. 9, 1912. The immediate growth of the town was from the narrow-gauge Norfolk and Western Railroad completed in 1881. At that time there were four general stores, one drug store, one blacksmith shop, a saw mill, stave factory and warehouse, and a population

First and second grade of Jackson Township School in 1937 with teacher Martha McIlwain. (l. to r.) Front: Paul Hainlen, Jr., Dewayne Moorman, Eugene Schaaf, Billy Hochstedler, and Tom Harper. Middle: Jim Summers, Ruth Rennaker Young, Vivian Achor White, Mary Moorman Buroker, Ruth Moss Roach, unidentified, Sue Hullinger Summers, and Delores Rust. Back: Mildred Middlesworth Clevanger, Eloise Powell Newhouse, Phyllis Rogers Prickett, Dan Cranor, Meda Froflich Osborne, Martha Jean Pyke Lavengood, and Wilberta Riggs.

Jackson Township School

of 100. At one time there were two grade schools at Sycamore. The schools were closed in 1922 when the Jackson Twp. School was completed and used for all grades. 1922 was also the last year that a horse drawn school bus (hack) was used. In 1924 Paul Kendall purchased a general store from Claude Ellis. Paul and his wife, Velma, operated this general store until 1965 when it finally closed its doors. His merchandise included groceries, meats, ice cream, hardware, farm supplies, patent medicines for humans and livestock, clothing, gasoline, oil and lots more. He also operated a school bus taking children to Jackson Twp. School. It was one of the last businesses in Sycamore. From 1903 until the early 1930s the interurban line ran through the south end of Jackson Twp., stopping at Sycamore for freight and passengers. Residents would ride their buggies to Sycamore, and take the train to shop in Kokomo, Marion or Frankfort. In November of 1943 a fire destroyed the Sycamore Farm Bureau Elevator. The elevator was known as the C.C. Currens Elevator, before being purchased by the Farm Bureau organization. It was rebuilt by 1945 and operated by Farm Bureau until 1978 when it was purchased by Mr. Ortman. It is now owned by Kokomo Grain and is used for storage only.

The train still goes through Sycamore once a day traveling from Marion to Frankfort.

Schools

The first school was taught in a cabin on William Braden's farm in the fall of 1849. David Stanfield was the teacher. The cabin, a log structure, was 12 x 14 feet, had one window and one door, a puncheon floor, a stick and clay chimney, and a roof of four-foot boards, held on by weight-poles. It was located near the center of the southwest quarter of Section 5, Township 24, Range 6.

In 1876 there were six frame schoolhouses in Jackson Twp. In 1900 there were five one-room schools, and one four-room school in which two years of high school work was given. In 1922 Jackson Twp. School was built by Douglas Moore. The township trustee was William F. Morton. The first graduating class was in 1923 with three graduating. In 1937 there were three grade school teachers and six high school teachers. The last graduating class from Jackson Twp. School was 1949 with 14 graduating. The total number of graduates from Jackson Twp. School was 183. The school team name was Stonewalls and their colors were blue and white. The basketball team won the county title in 1931 and 1949. They were sectional champions in 1932. The school's electric power was a 32V system with a four cylinder motor and large wet cell storage batteries. In 1930 Public Service and REMC brought 110 volt power through Jackson Twp. In 1950, Liberty, Jackson and Union townships voted to form Eastern School Corporation. The high school students went to Eastern High School at Greentown and the Jackson Twp School was used for a grade school. It continued as a grade school until 1974 when it was closed and the students were sent to Greentown Elementary beginning with the fall semester. The Jackson Twp. School was sold at auction in October of 1974 and was torn down several years later. The school building had been used for 53 years. There are no old school buildings left standing in Jackson Twp.

Farmers Institute

After the Civil War, Land Grant Colleges were established throughout the United States. Purdue University was chosen for Indiana and three branches were designated: Resident, Research, and Extension. The Extension Service's job is "to take the College out to the folk." The Farmers Institute was the first method used. Jackson Twp. started the Farmers Institute in 1921 and it was held annually till about 1949-1950. The members would display their agricultural products, baked goods or handwork. They had speakers on various subjects. Every year a play was presented to raise funds to support the program. The meetings were held in Jackson Township School. Each member also paid a small membership fee. Officers for year 1949-1950 were as follows: Harold Schaaf, Bob Johnson, Armem Warnock, Wilbert Riggs, W. Powell, C. Thompson, H. Woodmans, Everett Johnson (County Agent), Dorothy Johnson, F. Woodmanse, Mary Warnock, L. Shockley, M.D. Winegardner, B. Riggs, Bert Hainlen, L. Brunk, Guy Johnson, L. Schaaf, E. Powell, N. Schaaf, and M. Winegardner.

Meeting of the Farmers Institute.

Elevator in Sycamore

Curry Chapel Cemetery

Honey Creek Church at 1100E and 400N

Curry Chapel Cemetery

There is but one cemetery in Jackson Twp. It is located on the east side of county road 1100E about one-fourth of a mile north of road 500N. In the 1876 atlas it was shown next to Cuppy/Curry Chapel. By some it is called the Powell Cemetery and others the Jackson Twp. Cemetery. A book titled *Cemetery Inscriptions of Eastern Howard County, Indiana* by James L. Gorman includes the following interesting story:

About the turn of the century the town of Xenia (now Converse) a few miles to the north decided to abandon and move their cemetery to make room for more residences. Many of the bodies in this cemetery were re-interred in Curry Chapel Cemetery including those of Jimmy Powell and Lemuel and Sarah Powell. Still later some of these were moved again to the Greenlawn Cemetery at Greentown. The following story was told by Mr. Warnock and several months later by Mr. Powell, neither of whom have seen each other in many years. (They both lived in Jackson Twp.) According to Mr. Powell he was working in the field across from the cemetery one day when he noticed Ed and El Warnock attempting to pull a coffin out of a grave. Since they seemed to be having a lot of difficulty with it, he went across to help. They told him they had been asked to move it to the Greentown Cemetery but that the coffin felt like it had been loaded with rocks and "weighed a ton". They mentioned that it was Jimmy Powell's wife who was to be re-interred next to his grave in Greentown. Mr. Powell, who had attended the funeral of the lady, knew that she was not a large woman and also could not understand the coffin being so heavy. When it was finally removed from the ground, they could contain their curiosity no longer and opened the coffin. The bottom of the coffin was full of water and the woman's body was petrified. Mr. Powell said every detail was recognizable from the "ruching" on the blouse to the combs in her hair. The writers have no explanation, scientific or otherwise, for the "petrified body" story. We repeat it only for the reader's interest and because it was told to us by two different men widely separated by time and distance. We can only add the old saying "Truth is stranger than fiction".

In May 1941 the *Kokomo Dispatch* reported that there were several Civil War Veterans buried in Howard County, one being buried in Curry Chapel.

Churches

The Wesleyan Methodists organized the first church at the house of Joseph Hockett one mile south of Xenia. Among the first ministers were Alfred Thorp, Abraham Lee, and Emsley Brookshire.

In Blanchard's *History of Howard County* published in 1883, there were two churches listed in Jackson Twp. Curry's Chapel, a Methodist Episcopal Church, was located to the north of the cemetery. It was a white frame building with a white fence along the road in front of the building. A platform was built on the north wall of the building, so that the ladies could get out of the carriages directly onto the platform without getting their skirts dirty in the dust of the driveway. The building was later purchased by a farmer who lived on the Plevna Road; he moved it to his farm and for years used it as a barn. The Poplar Grove Church was in the southwest corner and was Protestant Methodist. It was erected in the year 1873 on the farm of Isaac Jesiop.

At the present time there are only two churches in Jackson Twp. The Honey Creek Church was built in 1898. In 1925 the building was purchased by Sherman Kendall. He was the minister until his death. His daughter Mrs. Elmer (Ada) Miller has continued his ministry. Services are held on Sunday mornings and eve-

Paul Kendall

Velma Kendall

Paul Hainlen Orchard

Earl Hainlen Orchard

nings. The Sycamore Friends Church was built in 1890. The first minister was J. Hammer Ellis. The church celebrated its 100th anniversary in August of 1990.

Hainlen Orchard

This is the fourth generation of the Hainlen family who have operated the Hainlen Orchard which was purchased in the early 1930s by A.C. Hainlen. He had three sons. Paul and Earl continued to work in the orchard business and Lloyd operated a nursery. A.C. Hainlen retired in 1946. Paul Jr. and Carolyn Hainlen now own and operate one orchard. They have approximately 50 acres of a variety of apples, peaches and pears. This orchard is located at 1250E and 5588N. Len Hainlen is the fourth generation to work at the orchard. Earl Hainlen owned the other orchard of 27 acres at 1300E and 4804N. They have apples, pears, and "you pick" strawberries. It is currently operated by Gene and Jackie Hainlen and the fourth generation of Hainlens, Mike and Karen.

Prominent Traits of the Boys

J.D. Gossett never attempts to appear other than he is. He says nothing of his ability. He is always attentive however dull the subject under consideration. Has consistent power in numbers. He is prompted to study by the love he has for knowledge.

A.W. Harper is slightly egotistical. He has an admiration for persons of culture and learning, which may prompt him to be one of their number.

H.C. Applegate is prompted to the attainment of knowledge by the financial benefit there is in it, as well as the desire for knowledge. He can comprehend from an explanation more readily than from study. He has fully as much confidence in himself as his power deserves. He is an agreeable scholar, never giving trouble to his teacher or school-mates.

George Allison possesses power of quick understanding. He is attentive and is quick to form an opinion which he does not like to have criticized by everybody. He likes the girls and the girls like him.

Oscar Pickett is inclined to be discontented unless there is something of an interesting character going on. He says little in company, and never tries to appear other than he naturally is. He has hardly enough confidence according to his ability.

Elsworth Cranor likes something of an exciting nature and will generally manage to have it. He studies but little comparatively, but studies for life while at it. He possesses the power to command. His playmates will walk to his talk as though he were a general and they his privates.

Grant Pickett is of a quiet disposition and if he were to attend school 20 years a teacher would never have cause to correct him. He is agreeable to his playmates, and is firm in his opinion when once formed. No boy has more power in discriminating right from wrong than Grant.

Emery Weeks possesses considerable power in the principles of arithmetic. He makes no attempt at display. He will agree with anyone on any subject, but at the same time he has his own opinion about the matter. He is like his father in this respect.

Noah Thompson possesses no extreme trait of character, but has a well-balanced mind. He attempts to obey his commander, Elsworth.

No boy can make more bluster than Elisha Gentry. He is kind-hearted and agreeable to his playmates. He has a lack of interest for school which is made up by his like for his calves, pigs and goat.

Sherman Hollingsworth possesses a good general knowledge which he has obtained by observation rather than study. He has good judgement for a boy of his years, and is of an ingenious term of mind.

Monte Hollingsworth has a quick understanding. He is industrious both in mental and physical labor. He is of a suspicious term of mind.

Take it all in all the boys at Sycamore Corner are rather an agreeable set. But two or three ever need to be watched in school. In intelligence they are equal to the boys of ten years ago. In morality they are superior to the generation preceding them, yet there is room for improvement in this respect yet.

Written by Clarkson Cate, a teacher at Sycamore School ca 1875. The following information on Clarkson Cate is taken from Blanchard's History of Howard County. Clarkson L. Cate was born on 31 Dec. 1853. He was the son of John and Rachel (Pierce) Cate. He began teaching school in 1872. In 1877 he married Mary Alice Gentry. He died 25 Sept. 1935.

LIBERTY TOWNSHIP

Plevna, IN, a little hamlet founded in either the late 1860s or early 1870s, is located at the intersection of two roads, four miles north of Greentown or 11 miles northeast of Kokomo. The east-west road is now (and has been for many years) known as Touby Pike. At the time of the founding, the southwest section was a total mass of native trees and brush, while portions of the other sections near the intersection were cleared of brush and trees, and the ground was used for farming. A long farm house stood about 40 rods north on the NE section owned by Ben Rogers, later by Peter Kingseed and Chris Lantz, and finally by H.J. Weisenauer. Also a log cabin stood on the west side of the road on the N.W. section, owned later by George Saul, a cousin of my mother. A little log building used for a store, and a log cabin nearby, stood on the N.E. corner of the intersection.

On the southeast section there were more houses. The Dawson farmhouse stood about 20 rods east on the S.E. section. The Dawsons owned the land on that section. At the corner was a doctor's office and his house was immediately south of it — a house made from lumber and is still standing there. Further on the south of the corner were three or four more houses owned by the Dreyer brothers, Sam, John and Bill, and Sam's father-in-law, Sam Irwin. The man who owned the store and lived nearby was a Mr. Bishop, and the Dr., a Mr. Steve Colescott, owned the office and house nearby on the S.E. corner. So this was Pleasantville (a former name for Plevna at that time) approximately 100 years ago.

Some of the early settlers around Plevna at that time were the Kingseeds, Rogers, Kennedys, Kaufmans, Kendalls, Murphys, Sproals, Yoders, Millers, Lantzs, Shrocks, Troyers, Zooks, Masts, to the north. To the east were the Lorenzs, Ooleys, Fays, Kirbys, Michaels, Dicks, Gossetts, Warnicks, Peters, Holsteins, Olwins, Odumus, and a few more. To the south were the Howells, Fishers, Loops, Nuners, Pettys, Julows, and Uncle Abe Saul (my mother's uncle). To the west there were Zerbes, Marquois, Grafs, Schaafs, Henslers, Strausses, and Dotterers. So it was quite a community after all, and most of them did their trading in Plevna.

Sometime in the late seventies Mr. Bishop sold his store to a Mr. Henry Miller who enlarged it and built a house nearby. He operated the store for four or five years and then sold it to Alfred Troyer, who after a few years sold it to Eli Miller. Troyer had four boys. The Troyer family moved to North Dakota after selling the store. Eli Miller operated the store until it burned down in the late 1880s. It was never rebuilt and that corner remains absent of any other building to this day.

About the time this store burned, a new store building was built across the road on the northwest corner. This was quite an imposing building. It was a long, two-storied building — quite an addition to the town and community. It was built by a Jerry Mast, a native of the area, and who also operated a saw mill west of town just across the road from the White schoolhouse where the youngsters of the area went to school. This store was run by Mast for a few years and was eventually sold to a newcomer from Ohio by the name of Pete Remington. Mr. Remington, wife and daughter lived in quarters at the rear of the store that he added on the main building. They were very popular people and did quite a lot of business. Mr. Remington operated the store for several years. He sold it to Henry Lorenz, a farm boy who grew up in the area. Lorenz also did a thriving business. In addition to running the store, he ran a huckster wagon every day to outlying districts. He also became a very popular merchant. Unfortunately this store building burned down one night with all its contents. This happened along about 1917 or 1918. It was quite a loss for Lorenz and the community, but he went to work and built a new building, the one that is now there on that corner. Lorenz sold his store in 1924 to Lantz Bros., Floyd and Fred, who operated it until a few years ago when they both retired. It is now operated by Jack Lantz, Fred's younger son.

After the Miller Store on the N.E. corner burned, Miller traded his house and lot for an 80 acre farm. The man who owned the farm was Noah Yoder, who ran a saw mill and sorghum mill. Yoder also operated a cider mill in connection with his saw mill and sorghum mill. His cider mill became a popular place for certain people of the area, as he always had huge quantities of cider on hand in season, both sweet and hard cider.

On the S.E. corner Dr. Colescott's office was next to the corner and his house just to the south. He was doctor in the early days of the town and a very popular man. He and John Saul (Amos's father) worked together to attain a post office for the town, which was finally granted. Colescott became the first postmaster, and he remained so until he sold his home and practice in about 1880 and John was appointed to suc-

West Main Street in Greentown

East Grant Street in Greentown

39

ceed him. John was postmaster for several years and was later succeeded by Pete Remington, in the 1890s.

Colescott sold his home and practice to a Dr. Albert Miller (no relation to Miller who owned the store) but Miller sold the house and built a new one just east of the office. It was a two-story square house, a very fine addition to the town. They had two boys. Miller was a big, portly man with a huge red beard and mustache. He was well liked in the community and had a good practice. Miller served as doctor here for several years and finally sold out to Dr. Gordon and moved to Anderson, IN. His boy, Don, became a doctor and practiced in Indianapolis; the younger boy, Lora, became a civil engineer and was killed in an accident on a bridge construction project.

Dr. Gordon remained here as a doctor for several years and in 1903 moved to Converse and lived there until his death in 1930. Before he left Plevna, another doctor had come in the person of Dr. Rinehart, who also was a good doctor. He was a doctor here for about 20 years. He moved to Frankfort and died. During the 1890s two other doctors practiced here for short periods. They were Dr. Abbott and Dr. Foust. Abbott was no good and did not stay long, but Foust was a young man and had great promise of good practice, but he heard of another town with no competition and moved there.

Dr. Gordon sold his house and lot and office building in about 1899 and moved to a 17 acre tract of land just west of town. The buyer, a George Smith, tore down the office building and built a new store building right on the corner and went into business, which meant that Plevna had two stores now. Smith operated this store for about 15 years. Other owners of this store afterwards were Willie Kennedy, Arthur Gross, Wm. Muncie and Ed Drinkwater. After Drinkwater, Lantz Bros. obtained the building and converted it into a hatchery and feed store. It is still used by Jack Lantz as a storage room for foodstuff and supplies for his grocery store on the NW corner.

Now we go to the SW section, wherein lies the Saul farm. Years ago Edward Saul (my grandfather) and his brother, Abe, hearing of yet government land unsold, came by horse from Ohio to investigate this land. It probably was in the late 1850s or early 1860s. I have heard the deeds were signed by James Buchanan, who was then President of the United States.

Edward Saul bought 160 acres on the southwest section of which is now part of Plevna, and 80 acres on the northwest section, while Abe Saul bought his land two miles south of Plevna, nearer to Greens Village, which is now Greentown. At that time it was a little village of very few houses. They bought their land and rode back home to Seneca County, OH. After a year or so Abe decided to sell his land in Ohio and move to his newly bought land in Indiana. He did this and began clearing his land and built a log cabin to live in. Edward Saul hesitated about moving to Indiana and decided to stay in Ohio, mostly because of ill health, and a year or two later he died. That left Grandmother Saul with nine children and 240 acres of land in Indiana to care for. So Uncle John, a strapling young teenager (her second child and son) said he would go out to Indiana and take care of the land, build himself a log cabin, and begin clearing the trees and brush. He did this and never returned to Ohio again. After a year or two in Indiana, he wrote back home to his oldest sister, Martha, to come to Indiana and be his housekeeper. She came, then they both lived in his new log cabin and she helped him do some clearing. The Kingseed family lived close by over on the northeast section at the place my father later bought. She got acquainted with Alec, a young man of the family, and they were soon married. In the meantime, my father had come out here on a visit and while here he bought the Kingseed farm, and they moved here in the spring of 1883. I was 14 months old at the time.

So after Aunt Martha got married and left, Uncle John wrote back to Ohio to his youngest sister, Aunt Hannah, to come to Indiana and be his housekeeper. She came and also helped him, and in a year or two she married a young man of the neighborhood, Wm. Smeltzer. John was eventually married and built a big two-story home. Hannah Smeltzer had bought the west 80; Steve Saul (John's youngest brother) had bought the 80 acres on the northwest corner, all from their mother. In the meantime, Plevna had grown some. So Plevna was beginning to be a boom town.

I mentioned before that a post office was established here through the efforts of mainly Dr. Colescott and Uncle John Saul, but the naming of the town or post office has to go to Uncle John's credit. The first name submitted was "Pleasantville", but that name was rejected for the reason that another post office by that name was in existence. So the name Pomroy was submitted, and was also turned down. At this particular time an awful war was going on in Europe between Bulgaria and Turkey. The Turks had invaded Bulgaria and were laying siege on a Bulgarian City by the name of "Plevna." Plevna was quite a large city in Bulgaria and the

Bird's-eye view of Greentown

Meridian Street in Greentown

people of the city were starving and dying for want of food. The news of the people's plight and suffering was front page news in all the leading newspapers of the time, and practically all the world sympathized with them. So Uncle John, an avid reader, submitted the name of Plevna, which was accepted and thereby became the name of the new post office and town. The city in Bulgaria is still in existence, but is now called Pleven, as you can see on the map of the country.

The town was enlarging, and the farmers around and in the area were progressing rapidly to the extent that they needed a blacksmith very badly, mostly for shoeing horses and repairing machinery. So Uncle John, sensing the urgent need for a blacksmith, donated a parcel of land right at the corner of his farm to build a shop. So a new business was started. A Mr. Tyre operated the shop a few years then moved away and the shop was bought by Nick Richer, who operated it many years. Mr. Richer finally bought a lot off my father's place on the N.E. section, just north of the Miller store, and built a much larger building for his business. He later made farm wagons and other items that the farmers needed and used at that time.

Mr. Richer sold his shop to Simon Kendall in 1900 and moved his business to Greentown where he continued wagon making operations on a much larger scale. Mr. Kendall ran the shop a few years, then sold it to Noah Hughes, a neighborhood young man who had married into the Abe Saul family. Mr. Hughes ran the shop a few years than sold it to Wesley Summers, who converted it into a garage as automobiles began to appear. That left the community without a blacksmith, so a few of the farmers around the area organized a company to build and operate a shop. A brand new building was built on the southwest corner that originally had been used for that purpose. Some of the smiths that were hired were Harry Shrock, Charley Miller, and Bill Lucas. This shop prospered for a few years and finally was abandoned for lack of business as tractors were taking the place of horses, and machinery repairs were made at garages and implement stores. Another early blacksmith in Plevna was Walter Caylor who lived in a house in the northeast section directly east of the Miller or Troyer house. He also had a boy, Johnnie, my age. The Caylors were very fine people and were good friends of my folks.

Eventually the Summers garage was sold to Roy Ebersole and later passed on to Ralph Bogue. Shrock Bros, Emerson and Jim, with Bogue ran the place a few years then built a building on the northwest section a few rods west of the corner and took agency for the Oliver implement line, along with car and tractor repair. They are still there doing a thriving business, although they no longer work on cars, but do tractor work on all makes. Bill Meyers owns and operates the former garage on the northeast section now. He also has a good business.

Mr. and Mrs. Joe Dilts operated a little store here in the late 1890s for a few years. They sold candy, tobacco and ice cream. The store was in a small building on the southwest section near the blacksmith shop. The Dilts had two daughters, Ona and Zenna. The older one married a local boy, Frank Fay.

Three Greentown men in front of store in Greentown.

This is about the end of business life of the community, both past and present, except that there is a veterinarian here at present, Dr. A.L. Keim. He has a wide practice and is very capable.

There has always been since I can remember and at present, a religious sect known as Dunkards or German Baptists. During the late 1880s, or nearly 80 years ago, they built a church here in Plevna on the west side of the N.W. section, about half way from our house to the stores, and that church is still standing there. Only a few alterations have been made on that building in all these years. This church has always been well attended.

Plevna was the home of another church at the east end of town, known as the Wesleyan Methodist Church. This church thrived for about 20 years and was finally abandoned, after which the building was bought by Ralph and Albert Kingseed and moved to Ralph's place and converted into a machine shed. The Christian Church was built 3/4 mile east of Plevna along in the 1890s. It was also abandoned after a few years' use. The congregation of this church joined the one in Greentown and is now one of the leading churches of that town.

Earlier in its history, Plevna has had some minor industry. There were two tile factories in the area for a number of years, namely, the Klingman to the northwest and the Howell to the southeast of town. These two factories made drainage tile for farmers of the area to drain their swamps and ponds, which by the way, were many.

Then there were sawmills. Jerry Mast owned and operated a sawmill one mile west of Plevna for a number of years. It was located across the road from the school I used to go to, and at recesses and noon we kids would often play on and about the large supplies of logs that were stacked in the mill yard, and also would watch the men saw the big logs into lumber. Noah Yoder owned and operated a sawmill 1/2 mile north of Plevna for a number of years, and the Kendall brothers ran a sawmill two miles north of Plevna. Also there was a mill one mile east and a mile north of town, also one southeast of Plevna on one of the Howell farms. Yoder also owned a sorghum mill, as well as a cider mill in season, but these industries faded out years ago and are no more.

Sorghum mills are a thing of the past. Nearly every farmer in the community raised sorghum for sugar and molasses. There is one cider mill still in the area of Plevna. It is 2 1/2 miles southwest of town, owned and operated by Clarence Willetts.

Every farm used to have an orchard and the farms around Plevna were no exception. Every fall we would gather up apples and take them to the Yoder Mill, which was about 1/4 mile away, to have cider made, which in turn would become vinegar. But the apple trees are gone, along with the mills, as well as the sorghum and mills.

Another industry that was popular and profitable at one time in Plevna has faded out. That was the Lantz Bros. Hatchery. They did a big business in hatching chicks for farmers in a wide area around the town, but farmers don't raise chickens any more.

Another ancient industry of former days in Plevna was cutting and storing ice in winter for summer use. Ice was easily available on numerous ponds in the area in winter and was stored in an ice house directly south of the building on the southwest corner on Uncle John's farm.

Plevna had its social events along with its daily duties. Probably the most conspicuous was the homemade ice cream festivals that were held in the summertime at someone's home in the community. The Woman's Aid Club looked after and administered to the poor, unfortunate people of the area. In later years there was the Sewing Circle that met often in someone's home. Then there were the Spelling Bees and Cyphering Matches of the various schools of the community, which were popular in those days.

The Plevna area had a group of fine singers along about the turn of the century — a men's quartet, soloists, trios, duets, also a chorus of both men and women. The Dotterer brothers,

41

Men transporting pipes in the Greentown area.

Manny and Willie, Frank Graf, Monroe Kendall and Milt Troyer were some of the best men singers, while Verna Schaaf, Pearl Olvin and Myrtle Michaels were among the best women singers. They sang at many social events and gatherings, and were very much in demand at other events.

In 1927 a group of people of the area organized a Plevna homecoming event and invited all former Plevnaites to come home and visit with relatives and former friends. The first homecoming was held in Myers Woods, one mile north and 1/2 mile west of Plevna on the second Sunday in September. It was a big success; several hundred people attended from far and near. It was decided to have them every year. They held them until World War II and then abandoned them.

A few people who grew up in the Plevna area and got to be famous later on in life are: Johnnie Zerbe, born and raised 1/2 mile west of Plevna, was a noted Methodist clergyman. Grace Sloan Overton, who grew up 1 1/2 miles northeast of Plevna, became a nationally known lecturer and educator. Others who were well known in the educational field were John Huner, Frank Bagwell, and Ben Johnson. In the political field, Laird Troyer, a former Plevna boy, was mayor of Lansing, MI. Five Plevna men have held the Liberty Township Trustee office, namely, Wm. Howell, Rolla Dawson, Wm. Fay, Wm. Myers, and Kenneth Shrock. One of our present County Commissioners is a Plevna man, Ross Ingells, and Wayne Powell also held the office a few years ago.

The political life of our community has been varied. There was a time in the early days that almost everyone was a Democrat, but in recent years it has almost evened up between Democrats and Republicans.

Plevna has always been in the limelight of sports, especially baseball. There have been three or four quack ball teams here in the time that I can remember. In the early 1890s Plevna had perhaps the best teams for miles around. (In those days every little town had its Ball Club). Some who played were the Nuner brothers: Bob, the catcher, Jim, the pitcher. Jim Kirby was another pitcher. Some of the other players were Tim Kirby, Chas. Sloan, Ed Schaaf, George Lantz, Bill Dawson, Lew Murphy, Wes Schrock, and a few more that I can't recall at the moment. Then around 1900 there was another club that had a good reputation. Some of the players in this club were Andy and Harry Shrock, Fred Rody, George Lorenz, Frank Bagwell, and Clarence Kauffman. Another good club later on was composed of Ralph Kingseed, Dude and Peck Bagwell, Bill Julow, Mose Irwin, Spike Kendall, Fred Lantz and a few more. Later and more recently a few Plevna boys were members of a Greentown Club that had a state-wide reputation. The Plevna members of the team were Herman Kern, Floyd Shrock, Dick and Chuck Weisenauer, Paul Cheek. Some of these boys also were members of the Greentown High School basketball team that had a good reputation.

Disaster has struck Plevna a few times in its history, especially as to fires. The Miller, Lorenz and Smith store buildings burned, the Keim barn and animal hospital building, the Frank King barn, Shrock and Murphy barn fires, and Julow, Beachy, Powell and Kendall, and Percy Shrock house fires. The King barn 1/2 mile east of Plevna, one of the largest barns in the whole area, burned one night in the 1890s. The Murphy barn, another large barn, was struck by lightning in 1899. The Powell house just south of town burned just recently.

A record snowfall in February, 1912, isolated the community for a whole week by blocked roads. No mail was delivered the entire week. A killing frost and freeze occurred on the night of June 22, 1918, killing about all vegetation. Thousands of acres of corn were ruined in the area. A severe storm of wind, rain, and hail on July 12, 1925 did extensive damage to crops in this area. The floods of 1913 and 1943 did considerable damage to crops also. Plevna escaped the terrible tornado of April 11, 1965 which passed four miles south at Greentown where great damage was done.

Accidents and misfortunes were no strangers to Plevna. Perhaps the worst of these occurred on the 26th of June, 1926 when Hamilton Lantz, aged 12, was fatally injured in a two truck collision in front of the Lantz Brothers store. The boy died a few hours after the accident. Fred Lantz and a salesman named Willowby were critically injured in the accident, but both finally recovered. On Dec. 13, 1895 Bob Nuner was fatally injured in a corn shredding accident on the Eli Michael farm east of Plevna. A year or two later Joe King, 15-year-old son of Mr. and Mrs. Charles King, lost an arm in a hunting accident by the accidental discharge of a shot gun. On May 25, 1953, Mrs. Afton Kingseed was killed in an automobile accident at an intersection of two roads two miles northeast of Plevna. A few years earlier a young man, Woodrow Mast, was killed at this same intersection. Three years ago Mrs. Emanuel Troyer was killed in a car accident two miles north of Plevna. On May 7, 1963 Bob Kingseed was killed in an industrial accident in Kokomo. A few years ago the little son of Mr. and Mrs. Lowell Lantz was killed in a freak accident at the home of Emerson Shrock here in Plevna. A few years ago Mrs. Harry B. Shrock was fatally burned in a fire at their home in Plevna. On July 3, 1934 two local men, Gus Schaaf and Clarence Hamler, died in a boating accident on a lake in Michigan. Their bodies were never recovered. Three years ago last February 16 a six-year-old girl, daughter of Mr. and Mrs. John Garr, and a salesman by the name of Tenneson, were killed two miles east of Plevna. This accident was only 80 rods east of where we used to live. Perhaps the most appalling thing that ever happened in the Plevna neighborhood was the murder of Ben Dotterer, a retired farmer living southwest of Plevna. This crime occurred on the night of Sept. 2, 1901 when robbers invaded his home. Mr. Dotterer resisted their efforts to rob him and he was fatally beaten and mauled and died the next day. His wife was also badly beaten but recovered. This crime caused great excitement in the neighborhood, but the robbers were never caught and it remains a mystery to this day. I remember this incident very well.

Would you believe it that Plevna had a saloon at one time? In the late 1880s and early 1890s a man by the name of Dan Bowland, who lived a few miles north of Plevna, operated a gin mill for a few years. He had a fairly good business going until some of the church people of the community remonstrated to the extent that he was finally refused the license to operate and was forced out of business. This saloon was located just west of Jack Lantz's store.

Plevna was the scene of an auxiliary Air Force Base during World War II. The main base was located near Bunker Hill and is now called Grissom Air Force Base. During the war a number of auxiliary bases were established about 20 miles around the main base for training purposes, and Plevna happened to be in line for one of these bases. This base consisted of 320 acres and comprised the Amos Saul, Wm. Smeltzer, and part of the Spangler and Shrock farms. The farms were cleared of woods and fences and were tiled so many rods apart and paved runways were made. Hundreds of young men were trained here during the war and no doubt many of the ace fliers of the war got their training here.

After reading this story, one will no doubt wonder how Plevna got its mail. Living at the extreme east part of town was a family by the name of Mills who had a team of horses and covered wagon, or hack as we called it then. At first he would make a trip to Kokomo once every week to bring back supplies for the store and other articles that people needed, also the mail, and he hauled people there and back. Finally he got to going two times a week, then three times. Then in the late 1890s he sold his property and moved to Burlington, a town west of Kokomo. So two men of the town, John Peters and John Zerbe, rigged up hacks and made alternate trips every day of the week. They kept this up until rural free delivery was started in 1898, I believe. At this time the post office was abandoned and everyone got mail from free delivery service. About this time telephone service was established. This was another exciting time for Plevnaites, and the people thought, "What next?"

Up until the early 1890s what is now known as the Touby Pike was a dirt road. This road running east and west was graded and graveled about this time and remained a gravel road for several years. Finally it was blacktopped and is now a well travelled road. The north and south road was graveled in 1897. The Touby Pike was widened in 1958, ten years ago.

In the early days schoolhouses were every two miles apart, and the children in Plevna had as their nearest school a building one mile west of town. We all went to this school until 1894 when a schoolhouse was built 1/2 mile east of town. The ground for this school was donated by my father. It was known as the Plevna School and had a large attendance. In going to the White School before the Plevna School was built, we sometimes had to walk the mile in bitter cold weather. Sometimes we were lucky to ride the hacks, but most of the time we walked, rain or shine, cold or mild. These one-room schoolhouses are long since gone.

So after having lived in Plevna and community for over 80 years, I can justly be called an old timer. I have seen many changes made in the town and countryside around, from primitive to modern, examples of which — dirt roads to paved highways, log houses to near mansions or ranch house, from forests and swamps to fine well-tilled and productive farms; modes of travel from horseback to automobiles and many more mechanical items for household and farming. Not only these changes, but I have seen many friends and people come and leave our community, many by death and others by better environment elsewhere.

Not many people of my age remain here yet. As I can recall, Mr. and Mrs. Fred Rody, George Lorenz, Arthur Clingenpeal, and myself are the oldest, all of which lived in the community practically all their lives and have seen the many changes made and seen generations come and go. Many people who grew up in the Plevna community moved to other places in later life.

Plevna was a great loafing place for farmers and local townspeople in the old days. Checkers and gossip were the main attractions. Almost every night the stores were full of loafers who came to spend the evening and play a few games of checkers, shuck a few hundred bushels of corn or shock a square mile of wheat or oats.

Well this just about covers the early and later history of Plevna and community to the best of my knowledge. Some of the earlier history recorded here is hearsay as it occurred before I was born, but most of the later history and items I know to be factual, because I remember them. No doubt the earlier history is true as I have heard it related many times in my life by reliable persons who were much older than I. There has been quite a range of progress from Plevna's beginning until now, and from present indications that progress will continue as evidence to the fact that new houses are being built in and around the places. *History of Liberty Township by John Edward Weisenauer written in July 1968. Submitted by Joan Smith Beheler, Greentown, Indiana 46936, granddaughter of John Edward Weisenauer.*

Plevna School in District #4 with Bud Fisher as teacher.

MONROE TOWNSHIP

Location

Monroe Township is the smallest township in Howard County and is located in the west-central part of the county. It is bordered on the north by Wildcat Creek, on the west by Carroll County, and on the southwest by Clinton County. The southern border adjoins Honey Creek Township, and on the eastern edge it touches against Harrison Township. Part of Monroe Township used to be in Carroll County, but in 1844 it became part of Howard County. The township is named for the fifth President of the United States, James Monroe.

Monroe Township has always contained good farm land, the main attraction to early settlers. As the first pioneers entered this region, it was part of "The Seven Mile Strip" which was opened up to buyers in 1841. This was the land the U.S. Government made available for sale (through a treaty with the Miami Indians) to help finance the building of the Wabash-Erie Canal.

Early History

The first white settler in the county was David Landrum who, with his wife, came from Tennessee to settle in Indiana. In 1837 he erected a little cabin west of present-day landmark, Stonebraker Bridge, in the far western portion of the township, not too far from the town of Burlington. There were no roads at the time, only paths between Indian villages, and travel was quite difficult. In February 1839 other settlers came to build their cabins. These included Robert Walker, George A. Taylor, and Isaac Price.

The first marriage was that of William Walker and Nancy Price in January 1841. Nancy became a widow about a year later. The first white child born in the township was Mary Katharine Price, born Aug. 15, 1839, to Isaac and Katharine Price. Mrs. Price died later that year on November 10. The first death and burial of a white person, however, had been in the spring of 1839. The deceased was Thomas Landrum.

The first trader in the county was Joshua Barnett who also came in 1839. His supply of goods included a few groceries, liquors, and small notions.

The nearest trading post was at Burlington where people took their furs to exchange for what goods they could. Also, a water mill was located west of Burlington where Monroe settlers could take corn to be ground unless the water was frozen; the alternative was to take one bushel of corn to Logansport on horseback. About 1840, though, John Lamb built the first flour mill in the county, just east of New London on the east fork of Honey Creek. Other mills sprung up also, one of which was the Thompson Mill built in 1850 by owners Benjamin and Samuel Thompson. A flour mill, it was located northwest of New London on Honey Creek. One of the best mills and one that lasted a long time was the mill built in 1848 in the northwest part of the township for grinding grain and sawing lumber. Oliver Young owned it at one time, but later owner, J.W. Stonebraker, is the one whose name the mill has usually been known by.

Another type of mill, a tile mill, was built by Dick Cunningham in 1885 on land west of New London. A slave in the South when he was a child, he married Mary Reed of Ohio. They are both buried in the New London Cemetery.

The Town of New London

The only town Monroe Township has ever had is the town of New London, located in the eastern end of the township on the forks of Honey Creek. It sits on an elevated piece of ground surrounded by good farming country.

The town was laid out in 1845 by John Lamb and Reuben Edgerton. In 1845 John Lamb offered a lot to any blacksmith who would move to New London. William Gifford accepted and moved there Dec. 18, 1845, with his wife Esther and family. He died January 1849, leaving her with ten children to raise. A weekly mail service started in 1846 with Nathan Hunt as the first mail carrier. Within a few years, however, the United States government established a post office at Russiaville and the one at New London was discontinued. In 1854 postal service began at Shanghai, a country store located three miles west of New London.

Early businesses included a dry goods store, a grocery store, and a mercantile business. Little Jonathan Haworth was the first storekeeper in New London. John B. Miller came from east Tennessee in 1839 and was the first harness maker in the county. He brought hides to the tannery at New London to have them made into leather. The town also had an inn. Known as The Tavern, the two-story building was built by Big Jonathan Haworth next to the town hall.

The first newspaper in the county was started at New London. It was a Free-Soil paper called The *Pioneer,* published by Moses Wickersham. It lasted from 1848 to 1850. Financial troubles resulted in the press and type being sold and moved to Kokomo, and *The Kokomo Tribune* grew out of that.

There were no gravel roads in the area until 1867 when the New London to Kokomo Toll Road was started. It was finished in 1870 at a

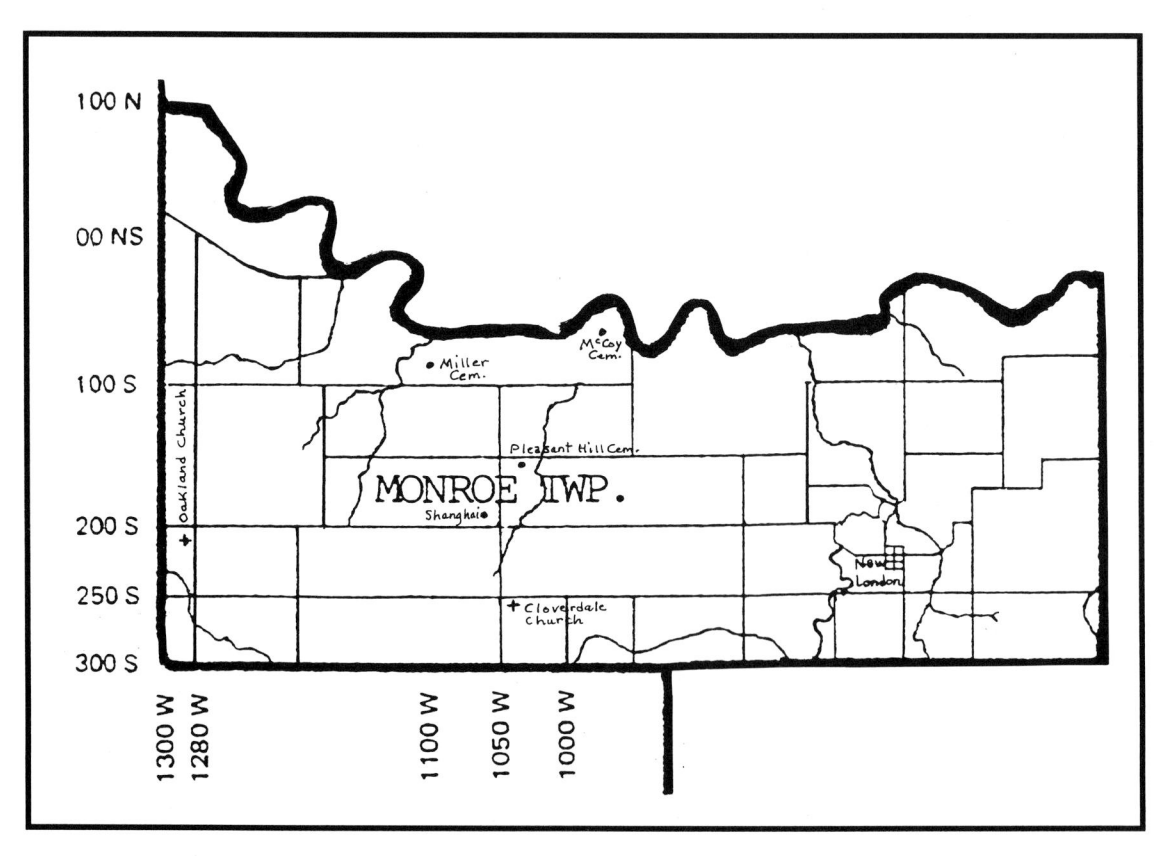

Men digging Johnson's Gravel Pit in 1904.

Will Herrington and family in front of the New London Garage in New London.

cost of $27,000. The ten-mile road ran east and west, crossing Wildcat Creek on a fine, iron bridge built at a cost of another $3500. The road remained a toll road for several years, and the toll gate stood one-half mile east of the landmark still known today as Shirley's Corner. The gate was erected on land belonging to Reuben Jessup.

By 1877 New London had become a thriving town, with a population of about 300. It had one dry goods store, one drugstore, one grocery store, two harness shops, two blacksmith shops, one wagon and buggy shop, one boot and shoe shop, one wholesale produce dealer, three physicians, one barbershop, one tin shop, one hotel, one gristmill, one saw mill, one tanning yard, one butcher shop, a Masonic lodge, an Odd Fellow's lodge, one high school building and two churches—one Methodist and one Friends. According to the 1877 Atlas, the town had no saloon in the place and was not likely to have one soon. One must keep in mind that many of the residents were Quakers and promoters of total abstinence.

One hundred years later, at the time of the country's bicentennial, New London had approximately 60 homes, one barbershop, one filling station, a recreation center called the "New London Barn," and one church, the New London Friends Meeting. The school had been torn down, and the school property was leased to the Howard County Park Board. Bud Temple has in recent years purchased the park land. Today, there are 67 homes in New London and many more have been added in the surrounding territory. Township trustee David M. Reser reports that Monroe Township has a population of approximately 1400, 150 of which live in New London. The number of businesses today in the town has decreased immensely. There are two auto body shops, Steve Johnson's in the middle of the town, and the Watkins & Son Body Shop on the south edge of town. The other businesses are Farlow's Orchard just one-half mile east of Shirley Corner and Kim's Country Salon.

One of the most memorable sites of New London's history is the little spring that exists between the church and the park. For over a century residents enjoyed their visits there and had memories of crossing the foot bridge of poplar logs (in the early days) or the hickory-elm logs of later years that helped one to cross the ravine leading to the old spring. Today the spring is overrun with bushes and other growth, but the water is still running. The foot bridge is long gone, however.

Education

The first school in the township was taught in 1840 by Thomas Stubbs, a 47-year old, well-educated bachelor from New York. The structure used was a very small log building located north of the Friends' Meetinghouse at the top of a hill. It was furnished with benches made from oak logs and had a large fireplace. Only one term was taught at this location. Mr. Stubbs built a house for himself about one and one half miles northeast of New London and taught again the next winter in his new home. Mr. Stubbs' income was mainly food items.

About the year 1842, a small log hut was erected for a schoolhouse near the north central part of the township. It was a subscription school with the teacher, William Miller, receiving room and board a week at a time from his pupils' families.

The Quakers in the community founded a school in 1844. It served as both a church and a school, and Hiram Newlin was the first teacher there. When the structure was destroyed by fire in 1851, another frame building went up nearby. From 1856 until 1876 this was used for school purposes only. Since New London was well-respected for the educational opportunities provided to its youth, the school was crowded and even had some out-of-state students who came to live with relatives and attend school here.

Norman Newton taught the first public school in the township. By 1853 there were only two public schools, and they were crudely made. By 1876 there were seven public schools, more sturdy than former ones, that employed nine teachers. The first school board was comprised of Thomas Easterling, James Fortner, and Isaac Bates.

From the years 1862-1870 Jeremiah Hubbard taught at various district schools in and around New London, including Black Hill, Porcupine, and the Lewis Jones Schoolhouse. He then went to teach in Russiaville. These school terms were about three and one half months long with the teacher being paid up to $45 per month. Sometimes there were 40 students in the classroom.

The Friends School came to an end in 1874 when the township bought the old frame building and the grounds. The New London Public School thus commenced with Horace G. Woody as the first teacher. He was a very educated man who had graduated at Ohio Normal College and was a master of grammar and languages. He went on later to be-

New London School as seen in 1954.

come principal as well as superintendent at Kokomo and later at Greencastle.

New London School got a new brick building in 1876. The bricks were made on the ground as the building was constructed. Eli Carter was trustee at the time. The school had four large rooms besides hallways, cloak rooms, and recitation rooms. It was said to rival any school in the county. This school lasted until 1913 when another new building was built. New London School was made a four-year high school in 1895. At the end of the school year Eighth Grade Commencement was held in the morning at the old town hall followed by a picnic; then High School Commencement was held in the afternoon. As evidence to show how respected the New London schools were, it is said that a Reverend E.D. Simons of the Newlight Christian denomination came to this area in 1891 purposely to give his children the advantages of a good education.

The last school at New London was built in 1913 at a cost of $30,000. Dr. W.H. Newlin was the trustee at the time. Wilmer Lindley, who had graduated in the Class of 1903 and went on to graduate from Earlham College, was principal for a while. Others included Paul Kelsey, R. Lamb, A. Benge, Lloyd Keisling, E.C. Crider and George Connelly. Mr. Connelly had a long tenure, serving during the 1930's and 1940's. New London became a grade school in 1948-49 when Monroe, Harrison, and Honey Creek Townships consolidated to become Western School Corporation. The high school was then located first at West Middleton and then at Russiaville (see Western School History.) When New London was still a high school, there was a gymnasium located a block south and two blocks west of the school where basketball was played by the "New London Quakers" wearing blue and gold uniforms.

Whites have not been the sole residents of Monroe Township. For many years and still today, various members of the Russell Reed and Cecil Reed families have lived at the eastern edge of New London. Early histories tell of their relatives, the Dick Cunningham family, who had a tile mill west of town. In the 1840's and 1850's there were two Methodist Churches in New London, one for whites and one for blacks. Another history states that Samera Newlin, a Quaker, was one of the teachers in the colored school; she taught at the Friends School, too.

Underground Railroad Activities

During the days when the Abolitionist Movement was strong in the 1850's, many in the New London community, especially Quakers, helped the Freedman's Aid Committee to assist runaway slaves. As slaves escaped from their plantations in the South and crossed the Ohio River, many were aided on their way north to their ultimate destination in Canada. These series of stops were known as the Underground (secret) Railroad which had a number of "conductors." In the New London area, one such conductor was Daniel R. Jones, known as "Uncle Dan." As slaves came from Westfield to New London, sympathizers would give shelter and food to those in need of safety before being sent on to Poplar Grove in Ervin Township and on north until safely out of the United States. The Underground Railroad has always been a highlight people relate when telling the history of New London.

Cultural Activities

In the early 1870's some students at New London School were interested in creating a literary society, and, as a result, the Junta Literary Society was born. It grew from about ten members to 40. Their meetings included a variety of presentations such as charades, debates, plays, and lectures. In addition, they built up a library of more than 300 volumes by the late 1890's. Also out of their efforts to build a hall for their activities came the New London Hall. A literary paper called *The Junta Star* was published by W.H. Newlin and C.G. Taylor in the 1890's. Nathan Cosand's poems were often published in this paper.

Steve Wilson's Singing School was held in the 1880's at Pleasant Hill Meeting House. Later he held one at Cloverdale Methodist Church. Mr. Wilson was a teacher of music for many years.

Fairs were another amusement held back in olden days. In the early 1860's and for 10 or 12 years thereafter, a fair was held west of Shirley Corner on Rev. J. E. Hartsuck's farm. Supposedly Tom Thumb, the famous midget, was an attraction there, along with his wife.

In time, a telephone service was started in New London, and Prior Comer (grandson of John Prior Wright) had charge of the exchange. The switchboard operated until Indiana Bell went on the dial system in the 1950's. The last operator was Opal Shepherd who had taken over the job in 1944 from Lloyd and Reba Carter.

Churches

The first minister in the township was Job Garner of the Newlight Christian denomination. He and his wife Rebecca came in 1840, and since there were no church buildings yet, services were held in the log cabins of the early settlers. Sometime later a meetinghouse was erected and called the Sugar Grove Union Church. It was located in the western part of Monroe Township near present-day County Road 1280 West and a short distance north of 250 South. This church was destroyed by a suspicious fire in January of 1888. A *Kokomo Dispatch* account at the time suggested there were conflicts among the Methodists and the Newlight Christians and that the fire might have been intentional. The same year the Oakland Christian Church was built and has been in use up to the present time. It is located just a little farther north at 1280 West - 200 South.

Through the years the Sugar Grove Union Church was shared by a variety of denominations including United Brethren, Newlight Christians, Methodists, and the Progressive Brethren (1883-1886), who were a group that divided from the German Baptist Brethren denomination northeast of them.

The German Baptist Brethren "Taufers," sometimes referred to as "Dunkards," settled in Carroll County by 1828, and by 1845 four or five families had come to western Howard County. In 1852 they desired to form a separate congregation, and the Howard County German Baptist Brethren Church was organized. After meeting in homes for several years, the group built their own meetinghouse in 1865 on land owned by Jonas Brubaker. The wooden church was located south of Wildcat Creek on a hill just west of Stonebraker's Mill. The church was moved to Ervin Township in 1886 where services were held until September 1993. At that time it was sold to another denomination.

A major denomination in the township was the Society of Friends, known as the Quakers. Two churches existed. One was at Pleasant Hill Friends Meetinghouse which was established in 1852 and stood at 150 South-1030 West. The first recorded Friends minister in the county, James Owen, served there. The church is long gone, but the cemetery still exists.

The majority of Quakers in the area attended services in New London. The very first

New London Friends Church 1856-1905

New London Friends Church which was built in 1952.

Oakland Christian Church, one of two active churches in Monroe Township in 1994.

service was held in a grove west of the town with six people attending. As was the custom the service was silent throughout. After that, services were held in houses. Then John Prior Wright and his wife led efforts to erect a building for worship which was completed in the early 1840's. It was made of rough logs and doubled as a school. The building was destroyed by fire in the 1850's. A very large church was next constructed which lasted from 1856-1905. It had a basement with a well-equipped dining room and kitchen. The women often held "penny suppers" to help with church expenses such as the purchase of songbooks. Usually $30 or more could be raised at each supper. Many patrons came to these suppers from Kokomo. Another event that occurred in this church was New London's first revival. Jeremiah Hubbard and William Pinkham were leading the services at the Methodist Church, but an overflow crowd required a bigger building. Rev. Hubbard arranged to have the meeting moved to the Friends Church.

In 1905 the large church was replaced by another structure. Jehu Reagan was pastor at the time. This church served the community until 1951 when it, too, was destroyed by a fire. By 1952 the members had erected a beautiful stone building which approximately 50 people still worship in today. Instead of penny suppers, the congregation has gained a reputation for the fish frys they hold in the spring and sometimes in the fall of the year. Ann Carter is the current pastor.

William Wilson was the first Methodist minister in the township. At first services were held in homes, but in time a church was built in the town. Years later it was moved to a different location in New London, and eventually it was sold to the Baptists and moved to Russiaville. Another Methodist church, one for the blacks in the community, also existed. Thomas Roberts was the minister.

In 1888 Cloverdale Methodist Church was built where County Roads 1050 West and 250 South intersect today. It was dedicated in September of that year; L.E. Knox was their first minister. The church was painted white and had a bell tower. The floor elevated upwards, leaving two side aisles. A stove was located at the east and west ends of the building. Cloverdale was home to its congregation until 1968 when it closed. It was deeded back to the Methodist Conference in 1968 who then sold the land back to Nolan Miller. Today the building still stands, and out in front is the old pump that people used to quench their thirst. Just down the road north at the next intersection used to stand the old country store called Shanghai. During threshing season back in olden days the women of Cloverdale Church used to cook dinners for the threshers and serve them in a hall on the north side of the country store. Shanghai also had a post office and one gas pump. Mr. and Mrs. Preston Crawford operated the Shanghai store during the Depression years.

Two other churches existed in the New London community for a few years. The Seventh Day Adventists organized their church in 1878 when their members purchased the old district school building no longer needed. This church continued until 1912. The Holiness Christian Church was built in 1898, and it, too, continued for several years.

47

Medical Facilities

Over the years, New London had a number of physicians who served the citizens. Around 1846 there were three: Drs. Stoneman, Wickersham, and Barrett. A little later, Dr. J.F. Henderson, Dr. Pettyjohn, and Nathan Mendenhall practiced there. One whose name has left its mark on the community was Dr. D.J. Shirley. The location of his home is a landmark people still recognize today. The area where Alto Road (250 South) intersects with the New London Road (750 West) has been referred to for many, many years as Shirley's Corner or just Shirley Corner. For a few years that area was also referred to as Brantown because a Dr. T. Volney Gifford had a sanitarium in that location in the early 1860's, and because the sanitarium was known for its nutritious bran bread, the nickname was used. A few years later, Dr. Volney opened the Invalid's Home at Kokomo. Several doctors worked for Dr. Voley at the sanitarium.

Another well-known doctor at New London was Dr. W.H. Newlin who was a physician for 46 years. He died in 1935 at age 70, and at his death, he was the oldest practicing physician in the county.

Years later Dr. John R. Ware came to the community and had a general practice from 1959 until his death in 1979. His office was located next to his home at 700 West - 250 South.

Cemeteries

There are five cemeteries located in the township. The oldest one is located behind where New London High School stood and has pioneer graves dating back to 1841. On the north of the New London Friends Church and also across the road from the church is the New London Friends Cemetery. The other three cemeteries are in the western part of the township. McCoy Cemetery is located on private property at 50 South - 975 West; Pleasant Hill Cemetery is at 150 South - 1025 West; and the Miller Cemetery is at 100 South - 1100 West.

Social and Educational Organizations

For more than 50 years, the people of Monroe Township have had several opportunities to involve themselves in activities of a social or educational nature. Home Economics Clubs started forming in the 1920's to expose housewives to better ways of homemaking. These continue today, and in Monroe Township several women are involved in the Monroe Extension Homemakers, the Happy Homemakers, and the Sugar and Spice Club.

With this being a farming community, many have held membership in the Farm Bureau organization. The Masonic Lodge at New London, which dates back to the 1840's, continues to have meetings every second Wednesday of the month. And those who have joined the Russiaville Lions Club find plenty of involvement in worthwhile service projects that benefit many in the community.

Since mid-century the youth in the township have been invited to join 4-H clubs that offer projects dealing with a variety of educational topics. Their completed projects are exhibited at the Greentown 4-H Fair in July of every year. For the sports-minded boys and girls, too, there are Little League baseball or Pixie League softball teams which offer summer fun.

Friendship Home

In the late 1960's Bette Bannon spearheaded an endeavor to create Friendship Home for Girls. It was founded to provide a better atmosphere to girls whose own home environments had been determined by the local welfare department to be unsuitable at the time. In 1966 Dwight and Lillian Bennett donated three acres of land on which the home was built. The home is located at 6412 West - 90 South. It houses up to 14 girls who may stay until they reach the age of 21.

(This history was compiled by Carolyn Wheeler with the help of the early history written in the 1877 Atlas, Blanchard's 1883 history, and the New London history written by Edna Jones Payne.)

TAYLOR TOWNSHIP

Taylor Township was first plotted the winter of 1846-47, so all the history books tell us. There was rich rolling land along the creeks and smaller streams that seemed perfect for the production of many good crops. Farm land is what Taylor Township was for the first 100 years, or so. It included three communities, namely Fairfield, now known as Oakford; Terre Hall, now known as Hemlock; and Tampico, now known as Center. Each of these communities was well equipped to serve its neighbors.

The year 1852 saw the township grow by leaps and bounds. All three of the villages were laid out — Tampico, by Ephraim Trabue; Terre Hall, by Asa Parker; and Fairfield by Stephens & Miller. Fairfield had additions in 1852, by Frazier and Puckett. The 1854 addition was done by Osborn & Thomas. In 1855 Joseph Lowry laid out the third addition. Tampico had one addition done in 1858 by Elizabeth Trabue.

Center has seen three name changes. At first it was Tampico, then it became Centre. Now of course it is known as Center.

Although farming was the mainstay for this township for many years, it has become a small business haven. The farmers now total only 50. The current farms in the township are: Brian K. Adair, Robert L. Adair, Russell W. Adair Jr., David Blazer, Richard Blazer, Lannie L. Bogue, Scott Bogue, Richard Cannon, Michael Cobb, Max Cole, Tracy Cole, Fred David, Dale Fawcett, Eugene Fenn, Jerry Gates, John Grinslade III, James Hoppes Jr., John Ingels, C. Ray Lamb, Ned Lamb, George Lohrman, David Long, Maple Farm, Inc., Francis E. McClain, William Mugg, Francis E. Osburn, Edgar Richards, John Rickey, Everett Smiley, William A. Stafford, Charles Strawback, William Trine, Bradley Webber, Jonnie Webber, Joseph Vern Williams, Wayne Wyrick, Stan Rush, Larry D. Johnson, Delores Saul, Richard Saul, Artie Scruggs, Gene E. Sellers, Jerry Sellers, E. Wesley Smith, Wayne Stiner, Roy Taylor, Ralph Wal, Joetta Webber, Gary White, Jessie H. Windlow. These few farms and farmers keep alive the heritage of this township.

Only the name of Cobb, Ingles & Mugg have survived the 148 years of farm history in this township. A list of the early settlers for the township include William S. Rodman, said to be the first white man; he arrived between the spring of 1841 and the winter of 1842. His brother-in-law Charles Harmon followed soon after. 1842 saw the arrival of Alexander Thatcher and Allen Sharpe. As the area become known and populated the changes and development started. 1843 brought Laomi Ashley, David Thatcher, Job and Henry Garner, Elias Wilson, Thomas & Isaac Miller, Matthew, William & Samuel Poff, Nathan E. Beals (Bailes). 1844 brought Mordecai Overman, who built the first brick home about 1854. He left the area about 1856. Peter Kirkman, Robert Bracken, Robert Morrison, C. Smith, E.S. Apperson, John Albright, J.H. Hatton and Dr. J.A. Horine were also new residents in 1844. The following year of 1845 brought Isaac Eads, Jesse D. Scott, Reason Lackey, Washington Baumgardner, Peter Daniels, James Smith, John Dillman, Joseph Skeen and Jacob Baumgardner (brother of Washington). 1846 was a slow year for growth as only five new families came to the area; they were B.W. & Jacob Applegate, G. Ingles, Sr., J.W. Morris, John Welty and William Helms. 1847 brought Abraham Ingles, John Alexander, Sr., John Dillman, William Mugg, Edward C. Albright, John Moulder, Thomas Beard, Myron Beard, Ezekiel Parker, Asa Parker, William Hughes, Jesse Thatcher and Ephraim Trabue.

Now that the township had been plotted and the families busied themselves clearing and planting crops, the area began to develop and prosper. The usual stores and mills appeared as well as churches and schools. Civilization had begun. A partial list of the known families that arrived 1848 and later were: Thomas Kimball, Arch Gilson, David Foster, Wm. Coons, John Goyer, J.G. Templin, John G. King, Henry Ryan, Silas Andrews, David Sawyer, John Ingles, Wm. Morton, John Street, John Lindley, Theophilus Manuel, Simeon Mugg, John Spencer, W.G. Elliott, R.C. Cobb, Gideon Stevens, Ezra Pierce, Luther Hall, John Hastie, James Surry, Robert Kingsley, John Seawright, Jeremiah Bassett, Wm. Currens, George Duinette, George and Thomas Plankenstaver, L.L. Bennett, John T. Cobb, Joseph Imbler, David Jackman, T. Millikan, Reuben Shenk, Denton Simpson and Thomas W. Smith.

The 1850s brought more families to the township, and along with them came more business and farms. Some of those families were: J. Keck, Enos Neal, Isaac N. Knight, M.T. Patten, John Brummett, J.J. Duncan, H.T. Thomas, R. Thomas, Dr. Reuben Thomas, Bennett H. Chandler, Wm. Rex, Levi Pearson, J.T. Dyar, A.J. Duke, W. Darrough and Joseph Haskett.

The results of a big snow storm on February 25, 1961.

The trees were laden with ice after an ice storm on January 26, 1967.

As the city of Kokomo moved south and expanded, portions of the township became a part of the city. Therefore, the business base and population of the township have grown tremendously the past 40 years or so. A list of the township subdivisions include:

Alexander Acres, Booth, Coles Acres, Cook, Dillman's, Fairfield Acres, Hartsfield, Hochstedler's, Jones Manor, Kelsay, Meadowlark, Orem, Parsons, Porter, Raymond's, Springdale, Swinney Minor, Terrace Meadows, Walton Woods Minor, White Minor, Cardinal Point, Indian Heights, Alfrida, Cammerers, Coles Minor, Davis Manor, Donald, Flowing Wells, Hendershot Minor, Ingleside, Karnes Acres, Keyton Acres, Moree's Minor Manor, Oscars, Plantation, Pumpkin Vine Meadows, Robinson, Stoneybrook, Tarrytown Estates, Walton Lake Estates, White's Minor, Winding Brook, Worthley Estates, Baker, Chateau East, Cobb, DeBusk, Duncan Acres, George Karns, Hipp, Jesse Kelly, Lou's Minor, Lytle Minor, Newlin, Ostler, High Bend, Randolph's, Southwood, Stoneybrook East, Taylor Meadows, Walton Woods, Wooley Minor, Timme, Hodson's Minor.

Indian Heights is the largest and most populated. It is the home of many home-operated businesses and, of course, the Indian Heights Volunteer Fire Department. The department began in about 1959. It is still an all volunteer department. The first fire station was built on land donated by National Homes, the developer for the subdivision. It has steadily grown. The current station was built in 1974 with a second station built in 1988. This volunteer fire department serves the township and is available to assist the surrounding areas when requested. Station #2 is located just east of Center and across from the high school. It also houses a community center that is used by residents for various events.

Some of Its Citizens

Fredrick Youngman came to Taylor Township in 1866 and commenced making tile for the Braden & Byers Co. Mr. Youngman bought the factory soon after he arrived. The factory was located just east and south of Fairfield. He claimed to have made the first machine-made tile in the state. About 1870 he built a stately two-story home in which to raise his family of three daughters. This home was a constant piece of history until the night of June 18, 1992 when lightening hit it and the following fire devastated it. The home had never been out of the family and was unaltered. It was listed on the Indiana Historical Society Register and is pictured in their book titled *Indiana Houses of The Nineteenth Century*. It was also placed on the **National Registry of Historical Places**. Mr. Youngman laid his manufactured tile on his farm of 375 acres and it was deemed the best drained farm in the area. This farm is still prosperous and is still in the Youngman family.

J.H. Martin was a native of Decatur County, IN. He married Elizabeth Caldwell, a native of Kentucky. They had a family of six sons. In 1866 they came to Taylor Township, a short distance south of Fairfield, where he built a fine brick home on their farm of 144 acres. In 1870 he and a son erected a large brick building in Fairfield for the purpose of operating a merchandise store. This home still stands as well as the business building. The home is still a residence and the business building now houses Hayes Bros. Contractors.

Rev. Denton Simpson came to Howard County in 1848. He was an educator. In the summer of 1849 he began farming in Taylor Township. He married Melissa Trabue and they had nine children. He was a licensed Baptist minister and preached for free in the Baptist society.

Nathan C. Beals was the first probate judge of Howard County. His arrival date cannot be documented. He built and operated the first mill in the township, just northeast of Fairfield.

Henry E. Rakestraw reached his 100th birthday July 21, 1961. He was born in Clinton County but spent most of his 100 years in Howard County. He was a resident of Oakford from 1902. He owned and operated the Oakford Elevator until it was destroyed by fire in 1946.

Cemeteries

The township does not have many cemeteries. The largest and most known is the Albright Cemetery. It is still active and has become one of the finest in the county. Its quite peaceful country setting makes it a popular final resting place. The Randolph Cemetery is located on the U.S. 31 Highway on the northbound side. It is just north of St. Rd. 26 and south of the Indian Heights entrance. This cemetery was a part of the Oakford Separate Baptist Church. The church is in Oakford now as it has been for many years. The Upper Kokomo Church Cemetery is located at 400 East and 200 South. The Lower Kokomo Church Cemetery is located on 400 East and 300 South behind the homes there. It cannot be seen from the road; unless you know just where to go, you would never find it. The Upper Kokomo Church Cemetery is also known as the Poff Cemetery, for the obvious reason that the Poff family is buried there. The Chandler Cemetery is located about 700 East and 300 South. There was a small cemetery just east of Oakford, called the Fairfield Burial Ground, but no trace of it exists today.

Railroads

Each of the three communities had railroad lines. These were used to transport the grain and goods from place to place. The mail also arrived by rail. Of the three towns, only Oakford still has its rails. However it is not used often and is in a bad way.

There was an interurban that ran for some time from Oakford. The old interurban station still stands as a private home.

Churches and Religion

The first church to organize in the township was the Lower Kokomo Church. It was a Christian denomination known as the New Lights. The year was 1843. The Upper Kokomo Church was organized in 1847. In the spring of 1846 the Union Separate Baptist Church organized. The elders responsible for the organization were Jacob Baumgardner and Uriah McQueen. They began in Harrison Twp. but moved to a Taylor Township location in 1849. The church began with eight charter members: Mr. and Mrs. Peter Kirkman, Mr. and Mrs. G.W. Baumgardner, Mr. and Mrs. Jacob Baumgardner and Mr. and Mrs. Charles Harmon. The Albright Chapel Methodist Church organized in 1847. In October of 1849 the Bethany Missionary Baptist Church was established. In July 1854 they changed their place of worship to the Christian Meeting House.

Fairfield Christian (New Light) Church was organized 1853 in a little cabin on the northwest corner of the Fred Youngman farm. Abandoned for a while, it reorganized in 1860 and is still a part of the Oakford history. The Methodist Church of Tampico was organized Nov. 5, 1857. The Friendship Baptist Church, an offspring from the Bethany Baptist Church, organized Jan. 17, 1877.

The list of current churches in the township includes: Brookside Free Methodist, Oakford Separate Baptist, Hemlock Friends, Mt. Zion Wesleyan, Indian Heights Grace Brethren, Cornerstone Christian, Southview Assembly of God, Fairfield Christian, Mt. Gilead Baptist, Indian Heights Baptist, Family Worship Center, Macedonia Christian.

Grades one through four at Oakford School in 1929 with teacher Naomi Ray. (l. to r.) Front: Ralph Maish, Ernest Powell, unknown, Ray Burger, James Lucas, unknown, George Lucas, unknown, Wilbur Burger, and Elmer Lee. Middle: Unknown, Unknown, Allie Lee, Oleta Kelley, Ruth Maish, Leona Kelley, Florence Maroney, Dorothy Radabaugh, Wilma Kelley, and two unknowns. Back: John Lee, Bill Maroney, unknown, unknown, Marion Radabaugh, unknown, Mary Katherine Longfellow, unknown, unknown, Betty Myers, Betty Hancock, Joanna Glunt, and Katherine Dunn.

Education

Education in this area was much the same as in other farm related areas. The towns each had a school house. The buildings in Oakford and Hemlock were brick structures. The one in Center was a good framed building. The one in Oakford still stands and has been converted into the home of Brenda and Jerry Schave.

The consolidation of the township schools was done and they are now the Taylor Community Consolidated School Corp. This system consists of three buildings, an elementary building in Indian Heights and two buildings at Center, an elementary and a junior high school.

There were four known one-room school houses in the township. They were the Eads School, located one mile east of Highway 19 on Center Road; the Lorts School, located near the Mt. Zion Wesleyan Church on State Road 26; and the Helms and Brown Schools.

Hemlock School about 1907

The home of Jerry and Brenda Schave was formerly the Oakford School building.

Oakford Post Office Postmasters

William Tryberger	Aug. 23, 1854
Robert C. Foor	Feb. 8, 1855
William A. Croddy	Jan. 6, 1859
William H. Thomson	Aug. 31, 1861
John Evans	May 22, 1866
Seth W. Chase	June 2, 1868
Lemuel E. Boyd	June 17, 1868
Henry Boyd	April 4, 1870
Andrew W. Caldwell	Feb. 23, 1871
Aaron Vanhook	Sept. 4, 1873
Franklin Hancock	Sept. 18, 1874
Lucius L. Bennett	Oct. 27, 1876
Daniel W. Martin	Jan. 31, 1881
Margaret E. Jennings	March 16, 1887
John N. Croussore	April 13, 1887
Silas F. Randolph	Feb. 28, 1888
Daniel W. Martin	Jan. 9, 1890
John G. Martin	Feb. 25, 1891
Charles M. Randolph	April 29, 1893
Jehu Hancock	June 25, 1897
Samuel A. Lowry	Jan. 19, 1899
William P. Jones	March 24, 1908
Jacob Whitman	Feb. 16, 1911
Clinton B. Tudor	April 20, 1915
Russell E. Tudor	Dec. 11, 1928
Clinton B. Tudor	Aug. 24, 1932 (assumed charge)
	Sept. 9, 1932 (acting)
	Jan. 10, 1933 (confirmed)
Laurel J. Beck	Nov. 1, 1934 (assumed charge)
	Nov. 7, 1934 (acting)
	Dec. 15, 1934 (confirmed)
Nora Hale	Aug. 27, 1935 (assumed charge)
	Aug. 31, 1935 (acting)
	Oct. 1, 1935 (confirmed)
Flossie P.E. Mason	Aug. 15, 1942 (confirmed)
	Sept. 14, 1942 (assumed charge)
Helga Summerton	June 30, 1947 (assumed charge)
	Sept. 15, 1947 (confirmed)
Joyce Sparks	February 1977 (assumed charge)
	Aug. 13, 1977 (confirmed)

Hemlock Post Office Postmasters

Andrew J. Cole	May 2, 1881
Benjamin F. Farmer	May 14, 1889
Amasa B. Seward	March 2, 1892
James W. McIntosh	April 10, 1892
Benjamin F. Farmer	Sept. 21, 1893
John C. Huntsinger	Aug. 6, 1895
Benjamin F. Farmer	Feb. 12, 1896
William T. Pugh	May 29, 1899
Jonathan R. Pickering	Feb. 28, 1900
James F. McInturf	June 30, 1905
Minnie Jackman	April 22, 1913
Mrs. Iva Snyder	April 30, 1935 (assumed charge)
	May 3, 1935 (acting)
Howard Duncan	May 31, 1935 (assumed charge)
	June 8, 1935 (acting)
	Aug. 28, 1935 (confirmed)
Ruth M. Sutton	Aug. 27, 1965 (acting)
	July 25, 1966 (confirmed)
Christina A. Bogue	Nov. 30, 1990 (officer in charge)
	Dec. 15, 1990 (confirmed)

Post Offices

Each of the three communities formed had their own post office, with two of the three still in operation. The Oakford Post Office was established Aug. 23, 1854, with William Tryberger the first postmaster. Hemlock's Post Office was established May 2, 1881 with Andrew J. Cole as its first postmaster. The post office in Center was closed Sept. 15, 1972. It was established Aug. 26, 1854 as Tampico, changed to Centre and the final change to Center came July 31, 1893. All that is known about this post office and its postmasters is that in 1882 J.B. Skinner was postmaster.

UNION TOWNSHIP

In 1844 the area that is Howard County was organized and named Richardville County, after a prominent Miami Indian chief. The land had previously belonged to the Miami Indians and was known as the Miami Reserve. Because this area was the last section of land given up by the Miamis, it was one of the last sections in the state of Indiana to be opened for settlement.

General dissatisfaction with the name Richardville—it was too cumbersome to use—caused the name to be changed to Howard County two years later in 1846. The new county was named for Indiana politician Tilman A. Howard. At this time there were three townships: Monroe, to the west; Kokomo, in the center; and Green, to the east.

In 1846 a subdivision took place, and the resulting townships were: Center, Ervin, Monroe, Clay, Harrison, Taylor, Howard, Jackson and Green. In 1853 one further division occurred; the territory of Green and Jackson Townships became Jackson, Liberty and Union Townships.

The first settler to arrive in the Union Township area was a man named David Bailey in 1842. He settled on land at the forks of Wildcat Creek, the principal waterway in the township. Thomas Moorman, C.P. Baldwin, C.O. Fry, James Lancaster and Elliott Mason cut the first road through the thick forest to the township from Grant Country.

The first log house was erected by Robert Felton, and Joseph Brown put up the second one within the township boundaries. Joseph Brown also planted the first nursery, bringing fruit trees to his new home from Wayne County in April, 1850. Other settlers followed, building cabins and clearing patches of ground where crops could be planted.

James Frazier and Jesse Dennis burned the first brick kilns about 1849; in 1848 Timothy Garrigus built the first sawmill at Jerome for Hampton Brown; James Lancaster had the first hand-mill on Lilly Creek just before the Brown sawmill.

In 1846 Reuben Hawkins built the first mill for grinding corn on Lilly Creek. The first brick house was built in 1852 by Phillip Barkdull; the second, still standing on SR 213, was put up by Aaron Coppock.

The first election was held at the home of Henry Bailey; the 1844 Presidential Election took place 1 1/2 miles south of Greentown at the Indian village of Shocomo; the polls consisted of a hat placed on an oak stump, where 15 votes were collected.

The first schools were subscription schools. Mrs. Rachel Baldwin taught the first school at her home 1 1/2 miles east of Jerome in 1845. Her husband, Charles P. Baldwin, taught the second school in 1848-49 in the vacant house of William Jones (later Hoover) 1/2 mile north of Jerome. The first school averaged 3 to 8 pupils; the second, about 25 pupils; by 1876 the township had 665 students. The first building built especially for school purposes was a hewed-log structure with slab seats, located just north of Jerome and built in 1850. It was shortly replaced by a two-story frame building, the upper level devoted to a Masonic Hall. This was the first frame school in Union Township.

The first blacksmith shop was established by Anderson Houston; in Jerome, by Smith C. Todd. The first doctors were J.N. Horine (a root doctor), Isaac Fisher, John Summers, Jonah Pierce; one of the more prominent conditions they were required to treat in the early days was ague, caused by the swampy conditions of the land before it was adequately drained. The first tanner was Francis Galway at Jerome in 1849; C.P. Baldwin was the first Postmaster (at Jerome). The first wedding was Phillip Barkdull's son Albert, to a daughter of Reuben Hawkins — another early pioneer. It is said that Levi Bailey, Justice of the Peace and a bachelor, encountered some difficulty performing his duties at the ceremony, and nearly fainted.

The first child born in the Union Township area was a child of Phillip Barkdull in 1846. The first death was a child of Thomas Moorman in 1845; the Moorman child was buried on land north of West Liberty, the burial ground later becoming the Simpson Cemetery. In 1846 the Barkdull family also suffered the death of a child, the burial being made at a location west of Jerome.

Establishment of Jerome

The village of Jerome was laid out in December, 1847, by Hampton Brown, who had arrived in the area the year before. He named the new village "Jerome" after one of his sons.

Jerome came into being because of the need of the people in the area for a place to do their trading. The closest trading points to them were New London, Russiaville, and Jonesboro, all too far away for convenience in a day when travel was over poor roads.

The first of Hampton Brown's lots were sold to Smith C. Todd for his blacksmith shop, and to Thomas Banks, who became the town's first merchant when he built a combination storehouse and residence on the west side. Many other businesses and families came to Jerome, and for a time the hamlet was a thriving place. In 1877 Jerome was incorporated, and a town government was maintained for three years.

The greatest single thing that would have made Jerome great also caused its demise. With the coming of the narrow gauge Toledo, Delphos, and Western Railway through Howard County, great effort was made to bring the railway through Jerome. But the town of Greentown (incorporated in 1873) stood more on a line between Kokomo and Marion, and though it was only a couple of miles south to Jerome, the railroad built the track through Greentown. After that, with business and interest in Jerome on the decline, concurrent with the rise of the same in Greentown, the prospects and career of Jerome began to fade.

The Establishment of West Liberty

Another village inside the Union Township territorial lines is that of West Liberty, situated a few miles southeast of Jerome. In 1847 Israel Zentmyer entered (claimed) the land where West Liberty is located; the following year he built a dwelling and blacksmith shop. In the spring of 1849 Zentmyer sold out to Moses Jones, who added a large water mill, and who had the site surveyed and platted in 1849. He then put the lots on the market.

John Barr, a son-in-law of Jones, erected one of the first houses in the town; Moses Rich established the first store about 1850. Other merchants over the years were: David Macy, a storeowner for five years; Lewis Sharpe; Allen & Goff; and Jacob Harvey, all early storekeepers. Hood & Becket built a large store; Beckett & Weaver had one of the largest stores in the village; D.S. Swan built a two-story building in 1868; and the three story Jones Mill was the largest in the county at the time.

The prospects of West Liberty seemed great. But like Jerome it too had no access to a railroad line; gradually business interests seemed to move on, leaving behind another little village on the prairie.

The Village of Phlox

The village of Phlox began as a crossroads in the south end of Union Township. Nothing but farms abutted the four corners of the intersection until 1862, when Edmund Peele donated one acre off the northeast corner of his farm—which would be the southwest corner of the intersection—for the erection of a log building to house a Friends church congregation.

In the late 1860's a frame building was built to replace the log church. About 1875 a frame school house was built on the southeast corner of the intersection. After a few terms of schools, this building burned; in 1878 a brick one room school was completed.

Gradually houses began to be built; in the 1880's a store was opened on the northeast corner. When a post office was proposed for the settlement, the name of Phlox was chosen; the post office remained until 1898. In the 1890's a larger store was erected on the northwest corner of the intersection.

In 1900 a large addition was made to the brick school, which served until 1915 when it was closed; later it was used for farm implement storage; it burned down in the early 1970's.

In the 1930's electricity came to Phlox; also the State of Indiana made the east-west road into SR 26. In the late 1930's the Friends Church was moved back from the road and enlarged.

In 1937 Henry S. Hatton opened a Standard Service Station and grocery on the west edge. His son James M. Hatton put in a sand croquet court behind the store and rigged it with lights; many matches were played there night and day. The store was closed in the 1940's.

Willie Wines operated a tomato canning business in Phlox a few years. Leo "Bud" Wunder opened a garage on the south side and did light mechanical work; Lloyd Lee had a similar shop on the north side of town. In the late 1940's Center Grove Baptist Church moved a building

Jesse Nash, Jr. and Mary A. (Batey) Nash, with their daughter May Nash standing on right side of gate in front of their log house near West Liberty in Union Township.

View of Phlox in 1940.

from west of town into a grove at the west edge of Phlox; later they built another building there.

The Cook family moved to Phlox in the 1960's and chronicled a sad story. Oldest son Bill was sent to Korea with the U.S. Army in 1967. He had recently been married to Barbara Johnson, and their son, Nick Joseph, was born after he left. Bill never got to see his son; he was killed just short of his twenty-first birthday when his jeep ran over a land mine and was fired upon.

Ross and Wilma Davis were the last merchants in Phlox, closing the store on the northwest corner in the early 1970's. Today there are 26 homes within the town limits. Boyd R. Dutton, who lives just south of the intersection, rebuilds old John Deere tractors in his garage in his spare time, and that just about constitutes Phlox's commerce these days. James Hatton, since 1920, has resided there the longest.

One final fact: few phlox flowers grow in Phlox.

Churches

The first preachers in Union Township were of the Methodist denomination, coming in 1844. Services were held in homes, the home of Charles O. Fry being the site of the first service. Sometimes, when the weather permitted, services were held out of doors, in groves of trees.

The first building to be built as a place of worship was a small log meeting house erected in 1847 by Friends settlers near the Forks of the Creek area. Services there were well attended for a time; gradually the congregation dwindled through deaths and people moving away, until the church was abandoned, with remaining members worshiping at other places. The log structure existed until 1871, when it was dismantled.

A Methodist Episcopal congregation was organized at Jerome in 1847; services were held in homes, then in a school house until 1853, when a new building was built on Jerome's east side. This building burned in 1874, and a second frame building capable of holding 300 worshippers was built on the same site; later the building was abandoned.

New Hope Friends Church was organized in 1858 at the home of Jesse Ellis, who lived near West Liberty. In 1862 the congregation moved to a new log building on land donated by Edmund Peele, at the crossroads that became the center of the village of Phlox. A frame building replaced the log structure in the late 1860's. Early ministers were Mary J. Peele, James A. Ellis, Jesse Hammer Ellis and Jefferson Jackson. This church exists today, in the same—though many times remodeled—building at the same location.

Center Grove Baptist Church came into being on March 21, 1869, through the efforts of Elders Jary Randolph, Hamilton, and Jacob Baumgartner. That year a frame structure was built at a location one mile west of Phlox, on the southwest corner of the intersection there. Services were held at the crossroads location until the late 1940's, when the congregation purchased a wooded plot of ground at the west edge of Phlox and moved the building there. Today, services are still held in the building.

The Jerome Christian Church had a flourishing congregation for many years. Their frame building, built in 1860, stood at the southwest corner of the village, not far from the bridge over Wildcat Creek. A tragedy occurred in the building in January, 1962, when Bradley Foland, infant son of church janitor Franklin Foland, was accidentally drowned in the baptismal while the elder Foland was cleaning the building. In the 1970's the congregation moved from Jerome to a new modern building two miles northwest of town. The old building was later torn down.

In 1892 C.D. Covalt, under conviction to build a church at West Liberty, donated $200 and a plot of land—100 days later the Methodist Episcopal Church opened in that fair village.

In 1893 a new United Brethren Church building was built 1 1/2 miles southeast of West Liberty. The congregation of 30 families had been meeting in school buildings. The 28 by 40 foot building was dedicated on Sunday, August 13, 1893, by Bishop Castle of Elkhart and church pastor J.A. Bushong. A church still exists at that location.

Cemeteries

The first burial in Union Township territory was a child of Thomas Moorman, buried in 1845 on a farm one mile northwest of West Liberty. Later Dr. S. Simpson purchased the land and the burying ground became known as the Simpson Cemetery. Among the graves is that of Robert 'Bob' Johns, a well known resident living just north of the area.

The second burial ground was just west of Jerome. The land, situated on a bluff between the forks of Wildcat and Lilly Creeks, was selected for a burying ground in 1846 by Joseph and Elias Brown. The site contained less than an acre, and no deed was ever written for it; the surrounding land belonged to William Laden, and thereafter whenever the land was sold, the cemetery acre was not included. Almost all of the people who died in the neighborhood were buried in that plot. As time went on the available space became depleted, and old graves were re-opened for a new burial.

In 1910 C.B.F. Clark, who then lived in Kokomo but who formerly lived at Jerome, saw the need for more room and bought 2 1/2 acres from landowner William Voorhis, the land being on the east side of the cemetery. Clark surveyed the land, laid off the cemetery plots, and put in ditching and a gravel driveway. He laid out 175 lots, many of which were sold before the work was finished. The grave of William Tolle, a farmer who lived three miles east of Jerome, was the first made in the new section. Others buried in the Jerome Cemetery are Hampton Brown and most of his children, William Shrader, and Cornelius Cullins.

Over the years the Jerome Cemetery did not receive the care it needed. The land around it grew up in trees and brush, and the accessibility of the burial ground back a long lane made it a somewhat isolated spot ripe for vandalism. Trees and bushes grew up around the tombstones; older stones crumbled or either fell or were knocked over. But today a fence and gate are in place, the trees have been kept in check, and the old Jerome Cemetery is well cared for.

The third burial ground in Union Township was made on a plot of ground between the forks of Wildcat Creek, a few miles northwest of West Liberty, and about a mile west of the Simpson Cemetery. This Cemetery, commonly known as the Forks of the Creek Cemetery, was begun in 1847 by members of the Friends congregation then worshipping a mile east of the location. This cemetery contains many old graves and is seldom used anymore. Among the people buried there are Amanda Hobbs Moorman, first wife of

Friends minister Chuza Moorman; Okey Shockney, son of pioneer Stephen Shockney; and John Fellow (d. 1927), prominent farmer and Friends worker in Tipton and Howard Counties. This cemetery is well cared for by the township trustee, as is the Simpson Cemetery.

The fourth and newest burial ground in Union Township is the New Hope-Ellis Cemetery, located 1/2 mile south of Phlox. This cemetery was established in May, 1885, by members of the New Hope Friends Church in Phlox. James A. Ellis owned land on the north bank of Wildcat Creek, and he was a preacher at New Hope Church. He gave two acres of land for a burial ground, on condition the church would fence and ditch it. The church agreed to do so and the donation was accepted.

A story has been handed down concerning the establishment of the cemetery. In early May, 1885, at the church's monthly meeting, while discussion was going on about starting the cemetery, someone suggested that action be postponed until the next month's meeting. But Miriam Overman requested that the matter be settled in that meeting, giving as her reason that the burial ground might be needed by someone before another monthly meeting could be held. Miriam Overman died a few days later on May 10, 1885, and her grave was the first one made in the new cemetery. Two days later Joel Adams became the second burial there.

Over the years an iron fence with gates was placed in front of the cemetery, and a horseshoe drive was made. In 1919 the cemetery was incorporated and a board of directors named to provide for its maintenance; in the 1960's, with most of the available lots in the cemetery having been taken, a strip of ground was added to the east side, making room for several more rows of lots. For the time being, with the additional space, availability of lots has been sufficient to meet the need. Among the people buried in New Hope-Ellis are Henry S. Hatton, J. Roscoe Shockney, and of course, James A. Ellis.

Francis Hannah uses machinery to dig the graves in New Hope-Ellis; in February 1993, he dug the grave of Robert Hannah, the hardest of all graves he has been called upon to dig. Robert Hannah was Francis Hannah's dad.

Union Township School

The first school session in Union Township was conducted in the home of Charles P. Baldwin in 1845. Gradually several brick one-room school buildings appeared around the township; these served until 1915 when two of them were condemned by the State Board of Health.

Two options were available: 1) Build new one room buildings, or 2) build one central unit to serve all the township. At the time the concept of centralizing rural schools was sweeping the country. Many Indiana counties were building centralized buildings; there were already five commissioned high schools in Howard County. Union Township opted to centralize its schools too.

The new building would be built near the center of the township, about 1 1/2 miles north of Phlox. The Elmer E. Dunlap architectural firm, with offices in Indianapolis and Kokomo, was given the job of drawing the plans. Greentown contractors Smith and Allen were awarded the contract to build the building, which was to cost $26,000; work was begun in the spring of 1916.

The brick building would have two stories over a raised basement; the basement would have a combination gymnasium and assembly room, a stage, rest rooms, and boiler room.

On the first floor were four large classrooms; the second floor contained three recitations rooms, a large domestic science room, and several offices. Modern in every respect, the building boasted its own heating plant, wash basins, and sanitary drinking fountains.

By August work had progressed to the point that plans for the laying of the cornerstone could be made. On September 12, 1916, in an elaborate ceremony under the auspices of the Greentown Masons, the cornerstone was put in place. Principal speaker was Warren Voorhis, who spoke for an hour on "The True Greatness of a People".

A box placed in the cornerstone contained several articles of interest, including a history of the township written by C.B.F. Clark, and several township plat maps.

The new Union Township central school building was completed in the summer of 1917, in time for the start of the school year. There were classes for all twelve grades, with the first graduating class being that of 1921.

In 1969 Union Township school itself was closed in yet another era of consolidation; eventually Union, Liberty Township, and Greentown combined to form the present Eastern Howard School Corporation. The Union land was sold to C.C. "Bud" Williams and the building was torn down. Today two homes occupy the site.

But the building remains in the memories of those who attended Union; the footsteps still tread the classrooms, and climb the stairways that rise from the halls of learning into the realities of life. Union will always be a part of her students.

Stories of the Township

When the first pioneer arrived in the area that was to become Union Township they found Indians of the Miami tribe still around. Charles O. Fry came in 1844 and settled on a claim in the vicinity of what would soon become Jerome. But Fry found he was right in the middle of an Indian sugar camp.

The Indians, incensed at this intrusion, gathered up some braves and terrorized the countryside, tearing down some unused cabins, pulling up the settler's fences, and running off their livestock. Charles Fry went to the chief with an offer to buy the land, but the chief declared it would take a load of hay to feed his ponies before any deals could be made.

Fry set out for the hay, but found that getting it was not going to be as easy as he thought. The nearest hay was in Marion, some distance away through a thick forest with relatively few roads. Fry had to cut his own trail but eventually made it back with the hay, and peace was restored. This was the last incident in Howard County involving the Indians.

As time went by Union Township was gradually built up. The heavy forests were cleared, the once plentiful wild game all but disappeared, and houses and farmsteads appeared. Fields were fenced off, roads were laid out—and sometimes re-laid out over a more favorable and straight course; bridges, both wooden and iron, were built over the waterways. In 1884 a 60-foot clear iron span was built over a creek at West Liberty; south of Phlox a wooden covered bridge spanned Wildcat Creek.

With the discovery of natural gas in Howard County in the mid 1880's, and the businesses that came to Kokomo to take advantage of it, gas wells were sunk all over the county including Union Township. The gas from the wells was pumped to Kokomo and used in industry. In 1889 a powerful gas well was drilled on the James A. Ellis farm 1/2 mile south of Phlox, and

Union Township School in 1940.

that fall this well figured in the death of pioneer Friends minister Chuza Moorman.

Chuza (pronounced Coo-za) Moorman was one of the very first brick masons in Union Township. He lived on a farm of 140 acres one mile south of Phlox on the Howard-Tipton County line. His house stood far back from the road, and in front of it stood a bank barn. Chuza Moorman and his in-laws, John and Abigail Fellow, all Quakers, were opposed to slavery in the days before the Civil War, and their farm was a stop on the famous Underground Railroad of that time. Slaves on their way to Canada and freedom were hidden in the basement of the bank barn, in an area accessible through a hidden door on the barn's main floor. A stream near the barn afforded the slaves the opportunity to lose their scent to the dogs that usually accompanied slave hunters.

But neighbors of the Fellows and Moormans were unsympathetic to their work. One dark night, as the Moormans lay sleeping in their beds, a party of disgruntled people made their way to the house and proceeded to stone it. One of the stones hit the headboard of the bed where Chuza and Rachel Moorman were sleeping; between them was their young daughter Amanda. The stone split the headboard apart, and fell—just missing Amanda.

Later on these buildings were moved closer to the road, and the barn no longer had a basement. But they are still standing, the property of Leonard Smith, and are still in use.

In October, 1889, a party of people including Chuza Moorman arrived at the Ellis farm to see a demonstration of the gas well. The occasion was for the benefit of a visitor from Kansas who had never before seen a gas well. Inexperienced William Kepler was to light the flame from a pipe that extended about 60 feet from the well house. At the end of the pipe was a four foot elbow that turned upward. The plan was to turn the elbow so the flame would shoot out onto the waters of nearby Wildcat Creek.

But the elbow was too loose, and when the flame was lit it fell to the ground; the force of the flame turned the pipe into a giant blow torch, and the pressure pushed the pipe around in a huge arc. Several men were injured, and Chuza Moorman was pinned to the ground by the flaming pipe. He was killed, and the body partly consumed before the pipe could be turned away. Chuza Moorman was buried in New Hope-Ellis Cemetery beneath a monument with a stone Bible on top—the book from which he lived and taught.

In November, 1892, a gas pipeline exploded near Phlox when workers pulled out a plug; several men were badly burned.

In May, 1896, during a spring storm, lightning struck a gas well southwest of West Liberty. The well, owned by the Lafayette Gas Co., was set on fire, and gas in a building over the well exploded, destroying the building. Men were sent out at once to contain the fire, using eleven pounds of explosives to blow it out. Natural gas had been a boon to growth of the county, but it was not without its perils.

In December, 1888, Jerome was the scene of a shooting. The victim was Grant County Sheriff Robert L. Jones, who had come to arrest John Fleming.

John Fleming, age 22, son of a well-to-do eastern Howard County farmer named William Fleming, had in September, 1888, hired a horse and buggy from Swayzee liveryman Perry Zirkle. He went to the home of a girl he was seeing, Ida McQuistan, and asked her to go with him. But he was rebuffed and threatened by her family. He then drove the rented rig to Marion, where he sold the horse. He was arrested, tried as a horse thief, and was convicted and sentenced to two years in the penitentiary. Later in September, just before he was to be moved to Michigan City, he escaped. Nothing more was seen or heard from him until December of that year.

Ida McQuistan was a daughter of Robert McQuistan, whose home was near the Howard-Grant County line. Although the family's wishes were for her not to see Fleming, those wishes she disregarded; 16-year-old George McQuistan, her half-brother, went to Marion and informed the sheriff that Fleming was to meet Ida McQuistan in Jerome that Sunday night around 9 o'clock, at the home of a widowed sister Jane Hopkins.

Sheriff Jones, only one month in office, started out for Jerome with Deputy Frank Fagan, George McQuistan and liveryman Zirkle. At the appointed time they approached the house, a log home; Fagan was to enter through the front door and Jones through the back door. The front door was blocked, slowing up Fagan, but Jones gained access to the house rather easily and confronted Mrs. Hopkins. He asked if Fleming was there and got no reply; at that moment Fleming sprang forward and shot Jones in the left arm.

Fleming and the girl retreated to a bedroom where they hoped to escape through a window. Jones followed and Fleming fired twice more, one shot missing and one shot striking Jones in the stomach. Jones used his only weapon, a club, and knocked Fleming onto the bed, then got on top of him and began putting handcuffs on. Deputy Fagan succeeded in entering the house, and he assisted Jones in subduing Fleming.

Deputy Fagan took Fleming back to Marion to jail, and Sheriff Jones, mortally wounded, remained at Jerome where he died from his wounds a short time later. He was only 39 years old.

Fleming was taken to Michigan City to avoid being lynched by a mob in Marion. In June, 1889, he was brought back to Howard County and tried in Howard Circuit Court on a charge of murder, was found guilty, and was sentenced to life in the penitentiary. He was paroled after serving about 25 years of his sentence.

In October, 1886, a young Albert Beveridge, later a U.S. Senator and author, made the first of many of his speeches in Howard County at West Liberty. Fresh out of college, he was on the campaign of 1886 speaking tour. Kokomo's O.A. Somers needed a speaker out at West Liberty and booked Beveridge for the occasion. When the good-sized crowd saw the youthful Beveridge they didn't expect much and indicated so, but Beveridge spoke clearly and eloquently and won the crowd over. Over the years until his death in 1927 he made many other appearances in Howard County.

On February 20, 1892, the Ellis store in Phlox was robbed by a pair of particularly vengeful thieves. Expecting to find the week's sales money, or perhaps the sales money for the store itself—Ellis had sold the store to E.C. Adams only a few days before—the thieves pulled the heavy safe out of the store into the street. There, they tried to open it, but only succeeded in ruining the safe. The thieves then took 400 yards of dress goods, unrolled them, and tramped them into the mud of the street. They did the same with linens, table cloths, and other items. They took with them clothing, boots, shoes, and groceries—and left the tools they used in the store. But they were frightened away before they could crack the sturdy safe; had they succeeded in opening it they would have found that the store sale money was not there—it had already been safely deposited in the bank.

Later in the year at Jerome a strange and disturbing phenomena was first noted on Sunday morning, August 28, 1892. In a 1/2 square mile area the wells and springs were showing a strong volume of muddy water. The same was true for Wildcat Creek, and for the smaller streams that emptied just below town. They were freshening and showing a much greater volume of water than was usual for them. The springs were increasing their flow, and there were several streams of water that had burst forth from the dry clay banks.

More disturbingly, there was a considerable amount of gas seen bubbling up in the affected streams and springs; some of it was strong enough to burn. In the streams the gas was boiling up and bubbling on the surface of the water, and everywhere there was a strong, pungent odor in the air.

It was believed one of the many gas wells in the area had burst its casing underneath the ground, and was leaking out the excess water and gas that was continuing to grow in volume with each passing day. Many people were beginning to fear that the entire town might explode.

It was all the more peculiar, all the excess water that saturated the ground, because there was a drought going on and there had been no rain for a month. But still the water and the gas kept coming, oozing and bubbling up. It found its way into the cellars of the homes and buildings, making it hazardous to light fires. Town residents sat in the dark, ate cold food, and remained fearful of striking even one match for fear it would be their last.

Then on Friday morning, September 16, there was a huge explosion, and a lake of fire that covered two acres appeared. Upon investigation the cause of all the difficulty was discovered, and it was as suspected—a farmer's gas well which had never been properly cased had been leaking for three years, until the ground could take no more. Workmen were sent to repair the well, and it was thought that all the problems were solved.

But the residents of Jerome soon found themselves without water. The gas well had been the only source of supply for Jerome's 50 families and local farmers; now, it was ruined. Water was flowing from the well and was flooding the area; water was going down into wells and cellars. But finally the whole mess was rather easily cleared up with the drilling of a new gas well—for the time being.

In September, 1894, a claim was made that a huge apple tree on the Anderson Conway farm two miles southeast of West Liberty was the largest such tree in Indiana. And it was indeed a large tree for an apple tree. Planted in 1846 by James Dean and his wife, the tree was 49 years old. It measured 9'6" in circumference, was 3'2" in diameter, the first branch was 9 feet above the ground, and the crown of the tree had a 54-foot spread. It was of the Vandever variety, and may have been the biggest, but it has long since been reduced to firewood or a pile of brush, or whatever end it was fated to.

For many years the educational needs of the township were met by building a number of one-room schools all over the township; seemingly there was one every mile or so. In 1883 Blanchard's history states that there were twelve such buildings at that time. In 1897 Trustee Echelbarger advertised for bids on yet another brick one-room building to be built that summer just south of West Liberty. The contract for the 25 by 35 foot building with additions, valued at $1,598, was awarded to Brown & Brown/(Manny and Grant Brown). In 1923 the building, no longer in use, was sold at auction; later it was used as a private residence. Today (1994) it still stands on its half-acre lot in pretty good condition—but unused.

In 1900 Trustee Jarret Echelbarger let a contract to the firm of Smith & Hostetler to build a rather large—but substantially only one room—addition with bell tower to the existing brick one-room school at Phlox. This building, too, became obsolete, and with some remodeling became a farm machinery storage facility. James M. Hatton can remember as a boy fondly watching William and Elden Kepler backing their huge threshing machine and steam engine into the building. Later on, this writer, the son of James M. Hatton, as a boy fondly watched Orville Passwater and his son-in-law Phil Hueston backing in their combine, wheat drill, corn picker, Farmall F-20 tractor, and other equipment for winter storage. Basil McClain stored farm equipment in the building for a year or two, and so did Wayne Krupp.

In the early 1970's the picturesque abandoned building burned. The remaining brick walls were torn down and hauled away; today the site is a private lawn.

In 1916, with the great improvements in roads and transportation, the trend of taking the schoolhouse to the students began to turn the other way of taking the students to the schoolhouse. That year, with four of their one room schools condemned by the state board of health, the people of Union Township voted to erect a single consolidated school building, and follow the trend toward consolidation of schoolhouses that was then sweeping the state.

A site was chosen near the center of the township, which was about 1 1/2 miles north of Phlox; the Kokomo architectural firm of Elmer E. Dunlap and Co. was put in charge of planning the building; Greentown contractors Smith & Allen were awarded the contract to build the building; and in 1916-17 the Union Township Consolidated School got itself a single building in which to educate all the students in the township.

This building served until 1969, when yet another consolidation closed Union School; the township's students were sent to Greentown along with students from Liberty and Jackson Townships, and the town of Greentown itself. The new school consolidation was named the Eastern Howard Consolidated School Corporation. This is the present system of education for students from Union Township.

The Union Township Consolidated building was sold to Greentown businessman C.C. "Bud" Williams. On a cold day in February, 1972, he recovered a black metal box full of documents from the cornerstone located inside the northwest corner of the ground floor classroom. A year or so later the building, with its windows already knocked out by vandals, was torn down. Today two homes occupy the site.

Another big day in the story of Union Township was the arrival of the first farm tractor in the entire county. The tractor was purchased by Howard and Fay Cullins, farmers around Jerome, and it arrived in late February, 1915. The tractor was an International Harvester, with a 40 horsepower gas and kerosene engine. It cost $650 and was delivered by Greentown's Herman Wagner, who declared it to be the first tractor in central Indiana. Before it was taken out to the Cullins' farm, Wagner gave a demonstration of it on the streets of Greentown before a crowd of interested farmers. The tractor was designed to take the place of two teams of work horses; it could plow, pull a binder, a manure spreader, hay todder, harrow or wagon. Any farm with four or more horses could use a tractor, it was said.

In about 1936 the large electric towers running southwest to northeast across the northern end of Union Township were constructed; at the same time electricity became available to rural customers for the first time.

In 1932 the main road running straight through the southern end of the township was taken over by the State of Indiana and designated State Road #26. Shortly thereafter, with the public works projects of the FDR Administration, the former gravel road bed was blacktopped for the first time. In 1992-93 the road was widened to its greatest width yet, to make the road more useable for semi-trucks.

Most of the secondary roads of the township remained gravel, and a familiar sight was the yellow road grader that made the rounds of grading out the gravel and keeping the road beds reasonably smooth. In the late 1960's to early 1970's an aggressive upgrading program replaced every gravel road in the county with a blacktop mixture. These roads set Howard County apart from neighboring counties, where roads were not so rapidly upgraded. But by the 1990's some of Howard County's roads—including those of Union Township—were reverting back to their earliest gravel status, as the high cost of maintenance for the higher quality roads began to tax the resources of the county.

Among later business ventures in Union Township were the McKinney Gravel Pits, a large gravel operation on the Howard-Tipton line two miles southwest of Phlox. Begun in the 1940's, the company continued to dig gravel out of the water-filled pits until the 1960's; today, the gravel equipment is gone, and positioned around the pits are the mobile homes of the Beaver Point Trailer Park. Two miles southeast of Phlox, also on the Howard-Tipton County line, the Dean Grain Co. was established in the 1960's on the farm of Lamaar Dean. Three miles west of Phlox on SR 26, on the Lanning farm, was established the Howard County Airport. Here, during the 1960's and on, the Lannings flew their own craft and also gave flying lessons to beginners. Other flyers boarded their small planes there, and in the 1980's and 1990's a new breed of flyers with ultra-light aircraft began to use the facility. One mile east of Jerome the Petty Campground was established in the early 1970's as a stopover for people with recreational vehicles.

Years ago people used to hold family reunions and gatherings at the Forks of the Creek area; the concrete base of the bleachers can still be seen in the brush.

A short distance east of Jerome the Country Cook Inn Restaurant was started by Gary and Arlene Voorhis in 1979. The building was unique in design, incorporating passive solar heating into the plan, with a wall of windows on the south side and a long sloping roof covered with sod on the north. The popular restaurant continues to do a very good business.

In the summer of 1967 huge 100 foot tall steel towers were built across Union Township, passing just east of Phlox as they wended their way from southern to northern Indiana. The heavy cables carried 765,000 volts of electricity. A large booster station was built on a tract of land at the corner of SR 22 & 35 and county road 1100 East. In the great ice storm of March, 1991, the weight of ice became so great that these towers were pulled down all the way from a point several miles south of Union Township right up to the booster station. The once tall towers became heeps of twisted metal; that summer even taller towers were put up to replace them, towers dismantled from a never completed line in southern Indiana, and hauled to the new location on flat bed semi's. A huge crane lifted the fully assembled towers into place, and they were guy-wired to the ground and set on their new base in a surprisingly short amount of time.

Charles and Katie McCoy operated the store in Phlox for several years, and they lived beside it in the same house originally built by the store's first owner. When Katie died on January 18, 1975, she had outlived her husband by 17 years, and she left 156 descendants: 3 sons, 6 daughters, 31 grandchildren, 67 great-grandchildren, and 49 great-great grandchildren.

Craig Foland, a gifted student and noted athlete at Eastern High School, lived with his family two miles southwest of Phlox. In the fall of 1972 he was killed in a hunting accident; the next year the Greentown News inaugurated the Craig Foland Mental Attitude Award, to be presented to the graduating senior athlete who, in the opinion of the selection committee, displayed an outstanding mental attitude. The first recipient of the award, which was continued every year afterward, was 1973 graduate Doug Robertson.

The current Union Township trustee is Jerome resident Paul Schini. He is in charge of a township that has come quite a long way from the solid forest and Indian trails that greeted the first pioneers. If they could come back and see what the township is today they would be amazed, and they would be proud; for this is their legacy; they made the beginning here and we have taken it to what it is now—

A township in which we can all be proud.
Submitted by Jeff Hatton

CHURCHES

Sycamore Friends Church in 1940.

HOPEWELL METHODIST EPISCOPAL CHURCH

Early religious meetings in Howard Township were held at Barnhart Learner's cabin in the southwest part of Section 26 near the present Kokomo reservoir dam. By 1845 a small group of believers had organized a Methodist class under the leadership of an itinerant minister named Burns. They planned to build a house of worship in the summer of 1849. It was announced that protracted meetings (a revival) would begin on a certain Saturday. On the Monday before the meetings were to begin, the settlers met to construct a log church on a half acre donated by Salathiel Good. (Southeast corner of County Roads 400 E and 50 N.) Before they could get started, it began to rain. However, bad weather did not stop these hardy pioneers. The preacher, Henry Bradley, pulling off his coat and rolling up his sleeves, said, "Come on, men. Methodists and ducks are not afraid of water. It rained for four days, but they were able to erect a 25'x30' hewed log cabin, and the meetings began on schedule.

They adopted the name Hopewell Methodist Episcopal Church. The charter members were Barnhart and Phoebe Bates Learner, Salathiel and Ulilah Good, Martin and Lucinda Smith, Timothy and Delilah Templin, Polly Thrailkill, and Mrs. Hays. The church was placed on the Kokomo Circuit and was ministered to by a circuit rider who held services there about twice a month. In this log church one of the earliest Sunday Schools in the county was organized under the direction of Pollard Brown.

As the years passed, the congregation outgrew the log cabin and wanted to build a new church, but could not agree on its location. Those members who wanted to relocate to Sycamore Road north of Wildcat Creek, broke away and organized the Vermont Methodist Episcopal Church. It was located on the site of the present Hillsdale United Methodist Church. In 1873 the people remaining at Hopewell constructed a new brick building across the road north of the log church on land donated by William S. Sale. The bricks were manufactured by John M. Leach from clay dug at the old Pittsburgh Plate Glass factory site in Kokomo. The total cost of the new building was about $2,500. Claudius Goyer, a church trustee, donated a bell purchased from the McShane Bell Foundry at Baltimore, Maryland. The new house of worship was dedicated on January 17, 1874, by Rev. S.N. Campbell of Newcastle, Indiana. The local minister at that time was J. Wesley Miller.

Hopewell Methodist Church, located south of the dam 400 E – 50 N, in about 1900.

For about forty years Hopewell was one of the religious and social centers of Howard Township and eastern Howard County. Its location on the new Kokomo-Greentown Gravel Road made it an attraction to people who wanted to take a Sunday drive. This trend was reversed with the coming of the automobile and improved county roads. Many rural churches were forced to close when their members were attracted to the larger congregations in Kokomo and neighboring towns. Attendance at Hopewell dwindled, and the building was finally abandoned around 1915. In 1925 the church and three-fourths acre were sold at auction to Oscar Allen for $200. Mr. Allen remodeled the church to make the dwelling that still stands on the northeast corner of County Roads 50 N. and 400 E. For many years it has been owned by the Hemmeger family.

Northeast of the remodeled church lies the Hopewell Cemetery near the spillway of the reservoir dam. This small burial site was donated by Salathiel Good, who had given the land for the original log church. The first known burial was Salathiel's father, Jacob Good, who died April 5, 1851. There are 112 known burials in this cemetery and probably more that were not recorded. Most of these people were early settlers of the community and members of the church. Several Civil War soldiers are among the dead. The last known burial was Mary Tolle in 1927. For a long time the Hopewell Cemetery was well-kept and mowed, but in recent years it has become another casualty of modern times. Vandals have broken and scattered the stones, and the graveyard has been allowed to revert to nature. This and many other small pioneer cemeteries throughout Howard County are an "endangered species" —a vanishing bit of local history. *Submitted by Ed Riley*

TWIN SPRINGS METHODIST EPISCOPAL CHURCH

The Twin Springs Methodist Episcopal Church was among the first of the denomination in the county with the first class meetings being held as far back as 1843. A class was formed with Thomas McClure as the first leader. Some of the first families were the McClures, T.A. Longs and John Lowes. The name was derived from the flowing of two springs from the opposite banks of two hills located near the church. The location was approximately five miles west of Kokomo on the road now designated as West Deffenbaugh. A building was completed about 1849 on the south side of the road. In 1873 a new facility was built on the north side of the road in front of the cemetery. The church was located in a prosperous farming community and served the religious needs of the area until 1934. The first pastor is listed as Rev. Taylor and the last to be appointed was Rev. C.B. Thomas with many pastors and presiding elders serving in the intervening years. Family names associated with the membership rolls include Dimitt, Tarkington, Long, Thorne, Wilson, Boyd, Honey, Bowen, Hamilton, Jackson, Nesbit, Miller, Irvin, and Spraker.

THE GERMAN BAPTIST BRETHREN "TAUFERS"

The "Taufers", sometimes referred to as "Dunkards", were founded at Schwarzenau, Germany by Alexander Mack in 1708. In 1836, they called themselves "The Fraternity of German Baptist" and in 1871 the name was changed to "The German Baptist Brethren". Members of this denomination had settled in Carroll County by 1828 and by 1840 there were many German Baptist Brethren in that county.

By 1845, about four or five German Baptist Brethren families had come from Union County, IN to live in the unbroken wilderness of western Howard County. Among these were Christian Kingery, David Overholser, and Joel Brower. These early German Baptist Brethren worshipped with the Bachelor's Run congregation in Burlington Township, Carroll County.

In 1852, these Howard County members desired to form a separate congregation. The Howard County German Baptist Brethren Church was organized and included all of Howard, and parts of Clinton and Tipton County. Heil Hamilton, one of the first preachers in Ervin Township, became a strong leader of this group. Other early leaders were: Joel Brower, Christian Kingery, John Rinehart, Jacob Hamilton, Daniel Welty, Josiah Woods, Alvin Eikenberry, Samuel Bock and his son Daniel.

For the next 13 years the Howard County German Baptist Brethren met in homes, but in 1865, they built their own meetinghouse on land owned by Jonas Brubaker, a German Baptist. The wooden church house was located south of Wild Cat Creek, on a hill just west of Stonebraker's Mill on the "Old Sycamore Road", in Monroe Township. This meetinghouse was moved in 1886 to its present location about a half mile north of State Road 22 on 1150 W. in Ervin Township. The meetinghouse continued to be used by the Howard German Baptist, "Howard Church of the Brethren", until September 1993, when it was sold to another denomination. Those who were still active in the church at that time were: Paul Kirkpatrick, Hazel Coy, Harold and Marjorie Eller, Pauline Eller, Oscar and Pat Metz, Norman and Martha Cory, Bud and Phyllis Dutton, and Olive Zering. Ada Sibert, a vital part of this church, died on June 5, 1993.

In 1881, there was a major division in the German Baptist Brethren denomination. At this time there were 160 members in the Howard Church and one third of these left to join the new group, "Old German Baptist Brethren", sometimes called "Old Orders". Among those who left were: John Rinehart, Amos K. Flora, Joel Brower, Jonas Brubaker, and Ephraim Woods. In 1882, this group built a meetinghouse on St. Rd. 22, about half a mile west of 1050 W, on the farm of Peter Miller. Services were discontinued here in 1944, but the building is still standing, and is used for storage.

Just two years later, 1883, there was another division in the German Baptist Brethren denomination. This group was referred to as the "Progressives" and is now known as "Brethren" (the Burlington First Brethren is of this group). Those from the Howard congregation who left to join this new group were: Simon Peter Woods, Luke Gregory, Samuel Eikenberry, Nancy Ann Gregory Eikenberry, Lenora Miller Gregory, and Mary Anna Miller Woods. Lenora was the daughter and Mary Anna the granddaughter of Howard County pioneer, John Benton Miller. The "Progressive Brethren" held their services in the Sugar Grove Union Meetinghouse in Monroe Township for three years before building their own church, "Salem", in Carroll County.

In 1908, the original denomination, "Taufers" or "German Baptist Brethren", changed its name to "Church of the Brethren" (the Kokomo Church of the Brethren is of this group). *Submitted by Cindi Stout*

THE QUAKER TRADITION

"I heard a voice which said, 'There is One, even Christ Jesus, that can speak to thy condition,' and when I heard it my heart did leap for joy."

-George Fox, Journal

It was in 1647 that George Fox, a humble shoemaker in the north of England, began to know God as a vital Spirit who could dwell in each heart and direct every living being in the Truth and Light of His Word. From that moment that fire spread, and in 1652 gave rise to The Religious Society of Friends—"Quakers." In 1656 this enlightenment was brought to America by Mary Fisher and Ann Austin. In 1681 William Penn's "Holy Experiment," Pennsylvania, became a working model of this faith.

New England Yearly Meeting was formed in 1661, followed by Baltimore (1672), Philadelphia (1687), New York (1695) and North Carolina (1698). Friends were drawn westward by 1800, from slavery and with the promise of new land, and Miami Monthly Meeting (Warren Co., OH) was set up in 1803. West Branch Monthly Meeting (Miami Co., OH) was set up by Miami in 1807, which set up Whitewater Monthly Meeting (Wayne Co., IN) in 1809. Ohio Yearly Meeting was set up by Baltimore in 1813, which set up Indiana Yearly Meeting in 1821. Whitewater gave rise to New Garden (1815), which set up Cherry Grove (1821), which set up White River (1824), which set up Mississinewa (1832) in Marion, IN.

Honey Creek (now New London) Monthly Meeting was set up by Mississinewa in 1846, and was the first organized Friends meeting in Howard County. Indiana Yearly Meeting established Western Yearly Meeting in 1858, and Honey Creek was transferred to its jurisdiction. As early as 1856, Friends were meeting in Kokomo (Mary Ann Rich, Richard Nixon, Robert Coate, Jesse Turner, Willard Moore and William Wooten) and on July 10, 1865, Kokomo Preparative Meeting became a reality. On October 19, 1867, Honey Creek Quarterly Meeting gave approval for Kokomo Monthly Meeting, which was instrumental in organizing the other Friends Meetings in Howard County.
Submitted by Ronald L. Tetrick

BETHEL FRIENDS CHURCH

On February 7, 1859, William T. Griffith and Catherine his wife, transferred one-half acre in Ervin Township, Howard County, Indiana, to the trustees in trust, for the Methodist Episcopal Church, known as the Baldwin Church of Howard County, for the sum of $5.00. The Trustees were Silas S. Baldwin, George Griffith, William Tatem, William T. Griffith and Washington Gwinn.

The Baldwin Church was originally at the northwest corner of Co Rd 800W and 400 N. It is not known whether the original building was moved to the new site, or just the congregation or both.

On April 28, 1886, O.L. Evans, Thomas M. Moulder, William O. Jeter, B.B. Richards, Peter Y. Blair; trustees of Bethel Methodist Episcopal Church of Howard County, Indiana, conveyed to the trustees of Honey Creek Monthly Meeting for the sum of one-hundred dollars, Bethel Methodist Episcopal Church. The trustees of Honey Creek Monthly Meeting were Silas Stout, Benjamin Tucker and Henry Mendenhall. (Honey Creek Mtg. became New London Monthly Meeting). At this time there were forty members who transferred and were accepted into the Society of Friends. Thus it became Bethel Friends Church.

On June 13, 1903, it was decided to build a new church. The committee appointed consisted of Tatman T. Griffith, Robert Wilson Merrell, Ellis Merrell, Myron Edward Gannon and William C. Jones. It was to be paid for by voluntary donations.

The church at this time was a white frame structure. The altar was on the north side. There were two doors on the south

Bethel Friends Church

New London Friends Meetinghouse

NEW LONDON FRIENDS MEETING

In the 1840's Friends came to New London from Ohio, Tennessee, Kentucky, North Carolina, and southern Indiana. Initially meeting for worship in a grove west of the present town, Honey Creek Preparative Meeting, now New London Meeting, was established June 21, 1845. It is one of the oldest organized religious groups in Howard County.

The first meeting house was built of logs and doubled as the school house. The meeting experienced rapid growth. Plans that started in July, 1851, resulted in a new meeting house in 1853.

It was a frame structure, typical of the Friends, with a seating capacity of one thousand. A partition with shutters divided the room. Men met in the east room and women in the west. Shutters were opened when there was a need to act in unison on important business matters. On Oct. 14, 1876, it was decided to begin meeting together. This meeting house was used for 50 years.

side. If I remember what I was told, the women went in one side and the men the other. At least they sat apart.

In March 1904 the church work was finished and accepted. The cost was $4000-$5000. The dedication was held March 13, 1904, with Rev. Thomas Brown of Carmel, Ind., Superintendent of Western Yearly Mtg. at that time, and Jehu Reagan as speakers. The membership at this time was one hundred.

On September 14, 1944, the property was deeded to the trustees of Bethel Friends Church, consisting of Clarence Merrell, Mazie Porter, and Walter Diller, by the trustees of New London Monthly Meeting. They were Kenneth Newby, Benjamin Tucker and J. Frank Kile.

In 1989, one hundred and thirty years later, the meeting was laid down and the property was sold. It went back into the property from which it came.

The semi-circle stained glass window dated 1903 that was over the entry way, was taken to First Friends of Kokomo, Ind, to be preserved. *Submitted by Mary Blangy*

In 1903 the decision to tear down the structure and erect a more modern facility was made. This white frame structure was used until it was destroyed by fire in November 1951. Within a year the present stone building was finished.

New London Friends have been responsive to the needs of people in distress. In the 1850's the Freedman's Aid Committee was busy assisting the "people of color". Old records report of clothing and money sent to Levi Coffin for Negroes seeking freedom from slavery. In fact community men were active in the operation of the Underground Railroad.

This Monthly Meeting established several meetings: New Salem - 1851, Lynn - 1852, Pleasant Hill - 1852, Reserve - 1853, Kokomo - 1863, Antioch - 1891, Kempton - 1899, and Bethel - 1903.

The Meeting's interest in service, school, and the community all proclaim the devotion of Friends. Twenty-seven ministers of the Gospel have been recorded by this Meeting.

COURTLAND AVENUE FRIENDS

In the Meeting for Business of Kokomo Monthly Meeting in fifth month (May), 1898, a committee was organized "to purchase a building for the use of the Mission Meeting and Bible School in the south part of Kokomo." It was reported in seventh month (July), 1898, that "the work was progressing" and that there were "about 40 in Bible School." A request for a meeting for worship was read in ninth month (September), 1898, and Courtland Avenue Friends Church was allowed without establishing a preparative meeting, in July, 1899. This meeting became an established monthly meeting on January 15, 1925. To its charge was given, in 1926, the work of the Sabbath School on North Buckeye, and the Mission at Wheeler and Main Streets. The former became North Buckeye Friends in 1947, and the latter was discontinued and sold after a few years.

A Meetinghouse was dedicated on the southeast corner of 1300 South Courtland Avenue and State Street in June, 1905, and an addition was completed in 1939. Ground was broken in late September, 1962, for the present structure, dedicated January 26, 1964. The educational unit was dedicated April 13, 1969. The addition of a Sunday School room on the south side of the Narthex in late 1981, installation of a carillon, central air-conditioning units and other improvements have followed.

The Meeting has been well served by dedicated ministers, too, beginning in 1898 with Josephine Hockett. Others have been Calvin Choate, David Commons, Jessie Snow, Sammie Talbert, Gurney Lee, Mary Hiatt, Orin Hutchins, Homer Biddlecum, Ralph Lawrence, Arthur Haworth, Luther Addington, Andrew Starbuck, John Retherford, Forrest Lamneck, Ray Morford, Carl Darnell, Paul Reish, Gordon Clarke, Isaac and Esther Phillips and James Walters. The pulpit is currently supplied by Rod Dennis. Pastoral counselor is his wife, Judy Dennis, also a recorded minister, and Anita Hunt, Christian Education and music director. Current membership stands at 181. *Submitted by Ronald L. Tetrick*

Top photo: The sanctuary of the Courtland Avenue Friends dedicated on January 26, 1964.

Middle photo: Courtland Avenue Friends Church 1905-1963

Bottom photo: Courtland Avenue Friends Church today.

Original Meetinghouse on Union St. and Mulberry, built in 1871.

Second church built in 1930.

FIRST FRIENDS MEETING OF KOKOMO

First Friends Meeting of Kokomo originated as a concern of Mary Ann Rich, a minister of the area. On Eleventh Month 8, 1856, she requested a minute from Honey Creek Monthly Meeting (now known as New London Monthly Meeting) to come to Kokomo to start a meeting. From this effort a Preparative Meeting was established Eighth Month, 1865. When the request was made Seventh Month, 10, 1867, to establish the Kokomo Monthly Meeting of Friends, the Honey Creek Monthly Meeting and Honey Creek Quarterly Meeting soon gave approvals and the first business session was held on Eleventh Month 6, 1867. Nathan Dixon was the first clerk and Richard Nixon was the first treasurer, with a proposed treasury of $10.00, and Mercer Brown as the first statistical recorder. The Meeting moved steadily forward and had an enrollment for Sunday School of 175 by mid-1868.

During this time a committee was able to obtain a lot on the corner of the three hundred block of North Union Street for $500 and the first true meetinghouse was built for about $5500 in the summer of 1871. The Meeting membership was 134 at this time. Additions to the buildings, remodeling, rebuilding after a fire, and other improvements were made through the years. In 1929 the Federal Government requested the location for building a post office and offered $20,000. The Monthly Meeting asked $50,000. After threats of condemnation proceedings, President Hoover was contacted and at his request for review, negotiations were concluded with a price of $40,000, plus retention of stained glass windows and other items. A new meetinghouse was built in the five hundred block of North Union Street and was occupied October 12, 1930. Recently that building was sold and a new meetinghouse was built and occupied at the present location of 1801 W. Zartman Road in July, 1984. The Meeting was able to incorporate two of the original stained glass windows from the 1871 meetinghouse into the new meetinghouse. The names through the years have been Kokomo Monthly Meeting of Friends, Union Street Monthly Meeting of Friends, and now First Friends Meeting of Kokomo.

Members have always held strong Quaker Beliefs and relied on Faith and Practice, the Friends' Book of Discipline, although certainly the Meeting has been open to innovations. The early meetings were silent, without formal leadership, with spirit-led comments and hymns. To help in leadership, the Meeting called Robert W. Douglas in 1875, who became the first paid Quaker pastor in America and Europe, an event which caused the London Yearly Meeting to visit Kokomo. The Meeting was also a leader in using music - organ, piano, choir, and a Sunday School orchestra.

Members of the Meeting have always been interested in education and were instrumental in starting Kokomo High School. Some members have served as board members, superintendents, principals, teachers, and have been affiliated with Earlham College.

The Meeting supports various outreach programs. The women support the United Society of Friends Women with an annual bazaar for support of various missions, the Kokomo Rescue Mission, Indians, and other missions and needs. Much work is done in making comforts and other items for the mission field and collecting clothing for the Indians. At present, extra effort is being made to support the Choctaw Mission in Alabama.

Most of this history is summarized from the history written by Lela Hardy, with assistance from Lilith M. Farlow, Marie S. Hadley, and Fleta P. Newlin. We close with a quote from that booklet, taken from the closing minute of the December 1, 1932 Monthly Meeting.

"We look back to blessings received and forward with faith and hope to the future with its opportunities. We lift our hearts in silent prayer for help and strength to meet what the future may bring, dedicated to spiritual growth with God's guidance."

The third building of the First Friends Meeting of Kokomo built in 1984.

NEW HOPE FRIENDS CHURCH

New Hope Friends-400 South (St. Rd. 26), 1100 East, Phlox, IN., became an indulged meeting in 1858, organized by New Salem Monthly Meeting. Services were held in the home of Jesse Ellis.

In 1862, Edmund Peele donated one acre of land, four miles south and two miles east of Greentown, for the location of a meeting house. New Hope Meeting received the deed from New Salem Meeting March 9, 1912.

In the late 1860's a new frame structure, built according to the usual Friends Meeting House 30'x90', replaced a log meeting house. New Hope Monthly Meeting was established and directed to be opened the first 7th day and third month.

A concern for burial ground was presented to the first Monthly Meeting. James A. Ellis donated ground one half mile south of the church.

Kokomo Quarterly Meeting was held at New Hope the third Friday and Saturday in June and was always well attended. The red brick school house across the road from the church not only provided the accommodations for the overflow crowd, who were ministered to by visiting preachers, but also the dining area for the bountiful noon meal.

On Fourth day, 10:00 A.M. teachers dismissed classes, farmers came in from their field work and all attended services. The Lord's Day services, as well as the midweek services were held in silence unless the Spirit moved someone to speak according to a custom peculiar to the denomination.

New Hope Monthly Meeting was authorized by Kokomo Quarterly Meeting to open and establish a Preparative Meeting at Hazel Dell (Tipton Co.) 5th Month, 9, 1885. Hazel Dell became a Monthly Meeting in 1894.

A preparative Meeting was set up by New Hope Monthly Meeting at Evergreen (Tipton Co.) 5th Month, 19th, 1902. Friends attended service at New Hope after Evergreen Meeting closed.

In the early church, discipline was strictly observed. Home missionary work was not neglected.

Jefferson Jackson, on 10th Month, 4th, 1873, became the first recorded minister from New Hope Monthly Meeting. Others were James A. Ellis, 1874; J. Hammer Ellis, 1876; Chuza Moorman, 1874; William Hunicutt, 1885; George Bragg, 1885; Walter Perry, 1917; Lindley Hiatt, 1921; Willie Wines, 1923; Minnie Kepler, 1933; Sterrett L. Nash, 1936.

The first report of a pastor, James A. Ellis, serving the meeting was 9th Month, 1899. Others who served were Rebecca Ruth Ellis, 12th Month, 1899; J. Hammer Ellis, 10th, 1990, 1903; James A. Ellis, 1901, 1902, 1908. Visiting ministers, as well as the ministers of the congregation, filled the pulpit when there was no pastor.

Blaine Starbuck was the first pastor, 1919, to receive a salary. Other pastors were Mary V. (Polly) Couch, 1920; Mary (Cox) Fox, 1923; Willie Wines, 1924. Other pastors and length of service are as follows: Josephine Hockett, four years; Ola S. Oatley, one year; Kenneth Eikenberger, two years; Lenna Chamness, three years; Luther Addington, one year; Fanny Roberts, two years and after marriage to Charles Gentry, Nov. 27, 1938, continued four more years; Roger Wood, one year; Arthur Haworth, 3 months; Inez Batchelor from Sept. 1, 1942 to June 1945. Fanny Gentry finished 1945 and continued three years. Others were: Sterrett L. Nash, one year; Bertha Kistler, Sept. 1, 1949-Sept. 1, 1965; Roy King, Sept. 1, 1965-Sept. 1, 1968; Sharlott Scott, 1969 for three months; Robert Garra, 1969; David Petersen, Sept. 20, 1970-July 1, 1972; Arthur Hollingsworth, Sept. 1, 1972-1977; Charles Hill, 1977-1984. Since 1984, John P. Clark has served as pastor.

With the provision she have possession her lifetime, Rhoda Cole deeded her property, Aug. 1937, to the church for a parsonage.

The widening of the east and west gravel road by the state (St. Rd. 26) caused concern for the safety of the people attending meetings. A building committee was appointed at the 7th Month, 1939, Monthly Meeting to consider the relocation of the church. The last services held at that location were on Sept. 17, 1939.

The church was moved to the west side of the lot until a basement was excavated and finished. A cement block foundation was laid after the church was moved over the basement. A pulpit was built on the west side. A vestibule with front entrance and a basement entrance was built on the east side. Stained glass replaced the clear glass windows and a new roof replaced the old. In 1950, the poplar siding was replaced by brick veneer. Services were held in the home of Rhoda Cole during the remodeling.

Dedication services were held Sunday, Dec. 17, 1939. Fredric Carter, Western Yearly Meeting Superintendent, delivered the message and offered the prayer of dedication; Sterrett Nash had charge of the music.

New Hope Friends Church continues to proclaim Jesus Christ as Savior and Redeemer to all. *Submitted by Margaret K. Dean*

The original New Hope Church.

New Hope Church as it looked in 1994.

NEW SALEM FRIENDS CHURCH

A few Friends from North Carolina opposed to slavery settled with the consent of the Indians in the Reserve and built cabins. They were established here, laid claim to the land in 1849 when the government opened it for settlement. Other Friends from North Carolina, opposed to slavery, soon joined the group south of Greentown across the Wildcat Creek.

These Friends were God-fearing people who stressed the importance of rearing and training their children in righteousness as a devine command. While they were erecting homes they met weekly for worship in Absolem Lamb's home. As soon as their homes were built, they built a place for worship, a log building 22' x 44'. In a short time the meeting place was too small and an addition was added to double the size. As soon as the first building was completed, a petition was sent to Honey Creek Monthly Meeting, near New London, asking to be an indulged meeting to meet on first and fifth day and to be known as New Salem Friends. In September 1850, a request was sent to Honey Creek and Northern Quarterly Meeting to establish New Salem as a preparative meeting. In January, 1855, New Salem was established as a Monthly Meeting by Concord Quarterly Meeting. The original membership was Absolem Lamb, Isaac Ratcliff, Nathan Freeman, William Rich, Naaman Colyar, Nathan Hodson, Zarchiriah Hodson, John Healton; the single members were Nathan Freeman, Jr., Moses L. Rich, Benjamin F. Lamb, Mrs. Abigail Hockett, Rachel Carr, making a total of 75.

Wherever Friends established meetings they also founded schools. New Salem was no different. The first school in Eastern Howard County was south of Wildcat Creek and met in the log meeting house. Anna Rich was the teacher.

Our Friends discouraged reading of scripture during worship services believing the message would be given to a messenger by the Holy Spirit. When visiting Friends were to be present, word was sent by runner. They used the plain language, had no night meetings, had no singing, wore plain clothes, were admonished to live within their incomes, taught to give aid when needed and to settle differences peaceably without recourse to law except when legal records were required. A member was disowned if conduct was unbecoming for a Christian unless he confessed his error and promised to do better in the future. All work ceased so all could attend fifth day meetings.

Three monthly meetings were set off by New Salem: New Hope, Hemlock and Greentown (now abandoned). New Salem and nine other meetings made up Kokomo Quarterly Meeting, New Salem being the oldest.

In 1876, a new meeting house was built. It was located across the raod from the first meeting house. It was built of bricks that were made and fired on the site. The foundation was measured at night with the North Star as a guide. Total coast of the building was $1,827.

In 1924, a sum of money left by a former member was used to build additional room on the east end of the building. The addition was used for a kitchen, educational and recreational purposes.

In 1954, a need was sensed for additional educational space and a modern kitchen, heating system, installing rest rooms, rearranging the sanctuary, buying new furniture, building a new entrance, enlarging the east room, and covering the entire outside with Bedford limestone. A committee of Charles Lamb, Norman Davis, Melba Parsons, Ola Petty, Jack Myers, Chet Wright, Jr., Charles E. Evans, and James Ellis, Pastor, was appointed to assess the concern and make recommendations to the Monthly Meeting. In 1956, the remodeling was completed and dedicated to the Lord's service. Total cost was $23,000. The mortgage was burned August 1, 1965.

Pastors who have guided us are: Amos Kenworthy, William Healton, Jonathan Healton, Milton Cox, George Bragg, Nathan Freeman, Laura Evans, Anna Jane Cook, W.A. Freeman, Daniel Freeman, Samuel Talbert, Lottie VanBibber, Josephine Hockett, Jesse Snow, Sara Jane King, Ora Thomas, Polly Couch Bowman, John Walters, Frank Stafford, Fanny Gentry, Ruth Lindley, Philip Dermond, Murray Kenworthy, Clyde and Lenna Watson, James Ellis, Richard VanTyle, Dorothy Pitman, Elmer Merrill, Lowell Nicholson and Kenneth Tost.

New Salem is now in its 154th year. The entrance has been enclosed, a new side walk, and new furnaces installed and the sanctuary repainted.

We pray that we will continue to do good to the bodies and souls of men so men will respect, believe, and accept the teachings of our Lord.

RUSSIAVILLE FRIENDS CHURCH

A request from Friends residing in the Russiaville area was presented first month 1877 to Honey Creek Monthly Meeting for the privilege of holding an indulged meeting for worship at Russiaville. At fourth month meeting the privilege was granted and Zimri Newlin, Nancy A. Newlin, Luna Wright, Gulielma Wright, Willis Kenworthy, Abigail Johnson, Joseph Peacock, and Elizabeth Stout were appointed to have care of the new meeting to be known as Russiaville Meeting of Friends.

For one year services were held in a place of business in Russiaville. Then a meetinghouse, partially erected by Jared Marshall at the southwest corner of Liberty and Marshall Streets, was deeded to the Russiaville Meeting. The original one-room building measured 26 by 36 feet and cost $565.07. The pulpit was located in the west end with two facing benches on each side and the door at the east end. A broad aisle passed through the center with benches on each side. The men sat on one side and the women on the other. In the center of the room stood a large box stove on which were kept bricks for the purpose of lending comfort to the feet of many who came from a distance in the cold, either on horseback or in a wagon. John T. Ratcliff was authorized to procure a bell for the church. (It is now mounted over the outside bulletin board.)

A request sent by Russiaville Indulged Meeting to Honey Creek, now New London Monthly Meeting, on six month, 14th, 1879, to establish a Preparative Meeting was granted. As a result of a suggestion by David Hadley who had conducted a Revival meeting at the little church, it was decided to enlarge it by adding two small rooms on the east side measuring 10 by 16 feet. With greater increase in membership, an addition to the north was built in 1889. In December 1879, John P. Wright and Rebecca Ratcliff were appointed timers of the meeting. Wright was later replaced by Marshall because of ill health. Following these were Jonathan Dixon, Robert Barclay Johnson and William G. Thompson.

The Bible School was established in 1883. Early marriages recorded in the church were those of Sherman Nichols and Emma McGrath on April 12, 1886, and William Carter and Alice Holiday, May 15, 1892.

On June 25, 1911, a Monthly Meeting was established by a committee from New London Monthly Meeting. At this meeting Thomas E. Newlin was appointed to fill the office of recording clerk and Mira Small reading clerk.

On January 29, 1914, the deed to the lot on which the present church stands was executed and soon afterward the parsonage was built. Asa Woodward was the first pastor to occupy it, moving there about Christmas in the same year.

In 1921 a committee including Manville Rayl, Walter Carter, Samuel Talbert, Charles E. Carter, William Thompson, T.E. Newlin, Owen Ratcliff and Wilmer Lindley solicited subscriptions for the new church. In a short time $17,500 was pledged. After many disappointments, but with steady advance, the large new Friends church on the corner of Main & Carter (now East) streets was completed and dedicated on September 30th, 1923. Those who contributed materials, services and labor to the new structure were Allen Newlin, Charley Carter, Cappy Hollingsworth, Sam Hollingsworth, John Bowers the contractor, and John T. Ratcliff who furnished quarter-sawed oak finish for the entire building.

Some of the early ministers were Elsie D. Wright and Thomas E. Newlin. Lewis I. Hadley was the first hired pastor, beginning in the fall of 1894. Following him were E. Howard Brown, Elwood C. Siler, James Mills, Earl Forbes, Nathan D. Night, Frank Stafford, Austin Osborn, Asa Woodward, Walter Brown, James A. Parr, Samuel P. Talbert, and Richard L. Wiles who was pastor when the church was dedicated in 1923. Other pastors who have served are Homer G. Biddlecum, J. Grant Johnson, John Compton, Paul Hicks, Allen Reynolds, John Retherford, Bernie Cook, William A. Wagner, William R. Abrams, Mary Hiatt, Herbert D. Pettengill Jr., Robert E. Heavilin Sr., and Hubert Mardock.

On April 11, 1965, the church structure was severely damaged by the Palm Sunday tornadoes which tore through the entire town. Meetings were held at Lynn Friends Meeting and the Western High School during the rebuilding of the church. The members of the rebuilding committee were Lewis Taylor, Oakley Carter, Russell Robertson, Jeaneen Waddell, Arline Darby, Lee Edwin Carter, Clyde Lindley, I.A. Hollingsworth and Ralph Pollock.

With nearly all of the interior removed the church was completely remodeled and refurnished with major changes in the floor elevation and in the front entrance which features a tapestry brick cross occupying a paramount position between the two sets of doors and reaching up into the peak of the A-line roof. A rededication service was held on May 22, 1966.

Pastors since that time have been Dwight and Gladys Smith, Dennis Mote (student pastor), John Bond, Delano Cunningham, Hugh Spaulding, Jeffery D. Blackburn, Morris R. Jones, Kenneth Tost (interim) and Brooks Martin.

Russiaville Friends Meeting is still reaching out to Christ, to His Church and to the World.

Russiaville Friends 1878 – 1923

Russiaville Friends 1923 – 1965

Russiaville Friends since 1966.

SYCAMORE FRIENDS

Recorded history often does not include the many things that truly reflect the life of a church. Yet our very presence today testifies to the vision of those who went before us. More important than history of heritage, however, is the purpose of our fellowship-that we bring the message of the Gospel of Christ to a lost world. With those thoughts in mind, look back over the years of the "life story" of Sycamore Friends Meeting.

Sycamore, located in Howard County at 1100 East and 100 North, was surveyed in 1881 and given the name because of the sycamore trees at the intersection. In its first years as an "official community," the town acquired a post office, four stores, and a schoolhouse but no meetinghouse, although at least seven denominations had held worship services here.

In the late 1880's many revival meetings were being held in this area. A young man from the Marion area, Constantine Shugart, came to Sycamore to preach. As a result, a sizeable congregation was established. Meetings were held at the schoolhouse. In early 1890 following a business meeting at the town's sawmill office, money was pledged and ground was broken for a Quaker Meetinghouse in Sycamore. The building, ground and furnishings were completely paid for by the day of dedication, August 24, 1890.

The next few years showed many revival meetings, often lasting three weeks, with meetings twice a day. Many conversions resulted.

As Sycamore Friends entered the 20th century, an annual salary for the pastor was approved, hitching rails were added to the grounds and discussions began about securing a parsonage.

The years of the Great Depression were reflected in the minutes as the meeting sought a "cheap, secondhand" heat plant to replace the old stoves. Another sign of the economic times was that Sycamore shared a pastor with New Hope Friends Meeting at Phlox, a meeting just five and one-half miles south of our meeting.

In 1940, the 50th Anniversary was observed. Many charter members were present for this occasion. During this decade modern improvements were added including indoor restrooms and the addition of a basement under the church. A furnace was installed making it possible to remove the stoves from the sanctuary. A small frame house across the road from the church was purchased for a parsonage.

A slow but steady growth pattern began in the 1950s. The State of the Society Report shared that members had caught the vision of the power of prayer and the importance of being guided by the Holy Spirit in carrying on the work of the church. A special project in this decade was the addition of leaded stained glass windows. (These windows were releaded and used when the new church was constructed in 1988.)

In 1965 Sycamore completed another remodeling project. A new furnace, hardwood floors, carpet, paint and new pews, as well as dividing the basement into classrooms, completed the redecorating. This was just in time. On Palm Sunday, 1965, a tornado devastated Greentown destroying the school. For several weeks, the new rooms at the church housed the second grade classes of Eastern Elementary.

The 70s and 80s brought more active ministries in the church: Lay Witness Missions, a strong Sunday School program, large Daily Vacation Bible Schools, an active United Society of Friends Women, Quaker Men, and weekly youth programs for ages 3 through high school (5 age groups). New ministries brought new physical needs and a Fellowship Center was planned and built. More ground was acquired and plans were set for a new meetinghouse. This church would have a 260-seat sanctuary, nursery, office, and library. This new building would be joined to the now existing Fellowship Center.

On Palm Sunday, 1989, the congregation moved from the original Meetinghouse that served us well for ninety-nine years into the new facility. The Centennial Celebration was held on August 19, 1990. Many reminisced through the pictures and relics of earlier days.

A long term goal for the building committee includes the addition of a Christian Education wing. Presently, eight of our fifteen Sunday School classes are held in the Original Meetinghouse. Many opportunities for ministry are opening for us.

Our purpose can be stated in the verse from John 15, "I have called you friends... go forth and bear fruit." It is our desire to bear fruit for Christ and His Kingdom.

Sycamore Friends Meetinghouse from 1890 to 1989.

The Sycamore Friends Meetinghouse since 1989.

FIRST CHRISTIAN CHURCH DISCIPLES OF CHRIST

First Christian Church of Kokomo, a congregation of the Christian Church (Disciples of Christ), was established as the Christian Church of Kokomo on February 21, 1851. Lewis Anderson, one of the founding forebearers, had traveled to Indianapolis where he heard Alexander Campbell preach to what he called "the largest gathering ever held in the city." Campbell, the founder of the Christian Church (Disciples of Christ), was a dynamic preacher and teacher who had come to Indianapolis hoping to rouse people to take up the flag of Christian unity and New Testament Christianity. So inspired was Lewis Anderson that he came back to Kokomo and met with Thomas Shepherd in a crude log cabin on High Street (now Superior Street), a place of much religious discussion, and together they set in motion the beginnings of a congregation in our city.

The church officially began on a Friday evening, February 21, 1851, in the home of Lewis Anderson located just east of Washington Street. There were seven in attendance, and Lewis Anderson and Thomas Shepherd were appointed to serve as Elders. Since it was nearly impossible to secure a full-time preacher, the little band decided to contact any traveling preacher who might stop and hold services. In closing the meeting, the first communion service was held, amidst the furnishings of a pioneer home, with the following charter members participating: Mr. and Mrs. Lewis Anderson, Mr. and Mrs. Thomas Shepherd, Mr. and Mrs. John Lindsay, and Edward Shepherd. Thus, First Christian Church was launched as the third congregation to be established in Kokomo and stands today as the second longest standing congregation.

In the early years the church met in various homes under the leadership of elders. In the spring of 1857, being inspired by a sermon of William Griggsby, the congregation envisioned the building of their first meeting place. Working diligently through the summer and early fall, a building was erected on Mulberry Street at a cost of $1800.00 on a thirty dollar lot. In October of 1857, the church building was dedicated "a chapel for humble souls to meet and nightly sing in voices sweet." (*The Kokomo Dispatch* - September 18, 1890).

Throughout the history of First Christian Church there has been a train of excellent ministers, the experience of growing pains in both good times and bad times, and a series of crises which posed turning points for the church. In the 1800's it was rare to have a minister stay with the congregation for more than two or three years. Nevertheless, the church grew steadily and even weathered many a controversy. For instance, in the latter part of the 19th century the use of a musical instrument in worship became an issue for debate, an extension of a controversy occurring in the denomination as a whole. In December of 1865, Brother R.E. Pearre became the pastor, and having a progressive spirit, he preached one Sunday morning on *"Positive Christianity"* and introduced into the sanctuary worship a melodeon. It stirred up so much trouble in the congregation that it forced his resignation by mid-summer. Nevertheless, despite Brother Pearre's leaving, the melodean managed to stay so that the congregation set the course for a diverse as well as excellent music ministry.

While the War between the States had divided many a denomination and congregation, the Christian Church in Kokomo held together in a noble way. Following the Civil War, the church became inter-racial with the membership of Joseph A. Brabay. Through these years several African-Americans became members, one being Ezra Roberts who graduated with honors from Kokomo High School and went on to become a professor at Tuskeegee Institute and the first assistant to Booker T. Washington.

Crises have also been difficult and yet strengthening factors in the growth of First Christian Church. In the latter part of the 1800's, it became apparent that the "little white church" was no longer adequate to hold the congregation. Thus, the decision was made to purchase three lots at the corner of Main Street and Jackson for $3,000.00, and a building committee was appointed. On December 2, 1875 the *Kokomo Democrat* reviewed the specifications of the building plans and carried the news:

"The New Christian Church"
'One of the Largest and Most Elegant Church Buildings in the State'

With this announcement began the efforts towards construction of a new building. With sweat, blood and tears the structure took shape, and though unfurnished, the first services of what would be called Main Street Christian Church were held in February of 1880. Soon after the reality of indebtedness confronted the congregation. Being unable to meet obligations, the board eventually proposed selling the building to the city of Kokomo. On March 4, 1881, the city council rejected the proposal because it did not meet with the approval of the tax payers. With this decision, the church was forced to come to the helm. The following Sunday a meeting was called and Dr. Edward A. Armstrong took the floor saying, "We have demonstrated to our community a church of little faith..." and he inspired them to give the finances necessary to eradicate the debt. This crisis was followed by twenty years of progress until February 27, 1904 when the building went up in fire. Again the congregation was faced with both struggle and challenge. Describing the hour, Rev. Jo Riley writes in his history of the church, "The Main Street Christian Church building was still in smoldering ruins when the first money was being solicited for a new building." On August 6, 1905 the new building, an akron style Indiana limestone structure, was opened for formal use. Underneath the majestic dome in the sanctuary the twentieth century was at hand.

Main Street Christian Church witnessed to an era of splendid work. The first twenty-five years of this century resulted in the development of strong Christian education programs. A departmentalized Church School was established on Sunday mornings, *Christian Endeavor* became active, and the first Boy Scout Troop was organized. Women's work began with the *Ladies' Aid Society* and eventually became the *Missionary Society*. Inter-church fellowship and outreach were undertaken, witnessing to the Disciples' commitment and unity and Christian service.

The second quarter of the 20th century brought the tradition of *The Birthday Dinner,* an annual memorial/missionary endeavor of the women. In the early 1940's, the Christian Youth Fellowship was organized, and one of the main activities was the Easter Sunrise Service. The entire church organization was also restructured with a manual of instructions being set forth by the Official Board. In February of 1951, the church passed the century mark with a pageant and centennial celebration dinner. Rev. Jo Riley was pastor at this juncture and became the first minister of Main Street Christian Church to be honored in the community with the *Distinguished Service Award."*

Following major remodeling projects in 1951 and 1966, crisis once again visited Main Street Christian Church on December 16, 1970. In the middle of the night fire destroyed the sixty-five year old structure, shocking the congregation and the community. Being without a building, the congregation was invited to share the facilities of First Congregational Christian Church until a decision could be made about the future.

During this interim period the congregation made the decision to relocate from the downtown to the west side. On September 9, 1973, Main Street Christian Church became First Christian Church and a new colonial style church structure built on a nine acre tract was dedicated to the glory of God. Though relocated, the First Christian Church has continued to be community oriented as well as active in the work of the Christian Church (Disciples of Christ). In recent years the church has done landscaping in addition to a remodeling and building completion project. As the congregation approaches the twenty-first century it is marked by a strong family ministry, a diverse music program, and significant outreach. The Christian Women's Fellowship ranks 33rd among all Disciple women in giving to outreach. In 1988, First Christian Church was recognized as *"Positively Kokomo"* with the lighting of the steeple on November 29, 1987. In 1991, the congregation celebrated 140 years through a Miracle Sunday campaign and the constructing of an attractive monument with the original cornerstones of the Christian Church in Kokomo and Main Street Christian Church and a marker designating First Christian Church. Today First Christian Church (Disciples of Christ) in Kokomo takes pride in being a vital congregation with a rich heritage and a promising future. *Submitted by Rev. Fred. W. Dorisse, Sr. Minister*

GRACE UNITED METHODIST CHURCH

Grace United Methodist Church of Kokomo, the oldest religious congregation in this city, is celebrating its 150th anniversary this year and the Rev. Charles I. Johnson, pastor, and a special sesquicentennial committee are planning a series of events to mark the milestone. The observance will extend through the year 1994.

To open the celebration, the church published an illustrated history entitled "150 Years and Counting, the Story of Grace United Methodist Church of Kokomo, Indiana, 1844-1994." The book was released in February. Tracing highlights in the church's life, the volume begins with the first evidence of the Methodist faith in the community in 1844. In that year the earliest settlers in the area began meeting in one another's log cabins for prayer and meditation.

Their first meeting place was the cabin of David Foster, a fur trader who had paddled his canoe down Wildcat Creek from Burlington and had chosen a spot for a trading post. The site he selected was on the north side of the creek west of what is now Kokomo's Main Street.

The settlers were followers of John Wesley, the founder of Methodism. Prominent among them was David Foster's wife Elizabeth, who invited her neighbors to gather for prayer in her home. There were fewer than a dozen of them and their religious venture took place in a primitive environment surrounded by forests and inhabited by the Miami Indian tribe.

Mrs. Foster invited an itinerant preacher named Jacob Coldazer to visit the little colony and with his help the settlers organized a church, the first in the Kokomo area. Outgrowing the Foster cabin, the group transferred its meetings to the settlement's log courthouse. Then they built their own church on what is now the southwest corner of Washington and Superior Streets. The site is part of the present Foster Park.

Foster meanwhile had donated ground around his trading post for the establishment of a town. He specified that it be named Kokomo, after the Miami Indian chief Ma-Ko-Ko-Mah, with whom he was friendly.

The church built by the Foster group in 1844 was the forerunner of today's Grace United Methodist Church. In 1845, the church organized the first Sunday School in Howard County, and it had an average attendance of fifteen.

The Indians were friendly to the settlers, but the forests were full of wild animals of various kinds and they made life somewhat precarious.

In 1851 the little log church was sold for $75 and the east half of the lot on which Grace Church now is situated was purchased. Soon afterward, in 1852, the congregation built a modest frame building which became the center of many community activities such as anti-slavery rallies and meetings to enlist men in the Union Army.

With the end of the Civil War in 1864, the church had grown so much that it needed larger accommodations. The little frame meeting place was torn down and a brick building was erected. The first church choir in Howard County was formed in that building and since this was in a time when many people frowned on music in church the organization of a choir was a bold and courageous act.

The church continued to grow and in 1893 it decided to construct a large and imposing edifice. Now known as Grace United Methodist Church, this building was constructed in 1895 at a cost of $33,000, a formidable sum in those days. The pastor at the time was the Rev. W.D. Parr, one of the most picturesque clergymen in Kokomo's history.

In 1944 the church celebrated its 100th anniversary with an elaborate program of events that lasted a week. In 1987 the congregation subscribed $706,000 for a major restoration of the sanctuary which included installation of an elevator, additional education offices, redesign of the main entrance on Mulberry Street, new landscaping and lighting, upholstering of the pews and other improvements.

Among the outstanding pastors the church has had were W.B. Freeland, William T. Arnold, F.F. Thornburg, J.W. Potter, LeRoy W. Kemper, S.H. Turbeville, Jesse W. Fox, Thurman B. Morris, Donald E. Bailey, John M. Sayre, Samuel E. Carruth, Donald Barnes, Wilburt Littrell, Walter Mayer and Charles I. Johnson. Rev. Johnson became pastor in 1988 and is now completing his fifth year as senior minister.

Events scheduled for the sesquicentennial year include the publication and distribution of the history book; a retreat for church leaders on May 21 with Bishop Sheldon Duecker of the Northern Illinois Methodist Conference as speaker; an original music composition directed by William H. Brown, Jr., music director at Grace, on May 22; a homecoming and open house in July; and an address by the Rev. Leonard Sweet, chancellor of the United Theological Seminary in Dayton, Ohio, on November 6.

Rev. Charles I. Johnson, current pastor of Grace United Methodist Church, has served in that position since 1988; was associate pastor from 1957-1960.

· 1845 ·

Kokomo's first church was a tiny log cabin located in Foster Park at the southwest corner of Superior & Washington Streets.

A wood frame church was built on the corner of Mulberry & Washington Streets to replace the tiny log cabin. · 1852 ·

· 1865 ·

The first brick church was built on the Washington & Mulberry Street corner to accomodate a growing congregation.

· 1896 ~ Present ·

Kokomo's oldest church building in its original form with the education wing added stands at the corner of Washington & Mulberry Streets.

71

Welcome to EASTER SERVICES AT THE CHURCH OF CHRIST Meeting at MEMORIAL HALL — Use South Door of Courthouse. Hear Edwin B. Strong Speaks at Three Services Next Lord's Day. Sunrise Service 7:00 A.M. Morning Worship 10:30 A.M. Evening Worship 7:30 P.M.

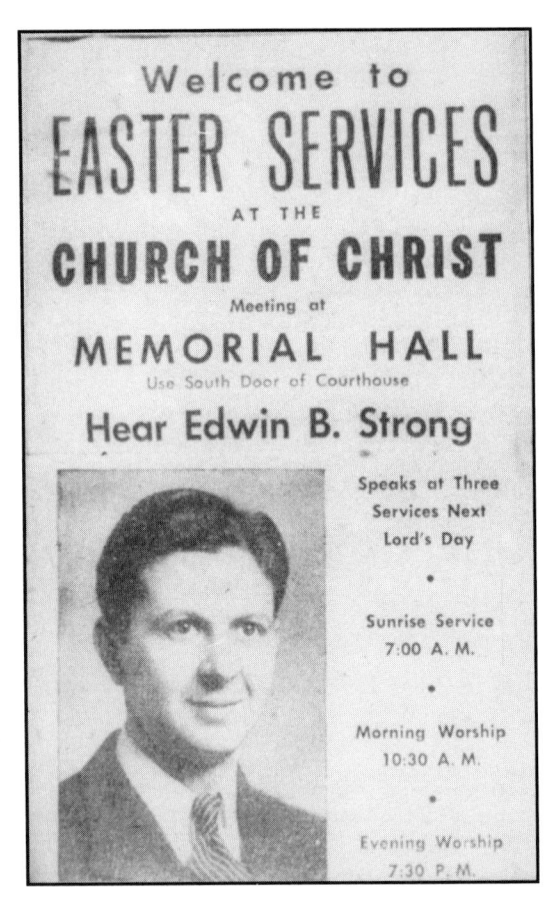

KOKOMO CHURCH OF CHRIST

Forty-eight years ago on February 17, 1946 a group of 75 men and women who wanted to be known simply as Christians, met together to form a new congregation. With the help of Edwin B. Strong, then president of Ozark Bible College, Joplin, Missouri, they chose the name "Kokomo Church of Christ." Their plea was to stand upon God's Word alone as their guide. Their goal was to build a strong body of believers who were well established in their faith and very active in demonstrating their love. The charter was signed in the home of Herbert and Gladys McFall on East Defenbaugh. Services for the first six months were held in Memorial Hall in the city court house with Edwin Strong preaching each week. Dale Storms (Kokomo native) would fly a private plane to Joplin each weekend to bring Mr. Strong to Kokomo.

In the fall of 1946, the meetings were moved to the house at 618 South Main Street. Rolland and Ethel Steever were then called to serve the congregation full-time. His initial salary was $50.00 a week and $10.00 for the parsonage. During his ministry the congregation grew both in numbers, spirit and faith. As a result of this strong growth, a larger brick structure was built next to the old house. The move was made in the fall of 1952. Rolland and his family remained in Kokomo until 1956 when he was called to serve as president of Eastern Christian College in Bel Air, Maryland.

Kenneth Washburn came preaching and teaching, with his wife Nancy, in September of 1956. During his ministry many families were added to the congregation and various new outreach programs were initiated. During a time in our country's history when many fellowships were led to compromise their faith, the Kokomo Church of Christ became famous for "Gospel Preaching." Brother Kenny, as he was affectionately known, left Kokomo in 1972 to travel full time as a revival preacher.

In the spring of 1972, the first full time youth minister, Stan Sutton, was called. He and his wife Jan organized the social and educational programs for kindergarten through senior high. He left in August of 1974 to serve with another congregation.

The Washburns were followed in 1972 by Ben and Mary Wilson. Mr. Wilson's teaching and detail with the Word of God encouraged and challenged many. He continued the strong gospel preaching along with starting the congregation's first choir. When the Wilson family left Kokomo in 1981, Ben went to work as a writer for Good News Productions International.

Gary and Linda Carpenter moved home to Kokomo in October of 1981. Gary is a 1968 graduate of Kokomo High School. In fact, he was president of his senior class. As a home grown boy, he knew very well how Kokomo natives think. Even after training at Ozark Bible College, Lincoln Christian Seminary and Trinity Evangelical Divinity School, he spends much time each week diligently studying God's Word. His strength in both the pulpit and the classroom has led many souls to our Lord and has refreshed many tired saints. In the last thirteen years, under Dr. Carpenter's ministry, the leadership of the congregation has been strengthened and the congregation has been blessed. New families are joining this fellowship on a regular basis.

In the fall of 1986 the second full time youth minister, John Piotrowicz, joined the ministry team. His wife Brenda grew up in Kokomo at another local congregation. During his three years with the Kokomo Church of Christ, a well organized graded youth program was established. In 1988 the senior high youth group traveled to Arizona to lead a Vacation Bible School program for grade school children on a Navaho Indian reservation. In 1989, the group went to New Brunswick, Canada, to help teach in a week of Christian service camp. These were weeks which the youth shall never forget.

On April 1, 1990, Frank and Tracy Weller, both Hoosiers, moved to Kokomo. Frank was called to be the first youth and music minister with the congregation. His experience in youth work has allowed a good youth program to continue to improve. His extensive training in church music has helped to establish a vibrant and energetic music program which involve many from within and several from outside the congregation.

All these ministers have had a tremendous influence on the steadfast spiritual

Members exiting the house at 618 S. Main after church service around 1949.

growth of the congregation and its respect in this community. All those who have since left Kokomo do return to visit lifelong friends quite often.

During these past 48 years this congregation has sent over 50 young people to various Bible colleges all over the country. Some have attended only one or two years, but others have graduated with degrees and now serve with numerous congregations as preachers, ministers' wives, youth ministers, teachers and cross cultural missionaries. This is the result of an emphasis by the leadership for spreading the good news and making a total commitment to Christ Jesus.

Charles Luttrell and his wife, the former Henrietta Storms, who is a native of Kokomo, left for Hawaii in the early 1960's as missionaries. They served for over twenty-five years, until Charles' death in 1986. Henrietta is continuing to serve by directing a preschool and teaching Sunday School classes in Waianae, Hawaii. She currently plans to remain as long as the Lord allows.

Mike Herchenroeder, a former Kokomo native, and Eunice, his wife, are serving in Papua New Guinea with Pioneer Bible Translators. Their work includes reducing a native language to writing and translating the Holy Scriptures into this language. Mike is a former Delco Electronics employee, trained in computer technology. He is currently using this training to prepare computer software that will aid all Bible translators to complete their work with greater efficiency and accuracy. The primary purpose for their work is to introduce souls in the jungle villages to Jesus Christ.

Along with those from within the congregation, several other full-time missionaries are supported with prayers, letters and funds. These include workers in Jamaica, Great Britain, Hong Kong and Manila in the Philippines. Support is also sent to Bible colleges, the Mission Services Association, the Howard Community Chaplain Program, and Rainbow Christian Camp in Converse, Indiana. The camp is sponsored by over 70 central Indiana churches and hosts over 1200 campers in more than 20 intense Bible-based, Christ-centered and Mission minded life changing weeks each summer.

Through the years many members of this congregation have served with mission works all over the country. Bill McGilvrey moved to Kokomo in the early 1970's while working with Mission Services Association. Even in his retirement he is well-known by maintaining communication with missionaries all over the globe. Ed Berndt served for several years as director of MSA after it moved to Knoxville, Tennessee. This is an organization which aids churches and missionaries in clearly communicating

Church elders in 1969 (l. to r.) Kenneth Washburn, Walter McFall, Wayne Ingels, Lyndall Jordan, Dale Storms, Eddie Berndt, and Ray Storms.

with each other. Dale Storms left his home in Kokomo with his family to serve as the business manager of Ozark Bible College, Joplin, Missouri. During his many years of diligent service, the college became one of the most financially stable educational institutions in the country. Even though many families and individuals have left Kokomo to serve Christ in other places, the congregation continues to grow.

Although few of the original 75 charter members are still with us, the congregation has grown to include over 140 households. The programs of the congregation still include Bible classes for all ages, but more programs have been added over the years. One of the most dynamic programs is the "B" team. This is a group of caring individuals who do tedious chores for cherished senior saints and those who just need an extra hand. The projects have included raking leaves, painting, and spring cleaning. An annual Vacation Bible School program is sponsored each spring to teach children from the community the impact of the life of Jesus Christ. A recent addition to the program is the Summer Concert Series. The congregation sponsors four to five concerts by Christian artists each summer for the congregation and the community.

As the congregation continues to grow, plans are being made to leave the aging property on Main Street and build larger, more efficient facilities elsewhere in Kokomo. It is the mission of this congregation to continue to proclaim the powerful name of our Lord, Jesus Christ to this city and the world while strengthening the faith of its members. Although the faces may change over the years, the spirit and purpose of this "family" remain constant through the direction of God's Holy Word.

Dr. Gary Carpenter

Alto Road Church of Christ under construction in 1962.

ALTO ROAD CHURCH OF CHRIST

The Alto Road Church of Christ traces its history in Howard County back to the early 1940's when Mr. John Young from Van Dyke, Michigan became concerned for the spiritual well-being of his mother and sister who lived in the Kokomo area. Young was born and raised in Kokomo. He later moved to Van Dyke and worked for the Ford Motor Company. He traveled from the Detroit suburb to Kokomo every week and after studying with them from the Bible, his mother and sister both became Christians. John continued to travel to Kokomo each week so that he and his family could worship God together.

Unknown to Mr. Young...there were other members of the Church of Christ who lived in Kokomo, the Roy Skomp family and the Frank Harmon family. Young, in 1944, sent a notice to a religious paper in which he sought the identities of people interested in starting a congregation here. Roy Skomp heard about the article and made contact with Young. This thrilled Young. He and Mr. Skomp began making plans to start a congregation in Kokomo.

The Church of Christ in Van Dyke offered to send their preacher, Mr. W.C. Anderson, here for a two-week gospel meeting to get the church started.

Three months went into the planning of this meeting. The group made contact with the officials of the city to assemble at Memorial Hall in the County Court House. Arrangements could only be made for one month.

The first meeting of the little church took place in Memorial Hall on October 8, 1944. There were only 10 people present. Mr. Anderson preached during that meeting.

On Monday, the struggling church received word that they could not use Memorial Hall for the whole month. An old store building was found to rent at 1217 South Courtland Avenue, ultimately becoming the permanent address for the congregation.

In 1950 the old store building was torn down and a new building was erected. The Delois White family worked full-time with the congregation. By 1957 the new church building was filled to capacity and two services had to be held each Sunday. So, in 1961 plans were made to start a congregation on the south end of the city.

On Wednesday night, August 29, 1962, seventy-five people attended the first meeting of the Alto Road Church of Christ. On the following Sunday, there were about 150 people present. The W.C. Anderson family worked full-time with this new congregation until 1968. Other ministers have served this church including: William Curry (1968-1973), James Dando (1973-1976) and Lynn Brust (1976 to the present time). In 1985 a beautiful Fellowship Hall was built on the property and serves the church's many needs.

Today, the Alto Road church numbers about 300. It is served by four elders: Rob Millspaugh, Bob Wavra, Phil Baskett and Walter McIndoo. David Yasko and Lynn Burst serve as its full-time ministers.

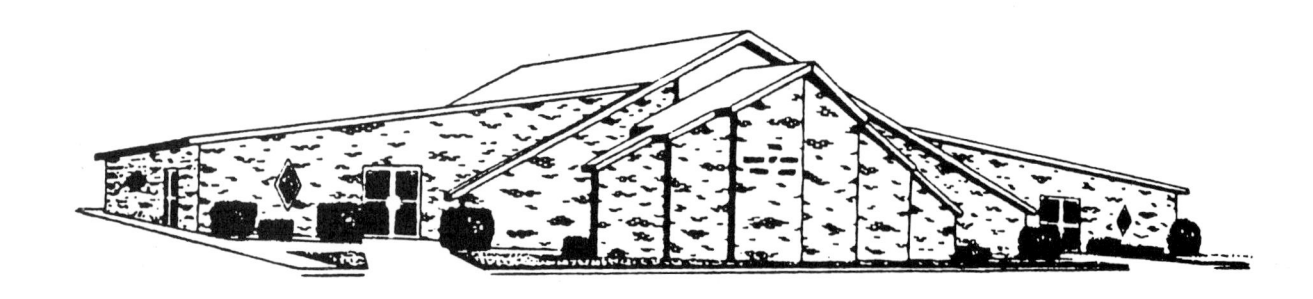

BIBLE BAPTIST CHURCH

Bible Baptist Church of Kokomo, Indiana, began in June 1944, at the downtown YMCA, with thirty-three charter members who had a vision for a strong Bible-centered ministry. Mr. Paul Myers was selected chairman; Mrs. Harry Wible, secretary; and Mrs. Homer Johnson, assistant secretary. A Service Committee was composed of Mr. George Shepherd, Mr. Ralph Adams, Mr. Ralph Myers, Mr. Harry Wible and Mr. Stacy Davis. Mr. Harry Wible was elected treasurer; Mr. Homer Johnson, Sunday School Superintendent; and Mr. William Paul, Assistant Sunday School Superintendent. The members called the first pastor, Rev. Patrick Henry.

In 1946, the growing membership purchased a large house at 404 West Jefferson. Construction began on a church building at the West Jefferson location in 1952, during the ministry of Rev. John Balyo. Sensing the leading of God, the church voted to fellowship with the General Association of Regular Baptist Churches.

Rev. Herbert Orman also ministered to this growing congregation and during his pastorate a youth program was begun - AWANA for girls and Christian Service Brigade for boys.

The Rev. Eddie Smith was the Pastor when the church building was completed in 1958. Additional educational units were added in 1960, and in 1962 a kindergarten started with 17 students.

While Dr. Ernest Pickering served as Senior Pastor, more educational units were added in 1968. During that same year the church gratefully received donated property near Young America to be used as a church camp, and Deer Creek Baptist Camp began. A lodge was built but later destroyed by fire in 1979. Deer Creek Baptist Camp is still in use and a portion of the camp is presently leased by Moody Bible Broadcasting as the tower site for Christian radio station, WIWC.

Dr. Ben Strohbehn assumed the senior pastorate in 1970. Under his leadership the church family grew to the point of needing two morning services during the mid-70's. In the spring of 1974, a School Committee was selected to inquire of the possibility of beginning a Christian school. The school became a reality in August 1974, under the supervision of Rev. Robert W. Belt along with a faculty of nine teachers. One hundred students in kindergarten through the 8th grade enrolled the first school year. The first graduating class participated in commencement exercises in May of 1983. Kokomo Christian School continues to be a ministry of Bible Baptist Church and strives to be God-honoring in everything from basic academics and college prep courses to extracurricular activities. The school's mission statement is: "For God's glory, Kokomo Christian School provides students a setting for academic excellence in the Christian perspective, builds character and develops students' gifts for service in their world."

In 1977, during the ministry of Joseph M. Stowell III, the church decided to relocate and purchased eighty acres at the intersection of S. Dixon Road and W. Lincoln Road. The ground breaking service June 3, 1979, signalled the beginning of construction. On June 29, 1980, the congregation held the first service in the new facility. The official dedication service was held on September 14, 1980.

Rev. Richard McIntosh served as interim pastor in 1983, and in January 1984 accepted the position as senior pastor. His ministry was centered on expository Bible teaching with an emphasis on Christian counseling and was actively involved in the AWANA ministry.

In August 1991, Rev. Daniel R. Johnson was called as senior pastor. Interestingly, his mother and grandmother were charter members of Bible Baptist Church. Due to continued growth in the ensuing years, once again two morning services were instituted in October 1993. Serving with Rev. Johnson as associate pastors are Rev. John M. Sitton, and Rev. Jonathan Tice. Serving as assistant pastors are Mr. Dana Neer, youth pastor; and Mr. Donald Criss, KCS Administrator. The church has been well served through the years by nine other men through Christian education, visitation and youth ministries.

The youth of Bible Baptist have many opportunities to participate in church-sponsored mission trips each summer in addition to teaching Bible classes, visiting the elderly, and helping with maintenance projects.

From its inception the church has had a desire to spread the gospel of salvation to mankind and supports thirty-nine home and foreign missionaries along with thirteen agencies and four Christian Colleges.

Through the years, many outstanding speakers and authors such as Dr. Walter Wilson, Dr. Harry Ironside, Dr. R.T. Ketchum, Dr. Vance Havner and Dr. Bob Jones, Jr. have shared the pulpit.

It is evident that God has empowered and blessed Bible Baptist Church during the last 50 years, and to Him belongs the glory for the great things He has done.

"Great is the LORD and most worthy of praise; His greatness no one can fathom." (Psalm 145:3)

B'Nai Israel Temple

B'NAI ISRAEL TEMPLE

Records indicate that clothing merchant Samuel Rosenthal was Kokomo's first Jewish citizen in 1845. Settlement of business and service persons led to the formal building of a Jewish house of worship in 1942. B'Nai Israel Temple has served the fluctuating congregation in all capacities—a place of assembly and education, as well as worship and celebration of life cycles.

A handful of Jewish residents functioned in previous years and took an active part in Kokomo life. In 1931, the women affiliated with the National Federation of Temple Sisterhoods, under the umbrella of the Reform movement of Judaism. Max and Lottie Gerber assumed leadership with Irv and Esther Andich to begin building the sanctuary. Student rabbis from the Union of America Hebrew Congregations, Cincinnati, have served the Temple on a bi-weekly basis. Harriet Gerber Lewis, daughter of the founders, is honorary chairman.

Fund-raisers support such community functions as relief for the homeless, local hospitals and Bona Vista. Grissom Air Base members were welcomed. The Temple art auctions brought internationally recognized items to the local scene. Misch Kohn, Kokomo-born artist, celebrated a weekend of outstanding recognition from the Temple and community. Tours are available for educational purposes.

The Honor Garden and back corner of the Temple during the celebration of its 50th Anniversary.

CHAPEL HILL CHRISTIAN CHURCH

One church with a vision provided the momentum to start another. It was 1969 and Kokomo Church of Christ, located on South Main, had decided there was a great need in southwestern Howard County for another Christian church (Independent). During a meeting on June 8, 1969, the Church of Christ determined that a new church would begin and be located in the Alto area.

But to start a new church and have it succeed requires a good nucleus of committed members. For this reason, 45 members of Kokomo Church of Christ willingly volunteered to make the move, and so Chapel Hill Christian Church began.

However, Chapel Hill Christian Church, as it is known today, has made many changes form its original beginnings. Having no building in 1969, the church, under the name "The Church of Christ at Alto", met at the Wray of Sunshine Kindergarten, which was located at the intersection of Alto and Dixon roads. The first service was held August 3, 1969.

By late December 1970, The Church of Christ at Alto was averaging 70 members and it was becoming evident to all that a permanent home would need to be built. In order to continue growing, however, a church constitution was needed. With the first constitution being ratified on November 10, 1974, the Church of Christ at Alto was now set to begin the first phase of what would become a major building program.

With the change of the name from The Church of Christ at Alto to Chapel Hill Christian Church, came the builders. The original building's plans designed by Goodman Church Builders of Joplin, Missouri, included an auditorium for 300 people, eight classrooms, a fellowship hall, kitchen, bathrooms and one nursery. Groundbreaking for the new church building began Sunday, April 6, 1975, with the dedication service taking place on May 2, 1976.

By 1982, however, the first building was bursting at the seams. During this time, another section was added to the original building incorporating more rooms for Sunday School classes. Attendance was increasing rapidly, now averaging 130 in Sunday morning worship and more and more programs were being provided.

The Worship Center was designed and built in 1985 as attendance finally reached proportions that the original sanctuary was not built to handle. This multi-purpose room is both a center for worship services as well as a sports and other programs facility. In addition, Chapel Hill Christian Church now has numerous rooms for Sunday School classes, a baseball diamond, a full kitchen, a larger fellowship hall, and a pre-school.

Extensive remodeling during 1993-1994 has created an atmosphere of beauty and continuity throughout the church. In addition, landscaping taken on by members of Chapel Hill Christian Church has added pleasure to the outside of the church as well.

Chapel Hill Christian Church now averages 300 in Sunday morning worship and has an extensive range of programs for all ages. Children's programs are available from infants through high school, and meet Sunday mornings and evenings, as well as Wednesday evenings. In addition, several adult Bible studies are held regularly, as well as, Chapel Hill Women's Fellowship and the Chapel Hill Worship Choir. Athletic programs include a volleyball league, basketball team, softball team and an annual golf outing. Sunday mornings find Sunday School classes for all ages meeting at 9:00 a.m. and then joining together at 10:00 a.m. for morning worship.

The vision that originally created Chapel Hill Christian Church in Kokomo, Indiana, is indeed alive and well and living at 2600 West Alto Road! *Submitted by Ann Kettering Sincox*

The original building of the Chapel Hill Christian Church.

Main entrance to Chapel Hill Christian Church.

Worship center and multi-purpose room.

CHURCH OF JESUS CHRIST OF LATTER-DAY SAINTS (MORMONS)

The members of the Church of Jesus Christ of Latter-Day Saints are often called Mormons because they believe that the Book of Mormon is scripture in addition to the Bible. The members of the church believe that God, Jesus Christ and the Holy Spirit are separate beings and that a living prophet receives revelation for today's world. The Mormon Church emphasizes the importance of the family, genealogy work, missionary work, self-sufficiency and assisting one another temporarily and spiritually. Every member has a calling or job in the church and all serve without compensation.

A branch of the Mormon Church was established in Kokomo around 1910. However, persecution became so intense that the missionaries were withdrawn and the church disbanded in 1917 or 1918.

In 1951 the Mormon missionaries once again established a church in Kokomo. The members met in many different places namely: Republican Headquarters on South Main, the YWCA, the dance hall above McLellan's Dime Store and in members' homes. In the late 1950's a house in which to have services was purchased at 1036 North Indiana at the corner of Broadway and Indiana.

In the early 1960's efforts were begun to build a church building. The leadership of the branch found a location on West Center Road that they felt would be the ideal location for a church building, but the owner of the land refused to sell. After a branch fast on Sunday for the purpose of acquiring this land, the owner called the branch president on Monday to say he had changed his mind and the Saints could purchase the land.

The house on Indiana Street was put up for sale and it was sold within a week. The members met temporarily in the basement of the Masonic Lodge and in members' homes.

Chester Berry served as a building missionary to help the local members build their new church building. Every evening the brothers met after their work to construct the new church. Each evening, two sisters were assigned to bring supper to the men who worked until 9:00 p.m.

The small branch had many money making projects to help finance this building. These included Friday night dinners and fudge making. Also, the Relief Society (the women's organization of the church) had bazaars to sell items that they had made. Some of the items sold at the bazaars were dough boys, ducks, infant carrier covers with matching quilts, pin cushions, machine knitted children's ponchos and aprons.

In 1966 the Kokomo Branch basketball team won the Indianapolis State Tournament. No team came within twenty points of the Kokomo team. They then advanced to the Regionals held in St. Louis. After winning there, the team advanced to the Area Tournament also held in St. Louis. The Kokomo team finished as runners-up in the Area Tournament two years in a row, losing out on an opportunity to play in the all church tournament in Salt Lake City. It was somewhat astonishing to the other teams how a small branch of the church with only eight players from a town named Kokomo could do so well.

In the early 1970's two additions were added to the church building which included the chapel and cultural hall. The members at this time - about thirty-three families - made the necessary financial donations to build these additions. They also had fund raising projects of raising and selling crops and bazaars (held twice per year).

When a Mormon Church reaches a certain level of membership and development, it is referred to as a ward instead of a branch. This event occurred in 1973 for the Kokomo Latter-Day Saints.

In the late 1970's, the Kokomo Ward hosted several food storage seminars that were open to the public. Since this was a time of recession in Kokomo, they were very well attended.

In the mid 1980's a fourth addition was added to the building which included classrooms and a new office for the bishop. This addition also housed the genealogy library that was opened in the early 1990's.

The local men who served as branch presidents in the Kokomo branch were Jack Spicer, Merlyn Jones, Paul Sutterfield, Lyman Marler and Richard Forbes. Those who served as bishops in the Kokomo Ward were Richard Forbes, Robert Adams, Bruce Myers, Larry Rhoades and Noble C. "Skip" Name.

The Relief Society Presidents from 1953 to 1994 were Locky Epperson, Arlene McNally, Annette Mitchell, Pat Burton, Mary Jane Collins, Rosemary Jones, Lulu Belle Koenig, Carol Dillman, Sammy Roark, Charlotte Haus, Lynn Pasquale, Ethlyn Dwigans, Virginia Moore, Pauline Forbes and Audrey Marler.

From twenty members in 1951, the Mormon Church in Kokomo has grown to five hundred fourteen members in 1994. The Latter-Day Saints in Kokomo look forward to the day when their ward will be divided to create two Mormon churches in Kokomo.

FIRST CONGREGATIONAL CHRISTIAN CHURCH UNITED CHURCH OF CHRIST

The guns of Gettysburg had barely silenced when the First Congregational Church of Kokomo held its first worship service on August 23, 1863. The church had been initiated through the work of the American Home Missionary Society. Meeting in Ecclesiastical Council with other Congregational churches in the state on September 8, 1863, First Congregational Church was officially organized. The fourteen charter members were Rev. and Mrs. J.L. Jenkins, Mr. and Mrs. M.R. Andrews, Mr. and Mrs. H.L. Kelso, Mr. and Mrs. James M. Patterson, Mr. and Mrs. Joseph Fleming, Mrs. Elizabeth Davis, Mrs. Margaret Murray, Mrs. Lucinda Hathaway and Mrs. Johanna Kaufman.

The war made for difficult times and after long delays the first church building was completed on the southwest corner of Mulberry and Union Streets. On July 15, 1866, the day the building was dedicated, two other churches in Kokomo cancelled their services and joined the celebration at First Congregational. The collection of $1300 that day more than cleared the indebtedness on the building. The Gothic building was sixty-five by forty feet with stained glass windows and varnished ash and black walnut interior.

In the 1870's the congregation grew rapidly to more than 150 members. A parsonage was built and a pipe organ was installed. In a progressive and inclusive spirit, four female members were added to the Board of Deacons in 1875. By the late 1880's the building was in need of repair, and significant improvements (including a natural gas furnace) were made with the assistance of the church's Ladies' Aid Society. In December, 1887, a fire damaged the interior but repairs were made quickly while the congregation met at the Methodist, Friends and Christian churches.

During the 1890's First Congregational Church founded three Sunday School missions. Two of these missions developed into Beamer Methodist Church and Courtland Avenue Church of Christ.

After the natural gas discovery, Kokomo's population tripled and First Congregational Church likewise grew. The church building was expanded with the addition of a pastor's study, Sunday School rooms and vestibule in 1896.

The congregation continued to grow and in 1923 voted to relocate. They purchased the present site at the southwest corner of Mulberry and Webster (505 W. Mulberry St.) and dedicated the present neo-classical building on December 9, 1924. Unique in the church's design for that era was the inclusion of a basketball court in the church's basement. The room could accommodate social gatherings and became known as Pilgrim Hall. Over the years, many future Kokomo basketball stars have developed their skills in Pilgrim Hall.

The church facilities were expanded in 1959 by the gift of the Fredrick home on Walnut Street. The home was used for Sunday School rooms and social gatherings. An educational wing, which included a chapel, nursery and church offices as well as Sunday School rooms, was added to the church edifice in 1963. The Fredrick home was later sold to serve as a transitional home for mental health patients. Adjoining lots to the church have since been purchased to provide for additional offstreet parking.

First Congregational Church has always been an active participant in the life of the Kokomo community. In the 1940's the church sponsored the Congo Club dances on Saturday nights in Pilgrim Hall for the high school youth of the city. As many as 300 teenagers on a given night enjoyed the chaperoned dances. Also, during the 1940's, the church sponsored "The Talk of the Hour" series through which national personalities were invited to speak in Kokomo, and Rev. Perry Avery and a layman escorted a boat load of livestock to war-torn Poland with the Heifer Project. Interracial Vacation Bible Schools were held long before the civil rights movement and pulpit exchanges with the black churches and dialogues with the Jewish synagogue have also been frequent in the church's history. When the church received the Tynan Woods as a gift, it gave the property to the YMCA through a 99 year lease enabling the development of Camp Tycony (Tynan Congregational YMCA). The church has also sponsored the Open Horizons program in which youths from the Juvenile Court were selected for a week's survival canoe excursion in the Boundary Waters Area near Ely, Minnesota.

Since 1960 the Women's Guild of the church has operated The Nearly New Shop. Originally begun to raise money to furnish the kitchen and the pastor's study, The Nearly New Shop has continued to sell clothes on consignment and to donate the profits to the church and to community projects and missions. For several years now The Nearly New Shop has been located at 115 W. Deffenbaugh.

A First Congregational Church Foundation has been established for the sole purpose of benevolence to the community and Christian missions. The Foundation often provides seed money for new projects and outreaches.

First Congregational Church has followed other Congregational churches in joining with the Christian Church (New Light) in 1931 to form the Congregational-Christian Churches. In 1957 Congregational-Christian Churches joined the Evangelical and Reformed churches to form the United Church of Christ.

Rev. Neal R. Sadler, the 25th minister, has served the congregation since 1988.

The original church building was dedicated July 15, 1866 and the present church building was dedicated December 9, 1924.

The original church building, dedicated July 15, 1866.

The present church building, dedicated December 9, 1924.

FIRST CHURCH OF GOD

The First Church of God at 2222 West Sycamore Street in Kokomo was formed in 1930 when three couples began holding prayer meetings in their homes. These founders were Rev. George Aner Gooch and his wife Dessie Mildred (Brown) Gooch, Dorsey Pearl Browning and his wife Sylvia Pearl (Cunningham) Browning, and James Silas Meacham and his wife Lula Josephine (Mossholder) Meacham.

Around 1931 the congregation had grown and began meeting at 910 East Superior Street in a small frame building formerly used as a grocery store. Rev. George A. Gooch served as the first pastor, and his wife was the first church organist. The first song leader was Sylvia Browning. The earliest Sunday school teachers were Dessie Gooch, Sylvia Browning, Lula Meacham, Wilma Meacham, and James S. Meacham.

Having outgrown the Superior Street building, the congregation moved on November 17, 1935, to 126 East North Street. Here they worshipped for over six years in a white frame building previously used as an office building for the Kokomo Steel & Wire.

In August 1940, Rev. Henry William Hartman of Battle Creek, Michigan, became the first full-time pastor and served until poor health forced him to resign in May 1941.

Rev. Kenneth C. Tabor became the pastor in June 1941, and under his capable ministry, the congregation built its first new sanctuary at 816 East Mulberry Street in 1941, using lumber from the old East North Street building. The church was built entirely by men of the church except for laying the blocks. While the old church building was razed and the new one built, the congregation held services at the YMCA. The new sanctuary was dedicated on November 1, 1942.

Besides Rev. Tabor, other pastors who served while the congregation met at 816 East Mulberry Street were the Reverends J. Herschel Caudill (1944-1945), Lawrence E. Foudy) 1945-1946), Edward E. Williamson (Jan. - March 1947), Merle W. Squier (1947-1952), John H. Williams (1952-1955), Elza F. Brown (1955-1959), and Leonard A. Walker (1960-1963). On March 1, 1963, Rev. John H. Williams returned as pastor, and he served until July 1, 1972.

Construction began on a new sanctuary at 2222 West Sycamore Street in May 1964, and dedication services were held on November 22, 1964. In March, 1965, a new brick veneer parsonage was completed adjacent to the church on the four acre tract. In 1978, a major addition to the church was completed.

Pastors serving the congregation since Rev. John H. Williams have been the Reverends Melvin Morace (1972-1974), Ronald E. Crump (1974-1986), David E. Bowerman (1986-1992), and C. Raymond Houser (1992-present).

During the years there have been a few interim pastors, namely, Everett Byrum (1935-6), Allan D. Combs (1972), Dr. Boyce W. Blackwelder (1974), and D.J. Davis (1992).

Ministers of music who have served the congregation through the years are Doug Yockey, Lloyd Larsen, Randy Bargerstock, David Tate, Richard Wheeler, and Grant Alford.

Current members of the Board of Elders are Truman Burger, Stephen Byes, Della Clouse, Larry Dailey, Cecil Mason, Marty Minton, Barbara Moore, and Richard Wheeler. *Submitted by Allen W. Moore, Church historian, and sponsored by the Fellowship Class*

FIRST PRESBYTERIAN CHURCH

In the early 1860's in Kokomo, Indiana, a few "Calvinists," as Presbyterians are sometimes called, gathered in their homes, in Jesus' name, to chat with visiting preachers from Presbyterian churches in nearby Lafayette, Logansport, and Delphi. By 1863, a handful of these Presbyterians joined the newly formed Congregational Church believing it to be doctrinally similar to Presbyterianism.

But five years later these same Presbyterians formed a separate group, meeting above a livery stable in a fine new building at the corner of Main and Mulberry Streets. Their first recorded meeting was a fund-raiser for Kokomo's needy children. Formal religious services began at that location on November 22, 1868 with a Presbyterian minister presiding over the enrollment of four members. Meetings continued regularly with Indianapolis ministers supplying the pulpit throughout the winter of 1869-70. During that time, as in other local congregations, the membership grew rapidly. However, in the 1870's interest in the church waned and it finally became inactive although it never actually dissolved.

Then in 1886 the discovery of natural gas in and around Kokomo changed the economic, social and cultural picture for the better as many newcomers flocked to the area from eastern states, especially Pennsylvania. Earlier migrations had been primarily from southern states where Methodist and Baptist churches dominated, but in 1886, five ardent Presbyterians arrived with their families for work in the glass factory which prospered with the gas boom. Those families, with the remnant of the original group of Presbyterians, spearheaded a drive to revive the church.

By September of 1888, they were meeting regularly, had an active Sunday School, and had paid $1250.00 for three lots at the southwest corner of Walnut and Washington Streets. Retaining the lot facing Walnut Street, they sold the other two lots to support the cost of building. Legend has it that some members were unhappy with the sale because they were again near a livery stable which was built on one of the lots they had sold and distracted worshippers by emitting unpleasant noises and odors.

Nevertheless, the congregation had raised the money for the building and lot ($12,518.07) by the time of the church's dedication on February 9, 1889. That building served First Presbyterian Church for sixty-nine years with one extensive remodeling and several redecorations until it was sold to Calvary Baptist Church in 1958. Calvary's occupancy ended literally in flames in 1989. Today, only the stately Victorian red brick facade, including the beautiful stained glass window, remains, a testimony to the building's long history as a house of worship.

First Presbyterian's "new" building, erected thirty-five years ago on West Jefferson Street, is of Indiana limestone in an architectural style sometimes called American Gothic. Its membership today numbers almost eleven hundred. It is administered by a staff of nineteen under the leadership of Rev. Dr. Walter J. Ungerer. Average attendance at two Sunday morning worship services is nearly five hundred. Despite a recent expansion of the physical plant, its classrooms are full each Sunday with seven adult classes and eleven classes for children and youth. During the week, a daily pre-school, a "Kids' Club" for school age children, and numerous adult study groups and church-related service groups maintain a high activity level every day from early morning until late afternoon and many evenings. "Youth Club," with approximately 100 teenagers, meets every Wednesday from 5:30 p.m. to 8:30 p.m. The Women's Association reaches out to support local, national, and international missions, while God's Helping Hands, an arm of the Board of Deacons, anonymously meets emergency and ongoing needs of local families and individuals. A small group ministry nurtures the shared faith of its members through fellowship and friendship. On a wider scale, fellowship and friendship thrive in such diverse activities as hog roasts and square dances, dinners, ice cream socials, and picnics, songfests and hymn sings: all this under the aegis of the church's current slogan, a promise to "Serve the Lord Boldly."

One wonders if the handful of Calvinists who gathered together in Jesus' name in their Kokomo homes in 1860, would find much in common with their descendants in 1993. Certainly they would be baffled by the commercial-size refrigerator in the kitchen, the whirring computers in the offices, and the elegant mauve decor of the air-conditioned sanctuary. But if they lingered a bit they would hear the reverberating echoes of the 1868 fund-raiser for Kokomo's needy children; they would recognize the strong Bible-based preaching, the adherence to Calvinist doctrine, the emphasis on education, the pervasive and vocal concern for social issues by believers united even in disagreement, the focus on the family, and the dedication to missions and evangelism. Surely they would be touched by the comprehensive music program.

Such visitors might enjoy reading the centennial history written in 1968 entitled "The Unfinished Story" which described their struggle to start the church. While they would feel pride in what had been accomplished from their seed-bed, they would also agree with the present members of First Presbyterian Church that the story is still unfinished.

GREENTOWN FIRST UNITED METHODIST CHURCH

[The first fifty years of this history is taken from the *Fiftieth Anniversary Souvenir* of the Methodist Episcopal Church at Greentown, Indiana, October 25-28, 1894.]

"The early history of Greentown proper bears the date of April, 1848, at which time the plat was placed upon record, and the principal causes which led to the origin of the village was the outgrowth of the neighborhood demand for a trading post. The town was laid out on the site of an old Indiana town, known as Green's Village, from which the name of Greentown is derived..."

"The class at Greentown was organized in 1844 by Rev. James Burns. The class comprised, as near as can be ascertained, the following persons: Jane Jones; James Morton and wife and daughter, Elizabeth; Mrs. Tempa Brown; Charles D. Fry and wife; Reuben Hawkins, wife and two daughters, Ellis Pickering, and Eliza Felton.—a membership of thirteen—and who will say that it did not take courage and heroism of an exalted type to brave the wilderness surroundings, to go from house to house to hold meetings, to endure the privations of pioneer life that the banner of the Cross might be reared, that the Redeemer's Kingdom might be built up and perpetuated for those who came after?"...

"Greentown Mission was organized in 1852, being set off from Kokomo Circuit. The preacher in charge the first year of the Mission was Rev. J.W. Doyle. The Circuit became known as Jerome in 1858, continuing under that name until 1884, since which time it has been known as Greentown."

"Meetings were held at private residences until the schoolhouse was built in the village, and that was then used as a place of worship for a few years, until Joel Stephenson built the 'Three-Story,' as it was called, and one room of that building was used as a meeting place until the church was erected (on the north-west corner of Meridian and Walnut Streets), which occurred in 1854, the site being donated by Charles O. Fry."

This first "building was a frame structure, capable of seating about 300 persons, and cost about $1,200...The house was enclosed, receiving one coat of plaster. The seats were of boards laid on blocks, which were so used until the winter of 1860-61, when a sum of money sufficient to replaster, comfortably seat the house and purchase a bell was raised, when the house was formally dedicated to the service of God."

"The old frame structure was used until 1892, when it was purchased by the Friends," and moved to its present location at the south-east corner of Grant and Washington Streets. It is of interest to note that this original structure is the same building that the Wesleyan Church remodeled in the year 1927, and used until building their present building.

"The commodious brick edifice in which we today meet was erected on the original site (on the north-west corner of Meridian and Walnut Streets) at a cost of $6,500" in 1892.

In 1917, twenty-five feet were added to the rear of the building to make room for the Dorcas class, choir loft, and two rooms back of the choir loft. The original tower was torn down, and a larger tower and entrance were built to access the basement, which was also added at this time.

The limestone facing was added to the building as part of an extensive remodeling in 1951.

Groundbreaking ceremonies for a new parsonage and fellowship hall on the south-west corner of Walnut and Meridian Streets, across from the church, were held on April 4, 1965. It was on the following Sunday, April 11, 1965, that the Palm Sunday tornado struck and caused extensive damage to the east end of the sanctuary.

Consecration services for the newly built fellowship hall and parsonage, and the renovated church building were held the following spring on May 15, 1966.

The church officially became the First United Methodist Church of Greentown in 1968, the year in which The Methodist Church and The Evangelical United Brethren Church merged to become The United Methodist Church.

In 1993, the 100-year-old church structure was fully renovated, so that we might better serve our growing community and its families in the name of Christ. The sanctuary and chancel areas were enhanced, the children's programing facilities saw major revisions, with improved rest room facilities on both levels and a more functional office layout.

Greentown First United Methodist church around 1906.

Greentown First United Methodist Church in 1994.

JUDSON BAPTIST CHURCH

By request of Brothers and Sisters in Ervin Township, Howard County, Indiana, an Ecclesiastical Council convened at the Stetler schoolhouse seven and one half miles west of Kokomo on May 21, 1859 for the purpose of consulting the propriety of recognizing them as a Regular Baptist Church. Delegates from the Sharon, Springfield and Deer Creek churches met with them.

Samuel Gearhart, Sara Gearhart, John J. Arthur, Alexander Robertson and Elizabeth Robertson presented their letters, and the Articles of Faith were read and adopted and the Council resolved to recognize them as a Regular Baptist Church.

Price Odell was ordained in 1860 and became the first pastor of Judson. There are still several descendants of Price Odell who hold membership at Judson and are faithful attendants there. He served for twelve years continuously and then at two-year intervals for a total of eighteen years.

Protracted meetings were usually held in mid-winter where many people either joined the church by letter or baptism. The baptisms were held in one of the creeks close by—sometimes even in the winter. These meetings were an enjoyable time for the young and the old. Many came either by bobsled pulled by horses or by walking through deep snow drifts.

Judson was moved across the road to its present location and has been remodeled several times.

Every church, like an individual, has its up and downs, health and illnesses. If a church cannot meet its obligations sometimes a persistent layperson has to take over and keep the spark of light alive.

For six years commencing in 1902, William J. Arthur literally kept it alive, as superintendent, chorister, organist, sexton and moderator. He also gave singing lessons at the church and in the school houses near by.

With renewed vigor in the church in 1908, Rev. W.P. Tedford began preaching on Sunday afternoon while he was still pastor at Young America. There was a real spiritual awakening during his six years at Judson. He came from Frankfort on the old "Interrurban Line" and was usually met by J.W. Haak, one of our first members to own an automobile. There are many stories told of these "machine rides". Rev. Tedford was often paid in produce which he carried home in sacks.

The church felt the great loss of Will Arthur and his help in so many things-especially in singing so it was fortunate that Rev. A.S. Shook was also an enthusiastic song leader. He drove thirty miles from Windfall to conduct weekly choir practices. He was always present at our annual Homecoming and ready and eager to give his testimony in song.

Rev. Price O'Dell standing in front of the first Judson Baptist Church.

The Judson Baptist Church in 1994.

Jack Yarian served Judson for a total of twenty-five years. This was the longest time any pastor served Judson. During his pastorate, J. Franklin Arthur, grandson of a charter member, was licensed to preach and, after study and experience, he was ordained in Judson on August 31, 1927. Spiritual life was added with the licensing of Kenneth Freeland and Jerry Cook to enter the Gospel Ministry following their graduation from Franklin College.

"The Faith of our Fathers" gives us the courage to look down the road to the future with hope that our children and grandchildren will always be able to look to our church for the same guidance and inspiration that has been enjoyed for one hundred thirty-nine years.

Judson is affiliated with the Judson Baptist Association, Indiana Baptist Convention and American Baptist Churches of the U.S.A. It is an active church, with a Women's Missionary Society, Judson Men's Fellowship, Baptist Youth Fellowship, Bible Study Groups, Adult Choir, Adult Bell Choir, and Junior Bell Choir.

Judson Church Ministers serving from 1859-1994 were: Rev. Price Odell, Rev. J.V. Knight, Rev. O.H. Hanna, Rev. R.H. Todd, Rev. J.H. Storms, Rev. J.K. Carson, Rev. E.W. Bowles, Rev. T.C. Smith, Rev. I.C. Tedford, Rev. T.C. Ploughe, Rev. Clem Ricketts, Rev. W.A. Kleckner, Rev. H.F. Perry, Rev. Willard P. Tedford, Rev. C.L. Merriman, Rev. A.L. Shook, Rev. A. Edrington, Rev. J.E. Yarian, Rev. B.T. Perviance, Rev. W.H. Harris, Rev. William Rix, Rev. Dale Heinbaugh, Rev. Harry Cubel, Rev. Dan Mattox, Rev. Chuck DeRolf, Rev. Arnold Maggard, Rev. Henry Hawkins, Rev. Wayne Dungan, Rev. A.E. McKenney and Rev. Tom Webber. At present we have an interim pastor, Rev. Bob Hammond.

During the tenure of Rev. Henry Hawkins' pastorate, one of the young women of Judson, Luann Young, felt the call to Christian Ministry. While Rev. Wayne Duncan was our pastor, Luann enrolled in Eastern Baptist Theological Seminary in Westchester, Pa. and graduated with a Masters of Divinity Degree in 1993. She was ordained in the Baptist Church of Westchester, Pa. where she is currently the associate pastor.

Our prayer is for the "Little Church on the Corner" to remain forever as a symbol of hope and faith for future generations.
Submitted by Mrs. Donald G. Mason

LUTHERAN CHURCH OF OUR REDEEMER

Lutheran families of Kokomo were cared for as a mission from 1885, to September, 1916, by several circuit riders who were Lutheran pastors of the area. Reverend George H. Kase of Emanuel Lutheran Church, Tipton, began caring for five families (20 souls) who met in the old Puckett Church on North Armstrong Street. Only two meetings were held there when the trustees of the church were requested to look for another place of worship. The Council Chamber of the City Hall was a large, comfortable room where the pastor came regularly every second Sunday afternoon and one day a week for personal work with the people, looking up new addresses furnished by the more enthusiastic members of the flock. On February 4, 1918, this group met to organize a congregation. After three meetings, the organization, (consisting of 14 voting members, and 48 communicant members) was perfected. The elected officers were elders and collectors: serving the north side was Gottleb Herkomer—the south side, Hugh Schroeder; serving as secretary was Fred Fiess; Treasurer, Frank Ulrich; Trustees, William Scheidt, Frank Ulrich and George Bergman. All meetings were held in the hospitable home of Mr. George Bergman, 1619 S. Main St., and his loyal daughters Lydia and Myrtle Bergman, added much beauty and impressiveness to the services with their splendid rendition of special music and song. The members chose to acquire and own property, having outgrown their facility which required members to ascend two flights of stairs. They were often disturbed by nerve-rattling noises, especially when the fire department was called out during services, which frequently happened.

The members took counsel from Synod's expertise. They were advised that mission work was most effective when a church had its own home—they also were advised not to go to the outskirts of the city. No lot could be found near the public square under $2,000.00, but property was located about four blocks from the public square to be sold to the highest bidder with sealed bids by March 4, 1918. The General Extension Board of Synod was contacted and advised they would support the congregation. A bid of $7,525.00 was offered and accepted and consisted of three houses on the corner of Union and Jefferson. The corner house was converted into a place of worship with the other two to continue as rentals for $300.00 annually which was used as repayment on the loan.

The church was dedicated on Sunday, May 12, 1918, with guests arriving in disagreeable rain. They came from Arcadia, Peru and Tipton, in their "machines and on the Traction having to walk four blocks north to the church from the station in the rain. Their churches had dismissed Sunday services so they could attend the dedication and celebration. Dinner was served (500) by the Ladies Aid. Collections taken in the services amounted to $120.00 and the table brought in about $90.00—most of this was 'pure profit.'"

After several "Calls" were extended, The Reverend Adolph J. Stiemke, a recent graduate from Concordia Seminary, St. Louis, was installed at Redeemer Lutheran Church at 208 E. Jefferson St., on Sunday, August 25, 1918, and served the church until 1924.

Reverend Walter J. Lobeck began his ministry January 11, 1924, through April, 1935. During his ministry, the second church building was erected in 1925, and the "old" church building was moved next to the new church, was renovated, and served as the parsonage.

Reverend Carl Ahlbrand was "called" April 26, 1936, and remained with the congregation until 1957, with the "Mortgage Burning Service" held September 9, 1945. The celebration service listed George Hartmann, Chairman of the Congregation, heading the committee, with trustees Frank Mullen, Ralph Snider and William Ullman in charge of the "burning of the mortgage" service.

On September 1, 1957, Reverend Rudolph A. Ritz was installed with 199 communicant members and served until March 10, 1967. The present church at 705 Southway Blvd. E., was built, with the Cornerstone Laying Service held on October 11, 1964, with 418 communicants and 209 families. The official name of the church became Lutheran Church of Our Redeemer.

Reverend A. Herbert Muhl served from September 1, 1967, until his death on May 8, 1993. Under Reverend Muhl's guidance, five sons of the congregation became Lutheran ministers. They are: Reverend Walter Ullman, Thomas Colley, Kent Umbarger, Timothy Muller, and the congregation's present Senior Pastor, William Allison—installed November 7, 1993. Also a "daughter" congregation was planned with the gift of land from a church family—thus Good Shepherd Lutheran Church at 121 Santa Fe Blvd, held their first worship service on July 15, 1979. The Redeemer Lutheran School was formed and began holding its first classes in August, 1984.

At the end of 1993, the Church Journal reflected a membership of 1,340 baptized members, 1,015 communicant members, and 517 families. *Submitted by Grace Jay*

Macedonia Christian Church in 1916 with Grange Hall in the background.

MACEDONIA CHRISTIAN CHURCH

Macedonia Christian Church began in 1882, when the Taylor Township Grange #688, voted to disband and offered its building to a religious group for services. The small frame Grange Hall was located on the present church property, in Section 12 of Taylor Township, land owned by John and Mary Hinkle. They donated the small corner tract on their farm to be used for church purposes. This land had been purchased from the government May 2, 1848, by Mary's father, Samuel Whisler, Jr.

With the aid of Brazilia M. Blount, who was preaching at Jerome, Macedonia was organized on November 24, 1882. Charter members were John Rich; his sisters—Rebecca Pero, Elizabeth Saul North, Leannah Scott, and Margaret Curlee; the latter's husband Abraham Curlee; and William F. Meranda and his wife Margaret. These Christians, reminded of the vision of the Apostle Paul at Troas, named the church, Macedonia. Other early members were the Duke, Helms, Himes, Saul, Smith, Thomas, and Willits families.

The Grange Hall was heated with wood stoves and lighted with oil lamps. There were no paved roads, and the minister who came one Sunday each month from Indianapolis, was met at the train station in Kokomo and transported seven and a half miles to the church by wagon. He would stay overnight at the home of a church member and would return to Indianapolis the following day.

After worshipping in the Grange Hall for 32 years, the congregation voted to build a new church at same location. This structure was dedicated May 21, 1916. It remained a part of the present church complex until 1993. The Grange Hall was moved a short distance northwest where it became a farm shed.

In 1957, a parsonage was built and dedicated as a part of the 75th anniversary on November 24, 1957. It was relocated and remodeled in 1973.

On June 13, 1964, Macedonia's congregation broke ground for a new sanctuary, fellowship hall, and classrooms. Additional land for this was donated by Elbert Cole and Paul Johnson, and the new edifice was dedicated May 2, 1965.

In 1979, a larger sanctuary was built along with classrooms, kitchen, fellowship hall/gym, and offices. This facility was dedicated on June 22, 1980.

In 1993, the congregation razed the 1916 building and remodeled the 1964 addition to include a chapel and classrooms. Also, improvements were made in the 1980 wing, the parsonage was enlarged, and parking was expanded.

From 1882 to 1962, Macedonia was served by circuit riders, seminary students, and parttime ministers. Some of these were David A. McDowell, T.A. Cooper, Arthur C. Patton, Aaron W. Havens, Leland Emerson, John W. Wittkamper, George W. Wise, William Shewman, and Charles Luttrell. In 1962 John H. Brownlee was hired as the first full-time minister. Other former ministers or associate ministers were Bruce Wotring, Stanley Sutton, George Mendez, Larry Johnson, Darrell Stout, Michael Percifield, Hondel Adams, Richard DuBose, and John Piotrowicz.

During its early years, Macedonia was the center of an agricultural community, and most of its members lived near the church. Although its membership was small, Macedonia was an active congregation. The women participated in the Missionary Society and Ladies' Aid Society. The youth had the Christian Endeavor organization and went camping at Bethany Park. There were special programs, Sunday School conventions, and the annual picnic at the park.

When World War II came, Macedonia's young people served in several branches of service. They all returned, but not to stay. The migration was to the cities for occupation and residence. The fate of the country church was doubtful, but the dedication and faith of Bessie Lovejoy carried Macedonia through hard times. Then came a spiritual revival, and the same conditions that took people away, brought others to Macedonia. People who moved here from the South, added strength to the congregation, and the church took on new life.

Although Macedonia had been organized as an independent church, the congregation affiliated with the Disciples of Christ during its early years. Later the membership voted to become independent again and incorporated on September 11, 1963.

Today Macedonia Christian Church is an independent, nondenominational church that conducts services according to the pattern in the New Testament scriptures, which include the ordinances of immersion as the form of Christian baptism, and the weekly observance of the Lord's Supper. The congregation fellowships with other independent Christian churches that are part of the North American Christian Convention and helps support eleven home and foreign missions. It also sponsors Little Lambs Preschool and Christian counseling.

The 1994 membership is 115 families with a weekly attendance of 260. The present ministers are Rick Keck and Ron Whitacre. The elders are Wayne Cannon, Larry Johnson, Paul Johnson, Corum Peck, and Rod Mason. The deacons are Walter Bliss, Terry Buckley, Steve Cusick, Don England, Robert Fague, Alan Gillogly, Larry Howell, Randy Keck, David Ray, Ed Riley, Vernon Sewell, and Eldon Terrell. Walter Bliss, Don England, and Vernon Sewell are trustees. *Submitted by Ed Riley*

Macedonia Christian Church in 1994.

MAIN STREET CHRISTIAN CHURCH

On June 25, 1848, several persons formerly belonging to the Church of Christ in other parts of the country came together in Russiaville and pledged themselves to the Lord. They vowed to keep the commandments of God and the Lord Jesus Christ, to take the New Testament as their only rule of faith, to renounce all traditions of men and to be known as the Church of Christ, Russiaville, Indiana. Those persons were Adam Conrad, Benjamin Jones, William Draper, Jonathan Spealman, Eli Avery, Enoch Avery, Jonathan Styles, James McKowan, Andrew Pennington, Nicholas Trobaugh, Mary Jones, Catherine Conrad, Nancy Draper, Margaret Spealman, Dorcas Avery, Louise Fox, Cela Draper, and A.M. Beard.

The church building was not erected until 1858. Adam Conrad served as the first minister. Preaching services were held once each month; social meetings were every Lord's Day and Sunday School every Sunday afternoon.

On April 11, 1965, the town of Russiaville was devastated by tornadoes. The church building was left with only three walls standing, and the parsonage was damaged beyond repair.

Until a new church was built, the members of the Russiaville Methodist Church allowed us to meet in their church building to hold Lord's Day services.

The congregation voted to rebuild the church and parsonage buildings on the original sites. Construction on the house was started in September 1965. The Coffman family moved into the new parsonage in January, 1966.

Ground-breaking for the new church building was held on April 3, 1966. On this day 176 persons were present at the worship service at the Methodist Church, after which all walked to the building site where an old walking plow, painted gold, had been placed. The assembled members, by joint effort, pulled together to break the ground. Actual construction began in May and was finished in late October.

The first worship service in the new building was held on November 6, 1966, with 203 present. The sanctuary was expanded in 1974 and a Fellowship Hall was built across the street, on the east parking lot, and dedicated on September 28, 1975.

Persons who have filled the pulpit are Messrs. Adam Conrad, Hodson, Grisso, Courter, Welch, Lowe, Brewer, Honeywell, Thompson, Walker, McClure, Watkins, Sailors, Johnston, Shaul, Brown, Whitcamper, Wolf, White, Hotaling, Payne, Rodgers, Edwards, Caloway, Pyle, Knox, Sholtz, Alford, Scott, Fenton Messenger, Orval Morgan, George McCoy (Elder), Gerald Gearhart, William Tullis, Gene Dye, Robert Powell, Fred Couch, Walter Kelly, James Coffman, Ron Waggoner, David Woods, John Jeffries, and presently, Mark Matthews.

Summer interns and associate pastors who have served the congregation are Kenny Hill, Al Michael, Bob Hicks, Kim Moe and presently Craig Taylor.

Several of our members have gone to Bible colleges. Also, some of our members have entered fulltime service for the Lord: Judy (Krajewski) Porter, minister's wife; Jerry Gragg, pastor; David McMillin, business manager, Ozark Bible College; Rich & Kathy Walden, missionaries to Thailand; Glen & Sherri Capps, missionaries to China; Kim (Mickelson) Baer, minister's wife; and Sherri (Milburn) Roberts, minister's wife.

View of Russiaville Christian Church in 1964.

Russiaville Christian Church in 1990.

MAIN STREET UNITED METHODIST CHURCH

For over one hundred years, members and friends of Main Street United Methodist Church have been led by 31 pastors and 14 associates to "Come Home to Faith."

In 1888, Rev. C.H. Brown, the local Methodist Pastor, with Oliver Albright chose a storeroom on Markland Avenue for a new South Kokomo Sunday School. A group of members from Rev. Brown's Church provided and furnished the room.

The first Sunday School was held in February 1889, and a year later church services were begun on Sunday afternoon. The church grew rapidly and an auxiliary pastor, the Rev. J.W. Oborn, was named.

In May 1890, a lot was purchased on the southwest corner of Markland Avenue and Union Street and a handsome frame structure was constructed at a total cost of $3,670.62. The first services of the new Markland Avenue Methodist Episcopal Church were held December 13, 1890, with the sanctuary beautifully decorated with fresh flowers.

The growing congregation soon needed a larger sanctuary with auxiliary rooms. In 1909 a lot at the corner of Harrison and Main Streets was purchased, and a structure of brick and stone was erected.

The church had a large sanctuary with galleries on three sides, a pastor's study, a choir room and a basement divided into classrooms. The pipe organ was donated by Andrew Carnegie. With the new location, it became the Main Street Episcopal Church with the first services held November 27, 1910.

The North Indiana Annual Conference held its sixty-eighth session April 5-11, 1911 at the new Main Street Church.

In 1939, during a ten-day conference, the Methodist Episcopal, the Methodist Episcopal South and the Methodist Protestant Churches united and became the Methodist Church. This Church was now the Main Street Methodist Church.

In 1949, a new addition was dedicated. It contained two auditoriums, a kitchen and several other rooms. Because of the growing membership an associate pastor was named to the staff.

A new chancel and other changes were made in 1958, and two years later, new pews and carpeting were installed. In 1964, a large education wing was added, containing a chapel and many multi-purpose rooms.

In 1968 the Methodist Church and the Evangelical United Brethren Churches united to become the United Methodist Church, bringing about the present name, Main Street United Methodist Church.

In 1968, the Senior High Youth Fellowship set up a corn dog booth at the

The original Main Street United Methodist Church

Howard County Fair to raise funds for a Memorial Plot. The Memorial Committee in 1986 built a large Memorial Garden on a lot south of the church.

On February 23, 1968 the parsonage next to the church was destroyed by fire. Six months later, August 28th, a three-alarm fire consumed the sanctuary, parish hall and most other areas. The new education wing was saved but had extensive smoke and water damage. Church and Sunday School were held at Indiana University Kokomo, and the office staff was provided space at the Church of the Brethren during the rebuilding.

The section containing the parish hall, kitchen, and other rooms was rebuilt first and on April 26, 1970, members returned to the hall for worship services. The first service in the newly built sanctuary was on January 17, 1971. The large cross over the altar was carved from the timbers saved from the ruins.

Main Street has supported a variety of mission projects throughout its history: bringing comfort and the tape ministry to the shut-ins, supporting an Iron Curtain refugee family, rebuilding a church in India, providing food, clothing and home repairs for the needy, and many other foreign and local projects.

In 1984, with a gift to the Music Department, bells were purchased for the Bell Choir. With later donations, four octaves of bells were added and two more choirs organized.

The Boy Scout Troop 530 (#30) celebrated fifty continuous years of scouting in 1985 with 74 Scouts receiving the Eagle Scout Award.

Also in 1985, funds were pledged, and a cottage was purchased at Epworth Forest. It has been used for retreats and family vacations.

At the present the 600 member congregation is a leader in supporting community ministries. For the past eleven years, the Main Street Congregation has presented an Easter pageant, with a cast of over 60 characters, live animals, and a 30 member choir, portraying the life, death and resurrection of Christ. The church is also the home of the annual Main Street Bazaar. This one-day event has been held as a missions fund raiser for nearly 50 years.

Through these programs and in many other ways, Main Street United Methodist Church continues to share the gospel of Christ, and invites people to come home to faith.

The present day Main Street United Methodist Church as it was seen in March of 1971.

MORNING STAR CHURCH

In the year 1942, because of national difficulties, it became necessary for our government to expand her war-time industries. Because of the war, there was perhaps one of the greatest movements of people that has ever taken place. In this great turmoil, amid the building of miles of assembly lines and the turning out of ships, planes, tanks, motors and ammunition, there were also those people who waged a war not with guns, ammunition, tanks, and planes, but with the Sword of the Spirit, the Word of God.

This great migration not only affected those who were not engaged in Christian work, but in some cases those who were actively engaged in preaching the Gospel. Being an employee of the General Electric Company and also an active minister of the Gospel, it fell to Pastor Luke Martin to be one who was requested to move. After much prayer, inquiring of the Lord and church leaders, it was decided that he should serve one of the United Brethren churches which was in need of rehabilitation both materially and spiritually. Consequently, in the month of August, 1943, he left Decatur, Indiana, with his wife and children and followed a moving van until it finally stopped at 704 E. Vaile Avenue, Kokomo, Indiana. Here the family began to adjust to new surroundings, new people, new jobs. Pastor Martin's job in the factory was one of taking charge of all windings in the huge General Electric wartime plant which manufactured large motor generator sets for Uncle Sam's Navy. His other job was one of preaching, teaching, and visiting the people of North Grove.

During this ministry at North Grove, many of the people under Pastor Martin's supervision at the factory, especially during revival times, would drive the seventeen miles Sunday evenings to be in the service. It was there that some of them felt their need for Jesus Christ, and soon a request was made for a Bible Class in Kokomo. Since there was no meeting place, Bible school was held one night a week in different homes. Those were busy yet wonderful days; the Lord blessed in many ways.

The house in which they lived was not adequate for their family. It was small and it became necessary for him to move. God made it possible for Pastor Martin and his wife to purchase a home for their family of six children. Pastor Martin and others had been praying for a church location, the kind of which would please the Lord. Two lots were purchased. From this point, while he was still pastor at North Grove, a tent was purchased by the conference and was brought to Kokomo and placed on the lot. A tent meeting began which lasted three weeks with several conversions. Many people attended the tent meeting and heard that there would be a basement church at the corner of Foster and Waugh Streets. In the fall of 1944, Pastor Martin was assigned as pastor of the Fairlawn United Brethren Church.

There was no place for worship, so the pastor's living room was converted into a chapel each Sunday morning and evening. The dining room and kitchen were used for Sunday school rooms. For nine months this was carried on with a full house each Sunday. During the month of June 1945, they had their first services in the basement.

July 15, 1945, the basement was dedicated. This was a great event for it opened the way for greater service for the Lord. However, it was soon apparent that the basement was fast becoming inadequate. Souls had been saved and families and children reached for Christ. Those were trying days, but the Lord sustained and the church was erected at a cost of approximately $28,000 for the grounds and building. It was a beautiful light blonde brick structure with a full basement, warm air heating, modern restrooms, fluorescent-lighted auditorium, artistic plastering, stained glass window, acoustical ceiling, radio room and office. It was built at the corner of South Waugh and Foster Streets just one block south of Markland Avenue.

In September 1974, God provided yet another miracle and the church relocated to its present facility at 2900 E. Markland Avenue and changed its name to Morning Star United Brethren Church.

MT. PISGAH MISSIONARY BAPTIST CHURCH

In early 1924 the Rev. Frank Roy Hatcher, a young associate minister of New Bethel Baptist Church in Indianapolis, came to visit his sister, Mrs. Louella Tyler. While here he found that a lot of Baptist believers were not attending church in the neighborhood known as the Plate Glass Addition.

He organized a Sunday School in the home of Horace and Birdie Johnson. The list of those attending include: Rev. Hatcher, Birdie, Bernice, Mattie and Patricia Johnson and John and Gertrude Talley.

They continued to meet in homes but in the spring of 1924 Rev. Hatcher, Charlie Johnson and Green Woods set out to buy a tent. They were not able to meet the purchase price of the tent so Rev. Hatcher got a loan from his place of employment, the Eli Lilly Company. When he was to make a payment on the loan, the company told him it was a gift.

The state moderator, Rev. Thomas of Muncie, came and organized the church and the Rev. Hatcher was called as the first pastor.

Rev. Hatcher served 16 years as pastor of Mt. Pisgah, commuting from Indianapolis. After leaving Mt. Pisgah he pastored Emmanuel Baptist in Indianapolis until his death. The ministers who came after him were the Reverends McBride, Ray, Burrus, and our present pastor, F.S. Kemper, who is in the midst of his 33rd year.

Rev. Kemper came to pastor in 1961 and under his leadership we have been greatly blessed. In 1967 six acres of property were purchased at 1599 E. Sycamore St. for $18,000. Groundbreaking services took place May 4, 1969. On March 8, 1970, we marched from our old place of worship at 219 S. Cooper to our new church home.

In August 1981 we burned our mortgage five years ahead of time. In 1984 property on the west side was purchased and paid for in full. In 1985 a new parsonage was built, dedicated and paid for in cash.

In 1993 a $400,000 Family Life Center was built and a new roof and lighted steeple were added to the church. The church hired the Rev. Wm Paul Barrett as assistant to the pastor.

The interior of the Mt. Pisgah Missionary Baptist Church.

NORTHVIEW CHRISTIAN CHURCH DISCIPLES OF CHRIST

The Northview Christian Church was founded May 6, 1962, with ninety-four charter members, as a congregationally governed body eager to respond more effectively to the power of the love of God in Jesus Christ our Lord. It was established to fulfill a needed ministry in this community and the world. The roots of Northview Christian go back to the Rich Valley Christian Church who saw its mission at the edge of a growing city. Together with the membership of this rural congregation, persons were commissioned from South Side Christian and Main Street Christian Churches of Kokomo, along with Meridian Street Christian of Greentown, Fairfield Christian and Macedonia Christian churches in the surrounding community, to begin a new corporate life. The congregation first met at Rich Valley Church and then at the Howard Township grade school cafeteria. On Nov. 17, 1963, the congregation moved into a new church building. The church is located on a ten-acre square of land at East Morgan and 100 East. The site was purchased from a member of the congregation, Mrs. Eva Buchanan. Richard Lauer, the last minister of Rich Valley Church, became the first minister of Northview Christian Church. A new parsonage was built on an adjacent one-acre plot and dedicated on June 12, 1966. Plans are being made this year to build a permanent structure to house the bell used at the Rich Valley Church which was given to the church by the congregation of Main Street Christian, Kokomo. Northview continues to be a small rural church working to fulfill its ministry as a congregation willing to accept God's leading for His people. In 1996 the combined ministry of Rich Valley and Northview will be 100 years old. Assuming its role in the ministry of the Lord Jesus Christ, the Northview Christian believes that it is a fellow laborer with all who are Christian. As a part of the Christian Church (Disciples of Christ) it is Christ-centered, evangelical in proclaiming the gospel, adheres to the missionary commission, and seeks the unity of the church's spirit. Truly, it is a congregation growing, building, and serving you.

CHRISTIAN CHURCH AT RICH VALLEY

On August 23, 1885, several citizens met at Rich Valley Schoolhouse and organized an association for the purpose of promoting the religion of Christ, and in the future erecting a building for the worship of God and the teaching of religious principles in the community. Said building was to be known as "The Christian Church at Rich Valley".

Names of the members of the association are as follows: T.M. Buchanan, J.C. Yager, Samuel T. Scott, L.M. Yager, M.E. Grinslade, Joseph Fahl, Joseph H. Kuhns, N.H. White, D.A. White, Aaron Crumley, J.P. Yager, A.C. Touby, H.K. Johnson.

Several meetings followed. A committee composed of A.C. Touby, S.T. Scott and Aaron Crumley were appointed to find a location of a one-acre plot for the building. Mrs. Clara Grinslade Bruce agreed to sell to the association one acre of ground on the southwest corner of her farm across the road east of Rich Valley Schoolhouse, for the sum of $75.00, for church purposes. James S. Colville contracted with the trustees to construct the building. G.A. Kendall, T.J. Buchanan, Joseph Kuhns and Wm. Buchanan were his helpers. T.J. Buchanan excavated for the foundation; Frank Falk plastered; Ed Shaef painted. The bell was a gift from Main Street Christian Church. The building was completed in January and all indebtedness was paid, $1772.06. It was dedicated Sunday March 1, 1896. L.L. Carpenter officiated. Ten people responded to become charter members: Jesse C. Yager, Lawrence M. Yager, Thomas J. Buchanan, J.P. Yager, M. Catherine Yager, Sarah M. Locke, Cora Buchanan, Leora K. Yager, Mary Buchanan, George Kendall.

One of the first ministers was D.A. McDowell. In 1946 the congregation celebrated its 50th anniversary. In 1962 Rich Valley Church building was sold to a Mennonite Congregation. Rich Valley was then 66 years old.

Christian Church at Rich Valley

Northview Christian Church

ST. ANDREW'S EPISCOPAL CHURCH

"A nurturing, transforming community, reaching out in the name of the Lord"

It was many years after the Episcopal Church had been established in the State of Indiana that it made its way into the life of Kokomo. In October of 1885, the Rev. David Buel Knickerbacker D.D., Third Bishop of Indiana, came to Kokomo and held an Episcopal service in the Congregational Church. This small beginning soon resulted in the Mission of St. Andrew's being organized. Although the services were on an irregular basis, using supply clergy, two candidates for confirmation were presented to the Bishop on September 8th, 1890.

The embryonic church flourished and just eight years after its beginning, on March 3rd, 1893, the cornerstone of the church was laid on property at the northeast corner of Taylor and LaFountain (Apperson Way) Streets. The Church was accepted and dedicated for the purposes of Christian worship on May 1st, 1893.

Everything indicated a rapidly growing mission, with thirty-three confirmed within the space of six months in a mission that was but eight years old. With a new Church erected, and with another property at the corner of Harrison and Fort Wayne Streets, one could see a most promising future for St. Andrew's, Kokomo.

Unfortunately for the Church and those who had worked so faithfully to insure its growth and success, a very serious financial loss came to the mission. Through unfortunate investments, the funds raised and collected to pay off the indebtedness against the church properties, was lost in the financial depression of 1893 and the mission had to surrender its property and its new Church. Naturally there was much discouragement among the members and little desire to begin again.

The next six years were difficult ones as the mission continued meeting in various places. A request was made by the Rt. Rev. John Hazen White, then Bishop of Indiana, that the name of the mission be changed to St. John hoping that this new beginning would result in growth and stronger financial stability. This change did not bring about the growth that had been hoped and so the name was changed back to the old and familiar, St. Andrew's.

In 1902 the Rev. and Mrs. Henry Neeley came to St. Andrew's. Realizing at once that the mission needed a church plan adequate to its needs, Father Neeley arranged for the purchase of property for the church at 111 North Market Street and proceeded with the erection of a mission house that would be of real service to the congregation, bearing all the financial obligations personally. (A portion of this building is still in use today.) Father Neeley continued as priest of the parish until 1911.

The summer of 1912 was a difficult time but the parish continued its work under the leadership of Mr. Cleon E. Bigler, a dedicated lay reader.

The Rev. John F. Plummer became priest in September, 1912, and under his leadership, the mission grew to parish status and was recognized as such by the Diocese on March 19th, 1922, with Father Plummer serving as the first rector. In his tenure, the years saw the financial burden lightened until finally it was eliminated and the debt fund became a building fund. With its change of purpose came the desire for a much needed church building.

The Rev. Cleon E. Bigler, mentioned above, was instituted as the second rector on March 12th, 1923. Under his leadership, the Vestry purchased land on West Superior Street and undertook ambitious plans for this new building. Writing to the congregation, Fr. Bigler noted that. . .

. . . forty years have passed since the first services of the Church were held in Kokomo. Those forty years have witnessed many changes in the community as a whole and in the local congregation. During those years, there have been many trying experiences, many discouragements and many happy and joyful occasions as well. Has the Church justified her labor and sacrifice in those years? Here is the answer. 441 souls have been made "Children of God, Members of Christ, and Inheritors of the Kingdom of Heaven." 371 men, women and children have received "The Laying on of Hands" in Confirmation. It has kept hundreds to the faith of their fathers, who, had there been no Church here, would have drifted away . . . To the community this Mission and Parish has contributed that which is particularly her genius to contribute. Were the Church to be taken out of the life of this community we are confident that Kokomo would distinctly feel an indescribable and irreparable loss.

It was a great disappointment when the financial support of the congregation was determined to be inadequate to provide the $150,000 needed for such a vast project. In the end, the drawings were abandoned.

After the departure of Fr. Bigler, the Rev. Harry M. Kellam served briefly as third rector until a permanent replacement could be found.

In 1929 the fourth rector, Father Jewell, the Vestry, and the congregation proceeded to move the Market Street building across town to the 602 West Superior Street property.

The Rev. Gerald Lewis succeeded Father Jewell in 1938 and served during the difficult times of World War II.

In 1948 the Rev. Peter Dennis became the rector of the parish and almost immediately started planning the new church building to adjoin the old one. Much simpler than the 1925 design, the shell of this structure was completed in 1952.

The Rev. Richard Cooper became the seventh rector of the Parish. Under his leadership the interior of the 1952 structure began to be transformed. The altar and chancel area were completed and stained glass windows were placed throughout. The parish continued to grow under the leadership of Father Cooper as well as his successor, the Rev. George M. Davis, who was instituted in October, 1973. Under Fr. Davis' leadership, the nave of the 1952 structure was also completed and a Wicks pipe organ installed. Our present rector, the Rev. J. Dereck Harbin, was instituted in September of 1992.

Today St. Andrew's is a dynamic congregation of 210 families which seeks to be a nurturing, transforming community reaching out in love to others in the name of Jesus Christ our Lord. With thanks to God for those who have gone before, we eagerly look forward to our future as we serve our Lord and the people of Howard County.

St. Andrew's Episcopal Church

ST. JOAN OF ARC

St. Joan of Arc emerged as a mission parish from St. Patrick's. Erected as a mission church/school in 1922, it began to serve the Catholic community on the south side of Kokomo. In 1927 Rev. John Dapp was appointed as a resident pastor, at which time St. Joan of Arc became a separate parish. Italians, Romanians, and Belgians formed the major ethnic groups during the early years of the parish.

The Catholic School at St. Joan of Arc has been an integral aspect of the parish from its beginning. The "Red Brick" building which housed the first school and chapel was opened for school on November 10, 1922. 121 children transferred from St. Patrick's and entered St. Joan of Arc School under the direction of the Sisters of St. Joseph.

The priest that served as pastors during the early history of St. Joan of Arc were Father Dapp (July 1927-April 1929); Father Huemmer (April 1929-1935); and Father Franz (1935-1946). Father Francis Niesen began his pastoral duties at St. Joan of Arc in July 1946. His pastorate extended until June of 1970. It was during his long tenure that many changes took place at St. Joan: 1) The changes that affected the church as a result of the Second Vatican Council; 2) The major population influx that affected Kokomo with the expansion of the automotive industry. Under his direction, the present Church facility was built and dedicated in 1950. Many currently active diocesan priests got their start under his guidance as associate pastors. In the 1950's the school had its peak enrollment of approximately 500 students. Most of the property on which the St. Joan of Arc facility is situated was purchased during his tenure as pastor. Parish membership rose from about 500 to 1300 families. He is remembered as speaking his mind on issues and even letting civil officials know what needed attention.

Succeeding Father Niesen on June 17, 1970, was the Rev. Thomas Zimmer, whose mission was to eliminate a $216,000 debt. By the fall of 1973, Father Zimmer had accomplished his mission, and he was then transferred to Frankfort on May 1, 1974.

An experiment in a new style of leadership was begun in 1974 when Bishop Raymond Gallagher named a pastoral team to steer St. Joan of Arc. The three-man pastoral team was composed of Revs. Melvin Bennett, Leroy Kinnaman, and Edward Dhont. On June 23, 1976, Father Kenneth Bohlinger replaced Father Dhont as a member of the pastoral team.

Fire destroyed the rectory, meeting rooms, and school library in 1976. The Golden Jubilee of St. Joan of Arc Church was celebrated in 1977, the same year that the new rectory and education center structures were completed. Additions to the present school building at the corner of Purdum and Harrison Streets were completed in 1978. They consisted of two classrooms, a library, and a multi-purpose room that also serves as a gymnasium.

When the pastoral team was abolished in 1980, Father Bennett was named pastor. Father Robert Moan was pastor from June 1982 to July 1988. While under his direction, the parish purchased the Palmer Building at the corner of Webster and Markland Streets (July 1985). The historic "Red Brick" building was torn down in the summer of 1986.

As we prepare this church history for our community's 150th Anniversary in July 1994, our pastor is Father David Hellmann who came to Kokomo in July 1988. We have two newly ordained associate pastors, Father Michael McKinney and Father Joseph Westfall.

Presently, St. Joan of Arc School has 286 students in pre-school through seventh. Mrs. Ceceilia Smith has been the principal since 1986. Mrs. Smith attended St. Joan of Arc School from 1951 to 1959 and has taught at the school since 1971.

The religious education program is under the direction of Marilyn Chavez and Marinell High. Enrollment for pre-school through high school is 385.

The Parish has committed itself to assisting others in the community. Through the Ladies of Charity and the Good Samaritan Store, many within the community have been assisted when other agencies are unable to help. There has been a strong ministry to the migrant community of this area, especially working with area farmers to improve housing utilized by the farm worker. St. Joan of Arc also sponsors a Catholic parish in the country of Haiti.

Spiritual growth is encouraged in the parish through the Christ Renews His Parish program, Scripture sharing, prayer groups, and an annual parish Lenten retreat.

Greater attention has been given to the Youth Ministry program with the staffing of one full time and one part-time youth minister. The recently acquired Youth Center provides a gathering space for the youth away from home. As a Catholic faith community, St. Joan of Arc is committed to active concern for the broader community of Kokomo. The aim of St. Joan of Arc is that its presence in Kokomo be a source of life, love, and healing to the greater community through our union with Christ.

ST. LUKE'S UNITED METHODIST CHURCH

St. Luke's United Methodist Church of Kokomo had its beginnings with a small group called Daniel's Band. They were drawn together by the preaching of Mrs. Maria B. Woodworth, an itinerant evangelist, who came to Kokomo on May 23, 1885. Her message must have been clear and compelling, for hundreds of people attended.

On June 24, Daniel's Band met to discuss the possibility of organizing a new church. A committee was appointed which decided that such a church was indeed needed to take care of the work being accomplished by the revival meetings. The new church was known as "The Union Mission Church of Kokomo". Sixty-one names were submitted for membership. Interested persons of the community were invited to meet on July 1, 1885, and church organization was completed. It was decided the church be missionary in design taking the Bible as its creed and Christian character as the only test for church membership.

Soon a frame building was constructed on a vacant lot on the northeast corner of Madison and Freemont (now Armstrong) streets.

For five years they prospered as an independent organization but feared it would be difficult to continue without access to a ministerial supply. Therefore, the Union Mission Church asked the presiding elder of the Lafayette District of the Church of the United Brethren in Christ, to receive them into that denomination. The St. Joseph Conference sent them their first United Brethren pastor in September, 1891.

The Conference of 1898 appointed the Rev. W.M. Karstedt to the Kokomo church. He came with vision of a new and larger building. A lot on the northeast corner of Monroe and Washington Streets was purchased and construction began in August. The work proceeded slowly amid financial difficulties. Finally, in December 1900 the new structure was completed at a cost of $15,000.

The early thirties were the Depression years and finance committee reports reflect that era. They show a reduction in salary each year for the pastor, the janitor, the choir director, and the organist. By May, 1932, the recommended yearly salaries were $1,800, $360, $100, and $84, respectively. The committee recommended that the leader of the Sunday School orchestra be paid $1.50 per Sunday and fifty cents per week be given to the drummer!

A major church reorganization took place in Johnstown, Pennsylvania, on November 16, 1946, when the Evangelical and the United Brethren Church merged to form the Evangelical United Brethren Church. Church names had to be changed to reflect the new denominational name. The First United Brethren Church became St. Luke's Evangelical United Brethren Church.

In 1951, plans to remodel the church building were approved. The sanctuary remained unchanged but all other areas were reworked to produce the Memorial Chapel, a parlor, a new kitchen, and all new Sunday School facilities. The cost of the project was $44,000.

Although long range plans in 1951 had been to add a fellowship hall to the north of the building, current situations in 1959 called for further assessments of needs and options. In June, 1960, the results of all the surveys were presented to the congregation which voted to build a new church building on a five-acre lot owned by the Conference southeast of the city. Groundbreaking ceremonies were August 12, 1962 and the first services in the new church were September 15, 1963.

A second world-wide church reorganization involving St. Luke's occurred April 23, 1968, in Dallas, Texas, with the merger of the Methodist and the Evangelical United Brethren denominations. Few changes were felt locally with the exception of the name, which then became St. Luke's United Methodist Church.

In September, 1983, a church conference decided to expand the facilities to ease crowding and make room for future growth. Ground was broken May 13, 1984, and the congregation moved into the new building on March 3, 1985.

The history of a church is more than a story about buildings and budgets, dates and data, even pastors and programs. A church is the people, and its history should also tell the story of spiritual progress through the years. Recorded here are the results of the progress, the manifestations of God's working through the people of Daniel's Band and St. Luke's and all those in between.

From the beginning, its reasons for being were to minister to its members and to bring others to Christ. To that end, this church, through the years, has had a strong Sunday School program staffed by dedicated teachers. It has provided Bible School every summer and supported church camps. Depending on the era, its spiritual emphasis services were called camp meetings, revivals or evangelistic crusades.

St. Luke's has supported missionaries in addition to its regular contributions to United Methodist mission programs. The church has participated in many programs of outreach: a migrant clothing and food program, scout troops, basketball leagues, benefit courses, and district handbell festivals, to name a few.

Through the years the church as been blessed with excellent pastors, faithful choir directors, organists, and pianists, and talented singers. They have ministered to the congregation week after week and have presented programs of inspiration for the church and the community.

To God, for whom St. Luke's exists and from whom it draws its strength, it gives thanks and asks His continued blessing.

St. Luke's
United Methodist Church
1891 - 1991

SAINT PATRICK PARISH

The Catholic community in Kokomo began about 1850, when a half dozen families were visited by Fr. Doyle and Fr. Maloney to celebrate mass. Following the incorporation of Kokomo in 1855, and the establishment of Fort Wayne as a Diocesan See in 1857, Fr. Hamilton began efforts at establishing a mission in 1859. Dr. Richmond donated a lot in the Richmond Addition, and the congregation purchased an adjoining one. The first St. Patrick Church, a frame building, was built.

For the next ten years the congregation was served by priests from surrounding towns. It is difficult to appreciate the struggle of the faithful in those pioneer times and during periods of prejudice.

In 1869, Bishop Luers appointed Fr. Francis Frawley the first pastor, and Fr. Frawley added a vestry to the mission chapel. Fr. J.H. O'Brien, Fr. John Grogan, and Fr. Kroeger each had brief assignments at St. Patrick Parish.

In 1873, Fr. Francis Lordemann was ordained, and named pastor. He led the congregation of forty families into an ever-growing and influential parish.

In 1874, the first rectory was built, and in 1875, a lot north of the rectory was purchased and preparations were begun for a new church building. The old church was moved to an adjoining lot, and the new building was erected on the original site. Completed in 1877, it was the largest church in Kokomo with a seating capacity of 650.

The first school was also begun in 1874, with about thirty-five pupils. Part of the church buildings was partitioned off and used for educating pupils after Mass each weekday. In 1877, the old church, now moved and replaced by a new brick building, was remodeled to accommodate up to 130 students. Enrollment in 1877 was 60 students. By 1893, these facilities were inadequate, so a new, two-story brick building was built at a cost of $11,000. Named St. Francis Academy, it was dedicated by Bishop Radmacher of Ft. Wayne.

The Sisters of St. Joseph, Tipton, came to staff the school in 1894. Sisters Theresa Thistlewait and Seraphine Herlihy were the founding principals. St. Francis Academy consisted of eight grades and a complete three-year high school until sometime between 1911 and 1918. At that time, the name changed to St. Patrick School, and the high school was reduced to two years until it was closed in 1928.

Early in the new century the Catholic population had again outgrown its church building; Fr. Lordemann and the Parish decided to proceed building a third St. Patrick Church - our present structure.

Fr. Lordemann died May 22, 1910, after a long illness. His energy, business tact, spiritual and temporal guidance, and devotion to his Church won attention and respect of the whole community. In tribute, Kokomo businesses, even the post office and the bank, closed for his funeral.

Reverend Robert J. Pratt was appointed pastor and completed the building project within a year. He died in 1929.

The next pastor of St. Patrick Parish was Fr. Robert Halpin. In November 1944, the Diocese of Lafayette-in-Indiana was formed.

Fr. Leo A. Breitenbach became pastor in 1949, and, during the 1950's, he started a vigorous and continuing program of maintaining and modernizing the church property.

Fr. Breitenbach was named Monsignor in 1963; and, in this same year - after several years of fund-raising events and generous contributions of parishioners - the present St. Patrick School building was dedicated.

In the late 1960's, the total attendance at St. Patrick School exceeded 300 students. The school remained eight grades until 1972, when it dropped to six grades during an attempted consolidation of 7th and 8th grades with St. Joan of Arc.

All classes at St. Patrick were taught by Sisters of St. Joseph until the first lay teacher was hired in the 1950's; and gradually, after 1967, more lay teachers were hired. Some Sisters of St. Joseph remained until 1990. The school continued with six grades until 1990, when kindergarten classes and a pre-school program were added.

Under his supervision Msgr. Breitenbach's final addition to the church building was the central Altar of Sacrifice, selected after painstaking consideration of designs appropriate for the architecture and in the spirit of the Constitution on Sacred Liturgy. Msgr. Breitenbach died on May 19, 1965, and his funeral was a tremendous tribute from all who knew him.

The assistant pastor, Fr. Richard T. Villa, was appointed administrator and Fr. Paul W. Dehner was appointed assistant. Through their efforts the liturgical decrees of Vatican II were begun.

Monsignor Maurice D. Foley became pastor on September 1, 1965.

Reverend Monsignor Arthur A. Sego, J.C.D., accepted the pastorate in July 1969 following Monsignor Foley's resignation.

In 1972, a major renovation of our church began. The church proper was redesigned to meet liturgical requirements, including the Blessed Sacrament Chapel. The foyer area was enlarged and made suitable to handle gatherings of the faithful for funerals, weddings, and other special liturgies. All painting and decoration were kept simple to support - not conflict - with the beauty of the windows.

Our present Pastor, Fr. Maurice R. Miller, came to St. Patrick Parish on July 1, 1984 after Msgr. Sego was appointed Chancellor of the Diocese. Fr. C. Alan Funk was appointed associate in August 1993.

Today St. Patrick Parish serves 1077 families. Space does not allow for listing of the countless names of the faithful - lay people and religious - involved in the growth and life of St. Patrick Parish; indeed, several of today's names would include those whose families helped to begin our parish so long ago.

WAYMAN CHAPEL AFRICAN METHODIST EPISCOPAL CHURCH

TO THIS TEMPLE
To Thee This temple we devote,
Our Father and our God;
Accept it thine, and seal it now
Thy spirit's blest abode

Here may the prayer of faith ascend,
The voice of praise arise;
O, may each lowly service prove
Accepted sacrifice.

The history of Wayman Chapel A.M.E. Church goes back a hundred years, when African Methodists first began to hold services in the homes of their members under the leadership of stalwart men and women of the faith. The first sanctuary was a rented hall in the Armstrong-Landon Building in the downtown district, the heart of the city. This hall was rented under the administration of the first pastor, Rev. Johnathan Burden, in 1869, during the period of the circuit rider. Rev. H.F. Thompson succeeded him and became the first pastor to live in Kokomo. It was while he was pastor in 1872, that the first church property was purchased near the corner of East Richmond and Lafountain streets. The original building still stands. The father of John Milton, now serving on the Trustee Board, was the builder. One of the sidelights of human interest is that Rev. Thompson, who was assisting in the actual building, broke a leg in the process. The present property was purchased in 1909, and the present edifice was erected under the pastorate of Rev. W.C. Irvin. S.D. Hughes, now a trustee, and E.H. Gaston, who is the Director of Religious Literature, tell interesting incidents of the hole in the ground, which was filled with water. There were some who said it could not be done, but the architectural style of the building stands today as a monument to the faith, vision, courage and hard work of those earlier saints who made this day possible. The main part of the house formerly used as a parsonage and still owned by the church was constructed under the pastorate of Rev. McDaniel. Rev. S.M. Smothers remodeled the old church. The first pews were purchased under Rev. P.J. Lewis. Rev. E.E. Gregory added facilities for entertainment and youth. The present parsonage at 1025 N. Apperson Way was purchased under Rev. G.W. Williams. The organ was purchased and paid for during the pastorate of Rev. W.D. Shannon. Dr. J.P.Q. Wallace, present presiding elder, served one year, forty three years ago. Fifty three members were taken in during his administration and a Men's Class of 87 was organized and taught by him. Mrs. Almary Wallace, his wife at that time, organized the primary department, which now flourishes under the leadership of Mrs. Merle Rush.

Former Pastors of Wayman: Johnathan Burden, James Ferguson, S.M. Smothers, C.H. Hackson, G.H. White, W.D. Shannon, J.F. Pettyford, D.A. Graham, M.A. Lowe, C.T.H. Watkins, David Perry, Rev. Anderson, H.H. Thompson, Samuel B. McDaniel, W.C. Irvin, E.E. Gregory, Geo. W. Williams, J.S. Matherson, H.A. Perry, H.H.P. Jones, L.S. Parks, W.H. Robertson, Sidney Tate, Robert Kirk Sr., Johnson Burden, B.J. Coleman, P.M. Lewis, T. Price, Alexander Smith, W.H. Giles, W.H. Taylor, M.R. Dixon, F.B. Jones, C.H. Curry, H.L. Johnson and Michael Carson.

Our present pastor is Rev. Michael C. Carson senior minister, and his family. Under his great leadership we are growing and doing great things. We are sure that you will receive your blessings here. We meet no strangers.

Welcome - Welcome - Welcome

Groundbreaking Ceremonies - August 22, 1982. (l. to r.) Henderson Davis, Presiding Elder; Kokomo Mayor Stephen J. Daily; and Rev. Robert Kirk, Sr.

Wayman Chapel AME Church

POPLAR GROVE UNITED METHODIST CHURCH

This old landmark of Ervin Twp. has stood as a memorial to our ancestors for one hundred twenty-two years and is located at 1150 W - 500 N.

Four years of meeting in homes, churches and schools in the Poplar Grove area has brought these devoted people to this point in time.

It was first known as the Poplar Grove United Brethren Church. Dedication was 6 October 1892 to the service of the Lord. The ceremony was conducted by George Sickafoose, Rev. Robert Cummins, the first minister (1872-1874), and Rev. J.V. Terflinger, along with some thirty-six charter members.

Improvements in the church have been numerous over the years, and the frame building still stands with the bell tower on top of the gabled roof. An alcove was built on the east end of the church in 1901, and a new basement was added in 1952. The focal point in the sanctuary is a cross made especially for the centennial celebration in 1972, of walnut by Rev. Robert Weaver, who then served as pastor. The walnut came from a pulpit given many years ago to the Center United Methodist Church in Deer Creek Twp. Rev. Weaver served the congregation there, also.

The Poplar Grove Evangelical United Brethren Church became a member of the United Methodist Church with the merger of the two churches in 1968, and became known as The Poplar Grove United Methodist Church.

Oakford Separate Baptist Church

The present members are:
The Allen family – Clyde, Muriel, John, Margaret, William, Jeanne. Dena Bell, Ruth Brower, Karen Courts, John and Mary Downhour. Rose Freeman, Lillian Fording, Ronnie Gilbert, Vera Gillam, Rosabelle and Vernis Kirkman. Rose Patton, Lottie and Richard Ridenour, Lois Smith. The Summe family – Claris, Esther, George and Rolla; also Mabel and Earl Yater.

The current minister is Rev. David Abel, and the trustees are Lillian Fording, William Allen, and Brian Allen.

OAKFORD SEPARATE BAPTIST CHURCH

On-the-move and ever-growing are two adjectives which best describe Oakford Separate Baptist Church and its congregation.

In its 148-year history the congregation has out-grown five sanctuaries as membership increased from eight to over 400.

The church got its humble beginning in 1846 when elders Jacob Baumgardner and Uriah McQueen organized Union Church of the Separate Baptists in Christ and met in a log schoolhouse on Charles Harmon's Harrison Township farm.

Three years later an 18 by 20 foot log church was constructed in Taylor Township on the Reason Lackey property, approximately one mile east of U.S. 31 about one-half of a mile north of modern-day Ind. 26.

There were eight charter members: Mr. and Mrs. Peter Kirkman, Mr. and Mrs. G.W. Baumgardner, Mr. and Mrs. Jacob Baumgardner and Mr. and Mrs. Charles Harmon.

In 1862, that structure was moved and replaced, at a cost of $400, with a frame structure measuring 30 by 36 feet. The congregation was growing; in 1883 the church claimed a membership of 80 and a Sunday School attendance averaging 50.

In 1895 the church moved one-half of a mile south to a half-acre parcel, donated by Jay Randolph, just west of what was then Fairfield (currently Oakford). A schoolhouse at the site was demolished but some of its materials were used to build the church.

Many structural changes were made to the building over the years before it became the "little white church" in Oakford. However, once finished, the structure looked like what one pictures when thinking of a traditional-looking church. As the congregation continued to grow church officials agreed a new building was needed.

In 1976 a brick-veneer building, costing over $80,000 and built to seat about 250, was constructed on six acres directly across the road from the former church house. The two-story structure measured approximately 5,000 square feet per floor.

But once again the congregation grew. A 10,000-square-foot addition was added to the east end of the building, at a cost of nearly $370,000. In the spring of 1984 the doors to the present-day sanctuary, which can seat up to an estimated 650 people, opened.

Those who have served as ministers over the years include Jacob Baumgardner, Josiah Randolph, John Layman, M. Sharpe, James Hamilton, Andrew White, William Randolph, G.W. Baumgardner, George W. Turner, Wilfred Spurlin, George Bagwell, Noley Hughes, Jay Randolph, Omer McCoy, A.A. Fletcher, Ed Springer, Charles Brubaker, R.L. Farr, Thomas Woods, Chester Mitchell, Lora Eads, Glen Naphew, Lee Springer, Emil Freeman, Leslie Batey, Wheeler Davis, Eddie Sewell, Roy Nash, Albert Kimbler and Russell Peterson.

Jeff Harlow has served as pastor from 1974 to the present. Submitt*ed by Lisa D. Fipps*

Poplar Grove United Methodist Church

SCHOOLS

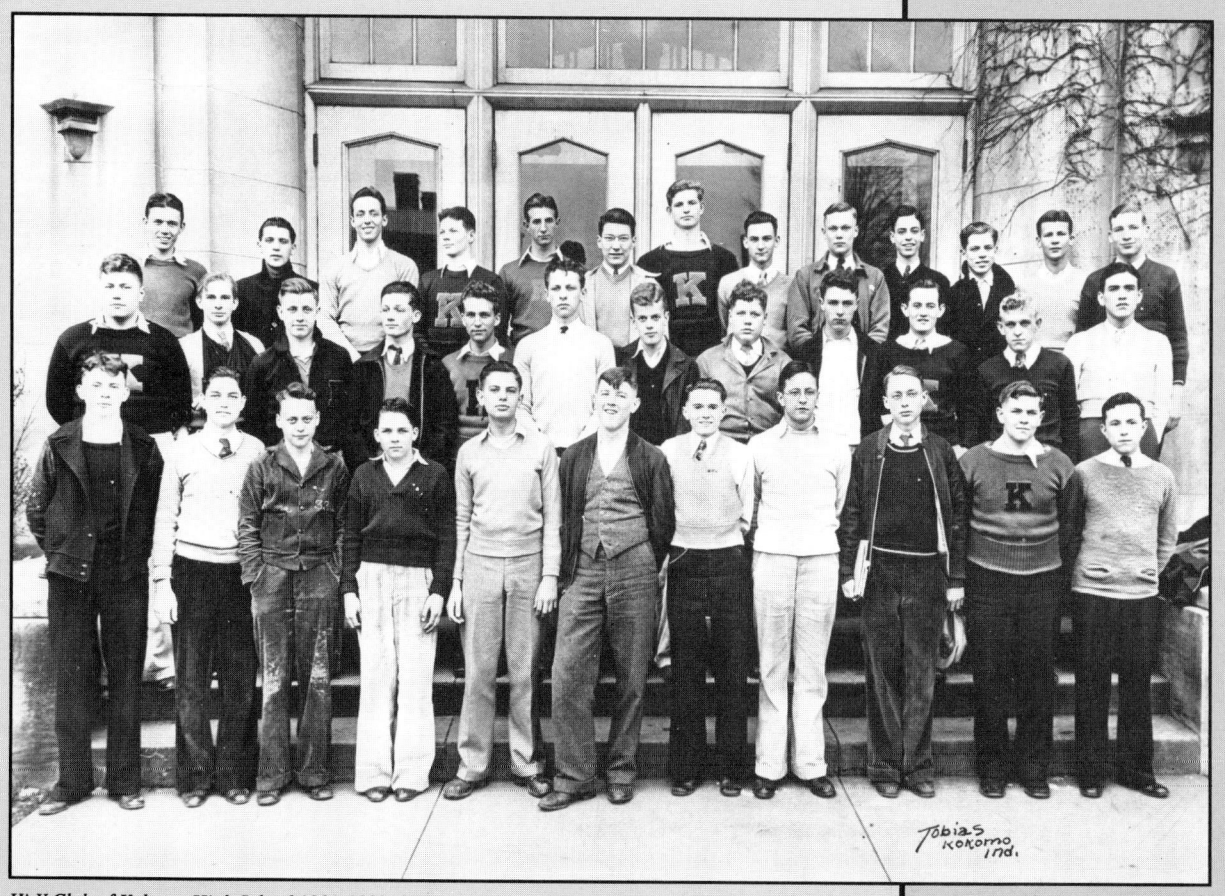

Hi-Y Club of Kokomo High School 1931-1932 (l. to r.) Top row: Chet Warman, Ron Rolfe, Bob Ellis, Joe Boughman, James Edwards, Bob Schuler, Norm Talbert, Jack Hite, Bob George, Ernest Davis, Bob Boyd, Bill Politz, and Bill Ashburn. Middle row: Guy B. Watson, Jack Taubense, Carl Learner, Dick Michner, Harold Moss, Nat Hamilton, Judd Wright, Max Shirley, Bernard Quinn, Ted Riffe, Marion Brower, and Bob Whitehead. Front row: Junior Duncan, Lowell Henderson, Roscoe Norman, Bob Hamp, John Jessup, John Joyce, Truman Kellie, Bob Page, George Schwenger, Dick Gerhart, and John Seagraves.

GRANGE HALL SCHOOL

Grange Hall School stood at the corner of East Hoffer and Home Avenue. It was replaced by the Jefferson Elementary School*, which was built east of the Hall.

It was built about 1875, by William Burgess 'Bird' Albright and his crew, which consisted of many Albright relatives (sons, cousins, nephews etc.) The Albright Crew built many brick buildings in Kokomo and Howard County. Among them were the old Brouse building, the N.W. 1/4 block on the west side of the Square (it burned), many of the one-room schools throughout the county, and, in Center, the Masonic Building, which was struck by lightning and burned a few years ago, and the Center Christian Church.

'Bird' learned his trade from his older brother, John Albright, who operated a brickyard (one of 65 in Indiana) on his farm in Taylor Twp., on S.R. 26, west of Center. The brothers were partners in the contracting business for a number of years. After John closed the brickyard, he sold his farm to 'Bird', who raised his family there.

*Bird's son, Lacy Albright, lived just three houses east of Grange Hall, on Hoffer. All of Lacy's children went to school at the Hall. Lacy was custodian at Jefferson School for many years; he loved the children and they loved him.

Grange Hall School

Members of the Class of 1889 as listed in the Kokomo High School Alumni Register. Walter E. Ervin, Allen O. Garrigus, V.S. Hillis, Bertha (Hughes) Connell, Alma (Lovett) Garrigus, Dora (Martz) Symons, Lora (McLaughlin) Hazeltine, Ed S. Moore, Nellie (Rayl) Blount, Aurora (Scoven) Critchlow, Mame (Styer) Marks, and George E. Thorne.

Third and Fourth Grade of Wallace School during the 1925-1926 school year. (l. to r.) Front: Raymond Bostic, Edward, Edward Ford, Lorain Garbert, Frederick Smith, Joe Rysong, Bernard Ortman, Howard Parsons, unknown, unknown, William Politz, unknown, Everett Newton, Orville Oakley, and Paul Bennett. Middle: Robert Washington, Dorothy Mae Sharp, Mary Alice White, Helen Parsons, Juanita Little, Allen Cuttriss, Alice De Lon, Thelma, Ruby, unknown, Earl Jones, Elenor Obermeyer, Freda De Vore, Helen Wyrick, and Mrs. Gussie Crider. Back: Evelyn Jordan, Lillian White, Mary Jo Young, Francis Rysong, Mary Floys, Madge Irene Morrison, Mary Duncan, Charles, Emma Ortman, Betty Harness, Theida Gifford, and Irene Hardebeck.

Grades First through Eighth at Center Schoolhouse in 1916.

HOWARD TOWNSHIP SCHOOL

On September 7, 1917, the new Howard Township School opened its doors to students in grades one through twelve. Built in 1916-1917, it is now the one of only two of the original township consolidated schools of Howard County still serving the community. The one-room schools consolidated into the Howard Township system were Rich Valley, Holler, Vermont, Cassville, Prairie, Loop, and Brown.

Architects for the building were the Elmer E. Dunlap Company. The Township Trustee was W.E. Grinslade, and the Advisory Board consisted of David A. Shenk, J.W. Clark, and Isaac Showalter.

The style and plans for the red brick structure were much like other schools built during that period. Careful attention was given to providing a facility that would serve well the people of the community. The building is still structurally sound and has been exceptionally well cared for through the years. The grounds are beautifully kept.

High standards of scholarship have been consistently maintained through the leadership of administration and faculty. In 1917 the school was accredited by the State Board of Education. In 1919 it was commissioned as a six-year high school, and in the ensuing years had held a continuous commission, the highest classification given a school. The principals serving Howard High School were Carol Beard, Edgar Botts, A.E. Benge, Clifford Lineback, Albert F. Hutson (the latter two having also served as County Superintendent), and Dwight V. Singer.

The last high school class to graduate from Howard was the Class of 1948. In 1949 the building was converted to an Elementary Jr. High School as a part of what was then known as the Clay-Ervin-Howard Consolidation, now the Northwestern School Corporation. Later Howard was maintained as an Elementary School, grades K through six. Principals serving through the Jr. High and Elementary years were George Davis, Lewis Fouts, Gene Alberson, David DeWitte, and Deborah J. Glass. It is interesting to note that the current principal, Deborah J. Glass, is a great-niece of two of the early high school teachers.

There are many instances of students whose parents and grandparents attended Howard, and also of former students who became teachers at the school. Others served on the staff. Some were elected Township Trustee, and a number served in various other capacities. Many Alumni became outstanding leaders and achievers, not only in the local community but throughout the country.

School pride and loyalty continue to the present day. Of recent interest is the fact that the old hand-operated basketball scoreboard from the first gymnasium was donated to the Indiana Basketball Hall of Fame. The Howard School Alumni Association meets in the school gymnasium each September for a carry-in dinner, fellowship and a brief program honoring the 50 year graduates. Former students and friends come from many states for this occasion. We celebrate with pride our heritage.

NORTHWESTERN SCHOOL CORPORATION

The Northwestern School Corporation is made up of three townships, Ervin, Clay, and Howard, and is located in the northwestern part of Howard County.

All the lands of the county were once a part of the Great Miami Reserve. By 1846 the Indians had sold their last remaining lands in Indiana and moved west, and Howard County was officially organized on June 13, 1844, one of the last counties in the state to do so. Small one-room log schoolhouses were built throughout the three townships and were later replaced by frame and then brick buildings. Students who desired to go to high school were sent to high schools in neighboring towns.

In the 1910's all three townships began to consider township consolidation for grade and high school. The decision to consolidate first came in Howard Township. The Howard building was built in 1916, the Clay building in 1921, and the Ervin building in 1926. Already the rural population was decreasing. People began thinking about a larger consolidation. There was some discussion of consolidation across the western end of the county, but the creek formed a natural barrier which had to be taken into account. The three school buildings had been built within ten years of each other and were much alike. In 1948 consolidation of these three townships was accomplished. The corporation was known as the Clay-Ervin-Howard School Corporation. In the 46 years since consolidation, the school system has grown considerably. This is due primarily to the increasing number of non-farm residents who are moving into the county areas.

The Clay building served as the entire high school until 1956 when a large addition was made to the rear of the old building. In 1962 the present day Northwestern High School was built as an addition to the former structure. At this time the 7th and 8th grades were moved from the Ervin and Howard buildings into the old school creating a junior high. The junior high students are now housed in the newest addition which was completed in 1980. Howard added a wing in 1953. A similar addition was made to Ervin in 1958. In 1965 a third elementary school was built just west of the high school, and in 1967 an addition to it was made. In 1966 a kindergarten program was begun, the first in the county.

Prior to the consolidation in 1948, the administrator of each school was the principal aided by the civil township trustee. After the consolidation in 1948, the school board consisted of three township trustees. Each principal was responsible to the county superintendent. In 1961-62 the state mandated consolidation throughout the state in order to eliminate the one room schools which still remained in some areas. After exhaustive study and investigation into such matters as curriculum, finance, population distribution, etc. their recommendation was for a single administrative unit for all the schools in the entire county.

The Clay-Ervin-Howard Corporation was judged to have fulfilled already most of the requirements for consolidation set forth by the state, with the exception of the method of choosing the school board. The state felt it should be made up of members elected specifically to the school board rather than as civil township trustees serving on the school board. In 1965 a referendum was held to determine whether a seven-man board should be formed, or whether the three township trustees would continue as the school board. The seven-man proposal was voted down. In the next county election there was a change in the township trustees, and the resulting three-man board exercised their right to determine by agreement whether a change should be made in the make-up of the school board. They decided that a five-man board would be preferable and in 1968 turned over their duties to the newly-elected five-man board.

Northwestern Elementary School

Northwestern Junior High School

Northwestern High School

In 1965 the office of county superintendent was abolished, and the corporation hired its own superintendent. The Northwestern School Corporation now consists of two elementary schools and the junior/senior high school, which are all accredited by the state.

INDIANA UNIVERSITY KOKOMO

Today Indiana University Kokomo has nearly 3,900 students, including about 400 students in Purdue University Programs at Kokomo, who have more than 30 associate, baccalaureate and master's degree programs to choose from. These students — and more than 250 faculty and staff — enjoy a 57-acre campus with seven major buildings and a new library under construction. When the campus began, the situation was quite different.

In 1945, local civic leaders asked Indiana University to take over the operations of Kokomo Junior College. The university agreed and assumed both the functions and property of the junior college. Within two years, enrollment exceeded the capacity of the single building at 508 W. Taylor St. and the university purchased the larger Seiberling-Kingston Mansion at 1200 W. Sycamore St. The mansion — and the neighboring Brown-Elliott house — was home to the IU Extension Center in Kokomo until 1965. In that year, the center moved to its present location at 2300 South Washington Street following completion of the Main Building. Since 1965, additional property has been purchased and the East Building, the Observatory, and the Kelley Student Center and Laboratory Wing have been built. The buildings occupied by External Relations, the Division of Education and the Division of Continuing Education have been converted from other uses. In 1992, the Paris home, on the northeast corner of the IUK property, was renovated for use as a campus hospitality center and named Kelley House in honor of benefactor E.W. Kelley. The new library facility, with a high-tech auditorium and exhibition gallery, is to be completed in December 1994.

As the campus has grown physically, so it has developed academically. Like other IU extension centers, the one in Kokomo focused on providing the general education courses for liberal arts programs. The university assumed that students would transfer to the Bloomington campus or to another university for advanced work and to earn degrees. By the mid-1960s, that philosophy was changing; the extension centers evolved into regional campuses with full degree programs. In Kokomo, a program to earn an Associate of Science in Nursing degree began in 1967, soon followed by a baccalaureate program in Elementary Education. The campus awarded its first degrees at its first commencement in 1970. During those years, Purdue University began to office associate degree programs in technology on the IUK campus. Over the past 20 years, the number and range of degree programs have continued to grow. In 1991-92, for example, the campus initiated baccalaureate degree programs in Speech Communication and Sociology and a long-awaited Master of Business Administration degree program.

IUK could not have grown as it has without able leadership. Four individuals supplied that leadership during the first 45 years of the campus' existence. Virgil Hunt, the first director of the extension center, served for 11 years, recruiting the first faculty of the center and overseeing its move to the Seiberling-Kingston property.

The Main Building
2300 South Washington Street (Opened 1965)

From 1956 to 1959, Smith Higgins directed the development of the campus, though his real impact came later. After leaving Kokomo, Higgins became dean of the IU Extension Division and engineered the transformation of the extension centers into regional campuses. Victor Bogle succeeded Higgins and became the last director and first chancellor as titles changed to reflect the new mission of the regional campuses.

The Seiberling–Kingston Mansion
IU Extension Center (1947-1965)

As head of the campus for 20 years, Bogle directed the move to the present campus, the expansion of degree programs, and the addition of Purdue programs. In 1980, Hugh L. Thompson became the second chancellor of IUK, beginning a decade that saw a doubling in the size of the campus, the acquisition and construction of five major structures, and further development of academic programs. In April 1991, Emita B. Hill became the third chancellor, assuming the challenge of leading IUK as it prepares students for the 21st century.

In 1945, Indiana University founded an extension center in Kokomo to expand the educational opportunities available in this region of the state. Today, IUK remains dedicated to providing the people of North Central Indiana with access to post-secondary education of the highest quality. The mission of IUK is to meet the changing educational needs of the people of its 11-county service area through a broad spectrum of undergraduate programs and a limited range of graduate offerings. As it readies to celebrate its golden anniversary in 1995, IUK remains committed to the attainment of excellence in all its endeavors.

The Kelley Student Center
IU Kokomo (Opened 1989)

KOKOMO-CENTER TOWNSHIP CONSOLIDATED SCHOOL CORPORATION

Fortunately for Kokomo, its first settlers were men and women who believed in both religion and education. Only three years passed before education was available in 1845 for Howard County children.

Dr. Adam Clark, the county's first teacher, established the first school in a rough log church that had been constructed in 1844 on the east side of Washington Street near Superior Street. Tuition was $2 per pupil for a 13-week term.

Subscription schools continued until 1853 with the annual attendance ranging from 16 to 38 pupils. Among the subscription school teachers, who usually boarded with different families for one week at a time, were General T.J. Harrison, John O. Heaton, George A. Gordon, Julia Barrett and Judge T.H. Palmer.

By 1850, a general movement was underway to establish free schools, and in 1853 the township trustee erected a log schoolhouse at the corner of Washington and Walnut Streets. This was the first building specifically constructed for use as a school, and the first free school in Howard County. The Rev. Denton Simpson, a Baptist minister and farmer, was the teacher.

In 1855 when Kokomo became a town, free schools were continued under the supervision of the town board. In 1856, 145 children were enrolled in the free schools.

Center Township subscribed $3,000 to the erection of a Normal Building on the south side of East Sycamore Street between Market and Lafountain Streets on the condition that the township would have the use of the four lower rooms for a free school known as the Indiana State Normal School of Kokomo.

In 1860, T.C. Phillips was School Examiner and Samual L. Rugg was Superintendent. In 1864, tuition in the Normal Department was $6.50 for the 11-week term and board was $2 per week.

Free schools were established officially when the Constitutional Convention of 1859-61 declared, "Knowledge and learning, generally diffused throughout a community being essential to the preservation of a free government, it shall be the duty of the general assembly to encourage, by all suitable means, moral, intellectual, scientific and agricultural improvement and to provide, by law, for a general and uniform system of common schools, wherein tuition shall be without charge, and equally open to all."

In 1865, Kokomo was incorporated as a city and the first Board of School Trustees—Richard Nixon, President; Gabriel McCool, Treasurer; and John Bohan, Secretary—was selected by City Council. The Board constructed two schools, including the original Columbian School, before Howard College was organized in the Normal Building in 1870 with M.B. Hopkins as President. With no high school available, advanced students were sent to college and their tuition was paid from school funds.

After Professor Hopkins was elected State Superintendent of Public Instruction in 1872, Howard College was closed. The high school building at the corner of Armstrong and Taylor Streets was sold to the Baptist Church, and the city school board purchased the Normal Building in 1873. Once the Normal Building was refurbished, Professor Sheridan Cox was elected superintendent, and he held the position for 20 years until 1893. H.G. Woody took over as superintendent from 1893-1898 before R.A. Ogg took charge of the city school from 1898-1910.

The discovery of natural gas in Kokomo sparked unprecedented growth for the city and the school system. By 1902, two more schools had been built, including Central Junior High School.

Kokomo pupils entered the new building March 22, 1898, and then the Old Normal Building burned the Sunday after Thanksgiving in 1898.

C.V. Haworth began is 33-year career as superintendent in 1913, and is considered one of the great contributors of education in Howard County. With Haworth in charge, the Board secured ground on Superior Street just south of the high school. This was a fortunate purchase since the high school building burned on March 24, 1914. For the remainder of the school term, school was conducted in half-day sessions in the Library, Y.M.C.A. and City Hall. Students attended school in the Tabernacle Building during the 1914-15 school year.

In addition to expanding the role education played in the community, Haworth oversaw the building of Jefferson, McKinley, Riley, Roosevelt, Wallace, Willard and Douglass schools, as well as additions to the high school. A gymnasium that bore Haworth's name was opened in 1925 and it burned in 1944. Memorial Gym was built to replace the Haworth gym in 1949, and the dedication game was November 18.

Second Kokomo High School built in 1898.

In 1929, through the generosity of A.J. Kautz, who served many years on the Board of Trustees, the school was presented with Kautz Field.

The establishment of a $1 tax rate in 1946 to amass a cumulative building fund for remodeling, expanding and replacing buildings was one of the first acts by Haworth's successor, O.M. Swihart. Over the next 25 years, that action resulted in the construction of Bon Air (1956), Elwood Haynes (1955), Lafayette Park (1957), Maple Crest (1956), Pettit Park (1953), Sycamore (1962/68), Boulevard (1965) and Haworth High School (1968).

In 1953, the Center Township and Kokomo School System consolidated to form Kokomo-Center Township Consolidated School Corporation. The district measures 25.5 square miles and its boundaries follow the Center Township line.

In the fall of 1968, enrollment in Kokomo-Center peaked at 13,230 students. As Howard County prepares to celebrate its Sesquicentennial, the official 1993-94 Kokomo-Center enrollment is 7,478.

As the enrollment decreased, several older buildings became obsolete and were closed, including Jefferson, Riley, Willard and Douglass schools. McKinley now houses the alternative programs while Roosevelt is home to the preschool programs.

In 1984 Haworth High School and Kokomo High School were combined. The Haworth building serves as home for students in grades 10-12, while the Kokomo building houses eighth and ninth graders.

With the enrollment stabilizing, Kokomo-Center Schools is presently in the midst of a community-wide visioning project for the 21 Century. Kokomo-Center Schools continues to be a force in the development of Howard County by providing a well-rounded quality education for students.

Special acknowledgement goes to longtime Kokomo High School Principal Frank Moore for his help compiling this school history and to the Kokomo Tribune for the photo.

WESTERN SCHOOL CORPORATION

In 1948 the Western School Corporation came into being. The year before, the local schools in the southwestern part of the county received a state inspection and were given a below-average rating. This was done for two reasons: the enrollment was too small to offer an adequate program of learning and the buildings failed to meet the health, safety, and educational requirements of the state. Thus the Howard County Board of Education, under the leadership of W.W. Lindley, moved to reorganize itself. In August 1948 the Harrison-Honey Creek-Monroe Corporation (now Western School Corporation) was formed. Similar corporations were formed in the other areas of the county.

During the year 1948-49, the student body consisted of students from New London and West Middleton areas. The first Western High School was located at West Middleton; grade schools were conducted at Alto and New London. Russiaville maintained its own high school that year, and joined Western in the 1949-50 school year. At that time Western High School was located at Russiaville, and the West Middleton building housed junior high students.

The name "Western" was chosen by the first School Board which consisted of Mr. Frank Bishop, Mr. Lowell Rich, and Mr. Leroy Kuhns. The school song was written by a student, Lucy Blodgett, with the help of Mrs. Lowell Townsend. The mascot name of "Panthers" was selected by the students from a suggestion made by another student, Arvilla Talbert. School colors of black and white were chosen, but a few years later the color "red" was added.

The small communities contributing to the establishment of the Western School Corporation have a solid background for good schools. Already the people had moved from several one-room school buildings scattered throughout the three townships in 1875 to the four buildings. The organization of New London's building as a high school dates from 1884 and was the second in the county. Russiaville's first graduating class was in 1898 and West Middleton's in 1910. Alto's school dates from 1920.

From those solid foundations, the progress of Western School Corporation has continued to express the community's goal of providing excellence in facilities and equipment, teachers, administrators, support staff, curricular and extra-curricular opportunities. Highlights of the school's forty-year history include construction of the first new building in 1954 and the decision to locate that and all subsequent buildings at the junction of the three townships.

A north building was constructed in 1962, the West Middleton building was sold, and grades seven through twelve were brought to the central location at 600 West - 250 South.

In 1965, the buildings at Russiaville and Alto were destroyed by the April 11 "Palm Sunday" tornado. Emergency measures such as half-day classes allowed the corporation to complete the school year, and the new elementary building was constructed as quickly as possible. As the population continued to grow and the New London building was no longer able to meet code standards, a decision was made to add on to the north building and close the New London building, bringing all students to the central location. To relieve overcrowding, a study was made concerning year-round school. There was not enough support for that concept, however, and the Board made plans for building a Primary school and adding a physical education facility. By 1981 students were housed in their present location: kindergarten through second grade in the Primary Building; third through fifth in the Intermediate Building; sixth and seventh grades in the Middle School; and eighth through twelfth grades in the High School.

As one looks back over the history of the Western School Corporation, there is one man who must be recognized for his leadership and service over a 35-year period. Mr. Richard R. Rea was the first principal of Western High School, and he became the school's first superintendent in 1966. The present high school gymnasium bears his name as a reminder to the community that Mr. Rea involved himself in the growth and successful development of this school corporation until his retirement in 1979.

The current superintendent at Western is Ron Wilson who replaced the late H. Dean Resler who died in 1993. J.O. Smith, a former superintendent at Western, had filled in as interim superintendent until July of 1994. Western's personnel consists of 13 people in administrative positions, 118 teachers, and 101 in the support staff. *History donated by former Western students who are now Western employees*

The first Western High School at West Middleton.

The second Western High School at Russiaville.

The third Western High School which was completed in 1955.

The fourth and present Western High School.

CLUBS, ORGANIZATIONS & MEMORIALS

The charter members of the Kokomo Chapter No. 414 Navy Mothers Club of America in 1944. Mrs. Esther Buckner (6th from left) was the founding president.

Kokomo Shrine Directors in 1948.

KOKOMO SHRINE CLUB

The Kokomo Tribune, December 8 and 12, 1919, reported a newly-formed Kokomo Shrine Club with the officers: Pres. Frank G. Hughes; V.P. O.H Buck; Scty. Will D. Tarkington; Treas. Harry J. Meck and Constitution and By-laws Committee: O.H. Buck, Fred J. Byers, George C. Davis, Willis B. Dye and Kenneth C. Rich. The first social function of the new club was "A Family Fun Frolic," held in the Elks Lodge club rooms on February 23, 1920, with 325 men, women and children in attendance. A five-course dinner, topped-off with cake, ice cream, coffee and cigars, was accompanied by music and entertainment. The remainder of the evening was devoted to dancing and card games, with special entertainment for the children. The second annual public fund-raiser was a show of local talent at the high school auditorium on September 25, 26, & 27, 1922 titled "The Melody Minstrels and Fun Frolic." During that period, the Kokomo Tribune reported each day the huge success of the night before.

Sometime between 1922 and 1946 the club became inactive. Reformed and chartered in 1946 (after WWII) it was incorporated as an Indiana not-for-profit corporation in 1948. Officers and Board members as pictured from left to right standing - William White, Robert Brauer, Ezra Coffell, Edwin Krull, Lavon Hawkins; sitting - Gerald Rybolt, Leon C. DeCroes, Paul J. Mills, Max Pross (Photo courtesy of Noble Leon C. DeCroes). This new club met in rooms above the Coney Island Restaurant and Fox Theater on West Mulberry Street. The Knights of Columbus also rented rooms in the building. It was customary for members of one club to invite members of the other for refreshments. In 1946 the K of C's first invited the Shriners to a stag party and then later the Shriners reciprocated with a party for the K of C's. This year (1993) celebrates the 47th annual Brats and Beer Bash at the K of C in March, and the B-B-Q Rib Roast at the Shrine Club in October. The two charter members of this reformed club, Robert Brauer and Leon C. DeCroes, are still active in the club.

From 1964 to 1966 Tipton County Shriners joined with Howard County in the Kokomo-Tipton Shrine Club. Tipton Shriners then formed their own club, meeting in the Tipton Elks Lodge club rooms.

In addition to the Mulberry Street location, Kokomo Shrine Club has occupied a Delphos Street address; held meetings in the Casa Grande Restaurant on Markland Avenue and US 31 By-pass; at the Ibn Saud Grotto on US 31 By-pass; and at the present location, Hwy 22/US 35 three miles east of US #31 by-pass, which was purchased in 1973. A few dedicated volunteer workers transformed the "old hog barn" into a respectable Shrine Club. This facility sufficed until 1980 when an addition of equal size was built. In 1989 another room and garage were added.

In 1969 Kokomo Shrine Club Mini-T parade unit was formed with nineteen members and sixteen half-size 1910 Model-T Ford replicas. This unit has grown to forty members and twenty-six cars and a semi-tractor/trailer rig for storage and transportation.

The Kokomo Shrine Clown Unit was formed in 1972 with six members and now consists of thirty-eight members and various vehicles for parades. They are also available for Clown antics and balloon art at schools, churches, and children-oriented assemblies.

The Kokomo Shrine Hillbillies Unit was formed in 1982 and has grown to include sixty-four members and twenty-five spouses. They are strictly a social group dedicated to raising funds for Shriners' Hospitals.

MAHA Shrine Guild, a unit of National Shrine Guilds of America, was formed in 1973, for wives and widows of Kokomo Shrine Club members. They, too, are dedicated to raising funds for Shriners' Hospitals and other local charities.

Kokomo Shrine Hospital Transportation Unit is a group of volunteer hospital van drivers dedicated to transporting patients and their parents to the Chicago Shrine Hospital (one of 22 nationally) and to the Cincinnati Burn Center (one of three nationally). The Shrine Club owns the hospital van, and the Murat Shrine Temple in Indianapolis pays expenses for these trips. The patient's family, or their insurance, is never charged for services of a Shrine Hospital. This is what a Shrine is all about.
Submitted by James D. Ingle

KOKOMO WOMAN'S DEPARTMENT CLUB

The Kokomo Woman's Department Club was organized June 3, 1912, by Mrs. John E. Moore and at one time had 400 members.

The Department Club has made several civic contributions that still benefit Kokomo.

The Club purchased their Club House in 1928, located at 314 W. Walnut. With a small down payment a mortgage was secured and was paid off in 1948.

Mrs. Moore's concern for the cultural and social life of the community women resulted in ladies playing a prominent part in civic affairs, education and civic promotions of Kokomo. She was never afraid to speak up for the rights of women. One of the speakers for Dept. Club related a quote from her grandmother, saying, "In 1850, there was a period when women were females, with no brains or rights. In 1900 they became ladies—best described as retiring ladies and then finally they became women and participated in public affairs."

The Department Club established the first County Museum in the basement of the old courthouse in order to preserve the history of the county. Curator was Mrs. E.O. Richardson.

The Club carried out a campaign for more sanitary conditions in grocery stores, fish and meat markets and advocated better lighting in park areas. They also assumed responsibility for getting home economics and gymnastics into high school, obtaining a city school nurse and even paying her salary for a time. They established a Red Cross chapter in Kokomo, campaigned for the YWCA, and planted trees and shrubs on the courthouse square and in parks.

Finally the membership of the Club declined and maintenance of the house became too much for the small group. It was a sad decision for the president, Carolyn Kempe and her board of directors and members, but in 1989 the club house was sold to Fortune Management and has become "The Bridge".

Scholarships have been awarded for the last five years. The last three years the recipients Kari Wells and Mark Dailey have received them.

The club, as well as a junior club that was active for a time, were active in several departments. They included the Arts, Public Affairs, Bible Studies, Music, Civic Affairs, Health, Culture, Drama and International Affairs. Mrs. B.D. Mitchell helped organize the first Junior Department Club.

Currently the club contains five departments: home life, education, the arts, public affairs and international affairs, and now meets at 1 P.M. on the first Thursday of every month at First Friends Meeting.

Many memories will always be with us but we definitely intend to exist and educate ladies in various fields with outstanding programs, as has been the objectives for which the Kokomo Woman's Department Club was formed: for mutual sympathy and counsel, a united effort toward higher civilization of humanity, religion, education, general, philanthropy and literary work.
Submitted by Theda Sallee, President 1994

If anyone wishes more information, all scrapbooks and other information have been donated to the Howard County Museum.

Kokomo Woman's Department Club members in 1984. (l. to r.) Back row: Lillian Kingery, Dorothy Kennedy, Guest, Dorthea Ahlbrand, Barbara Moore, Marie Hadley, Elsie Seagrave, Kathryn Grau, Carolyn Kempe, Madella Fernung, Myrtle Mason, Clara Bartlett, and Mabel Fleenor. Second row: Helen Cook, June Fleming, Marybelle Moore, Betty Talbert, Theda Sallee, Gladys Caylor, Mildred Ellers, Eleanor Barrick, Mabel Hill, Jane Pitzer, Lucille Nicholson, and Marie Booher. First row: Guest, Euretta Russell, Charlotte Benge, and Ruth Castle. Some members not pictured or that joined after 1984 are: Rosella Ashburn, Mary Thatcher, Gladys Hall, Susan Baldwin, Dorothy Haynes, Kathryn Fell, Glendola Newby, Ruth Ridnour, Phyllis Plona, Beverly Downey, Mary E. Cedars, Martha Craig, Ruth Dillman, Verla Dyer, Frances Gordon, Mary Gunnell, Anna May Hamilton, Mildred Kingseed, Gretchen Kurtz, Edith LaRowe, Irene Merrel, Helen Pasley, Audrey Schaaf, Louise Schaaf, Rose Russell, Hazel Teter, Helen Yater, Sandy Zell, and Martha Johnson.

Phi Beta Psi Sorority Chapter Members 1993-1994: (l. to r.) Seated are 50 year members Ruth Alice Jennings, Grace Jay, Katherine Witham, and Theda Sallee. Back row: Sara Leonard, Martha Maris, Kim Brewster, Mary Brewster, Katy Johnson, President Kathy Brockman, Martha Craig, Nancy Eckles, Mary Pickett, and Hazel Shuck. Missing from photograph is member Alvera Paskell.

RESEARCH CLUB

October 6, 1916, a number of women in the Greentown area decided there was more to life than housekeeping, family rearing, and farm tending, so they formed the Research Club.

The purpose of the club was to allow members to research subjects and share their findings with others at meetings once a month from October through May. Subjects were educational and cultural and covered a wide span of interests. The club joined the General Federation of Women's Clubs in 1917.

Our club has gone through the wars, depressions, voting rights and now modern life and changes of homes, transportation, clothes and appliances.

In 1916 Main Street had an interurban that ran to Marion and Kokomo on dirt streets. In 1942 Main Street was made of brick. The interurban was gone, but there were buses. Gas, tires, shoes, sugar, soap, and meats were rationed because of World War II. The livery stable was gone and was replaced by three auto sales lots.

Our town survived the 1965 tornado when it took down our school, homes, and businesses, but the Research Club celebrates its 78th year this year. We meet in our homes and churches and now have our meetings at 9:30 A.M. the 2nd Thursday of each month September through June. We have 36 members. We have interesting programs and help the library and other worthwhile community causes. We are proud to be part of the history of Howard County. *Submitted by Helen Hickman*

PHI BETA PSI SORORITY PI CHAPTER

Phi Beta Psi Sorority was founded by six high school girls at North High in Columbus, Ohio, February 15, 1904. It became a national non-academic sorority with Pi Chapter of Kokomo chartered June 30, 1922, by eleven girls.

Pi Chapter is active with 15 members fulfilling the purpose of the sorority in promoting sociable, benevolent and civic projects, to promote fraternal relationship among its members with cancer research being the national, state and local project.

Memorial

John "Earl" Jones, Sr.

JONES
John "Earl" Jones, Sr.
10-4-14 to 5-14-94

We started our marriage with five flat tires. Times were tough, but our love pulled us through. Papp (Earl) worked hard to provide for our family. Our son, John, helped Papp sell used tires. John would say, "Tires for nanners." Papp worked at Continental Steel, Mohr Construction for 24 years, and was owner of Jones's Garage. Papp served in WWII. Our 60th anniversary was celebrated on 2 Apr 1994.

Thelma Mae (Hughes) Jones

John Earl Jones III
Son of John E. &
Freda J. (Bradley) Jones Jr.
B. 1-31-63 Kokomo, IN
D. 12-24-78

My spouse and I were sitting on our lounge chairs on our front patio on a warm summer afternoon when we heard the whining of a dirt bike engine in the distance. I squinted my eyes in the direction of the sound to see a dirtbike and a rider rounding the corner and then going on by. My mind races back to a point in time when a young boy, my son, on a dirtbike would pull into our drive. A time in our heart that feels like only yesterday, but was actually over fifteen years ago, that the bike and its rider, Johnny, pulled into our drive.

I could see Johnny running out of the house toward the creek with Duchess, our Bassett Hound, and a fishing pole in his hand yelling, "I'm going to check my traps and catch some fish."

Soon he was out of sight, hidden by trees and brush that surrounded the banks of the creek behind our home. I kept a watch out the window and every now and then I could see the dark hair above the brush next to the creek. All of a sudden, I saw Johnny and Duchess making a mad dash for the house, with his fishing pole bobbing and a fish dangling on the end of the pole.

He started yelling with excitement, "Look what I caught!" I did look at what he had caught. The fish might not have been a trophy in most fishermen's eyes, but in his and my eyes it was the best job of fishing ever.

Johnny played flag football at Sycamore School in about the year 1970 and Little League at Bunker Hill about 1972-1975.

When Johnny became thirteen years old, he decided to detassel corn to buy him a dirtbike, because his love for dirtbike racing was great. He woke up very early on the summer mornings when most other boys were still asleep. He worked in the hot summer sun thinking all the time about the bright orange Suzuki 125 sitting around the corner for sale in our neighbor's drive. By the end of the season he had saved enough money for that goal in his young life.

After Johnny bought his motorcycle, he rode it everywhere around Cassville. Up and down the railroad tracks and back in the woods he would blaze trails. He would take his sister, Robin, with him on some of those expeditions.

Johnny's love of motorcycles grew with the fascination of small engines, that came from the necessity of keeping his Suzuki running, because he was the one that had to pay for most of the repair work. When Johnny was fifteen, he was offered a job working on small engines in a motorcycle shop as soon as his sixteenth birthday arrived.

I never wanted Johnny to race motorcycles because I was afraid that he would be hurt. Johnny was never hurt riding a motorcycle. All he ever derived from it was pleasure and I am glad I let him have it. Looking back I wish I would have let him race.

Johnny was a sophomore at Maconaquah High School in the fall of 1978 and attended First Assembly of God Church with our family. School was going very well for Johnny when he was dismissed for Christmas break; it was December 21, 1978.

Johnny and a friend were leaving to go Christmas shopping and to see a Clint Eastwood movie. He had put on his jeans and a T-shirt, as most teenage boys wore; he did not like dressing up. When going out the door, he kissed both of us good-bye and teased Robin, "Bye Shorty." Then he left.

I realized that the movie was over at 9:30 p.m., and that Johnny should be arriving home very soon when the phone rang. I answered the phone and spoke to the person on the other end. "Your son has been in a car accident," the voice said.

We rushed to the hospital and a doctor came in right away. He said., "Your son needs to be taken to Saint Vincent's Hospital in Indianapolis." The doctor continued talking, but I believe we were all in a daze wishing this was only a nightmare.

Johnny never regained consciousness during the next three days. We stayed with Johnny continually never leaving his side.

On December 24, Christmas Eve 1978, my son who was also my friend left this world to a better one.

Johnny was a friend to all people, young and old alike. He had a love for life that many people admire. I share his stories with my grandchildren and keep the memory of his life in my heart. So every time I see a boy on a motorcycle, I think of my son riding his in heaven.

Loved and missed,
Dad, Mom, Sister
Friends and Relatives

John Earl Jones, III

Memorial

IN LOVING MEMORY OF
FEROL STAHL

A DEVOTED WORKER, MOTHER, WIFE AND FRIEND

Betty, Marge, Sheila, and Kim

BUSINESSES

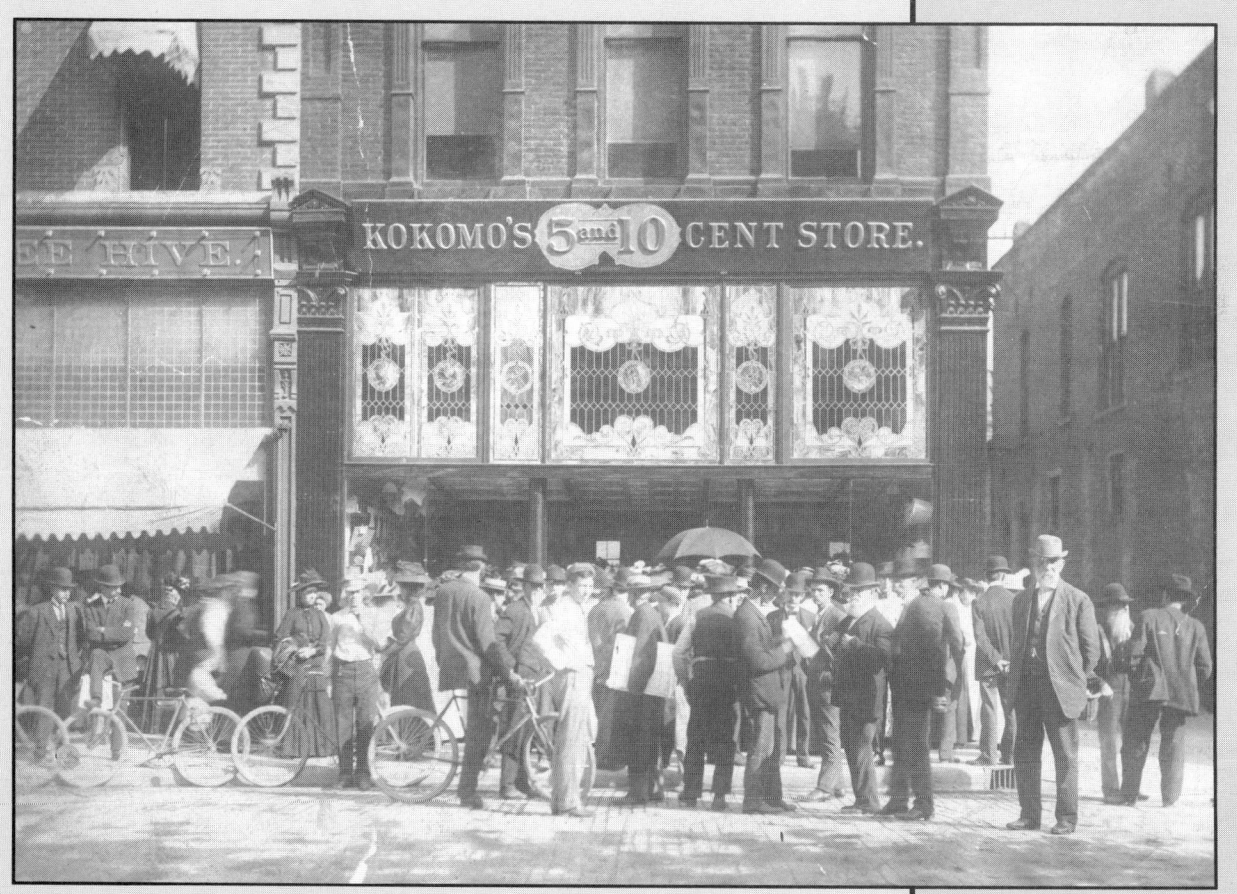

A five and dime store in Kokomo in the early part of the century.

CITY OF KOKOMO

It arose from a swamp and thicket of trees once inhabited by a tribe of Algonquin Indians, known as the Miamis.

Named for the orneriest Indian he ever knew, Indian trader and pioneer, David Foster, so named the orneriest town he'd ever known.

In the 150 years since pioneer traders first settled in this once small, isolated backwoods village, Kokomo — or "Co-co-mo" as the Indian chief bearing the eponym might have spelled it — has grown to nearly 50,000 people and covers more than 15 square miles.

In the early 1840s, however, Kokomo was just another countryside town in the middle of nowhere. Maps of the era show much of North Central Indiana, including Richardville County, later renamed Howard, as being in the middle of Indian territory. Had the Miamis not been a friendly tribe, historians believe Kokomo would not have survived in those first few harsh years.

Kokomo officially became a town January 1, 1844, after the Richardville County officials, who were eager to find a location for a county seat, accepted Foster's offer of 40 acres along the Wildcat Creek in the general area of what we now call Washington and Superior Streets. History books say Foster would have donated 80 acres, but County Commissioners of the day did not believe that 80 acres ever would be inhabited. Commissioners also considered Burlington, Sharpsville and Harrison as possible county seats, but chose Kokomo because of its centralized location.

For a then-salty $30 price tag, an early Kokomoan could purchase a lot in this new town. In the first sale of lots, 29 of the original 100 were sold in the first year. For the first 10 years, Kokomo residents of the day struggled with clearing out dense woods and undergrowth so thick that one history book noted that a "bird could scarcely fly" through it. Early settlers suffered through drainage problems until tile was laid to carry the overflow. Today, Kokomo covers more than 16.6 square miles, or almost 10,000 acres.

One of Kokomo's first established buildings was a log courthouse in which criminal court was held and county offices were located. As part of his deal with the commissioners, Foster agreed to construct the 24-foot square log courthouse on the central square, bounded by Sycamore, Main, Walnut and Buckeye Streets, where the current courthouse now stands. A log cabin jail was constructed at the present-day location of Superior and Washington Streets, from which no prisoners ever escaped, a feat that has not been accomplished with even our present day jail. Once regarded as lawless and without redemption, the City of Kokomo once was a part-time home to notorious felon John Dillinger and was the site of a courthouse square lynching of a man accused of killing a sheriff's deputy and a prominent reverend. Kokomo's history also includes the 1881 murder of Mayor Henry C. Cole, a man who had been acquitted of murder several years earlier on the grounds of temporary insanity. Kokomo's reputation was so bad, one Ohio journalist described early-day Kokomo as "the combined Sodom and Gomorrah of modern times, and the average Kokomoke is beyond redemption." Proving to be a diamond in the rough, however, Kokomo has emerged some 150 years later to be regarded as one of the safest and most livable cities in the nation.

Kokomo elected its first mayor, Nelson Purdum, in 1865, during the Civil War. At least 2,000 Howard County men, many teenagers, volunteered to fight for the Union. The first group of Howard County soldiers to volunteer for the war effort were the first group in the state to go into battle.

The first City offices were located in upstairs rooms on the west side of the 300 block of North Main Street, above the fire department's original station. Fire equipment of the day was horse-drawn, and fires were fought with buckets and some hose. Fires, such as the great fire of 1871, which destroyed the entire west side of the Courthouse Square, were forces to be reckoned with. Today, there are five fire department stations located around the city.

In 1894, City offices were moved to a newly constructed building at the southeast corner of Washington and Walnut Streets. The stone building, topped with turrets, also housed the fire and police departments.

Kokomo's first City Hall as it appeared in the mid-1800s.

After the City moved into its current building at Union and Sycamore Streets in 1983, the former City building was renovated. Now 100 years old, the original City building is used for office space, housing a variety of businesses and agencies, including the Kokomo-Howard County Chamber of Commerce.

Kokomo's growth in those early days was slow and arduous, and the businesses that did take hold primarily were limited in scope to the 6,000 residents of Kokomo. Then, October 6, 1886, came the most important day in the history of the city. On that day, natural gas was discovered in a cornfield near what is now Park Avenue and Armstrong Street. Overnight, Kokomo was transformed from an isolated rural town to an industrial center. The lure of free gas, free land and cash bonuses to businesses brought at least 25 new businesses to the city and boosted Kokomo's population by more than 2,000 people.

The price of lots doubled and tripled in value, law enforcement tightened and the once corrupt city was beginning to live down its reputation for guns and alcohol. That is until the gas ran out and Kokomo struggled for its very existence. Fortunately for Kokomo, local resident and inventor Elwood Haynes was on the verge of putting the first automobile into production in the United States. That first car — The Pioneer — produced and first tested on Pumpkin Vine Pike in 1894, is now stored at the Smithsonian Institution in Washington, D.C. and will be returning to Kokomo during the city's Sesquicentennial Celebration. It is the first time the original Haynes vehicle has been in Kokomo since 1922. The car will be on display at the Howard County Museum (Seiberling Mansion, Carriage House).

Haynes enlisted the aid of the Apperson brothers, Elmer and Edgar, to help him put the Haynes into production. The Appersons worked with Haynes until 1901 when they broke away and formed their own company. The Haynes Company produced an estimated 50,000 vehicles during the 20 years it was in business. Haynes closed its doors in 1925. Elwood Haynes died that same year.

Although Haynes' vehicles were a monumental achievement, perhaps his greatest legacies were his experiments with steel alloys and his invention of stainless steel. Haynes developed the first stainless steel while reportedly tinkering with different alloys to make a better cookware for his wife. Haynes formed the Haynes Stellite Co., which still operates today as Haynes International Inc., where scientists continue to invent newer, more effective steel alloys for industrial, commercial and automobile uses. Kokomo's automotive heritage continues today with Kokomo's two leading employers, Delco Electronics Corp. and Chrysler Corp.

Kokomo's growth steadily increased as scientists and inventors continued searching for ways to improve life in Kokomo and around the world. Dubbed the "City of Firsts," Kokomo inventors have a long list of accolades, including the first pneumatic rubber tire, invented by D.C. Spraker in 1894; the first aluminum casting, produced by William "Billy" Johnson at the Ford Donnelly Foundry in 1895; the first carburetor, developed by George Kingston in 1902; first American howitzer shell used in warfare, made by the Superior Machine Tool Co. in 1918; the first mechanical corn picker, produced by John Powell in the 1920s; the first canned tomato juice, developed by Kemp Brothers Canning Co. in 1928; the first push-button car radio, developed by Delco Radio Division of General Motors in 1938; and the first signal seeking car radio and all transistor car radio, both produced by Delco Radio Division, in 1947 and 1957, respectively.

Industrial development skyrocketed in the 1930s, with the additions of Crosley Radio in 1935, which was purchased eight months later by Delco Radio Division of General Motors Corp., and Chrysler Corp., which came to Kokomo in 1937. Today, Delco Electronics Corp, employs more than 12,000 people and has operations in several states and at least four countries. Chrysler Corp. employs more than 6,200 people today. Few Chrysler automobiles are completed without automatic transaxles and other products produced in Kokomo.

The Haynes automobile was the first commercially successful gasoline powered automobile.

Today, under the leadership of Mayor Robert Sargent, Kokomo's 32nd mayor, Kokomo remains a leader in urban development, law enforcement and aid to disadvantaged persons. The City has grown to about 45,000 people. In addition to sporting one of the lowest crime rates in the country, Kokomo has been ranked in the top 100 places to live in the country by *Money Magazine*. Kokomo was ranked the fifth most affordable market in the nation in which to purchase a home. Kokomo's average annual salary of $28,676 is the highest in the Hoosier state, marking the 12th straight year that the City of Firsts has captured that honor. Kokomo ranks in the top 30 metropolitan areas for average annual salary in the country. In the last six years, Kokomo has gained a renewed momentum as business startups and expansions have exploded along U.S. 31, which links Kokomo to South Bend to the north and Indianapolis to the south. Kokomo has earned a reputation as North Central Indiana's commercial and retail hub.

Mayor Robert Sargent

Judging by today's standards, one might have a hard time imagining English-French trappers swapping animal pelts with the Miamis in what we know today as Uptown Kokomo.

ANDERSON LAND TITLE COMPANY, INC.

Anderson Land Title Co. shares a proud heritage with Howard County from E.R. Anderson, a prominent businessman, to Richard B. Moore, the great, great, great grandson of Chief Richardville, the original owner of what was to become Howard County.

E.R. Anderson started in business in 1899 as E.R. Anderson Abstracter, with his first office located at 18 E. Walnut St. Then in 1910 he moved to 112 E. Walnut St. in the building that was the first location of the Kokomo Trust Company and now the present location of Americantrust Federal Savings Bank. On January 12, 1912, he then incorporated with sixteen prominent businessmen who were also stockholders of Kokomo Trust Company. In November of 1926 E.R. Anderson sold out his controlling interest to the then-formed Anderson Abstract Company. In early 1927, Kokomo Trust Company consolidated with Citizens National Bank, and the Anderson Abstract Company was then moved to the Citizens National Bank building at 224 N. Main St., later to become the home of Union Bank and Trust Company, now Society National Bank. Anderson Abstract Company remained at this location from 1927 to 1938 under the guidance of E.R. Anderson from 1927-1931, Harry O. Davis from 1931-1934 and Wayne D. Croddy from 1934-1936.

In January of 1936, Louise Andrews, who had learned the abstracting business under the guidance and leadership of E.R. Anderson, purchased the company from the Citizens Corporation, the surviving corporation of the merger of Kokomo Trust Company and Citizens National Bank.

Mrs. Andrew kept the company at 224 N. Main St. until she moved it to 104 1/2 W. Walnut St., above the McClellan Department Store in 1938. In 1950 Mrs. Andrews purchased and consolidated the records of the Citizens Abstract Company that had been founded in 1883 by J.I. Moutray. Mrs. Andrews continued to operate the business at 104 1/2 W. Walnut St. until she purchased the building at 209 W. Walnut St. in October of 1959, which was at one time the location of the Kokomo Water Works Company.

In 1972 Mrs. Andrews sold the business and Richard Moore took over as the acting manager of the company. Then, because of increasing business, staff and lack of space, the company was moved to 115 N. Buckeye St. in May of 1975. On January 1, 1985, the company was purchased by Richard and Margaret Moore. For the following two and a half years the company stayed at the location of 115 N. Buckeye St.

Along with the revitalization of the "Uptown Kokomo" project a new home was established for Anderson Land Title Company to its present location at 212 W. Walnut St. The company has not only seen many changes in its location over the past ninety-five years, but it has seen many changes in the way business is conducted. It has gone from hand-written abstracts and records, to computer-generated records and searches, and to title insurance to protect both the home owner and the lender. The Moores are operating the company as a family business giving that personal touch to their customers, who are looking for a long time security into the largest investment in their lives, that of home ownership.

The Moores' son, Tyler, has recently entered the title business by working for Elkhart Title in Northern Indiana. There he hopes to gain a wide range of real estate knowledge and information in a larger company and area, that can be used to help increase and expand Anderson Land Title's service to the Howard County area.

Richard and Margaret Moore in front of their business, the Anderson Land Title Company, Inc.

Big R Store, located at the corner of U.S. 31 & North Street

BIG R STORE

In the fall of 1961, Emil, Teresa and Les Johanning opened the first Fleet Supply, a farm and home store in downtown Kokomo. Little did they know the seed they were planting would grow into a chain of retail stores, serving the central and northern regions of Indiana.

The seed that became the tree is now known as Big R. Although the name has been changed, the dedication to quality and service hasn't. Today, Big R is a store with something for everyone: hardware, lumber, home-improvement, clothing, automotive, lawn & garden, and much, much more. Like the slogan say, "Almost Anything.... Big R's got it!"

Progress is a way of life for Big R Stores and Kokomo has a lot to do with that progress. The Johannings still run Big R and have strong ties to the Kokomo area; only now they run eleven Big R retail stores, three "complete" furniture stores and a rental center located in Marion.

Progress is a product of decisions of the past, and the Johannings and Kokomo have made many good ones. THANK-YOU KOKOMO... for 34 great years...we look forward to many more in the future.

The original Fleet Supply was at 314 S. Union where the Salvation Army Thrift Store is located.

The Central National Bank building.

CENTRAL NATIONAL BANK

On February 20, 1947, Russiaville State Bank opened its doors for business. Russiaville had been without a bank since December 1930 when the Russiaville National Bank closed its doors.

In the summer of 1946 a group of Russiaville businessmen approached Donald B. Smith, President of First National Bank of Kokomo, who had just organized and opened that bank with a similar group in Kokomo, to do the same for Russiaville.

An application was prepared for a new bank and was approved by the Department of Financial Institutions on September 13, 1946. The directors of the new Russiaville State Bank were O.G. Marshall, Robert McMinn, J.H. Padgett, Max P. Sellars, all of Russiaville, and Harry O. Davis, William G. Harter, Dowell E. Shirley, Donald B. Smith, and John E. Fell.

The new bank purchased the brick building on the northwest corner in the downtown four corners that had housed the old national bank. The vault and many of the bank fixtures were still intact. The upstairs of the building was occupied by the Russiaville Telephone Company that was still using a switchboard with operators. Helen Waddell was one of the operators.

The officers of the bank were Donald B. Smith, President; Max P. Sellars, Vice President; and Leon Vandivier, Cashier, who was the Chief Operating Officer. The other employees were Mazie Vandivier and Arda Berle Cochran. The Vandiviers moved from Franklin, Indiana, where they had been employed by a bank in that city.

There were 3,500 shares of stock that were sold at $16.00 per share to the new shareholders in Kokomo and Russiaville. The total capitalization of the bank was $56,000.00 consisting of $35,000.00 Capital Stock, $15,000.00 paid in Surplus and $6,000.00 paid in Undivided Profit. Within a year the bank was making a profit. Opening day showed deposits of $123,000.00. Assuming that a new shareholder purchased 100 shares at $16.00 per share in 1946, that investment today would be 1,286 shares including stock dividends with a book value of $57,805.00.

The new bank was opened on February 20, 1947, on a cold but snowless day, without much ceremony, just coffee, cake and cookies in the lobby. The bank grew and prospered; by 1957 the total assets were $1,764,250.00. During that period several additional directors had been added to the Board of Directors: Donald B. Smith, Jr. in 1951, Leon Vandivier in 1952, Ancel Walker in 1954 and James P. Coplen in 1957. Elmer Watson had joined the bank in 1948 and was appointed Assistant Cashier in 1949.

April 11, 1965, was the day of the Palm Sunday tornado. Russiaville State Bank had just the year before built a new bank building 100 feet west of the old building. After the tornado, there was nothing left of the bank except the vault and the concrete pad that it stood on. The bank vault and the vault door withstood the winds, and the next morning, all the records and money were moved to First National Bank in Kokomo. Thus just 16 hours after the tornado, the bank was open for business, from the lobby of the Kokomo bank. Within a week a trailer was moved into Russiaville, and the bank operated out of a mobile trailer until the bank building was rebuilt.

In 1968 Leon and Mazie Vandivier retired to Florida and Elmer Watson became Chief Operating Officer. In 1970 Donald B. Smith, Jr., succeeded his father as President of the Bank. By this time the bank had grown to $5,000,000.00.

Three years later Russiaville State Bank converted to a national bank and became Central National Bank of Howard County and applied for a branch in Kokomo. The branch opened in Kokomo in August 1973 and operated out of a mobile trailer while the new branch building was being built. By the end of the year Central National Bank had grown by 50%.

Ten years later the growth was from seven and a half million to twenty-one million. Today, as of the end of December 1993, the bank is over $35,000,000.00.

Many, many changes have taken place in the banking field in Howard County since the Russiaville State Bank was started. Today, Central National Bank is the only locally owned and operated commercial bank in Howard County. One savings bank in the county shares that distinction.

CHARLES CONKLE MOTOR CO., INC.

In the infancy of the automobile industry there were no "showrooms" or repair shops. People came by train to purchase their automobile at the factory.

Later, they franchised the automobile industry and the agents started opening showrooms and repair shops.

In 1910, Charles Rayl was employed by Bob Conwell of Galveston to manage a Studebaker sales location at the 100 block of South Union, one of the first in Howard County.

In 1912, they moved to 315 N. Main with five franchises: Studebaker, Olds, Safon 6, Abil, and Maxwell. After franchising, the cars came by rail five to a box car and had much of the assembly to be done at the depot on Buckeye Street. Later, they had a "driveway," where the agent could drive the car off the train at the depot.

In 1910 they put the cars in the showrooms up on cement blocks to protect the tires.

In 1914, with the war, the auto industry went into the war effort. Mr. Rayl went back to work for Haynes Automobile Company and sold a few used cars on the side.

In 1917, Mr. Rayl and Tom Phelps formed a partnership: The Rayl/Phelps Ford Dealership. It was located on East Mulberry Street in the Spraker Building just west of the downtown post office (phone 623).

In 1920, they cancelled their Ford franchise and signed up with Chevrolet. In 1921 they took the franchise for Willy Knight.

In 1922, Mr. Rayl acquired the Oldsmobile franchise and moved to 318 N. Buckeye, the site of the present Pontiac dealership.

The Great Depression began and the demand for the new and used cars went to the wayside. He kept the store open, but lack of business forced him to give up the Olds franchise in 1931.

Shortly after he acquired the Studebaker agency, he decided to employ his son, Durwood Rayl, and his son-in-law, Charles Conkle. As Mr. Rayl's daughter, I served as bookkeeper and office manager.

After a while, Durwood Rayl decided to take the Hudson-Terraplane agency.

In 1938, Charles Conkle took the franchise for Pontiac, LaSalle, & Cadillac as they gave up the Hudson-Terraplane agency.

In 1955, Mr. Rayl died suddenly and Charles Conkle retained the dealership.

In 1965, Mr. Conkle became ill and could no longer work. His son Charles has since run the business and now his son Chuck had joined him in the operation. *Submitted by Waneata Conkle, April 27, 1994*

Charles Conkle (left) and Durwood Rayl (right)

Strongest man in the world pulling nine Studebaker cars July 2, 1914. The cars were part of the dealership owned by Charles Rayl on Union Street.

CHRYSLER CORPORATION KOKOMO COMPLEX

Chrysler Corporation opened its first manufacturing facility in Kokomo in 1937 at the then closed Haynes Automobile Plant. The plant was converted to manufacture manual transmissions. This Central Indiana location provides a highly skilled and experienced workforce. In addition, there is easy access to the national rail system and truck shipping routes.

Chrysler built the present facility in 1955 to satisfy the demand for 3-speed rear wheel drive automatic transmissions. The original structure's size was approximately 850,000 sq. ft. There have been (7) major expansions since 1955 and the facility covers more than 3.4 million square feet or 67 acres under roof.

In March 1956, the first 3-speed torque flite transmission was built using a cast iron case. 1959 marked the start of production on the current rear wheel drive family of transmissions which used a die cast aluminum case. A major expansion in 1977 launched Chrysler into the manufacture of front wheel drive transmissions - the A404. Another expansion started in August 1985, adding another 482,000 sq. ft. needed for the production of Chrysler's A-604. This was the first 4-speed **electronically** controlled automatic transaxle. Production of the A-604 was started in March 1988.

The 1991 expansion to the transmission plant was to accommodate the 42LE front wheel drive, 4-speed electronic automatic transmission that was introduced May 1992.

The Company changed iron transmission cases to aluminum to reduce weight in the vehicles. With this change came the decision to build an aluminum casting facility in Kokomo.

The Kokomo Casting facility was built in 1965 on 29 acres of land. The plant initially covered 400,000 square feet of floor space and was designed and constructed specifically for the production of aluminum die castings. The plant currently manufactures 111 different aluminum parts, ranging in weight from 1 1/2 ounces to 41 pounds. The plant has 107 die cast machines ranging from 500 to 3,000 ton capacity.

The casting facility was expanded in 1969 and 1986. The facility has approximately 500,000 sq. ft. of manufacturing space. In 1993, it poured 219 million pounds of aluminum.

The Kokomo Complex produces automatic transmissions and aluminum parts for Chrysler cars and trucks built in the United States, Canada and Mexico. Automatic transmissions are also supplied to other automotive manufacturers around the world.

Transmissions and transaxles are manufactured in an environment which utilizes state of the art equipment and modern management principles.

The employees at the Kokomo Complex are dedicated to the Chrysler Corporation objective of being the highest quality producer of automobiles and trucks in the world. Chrysler and all the employees of the Kokomo Complex are proud to be a part of Kokomo and the great State of Indiana.

Automatic Transmission/Transaxle Capital of the World

COCA-COLA BOTTLING COMPANY

Coca-Cola was discovered in 1886 in Atlanta, Georgia, by a pharmacist named Dr. John Pemberton. He first mixed it with carbonated water at Jacobs Pharmacy. He sold the new drink for 5¢ a glass and advertised it as "Delicious and Refreshing." In 1888 Asa Candler became a partner of Dr. Pemberton. By 1891 Dr. Pemberton had passed away and Mr. Candler became sole owner of all rights to the formula for Coca-Cola Syrup. His total cost for all rights, including his initial investment, was $2300. In 1894 Joseph Biedenharn, who had been selling Coca-Cola at his soda fountain since 1890, was the first person to bottle Coca-Cola in Vicksburg, Mississippi. Coca-Cola Bottling plants spread quickly throughout the United States. Coca-Cola was bottled in Kokomo sometime prior to 1915. However, the first bottler contract was dated 1919 and assigned rights to Roy Newsom. In 1921, a two-year renewal agreement was signed by Harry Wolter, the new owner of this company. The first known location for a Coca-Cola plant in Kokomo was 112 W. Jefferson. The operation was later moved to 600 S. Union. That building is now used as a warehouse by King's Heating and Plumbing. The next location was in the 400 block of W. Superior. That building was used until the move to the current location at 2305 N. Davis Road.

Records show the earliest contract to bottle Coca-Cola in this area was executed with Reuben Cottey of Logansport on July 27, 1907. In 1923 new owners acquired the Logansport company. These owners were Frank Enyart and Frank Etnire. Coca-Cola was bottled in Peru, also prior to 1915 until March 1932, but we do not know the name of the bottler.

On March 1, 1932, the Logansport company became the owner of the Coca-Cola Bottling works in Kokomo and Peru. By March of 1936 this merged company had been purchased by three brothers, Edmond, Frank, and Roy Severns. Roy was elected President and Manager. Edmond was employed by Continental Steel, where he was busy working his way up to the eventual positions of President and Chairman of the Board. Frank was a Vice-President with the Coca-Cola Bottler in Indianapolis.

In 1944 the Severns brothers purchased the Coca-Cola Bottling Company, Elwood, Ind., from Mrs. Lulu Vantine.

In 1959 the son of Edmond, E.P. Severns, Jr., was elected President of the Company. He is still serving in that capacity today.

By 1965 the operation was known as Coca-Cola Bottling Company, Kokomo, Indiana, Inc. Also in 1965 construction of a new production facility was begun in Kokomo by addition to the present warehouse on Davis Road. New high speed production equipment was installed in the remodeled building. In March of 1966 the bottling of Coca-Cola and other soft drinks resumed in Kokomo. The bottling was discontinued in Logansport and Elwood at that time. Logansport continued to be used as a warehouse until 1988 when the building was sold. At that time the Logansport employees transferred to Kokomo where they now do the pre-mix and post-mix filling.

In January 1977, Mr. Severns purchased the Coca-Cola Bottling Company of Plymouth from Robert Beiter. Bottling was discontinued in Plymouth, and Kokomo produced for Plymouth. A new warehouse was built in Plymouth shortly after the purchase, and it is still in use as a distribution center. Eighteen employees work at the Plymouth operation. Seventy-five employees work in Kokomo.

E.P. Severns remains as President and a third generation of the family has become active in the business. Craig Severns became General Manager in 1981 and his brother, Tim, recently was promoted to sales manager. A sister, Susan Severns Ellert, works at the Plymouth location. She is in charge of all fountain sales. The company does business in fifteen counties in north central Indiana and services the cities of Kokomo, Logansport, Peru, Tipton, Elwood, Delphi, Flora, Rochester, and Plymouth.

The product line has changed a great deal through the years. At one time the only product was a 6 1/2 oz. returnable Coca-Cola. We no longer sell any returnable bottles. We sell non-returnable bottles in different sizes ranging from 10 oz. to 2 liter. We also sell 12 oz. cans in 6 packs, 12 packs, and 24 packs. We sell pre-mix and post-mix fountain syrup. We also handle many different models of vending equipment and special event equipment.

Coca-Cola and allied products are available throughout the world. The Coca-Cola contour bottle is considered to be the best known package in the world. Coca-Cola continues to be "Delicious and Refreshing." We are proud to serve you our products.

HAYNES INTERNATIONAL INC.

The history of Haynes International, Inc. is one of continual innovation in the processing and development of high performance alloys. The Company was started in 1912 in Kokomo as the Haynes Stellite works. Its principal product was cobalt-chromium-tungsten metal-cutting tools, the invention of Elwood Haynes, who is generally credited with having invented the first mechanically practical, gasoline-powered automobile in the United States. His tiny car is now on exhibit at the Smithsonian Institution in Washington, D.C. Although Haynes' claim as the inventor of stainless steel is not as firm as that for cobalt-base alloys, many of the leading steel companies paid royalties, based on their stainless steel production, to Haynes and his American Stainless Steel Company for as long as his patents were in effect.

Union Carbide and Carbon Corporation bought Haynes' small Company in 1920 and infused it with even more technology in order to diversify away from the HAYNES STELLITE tool metals which were the company's sole product. One of the first developments under the aegis of Union Carbide was the nickel-base alloys HASTELLOY® alloy B. The name was coined from **HA**YNES **STELL**LITE al**loys**, and it remains one of the company's main trademarks today. It was used for rocket nozzles on the Viking I and II vehicles which made soft landings on the planet Mars.

HASTELLOY alloy C soon followed alloy B and gained rapid acceptance in the chemical process industry. In addition to playing major roles in the then-infant petrochemical industry, it was invaluable as a corrosion-resistant material of construction for equipment used in the nuclear and pharmaceutical fields. One of the most spectacular applications of alloy C was for the skirts of the huge F-1 and H-1 rocket nozzles which lifted the Apollo vehicles off for their journeys to the moon.

HASTELLOY alloys were so successful, because of their extraordinary corrosion resistance, that the Company built a rolling mill in 1948 to handle the increased demand. Shortly afterward, the development of HASTELLOY alloy X was the start of one of the most spectacular success stories in the saga of high-temperature metallurgy. Alloy X was timed exactly right to play a leading role in the age of jet aircraft. The market for both jet aircraft and alloy X expanded exponentially together. Alloy X had the best combination of high-temperature strength, oxidation resistance, and fabricability of any alloy available to jet engine builders for many years.

Parallel improvements were being made in the HASTELLOY corrosion-resistance alloy field. One of the major roadblocks to expanding markets for these alloys was their need for a complicated heat-treatment after welding to restore corrosion resistance. Welding, which is unavoidable in the construction of large process vessels, drastically decreases heat affected zone corrosion resistance. Heat-treatment to remedy this condition is expensive and sometimes causes unwanted dimensional changes.

HASTELLOY alloy C-276 provided an answer to this dilemma. It was produced with very low silicon and carbon. One of the tools for producing low-carbon, low-silicon alloys was a post-melting refining process known as argon oxygen decarburization (AOD). Haynes was a pioneer in the development of this important production process for nickel-base alloys.

In the 1960's, aircraft engine designers were asking for more and more heat resistance from alloys. To fill this need, Haynes went back to its original field of cobalt-base alloys and developed HAYNES® 188 alloy. By judiciously alloying with the rare earth metal lanthanum, plus chromium, tungsten and nickel, the new alloy gave engine builders a 300° F temperature advantage over any other alloy then available. One of the many results was the Pratt & Whitney F100 engine which powered the **McDonald Douglas** F15 attack aircraft in making a number of world speed and climbing records.

Cabot Corporation of Boston bought Haynes from Carbide in 1970. They continued the tradition of technical development for 16 years. However, in 1986 Cabot spun Haynes off as a separate entity in a corporate downsizing program. Ever seeking better and better products, the **Haynes** laboratories introduced **HASTELLOY** C-22™ alloy. This C-family alloy contains precise combinations of chromium, tungsten, and molybdenum which offer improvements in corrosion resistance over previous versions.

Developments in high-temperature alloys also continued, and the present day successor to **HASTELLOY** alloy X and HAYNES 188 alloy is **HAYNES 230**™ alloy, a nickel-chromium-molybdenum-tungsten alloy that combines high strength and oxidation resistance with excellent long-term stability and good fabricability.

Right up to the present day, metallurgical developments have continued apace at **Haynes.** Since 1967, with **HAYNES** 188 alloy, the company has won nine R&D 100 Awards for technical excellence. This award is given annually to the 100 top technical developments in the United States. The latest award was for ULTIMET® alloy in 1991. This new alloy has an extraordinary combination of wear and corrosion resistance.

A total of six Chemical Processing Awards have been received for developments of use in the chemical process industry. These include awards for HASTELLOY alloys B-2, C-22, C-276; **HAYNES** 214™ and 230 alloys; and ULTIMET alloy.

In addition to its technical prowess, **Haynes** takes special pride in its record of customer service and quality. In its worldwide service centers, **Haynes** maintains two-million pounds of finished goods inventory in over ten thousand combinations of alloy and forms to respond quickly to customer needs.

HOLDER MATTRESS COMPANY

Since Holder Mattress Company is nearing its 50th year in business, many people in the Central Indiana area have depended upon this company for most, if not all, their bedding needs for most of their lives. Founded in 1947, in Kokomo, the company has maintained a philosophy of premier bedding at affordable prices since its inception. Its founder and owner, Lyle Holder, has always emphasized high standards and good customer service and credits this mixture with giving the business its longevity.

Lyle Holder was born in Oklahoma in 1916. His father Floyd had been in the land rush of 1889 in Oklahoma. Having been reared with a pioneer spirit, he wanted to achieve more than was possible in the economically-depressed Dust Bowl area. During the Depression era, not many people could afford to buy new mattresses; thus, renovating old mattresses became the way to get into the business. Lyle's best friend, Virgil McClintock, had a father who was already in that business and taught Lyle what he needed to know. World War II interrupted his career as Lyle served in the Air Force from 1941-1945. Following the war, Lyle and his brother Wayne traveled to Ironwood, Michigan, to start a mattress business there. The winters were harsh not only for the winters but also for lack of business. After marrying Bonnie, in 1947, they decided to go somewhere warmer and more prosperous.

Lyle and Russell in 1941.

Heading down U.S. 31, they spotted smoke on the horizon. They knew this meant factories and economic prosperity. They set up shop first in Sharpsville; they later found a house in Kokomo complete with a separate building that housed a laundry business. They continued to run the laundry and began the mattress business that they started with a few innerspring units and less than $1000. Shortly thereafter they started working at Chrysler. With income derived from three sources, they started to build the mattress business. In 1951, Lyle and Wayne were laid off from Chrysler and were able to give full time to the young mattress business. They moved the business to the corner of Webster and U.S. 35 in 1956. The move to the company's current location came in 1961. The concept of building the finest mattresses and boxsprings made anywhere and selling directly to the public really started to catch on then. The second generation family came into the business in the late sixties and early seventies. In 1971, a second store was added in West Lafayette, Indiana. Other stores followed in Muncie in 1976 and Anderson in 1979. Wayne, Lyle's partner, passed away in 1979, and the original business was divided. The current Kokomo store and the business name was retained by Lyle Holder. Early thereafter, Lyle ventured into the Indianapolis market by opening a location in Carmel. Now Holder Mattress circles the Indianapolis area with additional locations in Greenwood, Castleton, Speedway and the East Washington Street area.

Today, Holder Mattress Company has even surpassed the hopes and dreams Lyle Holder had for it in 1947. Lyle, at age 77, is still active in the business. Other family members, Stephen and Lisa Holder, Tim and Linda McAshlan, and Tom and Tracey Buersmeyer, are active owners and participants in the current business. Holder Mattress has become more than just a bedding business. Today, it offers a complete line of bedding, furniture and accessories in its quest to become a complete bedroom store. Holder Mattress has become a household name in Central Indiana for the finest quality mattress and bedding related goods.

Holder Mattress Company

HOWARD COMMUNITY HOSPITAL

In 1953, the Howard County Medical Society advised local government officials that additional hospital facilities were needed in the Howard County area. A study committee was appointed and reported in June that the need was, in fact, there.

In May of 1956, a referendum on a $1.8 million bond issue passed by a two-to-one margin and the first Board of Trustees was appointed. Members included Viola Obermeyer, secretary; Carl Tyner; William McFerrin; Gene Pickett; LeRoy Lacey, attorney; and Walter Bennett.

The Trustees chose an 18-acre plot on the south edge of Kokomo between Lafountain Street and U.S. 31 as the hospital site.

The new Howard Community Hospital was completed in 1961 and admitted its first patient, Max E. Peel, on December 3.

Howard Community Hospital (HCH) brought many firsts to the "City of Firsts." Among them were the first radiation therapy treatment capabilities for cancer patients in 1969. 1970 saw HCH begin the first county-wide ambulance service. The service, which was initiated through the efforts of HCH, was made equally available to both of the community's hospitals.

In 1970, ground was broken for a major addition to the hospital which ultimately held the area's first inpatient psychiatric service. The 33-bed unit could support both inpatient and outpatient services. The outpatient services were started in 1971. The addition of inpatient services came about in 1972.

In 1973 the hospital started the area's first coronary intensive care unit providing special and intense services for the victims of heart attacks and other heart related problems.

Another first for the "City of Firsts" was the accreditation for Basic Clinical Pastoral Education programs in 1975. Howard Community Hospital accreditation for Advanced Pastoral Education came in 1981, one of a very few hospitals in the country to hold this accreditation.

Kokomo's first cardiac rehabilitation program was begun at HCH in 1978. The area's first birthing room opened in 1983 introducing a "homey" atmosphere to the mothers and fathers.

The new 60-bed, $5 million Psychiatric Unit for teens and adults was opened in 1985 with a $500,000 donation from Delco Electronics and the General Motors Foundation. This was a major addition to the community in addressing the psychiatric needs of the area.

The hospital also opened Community InHome Care in 1985. The home health service provides a staff of registered nurses, physical and occupational therapists, speech therapists, social workers, nurses aides, and chaplains to care for the patients at home.

HCH opened the first unit in the area attending to women's specials needs with the opening of The Woman's Center in 1986.

The Community Oncology Center, opened in 1988, gave the community, under a single roof, access to the three modalities of cancer treatment: radiation, chemotherapy and surgery.

In June of 1988, HCH became the first area hospital to provide Extracorporeal Shock Wave Lithotripsy, the exciting new non-invasive treatment for kidney stones.

The first Cardiac Catheterization laboratory opened in Kokomo at HCH in November of 1988.

In 1991, HCH established the first Diabetes Center. The Diabetes Center team consists of a dietitian, diabetes educator, a coping counselor and physical therapist.

In December, 1991, HCH was the first hospital in the area to computerize all orders for procedures and tests with its hospital-wide Order Entry System.

In February, 1992, Kokomo/Howard County saw its first Extended Care Unit in a hospital. The unit is a skilled nursing facility which is a step beyond hospitalization for patients with any condition that can't be treated on a daily basis at home, but do not require the acute care of the general hospital.

Peak Performance, the out-patient physical therapy services, opened its doors to the community in October of 1992. Peak Performance is conveniently located in the building with the Kokomo Sports Center. It's easily accessible by the public and some of the equipment and services of the Sports Center may be utilized in the therapy process.

Howard Community Hospital and Saint Joseph Hospital and Health Center entered a collaborative effort to bring a fixed Magnetic Resonance Imaging Center to Kokomo to provide patients access to one of the most effective new technologies at the lowest possible cost. The center opened in October of 1993.

Howard Community Hospital "exists to provide general and specialty health services which promote and restore good health in a setting dedicated to the dignity of each individual and the highest standards of care." With that mission leading the way, Howard Community Hospital is looking to continue to grow and care for its community well into the future as a vital part of the community it serves.

Howard Community Hospital humble beginnings in 1961.

Howard Community Hospital in 1994.

KOKOMO HOWARD COUNTY PUBLIC LIBRARY

When the legislature established Howard County in 1844, the State Constitution of 1816, article 9, section 5, mandated that ten percent of the proceeds from the sale of lots in the county seat be reserved for a public library.

In 1850, when Kokomo's population was 378 and the county's population was 6,657, Corydon Richmond, Kokomo's first physician and second mayor, with Reverend William Dale and N.R. Linsday purchased $99.57 worth of books in Cincinnati, Ohio, for the Howard County Public Library. Mud roads and a rural population, however, kept library patrons and library books apart. This statewide condition brought about the passage of the 1852 School Law which called for local schools and township libraries.

In 1854, therefore, the Howard County Commissioners divided the county into six districts to be served by township libraries. District One, Clay and Harrison Townships; District Two, Ervin and Monroe Townships; District Three, Center Township; District Four, Taylor and Howard Townships; District Five, Liberty and Jackson Townships; and District Six, Union Township. This network made library books more accessible, but when the state withdrew its funding, the system dried up.

Then in 1883, an amendment to the library law of 1881 permitted school boards in towns under 10,000 population to establish libraries supported by local tax.

Two years later the Kokomo Public Library was born on December 25, 1885, in the Normal Building of Kokomo High School. It stood on the northwest corner of Superior Street and Apperson Way, now a parking lot for Kokomo High School downtown campus. Joshua Clinton Leach, a 27-year-old English grammar teacher, became Kokomo's First Public Librarian from 1885 to 1898.

Olive Moreland, a Leach assistant, succeeded him in 1898, and with Belle Sherfy Hanna converted the book collection from the Perkins classification system to the revolutionary Dewey System it remains to this day.

In the spring of 1900, a small but mighty librarian from the State Library in Indianapolis took over, Eva M. Fitzgerald. She shamed the school board into seeking funds from Andrew Carnegie for a building to house the library which had to move four times into different rooms around town. Carnegie gave $25,000 and the Carnegie Building opened on January 30, 1905. It endeared itself to thousands of Kokomo residents until the wrecking ball demolished it in November of 1965, bringing tears to many.

During the years in the Carnegie Building, different head librarians served. Edith Trimble of Terre Haute and a member of the first graduating class of Indiana's library school served from 1906 to 1910. Isabelle Ford, a local young woman whose mother, Emma Alice Ford, became Howard County's first automobile accident fatality, was librarian from 1910 to 1917. Dana Hollingsworth Sollenberger, from 1917 to 1935, became the first head librarian to have been born in Howard County, and the first married woman to head the library. She took the library through World War I and through the Great Depression when light bulbs were of such low wattage that books were searched for on the shelves with flashlights. From Marion, Indiana came a University of Michigan graduate, Susan Erlewine, to resurrect the library from the poverty of the Depression. She later married Harry R. Fawcett. She served from 1935 to 1941. Finally, the last librarian to begin and end her year of service in the Carnegie Building was Kokomo High School Librarian, Aileen Scott Weiland. During her years, 1941 to 1957, she began pursuing county wide library service. Before she retired, she installed at curbside a gray metal box with bold black letters which read, "Auto-Page Drive-Up Book Return."

In 1957, the 52-year-old Carnegie Building was literally bulging and crumbling at its seams. A young librarian, Philip T. Hamilton, the son of two librarians, came to Kokomo. At first, plans were to add to the Carnegie Building, but as the foundation was dug for the addition, the north wall of the Carnegie began to move precariously causing the building to be closed and condemned. Hamilton built the present library building, updated library service, reached out with bookmobile service and a branch library, and pursued county-wide library service making Kokomo Public Library the Kokomo Howard County Public Library. He resigned in 1981.

Charles N. Joray came from the directorship of the Bluffton-Wells County (IN) Public Library to succeed Hamilton on January 11, 1982. His first official act was to close the library because mountains of snow and a temperature of 18 degrees below zero numbed and stalled the city and county. He added the Russiaville Branch, remodeled the main building making a room for genealogy and local history, and in 1994, he discarded the library's card catalog.

An automated system brought the Kokomo Howard County Public Library into the Twenty-first Century, when Howard County was 150 years old.

Carnegie Public Library from 1905 – 1965.

Kokomo Howard County Public Library from 1967 – Present.

KOKOMO RENTAL & SALES CO., INC.

Kokomo Rental & Sales Company Inc. was founded in late fall of 1946 by Jack Ashenfelter and his wife Viola in a 100 year old house at 915 North Washington. They started with $800.00, a handful of equipment, tools, and some scaffolding. Since Jack was a full time sales representative for Bil-Jax Scaffold Co., Viola ran the business during the week and he took his turns on the weekends.

In November of 1957, Jack's son Duaine L. (Bucky) Ashenfelter joined the firm and commuted to and from Swanton, Ohio until he moved his family to Kokomo in September of 1958.

In the early sixties the business was expanded to include party and hospital equipment. The site chosen was Sheen's Restaurant, now the home of the Nearly New Shop on Deffenbaugh Street. The party division continued to grow and was eventually moved to North Washington Street, now the site of Holder Mattress.

In 1967 Jack died, unexpectedly, and Bucky assumed all management responsibilities. Since traffic was beginning to become a problem at the Rental, it was decided in 1972 to move the tool division to 1915 E. North Street in the new Kokomo Industrial Park. In the spring of the same year, Bucky's daughter, Linda, was asked to join the firm for a new Kokomo Janitor Supply Division, which was later sold to accommodate the growing tool rental. She continued with Kokomo Janitor Supply and Bucky asked his wife, Betty, to join the firm to help manage. In the meantime, Viola decided to retire, and Betty brought the party division to the North Street address.

On May 25, 1989, Kokomo Rental was struck by lightning and burned to the ground. The only things salvaged were a modular classroom, the equipment out on rental and the accounts receivable. Not great but not hopeless. The classroom and the eleven semi trailers which had been used to store scaffold served until a new building could be finished. All new equipment was purchased and not one payroll was missed due to the Ashenfelters' perseverance and their loyalty to their employees.

In January of 1992, Bucky and Betty's daughter, Linda, was asked to return to the family business to assume the management duties and help expand and computerize. The Ashenfelters have retired from the rental business; however, Bucky is still an active sales representative for Bil-Jax and they both still consult from time to time. Linda is presently carrying on the tradition of family owned business dedicated to quality equipment and customer service.

KOKOMO TRIBUNE
TRIBUNE Has Been Serving Community 144 Years

August 17, 1993, the Kokomo Tribune began a new era of serving readers in central Indiana. That day, Jim Langschied, news editor, with the help of Linda Margison, special projects editor, and Tim Bath, assistant photo editor, paginated page one of the Kokomo Tribune.

Pagination allows news editors and other staff members to design pages of the newspaper on a computer screen. Cutting, pasting, copying and deleting of copy are done on a computer screen instead of on a board in a composing room. Photographs, graphics and illustrations also are imported onto pages using the new system.

Planning for pagination actually began in the fall of 1992 when the Tribune installed a new computer system for news and classified advertising departments.

The pagination system was developed by CText Inc. of Ann Arbor, Mich., using electronic publishing software from Quark Inc. Similar systems, using separate software, are used to produce the Tribune's classified and display advertisements.

Pagination was just another step forward for the Tribune, which made its first appearance in the Kokomo community on Oct. 30, 1850, when The Howard Tribune, a weekly newspaper, was first published for a handful of readers. With only two brief gaps, a newspaper bearing the name Tribune has been published since in the community.

Although the first Tribune appeared in 1850, its forerunner, The Pioneer, was published in New London, Ind., in 1848. It was a weekly newspaper and the first newspaper published in Howard County.

In 1850 its equipment and press were sold to John Bohan and Charles Ashley, who moved the operation to Kokomo. They published the first copy of The Howard Tribune from a log building known as "the old deadfall" on the northeast corner of Main and Superior Streets. After a few months, they moved to a building on West Walnut Street, on the north side of the square, where Johnson Title Co. is housed today.

At the time the Tribune was moved, its equipment included a crude hand press, a few cases of type, two or three makeup stones and a small assortment of tools. They value of everything connected with the paper was about $600.

The paper was published for about a year with Charles D. Murray as its editor. Economic circumstances in 1851 caused a temporary suspension.

In 1852, the paper was bought by C.P. Hensley of Logansport. He became the publisher and editor and got the paper out regularly until 1856, when he sold it to T.C. Philips, Hiram Newlin and J.H. Young. Philips bought out his partners in 1857.

Until his death in 1878, Philips was the Tribune. He brought the paper up from an obscure and inconsequential beginning to one of the best county seat newspapers in the state.

The paper was published on Walnut Street for a few years, then was moved to the northeast corner of Main and Sycamore Streets.

In 1862, a tornado overturned an adjacent three-story brick building which was under construction, onto the Tribune building, demolishing the smaller structure. The Tribune's equipment was ruined and salvage from it did not exceed $50.

Asking that 1,000 subscribers advance a year's subscription (1.50), Philips quickly obtained enough money to purchase new equipment. He installed it on the second floor of a frame building on the east side of the courthouse square, owned by J.M. Leeds. The building was where the S.S. Kresge Co. store once stood. A law firm now occupies part of the building.

For a brief period, the Tribune was in the hands of Col. N.P. Richmond and S.T. Montgomery. December 20, 1866, Col. Richmond took over the paper as editor, but only for a week. Montgomery assumed the duties of editor and publisher for about a year, then Philips again took over the editing.

In 1869, the Tribune moved into a building of its own on the southwest corner of Mulberry and Buckeye streets (now a parking lot). The paper had its home there for 23 years. It was known as the Tribune Block.

In 1892, the paper moved to the southwest corner of Walnut and Union Streets (now a parking lot). It was published there for more than 26 years when it moved to its present home on the northeast corner of Mulberry and Union streets. The first paper from the present building was issued Jan. 6, 1919.

After the death of Philips in 1868, his sons, A.F. and C.H. Philips, took control and operated as a partnership until 1881, when C.H. died. A.F. continued alone until 1883, when his younger brother, W.R., joined him under the firm name of A.F. and W.R. Philips.

In 1884 The Kokomo Gazette, owned by L.C. Hoss, was merged with the Tribune and published under the name Kokomo Gazette-Tribune until 1893. Then the Gazette portion of the name was dropped.

A.F. Philips sold his interest in 1885 to P.E. Hoss, son of L.C. Hoss. In 1885, B.B. Johnson purchased the senior Hoss's interest. The partnership of Hoss and Johnson lasted until 1886, when P.E. sold out to his partner. Johnson ran the paper until 1887, when he sold it to John A. Kautz and H.E. McMonigal. In 1897, Kautz bought out his partner.

During Kautz's ownership, Ed M. Souder directed the news operation. He survived Kautz by nine years, and continued as editor until his death in 1947. He was succeeded as editor by Dow Richardson. In 1970 John R. Barkley succeeded Richardson as editor. Bruce VanDusen became editor in 1978. The present editor, John C. Wiles, took over in 1981.

After Kautz's death in 1938, the Tribune was operated for ten years under a trusteeship with his widow, Blanche Kautz, and one of his three daughters, Mrs. Kent H. Blacklidge, as trustees. The general manager was Richard H. Blacklidge.

In 1948, after the closing of the trust, a partnership named The Kokomo Tribune was formed. Partners included: Richard H. Blacklidge; Cordelia Mayfield; Mrs. Robert J. Hamp Sr.; Robert Hamp Jr.; Elizabeth Newell; Juliana Mehlig; Dr. Arthur Hamp Jr.; Marian Nixon; David Hamp; Mrs. Lyell Doucet; Mrs. A.L. Williams; Mrs. Eugenia Fulkerson; Joan Nixon; Don Nixon and Joseph Nixon Jr.

In 1956, Richard H. Blacklidge was named publisher. He played a major role in the transition of the Tribune's production from the laborious methods of hot-lead typesetting to the sophisticated technologies of coldtype, photo-offset operations.

A sparkling new Tribune produced by the newer method made its debut on Sept. 7, 1967. The printing of that edition culminated many long hours of equipment changes and retraining, as the Tribune moved into the coldtype offset era. The center of the newer methods was the 48-page Goss Metro-Offset Press, only the second to be installed in the world.

In 1970, the Tribune opened a bureau office in Tipton, Ind. The paper opened a bureau office in Peru, Ind., in 1992. News stories are transmitted electronically to the Tribune's office in Kokomo.

In 1978, R.H. Blacklidge retired. His son, Kent H. Blacklidge, was named as his successor.

In 1981, Thomson Newspapers Inc. purchased the Kokomo Tribune. In September of that year, Kent H. Blacklidge resigned, and Richard D. Isham, general manager of the Tribune since 1976, was named publisher. In 1982, Isham left, and Gregory J. Ptacin, publisher of the Mining Journal in Marquette, Mich., was named publisher.

In 1983, Arden A. Draeger, publisher of the Herald-Times Reporter in Manitowoc, Wis., replaced Ptacin. Draeger continues to lead the Tribune today.

MARTIN BROS. SERVICE

In 1935 Eugene V. "Red" Martin took over a service station from his father-in-law, Chester Waddell. The business was very successful. William A. "Bill" Martin, moved back to Russiaville and went to work for Red; Bill's WWII draft number was 21 in Howard County. He worked for Red until he took his physical in November of 1943 and left for the Army thirty days later. When he left he told his brother that he wanted to go into the TV and appliances business when he came home. Bill was captured by the Germans in November of 1944 and spent seven months in a prison camp.

One evening a stranger came into the service station and purchased some gasoline. Before he left he asked Red if he knew of anyone who would like to go into the appliance business. Red quickly replied, "My brothers and I."

A week later a contract was signed to sell Hotpoint Appliances. Bill came home November 3, 1945, and another brother Carl came home from the Air Force December 3, 1945. "Martin Bros. Service" was formed.

In 1947 the business moved from the west edge of town to the present location, with a service station and a hardware and appliance store. The television line was added in 1949.

The business was destroyed in the Palm Sunday tornado, April 11, 1965. Business continued and we rebuilt the store without the service station.

Carl passed away in 1970, and Red and Bill continued the Martin Bros. business until the latter part of 1986 when Red and Bill decided that to better serve their customers, they would form two separate stores. Red and his son Max would take the hardware store and Bill and his son Bill, Jr. would have the appliance and television store.

William, Eugene and Carl.

MARTIN BROTHERS TV AND APPLIANCE

Martin Brothers TV and Appliance continues to serve Central Indiana from our store in Russiaville, which has 5000 square feet of sales area and 3200 square feet of warehouse. Today we still sell Hotpoint appliances and have added GE, Jenn-Aire, Crosley, Insinkerator, and Maytag appliances, in addition to Zenith and RCA television products.

Janet (Martin) Miller, daughter of Bill, Sr., is in charge of the office. We have three full-time employees to help with sales and delivery.

Martin Brothers TV and Appliance plans to serve the area for years to come with the help of Derrick, 13, the son of Bill, Jr. We hope that Derrick will choose to continue the Martin family tradition in Howard County.

MARTINS HARDWARE AND AUTOMOTIVE

Red and youngest son Max continued the hardware business with the help of Ed Martin and Anita (Martin) Kanable, two other children of Red's. Martins Hardware offered a complete line of True Value Hardware paints, plumbing supplies and water conditioning equipment from the 5000 square feet sales floor and 2400 square feet warehouse.

In the summer of 1988 it was decided to expand the business to include automotive parts. After several phone conversations and meetings, NAPA Auto Parts was selected and became a part of Martins Hardware. On November 17, 1988, the store received the first shipment of auto parts. The store became Martins Hardware and Automotive on November 18.

Since Red passed away (July 1990), Max, Anita and Ed still continue with the business at 175 E. Main Street in Russiaville. They have one full-time and three part-time employees.

With the possibility of passing the business to Max's son Cory, now 10, Martins Hardware and Automotive plans to be a part of Russiaville for a long time.

PSI ENERGY, INC.

PSI Energy, Inc., located at 1619 West Deffenbaugh, is significant because of its contribution to the economic development of Howard County, through the formation of a local utility company, which influenced trade, transportation, and the lifestyle of the public.

PSI's roots in Kokomo can be traced back to 1902 when the Kokomo, Marion and Western Traction Company was incorporated to build from Marion west along the Toledo, St. Louis and Western Railroad. It built from Kokomo to Greentown (9 miles) in 1903, but like many interurbans, was unable to make further progress until the second building boom. In 1905 it reached Marion (18 additional miles). In 1911 it organized a subsidiary, the Kokomo Frankfort and Western Traction Company to build to Frankfort. This extension (26 miles) was opened in 1912.

In 1912 the two interurbans merged to form Indiana Railways and Light Company. The line operated the whole system which included interurbans, streetcars, electric power and steam heat to various downtown businesses. In 1922 it became the Northern Indiana Power Company. The line was handicapped by running at right angles to the dominant pattern of interurbans radiating from Indianapolis. The entire interurban was troubled by the severe curves in cities that prevented railroad interchange except for very short distances.

In 1924 Northern Indiana Power Company was purchased by Samuel Insull, a personal secretary and working associate of Thomas Edison and an electrical engineering genius and a believer in consolidation of utilities. Northern Indiana Power Company consolidated with Interstate Public Service Co. which was organized in 1912 as an operating unit of Midland United-Midwest Utilities System. The Midland United-Midwest Utilities System was by far the most important of the holding companies in which the interurbans played a major role. This system was developed primarily by Samuel Insull, aided by the investment banking firm of Halsey, Stuart and Co. The company, based in Chicago, centered its attention on the Midwest, although it included properties in New England and elsewhere. Originally the company was primarily concerned with power companies and confined its interurban properties largely to a few power company affiliates.

In spite of its limitations, the interstate was among the most successful interurbans. It developed an extensive business that proved more profitable than the rail operations. In 1931 it was reorganized as the Public Service Company of Indiana, and its rail lines were thereafter operated by the Indiana Railroad.

Write-offs and losses from interurban operations topped $24 million between 1933 and 1941, which wiped out all of the common equity capital. No dividends were paid from 1933 until reorganization of the company in 1941. Obviously, the company was in deep trouble. The situation looked almost hopeless when in 1937 Robert A. Gallagher arrived on the corporate scene. He had been dispatched by Chicago bankers to see about arranging foreclosure and dispensing of the ailing properties.

But Mr. Gallagher saw what wasn't apparent on the red-inked financial statements. The basic electric utility system of the company was sound and had a good potential. He joined the company as vice president and in 1938 was elected president. On September 6, 1941 a consolidation took place aiming to bring stability to five companies. They were Public Service Company of Indiana, Central Indiana Power Company, Northern Indiana Power Company, Terre Haute Electric Company and Dresser Power Corporation. The resulting corporation, Public Service Company of Indiana, Inc., was a full-blown, major league utility. It represented the culmination of decades of consolidation of utilities throughout the service area. And it was a vast system.

It provided electricity, gas or water in nearly 600 areas in 69 counties, serving more than 225,000 customers. Its boundaries were Terre Haute and Vincennes on the west to Kokomo and Huntington on the north; from Jeffersonville and New Albany on the south to Castle, Connersville and Shelbyville to the east.

In 1945 gas and water properties were spun off into a separate company called Indiana Gas & Water Co., and the ice plants were sold to a non-affiliated interest. PSI became an all-electric utility.

In 1959 new offices were being built at 1619 West Deffenbaugh to house Kokomo's engineering and operations departments. In 1960 those offices were moved from a building across from Continental Steel Corp. In 1974 the customer service office was moved from an office on the northeast corner of Taylor and Main Streets to 1801 S. Park Road.

In 1990 Public Service Company of Indiana was renamed PSI Energy, Inc. as it is known today. PSI Energy remains as it has through its history, beginning with Kokomo, Marion and Western Traction Company - the lifeblood of society, with the public and private sectors relying more and more heavily upon the utility with each new invention and technological advancement.

SAINT JOSEPH HOSPITAL & HEALTH CENTER

The 80 year history of the health care ministry of the Sisters of Saint Joseph of Tipton, Indiana, at times reads like a Steinbeck novel. It chronicles the fight against prejudice and the triumph of hope over despair. It unfolds through a period of social and economic change in a midwestern community which was itself evolving into the automotive age. And, as it recounts this rich history, the singular lesson that emerges is that the ministry will survive only if its mission is embraced and preserved by those that are served and those that serve.

Originally called to Indiana to begin an educational ministry, the Sisters of Saint Joseph of Tipton were approached by Dr. Edgar Cox from Kokomo in 1913 and asked to respond to a desperate health care need in that community by starting a hospital. Thus began the health care ministry, in an unpretentious one and one half story converted homestead. It was called *Good Samaritan Hospital* and accommodated 12 patients. In 1923, amid a growing national tide of racial and religious prejudice, Kokomo was the site of a national rally of the Ku Klux Klan. In the book, *The Aspirin Age,* the author describes a Klan march through the center of Kokomo during which people threw money into an outstretched American flag. The funds were to be used to build a new hospital so that the citizens would not have to "suffer the indignity of being born and dying in a Catholic hospital." The "Klan" hospital was built in 1924 and called a "County Hospital," but was closed just four years after it opened due to financial failure. In 1935, the Sisters of Saint Joseph, having outgrown the *Good Samaritan Hospital,* purchased the vacated "County Hospital," which was renamed *Saint Joseph Memorial Hospital.* Ironically, the purchase was made possible largely through a bequest from a former Good Samaritan patient, Henry Fisse, Jr., who had been turned away from the "County Hospital" because he was thought to be penniless.

Since 1936, the Sisters of Saint Joseph have continued to provide the oversight and sense of mission which have made it possible for the hospital to grow and expand to meet the ever increasing needs of the community. The hospital has gone through many buildings additions, renovations, and in recent years, a name change to become *Saint Joseph Hospital & Health Center.* Each addition or expanded service has been in response to the mission of the Sisters to deliver high quality health care in an environment which recognized the dignity of the individual human person.

Today, *Saint Joseph Hospital & Health Center* is a 220 bed acute care facility which provides general medical, surgical, and emergency services. Over the years new programs and services have been offered to meet the health care needs of the community. Some of the expanded services include an adult and adolescent chemical dependency program, a stress unit, a home health care program, a skilled nursing unit, and a day care center for hospital associates. *Saint Joseph Hospital* has pioneered selected tertiary services such as renal dialysis and cardiac catherization by entering into joint ventures with St. Vincent Hospital and the Indiana Heart Institute, respectively. *Saint Joseph Hospital* is also proud of its other joint ventures with local hospitals to avoid duplication of services. Recent joint ventures include free-standing MRI and laundry facilities. *Saint Joseph Hospital* also offers a comprehensive regional cancer program which is one of the fifth most active programs in the state. Like the early Sisters who moved to Kokomo to provide nursing care where it did not exist, the staff at *Saint Joseph Hospital & Health Center* is committed to reaching out to the community to meet the current unmet needs.

SOCIETY NATIONAL BANK

The name Union Bank and Trust originated from the union of banks which had failed during the Depression. When Union Bank opened for business on June 30, 1930, there were thirteen employees and assets of $1,300,000. When opened, the only office of the bank was located at the southeast corner of Main and Sycamore, in the building which was formerly the office of the Farmers Trust and Savings Bank, currently Palmer's Jewelry Store. The second location served as the Main Office for thirty-nine years (1939-78). This building, which was located on the southeast corner of Main and Mulberry, was completed in 1915 and was originally the office of the Citizens National Bank. The employees of the bank transported its cash, furniture and records of the bank to the second building in a Model T Ford truck owned by Forest Zehring, an employee who retired from the bank in 1972. The only item that required extra assistance when being moved from the first main office building was the vault door.

For many years, the bank occupied only the basement of the building, with the remaining space being used as offices for professional and business enterprises. During the 60's, many businesses left the downtown area of Kokomo, and the bank began expanding to the other floors of the six-story building. The growth of the bank and the movement of businesses out of the downtown area, necessitated the expansion of the bank in the form of additional branch offices. In May 1950, the bank opened its first branch on Markland Avenue (1950-82).

In order to better serve the community, a seven-year expansion program began in 1978 with the opening of the new Main Office Plaza, which is the location used today. In the June, 1986 edition of *The Indianapolis Business Journal,* Union Bank & Trust Co. was named the 24th largest bank in Indiana, ranked by total assets of $287,300,000. On August 29, 1986, Union Bank & Trust purchased the State Bank of Greentown, which operated as the Greentown Financial Center until the merger with Ameritrust Corporation. The branch system has continued to grow, and on November 24, 1986, the Union Bank & Trust Company joined the Ameritrust Corporation, headquartered in Cleveland, Ohio.

Ameritrust Corporation was founded on September 20, 1894, under the name of Cleveland Trust Company with J.G. Cowels as its first president and $500,000 in capital. The company opened its doors a year later with four employees transacting the business in an office 12 feet wide by 26 feet long. In 1908, the Main Office was moved to the Rotunda Bank at the corner of Euclid and East 9th Street in Cleveland, Ohio. This national landmark is one of the most elegant and most visited structures in Cleveland. Cleveland Trust Company was one of the few banks that stayed open during the Great Depression to assure their customers the opportunity to access their deposits. In June, 1974, Cleveland Trust Company reorganized as CleveTrust Corp. and adopted the Ameritrust name in 1979. Union Bank began working under the name of Ameritrust Bank, Howard County on July 20, 1989.

On March 31, 1991, Ameritrust Corporation merged with Society Bank Corporation also from Cleveland. Society for Savings, founded by Samuel H. Mather and a group of prominent Cleveland businessmen, opened for business in a one-room office in the rear of the Merchants Bank in 1849. In 1867, Society constructed a three-story building on the corner of Public Square. Then, in 1898 on the same tract of land, the first skyscraper in Cleveland was built which was ten stories high.

In the mid-1950's, Society National Bank was formed as a companion institution to Society for Savings. Later that decade, Society was the first commercial bank in the United States to use the on-line teller terminal, one of the decade's most modern and sophisticated electronic data systems.

Following the 1958 merger of Society for Savings and Society National Bank, Society Corporation was created and became the first entity in Ohio formed under the 1956 Federal Bank Holding Company Act. Over the years, Society Corporation has had substantial mergers and acquisitions which gives them very strong presence in northwestern Ohio, southcentral Michigan and northern and central Indiana. On October 21, 1991, Ameritrust Bank, Howard County changed its name to Society National Bank, Indiana. When this merger was complete, Society became the 26th largest commercial banking organization in the nation with more than $25 billion in assets and more than $1.7 billion in equity capital. With more than 400 offices throughout Indiana, Ohio and Michigan, Society Corporation is a key leader in the financial industry of the Midwest.

Society's mission is to produce a superior return to shareholders, to safeguard depositors, to provide quality financial services to its markets, and to attract and retain quality employees dedicated to the performance of their duties in a highly ethical fashion.

Society National Bank lobby in 1921.

STOUT AND SON, INC.

For five generations, Stouts have sold furniture and provided personal funeral services in the western Howard County town of Russiaville. The business was started by a furniture maker by the name of Albert Stout in 1890. He began making caskets in addition to furniture in 1920. Albert then passed the business to his son Wallace. Wallace did not make the furniture like his father, but he did buy and sell it in addition to providing funeral services. In 1937 a block fire destroyed everything. Wallace rebuilt the store in downtown Russiaville on Main Street. When he retired in 1950, Wallace passed the business to his two sons A.B. and Kennard Stout. Again the store was destroyed. It was flattened by the Palm Sunday tornado of 1965. A.B., who was in his 60's at the time, did not want to rebuild. His younger brother Kennard, at the age of 50, went into debt to see the family name live on the through the furniture store and funeral home. He rebuilt the building at the current address of 200 E. Main Street. Kennard provided the store with many firsts. He was the first emergency medical technician in Howard County, because at that time the funeral director provided ambulance services for Russiaville. He also became the first person in Howard County to install wall-to-wall stretch carpeting. Kennard's son Denny worked in the store for about ten years before leaving to pursue a different career. The family chain was not to be broken, though, because Kennard's grandson Jeff Stout had taken an interest in the business. Jeff says that he had known that he wanted to be a funeral director since he was 12 years old. To accomplish this, he finished a year of general college. Jeff got married in June 1985, and he and his wife Bethanne then set out for a year of mortuary school together. After passing the first portion of the state test, they apprenticed for one year with Kennard. They passed a second part of the state test and both became licensed funeral directors. Kennard was not the only Stout man to achieve a first. In January 1991 a freak car accident claimed the life of Mike McKibben, Howard County coroner. At that time Jeff had been serving under Mike as a deputy coroner. Jeff was then appointed by the Republican Committee to serve out the end of that term, proving to be the youngest Coroner in the State of Indiana at age 26. Jeff was then elected to the position of Howard County Coroner in 1992. Kennard's other son, David, had recently joined the business as Jeff's helper since opting for an early retirement from Delco Electronics. Although the ownership has changed, the funeral home and the furniture store have changed little. The furniture store has always sold traditional style furniture of the best quality at a good price. The funeral home has always provided a more personal service. Jeff hopes that one of his children will take over the business. Even so, it will be a while before the business changes hands again. He has two daughters, Megan 6 and Morgan 4 and a son appropriately named Jeffrey Kennard Stout, who is only 2 years old.

ARMSTRONG – LANDON COMPANY, INC.

The Kokomo company of The Armstrong-Landon Company, Inc. had its beginnings in the 1855 hardware business of the Armstrong brothers, A.F. and Dr. Horace Armstrong and partner, Dr. J.A. James. The Armstrong partnership changed during its early years, thus the company's name also changed: in 1867, it was known as Armstrong, Beeson and Company; in 1869 or 1870, Armstrong Nixon & Company; in 1874, George Landon and Nathan Pickett joined the company under the firm name Armstrong Pickett & Co., and 1875, began construction of a building at the southeast corner of the courthouse square. During this time, the brothers E.S. and Henry Hunt were building lumber mill operations in the county, later developing a lumber yard and sash and door factory at 318 East Monroe Street. In 1882, E.S. took control of the lumber yard and his brother took the lumber mill. In 1883, E.S. Hunt merged his lumber yard with the Armstrong, Pickett Co. and the new, expanded operation was known as the Armstrong, Landon & Hunt Co.

The Armstrong and Landon families' interest continued through the 1940's, but the death of George Landon's son, Hugh McK. Landon, prompted the sale of stock to the Harry L. Moulder family and others. The Moulder family has continued to own and manage the operations now known as The Armstrong-Landon Company, Inc. H.L. Moulder and sons Thomas P. and Harry L., Jr. managed the company through the growth of the next few decades. The look of the current facility has changed greatly in the past decade, but not the service and commitment to the community. The mill expansions of the 1980's under the direction of the corporation president, John C. Moulder, and vice-president, Christopher L. Riesen, have resulted in the addition of a door assembly operation, stain finishing shop and an enlarged mill operation. The Armstrong-Landon Company has a long history of growth with Kokomo and the surrounding counties, and is pleased to be the second oldest continuously operated business in the county.

Armstrong-Landon Company, Inc.

CARL E. GREENO INSURANCE AGENCY

Carl E. Greeno was born and raised in Frankfort, Indiana, and graduated in 1956. He moved to Kokomo with his wife Patty and their three children in 1962 to go to work for the Colonial Baking Company. He won Salesman of the Year for the state of Indiana in 1964. He then started in the insurance business in 1966. He was with Commonwealth Life Insurance as a debit agent for five years where he won several sales awards and was Agent of the Year in 1969.

In 1971 Carl became associated with American Family Insurance of Wisconsin, and won several sales awards with them becoming Salesman of the Year in 1973. His wife Patty then became the first female agent for American Family in that same year. They operated their office at 215 W. Foster for ten years. In 1981 they became independent agents.

In 1983 they purchased the old service station at their present location, 600 E. Markland. After some extensive remodeling, they moved into this exceptionally exquisite office building in January 1985.

They have continued to grow, and Joe Fivecoate joined the agency in 1981. In 1985 the agency became a family business when son Kent joined the sales force after serving four years in the Marine Corps. The agency has continued to grow, and son Carl Greeno Jr. joined the agency in 1990.

Currently Greeno Insurance serves over 3,000 individuals and families and the insurance needs of 400 business concerns in Kokomo and Howard County. They now have a staff of seven agents and continue to grow.

Their office includes a state of the art computer system for record keeping. In addition, they have a special rating computer so that instant rate comparisons can be made of the country's finest insurance companies.

Carl E. Greeno Agency (l. to r.) Kent Greeno, Denese Johnson, Patty Greeno, Carl Greeno, Carl Greeno, Jr., Joe Fivecoate, and Angie Fivecoate.

DELCO ELECTRONICS

For more than half a century, Delco Electronics Corporation has supplied automotive electronics products to the automotive industry.

The Kokomo, Indiana–based company offers customers a full line of automotive electronics products — everything from steering-wheel-mounted air and radio controls, to an audio system with designed-in sound incorporating as many as eight computer-positioned speakers, to the Head-Up Display that projects vehicle speed and turn signal indictors up through the windshield, to an array of electronics under the hood that increase fuel economy and lower emissions.

Delco Electronics is a global company with 28,000 employees. Its products are designed, tested and manufactured in 12 countries, ranging from Singapore to Mexico to Luxembourg.

Delco Electronics was a division of General Motors prior to 1985. In that year, GM purchased Hughes Aircraft Co., made Delco Electronics a corporation and formed GM Hughes Electronics Corporation (GMHE).

GMHE's mission is to accelerate the application of advanced electronic systems and components in GM's products and plants; to lead in the design, manufacture and marketing of high-technology electronic products for worldwide automotive, defense and space applications; and to create entirely new business ventures.

Because of its long association as a supplier to the world's largest company—GM—Delco Electronics has brought high-volume manufacturing to new levels of sophistication and quality. Each day, Delco Electronics employees build more than 41,000 pressure sensors; 20,000 instrument clusters; 22,000 radios; and 30,000 engine control modules.

In addition to its product production, Delco Electronics also is a world leader in the design and manufacture of complex custom integrated circuits (ICs) for specific automotive applications. By providing about 40 percent of its own IC component needs, Delco Electronics ranks as the fourth largest in-house manufacturer of custom ICs in the United States.

With revenues in 1993 of nearly $4.5 billion, Delco Electronics continues a heritage as a major player in the automotive electronics marketplace that stretches back to 1936, when the newly formed Delco Radio Division of General Motors began assembling car radios by hand in Kokomo. Each decade since has brought technological innovation, pioneering manufacturing techniques and financial success.

Delco Electronics continues to build on this half-century tradition of innovation and development. One of the largest, most sophisticated manufacturers of automotive electronics in the world, Delco Electronics' strong, technically-oriented human resource base, its high-tech manufacturing and research facilities and its high quality of work life allow it to continue as a global presence and maintain its competitive edge into the 21st century.

Delco Electronics

FIRST FEDERAL SAVINGS BANK

First Federal Savings Bank of Kokomo, 200 West Mulberry, began operation as First Federal Savings and Loan Association of Kokomo, formed by local citizens in March 1934, promoting thrift and home ownership.

Founding President was J.E. Frederick. Asset size was $29,146. During his tenure, the association relocated from 109 East Sycamore to 113 West Mulberry, then to 107 North Buckeye.

In 1943, President Glen R. Hillis assumed an active role financing home purchases by World War II veterans. By 1951, assets reached $6,123,592, resulting in relocation to the Kokomo Dispatch Building, 200 West Mulberry.

Herbert E. Williams was named President in 1954. During his term, First Federal recognized unprecedented growth. The Dispatch Building was razed and a new building erected. In March 1960, with assets of $17,304,535, First Federal moved into its current building. In 1976, the first branch opened at Southway and Lafountain.

In 1977, Fred W. McClung was named President. Growth meant renovation downtown, adding two drive-up windows. July 1978, the Greentown Branch opened at 520 West Main.

Current President, Robert J. Heltzel, was elected in 1983. Celebrating 50 years in March 1984, assets totaled $134,939,584. April 1987, the Forest Park Branch opened at 2201 West Jefferson. July 1987, the association changed its name to First Federal Savings Bank of Kokomo. Going public July 1991, Central Indiana Bancorp, parent company of First Federal, sold 80 percent of its stock to Howard County residents. In January 1994, a merger with First Federal Savings and Loan Association of Peru, 2 North Broadway, created combined assets of $243,097,863.

Progressing from passbook savings and home mortgages, First Federal now offers checking, CD's, IRA's, money markets, annuities, commercial and consumer loans, ATM's direct deposits, tax deposits and payments, and numerous mortgage programs.

Old fashioned banking has gone by the wayside. However, First Federal Savings Bank of Kokomo remains true to its underlying purpose: making home ownership possible by innovative, creative financing and providing customers a safe and profitable depository institution.

The razing of the Kokomo Dispatch Building

First Federal Savings & Loan Association on N. Buckeye.

JOHNSON-WERT TITLE COMPANY

ESTABLISHED 1877

PHILLIP B. WERT
PRESIDENT

JOHNSON-WERT TITLE COMPANY

Johnson-Wert Title Company, 110 West Walnut Street, is celebrating its 117th year in business. The company was founded in 1877 by J.D. Johnson. Johnson had worked for Howard County Abstract Office and upon acquiring the company changed the name to *The Johnson Abstract Company.* Following his death in April 1909, his wife operated the business.

Later Dr. J.R. Morgan, a dentist and brother-in-law of Johnson, acquired the business. Morgan died in 1933. The next owner and operator was Mina Tharp, who worked in the Howard County Recorder's Office in 1900 and then joined Johnson in 1902. She operated the business until 1949. Ownership was then assumed by her daughter, Miriam Tharp Blake, who ran the company until June of 1969.

She then sold the company to a couple of abstractors who hired Phillip B. Wert to manage the company. He managed Johnson Abstract Company from 1969, acquiring the company January 1, 1985.

During his tenure the office records and systems have been modified to the level that its operation is considered to be among the best in the state.

Wert's son Andrew recently graduated from Manchester College, achieving a Bachelor of Science Degree with majors in both Business Administration and Computer Science. Wert says that the blend of these majors will work into the future growth of Johnson-Wert Title Company.

Wert said that he felt it was time to add his name to the company because it is known by its customer groups that he is the owner and that "obviously Mr. Johnson is not 117 years old."

Johnson-Wert Title Company's mission is to provide title insurance services to the Howard County real estate community with the highest levels of quality, professionalism, and timeliness possible.

To do so the company maintains a title plant which is a geographic system of maintaining records that refer to real estate. Johnson-Wert's title plant has records from the founding of Howard County in 1844 to the present which totals into the millions and is the most complete in Howard County.

PALMER'S JEWELRY

A family jewelry business that began in Europe and migrated to America with the arrival of Uncle Sol Freed to Marion, Ohio, at the beginning of this century is being carried on by two generations of Freeds in Kokomo, Indiana.

Robert Freed had worked with his uncle in Ohio prior to World War II. After serving 42 months in the U.S. Army Quartermaster Corps — 30 months overseas in Africa and Europe—Robert was released as a lieutenant with many honors. He met and married Frances Congress in Fairmont, W. Va., and the young couple purchased Palmer's Jewelry from Palmer Gevirtz two years after the store's founding in 1944.

The Freeds have been active and supportive of many community activities during their long residence here. Their five children, born and raised here, are now married and living elsewhere. However, Michael Freed, Bob and Fran's son, is a third-generation jeweler, who joined the business six years ago and has been very involved in the area activities. He is an avid golfer and competes in tournaments across the country. His knowledge of diamonds has been enhanced by his studies with the Gemological Institute of America.

The store's manager, John Martin, has been involved in the jewelry business since the age of 14. His knowledge of gold design, gemstones and diamonds has made Palmer's the leader in full-service jewelry in Central Indiana. By working with the customers' desires, Palmer's staff has pleased thousands of young and old over the years.

Palmer's is a complete jewelry operation covering a half-block of historical property at Main and Sycamore in Uptown Kokomo. The trained staff of 16 employees represent over 300 years of experience. Palmer's is the only store in the Kokomo area with a registered watch and clock repairman and two jewelers, one specializing in custom designing. Palmer's is a member of Retail Jewelers of America and the Chamber of Commerce. Hand engraving is also done on the premises.

Palmer's Jewelry

James and Edna King in the original store.

The current location of King's at 115 E. Vaile Avenue.

KINGS

In 1946, James King and Homer Johnson quit their jobs at Delco and opened an appliance store at 215 N. Buckeye Street. They heard about a supplier out of Kalamazoo, Michigan, called Kalamazoo Stove and Furnace Company. In order to sell Kalamazoo's appliances, they would also have to sell and install Kalamazoo's furnaces. This was the beginning of the heating business for King's.

Most of the sales, in the beginning, were replacing old coal furnaces with new coal furnaces. With new house construction on the rise, they soon began selling forced air systems.

The business consisted of four employees: James, Homer, and their wives. In 1947, they purchased a Ford flatbed with wood sides. This was not the vehicle they wanted, but it was much better than the car and wagon they had been using. In 1948, the partnership dissolved when Jim bought out Homer.

Jim and Edna's two sons, Ronald and Roger, have worked at King's from early ages. Ronald started installing furnaces at the age of thirteen and eventually started selling as well. Roger took his naps in the shop when he was a little boy. Now Roger works in the shop.

Due to the company's growth, in 1961, King's moved to its present location at 115 E. Vaile Avenue. In 1965, King's was incorporated under the name King's Heating and Plumbing, Inc. What was once a four employee, one truck company has grown to thirty employees and sixteen trucks.

The third generation of the King family is running the business now. Both of Ronald's sons work for the company. Jerry, since the age of eighteen, has worked his way up to Vice-President and is in charge of operations. Jay has recently returned, bringing his experience and new ideas to the company. Ronald is President and is still active in the business. Roger is also active at King's waiting on customers and purchasing parts. James is retired but can be seen, on occasion, waiting on customers.

H. E. MC GONIGAL INC.
BUICK, CADILLAC, JEEP-EAGLE

H.E. McGonigal Inc. was established in 1928 by Harry E. McGonigal. Harry first began selling Buick automobiles and a few years later acquired the Cadillac franchise. McGonigal began selling the dealership to Bill Wilson in the 1940s. Mr. Wilson owned and operated the business until 1968. He sold the business to Fenton Gingerich and Sid Golightly. They had managed the company for Mr. Wilson since the early 1950s. In 1978, H. E. McGonigal Buick, Cadillac bought the AMC-Jeep franchise. Mr. Golightly retired in the early 1980s and Mr. Gingerich later retired in 1986. At that time, Ivan Gingerich, Fenton's brother, became Dealer Principal. Ivan and Mike Raisor had been stock holders since Mr. Golightly's retirement. Ivan Gingerich is still the Dealer Principal and his son Rex is the General Manager.

H. E. McGonigal Inc. was located for many years on the corner of Buckeye and Superior in uptown Kokomo. Since 1977, the company has been located at its current location, 1220 E. Boulevard.

The company has over 70 employees. Many of the people have been with McGonigals ten, fifteen, and over twenty years. All the employees have done a fine job over the years and the dealership maintains high customer satisfaction indexes with Buick, Cadillac, and Jeep-Eagle. In 1993, H. E. McGonigal Inc. was presented with Buick's highest honor when they were named "Best in Class."

H. E. McGonigal Inc. is one of the older businesses in Kokomo and Howard County. They were honored by the state in 1994 in Indianapolis when they were presented with the Half Century Award. The company and its people support the community in every way possible. They are very thankful the community has allowed them the opportunity to serve their automotive wants and needs for so many years.

Rex Gingerich, who began full time with the dealership after his graduation from Purdue University in May 1987, standing next to Buick award and his father, Ivan Gingerich.

AMERICAN TRUST

AmericanTrust Federal Savings Bank, formerly Peru Federal Savings & Loan, first opened its doors for business in 1886. With assets of $58 million AmericanTrust currently offers full service banking to the communities of Peru, Warsaw and Kokomo. The branch office and parking garage in Kokomo was built at the corner of Union and Walnut Streets in 1979. Prior to the construction of this facility a mortgage loan office operated out of the Armstrong Landon building. Recent plans for improvement include enlarging the Peru office to expand the mortgage banking department and relocating the Kokomo office from the downtown area to the corner of Dixon Road and Boulevard (effective May 31, 1994) where we will service our customers from a modular facility until the construction of a new 4,000 square foot facility is completed in the fall of 1994.

RAYLS INSURANCE AGENCY

RAYLS INSURANCE began in 1947 when Bill Rayls opened his agency in a quonset hut. The agency was purchased after Mr. Rayls' death in 1980 by Jack and Judy Dean who are still running the business today at the present location, 701 North Washington Street.

Jack and Judy Dean, Debbie Plough, and Susan West.

STAHL WELDING, INC.
Crane Rentals – Machinery Moving
Rigging – Hauling
Fabrication and Repair
New and Used Steel

Globe American Corp., Kokomo, Indiana, about 1955. Globe American Corporation built the Maytag Stove. (l. to r.) Otho (Heavy) Delano, Custodian; James (Jimmy) Trayers, Supt. Emeritus; Alden Chester, President; Jesse (Jess) Jackson, Plant Manager; and Chalmer (Doc) Degler, Foreman, with Globe 52 years. These men total 209 years.

The Globe American crew that built the last lifeboat. Photograph taken November 6, 1945.

FAMILIES

John N. & Eliza Bennett Family circa 1899. Seated: Everett N. Bennett (a prominent doctor in Kokomo in the 1930s), Eliza Mow Bennett, John Nathaniel Bennett, and Jennie Maude Bennett. Standing: Catherine Victoria Bennett Crail, William E. Bennett, Malinda Evaline Bennett Mullikin, Edwin M. Bennett, and Dora Ellen Bennett Wooldridge.

RAYMOND ABNEY - Raymond Abney's parents William H. Abney (1874-1931) and Maude (Stephenson) Abney (1877-1958) moved to Kokomo from Hamilton County (Indiana) in 1917. The early ancestors of this family had settled in the Fall Creek Township area of Hamilton County in 1828 after a period of migration beginning in 1790 from South Carolina through several states (Georgia, Tennessee, Kentucky).

Several members of the Stephenson family (from the New Britton area of Hamilton County) preceded the Abney family's move to Kokomo. The flourishing economy from the discovery of natural gas years before had drawn several of Maude's sisters and their families to Kokomo in the early 1900's. Namely, Dan and Bell (Stephenson) Gray, Angelo and Ella (Stephenson) Reddick (in 1913 they homesteaded near Opheim, Montana), Harry and Magnolia (Stephenson) (Kitley) Higgins (Harry was her second husband and worked for the Kokomo Gas Company).

Edna and Raymond Abney on their wedding day.

William, Maude, and their four children moved to Kokomo after William quit his job at the Union Sanitary Plant in Noblesville. He was a molder and cast bathtubs and lavatories. He left the Noblesville plant when the workers went on strike and the owners closed the operation. At Kokomo he worked at the Hoosier Iron and the Globe.

Their children: Nona (1898-1974) became an x-ray technician in Indianapolis; Howard (1899-1962) married Mary Beymer, worked at the Neil Thomas Shoe Co. and later became a J.C. Penney manager; Ina (1901-1987) was a court reporter for Judge Marshall of the Howard County Circuit Court and married Ralph Leas; Raymond (1904-1987) worked for Kokomo Gas. He and Edna York (1905-1989) were married in June 1926 by Rev. J.W. Lake at the parsonage (now Rayls Insurance) of the United Brethren Church (now Save More gas station).

Raymond was in the 7th grade when his family moved here and he attended the Central School at the corner of Sycamore and Apperson. He met Edna at Kokomo High School and both graduated in 1923. While a student, Raymond worked several jobs. His first was for C.A. Remy who had a store in the 200 block of North Buckeye. He also worked for Leroy Stephenson who had a grocery at the corner of Kennedy (Apperson Way) and Richmond. He also picked up milk at the Newlon farm. Later he worked for Walter Remy who owned a grocery at the corner of North and Wabash. He delivered groceries in Mr. Remy's Model T Ford.

In 1920 Raymond bought his brother's 1918 Model T Ford for $100. He often skipped school to repair Model T Fords that belonged to his teachers Ray Peck and Virgil Fleenor.

After graduation Edna worked as a secretary for Mr. Pepka at the Kokomo Spring Company. She and other girls were often picked up for work in an open touring car. The men sat in the front and usually chewed tobacco. When they spit tobacco out the open car, tobacco juice came flying back where the girls were sitting.

After their marriage, Raymond and Edna moved to Hammond where Raymond worked for the gas company. Later he became an A&P manager. In Hammond their three children were born and raised: Nancy, Dick, and Judy. Dick and his wife Peg moved to Kokomo in 1957. Dick taught school at KHS until 1993. Peg has taught at KHS since 1968.

Dick and Peg have four children who graduated from KHS: Kevin, 1975; Kent, 1977; Karyn, 1980, Kriss, 1983. Karyn and Kriss lived in Indianapolis. Kent lives in Los Alamos, New Mexico, and has one daughter. Kevin is a night shift manager for Delco Electronics. His wife Kim works for the Howard County Adult Probation Department. Their two children are Kristopher (5th grade Lafayette Park) and Katie (2nd grade Wallace School).

ORANGE AND BLANCHE ACHOR - Daniel Achor (ca 12 Feb. 1830- 3 Aug 1900) was the son of George and Sarah (Ward) Dillon born in Highland County, OH. He married Emily King who was born 30 Oct 1848 in Ohio.

Gilbert Achor (1855-1932) was the third son of Daniel and lived in Grant County, Sim Twp. He was married to Catherine Smith (1856-1924). They had three children: Grace (Achor) Spears, Noah and Orange.

Orange Achor was born 19 Jan. 1885 in Grant County, IN. He was the youngest child of Gilbert and Catherine.

November 6, 1902 he married Anna Blanche Harper; she was born 21 April 1887 in Howard County. The youngest child and only daughter of Richard Harper (1845-1919) and Cynthia Cheek (1847-1909). Ervin, Oliver Earl, Marin E. and James R. "Pete" were her older brothers.

Orange and Blanche had seven children: Earl (1908-1988) married Mary Francis Newlin; Florence Catherine married James Cecil Calaway, (1908-1979); Wayne married Kathleen Shirar and have one son, Michael; Ethel Lillian married Gilbert Potts (1914-1971); they have four daughters: Karen, Marsha, Wilma and Brenda, and one son David; Paul (1918-1978) married Betty Jane VanMeter (1921-1942) they had two daughters: Peggy Jo and Rebecca who died at birth with her mother. He then married Dorthy Heuser (1923-1984) and had five children: Donald, Dean, Doloris, Patrica and Pamela; Robert (1923-1975) married Ruth Delrymple they had one son: Robert Gene (1950-1988); Vivian Christina married Richard Lawrence White; they have four children: Jerry Lawrence, Richard Joseph, Christina Ann and Joseph Edward.

Orange and Blanche Achor

The couple were lifelong farmers and raised their family on a farm east of Sycamore. For many years they made a home for Orange's father and Blanche's brother, Ervin.

In December 1937 they bought a 120 acre farm west of Burlington in Carroll County and moved there with their three youngest children. They lived and worked there for the rest of their lives.

Blanche died 9 Sept. 1959 after a heart attack. Orange then turned the running of the farm over to his son Paul. Orange suffered a stroke and passed away 2 Oct. 1963. They are buried in the family plot in the Burlington Cemetery.

Orange and Blanche had many friends and were active in the Methodist Church and the Burlington Community.

Vivian Christina (Achor) White was the youngest child of Orange and Blanche Achor. She was born 3 April 1931 in Howard County east of Sycamore, and moved to Burlington when she was six years old. She married Richard Lawrence White 9 Oct. 1948 in Howard County. He was born 6 Oct. 1927, the son of Howard and Ruth White.

Together they had four children: Jerry Lawrence married Karen Bacharach; they have one son Benjamin Howard. Richard Joseph married Barbara Irick; they have two sons: Joshua Joseph and Andrew Michael; Christina Ann married Barry Weaver; they have a son Brian Lawrence and a daughter Elizabeth Ann; Joseph Edward married Jennifer Moore.

Richard joined the Navy 16 Jan. 1945; being the youngest man on his ship he had many adventures. He served as a cook's assistant and was discharged 20 July 1946. Later he became a meat cutter and worked for Marsh Supermarkets for many years. Richard retired in 1989. Vivian was busy raising their children and working at Delco Electronics until she retired in 1993. They live in Kokomo, IN and are enjoying their retirement. *Submitted by Vivian White*

HERMAN D. AND R. MARIE ACHORS - Herman Delbert Achors was born in Green County, Indiana, on December 14, 1910. He moved to Howard County in 1927 to find employment and his future. Herman lived with a half-brother and sister-in-law, Cyril and Marie Dickey, on West Virginia Street. He started working at Continental Steel Mill's open hearth at age 17 and worked his way up through the ranks, retiring as superintendent of the Rod Mill in 1972.

In 1929 Herman and a younger brother, Orval Achors, moved their parents, Will and Emma Achors, from Green County to Clinton County. They moved all their possessions by horse and wagon traveling three days and staying in farmers' homes along the way.

Herman's ancestors date back to immigrants traveling by ship from Berne, Switzerland. His great-grandfather, Casper Hasler, was born in Berne in 1813. He left his wife Catherine and twins in Europe and sailed to America, living on cheese, crackers, and water for 38 days. He made his way to Bloomfield, Indiana, and worked as a stone cutter. The money he made was sent home for his family's passage to America in 1850. Herman's grandmother, Louisa, was one of their 14 children. She married Andrew Dickey in 1864 and Emma Mae Dickey, Herman's mother, was born in 1879. She married Will Achors in March, 1910, and Herman was their first-born son.

Herman & Marie Achors

Herman married Roxie Marie Shoemaker on Feb. 22, 1935. Marie worked as a cosmetologist at the Uptown Beauty Salon in Kokomo. Her parents were Calvin and Grace (Huffer) Shoemaker, life-long residents of Clinton County.

Herman and Marie had four children: Judith Kay (b. April 24, 1937), Herman Kent (b. March 7, 1939), Beverly Jeanine (b. Feb. 19, 1944) and Sherri Janae (b. March 16, 1955-d. Feb. 21, 1993). In 1946 the Achors family moved from Kokomo to Forest, IN to be near Marie's elderly parents. They moved back to Kokomo in 1959 and have continued to live in Howard County until the present time.

Their three surviving children also live in the Kokomo area. Judy and her husband Harold Orr have two children, Melissa (b. Feb. 23, 1968) and Matthew (b. Sept. 9, 1969), and one granddaughter, Kayla (b. Sept. 28, 1989). Harold worked at Delco Electronics as an engineer and retired in January, 1994, after 39 years of service.

Kent and his wife Kitty (Shaw) have two sons: Gregory (b. Jan. 22, 1964) and Jeffrey (b. Oct. 2, 1966). Greg and his wife Christie (Robinson) have two sons: Kyle (b. April 15, 1990) and Konner (b. Sept. 20, 1991).

Kent worked at Continental Steel for 27 years and is presently employed by Delco as a supervisor.

Beverly and her husband, Brig. Gen (USAFR) Boyd Ashcraft have three children: Darin (b. March 23, 1966), Stacey (b. April 1, 1967) and Darla (b. Sept. 12, 1969). Stacey and her husband, Randy Kammeyer, have a daughter, Annalissa (b. Aug. 11, 1993). Darin is married to Dr. Michelle Lecklitner. Beverly is employed as a school nurse for Western School Corporation.

Herman and Marie are very proud of their seven grandchildren and four great-grandchildren. Greg is a Navy pilot, Darin is an orthodontist, Jeff is a machine operator for Chrysler Corporation, Stacey and Darla are special education teachers, Missy works at E.D.S., and Matt is in timber procurement.

The Achors are active members of West Point Christian Church. They are avid fishermen and enjoy traveling and vacationing in Minnesota with their family. Herman and Marie enjoy living in the Kokomo area and are thankful for their family, home, employment, and the lifelong friendships they have found in Howard County. *Submitted by Beverly Ashcraft.*

RUSSELL WAYMIRE AND HILDA (THOMPSON) ADAIR -
Russell and Hilda were married July 24, 1926, in Kokomo. This union of 57 years brought forth nine children, a move from "city life" to the country and nearly 50 years of farming and raising Registered Purebred Hamshire hogs. All their children were born at home except Larry who arrived via St. Joseph Hospital. They are: Hilda Lucille (Mrs. Robert) Coghill (1927); Russell Waymire, Jr. (Bud-born in 1928); Joseph Edmund (Joedy - born in 1929); Ruth Ellen (born in 1933 - died in 1936); James Donald (Don - born in 1935 - died in 1992); Patricia Ann (Mrs. Keith) Swavey (Pat - born in 1940), David Francis (Dave - born in 1942); Robert Lawrence (Larry - born in 1945); Marie Elaine (Mrs. John) Brock (born in 1947). Most of them, as well as twenty-seven grandchildren and forty-four great-grandchildren, live within a short distance of the family home near Hemlock.

Russell (born Feb. 2, 1906 - died August 6, 1983) was born in Madison County, attended schools there and graduated from Elwood High School. He moved to Kokomo in 1924 with his parents, Francis Edmond (born in April 1886 - died in April 1958) and Maude (Waymire) (born in April 1876 - died in June 1944) Adair. He attended Indiana Business College where he excelled in bookkeeping (an invaluable skill during his business and farming years). He operated a Cities Service station in Kokomo before moving his family, in 1936, to a farm near Phlox.

Russell Waymire and Hilda (Thompson) Adair and Family - 50th Wedding Anniversary - 24 July 1976. Back Row: Don, Lucille, Hilda, Russell, Bud, Joedy, Pat. Front Row: Larry, Marie, Dave.

Hilda (born in September 1908 - died in 1992), the youngest of 11 children of Joseph (born Sept. 14, 1864 - died in September 1932) and Ellen (Simpkins) (born Dec. 4, 1868 - died Sept. 21, 1944) Thompson, was born in Alexandria, IN. Joseph and his family left St. Helens, Lancashire County, England, and sailed May 17, 1906, on the *Baltic*. Seven brothers accompanied the parents - Jack, Bill, Joe, Jim, Pete, Bob and Tom. Edwin was born in Kokomo shortly after their arrival. One sister Ellen, died of tuberculosis in 1903 and sister Ruth (whose smallpox vaccination hadn't taken) came later with relatives. Joseph was to begin work at Pittsburg Plate Glass Factory. In 1919, Hilda enjoyed a visit to St. Helens with her family.

The move to the farm was quite an experience for Hilda (a "city girl"). Modern conveniences were lacking - just a "privy", pump (water carried in and out), kerosene lamps, a big Globe kitchen range and the trusty Florence Hotblast heating stove. Both used wood, coal or corn cobs for fuel, and their ashes required removal daily. Everyone, including children, pitched in to do chores and crop harvesting.

In 1938, after two years of hard work and perseverance, they purchased the farm on State Road 19 southeast of Hemlock. Electricity eased household chores but a few years passed before the "pump and privy" were retired! Most of the family called this house "the Home Place". It is now the home of the youngest daughter, Marie and family.

After 24 years at the home place, Russell and Hilda purchased a larger farm west of Center. It was here they spent their last years together from 1962 to 1983. The land is now owned and farmed by the youngest son, Larry.

Those who may have known Russell and Hilda will know that their history includes more than is written here! *Submitted by Hilda Lucille (Adair) Coghill*

ALBAUGH - KELVIE - ROBERTS -
In 1891, after graduating from high school, Etta Wood and Lee Albaugh were married in the First Congregational Church in Kokomo, IN. Etta's parents had four daughters and one son. Lee Albaugh, an only child, was employed at the Albaugh Limestone and Coal Co. Together, the couple had one daughter Clara Alien Albaugh. Tragically, Lee Albaugh was stricken with tuberculosis. He was sent to Texas and warm climate for recuperation but died in 1907 at the age of 37. Clara Alien and her mother stayed in Kokomo where Etta owned and operated the Star Theatre. Her sister Mame Wood owned the Wood Theatre; Etta hosted grand theatre parties for different actors and actresses who performed in Kokomo.

Etta Wood Albaugh eventually remarried which was most unusual for a widow in that time period. Etta died in 1923.

Clara Alien Albaugh met Russell Kelvie while both attended Kokomo High School. Russell was a tall thin man proficient in basketball in high school and later enjoyed golf. His family had moved to Kokomo from Anderson where his father Wm. Kelvie was employed by the railroad. Russell's mother was Mary Jane Baskett Kelvie. They had one daughter Kathryn Kelvie who married Todd Beeching. They had one son, Charles.

Clara Alien Albaugh and Russell Kelvie were married June 29, 1916, in the First Congregational Church in Kokomo.

After employment with the Apperson Brothers Automobile Co., Russell was brought in as a partner with Vrooman - Smith Printing Co. This establishment soon became the Kelvie Press and still exists today in the original location on the corner of Buckeye and Sycamore Streets.

After eight years of marriage Alien and Russell Kelvie had one daughter, Patricia "Patsy" Albaugh Kelvie. While attending high school, Patsy met Hallie Roberts. He had moved to Kokomo from Whiting, IN with his parents, Gilbert and Lilly Roberts. They operated a restaurant on Lindsay Street across from the main office at Stellite Corporation. Both Hallie and Patsy graduated from Kokomo High School and attended college. Hallie served in the U.S. Naval Air Corps as a carrier pilot in the South Pacific during World War II. The couple married June 23, 1945, in the First Congregational Church in Kokomo.

Mr. and Mrs. Kelvie celebrated their 50th wedding anniversary to June of 1966. Alien Kelvie died in 1973 and Russell Kelvie died in 1980.

Patsy and Hallie Roberts reside in Kokomo where Hallie has worked at the Kelvie Press since 1951. The couple has two sons - David Russell born 1950 and Richard Gilbert born 1953. Richard currently resides in Houston, TX.

After college, David married Susan Kay Busby on June 24, 1972 in the Congregational Church in Kokomo, IN. Susan, the daughter of Janice (Fawcett) and Paul Busby, and David lived in the Chicago area for six years before returning to Kokomo to help run the family business. The couple has two sons, Matthew Paul - born 1975 and H. Andrew Kelvie born 1978. *Submitted by David R. Roberts*

ALBRIGHT -
Johnannes (John) Albrecht (died 1752) and his wife Anna Barbara arrived in Philadelphia on the *Johnson Gallery* on Sept. 18, 1732 from Amsterdam, Holland. They farmed in Berks County, PA and were blessed with six children: Magdalen, Barbara, Christian, Jacob, Ludwig and Judith.

Jacob Albright (born 1727-died 1791), the fourth child of John and Anna, married Sophia Welder (born 1749-died 1791). In 1764 they left Berks County for Orange County, NC. Jacob, a land owner and an elder in the Old Stoner Church, served as a drummer in the Revolutionary War. Their children were: Sophia, Catherine, Jacob Jr., John, Joseph, Daniel, Henry, George and Catherine.

George Albright (born 1761), Jacob's and Sophia's seventh child, married Barbara Catherine Holt (born 1770-died 1829), a wealthy land owner in Alamance County, NC. George donated land for the Mt. Harmon Cemetery in Alamance County where he and his wife are buried. They had ten children: William, Mary (Polly), Hannah, Alexander, Lattie, Nellie, Tamar, Alvis, Michael and Sallie.

William Albright (born 1791-died 1856), the first child of George and Barbara, married Louisa Wood (born 1798-died 1860). He farmed three thousand acres of land, and served as a Senator from Chatham County, NC from 1836-1848. He also helped to organize the Pleasant Hill Temperance Society. Their eleven children were: Elizabeth, Julia, Margaret, Tamer, Durant, William, Eleanor, Mary, Emily, Martha, and Henry.

Back Row - Robert Albright, Louise (Albright) Galloway, William Albright. Front Row: Glen Albright, Carol (Albright) Smoot.

Durant Albright (born 1826-died 1913), the fifth child of William and Louisa, married Sylvina Siler (born 1836-died 1870). They had seven children: Adolphus, William, Frank, Decie (Sarah), Henry, Loretta and Walter. His second wife, Mary Griffin (died 1887), and he had two daughters: Bertha and Maude. Durant, a land owner, was the first doctor to graduate from a medical school to practice in his home locality. His medical instruments are on display at the museum in Raleigh, NC.

William Albright (born 1856-died 1944), the second son of Durant and Sylvina, married Alice McCombs (born 1869-died 1964). He left Sandy Grove, NC in 1884 and moved to Cicero, IN. In 1889 he bought land in Noble Twp., Cass County, and farmed. Their three children were: Decie, Glen and Fon.

Glen Albright (born 1898-died 1993), William's and Alice's son, married Winona Herr (born 1903-died 1989). He farmed in Cass County, IN, was active in the Farm Bureau, and boxed in his younger days. Their four children were: Robert, William, Carol and Louise.

Robert Albright (born 1925), the first son of Glen and Winona, married Norma Long, and had three sons: James, Jerry and Terry (Jay). He married Nancy Way and

139

had a daughter, Susan. He served in the Navy (1944-1946), is retired from the Lake Havasu Street Department. They live in Lake Havasu, AZ.

William Albright (born 1928), Glen's and Winona's second son, married Bonnie Jones. They have three children: Belinda, Glen and Gary. He served in the Army (1946-1948) and retired from McMann's Const. They live in Logansport, IN.

Carol Albright (born 1929), third child of Glen and Winona, married William Gibbs and had three daughters: Teresa, Carol and Mary. She married Nathan Smoot and had a daughter, Cheryl. She is retired from Delco Electronics and lives in Kokomo, IN.

Louise Albright (1936), the fourth child of Glen and Winona, married Richard Galloway and has a son Bruce. She works for T.M. Morris and lives in Logansport, IN. *Submitted by Carol Albright Smoot*

HENRY J. LACY ALBRIGHT - Henry J. 'Lacy' was born 1862, son of William Burgess and Margaret Hodge Albright. He married Mattie Smiley (1882); she died in the 1894 flu epidemic. They had eight children:

Fredrick Arthur (1883) married Nellie Harris 1903. Died 1905. They had two daughters, Ruth and Rowena.

Jessie Irene (1885) lived in parental home 40+ years. Taught school at Meridian, 5th Ward & Darrough Chapel. Married John Colburn 1944; he died 1953. Married Walter Keiter 1954.

*Birdie Ellen (1887) Grandfather's namesake. See Clarence McCauley Family

Newton A. & Paul Robert (1889-'90) died in infancy.

Twins (1892) Claude Lewis (lived six months) & Maude Eunice. Maude married Richard Lee 1915. She died in the 1919 flu epidemic, leaving a two year old son, Richard 'Joe' Lee.

Henry J. "Lacy" Albright

Pauline Lucille (1894) When five weeks old, her mother died. She was raised by the Atrium Locke family, taught in Kokomo and county schools, married Ernest Bruce, lived much of her life in Center.

'Lacy' married Estella Day (1896). They had four children.

Margaret Elizabeth (1897) married Charles Fitzpatrick; both taught in Kokomo schools, moved to Indianapolis, where she taught at Indiana Deaf School, 14 years and Art and Special Ed in city schools. Died 1992; age 95. Family: Phyllis and Charles 'Albright'.

William Luther (1899) killed by the train at Taylor Street crossing at age 25.

Harvey 'Vern' (1901) married/divorced. Married Cecile Martin 1941. He was a farmer; an expert at raising tomatoes. Family: four loving stepchildren.

Kenneth Lacy (1908) Married Elizabeth Phillips 1929. A son stillborn. Divorced. Married 'Rene' Doran Fellows 1959. One stepdaughter.

'Lacy' was a devout Christian, staunch prohibitionist and deep thinker. He worked at Leach's Brickyard, was agent for 25 years for Metropolitan Life Ins., operated a grocery at Main & Deffenbaugh and at Wheeler & Lafountain for over 20 years and was custodian at Jefferson School.

After his house at 815 E. Hoffer burned, his father helped him build a large two-story home on the same site, where he lived until his death in 1951. Over a period of 25 years, 'Stella' opened the Albright home to approximately 500 'Wards of the Court', some for a short time, others for several years. For those who lived there for a long time, 'Grandpa' & 'Grandma's home was their home also. There were several fires which started in the chimney and damaged the roof over a period of years.

'Lacy' fathered 12 children, yet there was not one Albright grandson to carry on the family name. He was named for a Methodist preacher, Henry J. Lacy. The Lacy name has been carried on for at least four generations. The legacy of maintaining a Christian home is also being passed to new generations.

REV. WILLIAM (BILLY) ALBRIGHT - Rev. William 'Billy', was born May 22, 1799, in North Carolina. He married Elizabeth Snoderly (1798). He was a farmer, brickmaker, bricklayer and preacher. He followed his sons, John & 'Bird', to Howard County. He established ALBRIGHT CHAPEL METHODIST CHURCH in 1847 at the residence of his son, John. For 11 years the congregation met in various homes, then the 'Chapel' was built in 1858 on John's farm (approximately 150 yds. N. of intersection of Albright Rd. and Alto Rd.) The building was of brick, 35' x 45'; the cost was $1,500. 'Billy' was also a circuit rider for other country churches in the area.

ALBRIGHT CEMETERY came into existence just south of the Chapel, when there was an accidental death in the community, and no burial space was available. John Albright gave land for the burial. It is reported the first four burials in the cemetery were accidental deaths. Most of Billy's children, grandchildren and descendants are buried there.

ALBRIGHT ROAD was named for John Albright. He owned 112.5 acres on either side of Kokomo Creek. Albright Cemetery is part of that land. It remains a tribute to John, his father, 'Billy' and to Wm. 'Bird', and their descendants, who left a legacy of Christian faith and upright living to the community of Howard County.

WILLIAM BURGESS ALBRIGHT - William Burgess 'Bird', was born Dec. 2, 1833, in Campbell County, TN. He followed brother John to Howard County (1848), and became a brickmason. With bricks from John's brickyard, the two men built Kokomo's first brick building, the old Court House, schools and other buildings across the county.

He married Margaret Hodge (1857). They had eight children:

Hester Ann (1858) died at age 4.

James Newton 'Newt' (1860), married Jessie Butler. Studious and inventive, he built telephone connections between homes of relatives long before Canter community had general service. In 1900, he took wife, two children, and brother Joe, to Lake Ann, near Traverse City, MI, in a covered wagon. In three weeks they traveled 380 miles (about 20 mi per day). At one time three brothers and families lived in same house; all but 'Newt' returned to Howard County.

*Henry J. Lacy (1862) See Henry J. Lacy Albright Family.

Edmund Ephraim (1864) married Laura Reagan, Kokomo; had one son, Perle. A union bricklayer. Ed worked with his father and other Albright relatives as a builder.

William Burgess Albright family

George Nelson (1867) married Nora Seagraves, whose spiced peaches at a church social so pleased his fancy he quipped, "I'll marry that girl," and he did. He first farmed in Michigan, then Howard County, finally settling in Randolph County, near Winchester. His son, Dallas, had no children.

Dora Eunice (1870) was never a wife, mother or grandmother, yet she filled the duties of each for various family members during her life. A Christian lady, she raised two nieces after their mother died.

Joseph Skeen (1873) married Dora Humbarger, a Taylor Twp. teacher. As a brickmason, Joe worked with his father's crew on many buildings, including the Masonic Hall, in Center. His daughter, Mona Belle, worked at Carnegie Library, Kokomo.

Elizabeth Ann (1875) married Lon Amos. Farmed one mile south of Center on S.R. 26. He'd barely finished building a new home when Elizabeth died, leaving two small daughters, Mary Lorraine and Lacie.

'Bird's parents were Wm. 'Billy' and Elizabeth Snoderly Albright.

'Bird' was a God-fearing man, always careful never to 'take the name of the Lord in vain'. When building the old brick Court House, he found those contracted to cut the huge limestone arches for over the side stairs had cut one arch too short. 'Bird' called a workman to help him, he said to him, "Look at that! Some swearing needs to be done and I can't do it!" This incidence has been a favorite one to relate to each generation.

ALDRIDGE - The Aldridge family has its roots in Tipton County, although a third generation of Aldridges is now raising children in Howard County.

In 1853, Darlington Aldridge came from England with a Land Company and settled in Tipton County. Darlington had seven children: James, John, Jeremiah, Frank, Harvey and Lucinda (seventh child's name not known to author of this article.)

Jeremiah married Julia Hemerley and had three children: Newton Rutherford, William Edward and Porter. (Jeremiah had five more children with his second wife, after Julia died).

Newton Rutherford (1876-1965) and his wife Mary Jane Bitner had six children: William Clurid, Leona Mae, Luella Ruth, Edward Ralph, an infant who died at birth, and Lela Vivian. Newton owned and operated his own timber company in Tipton County, after having worked for a timber company in Kokomo.

Edward Ralph (1913-1985) married Bessie Berneice Greer in 1936. Edward ("Pete") had a chance to farm in Tipton County, but as he did not fancy a life of farming, he instead moved to Howard County to work at Chrysler.

Pete and Bessie had four children: Marjorie Jane, Fredrick Allen, Michael Edward and Judith Diane. Marjorie, Fredrick and Michael still reside in Howard County. Judith resides in Terre Haute.

Fredrick (born 1940) married Towana Kay Maddox in 1962. They have four children: Fredrick Allen Jr. (born 1962), Marsha Kay (born 1965), Gregory Edward (born 1969) and Douglas Eugene (born 1974). Fredrick has worked as Delco Electronics for 28 years.

Fred Jr. married Julie Ann Christian in 1980. They have two children: Beth Ann (born 1980) and Fredrick Allen III (born 1983). Fred Jr. served in the U.S. Army 1980-1985; he is currently manager of Harmon Boats in Sharpsville. He and his family reside in Clinton County.

Marsha married Joseph Jerome Santen Jr. ("Jerry") in 1988. She was head of Children's Services at the Kokomo-Howard County Public Library until resigning after the birth of her daughter, Gretchen Elizabeth (born 1992). Jerry, Marsha and Gretchen reside in Howard County.

Gregory married Michaele Kristina Thomas in 1992. He is a computer programmer at V/A in Indianapolis.

Douglas is currently serving a three year stint in the U.S. Army at Ft. Hood, TX. *Submitted by Marsha Kay (Aldridge) Santen*

ALVEY - Traveling south of Kokomo on the Park Road, crossing Little Wildcat, where the Indians once camped, across Duncan Road (300S) past Alto Baptist Cemetery, over the hill and just before Highway 26, on the east side of the road is the farmhouse of Howard and Betty Alvey.

Howard's parents, Charley and Emma, bought this farm in 1929. Charley was shipping clerk at Kokomo Pottery.

Charley (1891-1943) was born in Tipton County to Morris and Louise Fernung Alvey. Morris was a farmer from Franklin County and later farmed the Huston farm, now Huston Park in Kokomo.

Emma (1896-1973) was the daughter of the James and Lois McConnell Smallwood of Kokomo.

Charley and Emma had three sons: twins Howard and Harold (1915) and Glen (1918).

It was a great change from a modern house to an old farm house with no electricity, plumbing or telephone. Just barn, corn cribs, smokehouse, pump and privy. The boys attended Alto and West Middleton schools.

Howard and Betty Alvey

In 1936, the Alveys moved to the adjoining farm east called Kirtley farm. Howard farmed with his father raising corn, soybeans, hogs and a dairy herd. Horses gave way to tractors, corn pickers and electric milkers.

That farm was sold in 1942 to four different buyers, and later developed into South Downs, Country Lane and Ivy Hills subdivisions. Charley and Emma bought the west 102 acres joining their farm. Charley suffered a heart attack in 1943, dying at age 51.

Howard married Betty Jane Baker Feb. 26, 1943. Betty (born 1921), a 1939 graduate of Kokomo High School, was the daughter of Carl and Maude Baker. Carl (1886-1946) was the son of Harvey and Florence Bowman Baker. Maude (1893-1969) was the daughter of William and Alta Cooper Jones of Tipton County.

Howard and Betty farmed their farm and rented several other neighboring farms until 1982. Howard was also a partner in GW Invader Boats in Sharpsville for several years. Betty worked part-time at PSI, retiring in 1992. She served eight years on the Harrison Township Advisory Board. She is active in First Baptist Church-Kokomo, and is a past county president and district representative of IEHA.

They have two daughters, Marsha Burton of Carmel (1944) and Miriam Greeson (1955). Both attended Alto, New London, Russiaville and Western High School where both graduated.

Marsha has two children, James Edward Smith (1967) and Kelley Dyan Smith (1969).

Miriam is married to David Alan Greeson. They have one son, David Matthew (1987). They live in Miami County.

Howard and Betty celebrated their Golden Wedding Anniversary in 1993. They have seen many changes in the community: paved roads, dusk-to-dawn lights in every yard, bigger farm machinery and subdivisions and golf courses where once they farmed.

JACOB ALLEN ARNETT - Jacob Allen Arnett was born in Licking, MO on Aug. 25, 1874, the son of William H. and Mary (Cramblet) Arnett. On Feb. 3, 1895, in Licking, he married Ella Emma Granger, daughter of George W. and Margaret Lousaina (Wilson) Granger.

Jacob and Ella raised 10 children, one of whom was a granddaughter raised in their home. Children were: Martha Florence (Arnett) Doolittle, William Edward, Grant (1899-1904), Zora Ellen (Arnett) Sosbe, Susie Opal, Renna Bernice (Arnett) Hilliard, Joseph A., Lillie Mae (Arnett) Sherrill, Vera Helen (Arnett) Miller-Stockwell, Lemuel Ernest, and Harold Anderson.

L to R: Jacob Allen Arnett, Betty Jean Sosbe, Ella Emma Arnett, and Donald Sosbe.

Jacob brought his family to Indiana in 1912 to look for jobs. They lived in Elwood, IN from 1912 to 1917 or 1918 where Jacob was a glass worker. They moved to Kokomo where their youngest son, Harold, was born Sept. 27, 1919. On May 1, 1920, their daughter Susie Opal, age 17 years, died of tuberculosis at their home at 1823 South Purdum Street. She was taken to Elwood for burial.

In 1930 Jacob and Ella took their two youngest sons to Licking, MO to work the homestead of Jacob's father, William H. Arnett, who had died. They came back to Elwood, IN a year or two later, where they held a Christmas party with all of their children present.

In 1937, they moved back to Kokomo where they lived awhile in the Lenox Addition and on Goyer Road. In 1938, they lived at 1024 South Courtland Ave. Their sons Ernest (Bud) worked as a cook and Harold worked at the filling station known as the Hob-Knob Restaurant, 218 West Markland Ave.

Lemuel Ernest served in the Navy in 1940 and Harold Anderson served in the Air Force in California. On Sept. 10, 1938, both boys married their childhood sweethearts in their parents' home at 1024 South Courtland Ave. in a double ceremony. Maxine and Nadine Kofahl were the daughters of Harry Kofahl of Licking, MO.

Martha Arnett married Miles Doolittle in Elwood, March 22, 1913. They lived many years at 405 East North Street in Kokomo. They had four children.

William Edward Arnett married Amanda Ellen Julius on Aug. 7, 1915, in Elwood, IN. They raised eight children in the Elwood and Tipton areas.

Zora Ellen Arnett married Glenn C. Sosbe on Aug. 23, 1919, in Kokomo. When Zora died in 1938, Jacob and Ella brought her five children to live with them. They are: William C., Betty Jean, Donald, Glenn C., and Walter A. Sosbe.

Renna Bernice Arnett married Frank Leslie Hillard on April 15, 1922, in Elwood. They had no children.

Joseph A. Arnett married Mary Carney in 1926. They had two sons and lived mostly in Logansport or Kokomo.

Lillie Mae Arnett married Kenneth Sherrill on Dec. 5, 1929, in Sherrill, MO. They had four children and lived in Tipton and Kokomo.

Jacob and Ella eventually moved to 1424 North Waugh Street in Kokomo. Ella died on Thanksgiving Day, Nov. 25, 1943, at the age of 64. Jacob died on April 30, 1948 at the age of 74. *Submitted by granddaughter Imogene (Arnett) DeWitt.*

AMOS - William Amos was born in England in 1690, and came with his wife, Ann McComas, to Baltimore, MD in 1713. They were the parents of seven children. William died in 1759 and Ann died several years later.

Thomas Amos, born 1713, was the firstborn of William and Ann Amos. He married Elizabeth Day in 1735. They were the parents of six children. The dates of the deaths of Thomas and Elizabeth are not known.

Nicholas Day Amos was the fourth child of Thomas and Elizabeth Amos. He was born in 1742. He married Christiana Ditto in 1761. They were the parents of 14 children. Nicholas died in Kentucky in 1815.

Thomas Amos, born in 1765, was the third child of Nicholas and Christiana. He married Catherine Devore in 1788. They were the parents of ten children. Thomas died in 1830. Catherine died in 1853.

William Cook Amos, born in 1808, was the youngest child of Thomas and Catherine Amos. He married Antonette Endicott in 1830. They had three children. Antonette died in 1839. He then married Elizabeth Perkins in 1840. William died in 1868. They were the parents of nine children.

James and Elizabeth Amos

James W. Amos, born in 1859, was the son of William Cook and Elizabeth Amos. He married Elizabeth A. Young. They were the parents of five children. Eva died in infancy; Bessie was born in 1889 and married Renna Mason in 1935; Thelma was born in 1899 and married Herman Brown; Beulah born in 1901 and married Jess Hammer; Ray was born in 1903 and married Margaret Harbaugh.

Renna and Bessie Mason were the parents of four children. Arlene died at infancy; Donald (born in 1909) married Josephine Pollock in 1929; Wayne (born in 1911) married Arian Bulk in 1937; Robert (born in 1925) married Sara McHale.

Donald and Josephine Mason were the parents of four children: Dr. Joseph, David, Judith and Mona; they had 11 grandchildren and six great-grandchildren. Donald died Dec. 2, 1991.

Wayne and Arian Mason were the parents of one daughter, Marcia, who died in an accident. She was survived by four children. Wayne died July 19, 1969.

Robert and Sara Mason were the parents of four children: Jean, Sheryl, Dr. Robert and Susan. They also had several grandchildren. Robert died October 1983.

There are still many descendants of William and Ann Amos living in or around Kokomo or Howard County. They were sturdy pioneers with a love of God and country. *Submitted by Judith Eikenberry, granddaughter of Bessie Amos and Renna Mason*

WILLIAM C AND ROBERTA (CLEM) HARLAN ANDERSON - William Caywood Anderson is the grandson of Isaac Henry and Martha (Noel) Anderson from Kentucky and William Shephard and Martha (Hudson) Martin from Clay City, KY. Nannie, the 13th of 15 children of William and Martha, married Francis B. Anderson, son of Isaac and Martha, in 1903 and they moved to Edina, MO, where Raymond (married Pearl Nay) was born in 1904, and Frances Mae (married Albert Martin) was born in 1909. The family then moved back to Winchester, KY, where William was born Jan. 30, 1912. The family then moved to Kokomo in 1917.

William married Laura Shenks in 1929, and to this union a son, William Patrick, was born March 17, 1931. Pat married Norma Jane Harrison in Kokomo, Nov. 19, 1950, and they had three children: (1) David William, born Nov. 5, 1952, who wed Linda Dalton, May 27, 1978. Their children are Joshua David, born Oct. 5, 1978; Andrew William Joseph, born Aug 17, 1981; Krista Nicole, born Sept. 16, 1985; and Aaron Matthew, born Sept. 4, 1991; (2) Stephen Patrick, born July 30, 1955, who wed Deborah Maudlin, June 25, 1977. Their children are Chad Patrick, born Jan. 3, 1978; Tiffany Lynn, born Feb. 7, 1979; and Ashley Brooke, born July 6, 1985; (3) Pamela

Jane, born July 13, 1957, who wed Kenneth Carter, June 27, 1975. Their children are Brandon, born July 10, 1976; and Sarah Elizabeth, born Nov. 21, 1979.

William C. and Roberta (Clem) Harlan Anderson

William married Roberta (Clem) Harlan on July 2, 1971. She was born in Cutler, IN, Carroll County and graduated from Cutler School. Roberta and Francis Eugene Harlan had a son Brian John Harlan, born Dec. 8, 1958, who wed Carolyn Jean Harshbarger, May 12, 1984. Their children are Mary Elizabeth, born Nov. 13, 1987; Amy Nichole, born Oct. 12, 1989; and Mark Allen, born Feb. 18, 1993. Roberta was postmaster at Bringhurst for 27 years, from November 1965 until October 1993 when she retired. Her parents are Fred and Mary (Sandifur) Clem.

William attended school in Kokomo and Burlington. He worked as a Raleigh salesman from 1933 to 1939. He later worked for American Radiator Pottery where he helped organize the first union. He then went to work for General Electric in Kokomo where he was president of the local union. He later worked for Continental Steel as a machinist for 26 years where he was also Legislative Chairman of the Local 1054 and District 30. He has had a Rock and Gemstone Shop in his home on S.R. 18 & U.S. 31 for the past 30 years.

William has attended and been a member of Courtland Avenue Friends Church since 1917 and served on various committees. There are presently four generations of his family attending Courtland Avenue Friends Church. *Submitted by Roberta Anderson.*

ANSTETT - On March 10, 1920, two wagons and eight head of horses drove to an 80 acre farm located on 100W-300S. Christy and Lulu Anstett, man and wife, and Joe Anstett, a bachelor brother of Christy's, farmed in Benton County for four years raising draft horses. They had a sale selling thirty head of horses which gave them enough money to pay down on their new farm. It took two days driving their team of horses and two wagons to reach Howard County from Fowler in Benton County. Joe and Christy Anstett were the sons of Christiphor and Josephine Anstett of Fowler, IN. They were also farmers. Lulu, the wife of Christy, was the daughter of Eliza and Aden McGraw, farmers from Sharpsville, IN. After moving their other possessions from a railroad station in Fairfield, now called Oakford, they started a general farming operation with horses, cows, chickens, and hogs. Joe and Christy both worked with their teams and wagons to help build the Kokomo City Park. They had to drive their horses and wagons three miles to work each day and made five dollars per day. They also hauled gravel to put on the county roads in return for taxes on the farm. At the park they helped build the bear dens that are still visible today to those who remember where they were located. Joe worked at Greesons' Gravel Pit, where he hauled gravel by horse and wagon to build the Phillips Street Bridge in Kokomo. In 1925 a son, John Anstett, was born in the house on the farm. After years of Depression days and very hard times raising tomatoes for the Kemp Canning Co., they were finally able to keep the payments up and pay the debt off on the farm. John worked at home while attending Alto Grade School and West Middleton High School; that is where he met his wife Phyllis McKibben. She was the daughter of Ira and Nellie McKibbin who were farmers, and Ira worked at the Steel Mill also. After graduating in 1944 in the same class, John and Phyllis had a five-year courtship before marrying in 1946. Phyllis worked at Continental Steel and Miller Transportation, and John worked at General Electric until he started farming in 1948 on 199 acres known today as Emerald Lake. While living on this farm they had three daughters: Christina, Joene, and Lou Ann. In 1956 John, Phyllis and the girls moved to their own farm and home after renting previous farms. John continued to farm his 70 acres and rent other land. He was one of two Howard County farmers to put two tractors together to pull larger plows in 1960. In 1961 John and Phyllis planted their first single cross seed corn seed which grew into a seed business known as Anstett's Seed. It specialized in single cross hybrid seed corn and Indiana certified soybeans. All three girls graduated from Western High School and went on to become nurses.

Christy and Lulu Anstett

Christina Anstett Miller has two girls, Jennifer and Elizabeth. Joene has two children a girl Christie and a boy Bart. Lou Ann has two boys, Blake and Aden. John and Phyllis retired in 1988 closing the seed plant after 40 years of farming and seed production. They still live on the farm they bought and still own all the farm that belonged to John's parents except for 16 acres that was sold to Oakbrook Community Church, which is where all of the family attend.

JOHN V. AND BETTY J. ANWEILER - John was born in Otsego, MI just north of Kalamazoo on Dec. 4, 1915. His father was Otto Oliver Anweiler and his mother was Edna May (Nicholson) Anweiler. Otto was a papermaker by trade and had moved to Otsego when the paper plant closed in Kokomo. He died during the big flu epidemic of 1918 at Good Samaritan Hospital in Kokomo. Edna moved back to Kokomo to live with her father and mother, Benjamin Nicholson and Sarah Hannah (Carter) Nicholson who lived in Kokomo. Benjamin was a linotype machine operator at *The Russiaville Observer, Kokomo Dispatch,* and *Kokomo Tribune*. His mother also worked as typesetter at Russiaville. She died in 1975 at the age of 95.

John's paternal grandparents were John Otto Anweiler and Martha (Young) Anweiler who lived in Indianapolis, IN.

John and Betty Anweiler

John's ancestors on his mother's side were of Quaker faith and attended Russiaville Friends, New London Friends, and Union St. Friends. John grew up in Kokomo and graduated from Kokomo High School in 1933. He then went to work at Delco Radio. John spent three years in the Army in World War II and then returned to work at Delco. He started the first quick service laundry in Kokomo in 1947, running it until 1954. After serving 23 years working for the U.S. Post Office, he retired in 1980.

Betty Whited was born in Kokomo on May 29, 1922. Her parents were Harry Edward Whited and Delpha (Hammond) Whited. Harry was a molder who came from Coal City to Anderson and then to Kokomo. Harry worked at the Hoosier Iron and Globe American and he died in 1950. Delpha owned Peggy's Pie Shop on South Main Street for several years and she died in 1954.

Betty went to city schools and graduated from Kokomo High School in 1940. She worked at Mygrant's Candy Store and at Delco. She worked for the Kokomo-Center School Corporation as a secretary and bookkeeper, retiring in 1979.

John and Betty met at Delco in 1942 due to a narrow aisle and bumping into each other while going in opposite directions. The encounter ended in marriage in Nashville, TN on June 17, 1944, while John was in the service.

Their marriage has been blessed with two daughters: Vickie Sue (Anweiler) Getz of Kokomo who is married to Larry Getz; and Nancy Kathryn Anweiler of Somerset, NJ. They have one grandchild, Staci Leigh Getz of Kokomo. John has one sister, Catherine Anweiler of Kokomo. Betty has two nephews, Edward Whited of Lafayette, and James Whited of Jamie's fame in Kokomo. She also has one niece, Rebecca (Whited) Silvey.

John and Betty have been active in church work and are members of Chapel Hill Christian Church. They are both enjoying retirement and are enjoying living in Kokomo which has always been their home. John says that coming from before radio (except for crystal sets) to being able to see what is going on in the whole world is quite a change in a lifetime and the world is still changing. Life has been so good and we are looking for the joys of tomorrows.

ARMFIELD - The Howard County connection of the Armfield family began with Calvin C. Armfield who moved in 1858 to Howard County, locating in Liberty Township. Calvin C. was born in Guilford County, NC, son of Solomon and Thankful (Cimmons) Armfield. Calvin was married to Penninah Albertireson of North Carolina.

Calvin's great-grandfather, John Armfield, was born in northern England in 1695. He was a strict Quaker and a school teacher by profession. John and his young wife came with a colony of Quaker immigrants to Philadelphia in 1718. Afterward he moved to Bucks County, PA where he bought a farm and taught school. In 1765, John and his wife with their sons and a number of their neighbors, moved to Greensboro, NC.

William, the oldest son of John, was born in Pennsylvania in 1729 and married Mary Hamilton around 1745. Among the seven sons that were born was Solomon (Calvin's father). William was a strict Quaker who took no part in the American Revolution. That is, no active part until the British Tories took all of his livestock and food supplies. This act caused William to put aside his Quakerism for a day. At the morning of the Battle of Guilford Courthouse, he went to General Greene of the American forces and offered his services. When William reached home that night, weary and worn out, his wife asked, "William, where is thy game?" He replied, "The game I killed was not worth bringing home."

Dale and Mariruth Armfield

Calvin and his wife had six children among which was Joseph W. Armfield who married Samantha O. Chandler, daughter of John and Elizabeth (Hiott) Chandler. They had nine children: Lydia B., Leonard D., Lele Pearl, Lorina C., Lawrence W., Leo, Herman, Logan, and Lucy. With the second marriage to Grace (Davis) Armfield, three children were born: Walter M., Merrill, Mary Esther McAninch, the only living offspring of Joseph A. In his later years, Joseph was a Wesleyan Methodist minister who preached in Howard County.

Lawrence W. Armfield owned 110 acres of the original Armfield farm in eastern Howard County. The outstanding feature of his farm was his round red barn (which is still standing today) constructed in 1907 with the help of two men. Native oak and poplar trees on the farm furnished the lumber for the barn. Lawrence married Eva May Rhodes whose father Frank Rhodes was one of the pioneers of Taylor Township.

Russell J. Armfield, the only child of Lawrence and Eva May married Ella C. Fenn, a daughter of Edward Fenn and Dora (Meranda) Mugg Fenn. Dora Fenn was one of the founders of the Macedonia Christian Church on State Road 19. Russell and Ella had one child, Dale, born in 1924. At the beginning of the Great Depression of 1929, they moved to Boone Township, Madison County on a farm rented from Victor Swanfelt of Swedish descent. They later moved back in the early 1960's to Ella's family farm in eastern Howard County selling eggs and farming.

Joseph W. Armfield

Dale R. Armfield spent his early years of education in a one room school called Portable. Dale graduated from Summitville High School in 1942. In 1943, he married Mariruth Fouch who graduated from Frankton High School in 1942. Mariruth's parents were Cecil and Irene (Miles) Fouch. Cecil was born and raised in Tipton County. Irene was born and raised in Vermilion County, IL. She was educated as a school teacher and taught in Rossville, IL. Cecil and Irene farmed in Madison and Tipton Counties. Cecil was a real estate broker in his later years in the Elwood area. His children were Gene, James, Mariruth and Vera Juanita. Mariruth's grandparents were John and Lilly (Van Ness) Fouch, and Charles and Ella (Campbell) Miles. Both families were farmers. Mariruth's ancestors are descendants of the Huguenots, French Protestants who came to America during the 17th Century.

Dale and Mariruth moved to the Armfield farm in the spring of 1944 from Anderson, IN. They have four children: Diane Ruth Knight, Susan Marie Bond Ammerman, Brenda Jo Rogers, and Roger Dale Armfield. Roger is the sixth generation of the Armfield family to reside in eastern Howard County. Dale and Mariruth's grandchildren are Aaron David Knight, Traci Lynn Knight, Melinda Sue Bond, and Jessica Jo Rogers. *This small sketch of the Armfield family was compiled by Dale and Mariruth Armfield.*

ARNETT - Valentine B. Arnett was born in Ireland (1752-1801). He married Sarah (1756-1820). His children were Valentine, who married Celia Hancock; Edward who married Mildred Jacobs; John who married Catherine Arph; Mary Polly who married Joseph Cummings; Asbury who married Jemimah Weaver; Thomas was married first to Rachel Faulkner and second to Hannah Hudson; Willis married Elizabeth Mendenhall; Jesse married Margaret Williams; Charles married Susanna Graham; and Benjamin.

Asbury (1790-1870) was married in 1812 to Jemimah Weaver. Their children are: Sarah, James Henry, Rebecca, Valentine M., Tommy, Jesse, Winifred and Edward A.

James Henry Arnett (1816-1897), first married in 1839 Phebe Baldwin (1819-1861). They lived at New London, IN. Their children were Thomas, Jane, Valentine, Charlotte, Waldo, Eunice, Sarah Ann and Hannah. James Henry was married a second time in 1867 to Martha Wiltse, and they had Elizabeth, Rachel, Elbert L. and Jesse.

My great-grandparents were Sarah Ann Arnett (1855-1940) who was married in 1878 to Aubrey Flint DeLon (1855-1927), both of New London, IN. They moved to the west side of Kokomo, where they had a business 'DeLon Garden Home' where they raised produce. DeLon Street was named after them. Their children were William Pearl, Emma Lenora, Horace J. and Harry Everett, Fred King Sr. and Walter V.

My grandparents were Fred King DeLon Sr. (1893-1971) who was married in 1915 to Edna Alfloretta French (1895-1947). They had Gailen Louese, Fred King Jr. and Alice Lorene (1916-1981) who is my mother. She married in 1941 Myron 'Mike' Merrick (1910-1986). He was a deputy marshall with the South Whitley Police Department. They lived in South Whitley, IN. They were the parents of Beverly J. Schwartz of West Lafayette, IN and myself, Sara Ann Austin. I was named for my great-grandmother Sarah Ann Arnett DeLon. *Submitted by Sara Ann Merrick Austin*

SARAH "HARTWOOD" ARTIS - Sarah Hartwood was born on Dec. 4, 1827 in Rockville in Parke County, IN. She lived there until 1865. Sarah married John Artis. They lived in Howard County, near Ervin Township, for 10 years, then moved to Kokomo in 1871 on West Mulberry Street. The area was known as Haskett's Grove. They lived there for 25 years, when they sold their home and moved to 145 Western Avenue. Sarah worked for all the leading families in Kokomo.

Sarah and John had 10 children, all now deceased. They had four children when the Mexican War broke out and four more children when the Civil War started. These children were named: Victoria, Eva, Sarah, Duff, Bart, Burt, and two whose names are not known. Edna Martha, a granddaughter of Sarah and John, was born Aug. 25, 1886, in Kokomo, IN. She married Frank H. Black and they had four children: Martha Jackson (Indianapolis), Mary Beatie (Kokomo), Esther Davidson (Kokomo), and Ruth Moore (Cleveland, OH).

Esther Black Tuggle Davidson is the wife of Reed W. Davidson, a life long resident of Kokomo. She is the mother of one son, George E. Tuggle, and has two marvelous grandchildren: Derek Delon and Kelly Marie Tuggle.

Esther worked for nearly 40 years and retired from the Kokomo Howard County Public Library. She works diligently in our community and in the Wayman A.M.E. Church. *Submitted by Esther Davidson*

JOHN E. & LEONA M. ATKISSON - John Ellison Atkisson traveled to Howard County from Owen County where he met and married Jessie Snow. They joined the Oakford Separate Baptist Church where John was a lifetime trustee. He was a carpenter and contractor most of his life. Jessie was a housewife and took very good care in raising their seven children: Mable, Ethel, Edgar, James, Clara, Catherine and John Elbert, born June 16, 1923. John Jr. attended several grade schools in Howard County and was a 1942 graduate of Kokomo High School. He met and later married Leona Mae Kelley.

John and Ethel (Freeland) Kelley came to Howard County from Illinois. They lived south of Oakford and raised 11 children: Loren, Oleta, Wilma, Leona, Donald, Howard, Bob, Marjorie, Marlene, Shirley, and Gary. One son, Richard, died a few months after birth. John Kelley was taken from his family at an early age of 39, leaving Ethel to raise her family alone. There were some hard times, but she did a great job raising her children.

Leona was born on April 22, 1923. She attended grade school in Oakford and graduated from Sharpsville High School in 1942.

John Atkisson and Leona Kelley were married June 27, 1942. John farmed for 18 years and worked at Kokomo Spring for 21 1/2 years before retiring in 1985. Leona worked at Delco Radio for 30 years and retired the same day as John.

John is the oldest living lifetime member of Oakford Baptist Church. He is now serving as a deacon for life and is a fervent follower of the Lord. Leona has also attended Oakford Baptist Church for 52 years and has been a member for 30 years. She will always be remembered for her delicious cooking, especially her famous noodles.

John and Leona are the parents of three children. John Jr. lives across from Taylor High School with his wife Mickey and grandson Chris. He also has three step-children: Rocky, Linda, and Mike. Daughter Ellen lives west of Kokomo and has three children; Lori, Scott, and Cindy and one grandson, Andy. Steve lives in Fishers, IN with his wife Bonnie and his three children Michael, and twins Nikki and Chrissi.

John and Leona now reside 1/2 mile east of Oakford.

AULT - Jesse Ault is the son of Christopher and Phoebe (Sparks) Ault, who came to Marion County, IN in 1827. The Ault family had emigrated from Germany, and had settled in Baltimore.

Jesse was born in Marion County, five miles west of Indianapolis, and was one of 12 children. The Ault family moved from Marion County to Tippecanoe County where they resided on a farm.

Jesse Ault came to Howard County in 1846, and helped clear and develop the county.

He was married to Mary C. Kelley on Nov. 13, 1859. Two children were born to this union, namely, Sylvester E. and Margaret Lily. His wife died comparatively early in life, but he married again to Mahala Jane Dailey and had a daughter, Phebe. Later he moved to Tipton County where he was County Recorder. While there the Civil War started, and he enlisted in Company C, 101st Indiana Volunteer Infantry. At Missionary Ridge he lost his left arm in battle. This happened on Nov. 25, 1863, and he was discharged June 6, 1864. He returned to Tipton County, but came to Kokomo later where he resided until his death at age 74 on Aug. 22, 1910. Mahala died in September 1930.

Jesse's widow and daughter, Phebe, continued to live at 1122 E. Monroe Street. Phebe graduated from Kokomo High School in 1913 and went to Terre Haute Normal for one year, studying to be a teacher. She had to leave, as her mother opposed further education. Phebe worked at Thalman and Levi Department Store. Later, she worked at a canning factory and skate factory. When America entered World War I, Phebe went to Detroit, MI to live with her half-sister and husband. She got a job at Postal Telegraph, delivering messages to various factories in the vicinity. While doing this, she was seen by John Pyanowski who tested cars for Cadillac. He worked for Postal Telegraph previously so he asked the manager to introduce them. Soon after this, he joined the Army, but the war ended before he could be sent overseas. John and Phebe were married and returned to Kokomo and got jobs at Kingston Products. Later John worked for Con Carey vulcanizing tires. Eventually, he was able to start his own business, known as Horseshoe Tire Store. John and Phebe had six children. Their first child, Jessamine, died in infancy. Jean Antoinette was born Jan. 8, 1920. John Jr. was born Oct. 12, 1921. George Vincent was born July 23, 1923, and died in June, 1927. Partricia Eileen was born Sept. 20, 1926. Robert Adrian, born Feb. 7, 1929.

The family lived in Kokomo until 1942 when John and his daughters went to California. John had hay fever so that was the reason for moving. John and Jean got jobs at Lockheed so Phebe sold their home at 127 W. Elm Street. She and Robert moved to California in March, 1943. John Jr. was in the Air Force at this time. John Pyanowski died Feb. 12, 1974, and Phebe died Oct. 3, 1976. *Submitted by Jean (Pyanowski) Scott, granddaughter*

AUTER - Descends from Adriaen Hendrickse Auten who came to New Amsterdam (New York City) from Holland in 1651. Magdalena De Groff descended from

143

several Dutch and Huguenot families who came to New Netherlands (N.Y. State) as early as 1623.

Abram Auter was born in Pennsylvania in 1778 and Magdalena at Conewago, York (now Adams) County, PA in 1776. Abram rode with "Black Horse" Henry Lee (son of "Light Horse" Henry Lee of Revolutionary War fame) at the time the British ravaged the Niagara frontier near Buffalo in November 1813. Magdalena, becoming alarmed at the cannon fire, placed the children into a sleigh and started for Olean, 30 miles away. Abram came home, found the family missing and followed their tracks in the snow to find them. In the spring of 1814 he built a raft, made a cabin on it and took his family down the rivers to Cincinnati, where Auter and Voorhees relatives resided. They later moved to Preble County, OH.

Six of their children came with them. Their last child was born in Reading (now Cincinnati) in 1815. All of them were married at Eaton, OH.

Abram and Magdalena died within a week, July 25th and 28th respectively, during the cholera plague of 1849 and were buried in a common grave, with many others, in the Mound Hill Cemetery at Eaton. Their son Thomas and several other young men were cited for their public service during the plague. Thomas was baptized March 16, 1812 in the Dutch Reformed Church at Fleming, Cayugo County, NY. At Eaton he married Caroline Matilda Graham, born June 15, 1809 at Wheeling, VA (now W.Va.). They were married March 17, 1833, by Elder Levi Purviance, a famous early minister of the Christian Church. Thomas was a weaver and furniture maker.

The Auter Family - Juaneta Auter, Lela A. Caroline Auter, Thomas Atkins Auter, Sarah Sidella Auter, Abram Terry Auter, Lawrence Finney son of Juanita Auter, Edith Minerva (James) Auter.

About 1850, they moved to Kokomo, with three of their children: John VanTine (born Jan. 2, 1840), Abram Terry (born Aug. 13, 1843), and Caroline Atlanta (born Sept. 5, 1850).

Thomas was an elder at the Main Street Christian Church in Kokomo from 1853 to 1864. When the occasion warranted he was a preacher. He also served as its janitor and delighted in ringing the bells to call people to worship.

He was a Justice of the Peace in Kokomo and in May 1863 one John Thrall, a horse thief, while attempting to escape arrest, shot and killed one man and mortally wounded another. On Walnut Street, he encountered Thomas Auter, who picked up a brick bat and hurled it at Thrall's head. To escape the missile Thrall swung to one side whereupon the saddle turned on him and his capture ensued.

Upon the breaking out of the Civil War, Thomas Auter was appointed to an executive committee to solicit and collect funds for the support of the families of volunteers who were in the service of their country.

Their elder son, John Van Tine Auter, served a three month enlistment from April 18, 1861 in D Co. 6th Indiana Regt. He later served in A Co. 5th Regt., Indiana Cavalry. He was captured in Georgia and was a prisoner in the infamous Andersonville, GA prison from July 1864 to the war's end in April 1865.

Thomas Auter died Sept. 3, 1864 at Kokomo and was first buried in the "Old Cemetery". He was reburied in Crown Point Cemetery in 1902. Caroline Matilda Auter and her children moved to Cameron, Clinton County, MO about 1870. She died there on Oct. 7, 1872.

Abram Terry Auter, their young son, married Edith Minerva James (born Aug. 6, 1847 at Hillsboro, OH) at Kokomo on April 11, 1863. She was the daughter of Dr. Johnathan Atkins James of Kokomo. Abram was elected to the town board at Cameron in April 1870. He was a charter member of the Wildman Lodge #29, I.O.O.F., instituted at Kokomo Nov. 20, 1867. Abram T. and Edith Minerva Auter had the following children: Thomas Atkins (born Dec. 29, 1867) Sarah Sidella (born Sept. 2, 1865 Kokomo) Junieta and Junaneta (born June 26, 1870 Cameron) and Lella Carolina (born April 21, 1872, Cameron).

Prior to 1880 Abram T. and his family moved to Salina, KS, where he operated a hardware and sewing machine store.

The family was in Denver, CO by 1882 when they were listed in the Denver City Directory.

On Feb. 27, 1893, Thomas Atkins Auter married Mary Helen ("Ella") Mathews (born Dec. 10, 1872 in Marquette County, MI). She was the daughter of Charles Henry and Jane (Rule) Mathews, both born in Cornwall, England. They emigrated separately to Michigan in the 1860's to the copper mining area of Michigan. They moved to the gold and silver mining area of Colorado (Georgetown and Leadville) prior to 1874. Thomas and "Ella" had two daughters: Mabel Irine (born May 29, 1894 in Denver) and Edith Jane (born July 22, 1896) and a son Robert Leroy who died young. Edith was married on May 16, 1916, at Denver to Lawrence Franklin Cook.

BAKER - Watson Baker (1811-1879), son of Maurice Baker and Elizabeth Jenkins, and Nancy Rebecca Orr (1812-1885), daughter of Joseph Orr and Nancy Agness McIlheney, were married Dec. 23, 1831 in Ohio. The family moved from Washington Court House, Fayette County, OH to Kokomo, Howard County, IN about 1852. Watson Baker was a farmer on the 1860 census, Center Township, Kokomo, IN. Children, born in Ohio except the last two:

1. Isabel (1832-1913) married Joseph Bevington Bloomer (1830-1886) March 24, 1853 in Kokomo, IN. Burial, Lebanon, KS.

2. Mary (1834-1907) married Allen Trimble Bloomer (1828-1908) in Ohio. Burial, Newpoint, MO.

3. Joseph, born and died 1836, Fayette County, OH.

4. Melvina 'Bine' (1838-1873) married William Richard Shepard Nov. 15, 1855 in Kokomo, IN. Burial, Newpoint, MO.

5. William Harrison (1840-1916) married Harriet Francis Lindsey (1841-1878) April 5, 1860 in Kokomo, IN. Civil War, Cpl. Co. G, 43 MO Inf.

Marion Collins Skinner and Alice Baker Skinner

6. Elizabeth Jane (1843-1918) married Levi Thompson (1835-1924). Burial, Lebanon, KS.

7. Lucy Ann (1845-1925) married George Washington Kyger (1849-) Dec. 7, 1869. Burial, Pawnee, OK.

8. Samuel Maurice (1847-1912) married Miriam Josephine Van Dresen in Holt County, MO. Burial, Rathdrum, ID.

9. Nancy Belle (1850-) married James Wesley Kennedy (1842-1905). Burial, Daisy, WA.

10. Granville, born and died Kokomo, Howard Co., IN.

11. Luther Watson (1853-1932) born Kokomo, Howard County, IN, married Eliza Jane Porter (1862-1929) Oct. 30, 1877 in Kansas. Burial, Nowata, OK.

Child 5, William Baker and Harriet 'Frankie' Lindsey, daughter of Joseph Lindsey and Abigail Paist Whinery, lived with his parents in 1860 Kokomo, IN census. Her parents opposed her marrying 'Bill' Baker. After her death in 1878, he moved his family to Kansas to be near his parents. 'Bill' and Frankie' had 11 children, #1 and #11 born in Indiana; the others in Holt County, MO:

1. Alice (1861-1933) born Kokomo, Howard County, IN, married Marion Collins Skinner (1860-1944) in Kansas. Burial, Iola, KS. They were the parents of nine children and great-grandparents of the author of this article. Alice helped her father raise the children, except Florence, who remained in Indiana.

2. Florence May (1862-) married Tilman Sayles Aug. 17, 1881.

3. William Oscar (1864-1928) married his first cousin Maude Baker. Burial, Rathdrum, ID. Both were musicians.

4. Cora E. (1866-1875), killed at school when two boys were fighting, threw a stone and hit her. Burial, Highpoint, Holt County, MO.

5. Mary Adelaide (1867-1920) married Thomas Cline (1861-1937) in Lebanon, KS. Burial, Lebanon, KS.

6. Orville Mills (1869-1939) married Mary Carberry (1868-1955) Aug. 30, 1893 in Idaho. Burial, Otrano, IA.

7. Earnest (1870-1878) drowned at Billings Mill Race near Delphi, IN, four weeks after his mother suddenly took ill and died. Their graves have not been located. Within three years, death claimed two children and the wife of 'Bill' Baker.

8. Martha Frances (1872-1951) married three times. Burial, Eugene, OR.

9. Aura Belle (1873-1944) married three times. Burial, Eugene, OR.

10. Harvey 'Ted' (1875-) married Anna Stadt in 1902 St. Paul, MN. He was a soldier in the Spanish-American War in Cuba; went to the Philippines and fought in the insurrection; went to China to put down the Boxer Rebellion. He lost the sight of one eye due to a severed nerve; then was a barber in Detroit, MI.

11. Arthur Lindsay (1877-1961) was born in Delphi, Carroll County, IN, married Nora May Bevelhymer (1883-1973). He was in the mining and lumber business. Burial, Eugene, OR. *Submitted by Linda Grantham Stengele*

IVAN LAWRENCE BAKER AND WILMA D. SCOTT - Ivan Lawrence Baker and Wilma D. Scott were united in marriage Dec. 7, 1947, at the First Baptist Church in Anderson, IN. They resided in Anderson until their fourth son was born, and moved to Kokomo three months later. Ivan is a veteran of WWII and served with the U.S. Army in the South Pacific. He came to Kokomo as manager of the North Drive-In Theater, a subsidiary of the Alliance Amusement Company. He was later manager of the South Drive-In Theater and was affiliated with the Sipe Theater and also the first two McDonalds Restaurants that were opened in Kokomo. He later worked at Chrysler Corporation and retired from there in 1981.

Ivan Lawrence and Wilma D. (Scott) Baker

Wilma earned her real estate license in 1973 and later her brokers license. She was a salesperson at Pencek's Agency and Re/Max Realtors. She later worked in retail sales. She is a member of St. Luke's Methodist Church and also attends First Church of the Nazarene in Tipton.

Les, Karen, Lisa, Lauren and Lindsay

The oldest son, Leslie Camerson Baker, was born 1948 and graduated from Kokomo High School in 1966. He joined the USAF shortly after graduation. He served in Germany and in Guam. He met and married Karen Sue Sykes of Washington, D.C. (1975) upon his return to the States. They have three daughters: Lisa Nicole (1979), Lauren Renee (1980) and Lindsay Michelle (1981). Leslie earned his Bachelor of Science Degree in Management (1991) while in service. He retired from USAF in 1991. He and his family settled in Beavercreek, OH where he is employed as an engineer for LOGTC. The family are members of St. Mark's Lutheran Church of Fairborn.

Loren D. Baker, Leslie's twin, died shortly after birth.

Pete, Phyllis, Paul and Kimberly

Peter Lawrence Baker, middle son, born 1954, was graduated from Taylor High School in 1972. He then went on to earn his Bachelors Degree in EET at Purdue University in 1979, and later his Masters Degree in Business Administration from Butler University in 1973. This past year he passed his exam for Certified Quality Engineer. He is a manager at Delco Electronics, Kokomo, and is a member of Toastmasters International. He and Phyllis Jean Kellar were married in 1976. Phyllis has a Bachelor of Science Degree in Medical Technology from IUK (1976) and is a med tech at Howard Community Hospital. The have two children, Paul Robert (1980) and Kimberly Lynn (1983). They are members of First Church of Nazarene, Tipton - where Pete is Sunday School superintendent.

Brad and Mary Baker

The youngest son, Bradley Scott Baker, born 1957, was graduated from Taylor High in 1975, where he was on the Varsity Wrestling Team for four years. Brad earned his Associates Degree in Electronics from Ivy Tech of Kokomo in 1985, and is an electrician at Delco Electronics, Kokomo. He and Mary Beth Hurt, also of Kokomo, were married in 1978 and have four children: two daughters, Ginger Roselean (1980) and Cassie Johana (1983), and two sons, Luke Bradley (1990) and Levi Ivan (1992) - all named in part from maternal and paternal grandparents and father. Brad and his family are members of the First Assembly of God, where Brad works in the sound room.

SILAS AND SUSAN FRENCH BALDWIN -

Silas S. Baldwin was born Jan. 18, 1822, in Butler County, OH, the son of Thomas L. and Susan Stull Baldwin. He died March 9, 1898 in Warren County, IN and is buried at Locust Grove Cemetery, Warren County, IN. On April 4, 1844 in Montgomery County, IN, he married Susan French, the daughter of James and Abigail (McGilliard) French. Susan was born Jan. 14, 1830 in Montgomery County, IN. She died Sept. 5, 1910 and is also buried at Locust Grove Cemetery.

Silas had brothers and sisters which were, Indiana who married John Hart and Daniel Adams; Henry J. who married Margaret J. Weidner; Elizabeth married John Maze and later married her brother-in-law, Daniel Adams; and Rachel who married Jacob Ault.

Silas S. Baldwin; Susan French Baldwin

Susan's brothers and sisters were Alfred, Francis, Ralph and Ann Fisher. The children of Silas and Susan were: Indiana Ann who married John M. Wilson; Francis M. who married Harriett Boswell; Albert Benton who married Mavilla Warner and Jennie Troxwell; Ralph married ___; Orpha married George Rice, 2nd ___ Francis, 3rd ___ Andrews; Abigail J. married George T. Fewell; Laura Annis married Charles Horn; and Samantha A. and Charles A. who died in infancy and are buried in Price Cemetery in Ervin Township.

Silas was one of the early settlers of Ervin Twp. He was a justice of the peace, and founder of the Baldwin Church, which was located at the northwest corner of roads 800 W and 400N.

His father Thomas sent Ralph French, brother of Susan, to buy land in this area. Ralph purchased the land, where his niece, Indiana Ann Wilson, was later to live. The property is still in the same family.

Susan told her granddaughter Pearl Wilson that when they came to Howard County, they 'wintered' behind a huge log. It was near the property of Thomas Kirkpatrick. I imagine they must have built a lean-to beside it. I've often wondered how large that tree must have been! If it had been like the famous 'sycamore stump' they could have lived inside it.

Elias Jackson 'Lucky' Baldwin is also in this family. He was born in Butler County, OH and came to Montgomery County, IN. During the Gold Rush, he went to California where he struck it rich. Much is written about him in history. *Submitted by a great-great-granddaughter of Silas and Susan, Mary Blangy*

FRANK W. BALL -

My name is Sandra Beck-Lushin. I am the granddaughter of Frank W. Ball. In 1928, Frank Ball came to Kokomo to work for the Kokomo Diamond Plate Glass Company. In a letter, Frank wrote to his wife Rebecca Ann and family back home; he told of his new job and that he was making $20.20 per week. His room and board cost $1.00 per day. In the letter, he expressed concern about expenses back home and instructed his wife to sell their corn crop to pay their outstanding debts. One such debt was a doctor bill for $32.50. The corn crop, he believed, could be sold for $60.00. He went on to write that he had found a four room house, with three "good size" rooms and a kitchen. The property also included a 90 foot well and a large garden and could be rented for $10. His letter was postmarked in 1928 with a two cent stamp affixed.

His wife Rebecca Ann and five of his children, Lemoine, Veneda, Devella (Dee), Neoshia, and Beatrice joined him later after he rented housing and became familiar with the community.

When the Kokomo Diamond Plate Glass Company went out of business, Frank became employed by the Kokomo Water Works Company. One of his first jobs was installing a new water filtering system.

Besides being a housewife, Rebecca Ball was an excellent seamstress and helped supplement the household income with her talent.

Frank and Rebecca's daughter, Devella, who is their fifth child, is my mother. She met my father Whitney Beck, an Ohio building contractor, and in 1938 they married. They lived in Cincinnati, OH, where I was born. My mother returned to Kokomo in 1946.

In 1958, I graduated from Kokomo High School and married my husband, Jean Paul Lushin. We have five children. Our oldest son, Paul, is division manager for ECOLAB, Inc. in St. Louis, MO. He and his wife Sally have three sons. Vendala Dawn (Manfredi), our oldest daughter, is a computer specialist for Center Township of Howard County. She and her husband, Gregg, have two children. Our third child, Lori (Molden), lives in Evansville, IN and works for the Evansville Sheet Metal Company. She and her husband, Scott, have one child. Our youngest daughter, Kara Nikole, is a full-time student at Indiana University-Kokomo. Chad, the youngest child, graduated from Kokomo High School in the spring of 1994.

BARBER - Mark Barber (1813-1865) and his wife Mary Terrell Barber (1818-1893) left Clinton County, OH in the spring of 1853 for Ervin Township. Mark had bargained for 80 acres in the northwest center of the township from his relative, David Foster, who had trading post in Burlington. He acquired more land, cut the timber and built his house in 1864 and died the following year. Most of that land is still in the family, currently owned by Edwin and Norma Jean Barber Plank.

Mark and Mary raised seven of their nine children on this farm. Two died in infancy. The others were Robert Terrell (1847-1927) who married Rebecca Gates; Joseph H. (1849-1908) who married Emma Wilson and Melissa Coder; Nancy Jane (1850-1920) who married Benjamin Polk; Abner Ratcliff (1853-1944) who married Lydia Alice Riffe and Mary Beckner; Charles Henry (1856-1942) who married Sarah Elizabeth McCracken; Mary Sadona (1859-1940) who married Burns Cook and Jonathan Morris; and Martha Ellen (1861-1957) who married Levi Lenon and Lincoln Tucker. Abner and Charles Henry lived on this land until their death. Charles Henry had one living child, Alpheus Clifford. He and his wife Fay Platt, who had no issue, continued to live on a part of the farm until their death.

Abner Barber and his wife Lydia Alice Riffe (1861-1891) raised their five children on another part. They were Mark Allen (1879-1978) who married Mary Cripe and Eva Lenon Wikle, no issue; William Lester (1880-1964) who married Lillian McManama and had one son, Earl; David Ross (1882-1970) who married Julia Gladys Felton, had two children Norma Jean (Plank) and an infant son David; Mary Charlotte (1884-1969) married Dora Roach and had ten children: Laura Alice (Dunkin, Deane), Paul, Clarence, Earl, Thelma (Lybrook), Wilbur, Russell, Dora Jr. and twin infant sons; Minnie Zephel (1886-1965) who married Joe Teel and had four daughters: Mary Emily (Catron), Josephine (Clark, Haskett), Elsie Mae (Barrick) and Alice Louise (Maroney). After the early death of Abner's first wife, he married Mary Beckner and they had Walter Harold (1893-1982) who married Fleeta Mae Douglas, no issue.

145

Ross and Gladys Barber

Abner, a farmer, was very active in the community and the Young America Baptist Church. He served as administrator of many family estates, including his mother's. He was a staunch Republican and attended many of their conventions. He also served as a juror on both the local and state level. He traveled by car to Florida 18 winters until his death at age 91 in 1944.

The family of David Ross Barber, Abner's third child, lived on the original Mark Barber land. David was a farmer and road builder and very active in politics. His daughter, Norma Jean (Barber) Plank, author of this article, and her husband, Edwin Plank, purchased the David Ross Barber farm (her parents') in 1978 and the Alpheus Clifford Barber farm in 1959. These were both portions of the original Mark Barber land. *Submitted by Mrs. Norma Plank*

ROSS BARNARD - Ross Barnard was my grandfather and my father was Hobert Barnard. My father and Mary Johnson of Carroll County were married on June 20, 1937.

Hobert Barnard worked as a hired hand by the month on a farm in Howard County. Guy Wilson and his brother John Wilson owned the farm and farmed several acres of land with horses and tractors.

I, Donald Barnard, my brother Harold, and our sister were born on a farm owned by Mr. Wilson. This farm was on 900 West about 1/2 mile from the old Dogertown School which is no longer used as a school but part of it still stands.

My father and mother moved to a farm on Jerk Water Road in Howard County. The farm was on the south side of the road between 1050 West and 1180 West. Jerk Water Road is probably 100 South.

This farm was owned by Mr. Kingrey who lived in Burlington, IN. This farm has probably the largest hip roof bank barn in Howard County which was, as I remember, partly destroyed by high winds. It was rebuilt and still stands as of Jan. 1, 1994.

My father and mother had three more children born on this farm in Howard County: George, Mary Jane, and Robert Joe Barnard, the last born in 1947, which made six children in all, four boys and two girls.

My father owned his first farm machinery on the farm including a new Ford tractor and machinery which he signed up for at the fair in Flora. Tractors and new machinery could not be bought because of World War II and there was rationing of all goods short in supply because of war productions.

I remember my father sawing lumber from logs sawed on this farm back in the woods. The woods looked to be about like it is today in 1994 as it did when we lived on that farm. The saw mill was pulled by my father's tractor and an endless belt.

There also was a threshing machine on this farm which my father and a crew of men worked around the county area and on this farm. We had a grain binder which cut and tied bundles, then dumped them on the ground. Men, children and wives stacked them in shocks to finish drying.

After drying, the shocks were put on a wagon and hauled to the threshing machine which was driven by my father's tractor and a very long endless belt. The threshing machine separated the grain and blew the straw in a large stack over wood poles set in the ground and other smaller poles with random spacing which actually formed a barn of blown straw over the poles with a large opening underneath. The grain was then put in the barn.

I was large for my size and of course being the oldest child I must have felt in charge, for I carried water to the men and helped all I could in those years.

When the men worked together, the wives cooked lots of very good food. I remember my father and other men butchering hogs and beef in January and February when the weather changed and got cold. The meat was sugar cured and hung to cure in the smoke house. Other meat was canned and processed since there were no freezers in our homes in those days, only ice boxes.

When we lived on this farm I started school at New London School with my brother, Harold. We then moved from the area about 1940 or 1950. *Submitted by Donald Barnard*

WILLIAM WILSON BARNES - William Wilson Barnes was born Nov. 12, 1819, at Sherman, Fairfield County, CT, the son of William Barnes (1776-1853) and Susannah Fowler (1786-1860). His siblings were Sally, Andrew, Lybarthus, Jefferson, Garrett, Betsy, and Morris. His grandfather Stephen Barnes (1731-1816) emigrated from England and served under Washington in the American Revolution. After completing his education at age 13, William clerked in a store and worked in a lumber camp near Lake Champlain. In 1837 he visited a cousin at Palmyra, OH, and continued on to Cincinnati looking for employment. He settled in Highland County where he taught school, worked for local farmers and operated a blacksmith shop. August 5, 1841, he married Eliza Jane Littler, born Oct. 1, 1820, daughter of John Littler (1800-1855) and Nancy McClure (1804-1890) whose families were from Virginia.

William secured financial backing and opened a hotel and store in Centerfield, Highland County, OH. He hauled supplies from Cincinnati and sold them at a good profit. In 1844 William and his two brothers-in-law went to Kokomo to purchase land in newly organized Richardville, now Howard County, IN. After purchasing 560 acres, mostly in Howard Township and three lots in Kokomo, he returned to his home and business in Ohio.

William and Eliza had five children: Elizabeth Barnes (1843-1846); John William Barnes born Jan. 10, 1847, married Wyoma A. Brandon Jan. 9, 1879, died March 21, 1940; Cassius Lamantine Barnes (1848-1849); George M. Dallas Barnes born June 4, 1850, married Winifred Phillips June 25, 1879, died Oct. 7, 1906; and Stephen Titus Barnes.

Four generations of the Barnes Family. Sitting: L-R Stephen Titus Barnes, Edwin Barnes Riley, Wm. Wilson Barnes. Standing: Lillie Dallas (Barnes) Riley.

At the end of the Civil War the William Barnes family moved to Howard Township where William operated a sawmill on land he had purchased earlier in sections 14, 15 and 22. He became a leader in the farmers' Grange Movement and published the *Kokomo Granger* newspaper for a short time. He also bought over 4,000 acres in Saline County, IL, that yielded timber and coal, and gave each of his sons 500 acres.

After Eliza J. Barnes died July 12, 1890, William married 2) Fannie Justice of Bethel, OH. William died Aug. 29, 1910, and was buried beside Eliza in Crown Point Cemetery, Kokomo. Fannie returned to Ohio.

The youngest son, Stephen Titus Barnes, born April 4, 1853, married Rosella Lacey, daughter of James Lacey and Elizabeth Brandenburg of Grant County, IN. She was born Dec. 21, 1854 and died Dec. 25, 1882. They had four children: Charles Barnes, born and died 1875; Lillie Dallas Barnes, (1877-1951); Elizabeth Barlow Barnes, born 1880; and Rosa Barnes, born 1882. After Rosella's death, Stephen Titus Barnes married 2) Rebecca Ann Millikan Aug. 27, 1884. He later married 3) Sarah Jane Roper Sept. 7, 1889. They had three children: William Wilson Barnes, Jr., born 1890; Harry Roper Barnes, born 1892; and Mable Marie Barnes, 1896-1971. Stephen Titus Barnes died April 18, 1925, and Sarah died Feb. 9, 1946. They were buried at Crown Point Cemetery, Kokomo. *Submitted by Devin B. Riley*

BARNETT/DOWDEN/JOHNSON - Christopher Keith Barnett was born Jan. 8, 1962 in Johnson City, Washington County, TN, son of Kenneth Wayne and Barbara Ann McInturff Barnett. At the aged of three, he came to Howard County with his mother and stepfather, Walter Burton Johnson Jr. He was married Dec. 28, 1980 in Howard County to Gina Michelle Ellabarger (born Nov. 20, 1962), daughter of Carl Edward and Gladys Irene Minglin Harrell Ellabarger. Two children: Brandi Michelle (born March 19, 1983) and Logan Keith Barnett (born Feb. 27, 1988). Keith is a licensed plumber.

Robert Scott Dowden was born Nov. 12, 1963 at Kokomo, Howard County, IN, son of Robert Joe and Caroline Josephine Wilcox Dowden. Scott, not married, is an employee at Armstrong Landon.

Nikki Chantal Johnson Diaz Neal was born Oct. 9, 1969, in Kokomo, Howard County, IN, daughter of Walter Burton Jr. and Barbara Ann McInturff Barnett Johnson. Nikki 1/m Feb. 19, 1988 to David Leonard Diaz (born June 28, 1964), a son, Michael David Diaz, (born June 12, 1987). Nikki 2/m Aug. 1, 1991, to Mathew "Matt" Franklin Neal (born April 13, 1972); a son, Cody Mathew Neal (born Nov. 29, 1991). Nikki, other than living a few years in Connecticut has lived in Howard County; she is an employee of Ponderosa Steak House.

Kevin Wayne Dowden was born Dec. 3, 1954, Kokomo, Howard County, IN, son of Robert Joe and Virginia Barbara Leonard Dowden. Kevin, 1/m Jan. 12, 1980, in Salem, IL to Melinda Carol Shietze, two sons born to this marriage: Kevin Wayne Jr. (born Oct. 27, 1980) in Salem, IL and Kyle Robert Dowden (born Feb. 11, 1983) in Howard County, IN. Kevin, 2/m (March 9, 1985 in Howard County to Mary Ellen Ingle (March 22, 1962), daughter of Norman David and Sharon Sue Kendall Ingle. No children. Kevin is an employee of Jarrett Trucking Inc.

Top Row: L to R - Keith, Scott, Nikki, Kevin, and Michelle. Second Row: Teresa, Shellie and Karen.

Barbara Michelle Johnson Huskins was born Aug. 16, 1966, in Kokomo, Howard County, IN, daughter of Walter Burton Jr. and Barbara Ann McInturff Barnett Johnson. Married in Erwin, Unicoi County, TN April 4, 1994, to Ricky Allen Huskins (born Nov. 29, 1959), son of Harry Leonard and Florence Johnson Walker Huskins. Parents of a son, Jason Allen (born Aug. 19, 1992). Michelle and Ricky are first cousins.

Teresa Diana Barnett Vandergriff was born Feb. 28, 1960, in Johnson City, Washington County, TN, daughter of Kenneth Wayne and Barbara Ann McInturff Barnett;

came to Howard County with mother and step-father Walter Burton Johnson Jr. in the fall of 1965. Married in Howard County April 21, 1979, to Clyde Steven Vandergriff (born June 27, 1955), son of Clyde Horace and Shirley Marie Caldwell Vandergriff. They are the parents of two boys, Jeremy Steven, (born March 20, 1980) and Joshua Ryan, (born March 18, 1983). Teresa is employed at Hardee's.

Ann Nichelle Johnson Sterling was born April 30, 1974, Kokomo, Howard County, IN, daughter of Robert Joe and Barbara Ann McInturff Dowden. Shellie, as she is called, married Feb. 24, 1993, in Howard County to Richard James Sterling (born Dec. 5, 1973), son of Lester Lee and Sandra Kay Benge Sterling. A son, Jordan James was born to this union April 20, 1993.

Karen Elaine Dowden Degraffenreid was born Dec. 3, 1954, Kokomo, Howard County, IN, daughter or Robert Joe and Virginia Barbara Leonard Dowden. Married Oct. 5, 1985, in Howard County to Marty Lane Degraffenreid (born March 17, 1960 in Howard County), son of William Hale and Norma Jean Degraffenreid. *Submitted by Robert Scott Dowden*

WILLIAM JOSHUA BARNETT
William Joshua Barnett was one of the first white men in the Howard County area. He was one of seven children of James C. Barnett and Rebecca Jackson. He came here by waterway in 1839 from Cass County, when this county was first being developed. He built the first saw mill in the county, later known as Cromwell's Mill. Joshua was born in Ohio on Sept. 22, 1809, married Jane Voorhees in 1829, had four children - James, David Conner, John W. and Caroline. He died on March 13, 1844, in Ervin Township and is buried in the Barnett Cemetery, about seven miles west of Kokomo. It is written in the history books that he was acquainted with Peter Cornstalk. His Uncle Jesse was the first appointed sheriff of Howard County by the Governor and later asked to resign. His father in 1844 was appointed along with Isaac Price and Jonathan Hayworth as viewers for road construction.

David Conner Barnett served in the Civil War. Upon returning home, he became a doctor of medicine. He studied medicine in New London, and his practice included offices in Young America, Onward and Lincoln. He and his wife Rebecca had eight children (two died in infancy). The others were Lola Kinsey, Harry Barnett, Frank Barnett, Carrie Dunkin, Edward Barnett, and Fred Barnett. After Rebecca died, he later married Elizabeth Matlock of Hemlock. He lived to be 93 years old.

John Franklin Barnett was grandfather to my husband. He was born in Poplar Grove and moved to Kokomo where he lived the rest of his life. He and his wife, Margaret Edith Vance, had six children. Edith Marie Morrow was his daughter and my husband's mother. Her youngest sister, Dorothy, is the oldest living relative of this family. It is to her HONOR that I am writing this article. She has children, grandchildren, nieces and nephews living in Kokomo and is held in high esteem by all of them. *Submitted by Mrs. Donald (Jane Allman) Morrow*

BEAMAN
Three Beaman brothers early came to Howard from Owen County, IN, attracted by possibilities of better farm land and jobs in new industries. Their progenitors came from North Carolina in 1823. Theirs was a middle class contribution to developing the county - clearing land, tilling farms and serving time on production lines. Wright (1858-1933) and Samuel (1865-1941) came in 1888. With teams of horses they at first engaged in logging operations. Wright's family later settled on a farm near Hemlock. Lorenzo (1871-1954) arrived in 1891, took up work with factories, including 20 years with Continental Steel from which he retired.

This is the story of Samuel (Sam) Beaman's family. He married America Elizabeth Murphy (1869-1931) at Martinsville, Aug. 3, 1988. Their four children were born in Howard County. Garnettie and Claud died young (18 and 2 1/2 years). Court (1890-1985) and Paul (1906-present) grew up in the expanding economic and social life of Kokomo. After his logging experience Samuel, during the Panic of 1893, found himself digging ditches for a living. The growing Haynes Automobile Company eventually provided steady work. He may be seen in a blown-up picture of early Haynes employees in the Haynes Museum, wearing the black derby he usually sported. He later worked for Pittsburgh Plate Glass from which he retired in 1929 to a small farm near Haynes Monument which in those days was in the country.

America Elizabeth, Samuel Beaman with son Paul, Kokomo, about 1910.

Court's life, other than family, was marked by three interests: baseball, skilled machine production and association with fraternal organizations. As a young man he participated in boxing matches, but his consuming athletic endeavor was baseball which he pursued from 1905 until the 1920s. He was an outstanding player in the local Industrial League (in which he played on several teams) and two seasons in Toledo City League. Simultaneously he worked as a skilled machinist successively at Haynes and Apperson Automobile Companies and Kingston Products Corporation. His social endeavors centered around Masonic, Moose, Eagles, and, briefly, other fraternal organizations. He was most active in the Fraternal Order of Eagles, serving in a series of lodge offices and as a member of the Arie's National Championship Ritualistic Team. During World War II Court was a US Air Force inspector, Connorsville. Afterwards (1946-1963), he was Secretary for the Eagles Lodge. In honor of his life's work, the Lodge declared Oct. 23, 1982, Court Beaman Day.

Court married Gladys Ruth Pierce (1896-1972) April 3, 1915. They had three children. One, Dale, was killed in an auto accident in infancy. Chester (1916-present) was graduated from DePauw University (A.B. 1938) and University of Michigan (A.M. 1939), entered the U.S. Government, served as an Army officer in World War II and joined the U.S. Diplomatic Service (1949-1972). Subsequent to retirement, he set up a personnel management consultancy in Alexandria, VA. Chester married Mary Ruth Tyler (1915-present) of Missouri, Nov. 8, 1947. They had two children — Bruce Tyler and Mary Anina Ruth, who provided them seven grandchildren. Court's daughter Gladys (1918-present) was graduated from Kokomo High School in 1936. She married (1) Thomas Crull by whom she had four children (Betty, Thomas, Franklin and Robert), (2) Charles Smitherman (with whom she adopted a son Charles) and (3) Russell Bogue. She worked as hospital secretary and house mother at rehabilitation centers.

Paul, Sam Beaman's youngest son, first worked at Kingston Products, then joined the Prudential Insurance Company with whom he made a lifetime career. He married Ivaah Worthington (1911-present), Dec. 2, 1929. They had four children (Betty, Marlene, Judith and Paul Jr.) *Submitted by Chester E. Beaman*

RALPH DOWNS BEATY
Ralph Downs Beaty was born on a farm in Jennings County, IN, Aug. 2, 1881, to Joseph and Rachael Downs Beaty.

As a young man he worked for the American Express Company in Indianapolis. On Aug. 28, 1912, he married Ellen (Ella) B. Wohrer who was also from Jennings County. Their first child, Jane Elizabeth, was born in Indianapolis Sept. 6, 1916. Soon after her birth the family moved to Kokomo where Ralph worked for a time in the grocery store of C.A. Malaby, his brother-in-law. Ralph and Ella built a house at 1317 N. Purdum and a grocery store at 901 E. Markland Avenue.

December 24, 1918, a second daughter, Dorothy Ellen, was born. It was the terrible winter of the flu epidemic. Ella and Jane had been ill several times during the winter. Nine days after the birth of Dorothy Ellen, Ella died at the age of 33 years of influenza.

Ralph continued operating the grocery store, sold the house and lived in a boarding house near the store. The two little girls were taken care of by Ralph's sister, Bess Kendrick, and her family in Indianapolis. Ralph drove to Indianapolis every Sunday to visit his daughters.

Ralph and Pearl Beaty

In July, 1923, Ralph married a young widow, Pearl Findley Peek, and brought Jane and Dorothy back to Kokomo. On May 6, 1924, a third daughter, Rachael Louise, was born. They were a happy family for the next few years, then came the Great Depression! So many of the grocery customers were Pittsburgh Plate Glass factory workers who 'ran a bill' for groceries. Not being able to carry them any longer, Ralph was forced to close the store. The building was rented to Krogers for a few years, then sold to Ridgeways who still operate the South Side Feed Store at that location.

Ralph worked for W.E. Remy Grocery at the corner of Wabash and North Streets through the Depression and the years following. Shortly before his death of a heart attack Sept. 12, 1943, he worked for Kingston Products; the only time in his life spent working a 5-day, 40-hour week. He thought that was a vacation!

Ralph was a beloved husband and father with a great sense of humor. He was a respected businessman and was a friend to many people.

Pearl lived until Jan. 17, 1980, working as a practical nurse and keeping older persons in her home. She was a wonderful stepmother and mother to the three girls, was active in church, and had many friends.

Jane married Wayne E. Allen and has three children: Alice Jane Richey, Donald Wayne Allen and Mary Elizabeth Martin; seven grandchildren: Tamra Cravens Kwiatt, Anita Louise Woodring, Christina Lynn Richey, Daniel Allen Martin, Brian Kent Martin, Adam Joseph Martin and Sarah E. Allen. Jane and Wayne live in Kokomo and all the children and grandchildren live in the area.

Dorothy married James L. Lovejoy and has two daughters: Janet Lee Lovejoy-Sisson, and Jacque Lynn Lovejoy. They live in Los Angeles, CA.

Rachael Louise married Edward Wanca and has two sons: John Christopher Wanca and David Edward Wanca; one grandson, Stephen Christopher. They all live in the Akron, OH area. *Submitted by Jane B. Allen*

BEATTY-NEWBY
David Beatty had been a police officer for 27 and a half years when he died, June 27, 1989. As a small child he had dreams of being a policeman. He tried several times to join the Kokomo Police Department and the Indiana State Police but was rejected. Finally after much lobbying of Chief of Police, Elwood Luellen, he was accepted. At 11:00 p.m. Dec. 31, 1961, he realized his dream. He served the Kokomo Police Department as a Juvenile Aid Sgt., Detective Sgt., Radio Sgt., Desk Sgt. and as Captain in Charge of the Criminal Investigation Division.

On Oct. 19, 1956, he married Lou Ann Newby. They have five children: Karen Jo married to Steven Phillips, Michael Wayne married to Jane Arney, Janet Lyn married to Donald Davies, Samuel Todd, and Joseph

David married to Teresa Anthony. They have eight grandchildren: Lindsay Marie, Melissa Kay and Bryan David Phillips, Sarah Jayne Beatty, Marc Gregory Davies, Natalie Rochelle Beatty, Cory Johnathon Lay and Joseph David Beatty Jr.

David was born Sept. 28, 1934, in Kokomo to C. Paul and Helen Edith (Huston) Beatty. His grandparents were: Sanford and Dora (Anderson) Beatty, Leroy and Lola (DeWitt) Huston. His great-grandparents were John and Sarah (Purvis) Beatty, Perry and Mary (Henry) Anderson, Foreman and Magnolia (Ash) Huston and Alvin and Zella (Wilson) DeWitt, all of Tipton County.

Lou Ann was born July 3, 1937, in Kokomo to Leonard and Emma (Carver) Newby. Her grandparents were Merrill and Amel (Long) Newby and John W. and Frances (White) Carver. Her great-grandparents were Joshua and Louella (Neal) Newby, James Thomas and Eliza (Hamilton) Long, Mathew and Adeline (Vaught) Carver and William A. and Emma (Newcom) White.

Lou Ann is descended from several early settlers of Howard County including: Joseph and Frances (Reynolds) Taylor, Thomas A. and Margaret (McClanahan) Long, Thomas and Rebecca (Compton) Newby, Rev. John and Ann (Coverdale) Lowe, Benjamin and Susanna (Elleman) Neal, James and Mary (Stuck) Hamilton, and Jefferson and Elizabeth (Alder) White.

David and Lou Ann's ancestors include five Civil War veterans, three veterans of the War of 1812, five veterans of the American Revolution and one Hessian who defected.

Lou Ann is employed at First National Bank. She is a member of the Howard County Genealogical Society, Howard County Historical Society and the Indiana Historical Society. She also does volunteer work for the Kokomo-Howard County Library, Genealogy Room.

BECKOM-YAGER - William A. Beckom of Howard County, IN, married Helen Cedars of Howard County, IN. To this union four children were born: Donald Ray (married Esther Yvonne (Vonnie) Yager), Harold Wayne (married Mary Irene Padgett), Barbara Mae (married Allen McCloskey), and Mary Louise (married Edward Meadows). William was a mechanic; he ran a garage at his home in Harrison Township, IN.

Fredrick William Yager of Oakford, Howard County, IN, married Thelma Mae Unger of Howard County, IN. Four children were born to this union: Esther Yvonne (Vonnie) (married Donald Ray Beckom); Marsha Elaine (married Everett Rude); Charles Justin (married Sandra Sell); and Pamela Jolynn (married 1st Rodney Goode, 2nd Phil Miller). Fred was a farmer and also worked at Chrysler Corp. Thelma was a registered nurse. She lives near Oakford in Howard County, IN.

Donald Ray Beckom married Esther Yvonne (Vonnie) Yager. They have three children: Teresa Rae, Jan William, and Jay Donald. Don and Vonnie live near Oakford in Howard County, IN. Don drilled wells for several years; later he worked at Chrysler Corp. Vonnie worked at Delco Electronics Corp.

Teresa Beckom married Steven Charles Anderson; they have one child, Jeffery Michael Anderson. Jeffery married Consuella (Connie) Duffitt; they have one child, Austin Michael Anderson. Teresa and Steven divorced.

Teresa's 2nd husband is Arthur Cross. Teresa and Arthur have two children: Cody Christopher and Tayler Marie. They live in Howard County, IN. Arthur and Teresa work at Delco Electronics Corp.

Jan Beckom married Gyla Jean Merrifield; they have three daughters: Janelle Yvonne, Jamie Rae, and Jana Lynn. They live in Tipton County, IN. Jan works at Chrysler Corp.

Jay Beckom married Dawn Marie Laughner; they have one child, Monique Marie Beckom. Jay works at Chrysler Corp., and lives in Tipton County, IN.

BEEVER - Yvonne Jeannette Beever was born in Indianapolis Oct. 21, 1963, the only child of Skippy and Louise Beever. She attended Roncalli High School, where she played bells in the marching band. Her love of reading and the encouragement of a school librarian brought her to work at the Shelby Branch Library while she was in high school. She originally wanted to study architecture, but decided to get her Masters of Library Science instead. Yvonne attended IUPUI while working at Central Library, and received a BA in French. She spent the summer of 1985 at the Université de Dijon in France with the Indiana University language program. In June 1988, she married Norman Niehaus, who also worked at the public library. They divorced in 1991; they did not have any children. She received her MLS from IU in 1991, and remained in Indianapolis until the summer of 1993, when she made the trek north on US 31 to work as a catalog librarian for the public library in Kokomo.

Working next to the Genealogy Department, she was bitten by the genealogy bug and began her search in earnest. While she herself is an only child, she soon found many of her family lines flourished!

Skippy Beever, born April 20, 1931, joined the Army in 1954, but was given a medical discharge due to epilepsy. He married Louise Katherine Maier in Indianapolis Sept. 26, 1953; ten years later, Yvonne was born. Skippy worked for Frederick's Coal Co., Central States Bridge Works, Indianapolis Machinery and Supply; later, he laid carpeting and painted houses. Louise worked for 35 years with Bemis Bag; when it closed in 1984, she became office manager at Handschy Industries. Skippy died Aug. 11, 1984. Louise still lives in the same house where Skippy grew up, on the near-southside of Indianapolis.

L-R: Louise Beever, Yvonne Beever, Annie Brown Mallet, Anna Maier, Elinora Brown.

Louise's parents came from Germany: Josef Maier, born in Dunnigen, and Anna Angrick, born in Ostpreussen, both emigrated to the United States in 1928. Josef and Anna met at night school at Manual High School in Indianapolis, and married Oct. 1, 1929. They had two daughters: Elinora (born July 22, 1930) and Louise (born Jan. 27, 1933) grew up speaking German, learning English when they entered school. Josef and Anna became U.S. citizens in 1936 and 1937, respectively.

Skippy was one of ten children born to Carl Henry Beever and Ella Lounetta Hayden. Carl married Ella in Delphi, Carroll County, in 1920. They moved to Indianapolis after the death of their first baby, in 1922. At some point, the spelling of the name changed to Beaver, and Carl later changed his spelling to Beever, "to take the animal out of it." Carl was born in 1896 in Logansport, Cass County, to Henry S. Bever and Florence Stout (one of 16 children!) Florence's grandfather, Reuben Stout, was one of the early settlers of White County, IN. Henry was born in 1864 to Luke Bever and Catherine Mikesell. Luke was born in 1833 in Indiana, to parents who came from Ohio.

Ella's parents were John Hayden, born 1859 in Sweetwater, IL and Luanna Pile, born in 1868 in Tippecanoe County, to Ervin Pile and Laura Ann Philapps. The Haydens also had large families — Ella was one of 11 children. Intermarriage was common between the Haydens, Bevers and Stouts of this generation. It makes for some very confusing research!

BELCHERS - The Belchers live in Taylor Township, Howard County, Kokomo, IN. Steve was born in Troy, NY in 1951. He and his family moved to Kokomo in 1964. Steve's father, George Wheaton Belcher, was born in Hatfield, MA in 1922. He received his metallurgical degree from Rensselaer Polytechnic Institute in Troy, NY. In Kokomo he worked for Union Carbide prior to his death in 1965. His mother, the former Della Beale Barnes, was born in West Haven, CT in 1923. She had previously worked as a registered nurse at Howard Community Hospital. She passed away in Monmouth, NJ in 1973. His sister, Diane, is married to Jack Kaufman. They had their three children, Kim, Kristy, and Kyle, currently reside in Kokomo.

Sherri (Richmond) was born in London, KY in 1953. She and her family moved to Kokomo in 1965 from Lexington, KY. Sherri's father, Floyd Jonnie Richmond, was born in Williamsburg, KY in 1924. Floyd Jonnie Richmond, was born in Williamsburg, KY in 1924. Floyd first came to Kokomo in 1940. He worked as a farm hand for local farmers. He also worked at Gerbers (pottery), the Globe, and Turner Manufacturing. He served in the Army during WWII for three years. He served an apprenticeship in carpentry. For 18 years he worked construction in Florida and Kentucky as a carpenter and millwright. He was also a union brick and stone mason. Sherri's mother, Alberta Bernice Brooks, was born in 1927 in Williamsburg, KY. Alberta is a mother and a household manager. Floyd and Alberta made their permanent home in Howard County in 1965 when Floyd gained employment as a millwright for GM Hughes (Delco). He retired from there in 1987. Sherri has one sister, Sandra. She is married to Ronnie Deaton and they live in Williamsburg, KY. They have three daughters.

Steve and Sherri are both graduates of Taylor High School. Steve graduated in 1969. He served in the Army Reserves and worked for Cuneo Press. He received his Bachelor's Degree in Mechanical Engineering from Purdue University in 1980. He currently works for GM Hughes (Delco). Sherri graduated in 1971 from Taylor. She then graduated from Indiana University three years later with a Bachelor's Degree in Education. Sherri has taught at Taylor Community School Corp. since 1974. Steve and Sherri were married in 1972 at the First Baptist Church in Kokomo.

Stephen, Sherri, Shon Belcher

Shon was born in 1977 at Howard Community Hospital. Shon also attends Taylor High School. At the present time Shon holds a second degree Black Belt in karate under the guidance of Sensi Eddie Bethea who is an 8th degree Black Belt. Shon will graduate from high school in 1995 and plans to attend college. All during high school Shon has placed number one on his high school tennis team. Shon is planning to play tennis in college and his major is undecided at the present time.

Indian Heights Baptist Church has been the family church since 1965. Howard County has been a good place to grow up and raise a family.

BENGE - Benges of Howard County go back to Thomas Benge Sr. (bc1734-40-1811), married 1760 to Susannah Lewis (1742-1825), daughter of William Terrell Lewis Sr. and Sally Martin; Thomas Benge Jr. (born 1767) and wife Tempey Patsey Brown, a son, Obediah (bc1810/1811 North Carolina).

Not exactly sure when Obediah left his native state; he was in Alexandria, Madison County, IN in February 1841 and by 1850 he was in Clinton County, IN. His 1st wife was Eliza Jennie Goodwin. Ten known children: (1) Samuel; (2) Geneva; (3) Robert; (4) Martha; (5) Dorighert; (6) William A. (Aug. 16, 1851-March 17, 1928), wife

148

Sarah Long; (7) Harriet, wife of William Pratt; (8) James T. (March 2, 1855-Feb. 10, 1914), wife Sarah J. Pratt; (9) William Martin (Dec. 14, 1861-Feb. 11, 1915), wife Julia A. James; and (10) John J. Benge, wife Viola James. Obediah 2/m Jan. 29, 1868 to Mary Strong.

(3) Robert Benge (Feb. 18, 1841-June 10, 1927), Whiteman Cemetery, Sec. C., married May 24, 1863, to Elizabeth Huffer Floyd (March 8, 1838-April 21, 1916), widow of John Floyd, daughter of John and Anna Michael Huffer. Children known: (1) George Huffer; (2) William Henry (June 20, 1868-April 14, 1949), wife Margaret Elizabeth Harpold; (3) Phebe, wife of Charles E. Birden; (4) Martha, 1/m Frank M. Manoney, 2/m Omer Parker and (5) Pearl, wife of Milford Jenkins. Elizabeth Huffer had a daughter by her first husband: Elizabeth Augustia "Gustin" Floyd (born Aug. 18, 1857), 1/m Feb. 24, 1877 to Leonidas V. Heaton; 2/m Aug. 20, 1922 to Otho Dowden. She is buried in Elwood Cemetery in Elwood, Madison County, IN, but no death record has been found.

Richard James Sterling, Ann Nichelle, Jordan James

(1) George Huffer Benge (Sept. 15, 1864-Nov. 12/24, 1916), Whiteman Cemetery, married June 18, 1887 to Maranda Alice Haines (Jan. 29, 1870-Aug. 19/28, 1937), daughter of James M. and Maranda Parish Haines/Haynes. Ten known children, all born in Clinton County, IN: (1) Benjamin Harrison (Feb. 15, 1889-June 12, 1892); (2) Bessie Elizabeth (born Aug. 7, 1890), 1/m ? Burnell, 2/m William Franklin Holland; (3) Effie May (Sept. 23, 1892-June 27, 1977), 1/m Alva Clifton/Clifford Eikenberry, 2/m Elvy C. Sheets; (4) Robert Luther/Luther Robert; (5) Henry; (6) Roy Dean (June 29, 1897-March 1988), 1/wife Golda E. Rogers, 2/wife Buldah ?, 3/wife Sina Christina Persifall/Purciful; (7) female (born Aug. 1898-Oct. 28, 1898); (8) Jennie Alice (Dec. 15, 1899-Sept. 18, 1963), wife of Roy Myers; (9) Stanley Russel (May 31, 1905-1960); and (10) Dorothy Helen (born Jan. 13, 1910), wife of Gordon Lawrence.

(4) Robert Luther (Sept. 17, 1894-May 23, 1976), married Feb. 2, 1918 to Mary Christina Finney (April 17, 1899-Aug. 31, 1990), Fairview Cemetery; daughter of David A. and Mary Alice Ford Finney. Nine known children: (1) Lillian (Jan. 15, 1919-Aug. 22, 1982), 1/m William Levi Grissom, 2/m John B. Wade; (2) Irma/Elma, 1/m James I. Morris, 2/m Robert Wayne Ryan; (3) Howard Clayton (born Nov. 10, 1923), wife Mable Joan Clutick; (4) Richard Donald; (5) John Marvin (born Jan. 28, 1929), wife Barbara Jean Weatherford; (6) Wilma Jean (born Aug. 11, 1930), wife of Phillip John Carlson; (7) Luther Wayne (born Jan. 1, 1934), wife Maudie Louise Buslong Cook; (8) Georgia Arlene (born Nov. 1937), wife of Jewell Ray Richards; (9) Charles Vernon (born Nov. 6, 1939).

(4) Richard Donald (born Dec. 23, 1925), wife Frances Bell Herron, Greenlawn Cemetery. A daughter, Sandra Kay (born Nov. 1, 1949), married Lester Lee Sterling (born March 1, 1946), son of Ollie James and Ada Ion Brinson Sterling. Two sons, both born in Tippecanoe County, IN: (1) Eric Lee, born March 11, 1971, and Richard James Sterling, born Dec. 5, 1973, married in Howard County Feb. 24, 1993, to Ann Nichelle "Shellie" Johnson; a son Jordan James born April 20, 1993. Shellie, daughter of Robert J. and Barbara Ann Dowden. *Submitted by Richie and Shellie Sterling*

DWIGHT AND LILLIAN BENNETT

-Dwight Kermit Quentin Bennett was born in Prairie Township, Tipton County, IN, on Nov. 30, 1904, to William E. and Minnie Bell (Hamilton) Bennett. His parents moved to western Howard County when Dwight was small, and the family resided in Ervin Township where Dwight attended School No. 9 through eighth grade. He also attended new London School for a short while. He later attended Kokomo Business College and took correspondence courses through LaSalle University of Chicago.

Dwight married Lillian Irene Heaton on Oct. 20, 1923. Lillian was born Sept. 10, 1904, to William H. and Clara Inez (Shepherd) Heaton in Red Willow County in Indianola, NE. (See William and Clara Heaton History.) Lillian attended schools at Russiaville, Hillisburg, and New London.

Dwight's Christian faith was a dominating factor in his life. He became a Bible scholar and a lay minister and spent many hours studying the Scriptures. He considered himself an Evangelical Christian and served as a Sunday School teacher for much of his life. He belonged to the Christian Businessmen's group and served as treasurer of the Kokomo Rescue Mission.

Dwight and Lillian Bennett Family

Dwight was a farmer all of his life, but he had time to give to community service. He was trustee of Monroe Township from 1954-62; consequently, he served on the Western School Board. He served one term as Howard County Commissioner from 1966 to 1970. Dwight and Lillian donated land in 1966 for the establishment of Friendship Home for Girls, and they supported many charitable causes. They were active members of Farm Bureau.

Dwight and Lillian raised a large family of eight children. They included Bill, Maxine, Ted, Dick, Paul, John, Carolyn, and Judy.

Their firstborn, William Eugene (born 1924) was first married to Crystal Ruse of Forest, IN, and she and Bill had one daughter, Connie. A second marriage to Alice Marie (Peggy) Stewart produced four children: Bill, Jr., Becky, Laura and Barbara. Peggy also had a son Jimmy who was adopted by Bill. Peggy died Sept. 2, 1988. Crystal died July 30, 1991. Bill has spent most of his life farming and building fence.

Maxine (born 1926) married Carlous Jones of Clayton, GA. They have three daughters: Linda, Tina, and Lori. Maxine has been a homemaker all her married life while her husband has been a carpenter.

Ted, the second son, (born 1929) was married to Jane Ballard of Kokomo, and they had three daughters: Debbie, Lou Ann, and Cyndy. Ted's second marriage was to Marlene Potter of Detroit, MI. Ted is now retired from a career of truck driving, and he lives in Sebring, FL.

Dick (born 1931) was married to Joyce McDaniel of New London, IN. That marriage produced two children—Jackie and Rick. Dick is now married to Joan (Richardson), and they have a daughter, Glenda. Dick retired from Chrysler.

Paul Wayne (born 1933) was the fifth child. He married Mary Lou Bartley of Russiaville, IN. Their children include Jeff, Vickie, and Tami. Paul has made a career of farming, and Mary Lou has helped with the farm operation since retiring from Montgomery Wards in 1981. She had worked there 31 years.

John (born 1936) is married to the former June Stewart of Kokomo, IN. Their family consists of John, Jr., Pam and David. John works at Delco; June is a housewife.

Carolyn Sue (born 1938) married Charles J. Wheeler of Kokomo. They have two children, Steve and Cheryl. Carolyn is retired from teaching, and Charles is retired from Haynes International. (See Charles J. Wheeler History.)

The last child was Judith Ann (born 1944) who married Jerry Sellers of Kokomo. They have two children—Christopher and Tara. Judy is a teacher at Taylor School Corporation, and Jerry is engaged in farming.

Dwight and Lillian were married almost 59 years. Lillian died Oct. 1, 1982, and Dwight passed away on Oct. 17, 1984. They are both buried in the mausoleum at Sunset Memory Gardens at Alto, IN. *Submitted by Judith Sellers*

WILLIAM E. AND MINNIE BELL BENNETT

William Ehrman (born Dec. 6, 1869) and Minnie Bell Bennett (born Sept. 12, 1877) came to Howard County around the turn of the century. William married Minnie in Tipton County on Dec. 4, 1894. She was the fourth child of William and Francina (Smith) Hamilton.

William E. was a son of John Nathanial and Eliza (Mow) Bennett. John was a native of North Carolina having been born there Oct. 19, 1844, to Major and Malinda Catherine (Hagey) Bennett. Eliza, John's wife, came from Marshall County, IN, where she was born Jan. 8, 1843. Her parents were John Adam and Margaret (Martin) Mow. The Mows were descendants of Johan Mau who came to America from Wurtenburg, Germany.

William Bennett Family

William E. was the third child in a family of ten; only seven grew to adulthood, however. Edwin Murviel (1866-1939) was the firstborn, followed by Dora Ellen (1868-1911). After William were born Malinda Evaline (1871-1945), Catherine Victoria (1873-1950), Jennie Maude (1881-1913), and Everett Nathaniel (1886-1938). Three children died in infancy in 1876, 1878, and 1880.

While most of William's brothers and sisters chose professional careers, "Bill Ehrm" was a born farmer. In 1918 he bought a 118-acre farm in Ervin Township (located at 820 West - 00 NS), and lived on it until he died. It is still owned by family members. A Christian for all of his adult life, William was a member of New Zion Church located just down the road from the Bennett farm. His wife Minnie passed away on Dec. 11, 1913; he then married Mary Miller, the widow of John E. Miller in 1944.

William E. Bennett & Mary (Miller) Bennett

William and Minnie had four children who grew to maturity; their first child Agnes died at ten weeks. The other children were Nellie, Roland, Buell, and Dwight.

149

Nellie Grant (born Jan. 18, 1897) married Clarence L. McCormick in 1917, and to that union were born Howard (1917) and Ned (1920-1977). The marriage ended and Nellie started a rooming house which she named the Old Main Hotel. It was located at 718 North Main Street in Kokomo. She maintained it until her death on March 29, 1993.

Roland, the first son, was born Oct. 15, 1898. He married Lena Oyler Oct. 6, 1917. Their children were Kenneth (born 1920), Mary Catherine (born 1922), Roland Jr. (born 1924), and Dale E. (born 1937). Roland was a farmer and a bus driver at Ervin Township School for a while. He was killed in a construction accident in Indianapolis on Nov. 23, 1943. Lena died on July 10, 1991.

Buell Everett, the second son, was born July 13, 1900. He married Essie Mae Downey on Aug. 27, 1928. Their family included Betty Jo (born 1929), Ramona Mae (born 1931), Don (born 1936), Sandy (born 1939), and Kenny (born 1940). Buell was the owner of B&B Tire Store in uptown Kokomo for a number of years. His wife Mae has worked as a practical nurse and housekeeper most of her life since her children were raised. Buell died in 1984.

Dwight, born Nov. 30, 1904, was the youngest of Bill and Minnie's children. He married Lillian Irene Heaton on Oct. 20, 1923, and together they raised a large family of eight: Bill (born 1924), Maxine (born 1926), Ted (born 1929), Dick (born 1931), Paul (born 1933), John (born 1936), Carolyn (born 1938), and Judy (born 1944).

William Ehrman Bennett passed away on Oct. 27, 1948. He is buried at Albright Cemetery near Kokomo. His second wife Mary is also deceased. *Submitted by Paul Bennett*

EDWARD CHARLES AND DEBRA KAY BERNARD

Edward's position as an electronic engineer with Delco Electronics brought Edward and Debra to Howard County in 1988 from Columbus, OH. Both were born and raised in Ohio and met at the University of Toledo, Toledo, OH in 1980. They were married on Dec. 24, 1987, in Columbus, OH.

Edward was born in Allen County, OH on April 20, 1960. He grew up in Ottoville, OH where he graduated from high school in 1978. He enjoyed fishing at his family's cottage in Long Lake, Coldwater, MI. Edward graduated from the University of Toledo in 1981 with an Associate's Degree in Electronic Engineering. He then received his Bachelor of Science Degree in Electronic Engineering from Franklin University, Columbus, OH in 1986. Edward's present position with Delco is that of supervisor in the Product Reliability Department.

Debra was born in Sandusky County, OH on March 26, 1960. She grew up in Springfield, OH and Bellevue, OH where she graduated from high school in 1978. Debra then graduated with honors from the University of Toledo in 1982 with associate degrees in Law Enforcement, Correctional, and Social Services Technology. In 1984, she received her Bachelor of Arts Degree in Social Science from Ohio Dominican College, Columbus, OH. In 1991 Debra took a position as an adult probation officer with Howard County Adult Probation where she is presently employed.

William S. Sale Homestead, built 1879. Bought 1991 by Edward C. and Debra K. Bernard. Picture taken September 1993.

Although Edward and Debra have chosen to make Indiana their home, they are proud of their Ohio heritage.

Edward's parents were Richard William and Fern Olive (Hutchins) Bernard, both deceased. Richard was born in Mercer County, OH in 1914 to Henry and Matilda (Romer) Bernard. After serving three years in the Navy during World War II, he took a position as vice-president of the Ottoville Bank. Fern was born in Paulding County, OH in 1918 to Edwin and Olive Marie (Smith) Hutchins. She was employed as a cosmetologist for four years in Saint Henry, OH where she met her future husband. They were married in 1941 and together raised six children.

Edward's paternal great-great-grandfather Leon Bernard came from Alsace Lorraine, France in 1828 and eventually settled in Mercer County, OH in 1837. His other paternal great great grandfather John Joseph Romer came from Oldenburg, Germany in 1834. His brother Henry founded Saint Henry, OH in 1838 and John Joseph founded the Saint Henry Bank in 1905.

Edward's maternal great-great-grandfather Charles Hutchins came from England in 1853 and settled in Paulding County in 1858. His other maternal great-great-grandfather also came from England in 1849, eventually settling in Paulding County, OH in 1853. Both great great grandfathers were farmers.

Debra was adopted at the age of three months by Richard Leo and Mary Eileen (Dailey) Crookton. Richard, a Prudential Insurance district manager, died in 1971. Mary, a homemaker, was remarried in 1974 to Harold Joseph Siesel in Bellevue, OH.

Edward and Debra intend on restoring a portion of Howard County history. In 1991 they purchased a brick Italianate Victorian home built by William S. Sale in 1879 for $2,500. The restoration will take some time but Edward and Debra have put down roots in Howard County and are here to stay.

AARON L. BERRY - Aaron Leander Berry (1856-1944), was the son of Dr. Berry who lived at Greentown and was a 'Herb Doctor'. He married (July 28, 1883) Rachel Laney Lightfoot (1859-1950), the daughter of Newton and Nancy Margaret (Reeder) Lightfoot. They had nine children. My mother was Myrtle Berry who married Richard Rowland.

I was born 88 years ago, and was mostly raised in my grandparents' home. They lived at 1510 N. Jay. It was in their home that the North Side Wesleyan Methodist Church was organized. Meetings were held here until the church was built. My marriage in 1921 to Francis M. Randolph (1902-1966), was the first to be held in the church. Francis was the son of William and Melinda (Baker) Randolph.

When I was a child, the streets were dirt. We children played in the wagon tracks and would build houses out of the dust, only to see them destroyed when a buggy or wagon would go by. We didn't have the toys of today. It was fun to see the ladies selling lots next to our addition, which was called Tuxedo. They gave away plates, and our ladies would dress up and run down just to get a plate. I walked to the Ellis School (still standing on the by-pass), and later went to Riley after it was built.

Aaron L. Berry

My grandfather was a flagman for the railroad, at the corner of Walnut and Buckeye Sts. He walked from 1510 N. Jay in all kinds of weather, and never missed a day. The flagman's house had a pot belly stove and a chair in it. One of the old train engineers told us that they used to try and catch him off guard. They would roll the train up silently, but could never catch him off guard. He was run down by a team of mules and never fully recovered from it. He and my grandmother are both buried in Memorial Park Cemetery. *Submitted by Nellie Randolph*

BERRYMAN - George Albert "Al" Berryman (Oct. 13, 1913-Nov. 23, 1953) married Katherine "Kay" Marie Grady (Oct. 13, 1918-Aug. 23, 1993) on June 20, 1942, in Peru, IN.

After World War II they moved to Kokomo, IN, Howard County. Al became a Kokomo policeman. He was killed in the line of duty from a gunshot wound on Thanksgiving 1953. It was a family dispute call. He was the first policeman to be killed in the line of duty for 100 years in Howard County. After his death Kay became a beautician, and had her beauty shop at home so she could work and raise their two children. They had a daughter Linda Kay and a son Kenneth Allen.

Katherine "Kay" Marie Berryman and George Albert "Al" Berryman

Linda Kay was born May 22, 1943, married Daniel Lee Brock, born July 2, 1944. They were married Jan. 1, 1984. Linda worked at Delco Electronics and Dan was a realtor. They had two sons (Dan's by a previous marriage): Jeffery Allen born Dec. 21, 1963, and Douglas Lee born Oct. 29, 1966. They moved to Tipton County, IN.

Kenneth Allen, born Oct. 2, 1948, married Rebecca Jean Smith, born June 7, 1949. They were married Feb. 13, 1971. Kenneth became an art teacher at Western School. Rebecca taught fifth grade at Northwestern School. They had three children, including identical twin boys, Ryan Matthew and Scott Wesley, born Aug. 27, 1975, and a beautiful daughter Heather Nicole, born May 29, 1980. They attended Western School and are planning to attend college after graduation from high school. *Submitted by Linda Berryman Brock*

BITNER - Otho Ervin Bitner was born on July 20, 1905, and died on May 30, 1950. His parents were Charles and Lula (Dietz) Bitner. Otho worked as a well driller. He was killed in an accident while working in Monticello, IN. Flossie Stover was born on March 9, 1909, and died June 29, 1971. Her parents were Howard and Thursia Mae (Lewis) Stover. She was a homemaker and also worked in restaurant called The Cupboard. Otho was 19 and Flossie was 15 years old when they got married on Aug. 16, 1924. They had eight children together: Betty Lou born on Dec. 7, 1925; Paul Ervin Sr. born on Nov. 5, 1927; Ralph Eugene born on Aug. 11, 1930; Robert Clayton born on Oct. 17, 1934; Alton Leroy (Roy) born on Oct. 26, 1936; Patty Ann born on Nov. 20, 1938; Jean Elizabeth (Sis) born on Aug. 10, 1944; and Connie Sue born on Jan. 2, 1947.

Betty married Eugene Franklin Forbes Sr. on May 7, 1942. They had three children together: Saundra Lou, Eugene Franklin Jr. and Sharon Sue. They then got a divorce in 1952. Betty married Carson Hunley in 1953. They had David Lee Hunley together. He was born dead. Betty died on April 9, 1963.

Paul Sr. married Jane Ann Clark on Aug. 8, 1946. They had four children together: Paul Ervin Jr. born on Aug. 7, 1948; Marsha Ann born Oct. 10, 1951; Kevin Michael (Mike) born on Dec. 15, 1954; and James Eric (Jamie) born on June 10, 1959. Paul Sr. died Feb. 5, 1985.

Kevin (Mike) married Rhonda Jean Grammer on June 2, 1973. They had three children together: Stacy Marie, Brian Michael, and Erica Jane.

Ralph married Nancy Jean McClain in 1950. They had four children together: Jeffry Eugene Sr., Judy Kay, Jennifer Jean, and Janet Leigh. Ralph died on May 12, 1988. Nancy died in 1960.

Robert married Carolyn Lee Croxford first. They had four children: Mark Leslie, Charlotte Diane, Mavis Irene, and William Rodrick. He then married June Arlene (Carlile) Pusateri. She had Aaron James Pusateri from her first marriage. Together they had three other children: Sheila Lynn, Dawn Diane, and Tina Louise. Robert died on Aug. 18, 1992.

Alton (Roy) married Constence Sue Krise on April 9, 1955. They had five children together: Wesley Scott, Jocelyn Leigh, Steven Leroy, Anthony Shane, and Stephanie Sue. Alton died on July 5, 1988.

Patty married Joseph LaVerne Branch I on Jan. 1, 1955. They had six children together: Joan Claire, Kimmie Elaine, Joseph LaVerne II, Kathleen Anne, Jacob Andrew, and James.

Jean (Sis) married Carl Verlion Hughes on Sept. 12, 1964. Together they had David Carl. They then got a divorce on Feb. 19, 1972.

Connie had Todd Allen Bitner. She married Jack Lee Cardwell on Dec. 15, 1967. Together they had Angela Marie. They got a divorce in 1971.

BLANCHARD-BRADLEY - Laurence and Janice Blanchard have lived in Kokomo since 1967. Laurence is a watchmaker. He graduated from Elgin Watchmaking College in 1958. He is the son of Neil and Eveline Shepherd Blanchard, who moved to Kokomo in 1972 from Crown Point, IN. Neil Blanchard was born in Illinois in 1896. His father was Charles Blanchard. Neil served in WWI as a horseshoer. He died in 1989 and is buried at Calumet Park Cemetery in Merrillville, Lake County, IN. Eveline Blanchard came to America from England when she was nine years old in 1912. Her father, John Shepherd, had come a few months before the rest of the family. He had just missed passage on the *Titanic*. He worked in a mine in Southern Ohio before moving to Akron, OH where Neil and Eveline were married in 1922. She died in 1991 and is buried in Calumet Park Cemetery. They had four sons: The oldest Neil Jr. lives in Crown Point, IN; Richard lives in North Carolina; Laurence lives in Kokomo; and one son, Leslie, is deceased.

Neil and Eveline Blanchard

Janice Blanchard is the daughter of Ted and Mina Sprong Bradley. Ted Bradley was born in 1914, the son of Kay and Armelia Wardwell Bradley. They lived in Elwood, Madison County, IN. Kay Bradley was from Scottsville, KY. Armelia, his wife, was the daughter of Theodore Wardwell whose father had settled in Madison County in 1855 from Franklin County, IN. The Wardwell family has been traced back to Hugh Wardwell, 1490, in Lincolnshire, England. William Wardwell came to America in 1633 on the ship *Griffith* and settled in Massachusetts. William Wardwell's nephew, Samuel, was one of those wrongly accused and hung as a witch in Salem, MA in 1692. Mina Sprong Bradley, the mother of Janice, was born and raised in Elwood, IN. She was the daughter of William Sprong and Elizabeth Ertel. The Sprong family can be traced back to Johannis Sprough who came to America from Holland in 1650 and settled in what was then New Amsterdam (now New York City). William Sprong was the son of Milton and Gustie Lynch Sprong. Gustie's mother was Catherine Isenhour Lynch. Catherine was the daughter of Jacob and Rhoda Derry Isenhour. Jacob was a son of Benjamin and Catherine Becker Isenhour. Benjamin's father was Johannes Isenhour who came with his father Hans Nickolas Isenhour in 1741 on ship *Europa* and settled in Pennsylvania. This same ancestor Hans Nicholas in also the immigrant ancestor of former President Dwight David Eisenhower.

Patricia, Eveline, George, Norman, Laurence, and Janice Blanchard.

Laurence and Janice Blanchard were married in 1962 in Anderson, IN. They have four children: Patricia who is the kindergarten teacher at Indian Heights Baptist Day Care; George who lives in Minneapolis, MN; Norman who is attending Purdue University; and Eveline who is attending IUK and works at Hill Dept. Store. Both Laurence and Janice served in the military. Their sons both served in the military also. George served in the U.S. Army during Operation Desert Storm and Norman served in the U.S. Navy on the submarine USS *San Juan*.

BLANGY-WILSON - Ray Charles Blangy and Anna Pearl Wilson were married May 5, 1927 in Sharpsville, IN by the Rev. Thomas Newlin. Ray was born April 13, 1891 in Butler Co., OH, the eldest child of Jerry Benjamin and Mary (Frazee) Blangy. Ray's grandparents were Jere and Rebecca Ann (Kellis) Blangy, and Louis and Mary Ann (Tevis) Frazee.

Ray served in France and Belgium during World War I. During this time he and Pearl corresponded, but never met until several years later. After they were married they moved to Detroit, MI, where Ray was working at the Fisher-Body plant. In 1928 they moved to Ervin Twp. Howard County, where they remained the rest of their lives.

Ray Blangy (seated) Pearl Blangy

Anna Pearl was born March 8, 1891 in Ervin Twp., Howard County, IN, the second daughter of Roscoe and Laura Ann (Crites) Wilson. Her grandparents were John M. and Indiana Ann (Baldwin) Wilson; and Henry and Caroline (Foy) (DeMoss) Crites. Her great grandparents were John C. and Mary (McDowell) Wilson, and Silas S. and Susan (French) Baldwin. Both sets of great-grandparents were pioneers of Ervin Twp. Pearl's great-great grandparents were John and Mary (McElroy) McDowell; James and Abigail (McGilliard) French; and Thomas and Susan (Stull) Baldwin.

Richard Ray and Mary Blangy

Ray and Pearl Wilson Blangy were the parents of two children, Mary Elizabeth (1928 -), and Richard Ray (1931-1989). Ray, Pearl and Richard are buried in North Union Cemetery, Ervin Twp, Howard County, IN. *Submitted by Mary Blangy.*

BLOOMER - Joseph Bevington Bloomer (1830-1886) son of Jesse Bloomer and Sarah Bevington, daughter of Charles and Ann Rebecca Bevington, was born Dec. 2, 1830 in Fayette County, OH. He married Isabel Baker (1832-1913), daughter of Watson Baker and Nancy Rebecca Orr, March 24, 1853, in Kokomo, IN. Their families moved to Howard County, IN from Fayette County, OH in 1850's. Isabel was born Sept. 1, 1832. Joseph was a farmer. Children were born at Kokomo except the two youngest in Missouri. The family was in the 1870 Census, Holt Co., MO and moved to Smith County, KS before 1880.

1. Phoebe Ann (1854-1932) married in Smith County, KS 1st Wm. M. Clark (1850-1882), one son Joseph Wilson; 2nd John Crawford. Children: Nellie, Maida, Bryant, Frank. Burial Caney, KS.

2. Rebecca Alma (1856-193?) married George Kirk in Holt County, MO. Children: Ernest, Bertha, Chester, Jesse, Maude.

3. William Allen (1858-1951) married Nancy Jane Slater (1858-1930). He came to Smith County, KS in 1875 from Missouri. Children: James, Lloyd, Joseph B., Fannie, twins-Linnie, Lelia; Blanche. Burial Lebanon, KS.

4. Jennie Bell (1860-1941) married Rev. James Milton Allen (1855-1918) in Smith County, KS, 14 children. Burial Deerfield, KS.

5. Samuel Watson (1862-1890) married Annie Laura Gibbons in Smith County, KS. Children: Bertie, Ernest, Bonnie. Burial Lebanon, KS.

6. Emma Rosetta (1867-1892) married Charles W. Chelf (1863-1949), four sons. Burial Lebanon, KS.

7. Charles Edwin (1868-1953) married Mary Agnes Bush in Smith County, KS. They moved to Dewey County, OK in 1910 and the family settled near Seiling. Children: Emerson, Solon, Edith. Burial Seiling, OK.

BLOSSEY - Christian Albert Blossey B1830 Ger, D1877 WI was a miller and millwright. In 1864 in Germany, he married Bertha Marie Schmidt B1845 Ger, D1931 WI, a farmer. They had six children: Ida Antonio B1865 Ger, D1927 WI; Emma Ann B1867 Ger; Clara Agusta B1869 WI; Albert Frederick B1871 WI, D1951 IN; Mary Roberta B1874 WI, D1914; Ernest Carl B1876 WI, D1962 WA.

Ida never married; lived in Washington.

Emma M1898 Fred Zollner, and had two children: Bertha B1899, married Hugo Antl; and Paul B1906 married Erma.

Clara M1900 William Beucus, and adopted a child: Iva B1904, D1975.

Mary never married; was a nurse in Washington.

Ernest Carl, who worked for the railroad, M1902 Anna Cora Davis. They had two children: Mildred E. and Ernest Daniel.

Albert Frederick B1871 WI, D1951 IN was an engineer. In Kokomo in 1905 he married Ola Grace Ward B1880 IN, D1953, IN who was a teacher. Their three children born in Alton, IL: Carl Ward B1906, Rachel Louise B1909, and Zoe Alberta B1912. They lived in Wisconsin three years before returning to Kokomo.

151

Carl was a Delco engineer. In 1934, he married Sarah Fahnestock B1900 CO, D1974 FL, a college professor. They had two sons: Robert Gates B1939 IN; and Daniel Fahnestock B1942 IN; and a daughter, Elizabeth B1935 IN who died at birth.

Robert M1964 Betsey Kenyon. They had two children: Jean Elizabeth B1967 MI; and Peter North B1969 PA.

Daniel M1964 Glee Barber. They had three sons: Douglas Field B1967 IL; Ryan Fahnestock B1968 IL; and Cole Barber B1971 NY.

Rachel was a housewife. In 1929 she married William Henry Benson B1908 In, a Chrysler employee and farmer. They had two daughters: Nancy Lee B1930 IN; and Marilyn Sue B1933 IN.

Nancy, a Delco employee, married Robert Pope and had two sons: James Lawrence and Gary Lee, and they divorced. She then married Donald Hale and had two daughters: Kathryn Ann and Donna Annette.

(Marilyn) Sue, a factory supervisor, married Austin Fair and had two daughters: Victoria Louise and Sandra Joyce.

Zoe Alberta was a housewife. In 1934 she married Claude Clive Streeter B1904 IN, D1992 FL, a salesman and farmer.

The Streeter family is covered in another article in this book. *Submitted by R. Ann Nichols*

BOCK - Daniel Bock brought his wife Susanna (Erbaugh) and their seven children from Montgomery County, OH near Dayton to Howard County in 1874 where he purchased 160 acres at Ridgeway in Ervin Township. Daniel's parents were Samuel E. and Lizzie (Gable) Bock who raised their family on a farm near Dayton, OH. Rev. Daniel and Susanna Bock were of the German Baptist faith and in 1887 they deeded land at 1150 W., 150 N. to their church. Daniel (b. 1834 and d. 1922) and Susanna (born 1836 and died 1919) lived and farmed their land in Ervin Township until 1899 when they moved to Kokomo. Daniel was a skilled carpenter but lost his eyesight around 1909.

Samuel Abraham Bock (born 1858 and died 1925) was the second of seven children and 16 years of age when coming to Howard County with his parents. He worked on his father's farm and May 6, 1880, married Eliza Ann Eikenberry (born 1859 and died 1937) from Clinton County. They resided on his father's farm until 1893 when they moved to their own 120 acres in Ervin Twp. where his descendants still live. Sam was active in the community along with his productive farming, being trustee of Ervin Twp. for five years and then elected County Commissioner in 1906 on the Republican ticket. He retired from farming and moved into Kokomo where they resided at 502 N. Webster St.

Bertha May, born 1881, was the eldest of five children born to Samuel and Eliza Ann Bock. She married Orion Sylvester Flora and they raised six children on the family farm. (Fred Carlyle, Cecile May Carey, Wilma Bernadine Obermeyer, Dolly Mildred Tomlin, Carl Lawrence and Patricia Irene Gilbert). Their son Carl married Ruthadele Eller and Carl's widow and only daughter, Linda Johnson Reigel, presently reside on the old home place in Ervin Township.

Grace Mable (born 1883) was the second child who married Charles Price and they had no children.

Clarence Bock (born 1886) married Lenore Mercer and had two children, Frances and Martha. Clarence was graduated from Indiana University with an M.D. Degree and subsequently practiced medicine in Muncie, IN at Ball Bros. Memorial Hospital. Dr. Bock specialized in urology and died suffering a heart attack while in practice.

Daniel Lawrence (born 1888) married Ella Blanche Hobson and had two children, Anna Elizabeth Strawbridge-Bromley who resides in Kokomo and Dr. Daniel Hobson Bock, presently residing in St. Petersburg Beach, FL.

The two brothers, Clarence and Daniel, worked on their father's farm in order to support their respective educations at Indiana University in Bloomington. Daniel earned his LLB Degree and was instrumental in organizing the first "Indiana Union", being one of the first board members. His picture and name are displayed in the tower of the present Indiana University Union Memorial Building in Bloomington. Daniel became one of the Howard County prosecuting attorneys around the period of 1916-1917. He subsequently practiced law in Indianapolis, East Chicago and Hammond, Indiana. Before retiring to Alto in 1965, he served as Inheritance Tax Administrator for the Attorney General of the State of Indiana in the State House.

Blanche Bock, fifth child, died in infancy with no records and is buried in South Union Cemetery along with most of the Bock Family.

The Bock, Eikenberry and Flora families have contributed significantly to the development of Howard County throughout several generations. *Submitted by Anna Elizabeth Bromley*

HARRY AND LOIS BOGUE - Harry Bogue and Lois Hunsinger both attended at a young age the New Light Christian Church in Greentown, with their parents Charles and Stella LaRowe Bogue and Clyde and Dove Benson Hunsinger. They were active in the church and Young People's Class and began dating before Lois had graduated from high school. She was teaching the 4th grade in the Greentown School when they were married on Nov. 24, 1934. They started housekeeping two miles north and 1/4 mile east of Greentown on her father's farm. They spent $400 for a team of horses and about $800 for new and used furniture. Bread was five cents a loaf and liver 10 cents a pound. A good meal at a restaurant cost 25 cents which was what their wedding dinner cost. In 1939 they bought a farm 2 and 3/4 miles north of Greentown where they moved and continued to farm along with Harry driving a school bus and Lois teaching. They were blessed with two children, Ellen Sue and then Philip Wayne. Ellen Sue graduated and got her Masters Degree from Ball State before teaching in Kokomo. She married David Templin, the son of Ray and Dorothy Templin of Cassville, IN. Ellen Sue and David are now living in North Harbor near Noblesville with their two children Jennifer, a senior at Purdue and Christophor, a senior at Noblesville High School. David graduated from Purdue University and works at Delco in purchasing as Worldwide Procurement coordinator and farms their farm north of Kokomo. Philip Wayne attended Purdue University before taking over the farming after Harry retired and now lives on the home farm with his wife Debra, the daughter of Robert and Lois Turner of Indianapolis, IN with their children Bradley, Kimberly, Brian, and Brandon.

Harry's father, Charles, was a farmer and a carpenter. Lois' father, Clyde, owned the Hunsinger Coal and Lumber Company in partnership with his brother, Clint. Later, he sold his half to Clint and bought the farm north of Greentown and started farming. Later he moved back to Greentown, and he and his wife started the Hunsinger Hatchery in Greentown behind their home on Howard Street.

After Harry and Lois retired, they spent a good part of their summers at their summer home on Lake Webster and their winters at their winter home in Lake Placid, FL. They traveled extensively in the United States as well as several trips across both oceans and enjoyed a cruise, but were always glad to return to their home north of Greentown, in Howard County. *Submitted by Lois Bogue*

JAMES BOLEN - Burnell James (Jim) Bolen and Vera Louise Bolen were born in Anderson, IN and graduated from Anderson High School. Jim began his career with General Motors at the Delco-Remy plant in 1926. In July of 1936, Jim Bolen was transferred from Delco Remy in Anderson to work in the Accounting Department for the Delco Radio Corporation in Kokomo. With him came his wife, Vera, and their three children: Harry Douglas, James, Jr. and Margaret Elaine. He was employed from 1936 until Oct. 1, 1962, at the time of his retirement as supervisor in the Accounting and Payroll Department. They were active members of the Main Street United Methodist Church. Also, Jim participated in many of the Masonic activities and was awarded the 33rd degree in Masonry. They resided several years in Kokomo and later built their country home in Taylor Township. Jim passed away on Jan. 15, 1974, and Vera is a resident in the Americana Healthcare Center.

Their son, Harry, graduated from Kokomo High School in 1942 and then was employed over 38 years by Delco Electronics. He retired September 1979 from the Graphic Arts Department in the Engineering Building. His wife, Leanna Ade, came from Lafayette in 1941 to be employed in the Social Security office in Kokomo and worked there for five years before their marriage on May 6, 1945. She graduated from Montmorenci High School and Lafayette Business College. She retired from the S.S. Kresge Company (now K-Mart), as bookkeeper, after 35 years of employment when the downtown store closed its doors on Dec. 31, 1980. They are active members of the Main Street Methodist Church and participate in several of the senior citizens groups in and around Kokomo. Harry is active in the Taylor Township Lions Club and served as secretary for 20 years. They lived eight years in Kokomo and later built a country home in Taylor Township.

Burnell James (Jim) and Vera Louise Bolen

Jim, Jr. served in the United States Navy and did work temporarily at Delco Radio after the close of World War II. Later he attended and graduated from Stanford University. He married Betty Kay Job and they spent their entire married life in California. Both are 1942 graduates from Kokomo High School. Jim retired October 1986 from the SafeWay Food Stores being employed in the Legal Department in their home office at Oakland. She graduated from Purdue University as a pharmacist and retired in 1984 from the Kaiser Hospital and Health Care in Walnut Creek and surrounding area. Since their retirement they have done lots of traveling, both abroad and in the States. They have three children: Brent, Mitchell and Michael.

Samuel Abraham Bock and Eliza Ann Eikenberry Bock.

Harry and Lois Bogue

Margaret worked several years in the Mailing Department at Delco Radio. At one time four members of the family were employed there. She married Roy Long who was employed at Delco in the Machine Building Department. Both graduated from Kokomo High School. Also, he served time with the United States Air Force during World War II and Reserves. They live in Kokomo, although since his retirement in October 1974, they spend their winters in Florida. They have three children: James, Catherine and Alice. *Submitted by Leanna Bolen*

BOLINGER - Cornelius M. Bolinger (Dec. 27, 1862-Jan. 13, 1926) married Viola R. Blose (May 4, 1871-Dec. 24, 1969) in August 1889 in Darke County, OH. They came to Clay Township, Howard County, in March 1895, arriving by Pennsylvania Railroad and bringing with them one horse and Viola's prized cow. Cornelius traded land he had homesteaded in Kansas for 40 acres near Northwestern School. He sold the 40 acres and purchased another 100 acres in March 1901. This is now owned and operated by his youngest son Clifford. Their firstborn, Victor C., was born in Ohio; their other ten children were Clay Township births, and all survived well into adulthood. (See photo).

The children were: Victor C. Bolinger (June 30, 1893-April 2, 1971) who served in England and France during WWI, and married Corrine Coulter (June 4, 1897-March 8, 1978) on Aug. 20, 1917. They also had a farm near the 'Home Place' and raised two children: Eleanor, born July 26, 1922, who married Jay Norman Schneider (Aug. 8, 1922-Sept. 24, 1992). They had no children. Eleanor taught school until retirement. Donald John, born April 9, 1924, who married Betty Overton Leffert (Sept. 19, 1919-June 9, 1986) on June 8, 1951. Their only child is Donald John II. Donald John is an attorney-at-law and was a member of the U.S. Infantry during WWII.

Walter M. Bolinger (Feb. 24, 1896-April 9, 1984) married Ora Smith (Oct. 23, 1900-May 21, 1983) on Aug. 25, 1919, after serving with the Army in WWI. Their farm was south of Russiaville. Their four children were: Deloris Marie (Oct. 30, 1920-April 7, 1967) who married George Quick (Nov. 5, 1914-Dec. 19, 1969) on June 30, 1940. They had two sons, Robert Lee and Gary Jay. Mildred Ann (Oct. 22, 1921-July 1, 1971) married William Stringer, born Jan. 14, 1917, on Oct. 22, 1944. They had twin daughters, Sherry Lynn and Bonnie Lee. Their son, Wesley Earl, was killed in a motorcycle accident at age 26. Stella Mae (Sept. 24, 1922-July 11, 1985) married Paul Denton Long, born June 23, 1921, on Sept. 24, 1941. Their only child is Tanya Cheri. Roy W. (Nov. 17, 1923-Jan. 30, 1990) married Mary Angeline Straley, born June 3, 1926, on June 22, 1947. Their children are Peggy Lee and Phyllis Ann. Roy served in the Navy during WWII.

Marie Bolinger (Oct. 17, 1898-Sept. 26, 1981) married Russell Gillam (Jan. 25, 1899-Aug. 5, 1962) on June 1, 1924. Their farm was in Ervin Township. After Russell's death Marie married Edward Schirer, born Aug. 12, 1902, on April 12, 1973. Marie taught school for 39 years. She had no children.

Sherman Bolinger (Aug. 17, 1899-Oct. 19, 1962) married Phylora Fern Newman (Aug. 1, 1902-Dec. 13, 1932) on Feb. 7, 1923. She was killed when a train struck her car at a crossing in Windfall. Their only child is L. Owen Bolinger, born Sept. 7, 1924, who married Mary Ann Ericson, born May 16, 1930, on Aug. 13, 1950. Their children are: Michael Owen, Lisa Ann, and Matthew August. Owen was a fighter pilot in the Navy during WWII, and is now an attorney-at-law. Sherman, with his brother Howard, founded 'Bolinger Bros.', a farm equipment repair and manufacturing firm in Windfall in 1926 and remained a partner until his death in 1962. They also owned farms in Tipton and Howard Counties, which are still owned by Bolingers. Sherman later married Evelyn Lucile Sholty (Sept. 1, 1912-Jan. 5, 1994) on Dec. 25, 1933. Their children are: Marcia Ellen, born Dec. 7, 1935, married Jack Richard Dewitt, born Oct. 31, 1931, on Nov. 26, 1958. Their issue are Dustin Bryce, Diedra Ann, Darrick Leigh, and they adopted Darbin Munson. Sharon Sue, born March 14, 1947, married David Lee Voris, born Jan. 29, 1946, on Aug. 26, 1967. Their children are Clayton Gene, Carmen Gayle, Curt Gregory, and Christin Gae.

1945 Photo of the children of Cornelius M. and Viola Bolinger (with their mother). Front Row L to R: Betty, Victor, Viola, Clifford, Etta Louise. Back Row L to R: Walter, Zella Izola, Nina, Howard, Ruth, Sherman, Marie.

Nina Mae Bolinger (Feb. 24, 1901-Feb. 20, 1947) lived on the 'Home Place' and taught school all her adult life. She did not marry.

Ruth Bolinger (July 7, 1902-May 29, 1964) married Lowell Alexander, born Oct. 18, 1901, on Oct. 14, 1923. Their farm was in Ervin Township. There were no children from this marriage.

Howard Bolinger, born Sept. 20, 1904, was married to Bessie Marie Carney (March 13, 1906-May 27, 1990) on Oct. 15, 1927. Howard, with his brother Sherman, were partners in 'Bolinger Bros.', a farm equipment repair and manufacturing firm in Windfall from 1926 until Sherman's death in 1962. At that time Howard's sons, R. Wayne and Keith, became partners and are the current owners. Children from this marriage are: Ralph Wayne, born Aug. 19, 1928, and married to Lois Loy, born June 17, 1931, in Kokomo on Feb. 6, 1949. Their issue are: Stephenie Joan (killed in auto accident at age 19), Stephen Wayne, Terry Loy, Gregory Howard, and Jeffery Allen. Helen Louise, born Nov. 19, 1930, and married to Richard Dean Bergman on Dec. 22, 1950 (divorced April 4, 1967); their children are: Richard D., Kimberly Diane, and Troy D. Keith Allen, born Aug. 30, 1939, married Marilyn Sue Buller Whitacre, born Aug. 19, 1937, on July 25, 1962. Their children are: Cindy Ann and Brian Anthony (Marilyn's children by a former marriage and adopted by Keith), and Kay Tiffany, Gina Nicole, Kelly Sue and David Lee. Mary Ellen, born Aug. 18, 1944, married Leslie Martin, born Jan. 26, 1942, in Windfall on May 23, 1960, (divorced May 29, 1963). Their children are: Brent Jay and Cherie Beth, later adopted by Mary Ellen's second husband, Charlie Humphriss, born Sept. 9, 1944. This marriage: Aug. 19, 1966. Children: Andrew Arthur and Charles Jr. Divorced: Jan. 12, 1981. Rachel E. Camacho was born Sept. 8, 1984.

Betty Bolinger (Jan. 21, 1906-May 15, 1989) married Lawrence Maher (May 18, 1892-Feb. 5, 1958) on Dec. 25, 1931. Betty taught school for over 35 years. There were no children from this marriage.

Etta Louise Bolinger, born March 8, 1908, married William Ewing on May 1, 1928. (Divorced Nov. 13, 1936). Etta later married Marvin Hutchinson, born May 25, 1910, on Dec. 16, 1945. She was a public school teacher for 40 years. No children were born.

Zella Izola Bolinger (Oct. 14, 1909-Oct. 19, 1983) was married to Clarence F. Yater (May 17, 1910-May 20, 1988) on Nov. 28, 1931. They farmed in the Young America area and Izola taught school over 38 years. There was no issue from this marriage.

Clifford M. Bolinger, born Nov. 11, 1911, was married to Alma Koehler, born May 15, 1911, on Nov. 26, 1931. Their children are: Cornelius M., born Sept. 2, 1932, and married to Miriam Johnson, born July 21, 1934, on July 19, 1952. Their children are Linda, Susan, Cornelius Mark, Karen Kay (died as infant April 9, 1962), Christopher and Matthew. Carolyn, born Sept. 12, 1937, married Edward Boyce, born July 26, 1920, on Aug. 30, 1958. They have three adopted children - Carla, Jennifer Ann, and Nathan Edward. Michael, born Oct. 12, 1939. Benjamin, born July 30, 1941, married Cassie Ann Lambert,

born Nov. 29, 1944, on June 1, 1970. Their child is Jody Lynn. Michael and his brother Benjamin served in the U.S. Army 1963-1965. They and their father Clifford now live in houses on the 'Home Place' and still farm the ground purchased by Cornelius in March 1901.

It is interesting to note that the five Bolinger sisters that were teachers—Marie, Nina, Betty, Etta Louise, and Zella Izola—taught a cumulative total of 175 years in the Howard County area schools. *Submitted by Helen (Bolinger) Bergman from the research records of Mary Ann (Ericson) Bolinger*

LAWANA R. (PINKY) AND WILLIAM R. (BILL) BALLENGER - LaWana was born in Richmond, IN on Dec. 31, 1929 and came to Kokomo at 10 years of age when her father was transferred from Richmond where he worked for Montgomery Ward.

After graduating from Kokomo High in 1948, she met Bill on a blind date. Bill had been in the Army in Germany toward the end of World War II and was going to I.U. Extension on the G.I. Bill. The date blossomed into something special, and they were married on Nov. 4, 1950. By then LaWana was working at Delco and Bill was working at Sherwin Williams Paint Co. He was transferred to Shelbyville, IN where they lived for two years before moving back to Kokomo.

LaWana immediately went back to work at Delco and Bill soon followed suit, working 30 and 34 years respectively.

On May 15, 1955, their son Steven Paul was born. Steve graduated from Northwestern High in 1974, with a cast on his leg after being hit by a car when he had stopped to help a lady get her car out of a ditch. He had a cast on for a year. Steve didn't marry until he was 37 years old, and then to a nice little redhead named Kim Butler. They live and work here in Kokomo.

LaWana and Bill Ballenger

In 1956, the Ballengers bought an acre of ground from LaWana's parents and built a house on it, where they have lived for over 30 years.

Bill who is the oldest of three boys, was born in Ft. Wayne on Aug. 12, 1926, where his father, Ralph Armstrong Ballenger was a chiropractor. Ralph had been in World War I after graduating from two colleges and was halfway through another. While he was stationed in Kentucky in 1918, he married Sylvia Mae McKinney, who was born in Jerome, IN but was raised in Tipton. Ralph was raised in Sharpsville where his father owned a drugstore. Ralph met Sylvia at the Sharpsville Post Office where she worked. They were only married 23 years when Ralph died in 1941 leaving Sylvia a widow for 44 years until she died at the age of 89 in 1985.

LaWana's father, Everett Carroll Pickett, was born near Fountain City, IN in 1892. Her mother Edna Elizabeth Evans was born in Stark, KS in 1895. Everett left home at age 16 and finally ended up in Kansas where he met Edna, who was working in a store there. Her parents, Mary Jane and Lewis Ancil Evans, decided to move on to Montana where they homesteaded land. Everett followed them to Montana where he and Edna drove to Columbus, Montana by wagon and were married on Nov. 2, 1914. They lived in a one-room cabin where their three oldest children were born. After Edna became unable to walk from rheumatism, they decided to come back to Indiana where their other three children were born in Richmond. LaWana was next to the youngest.

LaWana doesn't know much about her grandmother Mary Roach Pickett, other than she was an orphan, left on a street corner, in a box, with her older brother in Cincinnati, OH. How she got over to Fountain City and adopted there, will probably never be known. LaWana's grandfather, Richard Oliver Pickett's origins go back to the early 1700's. *Submitted by LaWana and Bill Ballenger*

BOLTON-PLOSS - Jeremiah Bolton (Sept. 17, 1914) and Tempa Walden (June 6, 1912) were married March 27, 1937. They had 11 children: Bertha, Graylon, twins Josie and Jack, Jasper, Rose, twins Thomas and Conlas, Willard, David and Delphine.

In the mid-1950's, Jeremiah came to Kokomo from LaFollette, TN and obtained a job at Continental Steel. A couple of years later, he brought his family here.

Rose was born June 2, 1944, in Campbell County, TN. Before coming to Kokomo, the family lived for awhile in Kentucky where Rose attended a one-room school. She and two classmates made up the entire sixth grade. For grades seven and eight, she went to Washington School. Those two years and the four years at K.H.S. were with a perfect attendance record, despite the fact that she had about 22 blocks to walk to high school. There were no school buses in town at that time.

Michael and Rose Ploss

With the large family and many children in the West State Street neighborhood, there was always someone to play with (or fight with). There were no malls to hang out in, but there was Highland Park, where many fun-filled summer hours were spent.

After graduation in 1963, Rose worked various carhopping and waitress jobs. While working at Frisch's Big Boy, she met Michael Ploss.

Mike was born in Peru, IN on Oct. 17, 1938. His parents were Fred and Goldie Ploss. Mike and Rose were married June 9, 1967.

Rose started work at Delco in 1965 and took a leave of three and a half years when their first daughter Jennifer was born on Nov. 24, 1971. At this time they were living in New London, IN. Rose returned to work until June of 1977. A second daughter, Jodi, was born Sept. 30, 1977.

Presently, Mike is employed at Delco. The family owns a small farm near West Middleton, IN. Jodi is a sophomore at Western High. She is on the track team, is a wrestling cheerleader, and enjoys modeling.

Jennifer is a senior at IUK, majoring in education. Aside from her classes, she is busy with a job at Wendy's, substituting at various local schools, church activities—including youth leader, and planning her December wedding to Stephen Johnston.

Mike enjoys obtaining and restoring vintage motorcycles. For many years, he participated in motorcycle races and has several trophies.

In recent years, Mike and Rose have taken up square dancing and find it a very enjoyable pastime.

"We feel very fortunate to have grown up in this area with the job opportunities which were available to us; and we hope that our children fare as well should they decide to continue to live here."

NANCY AND WILLIAM BOUGHTON - Nancy and Bill Boughton first saw Kokomo when they came for job interviews in the summer of 1957, just before they married on August 18. While Bill was being interviewed for an elementary teacher's position with the Kokomo-Center Township School Corporation, Nancy was talking to the new director of the Kokomo Public Library, Phil Hamilton. Both were hired and moved to Kokomo following their wedding in Walhalla, SC. They had met at Indiana University where Nancy was getting her Master's Degree in Library Science and Bill had gone back to college to become a teacher.

William Stearns and his twin brother, Robert Scott, were born in Gettysburg, PA on March 22, 1930. The family, consisting of Dr. Jesse and Helen Stearns Boughton, Sibyl, Stuart, Bill and Bob, moved around during the Depression, but lived in Oakland City, IN from 1939 to 1943, where his father was dean and professor at Oakland City College, and minister of First Presbyterian Church. The family then moved to Salt Lake City, where his father was Dean and philosophy professor at Westminster College there. Bill finished high school there and graduated from Westminster College with a degree in Business in 1952. After trying the retail business for several years, he decided to go back to school to become a teacher. By then, his parents were back in Oakland City, and he returned to Indiana to pursue his teacher's degree.

Nancy Luella Harris Boughton was born on March 14, 1934, to James Henry and Elsie Drahosh Harris in Morristown, NJ (another historic town). Her father, James Henry Harris, owned Pocono Ice Co. When his health deteriorated, the family moved to Walhalla, SC, an area where many of the Harris relatives lived. Nancy has a younger sister, Lois, who has worked at K-HCPL since 1967, and two younger brothers, Bob and Don. Nancy graduated from Walhalla High School in 1951, worked one year in Anderson, SC, then left South Carolina forever with a degree from Furman University in 1956. She met Bill that fall in the Graduate Residence Center at I.U.

Nancy has worked at K-HCPL, either part-time or full time, for most of the intervening 36 years. Bill retired from teaching in 1990. All but one of his 33 years were spent at Lafayette Park School. They were charter members of Faith Presbyterian Church. Nancy wrote a brief history of that church.

They have four children, D. Scott, Ruth Lord, Carol Ramirez and David, all graduates of Haworth High School. Scott's degree is from Purdue, Ruth's from Ball State and I.U., David's from Cornell, and Carol has provided the three grandchildren.

The Boughton family history goes back to 1630; the Stearnses' to about the same time; the Harrises' to 1720's (all from England); and the Drahoshes' to 1890's (from Czechoslovakia).

Kokomo has been good to us, and we hope we have left a good mark on Kokomo.

HARLAN V. SR. AND MAUDE A. (FRAZIER) BOWERS - Like a lot of other people, Harlan and Maude came to Indiana looking for work. They moved here from Union County, TN on March 16, 1937. At that time they had a six-week-old daughter, Frances, the oldest of eight children. They settled in the western part of Howard County near Russiaville.

Harlan found work with some of the farmers, a Mr. Claude DeLong and the elder Doctor Evans. He then worked with the W.P.A. building roads.

To make ends meet, Harlan and Maude took in other people who had also migrated from the South to Indiana looking for work. Some were other family members, and some were friends.

One person they took in was Mr. Chet Atkins who is now known world-wide for his guitar playing. His brother Lowell also lived with them for awhile. Maude would do their wash by hand and cook and clean for them. They became almost like family.

Harlan had four brothers who also came to Indiana from Tennessee. They were Cliff Bowers, who was killed in a car wreck on Morgan Street in Kokomo; Bob Bowers, who went back to Tennessee; and Ulysses Bowers and Tom Bowers, who stayed in Indiana and raised their families here.

Harlan and Maude Bowers

Harlan went to work at Delco in 1942, and he moved his wife and family of four to Kokomo. Then in 1944 he was drafted into service for World War II. Maude was expecting their fifth child, and she moved back to Tennessee to be close to her family while Harlan was gone. Harlan Jr. was born in Tennessee and was 13 months old before his dad saw him for the first time.

After Harlan was released from service, they moved back to Indiana. Harlan then tried farming for himself in Clinton County. He got undulant fever from some cows he had bought from a sale barn and was hospitalized for a while. He then sold out and moved into Russiaville and went back to work at Delco. Later when he was laid off at Delco, he worked at the old Globe and Steel Mill.

In 1949-50 Harlan went to Detroit to work. He soon found he could not afford to live in Detroit and keep a family in Indiana. Besides, he missed his family very much. During those times there still were no jobs to be had, so Harlan sold shoes door-to-door. Lots of days he would go without food so he could bring home what money he made to feed his family. By this time there were eight children.

Maude went to work as a waitress at one of the restaurants in Russiaville to help make ends meet. She later went to work in a small factory in Kokomo until it closed. She still managed to take care of her home and children and always had time to show them the love they needed.

Harlan went back to Delco and retired in 1977 with 30 years of service. They now live near Russiaville. Their eight children include the following: Mrs. Kenny (Frances) Kidwell; Mrs. Larry (Jean) Tusing; Mrs. Eddie (Barbara) Tipton, who is deceased; Colin K. Bowers; Harlan V. Bowers Jr.; Mrs. Helen Turnpaugh; Dan D. Bowers; and Ronnie D. Bowers. *Submitted by Frances Kidwell*

LENORE HUNT BOYD AND DOROTHY HUNT KNIPE - The 1865 square Steinway piano in the music room of Lenore Boyd's home had its beginning in Kokomo when it was purchased as the 12th birthday present for Lenore Ellen, daughter of Cassie and Simpson Darnell, who came to Kokomo in 1859 to manage the Howard Drug Co. located at the northeast corner of the square. The piano was the second in Kokomo. Lenora

Darnall, in due course, grew up, married and moved to Andersonville, taking the piano with her. She became the mother of seven children, the youngest of whom was Ernest Martin Hunt who came to Kokomo after graduating from Whittier College, CA to work for the Kokomo Rubber Co. He soon met and fell in love with Julia Alberta Sumption. They were married in 1920. From that union came Lenore and Dorothy.

Ernest, after a few years with the Rubber Co., joined his brother-in-law and father-in-law in running the Sumption-Heady-Hunt Coal Co. on North Market Street. Ernest left the business in 1932. He was a highly regarded person in the community. He was a civic leader having served as commander of the American Legion, president of Kokomo Rotary Club and during his career he served as postmaster, Republican County Chairman, purchasing agent for the State Highway Department and finally bailiff of Howard Superior Court. He died in 1972.

Lenora Ellen Darnall 1872, 17 years of age, Kokomo, IN.

On June 20, 1863, William H. Sumption married Elmira Welsh in Kokomo at 6:30 in the morning. (The only train out of town left at 7:00 A.M.) Elmira had moved to Kokomo from Logansport. William had moved here from Ridgeville at the age of 20 to open a livery stable. Four months after they were married, William organized the 55th Indiana Volunteer Cavalry Company F and served as its captain and commanding officer for two years in the Civil War. He was mustered out in 1865 and resumed his business in Kokomo of harness making, manufacturing carriages, spring wagons and buggies. This building still stands on Mulberry St. and between Main and Buckeye. William served as Howard County Sheriff from 1894-1898. They lived in the brick house at 537 W. Sycamore which is one of the oldest houses in Kokomo.

William and Elmira had three sons, the youngest being John who married Julia Cora Cady (Dode) from Larwill, in 1889. John began his career as a lumber salesman, then went into the livery business with his father. For several years he sold purebred Belgian horses. He later went into the coal and building supply business with his two sons-in-law. John and Dode were the parents of Julia and Jeanness. Julia married Ernest Hunt, and their daughters are Lenore Boyd and Dorothy Knipe.

The lovely old Steinway came back to Kokomo in the late 20's and has stood in the same place for almost 70 years. Upon the death of Julia and Ernest, Lenore moved into the house she grew up in on Conradt Avenue, where, being a professional musician, she plays the piano almost daily.

Of the five grandchildren of Julia and Ernest, only one, Julia Knipe-Mills, lives in Kokomo. Perhaps her little daughter Virginia and the old Steinway will be the ones to carry on the family's Kokomo legacy.

CLARENCE (BO-DAD) BRADLEY - My grandfather John Henry (Poppy) Bradley, born Sept. 28, 1891, Bardley, Ripley County, MO, died Nov. 27, 1965 Searcy, White County, AR. On April 23, 1910 in Settlement, Van Buren County, AR he married Ethel Reams born December 1894 Franklin County, OH, died about 1919 Shirley, Van Buren County, AR. To this union were born two siblings: Helen Marie and Clarence Hiram (Bo-Dad). About 1924, my grandfather married Rosie Sara Smith, born March 17, 1905 died June 19, 1961. To this union were born eight siblings: Richard, Talmadge, Lois, Billy, Lloyd, Glanda, Inez, and Carolyn. My father, Clarence Hiram (Bo-Dad) Bradley, born Feb. 28, 1916 Shirley, Van Buren County, AR, died March 3, 1967 in Kokomo, Howard County, IN. On July 10, 1937 in Searcy, White County, AR, he married my mother, Flora Edna Jones, born May 31, 1919 in Walker, White County, AR, died Dec. 31, 1953. Her parents were George Thurman Jones, born Sept. 9, 1888 Smothersville, Franklin County, IL, died April 21, 1968 in Kensett, White County, AR and Sarah Elizabeth (Lizzie) Dunn, born July 14, 1895 in Waterloo, Lauderdale County, AL, died Aug. 11, 1987 Jacksonville, Pulaski County, AR. Both are buried in Searcy, White County, AR. They were married Dec. 4, 1916 in Walker, White County, AR. To this union of my parents, Clarence and Flora (Jones) Bradley, were born seven siblings (all daughters): Mary Edna Mae Bell, Freda Juanita, Martha Lorain, Helen Marie, Barbara Ann, Gladys Irene, and Janette (stillborn). My dad, mom and us children started making the harvest in the spring of about 1946.

Flora Edna (Jones) Bradley and Clarence (Bo-Dad) Bradley

We picked strawberries in Arkansas, then we would go to Michigan and pick cherries, then back to Indiana to pick tomatoes. We would leave Indiana just before the tomato season was done so we could get back to Arkansas to finish up the cotton crop. My parents were very hard workers. The year of 1952 we came to Indiana following the harvest and my dad and mom went to work at Haynes Stellite, so we stayed in Kokomo. In December 1953 my mother died of acute appendicitis and childbirth. At the age of 37, my father took on the reward of raising six girls. His goal was that we would always be together and today, in 1993, we all live within about 30 miles of each other, except our youngest sister lives in Florida. In 1958, my father married Barbara Hannah and they had one daughter, Rita Ann. My name is Freda Juanita Bradley, born July 25, 1940 in Higgison, White County, AR. On Sept. 27, 1959, I married John Earl Jones Jr, born April 17, 1937, in Kokomo, Howard County, IN. To this union were born two siblings: Robin Jo Jones, born Aug. 21, 1960 and John Earl Jones III, born Jan. 31, 1963. Robin Jo Jones on Aug. 14, 1981, married Dennis Jay Herrell born Nov. 8, 1961, Kokomo, Howard County, IN. To this union were born two beautiful daughters: Rachael Dawn Herrell, born March 1, 1983, and Rebekah DeeAnn born Oct. 18, 1986. Our son John Earl Jones III went home to be with Jesus on Dec. 24, 1978, after an automobile accident. At that time our family had to be very strong and really pull together, but with the help and love of our family, friends, and God, we made it. *Submitted by Freda Jones*

BRANTLEY - John Robert Brantley and his wife Rebecca (Nichols) came from Halifax County, NC, along with their children, to Tennessee in 1850. They settled later in Union County, TN where John Robert and Rebecca Brantley died in 1859 and 1861. Their children were William, James, Parlena, Joseph, Sarah, Benjamin, Elisha, Martha, Augustus, and Winifred.

Augustus Brantley married Charity Williamson on Aug. 7, 1862 in Union County, TN. Their children were William Harvey, Daniel Milton, Sarah Jane, Martha Ann, Benjamin, Louisa, Thomas, Easter, John, Freeman, Nancy, James, and Bessie.

Augustus and Charity's oldest son William was married four times, but he only had children by the first two. William's first wife was Tilda Ellison; they had four children: Silas, Rhonda, Prior Lee, and Hazel Catherine Brantley. His second wife was Hazel C. Boruff. Their children were Carlie Ann and James Harvey Brantley. Five of William's children moved from Tennessee to Illinois. Silas stayed in Illinois, but Prior moved to Denver, CO. Hazel Catherine, Carlie Ann and James Harvey all moved to Howard County, IN.

Hazel Catherine married Pryor Robinson and had five children: Clayton, Bertha, Helen Louisa, James Robert, and Donald. Hazel Catherine was better known as Aunt Katie, and was loved by everyone.

Carlie Ann married William Matthew Ellison. They had five daughters: Hazel Louise, Zettie Marie, Dessie Mae, Millie Maxine, and Marylin Louise. Hazel, Dessie and Marylin still live in Howard County, IN. Zettie lives in Windfall, IN, and Millie lives in the state of Alabama. Carlie Ann was always called Anne. She loved fishing, parakeets and religious music on the radio.

James Harvey Brantley married Iva Fern (Crousore) on Oct. 10, 1923, in Indianapolis, IN. Their children are Chester, Floyd and Robert Brantley.

The Brantleys came to Howard County, IN because it was where jobs could be found. James Harvey Brantley and William Matthew Ellison worked at the Steel Mill, and they also were farmers.

This story was written by Leanna Marie Davis, the granddaughter of Dessie (Ellison) Dickison, in memory of the Brantley ancestors. My great-grandmother Annie (Brantley) Ellison died in 1956, when my mother was only ten years old. I will always remember her through my mother's stories. *Submitted by Leanna Davis*

DICK AND JAN BREEDLOVE - Dick Breedlove, born Dec. 17, 1938, to Earl (Jiggs) Breedlove and Josephine (Cross) Breedlove. Attended St. Joan of Arc Grade School. Graduated Kokomo High School 1956. Worked at Standard Grocery on West Morgan 1953 to 1958. Went to Hank's Supermarket 1958 to 1965. Now has 28 1/2 years at Chrysler Transmission Plant.

Jan (Sutton) Breedlove, born July 8, 1941, to Max (Tony) and Mary Sutton. Attended Roosevelt Grade School Grades 1-5. Washington Grade School 6-8 grades. Graduated Kokomo High School 1959. Attended Glamour Girl Beauty Shop, Marion, IN, 1960. Worked at the Way to Beauty Shop; now housewife and babysitter for grandkids.

Dick and Jan were married April 8, 1961, at St. Joan of Arc Church. We have two daughters and four grandkids. Julie Breedlove married Mark Kuntz. They have two boys, Corbin-2 1/2 years old and Cameron-one month. Julie graduated from Haworth High School and works at Nasser-Smith and Pinkerton Cardiology. Jayne Breedlove married Mike Mock. They have two girls. Kylie is eight years old; Kelsie is five years old. Jayne graduated from Haworth High School and works at Burger King as assistant manager.

JAMES M. BREEDLOVE - James Madison Breedlove was the son of Henry and Nancy Agnus (Medsker) Breedlove. He was born April 8, 1844 in Marion County, IN. On July 28, 1867, he married his first wife, Mary Elizabeth McGuire, the daughter of John and Louisa (Williams) McGuire.

James and Mary moved to Kokomo from Boone County, IN between 1870 and 1872. He was a farmer and carpenter. He was also a skilled craftsman in woodworking, making many beautiful pieces of furniture and tastefully hand-carved intricate designs in the woodwork of his home at 719 N. Bell St., Kokomo. He also was mill superintendent for Armstrong-Landon Lumber Co. in Kokomo for many years. After Mary died Jan. 31, 1894, he married Malissa "Mame" Bauer—twice. He died Feb. 21, 1923, and is buried alongside of his first wife, Mary Elizabeth, in North Union Cemetery, Howard County, IN.

James and Mary had 10 children: William F. (1868-1869); Emma (1870-1874); James; Mary Ellen (Coy); Ira Ambrose; Fred; John Luther; Charles; Alfred "Jack"; and Nellie Louise (Mummert).

James M. Breedlove Family (1905) - Row 1: Alfred "Jack"; Nellie (Breedlove) Mummert. Row 2: Fred holding Raymond; Charles; Malissa "Mame" (Baur), James Madison's 2nd wife; James Madison; Ellen (Breedlove) Coy; Edward M. Coy holding Mary (Breedlove) Pierce; Ira holding his son James. Row 3: Lottie (McGail), Fred's wife, holding Eugene; John; James; Laura (England), James' wife, holding Naomi (Breedlove) De Witt; Melissa (McGuire) McCullough, Frank's wife; Frank McCullough; Lauretta (Horn), Ira's wife, holding Roscoe. Note: Melissa McCullough was a sister to Mary Elizabeth (McGuire) Breedlove, James Madison's first wife.

James was born Nov. 28, 1872, in Kokomo. On March 7, 1904, he married Laura Belle England. He died April 7, 1931, in Kokomo. They are buried in Union Cemetery, Forest, IN. They had eight children; only four lived to adulthood.

Mary "Ellen" was born Nov. 16, 1874, in Kokomo. On Aug. 20, 1894, she married Edward M. Coy. Although they had no children of their own, they helped raise many nieces and nephews. She died Feb. 13, 1946.

Ira was born April 15, 1877, in Kokomo. On June 25, 1899, he married his first wife, Lauretta Ellen Horn. They divorced in 1929. He later married twice: Ellen Moon (2nd) and Della Gordon (3rd). Ira and Mary had seven children.

Fred was born April 20, 1879, in Kokomo. He was raised to be a farmer and carpenter, but lost his right arm in a fodder-cutting machine at age 19. He established work in moving houses and heavy machinery. On Jan. 20, 1901, he married Lottie Ellen McGail. Lottie and Blanche (wife of Charles) became the only female professional paper hangers in Kokomo. They had six children.

John Luther was born Sept. 29, 1882, in Kokomo. He married Goldie Moore in 1909. He was a carpenter and builder. They had five children.

Charles was born Sept. 30, 1884, in Kokomo. He married Blanche Ann Kirken on Jan. 3, 1911 in Clinton County, IN. He worked as a carpenter, roofer, fisherman and old-time fiddler, winning many contests. They had two children.

Alf "Jack" was born March 5, 1888, in Kokomo. He married Rebecca Gill, March 27, 1912 in Frankfort, IN. He was a carpenter and in later years did beautiful miniature carvings.

Nellie was born Feb. 28, 1890, in Kokomo. She married Earl Elias Mummert, Aug. 22, 1913. They lived on farms near Galveston and Burlington, IN until he retired and moved to Kokomo about 1942. They had no children.

Other children of Henry that settled in Howard County were: Jeramiah (1840-1881); Eliza Jane (Parsons) (1842-1900); George Washington (1844-1928)—twin to James Madison and is mentioned in a history of Howard County by Jackson Morrow; Mary Ann "Molly" (Hayes) (1849-1920); Rebecca Margaret (Hurley) (1851-1903); Martha Moriah (Jones) (1854-?); Delilah Elizah (Turner) (1856-1911).

For further information see *Breedlove Genealogical History* by Olive (Breedlove) Smith (updated by Janet Gothard).

ISAAC NEWTON AND HANNAH BRENTON

- Isaac Newton was born March 12, 1840 in Johnson County, IN. He died Sept. 12, 1909 in Center. He married Hannah Hubble on Dec. 29, 1861. Hannah was born Dec. 7, 1841 and died Sept. 19, 1878. She is buried in the Chandler Cemetery.

Isaac and Hannah had seven children: Charles Cholafax, William McClain, Kizzie Jane, Sadie, Amanda, Callie O. and Mallie. Charles was born June 16, 1868 and died in 1959. He married Cyrena Reel April 11, 1891 and Stella Effie Hiatt, Feb. 16, 1893. Charles had nine children. William married Ellen Dora Eades on Aug. 14, 1890. Kizzie was born Sept. 30, 1874 in Howard County and died Sept. 11, 1939 in Ervin Township. She is buried in the Galveston Cemetery. Kizzie married Lewis Murphy on Nov. 27, 1890. Sadie married Charles Westfall on March 29, 1891. Amanda married Frank Behr Dec. 24, 1895. On June 6, 1899, Callie married Ira E. McIntosh. Mallie married a Murphy boy.

Joseph, Issac's father, was born Nov. 16, 1816 in Gallatin County, KY. He married Elizabeth Jane McGee on Feb. 26, 1838 in Johnson County, IN. Elizabeth was born in Kentucky in 1821. Joseph and Elizabeth had eight children, all who were born in Johnson County, IN: John born in 1838; Isaac (the subject of this article); Sarah born in 1841; Mary and William D. born in 1843; Oliver born in 1844; Samuel P. born in 1845 and Nancy C. born in 1848.

Joseph was the son of Robert and Sarah Brenton. Robert was born Nov. 13, 1772 in Washington County, PA and died March 2, 1840 in Marion County, IN. He married Sarah Brown Spillman Sept. 17, 1797 in Lincoln County, KY. Sarah was born Jan. 14, 1781 and died Sept. 11, 1827. She was the daughter of William and Mary (Spillman) Brown. Robert and Sarah had 14 children, all born in Kentucky except Washington, who was born in Marion County, IN. Mary born March 16, 1799; James born Nov. 26, 1800; Elizabeth born May 15, 1802; William born Feb. 15, 1804; Henry born Dec. 30, 1805; Rebecca born Dec. 6, 1807; Samuel born Nov. 22, 1809; John born June 22, 1811; Robert born Feb. 25, 1813; Sarah born Feb. 5, 1815; Joseph born Nov. 16, 1816; Phoebe born July 25, 1818; Nancy born Aug 22, 1820 and Washington born Feb. 5, 1823.

Robert was the son of Major James and Mary (Woodfield) Brenton. James was born in 1742 in Hampshire County, WV. He married Mary Woodfield (his second wife) in January, 1772 in Fayette County, PA. Major Brenton served in the Revolutionary War. He died on Nov. 19, 1782 at the Battle of Blue Lick (which took place in his front yard) in Shelby County, KY. Mary was born in 1750 between Wales and England, the daughter of Joseph Woodfield. She died in 1834 in Johnson County, IN and is buried in Marion County. James and Mary had five children: Robert, Mary, Nancy, Rev. Henry and William. Mary was born Oct. 3, 1773 and married James McClain May 21, 1792. She died in Marion County, IN after 1850. Nancy was born Oct. 8, 1777 and married Thomas Spillman Nov. 17, 1798. Thomas Spillman was Judge of Gallatin County, KY and was the brother to Sarah Brown Spillman. Rev. Henry was born in Harrodsburg, KY on Dec. 2, 1779 and died Oct. 11, 1846 in Marion County, IN. He married Esther Baird on June 14, 1814 in Knox County, IN. I have no information on William.

BROMLEY - Jay Myron Bromley, a molder of castings, met his family at the Interurban Station in Kokomo on Union Street in 1922. They had moved from Shelbyville, IN to Kokomo where Jay Myron was to be in charge of the foundry molders at the Kokomo Malleable Iron Works on Berkley Road. The family consisted of his wife, Susanna Kidd Bromley, sons Lee Myron and Jay Thomas and daughters Genevieve and Esther. Later, a son, Luman William and another daughter, Nancy Ann, were born in Kokomo where the family resided at 311 North Western Ave. for 33 years.

Jay, the father, was born in 1887 in Westons Mills, NY, the son of Alexander Thomas Bromley and Lillian Smith Bromley, along with five other children. When Jay was 12 years old (in 1889) and riding with his father, Alexander Thomas, in a horse-drawn wagon, the horses ran away, tossing Alexander Thomas from the wagon. Falling on his head breaking his neck, Alexander died as a result. Jay Myron went to work in a lumber mill to support the family and later moved to Norwood, OH where he learned the trade of a molder.

Jay Jr. Thomas Bromley - Esther Bromley, Jay Sr., Myron Bromley, Lee Myron Bromley, Susanna Bromley

Susanna Kidd Bromley, born in Cincinnati, OH in 1889, was the daughter of Irish immigrants from Belfast, Ireland, William Henry and Susanna Williamson Kidd. William Henry was a carpenter and built ships in Belfast and later helped build the skyscrapers on the Ohio River at Cincinnati. They had 12 children. He died in 1922 and Susanna died in 1909.

Jay and Susanna Bromley were members of the First Baptist Church in Kokomo. After retirement they moved to Clearwater, FL where they resided until 1965 when Jay died and Susanna in 1957, both being buried in Memorial Park Cemetery in Kokomo.

The eldest of Jay and Susanna Bromley's six children was Lee Myron Bromley who worked for Delco Electronics as an accounting supervisor. He graduated from Kokomo High School in 1928 and attended Purdue University. Lee and Virginia Knipe, daughter of a local florist, were married June 7, 1936 and had two sons, Thomas Lee and John William Bromley. Virginia died in 1986, and Lee married Betty Bock Strawbridge on May 26, 1990.

Jay Thomas Bromley graduated from Purdue University in Pharmacy in 1937 and later retired from Eli Lilly. He married his KHS Sweetheart, Catherine Albright, who died in 1975. They had three children: Linda, James and Janice. Jay later married Ethel Pena. Jay served in the Navy during WWII. Jay now resides in Palm Harbor, FL.

Genevieve died when seven years of age from diphtheria and is buried in Memorial Park Cemetery, Kokomo.

Esther was a secretary at Continental Steel and later a realtor/broker in Ramsey, NJ. She married Richard Morris Tunis and they had two sons, William and Richard. Esther's husband died in October, 1983.

Luman was an orthopedic surgeon practicing in Ft. Wayne, IN. He married a nurse, Beth Warren, and they had five children: Bruce, Joel, Matthew, Elizabeth and Daniel. Luman died in 1983 of cancer and is buried in Ft. Wayne, IN. Luman also served in the Navy during WWII.

Nancy Ann was a secretary at Delco Electronics and married Walter Finney who died in 1982 in Milwaukee, WI. They had one daughter, Susan Josephine Finney. Later, Nancy married Clarence Polaske and they reside in Safety Harbor, FL.

All the Bromleys moved away from Howard County except Lee Myron who loved Kokomo and Howard County and enjoyed the people and life there. (Lee passed away suddenly Feb. 13, 1994.) *Submitted by Lee M. Bromley.*

REGINALD & ELVA (SHIELDS) BROOKE -

Elva, daughter of Lee (1902-1975) and Lula (Weeks) (1905-1984) Shields, came to Howard County from Washington County in 1946 when her parents moved to a farm in Taylor Township. Lee, son of Otho (1871-1948) and Estella (1873-1941) (Ridlen) Shields, and Lula, daughter of Joseph (1867-1944) and Amanda (1864-1940) (Huckleberry) Weeks were born in Washington County, died in Howard County, and are buried in Albright Cemetery. Elva attended Kokomo High School, graduating in 1948. Her older brother Donald (1926-1978) was a veteran of WWII. He was employed by Fisher Body, Marion, when he died of cancer and is buried in Albright Cemetery. The youngest child in the family, Ora Elmer, (1935-1983) graduated from Kokomo High School in 1953 and was employed by 3M when he died of a heart attack in Hartford City and is buried there. Elva was employed by Shell Oil Company as a bookkeeper from 1948 until her marriage to Reginald Brooke on Aug. 18, 1951. They then moved to Anderson where he was employed by Delco Remy. In April of 1952 they came back to Taylor Township and worked at Haynes Stellite for a number of years. Reginald later owned and operated A&H Plumbing and Heating and Elva worked for Delco Electronics. Reginald is the organist at their church, Morning Star, near Kokomo. They retired in 1992 and live in Hemlock, IN. Their hobbies include music, genealogy and RV'ing.

Reginald and Elva Brooke

Reginald, son of Lindsey (1890-1975) and Correll (1892-1941) (Lutz) Brooke, was born in Marion, IN on April 9, 1932. Lindsey, the son of Isaiah (1887-1922) and Matilda (1857-1923) Heiser Brooke, graduated from Indiana Business College in Marion, IN. He served in the U.S. Army during WWI, owned the Marion Vault Works, owned and operated a grocery on the near south side of Marion, worked in an ice plant and was a farmer until he retired. His death occurred in St. Joseph Hospital, Kokomo, IN, and he is buried in Grant Memorial Park, Marion, IN. He married Correll Lutz, daughter of Charles (1869-1935) and Minnie (1870-1938) (Circle) Lutz, in 1922; they had two sons: Charles (1930) who was stillborn, and Reginald. Correll studied opera at both the Cincinnati and Chicago Conservatory of Music. After the death of Correll, Lindsey married, in 1948, Cecil Shaw who died in 1954. He married Rhea Unger in 1956; she died in 1970 in Marion and is buried in Lewisburg, OH. Reginald attended elementary school at McCulloch in Marion and Hendricks near Jalapa and graduated from Sweetser High School in 1950. He attended classes at IUK, Taylor and Butler University.

Reginald and Elva have two children, Susan (1953) and James (1957). They both attended Taylor Twp. School. Susan graduated from IUK and Indiana Wesleyan. She married Mike Smoker, son of Raymond (1918-1988) and Mildred (1920) (Allen) Smoker, in 1972 and they have four children: Jennifer (1974), Jason (1978), Lindsey (1980) and Sarah (1986). Mike graduated from IU in 1978 and is self-employed in the trucking industry. Susan is a nursing administrator at Marion General Hospital. They live near Marion, IN. James graduated from Purdue University in 1980 and married Beth (1959) Millard, daughter of Howard (1922) and Mary (1922) (Brubaker) Millard, in 1983. James is an engineer for Eli Lilly in Indianapolis. Beth is a 1982 graduate of Purdue University and is a member of the U.S. Treasury Department in Washington, D.C. They live in Indianapolis.

JONAS BROWER -

Jacob Brower, the forefather of the Brower family, came to the United States from Ameka, Holland, and he and his wife settled first in Virginia.

A son Daniel and his wife Sarah moved with their family of eight children to Preble County, OH. The children were Jacob, John, Joel, an infant who died at birth, Lyda, Betty, Katie and Barbara.

Joel was then 12 years old. He came to Indiana when an adult, married Deliah Parker, took a claim of 160 acres from the government in Ervin Township where he and his wife raised their family of six: Alfred, Jonithan, Jonas, Joel, Frank and Sarah. Joel was a farmer and an Elder of the Old Order Church.

Jonas was a farmer and owned threshing machines which he took over the country by train and threshed grain for farmers. He was also involved in politics and served as Democrat County Commissioner of Howard County. He married Cathryn Ford and they had a daughter Florence. After Cathryn's death he married Iris Farr and they had a son Leonidas and a daughter Minnie.

Florence married William Cooper. They had four daughters: Goldie, Fern, Hazel and Eva.

Minnie married Frank Disinger. They had one son Clarence.

Leonidas married Mary Rebecca Mason. They had three sons: Eldon, Ansel and Dale. Leonidas was a farmer and died in a hunting accident at age 48. Mary managed the farm for a few years and then was employed by the Indiana Girls School at Clermont, IN until her retirement. She lived to be 99 1/2 years of age.

Front Row L to R: Jennie Williams, Ruth Brower, Nancy Babb, Janet Williams, Dale Brower, Jaime Babb, Larry Babb, Jeff Williams, Jack Williams, Scott Babb.

Eldon married Agnes Beck and they lived in Detroit, MI. He worked in the automobile industry. They had two children: Marjorie and Robert.

Ansel married Ruth Marsh and he lived on the family farm in Ervin Township. They had two children: Phyllis and Nelda. Phyllis married Fred Henry and they had two children: Charles and Cheryl. They adopted a daughter, Mary Jane. Nelda married Robert Lovelace and had one daughter Beth Ann.

Dale married Ruth Gillam. They lived on a mink farm in Ervin Township. He also retired as Director of Indiana State Agency for Surplus Property. They had three daughters: Janet, Linda and Nancy.

Janet married Jack Williams and had two children: Jeff and Jennie.

Linda married Leo Leger and had one daughter Camela. Linda and Camela were killed in an auto accident.

Nancy married Larry Babb and they had two children: Scott and Jaime.

After seven generations the descendants of Jacob Brower live in Howard and Cass County. *Submitted by Dale Mason Brower.*

BROWN -

Hampton Brown, born Aug. 11, 1797, son of Quaker missionaries to the Indians, came to the present site of Jerome in Union Township on Wildcat Creek from Wayne County in 1846 to join two sons, Elias and Joseph. Other family members came later. He built the first cabin and a grain mill and proceeded to develop the village. He name it Jerome after one of his sons, but it wasn't recorded until 1867, because his home became part of a secret underground railroad through which slaves could escape.

He was the father of 15 children, 12 by his first wife Mary, and three by his second wife, Agnes. The village flourished as other settlers came, and the Brown brothers built a combination water mill at the dam which brought more people needing grain milled or timber sawed.

His son Jerome became a farmer, securing a land grant north of Jerome and raised a large family, also. He later became a county commissioner.

Jerome's son, Jonah, (1843-1923) was captured during the Civil War at the Battle of Stone's River at the age of 19. He was a member of the 39th Regt. in the Indiana Volunteer Infantry, 8th Cavalry, and was later released to Camp Carrington, IN. In 1869 he married Christina Mann (1850-1935) and lived on the homestead north of Jerome, building a new home in the late 1890's. Most of the lumber for the home was cut from the woods on the farm and hauled to Kokomo by horse and wagon to be milled.

Their children were Theron, Erie and Waldo. Jonah served as postmaster at Jerome for several years, ran a general store there and was active in the GAR encampments. Nearing retirement age they moved to Santa Barbara, CA and lived briefly at Eugene, OR, but returned in later years to the homestead.

Their younger son Waldo (1893-1952) served in WWII in the Infantry at Camp McClellan, AL until the Armistice came. Waldo married Anita Kribbs (1896-1969) in 1922. They lived on the homestead with the exception of three years spent in Chicago while he studied to become a pilot. The Depression forced them back to the farm where they took up farming again.

Mr. & Mrs. Robert Hill

They were the parents of five children: June (Mrs. Robert Hill) of Kokomo; Shirley (Mrs. Wendell Cartmell) of Greenwood, IN; Sonya (Mrs. Hayne Yarborough) of Saluda, SC. A son, Theron, resides in Lafayette, IN, who served as sergeant in the Air Force in the Korean War in 1952. He served in Company B of the 279 RCT.

Dr. Lindan and Connie Hill and sons, Robert and Lindan Jerome, have resided on the Brown homestead since 1984, and he is the son of Mr. and Mrs. Robert Hill of Kokomo.

The Hill family also includes son, Dr. Raymond and Gail Hill of Ann Arbor, MI and son Brandon; Lt. Col. and Roberta (Hill) Matchette of Lawton, OK and children, Daniel, June, John, Anne and Michael; Dr. Philip and Dr. Lucinda (Hill) Coulter and son, Eric, of Tuscaloosa, AL; and Mr. Bruce and Heather (Hill) White and sons, Clayton and Cody, of Noblesville, IN.

Mr. and Mrs. White are with the family business, COMP Corporation in Kokomo, with her parents, Mr. and Mrs. Robert Hill.

ALBERT W. AND TARITA A. BROWN -

Alberta Wendell Brown Jr. and Tarita Ann (Wilson) Brown were both born and raised in Howard County. At one time their families lived as neighbors. They were childhood sweethearts and can trace their relationship back as far as kindergarten. Tarita has a love letter written by Wendell in 1966 in which he says "I love you Therita, do you love me? I yours, Wendell." How special it must be to have kept something so sentimental as this.

Wendell was born March 14, 1960 in Kokomo, IN. His parents are Albert Wendell Brown Sr., from Tatum, TX and Mary Elizabeth (Lyle) Brown, from Coffeyville, KS. After graduation from Haworth High School in 1978, he went on to Purdue University in West Lafayette, IN to receive a degree in Mechanical Engineering Technology.

Tarita was born April 30, 1961 in Kokomo, IN. Her parents are Willie James Wilson, from Laurel, MS and Miriam Elizabeth (Hall) Wilson, from Thornton, AR. After graduation from Haworth High School in 1979, she attended I.U.P.U.I. School of Nursing.

Albert and Tarita Brown Family

After being engaged for one year, they were married on Aug. 16, 1980. From this union came three sons: Albert Wendell Brown III, born April 10, 1984, Quentin Terrell Brown, born Jan. 13, 1987, and Kyle Montgomery Brown, born April 5, 1991. Kokomo is their birthplace also.

Wendell's grandparents are (Maternal) Walter Lyle from Montgomery, AL and Channie (Bobbit) Lyle from Beggs, OK; (Paternal) Patrick Brown from Stonewall, LA and Mandy (Glaspie) Brown from Rusk County, TX.

Tarita's grandparents are (Maternal) Lewis Hall from Thornton, AR and Betty (McCoy) Hall from Fordyce, AK; (Paternal) William M. Wilson from Troy, AL and Mae Jewel (Evans) Wilson from Newton, MS.

Their church heritage has been traced back to the year of 1907. Each generation of their families have been in the Church of God in Christ, with many of them being deacons, missionaries, ministers, and pastors. They now attend Grace Memorial Church of God in Christ, where their pastor is Bishop Milton L. Hall.

During the years of 1990-91 Wendell received another degree in Business Management. He is presently employed with Delco Electronics, here in Howard County, as a supervisor. Tarita is a homemaker, and has a trade of sewing and crafts.

Their roots in Howard County started in 1941. They are proud to reside in Kokomo. Having lived in other cities for a short while, they are very glad to be back home. This community has proved to be a blessing to them.

POLLARD JACKSON BROWN -

Pollard Jackson Brown was born in 1814 in Limestone County, GA to Robert Coleman Brown and Nancy Brown.

In 1827 the family and some other close kin moved from Garrard County, KY to Putnam County, IN, where they began farming 320 acres.

Pollard's grandfather, William Brown, had served in the Revolutionary War, which perhaps influenced Pollard's decision to enlist and serve for one year in the Mexican War. For this one year of service, he received a grant of 160 acres of land from the government.

After his return from service, Pollard married Nancy Bacon, daughter of William and Deborah (Smith) Bacon and they set up housekeeping in Lawrence Township, Marion County, IN. Between 1850 and 1860 they had four children: William Bacon, Mary L., Nancy Ann and Pollard J. Jr.

In 1861, at the age of 47, Pollard enlisted in the Union Army, serving three years with the 3rd Indiana Cavalry. During this time, he and also his horse "Old Bob" were wounded but not put out of service.

After the war, the family settled down on the old Kokomo and Greentown Pike. The property is one half mile west of the Kokomo Reservoir Dam. Two more children were born to the family, twins Howard L. and Laura Frances. These children were raised and married in the Howard County area.

William B. married Mary M. Summers. Mary L. married Gideon T. Jackson. Nancy A. married J.F. Nichalson. Pollard J. married Lizzie Brown. Howard L. married Mary D. Templin. Laura F. married Richard M. Wiley.

Pollard was active in the GAR Post #31 and always rode "Old Bob" to the meetings, in parades and special events. His horse became a mascot of his fellow veterans.

According to the Kokomo Dispatch Aug. 18, 1877, "Old Bob" died at the age of 35 and was buried on the family farm with full military honors. A handsome picket railing was built around the grave.

During the last five years of his life, Pollard was blind. He spent much of his time visiting with friends, swapping stories about the war and politics. Pollard died on Feb. 2, 1899 at the age of 85. His wife Nancy died on April 25, 1914 in Indianapolis at the home of their daughter, Mrs. Richard Wiley. *Submitted by H.W. Knotts*

WILLIAM AND RETA BROWN -

William Brown - baseball player, politician, and veteran's advocate - and his wife, Reta Mae Horton, both came from Hoosier lineages.

"Brownie's" great-grandfather, James Brown, a farmer, was born in Indiana about 1813 and married a Hoosier woman, Elizabeth, born about 1816. They had seven children: the eldest was William Brown, born in Indiana (presumably Harrison County) in 1838. William, a laborer, lived near Jerome, IN and died in 1917. William and Emily had six children: Emma, Louie, James (March 1869), Charles, Rosy and Edith.

James Brown grew up near Jerome, but went to work in the coal mines of West Virginia. In 1892, he married a local girl, Leanna Pack, born in 1875. The couple journeyed back and forth between Indiana and West Virginia before Leanna's death in Kanawha County, WV between 1900 and 1907. Their first son, William, was born Sept. 24, 1893 in Acme, WV, but his brother, Carlos Guy, was born in Kokomo on July 26, 1895. Their third child died as an infant in Kanawha County in 1896. By 1907, James was working in Indiana. On Dec. 13, 1907 he was stabbed to death in an Alexandria saloon. His boys "Willie" and Carlos went to live with Uncle Charles Brown in Kokomo.

By the time "Willie" was 16 and Carlos (15), they had jobs in the glass factory. By 1916, "Bill" was working at the Globe Stove and Range Company. During World War I, Carlos enlisted with the Navy and Bill served in the Army's 1st Air Squadron, obtaining the rank of sergeant as a "doughboy" in France.

40th Anniversary - William and Reta Brown Feb. 5, 1967

After the war, Carlos moved to West Virginia, married Nona Cooper, and died in November, 1988. William returned to work in Kokomo and played semi-professional baseball in the old Midwest League. By 1926 he was a salesman with Globe. He later became general manager of the Kokomo Dodgers and Kokomo Highlanders baseball teams.

On Feb. 5, 1927 he married a secretary at Globe, Reta Mae Horton (born Nov. 11, 1905), daughter of Lindsay Oliver Horton (1871-1931) and Artie Melissa Skidmore (1873-1923) of Tipton County. Reta's paternal grandparents were George B. Horton (1836-1874) and Sarah Swing (1834-1897); her maternal grandparents were Isom H. Skidmore (1846-1908) and Sarah J. Unthank (1847-1934).

William and Reta had four children: William Horton (1927-1989), who married Barbara Ann Short in 1946; James Eugene (1930-1976), who married Eleanor Thomas; Robert Leon (1932-1989); and Gloria Ann (born 1935), who married Jerry Lee McQuiston in 1953.

Around 1926, William took a strong, active interest in politics and in the treatment of war veterans. He had leadership roles with the Veterans of Foreign Wars and American Legion and other fraternal organizations and public office. He was elected to the Kokomo City Council (1934-1939), served on the Election Commission, and served two terms in the Indiana State House of Representatives (1939-1943). He was a life-long Republican and booster of all things Hoosier! In 1967, William and Reta retired to Clearwater, FL. They returned to Kokomo in 1972 where William died April 10, 1972. Reta and son Robert remained in Kokomo. Reta died March 24, 1990, a year after Robert was killed in an auto accident. *Submitted by Gloria McQuiston*

BROWNING -

William Allen Browning (Jan. 12, 1869-June 27, 1942) married Louisa Tate "Ida" Milliken (April 10, 1878-June 14, 1962) on Dec. 14, 1902 at the Milliken family home in Napier, Lewis County, TN.

They became the parents of nine children. Five of the nine came to the Kokomo, Howard County area in the 1930's for work in the various plants. Two died as young children.

Their children were: Elzie Parker (Oct. 15, 1903-Jan. 8, 1967) who married Ila Graves, Dec. 31, 1924. They stayed in Tennessee and raised their family. They had six children, two of whom died as infants (E.P. Jr. and William). Their other children are Ruth, Daris Wayne, James and Joyce.

Louie Netherland (Oct. 17, 1905-Aug. 30, 1973) who married L. Faye Johnson (Nov. 27, 1934 in Howard County. They had a family of four daughters and a son: Lois A., S. Sue, Judy, Wm. Howard and Peggy I. Louie worked and retired from Continental Steel.

Martha Celine (Aug. 26, 1907-Nov. 11, 1929) lived and died in the family home in Tennessee. Her daughter Virginia came to the Kokomo area and married James Lindsay. He is retired from the military and they live in Nevada.

The Netherland Tait Home on the National Register of Historic Places

Mary Roxie (Sept. 14, 1909-May 23, 1943) came to Kokomo with her young daughter, Gladyce Rone, from a previous marriage. Nov. 3, 1935 in Peru, IN she married Edwin Marion Kraner. They had one son, Charles Allen.

Esther Lee (Aug. 10, 1911-March 4, 1984) came to Kokomo for a while. She then moved to Robinson, IL and married Hugh B. Johnson Dec. 25, 1936. They had two sons, William and John.

William Tait (July 10, 1913-July 4, 1915)

Charles Henry Smart (Dec. 31, 1915-April 30, 1926)

Fannie Mae (Jan. 28, 1918-Dec. 13, 1978) married William Howard Lamm, Nov. 2, 1935 in Kokomo, IN. They had three children: Phyllis O., Vivian Audrey and Michael Aaron. Fannie worked at Delco, and Howard was a guard at Chrysler Corp.

Alford McKinley "Mac" (Sept. 4, 1920-Oct. 24, 1974) came to Kokomo for a short while, he then went into the Army. While in the service he met and married Nancy Shaffer in Buffalo, NY. They had one daughter, Cherie. After their divorce he moved about a lot, returning to his brothers and sister here in Kokomo, where he lived the remainder of his life. Cherie now lives in California.

All the issue of Wm. Allen and Ida were born in the family home, as well as many of the grandchildren. There were four generations born in this home. It was built about 1840, by Netherland Tait, grandfather of Ida. This home is located just off the Natchez Trace in Lewis County, TN. We can cite a great deal of history with this home; that is why it has been placed on the National Register of Historic places. *Submitted by Candy L.P. Jones*

BRUBAKER - Judge R. Alan Brubaker was born in Howard County on Jan. 13, 1944, the son of Roy A. Brubaker, born in Howard County on Jan. 15, 1907, and Mary Waneta Haun, born April 21, 1907. Judge Brubaker spent the early years of his life in Carroll County where his mother's family had resided since the Civil War. Mary Waneta Haun was the daughter of Earl C. Haun and Iosa Ill Jacoby, and the granddaughter of Martin Gentry Haun, Civil War veteran, farmer, merchant, and auditor in Carroll County. His father is the son of Harley E. Brubaker and Malisse Ellen Bailey. Roy's grandparents, Louis and Hester Brubaker, migrated to Indiana with other German Baptist families from Ohio in the late 1800's. His maternal grandparents, Abraham and Mary Bailey, and six of their children, moved to Indiana from Franklin County, VA in 1895, with a number of German Baptist families who settled in Ervin Township. Judge Brubaker began his education in the Burlington Grade School; in the fifth grade, attended Ervin Grade School graduating in May of 1962 from Northwestern High School. He graduated from Purdue University, majoring in History and Political Science and received a degree in Secondary Education.

Judge R. Alan and Peggy Jo (Metzger) Brubaker

He married Peggy Jo Metzger of South Whitley, IN, on Dec. 24, 1966, the daughter of Joe C. and Dorothy L. (Shanahan) Metzger. Peggy graduated from South Whitley High School and holds degrees from Purdue and Butler Universities. The Metzger and Shanahan families have long been residents of Wabash and Kosciusko Counties, the Metzger family having arrived as early Indiana settlers from Pennsylvania along with other members from the German Baptist Church. The Shanahan family came to Indiana from Cork County, Ireland, in 1820 as immigrant workers on the Wabash-Erie Canal.

Judge Brubaker attended Syracuse University College of Law 1966-1969. He practiced law in Syracuse, NY before entering the Judge Advocate Generals' Corps, United States Army. He was stationed in Charlotteville, VA, the Panama Canal Zone and Fort Jackson, SC. In the military he prosecuted Military Courts' Martial and served as the youngest military judge in the United States Army hearing cases in the Southeastern part of the United States.

In May of 1976 the Brubakers returned to Howard County, taking up residence on the family farm in Ervin Township. They have three daughters: Melissa Ellen, born Syracuse, NY, June 11, 1970; Jennifer Lynn, born Ancon, Canal Zone, Feb. 12, 1972; and Mary Jo, born Columbia, SC, Oct. 12, 1974.

Both Judge and Mrs. Brubaker come from a long line of Republican families and were involved in Republican politics in Howard County until Judge Brubaker's appointment to the bench on May 5, 1985 by Governor Robert D. Orr. They have been active members of the Bible Baptist Church in Kokomo. Peggy has been engaged as a school teacher in the kindergarten and pre-school areas and is presently a school psychologist for Kokomo Center Schools.

BRUFF - James F. Bruff was known by many names: J. Frank Bruff, Frank Bruff, J.F. Bruff. He was also known as Kokomo's premier architect during the town's glory days as a gas boom rapid-riser.

James F. Bruff was born in Lafayette, IN, probably in 1868. He studied at Purdue University, graduating in 1887. He spent one year in Chicago, in the offices of leading architects; then he located in Kokomo in September, 1888. His first office was over Lea's Drug Store.

Bruff was a bachelor who lived in rooms in the Lindell Hotel. In January, 1890, he bought a half-interest in the Five Cent Store of W.F. Field, who afterward became his partner.

Bruff was a very good architect. He designed many buildings not only in Kokomo, but in other towns and cities around Indiana. Often he needed to beat out other architects and win a competition to get a commission; more often than not he won.

Bruff designed many of the older business blocks around the square and on the streets of downtown Kokomo. He was the architect for the old Carnegie Library building that used to stand where the present library is located on North Union Street. He designed both commercial and residential buildings, being equally at home with either type of design.

It was written of him that his talent was for the sightly and orderly, the symmetrical and simple; he shunned the opulently ornate. He was described as a thoroughly honest and reliable man; a weakness was his lack of diplomacy in dealing with men. But it was also said that he was a man of thorough integrity; and though his manner sometimes seemed distant, his speech abrupt, his was a person of kind heart and generous impulse. He lived a somewhat lonely existence, having no close relatives near him.

His memberships were in the Elks Lodge, the Sigma Chi college fraternity, and the Episcopalian Church—where his parents had belonged.

James F. Bruff was killed while riding the 'voodooed' street car—so named because of the many accidents it had been in—on April 7, 1906. He was on his way to supervise construction on the new Jenkins Glass Factory; when the car passed through city park, the wheels hit a bolt lying on the track; the car bolted and careened down a hill. Bruff tried to jump clear, but his head was crushed by the car's roof.

James F. Bruff's closest relatives were brothers John R. Bruff of Salt Lake City, and Charles Bruff of Denver, CO. While they were enroute to Kokomo, the Elks officials took charge of the body.

Funeral services were held in the lodge room, officiated by Rev. Henry R. Neely; then the body was taken to Lafayette for burial.

Joseph Coppage, an apprentice in Bruff's office, took charge of the work on hand. Thus came to a close the talented but singular life of one of Kokomo's greatest architects, James F. Bruff. *Submitted by Jeff Hatton*

BRUNNENMILLER-ARNOLD - Bruno Brunnenmiller was born into a farming family in Wurmlingen, Germany on Oct. 9, 1829. He was one of ten children born to Kaspar and Karolina Gross Brunnenmiller. Bruno left Rottenburg, Germany May 18, 1863, arriving in New York. While working in a foundry in Philadelphia, he contracted typhoid fever. He went to Cincinnati, OH to work on a farm while recovering from this illness. He met and married Catherine Arnold Feb. 27, 1859 in Decatur Co., IN. She was born Jan. 31, 1839 in Cincinnati, daughter of John and Louise Klensch Arnold. John was a stone mason who came to America from Germany about 1832. He worked on the capitol building in Washington, DC and settled in Decatur County, IN where he, along with others, constructed most of the original stone buildings there. His wife was also born in Germany.

Children of Bruno and Catherine Arnold Brunnenmiller. Left to R Front row: Pearl B. Miller, Evelyn (daughter-in-law), Barbara, his daughter, George B. Miller. 2nd row - Charles Miller, Mary Etta Miller, John A. Miller, Joseph B. Miller. 3rd row - Mrs. Waldo Miller, George Miller (son of Joe) Mrs Cora Manring Miller (Joe's wife), Waldo Miller (son of Joe), Beatrice Miller (Pearl's wife).

Bruno and Catherine Arnold Brunnenmiller settled in Howard County, IN about 1861, where they raised eight of their 11 children, three dying in infancy. These 11 children included: John A. (1859-1979, married Mary Goodwine and Frances Morgan Swain. He was a teacher and famous mathematician and astronomer, working at one time with Albert Einstein; Frank 1861-1956, a farmer who married Alberta Brobst; George (1863-1957) a teacher and President of Cogswell Technical College in California, married Mary Merrill Blood and Edna Grinnell; Louise 1864-1864; Joseph 1867-1946, a farmer who married Cora Manring; Charles 1870-1962, a farmer who married Dorothy Reamy; Mary Etta 1872-1954, married farmer Will Fawcett; Effie May 1874-1904; Grace 1877-1877; Pearl 1878-1970, a farmer who married Ida Ratcliff and Beatrix Colescott; Sam 1881-1881.

Pearl B. Miller was born Oct. 24, 1878 in Howard County. He and his first wife Ida had a daughter Aletha 1902-1913. After Ida's death in 1907, Pearl married Beatrix Colescott. They had Terrence 1910-1974; Mary 1912; Phillip 1914; and Barbara 1918. Mary was born Feb. 23, 1912 in Howard County, married Francis B. Ratliff May 1, 1937 and had four children: Earl Robert 1939; Larry David 1941; Mary Frances 1945; and Ruth Ann 1948. Francis died Jan. 9, 1986. Mary lives on Brunnenmiller land in Howard County. Pearl Miller farmed 180 acres of land and died March 30, 1970 from an accident while burning his fields. Beatrix Colescott was born Feb. 9, 1883 in Howard County, daughter of Wesley and Rebecca Crabtree Colescott. She helped raise her younger siblings after her mother died in 1903. Beatrix died Aug. 8, 1971. Wesley was born in Maryland (1848-1905) son of John W. and Celia Wooters Colescott. Rebecca was born in Ohio (1863-1903) daughter of Edward and Lurenna Goyer Crabtree. The Colescott line came to America from Scotland about 1770, while the Crabtrees came from England in 1819. John and Celia Colescott settled in Howard County about 1861, while Edward and Lurenna Crabtree settled there about 1871. These were farming families as were the Brunnenmillers and the Goyers.

BRUNO BRUNNENMILLER AND CATHERINE ARNOLD - Bruno was born Oct. 6, 1829 in the village of Wurmlingen, Wurtenburg, Germany. He immigrated to the United States in May of 1853 at the age of 24. He arrived at New York City, and found work at a foundry in Philadelphia for a short time. He lived at Lancaster, PA for a year or two before moving to Cincinnati, OH where he lived for two years. He moved to Decatur County, IN where he met and married Catherine Arnold in 1859. In 1861 they bought land and built a home in Eastern Howard County just south and east of where the Kokomo Municipal Airport is now located. The brick home is still standing as of this date (1993). To this union 11 children were born.

Bruno Brunnenmiller and his wife Catherine Arnold

Catherine Arnold Miller was born in Cincinnati, OH on Jan. 20, 1839, her early life was in Decatur County, IN. The name Brunnenmiller was shortened to Miller, and the Miller family farmed the land for many years.

Bruno died May 10, 1907, aged 77 years, at his farm home. Catherine Arnold Miller died Jan. 5, 1921, at the age of 82, at the home of one of her daughters. She and Bruno are both buried in Crown Point Cemetery. Some descendants of Bruno and Catherine who have lived and still live in Howard County are as follows: Frank Miller (son); Arthur Caleb Miller (grandson); George Franklin Miller (great-grandson); Arthur and George Miller built and operated the Miller Packing Company located on the west side of Kokomo (where the new juvenile detention center is now located) for over 50 years; Stephen Douglas Miller (great-great grandson); and Douglas R. Miller, Neal T. Miller, and Mark S. Miller, all (great-great-great-grandsons) of Bruno and Catherine Brunnenmiller.

The German history of the Brunnenmiller family is recorded for five generations before Bruno, dating back into the 1500's. The earlier generations were all farm people in southern Germany. The history of the Brunnenmiller family is woven into the history of Europe. Two of the Brunnenmiller sons served in Napoleon's Army in Russia from where they never returned. Others served in WWI and WWII.

HENRY P. AND JUNE M. BUCHHOLZ -
August 1963 found the Buchholz five moving to Kokomo from Madison, WI. Henry began teaching physics at Kokomo High School, and June did private-duty nursing and looked after their three sons. They met in 1951 at Huntington College where June was the college nurse. Following Henry's graduation they were married June 24, 1953 in Kitchener, Ontario.

Henry Percell was born in Huntington, IN July 9, 1929. After graduating from high school in 1947 and Huntington College in 1953, he served as communications officer aboard the USS *Taylor* in the South Pacific 1953 to 1955. He then taught physics and mathematics in Fulton and Rochester, IN. In 1961 he received a National Science Foundation Scholarship to University of Wisconsin. He received the Master of Science Degree in 1962 and remained one more year doing graduate work, then came to KHS.

June Marie was born in New Dundee, Ontario, June 2, 1929, grew up and graduated from Preston High School in 1947, Kitchener-Waterloo Hospital in 1950 and Huntington College in 1954.

In 1954 June joined Henry in Honolulu, HI and enjoyed island living for a year. June and Henry attended First Christian Church, Honolulu. David Frederick was born March 30, 1955 but didn't get to meet his Dad until he returned from a tour to Japan in July.

While living in Fulton and Rochester, June directed adult and junior choirs and did nursing at Woodlawn Hospital. Joining the family were Robert Henry on June 6, 1956 and James Richard on June 22, 1960.

Henry P. Buchholz and June M (Litwiller) Buchholz

In Kokomo the family became complete with the arrival of Laura Marie on Jan. 28, 1967 and Mary Elizabeth on Sept. 24, 1971. Henry retired in 1991 after 38 years of teaching; June completed 25 years as choir director at South Side Christian Church.

Henry's parents were Friederick Heinrich Buchholz and Effie Pearl Percell, married July 5, 1923; grandparents Heinrich Friedrich and Magdilena (Felton) Buchholz and James Robert and Elizabeth (Drabenstot) Percell. Great-grandparents Friederick Heinrich and Caroline (Sonnemaker) Buchholz (both born in Hanover, Germany) and John and Barbara (Christman) Felton; William and Nancy (Wilson) Percell and Fred and Martha Drabenstot. William and son James Robert came to Indiana from Kentucky with a cattle drive—James' shoes had worn out and he arrived barefoot.

June's parents were David Litwiller and Nellie Norene Hilborn, married July 14, 1927. He was a school teacher 40 years and she a church organist. Grandparents Christian and Maria (Miller) Litwiller and Amos and Laura (Reichard) Hilborn. Great-grandparents Peter and Elizabeth (Lichti) Litwiller and Christian and Maria (Roth) Miller. Peter and Elizabeth were born in Upper Alsace, France, and arrived in Upper Canada in 1827. Both Peter and Christian were Bishops in the Amish Mennonite Church. Jacob and Caroline (Witmer) Hilborn and John and Mary (Witmer) Reichard. Jacob, Caroline and Mary were born in Ontario, John in Michigan. They were farmers and of the Dunkard faith.

Our children now live in Ohio, Tennessee, California, and Indiana but still consider Kokomo "home".

BUCKLEY -
Buckley-Saul history tells that three brothers named Lindley came to the United States from England. They settled in North Carolina in about 1769. One of them married and had a son, James. The young parents were killed by Tories because they would not take up arms and betray their Quaker faith. James was raised by a neighbor.

James married Susan Stout. They moved to Hagerstown, IN near Richmond in 1811. That year they had John, the ninth of 12 children.

Gary and Karen Buckley

John came to Howard County in 1845, and James followed in 1847. James claimed Section 32 northwest of Greentown and paid $200 per acre. He used part of his land to lay out the Lindley Cemetery along Wildcat Creek. (It is separated from Greenlawn Cemetery by the westernmost road in the cemetery). Mary, John's wife, was the first person buried there. The early gravestones were still there in 1907, and later family graves can still be found.

John claimed land southwest of Greentown and cut trees to make a road to the bank of a stream where he built his cabin. Ralph McQuiston owned the land in recent years. John and Mary had 11 children including Samuel Lindley.

Samuel lived south of Plevna with his wife Lillis Cook Wilkinson. They later moved northwest of Greentown near the Chicago Pumping Station.

Lillis was the first teacher in the first school in Jackson Township. It was built in 1849 one mile north and three-fourth's mile west of Greentown. The log building was a subscription school as were the others in the area. Later it was moved and became the home of Ira Tharp.

Lillis and Samuel had one child, Walter, born in 1883. He married Nora Brobst, and they had ten children.

Walter attended Martin School, built in 1862 by William C. Martin on land Martin deeded to Liberty Township for five dollars. Martin School was used until 1917. Walter taught there in 1901 and 1902-03. In 1941, Walter, Rosa Dawson and Laura Chenowith wrote "A Brief History of Martin School" which includes many stories and lists of pupils and teachers.

Rowena Corrine, Walter and Nora's eldest child, married Fred Buckley in 1925. They lived in the Greentown area all their lives and had five children: Robert Buckley, Lillis Wright, Diane Vanderkolk, Gary Buckley, and Jennifer Jones. Lillis and Gary are still residents of Howard County.

Gary and his wife, Karen (Felt), now live on part of the farm where he grew up east of Greentown. They have two children, Alicia Buckley Brockwell and Matt Buckley. Gary is the owner of Felt Business Systems. He is active in Kiwanis, on the board of Junior Achievement and treasurer of the Greentown Glass Museum.

A.N. AND ESTHER BUCKNER -
Augustus Newton Buckner Jr. born Oct. 7, 1888 in Birmingham, AL. Son of Augustus Newton Buckner, son of Isaac Newton Buckner. His mother was Ella C. Lyerla. He died Sept. 6, 1974 in Ft. Myers, FL. He is buried in Kokomo Memorial Park Cemetery.

Esther Lily (Heisel) Buckner born March 25, 1894 in Terre Haute, IN. Daughter of Rudolph Herman Heisel, son of Lenhard Heisel, son of John Heisel. Her mother was Isabella Whitfield. She died Aug. 2, 1984 at Moosehaven in Orange Park, FL. She is buried in Kokomo Memorial Park Cemetery.

A.N. Buckner about 1922. He headed the Electric Motor Rewind Shop for the Carter Electric Company in Kokomo.

A.N and Esther Buckner were married Jan. 8, 1916 at the Little Chapel on the "Circle" in Indianapolis.

The Buckners moved to Kokomo in 1920 with three children: Lois, Robert, and Albert. Mr. Buckner, an electrician and electric motor re-winder, had been employed by Fairbanks Morse Company in Indianapolis. Six more children were born in Kokomo: Omar, William, Noel, Richard, Rebecca and Ruth. Sons Albert, Omar and Noel answered the call to the military in WWII.

A.N. Buckner worked for Carter Electric Co. of Kokomo for 23 years. In 1945 he established Buckner Electric Motor Shop in Kokomo. He was a Democrat and Union activist, a lifetime member of NISA (National Industrial Service Association), and IBEW (International

Brotherhood of Electrical Workers). He was business agent for the Kokomo IBEW Local Union 481. He received his 50 year IBEW Union Pin in 1970. Mr. Buckner retired in 1954.

A.N. and Esther Buckner

Esther Buckner served many Kokomo civic organizations. She was a charter member of Kokomo Navy Mothers Club, an active member of Red Cross Motor Club, YWCA, Kokomo Birthday Club, Star Needle Circle, Woman's Department Club, Women's Order of Moose and Eastern Star. On Jan. 18, 1944 she was nationally recognized and personally presented with two National Distinguished Service Awards, one from Henry Morganthau, U.S. Secretary of the Treasury, and another from U.S. Surgeon General W.E. King. The awards were on behalf of the Kokomo War Savings Program for sale of E-Bonds. She worked at Delco Radio during the war because of the man-power shortage.

The Buckners retired and moved to Ft. Myers, FL in 1957. They celebrated their "Golden" wedding anniversary there in 1966. Mr. Buckner was killed by an auto while crossing a busy Ft. Myers street in 1974. Mrs. Buckner moved into the Moosehaven Retirement Home at Orange Park, FL in 1980. She died there in 1982. They were both life members of The Moose Lodge of Kokomo and members of Wesley Methodist Church in Ft. Myers. They leave 23 grandchildren, 41 great-grandchildren, and two great-great-grandchildren, many who still live in Howard County. *Submitted by Carl Richard Buckner*

CARL RICHARD BUCKNER - Carl Richard (Dick) Buckner was born July 11, 1930 in Kokomo, IN. He was the son of August Newton Buckner, Jr., son of August Newton Buckner, Sr., son of Isaac Newton Buckner. His mother: Esther Lilly Heisel.

Educated in the Kokomo Public Schools, he graduated from Kokomo High School with the class of 1950, after sitting out two years recovering from polio in 1945. He gained an early interest in electronics and began designing and selling TV antennas while still attending high school. He operated Buckner TV Sales and Service at Kokomo from 1950 to 1956 when he moved his business to Naples, FL. There he purchased and operated Naples Radio and TV from 1957 to 1962.

Carl Richard Buckner

Dick closed his TV business in 1962 and enrolled at Olsen Electronics School in Atlanta, GA. He graduated and obtained his FCC First Class Broadcast Engineer License and was chief engineer at several radio stations in Georgia and Florida until October 1964 when he built and operated radio station WCOF in Immokalee, FL until 1972. He also built several cable television systems during his career.

Dick semi-retired in 1972, but returned to the broadcast business in 1978 as general manager of radio station WVOJ in Jacksonville, FL. In 1988 he received an honorary Bachelor of Science Degree in Broadcasting from Jones College in Jacksonville. In 1990 with the onset of post-Polio Syndrome and the weakness it caused, he was forced into retirement from WVOJ and active work.

Dick married Marilyn V. Rimes on March 3, 1957 in Naples, FL. They had four children: Kenneth Craig, born 1958; Beverly Ruth, born 1959; Elizabeth Jill, born 1961; and Ronald Joseph, born 1967. Dick and Marilyn have nine grandchildren.

On March 23, 1994, Dick departed this life and went home to be with our Lord. During his life, despite his physical disabilities caused by polio, he was not hindered or discouraged. He was determined to succeed, which he did, never complaining about his problems but rising above them. He was a success as a husband, father, grandfather, businessman and friend.

ROBERT LEE BUCKNER - Robert Lee Buckner was born May 6, 1918 in Indianapolis, IN. Died Dec. 3, 1938 in Kokomo, IN. Buried in Kokomo Memorial Park Cemetery. Son of A.N. and Esther Buckner. He received the blue ribbon for being the healthiest two year old baby in the "Better Babies Contest" at the 1920 Indiana State Fair.

Robert Lee Buckner (1918-1938)

The following from The Kokomo Tribune:

"He died at age 20 in the home of his parents. Mr. and Mrs. A.N. Buckner, 600 East Boulevard. He had been ill for the past eleven days of Sleeping Sickness. Buckner moved to Kokomo with his parents at an early age. He attended Jefferson Elementary School and graduated from Kokomo High School with the class of 1937. He had been employed at the Delco Radio Division of the General Motors Corporation at the time the fatal illness took him. Buckner was known widely among the younger set and was well-liked by everyone. He played three years on the varsity of the Kokomo High School football team (1935-36-37) and was prominent in Demolay work. He had held all the offices of the local chapter, and at the time of his death, was Master Councilor, the presiding position of the Kokomo group. He ascended to this office on October 1, 1938. Surviving Buckner with the parents are three sisters, Lois, Rebecca, and Ruth Ann, and four brothers, Albert, Omar, Noel, and Richard, all at home."

FREDERICK C. BULK - "Today, we all walk to church. The horses have worked hard in the field all week. They need the day for rest."

These were the words of one of the settlers in Ervin Township, Frederick C. Bulck, spoken to his family on a Sunday morning in the spring. The church, Zion Evangelical German Lutheran, located in Ervin Township, was two miles away. His family, which eventually grew to nine daughters and one son, looked forward to going to church. In the winter not everyone could ride in the sleigh. It became a contest to see who got to go to church and who had to stay at home.

Mr. Bulck was interested in community growth. His first interest was church. Along with other German settlers in the area, they organized a church based upon the teachings of Martin Luther. First services were held in the homes of members. On Oct. 27, 1871, they purchased ten acres for $200. There was a log house on the land. By removing a dividing wall, the congregation was able to use this house for their first church services. The first church building was built in 1887 and enlarged in 1911. An active congregation continues at that site today. They meet in a building that was dedicated in 1945.

Mr. and Mrs. Fred C. Bulk in front seat

With the purchase of the ten acres, the congregation soon built a one room church day school. Mr. Bulck was a teacher there for 16 years. The instruction for subjects was in German. Lessons from the Bible were taught.

Mr. Frederick Bulck, a Democrat, was elected to the office of Ervin Township Trustee for two terms. He was instrumental in getting several red brick one-room schoolhouses built. These were constructed in the late 1800's. The buildings were located so that no child had to walk more than two miles to class.

Frederick C. Bulck (1845-1921) was born in Westphalia, Germany. Mr. Bulck came to this country when he was ten years old. The Bulck family (two sons and four daughters) lived in Pennsylvania for only a short time. Soon they moved to Indianapolis. There the father was very successful in the draying business.

Frederick C. Bulck (spelling changed to Bulk) came to Howard County and Ervin township in 1867 from Indianapolis. He wanted to farm. He purchased his first 80 acres for $16 per acre. A short time later he purchased an additional 40 acres. He continually worked at improving his farm. It rated as one of the best in the county. On Nov. 30, 1870, he married Dora Pohlman. Miss Pohlman, (1849-1931) was born near Cincinnati, OH, and grew up in Indianapolis. Her parents had migrated to the States from Prussia.

Many of their children were better known by their nicknames. Caroline "Lena" (1871-1943), wife of Wm H. Hartman; Sophia "Soaf" (1874-1943), wife of George Schakel; Matilda, "Tillie" (1876-1964), wife of Henry Obermyer; Anna, "Mudder" (1878-1967) wife of Fred Lutz; Mary (1880-1959) wife of Harvey Sedam; Ida (1882-1939) wife of Carl Welke; Clara "Hale" (1884-1964) wife of Ross Hobson; Fred "Fritzen" (1887-1975) Bulk; Elsie "Shurp" (1890-1981) wife of Lloyd Hobson; Alma "Moose" (1893-1961) wife of John Beahrs, Mr. Frederick C. Bulk's death was caused by a car accident. His car was crowded off the road while he was returning home from Peru. As he worked to get his car back onto the road, another vehicle sideswiped his machine, injuring Mr. Bulk. He lived only a short time, never regaining consciousness.

Relatives living in this area descended from this hard-working civic-minded pioneer may be named Rossman, Mason, Hartman, Obermeyer, Prifogle, Beahrs, Hobson, Welke, and Pohlman. *Submitted by Leonard E. Hartman and Arian Mason*

BURGETT-STAFFORD - Homer Emanuel Burgett was born a triplet, March 12, 1881, in Clinton County, IN, a son of William Jacob and Sophia (Rader) Burgett. James Henry and Elsie Lenore were the names of the other babies. The baby girl died the day after birth.

Their mother died in October when the boys were seven months old. She is buried in the Stroup Cemetery in

Clinton County. Their father's sister, Nora, and her husband, Frank Wisehart, took the children to live with them in Frankfort. Uncle Frank taught "Dick" to play the violin which was a favorite pastime all his life. He liked to play for square dances and entertain his family. At one time he played an instrument in the City Band at Frankfort, IN.

Burgett Family - Standing: Anna Mae Taylor, Nora Earlywine, and Kathryn Conner. Seated: Lelah Cook, Homer E., Stella Burgett, and Beulah James.

"Dick" played football while attending Frankfort High School but for whatever reason he did not graduate from there. He went to work on threshing rigs, and later in life became a plumber.

Stella Effa Stafford became his bride on June 24, 1903, in Frankfort. They were the parents of five daughters: Lelah Evalyn, Mary Kathryn, Anna Mae, Nora Pearl, and Beulah Alice, who were reared in the Russiaville Community as the family moved there before 1915.

Stella was born Sept. 7, 1881, in Clinton County, IN, to Charles W. Stafford, Jr. and Senah Ann (Wisehart) Stafford. Frank Wisehart was Senah's brother. When nine years old, Stella's father died and she went to work as a hired girl, while some of the other children went to an orphanage for a time; then the maternal grandparents, Absolom and Mary (Keisling) Wisehart, took them in until the mother was able to care for them again.

She learned many domestic skills during this period and excelled in cooking, canning and sewing. She enjoyed crocheting rag rugs which she gave to every family member for a birthday present or a wedding gift. For many years she taught Sunday School at Russiaville Baptist Church and was active in the women's ministry.

Burgett Sisters: L-R Standing: Beulah James, Nora Earlywine, Kathryn Conner. Seated: Anna Lynch and Lelah Cook.

Stella died on June 30, 1970, in Kokomo, at 89 years of age. Her husband of 63 years died on Nov. 13, 1966, at 85 years of age. They are buried in the Russiaville Cemetery, one mile north of where they had lived for 40 years.

They were survived by their five daughters, who are still living, ten grandchildren, 22 great-grandchildren, and one great-great-grandchild.

BUSH - Rolly Franklin Bush came to Howard County in 1910. His previous residence had been Brown County, IN. His father had a farm and peach orchard; it was said to have been at the foot of Bear Wallow Hill. His parents were William and Viola Elizabeth (Conard) Bush. When locating in Howard County they farmed for the Learner family on Sycamore Road where Delco Park now stands. As a young man Rolly and his brother Roy worked for Deardorff's Flower Shop. When President-Elect Theodore Roosevelt made a whistle-stop in Kokomo the two boys presented him with a dozen long-stemmed American Beauty roses. Rolly went to Officer's School at Purdue in 1917. He served in the Army in WWI. In 1920 he married Iva Kimbel of Kokomo. They were married under an oak tree at Battleground Park which was said to be bad luck; they didn't believe it. One of his first places of employment was Pittsburgh Plate Glass. He also worked at Monardo's Fruit and Vegetable delivery firm. Rolly later worked at Continental Steel Corp. He operated the "transfer car", moving sheet steel from the Hot Mill to the Sheet Galvanize Dept. He retired from there in 1962.

Rolly F. Bush and Iva Kimbel Bush

Iva (Kimbel) Bush was the daughter of Charles Western and Rosa Ellen (Stewart) Kimbel. She was first violinist in the Kokomo High School Orchestra. Her class was the first one to graduate from the new Kokomo High School after the old one burned. Iva was employed at the Crosley Radio Plant (Delco) in the 1930's. Rolly and Iva attended the Main St. Methodist Church; it was said their Sunday School Class "Kings Sons and Daughters" was the largest in Kokomo. The ladies at the church made an "Irish Chain" name quilt for a fund raiser. Each name placed on the quilt cost ten cents and then the quilt was raffled off to the highest one. Iva got the quilt, and it is in the family today. Rolly and Iva had three children: Rolly Jr.; Viola Jean and Maryellen, the writer of this article.

ELVA RACHEL WILSON BUSTAMANTE -
Born April 15, 1899, in Kappa Corner (near Kokomo), IN, Elva Wilson began a life that would take her posterity on a journey that still continues between two worlds. This young brave woman did what few people in Kokomo never even dreamed of; she left her home, and started a new life in Colombia, South America.

Her parents: Laura Crites and Roscoe Wilson; sisters: Estelle Merrell, Pearl Blangy, and Crystal Elleman.

In 1917, she went to Marion College to study. There she met a Purdue student from Colombia, S.A.: Luis Bustamante, who worked with Haynes Automobile. Kokomo was the place where they chose to marry. Later they started their family when their first child Paul was born. Paul currently lives in Colombia, but his family is spread between the United States, Peru and Argentina.

Elva and Luis Bustamante

In 1921 they left for Girardot, Colombia. The sojourn began in New York City, where Elva left her country with her husband and her child. The United Fruit Co. ship would take them to Barranquilla. From there, they would travel again by riverboat to their final destination where Elva would meet her mother-in-law and father-in-law for the first time. Luis' father was a decorated general and an active member of the Liberal Party. Elva was ready to explore another country, another culture, and see the Andes Mountains (where Bogota is located). Also, Elva would see the coffee plantations, and experience the Magdalena River. Elva loved her new country and its people, and they loved her.

In December of 1923 their daughter Laura was born in the tropical town of Girardot. Laura spent most of her life in Colombia, but currently lives in Kokomo with her daughter Elva Lucia Mazabel. Two of Laura's children, Jose and Jorge, remain in Colombia, and Juan in Venezuela. Elva's return trip to Kokomo in 1927 was where her other daughter Caroline was born. Caroline is a life-long resident of Kokomo, wife of Nick DelVecchio, and mother of Sarah Bliss and Philip DelVecchio.

Elva made many trips between the two countries. She was an artistic woman who could capture the beauty of both countries on canvas using oil paints. Not only was the link between the two countries captured in art, but in the hearts of her descendants. Jorge, her grandson, obtained his degree at Indiana University-Kokomo; currently attending public school in Kokomo are her three great-grandchildren: Juan Gregorio, Carlos Jose, and Diego Arbelaez (sons of Elva Lucia); also Elva's eldest grandson's daughter, Carolina Mazabel, graduated from Purdue University-Kokomo. The bonds Elva created continue generations after her courageous venture into a place many can only dream of going.

Her husband Luis died in October of 1960, and Elva made her last trip to the United States in 1981. She died in Kokomo on Oct. 8, 1982, and is buried in the family plot in North Union Cemetery across the field where she was born. On her last trip from Bogota to Miami, quoting one of her favorite authors, she mentioned how good it felt to be back to her native land.

BUTLER - The Butler and Stratton families were a part of the great western migration of Quakers from Virginia, North Carolina and New Jersey.

Susan Mira Stratton was born (Dec. 4, 1858-March 6, 1943) in the log cabin on the Stratton family farm northeast of Russiaville in Honey Creek Township, Howard County, IN. She was the oldest child of Eli B. and Rebecca Mote Stratton. Her brother, Arthur Elvin, was born July 25, 1860 and her sister Rachel Ellen was born April 19, 1862. Eli died in 1864 at the age of 26 from a "chill" and pneumonia. He had ridden his horse to Fairfield to pay off the mortgage on the farm. Because of his death, Rebecca and her young children moved to Watseka, IL to live with her brother.

Jared Patterson Butler was born (Sept. 26, 1850-Aug. 13, 1923) in Rush County, IN the sixth child of seven of Joseph J. and Eliza Patterson Butler. The family moved to Henry County in 1867 and then moved to Ash Grove, IL in 1872. Jared attended Earlham College in Richmond, IN for a time.

Susan worked for the Butler family, as well as other families, before she and Jared were married Nov. 29, 1873. After Clarence Ora was born in 1875 they moved to the Stratton farm near Russiaville, eventually buying out the interests of Arthur and Rachel Stratton. Loura, Fred Otis, Eva, and Myrtle Ethel were all born in the log cabin and lived there until the frame house was built in 1887, just in time for the birth of Earl J. (Sept. 16, 1887-May 11, 1967) and then Rachel Elsie on Sept. 20, 1889.

Earl J. Butler attended Lynn Grammar School and graduated from New London High School in 1908. He graduated from Marion Normal School and taught for one year at Lynn before turning to farming.

Hazel Oveda Miller was born (Jan. 28, 1889-Sept. 15, 1982) on the farm in Monroe Township, Howard County, IN which was owned by her grandfather Hiram Fritz. She was the only child of Oscar (Feb. 18, 1867-Nov. 28, 1888) and Alice Viola Fritz (Nov. 17, 1869-Jan. 26, 1964) Miller. After her mother married Morgan C. Floyd (Feb. 18, 1857-March 23, 1935) she lived in Russiaville

162

on East Main St. Hazel graduated from New London High School in 1907. Before her marriage she worked as a seamstress and sold household products.

On Dec. 19, 1912 Earl and Hazel were married in the Friends parsonage in Russiaville. They lived with his parents until September 1914 when their new house, just west of his birthplace, was completed. Besides farming, he was Assistant County Road Superintendent for a time. For more than 40 years he was the State Farm Insurance Agent for the area.

Three children, Ralph M., Esther Lorene and Helen Lucile grew up on the family farm and all graduated from Russiaville High School.

Ralph M. Butler was born Feb. 26, 1916 and was married Aug. 17, 1935 to Mary Elizabeth Robertson (Oct. 31, 1916) of Forest, IN. Their daughter, Odel Ann Butler (Aug. 3, 1936) was married June 17, 1956 to David Strange (Aug. 12, 1934) from Clinton County. Their children are Michael Stephen Strange (May 22, 1966) married July 30, 1988 to Jill Bougher (Oct. 19, 1964) of Howard County, and Cynthia Ann Strange (Nov. 2, 1969) was married June 15, 1991 to R. Wynne Herrbach (Dec. 2, 1969) from Hamilton County. Ralph and Mary's son, Jared William Butler (Aug. 4, 1941) was married Sept. 20, 1963 to Martha Jane Harris (Oct. 4, 1940) of Clinton County. Their children are Julia Denise Butler (Nov. 23, 1964) who married Mark A. McCann (Aug. 5, 1964) of Howard County on Nov. 3, 1990. Their daughter Molly Michelle McCann was born Sept. 23, 1993. Jerry and Marty's daughter Jenny Michelle Butler (June 23, 1966) was killed in an automobile accident Feb. 18, 1989. Their son Peter Eric was born Jan. 26, 1968 and Stephanie Leigh Butler was born Sept. 19, 1970.

Esther Lorene Butler (Oct. 31, 1918) was married Aug. 18, 1938 to Ralph Wayne Davis (March 20, 1918) of Forest, IN. Their two daughters: Barbara Jane Davis (Feb. 19, 1945) married June 23, 1967 to Harry William Charles II (March 30, 1945-Oct. 3, 1988) of Clinton County. Their two sons ar Scott Allen Charles (Dec. 22, 1970) and Matt Edward Charles (Jan. 29, 1973); Beverly Jean Davis (Sept. 3, 1954) married on Jan. 3, 1976 to Wayne Allen Eppley (Sept. 30, 1953). Their two sons are Anthony Wayne Eppley (July 21, 1982) and Christopher Davis Eppley (Aug. 8, 1984).

Helen Lucile Butler (Sept. 28, 1921) was married Oct. 16, 1943 to Isaac Allen Hollingsworth (Sept. 21, 1914). They had two daughters, Peggy Ann Hollingsworth (Nov. 4, 1944) and Alma Sue Hollingsworth (June 8, 1953) who was married Dec. 21, 1974 to John Edward Pierce (Oct. 2, 1952) of Howard County. Their children are David Allen Pierce (April 7, 1981) and Holly Suzanne Pierce (June 27, 1984).

For more details see the booklet *Quakers On The Move,* May 1979 by Peggy Butler McAleese

JOHN ANDERSON AND SARAH ANN (OVERMAN) BUTLER - John Butler came to Howard County, IN around 1920 and remained here until his death on Dec. 29, 1947.

He was born in Tipton County, IN, Oct. 5, 1862 to Wills (born 1819) and Sarah (Dillner) Butler (born 1824).

Wills was the son of Eli (1778-1852), son of Noble Butler (1739-1799) and Susannah Beale (1742-1832), and Jane Buzan (1787-1873) Butler, natives of Georgia and Kentucky respectively. Eli and Jane came to Indiana, with their families, while it was still a Territory. Here they married and reared a family of nine children: Christopher, Noble, Sallie, Phebe, Susannah, Edith, Mary, Wills and Isabel.

Wills was born in Wayne County, IN, June 14, 1819. Sarah, daughter of Augustine Dillner, was born in Pennsylvania, Sept. 25, 1824. They married Jan. 1, 1845 in Marion County, IN. They had nine children: Elizabeth, Phoebe, George, Smith, Jesse, Susan, Marion, John and Sylvanus.

John married Sarah Ann Overman, Nov. 12, 1894 in Howard County, IN. Sarah, (born Oct. 2, 1876), was the daughter of Price Overman (1854-1919), son of Obediah Overman (1831-1898) and Sarah Hall (1823-1906), and Cynthia Baldwin (1860-1883), daughter of John, (born 1810) and Nancy (born 1817) Baldwin.

John and Sarah Butler

John and Sarah, the subjects of this article, had 11 children: Clarence, Anna, Glen, Obediah, Mary, Claude, Avan, Thelma, Wilma, Don and Dallas.

Clarence married Maggie Miller; their children: Morris, John, Virginia, Deloris, Marita, Robert, Denney, and Joyce. Anna married (1) Warren Hiatt; their children: Wanda and Arliss, (2) Hurshel Hethcote, who had three children: Hurshel, AnnaBelle and Merrill; then they had five children: Melba, Max, Merritt, Claude D. and Janice. Glen married Edra Hawkins; their daughter: Rosalyn. Obediah married Velma Quick; their children: Jack, Carol and Karen. Mary married Robert Reed; their children: Darrell, Doyle, Doris and Deloris. Claude married Leona Mills; their children: Betty, Ersalee and Dorsel. Avan married (1) Anna Clara (Dottie) McClain; their children: Patsy, Edward, Donal and Sarah, (2) Kate Brock, who had two children: William and Mary Kay. Thelma died at the age of eight. Wilma married Claude Glass; their children: Clyde, Francis, Charlotte, Sharon, Shirley and Duane. Don married Tressie Barnett; their children: Kenneth and Frieda. Dallas married Lillian Reed; their son: Danny.

John Butler died at the home of one of his daughters in Huntington County, IN. His wife Sarah died at their home in Greentown, IN, on Aug. 26, 1934. They are both buried in Ellis Cemetery in Howard County, near the little village of Phlox, IN. *Submitted by Anita K. Harrell*

JOSEPH ROBERT BYERS - Joseph Robert Byers, son of William C. and Laura Lillian (Woodard) Byers was born in Birmingham, AL June 1, 1934. He came to Kokomo, IN from Gary, IN where his family lived at that time. He was in the Air Force and stationed at Bunker Hill Air Force Base. He had previously been at Lackland Air Force Base, San Antonio, TX, where he had taken basic training. He also served in Wyoming, South Dakota and Okinawa. He married Linda Ellen Teter (born Aug. 10, 1938 - daughter of Lewis and Hazel Dickey Teter) on Nov. 29, 1958. Children born of this marriage are Joseph Robert Byers Jr. (born Nov. 26, 1959), Lori Lee Byers (born May 30, 1962), and Julie Lynn Byers (born May 10, 1967).

Joseph R. and Linda (Teter) Byers

After being honorably discharged from the Air Force, Joseph worked for more than 30 years at Chrysler Corp. until his retirement Dec. 31, 1993. He enjoys fishing and gardening.

Linda Ellen Teter Byers graduated from Kokomo High School in 1956 and attended Indiana University Kokomo. She was employed at Indian Heights Elementary School as a substitute teacher from 1963 until 1976, at which time she became the school's financial secretary until her retirement in 1993. She belongs to Heart and Home (Home Extension Club), volunteers at Howard Community Hospital, plays bridge and enjoys her family.

The couple are members of Bible Baptist Church and currently reside in Kokomo and winter in Vero Beach, FL.

JOSEPH ROBERT BYERS JR. - Joseph Robert Byers Jr.(born Nov. 26, 1959 - son of Joseph Robert and Linda Ellen Teter Byers) graduated from Taylor High School in 1978 and from Bob Jones University, Greenville, SC, in 1983. He married Denise Renee Petersen (born April 12, 1962 - daughter of Paul and Jeanine Petersen) in Kankakee, IL.

Joseph Robert Byers Jr. and wife Denise (Petersen) Byers

Joseph Jr. is currently attending Indiana University to gain a master's degree.

Denise also graduated from Bob Jones University. She graduated in 1984 with a degree in home economics. She is currently employed by Hills Communities Corp. in Indianapolis, IN.

They now reside in Indianapolis, IN.

JULIE LYNN BYERS - Julie Lynn Byers (daughter of Joseph and Linda Ellen Teter Byers) was born May 10, 1967. She graduated from Taylor High School in 1985 and graduated from Indiana University-Kokomo in 1990 with a Bachelor of Science degree in nursing. On Aug. 4, 1990 she married Paul Duane Beihold (born May 24, 1963 - son of Thomas Edison and Marjorie Johnson Beihold).

Paul and Julie Beihold

Paul graduated, with highest distinction, from Purdue University in 1991. Paul is employed at Allison Engine Repair Operation in Indianapolis, and Julie is employed at St. Vincent Hospital in Indianapolis.

They now reside in Brownsburg, IN.

LORI LEE BYERS - Lori Lee Byers (born May 30, 1962 - daughter of Joseph Robert and Linda Ellen Teter Byers) graduated from Taylor High School in 1980 and attended Indiana University-Kokomo. On July 27, 1984, she married Michael Karl Creighton (born Oct. 31, 1959- son of Robert and Phyllis Creighton).

Children born of this marriage are Kayla Ellen Creighton (born Jan. 17, 1988), Aaron Michael Joseph

Michael Karl and Lori (Byers) Creighton

Creighton (born April 23, 1989), and Cameron Lee Creighton (born Feb. 20, 1992).

They now reside in Spokane, WA.

BYRUM - Caleb Parker Byrum came to Indiana about October 1839 from Preble County, OH with Exum Byrum and Levina Byrum (older relatives) to the vicinity of Burlington, IN.

Caleb was born July 13, 1819 in Chowan County, NC. His home for a while was about three miles north of Burlington on the west side of the Old Michigan Road in what was later known as the Mack Robinson home. He married Susan Cline, June 16, 1842, who was born Feb. 28, 1821 in Harrisburg, PA. She was the daughter of George Cline and Hannah Wahl. Hannah was of half-Indian ancestry. They had ten children.

John Byrum, my grandfather and the second child of Caleb and Susan Byrum, was born Jan. 3, 1845. Later on they moved east of Burlington on the east bank of the Wildcat Creek. The family lived there until Caleb died April 20, 1880, and his wife Susan died Sept. 4, 1897. John acquired 80 acres of ground to the north of the home place and traded for the farm where I now live at 9923 W and 200 north and received $800 extra in 1870.

Mary C. Fegley, born Feb. 17, 1853 and died March 8, 1913, became the bride of John on March 14, 1872 in Howard County. Four children came from this marriage. For some years he was known and respected for his ability to make sorghum molasses and maple syrup. He was a farmer and cattle feeder. John died June 8, 1934. He and Mary were buried in the South Union Cemetery in Howard County.

The old home place on the east bank of Wildcat Creek is now a hunting lodge. *Submitted by Richard E. Byrum*

RAY AND MARGARET CAGE - On June 25, 1942 Ray Everett Cage married Margaret Josephine Mason Cage at the Baptist Church in Oakford, IN. Ray was born Dec. 21, 1917. He was the son of Everett Cage and Lilia Dale (Fisher) Cage born in Tipton County.

Ray, Margaret, Eddie and Becky Cage

Margaret was born April 2, 1926 in Michigantown, IN. They moved to Oakford when she was 14 months old. She was the daughter of Flossie Phoebe Ellen (Springer) Mason and Charles Otto Mason. To this union were born five children. Rebecca Lee Cage was born Jan. 23, 1944. She now lives at Billy-Bob Trailer Court on State Road 31. She has three daughters. She also has one baby girl and one baby boy who are deceased. Ray Edward Cage was born Aug. 2, 1946. He died on Jan. 21, 1990. He has two boys living in this area. Royce Leon Cage was stillborn on Aug. 9, 1953. Rhonda Ellen Cage was born July 17, 1954. She has one daughter and they live in Phoenix, AZ. Rozella Lynn Cage was born Oct. 16, 1963. She has one boy and one girl and they live in Indianapolis.

Ray and Margaret have eight grandchildren and five great-grandchildren.

WILLIAM COURETTE CALDWELL, JR. AND PEGGY ANNE HERRON CALDWELL - The Delco Radio Division of General Motors brought William (Bill) to Kokomo in 1952. He and Peggy lived on 1628 Kingston Road before moving to 205 South Hickory Lane in 1959.

Both were born in Evansville, IN and were married there on April 16, 1949 while Bill was a senior at DePauw University. Their parents were Dr. and Mrs. William Courette Caldwell (Mary Daves Mason Caldwell) and Mr. and Mrs. William Aaron Herron (Grace Martin Herron) of Evansville.

While at Delco, Bill wrote the first books and training manuals on semiconductors in automobile radios. Some of the material was published by Howard W. Sams and used by the U.S. Navy. Later, he was assigned to sales and marketing positions.

Peggy taught kindergarten for two years, and later served as foundation director for St. Joseph Hospital and Health Center. Active in civic affairs, she served as chairperson or president of Cheer Guild, Symposium, March of Dimes and PEO Sisterhood Chapter BU.

Bill served as president of the Northwestern School Board, Northwestern School Foundation, Friendship Home, Friendship Village Foundation, and the Firebird Amateur Radio Club.

As members of Grace United Methodist Church, they chaired various church committees.

They were the proud parents of a daughter and three sons:

Anne Caldwell Mershad, born Dec. 30, 1952; learning disabilities teacher in Centerville, OH; married to Martin Joseph Mershad; one daughter (Mary Grace Mershad).

John Martin Caldwell, born Oct. 16, 1965; manager-computer sales in Marietta, GA; married to Kristen Anne Lyslo; one daughter (Erin Anne Caldwell).

Douglas Daves Caldwell, born Sept. 4, 1954; died Sept. 5, 1954 (birth defect). William Stanton Caldwell, born Jan. 20, 1959; died Aug. 25, 1964 (traffic accident).

Bill and Peggy retired in 1988. They plan to remain in Kokomo and pursue numerous hobbies and interests.

Misc. Facts: William was born July 3, 1925, graduating from Bosse High School in Evansville (1943); served in U.S. Navy (1943-1946); attended Purdue and DePauw Universities (AB-Economic 1950); graduate studies, Purdue University.

Bill's sister, Martha Mason Caldwell Beeson, is deceased.

Peggy was born Jan. 13, 1929 and graduated from Bosse High School (1946); attended Winthrop College (1946-1947); Indiana University (1947-1949). Peggy's sister, Barbara Jean Herron Wolfe, is deceased.

They lived in Evansville, IN; Louisville, KY; Cuyahoga Falls, OH and Snyder, NY before moving to Kokomo in 1952.

GARY LEE AND JANET KAY CALVERT - Employment for Gary with Delco Electronics brought Gary, his wife Janet, and son Chad to Kokomo in May 1982. Gary is presently with Delco Electronics and recently received his 10 year service award. His current expertise is microprocessor programming. Gary was born in La Porte, IN Nov. 7, 1948. Attended high school in Monon, IN and graduated from Valparaiso Technical Institute in 1970. Gary was employed at several electronic firms in Indianapolis, IN before settling in Kokomo with Janet and Chad. Gary and Janet were married in Indianapolis, IN Nov. 26, 1976 and became proud parents on March 13, 1979 to Chad Lee Calvert.

Gary's father, Owen Calvert, was born in Calvertville, Greene County, IN where several generations of Calverts had lived. He was born Feb. 15, 1926 to Raymond B. and Tina Melvina (Stephens) and they later moved to Medaryville, IN where his father Raymond was a farmer and a carpenter. Owen moved to La Porte, IN to work as a machinist at Allis Chalmers and later became a truck driver transporting steel from the steel mills of Gary, IN to factories across Indiana, Illinois, and Michigan.

Gary's great-great-grandfather John Oscar Calvert served in the Civil War in the 53rd Indiana Regiment near the end of the war at Harrisburg, PA and was sent to the hospital at Beaufort, NC and then to a hospital on David's Island, NY before coming home to become the first postmaster of Calvertville, IN. Calvertville is no longer on most maps, but is about five miles north of Bloomfield, IN where road 157 turns to go to Worthington, IN.

Gary's mother Violet Mae Myers was born in Pulaski Co., IN June 9, 1930 to Charles Agustus Myers from Baltimore, MD and Nora Ireno Bullock of Wheatfield, IN. Violet was married to Owen Nov. 25, 1946 in Medaryville, IN and then moved to La Porte with Owen where Gary Lee, Randy Dennis (Nov. 1, 1956), and Connie Jo (May 25, 1950) were all born. Gary has a daughter Cathy Elaine, born in White County, IN, Oct. 3, 1971, from a previous marriage now living in Mulberry, IN. Gary's brother Randy has also settled in Kokomo to work for Chrysler. Gary's sister Connie is living in Palmyra, TN.

Janet Kay (Brummett) Calvert was born in Indianapolis, IN June 28, 1949, to Arthur and Beatrice Brummett. Janet recently received her 25-year pin from the American Legion Auxiliary. Arthur Francis Brummett was born in Columbus, IN March 26, 1915 and served in the Navy during World War II. Beatrice Burdette (Jenkins) Brummett was born in Dunkirk, IN Aug. 15, 1915 and was married to Arthur June 26, 1937. Arthur and Beatrice Brummett now live in Indianapolis, IN as does Janet's only sister Barbra Sue (Brummett) Garrod.

Seated (L-R): Anne Caldwell Mershad, Mary Daves Mason Caldwell, Peggy Anne Herron Caldwell. Standing: Martin Joseph Mershad, John Martin Caldwell, and William Courette Caldwell, Jr. (1986 photo).

Gary, Janet, and Chad Calvert 1993

Gary's many activities include being assistant scoutmaster for Troop 568 where Chad is a Life Scout, an amateur radio operator WB9SMX for 25 years, a member of Kokomo Shrine Club, Murat Shrine, Scottish Rite, Howard Masonic Lodge F.&A.M. No 93, Fraternal Order of Eagles #255, Moose Lodge #179, life member of the National Rifle Association, Indiana Genealogical Society, and Howard County Genealogical Society.

Gary's recent interest in Genealogy has lead him to a book "Descendants of the Virginia Calverts" by Ella Fay O'Gorman 1947 where his surname ancestors were recorded and documented from Sir George Calvert (First Baron of Baltimore) to as recent as his father Owen. *Submitted by Gary Lee Calvert*

CARTER - Levi Carter (March 23, 1838-Aug. 20, 1905) was born in Orange County, IN to Mary Ann Carter. Mary Ann and Levi moved to Parke County, IN in 1842, where Mary Ann married Lindley Robbins the next year.

On Oct. 23, 1858 Levi married Emily Jane Newlin (Sept. 10, 1839-March 7, 1898), the daughter of Calvin and Rebecca (Hadley) Newlin. Soon after their marriage the young couple moved to Fountain County, where the first two of their children, Charles Eli (Feb. 4, 1859-April 9, 1943) and William Andrew (Aug. 6, 1860-Feb. 3, 1913), were born. Sometime after the birth of William Andrew, Levi moved his young family to Illinois. While living in Illinois their little family grew by leaps and bounds to include: Laura Ann (Nov. 27, 1861-Nov. 6, 1905), Mary Alice (Feb. 22, 1864-Jan. 21, 1937), George (Oct. 1, 1865-Sept. 14, 1866), Ethleen (March 16, 1867-March 16, 1963), Enoch Lindley (March 21, 1869-May 13, 1958), Arvilla (March 22, 1871-April 1, 1920), Oliver Bales (Nov. 5, 1872-July 1, 1924), and Burton Calvin (Oct. 6, 1875-April 6, 1894).

Sometime about 1876 Levi and Emily brought their family to Howard County, finding residence east of Russiaville in Harrison Township. The Carter family grew even more with the arrival of Sarah Rozella (Nov. 30, 1877-Aug. 17, 1963), James David (Feb. 14, 1879-July 17, 1951), Clarence C. (Oct. 6, 1881-Aug. 6, 1964), and Florence Elsie (Oct. 6, 1881-Aug. 28, 1882). Throughout all the moves the family made, Levi and Emily remained steadfast in their Quaker beliefs and practices, raising their children in the faith of their forefathers.

Over the many years since the beginnings of Levi and Emily's life together there have been many descendants sharing memories of special family occasions. For a number of years there was an annual Carter Reunion held during the summer as well as a Cousins Dinner in the fall. Holidays and special occasions were also celebrated by the family. The reunion has been discontinued but the Carter Cousin Dinner is still held each fall. Of the 52 first cousins, about 10 are still living in 1994.

Descendants of Levi and Emily are living in several states, but the greatest number of them still reside in the Russiaville and Howard County area. *Submitted by Sue Bingaman Sheagley*

ROSEMARY AND ROBERT CARTER - The home pictured here was originally built around 1850; the frame work is all hand-hewed beams pen-framed together. Gravel was taken from two pits on the farm for graveling county roads.

Robert Carter purchased the farm in 1939 at $50.00 per acre, and it has been in the Carter family 54 years. Robert farmed and was active in community organizations until his untimely death at age 40, of a brain tumor, leaving his wife, Rosemary and three sons ages 13, nine, five, and soon to be the fourth son who wasn't privileged to know his dad, but seemed to sense his Dads drive to farm and make good use of farming skills his Dad used.

Rosemary Carter and Robert Carter

Meanwhile the older boys did the farming with help from uncles and grandpas. They managed a good dairy herd and raised hogs. As the boys attended school, they were involved in the usual activities and church youth groups; they did the farm work including milking twice a day, tending to hogs and farming on weekends.

Dan continued farming after graduation with his brothers' help, graduating from Earlham College, did post graduate work at Ball State; he married Elizabeth Ann Garbert from Kokomo. They moved a short distance away and help with the farming; they have two children Laurel and Will, both in college. Dan teaches at Northwestern; Ann is the minister of New London Friends.

Gene married Beth Ann Swift from near Plainfield. She is a nurse. They moved away, he taught school awhile, then went into the construction work. They have two sons, Dane and Tyson, both attending college and Jason, whom they raised, just married Michelle Loucks.

Four Carter sons- Dan the tallest; Max, Gene and Tim Carter

Max married Jane Deichler from Brockport, NY. They have two daughters, Maia and Lissa and a son Seth. Max graduated from Ball State, served two years teaching in a Quaker school in Ramallah, Jordon. He received his Master's Degree at Earlham College and his PhD at Temple University in Philadelphia. He is now professor at Guilford College, NC.

Robert and Rosemary Carter home SW of Russiaville; built around 1850

Tim is married to Kathy Cook from Fairmount. He took a two year accelerated farm course at Purdue, returned to the farm where he manages a hog confinement operation, farms other land besides the home place, drives a school bus and is teaching their sons Nathan and Nicholas farming, raising 4-H calves and hogs.

Mother Rosemary was busy in community and church work, keeping the house in order, raising chickens, dressing out fryers and hens, helping with chores when needed, attending school functions and later working in the school cafeteria. She really wanted to do beauty work, so night classes were offered, graduating in 1968 and has worked in shops in Kokomo and Russiaville.

The Lord has been good to us for which we are grateful!

CHASTEEN-TAYLOR - Don Fredric Chasteen was born Aug. 29, 1928, on a farm near Sheridan in Hamilton County, IN. He was the first born to Clarence "Jack" Wilson Chasteen and Charlotte Gladys (Davenport) Chasteen. The family moved to Howard County before 1930 where Barbara Eloise was born Nov. 18, 1930, and Jack Wilson was born Feb. 13, 1936. Jack was four days old when Clarence died. Gladys reared her children in Russiaville as a single parent. In 1966 she married Walter Butterworth. Gladys died March 31, 1979, at 69 years of age. She is buried beside Clarence in the Russiaville Cemetery.

Don played baseball and basketball for Russiaville High School where he graduated in April 1946. He worked for Continental Steel before beginning at Haynes Stellite Dec. 2, 1946. He left June 6, 1955, for Fort Leonardwood, MO, for basic training in the United States Army, 34th Regiment, 32nd Division. He was sent to Okinawa in October, then to Korea for 18 months and returning to America in April 1957, where he resumed his employment at Haynes and retired from Haynes International in 1984.

Levi and Emily (Newlin) Carter Family

Don F. and Jacqueline Chasteen

Playing softball on City Leagues in Kokomo and Frankfort and semi-pro baseball in Frankfort were favorite pastimes, as well as bowling. He has held memberships in the Masonic Lodge, Fraternal Order of Eagles, Phi Delta Kappa Fraternity-Beta Nu Chapter and the Association of Realtors.

Deidre, Stacy and Holly and David Mote

Don and Jacqueline Ann Taylor were married Oct. 15, 1955, by the Reverend Roy Helms in the Methodist parsonage in Russiaville. They have three daughters: Holly Anne, born Dec. 2, 1958; Stacy Jane, born Jan. 26, 1961; and Deidra (Dede) Beth, born Nov. 2, 1962. The girls were reared in the Russiaville and Alto communities. All graduated from Western High School, and Stacy graduated from Indiana State University and Indiana Wesleyan University. Dede attended Indiana State University and Professional Careers Institute. Holly married James Wallace Mote and they had one child, David Matthew Mote, born July 29, 1979. David attended Kokomo Christian School K-8 and is now a freshman at Kokomo High School-Downtown Campus.

Jacqueline Ann Taylor was born Dec. 19, 1931, at the home of her maternal grandparents, Homer "Dick" and Stella Burgett, in Russiaville. She was the only child of Cleo "Jack" Lavon and Anna Mae (Burgett) Taylor. After her parents divorced in 1939, she and her mother made their home with the grandparents.

Jackie attended school in Russiaville, Indianapolis and Kokomo. She graduated from Western High School on May 1, 1950. She continued her education at Kokomo Business College and Scarritt College in Nashville, TN. Bookkeeping and clerical positions were held until she gave up employment in 1960.

Upon profession of faith, Jackie became a member of the Russiaville Baptist Church on Aug. 14, 1951, where she taught Sunday School and the children's Joy Club; she also sang in the choir and held offices in the Women's Missionary Fellowship. She has been a member of the Bible Baptist Church in Kokomo for 21 years and holds memberships in the Howard County Genealogical Society, Kokomo Symphony Women's Guild and Heart "N" Home Extension Club.

CHEEK - In the spring of 1911, John W. and Theo Docia Cheek decided they wanted to be farmers in Howard County, IN. They put their three sons on a train and moved. Charles H. was oldest, Paul W. was two years younger and Edwin W. was the youngest. After they moved to Indiana in 1914, Wilbur (Bill) was born. The three sons went to the Plevna School. Uncle Bill spent 12 years in Greentown School. They are all gone except Uncle Bill, now 80, who lives in St. Louis with his wife, the former Lillian Vandenbark from Greentown. Grandpa was born in North Carolina in 1883 and died 1941 with a heart attack. Grandma was born in North Carolina in 1885. She died in 1971. They were married Dec. 25, 1903.

Grandpa and Grandma Cheek

I was named after John Walter. He and I spent lots of time together. I thought he was about the nicest person I had ever known. Grandpa would take me with him to the store in Plevna to sell eggs and I was sure there would be some candy for me. Grandpa lived on a farm three miles north of Greentown and moved to another farm one and one-half miles south of Plevna. We lived through the field one-half mile, so I could run across the field whenever I got ready. I loved to stay with Grandpa and Grandma. They spent the rest of their lives on the farm. Grandpa drove a school bus for 20 years, milked cows, and raised chickens. They were active in community affairs and Meridian Street Christian Church in Greentown. Grandpa would help other farmers when they were sick and behind on the farm work. The farmers would thrash the grain together and I can remember when they came to Grandpa's place, would do it all in one day, and have a big thrasher dinner. It was lots of fun; everybody knew each other. Life on the farm was good in those days and the people enjoyed it. Grandpa belonged to the Masonic Lodge in Greentown and his name can be found on the attendance record. Grandpa lived a full life and everyone spoke good of him. When he died, I was 15 years old; but I remember it and it was hard to lose him. There are 84 relatives of his still living in Indiana and most live in Howard County. He voted Republican and taught his sons to do the same. My dad was Charles H. Cheek, the oldest one of Grandpa's boys. I am proud and glad to be a member of the John Walter Cheek family.

GERALD CHEEK - Sycamore Friends Meetinghouse was full on this Saturday, Nov. 23, 1968. People were anticipating the start of the wedding. As the music started, a hush settled over the people. The new family of Gerald Cheek and Pam Powell was beginning.

Pam, second child and only daughter of Ronald "Red" and Pauline (Shrock) Powell was born Feb. 12, 1946, in Peru, IN. Her brothers are Ronnie and Jerri. Grandparents were Kenny and Pauline (Fansler) Powell, and Percy and Della (King) Shrock.

Gerald, first child and son of John and Eva (Hullinger) Cheek was born Oct. 19, 1946, in Peru, IN. His siblings are Fred, Bruce, and D. Kay. Grandparents were Charles Hershey and Sarah Eva (Ronk) Cheek, and Clyde Eli and Mary Ilo (Trott) Hullinger.

Pam worked at the lumberyard in Greentown until the birth of their first child. After their three children started school, Pam went back to work as a teacher's aide. In 1988, she became the secretary to the Veteran's Service Officer of Howard County. Upon graduation from college, Gerald starting teaching mathematics at Marion High School.

Stacy Jo, born Oct. 28, 1971, married Jeff Webb, an accountant, on June 19, 1993. Her high school softball team made it to the Final Four in the State Tournament. She will graduate from Manchester College in 1994. She has received many scholarships, and she's made the Dean's List three times. Her latest award was "Outstanding Future Elementary Educator." Her goal has been established to own and operate a daycare.

L-R: Gerald, Pam, Stacy, Jeff, Stephanie, John III June 19, 1993

Stephanie Kay, born on Dec. 7, 1974, was the child with the big eyes. Immediately after birth, while lying on her mother's stomach, she raised her head and looked around the room. In the sixth grade, her basketball talents were starting to bud. Years of practice in the elementary grades, and junior high, A.A.U., U.S.Y.B.L., and high school paid off. In 1988, her U.S.Y.B.L. team won the National Championship. From her freshman year of high school until her senior year, she started in every varsity game but three (Senior Nights). Stephanie has chosen to further her education at Wabash Valley College, in southern Illinois. Her goal is to play in a Division I school, and has selected a major in marketing.

John Walter III, born on Aug. 7, 1976, was our last child and only son. On his first birthday he received a pedal John Deere tractor, as do all grandsons in the Cheek family. On his seventh birthday, the family was fortunate to be able to celebrate in Disney World. In the fourth grade, John and Stephanie played basketball together. He continued to play football and basketball during his elementary years and through high school. His summer league baseball team won the State Championship. In Little League, he was the number one draft choice, and he hit a grand-slam home run over the fence. His eighth grade basketball team won the City-County Tournament. He earned his first athletic letter in basketball. He has worked for a farmer since starting high school.

CLARK - This is the history of the Clarks in Howard County, IN and their ancestors. Horace G. Clark was born on May 14, 1849 in Clinton County, IN. He moved to Howard County and married Viola J. Lawerence on July 8, 1882. He died Aug. 30, 1924 in Howard County, IN.

Horace's wife Viola was born June 6, 1864 in Miami County, IN, but she died in Howard County, IN on Feb. 17, 1954. Horace and Viola had six children: Albert, Ida Belle, Charles, William, Minnie, and Eva Clark.

Albert Clark was born June 6, 1883 and died Jan. 28, 1949 in Kokomo, IN. He married Nancy Florence McFarland on April 29, 1905 in Howard County, IN. They had one child, Bertha Jewel Clark. Albert's second wife was Rosie Tygart; they had no children.

Bertha Jewel Clark married James M. Massey on March 14, 1921. They had four daughters: Betty Jane, Maxine Mae, Virginia Joan, and Nancy Lee Massey. Betty married Charles Joseph Young on Oct. 9, 1941. They had four children: Joseph Le Roy, Steven Michael, Max Lee, and Susan Gay. Maxine married Edgar Lloyd Thomas on April 10, 1943. They had one child, James William Thomas. Virginia was first married to Keith Ewing on June 6, 1956, and they had two children, Melody Sue and Timmothy Kent Ewing. She later married Larry Gould on Jan. 9, 1971. They had two children, Matthew Jay and Andrew Clark Gould. Nancy married John Farthing on July 24, 1960 and they had two children, Penny Jolene and Jeffery Scott Farthing.

Horace Clark's parents were Elisha and Susan (Daggett) Clark. They had six children: Ranson, Merrilla, Joseph, Manuel, Lewis, and Horace Clark.

Horace's grandparents were Nathan and Jemina Clark. Nathan was married twice. His second wife's name was Rebecca; we do not know his wives' maiden names.

Nathan was born June 21, 1768; his birthplace is unknown, but he died in Delaware, OH. His children were Lettice, Nathan Jr., Nancy, Rhoda, Elisha, Betsy, Calvin, and Almira. Nathan's grandson, Albert, is the one that moved to Howard County and started the Clark line in Indiana. This was written by a descendant of Albert Clark. *Submitted by James W. Thomas*

C.B.F. CLARK (1860-1931) - The Clark family came to Indiana from a Pennsylvania Dutch background. Charles Benjamin Franklin (C.B.F.) Clark was one of seven children born to Alex and Rebecca (Fadley) Clark. The family lived on a farm near Jerome. C.B.F. married Mariam E. (Mayme) O'Neil and they had two children: Don R. and Edith and four grandchildren: Richard, Danny and David Durham and Mariam Clark. Aside from his family, C.B.F.'s best friend and constant companion was his coach dog, Pike.

C.B.F. Clark and Pike

Edith remembers her father as a man of many talents. He raised bees and also made maple syrup from the trees on the family farm. He taught school in several of the one-room school houses in the area, the last one being at Hemlock. In 1913 C.B.F., a staunch Republican, decided to enter the political arena and was elected justice of the peace, county auditor, and finally trustee of Center Township, an office which he held for many years. While he was trustee he took Edith to Indianapolis on the interurban to visit his friend, Governor Jackson. The interurban tracks ran along the Water Company Canal, and Edith received a history lesson about the canal. Local history was one of his interests and he worked with his friend C.V. Haworth, Superintendent of Schools, on several history- related projects. C.B.F. was also a mapmaker. Many of his original maps of Kokomo and surrounding areas were displayed in public offices.

The Knights of Pythias Lodge was another of C.B.F.'s interests. Every year before Decoration Day (Memorial Day) he and Edith would go to Crown Point Cemetery and repaint the red, yellow and blue markers commemorating the graves of deceased lodge members. Around 1920 C.B.F. sold the land where the family home stood at the southeast corner of Sycamore and Ohio Streets to the city of Kokomo in order that the city might enlarge Crown Point Cemetery. The house was moved to 919 E. Sycamore where it stands today.

He plotted out a section in the north part of Kokomo that is known as the CBF Clark subdivision.

CLARK - Howard County, IN was never home for either Howard or Janet Small. In fact, neither has ever visited there. But each has an ancestor for whom Howard County was home in the 1800s.

William Clark, Janet's great-grandfather, is said to have been born in Howard County in 1844. The first record located is the marriage license issued William H. Clark and Susan E. Leach in 1863. In 1870, the family lived in Harrison Township with their three oldest children, Lulu, Edward and Ernest. Their youngest child, Oran A., was born in 1874. According to newspaper accounts in 1876, William died at his home near Alto of consumption in the 32nd year of his life. The Odd Fellows Lodge No. 276 had memorial resolutions for him printed in the Kokomo newspapers. A history of Howard County, written in late 1876, states that William Clark was a charter member of the Union Grange No. 562, organized in 1873. Their meeting hall was one mile east of Alto. The same history mentions a James Clark as being in this area by 1842. Was he William's father? William's widow, Susan, and their four small children moved to Kansas in 1878. Who did this young family travel with? Were the Clarks Quakers? The family has not been located in the Howard County Quaker records. But in Kansas, Susan homesteaded land in Rice County near the new town of Sterling and gave a portion of that land for a Quaker meeting place.

Here Oran Clark met and married Nettie Beham. Their son Winston was Janet Small's father. Howard Small is a descendent of John and Lydia Lamb. The Lambs were early day members of the Quakers. Henry Lamb, known as "The Glove Maker," was in Virginia before 1739 as he and his family were mentioned that year in the Quaker records as being received in North Carolina from the Nansemond Monthly Meeting in Virginia. Henry's son Esau's youngest child, Josiah, was born in North Carolina about 1771. The family lived in Ohio for a few years before coming to Indiana. Josiah's oldest son, John, married Lydia Mendenhall in Wayne County, IN in 1814. Their oldest son, Hezekiah, married Hannah Small in 1836 in Grant County. John and Lydia Lamb were members of the Mississinewa Meeting, going to the Honey Creek Monthly Meeting when it began on the 14th of the eleventh month in 1846. The John Lambs, with their son Hezekiah, Hannah and their children were among the many Quaker families who decided to move west about 1852. The Lambs lived briefly in Fayette County, IA. Later they moved to Dallas County, IA where they lived until 1864 when they moved to Fremont County in southwest corner of the state, near the little town of Riverton. There the youngest of Hezekiah and Hannah's 18 children was born. Their daughter, Hannah Naomi, who married Henry Bowen Small, was Howard Small's grandmother. The Smalls also were Quakers who came to Indiana early in the 19th century.

CLEVENGER-HINKLE - Joseph E. Clevenger, son of Squire and Sarah (Gosset) Clevenger, was born on March 4, 1840. Margaret Ann Hinkle, daughter of Henry and Esther (Brock) Hinkle, was born on Nov. 11, 1844. Joseph and Margaret were married April 28, 1863 in Howard County while Joseph was home on furlough from the Civil War. Joseph served four years with Co. D, 39th Regiment of the Indiana Volunteer Infantry.

When Joseph returned from the Civil War in 1865, he and Margaret bought 40 acres of land about three miles from Greentown. There they built a log cabin. They had four daughters: Sarah Elizabeth, Mildred Louise, Leota Elmire and Dollie Alice. They also had six sons: Charles Henry, Walter Amos, Arlie Isaac, John William, Frederick Guy and Vern Ray.

Joseph and Margaret sold their farm in 1897 and moved to Greentown to retire. In 1914 they sold their home in Greentown and moved into Kokomo and lived at 1121 South Purdum St., to be near their children.

Joseph died Sept. 28, 1923 and Margaret died Jan. 24, 1930. They are buried in the Greenlawn Cemetery near Greentown, IN. *Submitted by Marty and Larry Thompson*

CLEVENGER-KECK - Frederick Guy Clevenger, son of Joseph E. and Margaret Ann (Hinkle) Clevenger, was born in Howard County on July 20, 1883. Hazel Lulu Keck, daughter of Michael U. and Catherine Ann (Poe) Keck, was born in Howard County on Oct. 3, 1888. They were married April 14, 1906.

Fred spent 40 years of his life as a minister and farmer. Fred and Hazel had three daughters: Jeannette Adeline, Naomi Ruth and Cecile Ann; and five sons: Arlie Unger, Gilbert Ross, Michael Joseph, Samuel Guy and Amos Blaine.

Fred and Hazel lived in several residences in Kokomo before moving to Sims, IN. After Fred's death on July 16, 1953, Hazel lived with her daughter, Jeannette, and family at 2124 Apperson Way North. Hazel died at her daughter's home on Dec. 28, 1958. They are buried in Albright Cemetery, just southeast of Kokomo. *Submitted by Marty and Larry Thompson*

CLOUSER-CONWAY-SUMMERS-MILLER - Fertile soil surrounding the eastern Howard and Tipton County lines was significant in the settling of their ancestors in Howard County.

Simon Summers (1822-1892) spent their first winter in this county (1865) lodging beneath a native log near Wildcat Creek at road 980 East. Born in Kentucky, he then purchased 220 acres. He was married to Elizabeth Wines (1818-1907) for 60 years. Both were pioneer residents and highly respected citizens. Their children settled farms and erected barns in the area.

Simon Jr. (1852-1927), born in Decatur County, married Mary Elizabeth Miller (1850-1934). Mary was the daughter of pioneers who operated an early day sawmill. They were active members of the Center Grove Baptist Church at 980 East. One son, Arthur Clifford (1872-1961), known as "A.C.", married Emma Luessa Miller (1870-1952) daughter of Peter Miller.

Clouser - Lamoine and Carolyn Sue

Peter Miller was born in Germany March 1, 1815. He came to the United States at the age of 12, smuggling his grandmother aboard ship. He enlisted as a private in Company I, 69th Regiment of the Indiana Volunteers at New Castle on Aug. 11, 1862. He was mustered into service in Indianapolis on Aug. 19, 1862. He was honorably discharged by reason of disability on Dec. 1, 1865. Upon his return from the Civil War, his second wife Mary Craig gave birth to their daughter Emma Luessa. Following her father's death in 1872 and her mother's in 1876 Emma Luessa was raised by a family on Wildcat Creek near Phlox. Emma and A.C. made their home on the county line.

Lema Summers (1895-1977) became acquainted with Leo Clouser (1894-1971) of Tipton County as he worked as a farm hand and she in a household on State Road 213. They married in 1915. Lema was the eldest daughter of A.C. and Emma Summers and Leo was the second son of Benjamin F. and Sadie Belle (Mitchell) Clouser. Lamoine (nicknamed Mush), ninth of 13 children, was born April 22, 1931. Lamoine met his future wife Carolyn Sue Conway (born Sept. 19, 1933) in the late 1940's while he was working on her father's Howard County farm.

Manville E. Conway still resides at this location. He was born June 28, 1909 in Tipton County near the corners of Howard and Grant counties. Manville, son of Everett G. (1885-1958) and Mazy (Keever) Conway (1890-1980), married Anabel Kleyla of Windfall. Daughter of Willard Raymond, known as Shine, (1893-1953) and Gladys Doggett Kleyla (1893-1975), Carolyn Sue's mother Anabel died Dec. 20, 1937 as a result of a housefire.

Benjamin F. Conway (1835-1915), father of Everett, came from Muncie with his brothers to scout the Howard/Tipton County are before the territory was opened to pioneer settlement. He returned with his wife Sarah Ellen Lawson (1845-1920) to the densely wooded useless swampland. Benjamin and his brothers cleared and ditched fertile fields on both sides of the county line, often laboring for others clearing timber for $1.00 a day.

167

Residing near Phlox, Lamoine retired from Continental Can in Elwood and continued to farm land settled by pioneer family members. Sue worked at the State Bank of Greentown. Together they raised three sons: Sidney (1952), Rodney (1954-1973) and Matthew (1957). They have one grandson Benjamin (1984).

COE-WYANT - John Coe (1794-1898) came to Indiana from Virginia with his family about 1840, settling first in Union County. While there John married on Oct. 10, 1848 Rachel Burke Ammerman (1816-May 2, 1905), a widow with three sons: William, Elisha, and Albert.

John and Rachel moved their young family to Harrison Township of Howard County in 1853. Elisha accompanied his mother and step-father on the move. John and Rachel were the parents of three children: Francis Marion (March 2, 1849-May 18, 1923); John Wesley (Oct. 10, 1851-June 7, 1934) and Andrew J. (1856-1865).

John Wesley married Cynthia Ann Nutter (Oct. 10, 1853-March 25, 1889), the daughter of Joseph and Nancy Ann (Gerhart) Nutter, on Dec. 1, 1874. Cynthia's father was a pioneer settler of Forest Township in Clinton County. John W. and Cynthia were the parents of Rachel Ann (Dec. 1, 1878-Dec. 24, 1934), Orpha Ellen (Dec. 13, 1882-Nov. 7, 1951 and a son who died as an infant.

After Cynthia's death, John W. married Minnie B. Hunt, daughter of Levi and Margaret (Cline) Hunt in 1899. They had no children.

Rachel Ann Coe married William R. Wyant on March 30, 1899. William was born in Boone County, IN on Jan. 19, 1865 and died in Kokomo on Sept. 23, 1955. He was the son of William Henry and Catherine (Straley) Wyant. Bill and Ann were the parents of 11 children: Vernida Ann, Chelsea Leo, Bermal Oscar, Cleola Catherine, Ruby Blanch, Velda Lorene, Maurice Elvie, Treva Irene, Clora Louise, Garnet Mae, and Hugh Kenneth.

Bill had been married previously to Miss Mary Ann Johnson of Tipton County and they were the parents of one son, William Franklin.

Two of Bill and Ann's children, Treva and Kenneth, reside in Kokomo. Many more descendants of the Coe and Wyant families currently reside in the Howard County area. *Submitted by the descendants of Bill and Ann (Coe) Wyant*

ANNIS B. COHEE - Annis Belle Cohee was born July 19, 1895 in Liberty Twp., Howard County to Frank E. Cohee (1866-1929) and Vesta M. McGraw (1867-1964); one of four children. Annis married Delbert Ray Bagwell on March 16, 1916 in Greentown, IN. Delbert was one of five children born to Milton Arthur ("Archie") Bagwell (1863-1931) and Dora Belle Olwin (1867-1956) who lived in Jackson Twp., Howard County.

Annis walked to school each day to attend a one-room schoolhouse. She attended Greentown High School, which was the only high school in the area for a number of years. In 1924 Union Twp. built their first high school and Jackson Twp. built theirs about 1925. Delbert had a three-mile walk one way to high school each day.

Annis and Delbert's first house was in the northern part of Greentown, where their first child, Gene, was born on June 1, 1917. Around 1918 they moved to another home very close to their first; in 1919 they moved to the old Brown farm (one mile north of Jerome in Union Township), and in 1928 moved to a farm they rented from the Hiram Wesley Lyons family until they purchased it between 1940-1942.

Annis Cohee-Bagwell, husband Delbert, children. Gene, Aggeleze "Toots" and Joan

Their children are: Wilford "Gene" born June 1, 1917 married Clydia Belle Buell on Nov. 16, 1940, children are Carol Ann born April 2, 1942 and Richard Gene born May 13, 1944; Doris Aggeleze Bagwell born Dec. 19, 1919 married Harry R. Plotner on April 24, 1948 had one daughter, Jody Kay born Dec. 17, 1950; Joan born Dec. 19, 1921 died March 13, 1977 (buried Alta Mesa Cemetery in Palo Alto, CA) married Irwin Trowbridge on June 15, 1946 had one son David Lee born Feb. 9, 1948; Archie Ray born April 24, 1931 married first Hildreth Anita Cox on June 20, 1953, then Sue ___, no children; Nancy Kay born Oct. 3, 1933 married Roger R. Mosser on Feb. 27, 1954 and has four children: Susan born April 25, 1956, twins Dean Bradley and Bruce David born May 24, 1959, and Diane born Oct. 24, 1961. All five of their children attended school and graduated from the Greentown High School.

Annis and Delbert were both members of the Meridian St. Christian Church in Greentown where Annis received baptism on Oct. 3, 1915 and Delbert the same in 1917. Annis worked as a seamstress at a local department store and carried out the usual "wife of a farmer" duties. Delbert worked as a drugstore clerk (1916), at Kokomo Rubber Works and as a farmer.

In 1965 Annis and Delbert's house and barns were destroyed by a tornado. They built a new home and a small barn, selling it around 1970 when they moved into Greentown. Delbert died there on July 17, 1973. Annis continued living in the home until it got to be too much to take care of, then she rented an apartment with a Mrs. Hill in 1975. She lived there until her death on Feb. 14, 1978. She was buried next to her husband in the Greenlawn Cemetery in Greentown. *Submitted by Cathie A. Sutterfield*

DELITE COHEE - Delite Cohee was born Nov. 11, 1901 in Greentown, Howard County, IN to Frank E. Cohee (1866-1929) and Vesta M. McGraw (1867-1964), the youngest of four children. Delite married Leo J. Renshaw on June 24, 1925 in a Catholic church in Kokomo. Leo was born June 23, 1898 in Elwood, IN, the son of John M. Renshaw (born 1862 Indiana) and Margaret Smith (born 1867 Indiana) of Center Township, Howard County, one of six children.

As newlyweds in 1925, Leo worked as a brass plate worker and Delite as a saleslady at a department store. They lived in an apartment within a few blocks east of downtown Kokomo. About 1930 they moved to Greentown and in with Delite's mother, Vesta Cohee, after her father's death. From here they moved back to Kokomo and lived in a brick home just a few blocks from Kingston Products where Leo worked as paymaster. Leo opened up a restaurant along this same block, moving an old railroad car to the lot and converting it into an eatery. Delite's mother was the cook and ran the restaurant with Delite's help. Leo ran the register during his lunch break. Vesta served breakfast and a noon day meal.

Delite (Cohee) Renshaw and daughter Maxine

Delite and Leo had three children: Maxine (Hancock); Jerry L.; and William J. All are still living in Kokomo today.

Delite converted to the Catholic faith when she married Leo. In 1935 Delite became pregnant with their fourth child and an infection set in. Delite died Sept. 15, 1935 at the Good Samaritan Hospital in Kokomo from complications. She was buried in the Memorial Park Cemetery in Kokomo. Leo remarried and died March 21, 1948 and was buried in Crown Point Cemetery in Kokomo. *Submitted by Cathie A. Sutterfield*

FRANK E. COHEE - Frank Edgar Cohee was born Dec. 19, 1866 in Union Twp., Howard County, IN to William L. Cohee (1839-1920) and Elizabeth David (1843-1918). Frank was one of seven children: George born 1864, John Elmer B. 1868, Laura born 1872, Flora J. born 1873, Eva Pearl born 1877 and William Burt born 1884. Frank married Vesta Martha McGraw on June 15, 1889 in Grant County. Vesta was born April 2, 1867 to Francis McGraw (1835-1926) and Nancy "Jane" Sutton (1837-1902) in Grant County (part bordering Howard County).

Frank E. Cohee and wife Vesta (McGraw)

Frank and Vesta had four children: a son who died at birth, Annis Belle (Bagwell) born July 19, 1895 died Feb. 14, 1978; Roxey (Shesteck-Johnson) born July 17, 1897 died Jan. 4, 1971; and Delite (Renshaw) born Nov. 11, 1901 died Sept. 15, 1935. Frank moved his family between Howard and Grant Counties for a time and settled

Wyant Family Reunion 1993

into a farm house just on the southern edge of Greentown on Meridian Street. He owned 60-80 acres of land in which the Wild Cat River ran through, which enabled him to dip gravel and sell it to the county for road improvement. Frank had two horses and Jersey cows, and he farmed two fields each year consisting of 15 to 20 acres each. Frank did little farming, sold his gravel, and made a habit out of going to town every day to the drugstore to sit and visit with the other men there. Frank also drove a school hack for several winters, carrying the area children to and from school. The hack was pulled by two horses and was heated with a kerosene burning heater, which never kept it warm. It has been said that Frank was kicked in the chest by a mule and had medical problems ever since that incident. Frank did own a car and let his first grandchild, Gene Bagwell, drive it before he was even old enough to go to school!

About 1927 Frank and Vesta moved from the old farmhouse to an apartment in Greentown, before purchasing a home on the north end of town where Frank died at the age of 62 years at 5:30 Sunday morning, Aug. 25, 1929 of a sudden heart attack. Frank was buried in the Greenlawn Cemetery in Greentown. Vesta died at the age of 96 on March 21, 1964 at Marion General Hospital and was buried next to Frank. *Submitted by Cathie A. Sutterfield*

ROXEY COHEE - was born July 17, 1897 near Greentown, IN; one of four children born to Frank Edgar Cohee of Howard County and Vesta Martha McGraw of Grant County. Roxey's siblings consisted of a brother who died at birth, Annis Belle (1895-1978), Delite (1901-1935). The family lived between Grant County and Howard County for some years as Roxey attended Taylor Township Schools of Howard County in 1907-8; then Common Schools of Green Township in Grant County. When Roxey graduated from Greentown High School Class of 1915 (21 students) her family was living on the southern edge of Greentown where they owned 60-80 acres where the Wild Cat River ran through it.

Around 1917-18 Roxey met a man named Joseph F. Shesteck, born March 29, 1896 in Latrobe, PA to Vincent Sistek and Marie Belsam, both from Austria. Somehow Joe found his way to the Kokomo area while serving in WWI. Roxey and Joe were married around 1920 and left the area. In 1922 they both worked for United Miller Shoe Company (place unknown). By 1923-4 they returned to Greentown and opened up a restaurant named the State Highway Restaurant. Roxey ran the business; her mother as the cook; while Joe worked at Kokomo Rubber Company. They lived in an apartment above the business and later purchased a home in town close to Roxey's folks place near the high school. Roxey and Joe were divorced and split their possessions. Joe left town and moved to northeast Ohio. Roxey began courting Glen Johnson (a high school sweetheart?) and they were soon married. Together they had one son, Edward Johnson, born July 22, 1925 in Greentown. By 1930 they had moved to Toledo, OH and shortly after to Detroit, MI

Roxey (Cohee) Shesteck-Johnson

Apartments were difficult to come by during the Depression years, especially when they had a child. Finally they settled into an apartment on Miller St. above a drugstore where Ed worked his first job. Glen worked for Chrysler Corporation as a general foreman and retired in 1959 at the age of 62. Roxey worked for Taylor Car Company around 1946 during the war years. In 1937-38 they purchased a summer home in Highland Township in Oakland County, MI; in 1946 it became their permanent residence.

Roxey devoted much of her time to her four grandchildren who lived nearby; playing cards with card club, garden club, crafts, sewing and crocheting. Time during the summers were spent at their upper peninsula home in Baraga. Roxey died of cancer on Jan. 4, 1971 in Pontiac, MI. She was buried in the Highland Cemetery in Highland, MI. Glen died March 14, 1984 of a heart attack and is buried next to her. *Submitted by Cathie A. Sutterfield*

WILLIAM L. COHEE - William L. Cohee was born Aug. 2, 1839 in Kent County, DE, the son of Hinson Cohee and Ann Longfellow of Delaware. William married Elizabeth David of Jackson Twp., Rush County on Oct. 28, 1862 in Rush County, IN. Elizabeth was the daughter of Jacob David of Kentucky and Catharine Kiplinger of Indiana. William and his new wife moved to Union Twp., Howard County in 1862 near Jerome in Section 18 purchasing 46.71 acres, where he made a living as a farmer.

William and Elizabeth had a total of ten children, but only seven lived to adulthood: George (1864-1946) who married first Ida _____, then Murl Pennington in 1907, he had eight children; Frank Edgar (1866-1929) married Vetsa M. McGraw in 1889, four children; John Elmer (1868-?) married first to ?, then Axie Crandall, three children; Laura (1872-before 1900) never married; Flora J. (1873-1933/4) never married; Eva Pearl (1877-1973) married Willis J. McCann in 1900, two children; and William Burt (1884-1944) married Julia M. Bennett, four children.

William died July 23, 1920; Elizabeth died July 10, 1918; both were buried in the Greenlawn Cemetery in Greentown, as well as most of their children. *Submitted Cathie A. Sutterfield*

COLE - In the early 1900s, Albert Clayton Cole came to Howard County from Hume, IL and settled in Taylor Township, on the Howard and Tipton County line. He was in his early teens and came with his widowed mother and bachelor uncle to settle on 80 acres and a three room log cabin. Clayton was born in 1892 in Nebraska where his father was a telegraph operator. Clayton was five years old when his father died and he and his mother moved to Hume, IL.

There were approximately 40 acres of tillable ground and the rest of the farm was heavily timbered and swampy. He later acquired more acreage.

Clayton married Elva Rawlings in 1913. Elva was born in 1894 to William and Mollie Rawlings, who lived on Road 31, just five miles south of the Courthouse in Kokomo. Her grandfather (also William Rawlings) owned a section of land acquired by a land grant, signed by President Taylor in 1840. His home still stands on Center Road, just west of road 31.

Clayton and Elva raised four children: Enid (Roler), Mark, Mary (Leap) and Max. All are still living in this area, except Enid, who passed away in Phoenix, AZ in 1962.

Elva 1894-1980, Clayton 1892-1969 married June 22, 1913

Five generations of the Cole family have attended the Oakford Christian Church at various times, beginning with Clayton's mother.

Early neighbors living in this area were the William Calhouns, Yagers, Sauls, Col. Wooldridge, Bill Forsythe and C.B. Tudors. C.B. had a large family and ran a local grocery store. Dolpha Saul furnished the local store with milk. Mr. Cole also helped furnish milk and later years with meat.

There was swamp and heavy timbers on the south of the farm land that had to be cleared. Timber was dynamited and land stripped so gravel could be taken out. Gravel was sold to Tipton and Howard counties for building roads. The gravel sold for .25¢ per yard. Later the pits remaining, were used for swimming holes and fishing. They have since been mostly filled in.

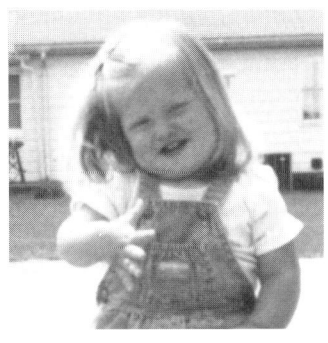

Laura Cole, daughter of Barbara Cole, granddaughter of Max Cole

Tillable ground was used for farming, raising oats for horses and corn for raising and feeding cattle and hogs. Sheep were also raised. At the same time Clayton was farming he was buying stock around the county and having it butchered at Aldolpha Saul's butcher shop, which was north of Fairfield (now called Oakford). He would then sell the meat, wherever he could, to stores like Tudors in Fairfield, Fretz in Sharpsville, and Vetters and Sokol in Kokomo. Later around the 1930s he built his own slaughterhouse, just over the Howard County line in Tipton County.

In the middle 1930s Stokley Canning Company leased an area around the gravel pits for a migrant labor camp and pea and lima beans shelling plant. They would shell the peas and lima beans for surrounding farmers in the area, who had raised them, and they would haul them to the plant. The remaining vines would pile up and ferment, and then the farmers would haul them away for silage to feed stock in the winter.

In later years as Mr. Cole's sons grew up, they married, built their homes on the farm, and raised their families. His older son Mark took over the butchering business and his son Max did the farming. Canning crops became some of the crops and in 1966, Max was chosen as Tomato King for the State of Indiana.

Today the butchering is still done by Mark's sons and the farming by Max's son, who also raises corn, beans and some produce.

CONNER-BURGETT - Leo Claude "Bud" Conner was born Feb. 24, 1911, in Kokomo, IN, the son of Howard Claude and Elva Louise (East) Conner. He had two sisters, Clotelle and Beulah. His parents were also born in Howard County, IN.

"Bud" attended school in Middlefork through the eighth grade; then went to Burlington High School finishing the sophomore year.

Claude and Mary Kathryn Burgett were married by a justice of the peace on Feb. 16, 1929, in Kokomo, IN. Two children were born to this union, Victor Dee on Nov. 13, 1930 and Stella Evelyn on Nov. 16, 1932.

"Bud" worked at the Continental Steel Corp. starting in 1936 and retired as a roller at the mill in 1971. He then worked for 10 years at Edden Corporation.

He held memberships at the Masonic Temple in Kokomo and the Shriner's in Indianapolis and Kokomo. He was a 32nd Degree Mason.

Claude died Oct. 11, 1986, from colon cancer. He is buried in the Russiaville Cemetery.

Mary Kathryn "Kate" Burgett was born Oct. 7, 1909, in Clinton County, IN, the second child born to

Homer E. and Stella (Stafford) Burgett. She has four sisters: Lelah Cook, Anna Mae Lynch, Nora Earlywine and Beulah James.

Katie attended school in Russiaville finishing her sophomore year then going to work in Frankfort, IN, for two years at the Bankable Cigar Factory before her marriage to Claude. She and "Bud" celebrated their 55th wedding anniversary at their residence at 1032 S. McCann where they had lived for 51 years.

Kate attended church at the Russiaville Baptist Church while a young woman and the First Baptist Church in Kokomo.

Their son Victor Dee Conner married Nina Dale Purdy of Indianapolis on Good Friday, March 23, 1951, in Indianapolis, IN. They have four children: Vickie Mavis, Theresa Brook, Kurt Victor and Sean O. Conner.

Stella Evelyn Conner married Paul Raymond Hosier Sept. 2, 1955, at the First Baptist Church in Kokomo, IN. Two children were born to this union, Kit Lee and Kathryn Dee "Kathy" Hosier. Evelyn and Paul were divorced after 15 years of marriage.

"Bud" and "Kate" have six grandchildren and nine great-grandchildren.

COOK - Cecil Cook (born on Oct. 5, 1911) was the son of Martin Seth Cook and Alta (Milburn) Cook. Alta's parents were Andrew Milburn and Catherine (Shaffer) Milburn, long-time farmers in Carroll County.

Catherine Dolores Coughlin (born on Sept. 11, 1914) was the daughter of John Coughlin and Lelah (Davis) Coughlin. John Coughlin's parents, Tim and Ella (Hooley) Coughlin had come from Ireland and settled in Logansport. Lelah's parents were Walter Horace Davis and Nellie Adessa (Trittle) Davis.

On Aug. 5, 1939, Cecil and Catherine Dolores (Coughlin) Cook were wed in Kokomo. Cecil worked for many years as a tool and die maker at Haynes Stellite/ Cabot. Dolores worked for 47 1/2 years at Delco and is a member of Delco's 35 Club. In addition, she received degrees from Indiana Vocational Technical College in 1972 and 1975. Cecil and Dolores were the parents of two sons, Michael Warren Cook (born on Feb. 4, 1946) and Rodger Wayne Cook (born on April 27, 1948.) Cecil died on June 8, 1988. Dolores still resides in Kokomo.

Michael Warren Cook was a 1964 KHS graduate and Delco employee. He joined the United States Air Force in 1965 and died on July 31, 1966 in Germany after a brief illness.

Rodger Wayne Cook is a 1966 KHS and 1968 ITT graduate. He accepted a job as outside plant engineer with Indiana Bell in 1968. On June 21, 1975, Rodger wed Jane Ann Allen. She is the daughter of Wilbert (born Nov. 23, 1916 in Greene County, IN and died Feb. 27, 1976) and Carrie (Emery) Allen (born Jan. 23, 1922 in Greene County and resides presently in Greentown.) Jane was a 1971 Haworth High School graduate and also received degrees from IUK and Indiana Vocational Technical College. Rodger and Jane are the parents of a son, Zachary Michael Cook (born March 3, 1988 in Indianapolis.) In June 1992, Rodger, Jane and Zachary moved from Windfall to Lafayette, CO.

BOB AND EDITH COOK - Although living most of their married life in California (Redondo Beach and San Jose), with additional residences in Massachusetts and Virginia, Bob and Edith Cook's roots were in the Midwest, centering around Howard County. Edith Joann (Parkhurst) Cook was born May 6, 1928, in Kokomo, daughter of Ora and Janice (Freed) Parkhurst. She married Charles Robert Cook Oct. 9, 1948, in Kokomo. Bob was born Dec. 18, 1925, in Rib Lake, WI, son of Ross C. and Merle Mae (Shuck) Cook. Bob was a tool and die maker (with a teaching degree for machine stops from Deanza College, Cupertino, CA), a master mason, Scottish Rite and member of the Eastern Star. He was in the U.S. Navy, 1943-1949, had a pilot's license and loved to fly. Bob and Edith moved to California in 1966; he died in 1984, in Indianapolis. Edith is a member of the Eastern Star and Navy Mothers and a homemaker. She moved to Florida in 1984 and returned to central Indiana in 1993.

Bob and Edith Cook have three sons. Kevin Thorton Cook, their first son, was born July 28, 1949, Kokomo. He had two years of business courses at Foothill Community College, in Los Altos, CA, is in sales and lives in San Jose, CA.

Blaine C. Cook, the second son of Bob and Edith Cook, was born Aug. 22, 1950, in Kokomo, and is a deputy sheriff for Siskiyou County, CA. He married Dixie Brink, Feb. 6, 1982, Yreka, CA. She was born Jan. 15, 1960, Lodi, CA, daughter of Dick and Carleen (Cox) Brink. She is a cosmetologist-esthetician.

Bryan J. Cook, third son of Bob and Edith Cook, was born Aug. 15, 1956, Culver City, CA. He was in the U.S. Navy, 1974-1980, as an electrician on board a nuclear powered submarine (USS *Henry Clay*, SSBN 625). He moved to Portsmouth, NH in 1980 where he is a supermarket employee. He married Michele York, in 1977. She was born Sept. 19, 1956, Portsmouth, ME, daughter of Emery and Carol (Ashcraft) York. Bryan and Michele and have two daughters, Chelsea Elizabeth, born Sept. 15, 1985 and Emily Ann, born Sept. 18, 1989.

The above history was abstracted with permission and modified from *The Mason-White Family* History, copyright 1990, by James M. Freed. *Submitted by Edith (Parkhurst) Cook.*

COPP - Copp family members were first settlers of Tipton County, in the area known as Slacum, a few miles west of Windfall. Harrison Copp was a carpenter and builder of several bungalow houses in the area.

His son John Copp (1867-1934) worshipped at the Windfall Church of the Brethren, which actually wasn't in Windfall but was located in the Slacum area, one mile east of SR 19. John Copp married Sarah Alice Stout; a farmer, he purchased 40 acres a few mile northeast of Windfall and moved his family to a new house he had built there about 1909.

The family consisted of sons Albert, John Paul and Jesse; and daughters Martha (Henry), N. Berniece (Turner), and Anna Emoline (Dutton).

John Copp was an industrious farmer; he got the land of area landowner John Milt Summers to farm simply because Summers had seen his crops and liked his work. John Copp was binding wheat in a Summers' field on the Howard-Tipton County line one June day in 1921 when Timothy M. Myers, a disturbed resident living across the road, came out of his house and yelled at him, asking if he would do him a favor. John Copp replied if it was such that he could, yes, he would do it. Myers said he could indeed do this for him, he could carry him back into his house. Then he took a shotgun he had concealed and shot himself. A horrified John Copp kept his word and carried Myers' body back into the house.

Family of John Copp 1908

John Copp eventually bought two farms of 40 and 48 acres in Howard County, one-half mile south of Phlox and down the road that passed by the New Hope-Ellis Cemetery. A house existed on one farm, but not on the other, so John Copp moved a house to it from a location west of Phlox. During the move the mail boxes had to be taken down, and Albert Copp was given the job of going to the door of the homes to obtain the necessary permission. Imagine his consternation when he encountered a deaf man who could not understand what he was trying to tell him!

John Copp became a rather large man physically in his later years. Deeply spiritual, he is remembered to have sat on a hillside at his last Tipton County farm and make the remark that the world could be a very good place if only people would live right. He died on his Howard County farm at age 66 in 1934.

Anna Emoline Copp married Floyd Dutton (1903-1983) and their children are: Alice C. (Hatton); John Edgar 'Bud'; Patricia (Metz); Boyd R.; and Kelta Dutton. Anna Emoline is the beloved grandmother of this writer— she has supplied him with many stories of her family and events of earlier years. A deeply spiritual person like her father, she has lived a long and useful life, encountering her share and more of life's trials, and overcoming them all she looks forward to the reward promised by the Master to all who endure to the end. *Submitted by Jeff Hatton*

JOHN COPPOCK - John Coppock was born Oct. 14, 1798 in Tennessee, a son of Aaron and Margaret (Tucker) Coppock. His third great-grandfather, Aaron Coppock, came to America from England in 1701. John met and married, on March 14, 1818 in Blount County, TN, Martha Patricia Williams, who was born March 14, 1800, in North Carolina. They moved to Kokomo, IN around 1850.

John and Martha Coppock had the following children: Aaron, born December 1819 and married in 1848 to Sarah Lamb.

Dorcas, born Oct. 31, 1820, married on June 25, 1838 to Jesse Mote. He died Dec. 22, 1868; she died July 17, 1902. Both are buried in Crown Point Cemetery.

Rachel was born in 1822 and married around 1840. Nothing else is known about her.

Margaret, born Feb. 15, 1824, married James Mote on Sept. 15, 1841. He died Jan. 4, 1873; she died March 1882.

Jane was born in 1826.

Sarah, born 1828, married April 2, 1846 to James Guilinger. She died Jan. 31, 1895.

Martha Patricia (Williams) Coppock died around 1860. John remarried in 1865 to Margaret Carroll. A son, David Grant Coppock, was born Aug. 22, 1868. He married Lydia Ann Corbin on Jan. 13, 1896. David died March 19, 1898. John Coppock died Feb. 26, 1880. John and Martha Coppock were the fourth great-grandparents of Rodger Smith. *Submitted by Rodger Smith*

JIM (KOKOMO) COUGHLIN - James Harold Coughlin was born Aug. 13, 1917 to John and Lelah (Davis) Coughlin. He was their fourth child.

When Jim was two or three years old, he and his brothers and sisters were surprised early one summer morning to see circus wagons with lions and tigers inside, being pulled by teams of horses, elephants following along or sometimes ahead, passing in front of their home, going to the circus grounds somewhere west of their residence. Jim never forgot!

One summer the circus was set up in Highland Park. Jim and his brother John (who was a year older) and some neighbor boys went to the circus together, but Jim never came home with them. Jim's parents reported a lost boy immediately. The next day, the police came to report Jim was in Anderson with the circus. That was just the beginning! Every summer when the circus came to town Jim would hurry there to see if he could water the elephants or just watch them perform.

When Jim was 17, he got a summer job, which turned out to be a permanent one. That same summer, he surprised his family by getting married. He and his wife rented a nice apartment from her aunt, bought a used Ford with a rumble seat in the back, and almost every evening on a hot day, they would drop by to see who wanted to go swimming with them. They both loved to dance. They were just two kids who loved each other and their families. About two years later their daughter Wanita was born. The circus was always calling him, and while he tried to talk his wife, Viola, into bringing their daughter with them and joining the circus as a family, he could not convince her it would work.

Eventually, Jim went with the circus. When he returned three months later, he learned his marriage was over.

170

Jim (Kokomo) Coughlin - Elephant trainer and owner, August 13, 1917-February 7, 1981.

In 1939 he joined the Ringling Bros. and Barnum and Bailey Circus. Every summer they would be on tour, often playing Kokomo. Through the years family relatives in other cities would always go to see Jim perform and ask him to visit them.

During World War II, Jim enlisted in the service, but because of a damaged ear drum, he was not accepted. During the war, he drove large transport trucks across the United States.

After the war, he rejoined the circus. In 1947 he joined the Clyde Beatty Circus as an elephant trainer. He stayed with them for several years. In 1964, he purchased a special truck and a baby (14 month old) elephant named Sabu. (Later, he purchased a second baby elephant).

Jim (Kokomo) and Sabu starred and had top billing at Radio City Music Hall, Acapulco Cabaret, Montreal, Quebec; Calgary Stampede, Calgary Canada; new Hawaiian International Center, Honolulu, HI. He appeared on T.V., night clubs, stage and variety shows, including Mike Douglas, Boss City, Hollywood Palace, Billy Barty and Baby Daphne. He also appeared on the Red Skelton Show and the Merv Griffith Show.

Jim began to develop emphysema and had to retire. Jim also had worked for Paul and Dorothy Kelly, who own the Circus Brothers Winter Quarters, which they purchased from Cole Brothers' Railroad Circus. (The Winter Quarters are across from Grissom Air Base). He had traveled with them while performing in The Shrine Circus. Paul and Dorothy Kelly purchased Jim's elephants, and Dorothy (now 82) finished training one of them.

Jim died Feb. 7, 1981 in Lakeworth, FL.

Jim's former wife, Viola, and their daughter, attended his funeral. Viola's husband died some time earlier, and she and Jim had resumed their old friendship. Jim, their daughter, Wanita, and Viola occasionally visited each other. *Submitted by Dolores Coughlin Cook*

COSTLOW-INGELS - Little Shelby Davis was born on Nov. 19, 1991 to Tom and Tanya Davis of Greentown and at the age of two is too young to realize the rich heritage she shares with families of the Costlow and Ingels line.

Patrick Costlow (1826-1899), along with two other men, started a brick kiln just east of Greentown in 1844. These were the first bricks made in Howard County. After marrying Malvina Woods (1833-1894) in 1848, Patrick bought a grocery store and decided to add some dry goods to his stock. Most were bought in New London and hauled by ox team. He and his wife began their lives together in a log cabin in the west part of Greentown.

Patrick and Malvina had six children, including John Ingels (1847-1924) and Susan Ingels (1851-1936). Susan married Frank Gideon. She and John worked together in a law office in Kokomo until Frank moved to Washington. John followed his interest in stenography and became the first shorthand reporter for the Howard Circuit Court and kept that position for 25 years. John Ingels would practice the shorthand needed for court reporting by quietly transcribing the preacher's Sunday morning service.

John Ingels and Henrietta Costlow (1851-1937) married in 1868 and set up housekeeping in a newly built three-room house. After their first two children were born, they moved into a house on the crest of a hill on South Union Street. There was no sign then that there would ever be any town on the south bank of the Wildcat as there were only a half dozen homes scattered over the entire area. They had nine children: Offa, James, Claude, Fredrick, Lulu, Hale, Logan, Lena, and Rosa.

Lulu Ingels (1880-1965) married Almon Hunt (1872-1946) in 1902. Almon began teaching in 1892 at one of the country schools for $40 a month. Most of their years together was spent in Greentown. They had one child, John Thomas Hunt (1903-1948) who married Dorothy Gallion (1906-1993) in 1923. Most of their years were spent in Greentown. They had three children: John, Sandra, and Sheila. Sheila married Max Estes in 1961 and they had three children, Mark Max, Tanya, and Nathan.

Tanya married Tom Davis in 1987 which completes the line down to the newest member, Shelby Rose. When she is a little older, she will learn of her ancestors who included the county's first court reporter among others who were a part of the early development of Howard County.

COWGILL - One local resident, born and raised in Kokomo, reflects on a half century of its growth and that of her family. Just as Kokomo has gone from dirt and brick streets to paved roads and highways, subdivisions and small towns that almost eliminate farm land from Howard County, allowing Kokomo to grow, that is how the Cowgill family has now spread.

Orval Farl Cowgill, the sturdy red-haired, freckled young man, born and raised in Kokomo during the time of nickel movies and trolley cars, met a blond, blue-eyed girl of 70 pounds, which he would later nickname "Runt", Ida Hazel Butcher, from southern Indiana. She had moved up here to get a job in the "big city" to help raise her 12 brothers and sisters. He worked at the Pottery and later the Continental Steel Mill. She worked at Thalman-Levi's, the jail, and later, Margaret Hayes' Day Care and Joy Ann Bakery.

They had four chldren. Their oldest, Othella Frances (Cowgill) Clymer Muzzio, is now residing in Pittsburgh, PA. Her daughter, Pamela Gale Clymer, and her grandson Scott, are now residing with Pamela's husband in the southern states. Her son, Jeffery Lynn Clymer, wife and four children are in Pittsburgh. Her other son, David, wife and children are in Virginia.

Their second child, Orval Aaron Cowgill, is residing with his wife in Malden, MO now that he is retired from the Air Force. His daughter, Susan Dawn, resides with her husband and children in Texas. His son, Stephen Corder Cowgill, and wife reside in Louisiana.

Their third child and writer of this article is Esther May Cowgill Cook, listed in *2000 Notable American Women*. She resides here in Kokomo with her son, Troy Andrew Cook, and his wife Loretta and child, Tia Alyssa. Her daughter, Royce Ann Cook Gomez, resides with her husband, James, and child, James Andrew, in Chicago.

Their fourth child, Gladys Jane (Cowgill) Brankle, resides in Sharpsville with her husband, son Robert, and his wife. Her son, Michael, wife and children live in Kokomo. Her daughter, Melinda, and husband reside in Oakford.

We know that the Cowgills were of English descent and arrived by boat 300 years ago. We know the Butchers or Phipps were of German-Dutch and/or Scotch-Irish descent and great-great-grandfather Phipps fought in the Civil War. We know that grandfather Fred Cowgill fought in World War I. He is listed in the 1920 edition of *Howard County In the World War* by C.V. Haworth. We know that our great-grandmother was a full-blooded American Indian. The writer knows that the records of the Russell-Raines and Griswold reunion were destroyed when her father died. She knows that her grandmother was Jeanetta May (McCartney) Cowgill Glover and is buried in Memorial Park Cemetery at Ohio and North Streets, along with several aunts, uncles and cousins. She would appreciate any further information from anyone who knew any part of her family. *Submitted by Esther M. Cook*

JAMES AND MARY (MASON) COY - Two pioneer Howard County families were united when Mary Jane Mason and James Henry Coy were married May 23, 1874. They were both born in Howard County. Mary on Dec. 13, 1853, daughter of Simon and Elizabeth (White) Mason, and James was born Sept. 19, 1853, son of Alexander and Mary (Smith) Coy. They lived in Clay Township when Mary died Sept. 22, 1919. James later remarried to Bessie L. Hooper. James was a farmer in Clay Township and later became an owner and manager of a feed store and a grocery store clerk. He was educated in a Quaker seminary in Iowa and was a member of Pathfinders Lodge. James and Mary Coy had six children (all born in Howard County) listed below that lived to adulthood and some of their descendants live in Howard County.

1. W. Oscar Coy, born Sept. 9, 1877; died July 10, 1974; he did not marry.

2. Eva Newcom, born Sept. 16, 1880; died Feb. 5, 1910; married William Newcom and they did not have children.

3. Anna Price, born Sept. 20, 1884. She was a school teacher and later worked at Delco Radio. She died July 25, 1980. On Dec. 29, 1906, she married Oscar Price who was born March 16, 1886, Howard County, son of Charles and Marinda (Gorden) Price. He was a farmer and at one time was a Standard Oil agent in Greentown and in Russiaville. He died Aug. 8, 1969. Anna and Oscar had six sons: Dennis, born May 27, 1908 and married Gladys Harter (lived in Brown County, IN); Harold, born March 1910, and married Ruby White (lived in Montgomery County, IN); Gerald, born March 8, 1910 and died Sept. 26, 1910; George, born Oct. 28, 1912 and married Emily Tubbs (lives in Ft. Myers, FL); Richard, born Jan. 7, 1920 and married Nellie Smith (lived in Hampton, VA); Robert, born Jan. 25, 1927 and married Joyce Pullen (lives in Howard County).

4. Emma Ellis, born April 28, 1887, was a housewife and died Feb. 22, 1935, Kokomo. On July 21, 1906, she married Arthur Ellis, who was born Oct. 1, 1881, Howard County, son of Isaac Ellis and Catharine (Jones) Ellis. He died Dec. 4, 1946. Emma and Arthur had three children (all born in Howard County): William Gale, born May 21, 1908 and died Jan. 17, 1911; Thelma Ray, born March 5, 1911, who married (1) Paul Jett and (2) Vernon Ray, and she lives in Howard County; Mildred Hosier, born May 16, 1915 who married Ted Hosier and they live in Wabash County, IN.

5. Hazel McGovern, born Oct. 3, 1889, was employed with the Kingston Products Corporation and lived most of her life in Howard County, dying Sept. 19, 1968. On Nov. 27, 1909, she married Arthur C. McGovern, who was born Oct. 28, 1886, son of Richard Elder and Sallie Reel and later adopted by Thomas C. McGovern. He was a businessman in Kokomo and died Sept. 1, 1942. Arthur and Hazel McGovern had two children, both born in Howard County: Kathryn Roy, born Oct. 22, 1910, who married (1) John Coapstick, and (2) Bernard Roy, and she lives in California; Thomas C. McGovern, born April 6, 1913, who married (1) Mildred Woodring and (2) Dora Hundley, and he lived in Howard County.

6. John Coy, born July 4, 1893, was owner and operator of a machine shop in Connecticut and later moved to Florida where he died Feb. 23, 1963. He married Margaret K. Washington of Kokomo, who was a homemaker and she died Sept. 22, 1976. They did not have children.

The above information was abstracted, with permission, from *The Mason-White Family History*, 1990, by James M. Freed. *Submitted by Robert W. Price*

LOUIE AND ERMA CRAIG - Louie E. Craig and Erma Gladys Crews came together in wedlock at the home of friends in eastern Howard County, IN on Dec. 5, 1943. Frank and Helen Frazier, of Greentown, hosted the wedding that was officiated by Rev. J. Lee Springer.

Both Louie and Erma were born and raised by their respective parents in other parts of the country before they moved to the Kokomo area.

Louie was born in Henryville (Lawrence County), TN on Dec. 5, 1905, to his parents Will Clark and Eva L. (White) Craig. He was the second child born of three sons.

Erma was born in Nashville (Davidson County), TN on April 7, 1911 to her parents Walter Barry and Willie Mae (Pennington) Crews. She was the first child born of two sons and four daughters.

Growing up on a farm in eastern Tennessee, Louie later worked at a local sawmill and even later for a steel mill in Wirton, WV. It was in that steel mill that he gained the knowledge that ultimately led him to Kokomo on July 29, 1929, when a Mr. Mossburg brought an experienced crew of 10 workers (including Louie), to start up and run the sheet mill at Continental Steel Mill. Louie worked there over 40 years, until he retired in February of 1970. His leisure time interest has always been in lawn and garden activities. Louie was baptized by the Rev. David Woods, Russiaville Christian Church.

Louie and Erma Craig...church directory photo

Being one of six children has always meant a great deal to Erma. Following her birth and pre-school years in Nashville, TN her family moved to Akron, OH where she went to school for 12 years. Many summers during her formative years were spent in Henryville, TN. It was then that she met Louie, who was her sweetheart for a short period of time. After graduating from high school, she worked at C.H. Yeager Department Store and for a time was co-owner of a restaurant that went by the name of Hobby Lobby. She then came to Kokomo to be married to her former childhood sweetheart. Her hobbies include gardening, oil painting and reading. For a number of years she taught the third grade Sunday school class at the United Methodist Church in Kokomo.

Donna Mae (Craig) Janner, their only child, was born on Aug. 9, 1945. They raised their daughter in the house at 725 W. Foster St., that they would live in for many years.

Shannon DeLei Janner, their only grandchild, was born on Feb. 9, 1970.

EDGAR L. CRAMER - Edgar L. Cramer was born Aug. 26, 1873 in Piqua, OH. In May 1894, he married Edna Maude Helmer, who was born Aug. 3, 1876 in Fairfield, OH. Edgar was a son of Henry and Eliza (Pierce) Cramer. Edna was a daughter of Martin Henry and Dora LaFrances (Collins) Helmer who came to Kokomo in 1900. Edgar worked for the Globe Stove Company and died Jan. 18, 1938.

She died July 17, 1930 and both are buried in Memorial Park Cemetery.

Edgar and Edna were the parents of the following children: Ethel Pearl Cramer was born Feb. 26, 1895 and married Robert Frazee Zimmerman on July 23, 1920. Ethel worked for the Hankow Tea Company. Robert was an interior decorator, born Jan. 22, 1894 and died March 1, 1949. Ethel died Dec. 7, 1945. They resided in Kokomo.

Roy Edgar was born Dec. 24, 1896. He first married Ruth Wimmer around 1919. He then married Grace McConnell in 1946. They resided in Marion, IN. He died Oct. 25, 1977.

Carl Collins Cramer was born in 1901. He married Georgianna Carey around 1935. He died Dec. 18, 1959. She died around 1975. They lived in Marion, IN.

Edgar and Edna were second great-grandparents of Rodger Smith. *Submitted by Rodger Smith*

HOMER B. CRISPIN - Homer Boyd Crispen was born a twin on Dec. 27, 1889, in Cass County, IN, the son of James A. Crispen and Matilda Edgar McKinney. His twin, Omer, died shortly after birth. Homer grew up in Cass and Fulton Counties. His father died when he was 10, so he had to assume many duties on the farm as a child. He

Homer B. Crispen Family - L-R Norma Stewart, Helen Soblotne, Wayne Crispen, Maude Crispen, Doris Kull, Homer Crispen, Loren Crispen, Betty Miller, Rosemary Mendenhall.

came to Howard County when he was 18 years old. He worked at the railroad station freight house. He married Maude Marie Zeigler on Nov. 27, 1913, at the home of her parents (William and Claudia Zeigler) in Kokomo. At the time of his marriage, he was working at the Kokomo Brass Works. Later he worked at Kingston Products where he made roller skates and at Kokomo Stamp Metal as a shipping clerk. It went out of business and he was laid off. He then worked at Malby's Grocery Store. He also drove a delivery truck for Kokomo Bakery on Ann Street. He worked for a time at the Studebaker plant at South Bend, IN. During the Depression, he was out of work, so he and his family made ice box cookies and donuts and sold them around Kokomo. At Thanksgiving they made mince meat to sell. He found a job working for the WPA at the courthouse in Howard County. He also worked at a furniture factory in Peru. In the late 1930's he worked at a grocery store/fruit market on North Washington Street in Kokomo where the Factory Connection is now located. In 1938-39 he worked at Clyde Ramey's grocery store. In the early 1940's he hired on at Continental Steel and worked there for 15 years until he retired. He died Nov. 5, 1975, in Kokomo, and is buried in Crown Point Cemetery there.

Maude was born Sept. 18, 1894, the daughter of William Joseph Zeigler and Claudia Evelina Reddin, in Howard County. She and Homer had seven children. Their children all born in Kokomo are: Loren Kenneth Crispen, born Nov. 24, 1914, (spouse-Audra Mae Ball); Doris Eileen, born May 13, 1916, (spouse-George Kull); Helen Louise, born Nov. 11, 1920, (spouse Roy Soblotne); Lawrence Wayne, born Nov. 13, 1924, (spouse-(1) Betty Zirkle, (2) Betty Duncan); Rosemary Jean, born March 15, 1928, (spouse-Warren Mendenhall); Norma Lucille, born May 9, 1930, (spouse-Jack Stewart); and Betty Jane, born Sept. 10, 1934, (spouse-Carl Miller). Maude was an accomplished musician. She suffered from the effects of diabetes later in her life and she died Jan. 12, 1974, in Kokomo. She is buried next to Homer in Crown Point Cemetery there.

LOREN CRISPEN - Loren Kenneth Crispen was born Nov. 24, 1914, in Kokomo, IN, the oldest child of Maude Marie Zeigler and Homer Boyd Crispen. He married Audra May Ball on Oct. 27, 1939. Audra was born July 6, 1915, to Anna Mae Fletcher and Frank Ball in Mitchell, IN. Audra came to Kokomo in 1935 and lived with her sister Mary Ball Tickfer. It was then that she met Loren and began dating him. They will celebrate 55 years of marriage in October 1994.

In his youth Loren worked as a paper carrier for the *Kokomo Tribune* and the *Kokomo Dispatch* newspapers for extra money to help his family, and in high school he worked at Ferriter's Market delivering groceries in the Forest Park area. Loren graduated from Kokomo High School in 1934 and began working at Chrysler Corporation. He worked at Chrysler as a laborer for 36 years until he retired in 1975. Since his retirement, he has participated in and won many medals in the Senior Olympics in bicycle racing, basketball free throw, racewalking and billiards. He is a volunteer caller for the American Red Cross blood drives. His mother was a charter member of North Street Baptist Church in Kokomo, IN, and he belonged to the Baptist faith until 1977 when he became a member of South Side Christian Church (Disciples of Christ).

Loren and Audra Crispen

Audra lost her mother when she was 13 years old and assumed the household duties of her family at an early age. She came to Kokomo after graduation to live with her sister and to get a job. She worked as a clerk at Zikers Cleaners and as a sleevesetter for her brother-in-law, Bernard J. Tickfer, at Reliance Corporation. She, too, was raised in the Baptist church. In 1977, Audra became a member of South Side Christian Church where she is a very happy member. She is known for her decorating skills, especially at Christmas, and her endless helping of people in need. She wanted to be a nurse, but her father discouraged it, so she became a devoted wife and mother to Karen Beth Crispen born May 30, 1950. (See related article.) Audra's hobbies are embroidery, handsewing, cross stitch, and interior decorating. She enjoyed croquet and tennis when she was younger. She belonged to Materian Club (YWCA) and to Intergroup Friendship, which was started to improve race relations in the 1950's. Today she enjoys cooking and being with her two grandchildren, Chris and Jennifer Sosbe. She and Loren went to Europe on their first airplane ride in 1990, and Loren celebrated his 75th birthday in London, England!

HERSCHEL AND VIRGINIA (SMITH) CRISS - Herschel William Criss was born May 14, 1886 in Lintner, Piatt County, IL, the second of nine children born to Clark Augustus and Mary Magdalene (Traxler) Criss. In 1901 Herschel's family moved from Illinois to Howard County, IN.

Herschel's brother and sisters are as follows: Millard Harrison Criss (1885-1885); Anna Beatrice (Criss) Smith (1888-1984), wife of Hugh Edwin Smith (1886-1973); Rayman Herbert Criss (1891-1900); Eva Irene Criss (1893-1913); Oscar David Criss (1896-1975), who married (1) Mary Elizabeth Hatton (2) Marie Vaughn Fry; twins Earl Bryan Criss (1899-1899) and Orville Dewey Criss (1899-1968), who married (1) Blanche E. Ratcliff (1898-1928) (2) Alice Cornthwaite Griner (1883-1933) (3) Ann Claire

Robb; and Clark Wayne Criss (1903-1988), who married Florence Vaughn (1908-1990).

On Feb. 26, 1908 Herschel married Virginia Cleveland Smith, born Dec. 16, 1884 in Crigglersville, VA, daughter of Joseph A. and Mary (Utz) Smith. Herschel was a farmer, a former Hill Standard Playground Equipment employee, and a retired Globe American Corporation employee. He enjoyed woodworking and carpentry. He was a highly respected member of the Shiloh Methodist Church. After nearly 61 years of marriage, Herschel quietly passed away on Jan. 7, 1969. Virginia lived until Aug. 22, 1972. They are buried in the Shiloh Cemetery.

The following four children were born to Herschel and Virginia, all in Howard County:

1. Ralph Henry Criss, a retired Globe American Corporation employee and a retired Friends minister, born July 12, 1909, who on June 6, 1950 married Avis Rachel Turner, born Dec. 2, 1907, died March 25, 1992, daughter of Samuel Edward and Margaret Elizabeth (Johnson) Turner. They have one son, Jonathan Dean Criss, born Nov. 24, 1951, who married Diana Lu (Prifogle) Curl.

2. Kenneth William Criss, a former highway construction employee, born April 21, 1911, died May 19, 1983, who in 1942 married Lassie (Johnson) Thomison, born Dec. 8, 1900, died Oct. 9, 1979, daughter of Calvin and Sarah Jane (Nelson) Johnson.

3. Helen Mary (Criss) Spence, a retired registered nurse, born Sept. 16, 1915, who on Sept. 11, 1943 married Frank Merrell Spence, born Jan. 23, 1904, died Feb. 7, 1979, son of Thomas S. and Audrey Leota (Merrill) Spence. They have six children as follows: Marilyn Jean (Spence) Klenck, born Oct. 4, 1944, who married William John Klenck; Joseph Steven Spence, born Oct. 31, 1946, who married Patricia Elaine Richason; Susan Virginia (Spence) Neuhauser, born Dec. 23, 1947, who married Larry Lee Neuhauser; Kathryn Ann (Spence) Disney, born July 15, 1949, who married Jerry Neil Disney; Timothy Criss Spence, born April 24, 1953, who married Brenda Carol Lemley; and Peter Glen Spence, born July 24, 1955.

4. Dan Maurice Criss, a former houseman for the Hotel Frances, born Dec. 26, 1916, died March 25, 1987, who on Nov. 12, 1942 married Dorothy Thomison, daughter of William and Lassie (Johnson) Thomison. They have two sons as follows: Dana Bryll Criss, born Dec. 31, 1948, who married Patricia Colean McGuire; and Daryll Kaye Criss, born Dec. 22, 1952, who married Nancy L. Birnell.

Submitted by Ralph Henry Criss

CRITCHLEY - James and Ellen (Gerrard) Critchley and family of 11 children immigrated from St. Helens, Lancashire, England in May 1906, coming to the U.S.A. on the *Baltic* ocean liner, arriving in New York, Ellis Island, then to Kokomo, IN where they had relatives.

It is my belief that the Pittsburg Plate Glass Company of Kokomo sent for people of England to come over to give them the knowledge of making good glass as they had worked at Pilkington's Glass Factory in St. Helens, England. It was the largest glass factory in the world. However, they worked in Kokomo for very small wages such as 11 cents per hour.

Three children were born in the U.S.A. The eldest son William liked sports and was a homing pigeon fancier, as were his brothers John and James Jr. They had pigeon lofts at their home, 1300 E. Vaile Avenue, Kokomo. Some pigeons won races by flying 400 and 500 miles a day. The birds were used in wartime to carry messages tied on their legs. Birds were shipped in cages by freight to other cities and released by a caretaker who fed and watered them. Birds then returned home, flying through mountains and such. Many of these birds won National Diplomas and prizes of red, white and blue ribbons at the Indiana State Fair. Some birds were named, such as Jimmie, and 400-mile day bird. Red Ash and Blue Chicker were other names.

Son James Jr., who was a beautiful penman, wrote the Lord's Prayer or the Twenty Third Psalm, on the back of a postage stamp. After retirement, he wrote hundreds of these stamps, sending over 350 to England, Queen Elizabeth, Charlie Chaplin and relatives. When released from World War I, he was the only soldier allowed to write discharge papers for his brother John and himself. Officers had seen his handwriting by censoring his letters. Both brothers were allowed to stay together in the war, a courtesy allowed, being requested by their parents.

Son Lambert was a lightweight boxer. He boxed in Ohio, Kokomo, IN and surrounding cities about the year 1920.

Daughter Lily brought Volunteer In Community Services into Kokomo, IN to help senior citizens through Congressman Hillis in about 1980.

All were members of St. Andrew's Episcopal Church, Kokomo, IN. *Submitted by Lily Critchley*

CRITES - The farm home of Dale and Mary Ann Crites is located on the Howard and Cass Co. Line Road. It will be a centennial farm in 1995.

The farm was purchased in 1895 by Benjamin and Rachel Mote Crites. Benjamin was the son of Valentine and Sarah Keck Crietz. Somewhere in the 1800's the spelling was changed to Crites.

Benjamin and Rachel had two sons, Charles and Roy. Roy was Dale's grandfather. Roy married Daisy Harness and lived on the farm in the early 1900's. Daisy was the granddaughter of George Harness Sr. George was a prominent landowner in Howard and Cass Co. He lived to be 108 years old. He moved in 1849 to what was known as the Indian Reserve in Howard County. One of George's daughters was the first of 150 white persons to be buried in the Indian Reserve in the state of Indiana.

George's daughter Susan married Andrew Forgey and on July 5, 1855 helped to organize a church on the Howard and Cass Co. line. It is known today as the Upper Deer Creek United Church of Christ. Several of the Crites and Harness descendants are members of the present church.

Roy and Daisy Crites with son Roy

When Daisy and Roy lived on the farm they drove a school bus pulled by horses for School No. 11 which was located one half mile west and two miles south of the farm. There were times when the school bus was a simple mud boat because of the terrible road conditions. Daisy and Roy had two sons, Oscar and Harold. Oscar died in early childhood. Harold graduated from Young America High School.

Harold married Lora Stover in 1924. They moved onto the farm and Roy and Daisy moved into Galveston. Harold and Lora had six children: LeeRoy, Dale, Dean, Laramie, Lucenia and Duane. Harold and LeeRoy were killed in an automobile accident in 1937. Dale at the time was nine years old.

Dale graduated from Ervin Twp. School in 1946. He married Mary Ann Mathis on May 9, 1948 and they moved onto the farm that was still owned by Roy Crites.

Richard Dale and Mary Ann Crites

After the death of Roy in 1956, Dale and Mary Ann purchased 63 acres of the original farm. Thirty-seven acres were purchased by Pete Moore, husband of Lora Crites Moore. After the death of Pete Moore, the 37 acres were purchased by realtor Ron Warren. Warren developed the road frontage to be known as Sunrise Subdivision. Dale and Mary Ann purchased some ground back from Ron Warren.

Today the farm consists of 88 acres. The 100-year-old house and barn have been remodeled. Dale and Mary Ann have four children: Rick, Mary, Peggy (Densmore) and Michael. They have 11 grandchildren and three great-grandchildren.

HENRY CRITES - Henry Crites was born Jan. 30, 1832 in Fayette County, PA, the fourth child of Valentine and Sarah Ann Keck Crites. He married Aug. 7, 1864, Caroline (Foy) DeMoss, who was born Feb. 9, 1840 in Perry County, OH. She was the daughter of Jacob and Nancy Shunk Foy. She had ten other brothers and sisters.

When Henry was about two years old, they moved to Starke County, OH. He remembered walking all the way. He said it took all day, to go up the mountain, and all day to go down.

His siblings were: Mary 'Polly' who married Lewis Priest; Fietta who married Lorenzo D. Alvord; John K. who married Margaret Mitchell; Benjamin F. who married Rachel Mote; Elizabeth married William Owen; Michael first married Harriet Foy, and second Frances M. Prame; Sarah 'Sallie Ann'; and Tobias, who died at birth. Sallie Ann was taken to Colorado by her sister Polly, after their mother died.

Henry and Caroline had Frankie who died in infancy; Jacob Elsworth (1866-1904) and married Cora Ann

Family of Mr. and Mrs. James and Ellen (Gerrard) Critchley - L-R Back - Edward, Lambert, John, James Jr., Thomas, Albert, Robert and Richard. L-R Front: daughters Elizabeth, Mary Ellen; sons William and George A; mother Ellen; daughters Lily and Margaret M. Critchley

173

Ronk; George Washington (1867-1934) who first married Dora Dean Holman, and second Bessie Lee Fickle (1884-1973); Laura Ann (1871-1947) who first married Roscoe Alvin Wilson and second Myron E. Gannon; Edward Louis (1875-1965) who married Mary Darcus Ronk.

Henry and Caroline Foy Crites; Myron E. and Laura Crites Wilson Gannon and 'Old Dan'

Henry enlisted under Capt. Thomas Kirkpatrick at New London, IN, April 25, 1861, in Co. E, 13th Reg. Ind. Vol. Inf. He was discharged Dec. 31, 1863 at Folly Island, SC. He reenlisted under Capt. Runnell, Jan. 1, 1864 as a Vet. Vol., at Folly Island. His final discharge was Sept. 5, 1865 at Goldsboro, NC. He was taken prisoner and served 120 days at Belle Isle, Richmond. He was aboard the vessel *Maple Leaf*, which blew up in St. John's River, FL. He was wounded in the right shoulder in the battle between Petersburg and Richmond. He was in the hospital at Hampton one month and at Newark, NJ two months. He was in the first battle at Bull Run and Rich Mountain, the last one being at Fisher, NC.

He also carried mail by horseback in early days, on a blazed trail, from Delphi to Marion by way of Kokomo. The trip took two days each way, for which he received a salary of ten dollars a month.

Caroline Foy first married (March 1, 1860) William Riley DeMoss. She had one son William Riley Jr., who married (July 26, 1879) Barbara Ellen Rusk. Their children were Frank DeMoss (1880-1953), who married (Oct. 10, 1900) Ina Belle Tolley (1880-1960) and had Grethel (1904-1920); and William Harvey (1902-1971) who married Esther Martin; Grace P. DeMoss (1885-1975) married Omer F. Long (1884-1970) and had Elsie Mae Krall, Chester Clarence and William Harry. Bertha DeMoss (1895-1971) married Orville Scott (1893-1967). Their children are Harold M., Max, Carmen Thompson and Betty Weaver.

Henry died Nov. 22, 1929 at the home of his granddaughter Pearl Blangy, in Ervin Twp. Caroline and Henry are buried at Sprinkle Chapel in Cass County.

Their daughter, Laura Ann, first married Roscoe A. Wilson. They had Estelle, Pearl, Elroy, Elva and Crystal. Laura Ann married second, Myron E. Gannon (1861-1944). *Submitted by Mary Blangy*

CULBERTSON - Russel Phillip graduated Kokomo High School, Purdue University, BS in Mechanical Engineering; and an MS Science in Engineering.

John Frederick master mechanic, Bethlehem Steel
Morton Colfax, farmer, paper hanger; Calvin Garrigus, farmer - Civil War.

Davidson, farmer, held several political offices in Grant County. He gave land from his farm to establish a United Brethren Church and Cemetery. The Bishop from Ohio came to bless and consecrate it.

David, farmer
John, presumed farmer.
William, probably farmer. He fought in the Revolution.

John Culbertson came from Ireland, having been forced to leave Scotland by King James II. They were Conventures - Presbyterians. His father, as far as we know, was William, who fought in the Battle of Londonderry (born in Scotland).

Calvin's mother was Bathsheba Losey Garrigus. The Garrigus(e)s were descended from French Huguenots and forced to leave France by Lewis XIV because they were not Catholic. They first went to the Hague, Netherlands, and then to New Jersey.

Martha Ellen Woods Culbertson and Calvin Garrigus Culbertson

Bathsheba's brother, Milton Garrigues, is named as an early settler in the "Kokomo Pictorial History of Kokomo," published 1990. He came to Howard County in 1852, taught school, practiced law, was Superintendent of Schools, and a State Senator for Howard-Miami counties in 1878. He served in the Union Army during the Civil War.

Their father, Timothy Garrigues, was born in New Jersey, later moved to Ohio, and Howard County. He was a "circuit rider" minister. General research tells us he was a fiery, well spoken man who had strong religious and political beliefs. He believed in "free land", etc., and went out to Kansas on horseback, with gun, to fight for his beliefs. He was gunned down and buried in Omaha, NE.

Timothy Garrigues' ancestors were: David Garrigues, New Jersey, fought in the Revolution; Jacob Garrigus, New Jersey, fought in the Revolution; Matthew Garrigues, France, the immigrant from Netherlands; Jean Garrigues, France; Count Arnald Garrigues, France.

In doing research, we have found them all to be outstanding, honest, hard working people devoted to their God and religious beliefs. *Submitted by Carolyn Culbertson Lavengood*

CURLESS - John Curless was born in Ohio in December of 1853. His parents were from New Jersey. He married Roanna Zentmeyer on March 6, 1884. She was born in Indiana in February of 1860. Her father was born in Pennsylvania. They were married in Howard County, IN and lived there for the rest of their lives. They are buried in Simpson Cemetery in Howard County.

They had five children: James Merrill, born in January of 1885; Frank born in July of 1886; Jennie E., born in December of 1887; Ruby, born in January of 1891 and Nettie, born in December of 1898.

After a career in the Navy, James Merrill Curless married Irene Kollath on Feb. 16, 1918. She was born on Dec. 6, 1895. They were the parents of two children. One was Elsie, who married Ben Olson. They are both retired from United Airlines and now live in San Mateo, CA. A son, James Merrill, married Doris Roberts. He has the franchise for the John Deere dealership in Lowell, IN and is retired as director from the South Lake National Bank at Lowell. They make their home in Lowell. James Merrill, Sr. is also buried in the Simpson Cemetery in Howard County. Irene, his wife, was cremated and her ashes are buried in Dolton, IL.

Frank died from drowning when he was around 18 years of age. He is buried in Simpson Cemetery in Howard County, IN. The inscription on his tombstone says the day before he died he gave this testimony in the churchyard: "I am constantly striving to live an earnest Christian life. I am ready to go whenever the Lord shall call for me."

Jennie Elma married Hurshel B. Hethcote on Nov. 8, 1914. They had three children: Hurshel Curless, born on March 8, 1919; AnnaBelle born on Sept. 9, 1920; and Merrill LaMarr, born on Jan. 9, 1924. Hurshel, Jr. lives at this time in Anderson, IN; AnnaBelle lives in Mt. Etna, IN; and Merrill lives in Warren, IN. Jennie and Hurshel, Sr. are both buried in Simpson Cemetery.

Ruby married Robert Hill. They had one child; Ralph, who retired as a chemist from Standard Oil of New Jersey. He passed away a couple of years ago. At the time of his death he was living in Green Valley, AZ.

Nettie married Vaughn Chaney. They had two children. One was Vaughn, Jr., who retired as supervisor from Kelloggs of Battle Creek, MI. He now lives in Florida. His sister Mary Catherine married Manford Neal and they live in San Diego, CA. *Submitted by AnnaBelle Friend*

CURRENS-ELLIOTT - Clarence C. Currens was the son of Robert J. and Eliza Rose (Fehrle) Currens. He was born July 9, 1896 and died Oct. 6, 1944.

Naomi Elliott was born to John Elliott and Rosa (Elliott) Elliott on Feb. 28, 1901, and died July 10, 1972. Smiley served in World War I, was active in the American Legion, marched in many parades, and was also active in the Masonic Lodge. Naomi belonged to the American Legion Auxiliary and Eastern Star.

Clarence was known as "Smiley" to his many friends and he and Naomi were married in June 1921. They owned the "Sweet Shop" in Greentown at that time. Smiley was elected sheriff of Howard County and served for two terms. They purchased the farm east of Greentown and owned the "Currens Cafe" on the corner of Union and Walnut Streets in Kokomo. He and son Jack later operated the grain elevator in Sycamore, IN.

Clarence 'Smiley' Currens and Naomi (Elliott) Currens on the farm in Greentown where they were happiest.

Naomi served as matron at the jail while Smiley was sheriff. She was later an antique dealer who specialized in Greentown Glass. She was on the original board of the Greentown Glass Museum.

Many good times were shared with family and friends at the farm. Several times they entertained the town of Greentown with special Halloween parties held in the barn.

When Smiley was sheriff, the family lived at the jail on South Main Street. The living quarters were in the front and upstairs, and the jail and kitchen were at the rear. At that time there were iron bars covering the windows, and there were cells in the basement called dungeons. They had iron doors, a place to put food and very little light.

They had two children: Jack Elliott Currens, (born July 23, 1923-April 19, 1991) and Nancy Ann Currens (born Jan. 15, 1930-).

Jack attended Butler University, served in World War II, and was president of the Realty Division of Union Carbide Company in New York City. He married Betty Hight and they had two children, Diana and Douglas. They later divorced and Jack married Dorothy Butler of St. Petersburg, FL, where he lived until his death.

Nancy married William Gressman of Janesville, WI and they had a daughter, Gay Ann. Bill worked for Delco Radio (Electronics) 39 years before his retirement. Nancy was secretary to Robert Whitehead, attorney; Raymon Gilbert, mayor of Kokomo; and later was employed part-time at Continental Steel in the offices. She and her daughter had antique shops in Kokomo.

The Currens family was a large one of nine children. Glen and Rufus had the Currens Brothers Grocery in Greentown and Wanda (Currens) Caldwell, who married Paul "Spid" Caldwell, had the "Highway Cafe" in Greentown.

174

The Elliott family lived in Sycamore and they had several children. Roscoe Elliott had the insurance company in Greentown. Cecil (Elliott) Cranor married Frank Cranor and Hammer "Mick" Elliott lived in Red Bridge, IN.

DAVID - George and Angeline David bought 60 acres in Union Township, Howard County, Aug. 29, 1874 from William and Ivy Gilson. They gave $400 an acre. This started ownership of the land to be in the David family name for 100 years and longer.

They had six children: Ivy A., Theodore E., John W., Jacob E., Edward E., and George W. David.

The father, George, died in 1889. Later all of Edward David's brothers and the sister sold their land to him. He married Clara Simpson in 1888. Around 1890, they built a house in a cornfield on their land. The framework was native lumber from their woods, and it cost around $500.

Edward and Clara had three children: Myrtle David, William David and Clifford David. Clifford married Inez G. Brunk, daughter of Nathan and Mary Kathryn (Zahn) Brunk, in 1916. Edward David bought another 20 acres to make a total of 100 acres in all. He died in 1929 and his wife Clara died in 1934. By the year of 1937 all the land was deeded to Clifford and Inez David.

They had two children, Doyle Edward David and Madonna Jean David. She married Frank Conway and they live in Greentown. Doyle married Janice Bryant, daughter of Carl and June (Fox) Bryant in 1941, and they started their married life in the David homestead.

Doyle helped his father farm their land plus some acreage they rented. They each bought more adjoining land through the years.

Doyle and Janice have two sons, Stephen Bryant David and Jan Edward David, who grew up on the farm, enjoying showing 4-H calves and helping with the farm work.

After Clifford David's death in 1965, Inez deeded land to her children with Doyle buying his sister's part in 1967. It now totals 273 acres. The David sons graduated from college, fulfilling their dream to coach and teach at various schools. They married and a new generation of sons were born.

Stephen married Carly Fox, daughter of Dr. James and Jane Fox, and they have two sons, Stephen Bryant David Jr. and Zachary Edward David. They live on the Isle of Palms, SC. Stephen is a self-employed real estate broker in Charleston, SC and Carly is vice principal at Trident Academy, Mt. Pleasant, SC.

Jan married JoAnn Voss, daughter of Wayne and Marcelle Voss, and they have three sons: Andrew Carlton, Nicholas Edward and Rocky Joseph David. They live in Kendallville, IN. Jan is assistant-principal, athletic director at Kendallville Middle School, and JoAnn is a guidance counselor at Carroll Junior High School, Fort Wayne, IN.

Doyle and Janice continue to live in the house built by his grandparents. It has been remodeled, but the original framework is still there.

On March 7, 1980, they completed the history of the farm and were given the Hoosier Homestead Farm Award.

The David families all share in the history and love to come home to the farm.

The David Family Farm, Howard County

DAVIS–COUGHLIN - Nathan James Davis was born Jan. 1, 1829, in Martinsburg, VA (now West Virginia) to Jeremiah Davis. Jeremiah Davis was born 1798 in Martinsburg, VA and died July 29, 1876, in Dayton, OH. He was buried in Woodland Cemetery. In 1848 James Davis married Anne Elizabeth Carlisle. Anne Elizabeth was born Oct. 13, 1831, Dayton, OH to John M. and Margaret A. Carlisle. John M. Carlisle was born in 1799 in Rockingham County, VA. He died Aug. 28, 1872, in Dayton, OH and is buried in Woodland Cemetery. His wife Margaret A. was born 1801 in Frederick County, MD. Margaret A. Carlisle died Feb. 9, 1881, in Dayton, OH and is buried in Woodland Cemetery.

James Davis, his wife and their children came to Kokomo in 1862. James was a contractor skilled in brick work. He died March 1, 1869, while he was engaged in the construction of the Howard County Courthouse. He held the contract for the brick work on the building. Other construction included the First Methodist Church.

Anne Elizabeth (Carlisle) Davis was a good businesswoman, also an accomplished seamstress. She opened a dressmaker's shop and soon became known for her fine work. At one time, she employed eight other dressmakers. She was reported to have had the first Singer sewing machine in Howard County. Anne Elizabeth died Feb. 14, 1923, age 91.

Anne Elizabeth and James Davis had nine children. Mary Susan 1850-1898 married Daniel Jenkins; Rosina Jane 1852-1928 married Perry Albright; Ellen L. 1854-1864; Sarah Elizabeth 1856-1877 married Abram T. Cosand; Laura Bell 1858-1908 married Ben F. Overman; Henrietta 1860-1875; George W. 1863-1936 married Lula M. Beamer; Orian N. 1865-1868; Horace Walter 1868-1935 married Nellie A. Trittle, and after her death, six years later married Martha Smith.

Horace Walter Davis married Nellie A. Trittle Aug. 18, 1890. They had two daughters, Nellie Edna Davis, 1891-1923 and Lelah Elizabeth, 1893-1968. Horace Walter Davis married Martha Smith Dec. 10, 1896. They had two children: Nathan James 1906 and Monell Olive, Feb. 1, 1911, who married Floyd Louks Dec. 3, 1942. Monell and Floyd have a daughter Beverly.

Nellie Edna Davis, 1891-1923, married Fred Crone. They had three daughters: Winifred, 1913-1993, married Harold Stevens. (KHS grad in 1931, 50 years in Eastern Star, retired from Cabot in 1974); Elizabeth, 1916- __ married Cecil Anderson, KHS grad in 1934, 50 years in Eastern Star, retired from Texas Instruments. She lives in Houston, TX with her seven children; Wanda Mae, 1922-1993, married Frank Williams. (Attended KHS, 48 years in Eastern Star, retired licensed practical nurse and surgical nurse, active in volunteer work). A son Richard Williams and grandson Adam live in Florida.

Lelah Elizabeth Davis married John Coughlin of Logansport, June 25, 1912. John's parents were Ella (Hooley) and Tim Coughlin. (Ella Hooley and her family came from Ireland and settled in Logansport where her father was a tailor). Tim and Ella were married Jan. 18, 1888. Their children were John, Marie, Kathleen, James, Cecil, George, Cornelius, and Edward.

Walter H. Davis and daughters Lela and Edna about 1900

Lelah Davis and John Coughlin were married by Father Quinn in St. Bridget's Church in Logansport, IN. They were living in Logansport during the 1913 flood, which did a great deal of damage. They moved to Kokomo before their oldest child was born; at that time John was a timekeeper for the railroad. During World War I, he worked in a munitions factory in Moline, IL. After the war ended, he worked as a machinist at Apperson, then later at Haynes. During a big lay-off at Haynes, John became a Metropolitan insurance agent; later he sold sweepers and then Maytag washers. About 1928 or 29, he went to work for Reese Tool and Die Shop. He was there all during "The Great Depression" and until the shop closed. During World War II, John worked at Cook's Tool and Die Shop in Indianapolis. John and Lelah had 13 children: Mary Carlisle, Catherine Dolores, John Horace, James Harold, George Edward, Patricia Elizabeth, Rebecca Edna, Frederick Timothy, Robert Patrick, Agness Ellen, Rosemary Wanda May, Virginia and Madaline Florence. (Rebecca, Virginia and Madaline died in infancy).

In 1927 our courthouse was torn down. Perhaps the city intended to build another one, but the times were bad; every one was just getting by. Each month seemed to bring further lay-offs and store closings. Empty store windows were coated with Bon Ami, and when the wind would blow leaves or debris into the empty store entrance, the leaves and debris would swirl and form little miniature dust storms. It was eerie! The courthouse square became a beautiful park, with shade trees and park benches. The park was always in use. At the edge of the courthouse lawn, there used to be cement ledge about 18 inches high. This ledge was always occupied by a group of men, usually talking about economic conditions. Every few minutes some one would leap from his seat and give an impassioned speech, trying to offer a solution to what was a nation wide problem. Catherine D. was lucky enough to work as an extra on Saturdays from 11:00 a.m. to about 10:30 p.m. for one dollar, at Woolworth 5 and 10¢ Store. (That one dollar was for about 11 hours.) After F.D. Roosevelt was elected in 1932, things began to improve, slowly but surely. Factories, business and stores began to rehire. In 1935 Kokomo made plans for a new courthouse. The basement was started Dec. 4, 1935. The cornerstone was laid Aug. 12, 1936. The year 1935 also brought Crosley Radio to Kokomo. In less than a year, Crosley was purchased by General Motors. This was a real blessing to Kokomo. In 1937 Chrysler came to Kokomo. Chrysler and Delco Electronics continue to be our leading industries, although we have many others. Our new courthouse was dedicated Oct. 20, 1937. As a city, we have continued to grow, with new malls and shopping centers, new homes, new restaurants, and eating centers of all kinds. The new courthouse helped to make Kokomo more prosperous.

In 1935, when Crosley came to Kokomo, most of the wages were 28¢ and 29¢ per hour for women. Perhaps the men were paid a little more, but probably not much more. They were paid twice a month and rarely got a full 40-hour week, but how happy they were to be working!

Mary Carlisle (Aug. 10, 1913) married Robert Johnson Oct. 29, 1932. They had seven children: Marilyn, Donna, Elizabeth, Benjamin, John, Dennis and Rosalee; Catherine Dolores (Sept. 11, 1914) married Cecil Cook Aug. 5, 1939. They had two boys Michael (deceased) and Rodger; John Horace April 3, 1916. First marriage to

Charlotte Holder. They had two children, Dolores and Daniel. Second marriage to Frances Beck. They had two children, Kathie and Timothy. Frances has a daughter Jane (Host) Deis. John is a veteran of World War II; he served in England. He is a retired electrician. James Harold Aug. 13, 1919-Feb. 7, 1981. Married Viola Webb May 18, 1934. They had one daughter Wanita (Coughlin) Reed; George Edward (Feb. 15, 1919- April 3, 1994) married Martha. They had four children, Edward, Barbara Ann, Robert, and Joseph Michael. Edward was World War II veteran who served in England; Patricia Elizabeth Dec. 26, 1920-Nov. 15, 1987. Married Edgar Archer. They had three children: Mary Lee, John, and James; Rebecca Edna March-1922-April, 1923; Frederick Timothy May 29, 1923-Nov. 9, 1993. Married Janet ___; they had one son. Frederick was a World War II veteran who served in Africa, Italy and Burma; Robert Patrick Nov. 3, 1925-April 7, 1945, a World War II veteran. He was injured going into France and received Purple Heart, spent the winter in Belgium, volunteered for infantry duty and was killed in hand-to-hand combat in Germany; Agness Ellen June 5, 1927 ____; Rosemary (Jan. 27, 1928) married Harold Davis. They had four children: Cynthia, Robert, Carol and Pamela; Virginia (July 11, 1933) died in infancy; Florence Madaline (Feb. 7, 1935) died about 1937.

John and Lela Coughlin were married 56 years when Lela died Feb. 28, 1968. John died 30 days later, March 31, 1968. Lelah Elizabeth (Davis) Coughlin was one of those rare people, who are always a pleasure and comfort to be near. She listened, felt empathy. She could always find something humorous in every situation. She would always tell her children "Happiness is within You."

(Lelah was born April 6, 1893 and John was born Jan. 27, 1889.) *Submitted by Dolores Coughlin Cook*

DAVIS - ROCKEY

John N. Davis, the son of Evan and Sarah Davis, was born April 30, 1841 in Carroll Co., IN. He died Sept. 21, 1920 in Howard County at the age of 79 years.

Isabelle Smith, the daughter of Tobias and Dorothy (Runnels) Smith, was born May 14, 1840 at Deer Creek, Carroll County, IN. She died at the age of 90 years on May 26, 1930, at her home in Ervin Twp., Howard County, IN.

John and Isabelle were married in Howard County on Aug. 26, 1864. They had two sons, Frank "Frankie" who died when he was six years old and Joseph Odessa "Dessie" who was born May 18, 1872, and died Sept. 27, 1946, at his home in Howard County.

George and Annabelle Rockey 50th Anniversary Feb. 3, 1990

Dessie and his parents moved to Howard County when he was seven years old. In 1888 they purchased 42 acres from Sarah Baer. Dessie's father, John, was a good farmer. One year he raised strawberries. They picked 900 quarts which cost one cent a quart to have picked and sold them for ten cents per quart.

Dora Esther Miller (July 9, 1884 - Feb. 15, 1959) was the neighbor girl who was the daughter of Thomas P. and Emma (Suit) Miller. Dora and Dessie were married Dec. 31, 1904 in Howard County. They had two daughters, Luella Merle who married G. Bright Hanna and Annabell born July 31, 1921. She met her future husband George Franklin Rockey at an uncle and aunt's house who lived where Chippendale Golf Course is now. Annabelle graduated from Ervin High School in 1939.

George Franklin Rockey was born Sept. 28, 1916 in Tipton County, the son of Clarence and Blanche (Kerby) Rockey. He graduated from Galveston High School in 1935. Annabelle and George were married Feb. 3, 1940. They remained on the Davis family farm.

Annabelle and George were saved Feb. 9, 1946, and later he became a minister serving in the Christian, Mt. Lebanon Friends and Pilgrim Church. They served in the prison ministry for 14 years and the Kokomo Rescue Mission.

George was a very good farmer and mechanic. He retired with 30 years from Cabot Corp. which is now Haynes International. He was a pilot for several years and died in an Indianapolis Hospital on Oct. 4, 1991.

Annabelle was a good farm wife by helping with milking cows, feed pigs, helped on the hay baler, cut hay, planted wheat and many other farm duties. She has helped at the Kokomo Rescue Mission for 20 years. One of the many things she has done is make lap robes for the Christmas boxes.

The Rockey's have two sons. Charles Vernon was born Nov. 14, 1942. He married Winifred Stroup on Feb. 15, 1963 and is living in West Middleton, IN. They have four children. Lesa Lynn who was born Dec. 24, 1963 and married Bryan Byers; they have one daughter Bethany. Monica Jo born June 8, 1965, Charles David born Nov. 17, 1968, and Jennifer Ann Dec. 15, 1971. Their second son John Thomas Rockey was born July 26, 1951 and lives in Jackson, MI. He married Alice Hardy Aug. 17, 1974. They have one son John C. born Jan. 8, 1977, and a daughter Andrea born Jan. 11, 1980. *Submitted by Annabelle Rockey*

DAYHUFF-LINDLEY

The history of our extended family has long meshed with the substance of vitality of Indiana! Pioneer planners and visionaries, my Quaker ancestors were of Dutch, Irish and German descent and came from Maryland, Virginia, North Carolina and Pennsylvania. They were aristocrats, politicians, bakers, hoteliers, farmers and soldiers. Their marriages, interweaving like a strand of DNA, made up the whole fabric of Indiana life.

Jonathan (1756-1828) Lindley's grandparents were Scotch-Irish and came from Ireland in 1713 and purchased land from William Penn in Kennett Square, PA. His wife, Deborah Dicks' (1757-1811) grandfathers, Peter Dicks and John Hiatt, were English. They arrived in 1684 with Penn and bought land in Bucks County, PA. By 1753, they migrated to North Carolina where Deborah's grandmother, Martha Hiatt had founded Cane Creek Quaker Meeting.

Alicia Dayhuff Frank, fourth great-granddaughter

Jonathan prospered in North Carolina and donated large sums of money in support of the American Revolution. He served six terms in the legislature, excelling in finance. He voted to charter the University of North Carolina, the first state university in North America, and served as trustee.

Quakers were the first religious group to condemn slavery 100 years before the Civil War and the only religious group in the South to take a stand against it. Jonathan sponsored an anti-slavery bill in North Carolina but it was defeated. Zachariah Dicks, Deborah's father, one of the most famous Quaker ministers of his time, urged Southern Quakers to move to free soil states. Some of the Lindley grandchildren were active in the "Underground Railroad" during the Civil War.

Around 1808, Jonathan visited his son Zachariah (1776-1841) in Indiana and bought land in Vigo County for a settlement. By April 1811, he had converted his extensive timber, turpentine and land interests into $100,000 in gold and set out for Indiana with his 11 children:

Hannah (1778-1859) and Tom Braxton; Ruth (1780-1854) and Joseph Farlow; Amy (Thompson) and Thomas (1782-1828); William (1787-1850) and 1. Michel Hollowell, 2. Anna (Fisher); Deborah (1789-) and Jonathan Jones; Mary (1792-1833) and Silas Dixon; Queen Esther (1794-1849) and Alexander Clark; Catherine (1794-1863) and Edward McVey; Sarah (1796-1829) and William Haley; Jonathan (1800-1865) and Mary Lindley and my ancestors, Elinor (1784-) and Samuel Chambers, Jr., (1783-1842).

Daniel Boone had lived near Cane Creek, and Lindley's wagon train probably followed the trail over the Wilderness Road via Western Virginia, through the Cumberland Gap into Kentucky and across the Ohio River. They stopped 40 miles NW of the river at the Half Moon Spring stockade. Governor William Henry Harrison visited them and suggested that they settle nearby because of Indian unrest along the Wabash. Jonathan chose Lick Creek for its fast-moving water. Deborah died August 1811. Jonathan married Martha Henley in 1812 and Guliema (1813-1909) was born.

Jonathan Lindley's influence was far-reaching: Indiana Seminary, (Indiana University) was established in 1820 at the site chosen by Jonathan Lindley and he became trustee. Terre Haute was founded on land owned by Jonathan's Terre Haute Company. When he was a state senator and finance chairman, the Indiana tax laws and other basic legislation were formulated. *Submitted by Alicia Dayhuff Frank*

DAYHUFF-PERRY

Charles and Monette Dayhuff's only child Charles Hal Jr., "Buck" (born 1906-) lives in Atlanta, GA. He graduated from Baylor Military Academy, Chattanooga, TN and attended Cornwall-on-the Hudson, and received an appointment to West Point and to Virginia Military Institute, Lexington, VA; he attended the latter.

Buck graduated with honors from Virginia Military Institute, 1931, and he was regimental commander and first captain of Corps of Cadets, the first "six striper" at VMI. He was commissioned in the Cavalry, as his father before him. He was tactical officer and taught English at VMI 1931-1937, then to Culver Military Academy, Culver, IN, until activated for World War II when he joined G-2, Army Intelligence and worked in Latin America. He served in the Pentagon, in England, and retired at Army War College, Carlisle, PA in 1961 as colonel. He taught at Valley Forge Military Academy, 1961-1972. He lived in Paoli, PA until 1992 when he moved to Atlanta, GA.

LCol Charles Hal Dayhuff III (VMI 59); Col Charles Dayhuff Ret

October 7, 1933, Charles Hal married Marian Weaver Perry, (born 1912) in Chevy Chase, MD whose ancestors came to St. Mary's, MD in the *Ark* and the *Dove*, 1634-1658. They have three children. Their two older children follow the family's tradition of military service to their country, beginning with the American Revolution and continuing to Desert Storm, 1991.

1. Marian Alicia Dayhuff Frank, (born 1935-) of Jacksonville, FL. Consultant, International Affairs,

specializing in cross-cultural medical civic action projects, naval officer, U.S. Naval Reserves, former assistant naval attache to Peru and to Algeria, 1986-1922. Serving in S. Korea, the Pentagon. She enlisted in 1977, rose to senior chief petty officer and was commissioned a naval officer in 1986.

Married (1) LCDR Richard Youngjohns, divorced February 1964, has two daughters: Marian Alicia (born 1954) (Mrs. V.R. Anderson), a son, Matthew; Stephanie Jane Bergeron, (born 1958) divorced, a daughter, Alexandra. Married (2) Thomas Paul Frank, CDR USN K.I.A. Vietnam, 1971.

2. Lt. Col Charles Hal Dayhuff III, Infantry, Ret., Atlanta, GA, Ranger/paratrooper. 1959 graduate, Virginia Military Institute. He served in Germany, two tours in Vietnam, South Korea, Panama-Jungle Warfare School. He married (1) Johanna Glass, divorced 1965, and in 1968 (2) Barbara Slade Cribb, widowed by the Vietnam War. They have a son: Charles Hal Dayhuff, IV (married 1991 Latrelle Harvey), a grandson: Charles Bradford Dayhuff.

He adopted Martha Cribb-Dayhuff, (Mrs. Riley Rhodes) and Richard Edward Cribb-Dayhuff, SSGT, U.S. Army Reserves. When Richard qualified as a paratrooper, he received his dad, Hal Dayhuff's, jump wings. It was a proud day. Hal and Barbara have six other grandchildren: Andrew and William Rhodes; Heather and Jason Dayhuff; Elizabeth and Jessica Harvey.

3. Jane Duke Collins (born 1940-), is the New Jersey, Connecticut, Pennsylvania, district director for Innisbrook Paper Company and her husband, Ronald Wayne Collins, a General Tire dealer in Merchantville, NJ, have two children, Ronald Wayne Collins and Monette Weaver (Mrs. Carmen DiTore); three grandsons: Ronald, Jeffrey, and Christopher Collins. *Submitted by V.R. Anderson*

DAYHUFF-BUTCHER - Charles Hal Dayhuff, "Duff" (1878-1965) Samuel and Ladie Dayhuff's eldest son, joined the Army in 1896, upon graduation from Kokomo High School. He was in Troop "B", 8th Cavalry in the Spanish-American War; and in the 14th Cavalry during the Philippine Insurrection, 1899-1905, and he became the regimental sergeant major, 14th Cavalry.

On Dec. 26, 1905, he married "the girl next door", Monette Butcher, daughter of John and Sarah Butcher. Charles Hal Jr. was born in December 1906, when they were stationed in Ft. Walla Walla, WA. They were sent back to the Philippines in 1908 and remained until 1912, when they went to Ft. Clark, TX with the 6th Cavalry. He rode with General Pershing in the Mexican Border Campaign against Pancho Villa and received a meritorious battlefield commission in 1917 to brevet major, Reserve Officers Corps. During World War I, he was deputy adjutant general of the Port of Embarkation, Hoboken, NJ and received a commission from President Wilson. He retired in Jacksonville, FL with the rank of major in 1934. Monette died in 1961 and he moved to Paoli, PA to live with his son.

He had closed the circle: Paoli, IN — Paoli, PA. He died on Feb. 28, 1965 and is buried with his wife in Arlington National Cemetery.

Monette Butcher Dayhuff and Charles Hal Dayhuff in Philippine Islands Occupation Forces

Monette's father, John Bryant Butcher's (1843-1919), parents were William (died 1868) and (2) Sadona (Brown) Butcher of Virginia. They settled in Decatur County early 1800s.

Bill Butcher moved to Howard County in 1853 and farmed 800 acres for over 50 years. Bill had five sons by his first wife and three by Sadona. The Butcher sons: Solomon T., George, Isaac N., A.P. and John fought in the Civil War. All returned safely. John became a sergeant in Co. H, 34th Indiana Volunteers 1861-1864. He was a commander of the T.J. Harrison Post, G.A.R. veterans. In 1867, Sarah (Thomas) and John were married and settled in Ervin Township where he farmed for over 30 years. He served a term as trustee. In 1903, he opened a livery business at W. Jefferson St. which he ran successfully until his death in 1919. Sarah and John Butcher had three children:

1. Monette Dayhuff.
2. Orville (1870-1950) married Grace Eicholtz (1873-1946): one son John Orville (1908-) of Victoria, TX, married Minerva Holbert, 1936; two daughters: Grace Jane (Mrs. Thomas Beck) and Johnnie Margaret (Mrs. Arthur Williams)
3. Myrtle married John Stewart, (divorced) Riverside, CA; a son: John Phillip (1910-1942) crashed his plane in Venezuela, while working on a mapping expedition for the U.S. Coastal and Geodedic Survey Dept., now Defense Mapping Agency. *Submitted by Matthew Randall Anderson*

DAYHUFF-DUKE - Originally from Pennsylvania, the Dukes moved from Carroll County to Kokomo in 1860, after an unsuccessful farming venture. Mr. Duke established Duke Bros. Bakery and Confectionery. They had seven children: Alexander, William, Charles, David, George, Hattie and Ladie.

Alexander fought in the Civil War in C Co., 46th Regiment, Indiana Volunteer Infantry, Army of the Gulf, and was discharged on Dec. 10, 1864. Upon his return, he became his father's partner. In 1869, he married Louisa Clattabuck and had two daughters, May and Georgia. Alexander was active in city politics and served as a city marshal, 1868; as a city councilman and one term as sheriff of Howard County, 1878.

Ladie Duke Dayhuff, wife of Samuel E. Dayhuff, widow 1889, with Dollie Lair Dayhuff, wife of Bill Dayhuff; William Dayhuff, husband of Dollie Lair Dayhuff

Hattie (1841-1910) married (1) G. McRoberts, (2) Maj. John Walsh; one son, Gary McRoberts, Gary, IN. She was postmistress of Eminence, KY after Maj. Walsh's death.

David L. (married Nannie, born 1865-1891), in partnership with his brother, George W. (born 1854), Duke Bros. Co., a real estate, lending and insurance company. George was appointed State Insurance Commissioner 1880-1885. He married (1890) Nannie (Littler) (1865-1891). Ladie, after her husband Samuel Dayhuff died in 1889, moved back to Kokomo with her sons, William Duke (1880-1956) and Charles Hal (1878-1965), my great-grandfather, to live with her brothers George and David until her death. *Submitted by Stephanie Frank Bergeron*

DAYHUFF-SMITH-HASKETT - Appointed as circuit judge of Washington County and land agent, Jonathan Lindlay founded and planned Paoli, Orange County, and named it for his North Carolina home. Paoli's first sheriff was Zachariah Lindley and the second, Daniel Dayhuff, a Dutch Quaker from Baltimore, MD. He married Rachel Smith, in Paoli in 1822. Their son Andrew F. was born in 1827. Rachel died in 1839. Three years later, Daniel married Mary Lindley Chambers, Jonathan Lindley's granddaughter. Andrew was reared with their six children: Ellen, Catharine, Hannah, Marietta, Lilly and Samuel. Both sons later became physicians.

Andrew F. Dayhuff, one of the founders of the Howard County Medical Society, attended State College, Bloomington and worked a year in a store in New Albany where he met his fiancee, Adeline Frazier. But his real vocation was medicine so he returned to Paoli and studied under Dr. William Sherrod for four years. He went to Rush Medical College in Chicago to study medicine and surgery. After his graduation in 1853, he returned to Kokomo to open a practice which lasted until his death in 1884. He also was one of the most extensive real estate dealers in the city and originated the Dayhuff, Sharp and Armstrong Block. Andrew built Essex House for his bride, Addie, in 1855. Four children survived childhood: Daniel F.; Jessie T. (Mrs. James H. Ellis); Mollie P. (Mrs. Frank Merill) and Sarah (Sallie) who married Byron Haskett in 1879. His father owned the Haskett Dry Goods Co., a forerunner of Woolworth's, and the largest and most successful mercantile business in the city at that time.

Byron's parents were Luvenia (Jones) and Thomas Haskett. His grandfather Joseph came to Taylor Township in 1860. He farmed for a few years after marrying Abbie Rickle in 1863. They soon moved to Fairfield where he founded Fairfield Mills, one of the largest mills in northern Indiana. Byron and Sallie's son, Thomas Dayhuff Haskett, married Mary Ann Kilkuski of Chicago, and Thomas Linn Haskett was born in Oak Park, IL, June 24, 1932. Tom is the Indiana Director of Vista, Foster Grandparents and the Federal Action Agency and lives with his wife, Elizabeth (Ralston) in Indianapolis. *Submitted by Thomas L. Haskett*

DAYHUFF-CHAMBERS-LINDLEY - Samuel Chambers, Jr. (1783-1842) and Elinor Lindley married in 1805 and came to Indiana where Samuel served as state senator, succeeding his father-in-law, Jonathan Lindley. Samuel was one of nine children of Samuel Chambers (1742-1809) and Sarah Thompson (born 1744):

Emay (May) (born 1757 North Carolina) married Aron Lindley (May 1, 1809); Richard, Elizabeth, Hannah, Mary, Sarah, James and Grace (born 1777 married 1798 Owen Lindley).

Originally from New Castle, PA, they migrated to North Carolina in 1753, with the Dicks-Lindley-Hiatt families. Samuel and Elinor's daughter Mary Lindley Chambers (born Sept. 9 1813-da Sept. 13, - Oct. 17, 1879) married Daniel Dayhuff (ba 1798 died Jan. 27, 1863). They had six children: Ellen, (ba. 1843-da 1930) who became a midwife; Catherine A. (born 1845-), Lilly C.J., Marietta (1840-da 1923) Hannah C. (1851-1924), and Samuel (born 1846-died Jan. 20, 1889), who became a physician. He died Jan. 20, 1889 and was buried under the auspices of Williamson Post G.A.R. and the Presbyterian Church.

Samuel Dayhuff

Daniel, a widower, had a son Andrew F. and also the responsibility of three young girls who may have been nieces: Ann Dayhuff married William W. Worrel October 1842; Martha Dayhuff married William Burke June 24,

1847; and Mariah R. Dayhuff (1840-da 1920s) married David Hudelson May 18, 1859. The Hudelsons celebrated their 61st anniversary May 18, 1920, aged 80 and 85 respectively. They had been married from the Dayhuff Hotel. Daniel was a large landowner in Orange County and his hotel in Paoli stood for over 100 years until it was razed in 1920 to build the Federal Building. He left it to his three daughters, Ellen, Marietta, and Hannah who ran it until then.

Daniel and Mary Chambers Dayhuff's son Samuel (1846-1889) married Ladie Duke (ba 1855-1931), daughter of David D. Duke (died 1884), and Jane McCoy Duke (born Kentucky died 1872 Indiana). *Submitted by Marian Frank Anderson*

CHARLES HAL DAYHUFF III - Charles Hal Dayhuff III was born in Rochester, IN on Oct. 8, 1937. He is the son of Charles Hal Dayhuff, Jr. (Walla Walla, WA) and Marian Perry Dayhuff, (Chevy Chase, MD) the grandson of Charles Hal Dayhuff (Paoli, IN) and Angie Monette Butcher (Kokomo, IN) great-grandson of Samuel Dayhuff, (Orange County) later of Howard County. Brother of A.F. Dayhuff, MD of Howard County. A.F. Dayhuff's father was Daniel Dayhuff, one of the original pioneers of Indiana, and his mother was Rachel Smith, natives of Maryland and Pennsylvania.

Hal III is the only son of Marian and Charles, Jr. There are two sisters: Marian Alicia (Lexington, VA) and Jane Duke (South Bend, IN). The family was raised around the world since all of the men were career military officers: Cavalry, Armor and Infantry.

Hal, III graduated from the Virginia Military Institute in Lexington, Virginia, in 1959. Was commissioned in the Infantry and began service around the world: Europe, Korea, Combat in Vietnam and Panama Canal Zone.

Left to right: Charles Bradford Dayhuff, Charles Hal Dayhuff IV, Charles Hal Dayhuff III, Marian Perry Dayhuff, Charles Hal Dayhuff, Jr.

In April 1966 Hal III met Barbara Angeline Slade Cribb of Columbus, GA, while stationed at Fort Benning. Barbara was a widow of Vietnam. Her husband Edward was the 52nd casualty of the war as an army aviator and Mohawk pilot.

She had two children Martha Claire and Richard Edward. We (Hal III) had one child Charles Hal IV. Today there are seven grandchildren, and the fourth generation Charles Bradford Dayhuff was born Nov. 25, 1992. Charles Jr. and Marian now live in Atlanta, GA near Charles III and his family.

While stationed in the Republic of Panama for four years, Hal was one of the Army representatives of the Panama Canal Treaty negotiation team. Barbara and Hal are active in the church, community and scouting program.

Upon returning to the United States, they moved to Concord, GA, where they opened a real estate company with United Farm Agency, and Hal III served on the City Council. In 1980 they moved to Albany, GA, where they sold commercial property and developed an office park.

Over the years Hal and Barbara have participated and held offices in many organizations of many different offices in the church. Hal is past president of the Abraham Baldwin Chapter Sons of the American Revolution, past president of the Georgia Society Sons of the American Revolution, director of Rotary and sat on the executive boards of several Boy Scout councils. He holds the Silver Beaver Award and is an Eagle Scout.

Charles Bradford Dayhuff, one year; Charles Hal Dayhuff IV, 25; Charles Hal Dayhuff III, 56; Charles Hal Dayhuff, Jr., 87, Atlanta, GA 1993

Barbara and Hal have worked together in real estate, development, appraisal and mortgage business. Hal is currently regional manager of Georgia Mortgage Corp. Inc. in Atlanta.

Their three children are in Albany, GA, Atlanta and Fayetteville, NC. Martha cares for children. Richard is an electrician. Charles is a residential appraiser.

DEAN - Jack and Judy Dean migrated to Howard County from nearby Hamilton County in the summer of 1968. Jack went to Northwestern High School as football coach while Judy settled in as a young homemaker with two small children, John and Jennifer. A year later, youngest child Jeff was born and the Dean family was ready to make their mark on Howard County. In 1972 Jack left the teaching field to enter private business as an insurance agent. Then in 1980, he left Woodmansee, Berndt and Dean to join the Bill Rayls Agency. Four months later, Mr. Rayls passed away and Jack took over the leadership of Rayls Agency. Three years later his wife, Judy, joined him in helping the agency continue to grow. The three kids were quickly growing and moving into their lives as adults.

John graduated from Northwestern in 1982 and went on to Anderson College where he met his future wife, Brenda Niles. They were married in 1985, and John graduated in 1986; then they moved to Bloomington, IL to start his career in the area of computer programming with State Farm. They now have three dean heirs, Aaron, Caleb and Eli, and are active in their church activities in Bloomington.

Dean Family - Front Row: Brad Priday (Kayla), Jennifer (Kelsey), Meredith and Jeff Dean; Back Row - Judy (Caleb), Brenda (Eli), John, and Jack (Aaron)

Jennifer is a 1984 graduate of NHS and also continued her education at Anderson where she met her husband, Brad Priday. She graduated in 1988 with a teaching degree and was married in that summer. Jen and Brad now live in Sikeston, MO with twin daughters, Kayla and Kelsey. Jennifer is teaching fourth grade while husband Brad is a buyer for a major food chain. Both are active in their church and continue with their musical background in the church choir.

Last son Jeff graduated in 1988 from Northwestern and went to Hanover College for his freshman year, where he became a panther instead of a tiger for one year. He then transferred to Purdue University to attain his degree in supervision in 1992. Jeff was the third Dean to work at Arrowhead Springs and while there, met his future bride, Meredith Trott. They did their courting at Purdue and were married in the summer of 1993. Jeff is currently an assistant manager at WalMart in Michigan City looking toward getting his own store while Meri is using her communication skills in an insurance agency in Merrillville. They are making their home in Chesterton, IN.

The Dean family has grown in Howard County and spread beyond into other states, but they still call Kokomo home. Jack and Judy are still running Rayls Insurance Agency in the same location on North Washington Street and are active in Courtland Avenue Friends Meeting. Jack is also completing his sixth year on the Northwestern School Board, the last four as president. Although not originally from Kokomo, this fine city is certainly their home with many great memories and dreams for the future.

DELON-DeLON-DILLON - Five Delon brothers sailed from France, early 1700's to Pasquotonk County, NC. My fifth great-grandfather was one of these brothers. He married Hannah Overman of North Carolina. Their known children are Francis, Ann, Charles and Mark.

My fourth great-grandfather Mark Delon (-1808), married Ann Taylor and had Henry (1780-1828), Rheuben (1782-), Simon (1784-), Hannah (1785-1871), Jesse (1788-), Ann (1790-), Penelope (1792-1870), Miriam (1793-) and Margaret (1798-1884).

My third great grandfather, Henry (1780-1828) married first Mary Bundy (1777-1817). The children were Sarah (1800-), Nathan (1802-1832), Mark Anthony (1804-1832), Jesse (1806-), Nancy (1808-), Henry (1811-1894), Josiah (1814-), and Samuel (1816-). Henry married second Peninah Morgan, and had Mary (1819-1820), David (1821-1822) and Johnathon (1822-1904).

My second great-grandfather, Mark Anthony (1804-1832) married 1824 Mary Pritchard (- 1832). The children were Penina (1825-1825), Joseph (1826-1901), William (1829-1857) and Mary (1832-1832).

My great-grandfather Joseph Delon (1826-1901) was orphaned in 1832 when his father, mother and baby sister died. Joseph age six and brother William age three, were moved from North Carolina to an orphanage at Newport, Wayne County, IN by the Quaker Church. William settled later at Chicago, IL, and Joseph moved to Washington County, IN, and married Rebecca King (1829-1886) of Orange County, where Benjamin (1849-1920) and Mary Delon Pritchard (1850-1913) were born. In the late 1850's the family moved to Howard County, IN, finally settling at New London, IN, engaging in the harness, saddlery and grocery business. Joseph eventually bought a farm two miles north of New London. The other children are John Anthony (1852-1933), William Homer (1854-1856), Aubrey Flint (1855-1940), Austin J. (1856-1860), Francis (1862-1921), Julia Emmagene (1866-1952) and Hannah Lenora (1869-1871).

My grandfather Aubrey Flint Delon (1855-1940) married 1878, Sarah Ann Arnett (1855-1927). Their children are William Pearl (1880-1955), Emma Lenora (1883-1883), Horace J. (1885-1914), Harry Everett (1890-1969), Fred King (1893-1971) and Walter (1897-1897).

My father, Fred King Delon Sr. (1893-1971) married 1915 Edna Alfloretta French (1895-1947). They had Alice Loren (1916-1981), Gailen Louese and Fred King Jr. When my father married, his folks asked him to bring his bride home to live. What a beautiful Christian Quaker home we were raised in.

I am Gailen Louese DeLon (1918-), married Neil Thomas Harris 1937. We have two sons, Everett Neil and Thomas Paul. I retired from Union Bank and Trust Co. and Neil worked for Med-O-Bloom Dairy. We have been married 56 years and have four grandchildren and ten great-grandchildren. *Submitted by Gailen Louese Delon Harris*

FELICE AND SERAFINA DELVECCHIO - Felice DelVecchio was born May 6, 1876 in Gallo, Italy. He came to the USA in 1901, after serving in the Italian army. In New Castle, PA, he worked with a man named Nicholas Zeppetella. Felice arranged with Nicholas to marry his daughter, Serafina. Serafina was born in Riardo, Italy on Aug. 15, 1890. In 1909, she arrived in the USA and married Felice.

They had ten children; four died in infancy and six survived. The DelVecchio family settled in Howard County in 1916, where Felice worked for Pittsburgh Plate Glass. Serafina and Felice lived the rest of their lives in Kokomo.

The oldest of their children, Victoria, was born in New Castle, PA Aug. 4, 1910. She married Charles Kolb and had one son, Fred. Fred married Carolyn Harrington and has one daughter, Natalie. Victoria, Fred and family live in Kokomo.

Their next child Nicholas was born on Nov. 6, 1913, in New Castle, PA. He married Caroline Bustamante and they have two children: Sara who married Steven Bliss and have three children, Mara, Neal, and Carlyn; and Phillip who married Jennifer Wood. They have three children, Eryn, Kristin, and Anthony. Nicholas retired from the post office as Assistant Superintendent of Mails. Nick and his family live in Kokomo.

Felice and Serafina Delvecchio

Jeanette was born in Kokomo on July 27, 1915. She married Robert Layton. Jeanette, Robert and their only son are deceased.

Mary was born in Kokomo on Jan. 18, 1917. She married Arthur Soots. They had four children: Mary Lou who married Richard Hasacuster; she has five children: Michelle, Monica, Marcia, John Michael and Bernie Taylor; Carolyn, who married William Carter and has four children: Bob, Dan, Steve and Doug; Patricia who married Dan Butler and has one son, Anthony; and Joseph who married Linda Lawrence and has four children Angela, Andrew, Andrea and Austin. Mary is deceased. Her son Joe and his family live in Kokomo.

Anthony was born in Kokomo on Nov. 27, 1921. He graduated from the naval academy and earned a doctorate in psychology. He married Mary Cruciani and they had seven children: Steve, Thomas, James, Nicholas, Mark, John and Ann (McDonough). Tony lives in Las Vegas, NV.

Dominic (known as Tom) was born in Kokomo on Aug. 27, 1926. Tom was an educator in Illinois. He married Mary Kistler. Their children are Thomas, David, Robert, and Richard. Tom died in 1972.

Felice and Serafina cherished their Italian heritage, but were very proud of the contribution their children made to the USA. All three sons served in WWII. Nicholas was in the Air Force and was awarded a Bronze Star for meritorious service in the China Burma Indian Campaign. Tony served as a lieutenant in the U.S. Navy aboard the USS *Duluth* in the Pacific. Tom served with the Armored Service in the Philippines. Their daughters supported the country by working in the munitions plant supplying the Armed Services.

Felice and Serafina left their native land in search of a better life for themselves. In Howard County they found that for themselves and their family through hard work and dedication. They lived their lives proud of their adopted country. *Submitted by Nick DelVecchio*

CLARENCE E. DE WITT - Clarence Elmer De Witt (1893-1984) was the fourth generation of his family to claim Indiana as his home. His great-grandparents, Henry and Sarah (Youngman) De Witt, had moved with their families from Clermont County, OH to Decatur and Bartholomew counties, IN in the 1840s. Henry died and was buried near Sharpsville in 1871.

Henry's son, George W. De Witt (1837-1906), married Sarah Shaw in Bartholomew County, IN (1859). They moved north to farm and raise their children: John W. (1863-1932), Joseph F. (1867-1927), Henry F. (1874-?) and Parthena A. (1877-1967). George was buried in Crown Point Cemetery, Kokomo.

Joseph F. and his wife, Theresa Hageman (1877-1910), had two daughters and two sons: Hazel G. (1895-1922) married Roscoe Deisch (more information can be found on page 388 of the *Deisch Family History (1560-1985),* Ruby D. (1897-1968) married George Meacham; Clarence Elmer (our subject); and Earl Edison (1908-1910). Earl was said to have mourned to death two months after his mother's premature death.

Clarence Elmer was born Feb. 12, 1893. On Easter Sunday, April 16, 1922, he married Naomi M. Breedlove at the Harrison Street Christian Church. She was the daughter of James and Laura B. (England) Breedlove. (For more about them, see the Breedlove section written in this book.) For most of their lives, they were active members of this church. They were also active members of the Howard County Democrat party. He worked for the Pittsburgh Plate Glass. Clarence's friends nicknamed him "Shorty" De Witt because he was 4'9" in height. They lived and raised their family at 1139 South Delphos Street, where five of their six children were born. Their children are: Doris, Lucy, C.R. (Bob), Joe, Jim, and Mark.

Clarence E. De Witt Family - Back Row (L-R): Clarence Robert, Doris Irene, Laura Lucille, Marcus Ray. Front Row (L-R): Joseph Eugene, Naomi M., Clarence Elmer, James William.

Doris married Harry W. Moore (1908-1982) in 1947. She was a registered nurse at St. Joseph Hospital. In 1973, they retired to Diamond City, AR. Their children are: William H. Moore of Kokomo, Beth Ann Moore and Beverly A. Leffler, both of Diamond City.

Lucy married John B. Tedlock (1924-1984) in 1946. She worked at Kokomo Optical Company for 28 years. She is retired in Kokomo. Their children are: Sally Carol (died 1946), Steven K. of Kokomo, and Cathy S. Hensley of Walton, IN.

Bob married Imogene Arnett in 1949. He retired from Delco Electronics after over 37 years. They live in Galveston, IN. Their children are: Janet E. (Eads) Gothard of Kokomo, Clarence Jeffrey De Witt and Joyce G. Corrigan, both of Indianapolis, IN.

Joe and Jim live in Kokomo, where they own De Witt Brothers Florist. They have travelled and studied plants throughout the Western Hemisphere. In their orchid collection, they produced and registered a hybrid named for their mother. In 1990, Jim married Alma Babago Berjame in Cebu City, Philippines.

Mark married Kay Fuhrman in 1968. He became ill while serving with the U.S. Army in Korea. In 1977, at the age of 30, he died in Indianapolis. He was buried near Churubusco, IN. Their two sons, Mark Allen and Chad Edward, both live in Ft. Wayne, IN.

Clarence died May 1, 1984, and Naomi on Oct. 18, 1984. They were buried next to his father at Albright Cemetery in Kokomo. Along with six children and 11 grandchildren listed above, the family of Clarence and Naomi now includes nine great-grandchildren and one great-great grandson and spans eight generations of Indiana pioneers and citizens.

DICKISON - Robert Abram Dickison was born in Howard County, IN on May 20, 1915. Robert was decorated for his service during World War II. He was the son of David Grandville and Ethel Ivy (Washington) Dickison. His grandparents were Abraham and Mary Catherine (Ellis) Dickison. His great-grandparents were Daniel David and Hannah (Kiger) Dickison.

Robert Abram Dickison married Dessie Mae Ellison on May 17, 1941. He died Jan. 6, 1987. Robert and Dessie had four children: William Abrum, Sharon Romain, Vonda Lou, and Wanda Sue (twins).

William married Lois Snyder; they have one daughter, Dawn Darlena. Sharon married Paul Davis, who is now deceased. They also only had one daughter, Leanna Marie. William and Sharon still live in Howard County. Vonda married Douglas Ryman. They have three children: Alisha Lyn, Michael Douglas, and Matthew Abram. Vonda and Doug now live in Claypool, IN. Wanda married Donald Funk and they have two children, Bryan Christopher and Melinda Sue. Wanda and Don now live in Danville, KY.

David Grandville and Ethel Ivy Dickison

Robert's grandfather came to Howard County between 1852-1856. Abraham first married Edna Irwin in 1857 in Howard County. After Edna's death, he married Mary Catherine (Ellis) Cartwright. Abraham came to Howard County with his mother, Hannah, and his brothers and sister, Virden, Griffy, James, Joseph E. and Lavina Jane.

Daniel died in 1852, in Rush County, IN. His son Griffy died in 1856; he was buried beside Daniel at the Pleasant Run Cemetery, in Rush County, IN. Daniel and Hannah Dickison were married in Franklin County, IN on July 26, 1823. They both came with their families from Kentucky to Indiana.

I do not know who Daniel's parents were; I have never been able to find out. There was a man named Amos Dickison that was in Rush County, IN with Daniel, but I have not been able to prove that they were brothers. Hannah's parents were John Kiger and Sarah Parrish of Mason County, KY.

Robert and Dessie Dickison

The parents of Robert's mother, Ethel Ivy (Washington) Dickison, were Thomas Jefferson Washington and Violena Clara (Golding) Washington. Her grandparents were George Washington and Matilda Cooksey. Her fraternal great-grandparents were George Washington Sr., wife is unknown. Her maternal great-grandparents were Zacheriah Cooksey Jr. and Mary (Case) Cooksey. The Dickisons, Kigers, Washingtons, and Cookseys were all in Franklin County, IN in the 1820's.

David and Ivy Dickison had several children, some died in infancy. Those children that lived were Alma, Omer, Esta, Lowell, Russel (died young), Glen, Raymond, Ella, Robert, William (died at age 16), Mary Catherine, Lucille, and Ned. All the boys are now deceased and the oldest girl Alma is also deceased.

The Dickison family were mainly farmers, factory workers and teachers. They were all hard workers and believed in God. *Submitted by daughter Sharon Romain Dickison in loving memory of Robert Dickison.*

DICKISON - Abraham Dickison (ca. 1825-1888), son of Daniel and Hannah (Kiger) Dickison, settled in Harrison Township, Howard County, near West Middleton, IN between 1850 and 1860. He was a farmer by trade. He, his mother, and brothers owned 320 acres. He was married twice - first in 1857 to Edna Erwin (ca. 1833-1871) in Howard County, IN, and second to Mary Catherine Ellis (1844-1927), daughter of Joseph and Nehushta (Miles) Ellis, in 1875 in Howard County, IN. He and Mary donated land for the building of Mount Zion Methodist Church.

His children by his first wife, Edna, were Martha (dying young), Harvey (dying young); James; Marietta who married Cary Moody and William Campbell; John; Elvina Jane who married Frank Kirby; and Flora who married James Enright. His wife Edna, mother Hannah, daughter Martha, son Harvey, and brothers Virden and Joseph are buried in Alto Cemetery in Alto, IN.

His second wife, Mary, was first married to William Henry Cartwright (ca. 1838-1873). Four children were born to this union: Joseph; Viola who married William Fristoe; Sallie who married Edward Summers; and Fred. Abraham and Mary had two children, David and Howard. Mary is laid to rest in Prairieville Cemetery in Tipton County. Both of her husbands died as a result of wagon accidents and are buried in Kansas. It is said that Abraham broke his neck in the accident.

His son, David Granville Dickison (1876-1956), married Iva Ethel Washington (1880-1959), daughter of Thomas J. and Vilena Claravine (Golding) Washington in 1898 in Howard County, IN. The children of this union are Alma who married Glen Carter; Omer; Esta who married Archie Swing; Lowell; Russell (dying young); Glen; Raymond; Ella who married John Rollins; Robert; Mary Catherine who married Benjamin F. Irwin; Lucy who married Floyd Williams; Ned; and an infant that was buried under a peach tree on their farm near West Middleton, IN. Both David and Iva are buried in Prairieville Cemetery.

Mary Catherine Dickison (1920-19) married Benjamin F. Irwin (1912-1970) in 1940 in Howard County, IN. To this union were born five daughters - Carolyn who married James F. Robertson, Phyllis Martin, Cindy Beasley who married Duane Hurlock and Robert Beasley, Joyce who married Jack Jewell, and Sherry who married John Eades. They also adopted a boy - Donnie Irwin. *Submitted by Cindy Beasley*

DONNELL - Alman "Everett" Donnell (Oct. 7, 1878-Nov. 16, 1953) married Gracie ("Grace") Frances DeFord (Jan. 16, 1888-July 4, 1977) on Dec. 24, 1907 in Hillisburg, Clinton County, IN. Everett was one of 11 children born to Alexander and Jane (Cox) Donnell in Clinton County, IN. Grace was born to Calvin and Harriett (Stuart) DeFord in Clinton County, IN. Harriett died when Grace was 14. Grace, being the eldest, was responsible for household duties and acting as a mother to her younger brother and sister. Everett and Grace lived and farmed in Johnson Township, Clinton County, IN. They came to Howard County, IN in October 1929 when they purchased a 40 acre-farm in Monroe Township on 200 South.

Their children are: Laura Evelyn (Dec. 3, 1909) who married Zack Roberts on Oct. 26, 1929, in Kokomo, IN. They lived in Belmont in Howard County, IN then in Monroe Township, Howard County, until they moved to Kokomo in 1953. They have four children, Donnell Bruce Roberts (Aug. 2, 1930) of Terre Haute, IN, married Ora Lee McDonald Jan. 3, 1948, (divorced), married to Dorothy; Sue Ann Roberts married James Smith (March 2, 1933) of Kokomo, IN, Dec. 23, 1950; Vera Maxine Roberts (Jan. 23, 1936) of Punta Gorda, FL, married Billy Joe Miller March 21, 1953, (divorced), married Robert Murphy in August 1983 in Kokomo, IN; Thomas Edward Roberts (Aug. 2, 1937) of Kokomo, IN. Thomas married Jane Croddy July 7, 1956. Zack is retired from Continental Steel Corporation.

Alman and Gracie Donnell

Helen Virginia (Feb. 12, 1912) married Reid Lambert on Sept. 29, 1934 in Frankfort, IN in the home of Minister A.B. Crossman. They lived and farmed in Monroe Township, Howard County, IN until 1941, when they moved to a farm in Clinton County, IN. In August 1945 they returned to Monroe Township on 1280 West, Howard County, IN to a farm (previously owned by Reid's great-uncle William Thomas "Billy" Jackson-recently deceased; then owned by Billy's brother Alfred "Alf" Jackson). They purchased this farm in 1948 (after the death of Alf Jackson). Their children are: Lawrence Reid Lambert (Nov. 9, 1935) of 600 E. in Carroll County, IN, who married Loretta I. Devore on Jan. 10, 1958 in Frankfort, IN. Marilyn Frances Lambert (Donald L.) Wooldridge (Sept. 24, 1937) of 4554 W. Co. Rd. 180 S., Russiaville, Howard County, IN, married Nov. 27, 1957 in Kokomo, IN. Linnie "Joanne" Lambert married Roger V. Glassburn of 7128 E. 00 NS, Greentown, IN, on June 6, 1965, in Kokomo, IN. Reid was a farmer until his death (April 12, 1988). He had retired from the city of Kokomo-Traffic Department in December 1975.

Thelma Ruth (Jan. 17, 1918) married Lawrence C. Bennett (a native of Florida) on Aug. 8, 1939 in Carmel, IN. Thelma then lived in Westfield and was employed by Social Security Administration in Indianapolis, IN. They lived and raised their family in Port Orange, FL. Their children are: Harriett J. Bennett (Alfred) Cave (divorced) Bennett (Dec. 2, 1940) of Seattle, WA. Lawrence William Bennett (July 17, 1943) of Port Orange, FL, married Thracy Cardovia May 22, 1965 (divorced August 1979), married Kathleen MacFarlane Aug. 31, 1979 (divorced March 1992). Ruth Ellen Bennett Bogart (John G.) Yuzzolin (Nov. 1, 1943) of Port Orange, FL, married Robert Bogart June 15, 1964 (divorced June 1970), married J. Yuzzolin May 4, 1972. James H. Bennett (Jan. 10, 1949) of Allendale, FL, married Judy Reed on Aug. 21, 1956. Lawrence served in the Navy C.B.'s during World War II. He was a retired plasterer and self-employed building contractor (deceased April 12, 1974).

Edward Everett (Oct. 15, 1922) married Eileen May Dunn on Aug. 2, 1942 in her parent's home (Forest and Mary Dunn) in Russiaville, IN. They have lived and raised their family in Kokomo, IN. Their children are: Sharon Eileen Donnell Walls, (Nov. 2, 1947), of Kokomo, married Richard Thomas Walls July 1, 1966 in Kokomo (divorced); Mark Edward Donnell (Dec. 17, 1949) of Kokomo; Lloyd Alman Donnell (June 5, 1952) of Kokomo, IN, married Diane Shoffner Dec. 28, 1972 in Kokomo. Edward served with the U.S. Army during World War II in the Southwest Pacific. He is retired from Continental Steel Corporation and Delco. *Submitted by Marilyn Wooldridge*

WILLIAM H. AND CAROLYN DONSON - William Harry Donson and Carolyn Joan Keim were married July 1, 1962, and have lived in Howard County, on the same farm since. They have known each other almost all of their lives as they have always attended and been active in the same church, Kokomo Zion United Methodist.

November 23, 1964, they had their first child, Linda LeAnne Donson. After she graduated from Eastern High School (Howard County) she graduated with a degree in Elementary Education from Indiana University. December 6, 1966, Jeffrey Alan Donson was born. He graduated from Eastern and attended J. Hines Technical School. On June 23, 1990, he married Ruth Ann Rydstrom from Greentown, IN. September 2, 1992, they presented Bill and Carolyn with their first grandchild, Blake Alan Donson.

Bill was born in Howard County on May 22, 1942, the only child of Harry and Esther (Bryan) Donson. Bill's father died in March 1989. After graduating from Northwestern High School in 1960, Bill worked at Vermont Feed and Grain. After he and Carolyn decided to marry, he began farming full time, one mile south of Plevna.

Bill's paternal grandparents, Edward and Nancy Jane (Colbert) Donson, were farmers in the Windfall and Kokomo area. His maternal grandparents were Samuel and Maude (Sale) Bryan. Sam Bryan farmed in his earlier years around Howard County.

Carolyn was born Jan. 17, 1942, in East Lansing, Michigan, where her father was about to graduate from Michigan State University. Her parents are Dr. A.L. Keim and M. Marjorie (Shrock) Keim. Shortly after graduation they moved to Plevna, Indiana, where Dr. Keim began a very successful large animal veterinary practice. Dr. Keim passed on to his heavenly reward Aug. 19, 1976. Her mother remarried in 1982 to John Naphew of Galveston, IN.

Carolyn also has a younger sister, Winifred L. Jones Wyant, than has lived in Greentown, IN since her marriage in 1963 to Kenneth L. Jones. Kenneth died in December of 1984, and in 1993 she married Charles Wyant.

Carolyn's maternal grandparents were John C. and Merle (Grau) Shrock. John and Merle farmed all of their lives. John also taught school and drove a school bus for Howard High School (Howard Township). Her paternal grandparents were Abe and Suzanne (Troyer) Keim. Most of their married life was in Miami County and Howard County where they also farmed. Abe worked with work horses in his earlier years. Carolyn's Grandpa Shrock taught her Grandpa Keim in grade school.

Living in the Plevna community is special to Carolyn. This friendly, caring community was a wonderful place to grow up and also raise her family. She spent many hours helping her father as they traveled over several counties doctoring sick animals.

We are very proud of our Christian heritage, as Bill's parents and Carolyn's parents and grandparents attended Kokomo Zion. Carolyn's paternal grandparents were raised Amish, but as long as she knew them they belonged to the Howard-Miami Mennonite Church.

DOWDEN - Otha Dowden, (May 26, 1857-July 2, 1937), son of George E. and Hannah Harpold Dowden.

Otha came to Howard County in 1880; he was recorded in the 1880 census of Tipton County with his mother and stepfather, Alexander Coy. Otha married four times, but only had children by his first marriage Aug. 4, 1880, in Howard County to Mary Elizabeth Shepherd (July 12, 1864-Feb. 17, 1915), daughter of Jesse Thomas and Lavicia Rayl Shepherd/Shepard. They were the parents of ten children: (1) George E. (July 29, 1882/3-March 14, 1952), married March 16, 1907 to Leota Mae Alley (Nov. 18, 1882-June 30, 1973), daughter of Noah H. and Margaret Louisa Balser Alley. No children; adopted two daughters, Mae and Pearl. Both buried in Albright Cemetery; (2) Clyde Morris (Sept. 22, 1885-April 29, 1966), married Jan. 2, 1909 to Grace Mae Medley (Sept. 10, 1889-Sept. 5, 1975), daughter of James and Mary Jane Bailey Medley. Both buried in Crown Point Cemetery, parents of nine children: Earl Dewayne; Erma Bernice; Mary Elizabeth; Doris Jeanette; Dorthea Ruth; Donald Ray; Beulah Jeane; Lois Fay and Lila Mae. Two of these children still living as of today, Mrs. Howard (Dorthea Ruth) West and Mrs. William Howard (Lila Mae) Hoover; (3) Jesse Curtis (Dec. 28, 1887-March 1, 1951), married May 26, 1924 in Muncie, Delaware County, IN to Geneva Sophia ? Kessell (Nov. 22, 1886-Nov. 18, 1925). According to her obituary she was married before, having two children, William and Edith. Jesse never married again, no children. She is buried in Crown Point Cemetery, and Jesse is buried in Twin Springs Cemetery. His grave was once dug up by vandals; (4) Walter William (May 13, 1890-Aug. 12, 1919), 1/married Jan. 18, 1908 to Minnie Myrtle Harris (June 14, 1892-Oct. 9, 1966), daughter of Thomas H. and Fannie Elizabeth Shepard Harris.

Otha Dowden

Eight children: William Clarence; Everett Darrell; Bertha May; Betty Jo; Wilbur Raymond; Mary Catherine; Esther Eileen; and George Ronald. Walter 2/married Aug. 4, 1967 to Hazel Katherine Brantley Robinson (Jan. 11, 1889-Feb. 6, 1983, Albright Cemetery), Walter and Minnie are buried in Sunset Memory Gardens; (5) Eva Blanche (May 17, 1893-Oct. 31, 1913), married Oct. 15, 1910, to Henry F.J. Shanks (born Feb. 14, 1890), son of George W. and Mary Nicholson Shanks. One child: Charles Dewayne (Dec. 4, 1911-Dec. 31, 1989). Eva buried in an unmarked grave beside her mother in Twin Springs Cemetery; (6) Lula Ethel (Jan. 22, 1896-June 14, 1979), married July 17, 1912, to Russell Lee Gardner (Feb. 4, 1894-July 7, 1969), son of Robert and Alma Lee Gardner. Buried in Sunset Memory Gardens, six children: Helen Irene; Ruth; Rosemary; Russell Lee; Phyllis and Janet; (7) Maria Rosena (Nov. 22, 1900-28/31 October 1977), married June 30, 1917, to Roscoe Alva Kline (April 25, 1896-June 4, 1961), son of William and Sarah Gano Kline. Buried in Memorial Park Cemetery; (8) Edith Cora (Jan. 18, 1902-Oct. 10, 1991), married July 17, 1920, to Harold Vance Benge (Sept. 6, 1902-July 1, 1979), son of William Henry and Margaret Elizabeth Harpold Benge. They are buried in Crown Point Cemetery; (9) unknown male; and (10) Otis Wayne Dowden (Sept. 22, 1907-May 20, 1951), married Sept. 21, 1929 to Marjorie Laverne Dunn (born Aug. 19 1913), daughter of Jackson and Daisy Dean Havens Dunn. Three children: Jackie Wayne Dowden, born July 30, 1930; Robert Joe Dowden, born June 19, 1932, and Barbara Dean Dowden, born Nov. 11, 1934, married James Richard Quick. Otis is buried in Memorial Park Cemetery. *Submitted by Marjorie L. (Dunn) TarTar*

DOWDEN - Robert "Bob" Joe Dowden, born June 19, 1932, here in Howard County, the son of Otis "Bud" Wayne and Marjorie Laverne Dunn Dowden; married Nov. 3, 1984, in Erwin, Unicoi County, TN, to Barbara Ann (McInturff) Kaylor; born May 29, 1944, in Unicoi County, TN, the daughter of Willard James and Pansy Inez Miller McInturff. Bob and Barb are the parents of eight children in all; (his, her and our) and the grandparents of nine grandsons and one granddaughter.

Bob was first married Feb. 26, 1954, in Howard County to Virginia Barbara Leonard (Jan. 25, 1933-March 4, 1961), the daughter of Horace Charles and Marie Elizabeth Pohl Leonard. Two children: (1) Karen Elaine (born Dec. 3, 1954), wife of Marty Lane Degraffenreid and (2) Kevin Wayne Dowden (born April 21, 1958). Bob's second marriage was June 17, 1961, at Mt. Carmel, IL, to Caroline Josephine Wilcox (born Sept. 22, 1937), the daughter of Samuel Willis and Frances Pohl Wilcox. (Caroline and Virginia were first cousins). Divorce - one son, (3) Robert Scott Dowden (born Nov. 12, 1963).

Bob and Barb Dowden and granddaughter Brandi Michelle Barnett

Barb was first married Aug. 12, 1959 in Unicoi County, TN to Kenneth Wayne Barnett (born Nov. 3, 1943), the son of Earl and Helen Pauline White Barnett. Divorce - two children: (4) Teresa Diana (born Feb. 28, 1960), wife of Clyde Steven Vandergriff and (5) Christopher Keith Barnett (born Jan. 8, 1962). Barb, second marriage was June 11, 1962 in Unicoi County, TN to Walter Burton Johnson Jr. (born Jan. 7, 1942), son of Walter Burton and Lucy Jane Lewis Johnson. Divorce - two daughters: (6) Barbara Michelle (born Aug. 16, 1966), wife of Ricky Allen Huskins and (7) Nikki Chantal (born Oct. 9, 1969), wife of Mathew Franklin Neal. Barb, third marriage was Dec. 27, 1978 in Howard County to David Waylon Kaylor, no children - divorce.

Bob and Barb's daughter was (8) Ann Nichelle "Shellie" (born April 30, 1974), wife of Richard "Richie" James Sterling.

Bob was a veteran of the Korean War and was an auto mechanic for the past 45 years. He is now employed at Western Auto as a tire specialist. Hobbies are ceramics, baseball cards, and computer; enjoys reading, bowling, fishing, and camping, any outdoor sports, though his wife can play him a mean game of horseshoes; Barb has been a hairdresser for 19 years, also employed at Taco Bell and editor of the *Howard County Roots*. Her hobbies are genealogy, ceramics, and stamps; enjoys working puzzles, reading, bowling, camping, any outdoor sports. They are both Gemini, Barb at the beginning and Bob at the end. *Submitted by Bob and Barb Dowden*

HENRY DOWNHOUR - Henry Downhour (1841-1914) and his wife Marietta (Addie) Blount homesteaded in Howard County sometime before 1869. He and Addie had married in Blackford County in 1863.

Henry was the sixth of 11 children, but he and his brother John were the only two to have children to carry on the Downhour name. His father George and 19-year-old brother John, were "bitten by the gold bug" and joined the rush to seek gold in Placer County, CA in 1852. George died of pneumonia soon after their arrival.

Henry Downhour farmhouse; Frank, Andrew, Addie and Henry

Henry and Addie were the parents of 14 children. Four of their little girls died within four years of each other and are all buried in the old Galveston Cemetery with a common headstone. On it the family name is spelled Downhower. The other children were Eliza, John, George, Minnie, Albert, Elizabeth, Charles, Andrew, Frank and Florence; all of whom were residents of Howard County or nearby counties.

Perry Downhour of Florida, a descendant of Henry's brother John, was able to properly place in the family line, all Downhours contacted throughout the country. *Submitted by Jean Simpson*

RUSSELL AND VESTA DOWNHOUR - Although Russell spent most of his working years farming in Wabash, Grant and Cass Counties, his beginning and the end of his life were spent in Howard County where he felt his roots were.

Russell's father, George Downhour, was born in Howard County in 1869, and married Eva (Swisher) in 1895. Their fourth child, Russell E., saw the light of day on a cold Jan. 16, 1903. His was a typical carefree childhood with happy hours spent playing with nearby cousins. Russell was educated at Jewell School in Clay Twp. and his religious training was at Jewell Church.

At the school, often a group of 10 or 12 Haynes cars would come by and stop at the schoolhouse to fill up their radiators. The drivers were dressed in duster coats, with goggles on and gloves with cuffs halfway to their elbows, which always drew an audience of curious boys. Every fall, a traveling man came by and gave all the school children little samples of Post Toasties or Grape-Nuts and a box to take home to their parents, an early advertising gimmick.

Russell and Vesta Downhour

Farming with his dad, they were among the first to grow tomatoes for the Camp Bros. Canning Co. in Kokomo.

When Russell heard workers were needed to work on the original U.S. 31 in the early 1920's, he applied; and he and his team of horses were hired. These earnings allowed him to be able to marry Vesta A. (Childers) on Aug. 31, 1924, at Loree in Miami County. Their first home stood along the road he was helping to build.

Russell and Vesta were parents of a son Russell Jr. born Sept. 29, 1927; and twins Ellen Jane and Edith Jean born May 18, 1934. When Russell and Vesta sold their farm in Cass County, they retired to Greentown and lived there for 15 years. They belonged to the Farm Bureau, the Greentown Senior Citizens group-Seniors on the Move, and to the Meridian St. Christian Church.

Russell died June 12, 1992, but Vesta is still living in Greentown and takes an active interest in the lives of family and friends. *Submitted by Jean Simpson*

DROLL - The end of World War II bought many new residents and changes to Kokomo and Howard County. Among new arrivals was Charles Malcom Droll in 1946. He had been discharged from the Army in December, 1945, after having served in the Criminal Investigation Division and taken part in the following battles and campaigns: Tunisian, Rhineland, Central Europe and with service in Pacific Theater and Philippines. Like many new residents, he found employment in the automobile industry. While working the afternoon shift at Chrysler, he took day classes at Kokomo Business College. February 22, 1947, he married Ritta Dean Bogard of Greene County, IN. Housing was in short supply for returning veterans starting new families. Their first home was a two-room apartment at 619 West Sycamore Street. Because of the war and conversion from manufacture of peace time products to war time armament, civilian goods were in short supply. Consequently, the kitchen of this apartment had only basic amenities (i.e., a three-burner gas stove and ice box. An "ice-man" would deliver ice on a regular basis. In the winter, one could keep food-stuffs cold by placing them in a kitchen window-box, a box built outside the window- just raise window to store items.)

Charles Droll

Over the years, Charlie and Ritta had additional residences on Vaile Avenue, North Kennedy Street (which became Apperson Way North on Oct. 22, 1955) and in August, 1956, moved to 1531 South Washington Street. This residence, according to the Sunday, October 19, 1975, issue of "*The Kokomo Tribune*", page 6B, was the site, in 1926, of Kokomo's first radio station, WJAK.

Washington Street, in 1956, was lined with many old and beautiful trees. It is so sad that very few remain today. During the 1950's, Charlie left Chrysler to take employment as bookkeeper for Main Supply Company where he worked until 1962. From 1962 until his death, March 23, 1978, he was sales representative for Schaeffer Mfg. Co. of St. Louis, MO.

Charles and Ritta were the parents of three children: Randall Bogard Droll, Michele Lynn Droll and Laren Charles Droll. Randy and Michele graduated from Kokomo High School in 1966 and 1968 respectively. Laren graduated from Haworth High School in 1976.

At the present time, Randy, with his wife, Joan DeBardeleben, and children, Andrew and Larisa, are residents of Nepean, Ontario, Canada. Michele lives in Durham, New Hampshire with her husband, James Swisher, and son, Jascha Droll Swisher. Laren resides in Highland Falls, NY.

Ritta continues to live in the family home on South Washington Street. *Submitted by Ritta D. Droll*

JOSEPH MORROW DRUECKER AND GRACE M. BRODESSER DRUECKER - Grace and Joseph Druecker, parents of Harold Joseph Druecker (1913-1961). Isabel Striebel (1914-1957), Grace Marie Durfey (1917-), and Mary Helen Smith (1921-). Grandchildren are Joseph Druecker, Ann (Druecker) Gore, Susan (Striebel) French, K. Joseph, Stephen and Michael Striebel, David and James Durfey, Diana (Smith) Halliburton, Lorene (Smith) Sandifur, David, Norman and Nelson Blaine Smith Jr.; and 23 great grandchildren.

Grace Druecker (1888-1993), born in Milwaukee, WI, to Theodore Brodesser and Isabelle (Hunt) Brodesser. My mother studied oil and china painting, piano, elocu- tion and voice. She performed in concerts and sang solo at the opera house. Her paintings were on exhibit at the Howard County Library. Her father, born in Cologne, Germany, was a graduate of Bonn University. His wid- owed mother and family moved to America in 1871. Theodore taught piano and languages at Notre Dame University. He moved to Milwaukee to be an accountant for Schlitz where he met his wife, Isabelle. Her parents were born in Bath, England and Dublin, Ireland. Theodore's mother, Annah (Birkhauser) Brodesser was a concert pianist and performed before the crown heads of Europe. Annah brought the first upright Steinway piano to America.

Joseph Druecker and Grace (Brodesser) Druecker

Joseph Druecker (1882-1942), was born in Druecker, Wisconsin. His father was born in Bissen, Luexbourg, Germany. The family moved to America in 1856. His mother, Annah McGrane, was born in Port Washington, WI. My dear father graduated from Syra- cuse University. He owned the second horseless carriage in upper New York State and was privileged to give President Teddy Roosevelt a ride. He acquired "Sitting Bull's" saddle and snow-shoes, given by Wild Bill Cody. My fathers great-great-great-grandfather was Vice Presi- dent Daniel Tompkins. We donated to the Howard County Museum Mrs. Tompkins' coverlet, "Sitting Bull" saddle and snow shoes.

In 1915 Mother, Dad, Isabel and Harold moved to Kokomo where Grace Marie and I were born. Dad operated Kokomo Sand and Gravel Company, Frankfort Machinery Company and Druecker Paving Company that paved Phillips and Markland Avenue. Dad fought the Klan for Saint Joseph Sisters to acquire the hospital. We lived on Wabash Avenue and Broadway and moved to Forest Park on Mulberry Street. Dad was called mayor of Forest Park. They asked him to do whatever was needed. Our families are graduates of Notre Dame, St. Mary's, Indiana University, Purdue, Ball State and Ten- nessee Temple.

In 1965 we (Smiths) moved back to Kokomo from New Hampshire. Their father was captain for Eastern Air Lines, based in Boston. I'll conclude with the oldest to the youngest descendant in Kokomo, my daughter's and grandsons' accomplishments that are also notable.

Lorene, Mrs. Gary Sandifur, teaches KEY math at Kokomo High School. She received the C.V. Haworth Award, was president of National Honor Society, and secretary of Student Council. Trent is president of his senior class, president of National Honor Society at Kokomo High School, elected president of K Club, but only two offices allowable. Travis, a sophomore is a member of the National Honor Society, Student Council; their main activities. Travis broke his brother's city and Howard County seventh grade track record. Played in all sports. Trent finished football and Travis cross-country.

We count our blessings for our loving parents, my 14 children and grandchildren's accomplishments and mainly, their high morals. Here's to our sesquicentennial. *Submit- ted by Mary Helen (Druecker) Smith*

DUMOULIN - Ernest Fredrick Dumoulin married Adria Nellie Kissinger Cunningham Feb. 5, 1918. They were the parents of five children.

Robert Eugene married Thelma Meeks on Sept. 12, 1942. Bob and Thelma had two children; their daughter Deborah Ann was born Jan. 26, 1947. She married John Milton Ecklund and has two children. Their son Michael Kent was born Oct. 7, 1951, and died March 5, 1972. Bob owned Bell Electric before moving to Califor- nia. He died ten months after his father.

Rosemary was born March 4, 1920 and died March 5, 1920.

Ralph Leslie was born April 3, 1921. He married May Caroline "Carrie" Kramer on Aug. 20, 1946. They have five children. Linda Kay, born June 24, 1947; she married Stephen Joseph Farrington, Oct. 26, 1968 and are the parents of three children. Leslie Allan born Oct. 16, 1948. He married Debra Lee Smith, Feb. 1, 1969. They also have three children. Patrick Keith was born April 7, 1952. He married Teresa Kynne MacDonald on Aug. 3, 1974. They have two children. Daniel Lynn was born Aug. 20, 1953; he married Joan Margarette Cardwell July 1, 1971. They have three children. Jayne Faye was born June 24, 1963. She married Gary Robert Reed, April 17, 1982. They have two children. Ralph formally owned and oper- ated the Nip & Sip and later The First & Last Chance.

Regina Louise was born Oct. 11, 1923. She married David Albert Heflin, April 17, 1946. They raised a family of eight children. Cynthia Louise born Dec. 21, 1946. She married Dennis Glenn Stover, June 5, 1965. They have two children, James Maurice and Cassondra Louise, "Sandy". Sandy married John Wayne Thatcher and has two children, Justin Wayne and Jonnah Whitney. Donna D. born Feb. 20, 1948, married Charles William Hale on Oct. 4, 1966. They have two daughters, Christine Renee and Andrea Lynn. Thomas David was born Oct. 19, 1950. On July 22, 1972 he married Cynthia Jane Wittig. They have three sons, Travis David, Sean Thomas and Troy William. Theresa Ann was born Nov. 18, 1951; she married Mark Jeffery Shea, April 11, 1985. They have a son Matthew Heflin. Sharon Kay was born April 16, 1953. She married Marvin Ronald Clark and has three children: Benjamin Rian, Anthony Michael and Jessica Leigh. Robin Lee was born Jan. 22, 1956. He married Karen Denise Palmer, Aug. 30, 1974; they have two sons, Cory David and Tyler Lee. William Robert was born Feb. 12, 1959. He married Kathy Jane Williams, July 16, 1983. They have one daughter, Bailey Louise. Susan Elaine was born Dec. 5, 1962.

Donald Dwaine, the youngest of Ernest and Adria's children, was born Feb. 2, 1925. He married Wilma Joan Westfall, Oct. 27, 1956. They have three sons, Donald Dwaine II, David Dean and Mark Alan. *Submitted by Cynthia L. Heflin Stover*

DUMOULIN - Frederick Ferdinand Dumoulin was born in Switzerland, May 28, 1862. He died in Kokomo, Aug. 3, 1912. Born the third son of Jean-Baptiste Marie Dumoulin (1825-1885) and Marie-Victorie Heritier. They married Dec. 1, 1847.

Frederick came to the U.S. in 1882 at the age of 20 and settled in Leopold, Leopoldville, IN. He married Mary C. Evrard on Oct. 29, 1887. She was born in Perry County, IN, May 9, 1871, the daughter of John Joseph and Elizabeth Justine (Peters) Evrard, both having been born in Belgium. Her death occurred Feb. 13, 1920, just ten days after her mother's death.

After their marriage, they moved to Crystal City, MO, where their first child was born. Mary Ellen, born Feb. 18, 1889. They then moved to Kokomo. Here he worked for the Plate Glass Factory as a polisher. Their second child, Alice Victoria, was born Dec. 28, 1892. Their third child was Edward John, born April 5, 1896, and the fourth, Ernest Fredrick was born Jan. 14, 1898.

Alice Victoria married John Hill, May 7, 1913. They had one child, Edward John, who married Jesse Mary Bence, Nov. 25, 1919, and had a family of five children.

The families of Mary Ellen Dumoulin-Vonderahe and Ernest Fredrick Dumoulin are featured separately. *Submitted by Cynthia L. Heflin Stover*

DUMOULIN-VONDERAHE - Mary Ellen Dumoulin and Lewis Vonderahe were married Oct. 26, 1909. They had a family of three children.

Mary Eleanor was born June 6, 1910. She married John Wayne Hicks. They had three children: Joan Lee, born Jan. 14, 1936, who married John William Daniel (they also had three children); Robert Edward, born May 14, 1937. He married Yvonne Carol Harl, and they are the parents of four children. Rita Ellen is the youngest, born Dec. 26, 1946. She married Chester Wayne Roaden, and they are the parents of two children.

Ernest Edward "Brub" was born Feb. 5, 1917. He married Jenevieve Evelyn Mills, July 26, 1944. They had a family of six children. Ronnie Lee, born Oct. 3, 1945; he is married with no children. Deanna Marie was born Sept. 12, 1946, she married Eric Lowell Shipley, Dec. 17, 1966. They are the parents of five children. Jan Ellen was born Oct. 28, 1951. Jan married John Pierce Cotner, July 11, 1988, and they have one child. Anthony Mills was born

July 21, 1954. He married Roseanna Sweet Forbar on Dec. 30, 1983. They have one child. Michael Lewis was born May 2, 1955. He married Kimberly Kaye Robinson, Aug. 9, 1988. They have two children. John Ernest was born May 21, 1958. He married Karen Kae Hornstien, Aug. 13, 1976. They are the parents of three children. Brub was a farmer in Northern Howard County, and he drove a school bus for Northwestern School Corp.

Dorothy Irene, the youngest child, was born Oct. 31, 1923. She married James Robert Smith, Feb. 5, 1942. They have a family of ten children. Karen Lynn, born Jan. 25, 1947 and died March 21, 1986. Stanley Kent born Sept. 4, 1948, married Nancy Jane Gill. They have one child. Patricia Elaine, born Dec. 31, 1950. She married Richard Charles Boes, April 18, 1970. They have three children. Mark Allen, born Jan. 29, 1953. He married Cynthia Jo McKinsey on Jan. 26, 1973. They have four children. Leo David born Dec. 2, 1958. He married Cathleen Joyce Gustafson on Oct. 5, 1985. They have two children. Bernard Ray, born Jan. 17, 1961. He married Brenda Sue Coffman, Jan. 20, 1990. Marianne Louise was born Oct. 16, 1963. She married Clint Allen Orr, Feb. 21, 1987, and they are the parents of two children. Monica Ellen was born Oct. 21, 1966. She married Richard Dean Ham Jr. on June 11, 1988. Thomas Kevin was born Oct. 22, 1968.

Ellen and Lewis were also farmers in Northwestern Howard County. *Submitted by Cynthia L. Heflin Stover*

DUNCAN - James Duncan (1809-1892) born in Stoney Creek, VA, married Matilda Cones, born in Kentucky (1816-1890). James worked for a short time on the river boats on the Ohio River, then moved to a farm in Rush County, IN, and later came to Howard County by covered wagon and located his family on Road 26 south of Kokomo. There they raised the following children: John James, George, Margaret, Robert H., Jacob A., William, and Mary Elizabeth. Three other children died young.

Mary Elizabeth married Thomas Carr. Her daughter, Myrtle Carr, was a teacher in Kokomo schools, resigning from Palmer School in 1939.

John James (1843-1904), a farmer living near the village of Fairfield, married Susanne Neal (1845-1890). To that marriage the following children were born: Henry Carlton, Mary Matilda, Nellie Lee. Susanne died in 1890 from injuries received by a natural gas explosion while making soap. James then married Maud D. Jones, and three more children were born: George Armor, Orange Lester, and John Francis.

Don and Betty Duncan

Henry Carlton Duncan 1865-1920 married Lauretta Rawlings (1868-1957) and lived on the corner of Duncan Road and 31 By-pass where the Shell gas station now stands. The first house west of the Shell station stands the old Rawlings home and is now owned by the Tom Bass family.

Henry and Lauretta had the following children: Charles Leslie, George Lee, Jesse Earl, Clarence Carl, Fred L., Howard (Beanie), Julie E. and Mildred S.

Howard (Beanie) Duncan (1902-1992) retired as postmaster at Hemlock after 38 years of service and was also a barber for more than 38 years.

Mildred Sue worked at Delco Radio from 1946 to 1973.

Clarence Carl married Mary Schuyler and the following children were born:

Betty Jean married Wayne Smith, Howard Edward married Naomi Troyer, Doris Eileen married David Greeson, Fredrick Carl married Agnes Newport, Donald Eugene married Betty Thieke, William Dale married Carolyn Gingerich, Larry Wayne married Nancy Freeman and Cheryl Kay.

Clarence Carl served in the World War in 1919. He trained in Camp Zachary Taylor and Camp Knox, KY as a truck driver for Headquarters Co., 70th Regiment, 11th Div. until his discharge Feb. 7, 1919. Howard and Frederick served in the U.S. Army.

Donald Duncan, author of this article, was born Sept. 11, 1935. He served in the U.S. Navy from 1953 to 1955 in the Korean War. Donald married Betty Thieke (born Sept. 24, 1935) daughter of Willie Richard and Anna Elizabeth (Wheeler) Thieke on Sept. 11, 1953.

Donald worked for Colonial Baking Company for many years and now own "Ducky's" Family Restaurant at 816 East Markland Ave. Their son, Bill Duncan, is married to Margaret (Baldridge) and they have four daughters: Amanda, Lauren, Elise, and Marlea. Bill is the "Youth for Christ", director for Howard, Tipton and Miami counties.

Our daughter Lisa is one of the managers at Ducky's Restaurant and has worked there for 15 years.

Most of the Duncan family still live in Howard County.

DUNCAN - John Eberly Duncan, known as John Ed, a 50 year resident and a prominent farmer of Taylor Twp., Howard County, IN, was the second son of John and Nancy (Sergeant) Duncan, natives of Virginia and Indiana. John Ed, born Oct. 10, 1842, died March 11, 1917. Born on a farm in Hancock County, IN, his father died six weeks later. John Ed helped support the family. At 21 he hired out and soon invested the proceeds in a threshing machine, and by this means made his start in life.

He married Elizabeth Delana North, a native of Rush County, and moved to a 160 acre farm west of Center, IN, on the south side of the road in Taylor Twp. where the house still stands. They were blessed with four sons: Omer C., Charles E., John Pearl and Roscoe Kern.

John Ed was an extensive livestock raiser and dealer, shipping to various points; took great pride in farming. He maintained a lively interest as a Democrat in politics was twice elected Taylor Twp., trustee, superintendent of roads, active in Baptist Church and Masonic Lodge.

Omer Caswell Duncan born Nov. 20, 1867 died Oct. 3, 1943. Married Rosa Elizabeth (Lizzie) Ingels; three children were born, Virgil G., Ermie Ruth and Estel G.

Home of John Eberly and Elizabeth Delana Duncan, early 1890's. L-R: Omer, Kern, John Ed, Delana, Charles and Pearl.

Omer and Lizzie farmed two miles east of Kokomo on Pumpkin Vine Pike with horse drawn tools hitched to their teams by ole "Dutch & Mearl" or "Bird and Flora".

Pumpkin Vine Pike, now (100 S. Rd. E.) is known for Haynes Apperson testing and perfecting their first motor-driven automobile. Many times Omer would use his horses to pull the automobile up a grade in the road. Several evenings the men would leave their automobile in Omer's barn lot and borrow his horses to ride back to Kokomo for the night, returning next day to work and perfect the automobile. By putting hot lard in the bearings the inventors would be able to start the motor and head back to town.

Virgil Glen, born May 14, 1892, died March 11, 1954. Married Zola LuAnna Dearinger. Two sons were born, Dwain L. and Dale E. Virgil retired from the Army after serving 23 years. After the death of his wife Zola in 1925, the two sons were raised by their grandparents Omer and Lizzie.

Dale Edward Duncan, born Aug. 15, 1923, married Glenna L. Warnock, daughter of Cletus and Delight (Renbarger) Warnock. Three children were born: Sandra Sue Duncan married James H. Folkening; Stephen Kent Duncan married Ramona Kirkman, then divorced and married Sharen S. (Tyner) Brincefield; Lisa A. Duncan.

Dale and Glenna have been long-time members of First Christian Church, Kokomo, IN. Dale is an active member of 389 Naphtaili Masonic Lodge, Center, IN, and farmed the same farm his grandfather Omer farmed; he is now retired here.

Our grandchildren - Ryan James Folkening, Rodney Bryce Folkening, Stacy Rene (Duncan) Fisher and Bradley Kent Duncan. *Submitted by Dale Duncan*

DUPLER - The marriage of Philip Dupler (1776-1861), son of Frederick (1754-1800) and Catherine Shell, to Elizabeth Anspach (1781-1855), daughter of John Adam Anspach (1754-1838) and Barbara Barrow (1760-1831), took place in Tulpehocken, Berks County, PA on Jan. 26, 1802. Soon thereafter, the family journeyed to the new state of Ohio, settling in Reading Township, Perry County.

One of their sons, Emmanuel (1808-1847), married Margaret Foy, daughter of Jacob Foy (1776-1856) and Elizabeth Binckley (1778-1856), daughter of Captain Christian Binckley (1738-1831) and Elizabeth Reid (1739-1814).

After Emmanuel's death, Margaret moved her family to Blackford County, IN. Emeline (1827-1913) remained in Perry County. Those who came to Indiana were:

Left: Reuben Dupler; Right: Jonathan Dupler

Clarissa (1830-1871) was the wife of Solomon Fisher. Their daughter, Lucy (1849-1931) married Thomas Herron (1843-1901), settling in Howard County. Their children were: Joseph (1866-1938), a judge of Howard Circuit Court, and Belle (1867-1963), wife of Ulysses Mills (1865-1936).

Solomon Dupler (1832-186?) married Elizabeth Foy, and were parents of Henry, Frank, and Jacob. Henry lived in Howard County and was killed by a train about 1900.

Reuben (1835-1921) was married to Margaret Russell Foy. They were the parents of Emma, who died in 1870; Della (1872-1919), wife of Harry Raines; Minnie, wife of (1) William Merrill and (2) L.E. Poet; and Edward (1876-1943). Reuben was well-known in Kokomo, and in his later years, on special occasion, he would don his silk hat, and greet his friends. He would show off his strength and agility by performing various antics. Jonathan Dupler (1845-1903) married Mary Walker (1850-1919), daughter of Thomas Walker (1820?-1860) and Mary Kelly (1825-1871), on March 12, 1868 in Cass County, IN. Their children were: Edward (1870-1871); Harry (1876-1953); Clyde (1883-1885); Woody (1886-1967); and Elizabeth (1887-1937). The family lived in Jackson Township. Woody liked to stand in the middle of the road with one foot in Cass County; the other in Howard County. Jonathan met his death when he fell from an open second-story window.

183

Those remaining in Blackford County were: Serelda (1839-?), wife of Henry Balsey; Charlotte (1840-1919), wife of Ira Casterline; and Perlina (1842-1854).

Woody settled in Clinton County, IN with his wife Thelma Kuhns (1905-1973) and their children, Marilyn (1934-), wife of Gene Jacobs, and Phil (1936-). A daughter from his first marriage to Daisy Lamberson, Georgia Arnold (1907-), resides in Detroit. A son, 1st Sgt. Harley Dupler (1909-1943), died in World War II.

Harry Dupler worked for the Crescent Dairy and operated a neighborhood grocery store on North Main Street. He married Clara Garbert (1881-1957). They were parents to: Plennie (1899-1923); Delilah Deakyne (1901-1966); Darrell (1906-1980); and Margaret (1908-1909).

Elizabeth Dupler married Fred Garbert (1887-1936). One daughter Ferol (1911-1991) was born to them. Ferol married Robert Street March 9, 1934, and were parents to James, Jack, and Joseph. They resided in Clay Township. *Submitted by Marilyn A. Jacobs*

EARLYWINE-BURGETT - Byron "Si" Earlywine was born Jan. 19, 1909, in Michigantown, IN, the youngest son of Charles William and Osa Bell (Harter) Earlywine.

Byron graduated from Michigantown High School in 1925 and attended Fort Wayne Business College. He married Nora Pearl Burgett of Russiaville, in Kirklin, IN, on April 23, 1931. They made their home in Michigantown where "Si" worked as a livestock buyer. They had one child, Rodney Lee Earlywine.

Later they moved to Russiaville where "Si" became employed as a plumber with his father-in-law, "Dick" Burgett. He was employed by Martin Brothers as a plumber at the time of his death on Aug. 3, 1965. He is buried in the Russiaville Cemetery.

Nora was the fourth child of Homer E. "Dick" and Stella (Stafford) Burgett, born on Aug. 20, 1915, in Russiaville. She attended school there and later graduated from Huffer Beauty College in Kokomo, where she taught for 15 years. Nora and Si had owned and operated a restaurant in Russiaville from 1951-1954.

Byron "Si" and Nora Earlywine

After the death of her husband, Nora moved to Minnetonka, MN, in 1972. She worked there as a beautician until her retirement in 1981, when she returned to Russiaville, where she and her sister, Lelah Cook, reside. Nora is a member of First Baptist Church in Russiaville.

Rodney Earlywine graduated from Western High School in 1950, and attended Kokomo Business College while employed in the office at the Nickle Plate Railroad. In 1952 he was stationed at Ft. Knox, KY, in the United States Army. After returning home he went to Bethel College in St. Paul, MN and also attended the University of Minnesota. He became president of Dennison Corp. of Minneapolis, a vinyl siding company.

December 23, 1961, Rod married Jeanne Mae Ortel of Minneapolis, MN, in the Methodist Church at Russiaville, IN. They have two children: Dawn Joy, who married Dean Hilgers, Oct. 12, 1988, in Waconia, MN, and Rodney Byron Earlywine who resides in Plymouth, MN.

EDWARDS - Elmer (Doc) and Etta Edwards moved to Kokomo from Curtisville, IN in November 1916 with their five children: James 18 months, Roscoe seven years, Mildred (Pat) 9, Mary 11 and Esther 13.

Doc was transferred from the Curtisville section of the Pennsylvania Railroad maintenance crew to work on the Belt Railroad. It began at the Markland crossing and went south and west past the Haynes Auto Factory and Jenkins Glass Factory to the Steel Mill on Deffenbaugh St. Doc took pride in his work and often worked long hours mowing grass on the right-a-way and sweeping snow off the switches often late at night. He had rented a house in the 1200 block of South Ohio Avenue. There was no electricity or indoor plumbing but there was a large yard and a garden lot.

During WWI the railways were very busy and wages were higher than usual. Etta took a job at the Haynes Auto Factory sewing side curtains for cars. She wore a one-piece suit with bloomer legs, unusual for those days.

The Edwards children walked a country road one mile to the old Darrough Chapel four-room school where Mr. King was principal. During a below zero snow storm they walked to school past fallen electric wires, dressed as warmly as possible, only to find that there was no school that day. Mrs. King who lived next door took them in and warmed them before sending them home again. Etta was very upset that she had sent the children out on such a day, but with no way of knowing just how cold it was she couldn't be blamed. The next year the children were transferred to Meridian School where Ray Peck was principal.

The family never owned a car. Recreation was limited. Etta had a brother who lived in the 1800 block of North Lafountain Street. The family walked from Ohio Ave. on the Pennsylvania Railroad tracks north past the Plate Glass Company, over the sand dunes made from discarded sands from the Glass Company, past the monument for Chief Kokomo on Purdum Street, over the viaduct over Wildcat Creek, over Sycamore Street, past the railroad station and on to Lafountain Street from North Street. It seemed like fun with the family together on a holiday.

The family moved a number of times over the years. The next move was to Deffenbaugh Street just west of Main St. While there Etta's brother Floyd Hackerd returned from France where he had served with the Rainbow Division as an engineer. It was a thrilling time for all.

The next move was to North Union Street. There the older children grew up and finished school. Esther worked for the Hutner family in the Modern Clothing Store until she left to get married. Later she worked at Woolworth Dime Store and as an office helper for Dr. Reuben Craig. Mary worked at the switchboard for the telephone company, Pat worked at the Carnegie Library for Dana Solenburger. When Roscoe left school he went to Detroit and worked for Ford Auto Company for $5.00 a day - a very high wage for those days.

In 1921 M. Glen Edwards was born, six years younger than James (Red) who was involved in sports in grade school and in high school. He set some records in track, played basketball and football. Glen grew up admiring his brother and he himself was involved in sports years later in high school. James worked at Haynes Stellite for many years.

Mildred (Pat) later went to work in Franklin College Library and from there transferred to Shurtleff College in Alton, IL. While there she met Leslie Garton who was on overseas duty from England with the Shell Oil Company. They were married in 1933 where they lived during WWII. In 1960 they retired and moved to Black Mountain, NC and lived there until Leslie died in 1965. Later Pat returned to Kokomo.

Esther became a nurse. When WWII was declared in 1942 she volunteered for the Army Nurse Corps. She was sent overseas with a field hospital and served in Africa, Sicily, Italy, France and Germany. Roscoe joined the Marine Corps and served in the South Pacific, and Glen joined the Navy Air Corps and eventually was sent to England and the Azores. In March 1945 Esther went on leave to England to see Pat at the same time that Glen arrived there. All three had a wonderful reunion with Pat and Leslie.

After the war Roscoe drove a bus for the Indiana Railway for years and also worked at Stellite. Glen worked for the Upjohn Company and then joined his wife in the Dorothy Edwards Realty Company. Esther became a school nurse in the Kokomo Schools and worked there for 22 years. Mary married a farmer and lived in Miami and Cass counties.

Doc died in 1948 and Etta in 1959. Their children are grateful for the loving family life they provided. *Submitted by Esther Edwards and Janet Miller*

EHRMAN - The first knowledge on our part of the Ehrman's in Indiana was through the 1860 census. George W., of whom I am a descendent and his brother John were living with, and were day laborers for a Girton family in Shelby County, IN. They were the sons and two of the 13 children born to George and Prainey (Eshelman) Ehrman of Dauphin County, PA. John C. Ehrman was enrolled and mustered in to Co. "D" 33d Ind Vol Sept. 16, 1861 during the Civil War. He married Etty Billingsley on May 28, 1863. His death was from natural causes on Oct. 8, 1864 while in the military.

George Ehrman, the father, apparently after the death of the mother, came to Indiana to join his sons sometime after the census was taken, as his death in Shelby County was recorded on Aug. 1, 1863. He is buried in the Winterowd Cemetery, Norristown, IN.

George W. Ehrman was born March 5, 1840 in Dauphin County, PA. He was 19 when he first appeared on the census. He remained in Shelby County until 1868. During that time he was married to Margaret Beeler, daughter of George and Elizabeth (Emrich) Beeler. Three children were born to this union. William A. married Helen Bell, and he later became surveyor of Howard County; Sarah C. Ehrman married Jeremiah Rider and died at the early age of 24; John Frank, married Lulu B. Garrett.

Ehrman Farm - seven miles west of Kokomo on Sycamore Pike. Vina Alta Carter and Margaret Ehrman in buggy. George Ehrman with one horse and Elwood Rider w/two horses in front of scale shed.

After leaving Shelby County, IN, they moved to Mercer County, OH where George purchased a 60 acre farm, living there three years. He came to Howard County, Ervin Township, IN in 1872 and remained until his death in 1915. He was a prosperous farmer and the owner of 120 acres of land. A small portion of this land was given to be used as what is now known as Barnett Cemetery on the old Sycamore Road west of Kokomo.

John Frank Ehrman, my grandfather, was born Dec. 11, 1865 in Shelby County, IN. On Feb. 9, 1890 he married Lula Bertha Garrett, the daughter of Leander P. and Mary Harrell Early Garrett. He was an influential farmer in Ervin Township until his death on Feb. 24, 1933. To this union were born seven children which included two sets of twins. Vina Alta, Lester Ray, George Loren, Marion J. and Mary (twins) and Nellie and Lillie (twins).

The old Ehrman homestead is still standing seven miles west of Kokomo on the Sycamore Pike with its "bank barn" and the name Ehrman and year 1884 are vaguely visible on the slate roof.

Lester Ray, my father, was born on Feb. 27, 1894. He married Esther Grace Parker, the daughter of Samuel W. and Celestia Fellows, on Jan. 7, 1917. Four children were born to this union: George Parker, Thomas Ray, J. Frank, and Rosemary Ehrman.

Following the death of John Frank Ehrman, the farm was sold and the Lester Ehrman family moved to another farm located two miles farther west. There, our family raised chickens which were dressed weekly and along with fresh eggs were delivered and sold every Saturday to households in the west end of Kokomo. Lester drove a school bus at Ervin Township for many years.

In the fall of 1937, Lester and Grace Ehrman purchased a restaurant in Burlington, IN where the family moved during that year. The family owned and operated Ehrmans' Cafe from 1937 until 1946 and it became known as a good place for the young and old to meet and eat. There was good clean fun. The restaurant had a soda fountain and juke box and the young people came from small towns in the surrounding area to join in the fun, both before and during World War II. It is still remembered by the local townspeople for having been a wholesome place for good food, homemade tenderloin sandwiches and ice cream sodas. Lester also drove a school bus in Burlington Township until his health failed and he retired.

George P. Ehrman married Beverly Jean Taylor to which there were born three children.

Thomas R. Ehrman married Helen Crume and there were two children born of this marriage.

J. Frank Ehrman married Nina Jean Morrison and there were two children born to this union.

Rosemary Ehrman married Charles (Tug) Sutton to which there were born two children. *Submitted by J. Frank Ehrman*

WILLIAM AND RONDA ELDRIDGE -
William (Bill) Eldridge began his Howard County residence in 1976, when he was employed at Radio Station WKMO, as a disc jockey. He has had a varied career in advertising, having worked with other local radio stations and newspapers, and is employed at the Kokomo Perspective.

Bill was born April 24, 1952 in Tippecanoe County, to Lorna (Nelson) and James Eldridge, and spent his boyhood in Brookston, IN. He graduated from Frontier High School and attended St. Petersburg Junior College in Florida.

Ronda was born April 5, 1954 in Howard County, the daughter of Ronald D. and Jean (Downhour) Simpson. She and Bill were married Oct. 1, 1977 in Highland Park, Kokomo, and are the parents of Alison, who was born Feb. 10, 1981. Alison is a student at Western High School, plays the oboe in the school band and is on the swim team. She played T-ball and Pixie League and has been a Girls Scout for seven years.

As owners of the Convenience Plus store for several years, they were well known in the southwest edge of Kokomo. Bill is a member of the Kokomo Park Board, Family Services Association Board and the Eagles. Ronda has been a Girl Scout leader for seven years and Girl Scout Western Service Unit manager for two years. She earned the 1992 Outstanding Leader Award. Ronda was a precinct committeeman for two years in Harrison Township, is a graduate of Eastern High School and attended IU-K. She is employed at the NBD bank as customer service representative.

The family is active at Oakbrook Community Church and enjoy golf, basketball, travel and reading.

ELLABARGER - All the Ellabargers that are in Howard County, IN can be traced back to Ephraim Ellabarger, son of Jacob and Mary Hoover Kolb Ellabarger.

Ephraim and his family came to Howard County in 1883 from Wayne County, IN and bought a farm in Taylor Township. There as a farmer and merchant in the town of Center, he prospered and was kindly known. He was a resident of Howard County for 61 years; the last 25 years he and his wife spent their winters in Florida and the summer months at a home in Center.

Ephraim was born in Cambridge City, Jackson Township, Wayne County, IN April 14, 1850 and died Aug. 7, 1944 in Howard County at the age of 94 years, three months and 23 days. He married first Oct.4, 1874 in Henry County, IN to Emma Shawhan (June 11, 1857-Dec. 20, 1940), daughter of Enoch H. and Malinda Humbert Shawhan. Ephraim and Emma are both buried in Albright Cemetery in Howard County, IN.

Six known children, the first four being born in Cambridge City, Jackson Township, Wayne County, IN; the fifth one, not sure where it was born or if it was a male or female or stillborn or miscarriage, for the sixth child (Arthur H.) birth record states he was the sixth child born. The five children known are as following and all are buried in Albright Cemetery, close to their parents' graves: (1) Ephraim Frank (January 1876-August 1948), married Maude M. Vornauf; (2) Orin Albert (April 24, 1878-Jan. 21, 1948); (3) Eva E. (Jan. 11, 1880-Dec. 8, 1941), married Claude F. Ingels; (4) Edith L. (October 1881-1962), first married Philip Warden Stevens, 2nd married ? Hatton; and (5) Arthur H. Ellabarger (Sept. 6, 1885-March 3, 1901), never married.

Keith, Gina, Brandi, and Logan Barnett

(2) Orin Albert Ellabarger (1878-1948), married March 30, 1902 to Lulu Garshwiler (Oct. 5, 1881-Aug. 15, 1946), daughter of Ara K. and Angeline Mary Utterback Garshwiler. They were the parent of three children: (1) Wayne Orin; (2) Mary Lois (Sept. 14, 1907-Sept. 29, 1891), who first married ? Clifford, second married Feb. 27, 1943 in Grant County, IN to Paul Adams; and (3) Carl Lester Ellabarger (Jan. 27, 1912-Feb. 2, 1912).

(1) Wayne Orin Ellabarger (Feb. 4, 1905-April 29, 1953), married May 14, 1925 in Howard County, IN to Lena Ruth Warden (Nov. 18, 1905-May 18, 1973), daughter of William Manford and Lulu Jane Henry Warden. Wayne and Lena were also the parents of three children: (1) Barbara Lee, born Feb. 5, 1920, married May 3, 1947 to Nathaniel C. Lauderbaugh; (2) Lowell Wayne, born Jan. 9, 1930, married Sept. 22, 1950 to Virginia Lee Grant; and (3) Carl Edward Ellabarger.

(3) Carl Edward Ellabarger, born Nov. 25, 1931, married March 20, 1960 to Gladys Irene Minglin Harrell, (born Nov. 22, 1927 in Danville, Vermilion County, IL), daughter of Lester Calvin and Grace Eden Whaley Minglin. Two daughters were born to this union: (1) Lisa Darlene, born Dec. 30, 1960 and (2) Gina Michelle, born Nov. 20, 1962 in Howard County and also married, in Howard County Dec. 28, 1980 to Christopher Keith Barnett, born Jan. 8, 1962 in Washington County, TN, son of Kenneth Wayne and Barbara Ann McInturff Barnett. Two children: Brandi Michelle, born March 19, 1983 and Logan Keith Barnett, born Feb. 27, 1988; both born in Kokomo. Gladys, first married Alfred Harrell, son of Richard E. and Minnie Jane Beatty Harrell, two sons by this marriage, Gregory Lee and Brad Harrell. *Submitted by Keith and Gina Barnett.*

ELLEMAN - Enos Elleman was born in Washington County, TN March 31, 1802. His parents had emigrated some years previous to his birth from North Carolina and in 1806 in company with other relatives and friends to Union Township, Miami County, OH had settled near the south fork of Ludlow Creek, about two miles northwest of Milton, OH.

The mother of Enos Elleman died in 1810 and was the second person buried in Union Cemetery, near Ludlow Falls, OH.

Enos Elleman born March 31, 1802 died Oct. 13, 1889, married Margaret Ward, born Jan. 28, 1808 and died Feb. 22, 1900. They settled on the east bank of Stillwater River near Versailles, OH, on an 80-acre tract of land purchased from a government land agency at Cincinnati, OH for $100.00. In 1831 he sold this land and purchased and moved to a home in Union Township, Miami County, OH where Enos Ellemen died in 1889.

After some generations the Ellemans moved to Cass County, IN. My great-grandfather, William Ellemen born Oct. 21, 1835 died March 15, 1895 married Esther Coppock born Aug. 17, 1837 died Aug. 16, 1861. They had five children all stillborn. After her death he married Kiturah Atwood born Nov. 29, 1842 died Oct. 11, 1910. They had four children, one being my grandfather Elmer Ellis Elleman born Aug. 14, 1868 died Jan. 3, 1923.

Ralph and Christina (Jones) Elleman

He married Minnie Augusta Harness born Oct. 22, 1871 and died in 1949. They are buried at Center Cemetery, Cass County, IN.

They had six children; three who lived were Theresa Pearl Elleman Yater born April 6, 1889 died Jan. 27, 1987; Ray Burdette Elleman born Jan. 11, 1903, died March 6, 1986; H. Ralph Elleman born Nov. 3, 1898 died Jan. 29, 1980. Ralph Elleman was my father who married Christine Opal Jones born May 24, 1900 died Sept. 25, 1976. They are buried in the Galveston, IN Cemetery.

They both lived in Galveston, IN and that is where they met and married March 2, 1919. They had three children: Margaret Loraine Elleman born Aug. 29, 1920; Harold Burdette Elleman born Aug. 8, 1923 died Oct. 10, 1981; Charles Elmer Elleman born May 10, 1935.

My father, Ralph Elleman, used to tell us he slept in the jail. That worried me until I found out his grandfather William E. Elleman was the sheriff and my father would stay overnight with his grandparents.

My father had three white horses he farmed with. One was named Steve and he used to pull the fire wagon for the Kokomo Fire Department and each time my mother would ring the dinner bell, Dad had to unhitch that horse fast, because he was ready to run.

My grandparents Elmer and Minnie Elleman moved to Ervin Township in Howard County, IN. My parents also moved to Ervin Township from Cass County in 1925, when I was five years old.

We lived on Uncle Charley Elleman's farm, which was across the road from my grandparents. I lived there until I graduated from Ervin Township School, then I married George F. "Dick" Stahl. We have lived all but four years in Howard County, IN.

We have three children, Mrs. John (Judith Kay) Helm, Steven Gary (Dian Kirby) Stahl and Karen Sue Stahl.

Dr. John H. Elleman, a prominent doctor in Kokomo, IN is the son of Uncle Ray and Crystal (Wilson) Elleman. *Written by Margaret Elleman Stahl. Submitted by Karen Sue Stahl.*

ELLER - The name Eller is of German origin and means literally "one who lives near an alder tree." Family tradition is rather strong that three brothers came from the Rhine Valley in Germany and settled in Pennsylvania.

One of the these brothers, Jacob, migrated to Virginia. On July 19, 1790, the Commonwealth of Virginia conveyed to him 150 acres and additional acres were added later. Jacob and his wife, Magdalene had eight children. Jacob was associated with the Brethren Church and is presumed to have farmed and probably died in 1830.

One of Jacob's children, Abraham, had a son, Abraham "Abram" who brought his wife, son Josiah and his wife and children, and son Elias and his two children to Howard County by train around 1904.

Josiah and his wife, Orpha, probably had with them six children—Flora, Nancy, Charles, Esther, Lena, and

Ruby. Flora recalled that they arrived during the rainy season and the carriage got stuck in the mud several times on the way to Ervin Township. Josiah built a log cabin not far from the main house on the 76 acres he purchased on Oct. 21, 1905.

Back Row L-R: Josiah, Charles Sr., Richard. Front Row: Robert, Charles Jr., Harold and David.

Josiah's only son, Charles Abraham Eller, was born in Roanoke, VA, on May 29, 1895, and was about nine when he came to Howard County. On Feb. 9, 1916, he married Faye Marie Brubaker, the daughter of Uriah S. and Emma (Harter) Brubaker. Eight children were born to this couple—Catherine, Pauline, Harold, Mary, David, Robert, Charles, and Richard.

Catherine married Harry Dishon and they had one child, Donna Kay. Harold married Marjorie Gilbert and they have two sons, Howard and Gary, a daughter, Judith, and nine grandchildren, and live on the Eller homeplace. Mary married Samuel Smith and they have two daughters, Beverly and Cynthia and four grandchildren. David married Jane Dow and they have two children, Lynn and Alan, and live in Ervin Township. Robert married E. Joan Oilar and they have two sons, Larry and Gregory and four grandchildren. Charles married Marilyn Rodkey and they have a daughter, Kym, and live in Ervin Township. Richard married Marion Rieger and they have two sons, Michael and Richard, and a granddaughter, and live in Ervin Township.

All five sons of Charles Eller are farmers or retired farmers and the farming tradition of the Eller family is being carried on by some of the grandsons, so the farming legacy of the Eller family continues.

ROBERT G. ELLIS - Robert George Ellis was born July 22, 1915, in Kokomo, IN to George Washington Ellis and Madge Elizabeth (Bassett) Ellis. The family did their best to survive the decade-long Depression. Robert's dad, a Trenton, NJ native, was a potter by trade. His mother was one of Kokomo's first beauticians. His brother, Jack Eugene Ellis, was born Feb. 25, 1929.

Robert graduated from Kokomo High School in 1934, having participated in several sports which provided him with many lifelong friends. His first year of college was at Kokomo Junior College. His second year, in 1936-37, was at Indiana University. He and Betty Stevenson of Linton, IN, also an I.U. student, were married Aug. 3, 1937 in Brazil, IN. Their children are Stephen Jay Ellis, born April 2, 1942; and Barbara Dianne (Ellis) Revolt born July 20, 1945.

In the early 40's Robert was employed as an illumination specialist by Public Service Utility at Huntington, IN. He was transferred back to Kokomo. An opportunity arose to be a police officer; and he spent the next 20 years with the Kokomo Police Department, interrupted only by World War II. He entered the U.S. Navy Jan. 20, 1944, and was sent to Treasure Island, CA, for additional training as a signalman. He was assigned to the General Omar Bundy, AP 152, an army troop transport. Honorable discharge from the Navy came on Feb. 14, 1946, when his rank was signalman petty officer third class.

A civilian again, he returned to the Kokomo Police Department where he worked until retirement in August, 1962. His highest rank as a police officer was assistant chief of police. His most rewarding experience in the police department was his appointment as school safety officer. He worked with the school patrol, giving talks to all grades through grade 7. During his police years, he joined the Benevolent Protective Order of Elks, Lodge No. 190. In 1961, he became the Exalted Ruler of that organization. Meantime, his wife had completed training at beauty college, and operated her own shop for 26 years.

Betty and Bob Ellis at their home at 6323 Sandpiper Dr. Lakeland, FL 33809

In 1967 he entered Indiana University at Bloomington, receiving his BS degree in education in 1968. While teaching at Elkhart Central High School in Elkhart, IN, he attended Indiana University at South Bend, receiving his MS in education in 1972. He retired from teaching in 1979. He and Betty moved to Holiday, FL, then to Lakeland, FL in 1984, where they live at this time.

Since 1984, he has volunteered at Lakeland High School, first in social studies, assisting 12 teachers with their paper work and with students needing extra help. Among other duties, he served as scorekeeper for all varsity basketball games. In 1989 he received a two-year temporary teaching certificate and began a program in "Exploratory Teaching," which he had taught at Elkhart, IN. It is now a part of Lakeland High School's regular curriculum. Currently, he spends approximately five hours daily at the school with the athletic office. In 1993, he received his 50-year pin from the Masonic Lodge No. 93, from Kokomo, IN.

The Ellises have a full, rewarding life in Lakeland with Betty's church and volunteer work, Bob's volunteer school work, and their bridge clubs. Among their greatest joys are visits from their children and grandchildren—son Steven, his wife Sherry (Kasey), and their daughter Stephanie; and daughter Barbara Revolt, her husband Robert, and their children Jeffrey, Christine and Debra Revolt; and great-grandson Christian Dickey. The Ellises will celebrate their 57th wedding anniversary Aug. 3, 1994, and feel they are very lucky people!

WILLIAM MATTHEW ELLISON - This is the history of the Ellison family. William Matthew Ellison was born on Aug. 28, 1893 in Union County, TN. He left Tennessee to follow the woman he wanted to marry. Matt followed Annie to Saybrooke, IL where he married her on Jan. 22, 1917. They moved to Howard County, IN seeking employment which he found at the Steel Mill. Matt also bought five acres of land which he farmed to support his family. Matt died on May 5, 1969 in Tipton County Hospital, and was buried beside his wife Annie in Sunset Memorial Gardens Cemetery in Howard County, IN.

Matt and Annie had five daughters; they are Hazel Louisa, Zettie Marie, Dessie Mae, Millie Maxine, and Marylin Louise. Hazel married Charles Ford; they had two children, Jamakie Ann and Jerry Allen Ford. Zettie married Raymond Wood; their children are Cecil Dale, Arletta, Annie Mae, and Connie Sue Wood. Dessie married Robert Dickison; they have four children, William Abrum, Sharon Romain, Vonda Lou, and Wanda Sue (twins). Millie married Ralph Everhart; they had four children, William Matthew (stillborn), Contina (died age two), Gloria Jean died Jan. 29, 1988 in a fire along with her son, granddaughter, and son-in-law; Laura Jean is their only living child. Marylin Louise married James Freeman on April 3, 1955 in Kokomo, IN. Their children are Jeffery, Brian, and Michael.

L-R: Marylin Ellison, Millie Ellison, Dessie Ellison, Annie Ellison, mother; Matt Ellison, father; Zettie Ellison and Hazel Ellison

William Matthew Ellison was the son of Joseph Lafayette Ellison Jr. and Louisa (Dossett). Joseph and Louise were married on March 14, 1892 in Union County, TN. Joseph died Jan. 22, 1970 in Union County, TN. His wife Louisa died June 21, 1947 in Union County, TN. They had 12 children: William Matthew, Sarah Melinda, Bessie Arminda, Dina, Joseph Ulyess, Ellen Lee, Bradley, Jefferson, Marley, Authur Swain, Finna Esther, and Edith Irene.

Matt's paternal grandparents were Joseph Lafayette Ellison Sr. and Margaret Melinda (Lyke). His maternal grandparents were Matthew Dossett and Sarah (Berry).

Matt's great-grandparents were Robert and Sarah Ellison, Michael and Dicie (Lyons) Lyke, James and Phebe (Lynch) Dossett, and Henry and Eliza (Ellison) Berry.

All of the Ellisons were from Tennessee, except for Robert Sr. and his parents James and Elizabeth Ellison (Matt's great-great-grandparents); they came from South Carolina. Michael Lyke's family came from North Carolina.

Matt also had two sisters and a brother that moved to Howard County, IN. Matt's sisters Marley and Esther married McBee brothers and moved from from Tennessee to Howard County. Marley married Lorrie McBee and Esther married Leonard McBee. Uyless Ellison also moved from Tennessee to Howard County; later Uyless moved to Walton, IN where his son Emerson and his family still reside. *Submitted by Dessie (Ellison) Dickison, daughter of Matt and Annie Ellison*

ENGLANDS - Born and bred in Howard County, Virginia (Winslow) England and Harry Eugene England were the children of Doris and Edgar A. Winslow and Vivian and William Pickney England. They both attended Kokomo High School and first met when in the eighth grade. Both Virginia and Gene were avid rollerskaters and spent many enjoyable hours at the Skaters Delight Roller Rink.

After graduating from Kokomo High School (Gene in 1945 and Virginia in 1946) they were married on June 21, 1947 in the Pilgrim Chapel of the First Congregational Church. Gene was employed at Reliance Manufacturing Co. while in high school - leaving there to work at the Bunker Hill Naval Air Station (now Grissom Air Force Base). After that he was employed by Chrysler Corporation for 32 years - retiring in 1978 as a supervisor. After retiring, wanting to use his time wisely, he learned to bevel glass from Russ Ragland and was employed by Mr. Ragland for four years. At the present time he is the manager of Freshens Yogurt in the Kokomo Mall.

Virginia was employed by S.S. Kresge's downtown during her high school years where she learned about the retail business and learned to love it working in different areas of it the rest of her life. In 1963 she was employed by the Mill End Fabric Store working for Glen and Vera Rayl and worked there until 1973 when they closed the store. She went to J.C. Penney's where she was employed for 20 and a half years, retiring from there to work for Freshens Yogurt.

The Englands were blessed with two daughters, Shannon Mae and Luwanna Kay. Shannon is married to State Senator Steven R. Johnson and is a first grade teacher at Lafayette Park School in Kokomo and is also a private piano instructor. Senator Johnson and Shannon are both graduates of Indiana University, Steve returning there to be a lab instructor in chemistry for 19 years. He and Shannon are owners of Freshens Yogurt in the Kokomo Mall.

Front row L-R: LuWanna Kay England, Virginia Lavon England, Shannon Mae Johnson. Top Row L-R: Harry Eugene England, Senator Steven R. Johnson

Luwanna works in Los Angeles where she has lived for ten years. A former dance instructor for Betty Hayes Dance Studio in Kokomo she was active in Civic Theatre and choreographed many productions. She is now employed at the Gene Autry Western Heritage Museum in Los Angeles.

Through the years we have enjoyed church work, camping, square dancing and many other activities. Howard County is a good place to live and raise a family and we have always loved it and treasured the many friends we have here. We are proud and happy to be called "Hoosier."

ERTEL - The Ertel (Urtel) family came to America ca 1820 from the area of Bavaria in Germany. They first settled in Philadelphia. Charles Ertel was born in Philadelphia in 1833. He was the son of Philip and Mary Ludy Ertel who married in Pennsylvania in 1829. They had four children: Philip and George (twins), Charles and Elizabeth. They came to Rush County, IN in 1834. Philip died in 1874 and his wife in 1887. They are buried in East Hill Cemetery, Rushville, IN. There is a picture of the farms of Charles Ertel and also his brother Philip in the Atlas of Rush County, IN. Also in the *Indiana Magazine of History* Vol 32, there is an article written about the Ertel Mills and Woolen Factory owned and operated by Philip Ertel 1846-47.

Silas Marion born 1859, Charles William born 1886, Charles Ertel born 1833 and the baby Ray born 1909.

In the 1850 census the occupations of the Ertel men is wool carder. Charles Ertel married Priscilla David in 1858. To this union were born three children: Silas Marion, Lewis and Harvine. His wife died about 1857. His second wife was Rowena Houston, daughter of John and Susan Houston, natives of Fairfield County, OH. This marriage occurred March 24, 1870. This union was blessed with nine children: Mary Leota, John Perry, Charles Delbert, Nettie Estella, Ida May, Lucy Almeda, George Franklin, Peninnah Elizabeth, and Joseph Benjamine. Some of Charles Ertel's descendants live in Rush, Madison, Grant and Howard counties. The four generation picture is the line through the oldest son of Charles and Priscilla David Ertel, Silas Marion. Some of this family's line live in Howard County. Also Janice Blanchard who lives in Kokomo is a great-great-granddaughter of Charles Ertel through the daughter of Charles and Rowena Houston Ertel, Peninnah Elizabeth. Charles Ertel died in 1921 and is buried in Zion Cemetery, Raleigh, IN. His second wife died in 1907 and is also buried at Zion Cemetery.

ETHERINGTONS - John and Francis Etherington came to Carrollton, KY from Virginia in 1801. They had two sons - one of whom was named Richard.

The Ramseyer family came to Switzerland County, IN, from Switzerland in Europe, to raise grapes. They had a daughter named Mariah.

Richard and Mariah were married sometime around 1825. They came to Howard County in 1840 and settled between Kokomo and Russiaville, IN, along what is now State Road 26 - four miles east of Russiaville.

Richard and Mariah homesteaded 80 acres and, on Feb. 15, 1848, they received a sheepskin deed signed by President Zachary Taylor.

Richard and Mariah had five children: four sons, Phillip, Robert H., William, John Thomas and a daughter Elizabeth.

Robert H. and Mary Lou Etherington (their son) purchased the homestead from Richard and Mariah in 1881.

Robert and Irene Etherington

Robert and Mary Lou had seven children: Harry Etherington, Jessie Saul, Leroy A. Etherington, June Cardwell, Elizabeth McIntire, Susie McCain and John Etherington.

After the death of Robert and Mary Lou, the homestead was purchased by their son, Leroy A. and Artie (Cardwell) Etherington in 1921. Lee (as he was known) and Artie had four children: Ward Etherington, Maxine Etherington, Helen Gable and Robert A. Etherington.

Ward and Berniece Etherington had two sons: William and Thomas.

Maxine is unmarried.

Helen married Richard Gable and had eight children: Marilyn, Richard, Sara, Cathy, Edwin, James, Mark and Miriam.

Robert A. and Irene (Terhune) Etherington, the author of this article, have two children: Judy Briscoe and Jack Etherington.

The Etherington family has farmed this farm for 141 years.

On Aug. 2, 1985, the Governor of Indiana declared the farm to be a "Hoosier Homestead Farm" for being farmed by the same family for over 100 years. Lt. Governor John Mutz presented the family with a certificate at the State House in Indianapolis.

After 150 years, the farm is in a family trust, "The Lee and Artie Etherington Family Trust". (Note: Irene Etherington passed away June 25, 1994.)

GEORGE AND ADELINE ETHERINGTON - George was born Nov. 18, 1881 and died at the age of 102 Nov. 1, 1984. He was the son of John and Rebecca (Moore) Etherington. On May 22, 1906 he married Adeline Lincoln. Adeline was born in Illinois and died Sept. 23, 1960. George and Adeline are both buried in the Sunset Memory Gardens Cemetery in Howard County.

George and Adeline had seven children: Glenn Thomas, Russell Howard, George Earl Jr., John Lincoln, Francis Willard and Paul Eugene.

Glenn Thomas was born Feb. 12, 1908 and married Edith Simpson Aug. 17, 1930. She was the daughter of David Lewis and Eva (Dixon) Simpson. They had two sons: Dale Edward born July 14, 1931 and married Althea Kinney June 3, 1951; and Beryl Dean born Sept. 27, 1934 who married Barbara Ellen Gentry Dec. 24, 1954. Dale and Althea had two children: Dawn Elaine born Dec. 15, 1953 who married Larry Smith Aug. 9, 1974; and Sheila who was born July 25, 1958 and married Bruce Taflinger Aug. 4, 1979. Beryl and Barbara had four children: James Glenn born Sept. 22, 1959 and married Ronda Everhart May 23, 1983; Daniel Dean born Dec. 31, 1961; Joseph Mark born May 4, 1964 married Rachel Vincent July 11, 1993; and Ruth Ellen born Oct. 23, 1965 married Mike Wikel July 8, 1989.

Russell Howard born Aug. 12, 1909 and died Oct. 9, 1984 and married Freida Coe Oct. 25, 1929. They had two sons: Donald B. who married Martha Barbara and they had seven children; and Bobby.

George Earl Jr. was born Nov. 5, 1920 and died June 9, 1935.

John Lincoln was born May 11, 1923 and died Nov. 23, 1977. He married Maxine Purvis and they had three children: Marsha, Gloria and Linda.

Francis Willard was born Oct. 29, 1906 and died September, 1954. He married Frances Gooch.

George was the third child of John Thomas and Rebecca (Moore-Jackson) Etherington. John was born in November, 1847 in Howard County and died in 1922. He is buried in the Prairieville Cemetery in Tipton County. He married Rebecca Sept. 24, 1875 in Tipton County. Rebecca was born in February, 1849 in Ohio and died in 1922. John and Rebecca had four other children:

Arthur B. born Oct. 22, 1876 who married Della Mae Miller Oct. 22, 1907. They had one son, Lewis C. born June 8, 1919.

Amanda E. born in 1880. She married Jay Griffith April 24, 1897.

Samuel P. born March 12, 1885 and died Feb. 15, 1945. He married Dora I. Cardwell. They had three children: Everett Merrill; Ralph who married June Tucker and Crystal who married Robert Chase.

Edith born April 3, 1887 and died in 1962. She married Lee R. Miller March 12, 1905.

Rebecca also had a son from her previous marriage, Franklin Jackson, born in 1863 and died in 1946. He married Alice Phelps.

John Thomas was the son of Richard William and Mariah (Ramseyer) Etherington.

JOHN AND VERGIE ETHERINGTON - John was born May 26, 1900 in Howard County. On Oct. 2, 1920, he married Vergie Opal Murphy. Vergie was the daughter of Lewis Ellsworth and Kizzie Jane (Brenton) Murphy. John and Vergie lived in Howard County until 1958 when they moved to Miami County. John formerly worked at Globe American Company in Kokomo and retired from Eck-Adams Company in Peru. Vergie was born Feb. 12, 1902 in Cass County and retired from Howard Community Hospital. She died April 1, 1978. John died Nov. 4, 1983 and both he and Vergie are buried in the Galveston Cemetery. They belonged to the South Side Christian Church in Kokomo.

John and Vergie had ten children: Mary Jane born June 3, 1921; Marjorie born Aug. 12, 1923 and married Charles DeVoe Dyer March 14, 1946; John Murphy Jr. born Feb. 3, 1926 and married Vonna Lou Hite Sept. 12, 1946; G. Sue born March 26, 1927 and married Donald R. Shepherd Feb. 16, 1946; Roberta A. born Jan. 18, 1931 and married Robert C. Lineback December, 1951; Conrad Dewaine born Sept. 10, 1933 and married Norma Lieutal Carter May 25, 1958; Linda Lou born and died Oct. 26, 1935 and is buried in the Prairieville Cemetery; E. Elaine born Feb. 24, 1937 and married Timothy R. Quinn May 15, 1955; Larry born Feb. 14, 1944; and Sandra K. born Sept. 27, 1947 and married Rodney E. Alspaugh Nov. 18, 1966.

John was the son of Robert H. and Mary Lela (Garrison) Etherington. Robert was the son of Richard

William and Mariah (Ramseyer) Etherington. He was born Feb. 21, 1862 in Howard County and died Sept. 27, 1918. He married Mary Garrison Sept. 16, 1886 in Howard County. Mary was born Sept. 27, 1863 in Carroll County and died Jan. 26, 1920. She was the daughter of Jacob and Damaris Jane (Shinn) Garrison.

John and Vergie Etherington

Robert and Mary had seven children: Harry born July 1, 1887 and died Aug. 9, 1889; Jessie Florence born Feb. 3, 1891 and died May 9, 1952; LeRoy Anson born Nov. 30, 1892 and died July 15, 1965; Damaris Jane born June 3, 1896 and died Feb. 13, 1987; Elizabeth born Feb. 26, 1898 and died in 1960. John Mark (the subject of this article); Suzie born March 14, 1902 and is still living at the time of this publication. Jessie Florence married Marvin Saul Feb. 11, 1912. LeRoy Anson married Artie Cardwell Sept. 26, 1914. Damaris Jane married Evan C. Cardwell July 27, 1918. Elizabeth married Aaron McIntire, Aug. 26, 1916. Suzie married Glen McCain Nov. 19, 1921.

PAUL E. AND MARY H. ETHERINGTON - On Aug. 21, 1949 after looking across both oceans and all over the United States Paul met and fell in love with his first and only true love, Mary. On this faithful day in August in a small church in Russiaville they started their own chapter of history.

He was born the son of George and Adeline (Lincoln) Etherington, one of six boys, in the house that his father built. Paul and his brothers were raised on the farm where he has lived and farmed all of his life.

After graduating from West Middleton High School in 1936 he attended the eight weeks winter course at Purdue. April 16, 1941 found him entering a new line of work; for the next four years, nine months and 17 days he would be cooking for Army's 85th E-Vac Hospital in Europe and different camps in the States. After leaving the army in 1946 he came back to the family farm. Over the years of farming he has collected several arrowheads from the different fields he has farmed in Howard County.

Paul E. and the old Ford

Paul's grandfather John T. Lincoln was the veterinarian in Alto for six years. He lived just west of Alto.

Mary was born Oct. 4, 1920 in western Howard County, one of 11 children, to Frank and Addie (Malicoat) Watson. Her dad farmed and worked at Globe during WWII. Her family came from Tipton and Clinton Counties where they farmed and worked on the railroad. Mary worked at Delco during the war. At this time when there was not much to do but work, she kept a scrapbook of all the people from Howard County who went to war. After looking through it one day we discovered she had left out one picture that was the man she would marry.

They have lived in Howard County all their lives, where they have kept busy over the years in 4-H, Rural Youth and Farm Bureau. They have attended church at West Middleton Methodist since they were married.

They have three children. (1) David, who has followed in his father's footsteps, is farming in western Howard County. He graduated in 1976 from Western High School and attended Purdue's eight weeks winter course. On June 11, 1977 he married Rhonda Zamberlan. They have two children, Chad and Mindy. (2) Ann, who graduated in 1968 from Western High School and Ball. State. On Aug. 13, 1972 she married Michael Rockwell and now lives and teaches in Henry County. (3) Becky graduated in 1972 from Western and lives in Howard County.

RICHARD WILLIAM AND MARIAH ETHERINGTON - Richard William was born Aug. 10, 1818 in Kentucky. He died April 4, 1905 in Howard County and is buried with his wife in the Prairieville Cemetery. Richard received a sheepskin deed for his farm in Harrison Township on March 20, 1849 signed by President Zachary Taylor. He married Mariah Sarah Ramseyer and they had seven children: Catherine born in 1844; Philip born March 5, 1845 and died Oct. 8, 1909; John Thomas born in November, 1847 and died in 1922; William born April 14, 1850 and died March 31, 1933; Elizabeth born in 1852 and died in 1923; Martha born in 1855 and died June 21, 1874; and Robert H. born Feb. 21, 1862 and died Sept. 27, 1918 in West Middleton. All were born in Howard County except Catherine. Philip married Anna Creason on Feb. 25, 1869. John Thomas married Rebecca Moore Jackson on Sept. 24, 1875. William married Celestia 'Lettie' Francis Low April 11, 1872. Elizabeth married George W. Suite on Sept. 8, 1870. Martha married Harrison Souvers on Feb. 27, 1873 and Robert H. married Mary Lela Garrison on Sept. 16, 1886.

Richard William and Mariah Etherington

Richard was the son of John and Francis (Yancey) Etherington. John was born around 1779 in Virginia the son of William and Catherine. William died in 1798 in Culpeper County, VA. John married Francis Yancey on Jan. 24, 1799 in Culpeper County, VA and died on Feb. 21, 1822 in Owen County, KY. After his death, Francis and her youngest children lived with her brother, Phillip Ramseyer. Francis was born in 1758 and was the daughter of John and Mary (Layton) Yancey who were married in Essex County, VA in 1753. John Yancey was the son of Lewis Davis and Mildred Winefred (Kavanaugh) Yancey. Lewis Davis was the son of Charles Benjamin Yancey and Mildred the daughter of Philemon Kavanaugh.

ROBERT H. AND MARY ETHERINGTON - Robert H. was born Feb. 21, 1862 in Howard County. He was the son of Richard William and Mariah Sarah (Ramseyer) Etherington. He died Sept. 27, 1918 in West Middleton and his buried with his wife in the Prairieville Cemetery. Robert married Mary Lela Garrison on Sept. 16, 1886 in Howard County. Mary Lela was the daughter of Jacob and Damaris Jane (Shinn) Garrison. Jacob was born in 1836 and Damaris Jan. 17, 1844. They were married Nov. 28, 1860.

Robert H. and Mary Etherington

Robert and Mary had seven children: Harry born July 1, 1887; Jessie Florence born Feb. 3, 1891; LeRoy Anson born Nov. 30, 1892; Damaris June born June 3, 1896; Elizabeth born Feb. 26, 1898; John Mark born May 26, 1900; and Suzie born March 14, 1902 and is still living at this time. Jessie married Marvin O. Saul Feb. 11, 1912. LeRoy married Artie Cardwell on Sept. 26, 1914. Damaris June married Evan Cooper Cardwell July 27, 1918 in West Middleton. Elizabeth married Aaron McIntire Aug. 26, 1916. John married Vergie Murphy Oct. 2, 1920 and Suzie married Glen McCain Nov. 19, 1921. Jessie Saul died May 9, 1952. LeRoy died July 15, 1956 and is buried in Sunset Memory Gardens Cemetery. June Cardwell died on Feb. 13, 1987 in Kokomo and is buried in Sunset Memory Gardens Cemetery with her husband. Elizabeth died in 1960 in Normanda, IN. John is buried in the Galveston Cemetery with his wife after his death Nov. 4, 1983 in Kokomo.

Roberts' father, Richard, settled in Harrison Township in 1844, receiving his deed on March 20, 1849.

EVERLING - Danny L. Everling and Joan Stone Everling were married Dec. 25, 1964. They moved to Howard County and took up housekeeping the very same day. They are at the same home 30 years later. Joan lived in Elwood, IN and Danny lived in Curtisville, IN. Joan graduated from Elwood High School and is a graduate of Apex Beauty College in Anderson, IN. Danny graduated from Windfall High School and is a Marine Corp. veteran.

L-R: Danny, Joanie, Lewis, John

They have two sons, Lewis Allen Everling born Aug. 27, 1966 and John Adam Everling born April 10, 1974. Both boys graduated from Taylor High School and attended Indiana University at Kokomo. While in high school Lewis was a yearbook photographer, and John won the Louis Armstrong award for jazz band. While in college Lewis was an alumnus of the Bowen Institute of Political Awareness and photo editor for the college newspaper. John was a writer for the same paper a few years later.

Lewis is a professional free-lance photographer and John is employed at Chrysler. Danny is employed at Chrysler as a toolmaker, and Joan is a self-employed cosmetologist and owns Joanie's Beauty Salon and assists Lewis with his photography.

FARRINGTON - In April 1848, North Carolinian John A. Farrington (1809) paid $320 for 160 acres of land in Howard County, IN. The U.S. Congress had granted the right of preemption to actual settlers on this land acquired by treaty from the Miami Indians. By 1846, the Farrington family—Sarah (North Carolina, 1824), Eliza Anne (Indiana, 1839), Albert (Indiana, 1841), Jabez (Indiana, 1842)—had already built a house and improved four acres.

Although it is not known if John and Sarah traveled directly from North Carolina to Indiana, it is possible that they were part of an exodus from that state between 1815 and 1850. One-third of North Carolina's citizens, including farmers, emigrated in search of better conditions.

Life in Howard County must have held promise because the Farringtons farmed for three generations. Throughout his remaining 16 years, John had two more sons, Alfred and Emesly, and purchased additional land.

By 1874 when Jabez (32), inherited his portion of the family farm, he had married Emily Knote in 1868. He had also lived in constant pain since being captured and confined at Andersonville, GA prisoner-of-war camp during the Civil War.

Farrington Family April 27, 1946, 50th Wedding Anniversary - Arlie M. and Mary Ella Jones Farrington. Back L-R: Maxine, Eugene, Delight, Melville, Clytice, Lloyd

Jabez served with the Indiana Volunteers, 118th, 137th and 40th Regiments, before capture at the Battle of Franklin, TN, Nov. 30, 1864. According to eyewitnesses, that battle was more difficult than Lee's at Gettysburg and the casualties were as high.

Jabez' wife, Emily, must have suffered tremendously in 1888. On March 18th, Jabez (46) died from injuries sustained as prisoner-of-war, sunstroke and spinal irritation. Thirteen days later their daughter Victoria (5) died.

Without Jabez, the remaining Farringtons were forced to negotiate life without their husband and father—a stiff price lasting long after the war guns were silenced. When women had no legal standing, Emily kept her family together for a while—Mary E., Ellen, John W., Arlie Monroe, Flora B., Laura L. She ran the farm, gave birth to their eighth child, Jabez L., and even convinced two congressmen to intervene for her before the U.S. Pension Office.

In January 1900, two years after wedding Elijah Stevens, Emily (48) died. A guardian was appointed for the two youngest Farringtons. Laura (15) went to live with a family in Jackson Twp., and Jabez (11) was placed at the Indiana Soldiers' and Sailors' Orphans Home, Knightstown, IN.

Jabez' son, Arlie Monroe, became the third generation to farm in Howard County. On April 27, 1896, he married Mary Ellen Jones (Ella) in Kokomo. They raised seven children: Lloyd, Clytice, Melville, Velma, Delight, Eugene and Maxine.

By 1915, changes occurring throughout the country were also occurring within the Farrington family; life on the farm had lost its appeal. Migration was toward cities and away from farms. Clytice, Arlie's second child, explained her reason for leaving: "Women were expected to marry farmers, raise lots of kids, and work the farm. They were old and worn-out before their time."

Fourth generation Indiana Farringtons left the farm and moved to Kokomo, Indianapolis and Lafayette. Arlie and Ella Farrington eventually sold the farm and moved to Jerome where Arlie died April 21, 1949. Ella died Jan. 16, 1954 in Indianapolis. *Submitted by Allyne Kell Pittle*

ALBERT AND IDA GULLION FAWCETT -

Albert Ellsworth Fawcett, born Jan. 1, 1863, married Ida Belle Gullion, born Aug. 25, 1865, on Aug. 30, 1883. They owned a farm in Taylor Township. Albert died of lockjaw on Aug. 12, 1932 and Ida died in May 1949. There were three children born to this marriage: Ernest William, who died at the age of eight years; Eva Merle, who married Paul Snow who died Oct. 3, 1940. There were no children born to this marriage. Later Merle married Claude Gasho, a Taylor Township farmer, who died Feb. 12, 1979. There were no children to this marriage. Merle died in 1981. The third child was Glen David, who married Ruby Olive Johnson. They had two children: Ernest W. and Glen Dale. Glen was also a farmer. Glen David died in 1938 and Ruby died in 1985.

Ernest W. married Geneva Jane Parsons in 1940. They owned the Higbee Body Co. in Kokomo. They had one son, John Edwin, who married Lillie Elizabeth Daffron in 1968. John is a Doctor of Optometry in Kokomo and Lillie is school teacher in the Kokomo system. They have one daughter, Patricia Ann, born in 1978.

Glen Dale married Margaret Elizabeth Little in 1940. They are Taylor Township farmers and have owned and operated the Country Market for several years. Dale and Margaret have one son and one daughter. The son, Gregory Bruce, is a research analyst for independent colleges. Gregory married Sandra Nickel and they had one son, Jason Aaron Fawcett. This marriage ended in divorce. The daughter, Peggy Jane, worked as a technician in the hospital prior to her marriage to Stanley Rush in 1970. They are engaged in farming and raising pure bred hogs. Peggy and Stan live on the original Fawcett farm. They have two children. One son, Todd Raymond, is a senior at Purdue University and one daughter Jody Kay, is a student at Taylor School System.

FAWCETT -
Fawcetts here in Howard County, IN, can be traced back to Benjamin and Ester Hinton Fawcett, natives of Rockingham County, VA, and of Irish ancestry. After their marriage, in Virginia, they emigrated to Clark County, OH, near Springfield, where Mr. Fawcett engaged in mercantile pursuits and in miscellaneous trading. In 1837 they emigrated to Indiana, first settling in Montgomery County; then in 1843 they came to Howard County, which section, however, had not yet been organized as a distinct political division of the state. Kokomo was then an Indian village. He took a claim to 160 acres of government land two and a half miles west of Kokomo. New London was the county seat, and the county bore the name of Richardville. Kokomo was just being "considered." He aided in the organization of the county and in laying out the town of Kokomo. Merchandise was brought into the county on wagons drawn by oxen, being brought from Burlington, a leading trading point. Ague, or chills and fever, the whole family suffered, the whole nine of them at one time, when they were too sick, feeble and poor to employ a doctor or obtain any medicine: they had to "shake it out!" The Hinton family remained in Virginia.

David and Earlene Fawcett

Benjamin died Sept. 16/23, 1870 and his wife shortly thereafter (Oct. 24, 1870), both, buried in Puckett Cemetery in Howard County. They were the parents of nine children: (1) Silas H., married Sept. 10, 1851 to Jemima Harland, he died in Nebraska; (2) Charles W., died in 1891; (3) Crawford, 1831-July 12, 1908, married March 19, 1868 to Pennina Patten (1839-Feb. 7, 1919), Puckett Cemetery; (4) John M.; 1835-Jan. 31, 1918, married Oct. 11, 1860 to Margaret Isabel Canine (1840-1931), Crown Point Cemetery; (5) David, (1833-1910). (6) Henrietta, married a Landreth; (7) Susan E., 1826-1898, married Dec. 25, 1856 to William McClellan (1832-1886), Puckett Cemetery; (8) Martha H., married Dec. 28, 1865 to Hutton/Dutton H. Jackson; and (9) Mary, July 23, 1839-Aug. 30, 1875, age 36 years, one month and seven days, never married, Puckett Cemetery.

(5) David Fawcett was born March 29, 1833 in Clark County, OH, died March 21, 1910; he married April 11, 1861 to Charity Ann Smith (1841-June 27, 1924), daughter of William B. (Dec. 1, 1818-Oct. 28, 1905) and Sarah Ann Canine (Aug. 10, 1819-June 2, 1896) Smith, all buried in Crown Point Cemetery. They were the parents of six known children: (1) Albert E.(?Ephraim); (2) William E. (?Ephraim), 1867-January 1920, wife Mary Etta (1872-June 1954), Crown Point Cemetery; (3) Charles B., (1869-1927); (4) Frank Omar, March 28, 1871-May 26, 1957, wife Emma Perry (Sept. 27, 1873/74-April 12, 1959), daughter of James W. and Mary Jane Hensley Perry, Crown Point Cemetery; (5) John P., died 1949, wife Alda Crown Point Cemetery; and (6) Nellie, married a man named Young.

(3) Charles B. Fawcett, 1869-Dec. 19, 1927, married in 1895 to Alice P. Gennebeck (March 15, 1876-Nov. 12, 1955 Logansport, IN), daughter of John (1844-June 6, 1925) and Lucinda C. Ozer (died February 1909) Gennebeck, all buried in Crown Point Cemetery. They were the parents of three known children, all born in Howard County: (1) Ralph Owen, Sept. 8, 1909; (2) David, May 24, 1919 and (3) Edna, May 24, 1914, wife of Wayne Powell.

(2) David, being a twin himself, married a twin, Earlene Agnes Durkes, born Oct. 26, 1918 in Miami County, IN; twin daughter of Chester Lewis (Oct. 16, 1890-April 3, 1961) and Cleo Eva Antrim (March 3, 1895-Oct. 15, 1971) Durkes. *Submitted by David and Earlene Fawcett.*

FAWCETT -
Arriving in Howard County in 1843, Benjamin Fawcett (1791-1870) and his wife Esther Henton (1796-1870) settled on a government grant of 160 acres two and a half miles west of Kokomo. Father and sons cleared and farmed this land, some of which is owned by descendants today. The former Rockingham County, VA merchant and his sons helped clear the land and cut timber for the first court house.

The Fawcetts were married in Augusta County, VA in 1818, and to this union 12 children were born, nine of whom survived into adulthood: Silas Henton (1821-1896), Henrietta Gay (1823-1912), Susan E. McClelland (1826-1897), Charles Warren (1828-1891), Crawford (1831-1908), David (1833-1910), John Marshall (1835-1918), Martha Jackson (1837-1884), and Mary Fawcett (1839-1875). Benjamin was elected commissioner in the county's first election in 1844. Benjamin and Esther were Presbyterians. They are buried in Puckett Cemetery.

Crawford Fawcett was born in Clark County, OH, as the family migrated to Indiana. Crawford served in the cavalry during the Civil War. Upon returning to Howard County, he was a road builder and a farmer. He first purchased a farm in Tipton County and later returned with his family to the original farm at the corner of Malfalfa and Sycamore Roads. He and his wife, Pennina Patten (1839-1919), had two children: William Benjamin and Melinda Piper.

William (1875-1954), born on the farm in Tipton County, continued to farm as his father and grandfather before him. He married a Howard County native, Minnie Robertson (1874-1946). Three children were born to this union: Levi "Lee" (1901-1980), Lillian (1904) and James (1911-1987). This family resided in Clay Township.

The fourth generation began with Lee, born in Howard County. A farmer, Lee married Marvel Shaffer (1902) of Galveston. They purchased a farm on the Howard-Miami County Line and raised their five children in Miami County. Born to this union were: Russell (1924), Mary Lou Harrell (1927), Elizabeth Grondalski (1930), Richard (1933), and Sharron McConnell (1941).

189

Jane, Kent, David and Dick Fawcett

Richard, author of this article, helped on this farm until entering the U.S. Army (1953-1955). He later attended Indiana University and Earlham College. He is an employee of Chrysler Corporation and at present is New Programs Coordinator for the Transmission Division.

In 1960 Richard married Anna Jane Willson (1939), the daughter of Lawrence and Geneva (Agness) Willson of Miami County. She has a brother Edward L. Willson of Bunker Hill and a sister Waneta Johnson of Galveston, IN.

Jane attended Indiana Central Business College. She has held secretarial positions with Indiana State Highway Commission, Indianapolis, Delco Electronics, Purdue University and Indiana University. Both are active in numerous civic organizations and are members of First Presbyterian Church.

Their two sons were born in Howard County. David Alan (1963) and Kent Evan (1966), graduated from Haworth High School and Purdue University. David, a consulting engineer with EBASCO Environmental Group, lives in Atlanta, GA. He will marry Yolande deGastyne of Alexander, VA, July 1994. Kent, an operations manager with K-Mart Corporation, lives in Roswell, GA. Kent married Ginger Edwards of Robbinsville, NC. They have a son Jordan Conner born 1993.

JOHN FELLOW - John Fellow was born Sept. 13, 1793 in Wayne County, NC, the son of Robert and Rachel Peelle Fellow. John was married in 1827 to Abigail Coleman, daughter of Elijah and Mary Parker Coleman. In 1832 they moved, with three small children, to Wayne County, IN where six more children were born. In 1852 John and Abigail purchased 115 acres of land in Howard County, IN, Union Township, later adding an additional 40 acres. Their children were Robert who married Elizabeth Hubbard, Mary who married a Reece, Rachel who married Chuza Moorman, Elijah who married Susanna White, Elisha who married Ann Eliza Bowman, John who married Ann Baldwin, Jane who married the Reverend Jesse Hammer Ellis, Bennett who married Ruth Ann Ridgeway, and Abigail who married Stephen Decatur Shockney.

There was an incident that occurred at their home that has been recounted many times in the family and is worthy of note. It happened during the Civil War, in the fall of 1863. John and Abigail Fellow still had their youngest son at home with them. Also living with them was their daughter Rachel who had married a widower, Chuza Moorman. Chuza had a son by his first marriage and they then had three smaller children. There was an older log cabin nearby. John Fellow allowed a black man, Davy Coplan, and his family to move into this cabin. One night a group of about 30 men came. They were described by John's granddaughter, Jane Shockney Thomas, as "southern sympathizers, democrats, bushwackers". They threw rocks at both the Fellow home and the log-cabin, breaking windows and hitting one of the black children on the head. One rock split the headboard of the bed where Chuza and Rachel Fellow Moorman were sleeping. When the family and friends went to check on them the next morning, they thankfully found them with no serious injuries. Davy Coplan, however, loaded up his family that very day and returned to their previous home. The Fellow and Shockney families were both upset and embarrassed by this incident. The Coplans lived near Jane Shockney Thomas' other grandparents, John and Jerusha Anderson Shockney in Randolph County, IN and she saw them when she would visit there. The Fellow home where this occurred is still standing. *Submitted by Joyce E. Bowman, great-granddaughter of Stephen Decatur and Abigail Fellow Shockney*

FISHER - John Fisher was born in Hesse-Cassel, Germany. He was one of the Hessian soldiers under the British government. John was under General Cornwallis and was taken prisoner by General Washington in the Revolutionary War. When he was set free, he located in Bedford County, PA and there twice married, reared a family of 15 children and spent the remainder of his life.

Jonathan Fisher was born in Bedford County, PA, June 7, 1815 and is the youngest of three children born to John and Hannah (Berriner) Fisher. Jonathan was reared on the farm, and having lost his father when he was quite young, he moved with his mother to Henry County, IN in 1832. He remained about two years at home with his stepfather, Jacob Houser; he then worked as an apprentice at the carpenter's trade for two years when he began to take contracts for himself. A few years later, he moved to Delaware County and on Aug. 11, 1836, was there married to Rachel Howell, a native of Wayne County. They have 10 children, seven of whom survived: Calvin, Mary A., William, Louisa, Marilla, Eli C. and Susan. Jonathan located in Howard County, IN Nov. 6, 1846 and in the spring of 1849 he went on foot to Fort Wayne to enter 80 acres of land which he had pre-empted in Liberty Township. He was among the large hunters, and the first year lived on the profits of hunting; he killed 125 deer in one year and as soon as he could get work at his trade, abandoned hunting and worked until his health failed. Jonathan enlisted May 24, 1864 in Company A, 137th Indiana Volunteer Infantry and was mustered in at Indianapolis. He marched south to Duck River Bridge (Tennessee) where he had guard duty for five months until he was honorably discharged. Rachel Fisher died April 8, 1873 and shortly after, Jonathan married Margaret (Weimer) Jones. Their children are: Jonathan, Estella, Frederick D., Mabelle, and James Blaine-our grandfather. Jonathan and Margaret were members of the New Light Church; he cast his first presidential vote for General Harrison in 1836; he was Justice of the Peace in Liberty township for one term; constable three terms; and supervisor one year. He was one of the earliest settlers of Liberty Township.

James and Anna (Davis) Fisher

James married Anna (Lydia Ann) Davis, daughter of Isaac and Josephine (Stone) in 1902. Both worked at the Indiana Tumbler and Goblet Company in Greentown until it burned in June 1903. It was never rebuilt. James then went to Lancaster, OH to work in a glass factory, returned home, and worked for Jenkins Glass Company. He was a glass presser when he started working at 11 years of age. When Anna died in 1989—just four months shy of her 108th birthday—she was the last surviving employee. James also worked in several other glass factories and the last one was Dunkirk. He was also employed at General Motors and retired in 1953.

Their children are Helen Moran, Omer-our father, Esther Rush, Ruth Twineham, Roy, and James.

Omer married Juanita Bessie Warner in 1929. He also worked for Jenkins Glass Company. Omer retired from Continental Steel Corporation in December 1974. Both of them have been members of the Kokomo Church of Christ since 1963. He was an avid hunter and still fishes at his age of 83 years. He enjoys working in his large garden which supplies him and his children with vegetables. Juanita worked at Delco Radio during World War II. She was also president of her World War Mothers Unit. She had several other jobs but the most important to her was her family. Mother died in 1986. Their children are: Juanita Mae, Robert Joe, Patsy Jean, Charlotte Sue, and Sandra Kay. "Peggy" (Juanita Mae) is married to Pat Daly. Pat is retired from Delco. Their children are Patrick Joe Daly, Mrs. Nancy Sue Drake (Rev. Kim E.) and Mrs. Cindy Gay Tino (Michael). Grandchildren are Cameron and Carah Daly, Summer and Aubrey Drake, and Clayton and Coty Marshall (Tino). Joe served in the Korean Conflict. He is married to Ollie (Purvis). He was laboratory supervisor at Howard Community Hospital for 32 years upon retirement. Ollie is a registered nurse and is employed at Taylor School Corporation. Their children are Walter Joe, Cynthia Diane, Mrs. Julia Lynn Miller (Douglas), and John Matthew. Grandchildren are Aaron, Nathan, Clayton (Walter's sons), and Kyle and Cierra (John's children). Patsy was born in Dallas, TX to Katherine (Harness) and Clarence Fisher-formerly of Kokomo. In the early year of 1949, Patty came into our family permanently as a loving daughter and sister. Patty is married to Tom Sanders who is a supervisor of the model shop at Delco. Their children are Mrs. Carol Reed (Thomas), Gary Allen (Diana), Mark Edward (Kathianne), and Paul Wesley (Monica). Grandchildren are Holly, Matthew, Abby Reed, Wendy, Benjamin, Nicholas, Jacob (Gary's children), Katy, Hannah, Isaac (Mark's children), Brandon and Jessica Carter and Ryne (Paul's children).

Juanita and Omer Fisher

Sue is married to Ronald Pelgen and they own and operate Printcraft Press. Their children are Peggy Denice DeBard, Teresa Ann Hintz (Jim), Michael Lee (Virginia), Cheryl Marie, and David Gabriel. Grandchildren are Kevin, Ronald and Robert (twins) DeBard, Jami, Tiffany, and Victoria Hintz. Robert (Michael's child) and Cody (David's child). One great-grandchild, Kevin Wilson (Jami's child).

Sandy is married to Thomas Maddox Jr. Tom is a pipefitter at Delco and Sandy is an elected school board member for Taylor Corporation serving a second term. Their children are Stacey Marie, Thomas Brian, Anthony Joe, Robert Scott, and Daniel Lee. Stacey has an associate degree from Purdue in electrical engineering. Brian is employed at Hewitt Tool and Die. Tony, Scott, and Danny are students at Taylor schools. They have one grandchild. Corey (Brian's child). *Submitted by Sandra K. Maddox and Peggy Daly.*

FISHER - Zachariah Fisher and Phebe Brackett were married March 1, 1791 in Shelby County, KY. They had a double wedding with Jessamine Boone and George Wilcox, performed by Joshua Morris, a famous Baptist minister.

Zachariah had slaves. Their son, John Benford (1800-1887) did not approve of slavery, so he and his wife, Abigail Montgomery (1809-1884) moved to Montgomery County, IN in 1832. Here, they encountered many hazardous experiences of pioneer days. Indians were frequent callers to their cabin. They later moved to Howard County in a settlement west of Kokomo, known as Kappa. Their children were William Montgomery, James Owen, and Eliza Ann.

James Owen (1828-1920) married Ann French (1833-1864), daughter of James and Abigail (McGilliard) French. They pioneered in Howard County on a farm inherited by Ann from her parents. James' sister, Eliza Ann (Lyda) Fisher (1830-1901), married Ann's brother, Ralph French (1827-1879).

John Benford and Abigail (Montgomery) Fisher, Kappa, Indiana

James O. and Ann (French) Fisher had John Benford, Harvey Allen, Abigail Eliza, James Montgomery, and William. After Ann passed away, James O. married Eliza Jane Kepner (1848-1924) and their children were Anna, Haskett, Reece, David, and Amos. James O. and Eliza Jane retired in Galveston.

John Benford (1850-1913) married Lydia Caroline Plank (1855-1887), daughter of Elias and Anna Catherine (Heinmiller) Plank of Young America. Anna Catherine was from one of Howard County's early families - Johannes and Anna Elizabeth Heinmiller. The children of John Benford and Lydia Caroline (Plank) Fisher were Ralph Thomas, John Elias, Martha Catherine, and Dora Sylvia.

John Elias Fisher (1875-1972) took a homestead in 1904 at Meridian, ID and married Estella Hensell (1878-1967). She was a teacher and faithful Christian. John was an active member, elder, and Bible school teacher in the Christian church for over 70 years. They had one daughter, Jean, author of this article, born 1922. Jean was active in gospel music and was a church pianist for 47 years. She married Scott Heinmiller and lived in Howard County for six years. *Submitted by Jean Fisher Heinmiller*

HENRY FISHER - Henry Fisher was born in Maryland around 1792. He had at least three brothers, William, Daniel, and Noah. In the early years of the 1800s, all four brothers left Maryland. Henry moved to Guilford County, NC, where he married Mary "Polly" Dillon about April 24, 1810. William and Daniel Fisher moved to Knox County, TN and Noah to Rhea County, TN. Noah married Polly Dillon's sister, Dorcas Dillon, both of whom were born in Maryland, daughters of John Dillon. It is thought that the Fishers and Dillons knew each other in Maryland and that Henry Fisher and John Dillon went to Guilford County, NC together.

Henry and Polly reared at least nine children in Guilford County, namely John D. (who married Nancy Trotter), Solathiel (who married Polly Northum), Noah (who married Polly Manship, and later Zelphy White), Lydia (who married Joab Leonard), Sarah (who married Lindsay Manship), Delia (who married William Manship), Henry, Mary (who married Daniel Coleman), and Martha Jane (who married Eli Leonard).

Henry may have been the owner of a gold mine south of Greensboro know as Fishers Mine. It is known that the family lived in the vicinity of this mine. Around 1839 or 1840, Sarah and Lindsay Manship became the first of the family to leave North Carolina for Indiana, relocating in Hamilton County. Next were Henry's sons John D., Solathiel, Noah, and Henry who left in the 1850s, and also went to Hamilton County. The place they lived came to be known as Fisher's Switch, and later Fishers, IN. Henry also moved to Indiana during the 1850s. His wife Polly died sometime between 1850 and 1860, and it isn't known whether she made the long journey with him to Indiana. Henry relocated in Taylor Township of Howard County, living with his daughter Delia Manship and her husband William. Only Henry's daughters Lydia, Mary, and Martha Jane remained in Guilford County. Henry lived in Howard County until his death on May 31, 1871. He is buried at Albright Cemetery. *Submitted by Paul Joseph Weaver*

JOHN F. AND GERNA J. FITE - Having worked in Howard County for 13 years, John and Gerna decided to move here from Madison County once their youngest child had graduated form high school in 1972.

John Frederick Fite Jr. was born in Omaha, NB on April 4, 1931. John's parents were John and Nellie (Ashby) Fite, both born in Madison County, IN. John was raised mainly in Madison County, graduating from Anderson High School in 1949. He married his high school sweetheart, Gerna Ellis, on March 4, 1950. John started working at the Chrysler Plant in New Castle, IN in 1950, eventually transferring to the Kokomo plant in 1959 where he worked his way up to the position of quality control analyst. John retired from the casting plan in May 1990.

Gerna and John Fite

John's parents were John Frederick Fite Sr. and Nellie Victoria Ashby. John Sr. was born n May 24, 1906 in Elwood, Madison County, IN to John Perry and Elizabeth (Rhuddy) Fite. John Sr. did a lot of traveling with his work, but he eventually went to work for the Chrysler Corporation in New Castle, IN as a tool and die maker. He married Nellie on March 29, 1924 in Tipton, Tipton County, IN. Nellie was the daughter of Jerimiah and Ida May (Lutz) Ashby. She was born on Aug. 2, 1909 in Elwood, Madison County, IN. John and Nellie raised five children, John being the second oldest.

Gerna Jeanette Ellis was born in the small town of Moonsville, IN in Madison County on Sept. 19, 1932. She is the daughter of Marvin and Nancy Violetta (Noble) Ellis. Both Marvin and Violette were born in Madison County, IN.

Marvin's parents were Flurry and Effie (Hightchew) Ellis. Flurry and Effie were natives of Owenton, Owen County, KY. Marvin worked at Delco-Remy in Anderson, Madison County, IN and also in construction. He married Nancy Violetta Noble on Oct. 4, 1930 in Madison county, IN. He died on July 27, 1953 from a car accident, leaving Violetta to raise nine children. Violetta was the daughter of Frederick and Leafy (Harrison) Noble. She was born on Jan. 21, 1913 in Moonsville, Madison County, IN. Violetta died on March 8, 1986 and is buried alongside her husband in the Moonsville Cemetery in Madison County, IN.

John and Gerna have four children: Marsha Kay who married Daryl Smith and has two children Brady and Valarie; Linda Gail who married Jerry Turner and has two children Jerry Jr. and Carrie along with four step-children, Tanya, Debbie, James and Michael; Sandra Jeanne who married James Hamilton and has two children Jason and Justin; and Michael Eugene.

John and Gerna are members of the Eagles Lodge in Kokomo where John was auditor for one year. Just about every Saturday night, they will be dancing at the lodge. Since his retirement John has taken an interest in woodcrafting. Gerna enjoys sewing and helping her daughter do genealogy.

Although they are not original natives of Howard County, they have been happy to call Greentown their home for the past 22 years.

IRL AND GRACE FIVECOATE - Irl Loyd Fivecoate (born April 13, 1903, Cass Co., IN) is the oldest of 13 children of Ira and Maude (Miller) Fivecoate. Ira is a son of Benjamin and Christenna (Kessler) Fivecoate (Refer to Benjamin Fivecoate). Although, Ira and Maude were hard working farmers, they found time to enjoy music. Ira played the violin by ear, taught his seven younger children to play several stringed instruments and they all played as a group for public events.

Irl was born near Hoover, Cass County, IN, living there until 1910, then moved to Miami County, IN, where some of his fondest childhood memories were "when the Circus came to town" (Peru, IN) and seeing Buffalo Bill's Wild West Show.

Grace and Irl Fivecoate

Irl had four sisters: Leona, Irene, Marie and Emmaline, and eight brothers: Glen, Russell, Harold, Raymond, Carl, Loren, Gerald and Kenneth, of whom Irl, Harold, Raymond, Gerald and Kenneth are still living.

Being the oldest son, Irl helped his father farm when most his age were in school. He was exceptional in arithmetic, sometimes solving problems his one-room school teacher could not. Later on in life he completed drafting and surveyor's courses by mail.

Grace Leona Stafford (born Dec. 12, 1908, died Aug. 1, 1975, Howard County, IN), was next to the youngest of ten children of George B. McClellan Stafford and Ella Mae (Yater) Stafford. (Refer to George Stafford).

She was a member of the Free Methodist Church, Kokomo, IN. One of her prized possessions was a framed picture of Christ given to her as a young girl for perfect Sunday School attendance.

Grace met Irl in May, 1924, "set up" by her sister Rettamae and his sister Marie. Irl and Grace's father were working at the same farm near Grace's older sister Lettie and husband Jake Metz. They were married Sept. 17, 1927 in Howard County, IN.

They lived near Mexico, IN, while Irl worked for the Chesapeake and Ohio Railroad out of Peru, IN, 1924-1928. In 1928 they moved to North Buckeye, Kokomo, IN next to Grace's sister Beulah and husband Jesse Fivecoate. (Refer to Jesse Ernest Fivecoate). Irl worked for the Kokomo Pottery until the Depression. In 1930 he worked for the WPA Org. making $8.00 a week carrying two 14 qt. buckets of water (225 lbs. a day) to workers on the construction of 11 miles of State Road 22 east of Kokomo for 12 hours, and three more hours watering "sack covered" cement. Later he worked for "Splint" Gilbert and then for Edwin Matlock for $6.00 a week, house and "found".

He worked for Continental Steel, Kokomo, 1936-1943. He started his own waste removal service on a small rented farm west of Kokomo. In 1941 he bought the 145 acre "Purdum Farm" south of Kokomo, where he continued his business and farming and raised some of the largest Berkshire-Hampshire hogs in the state.

Although Irl was a very busy man, he would take the whole family to a movie every Saturday night and a ride in the country or visit with friends and relatives on Sunday. Grace was a very quiet, gentle lady who worked very hard caring for their eight children, all born at home and "put up" large quantities of food each year and when possible, made sure they attended Sunday School. When she found time, she liked to "chord" on the piano and sing church songs.

Grace and Irl Fivecoate

In 1960 Irl's sons Clarence, Lloyd and Leonard took over the business, until 1973. Grace and Irl lived at Nyona Lake, Fulton County, IN until 1963 when they sold their farm to the city's rapidly growing business and industry. They later bought the 160 acre Newby Farm and Orchard west of Russiaville. As a retired farmer, he could spend more time doing what he loved best, gardening and caring for his apple orchard.

Grace and Irl's children:

Roy Almon, married Barbara Ray June 15, 1952, one son Mark and one daughter Malinda.

Catherine Joan married Charles Kraner Oct. 19, 1958 (Refer to Charles Kraner).

Clarence Edward married Connie Kiser Jan. 25, 1959 (died July 18, 1974), one daughter Christina and one son Chad (died July 18, 1974). Married Judy Edwards August 1975.

Lloyd Wayne married Sue Williams May 29, 1960, one son Brad and one daughter, Kim.

Leonard Max married Pat Herren Aug. 7, 1960, four sons, Bart, Brent, Mike and Steve.

Harry Ray married Candy Morgan September 1962 (divorced 1983), two sons, Troy and Todd.

Eldon Dallas.

Clyde Allen married Robbin Havens Feb. 14, 1976, (divorced 1980), one son, Josh.

Irl and Grace Fivecoate have 21 grandchildren and 31 great-grandchildren.

Irl married Gladys Sottong Oct. 28, 1978. There was a surprise celebration given for Irl on his 90th birthday, April 13, 1993 with over 175 attending.

JESSE ERNEST FIVECOATE - Jesse Ernest Fivecoate (1889-1971) grew up on a farm east of Logansport, between Adamsborough and Hoover, near the north bank of the Eel River. He located in Howard County in 1915.

Jesse's great-grandfather, Michael Fivecoat (1788-1866?), was born in Pennsylvania, and settled near the town of Cadiz, OH before 1809. Michael served two enlistments with the Ohio Militia fighting against the British during the War of 1812. After the war, Michael married Sarah ____ and they made their home in the Cadiz area until the 1840s.

In 1849, Jesse's grandfather, Thomas Fivecoate (1820-1863), (Michael's oldest son), his wife Susannah Rush (1823-1863), and their three daughters, Sarah (1844), Mary (1846-1877) and Susannah (1848-1878), left their home in Ohio and moved to Adams County, IN. Thomas and Susannah's sons, Benjamin Thomas (1853-1937) and James Almon (1857-191?) were born at the new Fivecoate home in Adams County. Thomas farmed and also purchased swamp and wilderness land from the State, which he drained and cleared and resold as farm land.

Thomas joined the Union Army in 1862 and was captured at the Battle of Mundfordville, KY. Susannah became very ill shortly after Thomas left for duty, and died in April of 1863. Thomas died on Christmas Day in that same year. The Fivecoate children were separated and sent to live with family and friends. Benjamin and James Almon spent the winter of 1864-65 with their grandfather, Michael (age 76-77), who had also moved into Adams County. They separated shortly after that and passed from family to family, working to "earn their keep."

At age 14, Benjamin began an apprenticeship and later became a shoemaker. He also worked as a farmhand throughout northeastern Indiana, southern Michigan and western Ohio. In addition, he cleared land, built cabins and canal boats, and, for a while, worked on the canal between Bull Rapids and Fort Wayne.

Benjamin Fivecoate married Christena Emaline Kessler (1863-1942) Jan. 1, 1878. They raised a family of nine children: Ira, Nellie, Nora, Edith, Charles, Florence, Jesse, Pearl and Lulu. Benjamin farmed and served as Justice of the Peace for Cass County. In retirement, Benjamin made extra income by making oak rocking chairs. Several of the chairs he made are still in service today. The "E" on the end of the Fivecoate name identifies Benjamin's descendants.

In 1917, Jesse Earnest Fivecoate enlisted in Howard County to serve in World War I. He served in France with the 104th Infantry Division and was a member of the renowned 40 and 8. Jesse was wounded twice and was seriously injured with poison gas. He was decorated and received the Purple Heart.

Jesse worked as a molder, and later as an electrician, for Hoosier Iron in the 1920's. He also operated a photography business and provided "while you wait" photographs in Highland Park with a mobile darkroom. He was appointed city electrician in 1936 and remained in that position until he retired in 1956.

Jesse married Beulah Marie Stafford (1901-1982) in 1918. (See George B. Stafford). They made their home at 2529 North Buckeye Street in Kokomo. They were life members of the North Buckeye Friends Church, and provided a Christian home for their children. Beulah enjoyed teaching Sunday School and working with the youth. Beulah and Jesse's seven children are George, Benjamin, Lowell, Grace, Dorothy, Raymond, and Jesse Edward.

George "Pete" served in the Navy during WWII as a chief petty officer. He served in the South Pacific and was later stationed in Washington, D.C. In the 1950's he joined Delco Radio where he worked as an engineering supervisor. George married Mary Pickett. Their five children are George (Bud), Dennis, and the triplets, Shirley, Sheryl, and Sharon.

Benjamin also served in the Navy and survived being on three ships which were destroyed in the South Pacific. Following the war he worked as a fireman and later became the fire inspector of the City of Kokomo. Benjamin married Betty Jo Leach. Gerald, Joseph, and John Craig "Jack" are their three sons.

Lowell served in the Navy as a gunner on Merchant Marine ships during the war. He received the Purple Heart for wounds received during a German bombing raid near Cairo, Egypt. He returned to Continental Steel in 1945, where he worked as supervisor of the Nail Mill. Lowell married Eva Hightower, and their children are Janice, Robert, Donald and Jane.

Grace "Teny" is a graduate of the Good Samaritan School of Nursing, and did her affiliate nurse's training with St. John's Hospital in Springfield, IL. She married Earl Quinn Jr. after he returned from the Navy following WWII. Thomas Michael, Susan Jane, and Timothy Mark are their children. (See Earl Quinn, Jr.)

Dorothy and her sister Grace sang at church activities and for special occasions. Dorothy was engaged to Norman Goshern. Dorothy drowned while on an outing at Nyona Lake.

Raymond "Smoke" has been with Delongs Auto Parts since the 1950's, working in the building where the first automobiles in Kokomo were built. He is an excellent woodworker, and makes cradles for the new babies in the family. Raymond married Wanda McGuire. Cynthia Lynn "Cindy" and Allen Ray are their children.

Jesse Edward "Ed," served in the USAF with the Strategic Air Command. While stationed in northern Greenland, he flew aboard KC-97 refueling tankers on missions over the polar regions to refuel reconnaissance aircraft patrolling the Russian border. Ed worked at both Space Centers: The Atlantic Missile Range at Cape Canaveral, FL, and The Pacific Missile Range at Vandenberg AFB, CA. He also worked with the Strategic Air Command's missile installations in Kansas and Arizona. At present Ed is a senior control design engineer with Delco Electronics. In 1962, Ed married Susan Sandifur. Ed and Susan's children are Jeffrey and Christina.

Christy is a senior at Purdue University, Kokomo Campus. She is a volunteer worker for the American Red Cross and also serves on the mayor's advisory board. Christy is a gifted pianist and poet, and is a member of the IUK Singers. Jeff is a graduate of the Purdue-Kranert School of Business Management, and is self-employed. Jeff married Chris McComas, a graduate of the Purdue School of Pharmacy. Their two children are Micah and Abigayle. Micah is an aspiring scientist, and Abigayle is the 1993-1994 Purdue Alumni Association poster girl, representing the class of 2013. *Submitted by J.E. Fivecoate*

IVA (BAKER) FLETCHER - Iva Baker Fletcher was born on a farm in Clinton County, IN on Oct. 16, 1896 to Andrew and Nancy Jane (Laughner) Baker. She was the oldest of the couple's five children and the only one still living. Her paternal grandparents were William and Phebe (Pease) Baker, who moved into Forest Township, Clinton County, IN from Darke County, OH about 1853. Her maternal grandparents, William and Elizabeth (Ottinger) Laughner, were originally from Greene County, TN. They had come separately to Boone County, IN, where they met and married.

Iva Baker Fletcher

On Aug. 22, 1916, Iva Baker married Thomas Dayton Fletcher, born Nov. 22, 1897, son of long time Clinton County residents, James and Dove (Adair) Fletcher. Thomas Dayton and Iva Fletcher lived on his grandfather, Thomas Benton Fletcher's, farm in Forest Township, Clinton County, IN, until moving into Kokomo in 1922. Dayton worked for P.P. Glass Co. until it closed in 1928 and then found employment at the Steel Mill as a sheet metalist, where he worked until he retired in 1962.

The couple had eight children, two born while they lived on the farm and six more after they moved into Kokomo. Of the eight children, six lived to adulthood and are all still living: two boys, Thomas Doyle Fletcher of Largo, FL and Harold Eugene Fletcher of Peru, IN; and four girls, Pauline Fowler of Russiaville, IN; Thelma Arlene McNally of Atlanta, GA; Norma Jean Mann of Kokomo, IN and Edna May Canard of Tipton County, IN. At last count there are 21 grandchildren, 37 great-grandchildren and several great-great grandchildren.

About the time the couple moved into Kokomo, Dayton took up the hobby of training, racing, and showing coon dogs, winning many trophies for his efforts. Iva felt the need for a hobby, as well, and in 1947 began to raise Red-factor canaries. She joined the Bird Fanciers Club and in the next 30 years won a great number of trophies for the canaries she raised, in the club's annual bird show. When Iva reached the age of 80, she decided to give up her hobby, as the strain of getting up before dawn to see to the feeding of newly-hatched birds and dealing with the day-to-day responsibilities seemed a bit too much for her. Today, she still lives by herself in the house that she and her husband, who died in 1964, bought over 70 years ago. At age 97, she enjoys visits from her family, friends and neighbors and remembers fondly the events of her long life - her family, her move into Kokomo, the changes in the world and world events. *Submitted by Nancy Callahan, granddaughter, and Thelma Arlene McNally, daughter*

FLUHART - Margaret Elizabeth Morris, found elsewhere in this book, daughter of Edward Isaac Morris and Margaret Eve Uhrig, died Aug. 5, 1959 at Mt. Vernon, OH and was buried at Calvary Cemetery, Mt. Vernon, OH. At one time she was employed by the Hocking Valley Railroad, until they merged with another line. Later worked at the Ohio State Office Building on Front Street, in Columbus, OH. Margaret was married July 17, 1935 in Columbus, OH to Daniel Odford Fluhart. He was born July 17, 1901 in Columbus, OH to Thomas Fluhart and Rose Starner. He died Jan. 11, 1974 in Columbus, OH. Burial was in Union Cemetery, Columbus, OH. Daniel, a gateman at the Union Depot in Columbus, OH, took and punched tickets from railroad passengers. Around 1938, they purchased a farm east of Marengo, OH, and in 1944 the family moved to a 113 acre farm in Wayne Township, Knox County, OH. In 1960 Daniel Fluhart sold the farm and moved to Lake Wales, FL.

Children of Margaret and Daniel Fluhart are: Danny Morris, born May 30, 1941 at Columbus, OH and Mary Patricia, born March 17, 1944 at Delaware, OH.

Mary Patricia Fluhart was married Sept. 21, 1963 at Jacksonville, FL to Richard Marlin Thomas. Richard was born May 11, 1943 at Phoenixville, PA. They reside at Powder Springs, GA. Their two daughters are Kathryn Ann Thomas, born June 30, 1967 in Jacksonville, FL and Susan Elizabeth Thomas born Nov. 9, 1972 in Austell, GA. Katherine Thomas was married Sept. 5, 1987 to David Lee Todd, born April 6, 1965 in California. Their two children are: Sarah Elizabeth, born Dec. 10, 1990 at Austell, GA and Charles Thomas, born Jan. 28, 1993 at Austell, GA.

Danny Morris Fluhart attended public school in Fredericktown, OH, where he graduated in 1959. He has been employed with the Federal Bureau of Investigation, Washington, DC, since Feb. 8, 1960. Danny was editor of the Meek-Meeks Genealogist for nine years and publisher of the Ogle/Ogles Genealogist for three years. He also compiled the 1,055 paged book "Meek Family of Washington County, VA" in 1989. He is currently vice president of Dr. Samuel A. Mudd Society and holds several offices in the Grange Organization. He is very active in genealogy and a member of several genealogy societies in Maryland and Ohio.

Danny Fluhart married Elizabeth Herberg Sept. 18, 1965 at Hollywood, MD. Elizabeth was born Dec. 3, 1942 at Nassiedel, Silesia, Germany, now part of Poland, and is the daughter of Richard Herberg and Elisabeth Beyer. The family arrived in America April 12, 1954 on the USNS *General C.C. Ballou*, T-AP 157. Their first 1 1/2 years of married life was spent in an apartment in Washington, D.C. They later rented a home in Aquasco, MD and in December 1969 moved to their present home, near Hughesville, MD, which is situated on 5 1/2 acres.

The Fluharts have seven children: Thomas Edward, born Oct. 21, 1968; John August, born Feb. 21, 1970; Margaret Elizabeth, born Sept. 23, 1971; Elizabeth Ann, born Feb. 8, 1973; Catherine Marie, born July 17, 1974; Sarah Ellen, born May 14, 1978 and Daniel Herberg, on Dec. 7, 1981. All children were born at Leonardtown, MD except Sarah who was born in LaPlata, MD. Margaret Fluhart was married Dec. 12, 1992 to Kevin Joseph Wetherald and Elizabeth Fluhart was married June 19, 1993 to Mark Stephen Custer.

The Fluhart family reside at Box 221E, Hoffman Road, Waldorf, MD 20601. They are members of Brandywine Grange #348 and Saint Francis De Sales Church, Benedict, MD.

FOLAND - Sherwood Foland owned about 100 acres at the corner of 300 S. and 900 E. in Union Township. He grain farmed the land for his living, and a handsome living it needed to be, for there were four boys and six girls in the family.

All of the boys' first names began with the letter "F". There was Frederick, Fletcher, Forrest, and Franklin. All the girls' names began with an "M": Mildred (Everling), Minardean (Graham), Miriam (Smith), Melinda (Metz), Madonna (Miller), and Melbadean (Downing).

Sherwood Foland was an ambitious farmer, always the first—or one of the first—to plant his crops in the spring. He liked a modern car too. At one time he drove a 1930 Nash "straight eight" cylinder, twin ignition engine. It was a sedan with big wire wheels, with spare tires mounted in the front fender wells, and headlights the size of small moons—a real classic.

The Folands' only livestock consisted of horses. Each spring Fred Foland would throw a plow onto a mud sled, hitch two horses to it, and come to the village of Phlox a few miles away, to plow gardens.

The Foland family suffered several grievous losses of family members over the years, particularly the Franklin Foland family. In January, 1962, young Bradley Foland accidentally drowned in the baptismal of the old Jerome Christian Church, where his father Franklin served as janitor.

In December, 1971, older brothers Craig and Curtis were out hunting near their home southwest of Phlox. While they were experimenting with an automatic safety on one of their guns, it fired, striking Craig in the side. He died the next day.

A gifted student, Craig had been enrolled in pre-med school at Indiana University-Kokomo. He was also an outstanding athlete at Eastern High School; each year the school presents the Craig A. Foland Mental Attitude Award to the most deserving athlete.

In September, 1980, Franklin Foland was severely injured in an accident at Cabot Industries where he was employed. He died from those injuries later that month.

A granddaughter of Sherwood Foland, Traci Everling, perished in an accident on the bridge over Wildcat Creek on the west edge of Greentown a few years ago.

Today the Sherwood Foland house is home to another family, and others tend the field he once farmed; but the Foland name is still prominent in the local area. *Submitted by Jeff Hatton*

FORD - Reeve Ford was born in 1909, in Union County, TN. Reeve married Minerva Summers and they had four sons, Lloyd Edgar, Marvin, Donald and Floyd.

Reeve and Minerva were in a fatal car accident on Aug. 12, 1939 in Howard County, IN. Reeve, Marvin, and Lloyd Edgar died in the car accident. About a year later, Donald, age three, died from injuries due to the accident. Reeve and Minerva was expecting their fourth child at the time of the crash. The child survived the wreck and was born on Oct. 5, 1939, two months after Reeve died. Floyd Ford married Betty (Massey) Young. Betty had four children by her first marriage. Floyd had no children. Floyd is Reeve's only living child.

Minerva was married to Walker McDaniels before she married Reeve. She had one son, Virgil McDaniels. After Reeve died, Minerva married Floyd Randall and they had three children: Thomas, Shirley and Alvin. Later she married again to Herbert Lester Davis, and they had four children: Lloyd, Morris, Herbert Jr. and Robert.

Reeve's parents were James B. Ford (mother's name unknown). James B. was born December 1884, in Union County, TN. James and his wife had two sons, Reeve and Brutus. James married again to Ethel Loy, and they had seven children: Parley, Dellie and Stellie (twins), Pauline, Lee, Milas, and Willie.

Reeve's grandparents were Thomas A. and Amanda E. (Nelson) Ford. Thomas was born in July 1857 and died in 1934, in Union County, TN. Amanda was born on April 10, 1870, and died in Union County, TN, and they are buried in the Nelson Cemetery in Maynardsville, TN.

Thomas and Amanda were married in Union County, TN in 1884. They had nine children: James B., Emily Lucreen, William Robert, Rufus, Ida J., Osco, Theodore Roosvelt, Nora, and Charles Lee.

William, Rufus, Theodore, and Charles Lee moved to Howard County, IN. They all died in Howard County, IN, but were buried in Union County, TN.

William Robert married Lucretia (Engle) Ford, and they had five children: Hattie, Mannie, James Parlon, Goldie and Charles F. Ford. William was married three other times, but did not produce any children. William was Reeve's uncle.

Charles F. Ford married Hazel Ellison; they had two children, Jamakie Ann, and Jerry Allen. Jamakie married Roger Riggs, and they had two children, David Lee, and Pamela La'el Riggs. Jerry married Sheryl Riffe on Oct. 28, 1990. Sheryl had four children from a previous marriage, and they are: David, Eric, Travis, and Jennifer Smith.

Reeve's great-grandparents were William Robert and Elizabeth Ford of Tennessee. The Fords all came from Tennessee for as far back as my research has taken me, and that's to the year 1825. *Submitted by Floyd Ford, son of Reeve.*

FORDING - The first immigrant of the Fording family was Christopher Fording of England. He came to America in 1776 and settled in Westmoreland County, PA. Known children are John, Thomas who married Esther Ewan, Christopher and Jacob.

John Wesley Fording was born Sept. 7, 1808 in Pennsylvania and died Aug. 24, 1877 in Cass County, IN. He was the son of Thomas and Esther (Ewan) Fording. John Wesley Fording married Christina Shellenberger Oct. 1, 1829. They were living in Columbiana County, OH in 1830. Children of John and Christina Fording were: Ewan; Catharine Fording married A.J. Sargeant; Margaret Fording married David Parks; Thomas Fording; Esther Ann Fording married Jacob Owens; William Henry Harrison Fording married Jennie S. Morley; Jacob Fording; Mary Elizabeth Fording married Joseph A. Scott; Priscilla Fording married Norman T. Laurence; and John W. Fording Jr.

Ewan Fording was born April 8, 1830 in Ohio, died June 3, 1895 in Burrows, IN. On April 7, 1848 he married Deborah A. Phillips born Dec. 29, 1829 in Ohio and died July 24, 1877 in Miami County, IN. After the birth of four children, Ewan and Deborah moved to Indiana. By 1870 Ewan Fording, his parents, brothers and sisters were living in Carroll, Cass and Howard County. Children of Ewan and Deborah Fording are Christina Fording; Mary Catherine; Margaret E. Fording (1854-1924) married Albert L. Oldfather; Ida Viola Fording (1858-1920) married Shannon Galbreath; Minnie L. Fording (1860-1897) married Clinton Dunn who was a member of the Mongosia Tribe of Miami, IN; David Frank Fording; Rosa Fording (1865-1885); Jesse J. Fording (1869-1939) married Hulda Mae Talbert and Pearl Fording who married Will Gibson.

David Frank Fording was born May 13, 1862 in Cass County, IN and died May 17, 1930 in White County, IN. Frank was a very active member of many worthy causes. Because of this energetic talent, he applied himself to many occupations. He belonged to the Red Man, Moose, Odd Fellows, Rebekahs and Pocahontas lodges. He was also baptized in the faith of the Progressive Dunkard Church. On March 17, 1886 he married Carrie Catherine Bennett, orphan of Samuel and Catherine (Kunkle) Bennett. They were blessed with nine children; only seven reached adulthood: Clyde Elmer Fording (1889-1916) married Alta Marie Hight; Ocal (Doc) Fording (1891-1931) married Frances Marie Plummer, Nellie D. Fording (1894-1930) married Hubert Cleveland Hood; Ernest William (Bill) Fording (1896-1966) married Daisy Marie Herron; Russell Fording married Ruth Marie Rowland; Mabel Mary Fording (1902-1935) married Paul Elsworth Gordon; and Thelma A. Fording (1906-1976) married Floyd McGuire.

Russell Fording, the youngest son of David Frank and Carrie Catherine Fording, was born Nov. 18, 1898 and died Dec. 9, 1944. He married Ruth Marie Rowland in 1927 and to this union was born three children: Imajean Marie (Fording) married Franklin Welsh Martin, Jack Richard Fording (died infancy); and Bobby Russell Fording married Janet Sue Dunn. Russell was a good and loving father. In his short life span he was a hunter, fisherman, played horseshoes and was an avid sports fan. He was the owner of a grocery store, a barber and a carpenter. Russell worked at the Kokomo Machine Shop during WWII and put in many hours making bomb-shell casings for the servicemen overseas. He was very dedicated to his country. *Submitted by Imajean Marie Martin*

FORDYCE-TETER - Zed Lewis Fordyce was born in Kokomo, IN Feb. 17, 1937. He is the son of Murrel and Catherine Fordyce. He married Dorothy Lee Teter, daughter of Lewis and Hazel (Dickey) Teter in Kokomo,

June 28, 1958. The children born of this marriage are Jeffrey Lewis Fordyce (born Aug. 28, 1963) and Diane Elaine Fordyce (born April 26, 1965).

Jeffrey Lewis Fordyce presently resides in Greenwood, IN.

Diane Elaine Fordyce married James Everett Sheron (born Oct. 1, 1969) in Marion, IN on Sept. 4, 1992. They currently reside in Fairmount, IN.

FOUST - Jeff and Karen Foust were both born and raised in Kokomo, IN. Jeffrey Scott was born Jan. 5, 1956 to Patti and Marvin Foust. Karen Elizabeth was born to Max and Elizabeth Comer June 10, 1956. They both attended Kokomo Center Schools. Jeff graduated from Kokomo High School in 1974 and Karen graduated from Haworth High School the same year. They met previous to their Junior year in August at Crescent Dairy through a mutual friend. After graduation Jeff joined his father in landscaping at Foust Nursery which was located in Elwood, IN at the time. Karen went off to school at Indiana State University majoring in Art Education. She graduated in May of 1978. That summer, August 5th, Jeff and Karen were married at Grace United Methodist Church. Subsequently, Karen was fortunate enough to get a job as an elementary art teacher for Kokomo Center Schools.

One of the most wonderful events that has happened to them was the arrival of their two sons. Adam Michael joined them March 28, 1982 and then Justin Thomas arrived three years to the day later - March 28, 1985. Adam was really excited to gain a brother for his third birthday. A few weeks later he told them they could take him back to the hospital. Fortunately, they kept him.

Adam and Justin Foust

There was some sadness along with the growth of the Foust family. When Adam was just a little over a week old, his grandfather, Max Comer, suffered a heart attack and died three months later on June 18, 1982. Max had an advertising agency in the old transportation building located on Mulberry Street across the alley from Grace United Methodist Church. He moved to Kokomo from Swayzee where he had been raised and graduated from high school.

Elizabeth Comer, Karen's mother, grew up in Newcastle, IN. She was a home economics and physical education teacher in Selma, Swayzee and West Middleton Schools. She continued teaching while Max served in the Army during WWII. When he came home after his stint in the military, they started their family. Jan B. Comer was born Jan. 12, 1947 and Kevin M. Comer was born Jan. 25, 1949. Jan was hit by a car in front of his home on West Sycamore Street and only lived to the age of seven. Two years after his death Karen was born.

Marvin Foust, Jeff's father, was born in Sharp's Chapel, TN on Oct. 28, 1928. His family moved here when Marvin was six years old. His parents were Stella and Floyd Foust. Floyd moved up during the Depression because he had heard there were employment opportunities. He started landscaping in 1932, working out of a pickup truck selling evergreens and shrubs.

Patti Foust was born March 26, 1932 to Irma and Charles Rose in Kokomo. Patti graduated from Kokomo High School in 1949. She also lived in Oklahoma, Arizona and California for brief stints. She worked at Globe American and Syndicate Sales as a secretary during the fifties. She was the choir director for Calvary Baptist Church for several years. She has sung at numerous weddings and funerals over the years and presently sells Avon. They also have another son Mark Allen born May 23, 1960.

FRAZEE - William Samuel Frazee was born Nov. 12, 1817 in Butler County, OH, a son of Jonas Joseph Frazee who came to America from France. William Samuel married Mariah Randell April 12, 1838 in Hamilton County, OH. She was born in Connersville, IN April 19, 1820, the daughter of John W. Randell. William Samuel and Mariah came to Kokomo in the 1860's. He was a brick mason. They had 12 children, all born in Piqua, OH.

Anna Mariah, born March 13, 1840, first married Fred Lording around 1858. She later married Allen Wells and resided in Indianapolis. Angeline, born Jan. 8, 1842, died Nov. 13, 1842. John N., born Feb. 7, 1844, married Jan. 25, 1865 to Sarah Jane Simonton. He died May 17, 1916. Theodore F. was born May 22, 1846, married Matilda Addings around 1867 and resided in Indianapolis.

William David (Aug. 3, 1848-May 30, 1927) married Verlinda Mote May 1, 1870 in Kokomo. She was born July 27, 1852 in Jonesboro, a daughter of Jesse and Dorcas (Coppock) Mote who moved to Kokomo in 1860. Verlinda died Aug. 2, 1918 and both were buried in Crown Point Cemetery. William David was a contractor, and with his father, did some major work on the original courthouse in 1863. William and Verlinda made their home at 409 West Taylor Street. They had seven children, including a set of triplets. Only two children survived infancy, Nellie and George Oscar.

Nellie (Aug. 26, 1873-April 23, 1940) married William Zimmerman Feb. 9, 1893, one of eight children. He was a son of Casper and Elizabeth (Ardner) Zimmerman. Casper was born in Berne, Switzerland. Casper and wife lived in Swanton, OH. William and Nellie had a son, Robert Frazee Zimmerman (Jan. 22, 1894-March 1, 1949, buried Memorial Park Cemetery) who married Ethel Pearl Cramer, daughter of Edgar L. and Edna Maude (Helmer) Cramer, on July 23, 1920. They had two children: (1) Paul Warren, born April 29, 1921. He is an internationally known artist residing in Hartford, CT. (2) Lola Belle, born April 7, 1927, married Harry Damon Smith, Jr., son of Harry Damon and Mary Mildred (Dexter) Smith, Sr. They had three children: Rodger Damon, Linda Sue and Gerald Warren. Harry Damon Smith Jr., father of Rodger Smith, died Jan. 23, 1993.

David and Verlinda Frazee's other child, George Oscar, was born Jan. 4, 1882, married 1905 to Golda Ridgley, born 1838 in Mansfield, OH. She died Nov. 29, 1946 and he died Sept. 29, 1943.

The sixth child of Samuel and Mariah Frazee was George E. born Oct. 26, 1850, married in Indianapolis, Sept. 25, 1877, to Laura McFarland. Marvin E. (Nov. 22, 1852-Aug. 30, 1852). Frank was born in 1854. Clark (Jan. 9, 1855-Jan. 4, 1894) married in Indianapolis to Mary Francis Newhouse on Sept. 10, 1882. They lived in Peru, IN.

Joseph G. (May 3, 1857-May 11, 1933) married July 1, 1880, in Indianapolis to Lola Lodosca Newhouse. Laura, born Sept. 8, 1859, married in Frankfort May 21, 1888 to Wesley A. Darling. Clara, born Jan. 1, 1862, married in Indianapolis Oct. 26, 1880 to Charles J. Young. They lived in Portland, OR.

William and Mariah Frazee moved to Frankfort in 1869. Mariah died Aug. 28, 1890 and is buried in Crown Point Cemetery in Kokomo. William Samuel died Nov. 29, 1899. William and Mariah were third great-grandparents of Rodger Smith. *Submitted by Rodger Smith*

RICHARD L. AND DELORES M. FRAZIER - A job change brought Richard and Delores to Kokomo in 1957. Richard left Farnsworth Electronics in Fort Wayne for a position with Delco Radio.

Richard, better known as "Rusty", was born in Centralia, MO, Feb. 5, 1922. His father, Leslie Dwight, a railroad telegrapher and station agent, moved the family in 1932, to Pearl, IL, where Richard grew up and graduated from Pearl High School in 1939.

Delores was born in Mellott, IN, Aug. 6, 1925. She lived her early years in Mellott and graduated from Richland Township High School in 1943.

Richard enlisted in the Navy in August, 1941, prior to the U.S. entering World War II. He attended radio school and was assigned to the battleship USS *Massachusetts,* a sister ship of the USS *Indiana.* He was part of the commissioning crew and also the decommissioning crew after the war. He participated in the landings at North Africa at Casablanca, Algiers, his ship sustaining some shell-fire damage. After repairs, his ship was sent to the Pacific where they participated in every engagement from Guadalcanal to the landings at Japan in the closing days of the war. He transferred, at sea, from his battleship to a troop transport and made the initial landing in Japan with the 3rd Marine Division. He spent one period of 27 months without touching land. The last portion of his enlistment was spent at the Naval Air Station, San Juan, Puerto Rico.

Frazier Family - Back Row - L-R: Melissa, Eric, Donna and Gregory Frazier. Front row - L-R: Delores, Richard and Kimberly Frazier; August 1993

Delores was born with a great artistic talent and spent a lot of her time with her painting. She worked, after graduating from high school, in the art department at R.R. Donnelley's in Crawfordsville, IN.

Richard and Delores met through a mutual friend during the war and were married in Mellott, IN, June 22, 1947, after Richard was discharged from the Navy. They lived in Crawfordsville, IN, Delores working at her job at Donnelley's and Richard working in a sheet metal shop. In 1948 they moved to Valparaiso, IN where Richard enrolled at Valparaiso Technical Institute. He graduated in 1949 with a certificate in radio engineering, and enrolled in the Engineering School at Valparaiso University. His education was interrupted from April, 1951 to July, 1952 when he was called back into the service during the Korean Conflict. This time was spent at the Naval Air Station, Trinidad, British West Indies. He completed his studies and graduated from Valparaiso University with a degree in electrical engineering in January 1955.

Richard's and Delores' first child, Gregory Wayne, was born Aug. 27, 1953, in Crawfordsville, IN. He graduated from Haworth High School, Kokomo, IN, in 1971. He attended General Motors Institute in Flint, MI, for one year and transferred to Indiana University, where he graduated, on the Dean's List, in May, 1976. He was married to Donna June Eisen June 29, 1974 in St. Clair, MI, which was Donna's home. They have two children, Melissa Erin, born Oct. 23, 1978 and Eric Michael, born Oct. 21, 1980. Greg is an executive with Indiana Lumberman's Insurance Corp. in Indianapolis. Donna is a nurse at St. Vincent Hospital in Indianapolis.

Richard's and Delores' second child, Kimberly Annette, was born Aug. 28, 1960, in St. Joseph Hospital, Kokomo, IN. She graduated from Haworth High School, Kokomo, IN, in 1978. She has been employed at Howard Community Hospital since graduation, and is currently in the accounting department.

Richard's father was Leslie Dwight Frazier, born July 7, 1887, in Missouri Valley, IA. He died Aug. 23, 1976, in Springfield, MO, and is buried in Greenpond Cemetery, Pearl, IL. His mother was Jennie Pearl (Clarkston), born Sept. 9, 1901 in Sturgeon, MO. She died Oct. 7, 1948, in Pearl, IL and is buried in Greenpond Cemetery, Pearl, IL.

Delores' father was Harry Leslie Stephens, born June 19, 1898, in Mellott, IN. He died Sept. 27, 1970, in Waynetown, IN, and is buried in Waynetown Masonic

Cemetery, Waynetown, IN. Her mother was Ada Pearl (Sowers), born Feb. 1, 1900, in Wallace, IN. She died Sept. 16, 1992, in Attica, IN and is buried in Waynetown Masonic Cemetery, Waynetown, IN.

FREED - World War II's ending produced a new generation of young couples seeking a life of peace in the USA. When Robert (born Canton, OH, 1917) and Frances Congress Freed (born Niagara Falls, NY, 1922) arrived in Kokomo, IN, as newlyweds, they were anxious to establish a life that reflected their backgrounds and training. Bob had served 40 months in the U.S. Army Quartermaster Corps in the U.S., Africa and Europe. His outstanding dedication earned him the third highest award, the Legion of Merit, and promotion to officer of his company.

Fran was a graduate of West Virginia University's School of Journalism and had experience in editing, retail sales and business. The couple purchased Palmer's Jewelry from Palmer Gevirtz (est. 1944 in Kokomo); soon they were carrying on traditions of retail jewelry which the Freed family had begun in Europe in the 19th century. The small operation in the heart of Kokomo's downtown was the springboard for their dedication and service.

In 1946, Susan, the first of five children, was born. Now Mrs. Robert Gadomski of Bethlehem, PA, she is a speech therapist who met her husband, a chemical engineer, at Purdue University. Their marriage has produced Andrew and Elizabeth. Stephen, Susan's oldest son, is a Indiana University graduate in business; he met and married Terrie Potter, of Grand Rapids, at IU. They live in Arlington Heights, IL. Susan has her masters from Lehigh University, and Bob gained his at Purdue.

Second daughter Marilyn, born in 1949, also is an IU grad in the field of primary education. She is married to University of Illinois attorney Stan Eisenstein, Chicago. They have three daughters: Leah, Mara and Alyssa.

The Bob Freed Family 1993 - Left to Right: Judy F. Carter, Frances Freed, Robert "Bob" Freed, Marilyn F. Eisenstein. Back row: Robert Carter, Robert Gadomski, Susan F. Gadomski, Michael Freed, Jane B. Freed, Cheryl F. Meisterman, Alan Meisterman, Stanley Eisenstein.

Bob was called back into service during the Korean War; he was released in May, 1951. Daughter number three, Cheryl, born 1952, was born while Palmer's renovated and expanded. Life in Kokomo kept them volunteering for responsibilities in their faith through Temple B'Nai Israel and memberships in their organizations: Elks, Masons, Shriners, Community Concerts, Civic Theatre, Symphony, Morning Musicale, Altrusa, Kokomo Country Club, Hadassah, National Federation Temple Sisterhoods, PTA, American Association of University Women, Lions, YMCA and YWCA, IU 400 Club, B'Nai Brith, Panel of American Women, Scouts, among others.

Cheryl (Freed) Meisterman, a social worker in Columbus, OH, is presently working on her doctorate. She and Alan met as graduate students in Western Reserve. They have three children—Mollie, Dan and Sam.

All the Freed children were honor students in the Kokomo High Schools and served as leaders: class officers, editors of the paper or yearbooks or athletic leaders. Six years after Cheryl's birth, Fran and Bob celebrated the birth of twins—Michael and Judith. Twice during the years, exchange students joined the family; a boy from Iran and a girl from Bolivia.

The deaths of parents, Morris Freed (Canton, 1880-1948) and Mollie Zeligman (1898-1984) and William Congress. (Kokomo 1897-1972) were great losses. Matriarch Ida Amarsky Freed celebrated her 100th birthday October, 1993.

Twins, Michael and Judith, born 1958, completed the family. Mike, an avid golfer, graduated from the University of Cincinnati in business and was captain of the golf team his last two years there. He is married to Jane Bowman (Michigan State, chemical engineering); Mike is VP of Palmer's.

Judy's survival from lung cancer at age 16 focused on the entire family; the positive blessings are not ignored. The family works with American Cancer drives, etc, and she and her husband, Robert Carter, work and live in Cincinnati. Bob, a chemical engineer (Northwestern) and Judy (IU) met when both were attending Duke University's master in business studies. *Submitted by Frances Freed*

JOSEPH MARTIN FREED - A prominent farm family in the latter half of the 19th century in Ervin Township was the Joseph Martin Freed family. Born Nov. 16, 1841 (Clinton County, IN), he was the son of Joseph Freed and Mary (Webb) Freed, and the grandson of John Freed and Regina (Rife) Freed. He lost a leg in the Civil War and was known by some as "Peg-Leg Joe Freed." A farmer at NW1/4, S26, T24N, R2E of Ervin Township, he raised race horses and had a race track on his farm. With his family he moved (by 1901) to Warren County, TN and then to Kimball County, NE by 1904. Later he moved back to Warren County, TN, where he died Dec. 4, 1917. Joseph M. Freed was married three times: (1) Martha Mason, daughter of Jacob and Rebecca Mason, Jan. 11, 1866; (2) Matilda C. Drake, Sept. 29, 1901; and (3) to Geneva L. Snipes April 21, 1914.

Joseph M. and Martha Freed had ten children, first listed below and the last two are children with his second wife, Matilda. The place of birth of all ten children of Joseph and Martha Freed is assumed to be Ervin Township, Howard County, based on their owning land in Ervin Township, and the 10th child was buried in Price Cemetery, Ervin Township.

1. Alice Belle (Freed) Walden, born May 23, 1866; died March 2, 1887; married George Walden. No children.
2. Frances Morton Freed, born Jan. 2, 1868; died Oct. 24, 1875.
3. Fernandes Freed, born Oct. 28, 1870; died Sept. 17, 1873.
4. Clarence Franklin Freed, born July 3, 1873; died April 30, 1943, Warren County, TN. Frank married Emma Novella Youngblood. Frank and Emma Freed had three daughters: Birtha Mae Redman, Alta Mae Ramsey and Martha Jane Jones.
5. Rebecca May (Freed) (Johnson) Thomas, born March 20, 1876, died Aug. 11, 1920, McMinnville, TN. She married (1) William R. Johnson and (2) William Thomas and had one daughter, Elsie (Johnson) Neal.
6. Bertha Dell Freed, born April 30, 1878 and died June 20, 1892.
7. Sallie Jane (Freed) Medley, born May 14, 1880, and died Feb. 15, 1972, Tacoma, WA. She married George Medley and they had eight children: Georgia Dunn, Jody, Hazel, Lucy Quaintance, Ross, Thomas Paul, Kenneth, and Martin.
8. Joseph Howard Freed, born Dec. 18, 1882; died Dec. 10, 1950, Huntington, IN. He married Elsie Lucinda Fordyce and they had five children: Joseph Gerald, Hubert Howard, James Martin, Elsie Leota Francar, and Leo Darwin.
9. Alta Daisy (Freed) (Fordyce) Naylor, born Jan. 25, 1885, died Dec. 30, 1980, Huntington, IN. She married (1) Jacob Henry Fordyce and (2) Joseph Naylor. With her first husband she had seven children: Charles, Lester Martin, Cecil Hubbard, Martha (Fordyce) Snider, Glenn, James, and Clifford.
10. Infant son, born and died Nov. 28, 1887.
11. Mary Emma (Freed) Bradshaw, born Oct. 23, 1902, McMinnville, TN; died Nov. 28, 1981, Lima, OH. She married Raymond Bradshaw and had five children: John Martin, Donna Cordelia, Lowell Ray, Phillip Curwood, and Thomas L.

12. Cordelia Isabelle (Freed) Grass, born Oct. 23, 1904, Atlanta, NB; died Aug. 9, 1968, Lima, OH. She married James Grass and had two children: Betty Jean and James.

The above is abstracted (with permission) and modified from *The Mason White Family History, 1900* (edited by James Freed). *Submitted by Leo D. Freed*

OSCAR L. AND VERA H. FREED - Oscar L., son of Mabel (Ketchum) and Robert Freed, was born in Daviess County. He came to Kokomo in 1935 having just graduated from Purdue University and receiving a B.S. in electrical engineering. Oscar began working at Continental Steel Corp. For many years, Oscar was in the engineering department, but later became general plant superintendent. In 1971, Oscar decided to take an early retirement.

Vera (Hadley) Freed, born in Miami County, was raised in Kokomo. Her parents were Amelia (Wolf) and Homer Hadley. She graduated from Kokomo High School and worked at Delco. Vera and Oscar met through mutual friends. After dating for several years, they married in July 1938.

Since Oscar had R.O.T.C. while at Purdue, he was among the first to be called into serving during WWII. While in Europe, he was a captain in the 3rd Army, 246th Signal Operation Company. Oscar and his men set up and tore down communication centers for General George Patton. Brig. General Charles de Gaulle awarded Oscar the Croix de Guerre for bravery. He also was awarded five Battle Stars. Oscar stayed active in the Army Reserves until 1956; at that time, he was a lieutenant colonel.

Oscar and Vera had two children, Jeffrey L. and Alexca A. Both children are graduates of Kokomo High School and Purdue University. Jeff and his wife, Doris (Webster), live in St. Charles, IL. Alexca lives in Garden Grove, CA. As of this writing, Oscar and Vera have three grandchildren and four great-grandchildren.

Both Vera and Oscar have been active in local civic, political, and social organizations. A few of these organizations are the Howard County Red Cross, precinct committee persons for the Republican Party, and the fraternal orders of the Masonic Lodge, the Elk Lodge, and the Moose Lodge. They have spent many hours collecting funds for various local fund raisers. Vera still stays active in the Women's Federation of Clubs. Oscar is still very much interested in Purdue sports and remains a member of the John Purdue Club.

THOMAS AND EMMA FREED - Tom Freed and Emma Mason had a storybook romance! They were neighbors in Ervin Township, Howard County, but in December 1893, she accompanied her parents to Oklahoma Territory (O.T.). Tom traveled 700 miles in 1895 to find Emma in Woods County, O.T. After their marriage, Jan. 9, 1896, however, they had a series of disappointments. Two infant daughters died, they could not purchase land, and their house burned. They soon boarded a train back to Indiana. The one humorous highlight of the trip was that their daughter, Hollis, rode on the lap of Carrie Nation, but as soon as Tom found out her name (known throughout the nation for her sometimes very violent attempts to stop the sale of alcohol), Tom would not allow Hollis to sit on her lap.

When Tom and Emma Freed arrived back in Howard County in 1906, they did not return to farming, but instead lived in Kokomo, where Tom became a brick mason. They resided in houses at 1231 W. Jefferson, 1020 E. Markland, and 1029 S. Ohio Avenue, their residence at the time of their deaths. Emma's special interest was in making quilts. Tom was very creative with his hands, loved to whittle wood, made linked chains, wooden puzzles and helped his wife make quilts.

Tom was born July 13, 1875, Howard County, IN, son of John Milton Freed and Matilda (Willis) Freed, grandson of Noah Freed and Elizabeth (Ramsayer) Freed, and also of David Willis and Lydia (Coggshall) Willis. Tom died April 28, 1945. Emma Elizabeth (Mason) Freed was born May 8, 1880, Ervin Township, daughter of Jacob and Alice Early (Mason), granddaughter of Simon and Elizabeth (White) Mason and also of William and Catharine (Burchfield) Early. Emma died Feb. 28, 1948.

195

In addition to the six children of Tom and Emma Freed listed below, they had daughters, Charlotte and Zelma Ruth, who did not live long. All children were born in Woods County, O.T., except John and Janice.

Hollis Galathia (Freed) Thompson, born Feb. 4, 1898; died May 13, 1971, Greensburg, IN. Hollis married William (Bill) Thompson, son of Joseph and Ellen (Simpkins) Thompson of St. Helens, England. Bill immigrated to the U.S. with his parents in 1906, and was a tool maker. Bill and Hollis had one daughter, Ellen, born March 19, 1919, Kokomo. She married Alfred Tibbetts and they lived in Brazil, IN.

Arley Mae (Freed) Howard, born Dec. 20, 1899; married Thomas Howard, son of Ernest and Bertha Howard. Arley and Tom lived most of their married life in Hartford City, IN, where she died July 11, 1975 and he died Jan. 5, 1970. They had four children, all born in Kokomo: Alice Koch (born Oct. 17, 1925), lives in Chicago, IL; Mary Oswalt (born Dec. 24, 1926), lives near Hartford City; Thomas Howard, Jr. (born Oct. 20, 1928) lives in Hartford City; and William Eugene Howard (born July 27, 1930), lives in Livonia, MI.

B. Leon Freed, born Jan. 3, 1902. About 1930, he moved from Indiana back to Oklahoma where he married Myrtle Moyers. They lived on a farm in Major County, OK, and they had four sons, Ronald, Merlin, James, and Robert. He died Jan. 13, 1977, and she died Feb. 5, 1977.

Dee Leo Freed, born Jan. 3, 1902 (twin to B); married Mary John McReynolds, daughter of James and Rachel McReynolds of western Howard County. They lived their entire married life in Kokomo, where he died Sept. 10, 1976, and she died July 25, 1982. They had two children: Mary Dee Freed (born Aug. 30, 1935), who lives in Chico, CA, and John Wesley Freed (born June 28, 1940). John W. Freed is a retired Kokomo city fireman and with his wife, Sharon (Cooke) Freed, they have retired to Presque Isle, WI. John and Sharon have three daughters, all born in Kokomo: Leslie (born Feb. 21, 1962) who lives in Pleasanton, CA; Tracy (Freed) Kalscheur (born Sept. 22, 1964), who with her husband Craig Kalscheur lives in Eden Prairie, MN; and Shannon Dee Freed (born Sept. 6, 1966), who lives in Madison, WI.

John Lovell Linley Freed, born Feb. 3, 1907, Kokomo; married Ruth Lehmann. John was in various management positions with F.W. Woolworth, Sears, and later in real estate in Arizona, where he died in Tucson, Aug. 23, 1991. John and Ruth had two daughters, Patricia Ann (Freed) Monte, and Mary Kathleen (Freed) Simpson.

Goldie Janice (Freed) Parkhurst, born Oct. 24, 1909, Kokomo; married Ora Parkhurst. (See their family history under Ora and Janice Parkhurst.)

The above information was abstracted and modified, with permission, from *The Mason-White Family History,* copyright 1990, by James M. Freed. *Submitted by Robert L. Parkhurst*

FREELAND - Alexander H. Freeland (1846-1935), son of Isaac (1807) and Hannah (1814) Freeland, walked north from Georgia in 1863. He was the youngest son and known later as the Freeland who went north during the Civil War. The musket and powder horn he carried with him are still in the family. He settled in Jennings County, IN where he met and married Mary Spaulding (1847-1918). They had five children: Clark, (1874-1946), Harry (1876-1891), Edward (1877), Myrtle, (1881) and Lora (1885). They came to Howard County in 1876.

Harry Freeland died at the age of 15. Edward remained a bachelor. Myrtle married James Henry and they had four children. Lora married Emerson Polk and they had two daughters. Clark married Minnie Rice (1872-1926), who was a young widow with two children, Rae and Hale Rice. They had two more children Madge Freeland Wilson (1905-1987) and Owen Freeland (1908-1982).

Minnie Rice Freeland died in 1926 and in 1929 Clark married Mary Ridgeway McClellan. Clark farmed and was also known for his woodworking skills. He built a large two story dwelling that still stands today in Ervin Twp. in 1917. He wired it for electricity which they didn't get until 1941 and put in a chimney from the basement up and put registers in for a furnace even though they burned coal stoves until the 1950's. His innovations were before his time.

Madge married Guy Wilson and they had two children, Lyndal and Sharon. Owen married Josephine Swaim in 1928 and they had three children. Richard (1930) married Donna Perkins and had a son and daughter, Mark and Linda. They were later divorced and he married Barbara Sals who had three children. He adopted the two oldest ones, Thomas and Trudy. Richard served in the Air Force from 1950 to 1960 and then worked in the post office in Sarasota, FL. He retired after 20 years, and he now resides in Arcadia, FL.

Carolyn (1935) was the middle child and she married William Young in 1955. They had four children (1) LuAnn, an ordained minister who lives in West Chester, PA; (2) Larry, an electrician; he also inherited Clark's talent for woodworking. He married Teresa Wagner and they have three children, Leigh, Reid and Jay. (3) Laurie, a nurse who works with the heart team at St. Vincent Hospital in Indianapolis. She is married to Charles Huston and they live in Westfield, IN. (4) Leslie is the youngest and she married Michael Eikenberry and they have two children, Kayla and Kevin. Leslie is very talented and she keeps busy making and selling her crafts, especially the folk Santas. They live in Carroll County.

Bill and Carolyn live on their farm, and Bill retired after 39 years at the Chrysler Transmission plant in Kokomo. Carolyn retired from teaching at the Carroll Elementary School.

Kenneth (1940), the youngest child of Owen and Josephine, married Aloha Yarian and they both taught school for many years. They adopted four children and they moved to Woodville, TX where they still reside. Kenneth is a minister in a church near his home.

Owen worked in a garage from 1926 until 1937 when he started at Chrysler and he retired from there in 1965. He also raised popcorn for many years and had a small repair shop at his home. Owen had a great interest in our heritage. He had many hobbies such as studying about the Civil War, researching and recording historical facts and antecdotes, and also putting into print the *History of Ervin Township* in 1971.

After six generations, there are still many descendants living in Howard County. Unfortunately, they don't have the name of Freeland - it has changed to Young. *Submitted by Carolyn Freeland Young*

NATHAN FREEMAN - Nathan (1793-1871) and Mary Buckingham Freeman (1798-1873) were married in Orange County, NC. Following the trek of the Quakers to Indiana they moved to Randolph County and settled in the Jericho community with their two young children, Rachel and Joshua. Three additional children were born to this union before the move was made to Howard County. They were Mary, Nathan Jr. and Oliver.

Rachel married and died in Randolph County and very little is known about Mary. Nathan (1828-1896) married Anna Rich of Howard County and was prominent in the New Salem Monthly Meeting near Greentown. His biography can be found in the original history book of Howard County. Oliver (1834-1863) lived in Tipton County, and died at Vicksburg, MS while serving with the 54th Indiana Volunteers in the Civil War.

Joshua and Elizabeth Lytle Freeman

Joshua (1814-1862), engaged in farming in Randolph County, and married Mary Warrick in 1832. They had four children before her death about 1844. The oldest was William and little is known of his life. Richard (1835-1917) lived most of his life at Windfall in Tipton County and died at Richmond, IN. Nathan (1839-1909) spent most of his adult life in Montgomery County. Mary Jane (1842-1917) married Wesley Lytle in Howard County and died at Wabash.

Joshua moved to Howard County, one mile south of Greentown, in 1844. Within a year he moved to Grant County and married his second wife, Elizabeth Lytle in 1845. They moved back to Howard County and this marriage produced seven children: Lindsey (1846-1912) married and died in Trigg County, KY after the Civil War; David (1849-1918) married Nancy Larow of Howard County, served in the 7th Indiana Cavalry and followed his brother to Trigg County in 1884 where he spent the rest of his life. Louisa Jane (1851-?) married Michael Marigan in Howard County. Sarah (1853-?) married David Robinson in Howard County. Oliver Winifred (1857-1874) and Winnie Olivette (1857-1895) were twins. Oliver died in his teens and Winnie married Mahlon Brewer of Grant County. No information has been found on Harriett (1862-?).

Joshua, although 47 years old, and two of his sons, Nathan and Lindsey, all served in the 26th Indiana during the Civil War. Joshua became ill and was discharged at Jefferson City, MO with the notation "recovery doubtful". He returned to Indiana and stopping at his father's house for the night, died there before he was able to return to his wife and family.

David Freeman   *Lindsey Freeman and wife Nancy Howard*

After Joshua's death, Nathan and Lindsey were captured in the Battle of Sterling's Farm at Morganza, LA. They were taken to Camp Ford at Tayler, TX where Nathan escaped, and after a year Lindsey was exchanged for southern prisoners. Lindsey then returned to Indiana and joined the 153rd Regiment.

Nathan and his wife, Mary, plus their children Joshua, Oliver, Nathan and his wife, Anna, along with some of their children, are buried in the Quaker South Graveyard (Freeman Cemetery) in southeast Howard County.

Descendants of Nathan Freeman still live in the Greentown area. *Submitted by Charles E. Morris*

FRENCH - James French (-1815) of Bedford County, PA and Allegany County, MD, married Jane ___. It is not known whether she was the first wife or not. James had: Daniel, Lot who married Elizabeth Miller, Jeremiah, Ralph, Benjamin married Deborah Gist (June 25, 1775 Md) Elizabeth married Judge James Martin. James married Hannah Deam (1907 Miami County, OH) and Mary married Isaac Lane.

Lot French (-1828) and Elizabeth Miller (1774-1835) came from Pennsylvania to Hamilton County, OH and then to Crawfordsville, IN. They had Ann who married Martin Cumberland, and second Samuel Fisher. James French married Abigail McGilliard; Pheamy 'Amy' married James Harvey Applegate; Adam Miller married Mary Wilson. Adam and Mary had a daughter, Martha J., who was a doctor in Indianapolis. Mary 'Polly' married James Cowan; Charlotte married Gabriel Trullinger; Jane married Enoch Richardson; Sarah French married John Cowan; and Elizabeth 'Betsey' married Frederick Moore.

James (1802-1835) and Abigail's (1803-1868) children were: Alfred who married Nancy Jane Royalty; Francis; Ralph (1827-1879) married first Amanda Jane

McDowell; second Eliza Ann Fisher (1830-1901); Susan who married Silas S. Baldwin; John; and Ann married James Owen Fisher.

Ralph and Eliza Ann Fisher had Andrew, Laura, Sylvia married James Diller, Alfloretta married Myron E. Gannon, Alonzo Lewis, and Hewitt.

Alonzo 'Lon' (1869-1933) married 1890 Lucretia 'Lula' Alice Weed (1871-1930). Their children were Charles Basil who married Mamie E. Gearhart, Evert Thomas married Ferne Malaby, Elsie Odessa married Hillary Turner, Myron Andrew married first, Neva Gott, second Gailen Jett (for whom my mother was named), third Agnes Radcliff and fourth Ruby Henderson Severs; Edna A. married Fred K. Delon Sr.; Eunice Ann married Basil Smith.

My grandmother was Edna Alfloretta (1895-1947) who married Fred King DeLon Sr. (1893-1971). They had Alice Lorene who married Myron Merrick; Fred K. DeLon Jr. who married Joy Delight Merrell; and my mother, Gailen Louese, who married Neil Thomas Harris.

Gailen and Neil had Thomas Paul and Everett Neil.
Submitted by Everett Neil Harris

CHRISTIAN FRITZ
Christian Fritz born Aug. 1, 1807 in Brothersvalley Township, Somerset County, PA.

Died Feb. 10, 1882 in Howard County, IN; buried in Russiaville. His father was Valentine Fritz and mother, Susan Elizabeth Palm.

Married Catherine Shultz, born March 4, 1804 in Pennsylvania, died May 8, 1879 in Howard County, IN.

Christian and his wife Catherine and children moved to Indiana in 1846. George Dunlap (Christian's sister's son) and George Shultz (Catherine's brother's son) also came with them.

Their children:
1. Josiah, married, died in the Civil War; Children: Nancy Hurley and Mary Hagen.
2. William, married Franie Bitner, died in Civil War; Children: Frank Fritz, wife Lou-lived in Tipton County, IN; John-lived in Clinton County.
3. Elizabeth, married Joe Humber. She died in Pennsylvania. Children: Harrison Humbert, wife Eliza, lived in New London. He had three children: Sam Humbert died in Kokomo; Frank Humbert, died in New London; Elsie married Robert Thompson. Children: Chester Thompson, Kokomo; Ralph Thompson-Anderson; and Ruth Thompson-Howard County.
4. John Fritz, married Miss Cool. Both died Howard County. Children: Benny Fritz, died Russiaville.
5. Mary Catherine Polly Fritz. Married Samuel E. Kanable. (This is my family tie to Christian Fritz).
6. Susan married Tom Vernon. Lived west of Kokomo. Children: Lydia and Maude both died young. Martha married John McCain; Mary died young; Anna married John Welker; Ross died in accident.
7. Margaret married James C. Shaw; both died in Russiaville; Children: (1) Christian Monroe Clinton married Rosa H. Bryan, lived by Russiaville; Children: Irene Virgil, married Joe Morrison. Beulah Lorea married Benjamin Harrison Friend. Children: Mary Lou; Bud; San. (2) Howard Shaw married ? Children: Mary Shutters, lives West Middleton; Elzie married Claude Gordon, Kokomo. (3) Maggie; (4) Letitia.
8. Chancy Fritz married Elizabeth; wife and children all lived in Richland Center, WI.
9. Hiram Fritz married Martha Ann Morris; died New London, IN. Children: (1.) Alice Vilola married Oscar Miller in Russiaville. One child: Hazel O. married Earl L. Butler. Children:
  – Ralph M. Butler married Mary E. Robertson. Children: Odel married David Strange; Jared married Martha Harris. Their children are Jenny, Julia, Denise and Peter.
  – Esther Lorene Married Ralph Davis. Their children are Barbara married William Charles; Beverly. All lived near Forest, IN.
  – Helen Lucile married Issac A. Hollingsworth. Their children are: Peggy and Alma. All live in Russiaville.
(2.) Ettie Lee married Elsworth Rishel; moved to Lafayette. Their children are: Claude, Arthur and Monsell.

(3.) Minerva married Gurney Cosand; lived in Howard County. Their children are Vern and Nigel.
(4.) Howard Monroe married Mary Brandon. One son Kenneth Fritz moved to Florida. Another son, James, Galveston, IN. Mary Brandon then married Rev. Sanders, Lebanon, IN.
(5.) Lillie married Ora O. Hodson from Russiaville. Their children: George married Grace, ? Indianapolis.
(6.) Lottie married Fred Plummer. Their children are Dale Plummer. He and his wife live in Syracuse, IN and have two sons. Dwaine Plummer and wife Louise live in Howard County. 2nd husband: George Lindley and they live in Kokomo.
(7.) Lessie married Earl Vogus. They lived in Russiaville. Children: (1) Dayton died young. (2) Edith married Lee Dixon, Kokomo. Children: Evelyn Keller, Greenville, OH and Carolyn married Ed Kasmeyer, Kokomo. (3) Russell married Mildred Chambers. Children: Betty Jo married Larry Durr, Lebanon; Jane Ann married Robert Heltzel, Alto; Linda L. married Frederick K. Pinkerton, Hannibal, MO; William M. married Regena Long.
(8.) Carl Fritz married L. Cora Duke. 2. Zella Presing; no children.
(9.) Maude, twin sister to Carl, died young.
(10.) Cleo married Rolland Lines, moved to Michigan. Children: Elaine Lines Titerikngton, Detroit (three children); Rolland, Battle Creek, MI (four children); Margaret Lines Hunt, Landing, MI (two children); Cleo 2nd marriage, Elmer Sager, Battle Creek, MI.
(11.) Walter O. Fritz, married Lillian Burton, Kokomo. Children: Virginia-Arizona; Leota, California; Cleo, married Wellinger, South Bend, IN; Walter, second wife, Evelyn, California. *Submitted by Patty Arline Bogan Locke.*

JACOB AND DAMARIS JANE GARRISON
See story and photograph on page 344.

J.H. GARRITSON - James Harvey Garritson (July 7, 1859-July 16, 1918) had the building at 121 W. Sycamore St. constructed to house the J.H. Garritson Co., a wholesale grocery business which he had founded about 1902. The Garritson name is on the front of this building, near the top. Before 1902 he was a salesman for the Indianapolis Basket Co. He was born on a farm near the village of Miami, in Miami County, IN. His parents, Reed Garritson (1828-1873) and Mary Ellen Long (1835-1907), were born in Ohio. On Aug. 4, 1880 he married Catherine F. Liston, who died four years later. They had the two children listed below, who were born in Waupecong, in Miami County and moved with the family to Kokomo.

1. Mayme (June 1, 1881-Jan. 7, 1960), who married Leon C. Martin in 1908. They did not have any children. After J. H. Garritson died, Leon managed the wholesale grocery business.
2. Mary Bess (Jan. 7, 1883-Aug. 7, 1977), who married J. Hugh O'Reair in November 1906. She was called Bess. They had two sons - Henry Garritson "Gary" and Robert Hugh. Gary had a successful insurance business in La Porte, IN. He did not have any children. Robert had two daughters - Beverly and Carroll Lou. He worked with his father in the Kokomo Kandy Kompany, a wholesale candy business. Later he managed his mother's orange groves at Winter Haven, FL after her second husband, Charles N. Hodgin, died in 1962. Charles had inherited the groves from his parents. Bess married him in July 1921 after she divorced J. Hugh O'Reair about 1918. Charles owned a stone quarry located northwest of the corner of Markland and Courtland.

James Harvey Garritson's second wife was Molly Williams (July 12, 1872 - May 7, 1893), whom he married about 1890.

James Harvey Garritson's third wife was Clora Alice Woolley (June 25, 1873-June 29, 1962), whom he married on July 3, 1898 in the house at 515 W. Taylor St. She was called Alice. She was born in Kokomo, and when she was a child, she lived on the corner of Jefferson and Phillips, where her father operated the toll gate and collected toll from people who traveled on Jefferson Road. It was the only road going west from Kokomo. Alice graduated from Kokomo High School on June 17, 1891, attended the State Normal College in Terre Haute, and taught at Central School for three years. She was very active in church work all her life and held every office at the Main Street Christian Church except minister. She taught a Sunday School class there for 63 years. Alice and J.H. Garritson had the four daughters listed below, who were all born in Kokomo.

1. Frances Camille (Aug. 31, 1900 -), who married Charles Edward "Ed" Anderson on Jan. 3, 1922. Elwood Haynes took her and her father for a ride in his automobile one Sunday afternoon in 1902 or 1903. Her mother was afraid to go; she was fearful they would be killed. The car went about seven miles an hour. Ed Anderson was in the grocery and meat business. Their first son, Charles Thomas "Tom", was an engineer at General Electric in Syracuse, NY. Their second son, Jerry Edward, was an engineer at Delco.
2. Margaret Ellen (Aug. 29, 1905 - March 23, 1980), who married Jack Carroll about 1929. They had one son, John Garritson. After divorcing Jack, she married Lum A. Morrow of Elwood, IN about 1937 and lived in Elwood until about 1979.
3. Martha Josephine (July 21, 1910 - Aug. 14, 1987), who married Raymond Floyd Maddox. He owned Maddox Finance Co. They built the house at 1533 W. Walnut. They had one daughter, Margot Josephine, who was a school teacher in Kokomo.
4. Dorothy Jane (June 28, 1912 - June 7, 1986), who married George Vincent Reed on June 2, 1934. She was called Jane. George was treasurer of Continental Steel Corp. Their only child, Rebecca Alice, lives in Eagle River, AK. *Submitted by C. Thomas Anderson*

GATES - Be it known and understood that the Jerry Gates family is truly at "home" in Howard County. Jerry and Leann Gates made their home in southeast Howard County in October, 1973. They are native Hoosiers.

Jerry was born in Hamilton County in September, 1940, the son of Robert Gates and Delores (Hicks, Gates) Leonard. He was educated at Walnut Grove for 12 years. After his graduation in 1959, he joined the USAF spending his four years in the states (3 1/2 years) in Maine). 1964 brought him to Howard County to be employed by Chrysler Transmission Plant. He resided in Hamilton County and attended classes at IUK (presently the Seiberling Mansion).

Leann was born in Johnson County in August, 1947, the daughter of Vivian (Short, Harrell) Mann and Frank Harrell. Her first through sixth grades were spent in Danville, IN. Howard County became her home in 1959. She was educated at Pettit Park, Lafayette Park, and graduated from Kokomo High School in 1965. She graduated from Indiana Business College in 1966, and Indianapolis Floral Design School in 1990.

(L to R): Leann, Jerry, Scott and Todd May 1992 in Highland Park in front of the Vermont Bridge. The 25th anniversary celebration of Jerry and Leann.

Jerry and Leann met in 1966 and dated briefly. However, their love grew and was evident by February, 1967. They were married July, 1967 in Parr United Methodist Church, and resided in Hamilton County. Their first son, Todd, was born in 1972 in Howard County. Howard County became their home on a 20 acre farm in 1973. Their second son, Scott, was born in 1976 in Howard County. Both sons were born at Saint Joseph Hospital.

At present Jerry has continued with Chrysler Corporation for 30 years, becoming a machine repairman in

1971. Leann is working for Bowden Flowers as a floral designer. Todd received his 13 years of education with the Taylor Township School System graduating in 1990. His further studies took him to Muncie to Ivy Tech, graduating in 1992. He is working for Kokomo Chrysler-Plymouth.

Scott has attended Taylor Township schools and is in the 11th grade. His future plans are to become a diesel mechanic and to farm. They are members of Macedonia Christian Church.

The four (Gates) love country living. Their hobbies include their family pets, beekeeping, antique cars and tractors, gardening, and each others activities and interests.

Past history: Jerry's father, Robert Lewis Gates, was born in Hope, IN. He was the son of Edward and Gusta Gates. Jerry's mother, Delores J. Hicks, was the daughter of Ray and Ruth Hicks.

Leann's mother, Vivian Berniece Short, was born in Johnson County. She was the daughter of Leroy T. and Marie E. Short. Her father, Frank E. Harrell, was born in Jackson County. He was the son of Lute and Effie Harrell. Leann's only brother was killed at age 18. Both Leann and Jerry have half brothers and sisters.

LAURENCE G. GETZ AND VICKIE S. GETZ

- Larry and Vickie Getz have lived in Kokomo all their lives. They met while cruising Frisch's Drive-In and they were married six months later on Sept. 14, 1968.

Larry was born at St. Joseph Hospital on Oct. 9, 1943. He went through grade school and graduated from Kokomo High School in June of 1963. After graduating from high school, he went to work at Continental Steel Corporation. He worked there for two years and then went into the Army, serving in Germany for one year. After returning to Kokomo, he went back to work at Continental Steel and worked there until the mill closed in February, 1986. He is presently employed at Kelvie Press.

Larry and Vickie Getz

Vickie was born at St. Joseph Hospital on March 30, 1948. She went to Central School and graduated from Kokomo High School in June of 1966. She worked at Prudential Insurance Co. until the birth of her daughter, Staci, who was born on March 23, 1971. Vickie then went to work at Kokomo High School-South Campus in August, 1986 and is presently working in the Media Center at the school.

Larry's parents are the late Robert Getz and Ruth (Davis) Getz. They have been life-long residents of Kokomo and were married Nov. 6, 1942. Larry's grandparents are Stacy Davis and the late Mary (Fye) Davis who came to Kokomo in 1905 and James Getz and Amelia (Dehne) Getz who came to Kokomo in 1919 from Marion, IN. Larry has two sisters, Carol (Getz) Candlish who lives in Grundy Center, IA, and Cathy (Getz) Hostetler who lives in Copley, OH.

Vickie's parents are John Anweiler and Betty (Whited) Anweiler. They were both graduates of Kokomo High School and were married June 17, 1944. They have lived in Kokomo all of their married lives. Vickie's grandparents were the late Otto Anweiler and Mae (Nicholson) Anweiler who moved to Kokomo in 1918 from Michigan and the late Harry Whited and Delpha (Hammond) Whited who moved to Kokomo in 1915 from Coal City, IN. Vickie has one sister, Nancy Anweiler, who lives in Somerset, NJ.

Larry and Vickie's daughter, Staci, lives in Kokomo and is a graduate of Ivy Tech Vocational College and is presently working at Kokomo Family Care.

Kokomo has been a wonderful place to live and raise our daughter. We enjoy being involved in community activities and rooting for the Kokomo Wildkats.

GIBSON - Bobby Gibson was born the fourth son, in a family of seven children, of George Stewart and Mattie Francis (Bell) Gibson on Oct. 8, 1935, in Fort Smith, AR. He is a twin to Betty Gibson. Bob was born at home, in a log cabin. His parents moved to the Los Angeles, CA area when Bob was two years old. He and his twin sister attended school in California to the sixth grade. In 1948, Bob's parents moved back to Ft. Smith, AR where he graduated from Fort Smith Senior High School in 1955.

In 1955, on the advice of his sister and brother-in-law (George A. and Francis E. Rayl), Bob moved from Arkansas to Kokomo in hopes of going to work with Chyrsler Corporation. He worked for Med-O-Bloom Dairy for three months. In October Bob was called to Chrysler to take a test for their apprentice program. He passed the test and started to work on Oct. 4, 1955, as a pipefitter apprentice, in the old Haynes-Apperson building, located at the intersection of Apperson Way and Home Ave. In November, he was transferred to the new Chrysler Transmission Plant on the Highway 31-Bypass. Bob married Shelby Jean Clark from Linton, IN on Dec. 12, 1955 at the Brethren Church on S. Market. Bob and Shelby had three daughters: Nancy Ellen Sept. 10, 1956, Susan Glenn Feb. 12, 1958, Elizabeth Ann March 15, 1963. Shelby Jean was a mother and a homemaker until her death from leukemia Jan. 5, 1977. She is buried in Sunset Memory Gardens Cemetery in Kokomo.

Bob married Judith Ann (Hawkins) Rinehart, on Nov. 25, 1977. Bob graduated from the Chrysler apprentice program in 1959. He served as a journeyman pipefitter until 1963 when he was promoted as an engineer following up piping, heating and ventilation, air conditioning and refrigeration and hydraulic and pneumatic systems installations in the plant engineering office. He served as supervisor over the power house in 1980 and plant engineering in 1982. In 1968 Bob became one of two mechanical engineers in charge of all of the piping etc., for the transmission plant. With the retirement of the other mechanical engineer in 1978, Bob became senior mechanical engineer in plant engineering for the Chrysler Corp., Kokomo Transmission Plant facility. Bob remained the senior engineer until his retirement in September 1992 after 37 years of service. Bob is doing part time consulting engineering work with some companies outside of Chrysler Corp., since his retirement.

Bob and Shelby purchased a home in 1957 at 2821 N. Waugh St. in Kokomo, IN where they raised their children, and he still resides at that address today.

Bob has been a member of Northview Christian Church in Kokomo, IN since 1969. He has served as board chairman, deacon, has sung in the church choir, and has served as a trustee for the church for the last several years.

Bob served in the United States Naval Reserves for eight years. In 1962 he received an honorable discharge from the Navy.

Bob Gibson is a 32nd degree, Master Mason and member of the Napthali Lodge #389, located at Center, IN.

Bob has been a member of the Moose Lodge of Kokomo, Eagles Lodge of Kokomo, a member of the Elks Lodge of Kokomo, and a member of the National Rifle Association.

GIFFORD - My immediate family has lived in Howard County since about 1800. My father was Harry Hendricks Franklin Gifford (Harry H. Gifford) born April 13, 1885 and died Nov. 7, 1977. My mother was Neva Catherine Floyd born May 22, 1890, died Sept. 28, 1982, both from Russiaville, IN. My brother is Arthur Floyd Gifford, retired from Cabot Corporation and living in Sarasota, FL, and was born July 9, 1910. My sister Joan Morrow was born in Kokomo, Oct. 7, 1928 and I, Theda Elaine Gifford Sallee, was born May 31, 1917. Our sister, Irene Esther Gifford, was born July 3, 1909 and died Dec. 3, 1909. I was married Nov. 16, 1941 to Francis Marion Sallee who was born in Philadelphia, PA Aug. 23, 1913 and died here April 30, 1977. He retired in 1976 from Delco Electronics as a superintendent of manufacturing. Our first child was Michal Elaine Sallee Dawson born Sept. 2, 1943 and her daughter is Suzanne Elaine Sharp, born Sept. 23, 1963; her stepson is Richard Craig Dawson born March 23, 1962. Michal married Robert Dawson in 1969.

Back row: Rick Dawson, Peter Sharp, Suzanne Sharp, Michael Newman. 2nd row: Robert Dawson, Tracy Dawson, Julie Newman, Lee Newman. Front: Michal Dawson, Theda Sallee, Pam Newman; June 1989

Pamela Lynn Sallee Newman was born Dec. 14, 1946. Her children are Julie Lynn Newman born May 5, 1971 and Michael Francis Newman born Nov. 5, 1977. His father is LeRoy Newman. Both girls work at Delco. My dad and mother were born near Russiaville, IN. We lived on the old Honeycreek farm near West Middleton until I was six years old and moved to Kokomo. Dad was a postman here until he retired, a farmer several years and during World War I was a harness maker.

My paternal grandfather, Arthur William Gifford, owned the Honeycreek farm before we did. He was born Feb. 22, 1852, died Nov. 16, 1930. He married Matilda Alice Francis March 7, 1876 who died Nov. 20, 1935. Both are buried at Crown Point Cemetery.

My great-grandfather was Thomas Gifford born in Rush County, IN Sept. 18, 1829 and died April 26, 1887 in Howard County. He is in the Russiaville Cemetery. His wife, Mary Jane Pentecost, was born March 28, 1829 and died Feb. 16, 1914.

Not all the Giffords in Howard County are closely related but the name Gifford was of Norman origin and is said to have meant "a freehanded or liberal giver". It was formerly written Giffart, Gyffard and Giffard, the last of which is still occasionally found, but the form most generally used today is Gifford.

It is said that the family is descended from Herfast, a noble Dane of the tenth century on one side from an ancient Norman family on the other. Herfast was the father of Gunnora who married Richard, first Duke of Normandy, and was the maternal ancestor of William the Conqueror. "The historic Giffords of Normandy" is the way the family is referred to in ancient documents. The story is that the Giffords are descended from the DeBollebecs, relative of Richard I, the Duke of Normandy.

William Gifford, my ancestor who came from England, owned land in 1654 at Sandwich, MA and was one of the first settlers. Gifford deputies were elected in 1639 to the 1st House of Representatives of Plymouth Colony. The Gifford Arms are: Gules, three lions passant in palo, argent; Coat of arms said to have been granted to Walter, Earl of Longueville, by William the Conqueror.

I have seen this coat of arms hanging in my father's house. Arthur Gifford has it now. *Submitted by Theda Gifford Sallee*

HAROLD W. AND PATRICIA F. GILBERT -

Harold W. Gilbert was born to Harold D. and Adda E. Gilbert, Young America, IN on April 11, 1923. They moved to the William Addison Gilbert homestead on 850 North in 1935. William Addison was the son of Henry W. Gilbert and Betsy Gwinn Gilbert. Gilbert was born in Tennessee May 17, 1833 and died in Howard County Aug. 20, 1909. Addison was the first of their six sons and one daughter. Addison married Anna Heinmiller on July 20,

1886. To this union two children were born: Ernest and Vera Chambers. After the death of his first wife, Addison married Malinda Petty on Oct. 7, 1897. Harold Deo was born to this union on Nov. 20, 1899. Harold Deo Gilbert married Adda Elizabeth Williamson, daughter of Mercelle and Flora Hyman Williamson of Young America, on Aug. 25, 1920. Harold W. Gilbert was the first of three sons born to this union. The two others, both Howard County residents a good part of their lives, are: Paul Stuart Gilbert, and Richard Deo Gilbert.

Pat and Harold Gilbert

Harold W. Gilbert graduated from Ervin Township High School in 1940. He entered the U.S. Air Force in November, 1942, and served in the 14th Air Force in China in World War II, and in Korea in 1952-55. He retired from the Air Force in 1968 at Wright Patterson Air Force Base, OH, after which he was employed by Air Force Intelligence at Wright Patterson Air Force Base until his retirement from Civil Service in 1981. He married Patricia Irene Flora on March 18, 1945.

Patricia Irene Flora was born March 24, 1925 to Orion S. (Ora) Flora and Bertha May Bock Flora. Joel Amos Flora and his wife, Elizabeth Huff Flora, parents of Ora, lived in Ervin Township all their married life. The Floras came from Roanoke, VA during the Civil War. Ora was a schoolteacher and farmer who lived on State Road 22 west in Ervin Township. Ora and Bertha Flora were also parents of Fred, Cecile Carey, Wilma Obermeyer, Mildred Tomlin, and Carl Lawrence, all now deceased.

The Bocks, Samuel and Eliza Ann Eikenberry Bock, parents of Bertha May, came from Montgomery County, OH in the late 1800's. They lived in Howard County all their lives, retiring to Kokomo in later years.

Patricia Irene Flora graduated from Ervin Township High School in 1943. She married Harold W. Gilbert on March 18, 1945. Their two children were Philip Alan, now a Tuscon teacher, and Elaine E. Lagge, a Fountain Valley, CA teacher. Patricia graduated from Miami University, Wright State University, and Ohio State University. She taught at Fairborn H.S. and Wright State University. Both now retired, Harold and Patricia now live at 2458 N. Quesnel Loop, Tucson, AZ.

MAYOR RAYMON (SCOTTY) GILBERT -
Raymon Gilbert was born July 12, 1891 in Ervin Township to Ell and Ella Gilbert. He was the oldest of seven children. On March 10, 1928 he married Margaret DeHaven and they had one daughter, Patricia Louise.

Raymon Gilbert

Raymon attended grade school in Ervin Township and graduated from Young America High School. He went on to college, attending Muncie Normal College which later became Ball State University and received his degree in teaching.

During World War I, he enlisted in the U.S. Navy and served two years. Upon returning home, he became a farmer and taught school for 20 years in the Ervin School District.

Raymon was very active in the Howard County Democrat Party. He was first elected Howard County Auditor in 1933 and served for two terms. It was during this time the present court house was built. He was also manager of the Howard County License Bureau in 1949 and 1950. He was the Democrat County Party Chairman from 1946 until 1951 when he ran for the Mayor of the City of Kokomo and was elected. Raymon was the first Mayor of Kokomo to be elected and to serve two consecutive terms, serving from 1952 to 1960.

He passed away in 1962, two years after leaving office.

GILBERT AND WILSON -
On Aug. 12, 1955, a third generation native of Howard County and an eighth generation descendant of a Scottish indentured servant were married in Kokomo, IN. Rosemary Gilbert born May 29, 1931, a lifelong resident of Howard County, and Glenn E. Wilson who was born in LaPorte, IN on July 19, 1930, were married in the Union St. Friends Church. Both Glenn and Rosemary graduated from Kokomo High School, Rosemary in 1951 and Glenn in 1948.

Glenn's ancestors go back to the late 1600s or early 1700s when a Scottish lad of 16 came to this country as an indentured servant. The family history follows the history of early America, the French-Indian War, the Revolutionary War, fighting the Indians in western Pennsylvania, traveling down the Ohio River by flatboats, and in 1796 settling near what is now Dayton, OH. As the settlers moved on, so did his ancestors, moving on into what is now Fayette County, IN. In 1836 Glenn's great-grandfather, Simeon Wilson, settled in southern Carroll and northwestern Howard County near Poplar Grove. He helped many of his friends and relatives to settle in this area. Glenn's father, Glen J. Wilson, was born in Poplar Grove. As a child, he lived in the same house as Rosemary's grandparents would later live in and raise their family.

Howard "Gib" Gilbert

Glenn's mother, Goldie K. (Bausum) was born in Burlington, IN where her family had lived for several generations.

Howard (Gib) Gilbert, Rosemary's father, and her grandfather Ell Gilbert were both born in Poplar Grove, Howard County, Gib in 1898 and Ell in 1867. Ell's father Henry moved to Howard County, IN from Tennessee. On April 7, 1931, Rosie's father was appointed as one of the first motorcycle officers on the Kokomo Police Department. After 20 1/2 years at the police department, became a parole officer, court bailiff, and adult probation officer. Raymon Gilbert, Rosemary's uncle, was the mayor of Kokomo for two terms. When Rosemary was two years old her mother, Luella (Addler) Gilbert, passed away leaving a family of one son and six daughters, one being four days old. Luella's mother was a full-blooded Irish lass direct from Ireland and her father's parents came from Osnabruck, Germany.

Rosemary and Glenn have always lived in Howard County, raising a son Brian and a daughter Brenda. They are both now retired, Glenn from Delco Electronics and the Kokomo Police Department, and Rosemary from Northwestern School Corp. Brian and his wife Kim (Bowlin), along with their son Brian II and daughter Amanda enjoy trying to imitate some of his forefathers' lives by taking part in re-enacting the French-Indian War period of time. Brenda and her husband, Scott DeFabritis, along with their three daughters, Stephanie, Laura and Kara, now live in Miami County. *Submitted by Glen and Rosie Wilson*

JAMES GILLAM -
Jonathan Gillam, the forefather of the Gillam family, was born in Lancaster County, PA in 1753. He was a soldier in the Revolutionary War. He had three brothers and was married twice. He had 17 children. He came with his family to Dearborn County, IN.

A son Robert and his wife moved to Carroll County, IN. He had six children: Rebecca, Mary, Henry Harrison, Sarah, James and Albert.

Henry Harrison married Harriett Bushon. He took a claim of 160 acres from the government in Ervin Township. They had five children: Jacob, James, John, Mary Jane and Morton. The four boys and their father had many hardships clearing their land and building a log cabin home.

Jacob had 19 children: Everett, Otto, Hattie, Ova, Bertha, Andy, Mabel, Hazel, Russell, Wardie, Clarence, Milton and Ethel. Six infants died at birth.

John had two sons: Harrison and James.

James and Jennie Gillam

Mary Jane married Reuben Barber and they had 11 children: Edward, Adelia, Wilson, Harriet, Mary, Reuben, Susan, Eva, William, Roy and Clara. They went to Missouri and raised their family.

Morton had two sons: Elmer and Chester.

James married Jennie Dale and they had two children: an infant daughter who died at birth and a son William Pearl. They lived in Ervin Township and their farm joined the Colored Settlement. Fire destroyed their first home while they were away, and the only thing the neighbors were able to save out of their house was William's little red rocking chair. James was a farmer and raised cattle and hogs. When the cattle were ready to sell, the neighbor men would help each other drive their cattle down the road to Kokomo where they loaded them on the train and shipped them to Indianapolis to the Stock Market.

William married Flora Kirkpatrick. He was a farmer in Ervin Township. He raised cattle and lots of hogs. They had three daughters: Lois, Ruth and Vera.

Lois married Raymond Crites and they had two daughters: Rosabelle and an infant daughter, Phyllis, who died at birth. After Raymond's death she married Clifford Smith.

Vera lived in the family home in Ervin Township. She retired from S.S. Kresge after 40 years of service.

Ruth married Dale Brower. They lived on a farm in Ervin Township. They raised cattle, hogs and mink. They had three daughters: Janet, Linda and Nancy.

Janet married Jack Williams and had two children: Jeff and Jennie.

Linda married Leo Leger and had one daughter Camela. Linda and Camela were killed in an auto accident.

Nancy married Larry Babb and they had two children: Scott and Jaime.

After seven generations the descendants of Jonathan Gillam live in Howard and Cass County. *Submitted by Ruth Gillam Brower*

GIVENS - Addison Givens went from England to Ireland where he married Margaret McClanahan and they moved to Virginia about 1654 and settled on a plantation not far from Jamestown. Their descendants migrated to Muncie, IN. James Givens, one of the clan, became a musician and played both a violin and French horn. He traveled with the circus, and one of his stops was at Kokomo where he met and married Mellie Neal. They lived in Kokomo and had five children: Bertha, Otto, Elizabeth, Edward and Charles. Bertha and Charles were stillborn.

At the start of World War I, Otto and Edward went together to enlist in the Army, but Edward had injured his leg the day before and was rejected because he limped on the sore leg. Otto went on to serve in the Expeditionary Forces in France. While there he was exposed to mustard gas which he suffered from the rest of his life. When he returned home he married Ava Allison. They had no children. He became a sign painter and his work appeared around Kokomo for many years.

"Givens" Hungrey Nine Ball Team - Front Row: John Chapin, Woody Peters, Carl Bourne, John Sholty, Paul Massoth. Back Row: Edward Givens, Collin Wetzel, Carl Bader, David Brown, Bill Norris, Carlton Hilton, Clarence Wagner.

Elizabeth Givens married Wade Quick, an insurance salesman from Indianapolis. They had no children.

Edward Givens owned and operated a neighborhood grocery store on West Elm Street for many years. The advent of the supermarket and their competitive advantage caused him to sell the grocery when the opportunity came.

Edward, while a grocer, was interested in baseball, and he organized a baseball team of neighborhood boys. He laid out the baseball diamond in Highland Park, and his teams played local teams as well as teams from neighboring towns. Some of the players were: Paul Massoth, Lewis Wagner, Carl Bourne, Bill Norris, Bob Cline, Carlton Hilton, Ed Fortney and George Critchley. He later worked at the Delco Radio factory and also at local men's clothing stores as a salesman. He married Edyth Jones and they had daughters Elizabeth and Nancy. Elizabeth married Louis Haynes and their only daughter, Mary Edyth, was stillborn. Elizabeth obtained an interest in music at an early age and she became a piano teacher and an accomplished organist in Kokomo. She has played several recitals as well as served as organist in several churches. Nancy studied nursing after high school. She was never married.

GEORGE CLIFFORD GIVENS - George Clifford Givens moved to Kokomo about late 1919 for employment with Haynes Stellite Co. He worked as a metal polisher at Ontario Silver Co. in Muncie before moving. He was born in Barnesville, OH March 3, 1893. He married Lola Grace Branson in Muncie on Feb. 25, 1914. George worked at Dirigold Co. after leaving Stellite and also worked at Delco Radio. He died Dec. 20, 1943. He was a member of AF of L. He was interested in carving, bowling, and playing cards. George and Lola had five children.

The George Clifford Givens Family - Front: James Jerry, Kenneth Earl, Lora Belle. Second Row: Harry Melvin. Top Row: Lola Grace, George Clifford. Insert: William Eugene.

1. Lora Belle Givens, born July 31, 1915 in Muncie and was married first to Lee Roy Slabaugh April 5, 1935 and divorced Feb. 7, 1941. Three children were born of which two are living. She married second to Theodore Commett Mitchell April 2, 1944. Theodore was an electrician and died Dec. 22, 1949. She married third Arlie Garnet Irby June 12, 1954. He retired from the U.S. Post Office and died Feb. 26, 1968. Lora Belle worked as a seamstress and is a member of Church of the Brethren.

2. James Jerry Givens born Feb. 10, 1918 in Muncie. He entered service in July 1941 and married Wilma Maxine Comer Feb. 7, 1942. They have three living children. Two children died shortly after childbirth. Jim has been active in sports. He retired from the post office and continues to deliver the Kokomo Tribune by motor vehicle. He has been affiliated with South Side Christian Church as elder and deacon.

3. Kenneth Earl Givens born March 4, 1920 in Kokomo. He entered military service in July 1942. He married Mary Jane Duddy Jan. 31, 1943. They have three children. He served as a city fireman from 1946-1950 and was recalled to the Air Force during the Korean War. He made the military service a career and retired after 26 years. Kenny was active and interested in sports. He lives in Saratoga, CA where Mary Jane died Dec. 30, 1991.

4. Harry Melvin Givens born June 11, 1922 in Kokomo. His military was November 1942 to late 1945. He married first Betty Ann Irwin Dec. 22, 1945. He belonged to the National Guard and American Legion. He was a member of the Legion Post 6 Color Guard and they won the national championship in 1950. He was employed at the post office when he re-enlisted and made a career of the military service. Betty Ann died May 27, 1964 and is buried in Arlington National Cemetery. On Nov. 22, 1964 he married second Ruth Joyce Prather Auvil. Together they have ten children. Harry and Joyce are living in Sebastian, FL after retiring.

5. William Eugene Givens born Aug. 4, 1926 in Kokomo. He entered the Army Air Corps in January 1945 and was discharged August 1946. He was employed at Delco Radio and the post office retiring in January 1984. He was married to Esther Eileen Graham June 24, 1951 at Liberty Mills, IN. They have two children. Bill does woodworking and clock repair as a hobby and part-time business. His religious affiliation is with South Side Christian Church. (See also the Grahams) *Submitted by William E. Givens*

CLAUDE AND WILMA GLASS - Claude Sherman Glass was born in Tipton County March 7, 1900 to Ulyssis Eubirda "Bird" and Sarah Amanda (Ogle) Glass. His brothers were Othel and Raymond. In 1905 Bird bought a farm north of Phlox across from Union Township School bounded on the south and west by Wildcat Creek. It remained in the family until 1945. Claude attended Union Township School through eighth grade.

Wilma Inez Pearl (Butler) Glass was born south of Phlox June 18, 1912 to John Anderson and Sarah Ann (Overman) Butler. Older siblings were Clarence, Anna, Glenn, Obadiah, Mary, Claude, Avan and Thelma. Donald and Dallas were younger. (Only Wilma is still living). She attended Greentown School through tenth grade.

Claude and Wilma were married in Tipton May 8, 1932 and lived briefly on the farm before moving to Phlox. Claude trapped and did odd jobs where pay was commonly "cash on the barrelhead" daily with no certainty of being chosen to work the next day. One day Claude cut his hand while harvesting spinach with Clarence Butler. They went to the farm house to get the wound cleansed with turpentine and bandaged. At day's end Clarence's pay was docked and Claude had to agree to work another half day to pay for the treatment. Wilma worked seasonally in the canning factories. They attended Howard Chapel.

Startled Phlox neighbors rushed to Claude's house in 1934 thinking it was on fire. He had decorated his Christmas tree with automobile light bulbs which he had colored and connected to a car battery. In 1936 Phlox was wired for electricity.

They had three children while living in Howard County. Clyde Eugene, author of this article, was born Sept. 12, 1932 at the home of Hurshel and Anna (Butler) Hethcote who were then living on 100 acres in Polk Township, Huntington County. Cloid Arthur was stillborn Aug. 25, 1933. Wilda Clare, born Oct. 30, 1934 died of zinc oxide pneumonia 21 days later; a babysitter mistakenly used foot powder instead of baby powder.

In 1936, Trell Conway, a neighbor, moved the Glasses to Hurshel's 80-acre farm in Polk Township, Huntington County. Trell was going up to attend livestock auctions and charged only five dollars leaving Claude with just 11 cents. Claude found little work; even PWA and WPA jobs were scarce. Farm products were bartered at the Monument City store. Francis Leroy "Frank" was born May 15, 1937 at Hurshel's farm on US 224 west of Markle. In 1939 the Glasses moved to Andrews. Charlotte Rose was born Sept. 10, 1939.

On the day before she was born a guitar salesman stopped by. Wilma told him Claude had been unable to find steady work although he had talked to all local employers. The salesman left, but returned two hours later to say he had talked to the Kitchen Maid cabinet factory owner. Claude had a job if he'd report for work Monday. Claude did and worked there 28 years. The salesman didn't leave his name.

From 1941 to 1946 the family lived on The Flowing Well Place alongside the Salamonie River southeast of Monument City. Sharon Kathleen was born March 10, 1942, Shirley Lynne April 24, 1944 and Duane Alan April 2, 1946. Then the family moved to Andrews. Wilma attended the Pilgrim Holiness Church and was very religious. All six children graduated from Dallas Township High School and five attended college.

Claude, an avid reader, routinely borrowed books from the Andrews Library. His knowledge of world geography, biblical geography, electricity and mechanics belied his limited formal education. He died of lung cancer in Bluffton, IN Aug. 25, 1968. His funeral was at the New Hope Friends Church in Phlox, and he is buried in the Ellis Cemetery south of Phlox.

Wilma moved to Albuquerque, NM in 1974 and lives there as do Charlotte and Duane. Clyde lives in Loveland, CO; Frank in Cheney, WA; Sharon near Rupert, ID and Shirley near Larwill, IN. *Submitted by Clyde E. Glass*

GEORGE AND NANCY GOETZEN - George William Goetzen III was born April 26, 1950 in Orlando, FL. He lived 37 years in various cities in Florida before moving to Kokomo in May, 1987. George attended Leesburg High School and one and one-half years at Lake Sumter College. He started at age 14 working in his father's car dealership and, after several years, became vice-president. George is currently employed at Tipton Ford Dealership. He belongs to the Kokomo Aviation Club and is pursuing his private pilot's license. He has a son, Jason, who was born Nov. 27, 1975 and will graduate from Leesburg High School June, 1994. George married Nancy (Etherington) Goetzen March 23, 1989.

Nancy has been a resident of Kokomo since her birth March 16, 1950. She graduated from Kokomo High School June, 1968 and is currently attending Indiana University - Kokomo to finish her degree. Nancy is working as a Workmanship Standards Technician for the Delco Electronics Corporation where she has been employed since November, 1974.

George and Nancy Goetzen

George's parents were George William and Ethel (Featherer) Goetzen, Jr. George Jr. was born March 15, 1916 in Jersey City, NJ. He was a pilot instructor during World War II, was a skywriter from the Pepsi Cola Company and started Plaza Lincoln/Mercury Dealership in Leesburg, FL in 1963. George Jr. passed away July 8, 1988 in Wildwood, FL. Ethel Featherer was the daughter of Walter and Reena (Smith) Featherer born Sept. 22, 1919 in Carneys Point, NJ and is currently living in West Palm Beach, FL.

George Jr.'s parents were George Sr. and Mary (Brohan) Goetzen. Both George Sr. and Mary were born in New York, George on March 16, 1875 and Mary on Jan. 9, 1897. George Sr. was the son of William and Barbarella Goetzen. William was born in Germany August of 1827 and had a butcher shop on Palisade Avenue in Jersey City, NJ in the 1880s.

Nancy's parents were John Murphy and Vonna (Hite) Etherington Jr. Both were born in Kokomo in 1926, John on February 2 and Vonna on May 3. Vonna passed away Nov. 17, 1984 in Wichita Falls, TX.

John's parents were John Mark and Vergie (Murphy) Etherington. John Sr. was born in Howard County May 26, 1900 and Vergie was born in Cass County on Feb. 12, 1902. John Sr. was the son of Robert H. and Mary Lela (Garrison) Etherington. Robert was a farmer and was born Feb. 21, 1862 in Howard County. He married Mary Lela Garrison (born, Sept. 27, 1863 in Carroll County) Sept. 16, 1886. Mary was the daughter of Jacob and Damaris Jane (Shinn) Garrison. Robert's parents, Richard Wm. and Mariah (Ramseyer) Etherington, were the original ancestors to settle in Harrison Township of Howard County. Richard received a sheepskin deed signed by President Zachary Taylor on March 20, 1849.

WILLIAM FREDERICK GOLLNER - William "Bill" was born May 23, 1897, in Wheeling, WV, to Frederick "Fred" William Gollner and Wilhelmina "Minnie" Charlotte Berrehsem. When Bill was just a boy the family moved to Kokomo, IN. He was one of 10 children. He told the story that on the first day of school he was looking all around him and he saw a bird fly into its nest. He climbed the tree and took the nest down. Someone saw him and called the principal. When he got to school, he was paddled for not leaving the nest alone! How times have changed.

Bill worked at Haynes-Apperson sweeping floors when he was only 16 years old. He also worked at the Spring Works. He worked as a tool maker at Kokomo Electric Company in the 1920s. He worked at Kingston Products for 42 years and retired from there as a tool and die maker. He was fortunate to have worked through the Depression. He loved to fish and he and a son, William Junior, built a house on Bruce Lake, near Kewanna, IN, for the family to enjoy the outdoors-especially fishing! He could tell some tall fish tales!

He married Gladys Lucille Lillard, the daughter of Jerry Lillard and Millie Justice, on April 19, 1921, in Brookville, IN. He met Gladys through his brothers.

He was 89 when he died on Aug. 29, 1986.

Gladys was born on Oct. 1, 1901, in Williamstown, KY. The family moved to Brookville, IN, where her father, Jerry, was the sheriff in Franklin County. She was secretary of the Howard County Democratic Party for 14 years and was employed in the Howard County Assessor's and Auditor's offices for 18 years. She was a member of the White Shrine and Order of the Eastern Star.

Bill and Gladys had five children, two of whom are still living. The oldest was Catherine Louise, born July 29, 1921. She died two days later and was buried at Crown Point Cemetery in Kokomo. Mary Elizabeth was born July 26, 1923, (spouse-Richard V. Harrison) and died unexpectedly on Nov. 27, 1987. She is buried at Sunset Memory Gardens Cemetery. Helen Lorraine was born Aug. 27, 1925, (spouse-Lewis Aeschliman) and died unexpectedly March 24, 1992. Wilma Lucille was born March 28, 1929, (spouse-Charles William Sosbe) and presently lives in Moore Haven, FL, where she is retired and is enjoying the warm weather. William Frederick, Junior, was born Oct. 25, 1931, (spouse-Roberta Ruth Riley) and presently lives in Carmel, IN, where he is retired.

JACOB AND SARAH (GODDARD) GOOD - Jacob Good was one of the very early settlers of Howard County. He was born Feb. 12, 1784 in Virginia. As a young man he moved to Sullivan County, TN where on Sept. 17, 1807 he married Sarah Goddard (born Aug. 15, 1785), the daughter of William and Elinor Goddard. In 1815 Jacob acquired land on Reedy Creek in Sullivan County, TN. He sold that land in 1822 following the deaths of Sarah's parents. The family likely moved to Indiana in the 1820's. Records indicate they lived in Union and Henry County, IN prior to moving to Howard County.

In 1841, Jacob Good came to Howard Township and made a treaty with the Indians to clear and cultivate a small patch of ground near Wild Cat Creek. The treaty was kept in good faith and the following summer a crop of corn was raised, being the first attempt at agriculture in the township.

Jacob and Sarah had nine children:

Delila, (born June 14, 1808-Knox County, TN) married Timothy Templin Sept. 8, 1831, Henry County, IN;

Drucilla, (born Dec. 9, 1810-Sullivan County, TN) married James Imel July 28, 1830, Union County, IN;

Lucinda, (born Nov. 30, 1813-Sullivan County, TN) married Martin Van Buren Smith Dec. 17, 1840, Howard County, IN.

Salathiel, (born March 31, 1816-Sullivan County, TN) married Eulila Templin Oct. 22, 1835, Delaware County, IN.

Mary, (born Aug. 17, 1818-Sullivan County, TN) married Leonard Wilson Jan. 25, 1842, Randolph County, IN.

Emma, (born Dec. 12, 1820-Sullivan County, TN) married James Stephens in Indiana.

Catherine (born Feb. 12, 1824) married Levi Hiatt.

William, (born Aug. 28, 1826) married Sarah Garringer June 4, 1846, Howard County, IN.

Jesse, (born March 31, 1829-Indiana) married Susannah Welty Oct. 17, 1850-Howard County, IN and after her death in 1852 married Minerva Stanley March 27, 1853.

Jacob Good died April 5, 1851, at the age of 67, and was the first person buried in Hopewell Cemetery, the site which was donated by his son Salathiel. Within two years Jacob was joined in this cemetery by six of his grandchildren ranging from one to ten years of age. They were the children of Timothy and Delila Good Templin and Martin and Lucinda Good Smith. Jacob's wife Sarah died Aug. 29, 1864 and is also buried in Hopewell Cemetery. *Submitted by Dick and Virginia Good*

SALATHIEL AND EULILA (TEMPLIN) GOOD - Salathiel and Eulila Good and their young family of four children followed Salathiel's parents, Jacob and Sarah Goddard Good, to Howard County in 1844. They settled on Wild Cat Creek, three miles east of Kokomo. He built his first cabin on the spot where the Hopewell Methodist Episcopal Church was later located.

Salathiel Jackson Good was born March 31, 1816 in Sullivan County, TN. October 22, 1835 he married Eulila Templin in Henry County, IN. Eulila (born May 14, 1816) was the daughter of Robert and Eunice Beals Templin.

In 1845 and 1846 Mr. Good served as a Howard County commissioner. When the first school was organized in 1845 Salathiel was elected teacher. The second schoolhouse was built about 1848 and Salathiel Good was among the early teachers. The first public schoolhouse was built in 1854. Good taught the first term in this building. The first election in Howard Township was held in 1848. Salathiel Good was elected one of the trustees.

In 1849 Salathiel donated 1/2 acre of his farm south of Wild Cat Creek for a church. It became the Hopewell Methodist Episcopal Church. He also donated the site for Hopewell Cemetery.

In the spring of 1854 Salathiel and Eulila Good sold their land in Howard County, IN and along with their eight children moved to Richland County, WI. They remained there only two years before they moved on with their now nine children to Nemaha County, NE.

Salathiel and Eulila's eight children all of whom were born in Henry and Howard County, IN were:

Jacob (born Feb. 12, 1838-Henry County, IN) married Barbara Lash Oct. 24, 1861.

Mary "Polly", (born Nov. 25, 1839-Henry County, IN) married Jonathan Higgins Nov. 26, 1857.

Catherine, (born Oct. 26, 1841-Henry County, IN married William Starr Nov. 15, 1861.

William, (born May 13, 1844-Indiana) married Irena Dundas Oct. 17, 1865.

Oliver, (born March 2, 1846-Howard County, IN) did not marry.

Eunice, (born Sept. 25, 1848-Howard County, IN) married Robert Dundas Oct. 25, 1865.

Sarah, (born Jan. 21, 1851-Indiana) married Jacob Starr Sept. 30, 1869.

Joseph, (born Feb. 22, 1853-Howard County, IN) married Rosalinda Phippenney Oct. 29, 1874.

Harriet who was born (May 29, 1855) in Wisconsin married Philip Starr Jan. 1, 1874.

Salathiel and Eulila spent the remainder of their lives at Glen Rock, NE. They both died within four days of each other (Feb. 23 and Feb. 17) in 1887. *Submitted by Dick and Virginia Good*

GORDON - William Gordon born North Carolina, married Sarah Reed daughter of Olive Reed and R. Cook, born in Virginia.

After their marriage they migrated to Jennings County, IN where their children were born. John 1824, married Frances Collins, settled in Ridgeway in western Howard County, as farmers raising seven children, Robert, Peter, George, Morton, Mary, Sarah and Albert, born 1862, married 1893 to Ladoska Thomas.

Albert and Ladoska had four children before her death in 1901. She left Simion, Roy, Ida and Milton Grant born Jan. 2, 1894. Albert seemed to be a very hospitable type, having a pot of beans on the stove and inviting all visitors to have a bowl. He met death in 1926 from an accident while driving a team of horses, the team running away, dragging him, and breaking his back.

Milton Grant and Agnes Blanche Miller, daughter of Calvin Leroy Miller and Elizabeth Ann Robards Miller, were married (See Robards). Milton was a part-time farmer and later was employed at Hoosier Iron in Kokomo.

Anne, Rick, Teena, Ken, 1952

Their children were Roscoe, John, Albert and Lewis (Chet). All were born and raised in Howard County.

John married Lilly Livingston and had four children, Jerry, Sondra, Kathy and Cindy. After Lilly's death he married Mary Lou Joyner. John was a shipping supervisor at Continental Steel; was proud to have been in the 1st Marines stationed in the Pacific during WWII. At one point he was listed "missing in action" but another John Gordon was the missing Marine. John passed on in 1978. Jerry, Kathy and Cindy and their families settled near Newberry, SC.

Albert met death due to a car accident in 1950, leaving his wife Betty (Smiley) and three sons Robert, Albert, and Thomas.

Chet served as bombardier in the Army Air Force during WWII, stationed in Italy. During the conflict his plane was shot down over Vienna, Austria, at which time he was a P.O.W. and later liberated. After being discharged he took schooling with General Motors, retiring from Delco Electronics. He married Mary Jo McKnight of Galveston. They have two children, Stephen and Janice, and one granddaughter, Holly Gordon, daughter of Stephen.

Roscoe, eldest son of Milton and Blanche, was born and lived in Howard County his entire life (see picture under Robards). He was one of many young men enlisting in the Civilian Conservation Corps. His time was spent in California and Lagro, IN, helping make state and national parks so all future generations can enjoy them. He retired from Continental Steel. He married Florence Elma Burke. They have four children (see picture).

Kenneth, an Indiana state trooper for 21 years, now supervisor of traffic systems, City of Kokomo, married Marcia Barthelemy, and had three children: Gregory, Jeffrey, and Kendra (More).

Erick, a tool design engineer, married Alma Ruth Bess and has one daughter, Anna Lee.

Teena, employed at Delco Electronics, married James Mills; two sons, Greyson and David; later she married Grady VanBriggle; they have one son, Chester Allen.

Anne Elizabeth, employed at Electronic Data Systems, married John Stout; they have one son, John Edward Stout II.

Numerous descendants still reside in Howard County. *Submitted by Florence E. Gordon*

GORDON - John Gordon was born in Jennings County May 17, 1824 and died Jan. 16, 1899 in Howard County. He was the son of William and Sarah Ann (Reed) Gordon. It's not known how long the Gordon family stayed in Jennings County; by 1845 they were in Ripley County. This is where John met and married a local girl by the name of Frances Collins. Frances was born Aug. 11, 1827 in Ripley County to Thomas and Mary (Young) Collins and died Jan. 20, 1921 in Blackford County, IN. Thomas and Mary Collins moved to Howard County in 1850. The move must have been between censuses because they were reported in Ripley County and Howard County in the same year. Sarah (Reed) Gordon followed with her fatherless children.

John (age 42) and his eldest son Henry Clay Gordon (age 18) joined the Civil War efforts on March 7, 1865 by joining Company G, 147th Regiment for one year. They got as far as Harper's Ferry, VA when the war ended. Both contracted ailments because of exposure and improper food which would eventually cause their deaths. Other children of John and Frances Gordon were: Pheba Ann Gordon (1848-1916) married Bill Yater; Thomas Randolph Gordon (1849-1900) married Sarah A. Dutro; John Taylor Gordon (1851-?) married Sarah E. (?); Mary Frances Gordon (1855-1929) married Daniel J. Weidner; Sarah Jemima Jane Gordon (1858-1939) married Jim Hethcote; James William Gordon (1860-1941) married Jane Sadie Peek; Albert Milton Gordon (1862-1926) married Ladoska A. Thomas; Robert Morton Gordon (1864-?) married Elizabeth Betty Hethcote; Peter Elsworth Gordon and George Grant Gordon (1869-1881).

Peter Elsworth Gordon was born in Howard County on March 8, 1867 and died Aug. 6, 1937. He was a firm Methodist. His granddaughter, Ruth (Phillips) Johnson, remembers him saying "A Methodist I am and a Methodist I'll be until the day I die". He met a beautiful redhead by the name of Matilda Alice Eldridge while singing in choir. She became his wife April 4, 1887 in Howard County. This loving and caring couple had seven children: Roy (1888-1888); Frederick Milton Gordon (1890-1957) married Martha M. Lowbert; Sylvia Ossie Gordon (1892-1982) married Homer Phillips; Flossie Blanche Gordon (1896-1957) married Warren Winingar; Paul Elsworth Gordon (June 7, 1898-Dec. 8, 1965) married Mabel Mary Fording; Lucille Gordon (1905-1985) married Henry Jones; and May Pauline Gordon (1907-1951) married Pete Crousore.

Matilda Alice Eldridge was born Feb. 14, 1868 in Indiana to John and Polly Ann (Morris) Eldridge. This beautiful lady was mother to her children and also her grandchildren. Matilda took on the responsibilities of helping care for four young children when her daughter-in-law Mabel Mary (Fording) Gordon died. Joan (Gordon) Pickard was one of these motherless children; she remembers her grandmother as a sweet and loving person. On June 1, 1935 while Matilda was walking her grandchildren home from Houston Park a car careened across the road and plowed into them. Killed instantly was Olive Lou Gordon, age nine, (daughter of Mabel Mary) and another granddaughter Pauline Elizabeth Crousore, age four. Olive Lou was buried just two weeks after the death of her mother. Matilda suffered back injuries and severe shock. She lived to the age of 85 and died Nov. 18, 1953. She was buried beside her beloved husband Peter in Shiloh Cemetery. *Submitted by Donnie M. Pickard*

GORTON/STONE - Samuel Gorton, born 1592, Lancashire, England, arrived in Boston Harbor in 1636, with wife Mary (Maplet) and some of their nine children. Samuel, known for his radical religious ideas, founded Warwick, RI.

Samuel's great-grandson, Joseph Gorton II, born 1755, married Susanna Hibbard and lived in Connecticut. Joseph fought in the American Revolution.

Joseph's great-great grandson, Alfred Edwin Gorton, born 1876, arrived in Howard County via Puerto Rico. Originally from Detroit, MI, Alfred was head clerk in the treasury in Puerto Rico after it became a territory. Blanch Ada Stone was a resident there, with her parents. She taught in the public schools. "They met. The usual result followed". (Detroit Free Press, circa 1908) Blanch and Alfred moved to Kokomo, where Alfred worked at the South Kokomo Bank. They had two children, Frances Ione (born in Puerto Rico) and Ashton Earl.

Blanch Ada Stone was born in Jerome, IN, the daughter of the Rev. John H. and Sarah Ellen (Brown) Stone. Dr. Stone was practicing optometry in Puerto Rico at the time Blanch and Alfred met. He was the son of Solomon and Mary Stone, who arrived in Howard County in 1857. Solomon and Mary both died in December 1917, after 73 years of marriage. John was one of four sons involved in some nasty litigation over the Stone estate and the subsequent burning of the Stone cabin, located two miles north of Greentown, IN. Dr. Stone died in 1942 and was the last surviving Union Civil War veteran in Howard County.

Frances Ione Gorton worked briefly as a cashier in the South Kokomo Bank and then joined an all girls band, called "The Ingenues". She travelled from 1925 to 1934 with the group, "playing in nearly every country on the globe" *(Kokomo Tribune,* Oct. 31, 1937). Later, she married Arnold Anderson and settled in Gary, IN. She was librarian at the Merrillville Public Library until they both retired and moved to Sun City, AZ. She died in 1979.

Frances and her dad Alfred were both working at the South Bank of Kokomo on May 27, 1925, when it was robbed. There is an extensive account of the robbery in the May 28, 1925, issue of the *Kokomo Dispatch.* The family dog, Speedy, was there and the account tells of his annoyance with and harassment of the robbers.

Ashton Gorton married Nila Josephine Duncan of Kokomo, IN. He was the publisher of the *Kokomo Sentinel,* beginning with the first issue, Aug. 23, 1935. The *Sentinel* was published every Friday and could be purchased for three cents a copy. He was a Civil Service investigator during and after WWII. In 1948 he became personnel officer for the Federal Narcotics Hospital in Lexington, KY, where he remained until retiring in 1972. Nila died in 1975 and Ashton moved to Sun City, AZ, where he died in 1984. They had two sons, Ashton Ellison and Charles Edwin.

Ashton Ellison married Dorothy Smith of Lexington, KY, and currently lives in Evans, GA. Ashton is a retired Army officer, and he and Dorothy are school teachers. They have three sons, Ashton Samuel, Benjamin Lewis, and Michael Gamble.

Charles married Linda Bowers of Circleville, OH. They live in Lexington, KY, where he is a public health administrator and she is a community volunteer/registered nurse. They have a daughter Abigail Suzanne and a son Clayton Charles. *Submitted by Charles E. Gorton, partially from the works of Ashton Earl Gorton*

MURL LEONA UNDERWOOD GOYER - Murl Leona Underwood Goyer, daughter of Thomas W. Underwood and Matilda (Hawkins) Underwood of Kokomo, IN. Married to Harry Elwood Goyer - deceased. They had two children: Rosemary Goyer Lovegrove lives in Naples, FL and Harry Elwood Goyer who lives in Hamilton, OH.

Murl Leona Underwood Goyer

Murl Goyer was recognized a "Volunteer of the Year" for the region, state and United States but she also earned another award, the Sagamore of the Wabash Award as designated by Indiana's Governor, Evan Bayh. The award is the highest honor given by the Governor. It has been presented to astronauts, presidents, artists and musicians in the past, but it was a special 92-year-old volunteer (Americanna Health Center, Kokomo, IN) whose lifetime of service to others garnered the highest honor. Goyer, shy and humble, accepted the award and stated, "I appreciate everyone. I've come a long way and I'm thankful." *Submitted by Rosemary E. Lovegrove*

GRADY-FORT - George Cornelius (Duke) Grady was the son of Emily Dunn and Louis Grady. He was born 1881 in Kentucky.

Emma Rene Fort was the daughter of Wilson and Harriet (Hatcher) Fort. She was born in Olmstead, Montgomery County, KY.

Emma and Duke had four sons: Isham, George born March 4, 1911, William Henry (Bill) born Feb. 1, 1905, and Josephus born Feb. 4, 1908.

Isham married the former Emma Fort. They had two sons, William E. (Shake) and Isham Jr. Isham owned Pea Pops BBQ Restaurant located at 301 S Cooper St.

George and Emma (Fort) Grady

George married the former Margret Smith. They had four children: George Edward, Jeannie, Margret (Lani) and Robert (Bobby). George retired from Continental Steel.

Bill married the former Anna Mae Kay. They had one son Stephen Grady. Bill owned the Blue Swan Restaurant and Record Shop located on E. North St. He also worked at Perfect Equipment.

Josephus married the former Bernice Johnson. They had two children Esterline and William R. (Billy). Joe retired from Penn Dixie. *Submitted by Josephus Grady*

GRADY-BROWNLOW - Ivan and Rosann met while he was stationed at Grissom Air Force Base as an air traffic controller. They dated two years and were wed Aug. 14, 1991 by Rev. Franklin S. Kemper at the church parsonage.

Ivan, the son of Doris E. (Black) and Richard L. Brownlow, was born June 23, 1956 in Tuscaloosa, AL. He graduated from Chattanooga City High School, Chattanooga, TN in 1972. He entered the Air Force in the summer of 1977. Ivan has been employed by Wilson Foods, Pittsburgh Plate Glass and is currently employed by Chrysler.

Ivan and Rosann Brownlow

Rosann a life-long resident of Kokomo, was born Feb. 1, 1959, the daughter of William R. and Barbara J. (Greer) Grady. She is a 1977 graduate of Kokomo High School. She attended Indiana University at Kokomo, Ivy-Tech and Chattanooga Community College. She is currently employed by Kokomo Center Township Schools.

Ivan and Rosann are the parents of two children, Evan Keith and Erika Lynn Brownlow. Evan was born June 9, 1983 at Erlanger Medical Center Chattanooga, TN and Erika was born June 9, 1984 at Howard Community Hospital, Kokomo, IN. *Submitted by Ivan Brownlow*

WILLIAM AND BARBARA (GREER) GRADY - Life-long residents of Kokomo, Wm was born May 4, 1928 the son of Josephus and Bernice Lily (Johnson) Grady. Wm attended Douglas Elementary School and is a 1947 graduate of Kokomo High School. Wm has been employed by Perfect Equipment, and retired from Chrysler Corporation with 34 1/2 years of employment. He served in the Korean War from 1950-1952.

William and Barbara (Greer) Grady Family

Barbara the daughter of Wm I. and Emma A. (Tanner) Greer, was born June 27, 1932. She attended Willard and Douglas Elementary Schools. She graduated from Kokomo High School in 1951. Barbara has worked at Dukes Restaurant, Stellite and Delco Electronics. She retired in 1988 with 23 years of service from Delco.

Wm and Barbara are the parents of three daughters: Suzette Rachel (Grady) Perrigen born Aug. 6, 1955, Ranita Ellen (Grady) Olive Meriwether, born Aug. 5, 1956 and Rosann (Grady) Brownlow born Feb. 1, 1959.

The Gradys attend Mt. Pisgah Missionary Baptist Church, where they have held various offices through the years such as Sunday School teachers, superintendent, trustee and choir member. *Submitted by Wm R. Grady*

GARY L. AND CAROL J. GRAF - Jobs brought Gary and Carol to Kokomo. Gary arrived in early 1967 with Lake Central Airlines. Later that year, he began working for Chrysler Corporation. Carol arrived in 1968 with Northern Community Schools of Tipton County. They met in 1969 while getting pictures developed. Not only did pictures develop, but also a romance. After a two-year courtship, they were married May 2, 1971.

Gary Lee was born in Morenci, MI, on Jan. 15, 1944. After graduating from high school in 1962, he joined the USAF (1963) and served four years in France and Germany.

Carol June (Corn) Graf was born in Oakland City, IN, on Nov. 12, 1944, but grew up in Spurgeon, IN. After graduating from high school (1962), her family moved to Oakland City. She graduated from Oakland City College in 1965 and taught third grade at Oakland City Elementary from 1965-1968. In 1968 she received her M.S. degree from Indiana State University and moved to Kokomo. She taught first grade at Windfall, IN, for ten years.

In 1975 Gary and Carol moved to Cicero, IN, to enjoy lake living. They lived there eight years before returning to Kokomo in August of 1983. The nicest thing that happened to them at Cicero was the birth of their son Kyle Patrick on Jan. 3, 1977.

Although Gary and Carol are transplants to Kokomo, their roots go back many generations in their respective home communities.

Gary's parents are Doyle Herbert Graf and Stella Beatrice (Heximer) Swartzendruber. His grandparents, Herbert and Fern (Berry) Graf, and great-grandparents, August and Anna (Schudel) Graf, were farmers in the Fayette, OH area from ca. 1872.

Gary's grandfather Gabriel Heximer (born Chippewa, Ontario, Canada) was a minister in the Evangelical Church. He came to the Alvordton, OH, area in the early 1920's. Gabriel had several churches there and used a horse and buggy to travel his rounds.

Grandmother Idella (Schweitzer) Heximer was born in Huron County, MI. This is where she married Gabriel on July 3, 1907. She died in 1980 in Wauseon, OH, at the age of 94.

Carol's parents, Sylvester and Nora (Hunley) Corn, were born and raised in Lockhart Twp., Pike County, IN. They were married on Oct. 2, 1924 and farmed for 20 years one mile south of Spurgeon, IN. When the coal mine opened up north of Spurgeon, Sylvester went to work there.

Carol's grandparents, William Pleasant and Minerva (Ambrose) Corn and John Thomas and Celia Jane (Fairchild) Hunley, were all farmers in Pike County, IN. Carol's great-grandparents were also farmers and early settlers of Pike County.

As with our ancestors, some being ministers or deacons, our Christian heritage is cherished. Chapel Hill Christian Church is our place of worship.

Gary completed 26 years of service with Chrysler Corporation in 1993. Carol is presently employed with the Kokomo-Howard County Public Library.

We have been happy to call Kokomo home for these past 25+ years. It is a friendly and caring community, a wonderful place to live and raise a family.

GRAHAM - Thomas Bell and Elizabeth (Lehman) Graham and their three children moved to Howard County in 1902 to farm the land owned by Elizabeth's father Franklin William Lehman. The farm was located northwest of the intersection of County Roads 500 West and 400 North. Their three children were:

Lavada Ellen born Jan. 3, 1890 in Champaign County, IL.

Charles Norman born July 7, 1891 in Champaign County, IL.

Maude Belle born April 20, 1895 in Champaign County, IL.

In 1926 Thomas and Elizabeth purchased the farm which they owned until their death in 1940 and 1944.

Front row: James, Robert, Charles, Bertha, Paul, John Graham. Back: Esther, Edna, Ruth, William, Mary, Norma, Carolyn in middle.

Lavada married Otto Bergman in 1911 and lived in Howard County until her death in 1979. Maude Belle married Charles Raymond Murphy in 1914 and they resided in Logansport until her death in 1931. Charles Graham graduated from Galveston High School and attended Indiana University, majoring in chemistry. He taught in the Macedonia and Patty one-room schools in Clay Township. Mary Donahue, a pupil he taught in the fourth grade, later taught ten of the Graham children in the third grade. After the Clay Township High School was built he drove the school bus for a few years. He worked for a sugar company in Puerto Rico, munitions plants in New Jersey and Alton, IL, and for Union Carbide in Niagara Falls, NY. After serving in the Army during WWI he married Bertha L. Zimmerman and returned to Clay Township in Howard County to farm. After renting several farms he moved to his parents' farm in 1935.

Charles Graham was a progressive farmer with a strong interest in conservation. He was active in the Farm Bureau, serving as chairman of both the Clay Township and Howard County organizations. He used the best known farming methods to improve the soil and crops. He was one of the first farmers in the county to use hybrid seed corn to improve yield. The last year he farmed in Howard County, 1945, his farm raised the highest corn yield in the five acre corn contest.

Charles and Bertha raised 11 children:

Mary Elizabeth born Nov. 29, 1918, Edna Grace born Nov. 10, 1919, Ruth Helen, born May 22, 1922, William Thomas born Oct. 25, 1924, Esther Eileen, born June 24, 1926, James Adair born April 1, 1928, John Richard born Sept. 28, 1929, Norma Louise born Oct. 8, 1931, Robert Lee born March 14, 1933, Paul Edward born June 30, 1935, Carolyn Sue born May 29, 1940.

The family were members of the Galveston Methodist Church. The six oldest graduated from Clay Township High School. The next four attended Clay until the family moved to Wabash County in 1946. All the children were active in 4-H clubs and Indiana Rural Youth.

Edna married Donald P. Smith and raised four children in Clay Township until his death in 1967. She was employed by several restaurants and the Kokomo School System. In 1971 she married Frank Jackson.

Esther married William E. Givens and resides in Kokomo to the present. She was employed by several banks and the Kokomo Post Office.

GRAMMER - William Edward Grammer was born on Feb. 11, 1931 in Lafayette, IN. His parents were William Earl and Nora (Harper) Grammer. William became deaf because of an illness. He attended Indiana School for the Deaf. He quit after ten years of schooling. Lena Mae Kendall was born on Jan. 7, 1933 in Marion, IL. Her parents were Carl and Pauline (Booth) Kendall. Lena was born deaf. She attended Illinois School for the Deaf. She went for six years and then quit. The two then got married on Aug. 23, 1952 in Marion, IL. They then moved to Kokomo because of jobs. William worked in a factory which is now called Haynes International. He retired from there. Lena worked in the laundry department at in Howard Community Hospital. She retired from the hospital. They had two children together. The first born was Rhonda Jean. She was born on Sept. 11, 1955 in Kokomo. The second born was Thomas Edward. He was born on Aug. 21, 1957.

Rhonda Jean married Kevin Michael Bitner. He was born on Dec. 15, 1954 in Kokomo. His parents are Paul Ervin Sr. and Jane Ann (Clark) Bitner. Both Kevin and Rhonda graduated from Kokomo High School in 1973. Kevin had a job with Kingston Products waiting for him after they were married. He worked there for 18 years, but the factory closed. After that he sought employment elsewhere. During this time they had three children together, the first being Stacy Marie born on July 26, 1975; the second being Brian Michael born on Jan. 20, 1978; the last being Erica Jane born on March 9, 1981. Rhonda did not start working until all three of her children were in school.

Thomas Edward married Carolyn Jeanette Mundy on May 27, 1989. Carolyn was born on Aug. 6, 1959. Her parents are Floyd and Virginia Mundy. Thomas went to Indiana School for the Deaf, but quit after nine years. Carolyn went to Indiana School for the Deaf and quit, too. Thomas worked at Kingston Products, but he was in a motorcycle accident and was too disabled to work. They had two children together, the first born being Troy Edward. He was born on Nov. 6, 1989. The second born was Sarah Jeanette, born on May 9, 1991.

GRAU - John A. Grau, our grandfather, was born in Germany in 1823. At the age of 26, after serving six years in the German Army, he came to the United States, leaving his parents, brothers and sisters in Germany. He was one of 11 children. He had little money to make the voyage across the Atlantic. His father loaned him $15.00 and some friends loaned him a little. He may have done a little work on the boat if it was available. The trip by sail boat was long and treacherous. He landed in New York, but we have no record of events until he came to Ohio, date unknown. In Ohio, he married Christina Henninger, date unknown. She died in 1855. They had three children. All are buried in Ohio. After his wife Christina died, he married Regina Kauffman, his housekeeper. To this second marriage were born eight children. Our father, Charles W. Grau, was one of the eight. John A. Grau is buried in Howard County. He died in 1883.

Charles W. Grau was born in Ohio (1863-1932). He came to Howard Township, Howard County with his parents at an early age. Mary E. Fisher was born in Ohio (1867-1929), the daughter of Isaac and Catherine (Strome) Fisher. She came to Howard Township with her parents at an early age. Both families settled as neighbors in the mid 1800s, in Howard Township. Charles and Mary were married May 25, 1890, and settled on a small farm owned by Charles, who was a farmer in Howard Township.

To this marriage were born ten children: Oaroe, Merle, Mae, Albert and Alberta (twins), Gladys, Miriam, Theodore, Kathryn and Richard Grau. Merle married John C. Shrock in 1915. They had two children: Eldon Shrock and Marjorie Shrock Keim Naphew. Mae married John S. Durr in 1917. They had four children: Mary Durr Richey, Wilford Durr, a son who died at birth and Norma Jean Durr Spangler. Gladys married Kenneth Kratzer in 1921. They had one son: Thomas Kratzer. Miriam married Harry Durr in 1924. They had three children: Eugene Durr, Wanita Durr Covalt, and Paul Durr. Theodore Grau married Glenda Quick in 1943. They had two children: Annette Grau Hyman and Jerry Grau.

Richard Grau married Miriam Dunlap in 1938. They had two children: Rebecca Grau McClure and David Grau.

The Charles Grau family is in its sixth generation and number approximately 60 direct descendents. Most of them live in Indiana, in Indianapolis, Plainfield, Lebanon, Lafayette, Boswell, Elkhart, Howard, Grant and Miami Counties. The farm in Howard Township has been in the family many years and is still owned by a grandson of Charles Grau. There are teachers, farmers, business persons, a doctor and attorney among the descendants of Charles and Mary Grau. *Submitted by Kathryn Grau, daughter of Charles and Mary Grau*

WILLIAM AND EMMA (TANNER) GREER - William Irving Greer was born July 31, 1888 in Morristown, TN the son of Jasper and Maggie Greer. He moved to Middletown, IN at the age of 12 with his father and step-mother Florence. The family eventually settled in Marion, IN where they raised a family. Jasper found work in the Iron Works Foundry and Florence was a homemaker.

William, at the age of 23, married Emma (Armanda) Tanner on Sept. 2, 1911. Emma was born Aug. 25, 1892, in Carthage City, Rush County, IN. She was the daughter of Joseph Henry and Arcena Iona (Watkins) Tanner. Joseph worked as a housemover while Arcena was a homemaker.

William I. Greer and Emma Greer

William was a barber and was co-owner of Hughes and Greer Barbershop located at 117 N. Union St. in downtown Kokomo. Emma was a homemaker. They raised 13 children, eight sons and five daughters: William Irving born Dec. 1, 1912, Jeanette Iona born Sept. 15, 1915, Rosemary born Dec. 16, 1916, Charles Edwin born March 18, 1919, Howard Jasper born March 5, 1922, Paul Arthur born Nov. 14, 1923, John Richard born May 17, 1925, Myrle Eugene born April 10, 1927, Ralph Louis born Dec. 26, 1928, Peggy Louise born Sept. 5, 1930, Barbara Jean born June 27, 1932, James Alvin born Aug. 2, 1934 and Shirley Ann born Sept. 5, 1936.

William was a member of the Secondary Missionary Baptist Church, where he was superintendent for 10 years. He was also a member of Masonic Order Keystone No. 40, and one of the patrons of Golden Link Chapter of Eastern Star. He died Aug. 20, 1939.

Emma was honored as Kokomo's 1957 Mother of the Year. Nominated by her son Charles, who spelled out the word Mother, beginning each line with letters of the word. His letter follows: M-Mom is the mother of 13 living grown children; O- of this there are 19 grandchildren and six step-grandchildren; T-through her teachings and guidance her children have become leaders and well recognized in their community; H-happy at all times and more than willing to do her part in charity and church work; E-ever ready at any call to come to our homes or any home to pray or give counseling to any remedy, in illness; R-religion and brotherly love is her daily teaching.

Emma was an active member of Second Missionary Baptist Church. She served on Missionary and Usher Boards, Senior and Missionary Choirs, Golden Age Club and Mothers of World War II. She died Aug. 20, 1963, and is buried alongside her husband in Crown Point Cemetery, Kokomo, IN.

GREESON - The first naturalized citizen in this family was Isaac Greeson born 1703 Germany, died 1774 North Carolina. He came on the ship *James Goodwill* in 1728. We know of four children.

Jacob (Isaac) Greeson, a Revolutionary War Vet, married 1765 Elizabeth. They had eight children, all born in North Carolina.

Isaac Greeson born 1766, died 1856, married 1787 Dorothy Turley Ingle. He was a farmer. They were Lutheran, and had six children all born in North Carolina.

Jacob Greeson born 1789 North Carolina, married 1813 Katricka Lefful born 1798 North Carolina, died 1873 Indiana. He was a farmer. They were Lutheran, and had 12 children, nine born in North Carolina and three in Indiana.

David Greeson born 1815 North Carolina, died 1906 Indiana, married 1842 Mary (Polly) Hodges born 1823 Indiana, died 1868 Indiana. He was a farmer. They were Methodist Episcopal. They came to Howard County in 1851, and are buried at Alto. They had four children who died in infancy, and seven who lived to adulthood.

Rachel Ann Greeson born 1844 Indiana, died 1919 Indiana, married 1866 Williamson Dixon Ward born 1841 IN, died 1917 Indiana. He was a farmer and a carpenter, and a Civil War Vet. They were Methodist. They lost two girls young to diphtheria in Kansas, and one to an accident. Their four other daughters were: Ida Izora was a secretary at KHS, born 1856, died 1933 Indiana; Flora Esta a teacher in Kokomo Schools born 1868 Indiana, died 1952 Indiana; Harriat Rebecca a principal, born 1875 Indiana, died 1952 Indiana, married 1912 Lawrence McTurnan; Ola Grace.

Ola Grace Ward, a teacher in Kokomo Schools, born 1880 Indiana, died 1953 Indiana, married 1905 Indiana Albert Frederick Blossey born 1871 Wisconsin, died 1951 Indiana, an engineer. The Blossey family is covered in another article in this book. *Submitted by R. Ann Nichols*

GRIM FAMILY OF JACKSON TWP. - Samuel Grim was the great-grandfather of Ferol Palmer Stahl. Both born on July 16, exactly 99 years apart. 1832 and 1931.

Sam was born in Preston County, WVA and died Jan. 5, 1909 Howard County, IN, the son of Nicholas and Susannah Jones Grim. He married Rachel Tibbets Aug. 4, 1859 Blountsville, IN. Rachel born May 9, 1840 Blountsville, IN and died Oct. 29, 1916 Howard County, IN, the daughter of Joseph and Margaret Tully Tibbets.

Jack E. and Ferol J. Stahl

Sam and Rachel came to Howard County soon after their marriage and settled on a 40 acre farm in Jackson Twp. Nine children were born to Sam and Rachel, but only three grew to maturity.

Catherine Elizabeth, 1860-1888. Married George Boston.

Joseph L. 1862-1862, age nine months.

John Samuel 1865-1942, married Amanda Weesner.

Henry L. 1866-1867 Age 10 months.

Margaret V. "Rett" 1869-1949 married Leondus M. "Lonzo" Palmer.

Levi died at birth.

Luther D. 1876-1876 age 10 months.

(twins) Willie O. and Tilla died at birth 1878.

Margaret and Lonzo were married in 1886, Howard County, IN. He was the son of Jonathon and Rebecca A. Brandon Palmer.

Three babies born and died in Howard County, Elmer and the twins Freddie and Eddie. They then moved to a farm in LaFountaine, IN. There, four more children were born:

Cora Bell 1889-1924 married Joseph Boucher and Hershel Land.

Emma Sylvia 1893-1956 married Estel Girton.

Jesse Samuel "Jim" 1896-1986 married Velma A. Roderick and Daisy Bilby Rench. Jesse was a veteran of WWI.

Russell Lee "Pete" 1898-1981 married five times.

By 1900 Lonzo and Margaret were back living in Jackson Township, Howard County, IN.

GRINSLADE - The research that I have put into the Grinslade ancestry has been very rewarding to me. My effort will be compensated just to be able to pass on some of the activities that have been told to me in the past so that the future generation can read about them.

Records inform us that Josiah Grinslade was born Dec. 21, 1797 in New Jersey. He was the son of John Grinslade and Rebecca Moore who were married at Upper Springfield, Burlington County, NJ and grandson of John Grinslade and Elizabeth Matson. They were married at Piles Grove, NJ.

Josiah (1792-1868) traveled with his family to Clay County, IN. Later he married Elizabeth Smith (1800-1863) and moved to Wayne County, IN. They then had several sons who migrated to several places in the U.S.

Thomas Grinslade (1820-1880) was one of the sons that migrated to Marion County, IN where he married Mary Elizabeth Wilson on Feb. 23, 1854 in Marion County.

Thomas and William Johnson, as young men, walked or rode horses from Indianapolis to a location which is now Howard Township of Howard County. Records show Thomas purchased 80 acres for $200 on Sept. 20, 1849. They then built their log house near a large rock, which is claimed to be the largest rock in Howard County; it was also used by the Indians for a meeting place. This rock is large enough to drive four head of horses upon it side by side. Later Thomas purchased more ground on the Sept. 25, 1871 which consisted of 40 acres for $400. They had four children: Samuel M., John William, Charles Luther, Thomas Schuyler. Then Elizabeth gave birth to triplets, two girls and one boy, on Oct. 31, 1866. One daughter, Sarah Jane, died shortly after birth. Elizabeth died one week later after having the triplets. The other daughter, Elizabeth Frances, died ten months later. The other triplet, Wilson Elmer, was the only child who survived of the triplets.

Thomas in 1868 married his second wife Clara Norton and built a house at the present location of 3154 East 500 North, Howard County. In 1895 Clara Norton donated one acre of ground for the present Rich Valley Church.

Wilson Elmer Grinslade married Rosa Alice Weaver in 1889. Then on Nov. 26, 1902, W.E. Grinslade bought the homestead from his stepmother. W.E. and Rosa had six children: Ersie Elizabeth (Grinslade) Yager (1890-1977), Dora Pearl (Grinslade) Ward (1893-1983), Lucy Marurette (Grinslade) Locke (1896-1937), Regina Ann (Grinslade) Powell (1898-1984), John W. Grinslade (1903-1989), Fern Alice (Grinslade) Draper (1907-).

During 1916-1917 the Howard Township School was erected under the supervision of W.E. Grinslade, at that time trustee of Howard. It was the consolidation of seven one-room schools: Cassville, Vermont, Holler, Brown, Loop, Prairie and Rich Valley. The school opened Sept. 7, 1917 and the last high school graduation was in the spring of 1948. The building is still used as a grade school. W.E. received a lot of criticism from patrons for construction of a gymnasium in the building.

John W. Grinslade (1903-1989) married Thelma Johnson (1904-1966) and had three children: Beverly (Grinslade) Downey, John II and Thomas Grinslade.

John and Thelma purchased the homestead in 1937 from his mother Rosa. John was a farmer and trucker all of his life.

John Grinslade and Carroll Odom were the original pioneers who formed the Northwestern School Corporation. John was on the school board at Howard, and Carroll was trustee of Clay.

John and Beulah Grinslade II on June 14, 1971 purchased the homestead and are the present owner-operators. The homestead has been in the Grinslade name for 146 years. *Submitted by John W. Grinslade II*

GRINSLADE - My grandfather wrote the "Grinslade Ancestor Family" and I began writing "The Grinslade Family" from where he finished writing. I will continue to share more about our family so that the future generations will know about their family history.

John II, who is my grandfather, has informed me of some of the events when he was a young man. In 1948 it was the last year for nine high schools in Howard County. The county basketball tourney was a big deal then as it is now. The Howard Hornets were the winners that year. John II was the center on the team and was a member of the All Tourney Team. His senior year 1949 was the first year for Northwestern High School.

John II married Beulah Walker on Dec. 30, 1951 at Greentown Methodist Parsonage. He was in the Air Force until 1955, then returned to Howard County to work at Continental Steel and to farm the home farm that his great-grandfather purchased in 1849. They had four children: Jennie Rose (Grinslade) Spencer, Dec. 28, 1952; John Wilson III, Dec. 21, 1954; Bernice Kay (Grinslade) Reser Taylor, March 25, 1956; and Timothy Joe, Sept. 20, 1958. The children were the third generation to attend Howard School. Jennie was the first student in the second generation of graduates of Northwestern High School. The grandchildren of John and Beulah make the sixth generation to attend the First United Methodist Church.

Jennie Rose married Virgil Lee Spencer on July 16, 1971 at Greentown First United Methodist Church after he returned from the U.S. Army. They had three children: David Lee, July 31, 1972; Brenda Lee, March 23, 1974; and Jody Lee, May 16, 1976.

Jennie is a bus driver for Eastern School Corporation, and Virgil works at Chrysler Corporation. Jennie and Virgil are both volunteers for Eastern Howard Emergency Service. Jennie is an EMT and driver, and Virgil is a First Responder and driver.

For three generations the family has been participating in 4-H. David and Brenda have received the "Key Club Award," and Jody will received the award too. David, Brenda, and Jody have all won Grand Champion Pigeon at the State Fair. Brenda currently holds the record for the most money brought in by selling her pigeon in the Highlight Auction at the State Fair.

In 1994 David is graduating from Vincennes University. Brenda is attending Purdue University and majoring in management. Jody is a senior at Eastern High School and will graduate in May.

One tradition that you might notice is that several of the children are named after relatives. Jennie Rose and Virgil Lee are both named after grandparents, so they continued the tradition by giving their children, David Lee, Brenda Lee, and Jody Lee, middle names that have been passed down for five generations. *Submitted by Brenda L. Spencer*

GROVE - High school sweethearts Kenneth L. and Linda A. Gill were married May 22, 1971 at Saint Mary's Church in Dunkirk, IN. They had a daughter Jennifer, in July 1973 and soon afterwards the family came to Howard County for employment at Chrysler Corporation. Another daughter Emily, was born in Howard County in May 1975. A year later the family purchased a home in Greentown.

August 2, 1921 - DJ, Dorothy, Aunt Emma, Avis, Mary Clyde, Ore, Carl, Jimmy

Linda's parents are James Manor and Barbara Joyce Gill. They were married in 1946 in Forest Hills, NY. They raised five children in Albany, IN. Jim and his only brother Bob began a lifetime partnership together there, first opening a successful LP gas business from 1947 to 1965. After selling the business, they decided to develop a 40-lot housing addition named after their mother, Alcyon Acres, and when that was finished they built two apartment complexes. They built a furniture store outside Albany and began a new business venture. It was very successful and they both retired in 1991. The store was a family run business from the start, employing all the children at one time or another. Their sons bought the store.

Jim and Bob's family history goes back to 1760 with the birth of Benjamin Manor. Benjamin's son Samuel, (1782-1804) also had a son and named him Caleb Manor (1806-1874). Caleb was one of 11 children born to Samuel and Elizabeth Manor of Berkeley County, VA. Caleb came to Richland Township of Jay County in 1838. Caleb and his wife Elizabeth had 11 children. They were one of the earliest members of Fairview Methodist Church. Caleb farmed and was a merchant. Later in life while visiting a son who moved to Iowa, Caleb's wife died and is buried there. His son David James "DJ" (1845-1923), who fought in the Civil War, married Sarah Woolverton and had two children. They moved to Albany where Sarah died and DJ became a widower. A few years later DJ married Mary Mann, also from a prominent family in Albany, in 1887. She was a teacher and had two children with DJ. Before her marriage, Mary taught school in Dunkirk and quite a few years at Albany. She was a loving wife, mother, teacher and grandmother. DJ owned quite a few businesses during his lifetime. Besides being a merchant in dry goods, he dealt in real estate and livestock. When he died, he left a farm for each child. DJ and Mary had two children together, Alcyon and Avis. Alcyon (1889-1954) graduated from Indiana University and taught English and Latin. Alcyon taught high school in Desoto and also in Albany for 25 years. She married Carl Gill (1886-1925), a veterinarian, and they had two sons: Jim (my father) and Bob Gill. After Carl died, Jim and Bob, along with their mother, moved from the farmhouse outside of town, to the grandmother's home on Main Street. Jim was raised in the same home that he raised his own five children. Bob still lives on the original family farm outside Albany, the same home Jim and him were born in. Today the brothers remain very close and talk with each other almost daily. *Submitted by Mrs. Kenneth Grove*

ORLA REX "PAT" GUGE - A descendant of hard Dutch-Scotch-Irish stock, Orla Rex Guge (born March 30, 1910), known as "Pat" to friends and family, was born and raised in Kokomo, IN. It was there he met and married pretty, young Helen Mae Imlay (born March 11, 1916) on June 13, 1933. Together they raised seven children - Richard Lee, Barbara Mae, Patricia Ann, Charles Robert, Judith Ray, Rex Loren and Donald Gene. And finally, after a lifetime of living in Howard County, Orla Rex "Pat" Guge was laid to rest beneath its soil.

Helen May (Imlay) and Orla Rex "Pat" Guge with first child Richard 1935.

"Pat's" parents, Oliver Franklin Guge (born Sept. 4, 1886) and Bessie Glee Barnhart (born June 26, 1889), were married June 26, 1909 in Howard County. Bessie brought with her to the marriage a daughter, Violet Annabelle Graham, and during the next ten years "Frank" and Bessie added five more children to their family - Orla Rex "Pat", Mary Louise, Donald Glenn, Charles Russell and Loren Oris. Times were difficult for the young family and in the early 1920's Frank and Bessie divorced. They each eventually married again. Frank married Ombra McVety. Bessie married Benjamin Harrison Newburn and gave birth to four more children - Doris Maxine, Benjamin Harrison, Jr., Everett Nathaniel and Robert Lewis. Oliver Franklin Guge died at the age of 82, Feb. 26, 1969 and was buried in Crown Point Cemetery in Kokomo. Bessie Glee (Barnhart) Guge Newburn died Nov. 18, 1975 at the age of 86 and was also buried in Crown Point.

David Wesley Guge farmed the land as did his father before him. David (born September 1856) and his wife, Alice (Smith) Guge (born June 1855) were married April 28, 1843 in Boone County. They had six children - Charles, Oliver Franklin "Frank", John, Martha, Archie Carl and Jesse. The family farmed first in Tipton County and then in the West Middleton area of Howard County. David died in 1917 and Alice followed him in 1938. They lie together in Prairieville Cemetery in Tipton County along with David's parents, Nicholas and Martha Guge.

Nicholas H. Guge (also spelled "Gouge" in several old legal documents) was an early pioneer of Tipton County. Born in 1807 in Kentucky, he migrated northward into Indiana in the 1820's. He married Martha Dickinson April 28, 1843 in Boone County and then moved on to Tipton County as early as 1849, only four years after Tipton officially became a county. They farmed and they raised ten children - James V., William, Martha, Francis, Margaret, Samuel, Nicholas, David Wesley, Ananias and Sarah. Nicholas was 61 years old when he died Nov. 23, 1868. Martha died in 1902. She was 77.

Orla Rex "Pat" Guge passed away Jan. 15, 1987 at the age of 76 and was laid to rest in Sunset Memory Gardens. Helen, his loving wife of 54 years, joined him there two years later March 17, 1989, six days after her 73rd birthday. They left behind three sons, two daughters, 23 grandchildren, 27 great-grandchildren and a history of a family six generations strong in Howard County.

HACKENBRACHT

Vohann Heinrich Hackenbraugh was born March 20, 1819, in the village of Diedenshausen Konigried Prensen Provine, Germany. His occupation was a weaver. On Oct. 20, 1846, in Germany he married Friederche Marie Spies. She was born Nov. 8, 1827 in Konigried Peresen, Germany. In 1848 they migrated to America, settling in Coshocton County, OH. They had three children. Yohann died Jan. 23, 1893 and Friederche died May 12, 1902. Both died in Tuscarauas County, OH and were buried in St. Jacobs Lutheran Cemetery in Tuscarauas County, OH.

One of their three children, George Daniel Hackenbracht, was my grandfather. He was born Aug. 24, 1849, at Port Washington, OH. On Dec. 29, 1876, he married Mary Phillips at Coshocton, OH. Seven children were born to them. My father, Frank William, was the oldest. He was born Jan. 5, 1878. On Oct. 20, 1909, he married Grace B. Swigert, of Black Run, OH. They had six children: Francis, Velma, Howard, Kenneth, Lillian and Mary Ellen. Frank died Sept. 28, 1959, and Grace died Sept. 29, 1932. Both are buried in Fairfield Cemetery, West Lafayette, OH.

Mr. and Mrs. Kenneth Hackenbracht

Howard Hackenbracht, born June 16, 1918 in West Lafayette, OH, came to Howard County from Texas in 1939. He had been working on a ranch there. He worked for his aunt and uncle for some time on a farm in Jackson Township. He married Lorena Trout in May 1941. They had three children, Nancy, Joyce, and Dennis. Lorena died Jan. 10, 1958. Later Howard married Bea Hurlock and they had one son, Carl. Howard and Bea both worked at RCA in Marion until they retired. She died Oct. 25, 1991 and is buried in the Jefferson Cemetery near Upland, IN. Howard still lives outside of Greentown.

Kenneth Hackenbracht, born July 31, 1922 in West Lafayette, OH, came to Howard County in October 1939 by hitchhiking from Ohio. He walked from Marion, IN to a farm two miles west of Roseburg where Howard was living at the time. Kenneth worked on a farm for his aunt and uncle and was farming for his Aunt Lillian when he entered the Army. He was a volunteer at Ft. Benjamin Harrison near Indianapolis. February 18, 1943 he went to Florida for training and then to California for school. He was sent to England in February 1944, and served with the 112th Airborne Signal Battalion attached to the First Airborne Army. He served in England, France and Germany with the last nine months spent in Berlin, Germany. He was discharged March 26, 1946, at Camp Atterbury, with the rank of Tech. 4th Grade. He returned to Howard County where he was employed by a cousin for a year.

On Jan. 1, 1947, he married Miriam Wyrick. She graduated from Jackson High School in 1942. They started farming by renting a farm from his aunt. They had two daughters: Sherrill, born Nov. 30, 1949 and Jo Ellen, born Feb. 21, 1953. Kenneth and Miriam lived and worked on the same farm in Jackson Township for 38 years. They also farmed for several other people. Miriam died Jan. 28, 1985 and was buried in Greentown Cemetery. Miriam and Rachel Jenkins organized the genealogy project and got it started as a 4H project for the Howard County Fair. Sherrill is married to Danny Jarrard and lives in Columbus, IN. She is an LPN and works at a hospital in Columbus. Sherrill and Danny have two daughters, Shannon and Heather. Jo Ellen resides in Greentown. She is a graduate of Indiana University-Kokomo and works at a Kokomo bank. Kenneth later married his sister-in-law, Betty Mullen Wyrick, who worked as a nurse in Phoenix, AZ. She had been a widow for eight and a half years. Originally from Kokomo, Betty graduated from Kokomo High School in 1944. They still live in Jackson Township where Kenneth has lived 46 years on the same farm. Betty is retired from nursing and Kenneth (the author of this article) still farms 80 acres.

DAVID K. AND NANCY SUE HARGISS -

David K. Hargiss first came to Kokomo fresh from graduating from high school (June 1959) after receiving a telegram from Chrysler Corporation offering him an apprenticeship. He accepted an apprenticeship in Machine Repair and moved to Kokomo in August 1959. That was the beginning of this Hargiss family in Howard County.

David K. Hargiss was born at Emerald Hogdson Hospital, Sewannee, Franklin County, TN, on Oct. 15, 1940, to William David (born Marion County, TN) and Bessie Lou (Blankenship) Hargiss (born Hazel Green, AL). David's early years were spent in the mountains and coves of beautiful southeastern Tennessee in the Sequatchie Valley. His grandparents were Abraham and Martha Jane (Culpepper) Hargiss and Benjamin and Linnie Mae (Crowe) Blankenship. Both families had been in Tennessee since the early 1830s. David's family moved to New Castle, Henry County, IN, in 1954.

David and Nancy Hargiss

Nancy Sue Reynolds Hargiss was born Sept. 21, 1943 at St. Mary's Hospital, Sabetha, Nemaha County, KS to Wilbur (born Rushville, IN) and Iva M. (Jordan) Reynolds (born Nemaha County, KS). Wilbur and Iva met and married in New Castle, IN. While Wilbur was serving with the US Army during WWII, Iva went home to Kansas where Nancy was born. Nancy lived in the same house in which her mother and grandmother Leona Bruce Jordan had been born. This house had been built by her great-grandfather, Charles W. Bruce, on their farm south of Sabetha. After WWII, Nancy's family moved back to New Castle.

Nancy and David graduated from Walter P. Chrysler Memorial High School, New Castle, IN. They moved to Kokomo in 1962. David finished his apprenticeship and became a journeyman at the Kokomo Chrysler Transmission Plant. He became the Tool Room Supervisor in 1968. He now has 35 years with Chrysler Corporation. Nancy has a real estate license and does volunteer work. They have two children.

Cheri Sue Hargiss was born Nov. 19, 1961 at Ball Memorial Hospital, Muncie, Delaware County, IN. Jeffrey David was born Sept. 17, 1964 at St. Joseph Hospital, Kokomo. From 1963 to 1970 the family lived in Galveston, IN. In 1970 the family moved to Ervin Township, Howard County, where Nancy and David still reside.

Cheri attended school at the Galveston Elementary School until the end of the second grade. Cheri and Jeffrey attended Ervin Elementary. Cheri graduated from Northwestern High School in 1980 and Jeffrey graduated in 1983. Cheri is a Majority member, Past Worthy Advisor (twice) and Past Grand Representative to Michigan in the International Order of Rainbow for Girls, Walton Assembly, Walton, IN. She attended Grand Assemblies in Michigan, Nebraska, West Virginia and Indiana. She received the Quill and Scroll award for journalism in high school.

Jeffrey was in the Northwestern Tigers Marching Band, stage, and President of VICA. In 1982 he received 2nd Place in the Indiana State Vocational Machine Trades Contest. He is Past Master Councillor and past State Officer of the Order of DeMolay, Kokomo Chapter. Active in scouting, he was a cub scout and member of Boy Scout Troop #534.

While attending Purdue University, Cheri met David John Patrick Kilty (born March 3, 1958). They were married Sept. 8, 1984 in St. Mary Cathedral, Lafayette, IN. Dave attended Little Flower Elementary School and graduated from Scecina High School, Indianapolis, IN. He has a Bachelor of Science Degree from Purdue University, Master's Degree in Business Administration from Indiana Wesleyan University, and an Associate Degree in Computer Technology from IUPUI. He is a Quality Assurance Engineer at Kokomo's Chrysler Corporation Transmission Plant and Secretary of UAW 1302. Cheri is the Director of the YWCA's Family Intervention Center in Kokomo. She attended Purdue University and St. Mary's of the Woods College. She is past State President and current board member of Indiana Coalition Against Domestic Violence. She has been Director of the Lafayette YWCA's Woman in Crisis program and Assistant Director of the Marion program.

Jeffrey currently resides in Colorado. He is a computer technician and a photographer. He is still interested in music and plays keyboard, all brass instruments, drums and electric guitar. Much of his musical training is self-taught. His hobbies include miniature trains and wood carving.

David is a member of Galveston F & AM Lodge #244, Life Member of the National Rifle Association, National Muzzleloaders Association, and Past Scoutmaster of Boy Scouts of America Troop #534. David, Nancy and Cheri are members of the Order of Eastern Star and are Past Matrons and Patron. Nancy is a Majority member and past WA & Rep. of International Order of Rainbow for Girls. Nancy and Cheri are members of Sigma Phi Gamma International Sorority. Nancy is a Life Member of the sorority and served as International President 1984-85. She was International Vice-President, Editor and Counselor. Nancy and Cheri are members of the National Association of Parliamentarians, Indiana State Association of Parliamentarians, and American Institute of Parliamentarians, holding the classification of Parliamentarian.

Some of Nancy's Quaker ancestors were in Indiana by the 1830s. Francis Pellett, Nancy's 4th great-grandfather was born 1765 in Moate, Leinster Province, Ireland and came to America in 1799. The Pelletts, Borams and Holloways were early settlers of Parke and Marshall Counties, IN, from Columbiana County, OH. Jordans were in Greene County in the 1860s. These families moved on to Kansas where the next three generations were born. Nancy's mother moving to Indiana completed the circle, bringing the line back to Indiana.

The Hargiss clan in America dates back to Virginia before the Revolutionary War. Abraham Hargiss is reported to have been a drummer boy in the War of the Revolution. David's ancestors of Culpepper, Owens, Pyburn, Anderson, Watley, Brooks, Floyd, Coffelt, Goodman and Bible were all early settlers of Marion and Franklin Counties, TN. Most of them came from Virginia, Maryland and the Carolinas.

Although Jeffrey Hargiss is the only one of our immediate family to have been born in Indiana, our families have long histories in Indiana, Tennessee and Kansas. *Submitted by Nancy Hargiss.*

HAINLEN - The Hainlen family of Jackson Township has a long history in northeastern Howard County. In 1915, A.C. and Lousetta (Louie for short) bought a 20 acre farm in Jackson Township, consisting mostly of fruit trees. They set up residence there with their three sons, Paul, Earl and Lloyd.

All three sons attended a one-room schoolhouse that contained eight grades. They later attended the Jackson Township school, which replaced the old one room Reynolds School that they had earlier attended (which stood in one of their orchards until the early 1980s). The new school also replaced the Powell and Sycamore Schools.

The first Jackson basketball teams - boys and girls - was coached by Claud and Dorothy Kennedy. The girls' team went undefeated that first year, but the boys' team was defeated by Union Township 60-1. (A few years later, Jackson made up by beating Union 75-16). The Kennedys were parents of former Kokomo City Councilman John Kennedy. Two members of that first girls' team are still living: Pauline Crandall Hainlen and Elsie Smith Schaaf. Harold Schaaf is the surviving member of that first boys' team, as Earl Hainlen (Pauline's husband) died in 1993.

Lloyd Hainlen on his 81st birthday.

The Hainlens grew apples, peaches, pears and various berry crops. They expanded their operation in 1926 and again in 1934. These expansions were necessary as the sons, now grown, wished to follow in their father's footsteps. A.C. and Paul continued their operation at the home place, while Earl, with the help of his brothers and father, set up another orchard a mile to the east. Lloyd then established a tree nursery another mile further east. A.C. was also a self-taught artist of some note, with his paintings still to be seen in some local public buildings.

A.C. and Louie died in 1955, within several days of each other. They had been married over 60 years. Paul and Alta, his wife of 53 years, operated their orchard until his death in 1985. Earl and Pauline, his wife of over 60 years, operated their orchard until his death in 1993. Lloyd and his wife Eloise, operated the nursery for many years, with him finally retiring in 1990. Today, Paul Hainlen, Jr. and his family operate the original home place, while Gene Hainlen and his family have taken over from Earl at the "new place" (established in the 1930s).

Today, there are 39 direct descendents of A.C. and Louie Hainlen living. Those residing in Howard County include Lloyd and his daughter Jennifer Kirkman; Paul, Jr. and two of his sons, Len and Lyle; Colleen Hardy and son Terry; Gene Hainlen and sons Randy and Mike, along with next generation Hainlens - Travis, Trent, Elizabeth, Kyra, Yonda, Mya, Eric and Brandon.

A.C. was always proud when his customers noticed that the apples on the bottom of the basket were just as nice as those on the top. He also said that there is no right way to do a wrong thing. He was also pleased to be at the head of a large family of Republicans. He would be proud to know that the apples are still nice at the bottom of the Hainlen baskets today, but he might be distressed to know that a great-grandson has been elected Judge in Howard County as a Democrat! *Submitted by Lloyd Hainlen (a registered Republican for sixty years) and his great-nephew, Judge Randy Hainlen, (a registered Democrat for twenty years).*

HALL - Alexander Hall (1846(7)-1936) was born in Pickaway County, OH, the son of Anthony Hall and Rebecca Prosser. Alexander married Joanna Sager May 9, 1901, Danville, IL. Joanna (1880-1937) born in Williamsport, IN, was the daughter of John Sager and Jane Bunch. Alexander farmed and worked on the railroad. He was 73 when they moved to Kokomo, about 1919, and worked in the brick yard. Alexander was a Civil War veteran and a member of the Thomas J. Harrison Post of the GAR. Joanna was a cook at Duke's Restaurant in Kokomo which was famous for their Old Fashion Cream Pie. She later worked at Dick's Pie Shop for $12/week. Joanna was in the Women's Relief Corps and elected president (1928). She was also Quartermaster for the GAR.

Hall Family—Front: Joanna, Alexander, Helen. Back: Katie, Meda, Arol, Opal.

Alexander and Joanna had six children all born in Chenneyville, IL. Catherine (Maddox) (1902-1992)—some of her descendents are the Bizjaks descended from a daughter Irma and another daughter Mary (Sweeney) of Kokomo. A son Lawrence died a day after birth Nov. 18, 1904; Arol (1906-1989); Meda (Dillman) (1909-1955), Kokomo. The next child Opal (Crume) (1912-) resides in Kokomo. Opal graduated from Good Samaritan School of Nursing 1933 and became the hospital night supervisor. Later she worked for Drs. Drudley, Spangler, and Schwartz before she took the position as supervisor of Three West, St. Joseph's Hospital. She retired in 1965 to care for her husband Glenn. Helen (Beck) (1916-) another daughter lives in Wabash, IN; her children are Jeanne (Wright), Wabash; Bill, Ohio; Ann (Hollinden), Indianapolis; and Mike, Arizona. Another sister, the daughter of Joanna, was Ruth (Klontz) died in Washington 1969. Her children: William and Harold Huntly; Ralph and Phyllis Kabrick (Brashear). Alexander's first wife Martha Harmon died about 1891; they lived in Warren County, IN. Their children were Ira (1871-1875), Vessa "Bessie" (Orcutt) (1875-1954), Janetta "Nettie" (1876-1963), Estella "Stella" (Albaugh) (1878-1938), and Myrtle (Wert).

Arol "Brownie" Hall was on the track, basketball and football teams at Kokomo High School and on the basketball team that went to state in 1925. He was a great sports enthusiast, sometimes listening to one game on the radio and watching another on television. At age 15 he worked shining shoes, cleaning tubs in a barber shop and working in a meat market. After graduation (1926) he worked for the Globe Stove and Range Corp. washing windows. Later he held administrative positions and when he left in 1956 he was Superintendent. He then worked for the O. Hummel Co. Pennsylvania (1956-1962) and was the Plant Manager of Active Products, Marion, IN 1962 until retirement in 1969. Brownie married Mary K. Trayers (1905-1986) June 9, 1930 (see TRAYERS). He was active in St. Patrick's Church Pastoral Council and Eucharistic Ministry. He cherished his friendships in the Knights of Columbus and was the Grand Knight in 1951. For many years he brightened the eyes and hearts of children and adults when he played Santa Claus. His grandchildren will always remember him as a special Santa who they called "Ho, Ho". *Submitted by Joanna (Hall) Edgerly*

HAMILTON, WILSON, STRINGER, MIDDLETON, MOULDER, STRATTAN, THOMAS AND LAMB - Hamilton: I am the daughter of Lex and Florence Middleton Hamilton. My father's parents were John and Mattie Wilson Hamilton. John was the son of James and Mary, residents of the Twin Springs community.

Wilson: Mattie Wilson was the daughter of Charles 1836-1907 and Harriet Stringer Wilson. Charles' parents were Samuel 1791-1836 and Eliza Wilson. The family came to Harrison Township in 1849 from Virginia because of the slavery situation. Charles promoted the latest developments in farming. The Wilsons were active in the Twin Springs and West Middleton Methodist Churches.

Stringer: Harriet Stringer was the daughter of Shadrach and Isabella. The family moved to a farm near Alto in 1856. Shadrach solicited funds for lumber for school furniture for Harrison Township Schools.

Middleton: My mother was Florence Middleton Hamilton daughter of John and Anna Strattan Middleton. John was the son of William 1840-1919 and Jane Moulder Middleton who moved to Howard County from Montgomery County in 1854. He was the son of Levi and Mary Middleton. William engaged in farming and had a keen interest in affairs of his community. The village of West Middleton bears the family name. The Middletons were New Jersey Quakers.

Moulder: Jane Moulder was the daughter of John 1805-1900 and Eleanor Maris Moulder. Mr. Moulder was one of the three commissioners who established the county seat for Howard County and later the family became county residents. The Moulder family migrated to Indiana in 1816.

Strattan: Anna Strattan Middleton was the daughter of Joseph and Jane Thomas Strattan. Joseph 1836-1901 was the son of Jonathan 1804-1879 and Prudence Edgerton Strattan. Joseph and his father Jonathan were anti-slavery Friends and were active in the New London Underground Railroad movement. Jonathan corresponded with Friends in Philadelphia ordering books and educational materials for the community. The family came to Howard County in 1849 from Henry County.

Thomas: The family came to New London in covered wagon in 1842 from Grant County. Jane Thomas Strattan 1838-1936 was the daughter of Snead and Miriam Lamb Thomas. She was interested in flower gardening and was an active member of the WCTU. She experienced riding in covered wagon and airplane in her lifetime.

Lamb: Miriam Lamb was the daughter of John and Lydia who came to the area in 1840. John Lamb is credited along with Reuben Edgerton in plotting New London in 1845 and in building the first mill there. The Thomas and Lamb families were active in the Honey Creek Monthly Meeting of the Friends Church.

Most of my ancestors derived their livelihood from the pursuit of farming. Charles Wilson, Shadrach Stringer and Joseph Strattan promoted development of their community being supporters of the Kokomo-New London Gravel Road.

I share my heritage with many residents of Howard County. This is the story of my ancestors as they were active in Howard County history. *Submitted by Anna May Hamilton.*

ARCHIBALD HAMILTON - 1860 Census Howard County, there was William Hamilton (70y); James Hamilton (22y) and wife Sarah; Archibald Hamilton (20y); and Mary Hamilton (16y). Archibald was listed right after William. One of the puzzles is age! 1870 census, Archibald (26y) and Anna (27y) were in Tipton County, with three children. 1880 census Archibald and Anna disappear; Henry, Archibald's son, was living in Howard County, Union Township with Cilles Nordyke and her three children; she was head of the household, listing Henry as her nephew. According to Howard County marriage records, James Nordyke, son of Daniel and Sarah Lindley Nordyke, married June 27, 1874 to Celia Burns, and this raises more questions. Was she married before? Is she Henry's aunt? Is she Archibald's sister?

Archibald (Archa) Hamilton, married Dec. 2, 1860 to Anna Elizabeth Martin, born circa 1843 (or 1839) in Ohio. Archibald and Anna were the parents of three children: (A) Louvinia/Lavina C. (Feb. 22, 1862-Oct. 16, 1928), married Oct. 14, 1882 to Alonzo Stamm (died August 1935), son of Jacob and S. "Letta" C. Eads Dulanty Stamm. Crown Point Cemetery Sec. 14 Lot 67; (B) Henry Seymor (April 15, 1863-Sept. 22, 1939), married Feb. 2, 1884 to Effie Nora A. Stamm (Dec. 12, 1867-Jan. 7, 1942), sister to Alonzo; Crown Point Cemetery Sec. 21 Lot 45. Eight known children, believe ten in all. (1) Ila Otto; (2) Clarence F. (born June 8, 1886), married Minnie B. Asbell; (3) Charles Monroe (July 3, 1890/91-May 8, 1956), married July 7, 1914 to Martha C. Duppengeiser (Feb. 3, 1895-Nov. 7, 1987), daughter of Frederick and Marie/Mary Schore/Shorm; Crown Point Cemetery Sec. 21 Lot 113. (4) Archibald S. (June 5/8, 1891/93-Aug. 28, 1953), first married April 27, 1912 to Tiny Coleman, second married Minnie Hoyt. (5) Margery "Madge" L. (born Nov. 1, 1895/96), first married April 6, 1912 to Edmond C. Roach, second married ? Templin, third married Henry Bontenall; (6) Eva (born July 5, 1897), first married Sept. 19, 1914 to George Gerhart, second married ? Brent, third married ? Myler; (7) Dorthy (born Oct. 16, 1902), married ? Wayne; (8) male, Sept. 30, 1905, stillborn; (9) ? (female), married Robert Reabel and (10) ? (female), married Howard Wines. (C) Orvina, born circa 1869, wife of John Hendricks.

Tom, Brian, Ernest and Chris Hamilton

Ila Otto Hamilton (Nov. 9, 1884-July 12, 1956), first married March 12, 1904 in Fayette County, IN to Dortha L. Gettinger (March 30, 1884-April 11, 1919), daughter of Charles C. and Anna E. Catheart/Kithcart Gettinger. Buried in Crown Point Cemetery, Ila, Sec. 21 Lot 45 and Dortha Sec. 14 Lot 67. Nine known children: (1) Anna Ruth, December 1904/January 1905-June 30, 1905; (2) Beulah Alice; (3) Elsie Gertrude, (Feb. 23, 1908-April 11, 1910), first buried in Randolph Cemetery April 13, 1910, these three were first buried in Randolph Cemetery, moved to Crown Point Cemetery Oct. 2, 1910; (4) Nellie B., Feb. 16, 1911, stillborn, Crown Point Cemetery Sec. 14 Lot 67; (5) Ernest Dale; (6) Doris Bernice, born Feb. 26, 1916; (7) Frank; (8) Harvey and (9) Martha, married Charles Chambers.

(5) Ernest Dale Hamilton, born July 19, 1913; second married Jan. 29, 1933 to Helen Biddle (born March 26, 1915), daughter of Grover and Leatha Robinson Biddle. Four children: (1) Thomas Dale; (2) Richard Lee; (3) Harry Leroy and (4) Rebecca "Becky" Sue, wife of Thomas Beane.

(1) Thomas Dale Hamilton, born March 13, 1933, second married April 21, 1957 to Barbara Ann Richards (born Aug. 15, 1936), daughter of Andrew and Thelma Hall Richards. One child by first marriage and four by second: (1) Cynthia "Cyndi" Louise Hamilton (born Nov. 15, 1953), married Aug. 24, 1973 to Mark Snodgrass; (2) Pamela Sue (born April 15, 1958), married Feb. 14, 1976 to Bob Hendershot; (3) Jeffery Dale (born Nov. 24, 1960), married July 11, 1981 to Donna Bevington; (4) Brian Lee (born April 11, 1962), married Feb. 12, 1983 to Stacy Morris and (5) Sally Ann (born March 29, 1964), married April 30, 1983 to Bob Duke. *Submitted by Thomas D. Hamilton.*

ROBERT HAMILTON - On a farm in Shelby County, IN, there was born a little babe, christened Robert Hamilton.

His great-grandfather and grandmother came from Ireland around 1772 and settled in South Carolina.

Robert's grandfather, James Hamilton, was born in South Carolina in 1775, and his grandmother in 1773. They were married Nov. 24, 1796, and had six children. In 1812 he sold 227 acres in South Carolina; and we next find him in Fayette, Rush, and Shelby counties in Indiana.

His father, Samuel Hamilton, was born in Fayette County in 1813. Samuel Hamilton married Lydia Shelton Sept. 7, 1834, and they had nine children. Samuel was a farmer and lay preacher. He donated ground in Shelby County for old Fairview Church. It was organized in 1841. When Robert was five years old, he moved with his family to Howard County. His father rode north on an old black horse, named "Old Nig", looking for land. When he returned he had purchased 160 acres in Howard County.

In March of 1850 they loaded all their belongings and left Shelby County in a schooner pulled by five yoke of oxen whose names were: Buck and Broad (lead oxen), Buck and Ben, Buck and Bright, Tige and Lion, and Buck and Berry (the wheel oxen). They came on the Michigan Road, which was corduroy with a puncheon top and very rough, reaching Howard County in five days.

There were three acres cleared and a log cabin built on this one hundred sixty acres. They slept on the floor. The children attended school three months a year.

When Robert was 16 his father agreed to furnish material to build Mt. Zion Church. Joel and Robert helped fell the green timber, haul it to the saw mill, and then to the site of the church. His boyhood was spent working on his father's farm and roaming the hills with his brother, Joel.

On Nov. 17, 1870, he married Ada A. Baker and they had seven children: Lex, Cy, Fred, Rile, Maude, Samuel and Charles. They lived on a farm northeast of West Middleton.

He worked hard to make his family comfortable. His main joy, other than his family, was his loyalty to his church, Mt. Zion. He always attended services unless ill health prevented and would say, "I expect to see every one of you boys in church this morning." He lived his life as the average pioneer, a simple honest life with a great faith and wisdom.

Family, friends and neighbors would gather at his home for a big dinner every year on the Sunday nearest his birthday. He had several nieces and was known affectionately as Uncle Bobbie. In the summer a Hamilton cousin reunion was held at one of his niece's homes and all attended.

My grandfather passed away May 20, 1937, and his wife died in 1903. They are buried at Twin Springs Cemetery. His descendants still live in the West Middleton area. *Submitted by Ruth Hamilton Newby.*

GARFIELD AND INEZ HANKINS - Garfield Hankins married a native of Howard County, Inez Frier, in 1925. They had three children, Dale, Helen, and Robert. Inez was a daughter of John H. and Bertha Jane Gillam Frier. Garfield was born in Clinton County, a son of John R. and Elizabeth J. Hankins, and came to Howard County in 1923. Being the youngest of 13 children, he spent some years in Knightstown, IN, Soldiers and Sailors Home following his mother's death when he was ten years of age.

Garfield lived with the Bailey family in Crawfordsville, IN, where he graduated from high school in 1911. Then he tended a railroad car carrying livestock from the Bailey farm on their homesteading venture to Montana. He enlisted in the United States Navy from Montana in WWI. A few years later he came to Howard County to be with family members, then was a letter carrier in Kokomo for 34 years. He walked mail routes primarily in Forest Park and later downtown.

Dale Hankins, author of this article, graduated from West Middleton High School, from which his mother had graduated, in 1944, served in the United States Navy in WWII, spent several years as a teacher in central Indiana, then retired from civilian service with the United States Air Force at Wright-Patterson Air Force Base, Ohio, in 1993.

Helen Hankins Wright graduated from one of the last classes at West Middleton High School before its consolidation into Western School District. She and her husband Alvie live in Howard County. Their three children and families live in Indiana.

Robert Hankins graduated from Western High School, taught school several years and now resides in New Jersey. He and wife Carolyn have two married children.

Our mother Inez Hankins, widowed in 1969, still resides in Kokomo. One grandson, Kevin Hankins, lives in Howard County with wife Amy and four children. Kevin is an electrical engineer at Delco Electronics.

Our Christian heritage is the greatest gift we have received from our parents, Garfield and Inez Hankins. *Submitted by Dale Hankins.*

HANNA - Around 1860, Joseph Lorenzo Dow Hanna rode horseback looking for a good location for land and staked out a farm in the southwest corner of Ervin Township, Howard County. He married Elizabeth Bright and built a house near the Stonebraker Bridge and raised a son, Palestine and a daughter, Josephine.

J.L.D., (as he was known), was an excellent mathematician, and he served two terms as Howard County surveyor.

Palestine married Mary Hopkins and lived on what is now SR 22 near Ridgeway. They raised four children: Glenn, Geneva, Winifred and Guy.

When J.L.D. was older, Palestine moved back to the farm, taking three of the children, and farmed with his father. The oldest daughter, Geneva, had married by this time and moved to Adams County.

Later, Palestine moved, taking his family to Burlington where he served several years as postmaster. Winifred worked in the bank there and Guy attended Indiana State College at Terre Haute.

Glenn was in high school when Guy contracted T.B. and as a result, the family moved to Albuquerque, NM in 1910, to secure a dryer climate. They lived there two or three years. During that time, Glenn met and married Ida Belle Lewis.

Since Guy's health was not improving, the family, except Glenn and Ida, moved back to Indiana in the fall of 1912. Palestine still owned the farm but had rented it to a tenant who was occupying the house. So they rented a house in Kokomo until spring when they could move back and resume farming.

Glenn and Ida moved back to Indiana the next year and lived in the same house with his parents in Kokomo. During this time in Kokomo, Guy passed away. Then in the spring of 1913, the whole family moved back to the farm, where they were all engaged in farming. The farm, which consisted of 139 acres, was legally named "The Stockwell Farm."

Palestine's wife, Mary, became an invalid and was confined the rest of her life, in a wheelchair.

Two sons were born, on the farm, to Glenn and Ida: Chester L. in 1914 and G. Bright in 1916.

Winifred stayed on the farm for some time, but later obtained employment in Kokomo as a bookkeeper.

Glenn moved his family to Decatur, IN for a period of about three years, but returned to the farm in 1923. Mary died in 1936 and Palestine in 1938.

Glenn and Ida continued farming, with the two sons helping. Chester married Alice Pullen and moved away in 1934. Bright married Luella Davis and continued living on the farm with his parents and helped farm.

This arrangement continued until WWII, when Glenn and Ida moved to Kokomo, where Glenn was engaged in manufacturing war material. Bright and Luella continued farming until 1950, when he was ordained a minister and moved to Oakville, IN to take up a pastorate. The farm was rented to Bob Ehrman, who later purchased it.

HARLOW - John Blout Harlow, better known as "Bud", was a fourth-generation pioneer. His paternal great-grandparents, John and Elizabeth Evans Harlow, emigrated from Manchester, England to Ohio in 1820. His grandparents, Orlando and Nancy Coleman Harlow, purchased land in Indiana in 1854.

John "B"'s parents, George Albert and Minerva Tyner Harlow, a most estimable lady, were married in 1871. They purchased 120 acres in Prairie Township, Tipton County and erected a log home. George A. received a good education attending both common and high schools, and taught school for 12 years. In addition he taught singing and did all of his farming, expanding it to 170 acres.

From the union of George A. and Minerva were born seven interesting children. Lawrence A., John B., the subject of this writing, Zenas L., Cora A., Ulla A., Clyde G., and Erasmus V., all provided good school privileges.

On June 17, 1904, John B. married Neppie Rickard, residing in Howard County where John B. was a police officer for the city of Kokomo, from 1905 to 1907. He resigned after arresting the lady friend of a Kokomo city councilman.

John Blout and Neppie Harlow

In 1910 John B. and four of his five brothers and one sister emigrated to Cactus Lake, Saskatchewan, Canada for the purpose of homesteading. They leased railroad cars from the Soo Line and Canadian National Railway to transport machinery, livestock and household items, departing from Kempton, IN in early 1910. Major items to travel by rail were a Huber steam engine, a 40 inch separator and registered shorthorn cattle. The four brothers accompanied the train.

Women and children followed sometime later, giving the men time to set up accommodations at Cactus Lake rail end. John B. and Neppie's three-year-old son Lester accompanied them.

By 1924 they returned to Indiana with their three children: Lester, born in Tipton County 1906, Katherine Minerva born 1911 in Canada and Grace born in 1924 in Canada.

John B. and Neppie purchased 80 acres of productive farm land with good out buildings in northern Howard County one mile east of Cassville. The family resided there actively farming until John B. retired in 1943. Their three children received educations from Howard County systems, Lester from Kokomo High School, Katherine and Grace from Howard Township High School. Katherine later became a registered nurse attending training in Springfield, IL and St. Joseph School of Nursing in Kokomo.

John B. and Neppie moved to Huntington, IN to reside with their daughter Katherine, until their deaths in 1967, their ages 93 and 87 respectively. Both were Democrats and were earnest and faithful members of the Primitive Baptist Church.

Lester married Mildred Rosalee McCoy and from his union were born three children: Lester Gerry, Doris Carolyn and Joey Bruce.

Katherine married Walter Moffitt and to this union one daughter Suzanne was born.

Grace married Bernard Bartrum and to them was born one daughter Diane.

As of this writing, all descendants of John Blout and Neppie Harlow, from children to six generations of grandchildren, are living in Howard County, IN or adjacent states, with fond, sincere appreciation of our heritage and of Bud and Neppie Harlow. *Submitted by Lester Gerry Harlow.*

HARMON - Harmon can be either an English or a German surname. The original German spelling is more likely to be Harman, but was sometimes changed to the English form.

Charles Harmon was apparently one of the earliest settlers in Howard County. He was born on Oct. 4, 1811, in Hamilton County, OH, and married Elizabeth Rodman on March 30, 1831, in Marion County, IN. He sold his land there in 1837 and moved to Shelby County, IL. He reentered Indiana and obtained land in Taylor Township, section 30, in Howard County in 1841. In 1850 he was 39 and living in Harrison Township of Howard County, close to the village of Fairfield, to the southeast of Kokomo. Charles helped David Foster, generally regarded as the first settler in the county, to build his cabin. One of Charles's daughters said that during her early years of marriage a rifle would be taken along to church in case there was any game available along the way. The Harmon children included Mary Ann (Smith), William M., John T., Nancy Jane (Randolph), James R., and Charles M. With the exception of James, who was born in Illinois, each of the children was born in Indiana. During the Civil War, William and James served in Co. D, 89th Indiana Inf., for three years. Charles's wife, Elizabeth Rodman Harmon, died on March 22, 1873, at age 57. Charles's second wife was Mary Pitzer, whom he married on July 22, 1873. Charles Harmon died on March 29, 1883, at the age of 72, and was buried in Howard County.

His parents were John Harmon, born about 1767, probably in Virginia, who married Elizabeth Byrd (Bird) circa Dec. 16, 1787, in Montgomery County, VA. Charles's four eldest brothers, John B., Richard, James and William, were still living in Marion County in 1830, approximately five years after their father had died in Boone County, IN. At least two of them moved to Boone County eventually. There was also a younger brother, Hiram, and sisters named Elizabeth, Nancy Jane, Mildred, and Mary. The widow of John Harmon lived on until approximately 1870, 99 years, and died in Knox County, IL, where her daughter Nancy Jane had settled with her husband, Chesley Ray or Wray.

The foregoing text was written by a descendant, J. Steven Bush., who must bear sole responsibility for any errors contained in it. But credit for nearly all of the research that made it possible belongs to another descendant, Leslie A. Harmon.

HARNESS - We trace this family back to Peter Michael Harness born 1700 and died 1782, who accompanied William Penn on one of his trips from Holland to the Colony of Pennsylvania in search of a home and freedom for his Quaker religion.

His wife Elizabeth Tepebo Harness came with him; she was also from Holland, whose maternal ancestors were said to be of royal blood. She was a cousin of William Penn.

They had religious difficulties in Pennsylvania and moved to the South Branch Valley of the Potomac River. With punk, steel, and tomahawk in hand, their daughter, Elizabeth, then 11 years old, helped blaze the way and was the first white woman to set foot in this valley.

Their wagon train had the first wagons in this part of the country. In this valley they built a fort in 1837 which is still standing.

Michael and Elizabeth Harness had 13 children. Three sons were scalped by the Indians.

John Harness was the oldest son. He was a great scout and Indian fighter. He was with General Morgan in his first raid in Ohio, being one of the famous Virginian Riflemen. He was present at the making of peace with the Indians, under Cornstalk, eight miles southeast of Chillecothe, OH.

John Harness also fought in the Revolutionary War and became a captain. His father furnished beef for the troops.

After several generations the descendants moved to Indiana. Our forefathers were deeply religious. The Presbyterian Church was spoken of most frequently, also, the United Brethren Church.

Soon after they moved to Indiana, they helped organize and build the Upper Deer Creek Christian Church in 1848, the church I attended while growing up. Some were active in the Popular Grove Brethren Church, south of Young America, IN.

In 1832 Jackson Harness came to Cass County, IN. He was my great-great-grandfather. His son William Lewis Harness born Dec. 28, 1847 and died March 30, 1927 and married Sarah Frances Williams born 1852 VA and died 1916 IN. They had four children, one being my grandmother, Minnie Augusta Harness born Oct. 12, 1871 and died Jan. 16, 1949. She married Elmer Ellis Elleman born Aug. 14, 1868 and died Jan. 2, 1923. They are buried at Center Cemetery north of Young America, IN.

Minnie Harness Elleman (born Oct. 27, 1871-died Jan. 16, 1949); Elmer Ellis Elleman (born Aug. 14, 1868-died Jan. 3, 1923).

They had six children. Three who lived were Theresa Pearl Elleman Yater, born April 6, 1889 and died Jan. 27, 1987; Harold Ralph Elleman born Nov. 3, 1898 and died Jan. 29, 1980; and Ray Burdette Elleman born Jan. 11, 1903 and died March 6, 1986. My grandparents lived in Galveston, IN where my parents met and were married March 2, 1919. They are buried in the Galveston, IN cemetery.

The Harness name is very ancient. It was originally spelled Harnies then Harges or Hargees. John Harness began to write it Harness in 1790. They were descendants of Count Harmon Court Unverzay of Holland.

There were all kinds of occupations in the Harness families, but it all began as farmers, who came from Holland. I am proud to live in America under the United States' flag made possible by all of our ancestors.

It is indeed a good thing to be well descended, but the glory belongs to our ancestors.—Plutarch. *Submitted by Margaret Elleman Stahl (Mrs. George Stahl).*

FOREST HARNESS - He was prosecuting attorney of Howard County two terms, commander of Post 6 of the American Legion, judge advocate of the Indiana Department of the Legion and state commander of the veterans' organization. All this added up to a public career that was one of the most distinguished any native of Kokomo has had.

For some 20 years, Forest A. Harness served in the government of the United States as a Member of Congress, Assistant U.S. Attorney, Sergeant-at-Arms of the U.S. Senate and a member of the American Battle Monuments Commission.

Harness was a vigorous and effective prosecutor who worked at the job diligently and achieved an excellent record. The same hard driving nature characterized his service as a U.S. Attorney in which he prosecuted a number of important cases successfully. His handling of the government's case against Samuel Insull, the Chicago utilities magnate, indicted for fraud in the sale of worthless securities, brought him national attention.

He was first elected to Congress in 1938, from Indiana's Fifth District, and was re-elected four times. When he ran for Congress there was no television, and campaigning was based almost entirely on personal contact with the voters. In those days Harness visited every small town in the district, making speeches and mingling with the townspeople. His campaign slogan was "Hitch Up with Harness".

Prior to 1938, the Democrats had piled up majorities of 7,000 to 11,000 in the district. The first year Harness sought the office saw him winning by 12,459.

In Congress he was a staunch conservative, noted as a firm exponent of a strong national defense and as a foe of socialized medicine and other movements toward socialism. He served on many important committees, one of them investigating expenditures and propaganda in the government. His position as a leading opponent of what he held was unlawful federal spending for propaganda led to his writing an article on that subject for the *Reader's Digest*. He recalled his service on the House Military Affairs Committee as his most memorable public service. The committee worked out the consolidation of the Army, Navy and Air Force into the Department of Defense.

When he was Sergeant-at-Arms of the Senate, the body's majority leader was Robert A. Taft and the minority leader was Lyndon B. Johnson. Harness knew many of the great national leaders of the period from 1938 to 1954. One of his responsibilities as Sergeant-at-Arms was policing the famous hearings in which Sen. Joseph McCarthy accused the U.S. Army of wrongdoing.

Forest Harness lived and worked in Kokomo and in Washington during some of the most colorful periods in the nation's history and was a part of American political and public life, both on a local and a national scale. He was outgoing, forceful and respected for his principles and his industriousness. He left an enviable record.

Among the committees of the House on which he served were military affairs, rules, sub-committee on expenditures and propaganda in the federal government. He also was chairman of a committee to investigate the Federal Communications Commission and a member of the Republican policy committee.

FORREST "BRUCE" HARNESS - Forrest Bruce Harness, one of three children, was born on Oct. 24, 1947, in Benton Harbor, MI, to Russell R. Harness and June Eileen Click.

While still in school he worked on Mt. Hood at the hotel, then was a cook on a shrimp boat in the Gulf of Mexico.

Forrest "Bruce" Harness

Upon graduation from high school, he signed up for deep-sea diving and drilling for oil. He has traveled the world over, several times, and his last off-shore drill was in Brunei.

He married Donna in India and they came to the United States and settled in Santa Monica, CA. She enrolled in gem cutting school and is now a gem cutter in New York City.

Forrest sometimes goes by his middle name of Bruce, or "The Tree", since his first name is Forrest.

He has a daughter, Summer Harness, living in Portland, OR, living with her mother, Suzie Pfaff.

Forrest has one brother, Russell Marvin, and one sister, Pamela June Rademacher. She is secretary and mansion coordinator for Governor Richard Bryan in Carson City, NV.

GEORGE W. HARNESS - The years of the honored subject of this memoir are part of the indissoluble chain which links the annals of the past to those of the latter day progress and prosperity, and the history of Howard County would not be complete without due reference to the long life he has lived and the success which he has achieved as an earnest, courageous laborer in one of the most important fields of endeavor.

The Harness family is of German origin and the first of the name to immigrate to America settled in Virginia at quite an early period and became widely known in various parts of the state. George Harness, the subject's father, was born on the ancestral homestead contiguous to the south bank of the Potomac River and remained in Virginia until his 27th year, when he left the parental roof to make his own way in the world. He first went to Ohio, making the entire distance of four hundred miles on foot, renting a piece of land, raised one crop, after which he returned to his native state the same way he left it—afoot and alone. Later he brought his parents to Ohio, where he continued to reside for some years, and where, in due time, he was married to Harriett Sowers, who bore him 10 children, of whom the subject of this sketch is the only survivor. Disposing of his interests in Ohio, Mr. Harness migrated in an early day to the new and sparsely settled county of McLean, in the state of Illinois, but fearing the Indians, who at that time occupied the greater part of the country and were not always on friendly terms with their white neighbors, he left that state after a brief sojourn and moved to Boone County, IN, thence, subsequently, to Carroll County, where he spent the greater part of his life. George Harness was a man of excellent parts and throughout a long and strenuous life made his influence felt for good and did much to promote the advancement of the different communities in which he resided. He was a typical pioneer of the period in which he lived, strong, agile and fearless and as an industrious tiller of the soil and praiseworthy citizen gained the esteem and confidence of the people with whom he mingled.

George W. Harness

George W. Harness was born July 19, 1819, in Fayette County, OH, and when quite young accompanied his parents to Indiana, where he grew to maturity, spending the greater part of his early life in Cass County. His educational advantages were exceedingly limited, but by making the most of his opportunities he acquired a fund of valuable practical knowledge and in due time became an intelligent and remarkably well informed man. He began life for himself on a quarter section of land in the southern part of Cass County, given him by his father, and at once addressed himself to its improvement—a task of no small magnitude, the land being covered with a dense forest, to remove which and fix the soil for cultivation required much hard and persevering toil. By laboring early and late he finally succeeded in transforming the forest into a beautiful and valuable farm, to which he made additions at intervals until he became one of the largest land owners of the county, his real estate holdings at one time amounting to 1840 acres, the greater part of which was afterward divided among his children.

Mr. Harness was married Dec. 6, 1839, to Drusilla Beck, a native of Augusta County, VA, where her birth occurred in the year 1821, and who bore him 16 children, 10 sons and 6 daughters, of which large family but one son survives in George W. Harness, Jr., one of the wealthy farmers and representative citizens of the county of Cass. Mrs. Harness departed this life in February, 1888, and later Mr. Harness married Alice Smith, who was born April 26, 1862, in Cass County, IN, the daughter of James W. and Mary Smith. This union has been blessed with one child, a son, by the name of Russell, who was born on Dec. 2, 1890, and is now one of the most highly esteemed youths of Kokomo, with a bright and promising future before him. He was graduated from the Kokomo High School with the class of 1908.

Harness Cemetery—This is a neat little burial ground, enclosed with a wire fence and fairly well kept, with a few good monuments. George W. Harness, Sr. donated the ground more than 50 years ago but never executed a deed of record until May 2, 1906, when George W. Harness, Sr., of Howard County, IN, deeded a piece of ground 108x147 feet on the north line of the northeast quarter of the northeast quarter, section 34, Deer Creek Township, and west of the schoolhouse lot, to his sons, George W. Harness, Jr., and Russel Harness and their heirs, to be maintained as a burial place for the dead now interred or to be hereafter interred therein. This conveyance was made with the restriction that no part of it shall be used for any other purpose than a burial ground.

First interment was Harriat Harness, April 3, 1855; Ida Florence Harness, 1859; infant of George W. Habne, 1853.

JUNE CLICK HARNESS - June Eileen was born July 28, 1922, in Tipton County, IN to Dick and Carmen Click. Her mother, Carmen, taught school and had her own beauty shop in Elwood and Kokomo. Carmen was "proof reader" for the *Kokomo Tribune*. Her father, Dick, owned Click's grocery store, across from Delco, and also owned the Markland Cafe. He was also a car salesman before moving to California.

June graduated from Kokomo High School in 1940. She is a nightclub singer and performs around the country. She started tap dancing at age three and sang for Tommy Dorsey, Tex Beneke, and Les Brown. June could have been a lead singer for a "big band" but chose to raise a family instead. She is still going strong today. She lives in Mexico and continues to sing down there.

L-R: Forrest Bruce Harness, Pamela June Harness, June Click Harness, and Russell Marvin Harness and Riff of Africa.

June sang at Harvey's "Top of the Wheel" at Lake Tahoe in 1983. Her husband, Russ, did his share of moving around. He was a traveling salesman and sold Cessna airplanes all around the country as he flew and delivered the planes for the Johnson Corp.

Although June enjoys show business, none of the children had any desire to follow in their mother's footsteps. Her daughter, Pamela, is mansion coordinator for Governor Richard Bryan, Carson City, NV, who formerly worked in the District Attorney's office. Her son, Russ, has his own race car and bicycle shop, formerly in Los Angeles, CA, but now recently located in Portland, OR. The youngest son, Forrest, is a deep sea diver and works for SEDCO-ECHO, offshore oil drilling and production presently in Borneo ("Brunei").

June always travels with her beautiful German shepherd dog, named Riff, by her side. Riff was born in 1953 in Africa, and is very protective as a guard dog.

RUSSELL R. HARNESS
December 2, 1890, Russell R. Harness, was born to George W. and Alice Smith Harness, and was the one and only child born to that marriage. However, he had 16 half-brothers and sisters, who were fathered by George W. Harness. In 1908, Russell graduated from Kokomo High School with honors. On July 11, 1911, Russell married Gladys Eva Todd. In 1912, Russell graduated from the University of Michigan, Ann Arbor, MI. Also in this year, his daughter Eleanor Louise was born on campus. In 1914, Russell graduated from Purdue University, West Lafayette, IN and was a member of the Alpha Zeta honorary scholastic fraternity- having been initiated during his residency at Purdue University. Russell served as assistant cashier of the Kokomo Bank and Trust Company located at southeast corner of Main and Sycamore Streets-Uptown, Kokomo, and across from the Armstrong Landon Building.

Russell was a member of the Masonic Order, holding the honor of 32nd degree of that organization, and a birthright member of the First United Brethren Church, at the northeast corner of West Monroe and North Washington streets.

L-R: Russell R. Harness and Gladys Eva (Todd) Harness

On July 11, 1911, Russell married Gladys Eva Todd and they lived on campus at Purdue University where their first born daughter arrived on Dec. 8, 1912. Russell had a beautiful and palatial home of 17 rooms, one of the finest and most attractive at the northwest edge of Kokomo, located on 10 acres of rich ground, address 1619 North Phillips Street. He subsequently entered the law department of Michigan University, where in due time he finished his professional course and received his degree, being graduated with a creditable record with the class of 1912. Returning to Kokomo, he entered Purdue University in West Lafayette, IN, this time taking an agricultural course, since he planned to farm 1840 acres. The land, known to be of the richest soil, was sold to Guy Wilson and used by Purdue University for experimental purposes. It had acres of well-improved land, being well-drained and under a fine system of fencing. He had skillfully rotated his crops so as to preserve the strength of the soil, and no farm in the county was looked after with any greater care.

No more patriotic or worthy character could be found in Howard County or within the borders of the Hoosier state than Mr. Harness. Well-known agriculturist of Howard County, Mr. Harness also had large numbers of excellent cattle, hogs, and other stock on his farm, having always been a good judge of livestock and delighted to handle the same. There was richness of soil and the soil was kept up to its high state of productiveness.

He was a supporter of the Republican ticket in national elections. (Germany has contributed some of her best citizens to the United States.)

Russell died at the early age of "47" in 1938.

Russell, being a man of generous impulses upon whose credulity the unscrupulous could easily impose, never refused to go surety for such as requested the favor, with the result that many allowed him to redeem their obligations when they became due. By this means, he lost much of his property and cash. Though never reduced to poverty, he was enabled to leave but a modest portion of his farm holdings to his family.

RUSSELL ROBERT "BUD" HARNESS
Russell Robert, known as "Bud" or "Buddy" Harness was born Dec. 9, 1920, in Howard County, the son of Russell R. and Gladys Eva (Todd) Harness. He attended Wallace Grade School and graduated from Kokomo High School in 1938.

Active in sports, he played on the Kokomo High School basketball team and ran track. Russell always maintained an interest in Kokomo High School sports and was especially pleased that a nephew, Harry N. Werbe III, "Stormy", was named manager of boys basketball in 1965.

Russell attended the University of Illinois and was a veteran of WWII, having served as an aerologist with the U.S. Navy. He was a member of the Masonic Lodge in WaterVliet, MI and the Columbia Aviation Country Club in Portland, OR.

Russell Robert "Bud" Harness

In June 1940, he was married to June Eileen Click, his childhood sweetheart, the daughter of Dick and Carmen Click. To this union were born three children, Russell Marvin, born in Kokomo, IN; Pamela June, born Aug. 19, 1943; and Forrest Bruce, born Oct. 24, 1947, in Benton Harbor, MI.

In 1964, Russell married Kay Hammann and added two stepdaughters, Martha and Mary Catherine Hammann to the family.

"Buddy" had two sisters, Eleanor Louise (Harness) Victorson, born Dec. 9, 1912; died February 1981; and Bette Jane (Harness) Werbe, born Sept. 29, 1916.

Russell was employed by Johnson Corp., of Portland, OR and flew Cessna airplanes out of Skyways Airport. He sold and flew Cessnas, flying company planes to Kokomo and taking one or two family members back to Portland, OR for vacations. His main love was the "Piper Cherokee". Russell was widely recognized as a man of unlimited energy and ideas for promotional campaigns throughout the western states during his affiliation with the Johnson Corporation.

Russell died on Jan. 10, 1969 at the age of 48 and is buried in Rose City Cemetery in Portland, OR.

RICHARD HARPER
Richard Harper was born near Hatters Corners, TN, April 26, 1844 and died Dec. 5, 1919. He was the oldest son of William C. Harper 1820-1901 and Priscilla Cates 1826-1867. William came to Howard County in 1867, and bought 80 acres east of Sycamore, IN. There he cleared the land for farming and built a log cabin and barn. He lived there and raised his family until his death in 1901.

Richard married Cynthia Cheek on July 23, 1874. She was born in Indiana Sept. 2, 1847 and died Oct. 3, 1909. She was the daughter of Jason and Catherine Cheek of Dearborn County, IN. They had seven children: Clarence Ervin 1875-1934; Oliver Earl 1878-1968; Marion Scott 1879-1924; James Robert "Pete" 1883-; Claud Sept. 26, 1884-Oct. 14, 1884; Anna Blanche 1887-1959; Josie June 5, 1890-Aug. 3, 1891.

Clarence Ervin Aug. 1, 1875-Aug. 31, 1934. After his father died he made his home with his sister Blanche and her family. He is buried in Lindley Cemetery, Greentown, IN.

Oliver Earl April 1, 1878-Jan. 6, 1968. On Jan. 21, 1915 he married Emma Killen May 25, 1878-1932. They had three children: Richard Clem July 2, 1915-and two daughters, one who lived one day, and one was stillborn. Emma is buried in Earlham Cemetery, Richmond, IN. Earl later married Hazel Barnes March 6, 1888-Nov. 16, 1967, on Nov. 14, 1933. Earl and Hazel are buried in Marion, Grant County.

Marion Scott July 25, 1879-Sept. 17, 1924 married Laura Alice Sharp Aug. 7, 1881-Nov. 20, 1978. They were married Sept. 4, 1907 and had three children: Carl Sept. 5, 1908-May 22, 1987; Edna Aug. 8, 1911-who married Lowell Burt Nov. 30, 1911-Jan. 5, 1992 and Garnet Feb. 3, 1916.

James Robert "Pete" May 9, 1883-married Ina Edith Rust 1882-. They were married on Dec. 24, 1907. They had three children: Lydia Mae 1910-; Charles M. 1916-; and Gerald March 31, 1919-Oct. 6, 1992.

Claud born Sept. 26, 1884 and died Oct. 14, 1884.

Anna Blanche April 21, 1887-Sept. 9, 1959 married Orange Achor Jan. 19, 1885-Oct. 2, 1963. They were married Nov. 6, 1907. (See family history "Orange and Blanche Achor").

Josie was born June 5, 1890 and died Aug. 3, 1891; she is buried in Lindley Cemetery, Greentown, IN.

Richard was a farmer and lived on the land that his father had cleared in Jackson Twp. He died of tuberculosis and is buried with his wife Cynthia in Greenlawn Cemetery, Greentown, IN. *Submitted by Vivian White*

HARPER
William C. Harper, son of James and Mary (Loughery) Harper was born in North Carolina. In October of 1842 he married Priscilla Cate in Tennessee. The family moved near Williamsburg of Wayne County, IN in 1856. In 1867 the family moved to Jackson Township of Howard County where they found the land in its native state. The land was cleared and the family farmed the property on what is now located along County Road 100 North near 1200 East. William and Priscilla were the parents of five children; Richard, James, Mary (Mrs. James D. Allison), John L. and William Andrew. Priscilla died in 1867 and William C. married Sarah J. Willis in 1870. William and Sarah were the parents of one daughter, Leona (Mrs. Tim Miller).

John L. Harper was born in Wayne County, IN and married Phebe West, the daughter of Joel and Mary West in Howard County. John was active in Republican politics of the eastern part of the county. He often led rallies in Greentown. He spent most of his life farming. John and Phebe were the parents of five children; Cora (Mrs. Curtis Scherer), James Omer, stillborn infant son, Glen and Howard Samuel.

Howard Samuel Harper was born and lived within the same half-mile stretch on County Road 100 North for his entire life. He held many jobs within the community and was also active in township politics. In 1910 he married Elva Grace Ball, daughter of Amos and Isadore (Whiteley) Ball of Union Township in Howard County.

Amos Ball came to Howard County in 1868 with his parents, Solomon and Sarah (Wilson) Ball from Rush County, IN. Solomon was a blacksmith in the Jerome community for many years. Amos was widely respected farmer of the eastern end of the county and was president of the Farmers and Merchants Bank at Greentown before its merger with the State Bank of Greentown.

Howard and Grace Harper had 12 children; Mary (Mrs. Lawrence Smeltzer), Mildred (Mrs. Harold Pence), George, Frances (Mrs. Glendel Marshall), Candace (Mrs. Ralph Simpson), Kenneth "Bill", Betty Charlotte (died at six months of age), Harold, Victor, Dale, Tom and Sue (Mrs. Gene Alexander).

Dale Harper married Wilma Jane Pendergrass of Howard County in 1955 at Kokomo, IN. Dale has also lived within the same half-mile stretch of County Road 100 North for his entire life. He retired after 39 years of employment at Chrysler Transmission Plant in Kokomo.

Jane, the daughter of Paul and Glessie (Parrish) Pendergrass, was born in Kokomo, IN and is the oldest of two children from this marriage.

Dale and Jane are the parents of three children; Paul Howard, David L., and Matthew Jay.

JEREMIAH HARRELL
Jeremiah Harrell, the son and seventh child of Jeremiah and Sara/Sarah (Osborn/

Osborne) Harrell, was born in Scott County, VA May 8, 1802. His grandfather is believed to be William Harrold/Harrell, and was a native of Ireland. He emigrated to America settling in Virginia. Jeremiah Jr. came to Brookville, Johnson County, IN on the White River with his parents at the age of eight.

The family came to Howard County shortly after 1850 following Lucretia and her husband, Robert Ritchey. Jeremiah was a very successful farmer accumulating several hundred acres in Ervin Township. He gave all of his children valuable and improved tracts of land. The famous Sycamore Tree Stump of Howard County, which is now located at Highland Park, came from the property just three miles from where Jeremiah first settled.

Elizabeth Glasco/Glascoe born ca. 1796 in Pennsylvania, her parents have not been found as yet, and died 1860 in Howard County. She is buried in South Union Cemetery. Jeremiah and Elizabeth were married and had 10 children. It is believed they were all born in Johnson County, IN except Henry G. and he was born in Marion County, IN. These children are as follows: The first child, Jeremiah R., died as an infant in Johnson County, IN; the second child was Jonathan (ca. 1825 and died in Howard County Jan. 5/11, 1905) married Mary Drear and is buried at the New London Cemetery; the third child Sara Jane (Oct. 12, 1826-April 22, 1863) married John Cagley; fourth child Lucretia Ann (Dec. 31, 1828-March 25, 1909) married Robert E. Ritchey; fifth child William Wesley (ca. 1833-1889) married Elydia A. Landrum; child number six Henry G. (April 7, 1836-?) married Nancy Jane Landrum; the seventh child James Edward (Dec. 13, 1837-March 6, 1918) married Lucinda Alexander; the eighth child Mary Elizabeth (June 8, 1841-Dec. 24, 1908) married Joseph B. Early and after his death she married Leander Garrett; child nine was Martin Van Buren (Nov. 10, 1844-Dec. 20, 1912) married Susan A. Uitts; the tenth and youngest child was Tighlman "Ted" Ashley Howard Harrell (June 22, 1846-Aug. 5, 1928) married Charlotte Elizabeth Harrison.

Jeremiah married Abba Jones July 21, 1867. They moved to Michigan in 1883 where Jeremiah is believed to have died in 1885.

Today, after several generations, descendants of Jeremiah and Elizabeth are still living in Howard County.

MOSES HARRELL AND FAMILY - Jeremiah (1756-1834) and Sarah Osborne (1765-1838) Harrell, parents of Moses, became early Indiana pioneers when they settled near Brookville in Franklin County (now Fayette County) about 1810 with all eight of their children, before Indiana reached statehood. With talk of another war and the promise of new land free from Indian raids, they moved from Dungannon, near the old Osborne Ford on the Clinch River in Russell County (now Scott County) VA, where all their children were born: William, Stephen, Jane, Jemima, Sarah, Moses, Jeremiah, and Comfort. Jeremiah served in the Continental Lines and militia of South Carolina during the Revolutionary War, and shortly after removed to Virginia where he and Sarah, daughter of Stephen and Comfort Langrum Osborne, married Dec. 17, 1781. In the early 1820s he entered land in Rush County and finally settled in White River Township, Johnson County, IN, where he and Sarah died and are laid to rest in Mt. Pleasant Cemetery.

Their son Jeremiah (1802-1879), was the first of these Harrells to enter land in Howard County, when in the 1840s his family settled in Section 33 of Ervin Township near Wildcat Road three miles east of Stonebraker's Mill. While living in Rush County with his parents, Moses (1800-1862) married Margaret Murray Street (1816-1876), daughter of James Murray and Margaret Helmich Street, May 22, 1831. In 1831 he was an original land owner in Johnson County where all 11 of their children were born: Sarah (1832-1917) married Hugh E. Surface Jan. 20, 1850 in Johnson County; Jeremiah (1835-1901) married Phoebe Jane Roland (1837-1870) Oct. 19, 1854 in Grant County; Margaret (1837-1915) married Daniel Dorrell (1832-1912) Aug. 23, 1854 in Johnson County; James Murray (1840-1925) married Tabitha Ann Davis (1845-1924) Oct. 19, 1862; Eliza Jane (1842-1916) married George Clinton Early (1838-1909) March 28, 1861 in Howard County; William Madison (1844-1934) married Mary Catherine Hoover (1840-1910) Aug. 3, 1865 in Peru, IN; Comfort Emaline (1847-1893) married Samuel Harvey Davis (1844-) Oct. 13, 1864 in Howard County; Mary Jemima (1849-1923) married Samuel Doty (1845-1912) Oct. 4, 1866 in Howard County; Clara Josephine (1852-1916) married Lewis Cass Cooper Dec. 25, 1870 in Howard County; John Fullen (1855-1873); and Shelby Moses (1858-1923) married LuEmma Sharp (1863-1913) Sept. 22, 1877 in Grant County.

In the 1850s, Moses followed his younger brother Jeremiah to Howard County. With the promise of new land and his father's itch to move to new frontiers, he entered land in Section one of Monroe Township. Moses and Margaret Harrell are both laid to rest in Ball Hill Cemetery in Carroll County, IN.

Ray Duncan Harrell, author of this article and great-great-grandson of Moses, was born Oct. 1, 1931 in Kearney, NE, son of Arthur Garland and Margaret Evelyn Weinle Harrell. Ray entered the USAF in 1951 and spent a year in Seoul during the Korean War. He earned his engineering degree at the University of Wichita in 1958. On June 3, 1955 he married Delores Faye McKay, daughter of Irving Leon and Iva Verna Athens McKay, in Wichita, KS. They have three daughters, Linda, Tracy, and Susan. Ray retired from Martin Marietta Aerospace in 1991 and lives in Littleton, CO. *Submitted by Ray Duncan Harrell.*

HARRIS - Nathaniel Harris (1805-1874), son of William, was born in North Carolina, and died in Grant County, IN. He married first Pinniah Elliott (1799-). They had Bartlett, who married Louviana Houser and second Rebecca Morris; Jonathan Pritlow; Mary; Henry; Christine; Rachel married Cyrus Baker; Christopher and Ida B. The parents and Bartlett came north to Greenville Township, Darke County, OH. They then came to Sims Township, Grant County, IN, except for Henry.

Jonathan Pritlow Harris (1831-) married 1852, Mercer County, OH, Susannah Kennard (1836-1856). They had Elmira Melissa (1853-), Mary Samantha (1856-). After the death of Susannah, Jonathan left his daughters with their maternal grandmother, and came to Sims Township, Grant County, IN, with his parents, where he married Melissa Lewellyn (1831-). Their children were: Victoria first married William Platt, and second John Thomas Power; William King married Sarah Alice Polk; Joseph (1864-1912), married 1891 Mahalla Emmaline Wilkerson (1873-1926); Sarah Ester; Charles married first Jennie Johnson, second Sarah ?; Homer married Elma Mae Scott; Jonathan P. married the third time, 1875 to Eliza Jervis Russell.

Joseph and Mahalla Emmaline Wilkerson Harris had Ross who married Mary McMillen; John Franklin (1893-1980) who married 1914 Hazel Marie Garbert (1897-1984); Velma May married Charles Zook; Walter Lee; Charles Arnel married Florence Murphy, and Mary Grace married Elmer McCune.

John Franklin and Hazel Marie had William Paul (1915-) married first Minerva Perkins, and married second Ruth Almon; Neil Thomas (1917-) married 1937 Gailen Louese DeLon (1918-); and Hyldred Glorene (1920-) who married first Bob Terris and second William C. Horton Jr.

Neil Thomas and Gailen Louese had Everett Neil and myself, Thomas Paul Harris. *Submitted by Thomas P. Harris.*

LOIS ANN HARRIS - In July, 1967, I flew to Indianapolis where I met my sister and brother-in-law, Nancy and Bill Boughton, to visit with them in Kokomo. Since Nancy was working at the Kokomo Public Library, I visited the library, filled out an application for a job and was hired, starting the first full week in September.

I was born in Morristown, NJ on Oct. 16, 1943, and grew up in Walhalla, SC, when our family - my parents, James Henry Harris and Elsie Ethel Drahosh Harris, my sister, Nancy Harris Boughton, my older brother, Robert Alan Harris and my younger brother, Donald Lawrence Harris, moved in September of 1947. After graduating high school in May 1961, I entered Furman University that fall. Although I did not graduate from Furman, I had more than two years of credit hours when I visited with Nancy and Bill in July 1967. Because of the amount of college credits, I became a librarian assistant in the Children's Department until the summer of 1986, when I was lowered to clerk status. Except for this, I still enjoy my work at the library.

Since moving to Kokomo I have been going to Calvary Baptist Church where I am in the church choir and am an organist.

The Harris family goes back to the early 1700s in Maryland of Welsh parents. This ancestor, John Harris, graduated from Nassau Hall in Princeton, NJ with an A.B. degree and was ordained as a Presbyterian minister in 1756. After the Revolutionary War ended, he and his family moved to South Carolina where he helped to start the Presbyterian Church in that state.

JOHN MARCUS (JR.) AND DOROTHY ANN HART - John and Dorothy Hart and their four children (Terri, Becky, John Gilbert, and Melody) moved to Kokomo in September 1969, a career move for John to Delco Electronics from CTS Microelectronics in Lafayette. The children, eight, seven, two, and one respectively, were excited about the move.

John, born in Anderson, IN, Dec. 29, 1938, to John Marcus Hart Sr. and HuWeen Veletta Zellar Hart, was a graduate of Anderson High School, where he was part of the band and orchestra. He has continued playing the trombone—participating in the Kokomo Park Band and Kokomo Symphony Orchestra and occasionally playing for the First Church of God, where the family has worshipped all 25 of their years in Kokomo. John received his Bachelor of Science degree from Valparaiso (Indiana) Technical Institute in 1966.

Dorothy was born to Gilbert Henry Hill and Edith May (George) Hill in Spencer, IA, Jan. 25, 1940. Her family moved to Indiana in 1947 where she spent her early years in the northern part of the state, moving from Cromwell to New Carlisle to Elkhart to Butler. In 1954 the family moved to Anderson. Dorothy played the French horn in the Anderson High School band and orchestra, where she met John. They were married June 11, 1959. Dorothy also played in the Kokomo Park Band and Kokomo Symphony Orchestra for several years. She has been involved in many church and community activities, including being a member of the board of Central Indiana Christian Broadcasting, Inc., the board which worked to bring WIWC radio to the area in 1992-93.

John and Dorothy Hart

It was with great surprise that Dorothy discovered that she had roots in Howard County. Upon the family's move to Kokomo, she received a letter from her 91-year-old grandmother in Iowa which said, "Your great-grandfather, William Davis [her father], was born May 3, 1850, in Kokomo, IN. He, with his five brothers, one sister, and their mother, were alone while his father was in the Civil War."

Further research showed that the farm on which the Davis family had lived was in Clay Township—the area in which the Hart Family presently resides. Although Dorothy, her father, and his mother (Louetta Davis Hill) had all been born in Iowa, there were roots right here in Howard County, IN.

Although John's roots are in Anderson, IN, he has two uncles in Kokomo (his father's brothers, Bill and Jim Hart, who were in the shoe business).

John is a senior project engineer at Delco Electronics where he has received several patents and recognition for over 25 years of service.

Dorothy is an executive secretary/office manager for T.L. Taylor & Associates, a financial planning firm in downtown Kokomo.

John and Dorothy are proud grandparents of Kirk and Mark Hofstrom, sons of Terri and Dana Hofstrom, South Daytona, FL; and Taylor and Delaney Archibald, son and daughter of Becky and Alan Archibald, Indianapolis. John Gilbert is married to Jill Dorsey and lives in Indianapolis. Melody lives in Nashville, TN. *Submitted by Dorothy A. Hart.*

HARTLEROAD - Ronald J. Hartleroad could call two counties home. He was born May 7, 1930, in Peru, the son of Ray and Ruth Brenton Hartleroad. On Aug. 7, 1949, he married Aileen Hoover.

He served with the U.S. Navy in Korea; afterward he located in Kokomo. From 1955 to 1960 he studied at Butler University; from January 1960 to 1964 he was Assistant Principal at Eastern High School, and he taught freshman literature.

He was a dedicated man. When a student lost a foot in an accident, Ron Hartleroad went to his home and tutored him after school. In the classroom his method was unorthodox but effective. He would tell stories, dramatizing them with props; he would give students assignments to come up with zany activities and then write about them; he would bring exotic foods in for the class to try.

Once, a fight broke out between a student and a teacher on the floor above his classroom; when he heard a thump on the floor Ron Hartleroad ran to the window to jokingly see if anyone had fallen out!

This writer was in his classroom on Nov. 22, 1963, the day Pres. Kennedy was assassinated. Ron Hartleroad was called out of the room, then returned to tell us the solemn news.

After his short tenure as a school administrator-teacher Ron Hartleroad moved on to the post of engineer at Delco Electronics in Kokomo. He worked in the same department as this writer's mother, Alice Hatton, and they had many meaningful conversations.

Ron Hartleroad owned a home at 741 E. Cassville Road in Cassville; in 1968 he sold it and moved to a Twelve Mile rural route. He continued to commute to Kokomo, and to the Cassville United Methodist Church, where he was a member. Often before work, he would participate in morning prayer with other workers.

When he learned he had cancer he faced it bravely, with a sustaining faith that everything is in God's plan; and this new road he was trodding that ended on the horizon, he knew there was life beyond. He told Alice Hatton he wasn't going to let his illness bother him, and yes, he would take some time and do things with his family he somehow hadn't gotten around to before.

Ronald J. Hartleroad passed away on Dec. 15, 1976. His family was wife Aileen, daughter Susie, and sons Jay and Tim. He was 46 years old—just about the current age of the students he once taught at Eastern so many years ago.

To others Ron Hartleroad was helpful, he was inspirational, and he was sincere; and to God he was ever faithful. In that was his greatness. *Submitted by Jeff Hatton.*

HATTON - James Madison Hatton was born in 1833, probably in Kentucky. He married Martha Reynolds (1848-1932) and ten children were born—seven girls and three boys. Sometime during the 1870s the Hattons moved north to Indiana; on Dec. 9, 1882, Henry Simon Hatton, the eighth child and second son, was born on a farm north of Waupecong in Miami County.

Henry was named for his granddad, Henry Reynolds (1818-1899). During the Civil War, Henry Reynolds was a pacifist who refused to fight and was imprisoned. When he returned home at the end of the war his clothes and body were so dirty, the family made him undress out in the weeds, burn his clothes, and bathe before entering the house.

His son-in-law James Madison Hatton fought, with his brother Francis Marion Hatton, for the North; Francis Marion Hatton died of sickness at Shiloh in 1862, and James Madison named his first born, a son, Francis Marion Hatton (1866-1943) after his deceased brother.

James Madison Hatton, a farmer, located near Phlox in Howard County, and died there Jan. 27, 1909; he was buried in New Hope-Ellis Cemetery.

Henry S. Hatton married Mary Effie Rittenhouse (1884-1913), and their children were son Loraine, and daughters Beulah (Herder) and Gwendolyn (Wright). Mary Effie died of tuberculosis and Henry S. married Karin Johanna Nelson (she later changed her name to Carrie Jane) (1890-1979) of New Bedford, MA. Their only child was James Marion Hatton, born Jan. 25, 1920.

Henry S. Hatton moved to Phlox in 1920; he worked as a carpenter, at the Tin Plate Works in Elwood, and in 1938 he opened a grocery store-gas station in Phlox. He was well read, and was known as a man of wisdom. He died March 13, 1969, and was buried in New Hope-Ellis Cemetery.

James M. Hatton operated the gas station a few years. He served in WWII; returning home, he drove a truck for awhile. He married Alice C. Dutton on Nov. 1, 1947, and remodeled the gas station into a home. He worked at Chrysler Corporation from 1947-1979; Alice Hatton worked at Delco Electronics from 1952-1980. James is well-known for his mechanical ability, especially on automobiles. He is always ready to lend a helping hand wherever it's needed.

James and Alice Hatton have one son, Jeffrey A. Hatton, born Sept. 29, 1949. He graduated from Eastern High School in 1967, and began working at the Kokomo Post Office in 1968. He married Janalyce K. Kendall (born Aug. 8, 1954), on June 15, 1974, and they have two children: Ryan Nathaniel (born Oct. 8, 1977), and Shannon Chere (born May 5, 1981). They live in a house they built in 1986-87 a short distance from Phlox.

Today the Hatton name continues with Ryan Hatton and perhaps only one other person named Hatton, to carry on the James Madison Hatton branch of the Hatton family. *Submitted by Jeff Hatton.*

HAVENS - Henry Bascomb (1822-1885) and Phebe Ellen Shockley (1828-1873) came from Rushville, IN to Kokomo in the 1840s. Mr. Havens was the son of Reverend James Havens, one of the first circuit riders and early leader of Methodism in Indiana. Their first home was located where Turners Department Store stood, and when it burnt, they rebuilt a second home at the present site of the Masonic Temple. Mr. Havens operated a hotel at Union and Sycamore Streets, was a Justice of Peace for Center Township and one of Kokomo's first real estate dealers. They had six children: Georgia Morrow, Mary Florine Leach, Emma, Charles H. (Goof), William Walton and Bessie Agnes.

Charles H. (Goof) Havens (1857-1927) was editor of the now defunct *Kokomo Dispatch* from 1888 to 1914, when he was appointed Postmaster by President Woodrow Wilson, until his retirement in 1922. He was active in many civic organizations, the Democratic Party and was also involved in bringing theatricals and vaudeville groups to Kokomo.

Charles H. (Goof) Havens

By his first marriage to Lula Ewing Coates (1857-1884) they had a daughter, Gretchen Florine Gerhard (Mrs. Paul M.) (1882-1963); she had five children: Charles L., Daniel, Henrietta Rohr, Richard P. and Elizabeth Jane Burkhart.

Mr. Havens' second marriage to Orpha Dean McKinsey (1868-1924), whose father, George W. McKinsey also had been a Postmaster of Kokomo; there were two children born to this union, George Cedric (1889-1894) and Clara H. (Mrs. Carl G. Yarling) (1892-1951). Mr. Yarling was an assistant then City Engineer until 1927; he designed the first National Guard Airport in Kokomo. They had three children, Mary L. Sprowls, Carl G., Jr., and Phoebe E. McMullen.

Richard P. Gerhard (1916-1985) was an assistant then Postmaster of Kokomo until his retirement in 1976. He was married to the former Doris M. Lavenduskie; they had three children: Charles John, Catherine Eades and Paul D. Mr. Gerhard's grandchildren are the sixth generation of the Havens family living in Howard County.

HAWKINS - Judith Ann Hawkins is a lifelong resident of Howard County, being born to Robert Edwin and Genevieve Agnes Hawkins, on Jan. 17, 1938, in Greentown, IN.

Judith Ann attended school through the seventh grade in Greentown, IN. In 1952, her parents moved to an 80 acre farm in western Howard County, on Highway 22, and 975 West. She attended the eighth grade at Ervin school in western Howard County, and went on to graduate from Northwestern High School in 1956.

Judith Ann Hawkins married Kenneth F. Rinehart April 14, 1957, at the Shiloh Methodist Church in Kokomo, IN. They had three children: Susan Kay—Nov. 14, 1958, Jeffrey Allen—Oct. 18, 1960, and Julia Ann—May 16, 1967.

Judith Ann attended the Kokomo School of Practical Nursing and graduated from there in 1971. She worked as a registered nurse for Saint Joseph Hospital in Kokomo, IN, and for the Burlington Clinic in Burlington, IN. She also did some private duty nursing.

In 1977, Judith Ann met and married Bobby Gibson from Kokomo, IN. They were married in the Northview Christian Church in Kokomo, IN, on Nov. 25, 1977. Judith Ann's daughter Susan Kay was married in 1977. Her son Jeffrey Allen was killed when a car fell on him on April 25, 1981. Bob and Judy raised Julia Ann in their home until she married.

Some of Judith Ann's activities include being a church organist for 36 years, part of which was at the Shiloh United Methodist, of Kokomo, the 1st Brethren Church at Burlington, and presently plays for the Northview Christian Church of Kokomo, IN.

Judith Ann sang with a gospel trio, called The Good News Trio, from Burlington, IN. She also sang with the Sweet Adelines, "Stop Light City Chorus" and The Hoosier Hunnies, quartet. Judith Ann sings periodically as a soloist for her home church, Northview Christian Church, and was the choir director for two years for the church. She has held various offices during her affiliation with these churches.

Judith Ann Gibson presently is doing volunteer work at Saint Joseph Hospital, in Kokomo, IN.

HAWKINS - James Perry Hawkins was born in Horse Cave, KY, son of Ebenezer and Susan Elizabeth Hawkins. Also two other children, Fred and Beulah.

James was employed at the Haynes Apperson Motor Co., and later as a Tool and Die maker at the Globe American Stove Company.

He married Blanche Howell of Kentland in 1899. They had seven children: Theodore, Kenneth, Mildred, Allan, Doris, Robert, and James.

James Hawkins died in 1956 and is buried in the Albright Cemetery in Kokomo, IN.

Blanche Howell Hawkins was born April 10, 1881 in Kentland, IN. She was a devoted mother and homemaker all of her life. She lived at 1721 N. Jay St., in Kokomo, where she died in 1963. Blanche is buried at the Albright Cemetery in Kokomo.

Robert Edwin Hawkins was born in Cassville, IN on Nov. 25, 1914 to Blanche and James. He was the fourth son in the family.

Robert E. Hawkins graduated from Greentown High School in 1933. He met his wife- to-be, Genevieve Agnes Seager, while still in high school.

Robert and Genevieve were married in Greentown, IN on Feb. 5, 1935.

Robert E. Hawkins served four years in the United States Naval Submarine Service, on the USS *Narwal*.

Robert and Genevieve made their home in Greentown, IN where they had two children: Judith Ann, born Jan. 17, 1938 and Robert Edwin Jr. born Oct. 5, 1940.

Robert and family moved from Greentown to an 80-acre farm in western Howard County in Ervin Township.

Mr. Hawkins was employed at Delco Radio in Kokomo, IN, where he became a Tool Room Supervisor, and retired in 1974, after 37 years of service.

Robert was very active in the Shiloh United Methodist Church, where he held various positions, including Lay Leader; he sang in the church choir, and was a Sunday School teacher.

In the early 50s, Robert served as president of the Northwestern Parent Teachers Association.

Robert was a 52-year member of the Greentown Masonic Lodge.

Robert Edwin Hawkins Sr. died June 13, 1992, with entombment at Sunset Memory Gardens, in Kokomo, IN.

CYNTHIA ANN STEVENS DWYER-HAYEN

- Cynthia was born in Howard County on Aug. 2, 1950, the eldest child of Warren Bryan Stevens and Shirley Ann Auten Stevens of Howard County. Cynthia is a lifelong resident of Howard County and is employed as a teacher with Kokomo-Center Township Consolidated School Corporation.

Cynthia received her Bachelor of Science degree in elementary education from Ball State University in 1972. She received her Master of Science degree in elementary education with endorsements in reading and learning disabilities from Indiana University-Bloomington in 1974. Cynthia received additional licensing in Public School Administration and Reading Specialization from Indiana University in 1977. Cynthia received the advanced degree, Education Specialist (Ed.S) in Language Education with a minor in School Administration from Indiana University-Bloomington in May, 1990.

Cynthia has served as a teacher and administrator in the education profession for 22 years and was principal at Darrough Chapel Elementary School from January 1987-June 1994. In that capacity, she modeled shared leadership with the staff as they developed an educational technology pilot program with portfolio assessment of writing across the curriculum. Cynthia has a copyright of a model of the process of change in leadership roles, is a frequent speaker in education circles, and serves as an adjunct faculty member of Indiana University-Kokomo.

Cynthia has a daughter, Meghan Ann Dwyer, born April 12, 1983, who resides with her in Kokomo. On Aug. 8, 1992, Cynthia married Lawrence Brad Hayen of Howard County.

LAWRENCE BRAD HAYEN

- Lawrence Brad Hayen, born Nov. 20, 1953 is the grandson of Lawrence Arthur Donelson who was an electrician and the first neon tube bender in Howard County. Lawrence Arthur Donelson was born in Howard County on Feb. 3, 1909 and was deceased in June 1982. Lawrence Arthur was the son of Loren Donelson and Artie Mesa Gullion Donelson whose families came to Howard County in 1868 from Switzerland County, IN. Lawrence Arthur married Jessie Waters Donelson, born Jan. 30, 1912 in Mt. Carmel, IL. They had three children. Their eldest daughter, Phyllis June Donelson, was born May 1, 1932 and married Warren Henry Hayen of Marion, KS who was born on July 11, 1934. They had two children, Lawrence Brad and Phyllis Kimberly Hayen Wyrick, born Dec. 4, 1957.

Lawrence Brad Hayen served in the U.S. Navy as a medical corpsman from 1973-1977. He received an associate degree from the University of California-Berkeley in Operating Room Technology in 1975. He received the Bachelor of Science degree in Business Administration from Indiana Wesleyan University in 1994. Lawrence Brad is employed as an electrician at Delco Electronics in Kokomo.

Lawrence Brad has a son, Aaron Matthew Hayen, born May 19, 1979, who resides with him in Kokomo. On Aug. 8, 1992, Lawrence Brad married Cynthia Stevens Dwyer of Howard County.

HAYNES - Enoch and Elizabeth Haynes were married in New York state after which they moved to Ohio. They had 10 children: Samuel, Wright, Charles, Deborah, Stephen, James, Elizabeth, Asa, Content, and Sarah.

James married Martha Harlan of North Carolina in Clinton County, OH, and they moved to Miami County, IN in 1854. They had 10 children: Milton, Lydia, Malinda, Eliza, Martha, Wesley, John, Franklin, Andrew, and a son that died in infancy.

Wesley married Rebecca Stevenson (of Warren County, OH) in 1843 in Miami County, IN. They had four children: Charles, Warren, Frank, and Joseph Wilbur. Both Charles and Warren died in infancy. Wesley enlisted in military service in March 1863, and he served in the Civil War until mustered out in August 1865.

In June 1877 Rebecca died leaving Wesley with two minor sons, and in 1878 he married Sarah Oren (of Clinton County, OH) who was the first lady to fill the office of State Librarian of Indiana.

Joseph Wilbur was married three times, but left no heirs. He became a rural mail carrier and lived in Colorado most of his adult life. He adopted a daughter Dorothy who lived in Kokomo all her life. She never married. His third wife was Elnora Golightly.

Frank married Nellie Ward and they were destined to have tragedy strike their children. First, they had twins Ward and Esther, but Esther lived only three months. Next, their son Paul lived only about three years. Finally, Edith lived about 26 years with a gland problem that left her very obese. Ward was the lone survivor only to lose his father at the age of 16. He took over support of the family, quit school because of that, and operated a home delivery dairy in Kokomo for many years.

Ward married Mary Jackson and they had sons: Lawrence, Louis, John, and David. His sons all fulfilled one of his wishes by obtaining college degrees. (Lawrence earned a Ph.D. and David an M.S.).

Lawrence married Louise Peterson, of Vermont, and they had daughters Beverley, and Marilyn, and son Peter. Beverley married Thomas Fotovich of Kansas City, KS and they had a son Benjamin and a daughter Emily. They live in the Kansas City area. Marilyn married Frank Caryl and had daughter Lisa. She then married David Sims and had daughter Sarah by him. Her third marriage was to Dean Macan. They live in Olathe, KS. Peter married Karen Eckman in Ephrata, PA and they had a daughter, Caitlin, and sons Tyler and Mitchell. He became a minister and held pastorates in Greencastle, PA and Glen Arm, MD where they now live.

Louis married Betty Givens and they had a daughter Mary Edyth who was stillborn. They live in Kokomo.

John married Maxine Spencer and they had no children. He then married Virginia Taylor and they adopted a son, Thomas, and a daughter, Janet. Tom married Linda Roberts and they had daughters Christina and Carrie. Janet married Kevin Bentley and they had sons Michael and Scott. All of John's family live in the Kokomo area.

David married Carol Lambert of Indianapolis and they had a son Anthony who now lives in Kansas City and has never married. They also adopted a son, Bobby, who married Mary Lennox and they had sons Zechariah and Jacob. He is in the U.S. Navy in the Pacific. David lives in Indianapolis. (See Ward and Jackson) *Submitted by David E. Haynes, son of Ward and Mary Haynes.*

BOB AND BERDINA REYNOLDS HEAD - Bob Head and Berdina Reynolds were married in Oakford at the Fairfield Christian Church, Jan. 15, 1960. It was the last wedding to be held in the old church building, located where the present church parsonage is built.

Bob was born in Clay County, TN April 15, 1935. He moved to Tipton County as a very young boy. He graduated from Sharpsville High School in 1955. Berdina was born in Howard County on Feb. 2, 1941, and graduated from Kokomo High School in 1959.

They have two daughters, Kelly Lynn, born May 9, 1964 and Bobette Lenae, born Dec. 11, 1965, and six grandchildren: Brooke Renee Edwards, July 12, 1985; Kari Lenae Daggett, Oct. 23, 1986; Kaylee Lynn Marchione, May 26, 1987; Cody Ryan Daggett, Sept. 23, 1988; Joshua L. Marchione, July 6, 1989; and Michael Drew Daggett, Sept. 5, 1990.

Bob and Berdina Head

Bob served in the U.S. Army from 1957 thru 1959 in Germany. After being discharged from the service, he graduated from Barber School and began cutting hair for Ned's Barber Shop in Kokomo. In 1965, he moved his barber shop to Sharpsville and cut hair there until 1977. He was employed at Delco Electronics in the Security Department retiring from there in 1992.

Berdina worked at Chrysler Corporation beginning in 1959 directly out of high school. After ten years, she quit to remain home with the children. After the children were in school, she worked for Davidson Construction Co. in Kokomo. In 1974, after completing real estate school, she began selling real estate for R.L. Tomlinson and has remained in that field for 20 years.

Bob and Berdina purchased the Clayton and Elva Cole home on 100E out of Oakford and restored it in 1992. That is where they presently reside.

HEATON - William Heaton was born in Washington County, PA in 1789. He married Polly Hart of Virginia and they had a daughter, Elizabeth, born in 1811. Tragedy struck when Polly died in 1813. Later that year William married Rachel Osborne in Columbia, OH. When she reached maturity, daughter Elizabeth married Martin Roads. They had a daughter, Rachel, and a son, Berton, after which the lineage was lost.

William and Rachel moved to a farm near Lebanon, OH where Andrew, Amelia, Daniel, John Osborne, Lucinda, and Henry were born. In 1829 the family decided to move west. They loaded their belongings and headed south to the Ohio River where they boarded a steamboat near Cincinnati. Steamboats were new and nobody knew what to expect of them. John O. related many years later that they stopped along the river where both passengers and crew debarked and went into the forest to cut and load wood to fire the boilers. That made a lasting impression on the young boy.

The steamboat went down the Ohio and then up the Wabash to Wyandotte, IN which is about eight miles south of Lafayette. The journey took about three weeks. At Wyandotte, during the period of the Blackhawk wars, the Heatons lived near an encampment of about 400 friendly Indians and they frequently went to the Indian campground to visit, trade, etc.

It was here that William Heaton erected a flour mill on the lower waters of Wildcat Creek. He also built a general store and became the first merchant and miller of the village. John O. Heaton grew to manhood here and acquired as much education as the little log schoolhouse provided. He later went to the academy in Lafayette, a village of about 100 residents. In 1832 William Heaton was sent to the State Legislature by his neighbors.

At Wyandotte, the family grew with the births of Louisa, James, William Robert, and Vanburen. Rachel died in 1843 leaving William with several still small children. In 1846 William married Sarah Burton who helped with raising his children even though they had none of their own.

In 1844 John O. Heaton married Louisa Blystone, and in 1847 they moved to the village of Kokomo where he and a brother operated a general store. He later taught in the village school, and held elective offices of school trustee and county commissioner. He bought 80 acres of government land in northeast Kokomo where he erected the first frame house in the area. (It was at the corner of Monroe and Orchard streets.) All the other houses at that time were log cabins. He told of the rank growth of smartweed in the area where the courthouse now stands and of how paths were cut in the smartweed to the residents' cabins.

John O. Heaton's daughters, Alice and Sarah, lived in a house adjacent to his frame house until the late 1940s. Studebaker Park is encompassed by the Heaton property.

Another daughter, Emma, married Orlando Somers and they lived on East Jefferson Street. For many years a cannon was displayed in their yard because of his participation in the Civil War and his membership in the Grand Army of the Republic veterans organization. The Somers property is now Somers Park. (See Orlando Somers)

Lucinda Mary, another daughter, married Ezra Jackson, former county commissioner, farmer, livestock trader, Civil War veteran, and active member of the G.A.R. (See Ezra Jackson and Somers) *Submitted by Russell Keiter, great-great-grandson of William Heaton.*

WILLIAM H. AND CLARA HEATON -
Heatons were among the first settlers to come to Howard County. In 1840, Joseph Heaton (1809-1879) arrived in Harrison Township to build a cabin for his family. In 1841 his father, Daniel Heaton (1780-1863)—also known as Colonel Heaton—arrived and became a permanent resident as well. Joseph was first married to Hannah Baxter (1808-1851), a Canadian, and they had seven children: Thaddeus B., Delia, Hannah, Daniel M., Henry C., Eli, and Cornelius. After Hannah's death, Joseph married Rachael Harrison in 1852, and they apparently had no children together.

Bill (William) Heaton; Clara Heaton

Joseph and Hannah's firstborn was Thaddeus Baxter Heaton (born June 1, 1832) who married Matilda Rayl (born Nov. 13, 1837) in 1859; she was his third wife. His first wife was Catherine Jacobs; the name of his second wife is unknown. Thaddeus and Matilda had 11 children: Adolphus (1860-1911); Joseph, Anna, and Clara, who died in infancy; William H. (1867-1943); Nathaniel McKinley (1870-1890); Lula Alice (1872-1948); Frank K. (1873-1956); David C. (1875-1945); Flora (1878-1946); and Charles (1882-1966). Thaddeus died Dec. 5, 1900, and Matilda died Dec. 31, 1912. Both are buried at Prairieville Cemetery in Tipton County. Alongside their graves is that of their son Nathaniel who died in a hunting accident. Another tragedy that occurred in their family was the accidental drowning in the Wabash River of Adolphus at age 51.

Thaddeus and Matilda's son, William H., was born Aug. 8, 1867. He married Clara Inez Shepherd (born Aug. 11, 1868) on Dec. 24, 1890. To that union were born six boys and three girls. First was Lucille (1891-1967) who married Owen Branstetter. Their children were Gerline, Helen and Morris. Next was Charles Eli (1892-1916) who died at the age of 24. The next two children were twins: Ed (1897-1917) and Freddy (1897-1900). The fifth child was Roy (1900-1989) who married Mary Leckrone. They had no children. Anna (1901-1987) was next. She married Herschel Grose, and their children were Herschel and Betty. The seventh child was Lillian Irene (1904-1982) who married Dwight Bennett and had eight children. These included Bill, Maxine, Ted, Dick, Paul, John, Carolyn, and Judy. The next child of William and Clara Heaton was Carl (1906-1976). He married Cecil Huffer; they later divorced. There were no children of this marriage. The last child was Pearl (1908-1986) who married Mary Evelyn Sheets. Their family consisted of Beverly, Bob, Peggy, Don, and Linda.

William Heaton's occupation was that of a tenant farmer. The family lived in Tipton County briefly, in Clinton County for a time (at Hillisburg and Forest), and at Russiaville. They also lived near New London once, and when Lillian was born, the family had traveled to Indianola, NE, to see how they would like it there. After Lillian's birth, they returned to Russiaville where they lived most of their years.

Clara died Jan. 4, 1932, and William died March 4, 1943. Both are buried at Prairieville Cemetery. *Submitted by Maxine Jones*

HEINZMAN -
The Heinzman families' connection with Howard County began in January 1951, when Luther (Boots) started working for the Howard-Miami County Dairy Herd Improvement Association as supervisor. D.H.I.A. was an organization of dairy farmers who kept production records on their cows.

The first month he worked in Miami County and on his 21st birthday he met a young girl who became his wife three-plus years later.

They were married in the Lutheran Church in Wabash Oct. 24, 1954 and their first home was in the Forest Lodge Trailer Park. They only lived there two years, since they already had Stephen, born July 16, 1955 and another child on the way.

They moved to a house on the old Forest Harness farm, south of Kokomo on U.S. 31, where James was born Oct. 12, 1956. They lived there until January 1959 when they moved to Plevna, to a farm house owned by Dr. A.L. Keim. Here their third son, William, was born Sept. 19, 1959. William had a severe R.H. condition at birth, and was the first baby to have a blood exchange in Howard County.

Here also they were saddened by the loss of a baby boy, stillborn, and a baby girl who lived one day due to R.H. difficulties.

In 1964 Shirley started working at Delco to help with the medical expenses, where she is still employed. In 1967 they moved to their present house, 413 S. Maple St. in Greentown, which they bought from Bob Elliot who had it built in 1951. It went through the Palm Sunday tornado in 1965 and received damage but was not destroyed, as were some of the neighborhood homes.

The Heinzman Family of Kokomo, IN—Boots, Shirley, Stevie, Jimmy, Billy.

Here their three sons grew up and graduated from Eastern High School. Stephen has a Ph.D. and has been a research chemist for Proctor and Gamble, in Cincinnati, OH, since 1983. In 1986 he married Sharon Bergman. They have two daughters, Rachel Feb. 17, 1988 and Ariana Aug. 9, 1991.

James worked for a short time at Millbank, Chrysler and H & M Electric before starting at Wilson Foods, Logansport, in 1979. In 1978 he married Theresa (Teddi) Baldwin of Kokomo. They have two daughters and one son: Jamey March 30, 1979, Jordan Aug. 23, 1982 and Katherine (Katie) March 9, 1985. They live at 4422 W. 300N Kokomo.

William started working at Wilson Foods in 1978. He married Cynthia (Cindy) Degraffenreid of Kokomo in 1981. They live in Logansport with their two sons, Derek Aug. 21, 1985 and Alexander (Alex) Nov. 28, 1989.

They have been blessed with a loving family, good friends and good neighbors for which they thank and praise God for his riches.

Luther was born in Cullman, AL Jan. 20, 1930 to Harry Heinzman (Hamilton County, IN) and Grace Neff (Crawford County, OH). In December of 1993 Luther will complete 20 years at Wilson Foods in Logansport and is looking forward to retirement.

Shirley was born in Wabash May 12, 1936 to John Nordman (Livingston County, IL) and Ethel Bolinger (Wabash County, IN).

The first church they became members together was Zion Lutheran. The second was Holy Cross Lutheran, Dixon Road and their third is Redeemer Lutheran, Kokomo, where they have been members since 1975. Their final resting place will be Sunset Memory Gardens but Heaven is their home. *Submitted by Shirley Heinzman.*

HOWARD FRANK HELMS -
Howard F. Helms is a direct descendant of a prominent pioneer family in Indiana and Howard County which included John Helms (GGGG/F); John Helms, Jr. (GGG/F); William Helms (GG/F); Arie Helms (G/F) as documented in Volume II, Cass, Miami, Howard and Tipton County, IN Family History, 1898, Lewis Publishing Company.

His father, Howard Foster Helms, son of Aire Helms, married Lela Mildred (Walker) Helms of Greentown, IN in 1917 prior to his entry into the Army for World War I. During their marriage, they gave birth to three children: Lucile Helms, Ralph Helms, and Howard Frank Helms.

Colonel Helms was born in Kokomo in 1925 and spent all of his formative years in his hometown. He married his local high school fiance, Marion Francis (Morrison) Helms in 1948. During their marriage, they gave birth to three children: a daughter, Karla D. (Helms) Dain, who currently resides in Kokomo and two sons, Jeffry S. Helms and H. Brent Helms, both deceased and buried in Sunset Cemetery, Kokomo, IN.

Howard Frank and Marion F. Helms

Upon graduation from Kokomo High School in 1943, Colonel Helms was inducted in the U.S. Army during World War II. He served as an infantryman with the 89th Division and participated in three European campaigns. Upon termination of the War, he was discharged in 1946 and returned to civilian life. He enrolled in Indiana University and pursued his undergraduate work when he was recalled for the Korean War in 1950. Based upon his class status, he was deferred to complete his academic and R.O.T.C. accreditation. He received a business degree and a Regular Army Commission in 1951 and re-entered the U.S. Army later that year.

Colonel Helms served 25 years in the U.S. Army serving in the Infantry, Armor, and Quartermaster branches. He retired from active duty in 1971 after serving in Europe during World War II as well as serving in the Korean Conflict; the Dominican Republic Campaign; and the Vietnam War. His decorations included Legion of Merit with Oak Leaf Cluster; Bronze Star with Oak Leaf Cluster; Army Meritorious Medal; Army Commendation Medal with Oak Leaf Cluster and Combat Infantry Badge.

Upon return to civilian life and re-establishment of residency in Kokomo, Colonel Helms involved himself in local Republican politics. As a result, he was appointed Deputy Mayor-City Controller by Mayor Arthur LaDow and served in that capacity from 1976-1980. After this, he ran successfully for Howard County Auditor serving from 1981-1984 and served as County Treasurer in 1985 and 1986. He resigned from this office in 1987 due to personal considerations and entered into full-time retirement.

Colonel Helms and his wife, Marion, currently reside in Rainbow Springs Country Club Estates, Dunnellon, FL.

RALPH L. HELMS - Prominent local descendant of honored and recognized early pioneer family in Indiana and Howard County which included John Helms, (GGG-G/F); John Helms, Jr. (GG/GF); William Helms (GG/F); Arie Helms (G/F) as documented in Volume II Cass, Miami, Howard and Tipton Counties family History, 1898 - Lewis Publishing Company - Available Kokomo Library. His father, Howard Foster Helms, son of Arie Helms, married Lela Mildred (Walker) Helms, Greentown, IN in 1917 prior to his entry into the Army for World War I. During their marriage they bore a daughter, Lucile Helms, and two sons, Ralph L. Helms and Howard F. Helms. After a long and fruitful life together they were deceased 1968, Lela Helms, and 1985, Howard Helms, both of which are interred at Sunset Memory Cemetery, Kokomo, IN.

Mr. Helms was born in Kokomo 1921 and spent his entire youth in his place of birth. He courted and married his high school sweetheart, Mary E. (Kellie) Helms in 1946. During their marriage, they bore one daughter, Sally Helms (Long), who currently resides in Kokomo. In addition they had two sons, R.L. Helms, Jr. who resides in Carmel, IN and George F. Helms, residing in Cicero, IN.

Ralph L. Helms

Mr. Helms upon completing high school in 1939 enrolled in Indiana University from 1940 until 1942. It was at this time that he felt the call to arms and volunteered for service with the U.S. Army. He was assigned to the Infantry Branch and received his basic training at Camp Walters, TX. Upon completion of his basic training in 1942 he was assigned to the Intelligence and Reconnaissance Platoon, 137th Regiment, 35th Division for advanced unit training. During this period he received a grievous leg injury which led to an extended hospital convalescent period of 18 months and an ultimate medical disability discharge from the Atlanta Army Hospital in 1945.

Mr. Helms returned to civilian life and re-entered Indiana University for the completion of his undergraduate business degree in 1947. Upon completion, he enrolled in Law School and his LLB and Doctor of Jurisprudence in 1949. Successfully passing the state bar examination, he established himself in the private practice of law in 1949, city of Kokomo, IN.

Mr. Helms enjoyed an early reputation as a successful young lawyer throughout Howard County and, also was recognized as a skillful and dedicated Republican organizational visionary. His legal and political qualifications were recognized in 1960 with his appointment as City Attorney which extended for over 13 1/2 years of unparalleled service. In addition, during this period, he was elected Republican county chairman in 1964 and served until 1980 which set a record for the state for the County Chairman. Mr. Helms has concluded his governmental service by serving as County Attorney for a total of six years and continues to serve at this time as Assistant County Attorney.

Mr. Helms continues to pursue an active private law practice in Kokomo. He and his wife maintain their residence in south Kokomo.

HEMMEGER - The Miami Indian Reserve, including Howard County, opened for land entry in 1848. Shortly after, there was a migration from the Phillipsburg, Clay Township, Montgomery County, OH area. They settled mostly along the present State Road 26, including Terre Hall, now Hemlock; Tampico, now Center; Oakford and New London. The migrators were mostly Quaker descendants including the Cox, Thomas, Snethem and Cashner families and John and Elizabeth Hollingsworth.

Johnathon Cox bought the 40-acre farm located at the southwest corner of State Road 26 and 400 E. Their son, Elisha Aaron Cox, returned to Phillipsburg, OH to marry Elizabeth Cashner. Elisha moved his family back to Tampico, IN. Their daughter, Rosetta Cox, was born in Hemlock during the Civil War. Elisha moved his family, including Rose, to the Marion, IN area. Rose Cox married Charles Marian Vermilion in Marion, IN. Charley and Rose Vermilion had a daughter, Edna May. Edna May married Fred Hemmeger.

Their twin sons, Earl and Elmer, were born Jan. 26, 1923 in Marion. Fred was hired as an iron molder at the Hoosier Iron Works at Morgan and Webster Streets in Kokomo. Fred moved his family to Kokomo in 1921.

In 1925, Fred bought the old abandoned Hopewell Church at the northeast corner of the Waterworks and Vansickle Roads, now 50 N. and 400 E. Fred intended to use the old church house to raise chickens and build a new house next door.

Earl and Elmer Hemmeger

The Depression came, the Hoosier Iron Works shut down, and Fred had to convert the shell of the church into living quarters. His twin sons, Earl and Elmer, converted the house into the existing house after returning from WWII. Earl, always a bachelor, still lives in the house.

Fred and Edna Vermilion Hemmeger had nine children, including three sets of twins and a set of triplets. The triplets and two sets of twins died in infancy.

Fred's five daughters were: Mary Wyckoff, living at Beaver Dam, IN; Bernice Record, living in Walton; Martha Ball, of Marion; Joan Swanson, deceased in 1993, lived in Kokomo; Virginia Hemmeger, of Kokomo; Elmer, deceased in 1992, lived in Kokomo.

There are several descendents of Jonathan and Elizabeth Snethem Cox in central Indiana. Their daughter, Susanna, married Perry Morris and they are the ancestors of many Morris families locally.

The Hemmeger ancestors lived in the Cumberland, MD area and migrated to New Philadelphia, Tuscarawas County, OH before 1810. Several Hemmeger families migrated from New Philadelphia to the Blackford-Jay County area of Indiana in 1846.

The Vermilion ancestors lived in Piscataway, Prince George's County in Maryland in 1680 and migrated to Newark, Licking County, OH about 1835, and then to Marion, IN about 1880.

Earl was a Purdue University civil engineering graduate, Class of 1950. He was a State of Indiana highway engineer, Tipton and Howard County highway engineer, but most of his engineering years were spent as the City Engineer of Kokomo.

Elmer owned Hemmeger Printcraft Press and Linens Mainly in Kokomo.

HENDRICKS-MIDDLETON - In 1856 James Emerson Hendricks(on) (1831-1899) married Mary Ann Caudle/Caudell (1842-1903) in Shelbyville, Shelby County, IN, and had four children—William D., Elijah, John E., and Malinda (Rakestraw). They were members of the Lewis Creek Baptist Church, where James' parents, Matilda Young and David Hendricks, were founding members and David had been the first clerk until his death in 1836. The second clerk of the church was Buckner Caudle, Mary Ann's grandfather. Her great-grandfather was a Revolutionary War veteran named John Thomas.

James Hendricks moved his family from Shelby County to Howard County and by 1876 they owned 80 acres west of Russiaville. Their eldest son William David Hendricks (1858-1927) married Rhodema Jane Middleton (1861-1917) in 1882. Their nine children were all born in Russiaville—John L., Cecile A. (Balker), Robert T., James M., Alice (Johnson), Edd B., Mary (White), R. Ruth (Wells), and L. June. As of December 1993, the sole surviving sibling, Ruth Wells, lives in Minneapolis, MN.

The Middletons were Quakers from Virginia and Ohio. Rhodema Jane's parents, Eli Middleton (1828-1898) and Ruth George (1829-1864), also had four sons—Joseph M., James L., Calvin W., and E. Francis. Ruth died shortly after baby Frank's birth in Iowa and three-year-old Rhodema Jane went to live with her Aunt Jane and Uncle William Middleton in the town he founded, West Middleton, IN.

Ruth's father, Enos George, was born 1797 in Virginia, got married in Ohio to Sally Carson who was part Algonquin Indian, and moved to Howard County where he was buried in Russiaville beside the log cabin he built. Eli Middleton was the son of Levi Middleton I (ca. 1797-1853) and Mary Postgate (1801-1870), pioneer members of the New London Friends Church. They had seven sons and one daughter—Allen, David, Eli, William, Lemuel, Levi, Ascenith, and Hudson/Bud.

James E. Hendricks, Mary Ann Caudle Hendricks, Eli Middleton, and Mary (Postgate Middleton) Butler are buried in the Friends Cemetery in New London, IN. Levi Middleton is buried in the pioneer section.

The eldest son of William David Hendricks and Rhodema Jane Middleton, John Levi Hendricks, was born Jan. 2, 1883 in Russiaville, IN, and farmed and handled horses. In 1906, he won a homestead lottery and moved to Presho, SD. After four years of hard work, he sold his 180-acre homestead for $1 and joined the railroad working west. In Lava Hot Springs, ID, he met and married Orra Elvira Potter in 1918. They bought an 80-acre farm two miles out of town and raised four children—R. Rex, Thomas Payne, Phynis Rhodema "Judy" (Clark) and John Levi II. After 53 years, John and Orra moved to Seattle, WA. He passed away at the age of 90 in 1973 and is buried in Auburn, WA. As of December 1993, Orra Hendricks lives in Seattle. *Submitted by Nancy Hendricks Sandrock, granddaughter of John Levi Hendricks I*

HENRY - Abraham Henry (born 1828 Pennsylvania; died Dec. 18, 1893 Howard County, IN) and wife Catherine _____, (1827; May 26, 1916 Howard County, IN) were the parents of Michael William Henry (Nov. 30, 1854; April 22, 1929). Michael Wm. married first, Anielisa Dearinger, who died in 1894. He married second, Fannie Ladoska Ridgeway (Jan. 20, 1877; Nov. 23, 1925). The children by his first marriage were, Everett Ehrman and Goldie. Goldie married Phenny A. Brubaker. They moved to North Dakota and then to California. The children of the second marriage were Mary Lucille (April 21, 1914; Feb. 23, 1979); and Cora Omega (Sept. 1, 1901; Jan. 3, 1927).

Everett Ehrman (Nov. 5, 1889; July 25, 1946) was born in a log cabin just south of 100N and 750 W, on the east side of the road. He married Flora Saloma Eller (Sept. 19, 1891; Dec. 10, 1983); the daughter of Josiah and Ortha (Brubaker) Eller. Everett and Flora are buried in S. Union Cemetery. They had Glenn, Russell and Vada.

Russell is unmarried and Vada married ___ Bryan and lives in California. She taught school at Ervin.

Glenn and Mabel Henry

Glenn (born June 22, 1913) married (Dec. 24, 1943) Mabel C. Holloway of South Bend, IN. She was the daughter of Herman D. Holloway. They have two children, Mark Eugene who died at birth and David. Glenn was born in a log house on 1150 W and 225 N. The house now stands at 400 N and 1200 W. Glen is the owner of the 'White Elephant Store'. They have ball cards and miscellaneous merchandise. *Submitted by Glenn Henry.*

ISAAC F. AND AGNES HENRY

Isaac F. and (Esther) Agnes (Hagerty) Henry were both born in Belle Vernon, PA, and married there on Sept. 22, 1897. Isaac (born March 1875) was a glass expert, and as such, was hired by Pittsburgh Plate Glass and subsequently transferred to Kokomo, IN, around 1920. They bought a modest home on West Mulberry Street where they saw both their children, Fred B. and (Mary) Virginia, grow to maturity and head off to college. Isaac was later transferred to Okmulgee, OK, where Agnes joined him. However, after some time in Oklahoma, Agnes decided to return to their home in Kokomo to be in a central location to see her children and grandchildren. She was active in several organizations, Eastern Star and the Round Table among them, as well as being a member of the Presbyterian Church. Isaac never returned to Kokomo, having died in 1952 shortly after retiring. Agnes was born on April 21, 1875, and died in Kokomo, IN, on March 23, 1954. She is buried at Crown Point Cemetery.

Isaac's parents, John Short (born 1831, died Dec. 21, 1909) and Martha (Barrett) Henry (born 1831, died 1911) spent their lives in North Belle Vernon, PA, John being a glass cutter at American Glass Company. Agnes's parents were James (born roughly 1810, died roughly 1902) and Mary (Corwin) Hagerty (born 1834, died 1913) also of Belle Vernon.

After Isaac and Agnes's children finished college, they began their lives elsewhere. Fred B. was a National Honor Society member at Ohio State, earning a degree in Mechanical Engineering. He took up residence in Columbus, OH, married and had one son. Virginia (born May 30, 1902) attended Illinois College (now University of Illinois), graduated in 1925. Although she taught one year in Kokomo, during that time she married Clark Matson Brown on May 22, 1926, and at the end of the school year they moved to Gary, IN, where Clark set up a dental practice. They had two children, Richard Henry and Jacqueline. Clark died in the late 1930s, and Virginia returned to teaching in Gary, IN. She remarried on Dec. 26, 1949, to Sidney Moffatt.

Virginia and her son, Richard, live in Phoenix, AZ, and Jacqueline lives in Homosassa Springs, FL. Sidney's daughter, Kathryn J., has always been a close member of the family and lives in Chicago, IL.

HERCULES/DUNCAN

William Hercules, born 1738 in Scotland, arrived in what is now New Jersey in 1774. He married Amy (Forest) Groves and together they had eight children, Jane, Catherine, Sarah, Esther, William, Mary, James and Samuel. He moved his family by wagon and on foot to the Ohio Valley. He settled in Cincinnati, and built the first brick house there. He was a weaver of flax, wool and silk and was probably lured to that area by experimentation being done by entymologists who were trying to raise silkworms on mulberry trees in the Ohio Valley. Silkworms were not successful, so he moved his family to what is now Mason, OH. He died in 1829 and is buried there.

His son James, born in 1795, married Rebecca Thomas Ashley. They moved to Taylor Township in Howard County and owned property there in 1891. Their son John Taylor Hercules was born in 1847 in Darke County, OH. John and his brother Lewis (Lute) brought one of the largest sawmills in Taylor Township to Tampico (Center) IN in 1876. The mill operated there until 1882 when it was moved to Frankfort.

In 1866 John married Catharine Woolley from Paoli, IN and the couple lived in the house that still stands six doors east of the old church in Center. Their great-great-grandchild, David Holt Thompson, and family lived in this house until 1993 when it was sold. During renovation, David found and removed a board from the house with John Hercules's signature on it. The board is being passed on to John and Catharine's heirs as a remembrance.

John and Catharine had three children, Otis Welby, Arrah Cornelius (Neil), and Ivy Pearl (Pearl). Otis died unmarried at the age of 23. Neil moved to California. He had a daughter, Mary Katherine McCullock, now living in Fairfax, VA. Pearl was a piano teacher. She married Charles Duncan, the school teacher at Center. Charles later operated the general store and post office there. Each day he would hang the mail on a high post. The trainmen would pick it from the post and throw the incoming mail down on a platform beside the general store, never stopping the train.

Charles and Pearl had three children, Simon Von (Von) born in Center, Esther Wanita and Nila Josephine born in Kokomo. Von died in 1905 at Center when he was three. He was the sweetheart of the community, and when he died it was especially difficult for friends and family to accept his death because rigor mortis never set in. They were able to set him in his wicker chair and take pictures of him. He looked as though he had only fallen asleep in his chair.

Von Duncan taken after his death in 1905.

Charles moved his family to Kokomo where he was a charter member of the South Side Christian Church. He taught the Kings Daughters Sunday School class for many years. He retired from the Kokomo Post Office in 1938 and died May 13, 1950. Pearl died in 1957. They are both buried in Albright Cemetery.

Esther married Ralph Wesley Thompson of Kokomo. She worked for the Chevrolet dealership and retired to raise five children in Kokomo. Later she worked for the Dolly Hat Shop. Nila married Ashton Earl Gorton, also of Kokomo. They raised two sons in Lexington, KY. *Taken from the genealogical works of Ashton E. Gorton. Submitted by Beverly J. Wheeler*

HERRELL - LOWE

John C. Lowe (born 1864, died 1946) was married to Minnie Pence (born 1868, died 1932) on Oct. 30, 1884 by Rev. Delp. They had five children: Edith Marie (born 1887, died 1969), Bessie, Edward, Mary (born April 11, 1899, died Oct. 28, 1988), Isaac Corneilous (May 14, 1904, died Aug. 5, 1983). Edith Marie married Clinton Weller on March 24, 1909. They had two daughters. Bessie married Chester Wybrew on Jan. 20, 1910. Mary married Ora Fisher. They had two sons.

James H. Dice (born Jan. 10, 1861, died May 6, 1945) married Kitura Bell Ray (born Nov. 20, 1865, died March 11, 1949). They had four children. One of the children was Cecelia Ray Dice (born May 7, 1906, died May 2, 1992).

Dorothy's father, Isaac Corneilous Lowe, married my mother, Cecelia Ray Dice, on May 19, 1923 in St. Joseph, MI. They had four children: Voris (Buss) Lee (born July 24, 1925, died Aug. 28, 1989), Dorothy Irene (born Dec. 1, 1930), Carl James (born Aug. 13, 1935), Patty Lou (born Aug. 13, 1938, died May 29, 1992). Voris had three children. Dorothy had four children. Carl had five children.

B. Joe Herrell Family—Joe and Dorothy Herrell. L-R: Cecelia, Bill, Dennis, Don.

Mary Catherine Justus married William Jefferson Herrell and had a son named Floyd Eldon Herrell. Minnie Mae Ghent married Clinton Edgar Baker and had a daughter, Jessie Pearl Baker. Floyd Eldon Herrell (born April 30, 1890, died Feb. 9, 1958) married Jesse Pearl Baker (born Oct. 29, 1895, died March 17, 1983) on Nov. 18, 1911. Floyd and Jesse are buried at IOOF Cemetery in Rochester. They had six children. One of their children is Bobby Joe Herrell.

I, Bobby Joe Herrell, was married to Dorothy Irene Lowe at Christian Church Parsonage in Rochester, IN on May 14, 1948 by Rev. Grant Blackwood. Dorothy and I both grew up around Rochester. Dorothy and I moved to Kokomo and made our home. We raised four wonderful children. William (Bill) Jefferson (born March 12, 1949), Cecelia Marie (born Aug. 31, 1951), Daniel Joe (born Aug. 31, 1953), Dennis Jay (born Nov. 8, 1961).

William married Deborah Sue Chiles (born June 4, 1954) on July 10, 1971 in Kokomo, IN at St. Luke's United Methodist Church. They have three children: Jeffrey Lee (born May 10, 1972), Jennifer Marie (born Dec. 20, 1975), Jason Kyle (born Dec. 9, 1979).

Cecelia married David Lawrence Ault (born July 19, 1946) at Northview Christian Church on July 19, 1969. They have three children: Richard Gregory (born Aug. 12, 1970), Carrie Ann (born Aug. 22, 1972), Aaron Lee (born July 15, 1975). Richard married Jennifer Goodman (born Nov. 11, 1970) in Galveston, IN on March 4, 1990. They have two sons: Zachary Jacob (born Dec. 30, 1990), Austin Matthew (born June 4, 1992).

Daniel married Sue Ellen Wagner (born Jan. 20, 1954) at St. Joan of Arc Catholic Church Kokomo, IN on Oct. 4, 1977. They have two sons: Derek Daniel (born May 16, 1985), Kevin Kyle (born March 27, 1987).

Dennis married Robin Jo Jones (born Aug. 21, 1960) at First Assembly of God Kokomo, IN on Aug. 14, 1981. They have two daughters: Rachael Dawn (born March 1, 1983), Rebekah Deeann Herrell (born Oct. 18, 1986).

Times and money were rough but Dorothy and I enjoyed the family wholeheartedly. We would always manage to have family get-togethers on birthdays, holidays, and take a vacation. *Submitted by Bobby Joe Herrell.*

HERRELL

The year of 1976 we heard the Bicentennial Wagon Train was coming to Kokomo. It started from the Rose Bowl in California and was going to Valley Forge, PA. Our youngest son, Dennis Jay, Joe, a neighbor boy (Danny Waiter), and I decided to go on the Bicentennial Wagon Train that came through Kokomo. We set out with a mule (Hickory) and a small covered wagon. Joe followed in a van. He was bothered with arthritis at the time. People would come and go from the wagon train. Along the way we had accidents, weddings, and many other things on the wagon train while we headed to Valley Forge, PA. We met a lot of wonderful people. We would get into different towns and people were just great. They fixed food for us and a place to stay, and we would also sign our autographs. You would never know what an experience and wonderful time that you would have unless you would be on the wagon train yourself. We traveled about 20 to 25 miles a day. We arrived at Valley Forge, PA on July 3, 1976. After a wonderful time in Valley Forge, PA, we headed back home and back to work.

Bicentennial Wagon Train 1976—Joe and Dorothy Herrell in wagon. Dennis on mule, Hickory, hitched to wagon.

Joe and I also have two great-grandchildren, ten grandchildren and Dennis and his wife, Robin, have another baby on the way the last of September or first of October. Joe and I are both now retired and we do a lot of traveling in our motor home. Joe retired from the Operating Engineers, and I retired from Accurate Parts of Kokomo. We always enjoy coming back home to see our children, grandchildren, and great-grandchildren. They are all very precious to us. I enjoy cooking, baking, quilting, crocheting, visiting, working in my flower gardens, and making bouquets for the sick, anniversaries, and birthdays. I also like to go elk and bear hunting with our sons and friends. We have our grandchildren over to spend a night whenever we can. The grandchildren are in a lot of sports, such as baseball, softball, swimming, basketball, football, 4-H projects, school and church. Grandchildren keep Joe and me busy. We love it. I could write a lot more. The Lord has been very good to us. *Submitted by Dorothy Irene (Lowe) Herrell*

HERREN/HERRON-JOHNSON - William Marion Herren born Feb. 25, 1839 in Indiana, son of William and Julia Ellsberry Herren/Herron, both born in Kentucky. William Marion married Nancy A. Hendricks/Hendrickson, guessing in Shelby County, IN. He died in Howard County Nov. 16, 1912 at the age of 73 years, 8 months, 22 days, buried in Randolph Cemetery; no marker can be found. Only been able to find one son, Thomas W.; sure there are more.

Thomas W. Herron was born June 11, 1858 in Shelby County, IN, married Oct. 12, 1885 in Howard County to Laura Jane Harrison. He died at his home on North Phillips Street of diabetes, Oct. 7, 1929 age 71 years, 3 months, 26 days, buried in Randolph Cemetery (unmarked grave). He had a very large family; he left his wife and six children living, at the time of his death. Eleven known children, all born in Howard County: (1) Daisy, first married a Fording, second a Coy; (2) Minnie, married June 29, 1904 to Eli Sites/Sipes; (3) Lela E., March 2, 1889-Jan. 10, 1951, married Aug. 14, 1905 to James M. Catt (March 7, 1887-March 12, 1941), buried in Memorial Park Cemetery, parents of seven sons: Ralph J.; William L.; Clarence M.; Russell L.; Harold L. and two unknown: (4) Jerron "Jerry" Isaiah; (5) Fred, born Feb. 1, 1893, married Dec. 31, 1912 to Mabel Britton; (6) Thomas W. Jr., born Nov. 17, 1894, married March 10, 1917 to Edna Collins; (7) Louisa, born Feb. 5, 1896, first married Dec. 15, 1913 to Fred Nolte Jr. (born Aug. 31, 1887), second married Sept. 15, 1919 to Paul D. Bennett (born June 23, 1888); (8) Jesse, born Jan. 14, 1898, married May 22, 1920 to Lilly E. McGuire; (9) female, infant died May 7, 1904; (10) Mildred May, died Aug. 20, 1907; (11) male, March 22, 1908-March 23, 1908; these three are buried in Crown Point Cemetery.

(4) Jerron "Jerry" Isaiah Herron, Oct. 23, 1891-March 22, 1919; he is also in unmarked grave in Randolph Cemetery; his marker has been missing for many years. Married July 13, 1910 to Grace Mildred Roberts (Nov. 26, 1892-Nov. 26, 1983), buried in Memorial Park Cemetery; she remarried Aug. 26, 1919 to Loren Youngman and then Albert Frank Conwell; she was a daughter of Albert and Harriett Poirier Roberts. They were the parents of three children: (1) George; (2) Esther Charlotte and (3) Viola, married Edward Obermeyer.

Greg, Penny Jean, Connie and Joe Johnson

(2) Esther Charlotte Herron, born May 18, 1916 in Howard County, married Jan. 19, 1935 to "Duke" Harold James Johnson, born Sept. 24, 1915 in Howard County, died April 23, 1973 in Bluffton, IN, buried in Memorial Park Cemetery, son of Virgil and Mary Ann Waits Johnson. Duke and Esther, parents of three children, all born in Howard County: (1) Shirley Ann, born Aug. 18, 1935, married Dec. 31, 1950 to Charles Cliff Mitchell; (2) Glen Richard "Dick" born July 1, 1942, married Gloria Jean Haworth; and (3) Joseph "Joe" Wayne Johnson, born Sept. 22, 1943, married Oct. 20, 1962 in Unicoi County, TN to Connie Ruth, born Feb. 20, 1946 in Erwin, Unicoi County, TN, daughter of Willard James and Pancy Inez Miller McInturff. Joe and Connie were the parents of four children: (1) Gary Wayne, born and died Feb. 3, 1964 in Camp LeJeune, NC; he only lived a few hours; he is buried in Jones Cemetery in Unicoi County, TN; (2) Gregory Alan, born Aug. 21, 1965 in Howard County, married Oct. 7, 1989 to Kathleen Annette Barton, born Oct. 2, 1964, daughter of Earl and Doris Barton (3) Penny Jean, born July 29, 1966 in Howard County, not married, living in Florida; and (4) Deborah "Debbie" Lynn Johnson, Sept. 25, 1971-March 4, 1973, Memorial Park Cemetery. *Submitted by Joe and Connie Johnson.*

JAMES EDMUND AND SARAH JANE (GORDON) HETHCOTE - Eli Hethcoat was born in 1833 in Indiana. His father came from North Carolina. Eli came to Howard County, IN and settled in Section 21 of Clay Township around 1850. He married Nancy Ann Overholser (born 1833), on Nov. 25, 1853 in Howard County, IN. She was the daughter of Daniel Overholser (1801-1875), and Mary Brubaker (born 1805), who came to Howard County around 1850 from Carroll County, IN, formerly of Preble County, OH.

In the ensuing years they had six children: Lucinda (born 1854), Mary (born 1855), James Edmund (1859-1934), Charles (born 1862), Hester (1865-1877) and Etta (born 1868).

Eli died in 1899 and Nancy in 1904. They are buried in Shiloh Cemetery, east of Kokomo, IN as is their daughter Hester, who died at the age of 12.

James E., the subject of this article, changed the spelling of his name from Hethcoat to Hethcote. He followed in his father's footsteps in becoming a farmer. On Aug. 14, 1880 he married Sarah Jemima Jane Gordon in Howard County, IN. She was the daughter of John Gordon (1824-1899) and Francis Collins (1827-1921). John Gordon's father, William Gordon, was born in North Carolina. Francis Collin's parents were Thomas Collins (1794-1878), and Mary Young (1802-1878), who were both born in Kentucky. John and Francis Gordon and her parents, Thomas and Mary Collins, are all buried in North Union Cemetery in Howard County.

James E. and Sarah J. Hethcote

James and Sarah Hethcote had six children: Clyde (1881-1932), Claude (1883-1944), Elsie (born 1886), Bessie (1889-1941), Hurshel (1890-1972) and Myrel (1895-1971).

Clyde married Henrietta Kress. Their children were: Hazel, Marie and Everett. Claude married Nora Maher - no children. Elsie married Chester Miller. Their children: Russell, Maxine and Marion. Bessie married Ben Crumpacker. Their children: Clealia and Donald. Hurshel married Jennie Curless in Howard County on Nov. 8, 1914. She was the daughter of John and Roanna (Zentmeyer) Curless. Their children, all born and living in Indiana, are: Hurshel born in Huntington County, in 1919, now of Anderson; AnnaBelle Friend born in Blackford County in 1920, now of Mt. Etna; and Merrill born in Wells County in 1924, now of Warren. Jennie died on Aug. 22, 1926 and is buried in Simpson Cemetery, Howard County.

In 1927 Hurshel married Anna (Butler) Hiatt in Howard County. She was the daughter of John Butler (1862-1947) and Sarah Ann Overman (1876-1934). Anna's husband, Warren Hiatt, son of Lindley and Maude (McCoy) Hiatt, had died leaving her with two daughters: Wanda Hunnicutt (1919-1982) buried in Star of Hope Cemetery, Huntington County, IN and Arliss Jean Drabenstot born in 1923 and is now of Huntington, IN.

Hurshel and Anna had five children, all born and living in Indiana. They are Melba Milar born in Grant County in 1928, now of Huntington; Max born in Huntington County in 1931, now of rural Andrews; Merritt born in Huntington in 1934, now of rural Warren; Claude D. born in Huntington County in 1937, now of North Manchester; and Janice Kellam born in Huntington County in 1939, now living in Mt. Etna. Hurshel and Anna are buried in Simpson Cemetery Howard County, IN.

Myrel married Perry Baker. Their children: Lucy and Arnold who died very young; James, Virginia, Helen, Ruth, Charles and Betty.

James Edmund Hethcote died in Huntington County, IN on Dec. 19, 1934. Sarah died in Kokomo, IN on July 8, 1939. They are buried in Crown Point Cemetery, in Kokomo, IN. *Submitted by Melba D. Milar.*

MARK AND MARY (GUY) HEWITT - Mark and Mary (Guy) Hewitt's ancestors have lived in the Howard County area for over 140 years. Born March 20, 1951, Mark is the son of James Lindley Marshall and Carolyn Joan (Bender) Hewitt. Mark graduated summa cum laude from Purdue University and is a software engineer at Delco Electronics. Mark's son Troy was born to his first wife, Cynthia Smiley, in 1970. Heather and Megan Hewitt are children of Mark's marriage to Mary Jane Guy. They were born in 1985 and 1987, respectively. Mary, the daughter of Arvelee Guy and Marie Newman, was born Jan. 25, 1957. Mary studies nursing at Indiana University-Kokomo.

One of Mary's maternal ancestors, David Greeson, came to Indiana from Guilford County, NC in 1832. In 1851, David bought land off an earlier settler on the east fork of the Little Wildcat and here, in Harrison Township, he built his home. David, who was the township trustee, bought the "Buckeye Farm" along what is now Alto Road for $2900. All totaled, he owned 380 acres in Harrison Township and 90 acres in southern Center Township. He was an exhibitor of fine cattle and Berkshires.

Mark's maternal ancestors, Jonathan and Jane (White) Pickering, arrived in Howard County in November of 1852. They were Quakers and had come north from Rheatown, TN to escape the practices of slavery in the South. The 508 mile trip had taken 27 days and cost $55 including toll roads. They settled on the north side of Alto, near Jonathan's sister, Mary (Mrs. Jesse Marshall). They were drawn to the area by relatives and other Quaker families that had previously come north. Jonathan, who was a blacksmith, was also the justice of the peace for Alto in 1860.

Mark's paternal grandparents were both attorneys. Mark's grandmother, Nina Lindley, was reportedly the first woman to graduate from Indiana University Law School. His grandfather, John Marshall, was a past president of the Howard County Bar Association, a Howard County Circuit Court judge, and the Kokomo City Attorney. Dr. Tom Marshall, John's grandfather, was born in Washington County, PA and had come to the area around 1851 on the Ohio and Erie Canal.

Mark's maternal grandfather, Floyd Harry Bender, came to Kokomo with his brother Roy around 1917. Floyd's father, Wm. Troy Bender, was born in Nashville, IN and had later moved to Linn Creek, MO. When the two brothers came to Kokomo, it was onboard a train they had "hopped". They were young and like other adventurous young men of their day, they had decided to see the U.S. on a rail car. Floyd met his wife, Lelah Pickering, at a Halloween parade in downtown Kokomo and decided to set up roots. *Submitted by Mark A. Hewitt*

HIATT - Wilson J. Hiatt was born in Randolph County, IN, June 29, 1843, the son of Richard and Charlotte (Coats) Hiatt. The Hiatts were natives of Virginia and the Coats family of South Carolina. Wilson served in the Civil War. He enlisted in Co. F, 134th Indiana Volunteer Inf. and also served in the 55th Indiana Volunteer Regt. He took part in the Battles of Richmond, KY in 1862 and was in the famous Atlanta Campaign, which resulted in his receiving a testimonial from President Lincoln, for his outstanding service.

After his army career he returned to Randolph County and resumed an active life engaged in agriculture. In 1865 he married Jennetta Hunt, who died in 1875. In 1877 he married Abigail Chamness (born 1855). They had two children, Lindley and Mary. Mary married Emery Ault. Also in this family was the son of Wilson's first wife, Howard Hunt, and Abigail's son, Elmer Chamness.

Wilson J. Hiatt and his grandson, Warren J. Hiatt

When Lindley was about three years old, the family moved to Howard County, settling on a homestead about seven miles northeast of Windfall, IN.

On Oct. 31, 1897 Lindley married Maude McCoy. Six children were born to this union: Warren J., Russell, Inez, Cordelia, Kenneth and Pauline.

Lindley's ancestors were Friends who left England in William Penn's time. His great-great-grandfather was Daniel Williams of North Carolina, a Friends minister. His great-grandfather, Jonathon Hiatt, left Virginia on account of slavery and came to Indiana, settling east of Winchester. His grandfather and grandmother, John and Sally (Wright) Coats, came to Randolph County when Indiana was taken in as a state.

Lindley was called to the ministry and was recorded "A Minister of the Gospel of Jesus Christ" by the New Hope Monthly Meeting of Friends.

Warren was born June 29, 1900, in Howard County, IN. He married Anna Butler on Sept. 8, 1918. They had two daughters: Wanda and Arliss Jean. Anna, born Feb. 19, 1897, was the daughter of John Butler (1863-1947) and Sarah Overman (1876-1934).

Warren died in 1926 and is buried in the Greentown Cemetery in Howard County. Anna married Hurshel Hethcote in 1927. She died in Huntington County, IN on Aug. 15, 1991 and is buried in the Simpson Cemetery in Howard County, IN. *Submitted by Arliss Jean Drabenstot*

HIATT - Levi Hiatt (born Ohio, Jan. 15, 1819) came to Howard County, IN, in early pioneer times. In 1850 with his wife Catherine Good Hiatt (born Feb. 12, 1824) they settled in the woods three miles southeast of Kokomo in what was known as the Crousore Settlement. Here they built a log cabin and raised nine children. These children were Mahala, Sirena, Sophrana, Clinton, Levi, Charlotte, Matilda, Morton and Dillon.

Mahala married George Stanley. They resided in Howard County. She is buried in Greentown Cemetery. Sirena married F.M. Crousore in Howard County on March 5, 1867. Son Clinton, born Feb. 12, 1853, married twice, first to Sarah Deberd in 1871 and second to Sarah Rich in 1874. Clinton died Dec. 17, 1875, and is interred at Greentown. Charlotte Hiatt married Dayton VanBibler Nov. 27, 1879, and Matilda married George Swisher, Feb. 16, 1876. Morton Hiatt, born 1864, married Emma Jennings on Dec. 4, 1881. Dillon Hiatt was born in 1866 and married Rose Ree, May 3, 1888. Dillon died Sept. 24, 1905.

The elder Levi Hiatt passed away Oct. 7, 1876. Catherine, his wife, lived until Jan. 25, 1901. Both are buried in Greentown Cemetery.

Levi and Catherine's son, Levi, was born Feb. 15, 1854, and like his father he was a farmer. On Feb. 7, 1875, Levi married Margaret Jane Nunn, the daughter of Solomon Loffer and Mary Whitaker. Levi and Margaret raised daughters Effa, Lovella, Zella and Gladys along with sons Salathiel, Omer, Charley, William, Everett, Leslie and Orla in Greentown.

Effa Hiatt was born Nov. 14, 1875, and died May 3, 1952. She was married to Charles Britton. Born Oct. 8, 1878, Omer Hiatt married Sarah (Sadie) Chew, Sept. 4, 1899. He passed away Nov. 21, 1960. Son Charley was born Oct. 22, 1880. He married four times and passed away Aug. 5, 1954. Lovella was born Jan. 15, 1883, and died Nov. 28, 1951. Her husband was Andy Paxton. William Everett was born Oct. 2, 1884, and married Katie Callien, Oct. 22, 1904. He died in Greentown on Jan. 17, 1960. Zella Hiatt, born July 10, 1886, married Charles E. Thomas on July 10, 1915. She died April 5, 1977, in Kokomo.

Born March 22, 1888, Leslie Hiatt married Ethel Howard on Nov. 29, 1911. He died Feb. 6, 1970. Gladys, born Oct. 13, 1895, married Robert Gibbs on Feb. 24, 1916. On Sept. 15, 1989, she passed away. Orla Hiatt lived less than two years. He was born Jan. 7, 1893, and died Sept. 6, 1894.

Levi and Margaret's second child Salathiel was born in Kokomo on Feb. 2, 1876. He married Flora Wilson (born March 16, 1879) on Oct. 29, 1898, in Kokomo. Flora died in childbirth at the age of 33. Prior to her death six children were born to the couple. Salathiel remarried twice, first to Belle Shaffer and then to Minnie Smith. Salathiel died Sept. 21, 1927. Both he and Flora are buried in Greentown Cemetery.

The children of Salathiel and Flora included Mable born May 27, 1898, in Greentown. She was married Jan. 27, 1917, to Oscar Oaks and then moved to Tennessee where she died May 4, 1963.

Son, Virgil, was born June 30, 1903. He died May 14, 1974, and is buried in Crown Point Cemetery in Kokomo. His widow, Helen Swisher Hiatt, still resides in Kokomo. Wilson Hiatt was born and died April 30, 1912.

The rest of Salathiel and Flora's children moved from Howard County. Elsie, born Oct. 27, 1905, later moved to Lafayette, IN. Blanche, born May 3, 1910, married Paul Sims on Nov. 25, 1937, in Muncie where she lived until her death in 1987. Ida Hiatt was born Dec. 15, 1907, and married Ray Goodman on March 1, 1924. After his death on April 26, 1940, Ida married Earl Grove. They resided in Muncie where she died March 19, 1988.

Among the several surviving Hiatt descendents are Joyce Goodman Kelly, Gaston, IN and Phyllis Goodman Wolfe, Fort Wayne, IN.

The original Hiatt farm still stands today in Howard County.

JOHN RALPH HICKS - John Ralph Hicks was born on Sept. 15, 1899, to Frank and Fanny Grace (Kemper) Hicks. After high school graduation Ralph went to work for Dodge Motors and retired from Chrysler Corporation. He married Agnes Smith Harness, born in Cass County to Samuel and Cynthia (Cripe) Smith, on Nov. 29, 1925. Agnes was a member of Grace United Methodist M.E. Church, although she attended United Brethren Church. She was a 1913 graduate of Kokomo High School. Ralph and Agnes had one daughter, Marilyn Agnes Hicks, born on Aug. 3, 1929 in Kokomo, IN. She graduated from Kokomo High School with honors and is librarian at the University of Wisconsin in Madison. Marilyn is an accomplished violinist.

Ralph's mother, Fanny Grace (Kemper) Hicks, was born Feb. 4, 1879 and married Albert C. March, May 16, 1914. Albert C. March was born Jan. 2, 1872. The parents of Grace were John E. Kemper, born in 1845, and Mary E. Kemper born 1855.

Ralph's sister, Emily Nancy March, was born Oct. 2, 1903. Ralph and Agnes have an extensive collection of Greentown Glass and a collection of gold antique watches. Their family pet was a pampered cat named Sadie, and she had her very own heated and air conditioned cat house.

Hiatt Reunion circa 1911. The adults seated in the center of the picture are: Flora and Salathiel Hiatt, Solomon Loffer, Margaret and Levi Hiatt and Omer Hiatt.

219

L-R: Albert C. March, John Ralph Hicks, Emily Nancy March, and Fanny Grace (Kemper) Hicks March.

Raymond and Ethel Hite

Ella Blanche (Hobson) Bock (Mrs. Daniel L. Bock)

Agnes (Smith) Harness Hicks died April 20, 1970. J. Ralph Hicks died Dec. 8, 1974. Ralph and Agnes are both buried in Crown Point Cemetery on East Sycamore Street in Kokomo, IN.

Death dates: John E. Kemper, October 1894; Mary E. Kemper, October 1934; Lola G. Ackley, November 1937; Marion R. Kemper, Feb. 29, 1944; Alonco Kemper, November 1944; and Albert C. March, April 9, 1962.

RAY AND SUSIE HILL - George Hill was born in Ohio in 1867, and at age six moved with his parents to Indiana. George married Addie Ballard on March 6, 1890 in Shelby County, IN. They moved to Tipton County very shortly after their marriage as that was where their first child was born in July 1891. The family was living in Madison County near Elwood in 1894 when their third child Raymond Isaac was born. By 1914 they had moved to Howard County to the village of Guy. George and Addie were charter members of the Greentown Wesleyan Church; all charter members were received on Aug. 6, 1920. They were living in Greentown when George died on Nov. 12, 1943 at the age of 76.

Raymond was married Oct. 31, 1912 to Susie Glenn Snyder in Tipton County, and they "set up" housekeeping in Guy. After living on several rented farms in Howard County, Ray and Susie bought a farm in Union Township about 1940, where they continued to live until his death Feb. 24, 1976.

Ray was a farmer and drove a school bus for the Union School and later the Eastern Howard School Corporation. He was an active member of the Wesleyan Church in Greentown.

Ray and Susie were the parents of Clara B., born in 1914; James F., 1915; Robert E., 1920; Phyllis J., 1922; Betty J., 1924; and Charles G., 1926. *Submitted by Jean Simpson*

RAYMOND AND ETHEL HITE - Raymond Vernon Hite was born in Kokomo May 10, 1893 the son of Julius and Lydia (Maple) Hite. He married Ethel Ita Bryant, daughter of James and Olive (Ladd) Bryant, Feb. 19, 1912. Before his death June 12, 1953, Raymond was assistant chief electrical engineer for Continental Steel Corporation. Ethel was born Oct. 1, 1895 in Sims, Grant County, IN and was a practical nurse. Raymond and Ethel had five children; Onda Lindley, Robert, Wanita Carson, Vonna Etherington and Patricia Walden-Heischberg.

Raymond's father, Julius Sheridan Hite, was born Aug. 24, 1867 in Sardinia, OH. Moving to Howard County, he married Lydia Letitia Maple Jan. 10, 1891. Julius was a farmer and a mail carrier using a horse and buggy to deliver the mail. Lydia was born Feb. 26, 1873 in Howard County and was the daughter of Elijah Grant and Sarah Elizabeth (Friermood) Maple. Julius and Lydia had five children: Raymond, Sylvia Comer, Maisie Lewis, Wayne and Gerald.

Raymond's grandparents were William Harvey and Nancy J. (Wills) Hite. William, born June 10, 1835 in West Union, OH; died Jan. 18, 1915 and married Nancy Wills April 14, 1865. Nancy was born in 1838 and passed away in 1872. Both are buried in the Sardinia, OH Cemetery. William and Nancy had three children: Julius, Noah and Joseph.

Noah and Elizabeth (Boice) Hite were the parents of William Harvey, Mary Huggins, Arminda Daily, John, Cassius Clay, Ada Curless, Minervia Kress, Lewis Kossuth, Ida Purdy, Samuel Bell, Julius and Rebecca. Noah and Elizabeth moved to Brown County, OH in 1836 and located on the White Oak Creek. Noah was born May 4, 1812 in Rockbridge County, VA and passed away Jan. 10, 1882 in Sardinia, OH where he is buried. He married Elizabeth, daughter of George and Eleanor Boyce (Boice), April 8, 1934 in Brown County, OH. Elizabeth was born April 7, 1816 in Maryland and died Dec. 8, 1904. During the Civil War, Noah once had to hide his livestock in the forest so the Confederate soldiers camping next to his barn couldn't slaughter them for food.

When Nancy (Etherington) Goetzen visited Sardinia, OH to visit a distant relative (Ralph Hite) in 1964, both William Harvey and Noah's original homes were still standing.

Noah's parents were Joseph and Magdaline (Rosenberger) Hite. Joseph was born in 1773 in Rockbridge County, VA and died between Ellicott's Mill and Poplar Springs, MD Dec. 10, 1814 from wounds he received during the War of 1812. Joseph and Magdaline had two children: Noah and Ann. Joseph married Magdaline May 31, 1811 after the death of his first wife.

Daniel and Appolonia (Keller) Hite were the parents of Joseph and seven other children: Abraham, Andrew, John, Reverend Daniel, Magdaline Hopwood, Ann Bear and David. Danial was born in 1752 and died in November 1829 in Page County, VA. Appolonia was the daughter of John and Anna Maria (Appolonia) Keller.

Note: There is a HITE FAMILY Reunion at BELLE GROVE PLANTATION, P.O. Box 137, Middletown, VA 22645 (703) 869-2028 once every three years.

HOBSON - Robert P. Hobson was born July 30, 1801, the son of William and Sarah Milburn Hobson of Shelby County, KY. Sarah died giving birth to their ninth child in 1803 and William remarried Betsy Cyphers in 1805. They moved to Clark County, IN in 1810 where William spent the rest of his life with several of his 18 children who lived a great many years in this area.

Robert was married in Washington County, IN on Sept. 26, 1822 to Sarah A. Hawn born in North Carolina in 1798. They lived in Jackson County, IN in 1830, then to Bartholomew County, IN in 1843/45. In 1848 they moved to Howard County where they lived until Robert died on Jan. 3, 1863 and Sarah died in 1871. Both are buried in the Alto Cemetery with three daughters: Martha J. - born 1829, Elizabeth Sarah - born 1831 and Nancy - born 1832. Their grandson born 1861 - died 1870, named Franklin Pierce, son of Jesse born 1840, is also buried in the Alto Cemetery. Jesse married Mary H. Cain and is buried in Wabash County at the Friends Church Cemetery. Another son of Robert and Sarah was James - born 1834 - no information.

Robert and Sarah's first-born child was Mary Ann, born 1824 - died 1911, who married John Bolivar Snyder (See Howard County Roots, p.46). Their second-born child was Absolon N. Hobson, born Nov. 2, 1825 in Washington County, IN and came to Howard County in 1848 with his parents. He married Martha Jane Foster on Dec. 23, 1858 (daughter of Vincent and Sarah Foster).

The Alto church.

Absolon and Martha Jane Hobson lived in the village of Alto in Harrison Township, Howard County, the Alto Road (250 South) being one of the first roads built in Howard County. Absolon was active in the I.O.O.F. Lodge, their building being erected in 1876 at the northwest corner of Alto. They were also active in the Methodist Church which was located just south of the corner on the east side, along with a brick parsonage and school building. Later Absolon and family moved to Clay Township where he was active in politics on the Republican ticket and elected a trustee. He died just south of Greentown on Aug. 11, 1905 at 80 years of age. Martha remarried Lewis Kern Dec. 5, 1907. Following are the descendants of Absolon N. and Martha Jane Hobson:

a. Anna E. - born 1859 - married Oscar Greeson, Howard County, IN.

b. Vincent - born 1861 - married Ida Meranda Oct. 15, 1891 in Howard County. Vincent died at Greentown Nov. 5, 1900. Had a daughter who died in 1911.

c. William Foster/Franklin? - born 1863 - married Anna America Thorne Dec. 21, 1887. William died 1938 and Anna A. born 1867 died 1953. Both are buried in Kokomo at Crown Point Cemetery.

d. Robert - born 1865 - died Feb. 18, 1893.

e. Florence - born 1866 - married May 13, 1885 to Edward Washburn.

f. Matilda (Tillie) - born 1869 - married Aug. 13, 1891 to William H. Foreman, M.D. who practiced in Indianapolis, IN.

g. Georgia - born Feb. 25, 1868 - married John Jessup Dec. 17, 1886. Died in 1956.

The writer's grandparents, who were farmers and eventually settled in Alto, third lot west of the corner on the south side, have great-great-grandchildren living on this site today. Grandparents William and Anna have their pictures hanging there on either side of the fireplace. The original homestead was destroyed in the 1965 tornado and rebuilt to its present state.

William and Anna had two children, Ella Blanche Hobson Bock (Daniel Lawrence) and George William Hobson. Blanche (born Feb. 15, 1892-died 1954) and Daniel had two children: Anna Elizabeth Bock Strawbridge-Bromley of Kokomo and Dr. Daniel Hobson Bock of St. Petersburg, FL.

Their second child, George William Hobson (born 1898) died in Evanston, IL. Married Melba Currey, classmate at Indiana University, Bloomington, IN and they had three boys, Richard C., William (deceased) and David and one daughter, Barbara (deceased) Simon MacAdam (Robt.) of Fontana, WI.

Anna Elizabeth Bock Strawbridge and Charles Thomas Strawbridge had two children: Charles Lawrence (Larry) of Indianapolis and Susan Elizabeth Strawbridge Dyer of Alto. *Submitted by Betty Bromley (Mrs. Lee M.)*

MARK AND PEGGY HOBSON - The Hobson Farm at 7816 West 100 South Road in Western Howard County is the oldest homestead in the county still owned and farmed by the original homestead family. The Hobsons came to Indiana by covered wagon in 1828, and settled in Parke County.

While prospering in Parke County, Jesse Hobson bought land from the State of Indiana on July 1, 1843: "the southwest quarter of Section 2, Township 23 N, Range 2 E, containing 160 acres in Richardville County, IN". The farm was worked and eventually willed to Jesse's son Elihu. Elihu's son, Alfred, and grandson, Paul, continued the tradition. Today the farm is still owned by Paul's wife, Ida, and farmed by his son, Mark, and grandsons, Mat and Abe. Mark lives on the remaining 97 acres with his wife, Peggy.

Peggy Ragland Hobson came to Kokomo in 1973 and operated Studio Stained Glass, which eventually became Ragland Stained Glass. The downtown business closed in 1988. In 1990 Peggy became Executive Director of The Howard County Convention and Visitors Commission.

Peggy's Hoosier roots go back to the last century, when her mother's ancestors homesteaded in the Alexandria area in the 1840s. Her mother, Lois (Barner) Krogh grew up in Anderson. Her father's families came to America from Norway to homestead in North Dakota in the 1870s. Peggy was born in Austin, TX and moved from there to Illinois, Fort Wayne, IN, West Virginia, Missouri, and Iowa before permanently settling in Howard County. *Submitted by Peggy Hobson.*

HOLDERITH - Peter H. Holderith married Cecilia A. Renie on Feb. 14, 1888 in Tipton County, IN. Peter was the son of Frances and Mary Holderith of Jennings County, IN and had seven brothers and sisters. Cecilia was the daughter of Augustus and Catherine (Gasper) Renie also of Jennings County and she had six brothers and sisters.

From Tipton County they moved to Marshall, MO. There they had four children, Joseph D. (1890-1916), Frank A. (1889-1985), George L. (1893-1970), Mayme M. (1895-1986) and Clarence P. (1906-1968).

In the early 1900s they moved back to Indiana settling in Kokomo at 1022 North Courtland Ave. Peter worked for Kokomo Brass Works and the Haynes Factory as a brass worker and machinist. Peter Holderith was struck by a car and died May 29, 1922 at the age of 70. Cecilia was a housewife and raised five children. Cecilia died Oct. 12, 1948 at the age of 83.

Joseph D. died at the young age of 26 from a long illness with tuberculosis.

Frank A. married Mary Reichert on Aug. 19, 1925. Together they had three children, Joseph, Martha, and Catherine. Frank had a grocery business with his uncle Charles H. Renie for many years at 823 West Jefferson. He also worked as a deliveryman for Hamilton Harris-Zapfe Paper Co. up until his retirement. He died of old age at 96.

George L. was a graduate of the University of Notre Dame in 1918 and ordained a priest in 1923. He was an associate professor of history from 1928 through 1952. He was also supervisor of university buildings and became the first golf coach of Notre Dame in 1933.

Mayme M. never married but helped raise her brother's children after the passing of their mother at a young age. She worked as a housekeeper for Judge Winslow for many years. She was always known as "Aunt Mayme" to everyone and was also known for being such a good cook, making wonderful cinnamon rolls and butterscotch pie. She lived at the family home all of her life until 1980 at the age of 86. She moved to Sycamore Village and was there for six years before passing on at the age of 92.

Clarence P. or "Pete" as he was known was the only member of the family born here in Kokomo. He married Nollie G. Smith in 1942, daughter of Samuel and Cora (Curry) Smith of Tipton County. On July 2, 1943 their only child was born, Patricia Louise. Pete worked at Allisons in Indianapolis for many years, and also at Continental Steel in the office. He also started his own business in his garage, eventually moving it to a large building he had built at 2109 North Wabash. The business was called the Hoosier Rack and Engineering Co. There he made racks for plating and anodizing. He did a lot of business with G.E., Delco, Chrysler and did quite well for himself.

The Holderith family were all members of St. Patrick's Catholic Church. *Submitted by Patricia (Holderith) Tracewell*

HOLLINGSWORTH-BUTLER - Isaac Allen Hollingsworth was born Sept. 21, 1914 in Russiaville, IN to C.W. "Cappy" and Mary Iona (Newlin) Hollingsworth. He was the youngest of four children and was named for his grandfathers, Isaac Hollingsworth and Allen Newlin.

His parents owned and operated the water works in this small town. When the word "FIRE" was called out by mouth or telephone, the water pump was started to give more pressure to the town water system. As a small boy, Ike would go along to the scene to help fight the fire. The roll of hose was attached to the nearest fire hydrant. The high school principal let the older boys leave school to help form the bucket brigade. A few people were ready to help carry out the furniture.

On Nov. 18, 1936, three years after Ike graduated from Russiaville High School, a house was burning on East Main Street and he was busy trying to fight the fire with the leaky hose. A deputy from the State Fire Marshal's office who was driving thru town, stopped and started telling him how he should be fighting the fire. Ike handed the squirting hose to him and said "Here, you do it." He got in his car and drove away!

In March 1937 a quarter block of the business section caught on fire from the Electric Chicken Hatchery and several stores were destroyed. The following day it was estimated that over 1,500 drove to Russiaville to see the smoking ruins.

On Jan. 8, 1942 the Methodist Church furnace overheated and the building burned to the ground. The following day the Township Trustee and Advisory Board opened bids to purchase a fire truck. The Russiaville Volunteers organized later that year when the new fire truck arrived and Ike was named Chief. This was the only fire truck in the west end of the county and the volunteers spent many hours fighting fires in other townships at any time of day or night. Some years later a former garage building was purchased by the township to house the fire equipment.

Helen Lucile Butler was born Sept. 28, 1921 on the Butler Farm in the northeast section of Honey Creek Township, the youngest of three children of Earl J. and Hazel Oveda (Miller) Butler. She was a birthright member of Lynn Friends Meeting located east of Russiaville. The Butler family moved their membership to Russiaville Friends Meeting in 1932.

After graduating from Russiaville High School as valedictorian of the class of 1939, she attended Kokomo Business College, then worked in the main office of the Continental Steel Corporation for three years.

On Oct. 16, 1943 Isaac and Helen were married in the Friends parsonage at Anderson, IN by the Rev. John Compton. They have lived in Russiaville since that time and he has supported the family as a self-employed electrician and licensed plumber in the local area. Ike is a birthright member of the Russiaville Friends Church and served as custodian for several years until he was drafted into the military service on Dec. 26, 1944. He served in the Medical Corps in South Korea in the occupational force at the end of WWII.

The family has been active in the community and church affairs and continue as custodians of the church.

Peggy Ann Hollingsworth was born Nov. 4, 1944 in Russiaville. She attended New London, Russiaville, and West Middleton schools. In the spring of 1958, dial telephone service came to western Howard County. Representatives of Indiana Bell came to school to train the students in the changeover from calling "central" to being self-reliant! She graduated at Western High School as valedictorian of the Class of 1963. At WHS, she was active in many clubs, including band (flute), choir (accompanist), and Future Teachers of America. She was a 10 year 4-H member.

Peggy attended the Kokomo Campus of Indiana University (1963-65) the last two years of its operation at the Seiberling Mansion (West Sycamore Street) location and was named the Outstanding Female Student in 1965.

Peggy transferred to the Bloomington Campus where she received the Bachelor of Education with High Distinction in 1967 and the Master of Library Science in 1968. She has worked as a high school librarian following college graduation and since 1970 at Connersville Senior High School, serving the students of Fayette County.

Beyond her membership in the Russiaville Friends Meeting where she has served as pianist and organist, she has had opportunity to serve the wider family of Friends as Historian of the United Society of Friends Women International and as Recording Clerk of Western Yearly Meeting with headquarters in Plainfield, IN.

Alma Sue Hollingsworth was born June 8, 1953 in Kokomo. She attended Russiaville Elementary School until it was destroyed in the 1965 Palm Sunday Tornado. She graduated from Western High School as valedictorian of the Class of 1971. She was a 10 year 4-H member and active in many school activities, choir, Future Teachers of America, Historical Society, Future Homemakers, including a term as State Historian of the Indiana Future Homemakers of America.

Alma attended the Kokomo Campus of Indiana University for two years and worked at Sears Roebuck & Company in her spare time. She transferred to the Bloomington Campus for one and one-half years receiving a Bachelor of Education with High Distinction in December of 1974. Her Masters in Education was from IUPUI in 1978. She taught at the Amo, IN Elementary School and is now teaching in the Avon Community School Corporation.

On Dec. 21, 1974 Alma married John Edward Pierce, son of Charles Edward and Dolly Mae (Ringeisen) Pierce. He was born Oct. 2, 1952 in Kokomo and attended first grade at Kokomo Central Elementary School. He was active in many sports and activities during his school years at Western and was president of his Western High School graduating class of 1970.

In the spring of 1972, Alma and John participated in the Indiana University-Kokomo Singers trip to Italy.

John graduated from Indiana University, College of Arts and Science in 1974 and received the Bachelor of Arts in History with High Distinction in 1975. He was elected to Phi Beta Kappa and in 1977 received the Doctor of Jurisprudence, from the Indiana University School of Law in Indianapolis. He is now an attorney in Danville, IN, and resides in Plainfield, IN.

David Allen Pierce was born April 7, 1981 in Danville, IN to Alma and John Pierce.

Holly Suzanne Pierce was born June 27, 1984 in Danville, IN to Alma and John Pierce.

Both children have attended Plainfield Central Elementary School and David is now in Plainfield Community Middle School. Both have participated in community sports. They are all members of Fairfield Friends Meeting near Camby, IN.

Ike was still Chief of the Volunteer Fire Department when a radio system was installed in March of 1965. On April 11, 1965 the firehouse and all equipment was demolished in the Palm Sunday Tornado that struck the entire community. Neighboring fire departments helped after this terrible disaster and thousands of dollars were collected to help buy new equipment as people drove through the town to see the path of the tornado. The firemen were still needed to help in the clean-up operation of burning the destroyed homes. Borrowed equipment could be seen near the homes of the volunteers as they were ready to roll on a moment's notice.

He has seen many volunteers give of their time, energy, and money to keep the fire department operating and he is now going to the fire station in full gear by riding his bicycle to answer the call, instead of running all of the way.

Ike received a Firemen's Clock with the following inscription: "To Ike Hollingsworth for years of Service and Leadership as Chief of The Russiaville Volunteer Fire Department. Presented by the Members of the Russiaville Volunteer Fire Dept."

In 1989 at the State Fire Marshal's Leadership Conference, Ike received the State of Indiana Meritorious Service Award.

At the State Convention of the Indiana Volunteer Firemen's Association held at Elkhart, IN in June 1994, Ike received the Ollie Sandberg Award.

For more family connections, read in the book "The Butler Family History" and "The Allen T. Newlin History." Also refer to the book compiled and published in 1947 by George L. Woody, "The Story of Russiaville and Honey Creek Township."

ARTHUR E. AND ANNA LOUISE CRIPE HOLLINGSWORTH
Charles Hollingsworth (1898-1963) was born in Howard County to Louisa (Comer) and Wilson Hollingsworth. His father met his death from a falling tree when Charles was 14.

Louisa operated the Center Telephone Company for many years and later resided with her son and family until her death in 1946.

Mary Lucy Elliott (1892-1993) was born to a Quaker family, Glenna (Woolen) and Wilson Elliott in Grant County. She married Charles Hollingsworth on Oct. 16, 1909. They had one son, Arthur Edward, Dec. 15, 1922.

Their home was always open to those in need and they had many family members and friends with them all their married life.

She lived with her son and family until her death, at 101, in 1993.

Samuel Cripe (1903-1991) was born to Susan (Wise) and Henry J. Cripe near Camden, IN. He was the youngest of seven children. They belonged to the German Baptist Church (Dunkard). The family has always been proud of these fine people and happy to be a part of this heritage.

Leona Ruth Campbell (1905-1978) was born to Perl and Alice (Johnson) Campbell near Deer Creek, IN; family of six children.

Samuel and Leona were married May 24, 1924 and to them were born three daughters, Anna Louise (Ann), Jeanette, and Charlotte.

They moved to western Howard County in 1928 from Carroll County. It was a struggle to survive "The Great Depression" with hardship of much family illness and a young family. They made it through those years because of hard work, prayers, and a positive attitude.

Their home was always open and welcome to all family and friends. There are so many happy memories of being together in the kitchen and around the piano. Leona was an excellent cook and hostess.

Arthur and Anna Louise Hollingsworth

Jeanette was an accomplished pianist and she and Anna Louise (Ann), accordionist, entertained for many events, church and school. They broadcasted from WKMO during summers while in high school.

All the girls graduated from Ervin High School: Anna Louise 1942, Jeanette 1944, and Charlotte 1946.

Arthur E. Hollingsworth and Anna Louise Cripe were married Jan. 24, 1947.

Arthur served with the Naval Air Corps during WWII (1942-1946) in the Pacific Theater as a naval pilot.

He graduated from Kokomo High School, 1941, and attended Indiana University.

In 1986 he retired from Haynes International Sales. For many years he was the Employment Manager at Haynes Stellite. He was also Personnel Manager at the Air Force Plant at Alexandria, IN (1955-1958) which was operated by Haynes Stellite.

Anna Louise had worked at Indiana Bell Telephone, Roger Briney Jewelry, and Haynes Stellite as PBX operator and receptionist. In 1989, she retired from Taylor High School after 25 years being secretary to the Principal.

They have two children: David E. Hollingsworth and Elizabeth Ann Guyer and three grandchildren.

They are retired to their home in Center enjoying their family and friends. They spend and enjoy much time with their grandchildren: Lauren and Spencer Hollingsworth of Huntington, IN and Rachel Guyer of Kokomo. They also enjoy gardening, caring for their home and traveling.

They're members of the Grace United Methodist Church of Kokomo and many other organizations. *Submitted by Arthur and Anna Louise Hollingsworth.*

HOLLINGSWORTH
Samuel P. Hollingsworth (1861-1940) was a famous person in Howard County in the 1800s. He was a high wheel bicycle rider and held the distinguished honor of winning the world's record for a 24 hour bike endurance, covering 280.9 miles. This occurred in June 1886 and took place on the National Road from Greenfield to the Cumberland Toll Gate at Indianapolis. His first bicycle was wooden and built by Sam and his brother, Ben. He entered a bicycle race at the Clinton County Fair and won, racing against a professional bicycle rider. Since Sam was an amateur, his fame spread overnight. The professional rider, Jack Prince, quit his own racing career and became Sam's trainer and followed him across the nation to keep him in shape and to give professional advice. Sam's father was a Quaker minister, so he was brought up in a strict home where he learned how to discipline his body and his habits. Later on, as his racing career developed, he found that not only were tobacco and alcohol to be abstained from, but coffee, tea and cocoa as well.

Sam Hollingsworth

Sam raced in many cities including Philadelphia, a non-stop endurance feat which amounted to 198 miles in 12 hours. He won five races in one day at New Castle, PA. He also raced in Macon, GA, Memphis, St. Louis, Omaha, Chicago, Boston, Cincinnati, Saginaw, Grand Rapids, Detroit, Buffalo, Springfield, MA, Hartford, CT, Madison Square Garden, NY, and in many other towns in Indiana and Ohio. He was an amateur high bicycle rider for less than 10 years winning no less than 20 gold medals, along with diamonds, silver and many other racing prizes. Some of his medals (donated by some of his descendants) are in a frame and on display at the Seiberling Mansion.

Sam was instrumental in founding the Indianapolis Athletic Club. Some of the well-known friends of his were Ed Souder, editor of the *Kokomo Tribune*, C.V. Haworth, Superintendent of Kokomo Schools, Elwood Haynes, and Clessie Cummins of Diesel Motor Fame.

Sam had three brothers: Benjamin, Lynn, and Calvin; one sister, Melissa; and two half-brothers, John and Harvey. The Hollingsworths are descendants of Valentine Hollingsworth, who came to this country from England in 1682, sailing with William Penn.

Sam was the son of Izaac Hollingsworth (1821-1902) and Peninah Cosand (1832-1887). He was married to Charlotte Haun (1869-1933). She was the daughter of George Haun and Frances McKensie.

Sam and Charlotte had four children: Tracy (1889-1936), Lucille, Karleen, and Ted. All were born in Howard County, near Russiaville. Grandchildren: Robert M. Hollingsworth, Daytona Beach, FL; Rosemary Redding Zimmermann, Chicago, IL; Rex Redding, deceased; Charlotte Hollingsworth Young, Kokomo, IN; Josephine Hollingsworth Michaelson, Tampa, FL; and Phillis Hollingsworth Ryan, Dunedin, FL.

ALBERT CLINTON AND KATE (LOCKE) HOSTETLER
Our grandfather and grandmother were lifelong farmers and residents of Howard Township, Howard County.

Albert Clinton Hostetler (Dec. 1, 1879-Sept. 29, 1966) was one of nine children, born in a cabin east of Cassville. After the death of his father, Jacob L. Hostetler (who died at age 41 from a sunstroke while making hay), Albert hired out at age 12 to Wilson and Rosa Grinslade for bed and board. He worked on their farm until he was 29. During this time his mother, Katie (Enders) Hostetler, married Moses Kauffman, and they and the rest of his family moved to Los Angeles, CA.

Kate Locke (Nov. 29, 1884-Nov. 2, 1970) was born on her grandfather Jesse Yager's farm, located one mile north of Howard Township School. Her father, Eli Locke, died when she was nine. Since she was four years older than her brother, Thomas, and her mother, Sarah (Yager) Locke, "was afraid of her own shadow", Kate became "head of the household".

Both Albert and Kate attended Rich Valley School, each walking about one mile. Albert attended through the sixth grade and Kate all eight years. Then she drove a horse and buggy seven miles to Kokomo in order to graduate from Maplewood School. Today Rich Valley School no longer exists. It was located just west of Rich Valley Mennonite Church, which was formerly a Christian Church and Albert and Kate were members there. In fact Kate's Grandfather Yager initiated the building of this church.

Albert C. and Kate (Locke) Hostetler Nov. 26, 1908 wedding.

On Nov. 26, 1908, Albert and Kate were married in the bride's home. Relatives and neighbors were served wedding cake and "toasted" with "float", a creamy fruit drink. They left on their honeymoon by train to Banff and Lake Louise, Alberta, Canada; Vancouver, B.C.; and down the Pacific Coast to Los Angeles, CA, to visit Albert's relatives. Along the way home they stopped at Grand Canyon, AZ; photos show them riding mules down the snow-covered canyon trail.

Through inheritance from the Yager and Locke families, Albert and Kate acquired 180 acres of farmland, located at 400 N.-100 E. Within this acreage stood an abandoned one-room schoolhouse, Union #4, on an acre of land. They purchased this building for $500.00 and remodeled it for their home. Later Albert purchased an adjoining 45 acres.

Albert was extremely proud of his big Belgian horses; however, a team of Percherons, Mandy and Dutch, were the workhorses and pets of all. He was a diversified farmer who raised grains, hay, Poland China hogs, and

Hereford cattle. The cattle herd began with two heifers received as a wedding gift from the Grinslades.

Kate was an "outdoor lady", with two huge gardens, lots of produce and flowers, which were generously shared with friends. She always took floral bouquets to church. She also raised many chickens. In 1936 Albert and Kate became members of Main Street Christian Church in Kokomo. He served as a deacon and she became known as "The Noodle Lady", making noodles for church dinners.

They were the parents of two daughters:

(1) Sarah Catherine (Dec. 10, 1917) - on April 9, 1944 she married James Doyle Rockey (July 26, 1917); they recently celebrated their 50th wedding anniversary. They are the parents of three children:

James Bennett (July 3, 1945).

Clinton Lewis, (March 16, 1947) - Married Aug. 8, 1970, to Nicole Lynn Pritz (March 1, 1970); they have one son, Christopher McClain (Feb. 27, 1979).

Kay Arden (Sept. 28, 1956) - married Oct. 10, 1981 to Brodrick Clayton Silence (April 3, 1956); they have one son, Clayton Rockey Silence (April 28, 1982).

(2) Fern Locke Hostetler (July 6, 1920): On March 27, 1941, married Harold Wilburn Tyner (Oct. 30, 1920) - died in an auto/truck accident May 20, 1966); they are the parents of four children:

Karen Lou (Dec. 2, 1942) married on June 13, 1967 to Thomas F. Adams (Nov. 19, 1942); they have one daughter, Annette Lynn (Nov. 15, 1975).

Sharen Sue (Dec. 2, 1942) - married March 7, 1969, to Gary Brincefield (Jan. 4, 1943 - died Dec. 11, 1986). They have two children: Jill Elaine (Jan. 27, 1970) - married Nov. 23, 1990, to William Kaiser (Feb. 18, 1968); parents of Kaitlyn Elaine (April 8, 1992). Gary Cash Brincefield (Dec. 19, 1973).

Jewel Lee (July 27, 1945) - married Aug. 17, 1969 to Charles Larry Bates (July 2, 1942) - they have three daughters: Beth Ann (Aug. 20, 1972); Katherine Lee (Dec. 27, 1974); Sally Jane (Feb. 18, 1977).

Mina Kay (Feb. 25, 1948) - married Jan. 9, 1977 to Donald Lowery (April 4, 1950).

On Feb. 14, 1981, Fern L. Tyner married William G. Nash and on June 29, 1991, Sharen Brincefield married Stephen Kent Duncan.

Affectionately known by their grandchildren as "Papaw Albert" and "Ma Kate", they gave many happy memories to all seven grandchildren. Together they would attend Saturday morning movies and often go to Highland Park. On weekend overnight events they would be allowed to concoct "exotic" foods in their back-porch pantry, using eggs, sugar and flour and lots of food coloring. There was always a big bag of bubblegum, popcorn, and comic books to share. Christmas Eve was always a special delight - remembered all year long. These grandchildren were the "Light of their Lives" and they instilled in them a love of Howard County soil. They retain an interest in the farm to this day, and I, the youngest grandchild, live with my family in that old Union #4 schoolhouse my grandparents called "home". *Submitted by Kay (Rockey) Silence*

WILLIAM HUGHES - William Hughes was my great-great-grandfather. William came from Tyrone County, Ireland, about 1797 and died on Sept. 10, 1850 in Honey Creek Township, Clinton County. Honey Creek Township was in Clinton County until 1859, then it was given to Howard County. William Hughes married Jane White in Ireland. They migrated from Ireland about 1830 with their three children: Alexander, Samuel, and William Jr. William and Jane and their three sons settled in New York where William and Jane had three more sons: Thompson, Hamilton and David. Then they moved to Tippecanoe County, IN. They had two more sons: Stewart and Richard, who were born in Tippecanoe County. Then William homesteaded 80 acres in Honey Creek Township in 1843. The land is on the southwest corner of 680 west and 500 south in Howard County.

My great-grandfather was Alexander Hughes born about 1822 in Ireland and died on Sept. 10, 1910 on the land in Honey Creek Township. Alexander and Elizabeth are buried at Prairieville Cemetery in Tipton County. Alexander had two marriages, first to Elizabeth Wallace; their union produced eight children. Elizabeth died Sept. 27, 1875. Then Alexander married Ellen (Boose) Wilson on Sept. 29, 1886 and Ellen (Boose) Wilson was born July 7, 1864 at Michigantown in Clinton County and died Jan. 19, 1932 in Kokomo.

Morris Edward Hughes and Ethel Mae (Elsea) Hughes

She is buried at Prairieville Cemetery also. To this union were born Elsie, Morris Edward, Frances Fern, Joseph, and James. My grandfather was Morris Edward Hughes born Feb. 4, 1890 in Honey Creek Township. Morris died Sept. 25, 1950 in Kokomo, IN. He married Ethel Mae Elsea on Feb. 9, 1911 in Howard County, Ethel (Elsea) was born July 7, 1892 in Tippecanoe County. She died on Oct. 1, 1960 in Kokomo. My grandfather and grandmother are buried in Prairieville Cemetery also. To this union were born Mildred Pauline, Edna Irene, Thelma Mae, Carl Leroy, Cleo Edward, Dorothy Opal, Francis, Betty Louise, and Wilma Pearl. They had two other children that were stillborn. My grandfather was a farmer and drove a school bus for Prairie School in the late 1920s. The first one was a horse pulling hack and then a motor bus. He died at the Globe Factory in Kokomo. My grandmother was one of the nicest, most loving persons I ever knew. My mother is Thelma Mae Hughes; she was born on May 6, 1917 in Prairie Township in Tipton County. She married John "Earl" Jones Sr. on April 2, 1934. They met at a swimming hole just west of New London and from this meeting, in 1994 they had 60 happy years together. John "Earl" Jones Sr. passed away May 14, 1994; he is buried at Memorial Park Cemetery. To this union two children were born: Barbara Ann and John Earl Jr. This is when I arrived, I am John Earl Jones Jr. I was born April 17, 1937 in Kokomo and I married Freda Juanita Bradley, who was born July 25, 1940 in White County, AR. We were married in Oakford, Howard County, IN on Sept. 27, 1959. This union produced two children: Robin Jo and John Earl III. Robin Jo was born on Aug. 21, 1960. Robin Jo Jones married Dennis Jay Herrell in Kokomo, Howard County, IN on Aug. 14, 1981; this union produced two children: Rachael Dawn and Rebekah Deeann. Rachael Dawn was born March 1, 1983 and Rebekah Deeann was born Oct. 18, 1986. John Earl Jones III was born Jan. 31, 1963, and after an automobile accident on the US 31 Bypass at the corner of Morgan in Kokomo, IN, he died Dec. 24, 1978. When little Johnny passed away it was the hardest and saddest time for the whole family. He may be gone, but he will never be forgotten. He is with Jesus now.

I was born at 1332 S. Jay St. in Kokomo and Howard County has always been my home and I am always proud to say "I am from Kokomo, IN" wherever my travels take me. *Submitted by John Earl Jones Jr.*

CLYDE AND DOVE HUNSINGER - Jacob Buchman and Obluna Stucky lived and married in Bavaria, Germany. Their boys, Balser and Henry, stowed their way on a boat to America in 1830. Henry married Catherine Fic who was also born in Bavaria. Their daughter, Obluna, married Peter Hunsicker.

Peter and Obluna Hunsicker had eight children. Laura married Lon Kemper. Their daughter Nada married Willard Ball and their son was Robert. Ora married Maggie Woodmansee. They had no children. Montie married Charles Ware. They had no children. Myrtle never married. Peter married Ethel Dawson and had a son, Homer. Clyde was born in 1885 in Chatfield, OH and at an early age moved to Howard County and married Dove Benson. His birthname was Clida Silvester Hunsicker but had it changed to Clyde Sylvester Hunsinger. Their children were Lois and Wayne. Lois married Harry Bogue. Their children were Ellen Sue and Philip Wayne. Ellen married David Templin. Their children were Jennifer and Christopher. Philip married Debra Turner. Their children were Bradley, Kimberly, Brian, and Brandon. Wayne married Roberta Greeson. Their children were Pamela and David and grandson, Shea. Clinton married Lela Ray who died at an early age. Later, he married Nellie Hodson. Their daughter was Mary Helen who married Ray Florea. Harry married Carrie from Cleveland. They had no children.

Clyde and Dove Hunsinger

Laura and her husband were co-partners of The Kemper Brothers Jewelry and Department Store in the center of Greentown. Ora farmed northeast of Greentown. Montie and her husband owned and operated The Greentown Hatchery and later were co-partners of the Mast and Ware Funeral Home and Furniture Store. Myrtle was a postal clerk. Peter was a minister. Clyde and Dove were co-partners with Clint in the Hunsinger Coal and Lumber Company and later sold their part to Clint and bought a farm north of Greentown and farmed before moving back to Greentown and built and operated The Hunsinger Hatchery. Harry was employed in Cleveland and entertained as a magician with magic shows as a hobby.

Clyde's and Dove's daughter, Lois, taught school in the Greentown Elementary and also in the Eastern Howard Corporation. Her husband farmed and operated a school bus for many years. When he retired, his son, Philip, took over the farming. After they both retired, they did extensive traveling. They spent their winters in their Lake Placid, FL home and their summers in their home on Lake Webster, IN while still maintaining their home near Greentown. Clyde's and Dove's son, Wayne, was in the Army and after graduating from Purdue University worked for IBM until he retired. They still live in Endicott, NY and have also traveled extensively.

In the early 1900s, there were many Hunsingers living in Howard County, but due to deaths and marriages, there are none in 1993 by the name Hunsinger of this family still living in Howard County.

HUNTER - Bob and Jerri Hunter have lived in Ervin Township, Howard County all of their married life. They built the home they now live in on a farm that has been in Bob's family for three generations.

Sylvester Wilson (1865-1940) married Ethie Brower (1870-1910) in Ervin Township, Howard County and they had six children: Orville (Bud), Claude, Edith, Ethel, Irma and Phoebe.

Irma Wilson (1903-1984) married William C. Hunter (1905-1979) and they had one child, Robert (Bob) Wilson Hunter born in 1927. Irma was a schoolteacher in the Kokomo and Howard County Schools for many years.

Bob spent most of his younger years in Ervin Township and graduated from Ervin High School in 1945. Incidentally, this school, which is abandoned, sits on the corner of the farm where Bob and Jerri live. Bob entered Purdue University and, after a stint in the service with Task Force Frigid in Alaska, graduated from the School of Agriculture in 1950.

Bob and Jerri Hunter

In 1951, Bob married Jerrel (Jerri) Towe after a long courtship. Jerri was born and raised in Burlington in neighboring Carroll County. Her parents were Dr. J.V. and Beryle (Metsger) Towe. She had one brother, Corwin (Doc) Metsger Towe and two sisters, Mrs. M.J. (Marda Gene) Catron and Mrs. C.C. (Joan) Joyce. Jerri graduated from Burlington High School in 1947.

The newlyweds settled into farming and Bob farmed for several years. He then decided to supplement his income by becoming a classroom teacher. He taught one year at Taylor School Corporation and 27 years in 6th grade, junior high and high school in the Northwestern School Corporation.

The Hunters had three daughters: Mrs. J. Andrew (Barbara Lynn) Cook who lives in Carmel, IN; Mrs. Dan (Beth Ann) Smith living in Plymouth, IN; and Mrs. Jon (Jennifer Jo) Huston residing in Lafayette, IN. All of the Hunter girls and their husbands graduated from Northwestern High School and went on to graduate from Indiana University or Purdue University.

After their children were born and mostly raised, Jerri also decided to become a teacher. She graduated from Indiana University at Kokomo in the School of Education the same year their older daughter, Barbara, graduated from Indiana University in the field of medical technology. This was also the year (1973) that second daughter Beth graduated from Northwestern High School. Jennifer still had several years before her graduation. Jerri went into teaching and taught at Western Primary School in Western School Corporation for 18 years.

After retiring, a few years ago, Bob and Jerri spend their winters in Naples, FL. The rest of their time they spend enjoying their children, eight grandchildren and friends and being on the farm in Ervin Township, Howard County, a nice place to live.

CARL HYNDS SR.
Carl Sr. was first married to Norma Young and they had two children, Raymond and Robert. Robert married Julia Heineman and they had a daughter Carol. Carol married Keith Shallenberger and they are the parents of triplets, Kevin, Kohl and Kiel. Raymond married Elvina (Barney) Padgett and they have three children, Russell, Jane and Sandra. Russell married Tonya Morrow and have a son Grant and live in Kokomo. Jane married D.C. Oliver and live in Flagstaff, AZ. Sandra married Mark Wright and have two children Wesley and Sara and live in Sanford, FL. Carl Sr. became both grandfather and great-grandfather on Nov. 12, 1967.

Carl Sr. came from Sandborn, IN, and after graduating from pharmacy school, came to Kokomo to work for George Kingston at Kingston Groceries, Meats, and Drugs. Harrison Mills, also a pharmacist for Kingston, purchased the store in the early 1930s. Carl Sr. purchased the store from Mills in 1944. In 1955, Carl Sr. and Ray Hynds formed a partnership. Carl Jr. became a partner in 1961, and the business was incorporated between Carl Sr., Ray and Carl Jr. The name of the business became Hynds Drugs Inc. Ray's son Russell became a partner in the corporation and is now manager of the business.

Carl Jr. worked for the family business until 1989, and on Jan. 16, 1989, went to work as assistant manager for Hook's Drug on Apperson Way N. in Kokomo. Robert Hynds worked for the family until 1956, and at that time moved to Muncie, IN to become assistant manager of Haag's Drug Store, until his death on Nov. 16, 1960, at the age of 38.

CARL A. HYNDS JR.
Carl, while working as a pharmacist for Hynds Drug Store, met a young beautiful lady, Elaine Granson. The following year, Feb. 10, 1962, they were married. There were five children born of this marriage: (1) Monica married John Eklem, and they are the parents of five children: Katherine, Philip, Domenica, Alexander and David. Monica and John live in Dearborn, MI. (2) Joseph married Shannon Morales, and they have one daughter, Elaine. Joe and Shannon live in Arlington, VA. (3) Philip married Ann Warner, and they have one son Patrick and are expecting their second child. Philip and Ann live in Plainfield, IN. (4) Bridget lives in Carmel, IN. (5) Mary Grace is the mother of two children, Jacob and Olivia, and they live in Wabash, IN.

Carl's parents are Carl Hynds Sr. and Beatrice Reames and his grandparents were John Perry Hynds and Lily M. Bolin and William Reames and Agnes Felker.

Elaine passed away on Dec. 27, 1992, after a long illness of heart disease. Elaine's parents were Frederick Jules Granson and Grace Beatley and her grandparents were Alfred Granson and Ernistine Guiot and Martin Beatley and Lucinda Cox.

Fred and Grace Granson had ten children, three died as infants. The surviving children are: Mary Louise (Renshaw), Richard, Fred, Joseph and David. Daniel is deceased.

MIKE AND BRENDA IMBLER
Mike and Brenda Imbler were both born in Kokomo, IN. Mike was born on Dec. 18, 1945 to Harvey and Maxine Imbler. Mike has one older sister, Sherry, who lives in Lafayette, IN. Sherry married Edward Mugg. She graduated from Kokomo High School in 1961 and from Saint Elizabeth School of Nursing in 1963. Sherry is presently a chaplain at Saint Elizabeth Hospital in Lafayette, IN.

Brenda's parents are Otis and Ilona Cook of Kokomo, IN. She has a younger brother, Ron, who lives in Salem, IL and a younger sister, Connie Holt, who lives north of Greentown, IN. Brenda, Ron and Connie all graduated from Kokomo High School.

Mike graduated from Kokomo High School in 1964. At that time there were many good paying jobs a high school graduate could obtain: Delco, Chrysler, Continental, Kingston, Cuneo and many more. Mike chose Chrysler because his father worked there. Mike took the apprenticeship test for skilled trades one month after he started working at Chrysler. In August 1964, Mike became an apprentice machine repairman at the Chrysler Casting Plant on Home Avenue. At this time the Chrysler Casting Plant was located in the old Haynes Automobile Plant on Home Avenue, Kokomo, IN.

Mike graduated as a journeyman machine repairman at the age of 22 years. In 1975, Mike graduated (with honors) from Indiana University-Kokomo with a degree in industrial management. Mike has held various jobs at Chrysler: production worker, machine repairman, maintenance supervisor, draftsman, civil and mechanical engineer. Mike currently is a mechanical engineer at Chrysler's Transmission Complex with 30 years seniority.

Mike and Brenda Imbler

Mike, like his father (Harvey Imbler) and father-in-law (Otis Cook), is a licensed Indiana state auctioneer. He graduated from Indiana College of Auctioneering and currently operates Imbler's Auction Service located in Kokomo, IN.

Besides being an auctioneer, Mike owns and operates Imbler's Enterprises which consists of renting out rental housing properties in the Kokomo area.

Brenda has been employed by Delco Electronics for 28 years. She and Mike own and operate the Merle Norman Cosmetic Studio that is located in the new Wal-Mart Plaza in Kokomo, IN.

Mike and Brenda have two daughters, Beth Ann Zirkle and Shannon Imbler. Beth Ann is employed at Chrysler Transmission Complex and is working toward a degree in business from Indiana University-Kokomo. Shannon is employed at the Merle Norman Cosmetic Studio and is working toward a degree in business from Indiana University-Kokomo. Beth has two daughters, Brittany and Brooklyn. The Zirkles live in Greentown, IN.

Mike's father and mother have lived in the Kokomo area most of their life. In 1946, the Imblers purchased a two-story house on a one-acre plot on the southwest side of Hemlock, IN. At this location the Imblers planted an apple orchard; some of the trees they planted are still producing apples.

Harvey Imbler was an auctioneer during the late 1940s and early 1950s. Harvey sold all of the Taylor Township's school buildings in Center, Oakford, and Hemlock, IN. Harvey also worked at the Dirylite Company and later at Chrysler's Casting Plant where he retired in 1982 as a furnace repairman and is currently living in Fort Myers, FL.

Brenda and Mike attend Kokomo's First Assembly of God church where they have held various positions as deacon, Sunday school teacher, and hospitality director.

The Imblers belong to the Kokomo Elks, Kiwanis, FGBMFI, Masons, York Rite, Scottish Rite, Eastern Star and Indiana Auctioneering Association.

The past four Imbler generations have lived in the Howard County area. Mike and Brenda plan to stay in this area after they retire but might go south for one or two months during the cold season.

INGELS
Originally from England, the Ingels family history in America dates back to 1731 when John and Susannah Ingels lived on a plantation near Philadelphia, PA, with their eight children, George, Matthew, John, James, Jean, Ann, Rachel and Joseph.

James Ingels Sr. (1713-1786) wed Ruth Harmer in 1737 and they had four children, Eleanor, James Jr., John and Ruth.

In 1777 James Ingels Jr. (1749-1815) married Catherine Boone DeHart (1752-1804) and they moved to Kentucky. They were buried at Paris, KY, and the cemetery was torn up in 1927. Catherine was a first cousin of Daniel Boone. They had eight children, Joseph, James, Elizabeth, Edith, Boone, Eleanor, Thomas and John.

John (1793-1859) and Rosa Garr Ingels (1803-1877) had nine children, Thomas, James, George, Abraham, Catherine, John, Joseph, Marion and Boone. John and Rosa moved from Kentucky to Wayne County, IN, and later to Fayette County, IN.

Born in Wayne County, brothers George and Abraham bought land in a virgin state on the Miami Indian Reserve, now Taylor Township of Howard County. The date of settlement in Howard County for George was 1846 and Abraham in 1847. They were listed as farmers in Taylor Township in Combination Atlas Map of Howard County, IN, published in 1877.

Abraham (1825-1906) and Nancy Jane Mugg Ingels (1835-1908) had six children, John, Emma, Henry Boone, Joseph, Rosa and George. They are buried at Albright Cemetery.

In 1877 Joseph Ingels (1865-1931) married Idella Alley (1870-1911) and they had five children, Iva Merle, Etha Monelle, Orval Verne, Eva Mae and Wayne. Joseph is said to have been a staunch Democrat.

In 1907 Merle (1889-1984) married Omer Orsburn (1836-1958). They had a son, Francis. Omer and Francis both were farmers and school bus drivers.

In 1935 Francis married Rosemary Etherington and they had two daughters, Janice and Carolyn. Francis is retired but still living on the original farm.

Janice, author of this biography, married Richard W. Johnson Jr. in 1957 and they had three children, Stephen, Diane and David. Janice works at the *Kokomo Tribune*.

In 1983 Stephen married Kimberly Baldwin and they live at Noblesville. In 1983 Diane married Kent Scott Bickel and they live at Walton with two sons, Kent Richard and Kasey Allen. In 1992 David married Rose Emma Herrera and they live at Jeffersonville with her son, Andrew.

The farming tradition continues by Carolyn and her husband Francis McClain and family. They were married in 1958 and he also drives a school bus. The McClain children are Sharon, Terry and Rex.

In 1983 Sharon married Doug Shane and they live at Greentown with two sons, Ted and Trey. In 1980 Terry married Laurie Marshall and they have two sons, Austin and Evan. They live in Taylor Township. Rex still lives at home. *Submitted by Janice Johnson.*

IRWIN - Joel Thomas Irwin (1847-1907) came to Howard County between 1860 and 1870 with his parents, Samuel and Priscilla (Morris) Irwin, and settled near Plevna, IN. Samuel and Priscilla's children were Joel, Sarah E. Powell, Nancy Whitaker, Thomas J., Matilda Drayer, Mary S. Wilson, Lucinda, Alice, and Daniel who evidently died young. In 1870, Joel married Emily Jane Snow, daughter of John M. and Sarah (Bundy) Snow. They had eight children - Benjamin Franklin (Frank), Mary Priscilla Lennington, Thomas Jefferson (Jeff), Samuel J., Jesse C. (dying at age seven), Sarah Olive Ritchie, and two sons dying in infancy. Joel and Emily are buried at Curry Chapel Cemetery in Sycamore, IN.

Samuel J. (1879-1940) was married twice - first in 1901 to Rhoda Langley (1880-1920), daughter of Silas and Mary (Swisher) Langley, and second in 1921 to Edna Aldridge. Rhoda already had a child, Archie, when she married Sam. Archie can be found on the census as Archie Langley and Archie Irwin. However, when he reached manhood, he took the name Archie Swing. Samuel and Rhoda had the following children: a son dying in infancy, Virgile Lee who died at age three, Della Olive Waits, Joel Thomas (Tom), James Edmond (Ed), Benjamin Frederick (Ben or Fred), and Mary Alice who died at age one. Samuel worked for the railroad and Pittsburgh Plate Glass. he was very strict with the children. Samuel and Rhoda are buried in Albright Cemetery in Kokomo, IN.

Benjamin F. (1912-1970), known by most as Ben or Fred, was a carpenter by trade. He worked for Dirilyte as a pressman, for Continental Steel, and also for Fenn Lumber Company. In 1940, he married Mary Catherine Dickison (1920-19), daughter of David G. and Iva Ethel (Washington) Dickison. They had five daughters and adopted a boy - Carolyn J. who married James F. Robertson, Phyllis Martin, Joyce who married Jack Jewell, Cindy who married Duane Hurlock and Robert Beasley, Sherry who married John Eades, and Donnie Irwin. Benjamin died of throat cancer in 1970 and is buried in Albright Cemetery in Kokomo, IN. *Submitted by Carolyn Robertson*

JACKSON - David S. Jackson was born in 1819 in Ohio. In 1839 he married Mary Louise Kennedy and they had six children before her death in 1853. David then married Margaret Ann Fansler. As second marriages sometimes go, she and David's children did not get along too well and some of them left home at an early age. Ozro, Margaret Jane, and Mary Ann migrated to Kansas while Ezra, Charles and Sarah Elizabeth migrated to Kokomo.

David and Margaret added to the Jackson clan with the births of Clara, Julia, Laura, David E., and Melvin. They became known as the second family. All of them lived in north central Ohio except David E. who moved to Garrett, IN.

Ezra enlisted in Company B, 135th Indiana Volunteer Inf. in May 1864 even though he was only 16 years old. He was honorably discharged in September 1865. He maintained his interest in veterans affair and was Commander of the Grand Army of the Republic (veterans organization) when he died.

In 1874 Ezra Jackson married Lucinda Heaton, daughter of John O. Heaton, Howard County pioneer. In 1877 they moved to a cabin on a farm belonging to Mr. Heaton on North Phillips Street Road. They later bought the farm and erected the buildings needed to farm it.

It was here that Ezra and Lucinda Jackson raised their family starting with Elda (she lived just short of 20 years). A son was stillborn and then Alice May, Osee, Ralph, Glen, Mary, and June followed. Alice May married Clarence Coate, Osee married Walter Keiter, Ralph married Ethel Amos, Glen married Maude Crousore, Mary married Ward Haynes, and June married Joe Fleming. All were farmers who lived northwest of Kokomo except Osee and Walter Keiter. Walter worked for F.W. Woolworth in Kokomo and, for a time, in Lockport, NY. He later worked for Kemp Brothers, tomato juice canning factory, in Kokomo. The others were grain and livestock farmers. Ward Haynes owned and operated a dairy with home delivery in Kokomo for many years.

Ezra Jackson served six terms as county commissioner of the second district where he became known as the "watchdog of the county treasury." He owned and operated the farm, traded livestock, and kept an active interest in politics.

There were 17 grandchildren of Ezra and Lucinda Jackson including: Roland, Irene, Raymond, and Thelma Coate; Russell Keiter; Ellen Louise, Frances, and Mildred Jackson; Charles and Betty Jackson; Lawrence, Louis, John, and David Haynes; and Mary Helen, Richard, and Ruth Ann Fleming.

All of the grandchildren were high school graduates; one, Lawrence Haynes, earned M.S., and Ph.D. degrees; another, David Haynes, earned an M.S. degree, while five others earned college degrees including Irene Cranmer, Raymond Coate, Russell Keiter, Louis Haynes, and John Haynes. Additionally Raymond Coate retired from the Air Force as a Colonel. *Submitted by John E. Haynes, great-grandson of David S. Jackson.*

JACOBS - Left an orphan at a young age, Ward Jacobs (1876-1917) came to Howard County from Johnson County, IN to live with his uncle, John Robards. His parents, Jackson (1850-1881) and Matilda (Robards) (1854-1881) Jacobs, died of typhoid fever in the year 1881 leaving three small sons, James Everett (born 1871), Milburn (1873-1895), Ward, and one daughter, Stella (1878-1903).

Ward was the great-great-grandson of Samuel Jacobs (1760-1840) a Revolutionary War soldier who served in the 2nd Virginia Regt. Records indicate he was one of about 11,000 men who made up the Revolutionary Army under General George Washington and was encamped at Valley Forge the winter of 1777.

About 1780 Samuel married Elizabeth Martin (1762-about 1830), daughter of Peter Martin (1741-1807) and Sarah Redding. About 1789 Samuel and Elizabeth came to Kentucky with her parents and settled in Shelby County. They migrated to Washington County, IN about 1822 settling near Martinsburg. They were the parents of 10 children. Their son, James (1785-1853) married Mary (Polly) Watts July 24, 1810 in Shelby County, KY. James was a veteran of the War of 1812 and served in the Mounted Military from Kentucky. He is listed among the first eight men to bring their families to Johnson County, IN in 1821. James and Polly were also the parents of 10 children among whom was Milburn Jacobs (born 1822). He married Martha Utterback (born 1825) March 19, 1846. Their issue of five children included Jackson, the father of our Howard County resident, Ward Jacobs.

On Sept. 24, 1899 Ward married Grace Smith (1874-1937) daughter of Jacob and Martha (Turner) Smith. They resided on the Smith homestead three miles southwest of Kokomo and Ward became a prominent farmer in Center Township. To them were born two children, Hurshel (1901-1973) and Dortha (born 1908).

Hurshel was a farmer and was elected for two terms as county commissioner representing the Second District. He served as president of the Northeastern Indiana Association of County Commissioners in 1953 and as a member of the board of directors of the Indiana Association of County Commissioners. He was a member of the Masonic Lodge and the Scottish Rite.

Ward Jacobs and Grace Smith Jacobs

In 1922 he married Elva Cole (born 1898), daughter of Perry and Estella (O'Bryant) Cole. They were the parents of two children, Kenneth (1924-1962) and Karlene (1929-1986), and the grandparents of six.

They formerly owned the land where the Lawndale subdivision is located at Boulevard and Dixon Road. Elva is memorialized as the street now known as Elva Drive was named for her and Elaine Court was named for their granddaughter. They were also involved in the development of Urbandale, located at Defenbaugh and Malfalfa Road. About 1968 they moved to Edinburg, IN to be near their daughter and her family.

Dortha chose to be a homemaker and in 1926 was married to Harry Kerby (1903-1988), the son of William and Emma (Smeltzer) Kerby. They were the owners of several apartment houses in Kokomo. Their only child, Phyllis (born 1928), was married in 1950 to Donald Woodward (1928-1969). They were the parents of three children:

Lezlie, married David Andrews. Children: Rachel, Leah (Mrs. Mark Madsen), Crispin, and Donald.

Ron and Cheryl (Andrews) Woodward are the parents of Matthew, Patrick and Elysia.

Thomas Woodward is the father of Chelsea and Westley.

After the death of her husband, Phyllis married Robert C. Oyler in 1972. They reside in Kokomo.

JAMES-BURGETT - Charles Wilson James was born Aug. 30, 1918, in Kokomo, the second son of Jesse and Jesse (Black) James. He has four brothers; James, Jesse, Frank and Richard. All were in the Armed Forces during World War II. Charles was in the Navy in the Pacific Theatre.

Charles married Beulah Alice Burgett on July 1, 1939, in Kokomo at the Calvary Baptist Church. He was employed at Continental Steel before entering the Navy and upon his return home from the war, he and Beulah moved to Miami, FL in February 1947, where he started his own construction business called C.W. James Construction Company, building homes and hotels. They were divorced in September 1959 in Miami, FL.

Beulah Alice Burgett was the fifth child born to Homer and Stella (Stafford) Burgett. She was born in Russiaville on August 19, 1918. She has four sisters: Lelah, Kathryn, Anna Mae and Nora.

Beulah attended school in Russiaville finishing the sophomore year. She was employed at Delco Radio from 1940-1947 when she moved to Miami, FL.

She was a certified dental assistant and upon her retirement in 1989 she returned to Kokomo. She is a member of First Landmark Missionary Baptist Church.

DR. JOHNATHAN ATKINS JAMES - Born Jan. 20, 1820 in Lancaster or York County, PA. In a series of 12 temperance articles in the *Kokomo Tribune* in 1871, he recounted his hardships during boyhood. His father, a farmer and "mechanic", in his 30s took to drink, squandered his money and abandoned his work and family and came to an early end. His wife soon followed and James and his sister were orphaned and brought up by his mother's relatives. He set forth that his mother was born and died a Quaker.

Dr. James was apprenticed and became a carpenter. He moved to Highland County, OH in 1838. He read and studied medicine and became a licensed doctor in Ohio.

He married Sarah Calhoon (born July 14, 1824, Highland County) Aug. 11, 1840. She was the daughter of William Calhoon (born Jan. 8, 1800, in Delaware). He was descended from James Calhoon, captured by Cromwellian forces at the Battle of Dunbar, Scotland in 1650. He was transported, as an indentured servant for seven years, to Block Island, MA (now Rhode Island) and learned the trade of brick maker. He was killed on the first day of King Philip Indian War, June 24, 1670 near Rehoboth, MA. His sons moved to Delaware. James was the son of Alexander Calquhoun (and Marion Stirling), the son of Alexander Colquhoun of Lusc, Dumbertonshire, Scotland, and Helen Buchanan. The Colquhoun are an ancient Scots highland clan seated on Lock Lomond.

William Calhoon's wife Martha McClure (born Aug. 26, 1808 Grayson [now Carroll] County, VA) was the daughter of Samuel McClure and Sarah Baldwin. Samuel was the son of Capt. James McClure (and Martha Chalfant) of the Pennsylvania Flying Camp, captured in November 1775, during the Revolution, upon the taking of Ft. Washington, New York City. He was a prisoner of war until September 1780 when he was exchanged. After the revolution he and his family moved to Virginia, where he died in 1821.

Sarah's family (parents and two brothers) also moved to Kokomo where they resided until 1865 when they moved to Marion County, IA. William and Martha died near Pella, IA Sept. 29, 1876 and May 9, 1892, respectively.

Sarah (Calhoon) James died March 16, 1865. She is buried in Crown Point Cemetery at Kokomo.

After Sarah died, Dr. James remarried (July 10, 1865) in Highland County, OH to Minerva Ann Giddings (nee Hixon) widow of Jay Giddings. She was the cousin of Dr. James' first wife. After the death of Dr. James, Minerva remarried (Nov. 23, 1876) to Andrew Brouse.

Dr. James moved to Kokomo in 1848, where he practiced medicine for a short while and then returned to Ohio. He returned to Kokomo with his family (wife and three daughters—one daughter born in Kokomo and two died young) in 1850 and resumed the practice of medicine. In 1853 he went to Chicago and graduated from the Rush Medical College. He was a founding member of the Kokomo Medical Society in 1854. He was in practice with Dr. A.F. Dayhoff from about 1853 to 1856, and also with Dr. R.H. Smith.

In 1856 he, along with Dr. H.A. Armstrong and Addison F. Armstrong, established a hardware company, one of the oldest businesses in Kokomo. In 1863 their building, a new three-story structure, was blown down. It was rebuilt and Dr. James continued in its co-ownership until 1867. In that year, with R.H. Smith, he established the Corner Drug Store at Main and Sycamore Streets.

Dr. James was a member of the Kokomo City Council 1st Ward, from 1865 to 1870, voluntarily retiring in 1871. He was largely responsible for the macadamizing of Kokomo streets and other improvements in the city.

He was almost solely responsible for the promotion and opening of the Crown Point Cemetery. When some opposed city membership, he offered to finance it himself. However, in the end, it was financed by the city. At the time of his death he was the superintendent of the cemetery.

He was, for a year prior to his death, deeply interested in railroads. He was elected president of one, but resigned because another person wanted the place.

He was a long-time member of the Masonic Order. He had been master of his lodge, Indiana #93, F.&A.M. Kokomo. At the time of his death, he was secretary of the lodge and owned the building where it held its meetings.

He died on Saturday, April 6, 1872, of a sudden massive internal hemorrhage. The obituary in the *Kokomo Tribune*, April 9, 1872 covered much of the front page. There was also a laudatory obituary in the *Kokomo Radical Democrat*, April 11, 1872. He was buried with full Masonic honors in the Crown Point Cemetery.

Dr. James and his wife Sarah had the following children all born in Ohio, except Lella: Martha (born May 18, 1842) married Harry Walker; Matilda (born June 9, 1843) married David P. Florer; Edith Minerva (born Aug. 6, 1847) married Abram Terry Auter; Lella (born Oct. 10, 1850 in Kokomo) married Joseph H. Littler.

MARJORIE (MIDGE) I. JANNER - Marjorie

Ione Schick was the next eldest child born to Benjamin Adam and Audrey Monica (Woodruff) Schick on June 31, 1918 in Kokomo (Howard County), IN.

Her older brother Wayne Paul was born May 8, 1914. He was killed in a tragic auto accident Feb. 3, 1937. Her younger brother Donald Eugene was born on Oct. 31, 1925 and another brother, Joseph Anthony, was born six years later on April 13, 1931. Joseph died of a brain tumor on June 13, 1947. Then Marjorie had a little sister, Nancy Loudica, born Sept. 4, 1932.

Marjorie attended school at Riley Elementary, St. Patrick's Elementary, and Roosevelt Jr. High, graduating from Kokomo High School in 1936. She then attended nurses training in Kansas City, MO at St. Vincent De Paul's School of Nursing, specializing in Obstetrics. Upon finishing her training, she worked at hospitals in Kansas City, MO and Kansas City, KS. Then, returning to Indiana, she continued her career in hospitals in Indianapolis, Kokomo, and Tipton.

Marjorie married William Joseph Janner Sr. at Holy Name Catholic Church, Kansas City, MO, on Dec. 2, 1939. He died in Kansas City, MO on May 14, 1971. This union produced two sons: William Joseph Jr., born March 1, 1941 and Wayne Carl, born Jan. 6, 1943. Two subsequent marriages to Louis E. (Bill) Allen and Eugene LeRoy Carr ended in divorce, with no children produced from either union.

Marjorie has six grandchildren: three from William J. Jr. (Theresa Lynn, Karla Ann and William J. III); and three from Wayne C. (Melissa Diane, David Wayne and Shannon DeLei). She has seven great-grandchildren: two sons from Theresa Lynn (Janner) Biddle [Shane Michael Crow and Justin Adam Crow]; two sons from Karla Ann (Janner) Myers [Brant Matthew Janner and Robert Reid Word]; two sons from William J. III [Zachariah Joseph Janner and Nathaniel Lee Janner]; one daughter from Melissa Diane (Janner) Kubly [Jennifer Ann Kubly].

1971-1993...Founded/published the *Kokomo Herald* newspaper.

1979...First woman candidate for mayor of Kokomo.

Marjorie has been a member of St. Patrick's Church all her life. She is a member of the Rosary Sodality, Women of the Moose, Lady of the Eagles Auxiliary, V.F.W. Auxiliary, A.A.R.P. and Women's Democrat Club.

She loves animals, of which she has several, and enjoys traveling. She still resides in the home place at 2123 N. Purdum St., Kokomo, IN where she was raised.

WAYNE AND DONNA JANNER - Wayne C.

Janner and Donna M. Craig were married on June 10, 1976 at the Russiaville Christian Church by the Rev. Gary Brown.

Wayne was born in Kokomo (Howard County), IN on Jan. 6, 1943 to his parents William J. Janner Sr. of Kansas City, MO and Marjorie I. (Schick) Janner of Kokomo, IN. He was the second child born of two sons.

Donna was born in Kokomo (Howard County), IN on Aug. 9, 1945 to her parents Louie E. and Erma G. (Crews) Craig. She was an only child.

Family members (left to right): Row 1...Donald, Benjamin, Audrey; Row 2...William J. Jr.; Row 3...Joseph, Marjorie, Wayne, Nancy.

Many of Wayne's early years as well as grades K-12 were spent "growing up" in Kansas City, MO and in Kokomo, IN. Local elementary and junior high, ultimately led to Kokomo High School and the Class of "61". An interest in aviation and an ongoing membership in the civil Air Patrol, first as a cadet at age 14, and then as an adult, has continued to this day.

Wayne and Donna Janner

Adult life included working for General Motors at the local Delco plant for over 31 years, the first seven of which were spent in hourly production activities and the next 24 were in skilled trades work as an electrician.

Becoming a Christian in 1978 at the age of 35, Wayne has since become involved in numerous church leadership responsibilities as well as publishing a monthly religious tabloid newspaper "The Christian Community News" from 1988 to 1990.

Wayne retired from General Motors on March 1, 1994 and became the publisher/editor of the *Kokomo Herald Weekly* newspaper (founded in 1971 by Marjorie Janner).

L-R: Melissa, David and Shannon.

The familiar neighborhood for Donna was Palmer and Washington Schools, followed by Kokomo High School and the class of 1963. She received vocational training as a hair stylist and then became employed by General Motors at Kokomo's Delco plant.

After becoming a Christian in 1975, she has volunteered her time as a: Sunday school teacher, church committee member, and church deaconess. Her hobbies are reading, flower gardening and travel.

Wayne and Donna have three children—Melissa Diane (Janner) Kubly; David Wayne Janner and Shannon DeLei Janner; and one granddaughter—Jennifer Ann Kubly.

JAY - Charles Woods and Naomi "Grace" Jay raised their three children in Kokomo, IN, in a home across from Highland Park overlooking the Kokomo Creek. Growing up, they thoroughly enjoyed playing all kinds of sports in the park and ice skating on the creek. All three children were confirmed in the Lutheran Church of Our Redeemer (Missouri Synod).

Firstborn, Joseph Walter Jay, was born June 24, 1944 in Athens, GA while Charles was in the Navy. Joe graduated in 1962 from Kokomo High School and January 1967 from Purdue University in mechanical engineering. His first job was at Continental Steel in Kokomo. On Feb. 14, 1970, Joe married Beverly Kay Robertson (born in Kokomo on April 24, 1943), a registered nurse in emergency room nursing. They had two daughters, Melissa Ann Jay (born July 21, 1971 in Kokomo, IN) and Juliellen Jay (born Nov. 18, 1974 in Anderson, IN). In 1974, Joe and family moved to Anderson, IN where Joe went to work at Guide Lamp. After a couple years, Joe was transferred to Monroe, LA where their family is still presently living. Melissa will be graduating from college in civil engineering the spring of 1994 and will be marrying on March 5, 1994. Julie is presently attending Northeastern Louisiana State majoring in elementary education.

Daughter, Cynthia Louise Jay (born on Oct. 29, 1947 in Kokomo, IN), graduated from Kokomo High School in 1965 and Marion County General Hospital School of Nursing in Indianapolis, IN in 1968. She is a registered nurse specializing in operating room nursing. After graduation, Cindy worked for one year at Howard Community Hospital. She then went to work as a private scrub nurse/surgeon's assistant for Dr. Sterling Tignor. She has worked with Dr. Tignor ever since (except for the four years she and her family lived in Germany). After dating for four years, Cindy married John Ernest Bernard (born Feb. 15, 1948 in Palmer, MA) who was a captain (a navigator) in the United States Air Force stationed at Grissom Air Force Base, Indiana. John's father was in the Air Force and he grew up in Europe as well as the USA. Cindy and John's first child, Jennifer Lynn Bernard, was born Nov. 17, 1978, followed by a son, Jason Edward Bernard, born on April 6, 1980. Both children were born in Kokomo, IN. After being stationed at Grissom for seven years, John got a new assignment. In July of 1980 their family moved to Ramstein Air Force Base in West Germany. For four years they lived in the village of Reichenbach-Steegen. In July of 1984 they were fortunate to get reassigned to Grissom AFB and to move back into their home in Cedar Crest. In 1985 Cindy once again began working with Dr. Tignor and is presently also working with his new partners, Dr. DeSanto and Dr. Seekri. On Oct. 1, 1993 John retired as a lieutenant colonel after 23 years of active duty with the Air Force. He is presently a full-time student at Indiana University-Kokomo working toward a post-graduate degree in computer science. Jennifer is a freshman and Jason is an eighth grader, both at downtown campus of Kokomo High School.

Front Row: Jason Bernard, Alex Jay, Gregory Jay, Jennifer Bernard, Andrew Jay. 2nd Row: Melissa Jay, Juliellen Jay, Kelly Jay, Beverly Jay, Grace Jay, Karen Jay, Cynthia Bernard. Back Row: Joseph Jay, Scott Jay, John Bernard.

Scott Thomas Jay, third child of Charles and Grace, was born Nov. 19, 1954 in Kokomo, IN. After graduating from Haworth High School in Kokomo in 1973, he took a four year apprenticeship in tool and die skilled trade at Lorentson Manufacturing in Kokomo. After becoming a journeyman, he remained at Lorentson's. In 1984, Scott went to work at Delco Electronics in Kokomo in the area of plastics and mold making where he continues to be employed. On Aug. 17, 1974, Scott married Karen Lynn Irwin (born Sept. 18, 1955 in Kokomo, IN). Karen worked for Mendelson Clinic an Dr. Watson before starting their family of four children, all born in Kokomo, IN. Daughter Kelly Nichole Jay, born July 14, 1978, is a sophomore. They then had three boys: Andrew Irwin Jay, born June 19, 1980, a seventh grader; Gregory Scott Jay, born July 29, 1982, in fifth grade; and Alexander Thomas Jay, born March 26, 1985, in second grade. Their family lives in the Ivy Hills addition south of Kokomo, and the children all attend Western School. *Submitted by Cynthia L. Bernard.*

JAY - Joseph Powers Jay born Feb. 16, 1881 in Kokomo, IN; died March 12, 1931 in Kokomo, IN; attended Culver Military Academy for his prep years of schooling and as a teen was a telegrapher for the local Western Union Office owned by his father. During the Spanish-American War, he took off the wire many of the stirring messages of that period. In 1905, he graduated from Purdue University Pharmacy School, second in his class. He purchased the old Bates Drug Store at Main and Mulberry Streets, later known as "Jay Bros. Drugs". In 1910, the brothers, Joseph and Thomas Jay, purchased Pictureland Theater on the southside of the square. Thomas Jay, purchased "Broadacres" in 1926, the country home (now 3104 W. Jefferson) once owned by A.G. Seiberling. On Sept. 9, 1908 Joseph Powers Jay married Mae Belle Wood (born Jan. 23, 1888 in Elwood, IN; died Aug. 28, 1953 in Muskegon, MI). They had two children born in Kokomo, IN: Winifred Joan Jay (Linn) (born March 20, 1913; died Feb. 9, 1973 in Pensacola, FL) and Charles Woods Jay (born Oct. 27, 1918; died July 26, 1984 in Kokomo, IN). Joseph became a prominent realtor in Kokomo. At his death on March 12, 1931, he was living at 912 W. Sycamore.

Joseph Powers Jay (born Feb. 16, 1881); Thomas Brush Jay (born April 14, 1887)

After graduating from Kokomo High School in 1936, Charles Woods Jay attended Indiana University and graduated from Kokomo Business College in 1938. On Sept. 22, 1940 Charles married Naomi Grace Johnson (born March 21, 1919 in Kokomo, IN and presently is living in Kokomo, IN across from Highland Park), a 1937 graduate of Kokomo High School. In 1942 he left his job at Delco to serve his country in the Navy during WWII for the next three years. Their firstborn son, Joseph Walter Jay, was born June 24, 1944 in Athens, GA. In 1947 Charles began working at Tenbrook Sales bottle gas company where he continued to work for the next 25 years. Cynthia Louise Jay, their first daughter, was born Oct. 29, 1947 in Kokomo, IN as was their third child, Scott Thomas Jay, born Nov. 19, 1954. In 1950, Charles was recalled into the Navy during the Korean War, serving with the 6th Fleet in the Mediterranean for three years. Charles was active in the local Boy Scouts and had a hobby/business involving horses. At one time he operated Horseway Trails, a horse trail riding business, and also owned a tack shop in New London, IN. After retiring from Tenbrook's, Charles worked as a bookkeeper at H.H. Gregg's appliance store until his death in 1984.

Naomi "Grace" Jay, an active 50-year member of Phi Beta Psi Sorority worked at Kokomo Gas & Fuel as a cashier (1937-1940), Kokomo High School as attendance officer (1961 and 1962), American Red Cross as administrative assistant (1962-1965), Howard County jail as a matron (1970), and Howard County Tuberculosis Association as executive director (1971-1973). Grace presently lives in the family home (since 1941) which is across from Highland Park. *Submitted by Scott Jay.*

JAY - Samuel Jay (born Jan. 13, 1784 in South Carolina; died Dec. 4, 1859 in Jonesboro, IN) married Bathsheba Pugh (born Dec. 28, 1788 in South Carolina; died Jan. 3, 1850 in Jonesboro, IN) on Jan. 15, 1806. They had five sons and four daughters. Thomas Jay, their eighth son, (born Sept. 11, 1822 in Miami County, OH; died Jan. 3, 1874 in Kokomo, IN) married Nancy Russell (born June 7, 1826 in Jonesboro, IN; died on Feb. 9, 1894 in Kokomo, IN) on Feb. 2, 1845. They purchased 1.28 acres between East Walnut and East Mulberry Streets, running from the West Rail of the Chicago and Cincinnati Railroad in December 1859. The purchase was from David Foster, the founder of Kokomo, IN. (The old Russell homestead stood on the northeast corner of Lafountain and Walnut Streets. The original land purchased by Thomas and Nancy lay to the north and east of the old Russell homestead.) Three sons and five daughters were born to them: Louise (Nov. 20, 1845); Charles Augustus Jay (born Sept. 1, 1848 born in Jonesboro, IN; died May 30, 1908 in Kokomo, IN); Gilbert "Gibb" D. (June 24, 1850); Bathsheba Ellen (May 11, 1853); Flora Alma and Nora Alliece (twins born May 5, 1856); William Oliver (Dec. 13, 1858); Maude Piles (Dec. 4, 1871). In 1861, Thomas opened the second bank in Howard County. This bank was privately owned by Thomas Jay & Co.

Charles Augustus Jay (born Sept. 1, 1848; died May 30, 1908); Anna Powers Jay (born April 17, 1856; died May 19, 1916). Married Sept. 23, 1879.

Charles Augustus Jay came to Kokomo, IN in 1859 with his family at 11 years of age. On Sept. 23, 1879 he married Annie E. Powers (born April 17, 1856 in Madison, IN; died May 19, 1916 in Kokomo). On Dec. 29, 1879, Charles and Annie Jay purchased a home in the 400 block of West Mulberry. They had two sons, both born in this home. Joseph Powers Jay was born on Feb. 16, 1881 (died March 12, 1931 in Kokomo) and Thomas Brush Jay on April 14, 1887 (died July 1974 in California). In 1887, Charles A. Jay & Co. was engaged in the egg and poultry business. A branch store was later opened in Danville, IL. Charles A. Jay leased land to the Chicago Gas Company so they could pipe gas from either Fairmount or Jonesboro to Kokomo in the 1890s. In addition, he owned the Clinton House, a hotel located on the northeast corner of Mulberry and Buckeye Street. The hotel, built by his father Thomas Jay, was later added on to by Charles A. Jay and renamed the Frances Hotel. The Citizens Telephone Company, located on North Main Street in the King Kennedy building was partially-owned by Charles A. Jay and Austin "Pan" Jay. The company, the first to install residence service throughout the city (1899), later merged into the Indiana Bell Telephone Company. In 1889, Charles A. Jay agreed to lease the main floor of the building he was

227

erecting on Mulberry Street, just east of the Clinton House, to the post office department. He was also a co-owner of a factory, the Kokomo Saddlery and Harness Company. *Submitted by Grace Jay.*

JENKINS - Howard G. Jenkins, his wife Irene and sons Frederick and Richard moved to Greentown from Pittsburg, IN (Carroll County) in 1949 when Howard accepted the call to be minister of the Meridian Street Christian Church. Howard, the son of Elmer and Lucy H. (Gray) Jenkins, was born March 7, 1906 in Winamac, IN. Irene, daughter of Harry Scott and Glennie (York) Golden, was born Dec. 18, 1907 near Idaville, IN. Howard and Irene were married Dec. 24, 1933 in Monroe County, IN. Soon thereafter Howard became minister of the Delphi Christian Church. Frederick Howard "Fred" was born Feb. 2, 1937 in Delphi. Richard Dean "Dick" was born July 1, 1942 in Lafayette while the family was living in a house Howard built in Pittsburg, across the Wabash River form Delphi.

Rachel and Fred Jenkins

Both Jenkins boys graduated from Eastern High School. Fred attended Purdue University. Dick attended Indiana Mortuary School and Kentucky Christian College. On Jan. 29, 1961 Fred married Rachel Louisa Jordan, daughter of David and Clara Louisa (Bartley) Jordan. Rachel was born July 25, 1940 in Johnson County, IN. Fred and Rachel's children are Mark Daniel, born Sept. 15, 1961 in Lafayette, Sarah Lucinda, born Jan. 24, 1963 and Heather Lynn, born July 10, 1964, both in Kokomo. Mark shares a home with his parents and is employed as a carpenter. Sarah married Michael P. Altman on April 27, 1985 in Kokomo. They live in Omro, WI with their children Eric Michael, born Oct. 28, 1988 and Abby Rose born Sept. 25, 1990, both in Oshkosh, WI. Heather lives in Indianapolis and is an insurance claims supervisor. She plans to move soon to near Kempton.

Fred and Rachel opened a photography business, Jenkins Studio, at 110 S. Meridian St., Greentown, in 1962. In 1967 the family moved east of town into a home-studio which Fred designed. They have photographed many Howard County individuals and families. Fred was president of the Professional Photographers of Indiana 1975-76.

Fred and Rachel have an interest in historic crafts. Fred has acquired the skills of tanning, spinning, weaving, blacksmithing, flintknapping and butchering. His small herd of Nubian goats provide the milk for many kinds of cheese. Rachel enjoys weaving, participation in the Greentown Research Club, the Greentown Area Business Association, the Indiana Gourd Society and several lineage societies. Rachel was instrumental in starting *The Greentown Grapevine*, a monthly newspaper.

On Aug. 14, 1965, Dick married Georgia Carol Miller in Ironton, KY. They have one son, David Howard Jenkins, born Feb. 11, 1967 in Grayson, KY. David married Pamela Ann Ouellette on Aug. 6, 1988 in Greeley, CO. They have a daughter, Tara Jean Jenkins, born April 7, 1992 in Aurora, CO.

Rev. Howard Jenkins died March 6, 1973 while serving as minister of the Walton Christian Church. He is buried in David Cemetery in Cass County, IN. Irene presently lives in Logansport, IN.

BENJAMIN BATES JOHNSON - Benjamin Bates Johnson was born Sept. 2, 1852 on his family's farm in Stark County, OH, the fifth of nine children to Jesse and Martha (Butler) Johnson. The family moved to Kokomo, IN Sept. 2, 1866. Jesse Johnson had been a farmer and retailer in Ohio. According to Johnson family history, he had moved to Kokomo to invest in what he thought was a promising business opportunity; however, he was swindled out of much of his investment. He was a strong Quaker but not a good businessman. He was broken-hearted the rest of his life, became an invalid, and died March 25, 1879.

Benjamin Bates Johnson finished high school in Kokomo, but lacked financial resources to attend college. He qualified academically to attend West Point, but was too short. His early employment history in Kokomo included Deputy Postmaster for three and one-half years and bookkeeper for the First National Bank for six years. In 1877, he was appointed Clerk in the House of Representatives at Indianapolis for both regular and special sessions. Next he opened an abstract and loan office with his brother, John D. Johnson, who took over the running of the business. In November 1878, he became Deputy County Treasurer. In 1882, he was elected Treasurer on the Republican ticket. He was subsequently defeated by a Civil War Veteran, although his competency was not in question.

In 1884, he bought half interest in the *Kokomo Tribune*, and became sole owner 14 months later. In 1891, he became part-time owner of the *Richmond* (Indiana) *Evening Item* with Charles F. Crowder. He and his family moved to Richmond at this time. In 1895, he sold his interest in the paper to John W. Barnes, because of ill-health. John Barnes was the father of Earl Barnes of the Barnes and Thornburg law firm in Indianapolis. In 1899, he established the Independent Ice & Fuel Company, which he incorporated in 1918. Like his father, he was not a good businessman and this business failed. From 1913 to 1917, he was appointed Secretary to Indiana Governor Samuel Ralston. Mr. Johnson was also on the Board of Earlham College.

Sometime in the 1880s, according to recollection of his son, Fred Bates Johnson, Benjamin Bates Johnson of the *Kokomo Tribune* and an editor of another Kokomo newspaper engaged in a scheme to boost their respective circulation by publishing some purportedly newly-discovered poems of Edgar Allan Poe. The two newspapers carried out a spirited dispute as to the genuineness of these poems, and boosted their sales at least temporarily. In fact, both knew that the poems were bogus and were actually written by the then unknown poet, James Whitcomb Riley. It is interesting to note that in some encyclopedias, references to Riley state that his early poems had appeared in several newspapers under the name "Benj. F. Johnson of Boone." Mr. Johnson had a mystical feeling about Poe, as Poe died in 1849, the year Riley was born.

In 1875, Mr. Johnson married Clara C. Albaugh, daughter of Aaron Albaugh of Kokomo. During the last years of his life he was estranged from her and lived with his lawyer son, Fred Bates Johnson, in Indianapolis. His wife lived in Bloomington with their daughter, Edna Johnson, an English professor at Indiana University. He died in 1924.

Mr. Johnson was perhaps best known as a newspaper owner and journalist, as well as a thinker on public affairs. He was, at least in late life, somewhat short-tempered. He seems to have evolved in his politics from the Republican Party to the Democrat Party. *Submitted by Gaar Johnson*

JOHNSON - Carole Ann White, the youngest child of Howard E. and Ruth Ella (Hunt) White, was born Jan. 3, 1939 in Kokomo, IN. As a small red head, Carole was a feisty little tom-boy known as "Corky" who was always tagging along after her older brothers and sisters. No one could discourage her, even though they tried very hard. Carole attended St. Joseph Academy of Tipton and then transferred to Kokomo High School. She became the Deli Manager at Krogers in the Markland Plaza Store. She later transferred to Lafayette and then on to Monticello where she is now employed.

One of Carole's hobbies is attending auctions, buying things which you might think worthless and turning them into articles of beauty. She married Bruce Neil Johnson Feb. 23, 1957 at St. Patrick's Church by Rev. Leo Brietenbach.

Bruce Neil Johnson, the son of Andrew Jackson and Helen Ruth (Phillips) Johnson, was born Sept. 25, 1933 in Fountain City, TN. He started working for Marsh Supermarket while in Kokomo High School, continuing on after graduation and eventually became a store manager. Bruce was transferred several times and decided to come back to Kokomo shortly before their first son was born. It was at this time Bruce went to work for Med-O-Bloom Dairy. He and Carole have owned two restaurants, one in Burlington and another in Greentown, IN.

Furniture refinishing has also become Bruce's hobby, as he is now retired. The two of them have turned out many beautiful pieces of furniture and other home accessories.

Carole and Bruce had three sons all born in Kokomo: Thomas Michael, born April 26, 1958 and he has one son Jeremiah; Craig Douglas, born July 26, 1962, married Tina Louise Gich April 4, 1985. They have two children: Michael Douglas and Kristina Nichole; Andrew Mark was born Nov. 6, 1964, married Cynthia Pearl Webb (Oct. 19, 1985; one son Andrew Neil came from this marriage.

For more information on the White family see the Howard E. and Ruth Ella (Hunt) White family also included in this publication.

JOHNSON - An early resident of Howard County was George Johnson. He was born in 1813 in Clinton County, OH the son of William and Mary Johnson. George married Ruth Moon in October 1840. Ruth died while giving birth to Robert Barclay Johnson in 1849. George and the two older children, Mary and Thomas, came to Indiana and Robert was left in Ohio with the Jake Hockett family who raised him until he was 21.

George first resided in Jackson Township, Miami County and then moved to Jackson Township, Howard County and took possession of a land grant farm signed by Ulysses S. Grant. That farm was passed on to Robert Barclay Johnson who married Elva Alice Saucer (1856-1950). They farmed the land and raised three children: (1) Gertrude (1877-1950) who married John Harvey and later lived in Kokomo. Their daughter Opal (1909-1989) was a first grade teacher at Washington School in Kokomo for many years. (2) William Earl (1880-1969) married Ethel Warnock and lived across the road from the original farm. Their two daughters married and reside in Howard County. (3) Everett Guy (1889-1966) married Mary Kingseed (1890-1978) and resided on the original farm his entire lifetime. He farmed and drove a school bus for Jackson School. Their three children were Robert (1910-1967) who married Dorothy Douglass (1914-1989); Mildred (1915-) married Virgil Smith; Wendell (1920-1936) died of leukemia while in high school.

This picture, taken in 1892 or 1894 is of the Robert Barclay Johnson family. Mr. Johnson was born June 19, 1849; Elva Alice Saucer Johnson was born March 19, 1856 and died Nov. 15, 1950. They were married Aug. 2, 1876. The youngest child is Everett Guy Johnson, born Jan. 31, 1889 and died Jan. 21, 1966. The daughter is Ethelyn Gertrude Johnson Harvey who was born Oct. 27, 1877 and died in 1950. William Earl Johnson is the oldest son and he was born Aug. 16, 1889 and died in 1969.

Robert and Dorothy lived two miles west of the original farm in Jackson Township where he farmed, drove a school bus and did electrical service in the community. They were also very active in the Farm Bureau organization. They had five children, four of whom still live in Howard County. Larry (1938) married Ada Reid and has served as a minister, child care administrator and has worked at McGavic Outdoor Power since 1981. Lelan (1939) married Martha Arnold and has worked for Howard County Farm Bureau Coop., Chrysler Casting, operated a furniture store in Kokomo and currently operates a truck for Cates Trucking. Roger (1942) married Carolyn Jackson, from another longtime Howard County family, and farmed, drove a bus for Eastern schools, and presently works for Diamond Distributors in Kokomo. They live on the original farm in Jackson Township. Rose Marie Varnetti lives in Kingman, AZ. Diane (1949) lives in Greentown and is a secretary at United Presidential Life in Kokomo.

Larry and Ada Johnson reside in Taylor Township and have three children: Kevin, Kenneth and Kristi. Kevin and his daughters, Brooke and Nichole, are residents of Howard County.

Lelan and Marty Johnson have four children: Timothy, Anthony, Amy and Thomas. They reside, respectively, in Chicago, Fort Wayne and students at Ball State University.

Roger and Carolyn have three children: Gregory, Bradley and Anne. Brad married Stephanie and they reside near the Reservoir and work for CSI in Kokomo. Anne is children's director at the Converse Church of Christ.

Diane lives in Greentown and her daughter Tammy is a student at Indiana Wesleyan University and Dawn is a student at Eastern High School.

JOHNSON - Barbara Michelle Johnson, born Aug. 16, 1966 in Howard County, IN, daughter of Walter Burton Johnson Jr., born Jan. 7, 1942 in Yancy County, NC and Barbara Ann McInturff Barnett Johnson, born May 29, 1944 in Erwin, Unicoi County, TN, daughter of Willard James and Pancy Inez Miller McInturff. Michelle has a son, Jason Allen, born Aug. 19, 1992 in Johnson City, Washington County, TN by Ricky Allen Huskins, born Nov. 29, 1959 in Unicoi County, TN, son of Harry Leonard and Florence Johnson Walker Huskins.

Rick Huskins, Michelle and Jason Allen.

Michelle's parents came to Howard County in the late fall of 1965. A tornado had touched down in April of that year and Kokomo and the surrounding area was still a mess. Walter Jr. was the sixth child, the second son, out of ten children born to Walter Burton Sr. (Jan. 3, 1902-Dec. 29, 1951) and Lucy Jane Lewis Johnson. Lucy Jane, still living in 1994 was born Sept. 16, 1912 on Spivey Mountain, Unicoi County, TN; she was also from a large family. Her father, David Adkins Lewis, was born in May 1872 and died sometime between 1910-1920. He is buried in the Lewis Cemetery I, on the land he owned at Spivey Mountain, in Mt. Dale Community; it is believed his father also once owned this land. David was the son of William (February 1830-????) and Harriet Adkins (1836-????) Lewis; they are also buried in the Lewis Cemetery I. William and Harriet were the parents of nine known children, all born in North Carolina: (1) William T., born in 1859; (2) James Mathew, born in 1860; (3) Sarah E., born in 1863; (4) Julia A., born in January 1865; (5) Elbert B., (Sept. 25, 1866-Sept. 16, 1951), wife Nancy Jane ?; (6) Aloma M., born 1869/70; (7) David Adkins Lewis; (8) Thomas G., born in 1873; and (9) Marthy J., born in 1877. Lucy mother, Deborah Vasta Justice, was born in Madison County, NC April/June 30, 1873, daughter of Jake and Harriett Roberts Justice; no information on this family. David and Deborah were the parents of ten known children: (1) Servania, born in August 1889, never married, buried in Lewis Cemetery II; (2) James Willard, Jan. 1, 1893-Sept. 27, 1974, wife Anna Lee Tipton (June 26, 1898-Sept. 28, 1966), daughter of Joe Berry and Bettie Louise Cooper Tipton; both are buried in the Lewis Cemetery II; (3) Harriet, born in May 1894, buried in Lewis Cemetery I; (4) Garrett, born in August 1895, died in 1967/68, wife Mary Crane, buried in Lewis Cemetery IV; (5) Samuel, born about 1896/97, still living in 1993, but he doesn't remember when he was born; his birthdate was recorded in the family Bible, but the bible was destroyed long ago. When he was a child and the family moved from North Carolina to Tennessee in a covered wagon, the wagon overturned in the water they crossed and the contents were spilled into the water including the family Bible. (6) David Jr., born about 1898/99, never married, buried in Lewis Cemetery I; (7) Toka May, July 8, 1901-Aug. 30, 1912, Lewis Cemetery I; (8) Betsy, March 18, 1903-Jan. 3, 1950, wife of Wolford Chandler, Nov. 18, 1895-April 14, 1969, both buried in Fishery Cemetery; (9) Massey Mae, June 1, 1905-1993, wife of Dock Witt Tipton; and (10) Lucy Jane Lewis Johnson. *Submitted by Ricky Allen and Barbara Michelle Johnson Huskins.*

JOHNSON - The first known progenitors of this branch of Johnsons was Philip and Susan Johnson. He was born in Scotland in the year of our Lord 1758 and died in Jennings County, IN in 1835 on July 11.

He was a soldier in the Revolutionary War. He enlisted at Hales Hale, VA, Essex County in April 1777 and served as a 'matross' for six years in Captain James Pendleton's Company. He was at the Battle of Bunker Hill and at Yorktown when Cornwallis surrendered. According to the records, in the Bureau of Pensions, Washington, D.C., Philip Johnson was in four battles: Monouth, Stoney Point, Camden and Pittsburg. He applied and received a pension on Sept. 12, 1818.

At that time he resided in Madison County, KY and was 60 years old.

After serving with Captain Pendleton, he also served with Captain Michael Boyer's Company, the 12th Virginia Regt.

He lived in Pittsylvania County, VA for 29 years before moving to Madison County, KY where he lived on the banks of Brush Creek.

Philip Johnson married after the war was over in 1782. His wife, Susannah Johnson (Maiden name not known), was born June 13,1766 and died Nov. 14, 1834 at the age of 68.

I will add that Philip's occupation during the Revolutionary War was a "matross". After searching for years for the definition of "matross" I came across the definition in an 1800s dictionary (this definition cannot be found in most modern-day dictionaries). A "matross" is a CANNON STUFFER and SWABBER and when not doing this, they are cook's helpers?

Now, Philip and Susan had 11 children, as follows: Jane born Sept. 15, 1783; William born Aug. 7, 1786; Giles born Dec. 14, 1788; Elizabeth born Feb. 22, 1791; James R. born June 11, 1793 (my fourth great-grandfather); Lennie S. born Nov. 14, 1795; Joel W. born March 24, 1798; Mary born March 2, 1800; Berry born Aug. 27, 1802; Langston born Oct. 25, 1804; and Clement born Dec. 27, 1807.

Philip Johnson and wife Susannah are both buried on the Mat Kibler farm. The place of burial is on the west bank of Big Otter Creek, Jennings County, IN, in an old garden. A three foot high stone wall has been built around the entire garden by John Butler, who owned the farm before Mat Kibler, the year being 1885.

This area is near the Jefferson Proving Grounds and is about 100 feet square, and is in much disrepair (I should notify the Jennings County Historic Society of this shame).

I will only briefly follow the direct lines that relate to me as space does not permit the following of others.

I would be pleased to help others if they think they relate to the 11 children aforementioned, offspring of Philip and Susannah.

Philip being my fifth great-grandfather, my fourth great-grandfather was James R. Johnson. He married his brother Joel's widow; Joel died in 1824.

Joel's widow as Martha Cauthorn; James died in 1846. His widow lived on a farm in Bigger Township, Jennings County, IN (being the entire Northwest Quarter of Section 13, Township 6, Range 9 East); besides this 400 acres, she also owned 120 acres. She paid taxes and was able to loan money to her neighbors.

Along with a large family, Martha raised fine livestock. After her children left home, she lived alone for a number of years. Her children, Anna and Mary B. Miles, lives with her for a time after which she was moved to Johnson County, IN, where she died on March 27, 1888 at the age of 83 years, 5 months and 20 days. She is buried in the Mt. Pleasant Cemetery near the Johnson and Shelby County, IN line.

Mark W. Johnson, Jack W. Johnson, Jody L. Johnson Lytle, Cara D. Johnson Smith - 1991.

Joel W. and Martha Cauthorn Johnson had two children, Anna (christened) Mary Ann S. and Martha. I will not follow their lines.

James R. Johnson and Martha Johnson (his brother's widow) had eight children viz: Frances (girl) born Aug. 17, 1829, died in 1880; Elizabeth born Feb. 9, 1831 (married surname of Ransdell) died 1895; James W. born Feb. 9, 1833, died 1861; William T. born March 13, 1835, died 1924; Henry Clay born Aug. 19, 1844; Amanda born July 20, 1937; Minerva (married surname Houghman) born Dec. 19, 1839; Melissa (married surname Williams) born June 17, 1840, died Dec. 4, 1880; and Sarena born June 26, 1842, died Dec. 2, 1925.

Of these children, I will follow one only, William T. Johnson, my third great-grandfather. He married Margret Armstrong and they raised nine children, most of which moved to northern Indiana and other areas. One of their children, Amanda, married a second cousin and they lived in Jimtown in northern Indiana. Joel Johnson and Isaac Rice were the first Johnsons to come to Indiana in 1818.

Of the early Johnsons there are many stories to tell, maybe some true and some hearsay; but room does not permit me to go into detail!

This branch of the Johnsons is scattered all over this great land. Early Johnsons were not highly educated, but were just and upright citizens; most were farmers and adhered to the Baptist faith, were industrious, and none of them were criminals or flagrant violators of the law (as far as I've heard)!

As with most early settlers to Indiana, they had to come here through the Cumberland Pass in Tennessee and most stopped off a year or more in Tennessee or Kentucky.

Now to jump back just a bit. James R., who was born June 24, 1793 and died in the 1840s and his brother's widow had eight children. One of his sons was an ordained Baptist preacher. They were raised on farms along Big Graham Creek.

Now for the more present day Johnsons. But before I get to this I wish to speculate on the surname of "Johnson".

During the Rebellion of 1745 many fought in this and then fled to America; perhaps the progenitor, Philip Johnson's father, was one such person, when Charles Edward, "The Young Pretender" Bonnie Prince Charlie, was defeated at Culladen Moor, April 16, 1745.

Many of the fugitives took their master's or lord's name and fled the area or sailed to the New World. Many,

229

many of these, peasants and serfs, assumed their owner's name and struck out in this new adventure.

The "Gaelic Clan" name of MacIan is equivalent to the English surname of Johnson.

I cannot relate to any famous Johnsons, but also cannot relate to any infamous ones either!

Now back to the direct lines:

One of William T. Johnson's sons was my great-grandfather, Richard Johnson, born 1862, died 1937. He married Mary McQuistion and they had a farm one and one-fourth mile east of Hemlock, IN on the south side of Highway 26. They had only one child, my grandfather.

John L. Johnson born 1882, died March 5, 1945 married Cora A. Tharp and they had two children.

Blanch born June 8, 1903 is a retired school teacher but has never married.

Hansel born Oct. 19, 1905 died Aug. 25, 1980 was a farmer and a high school math teacher and married Kathleen Swarts and they parented four children:

John born April 2, 1933 married and he and his family live in California and own an electronics factory.

Marilyn born Dec. 12, 1934 is married to Robert Taylor of Marion, IN and is a retired grade school teacher. They have two children:

Steve and Mike born 1955 and 1956 respectively.

John L. Johnson, John A. Johnson, Hansel Johnson, Richard Johnson (seated) - year 1933.

Jerry born Oct. 19, 1941, married Jeanne Myers and they have one child, Aimee. He is a heavy equipment operator.

Jack born Aug. 24, 1936 married Mary Halvie they have three children and he is a retired farmer and works for a land developer.

Mark born Feb. 14, 1957.
Jody born Nov. 11, 1960.
Cara born Dec. 19, 1964.

Mark married Lynn King; they have two children, Jennifer born May 27, 1974 and Justin, born Feb. 14, 1982, ages 19 and 10 respectively. Jennifer is a college freshman and Justin attends Eastern Elementary.

Jody married James Lytle and they have a son Wesley born Dec. 15, 1979 who attends Eastern Junior High School.

Cara married Richard Smith of Evansville, IN and they have no children at this writing.

This is a brief lineage of "my" Johnson branch; there are many other branches and lots and lots of untold stories or tales.

Many Johnsons have served their country in the Revolutionary War, Civil War, War of 1812, WWI, WWII, Korea, Vietnam and Desert Storm and wherever freedom was a cause. In the later generations of this family there are doctors, educators, farmers, business people and laborers, etc.

I will share any information I have obtained on any branch to those who pursue genealogy.

Some of this information was compiled in 1906 by Johnson and some by Charles Miles in 1935 and the rest by myself. *Submitted by Jack Johnson.*

AUSTIN L. JOHNSON - Austin Lincoln Johnson was born May 12, 1862 near Greentown, IN. He was the ninth child born to David and Belinda (Davis) Johnson of Howard County, formerly of Henry County, IN. Austin married Dec. 19, 1889 in Howard County to Ruth "Lorena" Penland, the daughter of Hiram Fernandes and Lettica (Price) Penland. Lorena was born Dec. 14, 1868 in Indiana. After her mother's death (age 31) in 1873, her father moved their family from Michigan to Indiana where he farmed and worked the sawmill on the Wild Cat River in Jerome.

Austin and Lorena made their home on Payton Street on the north side of Greentown. Austin made his living as a well driller to provide a much needed income for their large family of 13 children; *Charles F. (1891-1957), *Don (1892-1970), Emor (1894-1977), *Glen (1896-1984), Raymond (1899-1957), *Wayne Ted (1900-still living), Virgil (1902-?), Malcolm "Gig" (1904-1970), Leon Strangeman (1906-1972), Robert Edward (1908-1973), David Franklin (1910-1910), Mary Elizabeth (1911-still living), and Roscoe Carmony (1915-1990).

Children of Austin and Lorena Johnson. Top L-R: Charles, Don, Emor, Glen, Raymond, Ted. Seated L-R: Virgil, Gig, Pete, Bob, Mary, Roscoe.

Lorena spent her life having and raising children. She was heard to have said that at one time she wasn't away from her home, not even to Greentown, for a period of three years! She was known for her wit and sense of humor; many came to her for her wise counsel. On Sept. 21, 1940 Austin passed away and was buried in the Greenlawn Cemetery. In 1948 at the age of 80 Lorena was chosen as the Centennial Queen for Greentown's Centennial Celebration. The last five years of her life were spent in Windfall, IN at the home of her only daughter, Mary Ericson, a nurse. Lorena died Feb. 8, 1961 and was buried next to her husband in the Greenlawn Cemetery.

The Johnson children soon married, but did not carry on the tradition of uniquely large families. Charles married Wilma Young April 10, 1922; Don married Lorena Lowe Nov. 27, 1925; Emor married Harriet Mae Stiefenhoefor March 30, 1920; Glen married first Tressie Little July 1920 then Roxey Cohee-Shesteck; Raymond married Stella McWilliams in 1927; Ted married Lucille Kelly Aug. 7, 1937; Virgil married Annie Rajala Sept. 3,1 955; Malcolm "Gig" married Eleanor Lukoviak Oct. 31, 1936; Leon never married; Bob married Ruth Dunlap May 31, 1952; Mary married Dr. Harold Ericson Aug. 4, 1956; and Roscoe married Ruth Baker Feb. 6, 1949. Austin and Lorena had a total of 27 grandchildren.

Austin L. Johnson and wife, Ruth Lorena (Penland).

Several of the sons moved north to Michigan in hopes of making a better life for themselves and their families. Some continued the well drilling that they came by naturally; others hired on with the well-paying automaking companies. Those moving north to Michigan were: Charles to Baraga, Don to Bruces Crossing, Glen to Detroit then later to Highland, Ted to Warren, and Gig to Lake Orion. *Sons serving during WWI. *Submitted by Cathie A. Sutterfield.*

JOHNSON - When David and Belinda Johnson settled near Greentown in Howard County, IN, as early settlers of the area in the spring of 1848, they had two children and were expecting a third. In the years to come they were to reach a total of 10 children. Today they have great-great-great-great-grandchildren reaching adulthood. Many of these descendents are buried in the old part of the Greentown Cemetery.

David and Belinda had 10 children, one of which was John, grandfather of Mable, Clyde, Ruby and Blanche.

Mable married Charles E. Kurtz. Charles is deceased and Mable resides at Century Villa nursing home in Greentown. She is 98 years old. They have one daughter, Cathryn, who married Ralph Lausch and they have four children and five grandchildren.

Ruby married Glen Fawcett. Ruby and Glen are deceased but are survived by Ernest and Dale. Ernest married Geneva Parsons and they have one son, John, and one grandchild. Dale married Margaret Little. They have two children, Gregory and Peggy, and three grandchildren.

Blanche passed away at an early age.

Children of Clyde and Tressie Johnson. Front: Nancy Echelbarger, Charles Johnson. Back: Von Johnson, Beverly Keith, Wayne Johnson and Joan Hullinger.

Clyde married Tressie McClain who passed away at age 48. They are survived by six children, Joan, Wayne, Beverly, Charles, Nancy and Von. After Tressie's death, Clyde married Lilith Middlesworth in 1953. Clyde worked at Continental Steel for more than 33 years. Clyde passed away in 1967 and Lilith makes her home with her daughter in Greentown.

Joan married Ned Hullinger and they are the parents of two sons, Keith and Kent. Joan and Ned reside in the Kokomo area.

Keith is married to the former Linda Reeves. They are the parents of three children, Pamela, Scott and Bart. Keith is employed at Delco Electronics. Keith and Linda live in the Kokomo area.

Kent married Aneta LeMasters and they have two daughters, Stephanie and Carrie. Kent and his family live in Texas and he works for Delco in Mexico.

Wayne is married to the former Betty Jean Thompson and they are the parents of three sons, Wayne Eugene, Jay C. and Gary Michael. Wayne served in the U.S. Navy. Wayne and Betty live in Arizona.

Eugene married Deborah Fredrick and they have three sons, Christopher (adopted), Richard Chandler and Scott Franklin. Eugene is employed by Delco.

Jay C. married Elizabeth Kay Wermoff and they have two daughters, Kimberly and Courtney. They reside out of state.

Gary has two children, Callie and Cale, and they also live out of state.

Beverly married Robert S. Keith and Bob is decease. They have three daughters, Christie, Becky and Susan. Beverly makes her home in St. Joseph, MI.

Christie has one daughter, Hannah, and they live in Michigan.

Becky is married to Kevin Umphries and they have two children, Ashley and Ian. Becky and her family live in Maryland.

Susan is not married and lives in Michigan in the same area as Beverly.

Charles is divorced. He makes his home in Sycamore, IN. He is retired from the United States Coast Guard and is also employed by Delco Electronics.

Nancy is married to James C. Echelbarger. They make their home in Greentown. Nancy and Jim had four children, Bret, Lisa, Conde and Brian. Jim works at Delco.

Bret married Debbie LaCluyse. They have two daughters, Kristen and Brianne. Bret is deceased. Debbie and her daughters live in Kokomo.

Lisa died shortly after birth.

Conde is married to Lori Birdsong. They have one son, Tyler. Conde and his family live near Greentown and he works at Delco.

Brian has one son, Brandon, and they live in the Greentown area. Brian also works at Delco.

Von is married to Catherine Clement and they have two children, Melissa and Michael. Von is retired from Delco and he, Cathy and Michael live in Sycamore. Michael is a student at Eastern.

Melissa is married to Ernest J. Fipps. They have two children, Kiersten and Ernest Joseph IV. Melissa and her family live in Sycamore.

DAVID JOHNSON - David Johnson was born Nov. 7, 1821 in Iredell County, NC to Strangeman Johnson and Mary Whitacre. David married Belinda Davis on June 15, 1843 in New Castle, IN. Belinda was born Sept. 25, 1823 in Preble County, OH to Jacob Davis and Rhoda Barnett. The newlyweds set up household near their parents in the western part of Henry County not far from Knightstown, also near Shirley and Wilkinson. Desiring to establish a home of their own, they left Henry County in the spring of 1848 and took claim to 40 wooded acres in Howard County, near Greentown, paying $1.25 an acre and obtaining the deed on foot from Ft. Wayne, the deed having been signed by Zachary Taylor, President. Upon his return from Ft. Wayne, David erected a pole shanty on his property covering it with bark stripped from elm trees, which sheltered his family until the fall when he made ready a one-room log cabin. Here David and Belinda raised nine of their ten children; John (1844-1925), Hannah Jane (1846-1924), William (1848-1930), Louisa (1851-1851), Mahale Emmaline (1852-1891), Anderson (1854-1942), Mary M. (1857-1930), Isabelle (1859-1935), Austin Lincoln (1862-1940) and Oliver Morton (1864-1953). Besides caring for her own children, Belinda also raised Glen Lindley, the son of her niece who died.

Children of David and Belinda Johnson. Standing L-R: Jennie, Austin, Oliver and Isabelle. Seated L-R: William, Emma, John, Mary and Anderson.

The Johnson children all married and had families of their own. John married Elizabeth Harriet Covalt in 1866, the daughter of Jonathan and Rachel Covalt. To them was born Charles W. Johnson in 1867, the first grandchild. William married Eliza Emily Young, the daughter of Henry and Ellinor Young, in 1874. In 1881 Hannah Jane (Jennie) married Thomas Price. Emma married Isaac Murphy. In 1882 Mary married Dr. Daniel Peters, son of Pernell and Leona (Spanwell) Peters, both natives of Maryland. A son, grandson and great-grandson have become doctors also. Isabelle married Austin Willits in 1885, the son of Austin H. and Sarah Ellen (Lindley) Willits. Oliver married Elnora Turner, Anderson married Olive Colescott and in 1889 Austin married Lorena Penland, the daughter of Hiram Fernandes and Letitia (Price) Penland of Indiana and Michigan.

Three of the Johnson family members distinguished themselves in Howard County politics. John became a justice of the peace and William served a term as township trustee. Anderson Johnson served both as Howard County Treasurer and as State Representative. John served in the Civil War, enlisting in October 1864 at the age of 20, as a private in Co. I, 142nd Regt. of the Indiana Volunteer Inf. He was stationed in Nashville and engaged in the second battle there in December 1864. He was discharged in 1865 as a corporal. *Submitted by Cathie A. Sutterfield*

EDWARD JOHNSON - Edward Johnson was born July 22, 1925 in Greentown, IN to Glen Johnson and Roxey Cohee-Shesteck both of Greentown. Ed spent a very small portion of his life in Greentown with memories as a small boy riding his tricycle in the back of his parents' restaurant in town. By 1930 his parents had moved to Toledo, OH where his father worked for an automobile company, later moving to Detroit, MI where Ed began school. After he graduated from Denby High School in 1943, he entered the Navy Air Corps in July of that same year. By October 1945 he was a Naval Aviation Cadet, left the service, and began attending the Lawrence Institute of Technology in Southfield, MI in January 1946 and graduated June 1949 with a Bachelor of Science and Mechanical Engineering degree. He began attending the YMCA group in Pontiac, and there he met his wife-to-be, Helen Bullock, the daughter of Perry and Delia (Patterson) Bullock of Pontiac, formerly of Alabama. Helen was born March 29, 1928 in Pontiac, MI; raised in Flat Rock and Pontiac.

1963 Ed Johnson Family—Ed, Caryn, Cindy, Gary, Cathie, Helen.

Ed and Helen began dating the fall of 1948 and were married in Pontiac on June 23, 1950. They purchased a small log home near Ed's parents in Highland, MI. Ed was working as an engineer for Turner Engineering Electrical Construction Company in Detroit from 1949 until 1960, while building a new home in White Lake Township for his growing family of our children: Caryn Dawn born June 14, 1951; Gary Glen born Nov. 29, 1953; Cathie Ann born Jan. 9, 1955; and Cindy Lynn born July 10, 1959. In March 1960 Ed hired on with General Motors Company as an electrical and mechanical engineer at the Milford Proving Grounds. In April 1964 he was promoted to Manager of Plant Utilities and retired on Aug. 1, 1980 at the age of 55. Ed's love of flying led him to purchase the Lewiston Airport (northern Michigan) where he could fly and store his airplane. In 1961 he and Helen purchased lakefront property on East Twin Lake, near the airport, and had built a two bedroom cottage for family summer vacations and winter ski trips. Ed enjoys his time up north where he can relax and get away. Some of Ed's nicknames growing up were Rusty, Carrot Top and George. To date Ed and Helen have a total of 13 grandchildren, all living in Michigan. *Submitted by Cathie A. Sutterfield*

FLEMING AND RACHEL (BUNDY) JOHNSON - Fleming Johnson, son of Robert and Milley (Stanley) Johnson and grandson of Dempsey and Mourning Johnson, was born Sept. 24, 1833, in Marlboro, Stark County, OH, and died May 22, 1910. At the age of 19, his family moved to Howard County where they cleared the land for farming. On March 15, 1855, he married Rachel Bundy, daughter of Samuel and Priscilla Bundy, born Sept. 9, 1834, near Carthage, Hancock County, IN, and died March 27, 1904. They settled on a homestead near West Middleton, IN. Fleming engaged in sawmilling, farming, and carpentering. They were members of the Friends Church. Eleven children were born as follows: 1. Samuel B.; 2. Elva S.; 3. Laura S., who married Albert Lindley; 4. Charles W., who married (1) Dora E. Wilson and (2) Lillian (Stratton) Johnson; 5. John W., who married Lillian Stratton; 6. Milley P., who married Charles E. Carter; 7. Sarah Ann, who married John Bowers; 8. Joseph Bundy, who married Emma E. Rosenberger; 9. Abram L.; 10. Margaret Elizabeth (see below); 11. Martha R.

The Fleming Johnson Family—(seated L-R) Joseph B., Fleming, Margaret E., Martha R., Rachel B., Abram L. (standing L-R) Milley P., Sarah A., Charles W., John W., Elva S., Laura S.

The tenth child of Fleming and Rachel, Margaret Elizabeth Johnson, was born Jan. 6, 1875, in Honey Creek Township, Howard County, and died Nov. 3, 1962. On Dec. 20, 1906, she married Samuel Edward Turner, son of Rev. Jesse T. and Avis (Maddock) Turner, born Oct. 10, 1868, in Tonganoxie, KS, and died Dec. 23, 1964. Samuel was a graduate of William Pinkham School of Theology of Cleveland, OH and owned a farm midway between New London and Russiaville. Margaret was a loyal member of the Women's Christian Temperance Union. They were members of the Russiaville Friends Church and are buried in the New London Cemetery. Seven children were born as follows: 1. Avis Rachel (see below); 2. Harriet Esther, who died when she was 10; 3. Iryl J., who married (1) Wava Mae Maurer and (2) Mary (Stark) Givens; 4. Stanley Ward, who died at birth; 5. Milley Frances, who married Elmer Granville Merrill; 6. Fred Lewis, who married Sarah Evalyn Park; 7. Edith Marie, who married Frank W. Johnston.

The first child of Samuel and Margaret, Avis Rachel Turner, was born Dec. 2, 1907, in Howard County, and died March 25, 1992. On June 6, 1950, she married Ralph Henry Criss, son of Herschel W. and Virginia (Smith) Criss, born July 12, 1909, in Howard County. Avis graduated from Asbury College in 1932 and taught school for many years, was a missionary in China, and a loyal member of the Women's Christian Temperance Union and Friends Church. Ralph is a retired minister. One son was born to Avis and Ralph.

Jonathan Dean Criss was born Nov. 24, 1951, in Howard County. He is a 1974 graduate of Taylor University and is an insurance claims investigator. On May 31, 1980, he married Diana L. (Prifogle) Curl, daughter of Carl and Virginia (Rinehart) Prifogle, born March 3, 1950, in Howard County. They have two children, Stacey Marie and Jason Thomas. *Submitted by Dean Criss.*

GLEN JOHNSON - Glen Johnson was born Sept. 22, 1896 in Greentown, IN. He was the fourth son of Austin Lincoln Johnson and Ruth "Lorena" Penland. Glen was raised in Greentown and graduated from Greentown High School Class of 1915 (21 students). He enlisted for WWI Dec. 11, 1917 and served in active duty in Germany and France receiving a Victory Medal. He was honorably discharged on Aug. 6, 1919 at Camp Sherman, OH. His army records describe him as 21 years of age, gray eyes, brown hair, ruddy complexion, 5'7" tall, single, in good physical condition and of excellent character. His vocational knowledge was that of a tailor. His remarks stated that he would be returning to Greentown after his discharge.

Glen did return and married Tressie Irene Little on Jan. 31, 1920 (no record found). Tress was born Feb. 18, 1897 in Howard County to Sanford and Elizabeth (Mast) Little, one of nine children. Glen and Tressie had one son, Ernest Eugene ("Gene") born Dec. 10, 1923 in Greentown and died July 1, 1987 in Columbus, GA. Glen and Tress operated a restaurant in Greentown around 1921. Before 1925 Glen and Tress divorced, and their son, Gene, was raised by Tress' parents while she worked. She later remarried Harold Gebhart on Nov. 14, 1931 and moved to Ft. Wayne. Tress died July 26, 1944 at the age of 47.

Glen Johnson 1915 high school graduation picture.

Glen worked as a machinist and laborer after his divorce. He began courting Roxey Cohee-Shesteck who he married. Roxey was the daughter of Frank and Vesta (McGraw) Cohee, born July 17, 1897 in Greentown. Together they had one son named Edward, born July 22, 1925 in Greentown. Glen, Roxey and Ed moved to Toledo, OH before 1930 and then to Detroit, MI; living in several apartments during the Depression years. Eventually they settled in a Miller Street apartment above a drugstore where Ed worked his first job. Around 1937-38 they purchased a cottage in Highland Township, Oakland County, MI. This was used as their summer residence and became a permanent residence in 1946.

Glen worked as a general foreman at the Plymouth Division in Mount Elliott for Chrysler Corporation; retiring from there at age 62 in 1959. Glen was a member of the Masons' Greentown Lodge No. 341, F.&A.M. since 1920. In his retirement years he enjoyed his four grandchildren, fishing, reading, gardening, and listening to Tiger ballgames in his chicken coop. Roxey died of cancer on Jan. 4, 1971.

Glen contacted an oldtime friend, Helen Sdunek, who was his constant companion for the last 13 years of his life. He died of a heart attack on March 14, 1984 at his home on Lester Drive in Highland, MI. Glen was buried next to Roxey in the Highland Cemetery in Highland, MI. *Submitted by Cathie A. Sutterfield*

JESSE JOHNSON - In September of 1866 Jesse Johnson, Martha Butler Johnson and their seven children, ranging in age from one year old through approximately sixteen years of age, moved from the family farm of Dempsey and Martha Johnson, his second wife, in Marlborough Township, Stark County, OH to the young city of Kokomo.

Jesse and Martha, both being of Quaker backgrounds, were active with the Friends in Kokomo and both observed Friends' customs. The family was active in the newly established Kokomo Monthly Meeting of Friends which began in 1867. Martha Johnson became active in the newly formed Sunday School in 1868.

Jesse Johnson was born Sept. 29, 1803 in Nansemond County VA of Dempsey and Mourning Johnson of Isle of Wight, VA.

Robert, the younger brother to Jesse, born Aug. 20, 1806 preceded Jesse to Indiana by moving from Marlborough Township to Howard County, IN prior to 1866, purchasing a farm near New London, Howard County, IN. Robert married Milley Stanley in 1832 in Ohio and this union yielded nine children. Robert and Milley remained on the farm in Howard County until their deaths (Robert, March 30, 1891 and Milley, Sept. 30, 1892. The lives of the nine children are not known but some of the offspring are probably living in the immediate area.

Jesse married Martha Butler on Dec. 7, 1842 in Marlborough Township, Stark County, OH. They had nine children with two dying before the family moved to Kokomo, IN in the fall of 1866. Jesse purchased Lot 61 in the Sills and Richmonds subdivision in the City of Kokomo in June of 1866 prior to moving to the city. The family lived on this site for many years. Whether a house existed on the lot or a new building was constructed is not known. In November of 1866, Jesse purchased 22-1/2 acres of land outside the city in Section 31, township 24, Range 4 East. This land was developed into a productive orchard for the family.

Jesse Johnson (born Oct. 29, 1803-died March 1879; Kokomo 1866-1879); Martha Butler Johnson wife of Jesse Johnson (born Nov. 30, 1821; married Dec. 7, 1842; died June 22, 1888).

The older children received their early schooling in Ohio before moving to Kokomo but James and Albert Lincoln were educated in the Kokomo City School System. All seven of the children were fine students due to the basic emphasis the Friends put upon education at all levels.

Joseph D. Johnson, the eldest son of Jesse and Martha, died Oct. 11, 1875 at the young age of 27. Joseph was the City Attorney of Kokomo and he had established plans for marriage. Joseph is interred in Crown Point Cemetery, Kokomo.

John Butler Johnson, the second son of Jesse and Martha, became a successful educator and author in the engineering field at Washington University, St. Louis, MO and the University of Wisconsin, Madison, WI. John Butler married Phoebe E. Henby of Wabash, IN, Nov. 12, 1878. They raised five children.

Mary Mourning, the eldest daughter, was born June 14, 1844 in Ohio. Mary became a teacher in the Kokomo Public Schools. Mary moved to Wayne County, IN where she became the principal of the Bethel School. While there, Mary met and married Anderson Toms in October 1868 in Kokomo by the Friends' ceremony.

Margaret, who had left a sweetheart in Ohio when the family moved to Kokomo, was claimed by Robert Colton, a grist mill owner of Belfontaine, OH.

Benjamin Bates, born Sept. 2, 1852 in Stark County, OH finished high school in Kokomo. In March of 1868 at the age of 16 he became the deputy postmaster of the Kokomo Post Office. Benjamin married Miss Clara C. Albaugh of Kokomo July 4, 1875. They had three children, two surviving, Edna and Fred Bates.

James D. was born Jan. 18, 1860. He grew up and was educated in Kokomo where he remained in various pursuits in the business world including the abstract business and the insurance business. James met and married Miss Maud A. Anderson of Kokomo on Oct. 20, 1881. They had one child, a girl named Edith.

Albert Lincoln, known as Bert, was born Dec. 15, 1865 just prior to the family moving to Kokomo. Bert received his early schooling in Kokomo, but at the age of 16 moved to St. Louis to live with John Butler, his brother and wife Phoebe who moved to St. Louis in 1882. Bert was a student at the manual training school and then graduated as a civil engineer from Washington University. Bert married Marion Cox June 16, 1897 and had four children, Dorothy, Marian, Alfred Lincoln and John Crittenden.

Jesse Johnson, a farmer by experience, changed to the mercantile business upon moving to Kokomo. Through an unfortunate business relationship, Mr. Johnson lost his mercantile business and was beset by pleurisy from which he never recovered. He passed away in Kokomo March 25, 1879 at the age of 75 years old. Mr. Johnson is interred in the Crown Point Cemetery, Kokomo.

Martha Butler Johnson died June 22, 1888 in Marion, IN at age 66 years old. Mrs. Johnson is interred in Crown Point Cemetery, Kokomo.

Lovingly submitted: Robert Dexter Johnson, 2297 70th Street, (Lakeshore Drive) Fennville, MI 49408. "The Porches", built by John Butler Johnson, (my grandfather), in 1897 is currently a seasonal Bed and Breakfast owned and operated by Bob and Ellen Johnson. *Submitted by Robert D. Johnson.*

RICHARD L. AND CANDY JONES - Richard L. Jones was born in Muncie, IN, the son of Clifford D. and L. Helen (Roush) Jones. Reared and schooled in Muncie, he entered the U.S. Air Force after high school graduation. While in the service he was stationed at Pease Air Force Base in Portsmouth, NH. While there he met and married Carol Craig. They had four children: Anthony Edward, Timothy Joel, Thomas John and Kristin Marie. After their divorce he moved back to Muncie. While there he had a daughter, Misti Dawn Newman Walsh. In 1978 he moved to Howard County.

Candy L. was born and raised in Kokomo, the only daughter of Donald E. and Gladyce M. (Rone) Schick. She married Dwayne H. Propes in Silva, NC. They had three children: Angelia Ranae, Rachel Leigh and Jason Cole. Candy also had an older daughter, Lia Anna.

Richard and Candy Jones

June 1, 1978 Richard and Candy were married at the home of Candy's brother, Randy, by Rev. Ray E. Cage, long-time next-door neighbor and friend of Candy. Joining their family of children were a nephew and a niece, Bruce E. and M. Lee Ann Stevens, who along with another niece, Paula Lynn Swan, had previously made their home with Candy. This made a truly blended family.

Only Jason remains at home. All the other children are scattered across the country. Tony married Deloris (Knight) Williams; they have one son, Anthony Edward II "A.J.". Tim married Nannette Wyrick, and Tom is yet to get serious with anyone. They all live in the Portsmouth area. Kris married Timothy Phillips, of Mitchell, IN, and they live in Southern California. Lia married Mark Douglas Muir and they live near Pontiac, MI. They have a daughter, Meredeth Ann. Bruce lives in Mt. Vernon, IL while Lee Ann was married to Samuel Edwin Langley. They have two adopted children, Jessica and Dylan. They live near Jacksonville, FL. Paula was killed in a car wreck in August 1988. She leaves a son Anthony Bryan Light, who also lives in Mt. Vernon, IL. Angie married Peter Markopoulos and they live near Huntsville, AL with their son Nikolas. Rachel married Keith Stewart Heitzman and they live in Aiken, SC. Misti is a student at Vincennes

University and divides her time between Muncie and LaPorte, IN.

Candy worked at Delco for many years before going out on disability. She is the current president of the Howard County Genealogy Society. She is also Co-Director of the Indiana Adoption Coalition, as well as group leader for the Support of Search group. An avid genealogist, she has served the genealogy society in various offices. She is also active with the Gen. James Cox Chapter, NSDAR.

Richard's life work has been in the auto body and paint field. Old car restoration is his passion. They met in 1976 when they both were active with their own Van Clubs. They became officers in the state council and their mutual love of travel and camping brought them together. *Submitted by Candy L.P. Jones.*

JAMES "MARION" JONES - James "Marion" Jones was my great-great-grandfather. He was born Jan. 12, 1865 in Hawkins County, TN. Marion moved to Howard County, IN about 1914 and died on Sept. 1, 1940 in Kokomo. He worked at the Steel Mill and worked for the City of Kokomo also. Marion married Theodoria Jane (Dosha) Parker. Dosha was born Jan. 25, 1869 in Hawkins County, TN and died on April 10, 1911 in Hawkins County, TN. To this union were born three siblings: Martha Bell, James Lafayette, and Benjamin Franklin. After moving to Kokomo, James Marion married Maude (Brown) Cook on April 10, 1915 in Kokomo. He is buried at Crown Point Cemetery in Kokomo, IN.

My great-grandfather was James Lafayette "Fate" Jones; he was born Jan. 2, 1889 in Hawkins County, TN and died on July 5, 1966 in Center, Howard County, IN. He married Ida Bell Brown on Aug. 14, 1908 in Hawkins County, TN. She was born Oct. 30, 1890 and died on Nov. 20, 1920 in Kokomo, Howard County, IN. She was buried in Hawkins County, TN. Born to Fate and Ida were four siblings: Verna Hazel, Lawrence Arnold James, John Earl, and Nora Maxine. Fate married Nellie (Young) Gordon in 1928. He retired from Continental Steel in the open-hearth electrical department after 24 years. Fate Jones is buried at Albright Cemetery in Howard County.

Left to right, top row: James Lafayette (Fate) Jones, Ida Belle (Brown) Jones and Benjamin (Ben) Jones. Bottom row: James Marion Jones holding Verna Jones and Dosha Jane (Parker) Jones. Picture was taken 1910.

My grandfather is John "Earl" Jones Sr. He was born on Oct. 4, 1914 in Watonwan County, MN. He married Thelma Mae Hughes on April 2, 1934. She was born in Prairie Township in Tipton County, IN on May 6, 1917; to this union were born two siblings: Barbara Ann and John Earl Jr. My grandfather retired from Mohr Construction of Kokomo, IN. My grandfather and grandmother celebrated their 60th anniversary on April 2, 1994. Earl passed away on May 14, 1994; he is buried at Memorial Park Cemetery, Kokomo, IN.

My father is John Earl Jones Jr.; he was born April 17, 1937 Howard County, Kokomo, IN and married my mother, Freda Juanita Bradley, who was born July 25, 1940 in White County, AR. They were married in Oakford, Howard County, IN on Sept. 27, 1959. To this union were born two siblings: Robin Jo and John Earl III.

I am Robin Jo (Jones) Herrell, born Aug. 21, 1960 in Kokomo, IN. I married Dennis Jay Herrell in Kokomo, Howard County, IN on Aug. 14, 1981. Dennis was born Nov. 8, 1962 in Kokomo, Howard County, IN. To this union were born two siblings Rachael Dawn, Rebekah Deeann, and we are expecting another child in October 1994. Rachael Dawn was born March 1, 1983 and Rebekah Deeann was born Oct. 18, 1986.

My brother, John Earl Jones III, was born Jan. 31, 1963 and after an automobile accident on the US 31 Bypass at the corner of Morgan in Kokomo, IN, he passed away on Dec. 24, 1978. When little Johnny passed away, it was the hardest and saddest time for the whole family. We miss him very much; he may be gone, but he'll never be forgotten. He is with Jesus now. *Submitted by Robin Jo Herrell.*

CHARLES N. AND MARGARET A. JORAY - The Joray family moved to Howard County in 1982 when Charles began his work as the director of the public library in Kokomo. They live at 4606 Stratford Drive in the Devon Woods subdivision.

Charles, who was born Oct. 18, 1949 in Bluffton, Wells County, IN; is the second son of William and Delores (Egly) Joray. Margaret, who is known as Peggy, was born Nov. 4, 1951 in Evansville, Vanderburgh County, IN. She was the third of six children of Paul and Rosemary (O'Brien) Keil.

Charles received a Bachelor of Science degree in social studies from Ball State University in 1971 and a Master of Library Science degree from Indiana University in 1973. In 1974 Peggy received a Bachelor of Science degree in dietetics from Purdue University and also completed her dietetics internship at Indiana University Medical Center.

Charles and Peggy were married Jan. 24, 1975 in the Washington D.C. Temple of the Church of Jesus Christ of Latter-Day Saints.

They have four children: Craig Alan, born July 8, 1976; Bruce Charles, born Sept. 22, 1978; Elizabeth Erin, born May 21, 1981 and Molly Kathleen, born Feb. 6, 1984. The first three children were born in Bluffton, Wells County, IN while Molly, their fourth child, was born in Kokomo, Howard County, IN.

At the time of this writing, Charles has been the director of the Kokomo-Howard County Public Library for nearly 12 years. Peggy spends most of her time being a homemaker and mother, but she also works part-time as a consulting dietitian at long term care facilities in Logansport, Rochester, and Kokomo.

Charles enjoys playing the piano and has taken piano lessons for 20 years. He is a member of Kokomo Morning Musicale. He also likes to read, especially books and periodicals about the Amish. Peggy enjoys art and reading fiction and is a member of the Kokomo Art Association and the Delphian Reading Club. Peggy is also a Girl Scout leader.

Their children enjoy a variety of activities. Craig is an Eagle Scout and participates in scouting and his high school swim team. Bruce is also an Eagle Scout and in addition to scout activities, he enjoys playing the piano and is on the high school soccer team as well s the Kokomo Traveling Soccer Team. Elizabeth loves to read and she also takes piano lessons. Molly enjoys acting and singing and has participated in church, school and community drama productions. She is also a girl scout. Both girls enjoy playing with the family's two pets - a dog named Snickers and a cat named Mittens.

All four children attend school at Northwestern.

The entire family are active members of the Church of Jesus Christ of Latter-Day Saints in Kokomo.

JORDAN - The early Jordans who came to Howard County were Alexander (1823-1878) and Sarah (McClain) Jordan (1830-1919). Alexander was born in Pennsylvania, moving to Ohio and about 1845 to Jonesboro, Grant County, IN. Sarah McClain was born in Perry County, OH. With her parents John and Elizabeth (Mover), she came to Fairmount, Grant County in 1846. On Aug. 8, 1847, she and Alexander were married. They had six children, George (1848), who died in infancy, John J. (1851-1941), Mary Elizabeth (1854-1928), Moses Benjamin (1856-1938), Amanda F. (1861-1941), and Anna M. (1863-1950).

In the mid-1850s, the Jordans moved to Jerome, Union Township, Howard County, IN where he was employed as a miller. Later the Jordans moved on west to Kokomo where Alexander was employed as a machinist until his death in 1878. Sarah then moved with her children to Clinton County, just across the Howard County line near her son John who lived at Cloverdale.

Ross and Mary Jane Jordan

John married Lucinda Johnson (1848-1927) on Dec. 7, 1873. Lucinda came to Indiana from Somerset County, PA with her parents, Hiram (1825-1863) and Maria (Enos) (1827-1899) in 1851. Six children were born to this union: Clarence Elmer (1875) who died in infancy, Lewellyn (1876), Estella May (1880), Walter T. (1882-1965), Mandie (1884), and Grace (1887).

Walter T. and Mable Grace Shaw (1885-1965) were married Feb. 2, 1906. Eight children were born to this union: Ross G. (1906), Ralph L. (1908-1975), Violet Ione (1910), Vivian Irene (1913), Velma Iretha (1915), Herbert Leo (1920-1944), John Herman (1924), and Donald Joseph (1927).

Ross G. married Edith L. Fletcher (1907-1989) on Dec. 5, 1925. Three children were born to this union: Ross Glen, Jr. (1927), Lee Dwayne (1930-1990), and Mona Ione (1932).

Ralph L. married Helen Iretha Leckrone. They had one daughter Janet Elaine (1937-1988), and four sons: Larry Wayne (1940), Ralph L. (1944), Sumner Leo (1946-1947), and Rickie Dale (1953).

Violet Ione married Louis Lopez and they had no children.

Vivian Irene married Dallas B. Gross and they have four children: James B. (1935), Arthur E. (1937), Burl W. (1942-1951), and Bon E. (1955).

Velma Iretha married Herbert Carver and they have two children: Ronald D. (1939), and Janice I. (1942).

Herbert L. never married and was killed at Epinal, France in WWII.

John H. married Carmen Raney and they have four children: Bonnie Diane (1947), Robert G. (1948), John William (1956), and David E. (1960).

Donald Joseph married Sharon Redmon and they have two children: Jerry (1958), and Joseph (1959).

Ross G. Jr., author of this article, was born in Forest Township, Clinton County, and attended grade school in Forest, Russiaville, New London and Cutler. He attended Purdue University and served with the U.S. Navy Seabees in the Pacific area in WWII. In 1949 he married Annabelle Schafer and they have one son, Steven K. (1953) a computer systems analyst in Indianapolis. In 1957 he married Mary Anne Farley of Chicago, IL. They have one son Jeffrey D. (1959) a pharmacist in Batesville, IN. Ross retired from Delco Electronics in 1989 as a design engineer and Mary Anne retired as a high school teacher.

Over 100 descendants of Alexander and Sarah Jordan now live in Howard and adjacent counties of Clinton, Carroll, and Miami.

KANABLE - The Kanables came in a group of 52 to Howard County in 1845 from Somerset County, PA and settled around Russiaville. They were descendants of German immigrants. Jacob Kanable, Jr. (1781-1871) was the first to change the spelling from Knable to Kanable. His father, Jacob, Sr. was in the Revolutionary War. Jacob Jr. married Magdalena Enos (1786-1875) in

1803 and had 17 children. Magdalena was daughter of George Enos (Ennis) and Ann Guin, whose parents also migrated from Germany.

The 11th child of Jacob, Jr., Samuel Enos Kanable (1820-1874) married his third wife, Mary Catherine (Polly) Fritz (1830-1910) in 1857. Her parents, Catherine Shultz (1804-1879) and Christian Fritz (1807-1882), descendants of German immigrants, arrived in Howard County around Russiaville, in 1846 from Somerset County, PA. Christian's grandfather, Christian W. Fritz, was in the Revolutionary War. Christian Fritz was reported to be the wealthiest farmer in Howard County prior to his death. Samuel Enos and Polly had eight children.

Jim Graham, John Elmer Kanable, Loretta Fisher, Irene (Kanable) Taylor.

Their seventh child was John Elmer Kanable (1871-1926), born near Dow's Corner. He married Emma Cecil Hodson (1886-1956) in 1902. She was born in Russiaville, first child of David Benton Hodson (1866-1934) and Lenora Catherine Pixler (1868-1908). Lenora was daughter of Mahala Leming (?-1874) and Thomas Van Pixler (1838-1913). Thomas was in the Civil War in the Indiana Inf., 12th Regt. David Benton Hodson was the 10th child of David Hodson (1823-1898) and Delilah Hart (1828-1909). David Hodson was a minister, a school teacher, and a chaplain of the Indiana Volunteer Inf., 89th Regt. in the Civil War. He was the youngest of 13 children of George W. Hodson (1775-1837) and Sarah Powell (?-1855). Delilah Hart was the daughter of Miles Hart (1805-1875) and Amy Chaney (1806-1877) and wife of David Hodson. The Hart and Hodson families were Scottish-Irish and migrated to Howard County in 1849 from North Carolina by way of Highland County, OH and Madison County, IN. John Elmer Kanable and Emma Cecile owned a grocery store in Russiaville until 1919. They moved to Frankfort for three years, owning a grocery store and restaurant; returned to Russiaville in 1922 and owned a grocery store, then a restaurant.

Edith Josephine Kanable (1904-) was the first of eleven children born to John Elmer and Emma Cecile. She married in 1920 to Don Alexander, had son John C. Alexander, who was killed 1945 as a Marine fighter pilot. She divorced and married in 1930 to Roy C. Bogan (1902-1957) from Terhune, Boone County, who had one son, James Ragene Bogan. They lived in Terhune, had son, George Alfred Bogan, and daughter, Patty Arline Bogan. Jo and Roy owned a grocery store for two years in Kirklin; moved to Kokomo for one year, and in 1951 moved to Orlando, FL. Jo Kanable Bogan is still living at age 90 in Florida and has grandchildren and great-grandchildren living in Kokomo. *Submitted by Patty Arline Bogan Locke.*

KANABLE-FRITZ-HART-HODSON-PIXLER - We were always told we were related to half the people in Russiaville. Our ancestors came to Honey Creek and nearby townships. I want to give theirs and their children's names.

First my parents: John Elmer Sr. and Emma Cecile (Hodson) Kanable. Their 11 children: Josephine (Alexander) Bogan, Mildred O'hara, Catherine Heaton, Irene Taylor, Margaret Daniels, Ira, Mary (Merrifield) Smith, Helen Waddell, John Elmer Jr., Genevieve Huffer and Robert. All born from 1904 to 1924, in and near Russiaville.

John Elmer Sr. was the son of Samuel Enos Kanable and Mary Catherine Fritz. He was born in Clinton County. Mary was the daughter of Christian and Mary Catherine (Shultz) Fritz.

Great-grandparents: Christian and Catherine Fritz. They lived in Monroe Township near Russiaville. He was a farmer and stock raiser. Children: Josiah, William, Elizabeth Humbert, John, Susan Vernon, Margaret Shaw, Chancy, Hiram and their fifth child Mary Catherine. All were born in Somerset County, PA.

Grandparents: Samuel Enos Kanable, a farmer, lived in Warren Township, Clinton County. Married first: Catherine Masters. Four children: Milton Shakespeare, Charles, Isabelle Riggs and Ellen DeMoss. Second: Mary Jane Lawrence. Two children: Mary Catherine Craig and Sarah Moriah. Third (my grandparents): Mary Catherine Fritz. Eight children: Elmira Margaret Lape, Martha Baker, Levi Seward, Emma Jane Harland, Mitilda Connaway, Curtis, John Elmer and Lorretta Pavey. All born 1841 to 1874. Samuel died in 1874 and buried in Sims Cemetery in a woods, now overgrown by brush and weeds. Mary then moved with her family to near Russiaville. Sims Cemetery is in Warren Township.

John Kanable Sr. grocery store in Russiaville, north side of Main Street 1913. A short time later moved across the street to a larger room. People shown, left to right: Behind counter, John Cochran, Jim Graham, Dr. Morris, D.D. Summers, and the owner, John.

Great-grandparents: Jacob and Magdalena (Enos) Kanable. Lived west of Russiaville. Fifteen of their seventeen children: Salome Ambrose, George, John, Jacob III, Elizabeth Walters, Levi, Catherine (unmarried), David, Mary Weigle, Rebecca Gribble, Samuel Enos, Amy Shultz, Susanne Wiltrout, Martha Brumbaugh, and Phoebe Chandler. All born in Pennsylvania 1804 to 1829. Levi, Rebecca, Susanne and Salome moved to Viola, WI in 1854. Honey Creek Township became part of Howard County in 1859.

Great-great-grandparents: Miles and Amy (Chaney) Hart. Ten children: John M., Delilah Hodson, Mary Hodson, Sarah Gray, Anna Brittian, Emily Pickering, Clementine Conner, Francis Marion Chaney, Benjamin B., and Eveline Lindle.

Great-grandparents: Delilah married David Hodson. Eleven children: Miles Jefferson, Drusilla Buroughs, Emma Buroughs, John Luke, William Eli, Isabella Dillon, Mary Shuck, Martha Graham, Sarah Boyd, David Benton, and Laura Bolin.

Grandparents: David Benton and Lenora Catherine (Pixler) Hodson. First marriage. Four children: Born 1886 to 1894, Cecile Kanable, Minnie DeFord, Inez Lamberson, and Ruth (Tate) Kosnot. Third marriage: Ethel Goodnight. Two children: Ferris and Grace McElfresh born 1915 and 1919.

Great-grandparents: Thomas Van and Mahala Pixler. He was a mail carrier in Russiaville. Children: Sarah Emmaline, Rivers, Lenora Catherine, Hodson, Amanda Mae Butz, Myrtle Lewis and an infant. Van married second Lydia Wilson. Children: Charles, Lessie, Willard Earl, Blanche Boyer, and Ira. All born 1866 to 1885.

All grandparents buried Russiaville. *Submitted by Margaret (Kanable) Daniels*

KANABLE-HUFFER - I am the daughter (Genevieve Kanable Huffer) of John E. Kanable and Emma Cecile (Hodson) Kanable, of Russiaville, IN. They had 11 children, I was their 10th child. I had seven sisters and three brothers: Josephine Bogan, Catherine Heaton, Mildred O'hara, Irene Taylor, Margaret Daniels, Ira Kanable, Mary Smith, Helen Waddell, John Kanable, Robert Kanable. I was born May 5, 1923 in Russiaville, IN. In 1942 I married Harold W. Huffer December 23, while he was in the U.S. Air Force, Gulfport, MS. He was the son of Earl E. Huffer and Susie Mae (Weaver) Huffer, of Frankfort. He has two sisters, Mary Iris Henderson, of Mooresville and Susanne Scharff of Kokomo. One brother died at the age of 10 months.

We have two daughters, Phyllis K. (Huffer) Carberry and Joyce Ann (Huffer) Darnell. We have two granddaughters, Jennifer M. Turley, Jessica N. Darnell, one grandson, Mark S. Williams (Ball State). Harold and I lived in Russiaville 20 years and now living in Forest, IN (30 years). We both retired from Delco Electronics, Kokomo. We now spend our winters at our Florida home. We celebrated our 50th Wedding Anniversary in 1992, an Open House, from our daughters and grandchildren at Main Street Christian Church Fellowship Hall. We are members of Russiaville Main St. Christian Church.

KARNS - Loyle Dean Karns, born in Wabash County to Earl Jacob and Anna Dean (Yager) Karns on Sept. 23, 1934. (A twin to Lowell Dean Karns.) Attended Ervin School 1942-1944 then moved back to Wabash County. Married Dec. 12, 1954 in Urbana, IN to Bonnie (Hunter) Karns. Moved to Taylor Township in Howard County in 1965, working at Chrysler Corporation for 30 years. Families are members/attending the Grace Brethren Churches in Kokomo and First Baptist Church in Florida. All children graduated from Taylor High School at Center. Bonnie Karns, born in Fulton County to Clarion Elijah Hunter and Emma Majesca (Thompson) Hunter on May 14, 1936. Working as a homemaker and medical transcriptionist.

Jeffrey Dean Karns, born in Wabash County on Aug. 29, 1956. Raised in Wabash County and Howard County. On Aug. 11, 1978 in Orlando, FL married Linda Kay Hughes (born to Raymond and Betty Richards Hughes of Maitland, FL on Sept. 1, 1956 in Tiffin, OH). They moved to Florida in 1981, now residing in Lakeland, FL. Jeffrey teaches and also coaches the Girls Varsity Basketball Team at Lakeland Christian School, having led his team to the State Finals in four of the past five years. Linda is a homemaker and a Billing Coordinator for the City of Lakeland Electric and Water Utilities. Jeffrey and Linda graduated from Grace College, Winona Lake, IN. They are the parents of three children: Erin Renee Karns, June 24, 1980 (Warsaw, IN), Jeffrey (Dean) Karns, Jr., July 18, 1983 (Avon Park, FL) and Brandon Scott Karns, April 22, 1986 (Avon Park, FL).

Gregrey Gene Karns, born in Wabash County on April 20, 1959. Raised in Wabash County and Howard County. On Aug. 25, 1979, in Howard County, married Penny Elaine Julius (born to Philip and Lois Delong Julius of Greentown on Nov. 13, 1960 in Howard County). They are the owners of Karns Engineering in Greentown, which designs molds. Penny is a housewife and is a secretary at KE. They are residing near Greentown. They are parents of three children: Dustin Gene Karns, Feb. 2, 1982; Joshua Adam Karns, May 11, 1984; and Tyler Brandon Karns, Jan. 17, 1986.

Rhonda Beth Karns Januszkiewicz, born in Wabash County on Sept. 4, 1962. Raised in Wabash County and Howard County. On Aug. 3, 1985, in Howard County, married Walter Kyle Januszkiewicz (born to Joseph and Josephine Alexander Januszkiewicz of State College, PA on Feb. 8, 1955 in Elwood City, PA). Rhonda is a homemaker and self-employed medical transcriptionist. Walter graduated from Bowling Green State University and is employed by EDS at Delco; he is also Company Commander HHC 2nd BDE Indiana National Guard. They are residing near Windfall. They are the parents of three children: Samantha Jo Januszkiewicz, May 16, 1987; Joseph Kyle Januszkiewicz, April 18, 1989; and Alexander George Januszkiewicz, Aug. 23, 1991.

Kristopher Todd Karns, born in Howard County on Feb. 14, 1968. Raised in Howard County. On June 18, 1988 married Amy Lynn Grawcock (born to John and

Linda Bugher Grawcock of Kokomo on Sept. 17, 1969 in Laguna Beach, CA). Kristopher was discharged from the U.S. Marines in August 1990, graduated from Indiana University, P.U.I. School of Medicine in May 1994 with degree in Health Information Administration. Amy is a housewife, an accounting clerk at 1st National Bank of Kokomo and is majoring in accounting at Indiana University. They live in Greentown. They are the parents of two children: Emily Kristine Karns, April 16, 1991 and Heidi Breanne Karns, April 19, 1994.

KELLAR - William Agun (1820-1887) and Susan Garr (1822-1907) Kellar came to Howard County, IN in 1854 from Jefferson County, KY. They purchased 150 acres of land west of Kokomo. The land consisted of dense woods and a sawmill was built and operated. Logs made into lumber and hauled by oxen helped to build Kokomo. William also engaged in agricultural pursuits, purchasing many other plots of land totaling nearly 500 acres. Nine children were born to William and Susan: Jane (1843); Georgie Ann (1845), she married Cornelius Smith in 1861; Mary Elizabeth (1846), she married Andrew Clore in 1867; Sarah Kate (1848), she married A.W. Moore; Lewis Cass (1850), he married Martha Pennington in 1874; Edward Bryant (1853), he married Anna Smith in 1876; Rebecca Ellen (1855), she married George Sellers in 1877; Isaac Hite (1857), he married Addie Sellers in 1878; and Charles Richard (1860), he married Mahala Ray in 1881. Of his sons, Lewis was a farmer, the other three operated Kellar and Co., a furniture and undertaking business in Kokomo. Isaac and Edward handled the furniture and Charles was in charge of the undertaking.

William's ancestors came originally from Switzerland. William's parents were Moses (1786-1851) and Catherine (1797-1878) Kellar who lived near Louisville, KY. Moses' parents were Isaac (ca. 1750-1786) and Elizabeth Kuykendall Kellar. Isaac, a captain in the Revolutionary War, was killed by Indians near Jeffersonville, IN. Isaac's father was Abraham Kellar (ca. 1720-1787). Abraham spent his adult life in Virginia, serving as a justice, trustee, and represented Shenandoah County in the Virginia House of Delegates.

Lewis Cass Kellar (1850-1915) and wife, Martha Pennington (1855-1933), had 12 children all born in Howard County: Anna Lee (1875-1937); William Lloyd (1877-1879); Charles Frederick (1879-1924); Grace Maud (1881-1900); Claude Earl (1883-1949); Katie Adella (1885-1977) Pearl (1887-1887); John Homer (1888-1962); Paul D. (1890-1952); Leslie D. (1892-1977); Lewis R. (1897-1981); and Martha (1900-1932). Lewis was a farmer and a shoe cobbler.

Paul D. Kellar (1890-1952) and wife, Joyce Hester Hile, had two sons, Paul D. Jr. (1915-1971) and Raymond L. (born 1926). Paul Sr. operated Kellar Brothers Grocery in Kokomo with brother Leslie until 1924. Then he joined the Kokomo Police Department, retiring as Chief in 1952.

Raymond L. Kellar and wife, Mary Helen Carico, had two children, Kathryn Elaine, (born 1952), (author of this article) and David Wayne, (born 1955). After WWII duty in the U.S. Navy, Raymond followed in his father's footsteps working 27 years for the Kokomo Police Department, also serving as Chief. Kathryn married Ronald Byram and now resides in Miami County with daughters, Kelly (born 1977) and Amanda (born 1981). David married Janice Shockey and still resides in Howard County with daughters, Mary Ann (born 1982) and Susan (born 1986). A son, Michael, died in 1985. Following in the footsteps of his father and grandfather, he is currently a captain on the Kokomo Police Department. Raymond and second wife, Ruth Van Neman, currently reside on a small portion of William Kellar's original land. Many other descendants still reside in Howard County.

KELLY-BURGETT-COOK - Roy Ernest Kelly was born March 1, 1903, in Clinton County, IN, the son of Samuel Edward Kelly and Dessie (Rollins) Kelly. He married Lelah Evelyn Burgett on Oct. 13, 1920. To this union were four children born: Lowell Fredrick; Kathryn Eloise; Homer Edward "Dick"; and Lora Jane. They made their home in Russiaville and Roy worked on the railroad as depot master. This marriage was dissolved by divorce July 7, 1934. Roy moved to Linden, IN, and remarried. He died in 1978.

Lelah Evelyn Burgett was born Sept. 24, 1904, in Frankfort, IN, the oldest daughter of Homer E. "Dick" and Stella (Stafford) Burgett. She grew up in the Russiaville area and attended school there with her four sisters: Kate, Anna Mae, Nora, and Beulah.

Lelah E. Cook

Lelah married Russell Lowell Cook, who was born Jan. 1, 1893, the son of Dr. James and Emily (Ratcliff) Cook of Russiaville, IN. Russell and Lelah had one child, James Russell Cook, born Aug. 26, 1944. Russell died on Sept. 30, 1971, in Russiaville and is buried in the Russiaville Cemetery.

Lowell Fredrick Kelly married Rachel Owens and they had two daughters: Elizabeth Tracy and Sherrie Algeria. Kathryn Eloise "Kay" Kelly married Richard Merle Jarrett and they had three children: Richard Merle, Jr.; Deborah Kay; and Kent Allen. Homer Edward "Dick" Kelly married Estell Alverez and they had four children: Connie; Richard; Daniel; and Edward. Jane married Harry "Junior" Hosier and they had one child, Marsha Leigh Hosier. Jim Cook is unmarried. Lelah has 10 great-grandchildren.

Lelah was a soloist and member of the choir of the First Baptist Church in Russiaville where she also taught Sunday School and Vacation Bible School for many years until moving to Champaign, IL, to live with her daughter and son-in-law, Kay and Dick Jarrett. She returned to Russiaville in 1985. All four of Lelah's children of her first marriage are deceased. Jim Cook lives near Rochester, MN.

KELLY AND KELLY KLANS - Russell E. Kelly and Marjorie Joan Kelly were introduced to each other on a warm summer night, July 23, 1953, by a mutual friend. Russell was listening to records in his 1953 cream and flamingo Ford hardtop convertible on the north side of the square in Kokomo. He had installed a P.A. system, 45 RPM record player and a 110 volt AC system in the car long before such things were available commercially. During their two years of courtship they listened to records such as "Sentimental Journey", "I Really Don't Want To Know", and other great oldies by Glen Miller, Lawrence Welk, and Vaughn Monroe. They were married June 19, 1955 in West Point Christian Church, a small country church south of Russiaville, IN. They are still very active at West Point.

Russell, along with his older sister, Oneda, and younger sister, Reba, were the children of Marion Orval Kelly and Martha Alice Name Kelly. The family lived most of their lives in Howard or Clinton County, IN. Orval's parents, John and Harriet Keiver Kelly, lived near New London, IN. Martha's parents, Hillary C. Name and Eliza Jane Crockett Name, lived most of their lives in Kokomo, IN. However, at one time they lived in Pulaski County, IN where Martha was born.

Russell graduated from Forest High School in 1945 and received a B.S. degree in business administration from Indiana University in 1975. After graduation from high school he farmed for one year, served in the Navy, then worked for International Harvester in Indianapolis for three years. He worked for Haynes International in Kokomo for 38 years. While at Haynes he had a variety of assignments. In June of 1979 he took the position of Inventory Controller for their national warehouse system, a position he held until he retired in May of 1986.

Russell Kelly Family. Back row, L-R: Julia Kelly, Joanne Kelly, Phillip Kelly, Kimila Lowry, Jeff Lowry. Front row, L-R: David Lowry, Joan Kelly, Matthew Lowry, Russell Kelly, Christopher Lowry.

Joan's family lived in several places in Kokomo and Howard County. Joan's father, Jesse Marion Kelly, was born March 26, 1902 in Ripley County, IN near Osgood. When Marion was 12 his mother, Lucinda Belle Monroe Kelly, died from injuries received in a buggy accident. Jesse Holman Kelly, his father, died of a snakebite two weeks later. After his parents' deaths, Jesse Marion came to Kokomo to live with his sister, Lesta Ruth Kelly Brown, wife of Dewey Brown. He became employed at Continental Steel Corp. and remained there until he retired in 1961.

On Nov. 26, 1927 Marion married Ruth Helton. Ruth's parents were John Robert Helton and Harriet Rosetta Martin Helton. She grew up in eastern Howard County. Marion and Ruth had four children, Marjorie Joan, Marilyn Jean, Shirley Jane and Max Allen. The highlight of each summer was vacation time. Ruth's creativity was made known by the many handmade garments she made for those three little girls and herself in preparation for vacation.

Joan graduated from West Middleton High School in 1947. She was employed at Delco Radio for nine years. In the summer of 1956 she left Delco to become a full time housewife and soon-to-be mother.

While Joan and Russell were engaged, they purchased a house and 10 acres east of New London, IN. They spent a hectic last three months of their engagement remodeling the house so they could move into it after they were married. They had three children so the house was enlarged and more acreage purchased. Kimila Ann, their oldest daughter, obtained a degree in dental hygiene from Indiana University. Kim married Jeffrey Lowry, now an attorney in Kokomo, and they have three boys, Christopher, David and Matthew. Their son, Phillip Wayne, obtained his degree in electrical engineering from General Motors Institute and is an engineer at Delco Electronics. Phil married Joanne Hunkler and they live in Kokomo. Their youngest daughter, Julia Elaine, obtained a degree in elementary education from Johnson Bible College. Julie is a church secretary for Kingsway Christian Church and lives in Indianapolis. Russell and Joan still live in the house near New London, IN.

KENDALL - The Kendall name has been spelled many ways. Peter Kandel (1783-1849) married Elizabeth Drushel in Somerset County, PA. He moved to Holmes County, OH, in 1815; that same year his third son, Joseph Kendall, was born. Joseph married Lizzie Hostetler on Nov. 10, 1839.

In 1848 the U.S. government opened the last of the Miami Reserve in Howard County for settlement. Joseph Kendall came, bought 160 acres for $2 an acre, and returned to Ohio. In 1849 he brought his family and settled permanently two miles north and one mile west of the present village of Plevna. A farmer, he lived on this land until late in life, when he moved to land across the road in Miami County; he died there Jan. 26, 1892, and was buried in the Kendall Cemetery, for which he allotted ground.

Ten children were born to Joseph and Lizzie Kendall. Their first born was John Kendall (1840-1907), nick-

235

named "Big John" to distinguish him from his cousin "Little John" Kendall (1845-1921). Big John lived on the Joseph Kendall farm; he married Catherine Hershberger and they were the parents of seven children. After Catherine's death he married Alice Smith. Big John died April 8, 1907.

Family of Nathaniel Kendall.

Nathaniel Kendall was the first-born (May 10, 1864) of Big John and Catherine Kendall. He married Martha Gerhart on Dec. 17, 1885; four sons and four daughters were born to them. They worshipped at the Brethren Church in Plevna.

Nathaniel Kendall was an energetic man. Short and stocky, he worked the home farm, putting up the buildings that stand today, far back from the road. He operated a sawmill and a tile factory; he was usually the first to have any new device to make his operation more efficient.

He owned 150 well-improved acres of the home farm, and he owned another parcel in Miami County just down the road from his home. When the existing house burned, he moved his sawmill there and erected the house that stands today.

Nathaniel Kendall worked the home farm all his life, until he died Feb. 2, 1935; his grave is marked by a large gray tombstone in Kendall Cemetery.

Vern E. Kendall (1887-1967) was the second born and first son of Nathaniel and Martha Kendall. He lived across from the home farm in Miami County, where Joseph Kendall once lived. He married Dora Webb (1885-1958); their son Eugene L. Kendall (1917-1991) moved to the Nathaniel Kendall farm at the death of Martha Kendall, in 1957. Gene Kendall married Marcile Osborne, who now lives on the home farm.

Their children are Terry (born April 26, 1952), Janalyce K. (Hatton) (born Aug. 8, 1954), and Joanne E. (born Oct. 22, 1957), who presently lives in Dallas, TX. The Kendall family worships at the Howard-Miami Mennonite Church, down the road from their homes. Terry Kendall married Karen Yoder, and their children are Philip (born Jan. 2, 1983) and Joseph (born Jan. 1, 1989).

Today Terry Kendall works the soil of the Kendall homestead, which Joseph Kendall first homesteaded in 1848, and was built up by Nathaniel Kendall. *Submitted by Jeff Hatton*

KENDALL - William Harvey Kendall, son of Christian J. and Anna (Yoder) Kendall, was born Feb. 18, 1875 on a farm in Miami County, IN. On Feb. 27, 1898 in Howard Township, Howard County, IN, he married Cora Dell Templin, daughter of William Timothy and Cerena Florence (McQuiston) Templin, who was born Jan. 11, 1880 in a tiny cabin east of Hopewell Church, east of Kokomo, Howard County, IN.

Both families' ancestors migrated from Germany. William courted Cora by horse and buggy. Later years an open Model T Ford. Younger children sat on older children's laps. Put side-curtains on when it rained. Family had a bob sleigh to ride, "O what fun we had riding in a one-horse-open-sleigh". William and Cora lived their entire life on the farm in Howard County, with 62 years at the homeplace in Howard Township. They sold a section of land for the Howard Township School, built in 1916-17. Both died at their homeplace, William on Jan. 7, 1965 and Cora on March 24, 1965, and were buried in Memorial Park Cemetery, northeast part of Kokomo, IN.

Wm. Harvey Kendall, Cora Dell Kendall - married Feb. 27, 1898. Lived together over 66 years.

Both were members of former Rich Valley Christian Church. They were parents of nine children, all born at home in Howard County. First son stillborn; Elsie Fern, deceased; Merle Marie, deceased, married Charles E. Meadors; Lewis Ren, deceased, married Bessie Rockey, deceased; John William, deceased, married Mary M. Householder; Fred Earl, married Letha M. Dean; Mary Florence, married J.W. Whitezel, deceased; Martha Anna, married Chester C. Parker; Harold Richard married Mary K. Spangler, deceased, Esther Stine and Fayfern Dunkle.

All living children attended the Howard Township School. They participated in school activities, 4-H Club, Farm Bureau, Farmers Institute, Homemaker's Club and other community services. Boys were farmers and Fred and Harold served in WWII 1941-45. William Harvey raised corn, beans, and potatoes. Each child had his own bucket to pick up potatoes. He took part in Farm Bureau, Farmers Institute, Director of Farm Bureau Co-op, a fair exhibitor at local, county and state. William was elected, four year term, to serve on County Council of Howard County. He was chosen president of the council and held office beginning Nov. 4, 1930 and during construction of new courthouse. The council met in regular sessions, however, on account of construction of new courthouse and because of the many exigencies that had arisen throughout the economic period during which he had served; it had been necessarily requested to meet in many sessions in order to properly coordinate with the Board of Commissioners. All of these things the members of the County Council did faithfully and cheerfully and to them much of the credit must fairly go for the speedy construction of the new courthouse and the harmonious conduct of the county's business. The present courthouse was dedicated Oct. 20, 1937. Council officials took part in the dedication and Open House of the new building.

A few generations later, some of the family are still living in Howard County. *Submitted by Mary Florence (Kendall) Whitezel*

KENWORTHY - Clarence William "Willie" Kenworthy, son of Benjamin and Jennie Colburn Kenworthy, was born in Peru, IN on Sept. 15, 1890. "Willie's" grandparents, Uriah and Mary Carter Kenworthy, came to America from Oldham, Lancaster, England, in about 1849, first settling in Wayne County, IN, then moved to Noblesville, in Hamilton County, IN. The family followed the promise of employment by the railroad(s) and settled in Peru, IN before 1880. Benjamin Kenworthy worked for the railroad.

Clarence William Kenworthy served at least three years in the army before his WWI re-enlistment May 11, 1918. He was a member of the 168th Inf., 42nd (Rainbow) Div. He was wounded and subjected to poison gas attacks at the St. Mihiel salient in September 1918. After being hospitalized in France, he sailed from Brest in March 1919. For many years, he spent weeks at a time in veterans hospitals, fighting the recurring effects of the poison gas.

Clarence William Kenworthy and Maude Geneva Etherington, daughter of Oliver and Bertha Frier Etherington, were married Nov. 26, 1920, at the parsonage of the Congregational Church in Kokomo. They were the parents of two daughters: Bertha E. (Mrs. Robert J. Massoth) and Florence J. (Mrs. Russell B. Price). Their five grandchildren are: John, Mary Ann and Thomas Massoth; and Jeffery and Jerry A. Price.

Clarence William Kenworthy and Maude Geneva (Etherington) Kenworthy

"Willie" worked for several years at the Kokomo Rubber Works. Later he worked as an upholsterer and furniture finisher at the Hopkins Furniture Store in Kokomo. Maude Kenworthy worked at the Reliance Garment Manufacturing Plant on North Washington Street for several years during the Depression.

In about 1935, the Kenworthys purchased the large, two-story property at 418 North Union Street - immediately north of the A & P store - converted it to a five-unit apartment building and managed that facility until "Willie's" death in 1962.

As a youth, Willie worked odd jobs for several large circus organizations as they "wintered" in Peru. He never lost his fascination for anything "circus." He and Maude always were among the first to welcome the circus arrival, no matter the time of day or night. They were the last to watch the loading of the animals and the tearing down of the big tent. The Kenworthys really loved to fish the several lakes in central and northern Indiana, but only if the circus was not in town. "Willie" was a great storyteller and very often delighted friends, children, and grandchildren with ghost stories and tales of the circus, of cowboys and Indians and the Wild West.

Bertha E. Kenworthy married Robert J. Massoth, Feb. 22, 1941. See "Massoth" for details of their lives.

Florence J. Kenworthy married Russell B. Price, son of Marley J. and Grace M. Embree Price, on March 23, 1946. Their life story is featured under "Price".

Maude G. Kenworthy, who was married to John Wines in 1972, recently (October 1993) celebrated her 94th birthday at the Price home in Russiaville. *Submitted by R.J. Massoth*

MERRELL AND ROSALEA KENWORTHY - Merrell Kenworthy and Rosalea Farris were married at Faith Methodist Church in Kokomo on Oct. 19, 1974. Both have deep roots in the Howard County area. Merrell works for Electronic Data Systems at Delco Electronics and Rosalea does some substitute teaching in the Kokomo-Center Schools.

Merrell was born Aug. 11, 1946 at St. Joseph Hospital. He was raised on a farm in Taylor Township. Merrell was graduated from Kokomo High School in 1964. He received an S.B. degree in mathematics from the Massachusetts Institute of Technology in 1968. In 1983 he earned an M.B.A. degree from Indiana University. He is involved in many community activities including Kokomo Civic Theatre, Kokomo Kiwanis Sunrisers, Kokomo Men of Note, Curtain Call Theater for Children, Howard County Genealogical Society and Faith Presbyterian Church.

Although Rosalea was born in Hobbs, NM, her mother moved back to Indiana after her father died in a plane crash on Aug. 15, 1953 in Wichita Falls, TX. Rosalea was graduated from Kokomo High School in 1968. She received her B.A. degree from Indiana Central College in 1972 and her M.A. in art in 1977. She is active in the Orleanettes Homemakers and the Kokomo Mothers of Multiples as well as Faith Presbyterian Church.

Kenworthy Family

Merrell and Rosalea have been blessed with four children: David, born Jan. 25, 1978; Melody and Michelle, born April 3, 1980; and Jonathan, born Jan. 28, 1984. All of the children have been active in Curtain Call Theater for Children.

Merrell's parents, Wayne and Naomi (Henderson) Kenworthy, were married in Tipton County in 1926, but bought a farm in Taylor Township soon after they were married. Wayne's parents, Floyd T. and Lula (Terwilliger) Kenworthy, also lived most of their lives in Howard County. Floyd (1884-1957) was born in Tipton County and was married to Lula (1887-1942) in Tipton County in 1906. She was a native of Auglaize County, OH. They bought a farm in Taylor Township and lived the rest of their lives in Howard County.

Floyd's parents, William Riley and Marsella (Summers) Kenworthy, were married in Howard County, but lived most of their lives in the Windfall community. William (1862-1938) was a farmer and he and Marsella (1865-1935) are both buried in Albright Cemetery in Howard County. William's parents, Thomas and Martha (Layton) Kenworthy were married in Tipton County, IN, but both died in Howard County. Thomas (1834-1915) farmed in Tipton County for most of his life. Thomas and Martha (1839-1929) moved to Russiaville after their 50th wedding anniversary in 1909. Marsella's parents, Golvin and Eliza (Copeland) Summers, lived most of their lives in the Windfall area. Golvin (1841-1920) and Eliza (1839-1922) are both buried in Albright Cemetery in Howard County.

Golvin Summers' parents, Simon and Elizabeth (Wines) Summers, lived in Union Township, Howard County for most of their lives. Simon (1813-1892) and Elizabeth (1817-1907) settled in Howard County soon after the Civil War. Both died in Howard County and are buried in Albright Cemetery.

MICHAEL KERBY - Michael Kerby (1831-1911) and his brother Jeremiah (1828) came to America from Ireland in 1847, joining two brothers and two sisters; Catherine, Patrick, Margaret and James who had emigrated in 1845. In 1851 two other sisters, Hannorah and Julia also journeyed to the U.S. These were the children of Michael Kerby and Hannorah Connor of County Kerry, Ireland. Another brother, William, remained in Ireland.

Catherine Fahey (1826-1907) emigrated from County Galway, Ireland. On Nov. 1, 1854 Michael married Catherine Fahey and settled near Rushville, IN.

In 1852 Michael purchased 80 acres of land north of Greentown in Howard County. The title abstract shows he paid four dollars per acre. The land had to be cleared and drained for farming.

Michael and Catherine moved their family to Howard County in 1861, to their first house, a very small structure which was later used as their henhouse. Michael later built a large log cabin consisting of one room downstairs and one room upstairs. Their third house was built about 1900 and was a large frame house with front and back porches and seven outside doors. This house was replaced by the present owner in 1978, Michael's great-grandson, Bill Kerby.

In 1976, Bill received the Hoosier Homestead Award from the Indiana Dept. of Commerce. This award honors farms that have operated in the same family for at least 100 years. Ownership of the farm passed from Michael to his seven children, then to son William H., then to his widow Emma (Smeltzer), then Michael's grandson Leo Kerby, then today's owner, Bill Kerby.

Michael Kerby; Catherine (Fahey) Kerby

Michael and Catherine's seven children were:

Michael (1865-1940) married Olive Monroe with children Harley, Effie, Florence, Walter and Joseph. Michael and his family changed the spelling of their name from Kerby to Kirby.

Hannah (1857-1944) married James Lynch. No children.

Catherine (Kate) (1861-1941) married John Daugherty with children Ellen, Arthur, John and Mary Leona.

James (1864-1942) married Anna Mary Stahl with children Elsie, Clarence, Leona, Helen, James and Joseph.

Timothy (1868-1948) married Della Cranor with children Marie and Paul.

Mary (Molly) (1859-1928) married Bernard Hines. No children.

William H. (1860-1932) married Emma Smeltzer with children Alda (Rockey), Charles, Katie Pearl (Conwell), Nina (Moss), Leo, Josephine (Ortman), Vada (Moss), Everett, Homer (Gus), Harry and James Bernard.

Leo Kerby (1890-1967) was the operator and later the owner of the homestead farm for 45 years and was well-known in Liberty Township. Leo and Lydia (Crandall) (1890-1959) were the parents of Eugene (1917), Eva (Kratzer) (1921) and the present owner, William T. (1919).

William T. (Bill) retired from the U.S. Navy (1937-1957) after serving the entire WWII in anti-sub and convoy duty in the Atlantic and many other ships and shore stations. He then worked for the Standard Oil Pipeline Co. for 20 years, including a period on the start-up of the Trans-Alaska pipeline.

WILLIAM HENRY KERBY - William Henry Kerby (1860-1932) was born in Rush County, IN, the son of Michael and Catherine (Fahey) Kerby, Irish immigrants who came to America in the mid 1800s.

Michael had purchased land in Liberty Township and moved his family to Howard County in 1861.

In 1881 William married Emma Smeltzer (1862-1941), daughter of Robert and Sarah (Zerbe) Smeltzer.

After they were married they set up housekeeping on a rented farm close to Highway 18 in Miami County. In August 1892, William purchased 180 acres of farm land in Clay Township. It was to this farm they moved their growing family.

William and Emma Kerby

Through the years William bought and sold several parcels of land and added another 60 acres to the farm of his residence. He also raised Hereford cattle and enjoyed showing them and winning many awards at the New York State Fair in the early 1900s. His interest in Hereford cattle brought him in contact with Mike and John Murphy who were raising an unusual steer and son, Harry, recalled the time that he and his twin brother, Gus, as very young children, were allowed to sit on the back of "Old Ben" who is now a local point of interest in Kokomo's Highland Park.

William and Emma were the parents of 11 children:

Alda (1882-1977) was married to Clarence Rockey Oct. 23, 1912. Their children were Bessie, William, George, and Ralph. They lived near Galveston.

Charles (1883-1956) married Gaudeta Oden March 27, 1910. Mary and Robert were the names of their two children. They made their home in Kokomo.

Pearl (1887-1961) married Levi Conwell on March 2, 1905. Pearl and Levi had five children: Albert, Onas, Mildred, Howard, and Emma.

Nina (1889-1949) was married to Jesse Moss July 20, 1912. They were the parents of seven children: Edith, Herman, Doris, Esther, Russell, Dorothy, and Norma.

Leo's (1890-1967) wife was Lydia Crandall and they were married May 20, 1916. Their children were Gene, William and Eva.

On April 14, 1915 Josephine (1893-1940) married John Ortman. From this union came Emma, John, Robert, Richard, Ned, and Raymond.

Vada's (1895-1952) husband was Elmer Moss and they were married April 17, 1917. They were the parents of seven children: Elsie, Mary, Ray, Hershel, Betty, Gene, and Wayne.

Everett (1899-1980) married Grace Miller June 11, 1920. They had no children and retired to Florida where Grace is still living.

Homer (Gus) (1903-) is still living in Ft. Wayne where he made his home with his wife Dorothy Henley whom he married on June 27, 1936. No issue.

Harry (1903-1988) was married to Dortha Jacobs March 18, 1926. They had one daughter, Phyllis. Dortha resides in Kokomo.

Bernard (1906-1988) married Esther Duncan on July 21, 1933 and named their son Fred. They lived in Kokomo.

When William and Emma retired from the farm in 1922 they moved to Kokomo. Nina and Jesse Moss then took up residence on the "home place". They purchased the farm after the death of Emma in 1941. It was subsequently sold to Russell Moss, their son, who farmed it until he passed away in 1982. His son, Gordon, is now living there and farming the land.

During his lifetime William was a well-known and successful farmer. He was a member of St. Patrick's Church.

Emma was of kindly disposition and well thought of by all who knew her.

BENTON M. KIDWELL - Benton M. Kidwell, an only child, was born Oct. 11, 1885, in Tompkinsville, KY. He married Nora Helen Hagan in 1915. She was born in 1894. They had four boys: Bedford M. Kidwell, who died shortly after birth; Buford Marion Kidwell, born Nov. 11, 1918; James Kenneth Kidwell, born Feb. 10, 1929; and Clio Wilson Kidwell, born June 19, 1930. They also had one daughter, Beulah Mae Kidwell, born Sept. 11, 1920.

Nora Helen (Hagan) Kidwell died Jan. 9, 1941, at the age of 47. Benton was in poor health, too, and the raising of the two younger boys fell mainly to Buford and Beulah. Benton died Aug. 6, 1955, at the age of 70.

In the spring of 1942, Buford came to Indiana to look for work. He started working for Lloyd Hollingsworth on a farm. He brought the rest of the family to Howard County from Tompkinsville, KY, approximately six months later. They lived on Lloyd's farm. All had to work to make ends meet. Clio was 11 years old and Kenny was 12.

Buford Kidwell was drafted during WWII and served as an M.P. He transported prisoners of war from Italy to the United States. When discharged from the army, he continued to work on different farms for a while. Later he worked at St. Joseph Hospital and for Kings Heating and Plumbing. He moved back to Tompkinsville, KY, in 1974. In June 1977 he died.

Beulah Kidwell later married Otis Graves and moved back to Kentucky. She and Otis had one son, Roy Wayne Graves.

Kenny worked on the farms of Lloyd Hollingsworth, Loren Oakley, and Paul Garrison. He went to work at Continental Steel Corporation in Kokomo, IN, and retired from there in 1980. He married Frances Bowers in 1954. They had two children—Kenneth Randall (Randy) Kidwell, born March 22, 1955, and Deborah Louann Kidwell, born Jan. 31, 1956. Randy was killed in an automobile accident on June 22, 1991. He had two sons: Jason Kenneth Kidwell and James Eric Kidwell. Deborah Kidwell married Scott Pitcher, and they had two children: Amber Cheri Pitcher, born July 9, 1975 and Brandon William Pitcher, born Dec. 6, 1979.

Clio Wilson Kidwell, the youngest, also did farm work for the Hollingsworths, the Oakleys, and the Garrisons. He retired from Haynes Stellite Corporation with 30 years of service. He had three children: Steven Wilson Kidwell, Pam Kidwell, and Cynthia Kidwell. Steven married Rhonda Flora, and they have two boys, Chris and Derrick. Pam Kidwell married David Isaac, and they have two children, Benjamin and Ashley. Cynthia Kidwell married Dwight Dunmoyer and has one daughter, Angie. Clio later married Linda in 1988; he died in May of 1993.

When Benton M. Kidwell was about five years old, he had an aunt and uncle who were moving to Oklahoma in a covered wagon. They threw a little chair back across the creek to Benton. The chair is now in the possession of Kenneth James Kidwell and would be well over 100 years old. *Submitted by Amber Pitcher*

KENNETH A. AND PHYLLIS I. KIRK -
Kenneth and Phyllis both grew up in Kokomo; Kenneth was born here and Phyllis was born in Frankton (Madison County) IN. They both attended Kokomo schools. They were married June 19, 1952 and moved to Hartford City (Blackford County) IN, then to Grant County before returning to Kokomo in 1965.

Kenneth Allen was born in Kokomo, IN June 24, 1927. After high school he joined the USMC and served four years during WWII in the Pacific and was recalled to active duty for one year in 1950 during the Korean War.

Phyllis Irene (Bunnell) Kirk was born in Frankton, IN Nov. 5, 1926. Her family moved to Kokomo in 1931. She graduated from Kokomo High School in 1944 and was employed by Delco Electronics.

Kenneth and Phyllis have two sons born in Marion, IN. Jeffrey Allen (wife - Candace Kratzer) Kirk was born May 19, 1954 and Richard Dennis (wife - Teresa Culp) Kirk born Dec. 28, 1957. They also have two granddaughters, Laura Katherine Kirk born Jan. 28, 1984 in Teaneck, NJ and Tori Lynn Kirk born Nov. 26, 1992 in Kokomo.

Kenneth and Phyllis Kirk

Kenneth's parents were John Ernest Sr. and Mildred Marie (Haley) Kirk. John was employed in the machine shop at Continental Steel Corporation and Mildred was a department manager at Sears Roebuck and Company. His grandparents were John H. and Ida Belle (Clark) Haley and Elisah E. and Dora Isabelle (Jacobs) Kirk.

Phyllis' parents, Stephen Nelson and Blanche Tabitha (Kellenburger) Bunnell, were both born and raised in White County, IN. They married Oct. 17, 1905. Her grandparents were Harrison and Ellen (Hines) Kellenburger and Stephen and Nancy Ellen (Shields) Bunnell. Grandmother Bunnell's father (Joshua J. Shields) fought in the Civil War and died in Andersonville Prison in Georgia. Great-grandparents Nathaniel Bunnell was married to Susannah Runyan in 1831 and came to White County in 1833. Four sons and two sons-in-law were in the Union Army. John was at Vicksburg, Wesley died at Gettysburg, Abram was in Libby Prison and Thomas was with General Butler at New Orleans. Although circuit preachers held meetings in various homes, the Bunnell brothers helped establish and build the first M.E. Church in Reynolds, IN.

Kenneth retired in 1982 as Commander of the Air Section of the Indiana State Police after 29 years with the department. Phyllis retired in 1984 from Delco Electronics as a clerk with 30 years service. Both are happy to be living in Kokomo and Clearwater, FL.

ETTIS HENRY AND EDNA MOULDER KIRKENDALL -
Ettis was the second son born to James and Sarah Elizabeth Maish Kirkendall on Sept. 4, 1875, in Howard County, IN. He had two sisters and seven brothers. He grew up in Clinton and Howard counties. The family farm was one and one-fourth miles west of US 31, on the north side of US 26 in Harrison Township. The home is still standing. He married Edna Moulder, Feb. 13, 1896 in Howard County. Daughter of Henry and Martha Hadley Moulder. Martha was born Aug. 29, 1845, died April 16, 1923, buried at New London Cemetery. Not known where Henry is buried at. Edna was born Sept. 8, 1878, Reno County, KS, died April 26, 1951, Howard County. Ettis died July 17, 1951, Burlington, IN. Both are buried at New London Cemetery.

Edna and Ettis Kirkendall's 50th Anniversary. Married Feb. 13, 1896.

The family lived in Cass County, Johnson County, (where Ettis had a butchering shop), then to Scott County, IN around 1916, where they farmed. They moved back to Russiaville in 1920 and started a hardware store. Ettis later sold Conservative Insurance and advertising. They were members of the Russiaville Methodist Church, where Ettis was a janitor until it burned in 1941. They had seven children: Waldo Moulder, born July 17, 1898, Young America, IN, married 1) Faye Pound, 2) Nellie Gordon. Waldo and Faye have two sons, Waldo Jr. and Donald Winston. Waldo died Aug. 31, 1966, buried Crown Point Cemetery, Kokomo. Claude James born Dec. 7, 1900, Cass County, married Ida B. Harper, Jan. 2, 1932, Tipton County. He died Nov. 9, 1953, buried at Sharpsville Cemetery, Sharpsville, IN. John Neil born May 26, 1903, Cass County, buried at Young America, IN. Martha (Lucille) born Feb. 22, 1908, Greenwood, Johnson County, IN, married Robert Lee Rogers, Aug. 16, 1930, Howard County. She died Nov. 24, 1984, buried at Sunset Memorial Garden Cemetery, Howard County. She was a beautician. They had one daughter, Virginia Lee married Gary Harlow. Their children are Melinda, Tom and Elizabeth Ann. Sarah Elizabeth, born Oct. 26, 1909, Greenwood, married Melvin Earl Roler Aug. 28, 1927, Howard County. Their children are Dean and Leona Daught. Sarah and Melvin live in Greenfield, IN. Ettis (Howard) born March 25, 1912, Greenwood, married Martha Unger Feb. 11, 1934, Clinton County, IN. They live at Burlington, IN. He was a groceryman. Their children are Jane Ann married Allen Milburn, John Neal married Carolyn Long and James Vernon married Linda Rae Brethen. Robert Virgil born May 8, 1917, Scott County, IN married Clara Lillian Ratcliff Jan. 20, 1940, Howard County. He died Dec. 10, 1985, buried Russiaville, IN. They have twin daughters Marilyn Lue and Carolyn Sue, born June 11, 1947, Kokomo. Marilyn married Samuel Dennis Hennessee Dec. 28, 1969, Russiaville. Their children are John Robert, born Sept. 14, 1974, Indianapolis; Samuel Dennis II, born Oct. 14, 1976, Indianapolis; and Joseph Wesley, born Jan. 14, 1982, Indianapolis. Carolyn married Ted L. Salsbery July 7, 1968, Russiaville. Their children are Ann Clarissa, born Dec. 29, 1975, Indianapolis and Jefferson Leon, born Nov. 17, 1976, Indianapolis.

Many descendants still live in the surrounding counties.

CLAUDE JAMES AND IDA B. HARPER KIRKENDALL -
Claude was the son of Ettis and Edna Moulder Kirkendall. He graduated from Russiaville High School. In his later years he was a prominent farmer of Liberty Township, Tipton County, IN. He married Ida B. Harper, Jan. 2, 1932, in Howard County. She was born April 14, 1906, Tipton, Tipton County, IN, daughter of James Henry and Ida Gilliland Harper. Ida died May 13, 1969, Kokomo. Claude died Nov. 9, 1953, Sharpsville; both are buried at the Sharpsville Cemetery. Claude was a member of Russiaville Masonic Lodge #82 F. and A.M., Scottish Rite, Murat Shrine of Indianapolis, IN, Sharpsville Chapter #148 Order of Eastern Star.

They had three children, Marianna, born Aug. 18, 1932, Tipton County, married Marvin Gordon Bridgewater June 12, 1955, Tipton County. Second married Ora Kern May 5, 1973, Jackson County, IN, divorced from both. Marvin and Marianna had two children, Randall Lee, born June 20, 1956, Tipton County, married Karla Sue Adamson Nov. 23, 1975, Fishers, IN. Their children are Amanda Lynn, born April 26, 1976, Indianapolis and Aaron Jacob, born May 27, 1979, Noblesville. Randy is a mechanic and Karla is a typesetter. They live at Greenfield. Marcia Ann, born Sept. 15, 1957, Tipton County, married David Wayne Bode Sept. 4, 1976, Jackson County, IN. Their children are Klarissa Ann, born Sept. 6, 1980, Jackson County. She is an honor roll student and a Girl Scout Cadette. She has been in Girl Scouts for eight years and plays the clarinet in the school band. Kyle David, born May 15, 1983, Jackson County. He is active in sports, plays percussion in band, and has a been a Boy Scout for the past six years. They are members of Zion Lutheran Church, where Marcia is Sunday School Superintendent, member of Zion Women Fellowship, Lutheran Women Missionary League, Girl Scout leader for eight years, Member of Indiana State Quilting Guild and Jackson County, Jackson County and Scott County, IN Genealogical Societies. She enjoys quilting, crafts, family researching and serving the Lord.

Back: Claude James and Ida B. Harper Kirkendall. Their children James Richard, Jean Ellen and Marianna.

Jean Ellen, born Aug. 22, 1934, Tipton County, married 1) Robert Cannon, 2) Marvin Davis, 3) Henry Walker. She died June 13, 1978; buried at Sharpsville Cemetery. Jean and Robert's child is Karla Kay, born Oct. 3, 1956, Tipton County, married Timothy Bowser Aug. 3, 1975, Kokomo. Their children are Kristina Marie, born

Oct. 11, 1979, Howard County and Danielle Grace, born Sept. 13, 1983, Indianapolis. They live at Sharpsville. Jean and Marvin's children are Bradley James, born June 1, 1960, Frankfort, IN, married Donna Tatman June 1, 1985. Their children are Robin Michelle, born Nov. 6, 1985, Clinton County and Kimberly Brooke, born July 19, 1988, Clinton County. Timothy Jon, born Sept. 6, 1961, Frankfort, married Rebecca Harris Aug. 1, 1986, Madison County, IN.

James Richard, born July 9, 1936, Tipton County, married Carolyn Sue Hite, March 24, 1956, Kokomo. Her parents are Gene and Mildred Powell Hite. Their children are Cynthia Sue, born Oct. 1, 1956, Kokomo, married Todd Leon Cunningham Sept. 5, 1976, Sharpsville. Their children are Susan (Suzy) Tennille, born March 3, 1977, Tipton and Melissa Ann (Missy), born Feb. 19, 1980, Tipton. Cindy and Todd are farmers and live at Kempton, IN. Deborah Lynn, born March 3, 1958, Kokomo, married Walter Andrew (Andy) Destocki Jr., Sept. 14, 1991, Sharpsville. Their son, Andrew James (Drew), born April 22, 1993. Debbie and Andy live at Lancaster, OH. Jamie Renee, born Aug. 28, 1962, Kokomo, married Roy Rulon May 21, 1982, Sharpsville. Their children are Nicolas James, born Oct. 25, 1986, Noblesville, IN and Neal Alan, born June 23, 1988, Noblesville. They are farmers and live at Arcadia, IN.

FRANK AND SHIRLEY (KITTS) KING -

Franklin Gene King was born Nov. 21, 1938 in Tipton County, IN. He was the last of 10 children and his parents were Iva Ruth Love and Leslie Norman King. His brothers and sisters are Loeta, Ellen, Florance, Don, Ione, Geraldine, Darline, Ray and Roy.

Shirley Jean (Kitts) King was born Oct. 2, 1942 in Peru, IN. She is the oldest of three children. Her parents are Hattie Johnson and the late William Kitts. Her sister is Linda Hooker and her brother is Fred Kitts.

Back row: Terry, Alan, Frank, Shirley, Kamron, Leslie, Robin and Joan. Front row: Kelly and Aaron.

Frank and Shirley met through high school and were married Dec. 24, 1959. They are the parents of three daughters: Robin, Joan, and Leslie.

Robin married Terry Kingseed and they have a son named Kelly. Joan married Alan Wyant and have two sons, Kamron and Aaron. Leslie lives with her parents and attends grade school.

Frank retired from Delco Electronics and works part time at Keck's Gas Station in Greentown. Shirley works in the home.

A fine example of a Christian family, it has been their faith that helped them endure a tornado and a house fire. *Submitted by Terry Kingseed.*

KINGSEED -

The Kingseeds are of German descent. The first known Kingseed was Anton Koenigsamen who was born in Dreyson, Palatinate of Bavaria on June 26, 1796. On Jan. 26, 1816, he married Margaret Rauth, who was born on July 28, 1796 in Boerstadt. By trade a cabinet maker, Anton immigrated to the United States in 1832 and settled in Hamburg, Berks County, PA. The same year they moved to Pine Grove, Schuykill County, PA, and engaged in farming. In 1834, they sold the farm and came by wagon (a journey of six weeks) to Tiffin, OH. Located in Seneca Township, Anton Kingseed purchased 96 acres of land, which he cleared and farmed until his death in 1883.

Anton and Margaret Kingseed were the parents of seven children. They include: Martin, Peter, Christian, Margaret, Elizabeth, Sophia, and Anthony. Following Margaret's death, Anton remarried in 1847 to Catherine Baur of Seneca Township. Together they had three children: Joseph, Emelia, and Catherine.

Anton Koenigsamen; Peter Kingseed

Alexander Kingseed

Peter Kingseed, Anton's second son, was born in Dreyson, Bavaria, Germany on Jan. 18, 1822. Emigrating from Bavaria at the age of 10, they sailed to New York City from La Havre, France after a voyage of 30 days on the ship *Henry VIII*. Peter was a member of the Fort Ball Artillery in Seneca County, OH which organized on March 10, 1851 and served out its time. He was married Jan. 10, 1854 to Mary Duckwuler in Seneca County, OH.

Mary, Ralph, Milton, Lena, Charles, Rosa and Albert.

A History of the Indiana Farm

On Oct. 25, 1848, Peter Kingseed went to the land office in Fort Wayne and bought a patent of 240 acres located in Liberty Township, Howard County, IN. He arrived in Liberty Township June 2, 1854. Locating first in Plevna, he built a log cabin on his property. A few years later, he built the house which still stands and is known as the old summer kitchen.

What Peter found as he arrived was a heavily timbered land which included white oak, hickory, ash, sycamore, beech, sugar lynn, and poplar. The sycamore trees averaged 48 inches diameter and were 54 feet apart while the lynn trees were 14 inches diameter and 53 feet apart. Beech trees were 12 inches in diameter and 42 feet apart. By 1860, Peter had cleared 40 acres. His livestock comprised two horses, two milking cows, one wagon ox, four other cattle, six sheep, twenty-five pigs, totaling a livestock value of $275. The produce of the farm for 1860 was: 40 bushels of wheat, 400 bushes of Indian corn, 40 bushels of oats, 15 pounds of wool, 1 bushel of peas and beans, 5 bushels of Irish potatoes, 11 bushels of buckwheat, 50 pounds of butter, 2 tons of hay, and 20 pounds of maple syrup.

Peter and Mary's children were John W., Anthony, Lucinda, Henry, Alexander, Mary, Joseph, Rosa, Charles and Frank.

Alexander farmed the land after Peter retired to the city of Kokomo. During 1936, a covenant with the utility company allowed electricity onto the premises. The telephone arrived in the 50s.

Alexander married Martha Saul Sept. 20, 1883, and their children were Rosa May, Charles Edward, Albert Christopher, Mary Lovina, Ralph Alexander, Lena Elizabeth, and Milton Peter.

Albert and Ralph joined a partnership to buy and farm the land. When the partnership ceased, Albert acquired the land with the homestead and Ralph acquired 40 acres.

Robert Kingseed; Terry Kingseed

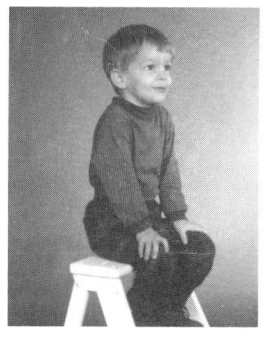

Kelly Kingseed

Albert married Afton Swingley in Amboy on July 30, 1909 and their children were Geneva Madge and Robert Lee. Robert helped farm and worked for Union Carbide until he was killed in an industrial accident in 1963.

Robert's children are heir to the farm, with the homestead belonging to his son Terry. Terry is presently employed in industry and the farming of the land is done by Max Kingseed, son of Ralph.

The next to inherit the family homestead will be Terry's son, Kelly Robert. *Submitted by Terry Kingseed.*

Original house.

239

ROBERT AND MILDRED (MODAK) KINGSEED - Robert Lee was born Sept. 5, 1918. His parents were Albert and Afton (Swingley). He married Mildred Ann Modak on June 5, 1943. Mildred was born July 1, 1923 in Youngstown, OH. She was one of five children. Her parents were Paul and Stella (Mitrovich).

Mildred and Robert met during WWII in Dayton, OH. She was working civil service and he was in the Air Force at Wright Patterson Air Force base.

Terry, Mildred, Robert, Beverly, Nancy and Jean.

Four children were born from this union: Jean Carolyn, Beverly Lynn, Nancy Lee, and Terry Lee. All four children were born in Marion, IN.

Jean married Duane Gesse of Kouts, IN on April 6, 1968. They have one son, Brad. Duane and Jean farm near Kouts.

Beverly married Kent Evans of Greentown, IN on Dec. 4, 1970. To this union two daughters were born: Amy Marie and Abby Lynn. Kent is a businessman in Kokomo while Beverly teaches high school.

Nancy works at Haynes International and is engaged to be married to Jim Meyers.

Terry married Robin King of Greentown and they have a son named Kelly. Terry works at Chrysler.

Albert Kingseed was born Nov. 18, 1887. He was a farmer until his death from a heart attack on July 16, 1969. His parents were Alexander and Martha (Saul) Kingseed.

Alexander was the son of Peter and Mary (Duckwuler) Kingseed and was born May 1, 1861. He was a farmer and died Feb. 4, 1953 from kidney failure.

Peter Kingseed was born Jan. 18, 1822 in Germany and died May 10, 1902 from pneumonia in Kokomo. He retired as a farmer.

On May 7, 1963, Robert Lee Kingseed was killed in an industrial accident at Kokomo, IN while working for Union Carbide. His older sister's name was Geneva Madge. Robert had an honorable discharge from the Air Force.

Mildred belongs to numerous community clubs and organizations. She was president four times for the Greentown American Legion Auxiliary. She was president three times for the Liberty Township Extension Homemakers Club. She enjoyed being social and government counsellor of Hoosier Girls State and is still active with that program. She is a member of a church in Youngstown. Mildred is retired and enjoys her family. *Submitted by Terry Kingseed.*

MAX AND PATRICIA KINGSEED - Max and Patricia Kingseed are lifelong residents of this area, both of them born and raised within the boundaries of Howard County.

Mildred Landrum, Max's mother, was a descendant of David Landrum, the first settler in Howard County of European descent. David and his family came to this area from eastern Tennessee, a true pioneer. They first settled in Burlington but moved into the western part of what is now Monroe Township. David built a cabin and in 1837 moved his family to the area not far from the Stonebraker Bridge in Howard County.

Max Kingseed; Patricia Kingseed

Max's father, Ralph, traced his family back to Germany. Ralph's grandfather, Peter, came to Howard County, Liberty Township in June of 1854 from Ohio to a farm of 240 acres which in those days was described as "in the green". Here he built a log cabin and began to clear the land. A few years later he built a frame house and he and his wife, Mary, became the parents of 10 children.

Max was born on March 29, 1933 on a farm one-half mile north of Plevna, IN. He is a graduate of the first class of Eastern High School in the year of 1951. Max's only occupation has been farming. Part of the land he farms includes the land on which he was born.

Patricia was one of three children born to Glenn and Ruby Kessler. Patricia's paternal ancestors came from Germany and lived in Allegheny County, VA in 1821. Three of the earlier ancestors fought in the War of 1812 and one was in a battle with Indians at Point Pleasant, VA. He was shot through the body, but lived to be 110 years old.

Patricia's grandfather, Oliver Kessler, spent most of his life farming in Howard and Miami Counties. Her father was also a farmer and a school bus driver for 32 years.

Her maternal ancestors came from Ireland and Germany settling in Frankfort, IN. Her grandfather, Walter Koontz, was a semi-pro baseball player in his 20s. They moved from Frankfort to Kokomo where he served as Center Township trustee for eight years during the 1930s and owned a grocery store.

Max and Patty are the parents of five children: Glen of Avon, IN; Greg, Julie, and Jim of the Kokomo area; and Jane of Lafayette, IN. At the time of this writing the grandchildren numbered nine.

Glen Kingseed; Greg Kingseed

Julie (Kingseed) Breisch; Jim Kingseed

Jane Kingseed

Patty is a 1952 graduate of Northwestern High School. When the youngest of her children entered school, she enrolled in nurse's training and realized an ambition to be a nurse which she had put on hold to take care of her family. She is an employee of Marion General Hospital.

Christian values have always been considered important to the people of this community and the First United Methodist Church in Greentown is Max's family's home church.

TERRY AND ROBIN (KING) KINGSEED - Terry and Robin were married June 12, 1982. From this union one child, Kelly Robert, was born April 14, 1991. Kelly is the sixth generation to have the family homestead which was patented to Peter Kingseed from the United States government and President Zachary Taylor on Oct. 25, 1848.

Terry, born Feb. 5, 1957 in Marion, IN, was the fourth and final child of Robert and Mildred (Modak) Kingseed.

Robin, born Sept. 27, 1960 in Tipton, IN, was the first child of Frank and Shirley (Kitts) King.

Robin has a Bachelor's Degree from Indiana University. She has performed with the Indiana University at Kokomo Singers. She plays a flute for churches,

Robert Kingseed's family as of July 1, 1992. Top row: Mildred (Modak) Kingseed, Duane Gesse, Kent Evans, Terry Kingseed and Jim Meyers (Nancy's friend). Middle row: Jean (Kingseed) Gesse, Beverly (Kingseed) Evans, Robin (King) Kingseed and Nancy Kingseed. Front row: Brad Gesse, Amy Evans, Kelly Robert Kingseed and Abby Evans.

orchestras, and various groups. During high school, she traveled to Europe twice.

Terry, Robin and Kelly.

Terry has a Bachelor's Degree from Purdue University and a Master's Degree from Indiana University. He served an apprenticeship program of four years as an industrial electrician. He maintains licenses for property and casualty insurance, life, accident, and health insurance, real estate broker, and state teaching certification. He has been involved with industrial and domestic maintenance. He served as vice president of Local 2958 United Steelworkers. He has worked as an electrician for Cabot Corporation which now is Haynes International. He presently works as an electrician for Chrysler Corporation at the casting plant.

Athletics has served as a major influence in Terry's life. He won 11 letters in high school and was the first pitcher from Eastern High School to defeat a Kokomo team. As a walk-on, it took five determined years to make the varsity football team at Purdue University. Now he assists various high school punters in this fine activity.

Terry met Robin in high school and dated for seven years before becoming engaged. They are pursuing their respective family genealogies. Both enjoy antiques. Their goals in life are serving the Lord and providing for their family and home. *Submitted by Terry Kingseed.*

KIRTLEY - The name Kirtley has been part of Howard County for over 100 years. Ottis Franklin Kirtley, the son of Lewis and Frances E. (Bland) Kirtley was born in Sharpsville, Tipton County, IN May 21, 1894. His parents, although both being born in Tipton County, lived in or around Kokomo much of their lives. They had four children: Noah Raymond; Lucille, wife of Joseph Estes; Lucy Mae, wife of Bernie B. Morgan; and Ottis Franklin.

The paternal grandparents of the subject were Lemuel and Mary Jane (Covert) Kirtley. Lemuel was born in Switzerland County, IN in 1826 and Mary Jane was born in Bartholomew County, IN in 1837. They had 12 children, 10 who lived to maturity. Lemuel did flatboating on the Ohio and Mississippi Rivers and made frequent trips to New Orleans. He served throughout the Mexican War and after that he went to Tipton County in 1854, and bought a farm of 80 acres in Prairie Township. He died three miles south of Sharpsville Feb. 27, 1910, at the ripe old age of eighty-three. Mary Jane died two years later on November 4, age seventy-three.

Jessie Agnes Branson Kirtley and Ottis Franklin Kirtley; taken about 1976.

Lemuel Kirtley's father, Abraham, and his wife, Lidea (Underwood) Kirtley, were married in Jefferson County, IN in 1816. Abraham was born in Orange County, VA in 1796 and Lidea in Indiana in 1801. They were parents of five children.

Abraham's parents, John (1764-1824) and Mary (Lewis) (1775-1820) Kirtley, were native Virginians. John's parents, Thomas, Sr. (1724-1799) and Judith (Calloway) (1736-1778) Kirtley, were born in Culpeper County, VA.

Thomas's parents were Sir Francis and Margaret (Roberts) Kirtley. Sir Francis was born in Wales in 1690 and came to America in 1710. He died in Culpeper County, VA in 1763. Margaret was born in Spotsylvania County, VA July 25, 1698 and died March 1781 in Orange County, VA.

Ottis Franklin Kirtley married Jessie Agnes (Branson) Dec. 20, 1914 in Howard County, IN. They were the parents of three children, all born in Howard County: Frances Elaine, wife of Guy R. Thomas; Laura Susan, died age 16 as a result of an auto accident; and William Franklin.

Ottis Franklin attended Purdue University, was a farmer and realtor. He was a 32nd degree Mason and a Methodist. In middle age he moved to Delaware County, IN where he remained several years, but returned to Howard County to retire. He died May 20, 1983, age 89. His wife, Jessie Agnes, had died Oct. 3, 1982.

His daughter, Frances Thomas, her husband Guy, two of their daughters and several grandchildren still live in Howard County.

WILLIAM KLINGMAN - William Klingman (Wilhelm Klingmann) was born July 23, 1854, in Binau, Mosbach, Baden, Prussia (Germany). He was the youngest and sixth child of Georg Peter Klingmann and Rosine Christine Endlich. His siblings were Johann Georg Klingmann, Christian Klingmann, Elisabethe Friedericke Klingmann, Luise Klingmann, and Katharine Klingmann.

William emigrated to the United States in 1872 at age 18. He left from Bremen arriving at New York City about March 15, 1872. He then took a train to Ft. Wayne, IN, where he met his older brother John (Johann) who had emigrated to Ft. Wayne earlier.

William Klingman married Mary Ann Troyer of Howard Township at Zion Evangelical Church (now Kokomo Zion United Methodist Church) on Christmas Day in 1873. She was the daughter of Andrew J. Troyer and Elisabeth Miller, an Amish family who had moved to Howard County from Holmes County, OH, in the 1850s.

William and Mary Ann Klingman lived one mile north of Zion Church in Section 12, Howard Township. In addition to farming, William operated a tile mill. They had 10 children: Cora E. Klingman, born Oct. 12, 1874, married John M. Lantz Feb. 9, 1895, died Feb. 25, 1904; Andrew Elmer Klingman; Edna E. Klingman, born Nov. 2, 1878, married Daniel E. Bryan Dec. 22, 1905; Albert Klingman, born September 1881, married Nellie Leona Kling Feb. 16, 1907, died July 20, 1958; Frederick Klingman, born Feb. 4, 1884, married Nora Klingelsmith Oct. 18, 1913, died 1971; Christina Klingman, born Oct. 19, 1886, married Charles D. Shockley Dec. 23, 1908; Erma E. Klingman, born July 6, 1892, married Frank Bugher Feb. 20, 1918; Letta M. Klingman, born November 1895, married Clarence Bugher Aug. 23, 1917; Olaus W. (Pete) Klingman, born March 14, 1899, married Mazie M. Hartman March 24, 1920, died Oct. 4, 1953; Ketric Klingman, born 1903. The Klingmans were active members of Zion Church for many years. The family was very musical; William and Andrew were church song leaders for over 50 years. They also played in the Zion community's Dutch Corners Cornet Band. William Klingman became a naturalized citizen in 1920 at age 65. He died Dec. 29, 1923, and Mary Ann died April 17, 1939. They were buried in Zion Cemetery.

Their eldest son Andrew Elmer Klingman was born Dec. 11, 1876, in Miami County, IN. On Jan. 18, 1906, he married Cora Ellen Shank, who was born Feb. 25, 1883, the second of eleven children of David W. Shank and Matilda Hershberger of Holmes County, OH.

In 1917 Andrew and Cora purchased 80 acres of his grandfather Andrew J. Troyer's farm one-half mile north of Zion Church in Section 12, Howard Township. In addition to farming Andrew also had a wood shop and did carpentry. They had two children: Bernice Roberta Klingman, born Dec. 12, 1907, married Edwin Barnes Riley, Sr. April 20, 1930, died July 19, 1940, and Titus Andrew Klingman, born Dec. 14, 1910, married Jewell Aldine Clelland Dec. 31, 1932, died Sept. 22, 1986.

Cora died Oct. 9, 1937, and on May 12, 1940, Andrew married Mary Jane Main, widow of John M. Main and daughter of William N. Howard and Hannah J. Wheeler. Andrew died Aug. 28, 1965 and Mary Jane died Aug. 9, 1976. They were buried in Zion Cemetery. *Submitted by Ellen J. Morris*

KNIPE - The Knipe family history starts back in Casterton, England in 1771 when John Knipe married Ann Browness. They had a son, Thomas, who married Agness Briggs on May 9, 1810, in Westmoreland County, England. They had 10 children and the son named Thomas Jr. came from England to Fayette County, IN and married Mary Meranda on Sept. 3, 1840. They had seven children and lived in Posy Township, Fayette County on a farm. A son Samuel was born May 30, 1847 and moved from Dublin, IN to Kokomo and married Sarah Jane Bowen on Oct. 26, 1876. They had two children, Thomas Landle and Zora Ethel.

Thomas Landle Knipe

Thomas Landle Knipe married Edith Joan Miller on March 3, 1910 and their two children were Virginia and John Richard. Edith Joan died in Detroit on June 14, 1922 and is buried in Memorial Park Cemetery, Kokomo. Virginia was 12 and John was 6 at that time. Thomas met Morna Mahala Hickam of Spencer, IN (sister of Col. Horace Hickam for which Hickam Field, HI was named). They were married on July 11, 1923 and had a son named Willis Hickam. Thomas Landle was a prominent florist in Kokomo, being active and an officer in many floral societies and civic affairs. He died Aug. 12, 1939 and is buried in Memorial Park Cemetery, Kokomo.

Virginia Knipe married Lee Myron Bromley on June 7, 1936 and they had two sons, Thomas Lee and John William. Virginia died on Dec. 24, 1986 and is buried in Memorial Park Cemetery, Kokomo.

John Richard Knipe married Cecila Jane Schueler in Mexico City on Feb. 7, 1941 and their three children are Julie Ann (lived one year and is buried in Memorial Park), Thomas Landle and Harry George. They all now live in Colorado. Prior to their move John was the owner and manager of a flower shop on West Jefferson Road.

Willis Hickam Knipe married his high school sweetheart, Dorothy Jean Hunt, on June 15, 1947 and their two daughters are Kathryn Ann and Julia Lenore.

Willis' career was military since he graduated from West Point and served in WWII, Korean and Vietnam wars. He was assigned to Moscow Russia as an Asst. Army Attache to the Ambassador and his assignment was terminated by an airplane crash which killed 37 with only five survivors, Willis being one of the survivors. After 20 years in the military, Willis retired as a lieutenant colonel to a second career as a math instructor at the high school level. Willis and Dorothy now reside on West Sycamore Road and are active in many church and civic activities.

241

The Knipes have had a prominent part in the history of Howard County and have contributed to its welfare. *Submitted by Lee M. Bromley.*

KRANER - Charles "Charlie" Kraner was born July 31, 1875 in Adams County, IN. He was the son of Augustus G. and Rose Ann (Fravel) Kraner.

He married Nov. 28, 1894 in Adams County, IN to Edna F. Rumple (Dec. 5, 1869-May 30, 1949).

With their two young sons they moved to Kokomo in 1912.

Edna was the daughter of Daniel and Adaline (Lorts) Rumple of Adams County, IN. She had been a life-long friend of popular writer Gene Stratton Porter.

Charlie worked at many types of professions. His favorites were police and fire. He died March 19, 1948. They are both buried at the Crown Point Cemetery in the family plot.

L-R: A.G. Kraner, Charles Kraner, Osa Kraner and Rose Kraner.

Their two sons were Harold Edger, born Sept. 7, 1896 and Edwin Marion "Liz", born May 17, 1902, both in Geneva, Adams County, IN.

Harold Edger married Osa Mae Howe (April 20, 1898-Feb. 6, 1984) July 8, 1922, they had three children, Jack, Jerry and Joan. Harold and Osa managed the Howard County Home for a while. Before that he had been employed with the IR & L-NIP Interurban Lines. He then went to the city and Cross Transit bus lines, where he became the assistant manager. After his leave from the county home he became a postal carrier. She was very busy taking care of the Howard County Museum. They were both active in the Republican Party, he having been a committeeman for several years. They were members of the Grace United Methodist Church. During WWI he served in the Army. They had seven grandchildren: Connie, Mark, Beth Ann and Michelle Kraner and Kathryn, Nancy and Judith Ingles. Harold died July 18, 1972. He and Osa are in the family plot at Crown Point.

L-R: Augustus G. Kraner Homestead, Adams County, IN about 1911—Edwin, Hugh and Harold Kraner.

Edwin Marion, or "Liz" as he was affectionately known, married Mary Roxie (Browning) Rone (Sept. 14, 1909-May 23, 1943) Nov. 3, 1934. They had one son, Charles Allen. Roxie had one daughter, Gladyce M. Rone, from a previous marriage, whom Edwin raised. Edwin worked and retired from the Continental Steel Corp. He died May 29, 1982. They had 11 grandchildren: Kurt, Karen, Karol, Karla, Kathy, Kelli and Kerri Kraner and Candy, Randy, Donald J. "Joe" and Fredrick Schick.

Edwin and Roxie are also in the family plot at Crown Point. *Submitted by Jerry L. Kraner, from the research of Candy Jones*

CHARLES AND CATHERINE KRANER -

Charles Allen Kraner was born in Kokomo, the only child of Mary Roxie (Browning) and Edwin Marion "Liz" Kraner. (refer to Charlie Kraner) An avid outdoorsman, he fishes and hunts with bow and gun. He has touched his roots by building his own gun, a trait he no doubt gets from his "Browning" genes.

As a young boy, he was a Boy Scout and played basketball for church league and was inseparable from his dog Laddie. In junior high (Washington School), he played baseball and won several ribbons in swimming. He also worked part-time for Carothers Grocery. A graduate of Kokomo High School in 1958, he won many ribbons in track and wrestling. He also played varsity football as a lineback and fullback.

Catherine Joan Fivecoate (refer to Irl Fivecoate) was the only daughter of Irl and Grace (Stafford) Fivecoate and was born in Howard County. She has seven brothers. Although she took music lessons for the clarinet and the Hawaiian electric guitar, she only continued a few years. She graduated from Kokomo High School in 1952. She was a member of the Howard County Rural Youth and held several offices. She started working at the Howard County Court House in 1953 in the Recorder's Office and then the Assessor's Office (County and Center Township) for whom she was the Howard County Deputy Assessor.

On Oct. 19, 1958, Charles and "Joan" were married and lived in Kokomo. Charles began working at the Chrysler Transmission Plant, Kokomo in 1959. Joan stopped working at the Court House when their son was born. In 1963 she worked for Delco Electronics, Kokomo for four years and then left to care for her growing family. Joan was den mother for her son's Cub Scout Pack. Later she volunteered in various capacities for her daughters' Girl Scout Troops. She volunteered as library aide, teacher's assistant and was active in the PTO at school.

In August 1975 when Joan's mother died, the family went to live with her father on a farm west of Russiaville, IN for two years. In 1977 they moved to rural route, Peru, IN. Charles is a tool and die worker at Chrysler and is a member of the Masonic Lodge 423, Walton, IN. Joan works at Thompson Elementary School in Walton, and still does volunteer work for Tribal Trails Girl Scout Council.

They have a family of seven children and fourteen grandchildren. The oldest and only son is Kurt Allen. Their daughters are Karen Yvonne, Karol Ann, Karla Yvette, Kathryn Jo, Kelli Lynn and Kerri Grace.

Kurt married Sarah West, March 27, 1981. They have three children, Elizabeth Ann, Zakary Allen and Katlynd Mary Jo.

Karen married Kevin Semrow, July 31, 1982. They have four sons, Kody Garrett, Kord Ahron, Kolton Theodore and Kolby Charles (twins).

Karol married Kevin Martin, July 23, 1983. They have two sons, Matthew Thomas and Michael Dean.

Karla married Todd Ault, Dec. 1, 1990. They have a daughter, Hannah Eileen and are expecting a baby in August 1994.

Kathy married Steven Swinford Aug. 1, 1988, divorced 1994. They have three children, Stacey Nicole, Steven Ray and Shawn Allen.

Kelli married Jeremiah Stevens Nov. 27, 1993.

Kerri graduated from Lewis Cass High School, Walton, June 1994 and will go into criminal justice at Indiana University-Kokomo in the fall.

Kelli and Jeremiah live in Hawaii, where he is in the U.S. Army. Karen and Kevin and family live in Port Huron, MI. Kevin was in the U.S. Air Force at Grissom AFB when they met. The rest of the family live close by.

KRING - The Kring family came to Howard County by way of Pennsylvania and Ohio. The family originated in Pennsylvania when Johan Jost Kring arrived with his brother from Germany in July of 1751. They docked in Philadelphia aboard the ship *Two Brothers*. While living in Lancaster County, PA a son, George, was born in 1766. George's grandson Elijah Kring was the first to come to Howard County. Elijah was born June 10, 1840 in Westerville, OH and at age 22 enlisted in the Ohio Co. G, 8th Calvary and 44th Inf. during the Civil War. He was discharged in June 1865 and in 1866 married Charlotte Young. She was born in Petersburg, France in November of 1848. Elijah and Charlotte moved from Fort Recovery, OH to Howard County in 1883. Elijah bought ground in the northeast part of Howard County and farmed there until he died. There were a large number of people of German ancestry living in that part of the county and being of like descent, he settled there also. Elijah died in 1926 and Charlotte followed him in 1934 and both are buried in Zion United Methodist Church Cemetery located northeast of Kokomo.

Roger and Sharon Kring

Elijah and Charlotte had five children, one of which was Frank Kring. Frank was born in Fort Recovery, OH in March 1882. In December 1904 he married Clara Gerhart. She was born in February 1883 in south-

Kraner Family, taken Nov. 27, 1993. Seated front row, l-r: Stacey, Shawn, Steven, Katie, Beth, Kord, Kody, Zack, Michael and Matthew. Row 2, l-r: Steve, Kathy Jo, Karla, Todd holding Hannah, Karen holding Kolton, Kevin holding Kolby, Karol and Kevin. Row 3, l-r: Kerri, Joan, Kelli, Jeremiah, Chuck, Kurt and Sarah.

ern Miami County. Frank bought and farmed 80 acres located two miles south of Zion United Methodist Church until he passed away. Clara died Dec. 20, 1959 and Frank died Sept. 30, 1964. Both are buried at Zion United Methodist Church Cemetery.

Frank and Clara had four children and their first son was Howard Kring. He was born in Howard County on Aug. 29, 1916. On Sept. 15, 1940 he married Betty Householder who was also born in Howard County on May 16, 1920. They had a son, Roger Kring. On June 10, 1957 Howard married Marjorie Brandt who was born in Tipton County on Jan. 18, 1917. They had a daughter Susan Kring who teaches school in Kokomo. In September 1988 Howard married Evelyn Heltzel and they reside in Kokomo. Howard Kring was co-owner and operator of Fenn Lumber Co. in Kokomo for 40 years until he retired in 1992.

Roger Kring was born in Kokomo on Sept. 10, 1941. On Nov. 28, 1982 Roger married Sharon Eikenberry who was born in Coloma, MI on May 23, 1947. Roger and Sharon are both employed at Delco Electronics and have been there 32 and 25 years, respectively. Roger is an electrician and Sharon is a machinist. They have four children and two grandchildren and reside in Jackson Township, Howard County.

KUNTZ - Jacob Elmer Kuntz (1867-1951) born Columbiana County, OH on May 31, 1867, the son of Robert Daniel and Juliana (Woolf) Kuntz. He was raised in Jennings County, IN. Jacob married first Theresa Margaret Fleming, (1876-1909) daughter of Samuel and Mary (McNew) Fleming. They were married Oct. 24, 1895 in Versailles, IN. To this union were born six children: Leo, Mary Leona, Robert, Otto, Harry and Russell (who died in infancy). To Jacob and his second wife, Mary Magdalena Spoleder, (1872-1946) daughter of Henry and Elizabeth (Traurbauch) Spoleder, was born one son, Elmer. In 1914 Jacob removed to Kokomo with his children and two step-daughters, Mary and Myrtle Schuyler. When he first came to Kokomo he was a fireman. He then worked as a machinist for Kokomo Steel & Wire Co. which became Continental Steel, where he was employed until he was forced to retire at age 75. He got gangrene and refused to have his leg removed saying, he came into this world whole and he'd leave it the same way.

Jacob (Jake) Kuntz; Jeannette McNabney and Otto Kuntz

Otto Elmer (1902-1970) was born Feb. 2, 1902 in Jennings County, IN. On Oct. 21, 1922 he married Jeannette McNabney, (1904-1992) daughter of James Ross and Mary Jane (Deshon) McNabney. Otto served in the U.S. Army 1920-1921 stationed at Fort Lewis, WA. After his discharge he went to work for the Kokomo Steel & Wire Co. as a mechanic. Later, he was moved to the Rod Mill Department of Continental Steel. He worked there until his retirement in 1967. Being born on Groundhog Day his family would call asking if he'd seen his shadow. Otto was very bald and his daughters and granddaughters would put very bright lipstick on and kiss the top of his head. Otto and Jeannette had four children: Theresa, William, Delores, and Mary Jane. Theresa and Mary Jane now live in Grants Pass, OR. William was a foreman for the Public Service Co.

Delores Mae was born June 29, 1931 in Peru, IN. She married Dec. 30, 1947, Jack Wayne Spicer, son of Marshall Harrison and Florence Charlotte (Ashby) Spicer. She worked at the J.C. Penneys Co. for 10 years in the Men's Department. Afterward, together they started Spicer's Upholstery Shop which they operated for 15 years until 1986. After Jack retired in 1988 they moved to Utah, where all their children live. They had five children: Jerry (who died at birth), Christina, Jack, Karen, and Mark. *Submitted by Delores M. Spicer.*

CHRISTIAN AND ELIZABETH KURTZ - On March 3, 1880, Christian A. Kurtz (1854-1935) married Elizabeth Grau (1859-1938) and brought her here to the 100-acre farm in Liberty Township, Howard County, which he had just purchased for $13.00 an acre. There was a small house and here they started their life together. Christian's parents, John (1819-1895) and Dora Hepperly Kurtz, (1819-1905) were both born in Wittenberg, Germany. It is not known exactly when they came to the United States but they had lived in Bunker Hill, IN for several years. Elizabeth's parents, John A. (1823-1883) and Rosina Kauffman Grau (1831-1902), were also born in Germany and had settled in Howard Township, close to the Zion United Methodist Church, about eight miles northeast of Kokomo.

The 100 acre farm which Christian and Elizabeth had bought had only one field cleared. The south end of it was a swamp with a corduroy road and the rest of it was still wooded. However, they were young and not afraid to work.

The children born to them were Harley, Charles, Arthur, Ira, Rosa and Roscoe. Arthur died when a young man and Ira moved to Delaware County near Summitville. All of the others stayed in Howard County, near their parents.

About 20 years later, Christian and Elizabeth purchased another 100 acres across the road to expand their farming operation. Elizabeth wanted a new house, so it was built, along with two big barns, chicken houses, hog houses, etc. Soon after this their children had grown and secured farms for themselves near their parents. Charles went into business selling feed, fertilizer, coal, etc. at Vermont, about a mile west.

After Christian and Elizabeth died, Charles lived on the home place with other members of the family doing the farming. Then in 1951, Charley's daughter, Catheryn, and her husband, Ralph Lausch, moved here from Indianapolis to take over the farm. Charley and his second wife, Mable, moved to Greentown. Ralph Lausch had grown up in a farming community in northern Illinois.

In 1979, there was another change when Ralph and Catheryn's son, Keith, who had a degree from Purdue in Aeronautical Engineering, moved back from Texas with his wife, Judy, to take over the farming operation. They have a son, Brian, who is interested in farming and may be the next generation to take over the farm.

Harley's grandson, Michael Jackson, farms his land; Roscoe's son, Robert Kurtz, farms his father's land, and Rosa's family still owns the farm that had been in her family. All of these farms join the original 200 acres that Christian and Elizabeth bought. Each family has gradually added more acres.

This means that there have been four generations living on and farming the same land. This probably will continue well into the next century. The other grandchildren and great-grandchildren are scattered over the country and are represented in many professions. *Submitted by Catheryn Kurtz Lausch.*

LAMBERT - Ora Lambert and Flora Flynt Lambert were one of the couples whose families lived in Howard County for many years. They were married March 10, 1905. Ora was the son of Jacob and Annis Preble Lambert, farmers living about eight miles southwest of Kokomo. The Preble family lived close by. Ora was brought up on the road on which the old one-room school called Patty School was located. In fact he recalled once that he lived directly across the road, so he hadn't far to walk to school. In later years a reunion of Patty School students was organized and Ora was president for several years.

Ora had three sisters: Madge, who died in 1982; Myrtie, who was married to Jim Merrill, and had three children, Hal, Leslie, and Ruth, who married Mark MacDonald. Myrtie died at a young age, before the children were grown. The other sister, Kate, was married to Lonnie Maddox and died sometime in the 1960s. They had a daughter, Alta, who married Walter Ammerman. They had two sons, Wayne and Dennis, the latter now deceased.

Ora Lambert at age 66; Ward, Annis, Flora, and Mary. Taken in 1942.

Flora was the daughter of John and Josephine Jackson Flynt and they lived in the Alto area. She and Ora attended Shiloh Church on what is now Road 22 and they are buried in the cemetery there.

Ora was a farmer too and was known for his interest in politics and national affairs. For a number of years he farmed the "homeplace" after his father died. When the sister, Kate, and her husband bought the family farm, Ora and Flora moved to a farm a mile east of Galveston, where they lived until Ora died in July 1945 at the age of 69.

They had eight children: Reid, who married Helen Donnell, and had three children, Marilyn Wooldridge, Lawrence, and Joanne Glassburn; Edna, who was married to Kenneth Fryback and had one son, John; Mary, who married Leonard Crockett, and later Ray Ritchey; Catherine, who died in childhood; John, who died in WWII; Betty, who married Wayne Schrepferman in 1945; Annis, who married Robert Poland in 1958; and Ward, who married Sherry Puckett in 1949. He died in 1977.

Betty's children are Katherine, Susan, Alan and Julie. Annis's are Thomas, Philip and Stephen. Ward's children are Deborah and John.

Flora moved into Galveston in 1946 and lived there until her death in 1953 at the age of 72. *Submitted by Annis (Lambert) Poland.*

JERRY AND PEGGY LAND - Ira Delere Land was the seventh of eleven children. He was born May 3, 1895 in Rose, TN and was raised in Sunbright, TN. He came to Indiana in 1928 as an engineer on the Nickel Plate Railroad. He met Dorothy Irene Davis at the grocery store in Bennetts Switch, IN. She had been raised by her grandparents and was working in their store. She was born Dec. 31, 1907 and had two brothers and two sisters. She and Ira were married and started housekeeping in Peru, IN before buying a house in Kokomo in 1933. They had one son, Jerry Lee, born June 29, 1930. He grew up in Kokomo and graduated from Kokomo High School in 1948. After graduation he worked at Cuneo Press. In the spring of 1950 he met Peggy Joy Wandle at a dance at Indiana Beach (formerly known as Ideal Beach) in Monticello, IN. Peggy had been raised in Logansport, IN, the daughter of Oren Denver Wandle and Nina Pauline Schaefer. There were two other children - Bonnie Jean (Pat) and Richard Lee.

Jerry enlisted in the Army January 1951 and had basic training at Camp Breckinridge, KY. After basic Jerry and Peggy were married in May. Jerry was sent to Ft. Sill, OK for Officers Candidate School. After his commission in June of 1952 he returned to Peggy who had remained with her parents in Logansport, and a son Jerry Lee Land, Jr. born April 27, 1952. He was six weeks old before his dad was allowed to come home and get acquainted. The three of them moved to Ozark, AL, near Camp Rucker where Jerry was assigned. They lived there until Jerry was ordered to Korea. While he was in the Korean Conflict, Peggy and their son stayed with both sets

(L to R) Back row: Sherry Bowman, Kerry Land, Kari Leah Land, Jerry Land Jr., Lee Land and Robby Land. Front row: Brian Bowman, Jerry Land Sr., Peggy Land, Chris Land, and Brandon Bowman.

of parents at different intervals. Jerry returned from overseas in time for Christmas with his family in 1953.

In January 1954 Jerry returned to work at Cuneo Press and Peggy went to work for a physician. They bought a home in 1955 and a daughter, Sherry Lee, was born April 15, 1956. Peggy returned to the work force in 1957 at Delco Electronics (formerly known as Delco Radio) and enjoyed a 30 year career. A third child was born April 16, 1961 and he was known as Kerry Lee. In 1973 Jerry Sr. went to work for the State of Indiana as a driver safety specialist.

Jerry Jr. married Lee Ann Hancock in 1975 and they have two sons, Robert Delere born Oct. 6, 1981 and Christopher Michael born Aug. 15, 1984. They live in Greentown, IN. Both parents are employed by Delco Electronics.

Sherry married George William Bowman and they have twin sons, Brandon Michael and Brian Christopher born May 26, 1987. She has her own business as a Mary Kay Beauty Consultant and lives in Kokomo.

Kerry married Sandra Ann Fulmer and they have a daughter, Kari Leah, born May 26, 1980. Kerry is an employee of the State Highway Department and lives in Kokomo in his grandparents' old home.

LANGLEY-SWISHER - Jonathan and Hannah (Smith) Langley came from North Carolina around the turn of the 18th century, stopping for a while in Clinton County, OH, then moving on to Delaware County, IN. The last known record is that they were in Clinton County, Honey Creek Township (IN) at the time of his death in 1853. By the year 1840 all of his children were married: Samual to Mary (Polly) Crousore, Curtis to a woman whose first name was Namomi, John C. to Ruth A. Adamson, and Rebecca to Edom Garner (a founder of Russiaville). Samual's family shows up in the 1840 census records (Delaware County), with his wife Mary and two children. In 1850 he is in Center Township, Howard County with Mary, a 13-year-old daughter Ellen J., 4 sons: Jonathon 11, John 10, Edom 8, William 3; and another daughter, Arminda A., age 3. In the year 1851, it is believed that a smallpox epidemic hit this family taking Samual, Edom, and William, all in one stroke. Silas was born this same year (the one who fought the railroad physically and in the courts and won). The 1860 census lists Mary 48, Jonathon 20, John 18, Ellen 22, Arminda 10, and Silas 9. All were still in Center Township, Howard County, IN. The location of the land that they were living on is now where General Motors has built several plants along the U.S. 31 Bypass.

Samual had accumulated land, stock in a railroad, and made loans to several businessmen in Russiaville and Kokomo.

Curtis Langley (Samual's brother) did not agree with the dispersion and the handling of the assets, so he came from around the Anderson area and filed suit in the Howard County Court, one of the first in this court. Curtis lost this suit against Edom Garner (the administrator of the estate). In the will Samual left several acres of land to establish a school (Darrough Chapel) for educational purposes only, that a school would always exist on it, and if a school ceases to exist, the property is to go back to the Langley heirs. The sad part is that Samual's children did not receive an education.

Tragedy struck again in 1853, Jonathon (Samual's father) died. Samual, his sons Edom and William are buried in the pioneer cemetery. There is no record of them ever being moved. Some believe Jonathon was buried with his son and grandsons but have no proof of it.

Mary and her family show up in Liberty Township in 1870. John had gone off to war and returned. This small farm was located just south and on the west side of what is now 750E and 100S.

This is where Mary and Arminda lived out the rest of their lives. Mary never remarried (1803-1895). Arminda was a pipe smoking, coarse individual, that never married (1848-1926). They are buried side by side in Greenlawn Cemetery.

Back west about one-half mile (southeast corner of 700E and 100S) lived a family of Cherokee Indians in a mud house on a dab of high ground jutting out of this swampy land.

The head of this family was Samual (we will refer to him as Sam) Swisher age 62, his wife Mary 60, a son Louis 30, (whose trade was a blacksmith), Jane 27, Mary 23, Samual 20, Rachel 16, and Elizabeth 14. Just prior to the time of "The Trail of Tears" that came upon the Cherokee Nation is when Sam and Mary got married. He had gone back to North Carolina to tell his family and friends and to bid them farewell. The walk back consumed one year of time. Apparently he had decided to enter the white man's arena as a white. Census records bear this out. Like the old saying "you can take a boy off the farm but you can't take the farm out of the boy", his Indian traits stayed with him. Because of this, he would be shot at while working his own fields or while hunting. Now Sam had a hunting dog that must have been a very good dog because he traded him for 40 acres of swamp ground which is located on the northeast corner of 600E and 100S in Howard County. This corner for years was called Swishers Corner. Being swamp ground, he cultivated the highest part located at the east end. He traded this property for a section of land in the state of Texas. Sam and Mary walked to Texas to settle their land, but when the local people perceived they were Indians, they tried to lynch them. They escaped by the narrowest of margins.

Death came to Mary after their escape. Sam cut a tree down, hewed a casket and buried her along the bank of the Rio Grande River. Sam made it back to Howard County (1808-1893). (Benjamin, his grandson, tried to find this grave from the description given him but couldn't find it).

Samual, Sam's son, spent a lot of time around his father's grave (Lindley Cemetery) killing ground hogs that molested the cemetery. When Samual was about 80 years old, a grandson of his was with him one day at the cemetery when Samual waded out into the deepest part of the Wildcat Creek and retrieved a large rock and carried it to his father's grave and placed it as a head stone. To look at this rock and judge the weight of it is awesome for a man his age to accomplish.

Those Langley boys, John and Silas, somehow, someway got acquainted with those Swisher girls, because John married Jane and Silas married Mary. Both families lived side by side along Goyer Road just south of 100S or Pumpkinvine Pike on the east side. Jane owned six acres and Mary owned seven acres. This came to be known as Langley Corner. They witnessed the great run of the first gasoline-driven car.

Silas and Mary bore Alice, Samual, Rhoda, Tence, and Elce. John and Jane bore Rosa, Mary Elizabeth, Louisa Ellen, Samual Gidion, Emmia, and Emeline (Cam). Rosa married George Konk from Jennings County (Oct. 6, 1892). They bore one son and five girls, Luther, Jesse, Lucy, Sarah, Jany (my mother), and May. George was a house mover by trade. He died July 20, 1915 after getting electrocuted while moving a home for the Harness family just north of Middlefork (July 15, 1915).

Sometimes Jany would tell us about her grandmother Jane. She would count and recall words in their native tongue. She would even quote some of the ditties the Swishers were known for. But most of all she would tell us about the times her grandmother would sit by the hour combing her hair and singing her Indian songs, sometimes recalling and singing them herself. Jane Swisher Langley (1843-1919), John Langley (1841-1912) Crownpoint Cemetery.

Jany married Basil Orem Martin (March 3, 1919), a native of Tipton County, whose grandparents were early pioneers of that county. Nine children were raised from this union.

Jany (1902-1960), Basil (1896-1970). I was the seventh born of these nine. Most of the descendents from John and Jane are buried in Howard County. Although we had all these relatives and not ever seeing a grandparent, I grew up in the western part of Howard County, thinking I had only my brothers and sisters, a few aunts and uncles as relatives, mostly on my father's side of the family. I now search records to find as many as I can, go to their graves and while standing over them, I ponder in my heart the hardships, the tragedies, the times of joy, and their relation to our Lord Jesus Christ that transpired in their lives.

LARUE - Mautice E. (Jack) LaRue was transferred to the Chrysler Aluminum Die Casting Plant in May 1966. (That was just one year after the Palm Sunday Tornado). He brought with him his wife, D. Jean (Smith) LaRue, and sons, Dan and Gary. They bought a new house at 1713 Gordon Drive, Kokomo, IN 46902.

Dan enrolled in Kokomo High School and graduated in May 1967. Gary enrolled in Maplecrest Middle School and graduated from Kokomo Haworth High School in 1972. They both attended Indiana University, Bloomington. Dan graduated BS in Finance 1975, Law School 1978. Gary graduated BS in Business 1976. In the fall of 1966 the LaRues joined Grace United Methodist Church where they have remained active.

Jack was born Oct. 18, 1913 in Girard, KS to: Bert Ray LaRue and Luna Wicks LaRue. He has one brother, Melvin Spencer LaRue, born May 22, 1917, and lives in Orlando, FL. Maurice graduated from Girard, KS High School, 1932 and from Pittsburg State University, Pittsburg, KS 1939 BS in physics.

Delma Jean (Smith) LaRue born Aug. 10, 1923 in Colorado Springs, CO to: Delmar Cleveland Smith and Myra Bell (Clark) Smith. One sister, Lameta Rose (Smith) Larson who lives in Prosser, WA. Jack and Jean were married Aug. 30, 1942 in First Christian Church, Independence, MO. He was commissioned Lieutenant (Jg) in the Navy January 1944. Served in Bureau of Ordnance Washington D.C. Discharged 1946. They moved to Chicago, IL in fall of 1947. Dan was born Sept. 28, 1949 in Masonic Hospital, Chicago, IL. Gary was born July 14, 1954 in Berwin Hospital.

RALPH AND CATHERYN LAUSCH - On May 9, 1937 Ralph Lausch and Catheryn Kurtz were married in the Hillsdale Chapel United Brethren Church, about five miles east of Kokomo. Catheryn was native to this area, with her roots going back to her great-grandparents. Her parents were Charles (1882-1978) and Bertha Conkle Kurtz (1883-1923); her grandparents were Christian (1854-

244

1935) and Elizabeth Grau Kurtz (1859-1928), great-grandparents were John (1823-1883) and Rosina Kauffman Grau (1832-1902); all of these lived in Howard County.

Ralph was from Orangeville, IL, a small town in northern Illinois just three miles from the Wisconsin line. They met while in college at what is now the University of Indianapolis.

Ralph and Catheryn lived in Indianapolis for a few years, but in 1951 moved back to take over the family farm, because of her father's illness. The farm had already been in the family since 1880. By this time they had four children, Eugene, Keith, Mary and Edwin.

Ralph and Catheryn Lausch, May 9, 1987, 50th Wedding Anniversary

Later, when there were three children in college at the same time, it seemed expedient for Catheryn to go back to teaching school. She already had a Bachelor of Music degree, so she now finished a Masters in Elementary Education and taught fourth grade in the Northwestern Schools for 20 years. Since retiring from public school teaching, she has given private piano and violin lessons to many students. She also played violin in the Kokomo Symphony for nine years.

Ralph was on the Northwestern School Board for nine years and has been active in many community and church activities.

Eugene went to Michigan Law School and is now an attorney in Indianapolis. His wife, Carolyn, is chairman of the English Dept. at Brebeuf High School. They have three children, Eric, Kristen and Jonel.

Keith has a degree in aeronautical engineering from Purdue and worked for General Dynamics for several years before returning to the farm to take it over in 1979, when Ralph retired. His wife, Judy, teaches nursing at Indiana University Kokomo. They have one son, Brian.

Mary went to Wisconsin Medical School and now is Chief of Infectious Diseases at Mt. Auburn Hospital in Cambridge, MA, one of the Harvard teaching hospitals. Her husband, Dr. Harvey Fineberg, is Dean of the School of Public Health at Harvard.

Ed lived in Florida for several years and has a degree from the University of South Florida in Tampa. He also returned to Howard County to help with the family farm, but gave this up because of physical problems. He is the owner of Lausch Photography and has a growing business taking wedding pictures, portraits, etc. He has one son, Joshua.

The family has been in Howard County for more than 100 years and is well established here. *Submitted by Catheryn Lausch.*

JOHN SHOWALTER LAWRENCE - John Showalter Lawrence was one of eight children born to John Lawrence (1794 Pennsylvania-1871 Fulton County, IN) and Sarah S. Showalter Lawrence (1804 Pennsylvania-1874 Fulton County, IN). John S. and his twin brother, Jacob S., were born March 31, 1830 in Dearborn County, IN. The paternal grandparents were Valentine Lawrence (1758-1827 Pennsylvania) who served in the American Revolution and Magdalena Bach Lawrence of Pennsylvania. The maternal grandparents were Christian Showalter (1771 Virginia-1825 Indiana) and Anna F. Funkhouser Showalter (1775 Virginia-1849 Indiana). John and Sarah Lawrence and their children moved to Howard County after 1850. Their parents then moved to Fulton County after the 1860 census.

Jacob S. Lawrence married Martha Chitwood on Nov. 16, 1852 in Howard County and his brother, John S., married her sister, Margaret Jane Chitwood (born 1836 Indiana), on Aug. 5, 1855. They were the daughters of John and Barbara Carlier Chitwood.

John S. Lawrence was a farmer who lived in Ervin Township, Howard County, about eight miles from Kokomo, where he raised his family. John S. and Margaret had nine children. They included Martha E. (1856-1894) who married Charles Lewis; John Frank (1857-1922) who married Jane Lenehan; Sarah (1859-1938) who married William H. Miller on April 2, 1879; Mary Catherine (1861-1927) who married Henry Milton Williams on Sept. 4, 1880; Margaret Jane (1863-1893) who married Henry Hudson; Waity Belle (1865-1871); Laura Etta (1868-1948) who married Aaron Deardorff on March 10, 1887; Anna Rebecca (1870-1961) who married Willis Andrew Eikenberry on Sept. 27, 1891; and Eva Lawrence (1874-1941) who married William Kidder on April 25, 1896.

John's wife Margaret died Sept. 20, 1888 at the age of 51. John continued to live in Howard County until his death at the age of 86 on Aug. 26, 1916. They were buried in Barnett Cemetery near Kokomo. A beautiful monument presently stands at this site dedicated to his family. Other family members were buried nearby.

Henry M. Williams (1857-1927) and his wife, Mary Catherine Lawrence Williams, (1861-1927) continued to live in Howard County. Their three children were born there: Edna J. in September 1882; Earnest Basil in September 1884; and Elsie C. in January 1890. The Williams family eventually moved from the area after 1900 to Wexford County, MI. They returned frequently to Howard County for family reunions. They died within a week of one another at the University of Michigan Hospital in Ann Arbor, Washtenaw County, MI. They were buried in Barnett Cemetery near the other Lawrence family members. *Submitted by Mrs. Earnest E. Griffin*

BALAAM AND SALLY LETT - Howard County was home to Balaam and Sally Lett for over 20 years. Farming land near Alto, Balaam and Sally are listed in both the 1860 and 1870 census in Harrison Township.

Balaam Lett was born in Georgia in 1798 to Daniel and Cynthia Lett. The family settled in Owen County, KY. There Balaam met and married Sarah (Sally) Osborn(e) on Sept. 28, 1819. Sally was born in 1802 in Kentucky to John and Elizabeth Osborn(e).

Not long after the birth of their son, Sampson, in 1824, Balaam and Sally moved to Jennings County, IN. Between 1829 and 1844, seven more children were born to this family. By 1850 they had moved to Tipton County.

Balaam and Sally Lett helped establish Baptist churches wherever they settled. Balaam's family included an uncle, son and nephew, all of whom were ministers.

Balaam Lett died Feb. 27, 1877 and Sally then lived with a daughter and son-in-law until her death, Sept. 6, 1886. Balaam, Sally, three daughters and two sons-in-law are buried in Clinton County, south of Kokomo, at the cemetery next to Hills Baptist Church.

Balaam and Sally's children included: Sampson, 1824-1892; John Osborn(e), 1829-1908; Luranna, 1831-1881; Sarah Ann, 1832-1895; Martha R., 1835-1856; Margaret Serilda, born 1837; Walter Goodhue, 1841-1919; and Thomas H., 1844-1866.

Sampson Lett married Nancy Hodges. They lived near Alto where he participated on the local school board. He is buried at Crown Point, according to his obituary. John Osborn(e) Lett married Elizabeth Mitchell and, after her death, married Rebecca Sutton. John Osborn(e) is buried in Albright Cemetery. He and his family lived for a time in Kansas but he returned to Indiana.

Luranna and Sarah Ann Lett married brothers—Preston Hopkins Ploughe and Isaac Newton Ploughe. These four are also buried near their parents, next to Hills Baptist Church. Martha R. Lett married Uriah Thomas but died at the young age of 21. Her sons were in Sampson and Balaam's households in the 1860 and 1870 censuses. Martha, too, is buried at Hills Cemetery. Margaret Serilda Lett married John Patton. They raised their family in Howard County.

Walter Goodhue Lett married Rebecca Ellen Wolfe Jan. 19, 1860. Their first son and this author's great-grandfather, Beverly Ward Lett, was born near Kokomo. After the Civil War, Walter pursued his calling to the ministry as an itinerate preacher in Missouri. Settling in McDonald County, MO, Walter and Rebecca had 14 children. Walter died March 17, 1919 and Rebecca on Nov. 25, 1924.

Thomas H. Lett died at age 22 on Sept. 6, 1866 and is buried in Alto Baptist/Cobb Cemetery. Thomas, Walter and brother-in-law, Preston Ploughe, all served in volunteer Indiana companies with the Union Army in the Civil War.

Balaam and Sally Lett, with their family, grew and were nourished by the farmland of Indiana. Family births, marriages and deaths, while working the land, tie them to Howard County.

LINDLEY - (Copied from a 1945 issue of *Kokomo Tribune* relating to Howard County Centennial.) The year 1945 marks the 100th anniversary of the coming of the Lindley family to the vicinity of where Greentown now stands. In the year 1845 James Lindley of Wayne County, near Hagerstown, IN, with his 12 children and in-laws, moved to a location just west of Greentown along the Wildcat Creek. His sons, Tence, John, James, William and Charles, and his daughters, Mary, Lydia, Jenny, Hannah, Rachel and Susannah accompanied him. These daughters married Elliot, Conner, Howell, Osborn, McMillen and Woods, respectively. Notice that most of these names are common around Greentown.

The son, John, settled west of Lamb Cemetery, the first house on the south side of the road to the Lindley School. There he finished raising his 11 children - his sons, Samuel, James, William, John and Thomas, and his daughters, Sarah, Susannah, Nancy, Martha, Mary and Hannah. These daughters married Nordyke, Reeder, Haworth, Martin and Watkins, respectively. These names are somewhat scattered over Howard and Tipton Counties.

Samuel Lindley bought a farm one mile south of Plevna, then called Pleasantville, raised 15 children and died on the same farm, having attained the age of nearly 94 years. He married Lillie Cook, the first school teacher in Liberty Township. His step-son, Benjamin Wilkinson, and his sons, John and Ambrose, and his daughters, Harriet, Louisa, Martha, Isabella, Lavina, Mary, Elnora and foster daughter, Maude Spencer and step-daughters, Josephine and Sarah, and step-son, Alazo Cook. Harriet married Dock Stone and John Larowe; Louisa married Charles Zerbe; Mary married A.R. Dick; Josephine married Frank Golding; Sarah married Elijah Gabriel and Maude married Evert Cass.

This brings the family history down to the memory of the now living descendants who are now widely scattered over Indiana and all over the world. The hundreds of descendant families can take up where this leaves off and construct their family genealogies from the above.

Their religion in the early days was that of the Friends, and John Lindley of the second generation was one of the founders of the New Salem Church south of Greentown. The original church was built about a quarter of a mile west of the present church. These old-fashioned Quaker principles are pretty strongly characteristic of his descendants.

The Lindley Cemetery is located northwest of Greentown. These early settlers are buried there. Later families of the Lindley family are buried in the newer cemetery adjoining the Lindley Cemetery.

JAMES LINDLEY - The first records of Lindleys to arrive in America were in 1639. They fled England because of persecution from the Civil War in England. Lindleys came from Lincolnshire, Yorkshire and Cheshire England.

The Lindley ancestors of Howard County came to Orange County, NC in 1775. There were three brothers, and records indicate that the Lindleys are descended from one of these brothers.

Simon Lindley was possibly the son of one of these brothers or he is one of these three brothers. Simon married between 1778 and 1779. Simon and his wife are believed to have been murdered because of religious

245

beliefs (Quakers) at "The Battle of Lindley Mill" in Orange County, NC in 1781. They left behind an infant son named James Lindley born Sept. 28, 1779. James was adopted by Robert Ray on May 27, 1783, possibly relatives of Simon Lindley.

Samuel Lindley, Martha Martin and Susan Reader.

James married Susannah Stout on Feb. 12, 1797 and had 12 children by the time they moved in 1811 to Wayne County, IN. Their children were Mary, Lyddia, Jonathon, Jenny, Hannah, Rachel, Tence, John L., James, William, Charles and Susannah.

In 1845, James and Susannah and their entire family moved to the area known as Greentown, Liberty Township, Howard County, IN. James died June 23, 1851 at the age of 72. Susannah died April 6, 1859. They are buried in the Lindley Cemetery which is part of Greenlawn Cemetery and two miles northwest of Greentown. This cemetery was laid out on James' land. John's wife (Mary) was the first Lindley buried in the Lindley Cemetery in 1847.

The Lindley name is well-known throughout Howard County and Greentown. They were among the first settlers and with 12 children who were married and living in the area they made up a majority of the population back then. Several of James' sons and sons-in-law were in the Howard County government when it first started.

Tence was a farmer, proprietor of a livery stable, dealt with real estate, was a County Commissioner for six years, City Commissioner for several years, and Ditch Commissioner. He was married four times and had five children.

Charles was a farmer, a Justice of the Peace and merchant. William was a farmer and he erected a sawmill along the Wildcat in Greentown that did a booming business for years.

John L. was the eighth child born April 22, 1811. He married Mary McMullen June 19, 1828 in Wayne County, IN. They had 11 children: Sarah, Samuel, James, William, Susannah, Nancy, Martha, John, Mary, Hannah and Thomas. John was a carpenter and was one of the founders of the New Salem Church of Greentown. All of his sons worked in the family sawmill.

The descendents of James and Susannah married and the majority of them are still in Howard County and surrounding counties. *Submitted by Christine Pickett*

JAMES ROBERT LINDLEY SR. - March 29, 1916-July 21, 1993. John L. Lindley is the son of James Lindley and the great-grandfather of James Robert Lindley Sr. John came to Howard County in 1845 with his father and family. His son, Samuel, moved to Pleasantville (now Plevna) in the middle 1800s and married Lillis B. Cook (Wilkerson). After Lillis died, Samuel married Amanda C. Thompson (Cook). Ambrose Eldon Lindley was Samuel's youngest son. Ambrose married Sarah Jane Lennington June 2, 1894 in Howard County. They had seven children: Samuel Arthur, Earnest, Mary Elizabeth, Doris Winifred, Wanita, Amanda Almeda and James Robert. Sarah Jane died Sept. 11, 1917 while James Robert was only a baby. Doris, who was 12 years old, quit school to help raise her younger siblings. She married five years later and James went to live with Samuel and Amanda. Three years later Ambrose married Louisa Aldine Clark and three years later he was killed in a farming accident. Shortly after his father was killed James quit school and went to work to help support the family.

Back row, l to r: Rita Walters, James Robert Lindley, Sr., Marjorie Lindley and Karen Jarrett. Front row, l to r: Keith Lindley, Bonnie Butler, Audrey Burkhalter, Pat Anderson and James Robert Lindley, Jr.

James met Marjorie Maxine Pearcy when Marjorie was 15 years old. James recalled taking Marjorie out and only buying one soft drink or ice cream because he couldn't afford to buy two and he would tell her that he didn't want any. They married Oct. 10, 1936 in Rochester, IN. They set-up house on Touby Pike where James was raised. They had eight children: Winifred who died in infancy, Bonnie K. (Butler), Patricia A. (Anderson), Audrey L. (Burkhalter), Karen S. (Jarrett), Rita M. (Walters), James R. Jr. and Keith D. James served in the Navy during WWII. On the day he was to leave Marjorie went into labor, causing James to get a three day pass. This marked the arrival of Karen. Jim went to work at Delco Electronics in January 1953. This income was supplemented by farming and various jobs Marjorie had. In the spring of 1955 the family purchased a 133 acre farm (Cherry Hill Lane) in Ervin Township and continued to raise their family. James later went back to school and got his GED with the help of the Navy.

James and Marjorie have 22 grandchildren: Deborah (Pickett) Hudkins, Tim, Christine and Chris Pickett, Tina Butler, Teresa, Andy Jr. and Tray Anderson, Mark, Andrea and Sheri Burkhalter, Heidi and Fred Jr. Jarrett, Rhonda, Rodney and Regina Walters, Michelle (Lindley) Lawson, Lisa (Lindley) Seward and Marsha Lindley, Troy and Matt Lindley; and 10 great-grandchildren: Justin Walters, Cory, Carlie and Cami Anderson, Jason Pickett, Courtney Walters, Alisha Lindley, Nathaniel Wayne Lindley Lawson, Brittany Johnson, and Zackery Pickett. James and Marjorie's family live in Howard County and surrounding counties and a few live out of state. James passed away on July 21, 1993.

Every precious memory we have of our grandparents, parents, brothers and sisters and all of our families can only live on if we share them with our children and grandchildren from now and forever. *Submitted by Marjorie Lindley.*

SAMUEL LINDLEY - The Lindleys fled England for religious reasons and came to North Carolina in 1775. Samuel is a descendent of Simon Lindley who was one of three brothers or a son of one of the three brothers.

Simon Lindley and his wife were murdered by Tories because of their religious beliefs as "Quakers". They had a son (James Lindley) born 1779, who was raised by some neighbors.

James married Susannah Stout in 1797 and had 12 children. They moved in 1811 to Wayne County, IN. In 1845, James and Susannah and their entire family moved to the area of Greentown, IN.

John L. Lindley was James and Susannah's eighth child. He was born April 22, 1811 in Wayne County, IN. He married Mary McMullen June 19, 1828 in Wayne County. They had 11 children: Sarah, Samuel, James, William, Susannah, Nancy, Martha, John, Mary, Hannah and Thomas. John was a carpenter and was one of the founders of the New Salem Church of Greentown. All of his sons worked in the family sawmill. Their lives were strongly focused on religion.

Around the middle of the 1800s, John's two eldest sons (Samuel and James) decided to head west. Samuel journeyed as far as Pleasantville, IN, now known as Plevna, where he homesteaded 40 acres. James, however, continued on to California, where it's rumored that he became a sawmill tycoon and his son was the founder of the Diamond Walnut Company.

Back row, l to r: Samuel Arthur Lindley and James Robert Lindley, Sr. Front row, l to r: Mary Elizabeth Endsley, Doris Winifred Hostetler and Amanda Almeda Miller.

Samuel Lindley was born Oct. 16, 1830 in Wayne County, IN. He moved to Howard County at the age of 16 with his father. Samuel married Lillis B. Cook (Wilkerson) who had a son from a previous marriage. Samuel's marriage to Lillis B. Cook was recorded as one of the first marriages to take place in Howard County. Their children were Harriet, Louisa, Isabelle, John W., Lavina, Mary Elizabeth, Elnora and Martha. Lillis died March 10, 1862.

Samuel married Amanda Thompson (Cook) Jan. 7, 1869. She was the daughter of the Honorable Michael Thompson of Harrison Township, Howard County. She had three children from a previous marriage: Josephine, Sarah and Ahaz Cook. Samuel and Amanda had a son, Ambrose, born March 18, 1870, and a foster daughter, Maude Spencer. Samuel died March 19, 1924 on the same farm he had homesteaded. Amanda died in 1933.

Ambrose Lindley married Sarah Jane Lennington June 2, 1894 in Howard County. They had seven children: Samuel Arthur, Ernest, Mary Elizabeth, Doris Winifred, Wanita, Amanda Almeda and James Robert Sr. Earnest and Wanita died in infancy.

Sarah Jane died Sept. 11, 1917 while James Robert was only a baby. Doris, who was 12 years old, quit school to help raise her younger siblings. She married five years later and James went to live with Samuel and Amanda. Three years later Ambrose married Louisa Aldine Clark and three years later he was killed in a farming accident. Shortly after his father was killed, James quit school and went to work to help support the family. Samuel was a well respected man and lived on his farm until his death at the age of 96. *Submitted by Rhonda Walters*

ELIAS LOCK - Elias was born in Preble County, OH in 1821, the fourth child of Abraham Lock and Rebecca Ott. Elias married Sarah Brown in 1845. She was born in 1824, the fifth of twelve children born to George Brown and Sarah Nethercutt.

Abraham's farm had become too small to support the continued increase of children and grandchildren. In the spring of 1849 Elias and two of his brothers, John Abraham and Michael, joined an early exploring expedition going to Howard County, IN. Their youngest sister, Mary, would later marry George Faulkner of Kokomo. They established large tracts of land in sections 30 and 31 in what is now Kokomo. Elias had 117 acres of land at a cost of $2.00 per acre. Parts of this same tract would be sold to the City of Kokomo 45 years later for $300.00 an acre.

After Elias had recorded the land and established a temporary home, he walked back to his home in Ohio. Loading only a few possessions on his horses, and with two small children, Louisa (married Harrison Reed) and Daniel (married Emma Demming), Elias and Sarah led the horses back through the wilderness to their new home in 1851.

Elias was a small man. He had only one name to his family, that of "Pop". Punctuality and thrift were the main characteristics of this man who came to establish a home in the wilderness. Elias paid little attention to his German Lutheran Church but he was a man of high ideals and principles, none-the-less.

Elias Lock, 1821-1891; Sarah (Brown) Lock, 1824-1907

In addition to improving his land, Elias sired eight more children: Antrim (Relta Leonard, Elizabeth McNutt), Eli (Sally Yager), Laura (Jacob Tressler), George (Settie Graf), Abraham (Molly Spangler), Edgar (Martha Penn), Sarah (died age seven months), William (Ada Carr, Daisy Lichtenwalter). Elias never disciplined his children; he left that task to his 180-pound wife. Sarah had a "goodly" amount of temper but she had a bright side that was liked by everyone. She wasn't given to making a show. An example was that she joined the Methodist Church in such a way that few knew until many years later. Elias died in 1891; Sarah lived until 1907.

As time passed their four-room log cabin became too small for a large family. Father and sons dug the cellar and laid the foundation in the fall, spring and summer. The bricks were made at his brother Mike's farm. The purchase price, transportation and installation by mason Bill Morgan, made a total bill of $9.00 per 1000 bricks.

The family cut all the wood to be used for the frame and the interior of the house. White and red oak were used for the framework and ash was used for the trim. Two years of spare-time work was spent on the house which was finished in 1880. It was a nine-room, red brick home, one of the finest in the county. Its sturdiness can still be seen standing at the corner of Locke and Madison Streets in east Kokomo.

After the turn of the century Sarah sold all but the house to the Miller Syndicate. She continued to live there until her death. The youngest surviving son, William, died in Fulton County in 1959, age 94. *Submitted by Ned Helmuth*

LOCKE-TOUBY, COAN, KEARNEY, COBURN - When Elsie Locke (1894-1975) and Emmett P. Touby (1888-1972) were married in 1914 they settled on a farm in Howard Township, Howard County, owned by Emmett's father, Albert C. Touby (1851-1931). The marriage brought together the descendants of two pioneer families who had come to Howard County when Kokomo was just a trading post.

Elsie's grandparents, Elias and Sarah Brown Locke, had traveled from Ohio to Howard County to stake their claim after the Miami Reserve was opened to settlement. As their family grew, they built the large brick home which still stands on North Locke Street in Kokomo. The sixth of ten children, George L. Locke (1856-1938), was Elsie's father. In 1891 George married the young school teacher, Settie Graf, and they began their life together in a log cabin on a farm in Liberty Township. Their children, Philip R. and Elsie, attended the one-room Martin School and later graduated from Greentown High School. The family were respected citizens of the community. George became known for his equitable handling as executor of family estates.

Emmett Touby's grandparents, Peter and Jane C. Touby, came to Howard County from Fayette County, IN in 1853. Their children were Leora, Mary, and Albert C. Touby. The Touby Pike which winds its way northeast of Kokomo followed a route which bordered the Peter Touby homestead. Peter was instrumental in getting the road built (originally a "corduroy" road), and thus it was identified by his name. In 1883 son Albert married Kate Willits (1858-1941), establishing their home on land acquired north of the early homestead. Here they lived in a log cabin until they were able to build a large frame home where they raised their five children, Alice, Emmett P., Jennie, Mary, and Bessie. Albert and Kate's concern for the character of the community was evidenced by the fact that in 1896 they helped to establish and build the Rich Valley Christian Church just one-half mile east of their home. Both the Locke and Touby families were influential in the early development of the county.

Upon the retirement of his parents and their move to Kokomo, Emmett and Elsie bought the home place and it was here that their five daughters, Louise, Dorothy, Frances, Virginia, and Joan were born and raised. They attended the Howard Township School and the family was very active in the Rich Valley Church and the community. Following marriage, three of the daughters established their homes in Howard County. Frances died in 1958.

Often when attempting to trace the history of a family, we are, of course, drawn into the lives of many other families. This is true of a number of pioneer families in Howard County.

Because of this, we are submitting the Locke-Touby history with subsequent generations and their family accounts following the common ancestry. *Submitted by Virginia Coan*

LOCKE, TOUBY, COAN - In 1928, the George W. Coan (1889-1961) family came from Grant County to become tenants of the Ashley Smith farm located on North Touby Pike. Both George and his wife, Mable D. Wimmer (1892-1965), were descendants of long-time Grant County families. The Coans soon identified with the community. They became devoted members of the Rich Valley Church, and their sons, Charles (1911-1990), Robert (1918-1982), and Arthur, attended the Howard Township School. Thus it was that the lives of the Coan and the Touby families became intertwined. Both families took seriously their responsibilities as stewards of the land as well as their responsibilities as citizens. Eventually two of the Touby daughters married two of the Coan sons.

In 1935, Louise Touby became the wife of Charles Coan and they became tenants of the farm which they later purchased on Touby Pike. Their children Patricia and Eugene, and their foster son, Robert, attended Howard Township and later Northwestern schools. Both Charles and Louise took very active roles in the community. Charles served as Howard Township trustee and as a member of the Northwestern School Board for two terms. Both he and Louise labored enthusiastically in the planning and building of the Northview Christian Church, the nucleus having developed from the former Rich Valley Church. Both served in many positions on the state and regional levels of the Christian Church in Indiana. Louise now resides in Robin Run Village, a facility of the National Benevolent Association of the Christian Church in Indianapolis.

In 1945 Arthur Coan returned to the Coan family farm after having served three and one-half years in the Army during WWII. He and his brother, Robert, had both served in the European Theatre. Arthur and Virginia Touby were married in 1946 following her graduation from Ball State University. They moved as newlyweds to the Locke farm in Liberty Township. It was here that their four children, David, Jane, Nancy, and Elizabeth were raised. Both parents and children were active in the Eastern School and community. Virginia taught music in the Greentown and Howard Township schools. The three daughters have married and now reside in other areas. However, David and his wife, the former Mary Neal of Tipton, live near Greentown with their son, Jason, who is a student at Eastern High School. Arthur and Virginia have retired from the farm operation but continue to live at the historic Locke farm which in 1989 was granted the "Hoosier Homestead" recognition. *Submitted by Louise Coan*

LOCKE, TOUBY, KEARNEY, COBURN - Dorothy Touby attended Ball State University and taught in Kokomo before and after her marriage to Fred Kearney. Fred was born in Chicago and reared in Shelbyville, IN. He became employed with Delco Radio, then left to serve in the Pacific Theatre of WWII. Upon his return they continued residency in Howard County, established their home west of Kokomo where their children, Caroline and Mark, attended Northwestern schools. Caroline's marriage to Kent Tudor took them to California and Ohio, while Mark's General Motors education resulted in his becoming a senior engineer at Delco Electronics. With his wife Pauline, secretary in Taylor School System, and son, Matt, they share enthusiasm for Taylor School activities, especially sports.

Dorothy and Fred spend much retirement time in volunteerism to preserve local religious and cultural heritage.

COBURN - After graduation from Ball State University in 1948 Joan Touby married Edver W. Coburn whose parents Rev. and Mrs. Walter H. Coburn had come in 1941 as ministers to the Rich Valley Christian Church. Edver had served in the U.S. Navy during WWII, and upon completion of his degree from Purdue University, they moved to Fulton County and later to Marshall County where both taught school for many years.

Their children are Charlotte, Marcia, Philip, Lesley, and Jonathon. *Submitted by Dorothy Kearney*

ABRAHAM LOCKE - Abraham Locke was born in Kokomo, June 15, 1858, to Elias Lock and Sarah Brown. March 6, 1884, he and Mary Louisa "Mollie" Spangler were the 730th couple married by Hayden Rayburn, Minister of the M.E. Church in Kokomo. Mollie was born Aug. 9, 1858, in Fairfield County, OH, to Peter Spangler and Hester Brumbaugh.

Four children were born to Abe and Mollie: Harry Paul died at two months of age, April 26, 1886; Hazel Lucy was born Feb. 14, 1887, at the home of her aunt, Carrie Betzner, in Marion; William Frederick was born March 18, 1889; Charles H. was born and died April 18, 1892. Abe was a farmer but spent many years working in the oil fields of Old Mexico. Mollie died of cancer at their home on East Morgan Road on Christmas Day 1925. Abe died Aug. 11, 1926.

Fred married Nellie (Chapman) Maple Oct. 14, 1918. He was an oil well driller most of his life, having worked on wells in southeastern Howard County, Adams, Wells and Miami counties. Fred and Nell had one son, Frederick Omada, born Sept. 20, 1919. He married Majesta Baumgardner Sept. 20, 1938. They have one son, Jerry Frederick, living in Evansville, and one daughter, Diane, who lives at Parma, OH. Diane has a daughter and a granddaughter. Omada and Jet are retired, living in Muncie.

Hazel attended grade school at the old Ellis School, corner of Morgan and US #31 Bypass. She graduated from Maplewood Classical School in 1905 and was a bookkeeper for Thalman & Levi Department Store. Hazel received her diploma from Deaconess School of Nursing in Indianapolis in 1909, after which she did private-duty nursing in Howard County, and later, during the typhoid and flu epidemics, in southern Indiana.

Hazel took laboratory technical training at the Washington Park Hospital in Chicago, after which she worked in Butte, MT and then at the Fort Harrison Government Hospital #74 at Helena, where she met and married a tuberculosis patient, Walter Zenor, Jan. 2, 1924. Walter was a civil engineer before WWI. They returned to Kokomo in 1925 where a daughter, Madeleine, was born Nov. 26, 1925. A son, Frank Allen, was born March 12, 1929. Walter died in 1938 of Bright's disease. Hazel sold the home place and moved to Burlington. She married Charles Arrasmith in 1943 after moving to Lafayette. Hazel died in 1972.

Frank Zenor went to live with his uncle, Howard Zenor, in Riverton, WY and never returned to Indiana. He married Bertha Snell Jan. 23, 1952, and she died Jan. 1, 1994, in Humboldt, NE. Frank retired in 1989, due to ill health, after 35 years of service with the Nebraska Public Power District at Butte, NE. He is living at Humboldt.

Madeleine married Owen Miller and they had a son, James Alan, born Nov. 11, 1954. She second married Dillard M. Holt, Jan. 26, 1963. He was a son of Virgil Holt and Etwol Williams. Dillard adopted Jim and they also

247

had a daughter, Jan René, born Oct. 23, 1963. Dillard died in 1978 and Jim died in 1983. Jan married Dennis Freidline and they have two children, Nicholas W., born Dec. 28, 1990, and Christina Marie, born Oct. 3, 1992. Jan lives southwest of Russiaville and Madeleine lives in Kokomo.

ELIAS AND SARAH (YAGER) LOCKE -
Jesse Clore Yager (1832-1916) and Margaret Catherine Shirley (1834-1916) came to Howard Township, Howard County area after their marriage in Oldham County, KY. They came in an open wagon, bringing tables, chairs, crocks, and utensils that have since passed down through the Yager family. Margaret was only 16 years old when she left home to settle in what was then, a wilderness. They built a home (which stands today) and farmed acreage located at 400 N and 250 E. They were the parents of five children: Lawrence, Sarah, Ida Belle, Pressly, and Eli. Sarah, our grandmother, was known affectionately in the community as "Aunt Sally".

In the spring of 1849, Elias Locke (1821-1891) and his two brothers, John and Mike, of Preble County, OH, pushed westward to Howard County, IN. They established tracts of land in what is now Kokomo and its vicinity. Elias purchased 117 acres at a cost of $2.00 per acre. Forty-five years later parts of this same tract were sold to the City of Kokomo for $300 per acre. After Elias recorded his land and established a temporary camp, he walked the distance back to his wife and home in Preble County, OH. Loading only a few possessions on his horses, and with his wife, Sarah A. Brown (1824-1906), and child riding, he led the family back through the wilderness to his new homestead. Later, they built a nine room brick house, which still stands, at 804 North Locke St. in Kokomo. They were farmers and to this union were born Louis, Daniel, Antrum, Elias, Laura, George, Abraham, John Edgar, Sara Catherine, and William.

Through the marriage of Elias Locke (1852-1893) and Sarah M. Yager (1857-1940) on Nov. 24, 1881, our maternal lineage emerged. They were the parents of Lula Belle, who died in infancy, Kate L. and Thomas Jesse Locke.

Paternally, our ancestors were Amish from Berne, Switzerland who landed in Philadelphia, on Sept. 1, 1736 on the ship *Harle*. They moved to a farming community near Hamburg, PA. Later members of the family migrated westward to Waupecong in Miami County. Our great-grandfather, Zacharia Hostetler (1813-1907) married Barbara Troyer (1818-1907) in 1835. To this union were born seven daughters and four sons. One of the sons was our grandfather, Jacob L. Hostetler (1851-1892).

Jacob Hostetler married Katie Enders (1854-1942) who was born in New York City. The Enders, William E. and Anna (Cline), were farmers west of Waupecong in Howard Township. Jacob and Katie had nine children: Willard, Albert, Maude, Carrie, Elmer, Anna, Ivory, and two sons who died in infancy. The last three sons and grandfather Jacob are buried in the cemetery at Kokomo Zion United Methodist Church.

Our parents, Albert Clinton (1879-1966) and Kate Locke Hostetler (1884-1970), were from this pioneer stock. They instilled in us their love for farming and the importance of a strong and caring home and family life. Above all, in tracing our heritage, we appreciate their examples of living wholesome and contributing lives in our community. *Submitted by Sarah C. Rockey and Fern Tyner Nash*

DAVID AND MARY ANN LONG -
My great-great-grandfather Long was an Irish potato farmer around 1800 during the potato famine. This problem caused him to come to the United States to settle in West Virginia. His son, Thomas A. Long, came from Kentucky up the Wildcat Creek looking for new territory to homestead. He settled in western Howard County in 1835, where he raised several children. His son, John T. Long, homesteaded in the south part of Jackson Township on what is now 1200 East. Here he raised two sons and three daughters and cleared the land. After a few years he sold the farm and bought a house and store in Sycamore. The store enterprise was unsuccessful due to bad credit so he became the Nickel Plate Railroad station agent. His son, Everett Long, my father, worked as a hired hand living on a farm nearby. In 1905 he passed the civil service exam and became a rural mail carrier on Route 5, Greentown. He used his income to purchase farm ground. In 1923 at age 45 he married Gertrude Brooke of Sims and they moved to a farm three miles east of Greentown. They lived here the rest of their lives having a daughter, Ruth, in 1925 and a son, David, in 1929. I was born on my father's 51st birthday. Ruth married Everett Putney and soon they moved to Florida where they still reside. I married Mary Ann Hodson in 1950 and moved to the farm east of Greentown on 100 South, where we still live. We are both retired from school teaching and are active with the farm work.

My mother was born in Iroquois County, IL and moved at age six in 1900 from their farm with her brother and parents to a 60 acre farm south of Sims. Mother's maternal grandmother was one of seven daughters of a man from around Moscow, Russia who moved to Berlin, Germany at age fourteen and married a German girl. He worked for a wagon maker then went in business for himself manufacturing lightweight buggies. All of his daughters migrated to the United States.

Mary Ann Long - Mary Ann's great-grandparents, Stevens, came to the United States from Germany having a baby on the ship. The baby was named Atlanta. The Stevens retired from farming in Taylor Township and moved to Hemlock. Atlanta married David Hodson and they lived on their farm south of Hemlock. Their son, Marble Hodson, married Alta Shepler and farmed west of Hemlock. Their oldest daughter, Winifred, died at age 29 leaving one son, W. Robert Wise. A daughter 14 years younger married David Long.

David and Mary Ann Long have three children and seven grandchildren that all live in Howard and Grant counties. *Submitted by David Long.*

JACOB T. LONG -
Jacob Thomas Long, the second child of Robert M. Long, came to Howard County in 1842 with his father, Thomas A. Long. In 1848, Robert married Mary Jane Thorne. They had nine children. Robert served as county commissioner for eight years. In 1893 he died from lock jaw.

Jacob was born on July 31, 1851. In 1875, he married Susan Elizabeth Murphy, daughter of Chester Murphy, a Civil War veteran. Jacob and his wife settled on a farm in Ervin Township, but four years later, moved to a new farm four miles northwest of Kokomo. There, he built a large barn, planted an orchard, ran a thresher and operated a sawmill. In later years, Jacob, unable to walk without the aid of crutches, moved into town, where he spent the last 20 years of his life.

Jacob and Susan had eight children: Blanche, Omer, Mazie, Madge, Grace, Carl, Roscoe, and Dale. Omer, the second child was born in 1884 and married Grace DeMoss in 1905. They had three children: Clarence, Harry and Elsie (Krall).

Mazie, born in 1886, married Butler Robertson in 1911. They had nine children: Twins who died at birth, Dorothy (Passons), Gene, Russell, Mary (Jeffries), Lois (Bowman), Ross and Neil.

Madge, born in 1888, married Elmer Rusk in 1912. Their children were Lloyd, Cloyd, Jay and Lewis.

Jacob Thomas Long and Susan Elizabeth (Murphy) Long

Grace, born in 1889, married John Wagner in 1914. They had two sons, John and Robert.

Carl, born in 1892, married Edna Mae Rader in 1914. Their children who reached adulthood were: William, Lola Mae (Seavers), Mary (Gardner), Carl, Donna (Goldkett), and Maxine (Munsel).

Roscoe was born in 1895. He married Roxie Roush in 1914. They had two daughters, Thelma (Roe) and Ellen (Hanger). Roscoe died in 1922. His brother, Dale (born in 1898), married Roxie in 1923. They raised Roscoe's daughters.

Blanche, the oldest child, born in 1883, married Charles Downhour, the 11th child of Henry Downhour of Howard County. Charles farmed in Howard County for a while, but later moved to Oklahoma, then back to Indiana, near Tippecanoe, and then to a farm near Bourbon, IN. Blanche died in 1955 and is buried in the Galveston Cemetery. Charles died 10 years later and is buried beside her. They had seven children, two of whom died in infancy. The surviving children were Eremel, who married Charles Havlin, an electrician; Susie, who married Everett Leiter, heating and cooling contractor; Esther, who married Floyd Gushwa, a truck driver. Floyd, the only son, married Nellie Lusher. The last daughter was Mary Jane, who married Edwin Butters, a farmer, who raised buffalo in Coldwater, MI.

Susie, the second oldest daughter, was working in South Bend when she met and married Everett Leiter. They had eight children: Devon, in Martinsville, Fred, in Bloomington, Arlene, in Goshen, Shirley (Lehr), Cloyce, and Ellen in Orlando, FL, Gerald, in Elkhart, and Gale, who moved to Kokomo in 1963. He has taught at Kokomo and Haworth High Schools for over 30 years. In 1970, he married Donna Niesse, who was also teaching in Kokomo. They have two children, Eric and Vicki. *Submitted by Vicki Leiter.*

JUDGE THOMAS A. LONG -
Thomas Ammon Long was born near Lexington, KY Oct. 16, 1796. When he was 13 he was bound out to Billy Barlow of Nicholas County, a gunsmith, to learn a trade. He worked six and one-half years for nothing; he returned to Bowden County and set up a shop as gunsmith.

His father was Robert Long who came to America from England in 1788. His mother was Margarate Ammon. Both families owned slaves. When Thomas was five years old, his father died and his mother remarried.

When he was 22 he married Margaret McClanahan. They had 13 children: Eliza Jane, Margarate, Martha, Robert, James, Polly, Sophronia, America, Eleanor, John Thomas, Esther, Mary Frances and infant.

Thomas' estate from his father's plantation, after his mother's death, was seven slaves, whom he freed. He, with his wife and five children, moved to Indianapolis. The land was swampy and three of the children died there.

In the spring of 1840 T.A. Long, with other pioneers, rode north on horseback in search of homes in the Miami Reserve, at that time a wilderness. He found a claim on Wildcat Creek in Clay Township. He bought the claim for $100.00. The claim had four acres cleared and had a small log cabin on it.

In March 1842, he and his family moved from Marion County and settled on his claim. The rest of his children were born here.

He built a small shop near his cabin and began repairing guns for the Indians. A small patch of corn was planted, the first in Clay Township and probably in the county. David Foster had built a cabin across the creek at a spring. Foster was trading blankets, guns and whiskey for skins with the Indians, so it was called Indian Springs.

When the county was organized Mr. Long was named one of the judges. His work as judge was mostly with the Indians as they would come to him for help when they thought they were not getting a fair deal from the settlers. The Indians called him "Old Specks" because he wore glasses. They counted him their friend.

In 1864 he moved on a farm in Harrison Township. He added nurseryman to that of gunsmith and blacksmith. He sold trees that gave his neighbors many kinds of apples that are now only a memory.

Knowing nothing in their earlier days but an open fire, Mrs. Long would still bake her corn pone over live coals and hang a pot in the fireplace to cook her dinner.

They were quite happy growing old together. They both passed away in 1890 and lie together in Twin Springs Cemetery.

He was counted quite a fiddler in his day and played for dances, but in later years he decided the violin was an instrument of the devil and refused to play.

T.A. Long was my great-great-great-grandfather, and I am very proud of him for being an influential man in Howard County. *Submitted by Sandy Newby Zell*

THOMAS A. LONG - Thomas Ammon Long was born near Lexington, KY, on Oct. 16, 1796. He was bound out to a gunsmith when he was 13. He worked for six and one-half years, learning the trade. On Jan. 14, 1819, he married Margaret McCleur McClanahan. Their marriage lasted 72 years, producing 13 children. In 1827, he moved to Indianapolis. In the spring of 1840, Long came to Howard County and bought a claim in Clay Township from a man named Hart for $100.

Long moved his family from Marion County to the claim in 1842. Here he built a shop near his home and repaired guns for the Indians. David Foster had built his home across the creek and was trading blankets, guns and whiskey to the Indians. Foster would interpret for the Indians and vouch for them, so Long would charge Foster for the repairs and Foster would charge the Indians three or four times the amount.

Thomas A. Long and Robert Ervin were named as the first two associate judges for "Richardville" (Howard) County. While they were serving their terms, court was held in the two-story log courthouse on the public square. When a jail was built, Judge Long, as a gunsmith, made the lock and key for the jail. The key is said to have been about 10 inches long and to have weighed about 4 pounds.

Long was known to the Indians as "Old Specks" because he wore glasses. Generally he got along well with the Indians. He was a close friend to Peter Cornstalk, who took a special liking to Mr. Long's youngest son, John. The Indians apparently trusted Judge Long and would come to him when they felt they were being cheated by white settlers.

One known conflict between Judge Long and an Indian involved the old chief Kokomo. Judge Long wanted to make some bells for his cattle, and went to see the chief to buy some brass. He was introduced by a Mr. Barnett as a Kentuckian. Kokomo left the wigwam, painted himself and returned, telling Mr. Barnett that he had scalped several Kentuckians and that he would scalp Judge Long also. Long informed Barnett that if Kokomo tried anything, he would shoot him on the spot. Kokomo changed his mind and Long got the brass he needed.

Mr. Long was a very religious man. In his younger days he was quite a fiddler, playing for dances when asked to do so. In later years, he decided that the violin was an instrument of the devil and never played again. When he was no longer able to attend church, he read the New Testament through every week, starting on Sunday morning.

The 72 years of marriage testify to the love between Thomas and Margaret. When Margaret developed cancer, Thomas began to worry that she would die and leave him alone. He began eating barely enough to keep up his strength and died on Oct. 19, 1890 at the age of 94 years and 3 days. The procession to the cemetery was a mile long. Ten days later Margaret died also. They are buried in the Twin Springs Cemetery.

JOSEPH MARSH LOOP - Joseph Marsh Loop, an early pioneer in Howard County, arrived in the fall of 1853 from Preble County, OH. He was born in Bativia, Clermont County, OH, Oct. 26, 1818. His father, Henry, and grandfather, Peter, were born in New York. On March 3, 1840, he married Margaret Elizabeth "Peggy" Link who was born in Virginia. They had 12 children and adopted their granddaughter. In September 1853, Joseph and Margaret sold their farm near Eaton, OH, and moved in two prairie schooners to Howard County with their eight children. They located temporarily in a log cabin on Wildcat Creek at a place then known as "Flabby," halfway between Greentown and Kokomo on the highway leaving Kokomo by Jefferson Street. They lived there about one year. Joseph Loop had taken out 640 acres of land 1-1/4 miles north of Greentown where he first built a log house on the east side of the road. About 1868 or 1869, across the road he built the first brick house in Liberty Township, making his own bricks. A young man, Hiram Pitman, just discharged from the Union Army, helped finish the house, met young Margaret Elizabeth "Maggie" Loop and married her there after the house was completed. This large dwelling has been continuously occupied and is currently the home of the Weir family.

Home built 1868-69 on 640 acre section 1-1/4 mi. north of Greentown by Joseph Marsh Loop, my great-grandfather.

On New Year's Day, 1928, John Nicholas Loop wrote his memories of the trip from Preble County to Howard County especially for his sister, Maggie Pitman. When the family moved, little Maggie was almost four years old and Nick was eight. Nick tells of the sadness of leaving their pleasant home, grandmother's orchard and little schoolmates that they would never see again. Tied to the back of one covered wagon was their black and white spotted cow "Barney", not acting in a friendly manner and unwilling to move on. This cow played an important part in settling and nourishing a large family in a new country. Every morning and evening Mother Loop would milk Barney and the chief food was mush and milk which gave the children health and rosy cheeks. Barney lived a long time and great floods of tears flowed from every eye when she died.

The third child of Joseph and Margaret was James David Loop who was born in Preble County, OH, Oct. 22, 1843. A Civil War veteran, he married Anna Breckinridge Crume (1857-1926). Anna was his second wife and helped raise his four children from his first marriage to Sarah Frakes and the five children from their marriage. Their oldest son was Joseph Brice Loop (Jan. 28, 1886-March 27, 1958) who married Minnie Mae Lovejoy on June 9, 1915. They raised five children - William Lowell, Mary Louise Doty, James Paul, Iola Mae Hankins and Helen Irene Webb. Mae Lovejoy Loop died in Kokomo, Sept. 3, 1992, at the age of 99 years. She was a grand Christian woman.

There are more than 70 Loops buried at the Greentown Cemetery and others at Crown Point Cemetery in Kokomo. *Submitted by James Paul Loop*

LOWERY-SUTER - Eileen Ruth Lowery was born on Feb. 19, 1916 in Kokomo, IN, the oldest daughter of six children born to Loyal and Nora Lowery. Her father was a carpenter by trade. Eileen lived and worked most of her adult life in Kokomo. She worked several years for First National Bank and Hank's Supermarket.

Robert Elhanan Suter was born on Oct. 9, 1912 in Martinsville, IN, the youngest son of six children born to Robert G. and Harriet Suter. He worked and lived most of his adult life in Kokomo. He worked for the Globe and participated in the building of the last lifeboat built at the Globe during WWII. He then worked for the Chrysler Corp. as a millwright for 27 years.

Eileen Lowery and Robert Suter were married on Aug. 21, 1936 in Logansport, IN. They had three children: Sandra Kaye, Robert James (Jim), and Pamela Jeanne. Eileen and Robert divorced in 1958; they each remarried, Eileen to Robert Crousore in 1970, and Bob to Bernice Schafer in 1961; he died on Aug. 5, 1976 in Kokomo, IN.

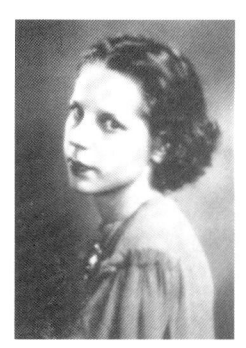

Robert Suter; Eileen Lowery

Sandra Kaye Suter was born on Sept. 8, 1939 in Kokomo, IN. She married Paul Gene Bowman on Nov. 8, 1959 in Forest, IN. They have five children: Paul Keith, Sheryl Lynn, David Cameron, Lisa Ann, and Mark Douglas. They have four grandchildren: Tiffeny Diane and Ashton Daniel Bowman; Stephanie Christine and Nicole Laraine Bennett.

Robert James Suter was born on April 6, 1942 in Kokomo, IN. He married Patricia Schafer in 1961; they divorced in 1968. They had three children: James Brian, Brenda Kay, and Robert Todd. He remarried in 1970 to Linda Shaff; they divorced in 1985. He has one stepdaughter, Sonya Shaff. He has three grandchildren and two step-grandchildren: Mandy Mae Suter, Jason Robert and Kyle William Martin, Jennifer Marie Wiseman and Kelsea Nicol Hudson.

Robert Todd Suter was killed in Swinfort, Germany on July 16, 1982 while serving in the Army Tank Div. He is interred at the Sunset Memory Gardens, in Kokomo, IN.

Pamela Jeanne Suter was born on June 23, 1948 in Kokomo, IN. She married Jack Fouch on Jan. 7, 1967; they divorced in 1974. She has one son, Scott Ashley Fouch, who married Michelle Pickett in 1988. They have two children, Brandon Scott and Curran Allen Fouch.

Of the Suter family, Pam is the only one still living in Kokomo. Sandy lives in California, Robert (Jim) lives in New Mexico, and Eileen lives in Bloomington, IN. The whole family still has fond memories of Kokomo and the people they know there. *Submitted by Pamela J. McDowell*

STANLEY A. AND FRIEDA A. LUCAS - The Air Force brought Stanley and Frieda to Kokomo in 1972 when Bakalar AFB, Columbus, IN, closed and transferred functions to Grissom AFB, Bunker Hill, IN. Stanley moved in January 1970 and finally moved his family to Kokomo on July 4, 1972.

Stanley and Frieda went to the same school, Nineveh High School in Johnson County, (the school which was used in the movie "Hoosiers") but really met in church and were married on June 8, 1952. Stanley joined the Air Force in January 1953 and was stationed in New Mexico and had a tour in England. They have three children, Donna L. Rund (March 19, 1954); Kevin A. Lucas (Dec. 1, 1957); and Brian K. Lucas (July 21, 1960).

After Stanley's discharge from the Air Force, he was in the construction business with his father in Johnson County. He and his family resided in Nineveh and Trafalgar areas during that time.

Stanley's parents, Lucien Bruce and Gladys Marie (Hogue) Lucas, moved to Johnson County from Casey County, KY in 1935. His grandparents, Azariah and Alice (Walls) Lucas and Joel A. and Lola M. (Brown) Hogue, were all from the Casey County, KY area. Grandpa Lucas worked and owned a sawmill. Grandpa Hogue was a farmer.

Frieda's parents, William T. and Audrey V. (McIntosh) Brockman, were born and raised in Johnson and Marion County, IN. They married Dec. 30, 1933, living in Johnson County until 1965 when they moved to Strawberry, AZ. They returned to Johnson County in 1978 and reside in Franklin.

Frieda's grandparents, Ira T. and Anna M. (Mitchell) Brockman, were farmers in Johnson County and Oscar D. and Frieda M. (Constable) McIntosh were from Greene County, but moved to Marion County, where they raised seven children. Oscar McIntosh worked for the New York Central Railroad.

Stanley retired from Civil Service and the Air Force in March 1993. In June, after living in Kokomo for 22 years—and becoming very attached to the area—Stanley and Frieda made the decision to move back to Johnson County (in the Whiteland area) to be closer to the majority of their family.

DALLAS F. AND LINDA K. LUNSFORD JR. -

Dallas started to work at Delco Radio (now Delco Electronics) in December 1965. He moved into a room at 315 East Taylor Street, Kokomo. Addie Sullivan (Linda's maternal grandmother) rented the room out to Dallas. One day he noticed a picture of me (Linda) on top of the TV, and asked who it was? Grandmother told him that it was her granddaughter, Linda, who lived in South Bend. He of course asked grandmother for my address. That was the beginning of our "Courtship", in June of 1967 we started dating. One year later on June 8, 1968, Dallas and I were married at Union Street Friends Church. His parents, Dallas F. and Mary R. (Lewis) Lunsford of Cambridge City, IN and his two sisters, Susan Blevins and Linda Kay Messer were present, plus other family members.

On Oct. 15, 1970 our daughter, Marilyn Sue Lunsford, was born and on Oct. 1, 1973 our son, James Franklin Lunsford was born, both in Howard Community Hospital. Now "Our Family" was complete with a daughter and son.

Marilyn graduated from Western High School in 1989 and was married on April 25, 1992, to Lloyd Arnold Rodgers II in First Friends Church. James "Jim" graduated from Western in 1993 and in the fall of 1993 started school at Vincennes University, majoring in tool and die.

My family roots for Howard County go back to about 1938 when my grandmother moved here from the Young America area. Before that, grandmother lived in Ohio and was married two times (Dennis), Floyd B. Bachelor and Lester C. Marston. When she moved to Indiana she was married five more times: Wm. D. Mummert, Ernest Mummert, Ott Collins, Frank H. Russell and Merl J. Sullivan. I spent most of my vacation time in the Howard County area. I loved to stay with Grandmother Addie.

My father, John Edwards, lived in the Howard County area about 1936 to 1943. My mother, Marian (Bachelor) Shaffer, used to work for Duke's Restaurant in 1939 which was located at 112 E. Sycamore. Mother met father while working for Bendix Corp. in South Bend. She and father were married on Sept. 25, 1943 in St. Louis, MO. On Sept. 4, 1946 I was born as an only child. I have many happy memories of Kokomo with family and friends, I have quite a few cousins both first and second, and two aunts and one uncle living in Howard County of my mother's line. *Submitted by Dallas F. and Linda Kay Edwards Lunsford Jr.*

PAUL KOSTA AND MARY HELEN TATE-LUSHIN -

In 1934, Paul K. Lushin, a Yugoslavian immigrant, migrated to Kokomo to seek employment with the Continental Steel Corporation. He had earlier worked in the Gary, IN steel mills, but because of the language barrier, he left Gary and came to Kokomo. Many of his Macedonian friends, from the same small village of Capri, Yugoslavia, had come to Kokomo the previous year and were now working for the Continental Steel Corporation. Paul was eventually hired and continued to work in the Kokomo mill until 1949.

Paul and Helen Lushin shortly after their marriage in 1936

Paul met and married a young lady from Russiaville, IN in April of 1936. Her name was Mary Helen Tate. She was 25 and he was 29. The following year the first of their four children was born, a son.

After working for the Continental Steel Corporation for 13 years, Paul purchased, in 1949, an old store building at the corner of Morgan and Webster Streets. They named their new business "Paul and Helen's Hoosier Bar Tavern". The Lushins owned and operated the Hoosier Bar, as it was known, for the next 25 years. One very unique and interesting item which was sold at the Hoosier Bar was his very own brand of "hot peppers". Paul had a talent for raising and canning peppers. He always had an ample supply and people would come from all over the city to purchase them. Even to this very day, individuals who remember the peppers and the special way they were prepared, tell how much they liked them and ask where they might purchase something similar. Unfortunately, his special talent with the pepper has not been duplicated.

The Lushins successfully operated the Hoosier Bar until the spring of 1975. They sold the business and retired. During their retirement years, they spent most of their time with friends, becoming active participants in several different senior citizens' groups.

Paul and Helen's Hoosier Bar Tavern as it was in 1963.

Helen passed away in August of 1986, at the age of 75, and Paul died less than two years later in 1988, at the age of 81. They enjoyed a full healthy life together and their marriage stood the test of time and spanned more than half a century. Throughout life, they dedicated themselves to family. Their children and grandchildren remember them with reverence and still can recall the tales their father and grandfather told about his years, as a young boy, in war torn Yugoslavia. He had been raised by his maternal grandmother and spent his youth tending sheep in the Macedonian mountains. The small village in which he lived was poor. The people's very survival depended upon their ability to raise and harvest their own food. While herding sheep on the mountainside, he would spend time with soldiers who were billeted nearby. Many times these soldiers made the difference as to whether or not young Paul had food. Battles were fought in close proximity to where young Paul lived, and "close calls" were not uncommon. Life in Yugoslavia in the early 1900s was, because of the war, both dangerous and harsh. Later, as a father and grandfather, Paul shared these experiences and stories with his children and grandchildren. He understood and related many times how much he loved and appreciated the opportunity to live and work in America.

Paul Lushin on the right tending his pepper plants (circa 1936).

Their oldest son, Jean Paul Lushin, is now the Center Township Trustee of Howard County. Their daughter, Kathryn Diane, lives in Bloomington, IL with her husband, and is a housewife. Another son, Stephen, is a tool and die supervisor at Delco Electronics, and their youngest son, Daniel, is a maintenance foreman for the Alaskan Pipe Line.

PEARL AND DOROTHY LYKINS -

Pearl S. Lykins, born March 15, 1893 to John and Mary Bell (Richardson) Lykins in Catlin, IL, one of nine children. John farmed and was Catlin Road Commissioner. They raised eight children (one died in infancy). Pearl served as sergeant in the Quartermaster Corps. stationed at Fort Leonardwood during WWI. After discharge from the army, he started working for Indiana Bell Telephone. He was employed as a lineman and line foreman for 38 years and before retiring was Supervisor of Building and Motor Vehicles in Kokomo. After retirement he worked as census taker and assessor of Howard County.

Dorothy M. Fort, born July 11, 1903 youngest daughter of Edward and Julia (Moran) Fort, Greenfield, IN. Pearl and Dorothy married Aug. 11, 1923 in Sacred Heart Church in Indianapolis, IN.

Edward and Julia owned and operated a slaughter house and butcher shop and farmed. Brandywine Creek ran through their farm that was the "Old Swimming Hole" of James Whitcomb Riley. They had a large apple orchard and shipped apples to other states.

Pearl and Dorothy Lykins

On Jan. 30, 1925, Pearl and Dorothy had a daughter, Barbara Ann, born in Shelbyville, IN. The family traveled and moved to several different Indiana towns for his work. When Barbara was old enough for school, they settled in Kokomo at 1530 S. Armstrong, and she went to Washington School in September 1931 from the first through seventh grade. Pearl still worked out of town during the week and came home on weekends. In 1933 they moved to 1718 S. Indiana, and then in 1935 moved to 1933 S. Buckeye where they lived for 59 years.

Their second daughter, Janet Sue, was born at home on June 8, 1936. Both Barbara and Janet are R.N.s. Barbara worked at Wolfcales' Drive Inn, Muir's Drug Store, J.C. Penneys and Kingston Products until entering nurses' training at Good Samaritan Hospital in 1943 and became a registered nurse in 1946.

Barbara married George W. Schmitt on March 15, 1947. Barbara worked at St. Joseph Hospital 10 years and as office nurse for Thomas W. Wachob, M.D. 22 years. She was treasurer of Good Samaritan Alumni and was chapter member of Lakeside Izaak Walton League in 1954. George was the youngest son of George and Frances (Terwische) Schmitt. His father was employed by Globe American until his retirement. George served three years in the army during WWII in the South Pacific. George and Barbara both graduated from Kokomo High School in 1943. George started working at Indiana Bell as a cable repairman for 38 years and retired in 1984. George is active in the Izaak Walton League; he was State President for four years and has been local president several times. He is also active in the Telephone Pioneers.

Janet graduated from Kokomo High School in 1954 and entered Holy Cross School of Nursing in 1954 and graduated in 1957 as an R.N. Janet worked several years for Dr. Alward and Dr. Michael. She is now working at St. Joseph Hospital & Health Center. Janet married Thomas S. Mutran on April 18, 1959 with them divorcing in 1978. They have three daughters: Theresa Dawn born March 20, 1960, Tamara Renee born Nov. 15, 1962, Terri Ann born Jan. 7, 1963. They had one son, Ted Thomas, born Oct. 14, 1965 and died on Oct. 15, 1965.

Dawn was employed by Kokomo Anesthesia Services, Inc. She has one daughter, Aubrey Meghan Smith, born May 3, 1983 and one son, Neil Joseph Smith, born May 11, 1987 from her marriage to Allerd C. Smith. They divorced in 1989 and she remarried to John C. Clark who works for Haynes International. John has one son, Ryan Joseph Clark, born May 1, 1982.

Tammy lives in Hesperia, CA and is married to Van Lawless. She has one daughter, Michelle Irene, born Sept. 12, 1984 and one son, Patrick Van, born July 29, 1988. Tammy is going to nursing school and is working part-time.

Terri has one daughter, Tiffany LeeAnn, born Sept. 15, 1983. Tiffany's father is Randy L. Vincent. Terri works at Red Lobster.

Pearl and Dorothy had a lake cottage at Beaver Dam Lake near Akron, IN for 18 years. They enjoyed fishing, entertaining and traveling. Dorothy belonged to the Tally Ho Bridge Club, helped at the Red Cross during WWII and was room mother at Washington School. Pearl became ill in 1972 and died on Aug. 17, 1973 of emphysema. Pearl has one sister still living, Ferne Hunt, 91 years old, in Danville, IL. Dorothy is still a resident of Howard County and has just celebrated her 90th birthday on July 11, 1993. She had met James Whitcomb Riley and contributed to a statue of Riley on Courthouse Square in Greenfield, IN.

LYNCH-BURGETT - William Edward Lynch was born in Kokomo, Aug. 5, 1925, to Paul L. and Mabel B. (Dillon) Lynch. Bill was nicknamed "BoBo" because he wore bow ties to school. He graduated from Kokomo High School in 1943.

Bill enlisted in the United States Marine Corps on Nov. 13, 1943, and served in the Pacific Area from April 8th to Oct. 25th, 1945. He was honorably discharged June 16, 1946, and went to work for the Nickel Plate Railroad as a clerk.

"BoBo" held membership in the Phi Delta Kappa Fraternity, Beta-Nu Chapter. He was elected National President of that organization in 1976, and his wife, Anna Mae, was elected National Sweetheart in 1981.

He was a devoted grandfather to his step-daughter's children: Holly, Stacy and Dede Chasteen, also great-grandson, David Mote.

Bill and Anna were married for 27 years before his death on Dec. 5, 1982. He is buried in the Russiaville Cemetery.

William E. and Anna M. Lynch

Anna Mae Burgett was born May 19, 1912, in Tipton County, IN, the third daughter of Homer Emanuel "Dick" and Stella (Stafford) Burgett. She was reared in the Russiaville community with her sisters: Lelah, Kate, Nora and Beulah.

Anna Mae attended school in Russiaville. At age 19 she married Cleo Lavon "Jack" Taylor on March 19, 1931, in Scirclevlle, IN. They had one child, Jacqueline Ann Taylor. This marriage ended in divorce in 1939.

William Edward Lynch and Anna Mae Taylor were married June 11, 1955, by the Reverend Roy Helms, at the home of Byron and Nora Earlywine in Russiaville, IN.

Anna worked at Delco Electronics for 38 years before retiring. She graduated from Huffer Beauty College while still working at Delco and got her high school diploma through the G E D program on May 5, 1985. She took art classes as a student of Florence Wright and holds memberships in the Phi Delta Kappa Auxiliary, Heart 'N' Home Extension Club and the First Baptist Church of Russiaville, IN.

KENTON AND MARY ALICE MADDOCK - Kenton Paul Maddock and Mary Alice (Sloan) Maddock have deep roots in Howard County.

Having farmed a number of years in Illinois, Kenton's grandfather, James Cletus Maddock (1846-1913), an Indiana Civil War veteran, settled in the county in 1893. James' fourth son, Harry Lee (1882-1968), Kenton's father, married Eliza Myrtle Young (1882-1978) in 1907, in Ervin Township. Among the earliest settlers of the county, Myrtle's family included the Youngs, Harrisons, and Masons.

Myrtle was the oldest of three daughters born to George Nelson Young (1861-1924) and Flora Ann (Harrison) Young (1861-1887). George's parents, Elijah E. Young (1823-1913) and Olive Melissa (Gordon) Young (1837-1915), moved to Howard County in 1856, and settled in the eastern part of Ervin Township. Flora Ann Harrison was the oldest daughter of John Wesley Harrison (1837-1915) and Eliza Ann (Mason) Harrison (1841-1892). Flora's untimely death at age 26 left Myrtle and her two sisters to be raised by their Grandmother Young.

John Wesley Harrison was born in Marion County in 1837, to Eli (1810-1848) and Rachel (Cruse) Harrison (1810-1890). In 1842, Eli moved his family to the Miami Reserve after it was opened for settlement. They initially lived on the south side of Wildcat Creek, two miles north of the present site of West Middleton. In 1844, Eli took a claim one-half mile east of Vermont in Liberty Township. When a relative, Capt. John Harrison (the first county sheriff) died in 1846, Eli sold his claim at Vermont and moved back to Ervin Township to assist with the estate. Two years later, Eli died, leaving his widow, Rachel, with a young family to raise. Rachel later married a widower, Joseph W. Heaton, a pioneer of Harrison Township, who also had a large family.

Eliza Ann Mason was the eldest daughter of Jacob Daniel (1812-1871) and Rebecca Ann (Showalter) Mason (1813-1897). Eliza's family moved to Howard County in 1850, purchasing land two miles north of New London in Ervin Township.

Thus, Kenton's forbearers were among the pioneer families of Ervin Township in Howard County.

Mary Alice's ancestors were also early settlers of Howard County, with origins near Plevna, in Liberty Township. Her parents were Virgil Todd (1891-1977) and Minnie Faye (Kilander) Sloan (1895-1992). Virgil was the second son of Charles Whitaker (1862-1941) and Julia Anna (Dick) Sloan (1866-1937). Charlie Sloan was a builder of many barns and houses in Liberty Township and the surrounding area. The sixth child of Andrew Jackson (1826-1870) and Catherine (Whitaker) Sloan (1832-?), Charlie was known for his craftsmanship.

Kenton and Mary Alice Maddock

Andrew, known as Jack, and Catherine were married in Howard County in 1851. They owned a farm one mile south of Plevna, where they lived until his death in 1870. Catherine later married Thomas Golding.

Julia Dick, Virgil's mother, grew up one mile east of Plevna. Her parents, Jacob (1820-1877) and Frances (Brand) Dick, (1824-1937) located there in the 1850s.

In 1892 Francis Marion (1856-1932) and Letta Ellen (Younce) Kilander (1864-1941) purchased a farm one mile south of the Dick residence near Flabby School. The Kilanders had four daughters. The second, Minnie Faye (known as Faye), married Virgil in 1913. They lived much of their lives in and around Howard County farming and raising pure bred Belgian draft horses.

Kenton and Mary Alice Maddock have a family history which is inexorably intertwined with that of Howard County. Family and local history remain a continuing interest with the entire family. *Submitted by Todd Maddock*

STEVEN H. AND SUSAN MADDOCK - Steven H., the second son of Kenton P. and Mary Alice (Sloan) Maddock, was born Dec. 15, 1946. He attended elementary school in Kokomo but graduated from high school at Forest View in Arlington Heights District in Illinois. Steven was married Jan. 13, 1968 to Judith Gillett of Rosendale, WI. He then attended I.U. in Kokomo for two years. In 1970 he transferred to the University of Wisconsin where he received his BA and MA degrees. In 1973 Steve and Judy divorced. In 1977 Steve married Susan Awe of Manitowoc, WI.

Steve and Susan Maddock

Steve is an artist. He taught art at St. Lawrence Seminary near Fond du Lac, WI for five years and was art instructor at Monona Grove High School in Madison, WI for ten years. At present Steven is a free-lance artist in the Denver, CO area. His work is primarily contemporary Western. A love of history, classical study, and a great sense of humor directs his work. At five and six years, Steve studied oil-painting with Geraldine Armstrong Scott. So his first awareness of fine art originated in Kokomo.

TODD L. AND PATRICIA MADDOCK - Todd L., son of Kenton P. and Mary Alice (Sloan) Maddock, was born Jan. 14, 1936 in the Good Samaritan Hospital in Kokomo, IN. He graduated from Kokomo High School in 1954. In 1955 he married Susan Morrison. From that marriage there were three children: Stanley C., Gail Marie, and Lezlie Sue. Little Gail passed away at 18 months. Todd graduated, with honors, from Purdue University in 1960, majoring in Forestry. After graduation he accepted a position with Potlatch of Lewiston, ID. The family then moved there in June 1960. In 1962 Todd and Susan were divorced. His second marriage was to Patricia Wygant and together they raised their four children. Pat's Susan and Margaret, and Todd's Stan and Lezlie.

Todd and Pat - June 1979

At present Todd is still with Potlatch. His position now is Head of Public Affairs for the Northwest Territory. He represents Potlatch in Congress, state and nationally.

MADDOX - James Thomas Maddox (1853-1923) was born in Kentucky. He married Rosa Greer (1858-1936) in 1875. They came to Howard County around 1880 to farm in Liberty Township. They were the parents of seven children: Grant, Inez, Thomas, Charles Courtland, Minnie, Leo, and Everett.

Charles (1889-1977) married Clara Milligan (1893-1947) in 1910. They had 11 children: Charles Edgar, James Woodrow, Cleo Sherman, Thomas Eugene, Lewis Fredrick, Marian Louise, Garland Solomon, Floyd Harold, Clarabelle Roselee, Lucy Jane, and Joseph Valentine.

During WWII Charles worked at General Electric, which was at that time producing war materials. He later owned Maddox Key Shop and Electrical Appliance Service.

Charles and Clara are best remembered for having the seven oldest of their eight sons in military service during WWII. The youngest, Joseph, was still in school. He later served in Korea and Vietnam.

Clara was Indiana War Mother of 1945. She was matron of honor at the christening of the S.S. *Kokomo Victory*, a U.S. cargo ship, named in the Maddox boys' honor after their hometown. Kokomo had the further distinction of providing the life boats and life rafts with which the ship was equipped. These were products of the Globe American Corporation which distinguished itself in such maritime construction work.

Another honor accorded Clara was that of christening the U.S.S. *YO* 222 at Jeffersonville, IN.

The Maddox boys served a total of 69 years in military service to their country.

Thomas (Gene) born July 25, 1917 married Opal Lucile Shrock in 1939. They had two children: Towana Kay born Dec. 26, 1943 and Thomas Eugene, Jr. born Nov. 15, 1946.

Gene joined the U.S. Army in 1943 and served in Europe during WWII as a Combat Medic. He received two Purple Hearts for wounds received in action and a Silver Star, one of the military's highest honors. After his discharge from the Army he joined the Army Air Corp, which became the U.S. Air Force in 1948, and served in the Korean War and during Vietnam. He retired in 1971 with 26 years of military service.

Towana married Fredrick Allen Aldridge. They have four children and three grandchildren.

Fredrick Allen, Jr. married Julie Ann Christian. They are the parents of Beth Ann and Fredrick III. Fredrick, Jr. served in the U.S. Army from 1980-1985. He is now manager of Harmon Boats.

Marsha Kay married Joseph Jerome Santen, Jr. They have one daughter, Gretchen Elizabeth. Marsha was Head of Children's Services at the Kokomo Public Library until the birth of her daughter.

Gregory Edward married Michaele Kristina Thomas. He is a software engineer at VIA Development.

Douglas Eugene is serving a three year enlistment in the U.S. Army at Fort Hood, TX.

Thomas, Jr. married Sandra Kay Fisher. They have five children and one grandchild: Stacey Marie, a student at Purdue University of Kokomo; Thomas Brian, a student at Indiana University of Kokomo; Anthony Joe, Robert Scott and Daniel Lee, students at Taylor School. Corey Stephen is the son of Thomas Brian. Thomas, Jr. is a pipefitter at Delco Electronics.

Six generations and 114 years later, the descendants of James and Rosa Maddox still live in Howard County. *Submitted by Towana Aldridge.*

MONTY CLIFF MAGGART - Monty Cliff Maggart was born in Logansport, IN on Aug. 27, 1951 to his parents, Vernon R. Maggart and Beverly A. (Rose) Maggart. Monty graduated from Northwestern High School in 1969 and received his BS and MS degrees in education from Indiana University of Kokomo. He is presently working on his administrative license. He has been employed by the Eastern Howard School Corporation for 21 years and teaches 6th grade math and science.

On Dec. 22, 1973, he married Joyce Caroleen (Meadors) Maggart. Joyce was born in Hamilton, OH to her parents, William B. Meadors and Edith G. (Bryant) Meadors. Her father died of lung cancer on Oct. 1, 1981. Her mother married Patrick L. Cummings in 1987. Joyce graduated from Fairmount (Madison-Grant) High School in 1970 and received her Associate's Degree in Nursing from Indiana University of Kokomo in 1974. She has been employed by St. Joseph Hospital for 21 years and is a staff nurse for St. Joseph at Home.

Monty and Joyce made their first home just north of Kempton.

On June 20, 1975, their first child was born. Heather Lynn Maggart was born at St. Joseph Hospital. Heather graduated cum laude from Eastern High School in 1993 and is a freshman in college at Calvin College and Seminary of Grand Rapids, MI.

On March 31, 1978, their second child was born. Daniel Cliff Maggart was born at St. Joseph Hospital. Danny is a sophomore at Eastern High School and is an honor student.

On Oct. 1, 1979, their third child was born. Joshua Seth Maggart was born at St. Joseph Hospital. Josh is an eighth grader at Eastern Middle School and is an honor roll student.

On July 9, 1981, their last child was born. Christopher Lee Maggart was born at Saint Joseph Hospital. Chris is a sixth grader at Eastern Elementary and has been an honor roll student.

On Dec. 11, 1981, the Monty Maggart home was burned to the ground. They moved to S. Armstrong in Kokomo, the former home of Monty's grandparents, Gladys and John V. Maggart.

In August of 1982, they moved to northeastern Howard County and reside there now in 1994.

Monty's family members are members of the Foursquare Gospel Church at 2020 S. Goyer Blvd., Kokomo.

ALICE PARSE MAISH - The farm on which we reside is a Hoosier Homestead farm (in the same family 100 years or more). So it was decided to trace Alice's lineage following that theme.

Borden Hanson was born March 6, 1800, in Wayne County, NC. At the age of five his family moved to Barnesville, Belmont County, OH, and grew up there. On March 30, 1819 he married Rachel Cox and 12 years later they and their six children joined a wagon train to Indiana and settled on a farm south of Economy, Wayne County. There, six more children were born. Borden died July 18, 1846.

In the spring of 1851 Rachel Cox Hanson moved to Howard County with her entire family and purchased a farm in Monroe Township. She died in 1853 and the farm went to her son, Thomas. Four other sons acquired farms nearby: Newton, Levi, Edwin and Elijah.

Myron and Alice Maish

Elijah Hanson (Aug. 8, 1835) married Mary Ann Morris (Dec. 21, 1839) and they had four children: Benjamin Franklin, Esther Jane, Florence and Martha. Elijah purchased a farm in 1860.

Esther Jane Hanson (March 15, 1860) married William Penn Hobson (March 15, 1862) on March 15, 1885. Yes, their birthdays and anniversary were all on March 15th! They had one daughter, Elsie Marie Hobson (Aug. 11, 1895), who married Jesse Hendricks Parse on Feb. 16, 1929. They had one daughter, Alice Lucille Parse (April 20, 1933). At least a portion of Elijah's farm was handed down so that the farm where we reside qualifies for Hoosier Homestead.

Jesse Parse (Oct. 28, 1900) was the son of Oliver Howard and Martha Parse. O.H. purchased a farm of 104 acres adjoining the Hobson farm when they moved to Howard County in 1927. Previously, they lived in Carroll County and North Dakota. Eventually Jesse purchased this 104 acres and with the 200-acre Hobson farm the current farm is 304 acres.

Alice was born in the house in which they now live. The house was built by Grandfather Wm. Hobson in 1916 and all of the wood came from their own woods.

After graduation from high school Alice worked at the Salvation Army in Kokomo. After marriage to Myron and moving to Indianapolis, she worked at the Community Chest and Salvation Army in Indianapolis until the birth of their children, first Paul and then Patty. When her mother, Marie, died in 1958, they returned to the farm. Two other children were born and Alice remained at home with them until it was time to think of college expenses. She has been employed in the high school office at Western High School for nearly 20 years.

Our children are: Paul Wade (May 5, 1957), a teacher at Frankton High School; Patricia Jo Kellett (Oct. 20, 1958) of Orland, IN, a housewife and mother of two boys and one girl; Diana June Schaaf (Aug. 14, 1963) of Kokomo, a 5th grade teacher at Howard School and mother of one son; and, Laura Marie Sheets (March 25, 1966) of Russiaville; she is employed by PSI and has one son and one daughter.

MYRON MAISH - Maish is an old German name. In fact, John George Maish immigrated from southern Germany and arrived at Philadelphia, PA on Oct. 16, 1751. This was apparently the start of the Maish family in America. He settled in Fairview Township, York County on a 200 acre farm. He married Catharine Ulp and they raised their family on this farm, located about eight miles southwest of Harrisburg. The Maishes remained pretty much in that community until 1836.

Then, David Maish, grandson of John George Maish, and his wife and family came to Clinton County, IN. David was born July 18, 1795, while George Washington was President. He married Hannah Tyson, born Jan. 1, 1800. Her descendants also came from Germany. Both the Maishes and the Tysons resided in York County.

David and Hannah had 10 children (7 boys and 3 girls) and felt all the land had been taken and they would not be able to afford to buy ground for so many children. They lived in Perry County and David operated a grist mill at Duncannon, PA. After deliberation, they decided to journey to Indiana, leaving June 1, 1836, in a covered wagon. It was quite a chore packing into one wagon all the provisions, clothes, medicine, and as many possessions possible. They obtained a Mitchells map and set out. They counted on the children to help. George was to help with the horses. Matt and David took rifles to hunt squirrel, wild turkeys and deer enroute, to provide for food. The two youngest and Hannah were permitted to ride and the others mainly walked. It was a long, hard trip across mountains and rough terrain. The trip was worsened by the children coming down with the measles while still in Pennsylvania. Nevertheless, they arrived in Frankfort on July 5, 1836, a trip of over 600 miles. One hundred years later, in 1936, a large centennial celebration was held at the Frankfort fairgrounds and this arrival was re-enacted.

The Maishes settled mainly in the Frankfort area and many engaged in farming, some becoming quite prominent. In fact, the current Frankfort High School is located on Maish Road and one of the Maish homesteads is nearby.

George Maish (one of the ten children) came to Howard County. His son, Willard Maish (Dec. 6, 1875) married Cora Roth (Aug. 30, 1876) and they had seven children: Katherine, Enoch, Floyd, Balford, Flossie, Donald and James. Willard was a farmer and lived on a 120 acre farm on Highway 31, just south of what is now Village Green Trailer Court. They eventually moved into Kokomo.

Floyd Maish (Oct. 27, 1898) married Laura Wade and they had five children: William, Ralph, Ruth, Thomas and Myron. Floyd and Laura lived in Sharpsville for a short time and then moved to Oakford. Floyd worked various places but retired from Stellite.

Myron was born Nov. 15, 1930. After high school graduation and working at Sharpsville cheese factory and Stellite, he was drafted into the army where he served in the Korean War. When he returned, he married Alice Parse on April 25, 1953, and moved to Indianapolis where he worked as a carpenter for approximately five years before coming back to Howard County where he farmed. He also started driving a school bus for Western Schools and has continued to do so for nearly 30 years.

MALABY-MERRELL - On April 9, 1846 Thomas Malaby purchased the farm at 6663 W 400 N in Ervin Township. In 1976 it was placed on the roster of Hoosier Homesteads. Thomas Malaby was born 1800 in Pennsylvania, and his wife Mary Wilson was born in 1801.

William Malaby, the son of Thomas and Mary, was born Aug. 15, 1826 in German Township, Fayette County, PA. He married Mary J. Kidder, Nov. 2, 1848. They were the parents of ten children.

Malaby-Merrell Homestead

One of these children was Martha Jane Malaby (1867-1943). She married Robert Wilson Merrell Dec. 22, 1885. He was the son of Benjamin and Harriett (Van Cleave) Merrell. Their children were, Erwin G. (1886-1948); Clarence C. (1888-1960); Ward C. (1890-1966); Edna Hoffman (1893-1970); Alice B. 'Allie' (1895-1976); Margaret Smith (1900-1973); Orman Benjamin (1897-1954); Dorothy Dean (1907-1980); Edith Loman (1910-1971).

Orman Benjamin married Mabel Jane Jones, (1900-1927) April 19, 1919. She was the daughter of Benjamin and Viola (Fair) Jones. Orman and Mabel were the parents of Lucille Heaton and Robert B. Merrell. Robert B. married Anita Karns (1927-1989), Aug. 11, 1946. They were the parents of two children, Rodney and Ryan Merrell.

Robert B. Merrell now owns and lives in the home place. *Submitted by Robert B. Merrell*

MALABY - W.B. Malaby (Mal) was born in Kokomo, IN Jan. 16, 1916 and lived there until he was nine years old when his family moved to Fort Wayne, IN where his father was in the bakery business. After graduating from The Chicago School of Commerce in Chicago, he returned to Fort Wayne where he met Norma Mayer, who had just graduated from International Business College. She was born in Defiance, OH on May 1, 1922. After their wedding in Defiance on Sept. 8, 1946, they moved to Kokomo where they lived for 35 years. Mal owned and operated a Sporting Goods Business - Mal's Out-O-Doors Store for 32 years. Norma worked at Delco Radio (Purchasing Dept.) and later in the office at Haworth High School. After retirement in 1981, they moved to Lake Manitou in Rochester, IN.

W.B. (Mal) and Norma Malaby 1991

Two sons completed their family. Thomas Albert Malaby, born July 19, 1957, is with television station WLFI in Lafayette, IN. David Carl Malaby, born June 23, 1962, is with Best Farms in Anderson, IN and lives in Alexandria, IN. He is married to the former Jama Granger of Alexandria. David and former wife, Linda Frazier Malaby, had two children—Malinda Jo Malaby, born Aug. 14, 1981 and Joshua David Malaby, born May 23, 1983.

Mal and Norma were active members of Grace United Methodist Church in Kokomo.

Mal's father, Carl A. Malaby, born Aug. 16, 1880 in Kokomo, was in the grocery business. His grandfather, Thomas C. Malaby, born in 1849 in Kokomo, was engaged in the buying and selling of real estate in the early 1900s. The great-grandfather, William Malaby, was born in Pennsylvania on Aug. 15, 1826 and moved to Howard County in the spring of 1845 where he taught school. Later he had a steam sawmill and was successfully engaged in the lumbering business in Ervin Township. His father, Thomas Malaby, was born in German Township, Fayette County, PA in 1800. With his family, William then two years old, he migrated in the spring of 1828 to Tippecanoe County, IN. From there to Clinton County in 1829 and finally in the spring of 1845 to Howard County.

The Malaby family has called Kokomo "home" since the pioneer days of 1845.

ABRAHAM LINCOLN MARNER AND MAGDALENA SCHMUCKER - Abraham's grandfather, Jacob Marner (April 2, 1798-Jan. 11, 1881) came to America with his mother as a teenager. His father was killed as a stable boy in Napoleon's Army in the retreat from Moscow. He settled in Scalp-Level, PA. Married 1823 to Susanna Eash (Aug. 28, 1801-Jan. 15, 1872). They had 12 children. Nine grew to adulthood. In 1811, he moved to Johnson County, IA, and his children who had families followed, all but one who moved to Elkhart County, IN. Abraham's father, Jacob J. (June 6, 1839-March 2, 1907), the ninth child, went along and the following year married the neighbor's daughter, Leah Knepp (Jan. 18, 1842-Aug. 12, 1900). They had 13 children: Abraham and Jacob Albert being twins, the third and fourth children.

Abraham, born during the Civil War, was named after the President. He met Magdalena Schmucker (June 15, 1864-May 20, 1929), the daughter of John Schmucker and Catherine Slabaugh; he as a hired hand, she a hired girl, working in Illinois. They married in Howard County, Dec. 26, 1897. They lived all their married life on the farm where she was born, 600 E - 525 N, Howard County, on the west side of the road. They were members of the Amish Church all of their lifetime, as were his parents and grandparents, and were all farmers. Abraham died in his sleep the night after helping erect an 8" x 8" frame barn. He was seen walking the perline plate on that occasion. They had two children: Joseph Elmer (Joe) (June 2, 1899-Oct. 10, 1978) and Dena Catherine (Katie) (July 3, 1901-May 28, 1987). Joe, a carpenter and farmer. Katie, a farmer's wife.

Joe married (Jan. 22, 1922) to Carrie Troyer (Sept. 18, 1900-June 28, 1968). They had six children: Eugene Francis married Audrey Birelay, Beulah Irene married Clarence Cobb, Kenneth Percy married Barbara Thomas, Thomas Wayne married Beverly Lee, Wilbur Joseph married Donna Trottier, and Larry Paul Dale married Lorine Roberts. Four live in Howard County.

Dena (Katie) married (Nov. 26, 1920) to Martin J. Troyer (April 23, 1896-Feb. 11, 1975). They had seven children: Almeda Lucella married Paul Hooley, Joel Abraham married Mary Ellen Haarer, Willard Allen married LaRue Quein, Sylvia Mae married Alan Roth, Miriam Caroline married Bernard Showalter, Omar Ray married Laura Miller, and Philip Lee married Marjorie Quiring.

Only Joel lives in Howard County today. All the Marners we know in the U.S.A. are descendants of Jacob Marner and Susanna Eash.

Abraham's brother, George (born April 12, 1870) married Feb. 3, 1918 Mattie Hochstedler (born July 20, 1873). He was a farmer and Amish Bishop and lived in Howard County as do some of his descendants. *Submitted by Joel Troyer.*

MARSHALL-FORD - Philip Marshall and Hannah Gifford were married Oct. 31, 1851 in Anderson, IN and early in 1852 came to Howard County locating just north of Kokomo at Cassville. Not more than a dozen white families were living in the area at the time. The rest were Indians. Hannah was born 1824 and raised in West Virginia.

Some of the Marner family 1987. Top L-R: Eugene and Audrey, Lorine and Larry, Orval Troyer, Wilbur and Donna, Kenneth and Barbara. Bottom L-R: Clarence and Beulah Cobb, Katie Troyer, Joel Troyer, Wayne and Beverly.

She went to New Paris, OH with her family where she met Philip Marshall, son of Hugh (1789 Kentucky) and Elizabeth (Pitts) Marshall. They had married in 1811 in Kentucky and emigrated to Preble County, OH in 1813. The only possessions they had were a horse, a kettle, and a feather mattress which was used as a saddle as Elizabeth rode carrying a child and the kettle while Hugh walked along side. Eleven children were born to them with Philip being the youngest. He was born Feb. 14, 1830 in Preble County. He served in the Civil War from August 1861 to July 1865 in the 39th Indiana Inf. and the 8th Cavalry. Philip was a farmer and plasterer by trade. In 1886 they moved to Kappa in Ervin Township where they lived until Philip's death in 1891. Hannah died October 1911 at the home of her daughter in Miami, IN. They are buried in North Union Cemetery in Ervin Township. They had four children: James, Balsora, Benton, and Oliver.

Marshall Ford family

Balsora Josephine Marshall was born May 3, 1859 in Kokomo and married to Arnold Ford on Oct. 2, 1881 in Kokomo. He was born Dec. 19, 1846 near Greensburg, IN to Johnson and Eliza (Walters) Ford and came to Miami County with his brother, Lafayette, where they bought land. Arnold was a farmer, butcher, and carpenter. He also kept bees and would go to fairs and Old Settlers Picnics and make ice cream using the honey. He died June 17, 1936 and "Belle" died Sept. 22, 1944. They are buried in the old Deer Creek Baptist Church Cemetery in Cass County. They had five children: Ambrose, Florence, Oscar, Olive and Ralph.

Ralph Ford was born July 4, 1891 in Miami County living there until his marriage to Rella Jacoby Bion on March 16, 1920. He worked on the interurban traction line that ran from Peru to Tipton. They moved to Tipton for a short time and returned to Kokomo in 1932 where he worked at Continental Steel and retired from there in 1958. Rella was born Dec. 11, 1898 in Mulberry, IN, daughter of William and Mary Elizabeth (Haas) Jacoby. She died Aug. 8, 1970 and Ralph on Jan. 17, 1976. They had three children: Donald, Mary, and William.

Mary Josephine Ford was born March 7, 1934 in Kokomo where she attended the Kokomo schools and married Robert W. Barnett on April 2, 1951. He was born Dec. 22, 1930 the son of Thomas and Elnora (Wilson) Barnett. Robert's ancestors were also pioneers in Howard County. His great-grandfather, Isaac Wilson (1848-1927), was one of the wealthiest farmers owning land from US 31 west to Dixon Road and Alto Road south to SR 26. His great-great-grandfather, was Dr. Thomas Batey (1824-1900), early physician who built the first permanent dwelling in Russiaville. Mary Jo and Robert have four children: Barbara, Vicki, Charles and Teresa. *Submitted by Mary Jo Barnett.*

MARTIN - Samuel Martin (1805-1870) and his wife, Elizabeth Wetterhold (1809-1848), were both Pennsylvania natives. They had five daughters and six sons. His parents (and apparently hers, as well) were "Pennsylvania Dutch"—a term commonly applied to German immigrants. After Elizabeth's death, Samuel married Nancy Grundon (1814-1904) and to them three sons were born.

One of Samuel's sons by his first marriage, Israel Watson Martin (1829-1889), married Sarah Cormany Light (1828-1901). They were both born in Pennsylvania, too, and had five daughters and eight sons. Sarah's parents were Christian Light (1792-1842) and Catherine Cormany (1793-1878) from Germany. I.W.'s father, step-mother and two of his half-brothers came to Howard County, IN and settled near Young America. It is not known what year this was but his third half-brother was deceased by that time. However, I.W., after studying medicine at Danville, PA, moved to Ervin Township in 1859 and located along what became the Judson Road. His wife and four oldest children followed a few months later. (One son had already died in infancy.) He continued to practice medicine there until his death. In addition, he owned the general store at Ervin and during 1863 was commissioned Postmaster for the village. His eldest son also became a doctor but died in early manhood.

Wayne and Carol Martin

Then in 1896, a younger son, Amos Addison Martin (1864-1943), graduated from the Medical School of Indiana. He had his office on West Jefferson Road—now State Highway 22—until 1926. He married Nettie Jane Daily (1868-1955) whose father, Wiley Daily (1843-1881), served two enlistments in the Civil War. (The first was with Co. G of the 89th Regt., Indiana Volunteers). After the war, Wiley operated a sawmill at Shanghai in western Howard County. Her mother was Louisa Catherine Foster (1849-1912) from the Ridgeway community. There were two daughters and three sons born to Amos and Nettie.

Their youngest son, Loren Ross Martin (1897-1983), was a farmer and lifelong resident of Ervin Township. He married Goldie Marie Crawford (1899-1989) from nearby Monroe Township. They had three daughters and a son. Her parents, James Preston Crawford (1857-1932) and Mary Elizabeth Hoagland (1864-1951), once had the country store at Shanghai.

Ross and Goldie's son, Earl Wayne Martin (1930-), is a third generation native of Ervin Township. He became an Indiana Conservation Officer and served 36 years in Crawford, Tipton and Howard counties. His wife, Carol Anne McCoy, (1931-), was formerly Administrative Assistant at the First Presbyterian Church in Kokomo. She was born in Russiaville to George Brant McCoy (1906-1991) and Melba Elizabeth Lewis (1910-). Her grandparents were Clarence Everett McCoy (1875-1955) and Maude Mae Brant (1879-1964); and Charles Kimball Lewis (1875-1950) and Iva Pearl Powers (1879-1975). Wayne and Carol have a daughter and two sons.

Gregory Brant Martin (1951-) was born at Kokomo. He attended DePauw University on a Malpas Scholarship graduating in 1973. He is married to Patricia Ann Manlove (1952-) who is a graduate of Indiana Wesleyan University. Their children are Stephen Brant Martin (1975-) and Elizabeth Ann Martin (1979-). Steve was born at Columbus, OH and Beth at Indianapolis. Greg has a computer consulting business.

Karen Anne Martin (1957-) was born at Corydon, IN. She graduated from DePauw University in 1979 and earned her master's degree at Indiana State University the following year. Since 1981, she has taught band and general music in the Arizona public schools.

Douglas Kent Martin (1958-) was also born at Corydon. He left DePauw University at the end of his junior year (as he did in high school) to enter the Indiana University School of Medicine. Doug and his wife, Danita Lynn Lively (1957-), both received M.D. degrees there in 1982. Their daughter, Katlyn Marie Lively-Martin (1988-), was born in Indianapolis.

In 1990, Wayne and Carol retired and moved to Arizona.

GLEN WARREN AND THERESA MARIE MARTIN - Glen arrived at Kokomo, in April 1976, to begin his engineering career at Delco Electronics. He established residence and found a local church. In November 1981, at an evangelistic crusade, in the Indianapolis Market Square Arena, he met Theresa. Periodic time together, at church events, soon increased, as both realized the relationship had more importance. They formally committed to exchange wedding vows on April 3, 1982, and traveled to Gatlinburg, TN, to spend their honeymoon time.

Glen is the first child, of three, born to Truman G. and Marjorie W. (Folkers) Martin, and arrived June 7, 1952, at Ames, IA, while his father was in South Korea stationed in the Army. Nearly three years later, a move to Indiana occurred, for his father's work at Purdue University.

Glen's early years were spent in Battle Ground, IN, where he developed interests in aviation, scouting, nature, sciences, and electronics. After high school graduation, May 1970, Glen entered Purdue University, and by December 1975, obtained a degree in Electrical Engineering Technology.

Glen's father, a geneticist, grew up in southeast Texas, in the small community of Lumberton. Grandparents, Reuben M. and Mary A. (Adams) Martin, continued to live and work in the area, until their passing. Reuben owned an oil well servicing business operated in the gulf area. Glen's mother originated from Ackley, IA and met Truman at Iowa State University, while he was working on an advanced education degree. She is the first child, and only daughter of Carl H. Folkers, a WWI veteran, carpenter, and later, a home delivery postman, and Helen (Warren) Folkers, a high school English teacher.

Glen, Theresa, Nichole, Tracy and Shane Martin.

Theresa is the first child to Merrill R. and Joan M. (Slusher) Mumaugh, and was Kokomo born, Aug. 12, 1962. She lived within the community, and stayed after 1980 graduation from Kokomo High School, and began fulltime employment, up until several months after her spring 1982 marriage.

Theresa's father, "Butch", is also a Kokomo native, and continued living here, as a carpenter tradesman, except during a period of Army service. Theresa's paternal grandparents were Clifford R. Mumaugh, a WWI veteran, tool machinist, and community barber, and Lillian M. (Spaulding) Mumaugh, who worked as an assembly worker in the factory that produced the "Haynes" auto. She retired in 1952, after working 20 years for American Laundry. Her maternal grandparents were Francis R. and Jeraldean J. (Fletcher) Mumaugh, and resided in central Illinois.

As marital years accumulated, Glen and Theresa became the parents of three children, all born in Kokomo. Nichole Yvonne was the first daughter, born March 16, 1984. Their second daughter, Tracy Leanne, was born July 27, 1986, and a son, Shane Matthew, arrived March 11, 1990. Family travels were generally to neighboring states, for friends and family. Glen does most all of the handyman work required, while Theresa takes care of quick family organization and coordination matters that arise. Though Glen and Theresa have jointly lived at three different addresses, all are located within the boundaries of Howard County. Life emphasis is steadfast on Christian living, family unity, good education, and U.S.A.

ANDREW JACKSON MASON

The immigrant Mason ancestors came to America from Germany in 1742.

George Mason was born in Virginia. He settled in Dearborn County, IN. He married Elizabeth Lawrence. They had 11 children: Philip, Daniel, Barbara, George, Jacob, Nicholas, John, Solomon, Susan, Izaac and Elizabeth.

Philip married Christina Everly. They had two sons: Jacob and John.

Jacob married Rebecca Showalter and they had 12 children: Philip, Simon, Martin, Andrew, Martha, Louisa, Eliza, Joe, Jefferson, Benjamin, Christina and a child who died in infancy.

Andrew Jackson Mason was a farmer. He married Amanda Jane Odell. She was the daughter of Rev. Price Odell. He was the founder of the Judson Baptist Church in Ervin Township. They had nine children: Lettie, Florence, Lillie, Omer, Ada, Mary Rebecca, Roscoe, Grover and Elsie.

Lettie married Frank Orr and they had nine children: three died in infancy, Estle, Cora, Lester, Audra, Florence and Otis.

Mary Rebecca (Mason) Brower

Florence married Omer Dearinger. They had no children.

Lillie married Harvey Lybrook. They had one daughter, Elsie, who was killed in an automobile accident when she was 20.

Omer married Tessa Marshall. They had four children: William, Lucille, Earl and Eva.

Ada married Ira Pearch. They had three children: Lovell, Ruth and Pauline.

Roscoe married Edith Griffith and they had six children: Virgle, Gerald, Garman, Carlyle, Martha and Wendell.

Grover was not married. He died at age 22 from an injury while playing football.

Elsie married Ernest Polk and they had two children: Orville and Ethel.

Mary Rebecca married Leonidas Brower and they had three sons: Eldon, Ansel and Dale. Leonidas was a farmer. He died at age 48 in a hunting accident. Mary managed the farm for a few years and then was employed as a house mother at the Indiana Girls School at Clermont, IN, until her retirement. She lived to be 99-1/2 years old.

Eldon married Agnes Beck and they lived in Detroit, MI. He worked in the automobile industry. They had two children: Marjorie and Robert.

Ansel married Ruth Marsh and they lived on the family farm in Ervin Township. They had two children: Phyllis and Nelda.

Phyllis married Fred Henry and they had two children: Charles and Cheryl. They adopted a daughter Mary Jayne.

Nelda married Robert Lovelace and they had one daughter, Beth Ann.

Dale married Ruth Gillam. They lived on a farm in Ervin Township. He was a mink farmer. He also retired as Director of Indiana State Agency for Surplus Property. They had three daughters: Janet, Linda and Nancy.

Janet married Jack Williams and had two children: Jeff and Jennie.

Linda married Leo Leger and had one daughter, Camela. Linda and Camela were killed in an auto accident.

Nancy married Larry Babb and they had two children: Scott and Jaime.

After seven generations the descendants of George Mason live in Howard and Cass County. *Submitted by Janet Brower Williams*

BENJAMIN AND NANCY MASON

Two early Ervin Township families were united when Benjamin Franklin Mason and Nancy Stetler were married Nov. 15, 1877. Ben, the youngest child of Jacob and Rebecca (Showalter) Mason, was born Aug. 6, 1853 in Howard County, and Nancy was born Oct. 15, 1854, Ervin Township, daughter of Daniel Stetler and Elizabeth (Glaze) Stetler. They were farmers and lived on the original Jacob D. Mason farm in Ervin Township. Ben died Oct. 27, 1933, and Nancy died May 1, 1931.

Benjamin Franklin Mason; Nancy Ann (Stetler) Mason

Ben and Nancy Mason had four children who are listed here, each with their own children and grandchildren, most of whom live(d) in Howard County: (1) Charles Jefferson Mason was born Sept. 13, 1878, lived his entire life in Ervin Township and died May 5, 1943. He married Pearl Price, April 6, 1898, daughter of Luther and Elizabeth (Miller) Price. Born May 21, 1878, she died Dec. 12, 1954. Charles and Pearl had six children listed below: (A) Orville Mason, born Jan. 12, 1899, married Inez Hauck (born July 26, 1899); they had two children, Elizabeth (Mason) Cole (born Jan. 22, 1922) and Ralph L. Mason (born Oct. 20, 1923). (B) Claude Mason, born Feb. 26, 1901, married Florence Niver (born March 31, 1898). (C) Glen Mason, born April 22, 1903, married (first) Stella DeGraffenreid (born Aug. 15, 1903) and (second) Edith (Miller) Stevenson; Glen and Stella had two daughters, Betty (Mason) Bayless (born Jan. 26, 1927) and Joan (Mason) Hall (born Dec. 14, 1930). (D) Howard Mason, born Feb. 5, 1909. (E) Helen (Mason) French, born March 31, 1914, married O. Dale French (born Nov. 10, 1913); Helen and Dale had two daughters, Marcheta (French) Price (born Feb. 23, 1942) and Anita (French) DeWitt (born March 31, 1947). (F) Virgil Mason, born Feb. 13, 1919, married Edith Rodkey; they had three sons, Mark (born July 20, 1944), Stuart (born May 24, 1946), and Dan (born Nov. 25, 1947).

(2) Flora (Mason) Wikle, daughter of Ben and Nancy Mason, was born April 10, 1880, lived her entire life in Howard County, and died March 31, 1960. She married Claude Wikle, April 15, 1905, also a native of Howard County. He was born Feb. 4, 1880 and died Oct. 27, 1940. Claude and Flora Wikle had one daughter, Mildred (Wikle) Wagoner, born July 13, 1905, who married Laurel Wagoner (born Aug. 7, 1903); Mildred and Laurel had two children, Raymond Wagoner (born June 6, 1924), and Virginia (Wagoner) Yoder (born Oct. 20, 1925).

(3) Elva (Mason) Greer, daughter of Ben and Nancy Mason, was born March 13, 1882, and also lived her entire life in Howard County, dying April 22, 1950. She married Howard E. Greer, Dec. 14, 1907, also a native of Howard County, born June 6, 1882 and died Dec. 19, 1965. Elva and Howard did not have children.

(4) Mertie (Mason) Rinehart, daughter of Ben and Nancy Mason, was born Nov. 16, 1883, and also lived her entire life in Howard County, dying March 6, 1969. She married A. Loren Rinehart, Dec. 22, 1906, also a native of Howard County, born June 10, 1884 and died Feb. 27, 1943. Loren and Mertie had two children listed below: (A) E. Gladys (Rinehart) Wolfe, born Feb. 3, 1910, who married Arthur Wolfe (born June 16, 1894); Gladys and Arthur had three children, Betty (Wolfe) Streeter (born Dec. 25, 1938), Linda Wolfe (born July 8, 1940), and Howard Wolfe (born Oct. 19, 1943). (B) Lawrence R. (Bud) Rinehart, born March 6, 1913, who married Margaret Ann Fouts (born July 9, 1912); Bud and Margaret had two sons, L. Keith Rinehart (born July 4, 1934) and Kenneth Rinehart (born Oct. 21, 1936).

The above is abstracted (with permission) and adapted from The Mason-White Family History, 1990, by James M. Freed. *Submitted by granddaughter Helen (Mason) French*

JACOB DANIEL AND REBECCA MASON

The Mason family history in Howard County began in 1850 when Jacob and Rebecca Mason arrived from Dearborn County, IN.

Jacob (April 6, 1812-Oct. 5, 1871) the son of Philip and Christina (Everly) Mason and Rebecca (Oct. 23, 1813-Jan. 12, 1897) the daughter of Christopher and Christiania "Ann" (Funkhouser) Showalter were born in Pennsylvania. They were married May 14, 1831 in Dearborn County.

Jacob purchased 160 acres of uncleared land in what was "the seven mile strip," land acquired by the federal government from the Miami Indian Nation.

They immediately set about to build their farmstead out of the Indiana wilderness by clearing land for their first growing season. A cabin was raised along with an animal shelter before winter set in. Each year more land was opened and buildings were added until at the time of his death Jacob and Rebecca had one of the finest farms of 225 acres in Howard County.

Home of Jacob and Rebecca Mason

Jacob was also a master carpenter. In 186? he began to build Rebecca's house. It took him and his sons seven years to complete. The structure was a masterpiece for its time. This beautiful home stands today (810 W.-00 NS, Ervin Township) on the Sycamore Road. The log foundation can still be seen in the basement. It is a monument to his craftsmanship.

Rebecca was a member of the Judson Baptist Church; she was a devout Christian who raised her children to follow its teaching and way of life. Even with the early deaths of six children and the heartaches she had to endure, Rebecca remained loyal to her beliefs until her death.

Twelve children came from this union. Christena (March 28, 1832-July 19, 1837), Simon Peter (March 7, 1834-Feb. 3, 1901), Phillip Lawrence (Feb. 7, 1836-Jan. 28, 1855), Jefferson (Dec. 5, 1837-Jan. 1, 1859), infant son (April 14, 1839), Eliza Ann (March 27, 1841-Oct. 30, 1892), Martha (May 8, 1843-March 13, 1901), Martin Van Buren (March 25, 1845-Sept. 1, 1901), Andrew Jackson (April 6, 1847-July 24, 1905), Joseph Wesley (Feb. 11, 1849-Feb. 18, 1931), Louisa (Nov. 29, 1851-Jan. 23, 1886), my great-grandmother and Benjamin Franklin (Aug. 6, 1853-Oct. 27, 1933).

The seventh generation of these rugged people still live in Howard County.

Taken from the Mason-White Family History by James M. Freed. *Submitted by great-great-granddaughter, Elizabeth White*

JACOB H. AND ALICE (EARLY) MASON -

The Jacob and Alice Mason family began in Ervin Township, Howard County, when they married in 1876. Both Jacob and Alice were from early Howard County families with both sets of Jacob's grandparents being among the early settlers of Ervin Township, as were both sets of Alice's grandparents. But Howard County was not to remain the home of this Mason family and their descendants, except for their daughter, Emma. In December 1893, with their first eight children, they moved west to settle land that had just opened for settlement in what was then Woods County, Oklahoma Territory (now Major County, OK), which already had gained members of both sides of their family (Jacob's dad and Alice's Burchfield relatives). Jacob died of tuberculosis within 10 years and Alice lived an additional 30 years in the new state of Oklahoma. The following is a brief summary of their family history:

Jacob Harvey Mason was born July 6, 1856, Ervin Township, Howard County, son of Simon Peter Mason and Elizabeth (White) Mason, the grandson of Jacob Daniel Mason and Rebecca (Showalter) Mason, and also of Jefferson White and Elizabeth (Alder) White. Jacob was a farmer in both Indiana and Oklahoma Territory and died March 7, 1903. Born Feb. 8, 1859, Howard County, Madora Alice Early was the daughter of William and Catharine (Burchfield) Early, the granddaughter of John and Margaret Early and also of Samuel and Elizabeth (Rider) Burchfield. She was a homemaker and farmer. She gave birth to 12 children with all surviving past childhood, except for one, and successfully met the challenge of raising the six children still at home after her husband died. She died Feb. 15, 1933, and was buried beside her husband in the Ames Cemetery, Major County, OK. The following is a brief summary of the 12 children of Jacob and Alice (Early) Mason, the first 8 born in Howard County, the last 4 in Woods County, Oklahoma Territory:

1. Lova (Mason) Lozier, born April 12, 1877; died July 26, 1942, Garfield County, OK. She married John Lozier and they had four children.

2. Mertie (Mason) Munkres, born Oct. 8, 1878; died Oct. 7, 1972, Blaine County, OK. She married James Munkres and they had 10 children.

3. Emma (Mason) Freed, born May 8, 1880; died Feb. 28, 1948, Howard County. She married Tom Freed and they had eight children. See their family history under Tom and Emma Freed.

4. Etta (Mason) Gander, born Nov. 1, 1882; died Aug. 5, 1981, Medford, OR. She married George Gander.

5. Anna (Mason) Montgomery, born Aug. 28, 1884; died Feb. 4, 1972, Garfield County, OK. She married Rhode Montgomery and they had nine children.

6. Alma (Mason) Burchfield, born July 26, 1886; died Sept. 4, 1909, Major County, OK. She married Clarence Burchfield and they had two children.

7. Lester Mason, born June 22, 1888; died May 11, 1966, Garfield County, OK. He married Susie Wysong and they had five children.

8. Lennie (Mason) Fyffe, born Sept. 25, 1892; died April 24, 1949, Garfield County, OK. She married William Fyffe.

9. Bertha (Mason) Nelson, born July 12, 1895; died June 20, 1963, Major County, OK. She married George Nelson and they had two children.

10. Clifford Mason, born Sept. 24, 1897; died March 13, 1982, Garfield County, OK. He married Ethel Morton and they had four children.

11. Lonzo Mason, born July 24, 1900; died Dec. 25, 1900.

12. Harley Mason, born Dec. 27, 1902; died May 28, 1993, Blaine County, OK. He married Ardell Wysong and they had eight children.

The above family history was adapted (and updated), with permission, from *The Mason-White Family History*, copyright 1990, edited by James M. Freed. *Submitted by Robert V. Freed*

J. FRANK MASON -

James Franklin Mason (known most of his life as Frank) was the eighth child of Simon and Elizabeth (White) Mason and lived most of his life in and around Howard County, IN. Born May 30, 1871, in Ervin Township, he was almost eight years of age when his parents pioneered in Sumner County, KS. He attended school at the Chikaskia School (Chikaskia Township, Sumner County) during the years 1880-1887. Although no civil records have been found to confirm the following, it is widely believed by a number of Simon and Elizabeth Mason's descendants that Frank Mason was the biological father of Rosa Mae Bymaster, born Feb. 23, 1891, in Kansas, and who lived most of her life in Major County, OK (died in Blaine County, OK, Oct. 16, 1990). Frank Mason returned to Indiana in the early 1890s, and after a brief period in the Dakotas he returned again to Indiana where he lived the remainder of his life. On Oct. 8, 1899, Frank married Clara Durfella Coy. She died April 26, 1908. Frank then married Julia Turley, Dec. 11, 1911. She died at the age of 100 years Dec. 11, 1969. The three sons of Frank and Clara (Coy) Mason are listed below, all born in Howard County:

1. Norman D. Mason, born Nov. 1, 1900; died at age 18 of pneumonia.

2. Andrew Jackson Mason (known as Jack) was born Nov. 13, 1902. Jack was a carpenter, lived in numerous areas of the western part of the U.S. and died April 5, 1977, Kingman, AZ. He married (1) Rachel Ray and (2) Mattie (Gentry) Harriman. He had eight children (five with his first wife and the last three adopted with his second wife): (1) Thelma (Mason) Nilmeier, born Feb. 25, 1924, Texas; (2) Loretta (Mason) Fomous, born July 5, 1926, Texas; (3) Beverly (Mason) Turner, born Jan. 19, 1929, New Mexico; (4) Dora (Mason) Nettleton, born July 17, 1932, Arizona; (5) Marvin Mason, born Dec. 7, 1934, Arizona; (6) Flossie (Mason) Pritzkau, born May 12, 1939, Oklahoma; (7) Carl Mason, born March 17, 1941, Oklahoma; and (8) Mary (Mason) Sanderson, born Dec. 12, 1942, Nevada.

3. Dema Leone Mason (known as Leon) was born June 17, 1905. He eventually moved to Wisconsin, was a painting contractor and died in Milwaukee, June 7, 1964. He married Elma Leona (Hellman) DuFrame, Rock Island, IL. She was born April 1, 1922, Gladstone, MI. Leon and Elma had six children all born in Milwaukee, WI: (1) Marco Mason, born Aug. 8, 1947; (2) Margo (Mason) Leonard, born Nov. 21, 1949; (3) Bonnie Mason, born June 22, 1952; (4) Jackie (Mason) Bissonnette, born April 27, 1954; (5) Carla Mason, born April 24, 1960, and (6) Dean Mason, born Oct. 30, 1964.

Frank made his living (as did many members of his family) as a painter and a carpenter. The home he built for his second wife, Julia, remains standing and continues to look very much as it did when first built in Ervin Township. It is reported by family, who lived within a few miles of Frank and visited with him often, that Frank disassembled an old building and hauled the lumber several miles by horse and wagon to acquire enough lumber to build the house. Frank and Julia lived in this house until shortly before each of them died.

Relatives report that Frank was known for his joyful disposition and humorous stories. He was first affiliated with the Methodist Church and later with Judson Baptist Church. He died Dec. 13, 1952, and is buried next to his wife, Julia, in the New London Cemetery, New London, IN.

Some of the above information was abstracted, with permission, from *The Mason-White Family History*, 1990, by James M. Freed. *Submitted by Willa M. Mills*

MARTIN V. MASON -

Jacob D. Mason and Rebecca Showalter migrated with their parents in the early 1800s from Pennsylvania to Dearborn County, IN. They were married on May 14, 1831 and had 11 children.

They migrated by covered wagon to Ervin Township, Howard County, IN and bought land eight miles west of Kokomo on the "Crick Pike" where they established a new home.

Their seventh child was Martin Van Buren Mason, born in 1845. In 1873, he married Acenith Davis. They had one daughter, Becky, who died of tuberculosis at 17 years. Acenith died in 1876.

Martin Van Buren Mason (58 years old), father of Renna V. Mason, grandfather of Donald G. Mason, great-grandfather of Joseph Mason, David Mason, Judith Eikenberry and Mona Lewe.

Martin then married Anna Bortsfield Belt in 1877. She was a young widow with two children (Ida and Charles Belt). They were farmers in Clinton and Howard County and staunch members of Judson Baptist Church.

Martin and Anna had five children, Eva, Ethie, Renna, Ward and Walter.

Renna, a farmer married Bessie Amos, June 30, 1907. They were the parents of four children, Arlene, who died at infancy, Donald, Wayne and Robert.

Donald, born April 16, 1909, was married to Josephine Pollock in 1929. They were the parents of four children, Dr. Joseph, David, Judith and Mona. Donald died Dec. 2, 1991. They had 11 grandchildren and 6 great-grandchildren.

Wayne, born Sept. 17, 1911, was married to Arian Bulk, May 9, 1937. They were the parents of one daughter, Marcia, who was killed in an accident in 1983. Marcia was survived by four children. Wayne died July 19, 1969.

Robert, born March 1, 1925, was married to Sara McHale. They were the parents of four children, Jean, Sheryl, Dr. Robert and Susan. Robert died Oct. 25, 1983. *Submitted by David L. Mason, great-great-grandson of Jacob D. Mason.*

OMER AND TESSIE (MARSHALL) MASON -

Prior to 1871, Andrew Jackson Mason (1847-1905) married Amanda Jane Odell (1848-1891), daughter of Rev. Price Odell, founder of the Judson Baptist Church, and Elizabeth (Cline) Odell.

The following 10 children were born: Lettie married Frank Orr; Florence married John Omer Dearinger (1872-1913) and after his death married Sylvester Wilson; an unnamed infant daughter; Omer Otto (see below); Lillie married Harvey Lybrook; Ada married Ira Pearch; Oscar Roscoe married Edith Griffith; Mary Rebecca married Leroy Brower; Andrew Grover (1886-1905); Elsie May married Ernest R. Polk.

Seated: Omer Mason, father, Eva, Tessie Mason, mother. Standing: Earl, William and Lucille Mason.

The fourth child of Andrew and Amanda Mason, Omer Otto, was born Jan. 28, 1875, Ervin Township, died Jan. 29, 1945. He married Tessie Ellen Marshall Dec. 30, 1894, the daughter of Newton and Lucinda (Moulder) Marshall, born Feb. 29, 1879, Howard County, died May 2, 1933. After the death of Tessie Ellen, Omer married Lela Pearl (Rice) Byrum, daughter of James and Harriett

(Young) Rice, born March 9, 1880, Howard County, died July 7, 1963. Lela was previously married to Charles Byrum and they had one daughter, Jean. Omer and Tessie had four children as follows:

William Andrew Mason born July 5, 1897, Tipton County, died April 30, 1983. August 25, 1916 he married Mary P. Gilbert, daughter of Elvadore and Ella (Gannon) Gilbert, born Nov. 29, 1895, Howard County, died Oct. 10, 1983. They were members of Union Street Friends Church. William owned Mason Realty, which his father founded. They adopted one daughter, Genevieve, who died a young woman.

Florence Lucille Mason born May 5, 1899, Howard County, died Nov. 29, 1984. She married Samuel Ross Rinehart Feb. 8, 1918 son of John and Susanna (Huddleston) Rinehart, born Oct. 3, 1887, Howard County, died May 19, 1960. After the death of Ross, she married Paul Alexander Feb. 18, 1967. Lucille was a member of Judson Baptist Church and retired in 1966 from St. Joseph Memorial Hospital, Kokomo, as a nurse's aide. Lucille and Ross had seven children as follows: Mason Rinehart, who married Evelyn Hensley; Maxine (Rinehart) (Stull) Kirby married Lilburn Stull (1918-1958) and had five children. After the death of Lilburn Stull she married Joseph Kirby; Paul Rinehart married Jo Ann Ingles and had four children; Nina Rinehart (1925-1943); Marilyn Rinehart (1926-1934); Virginia Rinehart married Carl Edward Prifogle and had four children; Buddy Rinehart married Emma Lou Fultz and had two children.

Eva Mason born Jan. 29, 1903, Howard County, died June 4, 1966. In 1919 she married Cecil Stonebraker, son of Horace and Lucy (Allread) Stonebraker, born June 5, 1902, Howard County, died Nov. 29, 1970. They had five children as follows: Wayne Carlton Stonebraker, who died at the age four months; Madalyn Stonebraker married Dale Templin and had two children; Gale Stonebraker married Patricia Winslow, they had two children, and died in 1983; Donna Stonebraker married Charles Sarver and had four children; Sharon Stonebraker married Jack Davis and they had three children.

Earl Marshall Mason, born April 29, 1906, Ervin Township, died Feb. 7, 1946. He married in 1924 Julia Betty Cotterman, daughter of Charles and Alice (Richard) Cotterman, born Dec. 21, 1904, Clay Township, died July 25, 1936. Then Earl married Arzell Titus, who died June 2, 1940. His third marriage in 1942 was to Irene Shaffer. Earl and Betty had two children as follows: Jack Mason, who married Dixie Rice, died in an automobile crash; Judy Mason married Don Parsons, they had three children, and divorced; then she married Don Towles. *Submitted by Virginia (Rinehart) Prifogle*

SIMON P. AND ELIZABETH (WHITE) MASON

Simon Peter Mason and Elizabeth White were both natives of Indiana, his birth occurring in Dearborn County, IN, March 7, 1834, son of Jacob Daniel and Rebecca Ann (Showalter) Mason, and her birth occurring in Hendricks County, IN, March 1, 1834, daughter of Jefferson and Elizabeth (Alder) White. The White family moved to Ervin Township of Howard County (E 1/2, SW 1/4, S35, T4N, R2E) about 1846 and their neighbors, the Jacob D. Masons, moved to the farm immediately west of them in 1850. As neighbors, Simon and Elizabeth met each other and married Oct. 28, 1852.

Simon and Elizabeth Mason established their farm home in Ervin Township and all 12 of their children were born in Ervin Township. They were members of the Judson Baptist Church. However, with most families having numerous children, it must have become apparent to Simon and Elizabeth Mason that in order to have sufficient land for themselves and their children that their future lay elsewhere. Consequently, in 1879 they migrated to Chikaskia Township of Sumner County, KS, leaving their three eldest children (married by then) in Howard County. Here in Sumner County several of their remaining children married, but Elizabeth died there Feb. 1, 1888, leaving their two youngest children (twelve and nine years of age) still at home. Simon sold his Kansas land in 1891 and on Sept. 16, 1893 he made the historic Land Run into the Cherokee Outlet of Oklahoma Territory, settling on land that became eastern Major County at statehood in 1907. However, Simon Mason did not live to see Oklahoma become a state as he died of smallpox Feb. 3, 1901.

The Simon and Elizabeth Mason family, Howard County, IN, early 1879, with married names given for the daughters. Back row, left to right: Martha Millsap, Mary Coy, Sarah Burchfield, Jacob Mason, Elizabeth Williams. Front row, left to right: Howard Mason, Charles Mason held by his mother, Elizabeth Mason, Frank Mason, Simon P. Mason, Ida Rice, Thomas Mason. Reproduced from the original tintype owned by Robert Price, of Russiaville, IN.

The 10 children of Simon Peter and Elizabeth (White) Mason (all born Ervin Township, Howard County), are listed below: 1. Mary Jane Coy, born Dec. 13, 1853; married James H. Coy and they lived their entire lives in Howard County. 2. Jacob Harvey Mason, born July 6, 1856; married Alice Early in Howard County. They migrated to Oklahoma Territory and settled near his father. 3. Sarah Ellen Burchfield, born between Aug. 1, 1857, and June 1, 1858; married Samuel Burchfield in Howard County. They eventually migrated to Oklahoma Territory and settled near her father. 4. Elizabeth Ann Williams, born June, July, or August 1861; married (1) William Harrison and (2) Joseph F. Williams. She died in Cleveland County, OK Territory. 5. Martha Catherine Millsap, born August 1863; married Ed Millsap. They migrated to Cleveland County, OK Territory. 6. Joseph Howard Mason, born March 18, 1866; married Alice Roberts. They lived in Hughes County, OK. 7. Thomas Jefferson Mason, born May 29, 1868; married (1) Elizabeth Young and (2) Martha Gearheart both in Howard County. With his second wife he eventually migrated to Alberta Canada. 8. James Franklin Mason, born May 30, 1871; married (1) Clara Coy and (2) Julia Turley in Howard County. They remained in Howard County. 9. Ida Mae Rice, born June 7, 1875; married Alfred L. Rice. They eventually settled in Oklahoma Territory near her father. 10. Charles Nelson Mason, born Oct. 17, 1878; married Martha Lozier and they eventually settled in Woodward County, OK. The above information abstracted from *The Mason-White Family History*, copyright 1990, by James M. Freed. *Submitted by James M. Freed*

MASSEY - Noah Wesley Massey was an old soldier in Co. F of the 70th Indiana Inf., under Benjamin Harrison's old regiment during the Civil War. Noah was born in 1823, in Green County, TN. He moved to Howard County, IN around 1858. Noah was married three times. Margaret Purcell was his first wife and they had three children, Amanda, Sarah Catherine, and James. Noah's second wife was Margaret Daughtery, but they did not have children. In October 1869, Noah married, for the third time, Mary C. Hall; they had 10 children, Mary Elizabeth, Belle, Martha, Stephen, Robert O., Pearlie J., Minnie, Gertie B., George F., and Noah Robert.

Noah died on Nov. 5th in 1893, and is buried at Soldiers Circle, Crown Point Cemetery. Mary died Jan. 25, 1937, and was also buried at Crown Point Cemetery.

Noah's son, James Manford, married Malvin Moore on April 18, 1892, and they had two sons, George W. and James Manford Jr.; two girls died in infancy.

George W. was born Aug. 31, 1893, and died July 20, 1900, in Marion County, IN. George had stepped on a thorn which became infected causing his death.

James Manford Jr. was born July 27, 1901 in Vermillion County, IN, and died Nov. 9, 1988 at Saint Joseph Hospital in Howard County, IN. James had driven a huckster truck for Massey Grocery Store. He retired in 1966 from Continental Steel Corporation after 38 years of service, as first stoker on the open hearth furnace. He married Betha J. Clark on March 14, 1921. They had four daughters, Betty, Maxine, Virginia, and Nancy.

Betty Massey was married two times. Her first husband was Charles Joseph Young; they had four children, Joseph Lee Roy, Steven Michael, Max Lee, and Susan Gay. Her second husband was Floyd Ford; they had no children. Betty and Floyd still live in Kokomo, IN.

Maxine Massey was married to Lloyd Edgar Thomas, and they had one son, James William Thomas. James William and his wife, Linda, still reside in Kokomo, IN.

Virginia Massey was married twice. Her first husband was Keith Ewing; they had two children, Melody Sue and Timmothy Kent. Virginia's second husband was Larry Gould; they had two children, Matthew J. and Andrew Clark. Virginia and Larry live in Lafayette, IN.

Nancy Massey married John Farthing; they had two children, Penny Jolene and Jeffery Scott. Nancy and John live in Arlington, OH.

Noah Massey came from Green County, TN, we believe he came alone, and we cannot find out anything else about Noah or his family at this time. We are still searching and hope someone, somewhere, can help us.

This history was written in memory of the Massey Family. *Submitted by Betty Ford*

MASSOTH - Howard County, IN, Health Records Book CH-6 page 78 details the Aug. 27, 1918 birth at 1024 N. Morrison Street in Kokomo of Robert Joseph Massoth. The parents were John Martin and Hazel Isabelle Mitsch Massoth. **On that same page**, the birth of Bertha Estella Kenworthy is recorded as Aug. 25, 1918 at 1801 N. Indiana Street. Her parents were Clarence W. and Maude G. Etherington Kenworthy.

Moving forward some 22 years and 6 months, those same two names are found on **the same page** again; this time in the Howard County Marriage Records (Book 65-page 554). Robert J. and Bertha E. are being married at St. Patrick's Church on Feb. 22, 1941. Bertha and Bob met while attending Kokomo High School.

(Bob and Bertha's three children - John W., Mary Ann and Thomas M. were born in Kokomo. Having moved "West" in November 1958, their family histories will be recorded as part of the Orange County, CA story.)

Left to right, standing: Massoths - John William, Robert J. Seated: Thomas M., Bertha E., Mary Ann.

Bob played baseball and basketball in the Kokomo area for several years. The 1935/1936 Kokomo Wildkats basketball team of Cleo Maddox, Lou Wagner, Ray Bennett, Tom Heckman and Bob - under new coach Alfred "Pee-Dad" Campbell - placed second (Frankfort was first) in the tough North Central Conference with an 8 and 3 record. (The Muncie game scheduled for January 1936 was "frozen out" by temperatures of minus 22 degrees and never re-scheduled.) The season's highlight occurred as the Wildkats beat the previously undefeated Tipton Blue Devils 24 to 21, in the Regional Tournament in the Marion Fieldhouse. That euphoria lasted just one week - the Wildkats lost to Fort Wayne 36 to 26 in the afternoon game at the Super-Regional in Muncie. The

1936 American Legion Baseball Team advanced to the final game only to lose 7 to 6 to East Chicago. Bob and his teammates agreed that if there is any truth in the old belief that athletic "ups and downs"/"highs and lows" contribute to an accelerated aging process, they aged considerably in 1936.

After 45 years in the work force - 15 with Haynes Stellite, 3 years with Michigan Steel in Muskegon, MI and the remainder in Southern California - Bob retired in early 1986. Bertha retired in 1985 after 23 exciting and rewarding years at Disneyland. Bertha had used her work-experience at J.C. Penney in downtown Kokomo (1936/1937) and her secretarial job at Delco Radio (1939/1940) to land a job at Disneyland in 1962. She became an Executive Secretary in the Marketing/Advertising Division. Edward Meck, an experienced newspaper man and a good friend of Walt Disney, was Bertha's first supervisor. Eddie, who might have been Walt's inspiration for Jiminy Cricket, had the job of keeping the general public advised of Disneyland programs, progress, coming attractions/expansions. Perhaps more importantly he had the job of teaching the employees ("Cast Members") Mr. Disney's expectations and philosophies regarding Disneyland "Guests". After Meck's retirement, and during the next 20 years, Bertha "passed the baton" so to speak, to at least six young aspiring Marketing/Advertising Directors. Small wonder she was affectionately called the "Aunt Bee of Marketing". On Bertha's last day at Disneyland, she was declared the Grand Marshal of the Main Street Parade. Her ambassador-type rose-colored sash was emblazoned "Bertha is Retiring Today." Riding in an open touring car and accompanied by Mickey, Minnie, Goofy and other "Cast Members", Bertha acknowledged the "Guests" along Main Street. At the conclusion of the parade, sad smiles and some tears were evident in "The Magic Kingdom"—"The Happiest Place on Earth".

After retiring, Bob and Bertha became interested in genealogy. They traced Bertha's family to the weaving mills of Lancaster, England. The Massoths, farmers and inn-keepers, were discovered in Burstadt, Germany. Both families came to the America in the 1850s. Because of Bertha's death in 1987, their dream of visiting England and Germany together was never realized. Bob did travel to Germany in 1991. In Lorsch, a small beautiful village just 10 miles east of Burstadt, he found a "Mom and Pop" Massoth grocery store. Many new relatives were found in the Burstadt/Lorsch area.

And in good times and bad, Bob remains an avid sports fan of the California Angels, the Rams, the Lakers and most recently the Mighty Ducks hockey team. *Submitted by R.J. Massoth.*

MASSOTH - The *Cedar Lake* (Lake County, IN) *Journal* in an article dated April 25, 1974 states: "Frank Massoth, general store owner and postmaster, and his wife, Mary Becker Massoth, raised eight children. One son, John Martin, exhibited family strengths when he grew up to be an acknowledged inventor. John had built a remote control gliding plane that he was asked to exhibit at one of Lowell's (Lake County, IN) Labor Day homecomings. He also improved a carburetor for the Ford automobile, invented a coil for the Model "T" Ford and made a "B" Eliminator for the battery radio before they were later completely electrified; however, the article failed to note that Frank Massoth had passed away in 1902 and that the Massoth family - widow Mary, daughter Catherine age 23, and sons John Martin age 22 and Joseph Conrad age 19 - had moved to Kokomo in early 1907. Both sons had been lured to the area because several industries - automobile, steel, rubber - offered great opportunities for growth and advancement. Both John and Joseph went to work for the Kokomo Brass Works/Kingston Electric Company. The inventions and improvements outlined above were developed at the Kingston Electric Company between 1907 and 1930.

The brothers divided all expenses equally at 1130 N. Washington Street, their first rental, until Joseph married Anna Rotheram June 14, 1911 at St. Patrick's Church. Joseph and Anna moved into a separate house as the brothers continued their careers at Kingston Electric.

Catherine Massoth (1883-1954) entered the Sisters of St. Joseph Convent at Tipton, IN becoming Sister Mary Petronilla. After graduating from the Good Samaritan School of Nursing in Kokomo and beginning her career at the Good Samaritan Hospital, she became the head of the Maternity Ward at Mercy Hospital in Elwood, IN, serving there until her retirement.

John Martin having kept the books at his father's general store, continued that habit for many years. His three meticulously kept Cash Journals, 1907-1930, were saved by the family and today offer a plethora, a super-abundance, of family and financial information. Several examples follow: "April 1907 started at 12-1/2 cents an hour; worked 72 hours the week of April 23 - 6 days at 12 hours per day - received 9 dollars; married Hazel Isabelle Mitsch of Cedar Lake at St. Patrick's Church on April 16, 1907.

The births of three sons, John Francis, Paul Edward and Robert Joseph are neatly recorded in the Journal(s). The first "Automobile Expense" was listed in 1913, almost seven years after the move to Kokomo. This first automobile, a used single seated, open "Empire" roadster, was followed in July 1917 by a used Saxon Six which had storable leatherette side curtains with small isinglass windows. Five gallons of gas cost one dollar. John's next car, and his last, was a new 1927 Buick Sedan, motor number 1813494, automobile 1754382. John Martin passed away in 1945. Other major events detailed in the Journal(s) include: the 1920 purchase of the house at 1025 N. Morrison Street which became the home place until 1975; the first "telephone" bill in 1926; and a 1926 Battery "B" Eliminator commission-agreement with George Kingston and "Billy" Johnson.

John Francis Massoth was born at 1130 N. Washington Street on Jan. 20, 1910. ("Birthing" was at home in the "good old days.") John, an avid 'ham' radio operator, worked at Kingston Electric for several years as an electrical engineer. The Great Depression forced him to look outside of Kokomo for employment. He landed a job with Chicago Telephone in Elkhart, IN in the middle 1930s. He was employed by Chicago Telephone until his death in 1967. John F. married Ethel Harmon Jan. 22, 1931 at St. Joan of Arc in Kokomo. Ethel passed away in Elkhart in 1989. Their only child, Rosemarie Massoth Martin, lives in Elkhart.

Paul Edward Massoth was born May 27, 1914 at 1206 N. Morrison Street. He was a member of the 1931-1932 Kokomo High School track team. Pole vaulting was his speciality. Paul also played semi-pro baseball in the Kokomo area, especially with the "IRMA" (Independent Retail Merchants Association) organization. Paul married Juanita Worthington on Sept. 7, 1940 at St. Patrick's Church. After the death of Juanita in 1953, Paul married Alean Bayer Feb. 27, 1960 at St. Joan of Arc Church in Kokomo. Both Paul and Alean enjoyed 45+ year careers at Kingston Products, retiring in 1980.

Robert Joseph was born Aug. 27, 1918 at 1024 N. Morrison Street. His story is presented as a separate item in this publication.

Hazel Isabelle Massoth passed away July 8, 1974. She and John Martin are buried in Kokomo's Memorial Park Cemetery. *Submitted by R.J. Massoth.*

MAST-HENSLER - The Larry Hensler farm two miles west of Plevna has one of the oldest and largest sets of farm buildings in the county situated on it.

Moses Mast (1823-1890) married Elizabeth Yoder (1819-1887); in 1853 they moved to Howard County from Holmes County, OH, and settled on the farm that now is the home of Larry Hensler.

In 1863 Moses Mast built the large 43x90 foot Pennsylvania Dutch styled 'bank' barn that still stands; in 1864 he built the two-story house between the barn and the road.

Somewhere along the line he set aside ground from his farm for a burial site; today it is known as the Mast-Hensler Cemetery.

Moses Mast belonged to the Old Order Amish Church. In 1880 a curious man known as the sleeping preacher made an appearance at his home. This man would lay down and appear to go to sleep; then, as if in a trance, he would get up and start to preach, complete with dramatic arm movement. He attained quite a following, but some wondered if he was possessed by a good spirit or perhaps, by a bad one.

Ananias Hensler (1849-1919) married a daughter of Moses Mast, and at the death of the latter the farm became the Hensler home. In about 1918 a tornado of short duration but tremendous fury touched down across the road from the Mast-Hensler farm. It moved across the road and tore into the buildings with devastating force. The roof of the house was lifted up, then set back down on the plates again; a garage was picked up and deposited in a pear tree; a chicken house was blown across the fields and slammed to the ground a half-mile away.

All the slates of the barn roof down to the purlin (roof support beam) were blown off; standing in the barnyard was a wagon with wooden spoke wheels; a slate blew into a wood spoke and shattered, the remaining part cutting halfway through the spoke.

After the death of Ananias Hensler the farm became home to his son, William A. Hensler (1872-1953). In 1954 his son, Lucius Hensler (1911-1976) took over. Today, Vera Hensler, widow of Lucius Hensler, and her son Larry Hensler and family reside on the farm built up by pioneer Moses Mast. *Submitted by Jeff Hatton*

MASTERS - CLUBBS - William Tilford Masters, "Bill", the son of Ira and Goldie (Krause) Masters, was born Jan. 1, 1918 in Kokomo and died Aug. 9, 1992. The second of four children, there were two sisters, Dorothy and Betty, also a brother, Robert "Bob". Bill attended Kokomo High School until Violet Clubbs and he were married Nov. 24, 1936 in Howard County by Rev. T.C. Savage at the Church of the Nazarene.

Bill and Violet Masters

Bill served in the U.S. Army during WWII. He was on the Kokomo Police Department, retiring in 1968 as Captain of Detectives after 20 years service. Later he was appointed Adult Probation Officer. At one point in time, he was employed by Chrysler Corporation and Stellite Division of the Cabot Corporation. Hobbies of traveling and fishing were enjoyed by the couple after their retirement. Winters were spent by taking their motor home to Pine Island, FL. Bill was a member of St. Joan of Arc Church and the David Foster Fraternal Order of Police Post 78.

Violet was the eldest of twins, the daughter of Charles and Rozelma (Meade) Clubbs, born July 5, 1920 and died April 28, 1991. She was one of six children. There were four sisters: Viola (her twin), Blanche, Rosalie and Addie, also one brother, A. Charles Clubbs. Violet attended Kokomo High School and was employed at Delco Radio which later became known as Delco Electronics. She retired in 1977 after 30 years. Membership was held in the St. Joan of Arc Church and also UAW Local 292.

Bill and Violet are interred at Memorial Park Cemetery beside their son Billy.

Three children blessed the marriage but the lives of two were taken at an early age. Judith Ann was born Oct. 27, 1937 and died at the age of four months; Sharon Sue born Dec. 21, 1938 and married William Paul White. (They are mentioned elsewhere in this publication.) Sharon and Bill have four children; William R. "Billy" born Oct. 24, 1943 died at the age of 29 on May 3, 1973 of a heart condition. He married Alyce Meacham and they had two daughters: Robin and Dawn. He was survived by his second wife Kathryn Cuttriss.

These loving parents and grandparents had six grandchildren and six great-grandchildren.

Their memory will be cherished for many generations. *Submitted by daughter, Sharon (Masters) White*

HENRY MENDENHALL - Henry Mendenhall was born Jan. 9, 1834 in Randolph County, NC. His Quaker parents were Jeramiah and Margaret (Young) Mendenhall. Jeramiah's branch of the Mendenhall family has been traced back to John Mendenhall, Sr. born Aug. 30, 1659 at Marredgehill, Wilts, England.

Henry was orphaned at an early age when both his parents died within a month of each other during the influenza and cholera epidemic. As was the custom at that time, Henry was "bound-out" to another Quaker family, and grew up as a farm apprentice to John Barker.

Due to slave conditions in the South, John Barker and several Quaker families in North Carolina decided to form a covered wagon train and migrate to Indiana. Only those who were physically unable to walk were permitted to ride. The men and even the women and children walked the rough terrain, enduring all types of weather and hardships for hundreds of miles. Henry, as a young man, was one of the "walkers".

The wagons found their way to Westfield, Hamilton County, IN. There Henry found Abigail Barker, whose father was a distant relative to John Barker. They were married May 10, 1855 in Westfield, IN.

They soon heard about the large Quaker church at New London, IN which seated 1000 people. This attraction convinced Henry to buy acres of farmland northwest of New London. There he joined other Quaker families to clear the land of forests and swamps for farming, built a family log-cabin, then added a frame-house later to accommodate their growing children.

Henry and Abigail were staunch believers in the old Quaker faith, and raised their children accordingly. On the first and fourth day of each week, without fail, Henry was always found at the New London Friends Church, often directing the meetings. His honesty, quiet unassuming manner and devotion to God, won people's respect and love throughout the community.

Nine children were born to Abigail and Henry Mendenhall:

1. Narcissa Ann, born Oct. 5, 1855, died Sept. 9, 1929, married Ossian Hobson Oct. 12, 1881.
2. Miriam Lucinda, born Oct. 6, 1857, died Nov. 1, 1858, diphtheria.
3. Ira J., born Aug. 7, 1859, died Jan. 5, 1861, diphtheria.
4. Delphina, born Aug. 19, 1861, died Oct. 6, 1960, married Oliver C. Beals Feb. 2, 1883.
5. Franklin, born Aug. 17, 1863, died Oct. 25, 1863, diphtheria.
6. Edwin Stanton, born Dec. 27, 1864, died April 28, 1954, married Neaty M. Crawford Oct. 10, 1889.

7. Elma, born May 2, 1868, died April 8, 1969, married John A. Hollett July 22, 1896.
8. Nathan Hobson, born March 9, 1871, died April 2, 1972, married Sally Dee Ponder.
9. Clara Daisey, born Aug. 14, 1875, died Feb. 14, 1961, married Theodore R. Haworth Feb. 5, 1903.

Henry died Nov. 11, 1907 at his New London farm, and is buried in the New London Friends Church Cemetery. The Beals family, the Hollett family, and the Edwin Mendenhall family remained in Howard County, but the Haworth family and Nathan Mendenhall moved on to California. *Submitted by Bobbie Nicholson (Doran)*

ABIGAIL (BARKER) MENDENHALL - Abigail, wife of Henry Mendenhall, was born Oct. 25, 1837 at Westfield, Hamilton County, IN. Her Quaker parents were Nicholas and Fanny (Low) Barker. Nicholas's branch of the Barker family has been traced back to another Nicholas Barker who was born May 8, 1787 at New Castle, DE and migrated to Randolph County, NC.

Abigail and Henry Mendenhall were considered one of the "pioneer families" in Monroe Township of Howard County. In later years, Abigail loved to tell stories of "real pioneer days" when the state and county was a swampy woodland in many big spots, and of the hard work it took to make it "different".

An article in the Nov. 25, 1892 issue of *The Kokomo Tribune* gave a descriptive interview of Abigail and her early pioneer life, whereby she laughingly stated "folks of pioneer times entertained themselves with hard work, instead of the frivolous modes of entertainment in vogue in later years."

Abigail (Barker) Mendenhall

In her early married life, she did all kinds of work: helped "daub" the cabin, worked in the field and garden, and at the spinning wheel and loom. She liked to ride a spirited horse, and took her child with her as she swung side-saddle, then traveled several miles to visit friends. But the family rode in the spring-wagon to the New London Quaker Church meetings.

She and Henry "lived off the land" and raised their six children through prayer, ingenuity, and hard work. Everything was done by hand (no electricity in the country until 1936), made her own laundry soap with family washing done on the "scrubboard", baked her own bread, raised her own meat, eggs, milk. The orchard yielded various fruits, plus numerous garden vegetables which were marketed weekly in New London, Burlington and Kokomo, sold or traded for necessities.

Abigail made many, many beautiful quilts, and she took pride in talking about her work with silk-worms and how she made skeins of silk. She enjoyed nature and taking care of bees, confessing she "really preferred bees to the care of chickens!"

Both she and Henry were strictly raised in the Quaker faith and were devout followers, but she once laughingly told how she and Henry broke the First Day of the Sabbath - "a day of rest". She had helped Henry build the big chimney of sticks and clay - the First Day of the Sabbath arrived - but they felt they must hurry the work on the cabin, so she proceeded to "daub" one end of the cabin while Henry fixed some much needed fence. The neighbors, alarmed at their absence in church, rode over to investigate in the afternoon and found them both working away!

After Henry died, daughter Elma Hollett (recently widowed) and children returned to the family homestead to live and care for her "pioneer mother" until her death on Jan. 18, 1928. Abigail is buried in the New London Friends Church Cemetery beside Henry. *Submitted by Rowena (Doran) Albright*

NARCISSA MENDENHALL-HOBSON - Narcissa Ann was the oldest child of Quaker parents Henry and Abigail (Barker) Mendenhall. She was born in Hamilton County, IN on Oct. 5, 1855. She, with her parents, came to New London when she was a small girl.

Narcissa became a member of the New London Friends Church, attended New London School, and enjoyed her membership in the W.C.T.U. activities.

Narcissa Mendenhall-Hobson Four Generation Family Picture Early 1910's. L-R Seated: Grandmother Abigail (Barker) Mendenhall; daughter Narcissa (Mendenhall) Hobson. Standing at back: Grandson Enos Hobson-son of Narcissa, great-grandson Howard Hobson-son of Enos.

Being the oldest child and oldest daughter, she grew up helping her mother with the younger children as well as learning the household chores. Family and relatives remember her kind ways and helpfulness.

On Oct. 12, 1881, Narcissa married Ossian Hobson. Three children were born to this union:

1. Grace, born May 11, 1885, died 19??, married Ellis Waldron on Dec. 23, 1906.
2. Enos Kaye, born Oct. 15, 1887, died 1971, married Bertha Hinshaw on Dec. 25, 1907.
3. Fannie Candice, born Oct. 18, 1889, died March 5, 1953, married Ray Jones Feb. 14, 1912.

Ossian Hobson was born 1857 to Sarah and Elihu Hobson.

Narcissa died Sept. 9, 1929 and Ossian Hobson died Nov. 9, 1935. Both are buried in the New London Friends Church Cemetery. *Submitted by Steve Doran*

DELPHINA MENDENHALL-BEALS - Delphina was the fourth child and second living daughter of Quaker parents Henry and Abigail (Barker) Mendenhall. She was born in Hamilton County, IN on Aug. 19, 1861. She, with her parents and sister Narcissa, came to New London when she was a small girl.

The Henry Mendenhall Family. L-R, front row seated: Henry, wife Abigail, Narcissa, Delphina. L-R, back row standing: Edwin, Elma, Clara and Nathan. Photo taken late 1800s, frame-house in background, steps covered with rugs Abigail made on her loom.

Delphina became a member of the New London Friends Church, riding in a spring-wagon with her family to church meetings and activities. She attended New London School, and participated in W.C.T.U. activities with her sister Narcissa.

Delphina (Mendenhall) Beals

On Feb. 2, 1883, Delphina married Oliver Cromwell Beals. Six children were born to this union:
  1. Colonzo Chelcie, born March 21, 1884, died Jan. 25, 1957, married Glendora Scudder Aug. 30, 1919.
  2. Jesse Franklin, born Nov. 25, 1886, died July 10, 1970, married Della Mae Snyder June 5, 1917.
  3. Sarah Eliza May, born Feb. 27, 1890, died Nov. 19, 1971, unmarried.
  4. Richard Henry, born Sept. 4, 1894, died April 26, 1922, unmarried.
  5. Arthur Edwin, born Jan. 14, 1899, died April 17, 1936, married Elsie Ridgeway 1922.
  6. Mary Esther, born Dec. 26, 1904, died Nov. 16, 1949, married Elisha Filmore Meredith Sept. 28, 1934.

Oliver Cromwell Beals was born April 10, 1859 in Hamilton County, IN to Sarah Jane (Symons) and Richard Beals. Oliver died July 8, 1913.

Delphina died Oct. 6, 1960. Both Oliver and Delphina are buried in the New London Friends Church Cemetery. *Submitted by Bill Doran*

EDWIN STANTON MENDENHALL - Two days after Christmas, Dec. 27, 1864, Edwin Stanton, the sixth child of Henry and Abigail Mendenhall, was born in a log-cabin in a clearing located a mile and a half northwest of New London, Howard County, IN.

Edwin was the first living son. At the age of 13, he began to assume the duties of elder brother, helping to clear the land, produce the food and tend the crops.

For Edwin, formal schooling had to be fitted in when the farm work allowed. Nevertheless, he succeeded in getting a partial high school education. Later, by working to pay expenses, he attended an Indianapolis Business College taking all courses on law. He took great pride in his penmanship.

Edwin devoted his life to his family and community, showing particular concern for community schools and township roads. He served many terms as Monroe Township Trustee, New London School Board of Directors, and Monroe Township Republican Precinct Chairman. He also served on the New London Telephone Company Board of Directors for 25 years.

Edwin Stanton and Neaty (Crawford) Mendenhall

His mental alertness during his advanced years was remarkable! At age of 82 years, he served on the Howard County Tax Review Board four years from 1944-1948.

Edwin was a quiet, warm, gentle man who loved to talk and listen to people. He possessed a keen sense of justice and civic righteousness. Many people came to him for counsel and guidance. He had a wide circle of friends in all walks of life.

He loved flowers and farming - the planting time, the growing of crops, and the harvest season. He became a well-known farmer in western Howard County, always seeking better ways to improve agriculture from Purdue University.

Edwin was a birthright member of the New London Society of Friends Church, following the same Quaker faith and beliefs throughout his life as his parents did before him.

On Oct. 10, 1889, Edwin married Neaty Marie Crawford at Michigantown, IN. Five children were born to this union:
  1. Mary, born July 9, 1890, died July 10, 1890.
  2. Paul Ancil, born Oct. 6, 1891, died May 8, 1913, married Mary E. Brennadon April 30, 1913.
  3. Owen Fowler, born March 4, 1893, died May 30, 1976, married Leora Maude Weaver March 17, 1922.
  4. Bertha Ann, born March 3, 1895, died May 27, 1965, married William Dee Doran March 20, 1915.
  5. Harry Loren, born Oct. 6, 1900, died Feb. 11, 1989, unmarried.

The Mendenhall home was well-known throughout the community for its warm hospitality. A skilled cook, Neaty was famous for setting a bountiful table of food at "threshing-time" and harvest-time. Unexpected guests at mealtime always received a warm welcome and an extra chair at the table, with a sack of food and a bouquet of flowers to take home!

Neaty was an active member in the Friends Women's Aid Society and the New London Quaker Church with her husband. She enjoyed sewing, and made many beautiful quilts, but most of all, she loved her flowerbeds and strawberry patch! Neaty was born on Aug. 3, 1865 at Burlington, Carroll County, IN, the 12th child of Martha Ann (LaDow) and James Crawford.

Neaty died at home on April 27, 1940. Edwin also died at home on April 28, 1954. Both are buried in the New London Friends Church Cemetery. *Submitted by Edith (Doran) Carpenter*

PAUL MENDENHALL - Paul Ancil, second child and eldest son of Edwin S. and Neaty M. Mendenhall, was born Oct. 6, 1891 at New London, Howard County, IN.

He was a birthright member of the New London Friends Church, following in the Quaker footsteps of his parents and grandparents, Henry and Abigail Mendenhall.

An avid reader, Paul became an honorary member of New London's Junta Library and Literary Association in 1908, and graduated from the New London High School with the class of 1910.

Paul Mendenhall and wife Mary (1913)

Paul grew up helping his father with the farm chores. After graduation he was employed with the Telephone Company.

On April 30, 1913 he married Mary E. Brennedon. A week later, a storm passed through the county damaging the telephone lines. Paul was among those called out to help. He fell from a telephone pole on May 8, 1913 and died while being driven home by his father, Edwin Mendenhall, from the accident.

The emotional shock to Paul's wife, a bride of one week, and to his parents, brothers, and sister was never forgotten. Paul is buried in the New London Friends Church Cemetery beside his parents. *Submitted by Margaret Doran*

OWEN MENDENHALL - Owen Fowler, third child and second son of Edwin and Neaty Mendenhall, was born March 4, 1893 at New London, Howard County, IN.

He was a birthright member of the New London Friends Church and graduated from the New London High School with the class of 1912.

Owen grew up helping his father with the farm chores, developing an interest in flowers and landscaping. He loved baseball and pitched for a minor league team and played in college.

He attended Greeley State College at Greeley, CO and Earlham College at Richmond, IN. In 1923, he moved to Goshen, IN and taught Industrial Arts in the junior high school until his retirement in 1959. He also attended Goshen College, graduating in 1947.

After Owen retired in 1959, he became a well-known landscaper, operating his own landscaping business until his death on May 31, 1976.

Owen and Maude (Weaver) Mendenhall

He never forgot his Quaker upbringing and possessed a deep religious faith. He was an active member of Goshen First United Methodist Church and later with the First Baptist Church in Goshen. He taught Sunday School at the Methodist Church for many years and was an active member of the Goshen Lions Club. Owen supervised the Airplane Model Club for many years and was often the court-appointed guardian for the Juvenile Correction System.

On March 17, 1922 Owen married Leora Maude Weaver at New London, IN. One child, a daughter, was born to this union: Ruth Eleanor, born Dec. 27, 1922, married Edward Allen Barrett on March 20, 1949.

Maude Mendenhall was born on Nov. 30, 1897 at New London, Howard County, IN with a twin sister, May. They were the youngest children in a family of 11 born to Jane Ellen (Hughes) and Peter VanNuys Weaver.

She graduated from New London High School with the class of 1916. Maude attended Earlham College and graduated in 1933 at Goshen College, Goshen, IN. She taught in Sharpsville, IN and Bluefield, WV before her marriage, and in the elementary schools and high schools at Goshen, Concord, and New Paris, IN after her marriage. She also taught French and Education Methods at Goshen College, and was a supervisor for Goshen College student teachers for many years, retiring in 1962.

Maude was a member of the Goshen First United Methodist Church, several Studies Groups, Women's Club of Goshen, Retired Teachers Association, and Daughters of the American Revolution. She died June 16, 1980.

Both Maude and Owen are buried in the New London Friends Church Cemetery in the Edwin Mendenhall family plot. *Submitted by Ruth Eleanor (Mendenhall) Barrett*

RUTH ELEANOR MENDENHALL-BARRETT - Ruth was born Dec. 27, 1922 on the 58th birthday of her Quaker grandfather, Edwin S. Mendenhall.

She was the only child of Owen F. and L. Maude (Weaver) Mendenhall. Ruth studied music, primarily violin, and played in the Goshen High School Band and Orchestra, Goshen, IN, and the South Bend Symphony Orchestra.

She was graduated from both Goshen High School and from LaSalle Preparatory Conservatory at South Bend, IN in the spring of 1941. Ruth was a Laura Kindig Science Scholar at Goshen College receiving her B.S. degree in the spring of 1944. She was active in many sports in school and later life, riding horses until her 60s, playing tennis, field hockey, basketball, and softball at various times. She was also a Red Cross certified Water Safety Instructor, and worked several summers as a life-guard.

Ruth was one of the six women admitted to Northwestern University of Medicine in Chicago in September 1944. After graduation from medical school, she was the first woman allowed to intern at Michael Reese Hospital in Chicago. She and fellow intern, Edward Allen Barrett were married March 20, 1949 at the University of Chicago Chapel.

Bertha and William Doran Family - 1940. L-R, front row, seated: Bertha (mother), Dee, William (father), Barbara June. Back row, standing: Bobbie, Edith, Max and Rowena.

Edward Allen Barrett M.D.; Ruth Mendenhall Barrett M.D.

After about two years of joint General Practice, Dr. Edward Barrett was called to active duty in the Army Medical Corps. Dr. Ruth Barrett started her four years of residency training in pathology at Alameda County Hospital in Oakland, CA while he served at the Presideo Army Base in San Francisco, CA.

Dr. Ruth was certified by the American Board of Pathology in 1956, and practiced pathology until retirement in 1988.

Dr. Edward completed two years of residency training in anesthesia, and practiced anesthesiology until he retired in 1980.

Dr. Ruth served about 10 years as Assistant Medical Examiner of Westchester County, NY, and 22 years as Chief Coroner of Orleans County, NY. She was the director of the laboratory and pathology service at Arnold Gregory Memorial Hospital, Albion, NY for many years. She also served as Consultant Pathologist to the FDR and Batavia Veterans Administration Hospitals.

Ruth served on many boards of directors, was vice-chairperson of the Mt. Kisco New York Public Housing Authority, President of Medical Staff, President of County Medical Society, Treasurer of Ninth District New York State Medical Society, and a member of the board of directors of the Medical Liability Mutual Insurance Company of New York State.

Dr. Edward Barrett was born in New York City, Aug. 31, 1914 to Morris and Annette (Schoenhaus) Barrett. Drs. Edward and Ruth retired to Bloomington, IN in 1988. They are the parents of four children:

1. M. Scott, born Aug. 20, 1950, married Ruth Nyenhuis July 10, 1975, now of Bloomington, IN.

2. Edward M., born Jan. 15, 1953, married Rosemary LaMar Oct. 27, 1984, now of Terrell, TX.

3. William W., born Oct. 1, 1962, unmarried, now of Greenwood, IN.

4. Elizabeth A., born June 15, 1965, married Timothy McCarthy Aug. 18, 1990, now of Albion, NY. *Submitted by Edward M. Barrett*

BERTHA ANN MENDENHALL-DORAN -

Bertha Ann was born on March 3, 1895 at New London, Howard County, IN. She was the fourth child and only living daughter of Quaker parents Neaty and Edwin S. Mendenhall.

She was a birthright member of the New London Friends Church, graduated from New London High School in 1914, and was a lifetime resident of Howard County.

Bertha loved music and enjoyed playing the piano, guitar, and singing gospel hymns. She also enjoyed drama, participating in school and church plays during her youth.

Bertha and her brothers either walked, rode horses, or traveled by horse and buggy or spring-wagon over narrow, dirt roads to their destination to visit friends, church and school social activities.

Her gentle, kind manner reflected the grooming of her Quaker heritage. As was the custom within Quaker families, the daughters learned all the fine arts of homemaking: sewing, crocheting, quilting, and cooking/canning recipes handed down from one generation to another.

Members of the Mendenhall family were early risers. Bertha and her brothers would waken at 4:30 AM each morning, help their father feed the livestock, milk the cows, then return to the house to eat breakfast and to get ready for school.

Even in later years, Bertha remained an early riser, doing a day's work by noontime then spending the afternoon leisurely crocheting, making quilts, or visiting friends. She was quite proud of her many quilts, sometimes selling one for $25 - a good price at that time! She was also a beautiful seamstress and dressmaker - a skill she utilized in clothing her four daughters.

Bertha inherited her parents' warm thoughtfulness of other people, and always lent a hand when called upon for help. She enjoyed doing mid-wife work when family responsibilities allowed. After her family was raised, she entered practical nursing at St. Joseph Hospital in Kokomo, then worked with private cases as selected by individual doctors.

The Quaker faith and beliefs ingrained in Bertha as a child remained with her during her lifetime. Her religious and spiritual faith in God sustained her through the years of raising children and personal illness.

On March 20, 1915, Bertha married outside the Quaker faith to William Dee Doran from Wirtz, VA. Seven children were born to this union:

1. Virginia Edith, born Jan. 12, 1916, married first James DeBoo on Sept. 26, 1937; married second Sid Carpenter in 1954.

2. Edna Rowena, born Oct. 10, 1917, married first Alvin Fellow on Sept. 14, 1938; married second Kenneth Albright, Aug. 30, 1959.

3. Dee William, born April 1, 1919, married first Virginia Newton on April 25, 1938; married second Dottie Whorell Nagle, April 13, 1962; married third Bernice Weeden May 9, 1981.

4. Charles Edwin, born June 13, 1922, died Jan. 18, 1926.

5. Max J., born July 15, 1925, died May 5, 1980, married Bonnie Kayler Aug. 11, 1946.

6. Martha Roberta "Bobbie", born Dec. 4, 1928, married Howard Nicholson June 19, 1949.

7. Barbara June, born June 23, 1936, married Arthur Miller, Jr. on Aug. 16, 1958.

Edith and June presently live in California; Max's family lives in Florida; Rowena lives in Indianapolis, Dee lives at Westville, and "Bobbie" lives at Rochester, IN. Bertha and William were divorced in 1951. He married second to Frances Ingle. William died Feb. 27, 1955. Frances died Oct. 27, 1979. Both are buried in the Ingle family plot at Dayton, OH.

Bertha died on May 26, 1965, and is buried in the New London Friends Church Cemetery in the Doran Family Plot beside Charles Edwin. *Submitted by Barbara June (Doran) Miller*

LOREN MENDENHALL -

Harry Loren was born Oct. 6, 1900 at New London, Howard County, IN. He was the fifth and last child of his Quaker parents, Neaty and Edwin Mendenhall.

He was a birthright member of the New London Friends Church, and remained an active, supporting member until his death on Feb. 11, 1989.

Loren Mendenhall

At an early age Loren lost his right eye in an accident. He developed an interest in music. Local music teachers instructed him with piano and voice lessons. Later he traveled to Chicago for further advanced lessons. The Mendenhall home always had music with sister Bertha playing the piano, brother Owen strumming the guitar, and Loren adding his tenor voice. Their gospel singing entertained family, friends, and neighbors throughout the community.

Loren graduated from New London High School with the class of 1919. He remained at home assisting his father with the livestock, tending the crops, and other farm chores. He was the owner and operator of the family farm for many years after the death of his parents.

Loren lived on the farm during his retirement years, and after death, his ashes were scattered over his beloved homestead. His gravestone marker is among those in the Edwin S. Mendenhall family plot in the New London Friends Church Cemetery. *Submitted by Dee Doran*

ELMA (MENDENHALL) HOLLETT -

Elma Mendenhall was born on May 2, 1868 in a log cabin on land cleared by her parents, Henry and Abigale

Mendenhall, near New London, IN. She was the seventh child of Henry and Abigale Mendenhall. A birthright member of the Society of Friends, she maintained a life long membership in the New London Friends Church. Elma grew to be a young woman in this Quaker community on her parents' farm.

Through the encouragement of her parents, Elma pursued an education and graduated from the New London High School not long after it was established, a major accomplishment for the period. It was Elma's ambition to become a doctor or a nurse, but because such training was virtually unobtainable for her in those days, she went to Normal School and became a substitute teacher for a short period of time.

Left to right, back row: Delite Hollett, Dwight Hollett, Lucile Hollett. Middle row, seated: Elma Hollett, Abigale Mendenhall. Seated on ground: Lloyd Hollett.

On July 22, 1896 Elma married John Alexander Hollett, a widower with four young children. She moved to Pierceton, IN with John to raise her four step-children: James Bertram, Orpha Dean, Cora Elizabeth and Opal Hope Hollett.

John bought a livery stable in Huntington, IN, and Elma and John moved to Huntington where their family grew with the addition of Lucile Abigale (May 2, 1897), Dwight Henry Hazard (Oct. 1, 1898), Clara Delite (Aug. 12, 1900), and Lloyd Lester (May 2, 1905). After nine years of marriage, tragedy struck the Hollett family on Feb. 12, 1905, when John died of pneumonia. He contracted this illness while traveling to care for his horses at his livery stable during a snowstorm.

Elma was pregnant and near term with Lloyd Lester at the time of John's death. After Lloyd's birth she returned to her parents' farm near New London. With the passing of her parents, Henry and Abigale, Elma acquired the homestead farm of 20 acres. From this farm her family was launched. A strong traditional value for education remained in the family. Her children Lucile, Delite and Lloyd all graduated from college. Dwight pursued a career as a mechanic.

Elma remained on the farm until 1948. She then made her fall and winter home with her daughter Lucile, in Chicago. Elma continued to spend the spring and summer season on the farm in Indiana accompanied by one or more of her grandchildren until near her 100th birthday. Elma Hollett departed this life April 8, 1969 and was laid to rest in the New London Friends Church Cemetery just one month before her 101st birthday.

The original Mendenhall homestead (and an adjoining 20 acres) remained in the family and was farmed by Lloyd until 1986 when ill health forced Lloyd and his wife, Virginia, to sell the farm.

Lucile married Jacob Harold Whitacre Aug. 5, 1928, died March 21, 1983.

Dwight Henry married Mary Price, June 12, 1920, died Oct. 12, 1981.

Delite married Bert Helm June 1, 1937, died Oct. 23, 1992.

Lloyd married Laura Virginia Anderson Sept. 20, 1946, died Nov. 17, 1990. *Submitted by John Whitacre, grandson*

NATHAN MENDENHALL - Nathan Hobson was born March 9, 1871 in a log-cabin northwest of New London, Howard County, IN. He was the eighth child and second living son of Quaker parents, Henry and Abigail (Barker) Mendenhall.

Nathan was a birthright member of the New London Friends Quaker Church. He attended the New London School and was an avid reader, becoming an honorary member of the New London Junta Library and Literary Association in 1892. Following in his footsteps, sister Elma became an honorary member in 1895, and sister Clara became an honorary member in 1896.

Nathan and Sally Dee Mendenhall

Nathan grew up helping his father and older brother, Edwin, with the farm chores and marketing of the vegetable, fruit and farm products. He married Sally Dee Ponder, daughter of Mary and N.V. Ponder at Marion, IN.

Nathan and Dee owned and operated a dry-cleaning business at Marion, IN for a few years, then moved to Rockford, IL where they owned and operated a dry-cleaning business for many years.

Nathan and Dee had no children. Shortly after Dee's death in Rockford, Nathan moved to Citrus Heights, CA. He made his home with sister Clara and her husband, Theodore Haworth, until his death at age 101.

Nathan died April 2, 1972 and is buried in the Sylvan Cemetery at Citrus Heights, CA. *Submitted by Janet Doran*

CLARA MENDENHALL-HAWORTH - Clara Daisey was born Aug. 14, 1875 in a log cabin a mile and a half northwest of New London, Howard County, IN. She was the ninth child and youngest child and daughter of Quaker parents Henry and Abigail (Barker) Mendenhall.

Clara was a birthright member of the New London Friends Quaker Church, participating in church activities with her parents, brothers, and sisters. She attended New London School, and grew up helping her family with the gardening and unending household chores. Housework was hard in the 1800s with no electricity, no bathrooms, no running water, no furnaces, or modern conveniences as we know them today.

Life and work were hard for Clara and her brothers and sisters growing up, but it became easier after the family moved into the frame-house their father built for his growing family. There was a large family kitchen, a parlor, spacious bedrooms to sleep everyone. Outside, Henry built a smokehouse to hang their cured meats, a woodshed to store firewood for the cook stove and heating stoves in the rooms, and the pitcher water-pump was placed over an underground spring just outside the kitchen door. Many a tin cup of cold, spring water was drunk on hot days throughout the ensuing years!

On Feb. 5, 1903 Clara married Theodore Robbins Haworth. Three children were born to this union:

1. Martha Esther, born Feb. 13, 1909, died Oct. 9, 1910, unmarried.

2. Mabel, born Aug. 3, 1910, died 1977, married Claude Finley on July 15, 1947.

3. Ruby Dee, born April 30, 1916, died November 1962, married Bernard Richards Sept. 5, 1937.

Theodore was born Jan. 30, 1876 to Mary Ellen (Robbins) and Stephen Haworth. He died June 13, 1953 and Clara died Feb. 14, 1961. Both are buried at Citrus Heights, CA where they had lived since 1920. *Submitted by Roy Doran*

CLARENCE AND ESTELLE MERRELL - Clarence Curtis 'Pat' Merrell, was born Aug. 26, 1888, in Ervin Twp., the son of Robert Wilson Merrell and Martha Jane Malaby. He had the following brothers and sisters. Erwin, Ward, Orman, Edna Hoffman, Margaret Smith, Allie, Dorothy and Edith Loman. He graduated from high school at New London. He was a farmer. He was also a very dedicated member and worker of Bethel Friends Church.

Clarence and Estelle Merrell-50th anniversary

On April 23, 1910 he married Tessa Estelle Wilson. She was the daughter of Roscoe Alvin and Laura Ann (Crites) Wilson. She was born Feb. 7, 1890 in Ervin Twp. She was also a dedicated member of Bethel Friends Church, where she was pianist and a Sunday School teacher. She attended #11 School in Ervin Twp., but did not finish high school.

On April 24, 1960, they celebrated their 60th wedding anniversary, with 80 guests present. On April 27, 1960, Clarence suffered a heart attack and died. Estelle lived to be 94 years of age, passing away Jan. 10, 1985.

They are buried in North Union Cemetery, Ervin Twp., just across the field from where they lived.

L-R: Clara Haworth, Mabel Haworth, Abigail M., Ruby Haworth and Theodore Haworth.

MERRILL - Roy Stanley (Stan) Merrill and Sharon (Sherry) June Osborn met in Howard County when both were young teachers in the Kokomo-Center Township Consolidated School Corporation. They were married June 21, 1964, in Wells County, IN.

Stan, son of C. Ralph and Myrtle Belle (Osborn) Merrill of Tipton County, IN, graduated (1952) from Sheridan High School, Sheridan, IN (Hamilton County); and Indiana University (B.S. 1956; M.B.A. 1961). Completing his student teaching at Kokomo High School, he was a business teacher at Sheridan High School for three years before returning to Kokomo High School in 1959, making a total of 38 years. Stan has been a business teacher, Coordinator of Cooperative Office Education at Kokomo and Haworth High Schools; presently, Counselor at Kokomo High School-DC.

Sherry, daughter of Herman Kenneth Osborn and Golda Irene First of Wells County, IN, graduated from Chester Center High School, Wells County, in 1955 and from Taylor University in 1959. She earned a master's degree in Elementary Education from Purdue University in 1964. After teaching six years at Jefferson Elementary School in Kokomo, she became a full-time mother.

Stan and Sherry are the parents of two sons, Anthony (Tony) Lynn and Eric Jerome.

Tony was born in Kokomo on April 13, 1966. He graduated from Haworth High School in 1984. He received his baccalaureate degree (1988) in Computer Science and his master's degree (1990) in Finance from Purdue University. On June 4, 1988, Tony married Paula Lynn Fischer, daughter of Theodore and Jacquetta Fischer, of North Aurora, IL. Paula also earned her baccalaureate and master's degrees in Human Resources from Purdue. Tony is Senior Products Accountant with 3M in St. Paul, MN. Paula is employed by Blue Cross.

Eric was born Aug. 31, 1969, in Kokomo; graduated in 1988 from Kokomo High School and from Purdue University in 1991 with a major in chemistry. Presently living in East Providence, RI, Eric is a chemist with Northwest Environmental Testing Lab. *Submitted by Sherry Merrill.*

MIDDLESWORTH-GRUBB - The first Middlesworth in Howard County was William, son of Joseph, Jr. and Susann Kern of Grant County and grandson of Joseph, Sr. and Harriett Hamilton of Fairfield County, OH. The father of Joseph Sr. was Abraham, son of John and Martha of Beavertown, PA.

William, with his wife Viola Malott and two sons, Homer and John, moved to Howard County in August 1849. A son, Glen, was born later in Howard County. John and wife, Mable, daughter of Della (Bradshaw) and William Golding of Howard County, had sons Clarence Wm., Robert G., Joseph Earl, John Jr. and daughter, Mary Doris (Winegardner).

The subject of this sketch is Joseph Earl, born July 4, 1920 in Jackson Township of Howard County. On Aug. 6, 1939 he married Bonnie Grubb, daughter of Marguerite Gillard and Russell Grubb, of Converse, IN. In 1940, the couple moved to the Joseph Middlesworth homestead in Grant County. Denny Lynn was born on Jan. 24, 1942. About two years later the family moved to a farm south of Sweetser, IN. On Dec. 19, 1944 Lonnie Rae was born. Then in 1946 Joe, Bonnie and family moved to Jackson Township, Howard County to the Schuyler Warnock farm. On April 11, 1949 Randy Joe was born and on May 13, 1954 the three boys had a baby sister, Jana Gae.

Raising a family on the farm was a good life. The children went to Jackson Elementary School and graduated from Eastern High School, Greentown.

Summertime was full of hard work but also funtimes with family and friends, which meant plenty of activity at Joe's house with the children of the neighborhood. All the children rode ponies, raced go-carts and played basketball, both outdoors or above the old hog barn. There was even a wooden tub in the upstairs bedroom corner for testing their basketball skills. This was after the farm "chores" were done.

Many evenings were spent visiting friends and relatives or entertaining company for meals or homemade ice cream. In the wintertime it was school, basketball, amateur hockey and lots of soup. The children often hitched a pony to great-granddad Middlesworth's sleigh and over the snow they'd go. What fun!

William Middlesworth - first Middlesworth to reside in Howard County.

Joe has farmed his whole life, just as four generations before him had done. Now in 1994, the children are all grown and have homes of their own. Denny, Lonnie and Jana graduated from Purdue University and Randy from Vincennes University.

At the present time Denny, employed at Boeing, lives in Kirkland, WA with his wife, Rosamond, and daughters, Kimberly Ann, Katie Lynn and Kelly Paris. Lonnie is employed at Reid Memorial Hospital in Richmond, IN and lives there with his wife, Charlotte, and two sons, Jason Rae and Evan Charles. Their daughter, Shawn Marie, and husband, James Tatone, live in Gainesville, FL. Randy, a contractor, lives in Howard County with his wife, Denise, and son, Joseph Trent. Jana, an architectural designer, is married to Tom Healy and they live in Danbury, CT. Bonnie is owner of The Red Sleigh Christmas Shop, Metamora, IN and co-owner of Carriage Manor Flower and Gift Shop in Kokomo, IN.

MIDDLETON - My family is originally from Howard County. My sister, Pam (Middleton) Challis, and I were born and raised in Kokomo. Our dad, Howard Middleton, (now deceased) was also from Howard County and born in Russiaville. Our mom, Dorothy (Shockley) Middleton, is from Anderson originally, but both parents graduated from Kokomo High School in 1939. Our paternal and maternal grandparents were born and raised in eastern Howard County before the turn of the century. My paternal grandfather, Ervin Middleton, was a machinist at Stellite, and in his younger years he built several homemade automobiles. My grandmother, Mae (Jackson) Middleton, attended one room schools of the day and later became a teacher and taught elementary grades at Ervin Township School in the Northwestern School District. My great-grandfather, Alvin Middleton, operated a machine shop in Russiaville in the late 1800s and early 1900s and was a key person in getting running water operating to the town of Russiaville. My maternal grandfather, Roy Shockley, was employed as a plating engineer by Dirlyte and Guide Division GM in Anderson.

Me, Steve Middleton, in my first car in 1955.

My dad was a navigator on a B-24 Liberator during WWII and he flew 21 missions from England, bombing rail yards and oil fields in Germany. He returned, married and attended Purdue. He and Mom moved to Texas and Iowa before returning to Kokomo where I was born in 1952. My dad worked as an engineer at Stellite, a shop supervisor at United Tool and Die, and manager of Hoosier Bearings (now Motion Industries). He died suddenly of a heart attack in 1976. My sister, Pam, was born in 1958, and is a nurse at Americana Healthcare. She is married to Marvin Challis and is mom to Kristen (12) and Bradley (10).

Our mom retired from Kokomo Center Schools after many years of service in the offices and is now enjoying retirement and community service work through the Cancer Society.

My dad, Howard Middleton, delivered groceries for Crothers Grocery on South Buckeye ca 1936. The delivery vehicle is a Hudson Terra plane (1936). This was his high school after-school job.

I am married to Tammy (Spotts) Middleton and am an engineer at Delco Electronics. We have a daughter, Samantha, aged six months. Due to my wife working outside the home in Carmel, we recently moved to Cicero so that our commute is evenly split. But my roots are here in Kokomo, and one day I would like to move back, even though we are only 30 minutes away from Howard County today.

CORBIN H. MILLER - Corbin Miller was born in 1833 on a farm in Ripley County, IN. In 1856, he met and married Barbara Ann Lung. They had three children, Charles, Isaac and Sarah, at which time the family moved to Howard County and began farming in Ervin Township. After the birth of another daughter, Ida, Corbin enlisted in the Union Army on Feb. 20, 1864 at Galveston, IN and served with the 21st Btry., Light Arty. until his discharge on Oct. 4, 1864. After returning home, Barbara gave birth to John E. on Aug. 5, 1866 and later Oscar in 1874, and Jessie in 1876. In 1880 the family moved to a farm in Clay Township. Shortly after, Barbara died and Corbin married Maggie Harley in Kokomo on Sept. 1, 1890. After suffering from palsy for several years, Corbin died in his home at 59 Orchard Street in 1907 and was buried at Crown Point Cemetery.

John E. Miller married Mary Cozetta Tow(e), the daughter of William Tow(e) and Jemima Collins Overholser on Oct. 25, 1890, in Kokomo. John was a farmer and a carpenter. To this union were born four children: William Chauncey, Harry Vane, Barbara, and John Corbin. Jemima had a daughter, Leona Fidilla, while married to her late husband, Tobias Overholser. John died on March 7, 1942 and Mary Cozetta joined him on May 1, 1963. Both were buried at Mound Cemetery in Howard County.

Harry Vane Miller was born in 1893 in Howard County. He was a farmer and later on a baker. He met and married Alta Collins in 1911 in Kokomo. They had one son, William Robert. On Sept. 30, 1916, Harry married Dulcinea Bassett in Peru, IN. Harry enlisted and served in the Army as a baker during WWI. While he was in France, Dulcinea gave birth to a daughter, Madonna Bell, on Feb. 20, 1918. After Harry was discharged and returned home, they had a son, Harry Van, Jr., on May 10, 1921. On July 22, 1926, another son, John Arthur, was born, followed by the birth of Richard Arlen on Aug. 27, 1932. The family lived in Kokomo for several years, Harry was working as a baker and Dulcinea operated a

263

beauty shop at their home on South Washington St., across from Foster Park. Harry died in 1978 and is buried at Mound Cemetery in Howard County. Dulcinea is presently living just north of Cassville, IN.

Madonna married Edward Howard Sullivan in Kokomo on Feb. 28, 1936. Howard worked at Globe American and later Continental Steel until his retirement. They had eight children, Donn, June Ann, Dulcenia, John, Donna Lynn, Barbara, Kathy, and Connie. Madonna later worked at Delco Electronics in Kokomo until her retirement. They are presently living just north of Kokomo near the Miami County line. With the exception of Dulcenia, who is living in Garland, TX and Barbara in Covington, LA, all the rest of the family lives in the immediate area. *Submitted by Madonna Miller Sullivan.*

DANIEL C. MILLER - Daniel C. Miller, a resident of Howard County for nearly half a century, was a native of the "Buckeye State". He was born in Tuscarawas County, OH Dec. 13, 1824. He was one of ten children born to Daniel Miller and Elizabeth Troyer. He was married in Ohio on Nov. 13, 1854 to Magdalena Frey, also a native of Ohio; born in neighboring Holmes County on May 12, 1832. Her parents were John Frey and Barbara Farmwald, both from Germany - Speyer and Elsass, respectively.

In 1854, Daniel bought a parcel of land located in Liberty Township a mile northwest of Plevna, at 500N 700E where in 1856 Daniel with his wife moved from Ohio.

Their five children were all born on that land. Amanda, April 5, 1856; Abner D., June 26, 1857; Sophia, Aug. 19, 1859; John D., Oct. 27, 1861 and my great-grandmother, Elizabeth (Lizzie), May 6, 1870.

Lizzie Kaser and Judith Morrison Shelton

He was a member of the Amish-Mennonite Church in which he was ordained to the ministry in 1867 and to the office of Bishop of Howard-Miami counties in 1873. From what little information I have found, he served his congregation faithfully and was quite concerned for peace.

When it was built and for how long it was used, I've not been able to find out; but Daniel Miller was responsible for the building of a small one-room brick schoolhouse on the land across the road from his farm. The bricks from this school were later used in part on the front porch of the Zion Church parsonage on Touby Pike.

In addition to being a preacher and farmer, Daniel was an excellent carpenter and built barns for 15 cents an hour along with his son-in-law, Eli Kaser. The house and barn he built still stands today, although the house has been remodeled and the barn is in great disrepair (*See photo page 344*). When built, the barn had been put together with pegs; and until the tornado in 1965, did not have a nail in it. But due to storm damage the roof had to be repaired.

Daniel died on April 7, 1902, aged 77 years, 3 months and 24 days, on this farm. Six years later, his wife, Magdalena, died. Daniel, Magdalena and children, Sophia and Elizabeth, are buried in the Mast Cemetery located in Liberty Township.

The youngest, Lizzie, lived her entire life on that farm, just four months short of 97 years. She married Eli Kaser on Nov. 16, 1889 and had four children. Everett, died in infancy from water on the brain; Goldie Magdalena, my grandmother, Hollie and Toby. She also raised a grandson, Richard Kaser.

As a child visiting my great-grandmother, I remember her having a mulberry tree in front of the house out by the road. I loved playing there, but after ruining a pair of white dress shoes I had to go barefoot and my feet would be stained for days. My brothers, sisters and I always loved going to Grandma's house.

MOFFITT - Lawrence Harvey Moffitt came to Kokomo, IN around 1900 with his parents, Franklin David and Martha O. (Dille) Moffitt, his brother Harry, and his sister Lena. They moved here from Thorntown, Boone County, IN. Franklin's family had settled in that area in 1841.

The family lived here for a few years, then they moved to Lawrence, KS. His sister, Lena, married Charles Gwinn. They had three girls, Francis, Mrs. Phyllis Jolly of Mesa, AZ and Mrs. Nellie Bacon of Esta Park, CO. Lena remained in Kansas when the family returned to Kokomo, IN.

Harry Moffitt married Anna Olson in 1923. Anna died in 1971. Harry married Lillie York in 1974. Harry died in 1981. He was an elephant trainer for the Wallick Circus, a truck driver, and a hod carrier. He was secretary-treasurer of Mason Tender Local 887.

Lawrence met a Miss Grace Belle Hallowell and took her to the Sipe Theater for their first date. They were married Sept. 30, 1912. Some of the places Lawrence had worked at were the N.I.P.-IR & L, Cloverleaf, Ward's Department Store, as a bus driver and supervisor for the Cross Transit, and was a custodian at the Howard County Court House.

Lawrence and Belle had five children: Walter, Robert, Martha, James and Homer.

Walter, his wife, Katherine (Harlow), and daughter, Suzanne, lived in Huntington, IN. He owned and operated the Huntington City Lines. His daughter now lives in Grand Rapids, MI.

Robert and his wife, Willodean (Owens), lived in Huntington, IN. He was a mechanic for his brother Walter's bus line. Robert died in 1969.

Martha is the widow of Lester Chapman. Martha and her two children, Dennis and Carol Chapman, live in Long Beach, CA.

James and his wife, Harriett (Whybrew), live in Kokomo, IN. He is retired from the Kokomo Police Department. They have three sons. James and his family live in Wisconsin. Robert lives in Kokomo, IN. Brian and his family live in Greenwood, IN.

Homer and his wife, Helen (Ridenour), live in Kokomo, IN. He is retired from the Kokomo Fire Department and Delco Electronics. They have four children. Ronald died in 1966. Janet and her family live in Kokomo, IN. David and his family live in Greenwood, IN. Lucinda and her family live in Kokomo, IN.

Lawrence Moffitt died Dec. 29, 1971 and Grace Belle Moffitt died Dec. 25, 1961. Both are buried in the Memorial Park Cemetery in Kokomo, IN.

WILLIAM HALL MOHR AND POLLY STEPHENSON MOHR - In the 1930s, Dee S. Mohr engaged in the road construction business under the name of Mohr Construction. Dee was married to Golda Mohr of Tiffin, OH. The Mohrs' children were George William Mohr, Stanton Mohr and Carolyn Mohr. George William Mohr became the most highly decorated soldier in Howard County because of his heroism in WWII. He and Stan

William H. Mohr and Polly Stephenson

continued with Mohr Construction, which Stan runs today. Carolyn Mohr studied acting and married Jack "Alvy" Moore who played Hank Kimball on the television show *Green Acres*. George William Mohr married Joan Goldsmith Mohr, of Indianapolis, IN. Their children include James Mohr, William Mohr and Doug Mohr.

William Mohr is a family doctor at Kokomo Family Care. He graduated from Indiana University and was student trustee of the university there. He married Polly Stephenson Mohr, daughter of Jack and Elaine Davis Stephenson of Leavenworth, IN. Polly attended Hanover College and Indiana University School of Law - Indianapolis. She engages in the general practice of law.

Polly Stephenson Mohr, William H. Mohr, Joan Mohr and G. William Mohr

Stanton Mohr, whose wife, Barbara, is deceased, had the following children: John D. Mohr, Daniel Mohr, Dee Ann Mohr and Tonia Mohr.

Carolyn Mohr's children include Barry, Janet and Allyson Moore.

MOORE - You can't go back much further in Howard County history than the Moores. Richard Moore, although a native of Huntington, IN, is a great-great-grandson of Francis and Catherine Richardville LaFountaine. The LaFountaines were son-in-law and daughter of the Great Miami Chief, Jean Baptiste Richardville, known in the Miami dialect as Pechewa, or Wild Cat, and for whom Howard County was originally named. Chief Richardville and Chief LaFountaine were the Miami chiefs who sold the land, that Howard County encompasses, to the white man. Richardville was born in 1761 and died Aug. 13, 1841. He built the family home that still exists at the forks of the Big and Little Wabash Rivers where the Huntington Bypass starts at U.S. 24 and IND. 37. His daughter, Catherine, married Francis LaFountaine, who was born in 1810 and known as Topewha. Francis died April 13, 1847, in Lafayette, victim of food poisoned by the Indians he led from Indiana to their new reservation in Oklahoma. The family stayed on at its Huntington homestead. Francis and Catherine LaFountaine's daughter, Archangel LaFountaine, married Christian Engelman; their daughter, Cecelia, married Howard Owens; their daughter, Juanita, married Roy Moore; and their son, Richard, married Margaret Seifert, also of Huntington County, on July 12, 1969.

Dick has retained his pride and interest in his Indian background while growing up in Huntington. He attended many Indian meetings and knew about the Miami connection in Peru and Wabash. It wasn't until they moved to Kokomo in 1972, to join the firm of Anderson Abstract Company, that he found the name Chief LaFountaine while reading a property abstract, and began searching even deeper for his ties to Howard County.

After Dick had worked as president and manager of Anderson Abstract Co., from May of 1972 to December of 1984, he and Margi purchased the company on Jan. 1, 1985. Then in August of 1986 they changed the name of the company to Anderson Land Title Co., Inc.

The move to Kokomo in 1972 came only three years after Dick and Margi were married. They came to Kokomo with their son, Tyler, age 22 months and their daughter, Terri, age 8 months. They purchased their first home in Kokomo at 1815 Versailles Dr. in Orleans Southwest. Shortly after the birth of their third child,

Mindy, in 1973 and finding they were out-growing their dwelling place they moved to 2241 Westdale Ct. There they had their fourth child, Shelly, in 1974. The Moores were active in the parish and school activities at St. Joan of Arc, where all four children attended school. The children began their active careers in sports and their lives were constantly busy. In 1980, just 10 years after their first child was born, they were blessed with just one "Moore" child, Michael. Again, the house seemed to shrink in size and the Moores moved to 1701 W. Mulberry St. where they reside today.

The Moores. Seated: L-R: Dick and Margi. Standing, L-R: Mike, Terri, Ty, Shelly and Mindy.

Tyler, following his graduation from the University of Notre Dame in 1993, is now living in Elkhart and is following in his father's footsteps by working in the title business. Terri graduated from Ball State University this year, 1994, with her degree in Elementary Education. Mindy is a senior in Nursing at Indiana University, while fulfilling her clinicals here in Kokomo at the surrounding hospitals. Shelly is a junior at Miami University in Ohio, and has enjoyed being a part of the volleyball team there. And Michael is now officially a freshman at Kokomo High School. Through all this Dick and Margi celebrated their 25th wedding anniversary on July 12, 1994 and have now lived in Kokomo for 22 years.

MOORE - Allen W. and Barbara E. Moore came to Kokomo in 1955 with their three-year-old daughter Colleen Ann when he began teaching at Kokomo High School. Three more daughters were born to them in Kokomo: Dione Elizabeth in 1956, Malinda Jane in 1962, and Martha Caroline in 1968.

The Moore family came to Indiana in 1814 when James Butler Moore migrated from Orange County, NY, to New Albany. He later founded Floyds Knobs in Floyd County, where he operated a saw mill, grist mill and general store. At Corydon, the territorial capital, he married Lura Belle Smith, daughter of Asa Smith, a Revolutionary War veteran from Glastonbury, CT.

Allen was born in Anderson, IN to Allen Wayne and Jessie Mae (Whitehouse) Moore. Barbara was born in Clarion County, PA, to James Caleb and Dessie Lovina (Rhodes) Tiley.

Moore Family. Seated, left to right: Martha Moore Pearson, Colleen Moore Craig, Barbara Tiley Moore, and Malinda Moore Johnson. Standing, left to right: R. Colin Craig, Allen W. Moore, and Michael A. Pearson. Taken on Oct. 21, 1991, 40th wedding anniversary of Allen and Barbara Moore.

Allen was graduated from Anderson High School and he attended Anderson University for two years before earning his B.S. and M.A. degrees from Ball State University, where he also completed one year's work beyond the master's degree.

Barbara was graduated from Clarion-Limestone High School and attended Anderson University and East Central Junior College.

For 40 years Allen was a business education and English teacher in Goshen, Kokomo, and Indianapolis. At Haworth High School, he was the only Chairman of the Business Education Department from 1968-1984. From 1984-1985 he served as Chairman of the Business Education Department of North Central High School in Indianapolis. He retired as an educator in 1992.

Through the years, the Moores have been active in many organizations. Allen is past president of the Kokomo Community Concert Association and has been serving on its Board of Directors for 16 years. He served as secretary of the Kokomo Teachers Association and as treasurer of the Creative Arts Council. At the First Church of God, Allen has served as secretary of both the Board of Trustees and the Board of Elders. A life member of Delta Pi Epsilon, Allen served as president of Pi Chapter at Ball State University.

A member of many hereditary societies, Allen is the current National Commander-in-Chief of the Sons of Union Veterans of the Civil War and a life member. He has been State President of the Sons of the American Revolution, President of the Huguenot Society of Indiana, and President of the Society of Indiana Pioneers. He is also a life member of the Order of Descendants of Colonial Physicians and Chirurgiens.

Barbara is President of the Marinda B. Dye Tent #17, Daughters of Union Veterans of the Civil War and is a Past-Department President. Currently, she serves on the Board of Elders at the First Church of God. Barbara is also a member of the Daughters of the American Revolution and Ladies of the GAR. She has also served as a Girl Scout leader and Sunday school teacher.

The Moores have five grandchildren, four of whom were born in Kokomo.

MORGAN - William G. Morgan, born 1808, married Ann Lowe, came from West Virginia to Howard County in 1852, by covered wagon to Indiana. They were parents of seven children. His uncle was the great Indian fighter.

Their youngest son, William B. Morgan, born in 1848 in West Virginia, continued to live in Howard County. He married Sarah A. Locke, in 1875, the daughter of Michael and Susannah (Lyons) Locke. They were parents of eight children.

Mr. and Mrs. John H. and Hazel Morgan, 50th golden wedding anniversary, Jan. 9, 1963; ages 76 and 74.

William B. Morgan learned craft of bricklayer at young age and became a brick contractor. He built his home which was off Morgan Street. The street was named after him. He manufactured brick there on the farm. He built the first brick Columbia School on North Street and first Armstrong Landon building in downtown, plus others in Kokomo and surrounding areas from brick made on the farm. He died in 1899.

Their sixth child, John H. Morgan, born in 1886, continued to live on the farm and married Hazel Costlow, daughter of William and Martha Costlow. John was a dairy farmer delivering milk to grocery stores and door to door customers. He raised tomatoes for the canning factory and had an acre of black raspberries, which their five children and neighbors were hired to harvest.

The farm seemed to be marked for modes of travel progress. The Pennsylvania R.R. located on the east side in his grandfather's time, then the interurban went through the middle of the farm in his parents' time. In about 1940 State Road 35 went through taking the barn and the stately old brick homestead. This is when the Morgan family had to pull up roots and move. They moved to a farm near Walton. John had always farmed with horses; now he changed to tractors. John H. Morgan died in 1977 and wife, Hazel, died in 1979; each were 91 years.

Their five children are: John W. married Frances Furedy, have one son, and live in Arizona. Eber, married Helen Carey and parents of eight children. They live near Young America. Marjorie, married Richard Dickensheets (deceased), lives near Winamac. They had five sons and one daughter. Lowell, married Helen Gray, lives near Walton, and the parents of four children. Lucille, the author of this article and a Kokomo High School graduate in 1939, married Charles Mills (deceased); lives near Roann, IN. We had one son and two daughters.

MORRIS - According to the obituary of Matilda Morris, the family lived and left Kokomo, IN about 1888 and settled in Columbus, OH. Matilda Morris was born Nov. 2, 1848 in Germany, the daughter of Jacob and Matilda Morris. She was married to Jacob Morris, born June 13, 1841 in Germany and died May 4, 1893 in Columbus, OH. Son of Myer and Henrietta Morris.

Matilda Morris died July 22, 1897 in Columbus, OH. At the time of her death she was a member of Pocahontas Lodge of the Order of Red Men; Ladies' Auxiliary, Woodmen of the World, Ladies' of the Maccabees and Knights and Ladies of Honor. Her work in these societies was well-known and appreciated. Both Matilda and her husband, Jacob Morris, are buried in Greenlawn Cemetery, Columbus, OH. They were the parents of two sons, Edward Isaac and Adolph.

Adolph Morris later in life became a patient at the State Epilepsy Hospital in Gallapolis, OH. Edward Isaac Morris was born in 1869 and died Jan. 16, 1910 at his home on East Long Street in Columbus, OH. Death was from tuberculosis at the age of 41. He graduated from the University of Cincinnati, College of Pharmacy in 1889. At the time of death, he operated his own drug store, located at the corner of Long Street and Grant Avenue, in Columbus, OH. His funeral was conducted at the Cathedral with burial in Calvary Cemetery in Columbus, OH.

Edward Isaac Morris was married Oct. 11, 1889 in Columbus, OH to Margaret Eve Uhrig, daughter of John Uhrig and Catherine Mingus. Margaret Uhrig was born Sept. 14, 1870 in Hillsboro, OH. Died June 23, 1961 at Mt. Vernon, OH with burial in Calvary Cemetery, Mt. Vernon, OH. After the death of her husband she supported herself by operating a rooming house. They became the parents of two children: Edward Howard, born Sept. 9, 1899 and Margaret Elizabeth, born Jan. 24, 1903 at Hillsboro, OH. Margaret Elizabeth married Daniel Odford Fluhart, and is mentioned elsewhere in this book. Margaret Eve Morris made her home with her daughter and son-in-law after their marriage in 1935.

Edward Howard Morris died Feb. 8, 1974 and is buried at Immaculate Conception Cemetery, Anchorville, MI. He was married June 25, 1920 in Columbus, OH to Alice Daugherty. Alice Daugherty was born June 7, 1886 in Columbus, OH and died Jan. 12, 1970. Her parents were John Joseph and Sarah M. Daugherty. They lived most of their life in Akron, OH. One daughter was born to them, named Marian Ruth on Oct. 19, 1921, in Columbus, OH. Marion resides in Fair Haven, MI.

MORRISON - Sometime between the years of 1827 and 1842, William Morrison and family emigrated from Ohio to the western portion of Howard County. Perhaps they were squatters when they first arrived as the earliest known land record is dated in 1842. Tradition suggests that the Indians begged for food in the days after their arrival. William was accompanied by his wife, Hannah,

265

nine children including Daniel, and his father, John. John resided in Howard County until his death in 1855.

John Morrison was born in either 1769 or 1770 in the state of Maryland according to the 1850 Census. He may have been of Scottish or Scotch/Irish descent. He matriculated to Ohio in either the late 1700s or early 1800s with perhaps a stop in western Pennsylvania but to date, we have no proof that John lived there. John's wife Mary, perhaps his second wife, died before the family departed from Ohio. John owned land in Knox County, OH and most of his children were born there.

William was born in Ohio, perhaps Fairfield County, in 1803 and wife, Hannah Nihart, was born in Northampton County, PA in 1804. They married in Knox County during 1823 and most of their nine children were born there. William's only known deed was for a two and one-half acre plot in western Howard County. The meager size of his acreage suggests that the family had little material wealth. William was both a farmer and a lumber manufacturer by occupation. He died in 1871 and is buried in Clinton County beside his wife.

Daniel Morrison (born 1822 Knox County, OH, died 1879 Howard County, IN) married Margaret Hazlett in 1849 in Howard County, IN. They also lived in the western section of Howard County, perhaps on the same land as father William. Daniel and Margaret had five children including William Alfred. Daniel was a veteran of the Civil War and served two years and one month in Co. G, 89th Regt. of the Indiana Volunteers.

William Alfred Morrison (born 1853 Howard County, IN) married Emma Jane Younkin in 1876 in Howard County and had 11 children including Homer C. After Emma Jane died in 1897, the children were orphaned and placed in a number of different homes. William Alfred then relocated to Whittier, CA and remained there until his death in 1912. Homer spoke very warmly of his mother and suggested that she was a woman that projected love and possessed the pioneer spirit.

The current generation started in 1912 with the marriage in Carroll County of Homer C. Morrison (born 1881 Howard County, IN, died 1930 Howard County, IN) to Mabel Cassandra Harmon. Homer and Mabel had eight children: Loree married Clyde Cross, Alice Carol married Earl Rodkey, Velma Ruth married Alton Eugene Kellar, Harold H. married Pearl Hasler, Gerald William married Ann Cheny, Nina Jean married J. Frank Ehrman, and Russell and Lois Catherine who both died young. Homer was a wonderful father who cared deeply for his children. He worked as a farmer on the Flo Miller farm until his death in 1930. Mabel and the children then moved to Burlington in Carroll County, IN. Mabel took full responsibility for raising the family and provided for her children while she often did without. Her sense of humor, her pretty smile and her warm heart touched everyone she knew. She remained in Burlington until her death in 1981.

The Morrison family have always been Christians. Daniel was a member of the Pleasant Run Friends Church while William Alfred and Homer C. attended the Christian Church in Burlington. The family has never been affluent and every generation has had to work diligently to provide for the next generation to leave a legacy of love.

Allied families include:

Hannah Nihart, born 1804 Northampton County, PA, died 1891 Howard County, IN, daughter of: John Jacob Newherd, born 1776, died 1851, Clinton County, IN, son of: Lorenz Newherd, born 1740, died 1817 Allentown, PA, son of: George Frederick Newherd, born Germany, died Northampton County, PA immigrant. Married families include Boyer/Berger.

Margaret Hazlett, born 1824, died 1893, daughter of: John Hazlett, probably Irish. Married families include Hamilton.

Emma Jane Younkin, born 1858, died 1897 Howard County, daughter of: Isaac Younkin, born 1814 Somerset County, PA, died 1861 Clinton County, IN, son of: Jacob Younkin, born ca. 1793, died ca. 1848, son of: Jacob Younkin, born 1761 Bucks County, PA, died 1811 Somerset County, PA, son of: Johann Henrich Junghen, born 1717 Germany, died 1787 Bucks County, PA, immigrant. Married families include Walters, Kitzmiller, Weimer, Nicola, Harbaugh, Ankene/y, Hornberger, Hartzell, Domer, and Somner.

Mabel Cassandra Harmon, born 1891 Carroll County, IN, died 1981 Carroll County, IN, daughter of: Samuel Roy Harmon, born 1842 Carroll County, IN, died 1898 Carroll County, IN son of: Stephen Harmon, born 1810 Greene County, TN, died 1885 Carroll County, IN, son of: Moses Harmon died Indiana. Married families include Pratt, Allen, Jervis, Patty, Russell, and Carter. *Submitted by Loree (Morrison) Cross*

CASWELL MORRISON - Caswell Morrison was born April 4, 1848 near Columbus, IN in Bartholomew County. He was the fifth of a family of ten children, seven boys and three girls, born to Enoch and Eliza (Marshall) Morrison.

On the 10th day of August of 1862 at the age of 14, he enlisted in the Union Army at Mount Healthy, 10 miles southwest of Columbus under the command of Charles A. Hubbard, Co. "A", 93rd Regt. of the Indiana Volunteer Inf. He was eager to join the army and fight for his country and, being a stout and robust lad, passed for 18 years of age.

"Cas", as he was known to his many friends, was the youngest of five brothers to enlist in the service, two of whom never returned, Miles Morrison being killed at Perryville, KY, in 1862, and Albert Morrison at Peach Tree Creek, GA on July 20, 1864.

Caswell and Emily Morrison

Cas's first military engagement as a member of the 93rd Indiana Regt. was on May 14, 1863 at Jackson, MS under the command of General Sherman. He then participated in the siege of Vicksburg, MS from May 18th to the date of its surrender to the Union Army on July 4, 1863. This decisive victory was followed by the capture of Jackson, MS on July 16th. Subsequent engagements in which "Cas" participated were at Memphis, TN (picket and provost duty), a fierce battle at Brices' Cross Roads, TN, battles at Pontotoc and Harrisburg, MS on July 15, 1864 (a strong enemy attack repulsed), and the capture of Nashville, TN on Dec. 15-16, 1864.

Cas participated in the additional battles of the siege of Spanish Fort in Alabama which fell to the Union Army on April 9, 1865 and the capture of Mobile, AL on April 9, 1865.

Cas spent three years in the military service, from Aug. 10, 1862 to Aug. 11, 1865, never missing a battle or a march with his regiment. He was proud of his military service and of his honorable discharge.

On Sept. 12, 1869, Cas married Emily Vickers in Bartholomew County. Their eight children included four daughters (Vida, Cora, Gertrude and Blanche), and two sons (William and Earl). Two children died in infancy.

Cas was a farmer for many years before moving to Russiaville from Tipton County in 1905. He served as Russiaville's mail carrier for several years, picking up the mail at the interurban station at the east edge of town early each morning and again in the evening, and taking it to the town post office in his two-wheeled cart. He mowed the Russiaville Cemetery as well as several lawns and he was a painter for the Eikenberry Brothers for 15 years.

Cas maintained his vigor and vitality well into his elderly years. Spry and enthusiastic in his 80s, he enjoyed giving demonstrations of his headstands and somersaults at the annual Morrison Reunions. He also gave demonstrations of his ability to spring over the woven wire fence that was in front of his home while he was about 85 years old. He was also an excellent marksman with a shotgun. Witnesses testified that he "shot from the hip" and that he rarely missed his target.

Cas was an active member of the Russiaville Friends Church and he assisted in its construction. He was blessed with the unique ability to memorize and quote many Holy Scriptures, giving the book and chapter where they could be found in the Holy Bible. He could recite some of the chapters of the Bible backwards. One of his favorite verses was II Cor. 5:1 which is "For we know that if our earthly house of this tabernacle were dissolved, we have a building of God, an house not made with hands, eternal in the heavens."

Caswell Morrison passed away Tuesday, June 27, 1933 at the age of 85 years, 2 months, and 23 days. He was the type of man who "made a difference" in the lives of many people. He freely gave of himself to help his community, his church, his family, and his country. *Submitted by Gene Parks, grandson of Caswell Morrison.*

RONALD L. MORROW - In July 1957, the promise of a job advancement with Chrysler Corp. brought Charles L. Morrow and his wife, Helen, from Flint, MI to Kokomo, IN to live, along with their young family, consisting of Ronald, then 11 years old, Richard 10, and Diane 4.

Charles, a tool and dye maker for General Motors since the age of 16, worked at Chrysler in Kokomo for six months before being laid off. After working at several other jobs over the next few years, he applied for and was hired at Delco Electronics, where he worked in skilled trades until his retirement in 1977.

Ronald Louis Morrow, the oldest son, was born in Flint, MI on May 10, 1945. He attended St. Joan of Arc School and graduated from Kokomo High School in 1963. While employed at Krogers on North Washington Street, he also attended Indiana University Kokomo. He married Rita Carol Schoner in September 1967, in Plymouth, IN.

The youngest of three children, Rita was born on Jan. 21, 1945, in Plymouth, IN to Adalene C. Xaver and Leo F. Schoner. She attended St. Michael's School in Plymouth, and graduated in 1963 from Ancilla Domini High School in Donaldson, IN. After completing her first year at Holy Cross School of Nursing in South Bend, IN, she was transferred to the Holy Cross affiliate at St. Joseph Hospital in Kokomo for the remaining two years of study. She met Ron at a youth dance held weekly at St. Joan of Arc Church. The young adult club (YAC) was formed to give Catholic singles between the ages of 18 and 30 a place to meet and socialize.

Ronald Morrow Family 1991. Front row, L-R: Kevin, Ronald, Rita, Stephanie, Steven. Back row, L-R: Scott, Jason, David, Brian, Karen.

In June of 1966, Rita graduated with a diploma degree in nursing, and returned to Plymouth to work at Marshall County Parkview Hospital, while her fiance, Ron, completed his basic training in the Indiana National Guard at Fort Leonardwood, MO.

Ron and Rita married on Sept. 23, 1967, at St. Michael's Catholic Church in Plymouth. They rented an apartment in Mishawaka, IN while Ron was employed as an insurance investigator for Retail Credit Company in South Bend and Elkhart, and Rita worked in the Emergency Department of St. Joseph Hospital in Mishawaka.

Ron transferred to Kokomo in July 1968, where they purchased their first home at 1420 Schuler Drive. Ron fulfilled his National Guard commitment over the next six years. Rita, meanwhile, began her career with St. Joseph Hospital in Kokomo in January 1969.

During the next five years, they celebrated the births of David, 1968; Brian, 1970; Scott, 1971; and Stephanie, 1973. The growing family moved to their current residence on Davis Road in 1973. Ron accepted a job at Delco Electronics in 1976, and eventually was accepted into skilled trades after completing training as an electrician. During these years they welcomed the births of Jason, in 1974; Karen, 1977; Kevin, 1978; and Steven, 1980. All of the children attended St. Patrick's School, then continued into the Northwestern School system. Those who have graduated have all gone on to Indiana University-Kokomo or the Purdue Technology Program at Indiana University-Kokomo.

Ron graduated from Indiana Wesleyan University in 1991 with a Master of Science in Business Management. In addition to his job at Delco, he teaches at Ivy Tech. Rita is a 25-year employee in the Emergency Department at St. Joseph Hospital. Ron and Rita celebrated 25 years of marriage last October with a Caribbean cruise.

Although our ancestors did not originate in Howard County, we are proud to call Kokomo "home", and we are grateful to all our friends for enriching our lives with so many memories. *Submitted by Ron and Rita Morrow.*

JESSE AND NINA MOSS - Jesse Ray Moss (Feb. 26, 1890-May 27, 1984) and Nina Julia (Kerby) Moss (Jan. 15, 1889-Sept. 2, 1949) were both born in Miami County, IN. Jesse was the second son of Moses (1863-1937) and Mary Davis (1864-1901).

Moses, as a boy, moved with his parents to a farm three miles northwest of Kokomo (200W). It was here he grew to young manhood. He was a farmer near Galveston. Moses and Mary were married in 1888. They had five children, Homer, Jesse, Mina, Clifford and Fred.

Fred was a baby when their mother died. Homer worked in the fields with his dad, while Jesse and Mina cooked and tended to household chores and took care of Clifford and Fred. Fred was a math teacher at Kokomo High School for many years. Moses resided with Fred in Kokomo and passed away there.

Nina Moss; Jesse Ray Moss

Nina Julia Kerby was the fourth daughter of William and Emma (Smeltzer) Kerby. She grew up on a farm in Clay Township in Howard County where her parents operated extensive holdings until 1922. They then retired and moved to Kokomo.

Jesse and Nina were married on July 20, 1912. They set up housekeeping in Galveston, but later moved to the "Harren Place", then to his father's farm in Cass County, IN. In 1929 they moved to the Kerby Farm in Howard County. After the death of Emma Jane Kerby, Aug. 15, 1941, they purchased the farm where they both lived out their lives.

Jesse and Nina were the parents of seven children: Edith (1913) who was married to Henderson Kendall (1910-1973) on June 9, 1934. They have one son, Joseph Terry. On May 30, 1981, she then married William Cotterman (1919-1986). He had three children: David, Sandy and Brian.

Orville Herman (1915) who was married to Virginia Kinsey (1915-1987) on July 22, 1939. They had three children: Robert, John and Kathy.

Doris (1917) married Donovan TenBrook (1918) on March 12, 1938. They have two children: Shirley and Sharon.

Esther (1920-1982) married Clyde Glassburn (1916-1985) on Dec. 22, 1940. Their five children were: Dixie, Diana, Donna, Jack, and Julia.

Russell (1923-1982) married Virginia Newport (1924) on July 13, 1946; they had four children: Gregg, Roma, Gordon, and Gayle. Russell purchased the "home place" and farmed it until his death in 1982. Their son, Gordon, purchased the land and is now living there.

Dorothy (1927) married William Aschenberg (1924) on Sept. 3, 1949. They are the parents of children: William, Barbara, John, Thomas, and James.

Norma (1930) married John Aschenberg (1934) on May 17, 1958. They have one son Michael. William and John Aschenberg are brothers.

During their lifetime, they were very hard-working people and were well-known. Jesse had a very good sense of humor. He loved reading Zane Grey books and told us all about the stories he read. He was always ready to play games with us. He was a member of the Deer Creek Church near Galveston.

Nina was a long time member of the Majestic Needle Circle in the community, and was well thought of. *Submitted by Dorothy Aschenberg*

DAVID AND KATHLEEN MOSS - David Earl and Kathleen Marie Moss live at 2001 Southway Blvd. E.

Dave was born in Kokomo Dec. 28, 1937 to Harry Earl Moss and Audrey Lucille (Dawson) Moss. He graduated from Kokomo High School in 1955 and received a B.S. in Physics from Purdue University in 1959. He began working for Delco Radio after graduation and later earned an M.S. in Engineering from Purdue University. He is still employed by Delco Electronics and holds five U.S. patents from semi-conductor research.

David and Kathie Moss

On July 1, 1961 he married Kathleen Edwards in Kentland, IN. Kathie was born in Watseka, IL on July 31, 1938, the youngest daughter of Alvin Harold Edwards and Ethel Marie (Weidert) Edwards. Her sister, Janice Carol Bergay, lives in Anaheim, CA. Kathie attended a one-room school for two years before Iroquois County began to consolidate schools. Her family moved to Kentland when she was 12 years old. She graduated from Kentland High School and worked at Purdue University as a secretary before she married Dave. She has studied china painting and specializes in applying raised enamel to porcelain bisque eggs.

Dave and Kathie have two children. Darlene Marie Moss was born April 22, 1962 in Kokomo. She is currently working as a hostess at Ryan's Steakhouse and as a housekeeper at Comfort Inn.

Glen David Moss was born in Kokomo Nov. 25, 1964. He graduated from Taylor High School and joined the U.S. Army. He is a veteran of Desert Storm. He recently returned to Kokomo and is employed by Steak n Shake.

Dave and Kathie are active members of Grace United Methodist Church. They are both members of Howard County Izaak Walton League where Dave currently serves as Chairman of the Board. Both serve on the committee for Ducks Unlimited in Howard County. Dave was a member of the Purdue Varsity Glee Club in college and still enjoys singing in the church choir and the Kokomo Symphony Chorus. He is past president of Kokomo Community Concert Association. Kathie is a past state treasurer of Indiana Rural Youth, past president of Kokomo China Artist's Guild, and treasurer of Kokomo Women's Aglow Fellowship.

MOTE - Jesse Mote was born in 1817 in Tennessee, a son of Jesse and Dorcas (Patty) Mote. He came to Jonesboro, IN as a boy. There he met and married Dorcas Coppock June 25, 1838. She was born in Greene County, TN, Oct. 31, 1820, a daughter of John and Martha Patricia (Williams) Coppock who came to Jonesboro in 1830. The Motes came to Kokomo in 1860. Dorcas ran a boarding house for employees of the Dolman Pork Packing Plant.

Jesse and Dorcas had the following children in Jonesboro: Rachel, born 1840, married Nov. 3, 1872, to Benjamin F. Crites, who was born Dec. 2, 1833. She died April 9, 1920. He died Aug. 31, 1915. They resided in Galveston. They had two sons, Charles Leonard Crites and Elroy D. Crites.

Alfred Mote was born Feb. 23, 1842 and died Feb. 10, 1917. He married April 11, 1872 to Sarah Elizabeth Sellers (Oct. 16, 1850, Chili, IN-April 23, 1923), daughter of Alfred Perry and Mary (Cole) Sellers, owners of Sellers Kitchen Cabinet Company which burned in 1904. They then moved cabinet company to Elwood, IN. They had three sons, Jesse Lee, Franklin Earl and George Roscoe Mote. Jesse moved to Riverton, WY, where he shot three wildcats which he had stuffed and sent to Kokomo High School. They became the school mascots. George R. Mote was a druggist.

Levi Mote, born April 26, 1847, married Martha Jane Fisher, March 4, 1884 in Tipton. Martha was born in 1850. She and a child died Dec. 29, 1891. Levi died Nov. 5, 1896.

Sarah A. Mote, born 1851, married Feb. 3, 1869 Allison G. Glover, born in 1848. A son, Ortho D., was born in 1870, married Aug. 21, 1899 to Sarah G. Shelley. Sarah and a child died June 9, 1875.

Verlinda Mote (July 27, 1852-Aug. 2, 1918) married May 1, 1870 to William David Frazee (Aug. 3, 1848-May 30, 1927). Only two children survived infancy: Nellie, born Aug. 26, 1873, married Feb. 9, 1893, to William Zimmerman. She second married Richard Sitgreaves, March 28, 1919; third remarried Sitgreaves, and fourth, married Rev. Benjamin L. Foster on March 11, 1936. He died in 1939 and she died April 23, 1940.

George Oscar Frazee (Jan. 4, 1882-Sept. 29, 1948) married in 1905 to Golda Ridgley, born 1888 and died Nov. 19, 1946.

Jesse and Dorcas (Coppock) Mote were the third great-grandparents of Rodger Smith. *Submitted by Rodger Smith.*

MOULDER - John and Eleanor Maris Moulder were two of Howard County's earliest pioneers. John Moulder, son of Jacob and Elizabeth Borland Moulder, was born in Orange County, NC on March 2, 1805. His grandfather, John Mohlar (later, Moulder), with brothers Lewis and Valentine, emigrated from Prussia about 1750 and first settled in Philadelphia. He married a Swiss emigre, Susannah Swingle, whose passage he had paid when she arrived in Philadelphia. John Mohlar and his wife left Pennsylvania before the Revolutionary War and raised eight children in Rowan and Orange counties, NC. They finally settled in Grainger County (now Union County) TN. John and wife, Susannah Mohlar, are buried there on the family farm near Maynardsville.

Sometime around 1815 or 1816, the Mohlars of North Carolina and Tennessee came together. The German name "Mohlar", often spelled "Moler" or "Mohler" was changed to the English "Moulder". No explanation has been handed down for the name change, though it might have been a move to fit in better with their Quaker friends.

Jacob Moulder and family, though not Quaker, moved with many Quaker families to Paoli, Orange County,

IN in 1816. There John Moulder and Eleanor Maris, of the old Quaker family, grew up together. They were married on Feb. 1, 1827 in Orange County and in 1828, settled in Parke County, where John was a wheelwright, harnessmaker and merchant, in partnership with Eleanor's brother, Aaron Maris. John and Aaron also ran a line of boats between Terre Haute and New Orleans, exchanging pork and livestock for rice, cotton and tobacco. John Moulder's farm became the center of the new town of Annapolis. John held the offices of postmaster and justice of the peace and all of the other offices Annapolis needed.

In 1842, John Moulder was one of three men appointed commissioners by the State Legislature to survey and locate land for the county seat of the new Richardson (later Howard) County. They negotiated with David Foster for the initial land donation that became Kokomo.

While on this assignment from the State, John Moulder scouted for land for himself; in 1843, he moved his family to a 160 acre tract of land on Honey Creek that was previously part of the Miami Reserve donated for the building of the Wabash and Erie canal. John and Eleanor raised their 11 children there, living long, full lives; a newspaper article of 1896 celebrated their pioneer spirit and that they "are the most ancient residents in the Hoosier State". John died at age 95; Eleanor at age 90 and are buried in the cemetery at New London.

The children of John and Eleanor Moulder were: Dr. Thomas Marion Moulder; Elizabeth Moulder Nixon (Mrs. Zimri.); Mary Moulder Vandenbark (Mrs. William); Jane Moulder Middleton (Mrs. John); Jacob Moulder (killed in the Civil War); Ann Moulder Ellis (Mrs. I.H.); Oliver Lewis Moulder; Henry Clay Moulder; Martha Catherine Moulder (died in infancy); Eliza Eleanor Moulder Evans (Mrs. O.L. Evans); and John Milton Moulder.

Their respected Howard County descendants include: Dr. J. McLean Moulder, Harry Louden Moulder Sr., Thomas Penn Moulder, Sr. and Harry L. Moulder, Jr. Descendants living today include John Evans of Russiaville; Miss Anna May Hamilton of West Middleton; Mrs. Benjamin W. Franklin (Sharon Moulder) of Bonita Springs, FL; Thomas P. Moulder, Jr. of Elk River, MN; Mrs. James S. Neave (Sally Moulder) of Kenton-on-Sea, South Africa; Mrs. Don Pletcher of Elkhart (Linda Moulder); Larry Moulder of Mount Dora, FL; John C. Moulder of Kokomo; Mrs. Steve Snyder (Joanne Moulder) of Indianapolis; Eleanor Rayl of Indianapolis; Allen B. Rayl of Waterford, MI; and Mrs. Christopher Riesen (Elizabeth Rayl) of Carmel.

The original Howard County farm of John Moulder is now owned by his descendant, John Evans. It is the only piece of land in the county that has never changed hands since its purchase in 1843.

MULLEN - Daily C. Mullen, born July 28, 1900 in Bunker Hill, IN of Frank and Ellen (Benner) Mullen. He came to Kokomo at age of 13 years, after the death of his parents.

He worked at Kingston Factory when he first arrived. He made his home at a boarding house with Mr. and Mrs. Smith on North Union St. In later years he worked at Crosley which later became Delco.

He married Nellie M. Fenn, daughter of David and Dora (Keeler) Fenn of Hemlock, IN, in 1923. Nellie was named after her aunt, Nellie Keeler, daughter of Ezra and Mariah Keeler. Nellie was a midget with the Barnum Bailey Circus. She was 28 inches tall at 30 years, when she died, June 1, 1903.

Daily and Nellie (Fenn) Mullen had three children. They have four grandchildren, four great-grandchildren. Daily died January 1956 in Kokomo.

Nellie lives in Kokomo, still active at age 88 years this October 1993.

Betty Jo, the oldest graduated from Kokomo High School in 1944. She married Guy Wyrick of Howard County. He served with the 15th Air Force in North Africa and Italy from 1942 to 1945. He was a staff sergeant on a B-24 bomber and flew 52 missions. Later he worked at Kennedy Space Center on fueling systems team for Apollo/Saturn V launches.

They had two sons, Roger Kent and Dennis E. Wyrick. They have a grandson and granddaughter.

Guy died in October 1977 in Phoenix, AZ. Later, in 1985 Betty married Kenneth Hackenbracht of Jackson Township, Howard County, where they now reside. Kenneth is a farmer, Betty is a retired nurse. She graduated from St. Mary's Hospital, West Palm Beach, FL.

Max E. Mullen still resides in Kokomo, where he has and still is in the realtor/appraiser business. He was married to Jane Cable. They had two children - Steven Mullen of Kokomo and Cynthia Mullen of Indianapolis. Two grandchildren reside in Kokomo.

Madonna was married to Bruce Shutt at Kokomo. She graduated from Kokomo High School. She now resides in Bloomington, IN, where she is employed by Indiana University. *Submitted by Betty Jo (Mullen) Hackenbracht.*

MULLEN/NEWCOM - I now live in Texas but my roots are in Howard County and it is still "home" to me. My forebears have been in the county many years.

I was born at Darrough Chapel to Agnes (Newcom) Mullen, 1900-1987 and Charles "Pete" Newcom, 1901-1981.

My maternal grandfather, Charles Newcom, 1879-1967, was born to William Newcom, 1832 Ohio-1902 and Frances Ann Gates, 1842 Ohio-1880. William's parents were Matthew Newcom, 1801 Pennsylvania-1880 and Mary Carey, 1810 Ohio-1916. All lived and passed away in Howard County.

My grandfather, Charles, and grandmother, Anna Catherine Ehrhard, 1882-1962, purchased a farm on 400 E in the early 1900s, which my husband and I now own.

My grandmother was known well as "Aunt Annie," a devout Christian. She spent much time visiting the sick and witnessing of her faith and what God had done for her. I miss her greatly. A few years before her death, she was struck by an automobile while visiting an ill friend and was from then on an invalid.

Her parents were John Ehrhard, 1852 VA-1918 Kokomo and Frances Hawn, who died in 1925 in Kokomo; her grandparents were Frederick Ehrhard, 1822 and Catherine, 1826, both born in Bavaria.

My paternal grandparents were Noble Mullen, 1870 IN-1935 Greentown and Zelma Howell, 1880 IN-1907, Howard County. My paternal great-grandparents were Emery Mullen, 1842 OH and Hannah Odom, 1843 IN. Both died in Greentown.

Hannah's parents were Lewis Odom, born 1802, SC and Hannah Golding, born 1805 PA. Both died in IN.

Zelma's parents were Matthew G. Howell, 1852 IN-1929 and Lucretia Nation, 1857 IN-1926.

Matthew's parents were Tense Howell, 1828-1897 and Eleanor Golding, born 1834 Indiana, died in Howard County.

Lucretia Nation, my great-grandmother, who raised my father and his siblings after their mother's premature death, came from a family we can trace to pre-Revolution. Her parents and ancestors are:

William Nation, 1832-1877 and Mary Jane Conn, 1828-1875; Judge Enoch Nation, 1804 TN-1865 IN and Sophia Thomson, 1807 VA-1876 IN; Sampson Nation, born 1775, NC and Susannah Johnson, born circa 1777 TN; Joseph Nation, born circa 1752 VA, died 1803 IN and Jerriter Vickery, born 1754 VA, died 1849 OH; Christopher Nation, 1717 VA-1799 NC and Elizabeth Swaim, born 1719, NC; and John Nation, born circa 1694 England, died circa 1774, NC and Bethia Robbins, born circa 1792, NJ.

Tradition says that John Nation, the first Nation found in the United States, was kidnapped as a child from his family in England, brought to the United States, and sold as a slave. The first written reference to him lists him as a 17-year-old servant boy in the household of William Beaks.

Christopher Nation was engaged as early as 1751 in riotous acts against the Crown. Joseph Nation fought in the Revolution and Judge Enoch Nation was a captain in the Civil War.

All my ancestors were farmers, but especially on my father's side, they were very active politically and held office in Republican politics and the Masonic Lodge, both in Greentown and in Kokomo.

Enoch and William Nation were also attorneys.

I am proud of my heritage. They were all good people. I pray my descendants can say the same. *Submitted by Betty Lou (Mullen) Culbertson*

LEWIS ELLSWORTH AND KIZZIE MURPHY - Lewis was born Aug. 19, 1866 in Howard County. He was the son of Chester Arthur and Polly Ann (McCoy) Murphy. He died Jan. 3, 1940 in Cass County, IN. On Nov. 27, 1890 he married Kizzie Jane Brenton. Kizzie was born Sept. 30, 1874 in Howard County, the daughter of Isaac Newton and Hannah (Hubble) Brenton.

Lewis Ellsworth and Kizzie Murphy

Lewis and Kizzie had six children: Herman E., Theodore 'Pete', Mary Ellen, Deva, Clarence 'Bud' and Vergie Opal. Herman was born in September 1891; died in 1971 and is buried in the Deer Creek Cemetery in Carroll County. He married Edith Bowman and then Dorothy Wright. Theodore was born in December 1893; died in 1972 and is buried in the Deer Creek Cemetery. He married Elsie Mae Little. Mary Ellen was born Oct. 10, 1899 in Howard County; died April 5, 1985 and is buried

Newcom Family Reunion circa 1908 or 1909. My mother, Agnes Newcom (Mullen), was the third child, first row, right side (large white hair bow). She was born 1900 so I'm guessing the date. My grandfather, Charles Newcom, first man, left side, back row, with a black hat. My grandmother, Anna Newcom - fourth woman from left, back row.

in Sunset Memory Gardens Cemetery. She married Charles Henry Roberts on June 1, 1923 in Kokomo. Charles was born Jan. 26, 1897 in Dillsboro, IN and died April 11, 1967 in Kokomo. Deva was born May 31, 1895 and married Fred Amos Dec. 22, 1917 in Howard County. Clarence was born in December 1896 and married Marie. Vergie was born Feb. 12, 1902 in Cass County, died April 1, 1978 in Kokomo and is buried with her husband in the Galveston Cemetery. She married John Mark Etherington Sr. Oct. 2, 1920 in Howard County. John was born May 26, 1900 in Howard County and died Nov. 4, 1983 in Kokomo.

Lewis' father was Chester Arthur Murphy. Chester was born in New York and died Nov. 9, 1874 in Jerome and is buried at Ellis Cemetery in Howard County. He was a saddler in Co. G, 13th Cavalry, 131st Regt. Indiana Volunteers during the Civil War. Chester married Polly Ann McCoy on Sept. 23, 1852 in Howard County, both being Missionary Baptists. Polly and Chester had eight children: Sarah A., William L., David C., Susannah Elizabeth, Margaret C., Lewis Ellsworth, Ada Mary and Oka Irene. Sarah, born Sept. 3, 1853 married Robert W. Hodson on Jan. 19, 1879. William L. was born Jan. 21, 1855. David was born May 2, 1858. Susannah was born Feb. 22, 1860 and married Jacob T. Long Feb. 25, 1882. Jacob Long, born July 31, 1851, was the son of Robert M. and Mary J. (Thorn) Long. Jacob and Susannah had eight children: Blanche, Omar, Mazie, Madge, Gracie, Carl, Roscoe and Dale. Margaret C. was born May 5, 1862 and married Melvin Hubbard Oct. 13, 1894. Ada was born Dec. 25, 1868 and married L. Wright Feb. 20, 1890. Oka Irene was born Aug. 23, 1873 and married Ollie Andrews May 17, 1891. All were married in Howard County.

Polly Ann was born April 8, 1834 in Jefferson County, TN and died Feb. 2, 1917 in Howard County.

MYERS - James M. Myers and Elizabeth Massena were married Dec. 22, 1847 in Ohio and came to New London area in 1850 with their oldest son, David, born Nov. 7, 1848 in Shelby County, OH.

James was born in Ohio Sept. 26, 1822. His parents are unknown to the author at this time. Elizabeth was born, in Ohio also, on Aug. 25, 1825 and like James her parents are unknown. They were farmers in western Howard County and had a family of eight children.

The children were as follows: David who married Mary E. Young Aug. 18, 1870; the second child William born Nov. 25, 1850 and married Martha Fortner April 21, 1876; third child a boy died at birth May 12, 1852; Mary Ellen born July 18, 1853 was the fourth; fifth John H. born May 1, 1857; number six was Sarah Elizabeth born Oct. 13, 1859 and married John F. Ritchey Nov. 30, 1878; Joseph, the seventh child, was born Feb. 5, 1863 and married Josephine Admell, Dec. 24, 1893; the eighth and last child was James Haworth born Oct. 13, 1867.

James died at 70 years, 11 months and 20 days, Sept. 16, 1893 and is buried in the New London Friends Cemetery. Elizabeth is also buried in New London Friends Cemetery and died Sept. 8, 1897. She was a member of the Seventh-Day Adventist Church of New London. *Submitted by great-great-grandson Robert Joseph White*

CLARENCE E. McCAULEY - Clarence Everett McCauley was born Nov. 23, 1886, in Clay Township to William Jefferson and Sarah Pruella Swisher McCauley. He married Birdie Ellen Albright, born June 7, 1887, to Henry J. Lacy and Mattie E. Smiley Albright, in Center Township.

Clarence, sister Lula, brothers Robert (Bob) and Burl, were raised by their father. Their mother, sister Blanche, and two infant brothers died before 1900. Bob and Burl became auto mechanics, but Clarence carried on the family tradition of farming. His education ended with 8th grade, yet he excelled in math and spelling. He was an honest, hard working, highly respected man.

Birdie graduated from Kokomo High School (1907), attended four semesters at Marion Normal College and taught at Palmer, Meridian and the first (newly built) Washington School in Kokomo, for nine and one-half years. She was a fine Christian who left a quiet legacy of service and love for God, family and country. At one time, five Albright sisters (Jessie, Birdie, Maude, Pauline and Margaret) were all teaching in Howard County.

Clarence E. McCauley and Birdie E. Albright McCauley.

Clarence and Birdie met at age 30, on a blind date, in September 1916. They were married Feb. 6, 1918 at her family home. As was the custom then, Birdie 'retired' mid-term to become a faithful, farm wife. They resided first in the Jeff McCauley residence, west of Cassville, then moved to Taylor Township, south of Center, on S.R. 26, for two years. In 1921, they moved to a 40-acre farm, 2-1/2 miles south of Galveston, (Clay Township), on Malfalfa Road, where they resided until 1952, when they moved to Miami County. Jeff McCauley was a member of their household until his death in 1932.

Life was hard during the Depression, but the farm provided abundant food for the table and for preserving. Clarence milked cows and raised tomatoes plus the usual row crops and share cropped for several neighbors. He drove a horse-drawn school hack for one year, then a school bus for 23 years for Clay Township School, including one year for the Northwestern Consolidation.

A son, Everett Lacy, was born Jan. 24, 1919; a daughter, Margaret Louise, died in infancy, and a daughter, Betty Lou, was born Nov. 25, 1928.

Everett graduated from Clay Township School in 1937; Betty in 1946. Everett married Helen Dye (Center Township), in 1940 and graduated Purdue in 1941. After serving two years as a Navy Medical Corpsman, he taught vocational agriculture at Cutler for two and one-half years and at Connersville for thirty-seven years. He became an outstanding teacher and community leader.

Betty married Ted Vaile, of Kokomo, in 1950. They became recognized leaders in the square dance recreation. They moved to Miami County in 1959.

Clarence and Birdie's descendants became a credit to the love, training and firm discipline taught in the home. Birdie's ardent faith in God was a strong influence in the lives of generations to follow.

JAMES A. McCAULEY - James A. McCauley, born in Virginia Oct. 2, 1823, came to Howard County in 1842 from Wyandotte County, OH. His parents were Alfred and Elizabeth Edwards McCauley, born in Virginia and both died in 1845. James A. was shown on the Ohio Census in 1845 one of eight children. He returned to Indiana, and married Elizabeth Pyle who was born Dec. 12, 1833. He bought 160 acres in the northeast corner of Clay Township, where they raised six children. The house has been replaced by a new modern house but it is on the corner of their farm. Their children were Milton Hamilton, William Jefferson, Cyrus Edward, Perry Morton, Margaret and James R.

The land was flat and in early years had much wet undrained areas; however, in later years the farm was more fertile and much better suited for row crops and cultivation.

James was an industrious, hard working farmer whose word was his bond. He adhered to the Methodist Church, was a Republican, and highly esteemed by all who knew him and one of the county's most progressive citizens. He died Oct. 29, 1890 of heart disease, age 67. Elizabeth, his wife, was one of the class of 13 persons that organized Cassville Methodist Church. She died July 27, 1917, age 84.

Milton Hamilton married Mary Emma LeMasters and they raised nine children just north of James' property. That house is still standing, back about 200 feet from the road on the east side. The children's names were Pearl, died at age 20, never married; Russell married Eva Merrill; Hazel Edith married Rev. Burl Bechdolt; Cecil married Tom Maher; Lola Mabel married Roscoe C. Coomler; Leslie, killed by train, age 39; Ernest married Hazel Edith Watkins; Blaine and Valerie died as infants.

Milton lived on his father's farm all his life where he died at age 67 from tuberculosis of the throat. His manner won him many friends because of his straightforward honest dealings and his many other fine traits of character.

Mary Emma McCauley, age 77, died of a complication of diseases. She was born May 12, 1859 and died at the residence, Aug. 22, 1936.

William Jefferson married Sarah Pruella Swisher and they raised seven children. They were Bertha Blanche who died at 17 of tuberculosis, having taken care of her mother. Clarence Everett married Birdie Ellen Albright; Lulu Mae married Glen Williams; Leora Lee was kicked in the stomach by a cow and died at age seven; Burley Cleon married Alice Vivian Maggart; Robert Otis married Mary Mills; and William Clayton.

William Jefferson was born Dec. 28, 1856 and died Sept. 1, 1932, at age 76 after having many strokes.

Sarah Pruella was born Sept. 30, 1862 and died Nov. 12, 1897 of tuberculosis. While William Jefferson had gone for the doctor, she called all the children together and told them she would meet them in heaven and asked them to pray. They prayed that the sun would shine and the birds would sing when they buried their mother, but the day was dark and very stormy, pouring down rain and they had to have a lantern to dip water from the grave.

Cyrus Edward married Addelia Pennington. They had two sons, Elmer and Leora.

Margaret married Harvey Lee Ashley. They had one son, Howard.

Perry Morton died at age 27. James R. died at age 30.

JOHN J. McCAULEY - John J. McCauley of Wyandotte County, OH, son of Alfred and Elizabeth Edwards McCauley, came to Howard County in 1842, at age 20. In 1845 he went back to attend the funeral of his father and mother. The Ohio Census record of 1845 shows eight brothers and sisters. Coming back to Indiana, he bought 160 acres of government land in the northeast corner of Clay Township. Being single when the Civil War broke out, he signed up with the Ohio Volunteer Inf., 33rd Regt., Co. "C" as proxy for his married brother. John took his own rifle with him, an eight-sided cap and ball muzzle loader, thirty-two inches long, patented in England in 1820, now owned by fifth generation Jon R. McCauley.

By the late summer of 1861, he was under the command of Colonel Joshua S. Sill, whose drilling and discipline rendered the regiment very efficient in battle. He joined forces of General Nelson at Maysville, KY in a battle in the invasion of the Blue Grass Region lasting about 60 days; then back to Louisville and brigaded under General Buell's Army until February 1862. At Bacon Creek, they suffered from measles, smallpox and camp diarrhea. They then went south to Huntsville, AL. The summer of 1862 found them on the march constantly, fighting fierce battles and finally set out to join the main army at Decherd, TN, during a torrential downpour and a fearfully dark night. They fought several battles back and forth across Kentucky and Tennessee. At Perryville the 33rd performed so gallantly it gained strong commendations. When General Rosecrans took over the command of the Ohio, he christened it the Army of the Cumberland. December 1862, they were on the move again. September 1, 1863 the Chickamauga campaign opened. They then went to Lookout Mountain and Mission Ridge. These battles lost the 33rd several men. Returning to Chattanooga he re-enlisted as a veteran and was given a 30-day furlough. Returning to Chattanooga in May 1864, he joined General Sherman's forces in the Atlanta campaign and on to the sea. At Savannah, GA, John was discharged May 27, 1865 on surgeon's certificate of disability.

Returning to Howard County, he built a beautiful brick home, still standing, on U.S. 31 just west of Cassville. His rolling farmland was best suited for pasturing horses and cattle. It was on this farm he lost his life, falling off a wagon load of corn fodder and broke his neck at age 72, as the horses bolted going through a gate. He was a good carpenter, and an industrious, hard-working farmer. He taught his nephew, William Jefferson, the art of making dynamite which was a must among every farmer clearing "new ground".

The early settlers, including John, bartered horses, cattle, grain and whiskey with Chief Kocomos to get the Indians to move to Miami town. They then helped them move.

John was born in 1822 in Virginia. Died Oct. 30, 1894 and buried in Crown Point Cemetery.

McDOWELL - Sometime after 1815, John McDowell and his wife, Jane (Young), moved their young family from Bourbon County, KY to Indiana. Their children were John, McElroy, Dabo, Cynthia, Jane, Samuel and Pine(?).

McElroy was born July 15, 1807 in Bourbon County.

While Dabo, my great-grandfather, and other family members lived for years in Ripley County, his older brother, McElroy, moved to Howard County.

McElroy McDowell on left, Dabo McDowell on right.

McElroy was married to Sally Sparks on Jan. 17, 1828 (in Howard County?); Armina Ernnez and Elizabeth. He and Sally Sparks were the parents of John D., Martha L. (born in Howard County), and Cintha A.

Upon McElroy's death Sept. 30, 1887, in Rippey, Greene County, IA, his wife, Elizabeth, signed a legal paper stating her husband spelled his name, "Muckelroy," and he was called "Uncle Muck" by other family members. McElroy was buried in the Mercer Cemetery in Rippey. His brother, Dabo, is buried in the Fairview Cemetery in Union, Boone County, IA.

Of all my ancestral photos, this one of Dabo and McElroy is my favorite. The photo is a copy of the original tintype. It looks as though the backdrop might be a tent, and that the two brothers might have been visiting a fair, and on a lark had their picture taken.

McFARLAND - David Nelson McFarland was born in Ohio, and died in New London, IN, on March 24, 1947. He was buried in Kokomo, IN. David married Missouri Ann (Woods) McFarland on Aug. 15, 1871.

David's parents were Timothy and Nancy (Moomaw) McFarland. Timmothy was born in 1825, and died on Jan. 26, 1892, in Clinton County, IN. He married Nancy Moomaw on March 31, or May 1849. Nancy was born on Feb. 27, 1829, in Ross, OH. She died in 1911, in Clinton County, IN. Nancy's parents were Henry and Ann (Gray) Moomaw. David was Timmothy and Nancy's only child.

David's paternal grandparents were Joshua and Sarah (Hixon) McFarland. Joshua was born on March 24, 1782, in Ireland. Joshua traveled from Ireland to Ross, OH where he married Sarah Hixon, on Feb. 9, 1819. Joshua died in Ross, OH, on June 19, 1863. He was buried in the Hixon Cemetery, along with his wife, Sarah, who died on Feb. 22, 1837. They had seven children: Sarah, William, Timmothy, Mary, John, David, and Rachel McFarland.

Joshua, Timmothy, and David were all farmers. It was told that Joshua gave his son Timmothy, 500 head of sheep, in order for him to get started in farming. Later David moved to Howard County, IN and started farming.

David and Missouri had eight children: Flora Jane, Timmothy Leonard, Robert Erwin, Bertha Pearl, Lilly Bell, Sherman Francis, Nancy Florence, and Lula McFarland.

Flora Jane was born Nov. 11, 1872, and died Aug. 13, 1874 (age two). Timmothy Leonard was born Aug. 23, 1874, and died Sept. 3, 1904. Robert Erwin was born Sept. 19, 1876, and died April 15, 1902. Lilly Bell was born July 28, 1882, and died April 7, 1902. Lula May was born June 12, 1895, and died 1895. All the above children of David's died young and never married. David and Missouri's three remaining children did marry. They were Bertha Pearl; she married first Elmer Murray and second to a Hickman. Pearl married Elmer on Sept. 27, 1897 in Howard County, IN. Pearl was born on Sept. 26, 1876 and died June 23, 1965 in Kokomo, IN. Pearl and Elmer had three children: Geneva Enda, Lula Martha, and Roy Murray. Geneva married Lewis Ralph Kellar on June 18, 1916. Lula married Leo Everett Crousore and Roy married Mary Stine.

Sherman Francis McFarland married Francis Alice Bowen on Aug. 14, 1933 in Howard County and they had no children.

Nancy Florence McFarland married first to Albert Clark on April 29, 1905 in Kokomo, IN, and they had a daughter Bertha Jewel Clark. Bertha married James Manford Massey on March 14, 1921. Bertha and James have four daughters, Betty Jane, Maxine Mae, Virginia Joan, and Nancy Lee Massey.

Nancy Florence married again to Tom Jones and they had adopted a son and named him Tom Jones Jr. Tom Jr. married Lila Durbin on Jan. 15, 1949 in Kokomo, IN. Tom Jr. and Lila have four children: Pamela, Stanley, Patricia, and Sandra. Tom Jr. married twice; Jeannice Ann Brown was his second marriage. Jeannice was married before to Levern Utterback; after his death she married Tom Jones. Jeannice and Levern had four children: Cynthia, Daniel, David, and Nancy Utterback.

The McFarlands came from Ireland to Ohio and later some of them moved to Indiana. They were farmers from way back. *Submitted by Florence McFarland*

HOLMES McFATRIDGE - Holmes McFatridge was born and raised in northwest Pennsylvania, moved first to Rush County, IN, later to Howard County.

Holmes was born, Mercer County, PA, May 20, 1799, son of Hugh George McFatridge and Catharine (Kitty) Holmes, both born in Ireland about 1761. They came to the United States about 1790, first to Carlisle, PA, later to Mercer County, PA and purchased a 200 acre farm near Greenville in 1799. The children of Hugh George and Catharine McFatridge were Hugh, Mary, Holmes, Nancy, George Gabriel, Elizabeth, Clarissa, Jane, and John. Catharine died Dec. 20, 1838 and Hugh George died April 20, 1839 and they were both buried in the Old Salem Methodist Church Cemetery, Mercer County, PA.

Holmes married in 1822, Mary Jane Wilson, daughter of Peter and Margaret Robinson Wilson and the sister of George and James Wilson who married Holmes' sisters, Mary and Nancy.

In 1836, Holmes, Mary Jane and their four children traveled across Ohio to get to their new home northwest of Rushville, IN where Holmes purchased 220 acres.

The six children of Holmes and Mary Jane were (1) Peter Wilson, born May 3, 1823, married Eliza Winston Clark, had Mary Abigail, John Wesley, Milo Minton; (2) George Washington, born Oct. 25, 1826, married Martha Ann Thomas, had Anna Elizabeth, James Winfield Scott, Lydia Ellen, Francis Marion; (3) John Wesley, born 1828, died about 1843; (4) Margaret Jane, born about 1835, married Daniel F. Noble, had Osa; (5) James Robinson, born about 1837, died 1853; and (6) Mary Ann, born May 28, 1842, married John J. Tarkington, had Laura, Lydia, George, Lewis, Oscar, Mattie, Arthur, Harry.

Mary Jane died 1845, buried in Balls Chapel Cemetery, Rush County, IN. Holmes married second April 30, 1846, Ann Mariah Endecott, daughter of Thomas Endecott Jr. and Mildred Grubbs and seventh-generation descendant of John Endecott who was the first governor of the Massachusetts Bay Colony in 1628.

Holmes and Ann Mariah had an additional six children. In 1858, Holmes, Ann Mariah, and seven unmarried children moved to Harrison Township, Howard County, IN where Holmes purchased 78 acres. They remained there for the remainder of their lives.

The six children of Holmes and Ann Mariah were (7) Thomas Henry Stockton, born April 10, 1847, married Nancy Ellen Leeson, had Mertie Ann, William Orla; (8) James Clayton, born Nov. 10, 1849, married first Lucinda J. Swisher, married second Sarah Francis Douglas, had Pearl William, Estella Anna; (9) Lewis Cass, born Nov. 10, 1849, married first Indiana King, had Mellie, married second Sophia Angelina Price, had Grace, Harry, Mabel, Edith, Belva, Emma, Hazel, Walter Price, Alfred, Elizabeth Ann; (10) Malinda Armilda, born Nov. 9, 1851, married John F. Wyatt, had Lura, William, Clarence Lester, Maude, Harry, Lottie May; (11) Franklin Pierce, born Jan. 10, 1853, married Clara Alvina Fouts, had Ira Lewis, Walter, Cleona Mae, Ethel, William Clancy; (12) William Jasper, born 1855, died 1870.

Holmes died April 10, 1871 and Ann Mariah died in 1881. They are both buried in the Twin Springs Methodist Church Cemetery, Harrison Township, Howard County, IN.

WALTER PRICE AND MARTHA WEGER McFATRIDGE - Walter came to Kokomo, IN in 1921. Martha came to Kokomo with her parents in 1908. They were married in 1922 and made their home in Kokomo for the remainder of their lives.

Walter Price McFatridge was born in Fairmount, IN, Dec. 11, 1895, son of Dr. Lewis C. McFatridge and Sophia Price and grandson of Holmes McFatridge and Ann Mariah Endecott (subject of another article in this book). Lewis was a physician, graduating from Indiana Medical College, Indianapolis, IN in 1880. He practiced medicine in the Indiana towns of Flora, Wheeling, Fairmount and for 25 years in Atlanta.

Walter married in Atlanta, IN, Aug. 12, 1922, Martha Magdalene Weger, daughter of Charles George Weger and Lily Eliza Elvin. Martha was born in Anderson, IN, July 6, 1900. Charley Weger was a foreman for Continental Steel Company and later operated a business called Staple Groceries and Fresh Meats. Lily died in 1910 leaving six small children. Charles moved to Pittsburg, CA about 1923 and died there in 1940.

Walter Price McFatridge and Martha Weger McFatridge

Walter, after graduating from Greencastle High School, worked in an automobile factory in Detroit prior to entering WWI service. He served in the U.S. Army from September 1917 until March 1919. He was a sergeant in the AEF 325th Field Arty., Btry. E, with six months in France. After the war, he attended Business College in Logansport, IN where he also taught English and mathematics. He then went to work for Kokomo Brick Company as a bookkeeper; then to Hoosier Oil Company which later became a part of the Shell American Petroleum Company where he worked as Auditor and Office Manager before retiring in 1957. He was a member of the Kokomo Country Club serving as Office Manager for 12 years. He was also a member of the Kokomo Rotary Club where he received the Paul Harris Fellowship Award. He was a sports enthusiast and participated in softball, volleyball, handball, tennis, bowling and most particularly golf, having five holes-in-one.

Martha, a Kokomo High School graduate, attended Indiana State Normal College and was a teacher in the Kokomo school system prior to her marriage. She was active in the American Red Cross and the Hospital Cheer Guild. She was a member of Phi Beta Psi sorority and served a term as its National President.

Walter and Martha were members of St. Andrews Episcopal Church where each served on the Vestry and as wardens. Martha also was active in St. Elizabeth and St. Anne's guilds.

Their three children were (1) Walter Price McFatridge Jr., born Oct. 31, 1926, married Eleanor Margaret Pond, had Ann Louise, David Alan (married Linda Sue Barkhaus, had Jessica Lauren, Andrew Jacob), Douglas Lee; (2) Nancy, born Nov. 2, 1931, died at birth; (3) James Charles McFatridge, born June 30, 1933, married Janet Gayle Williamson, had Jo Ann (married Michael Kent Smith, had Andrew James), Julie Ann (married John Bernard Rethlake).

Walter died Jan. 16, 1980 and Martha died April 17, 1992; both are buried in Sunset Memory Gardens near Kokomo.

FRANCIS McGRAW - Francis McGraw was born Dec. 2, 1835 in Fayette County, Waterloo Township to William McGraw (1787 PA-1871 IN) and Martha Higgins (1799 IN-1858 IN); one of eleven children. Francis met Nancy "Jane" Sutton and married her March 11, 1858 in Fayette County, IN. Jane was born Feb. 9, 1837 to Abe Sutton (born circa 1808-9 OH) and Sarah Conway (born circa 1809-10 SC). Jane was raised in Fayette County, Jennings Township which borders Waterloo Township.

Francis and Jane were living in Waterloo Township, Fayette County in 1860 with their first two children. By 1870 they had moved to Grant County, Green Township which was close to Greentown. Even though Francis did not settle in Howard County until his later years, many of his children lived there and most are buried in the Greenlawn Cemetery in Greentown.

Francis McGraw and wife, Jane (Sutton)

Francis and Jane's children consisted of: James Harrison (Harry) 1859-1937 married Mary M. Harper in 1878, they had two children; Laura 1861-1868; Annis M. 1863-1894 married John Wm. Devore in 1882, they had six children; Louella B. 1864-? married George P. Rowland in 1913, no children; Vesta Martha 1867-1964 married Frank E. Cohee in 1889, they had four children; John W. 1869-1958 married Minnie Belle Slaughter in 1895, they had eight children; Carrie D. 1874-1965 married Mr. Quinn, they moved to Chicago, no children; and Cora 1876-? married Frank L. Newkirk in 1898, they had three children and moved to California.

Francis built a small log home in Grant County and later moved into a larger frame home across the street where they raised their children and Francis farmed. Nancy died Feb. 28, 1902 and was buried in the Greenlawn Cemetery. The last years of Francis' life were spent with his daughter, Vesta Cohee, near Greentown. Here Francis died on Oct. 1, 1926 and was buried next to Jane in Greentown. *Submitted by Cathie A. Sutterfield*

VESTA M. McGRAW - Vesta Martha McGraw was born (one of eight children) April 20, 1867 in Grant County, IN to Francis McGraw (1835-1926) of Fayette County, IN and Nancy "Jane" Sutton (1837-1902) of Union County, IN. Vesta was born in a small log home in Green Township, Grant County where she remembers as a small child her parents found a snake curled up under her pillow. Later they moved into a farmhouse across the street and this home has been with the family for over 100 years; the last owners Waldo J. and Frances McGraw.

Daughters: Annis (left), Roxey (top), Vesta (McGraw) Cohee (right), Delite (lower)

Vesta married June 15, 1889 in Grant County to Frank Edgar Cohee, the son of William L. Cohee and Elizabeth David. They had four children: a son that died at birth, Annis Belle (Bagwell) born July 19, 1895, died Feb. 14, 1978; Roxey (Shesteck-Johnson) born July 17, 1897, died Jan. 4, 1971; and Delite (Renshaw) born Nov. 11, 1901, died Sept. 15, 1935. Vesta and Frank lived in Grant and Howard counties for a time and settled into a farmhouse on the southern edge of Greentown where they owned 60-80 acres with the Wild Cat River running through it. Vesta did all the milking of the Jersey cows, as well as all the other wifely duties that never ended. Her first grandchild, Gene Bagwell, remembers Vesta baking biscuits every morning before daylight. There was an outside pump for drinking water and an old cistern with a pitcher pump in the kitchen for washing hands and clothing.

As quoted by Gene Bagwell 1991, "If Vesta had any serious faults one would be that she was always wanting to give someone something. She always wanted to give each child a silver dollar, that if she had a dollar she wanted to give it to someone. She always wanted to live just long enough to see the next grandchild and then the first great-grandchild and the second and etc."

Vesta cared for her father in her home before his death in 1926. Around 1927 Vesta and Frank sold the farmhouse and moved into Greentown, first renting an apartment, then purchasing a home on the north side of town. Vesta worked as a cook in the State Highway Restaurant that her daughter, Roxey Shesteck, owned. Frank died of a sudden heart attack on Aug. 25, 1929 and was buried in the Greenlawn Cemetery in town.

Vesta's daughter, Delite and husband, Leo Renshaw, moved in with her. Leo invested in a restaurant in Kokomo and had Vesta run it for him. They all moved to Kokomo where Leo purchased a lot in the same block as Kingston Products where he worked as Paymaster, moved an old railroad car on it and converted it into a restaurant. Vesta served breakfast and a noon day meal, Delite also helped out and Leo ran the register during his lunch break. After the restaurant was disposed of Vesta moved in with her oldest daughter's family (before 1935).

"Vesta was always broke. She worked around wherever she could, staying with people, cooking their meals when they were sick or needed help. For the last several years, of course, she could not work. So she stayed with Annis and drove Delbert up a wall with her hands in the dishwater, leaving the stove on and water running." (Quote from Gene Bagwell 1991).

Vesta stayed between daughters, Annis in Greentown and Roxey in Michigan, during the last years of her life. She lived until she was 96, dying of old age on March 21, 1964 at Marion General Hospital. She was buried next to her husband in the Greenlawn Cemetery in Greentown. *Submitted by Cathie A. Sutterfield.*

McINTOSH/BECKER - Norwalk, OH, was the birthplace of Richard Thornton McIntosh, son of Alexander Frances and Ruth Caroline (Gilbert) McIntosh. Richard was born on April 22, 1930 and graduated from Norwalk High School in 1948. That fall he attended Bryan College, Dayton, TN, and it was there that he met Barbara in 1949. They were married in 1951 in Troy. Richard graduated in 1952 with a BA in English.

Barbara Ellen Becker was born in Troy, OH, daughter of Ralph Thomas and Leona Irene (Studebaker) Becker, on Dec. 9, 1931. After graduating from Troy High School in 1949, she attended Bryan College. It was noted by one professor that they were the most mismatched couple and had no chance of lasting. They celebrated their 35th anniversary in Kokomo on Sept. 15, 1986 and have nine grandchildren!

Richard and Barbara McIntosh

From 1952-54, they lived in Troy where Richard II was born Aug. 5, 1952 and Kathryn on April 8, 1954. In September they moved to Tippecanoe, IN. There Richard pastored a small church and attended Grace Seminary in Winona Lake. After four years in seminary, Richard received a BD, summa cum laude, and a MTh. Their third child, Michael, was born in Rochester on March 10, 1958.

They moved to Lima, OH, where Richard pastored a Baptist Church, 1958-60. He was ordained in 1958 at his home church in Norwalk. John Mark was born June 23, 1959 in Lima.

Richard became Dean of Students at Cedarville College in Cedarville, OH, and served in that position from 1960-70. He took post graduate work at Grace Seminary, 1970-71, and became a full-time Bible professor at Cedarville from 1971-84. Barbara became Director of Academic Records and Registration. Three of their four children graduated from the college and Michael became a fire-fighter paramedic.

Back to Indiana! In 1984 Richard became senior pastor of Bible Baptist Church in Kokomo. Barbara had been uprooted from her home of 24 years and found a "home" with the Howard County Genealogical Society and served as a volunteer. She has done research on both families and has traced her husband's maternal line back to 1066 with William the Conqueror.

It was time to move again! After six years, they moved to Galion, OH, where Richard is pastor of the First Baptist Church. Barbara is a part-time secretary-librarian at Galion Christian School and is a volunteer at the Ohio Genealogical Society Library in Mansfield.

Her hobby, of course, is genealogy, and she is on the committee of the Studebaker Family Association to put together volume three of the family history by 1996. It all started in Kokomo!

Richard's hobby is reading and driving Barbara from place to place. He is on the board of Evangelical Missions and attends meetings several times a year. He also serves as moderator of the Mid-Bethel Pastor's Fellowship and on the Council of Twelve for the Ohio Association of Regular Baptist Churches.

This is the saga of two Buckeyes.

McKILLIP - The Howard County (and Indiana) branch of the McKillip family began with the emigration of Alexander McKillip and his two brothers to the United States from Cork County, Ireland about the year 1800. Alexander settled in Bellefonte, Centre County, PA and became a member of the Pennsylvania Militia. In 1813 Alexander and his militia company marched to Lake Erie and volunteered to serve with Commander Oliverus Hazard Perry's fleet of ships which engaged with the

British fleet on Lake Erie on Sept. 10, 1813. The British were soundly defeated in the naval battle of the War of 1812. Alexander served aboard Perry's ship *The Trip* and was awarded one of forty-one silver medals by the State of Pennsylvania. (This medal is passed on to the oldest living male McKillip and is currently held by Arthur D. McKillip of Kokomo.) Alexander was also paid $209.32 1/2 for his service with Perry.

The McKillip Family of Howard County. Seated: Arthur D. McKillip. Middle, clockwise: Joan E. (Hirst) McKillip, wife of Donald, Donald C. McKillip, son of Arthur McKillip, Michael D. McKillip, Mark J. McKillip, Susan M. McKillip Johnson, Matthew A. McKillip, seated on right, children of Donald and Joan McKillip.

Alexander then departed for the "Western Country" and settled in Union County, IN near the town of Liberty. He married Elizabeth Skillman and they had 10 children. One of these children was James McKillip who married Margaret Weatherow and together they had seven children. Margaret died in January 1866 and in January 1872 James and the children moved to Howard County. On Aug. 6, 1874 James married Charlotte Sullivan, the daughter of Turner and Angilina (Bryant) Sullivan who were pioneer settlers in Jackson Township, Howard County. James and Charlotte had one son Ralph Vernon McKillip born Feb. 16, 1881.

Turner Sullivan was born Oct. 15, 1800 in North Carolina. His family moved to Tennessee where he married Maria Chandler and had four children. He had five children by his second wife after Maria died. After his second wife's death he married Angeline Bryant in 1845 and together had nine children, one of whom was Charlotte Sullivan. Turner Sullivan was the second settler in Jackson Township in 1847 when it was largely swamp. He cleared his own land and built a log cabin. He was the first Jackson Township trustee and built the first school house. He lived to the ripe old age of 91 years.

James McKillip founded a large farm just south of Converse in Jackson Township at 1350E 400N in 1872. A portion of this farm including the house and barn are still owned and occupied by the McKillip family.

On Feb. 5, 1902, Ralph V. McKillip married Nora Blanche Spencer, daughter of Square and Margaret Elizabeth (Clanorin) Spencer. Ralph farmed for several years and worked for Continental Steel in Kokomo for many years until his death on March 29, 1944. Nora died on March 16, 1963. Ralph and Nora had one son, Arthur Dale McKillip born Nov. 11, 1904. Arthur is still living and active, managing the family farm and enjoying his grandchildren and great-grandchildren.

Arthur McKillip worked for local companies including the Haynes Automobile Co., the Apperson Automobile Co., and the Bert Hubbard Co. During the Depression he joined the Western and Southern Insurance Co. where he worked until his retirement in 1965. On March 21, 1923 Arthur married Frances Andres King, the daughter of Edward Grant King and Ida Ellen (Werst) King. Frances was born March 9, 1904 in Wabash County. She died Nov. 19, 1992 after nearly 70 years with Arthur. Arthur and Frances had one son, Donald Gene McKillip, born in Kokomo on Sept. 27, 1926.

Donald McKillip graduated from Kokomo High School in 1944 and from Purdue University in 1949 after brief service in the U.S. Navy. On Dec. 31, 1950 Donald married Joan Elizabeth Hirst, daughter of Raymond M. Hirst and Marie Katherine (Schmidt) Hirst. Donald worked in plant engineering at Continental Steel for four years after graduation from Purdue and then at Delco Electronics. Donald retired from Delco in 1987. Joan retired in 1990 after serving as dietary director at area nursing homes.

Donald and Joan have four children and ten grandchildren. The children are: Susan M. (McKillip) Johnson of Mooresville, IN; Michael D. McKillip (who lives on the family farm); Mark J. McKillip of Kokomo; and Matthew A. McKillip who lives in Portugal. Susan and husband, Jim, have two children: Andreas and Adam; Michael and wife, Christine, have seven children: Michael, Aaron, Andrew, Rachel, Patrick, Brandon, and Gabriel; Mark and wife, Wanda, have one son: Zachary; Matthew is not married.

Our family has a long history of 122 years in Howard County which will be continued by the children and grandchildren. *Submitted by Donald G. McKillip.*

CHARLES ELMER McKINNEY - Over 100 years ago, my maternal great-grandfather, George McKinney, left Howard County, traveling westward, driving a team of oxen and living in a covered wagon, seeking fortune and fame. Included in his family was my maternal grandfather, Charles Elmer McKinney. The picture below was taken by his cousin, Miss Goldie McKinney, in her studio in Russiaville during his return visit here in 1896. During the winter months they traveled to Missouri then back to Texico, IL seeking better farm land. They remembered traveling through Texico, IL where the school boys threw snowballs at them when they passed the schoolhouse and also remembered the fertile farm land.

It seems strange that after 100 years, my brother, Bradley Tate, and I would arrive back in Howard County, Bradley as a salesman and myself as an engineer owning my own firm. We have found no other McKinney relatives living here but do find the Tate family represented.

Charles Elmer McKinney

In Texico, IL Charles raised his family of nine, including my mother, Verna Mable (McKinney) Tate, in truth and honesty. Verna presently resides in the Russiaville area and will be 91 years young on Dec. 11, 1994.

The following story, as told by my brother Bradley, proves that one's reputation is remembered for years (100 in this case) and travels for hundreds of miles.

During the year of 1983 while doing business in one of Lafayette's finer restaurants, a new chef had just come on duty. I asked him where he was from and he said, "West Frankfort, IL". I answered, "Oh, I'm from Texico. That's north of Mt. Vernon". To which he replied, "I know a lot of people there". Then to my surprise he said, "Did you know a Charles McKinney?" "Charles McKinney!", I cried surprisingly. "That's my grandpa! How did you know him?" He replied, "During WWII I was State Fruit Inspector and your grandpa had a fine apple orchard. If the truck of apples I stopped to inspect had Charles McKinney stamped on the basket lid, I wouldn't bother to inspect it because what Charles McKinney's stamp said, I knew was in the baskets. He was a very honest man! Sorry I couldn't say the same for the other apple shippers". That made me feel very proud, and confirmed what I already knew, as did everyone else who was acquainted with him.

My grandfather went to be with the Lord 37 years ago but his character of honesty was told to his grandson several hundred miles and three decades from where he lived, but back to where he was born. Character does make a difference and the story of his honesty quickly related to his daughter, my mother, who in 1976 at the age of 73, moved from her home in Texico, IL to where her father, Charles Elmer McKinney, was born and lived earlier in his life.

I once read, "Reputation is what men think you are; character is what God knows you are". Brad Tate, Kokomo, IN. *Submitted by Ted L. Tate, P.E. 1994.*

McNABNEY - James Ross McNabney (1876-1942) born Saline County, KS on Feb. 6, 1986, son of William James and Rebecca Catherine (Ladd) McNabney, died Oct. 14, 1942 Kokomo. His father owned and operated the Mercantile, Barber Shop and Bank in Summitville, IN. On Dec. 9, 1898 he married Mary Jane Deshon, daughter of James and Levina (Bright) Deshon. She was born Sept. 10, 1882 in Fairmount, died April 6, 1978(?), Kokomo. In 1916 he moved his young family of six children to Kokomo from Grant County, IN. He worked for Rufus Laymon as a clerk, for Haynes Auto Co. as a pipe fitter and cutter; he was a salesman for a fruit and vegetable distributor around the county, and for a short time he managed the A&P store. In 1926, with Herb Helms as partner, he started the City Fruit Store at 117 South Buckeye Street. Later that same year he became full owner, which he owned and operated until his death.

James Ross McNabney

A story passed down through the family that James as a consequence of his Irish ancestry was extremely frugal. If you squeezed a fruit or vegetable you bought it. After James's death the store was moved into the building just south on the corner of Superior and Buckeye Streets. The store was then operated by his wife, Mary Jane, and son, Ross. The city demolished this building; consequently, the McNabneys purchased Happy Owens Grocery on South Leeds and changed the name. During the Depression he opened the City Fruit Market in Peru, IN. One son and a daughter managed this store in Peru to support their families. For some reason he always had a toothpick in his mouth. James and Mary Jane (Mollie) had eight children born in Grant and Madison counties, IN: Paul, Ross, (twins) Jeannette and brother Jean, Elizabeth, Vivian, William and Mary. (Jean and Mary died in infancy.)

Jeannette (1904-1992) was born March 1, 1904 in Gas City, IN. She married on Oct. 21, 1922, Otto Elmer Kuntz (1902-1970), son of Jacob Elmer and Theresa Margaret (Fleming) Kuntz. She had a love for bridge, bowling and bingo which her family fondly called "The Three B's". For 24 years she operated Jeannette's Beauty Shop. Jeannette and Otto had four children: Theresa, William, Delores, and Mary Jane.

Delores Mae, was born June 29, 1931 in Peru, IN; married Dec. 30, 1947, Jack Wayne, son of Marshall Harrison and Florence Charlotte (Ashby) Spicer. They are the parents of five children: Jerry, Christina, Jack, Karen and Mark.

Christina, the submitter of this article, was born June 8, 1951, in Kokomo and graduated from Northwestern High School in 1969. Married Stevan Von Moon May 8, 1970 in Idaho Falls, ID. He is the son of Blaine and Viola (Dixon) Moon. They have six children: Cindy, Joseph, Charity, Jared, Jason and Celeste. *Submitted by Christina D. Moon.*

McNEAL - Making up the McNeal line of Howard County, were these ancestral lines: from Pennsylvania: Davis, Mellinger, Watts; from Virginia: Allen, Berry, Scott, Walker, also Eickenberry and Landis, but from Alsace and Switzerland before that; from Virginia and Ireland: Quinn, McMannis, McMahon; from England: Fulfer, Sparling; from New York and Holland: Ooley, Shipley; from Ohio: St. Clair. Most have been in America since the 1700s and a few since the 1600s, migrating from the Colony States and the South. They came through North Carolina, Tennessee, Kentucky, waiting on new lands to open into The Northwest Territory.

The McNeal line came from Virginia, and The Isle of Barra, of Scotland where Clan MacNeill began. McNeals were in Howard County for over 100 years.

Eli McNeal first came to Howard in 1866 after he was orphaned in Grant County where his father, John, died about 1862. His mother, Elizabeth (St. Clair) died on the moving trip from Ohio to Indiana, about 1852. Eli came to the Harrell farm in Erwin Township, to work. He met Martha Jane Davis, daughter of Benjamin and Elizabeth Jane (Watts), and after their marriage, they moved to Monroe Township, between Shanghi and Oakland. Eli helped found the Oakland Christian Church. Their children were George, Maude Parker (Mrs. Elda), and Auda Hendrix (Mrs. Charles).

George Lawrence McNeal became a medical doctor, graduating from colleges in Cincinnati and New York. He began practice in Deer Creek, later moving to Kokomo where his office was in the Spraker Building. He married Sarah Jane (Jenny) Allen, daughter of James G. and Lydia (Eickenberry), of Monroe Township. James was a farmer and brickmason, as was his father, James V. whose wife, Hannah Scott, was mother to James G. Allen. John and Nancy Allen were paternal grandparents of James G. Parents of Lydia were Isaac and Sarah (Mellinger) Eickenberry of Carroll County.

Children of Dr. George and Jenny were Marie James (Mrs. Charles), and Raymond Lawrence. Jenny died when Raymond was three and George then married widow, Jessie Slankard.

Raymond began studies of medicine at Indiana University, when WWI broke out. He lied about his age of 16 and joined the Army Medical Corps. Upon returning from France, he decided to farm in Monroe Township. He married Marie Walker, a teacher from Arcadia. They both were active on the farm, in Farm Bureau, and Sunday School teaching at New London Friends Church. She was appointed to the Ration Board during WWII; she was appointed by Governor Schricker as the first Farmer Field Woman to travel the state of Indiana, promoting the new Soil Conservation Program.

Their children were George Lawrence and Marjorie Ellen, graduates of New London School, and active in 4-H and Rural Youth organization. George married Mary Lou Phipps of Kokomo, a graduate of Indiana University. George graduated from University of California at Santa Barbara. They both were teachers in California. Their children were Cynthia Beede (Mrs. Glenn), who has two sons, Jordan and Nathan, all of the state of Washington; Steven Lawrence, a lawyer in California; and Brian and wife, Paige, also of California.

Marjorie met and married Raymond Clawson, of Boone County, when they were attending Purdue. He was an electrical engineer, and they made their home in Dayton, OH, where she was a teacher and genealogist. Their daughter, Melinda, an Indiana University graduate, married Ronald Emler of Wooster, OH, he is a graduate of Ohio State. He was a newspaperman and inn operator, and she was a writer and editor. They made their home in Massachusetts.

No matter how far away, Howard County and especially New London, have always been home.

Sources: Censuses (1790-1900), and County Records in Virginia, North Carolina, Tennessee, Ohio, Illinois, New York, Indiana and Kentucky; Family Records and Traditions. *Submitted by Marjorie McNeal Clawson*

JERRY AND GLORIA McQUISTON - Jerry Lee McQuiston and his wife, Gloria Ann Brown, were both born and raised in Kokomo.

Jerry's great-great-grandfather, William, was born Nov. 30, 1787, according to the date on his monument. A granddaughter wrote, "My father and his family lived in grandfather's home until I was 12 years old. Grandfather died about this time and I have heard him say that he was born in Ireland, and came to this country when he was eight years old, with his parents and a little sister, and his father's two brothers. Soon after he arrived, his father, mother, and sister died and he became separated from his uncles. He went to Tennessee, Kentucky, and Indiana." He married Sarah Gullion who was born in Kentucky Jan. 28, 1794 and died May 11, 1869. William died Sept. 18, 1872 in Decatur County, IN.

Born to William and Sarah were 10 children: Margaret, Jane, William, Lucinda, Rachel, Robert, Harrison, Barbara, Wesley, and John.

William's son, John, was born in Decatur County on Jan. 12, 1835. He was a minister at one time, came to Howard County in 1873 and died in Greentown on June 24, 1911. On June 21, 1868 he married Susan Julien (born March 22, 1841) in Rush County. They had seven children; Isaac, Cerena Florence, Everett C., Loren, Alice, Annie, and Simeon.

Jerry and Gloria McQuiston

Jerry's grandfather, Loren McQuiston, born Aug. 15, 1868 in Decatur County married Lida Armfield on Dec. 12, 1894 and resided near Greentown. They had one son, Everett Andrew (born June 13, 1897) and four daughters: Naomi McQuiston, Nellie Bennett, Neva Clevenger, and Alberta Wilson Bone Gordon. It was Loren's brother, Simeon, that built the large home west of Greentown.

Everett Andrew married Ester Overman on March 6, 1918. They had three children; Gilbert, Virgil, and Mary Lane Davis. Ester died in 1923 and on June 4, 1926 Everett married Hazel Fye (born July 8, 1904). Hazel was the daughter of George H. Fye and Harriet A. Young. Everett and Hazel had three children: Ernest Ellsworth, Delena Foust, and Jerry Lee (born April 15, 1935). Hazel died Jan. 4, 1940 when Jerry was four years old and his father died in September 1952 when Jerry was 17.

On Jan. 8, 1953 Jerry and Gloria were married in Kokomo and a year later moved to Galveston where they lived for nearly 40 years. Gloria (born April 14, 1935) is the daughter of William and Reta Brown. This lineage is listed elsewhere in this book. Jerry and Gloria have two children: Jerry Lee, Jr. (born July 25, 1955) and Tamara Lynn (born Dec. 7, 1959). Jerry, Jr. married Catherine Jump on Aug. 12, 1978 and have three sons; Jesse John (born Sept. 7, 1980), Jared Andrew (born April 8, 1983) and Tyler Lee (born Nov. 2, 1985). Jerry is manager and co-owner of DWF Retread Shop in Kokomo. "Tammy" married Jeffrey Lynn Keith on March 5, 1988 and they have one son, Jonathan Lynn (born Nov. 3, 1991). Tammy is head of Outreach of the Kokomo-Howard County Public Library.

Jerry and Gloria are both retired. Jerry was employed by Delco Electronics for 38-1/2 years, retiring from the position of supervisor in 1991. Gloria also worked at Delco for 10 years but her final position was that of secretary at Grace Baptist Church for 14 years. *Submitted by Jerry McQuiston.*

McREYNOLDS - Samuel McReynolds was born in Montgomery County, OH in 1820. He was ordained a minister in the Evangelical Lutheran Church in 1847; in 1850 he married Maria Deffenbaugh, oldest daughter of Kokomo pioneers George and Catharine Deffenbaugh. In later years he was agent for a New York nursery. He died in 1894, and Maria died in 1897; they were buried in the McReynolds plot in Crown Point Cemetery.

William H. McReynolds, the eldest of five children of Samuel and Maria McReynolds, was born at Camden, IN in 1851. He was 15 years old when the family moved back to Kokomo, and he spent the remainder of his life in and around the city. He was engaged in clerical work; at one time he was called upon to audit the city's books; and he owned and rented three houses in town.

Toward the end of the 19th century he purchased the 97-acre farm south of town near the Albright Cemetery; this later became known as the Albright Pit Farm because of a gravel operation there.

William's brother, Martin Luther McReynolds (1855-92), was a two-term sheriff of Howard County in the 1880s. Another brother, John McReynolds (1853-79), was an accomplished cornetist and bandmaster.

William McReynolds married Amanda Viola Meranda on Dec. 12, 1889. Three children were born to them: Clarence Samuel (born in 1890), Mabel Katherine (born in 1892), and George Martin (born in 1897).

About 1900 William McReynolds began rebuilding a three-room cottage on his farm because his wife wanted more room. She got it! The resulting house contained 21 rooms scattered about three finished floors and a partial basement. There were five outside doors, a basement entrance, an ornate front porch, three towering spindly chimneys, and a small attic room tucked away on top. A large 'bank' barn was built northeast of the house, and other improvements were made.

William McReynolds was a well-read man and daily made the trip into town to pick up the latest periodicals and newspapers. His wife, Viola, died in 1921 and William McReynolds died on Oct. 15, 1924, at age 73. He was buried in the family plot at Crown Point Cemetery.

Mable McReynolds married Edward Lucas and their children were Ruth Elizabeth (Longfellow, born 1917), James Edward (born 1920), George Charles (born 1922), and Mary Edna (born in 1924 - Mary is deceased). After the death of William McReynolds the Lucas family lived in the large frame house.

The vacant McReynolds house burned in February 1967; the barn also burned the following year. Today practically nothing remains of the fine old homestead of the pioneer William H. McReynolds family. *Submitted by Jeff Hatton*

McREYNOLDS - James McReynolds (1802-1853) and Mary/Pollie Phipps McReynolds (1802-1894) and their family of seven children came to Howard County in August of 1946, from Boone County, IN, where they had lived for one and one-half years. They had moved there from Allen County, KY, where all of the children were born. The traveled in a big, lumbering two-wheeled cart, pulled by oxen. On their journey they encountered many hardships and much suffering, as often occurred on such expeditions.

The children which accompanied James and Mary to Howard County were James (1830-?) married Lettie Davidson, Dec. 15, 1859, had at least one daughter, and farmed in Harrison Township for awhile. Raven (1832-1906) married Nancy Orem Feb. 19, 1854, and settled in Tipton County to farm, and had 11 children. Sarah (1835-1850). Robert (1837-1864) married Marilda Simpson, March 28, 1858, farmed in Harrison Township for a time, and had three children. Robert served in the 89th Inf. Div. during the Civil War and died in Memphis, TN. John (1840-?) married Hannah prior to 1860, and farmed in Honey Creek Township for awhile. Charles (1842-?) married Rachel Davis, Dec. 27, 1860, farmed in Honey Creek Township, and had at least two children. Peter Wesley (1844-1864). Peter served in the 57th Inf. Div. during the Civil War and died at Louisville, KY.

Of Raven and Ann's 11 children, most of them resided in Howard County. Samuel Wiley "Sammy" (1854-1924) married Ella Cunningham (1855-1941) July

6, 1880, and farmed near Kokomo. They had three children. James Robert "Jim Bob" (1858-1948) married Rachel Pence (1863-1938) Jan. 29, 1881, and the couple set up housekeeping in Tipton County where their six children were born. They lived in Tipton County until 1906, when the family moved to Howard County, where "Jim Bob" served as Democratic County Chairman in 1912. Sarah Matilda (1860-1933) married John West (1859-1943) and they set up housekeeping in Russiaville, and had one son. Charles William (1865-1940) married Mary Belle Henderson (1868-1918) Dec. 24, 1889 and the couple settled in Clay Township, where Charles became township trustee. Shortly after 1905, the family moved to Kokomo where Charles became prominent in local business and political circles. Charles and Mary Belle had four children. Thomas Calvin (1867-1959) married Leota Delphine Carter (1873-1944) March 3, 1897. Thomas and Lota had three children, and lived in Kokomo until they purchased the property that they named Sunnybrook Farm, located southwest of Kokomo. Thomas also became prominent in business and political circles in Howard County. He and his family moved to Phoenix, AZ in 1916. The last of Raven's children who resided in Howard County was Julia (1875-1961), who married John Custer Nov. 12, 1905. Julia and her husband lived in Kokomo.

THOMAS C. McREYNOLDS - Thomas Calvin McReynolds (1867-1959) was born in Prairie Township, Tipton County, IN, to Raven, a farmer, (1832-1906) and Nancy (Orem) (1835-1921) McReynolds. Thomas' grandparents were James (1802-1894), a farmer, and Mary/Pollie (Phipps) (1809-1899) McReynolds, who were early Howard County settlers, coming to Howard County in August of 1846 from Boone County, IN, and prior to that Allen County, KY, which is where the children, including Raven, were born.

Thomas married Lota Delphina Carter (1873-1944) daughter of John Braxton (1844-1925), a merchant, and Sarah Catherine (Fix) (1849-1929) Carter of Kokomo, in March of 1897. To this union were born three children: Thomas Calvin McReynolds, Jr. (1898-1975), and in March of 1908, twin girls Sarah Ann and Mary Catherine McReynolds were born. Both are still living in Phoenix, AZ.

Thomas attended college at Danville, IN, and graduated from law school there. After a year of teaching, Thomas returned to Kokomo and entered law practice, a vocation that he continued with until he became ill in late 1899. It was about this time that Thomas, along with his brother Wesley, was instrumental in starting Defiance College, Defiance, OH.

In 1896 Thomas ran unsuccessfully, on the Democratic ticket, for prosecuting attorney of Howard and Tipton counties. This was apparently his first and last venture into the political arena as a candidate.

After recovering his health, Thomas, along with Judge Kirkpatrick and two others, purchased the old Globe Stove and Range Company. He was involved with the company for two years. It was during this time that he became manager of the old Kokomo City Railway and Light Company, eventually becoming part owner in 1901 or 1902. The company built an interurban line to Greentown, IN, which was only the second or third interurban line built in the state.

Thomas was the first president of the Kokomo Chamber of Commerce, which was formed in 1912 or 1913, and he remained in that position until after he moved to Arizona, because of ill health, in 1916.

Indiana's Governor Ralston appointed Thomas a member of the Pan-American Exposition held in San Francisco in 1914-1915. Thomas's wife, Lota, was given the honor of decorating the Indiana building. During the Exposition, Thomas and Lota had the honor of listening to the first independent, long distance telephone communication between Chicago and San Francisco.

Thomas's son, Thomas Jr., married Mildred Clare and raised his son, Thomas III, in Phoenix. Daughter Sarah Catherine married Milton Sanders and raised her three children in Phoenix. Daughter Mary Martha married John Robert Mowatt and had one son, now deceased.

JESSE NASH, JR. AND MARY ADALINE (BATEY) NASH - Jesse Nash, Jr. born March 7, 1836 in Clermont County, OH to Jesse and Mary (Pike) Nash, he being the youngest of eight children. He was 11 years old when he moved to Howard County, IN with his parents.

Jesse Jr. and Mary A. Batey were married May 19, 1859 in Clinton County, OH. Mary A. Batey was the daughter of W.H. and Sarah Batey; both parents were born in Ohio. Jesse Jr. and Mary spent almost their entire life on a farm (log house) near West Liberty. Mary died Dec. 13, 1899 and Jesse Jr. March 6, 1908 in Union Township and is buried at Fork of the Creek Cemetery along with three of their eight children. Ferdinando born May 8, 1860 Clinton County, OH, died Jan. 19, 1941 in Matthews, Grant County, IN; Ellis born April 15, 1862 Clinton County, OH, died Dec. 10, 1937 in Wells County, IN; May born May 4, 1864 Clinton County, OH, died Jan. 14, 1945 in Henry County, IN; Joseph born July 30, and died Aug. 19, 1866 in Howard County, IN; Charles C. born Feb. 19, 1867 Howard County, IN, died Jan. 10, 1932 in Henry County, IN; infant boy died June 28, 1871 in Howard County, IN; Ernest born June 22, 1875 Howard County, IN, died Jan. 9, 1939 in Howard County, IN; and Everett born Nov. 29, 1878 in Howard County and died Sept. 15, 1880 in Howard County, IN.

Mary Adaline (Batey) Nash; Jesse Nash, Jr.

Ferdinando married Zien Ellen Law in Tipton County in December 1885. They had one daughter Bertha (1889-1968) who married Thomas Dorton (1890-1983) and they had two sons, John born 1917 and Howard Dorton born 1921. Both John and Howard live in Delaware County, IN. John and Bertha (Rooney) (1916-1989) have three daughters and five grandchildren. Howard and Betty (Wright) born 1921 have three sons and one daughter with eleven grandchildren and one great-grandchild.

Ellis Nash (see related story Ellis and Minta (Burns) Nash).

May Nash married James Conway (1859-1923) on April 8, 1903 in Howard County but lived on a farm in Henry County all their lives. They had no children.

Charles C. married Jessie (Burns) (sister to Ellis' wife, Minta) on Jan. 2, 1892 in Howard County, IN. They had four children, all born in Howard County. Roy (1892-1965) married Goldie Grissum (1892-1938) on Oct. 29, 1913 in Henry County. Roy was an agent for Cities Service Oil Co. in New Castle. Roy's second wife was Zola Boslaug. Grace (1894-1914) married Arthur Smith. Ollie (1896-1928) married Scott. Clifton C. (1900-1942) never married. Charles and Jessie had no grandchildren. Charles was a carpenter and built many barns in Howard County.

Ernest married Minnie Evans (1878-1960) on April 11, 1906 in Howard County. They had two children, Homer (1907-1932) and Burnett Marion (1912-1932). Both children died in their teens with tuberculosis. They lived most of their life in the Phlox community and were members of the Friends church. Ernest farmed and ran a saw mill. *Submitted by Estaleene Nash Suman*

JESSE NASH AND MARY (PIKE/PYKE) NASH - Jesse Nash born Feb. 2, 1792 in Westmoreland County, PA to Richard Nash IV and Jane (Barr) Nash.

Richard IV entered the Navy to voluntarily engage on board the Frigate *Trumbull* for the term of 12 months from Nov. 16, 1780. On Aug. 14, 1781 he was taken prisoner from the rebel ship *Trumble* near Delaware Bay and retained on the *Jersey* until Sept. 6, 1781 when he was discharged. Richard IV and Jane Barr were united in marriage circa 1785 and settled in Westmoreland County, PA. They left Westmoreland County, PA in 1804 to Mason County, KY, 1810 to Adams County, OH and 1822 purchased land in Fayette County, IN.

Jesse Nash and Mary (Pike/Pyke) Nash

Jesse Nash married Mary Pike/Pyke on March 28, 1816 in Adams County, OH. Mary was born Aug. 30, 1792 in Maryland to John Pike/Pyke and wife Mary. Jesse and Mary lived in Adams County, OH until 1829 then moved to Hamilton County, OH for one year. From 1830 to 1833 he rented a farm in Brown County, OH and from 1833 to 1847 he owned a 65 acre farm in Clermont County, OH. On April 24, 1848 he purchased 150 acres of land in Union Township near West Liberty from the government for $2 per acre. Mary died in 1850 and Jesse died in November 1855/56 in Union Township, Howard County, IN.

Hannah, Jane, and Mary Nash

To Jesse and Mary were born eight children: Jane, Feb. 18, 1817, Adams County, OH; William, Nov. 20, 1818, Adams County, OH; Richard, Oct. 12, 1821, Adams County, OH; John, Nov. 5, 1823, Adams County, OH; George W., April 28, 1826, Adams County, OH; Hannah, June 26, 1829, Adams County, OH; Mary Jane, Aug. 12, 1832, Brown County, OH; and Jesse, Jr., March 7, 1836, Clermont County, OH.

William, Jesse Jr. and Richard Nash

Jane married Joseph Jordon Aug. 10, 1845, Clermont County, OH; William married first Lucinda Brandenburg

274

Sept. 20, 1847 in Clinton County, OH and second Rachel Anna Harper Aug. 29, 1861 in Tipton County, IN. Richard never married; he enlisted in Co. "F", 11th Indiana Regt. Inf. Mustered in Aug. 31, 1861, appointed corporal, discharged Oct. 9, 1864. Wounds. I know nothing of John. George W. married Rachel Ann Shields on Jan. 9, 1853 in Clinton County, OH; Hannah married first Richard Jordon and second David Lewellen; Mary Jane married Theopolis Smith Jan. 15, 1851 in Howard County, IN and Jesse, Jr. married Mary Adaline Baty/Batey May 19, 1859 in Clinton County, OH.

Jane Jordon is buried in the Ellis Cemetery and William, Richard, George, Hannah and Jesse, Jr. are all buried in the Fork of the Creek Cemetery in Union Township. I do not know where John and Mary Jane Smith are buried. Neither do I know where Jesse and Mary (Pike) Nash are buried. I would be glad to hear from "cousins" or others, filling in blanks. *Submitted by Estaleene Nash Suman*

ELLIS NASH AND MINTA (BURNS) NASH -

Ellis Nash married Minta Burns (1873-1961) in Howard County on March 31, 1894. They had four sons: Raughlia (1894-1980), Herbert (1896-1963), Lester (1899-1957), and Oscar (1902-1992). Ellis and Minta moved from Howard County to Washington County in 1905, then to Wells County in 1916 where they lived on a small farm until their deaths. They are buried at the Greenlawn Cemetery in Greentown.

Lester, Raughlia, Herbert, Oscar, Ellis, Minta Nash.

Raughlia married Maggie Ellis born 1902 on Sept. 2, 1925 in Marion County, IN. They had two children, Johanna born 1927 in Washington County, IN and James born 1937 in Montgomery County, IN. Raughlia, a math and mechanical drawing teacher, lived in Campellsburg, Burlington, Brownsburg, Darlington, Valparaiso, Michigan City, IN, and Granby, CT. Johanna lives in Granby, CT with her husband Karl Van Valkenburgh and Jim lives in Essex, CT with his wife Elizabeth (Orr) and two daughters, Beth and Alison.

Herbert Nash married Addie L. Conwell (1898-1974) in Wells County on Dec. 21, 1922 after serving in Co. B, 4th Indiana Regt. and stationed in France during WWI. They lived in Wells County on a farm all their married life. They had two children, Estaleene born 1924 and Estel born 1925. Estaleene lives on the home place with her husband John Suman. She has three children, ten grandchildren and two great-grandchildren. Estel and Janice live on Monroe Res. near Bloomington in a home that he built and he has two sons, Frederick and Joseph, living in Wells County and five grandchildren.

Lester married Edith Keesling (1901-1987) in New Castle on May 19, 1923 and lived in Henry County and worked at the Chrysler plant. They had no children.

Oscar married Rena Beck (born 1908) on April 5, 1930 in Grant County and lived in Warren, Huntington County most of their lives. They had three children, Lois, Fred, and Marie. Marie, the only one living, with her husband, Richard Hirons, lives in Grant County near Van Buren; had two daughters. Cinthia Kay born Dec. 25, 1958 married Jerry Lee Evers in Fort Wayne, on April 20, 1991. Penny Susan born May 21, 1964 married Charles Slayton on June 22, 1985 in Grant County, IN. They have two sons, Andrew Charles and Luke Edward. Charles is a minister for Church of God and now lives in Pennsylvania. *Submitted by Estaleene Nash Suman*

CHESTER BALLARD NAY -

Chester Ballard Nay was born in Kentucky in the year of 1827. He married Sarah Calvert from Ohio. She was born in 1834. To this union were born seven children, four daughters: Martha, Laura, Melviene, and Icy, and three sons: John, Melton, and Harry Lee. The family came to Windfall in Tipton County. Chester passed away in 1888 at the age of 61, and is buried at Windfall. Sarah passed away in 1907 and is also buried in Windfall. Chester and Sarah Nay were my great-grandparents. Harry Lee was my grandfather. He was born in Windfall on April 15, 1872. He married Ormba McVety of Kokomo, on Aug. 26, 1905. She was born on Dec. 27, 1884. She passed away on May 19, 1952. She is buried at Crown Point. My grandfather worked at a brick factory in Windfall and Continental Steel at Kokomo. He passed away on Nov. 17, 1919. His cause of death was falling down an open elevator shaft at the Globe in Kokomo. To that union were born two sons. Chester Otho was born in 1906 and passed away in less then six months. Harry Leo was my father and was born on March 13, 1911 in Kokomo. In early 1920 he made his home at the Independent Order of Odd Fellows Home in Greensburg. He lived within three blocks from my present home. He worked at Hoosier Iron and Public Service at the time of his death. My mother is Edna Irene Hughes, who was born on Sept. 18, 1913 in Tipton County. They were married on Aug. 1, 1936 in Kokomo. He passed away at Public Service on Nov. 12, 1968. He is buried at Sunset Memory Gardens. My mother survives. To this union there are three children: Margaret Rose, Nancy Ellen (myself), and Edward Lee. Margaret Rose, born on Sept. 8, 1937, married David Louis Osborn on Feb. 4, 1961. They have one daughter, Cindy Diana, who was born on Jan. 15, 1968. She married Todd Koon on Sept. 17, 1988. After their child, Clinton Harry, was born (on Oct. 29, 1989), Todd passed away on Oct. 7, 1991. Cindy remarried Ron Coulter on Dec. 31, 1993. I was born on May 21, 1941. I married Samuel William Mathews on Sept. 1, 1967. To this union were born Douglas Lee and Mark William. Douglas was born on Nov. 18, 1968 and later married Cherie Renee Adams on May 23, 1992. Mark was born on July 10, 1970 and married Virginia Mae Chandler on Feb. 14, 1994. Sam and I divorced on Aug. 29, 1975. I remarried on Dec. 23, 1977 to James George Bessler. We have one son, Justin Edward, born on Oct. 13, 1979. Edward Lee was born on June 10, 1945 and married Mary Marie Shockney on July 12, 1975. To this union, there are three daughters: Heather Marie, Amy Michelle, and Angela Nay. Heather was born on July 30, 1976. Amy was born on Aug. 16, 1979. Angela Sue was born on Sept. 18, 1981. *Submitted by Nancy Ellen (Nay) Bessler*

NEAL - JOHNSON -

Mathew "Matt" Franklin Neal, born April 13, 1972 in Placer County, Roseville, CA, son of Cheryl Louise Voigt. He came to Howard County in July of 1990 from Connecticut; married Aug. 1, 1991 in Howard County, to Nikki Chantal Johnson Diaz, born Oct. 9, 1969 in Kokomo, Howard County, IN. Matt and Nikki, have one child, a son, Cody Mathew Neal, born Nov. 29, 1991 in Howard County. Nikki first married Feb. 19, 1988 in Howard County to David Leonard Diaz, born June 28, 1964 in Cook County, Chicago, IL, son of Benjamin Augustine and Marcia Lynn Ann Miller Diaz. David and Nikki are the parents of one child, a son, Michael David Diaz, born June 12, 1987 in Howard County. Benjamin Augustine, born Aug. 28, 1940 in Cook County, Chicago, IL is the son of Jesus and Socorra Esquivel Diaz and Marcia Lynn Ann, born June 18, 1943 at Lake Forest, IL, is the daughter of Leonard Wilson and Frances Ludwig Miller.

Nikki's parents came to Howard County in the late fall of 1965 looking for work; the tornado had touched down in April of that year and Kokomo and the surrounding area was still a mess from this. Nikki is the daughter of Walter Burton Johnson Jr., born Jan. 7, 1942 in Yancy County, NC, near the state line of Tennessee and Barbara Ann McInturff Barnett, born May 29, 1944 in Erwin, Unicoi County, TN, daughter of Willard James and Pancy Inez Miller McInturff. Barbara was first married to Kenneth Wayne Barnett of Erwin, TN. Walter and Barbara were married June 11, 1962 in Erwin, Unicoi County, TN.

Matt, Nikki, Michael and Cody

Walter is the son of Walter Burton Sr. and Lucy Jane Lewis Johnson. Walter Sr., was born Jan. 3, 1902 in Roan Mt., Carter County, TN/NC (they were living almost or was on the line of Tennessee and North Carolina), he was the only child born to Comer Johnson and Phoebe Markland. Walter Sr. died Dec. 29, 1951 in Erwin, Unicoi County, TN. He is buried in the Lewis Cemetery I on Spivey Mt. in the Mt. Dale Community of Unicoi County; this cemetery is close to the North Carolina line and it is straight up a hill on land belonging to Lucy's brother, Samuel Lewis. Lucy Jane, born Sept. 16, 1912 on Spivey Mt., still living in 1994, was the last one of ten children born to David Adkins and Deborah Vasta Justice Lewis. Walter Sr. and Lucy Johnson are the parents of a large family also, 10 children in all: (1) Florence, born April 13, 1932; (2) Servina, born Sept. 18, 1933; (3) Jackie, a son born in January 1935, died in 1938, buried in Lewis Cemetery; (4) Cleo, born Sept. 16, 1937-died in 1938, buried in the Lewis Cemetery; (5) Virginia Ann, born Sept. 10, 1940, never married; (6) Walter Burton, Jr.; (7) Arnold Nel, born April 20, 1944; (8) Mary Rose, born July 10, 1947; (9) Ruby Marie, born Nov. 22, 1948; and (10) Wanda Gaye, born May 10, 1950. *Submitted by Matt and Nikki Chantal Johnson Diaz Neal.*

NEWBY -

Thomas Newby came to Howard County, from Hendricks County, IN and settled on 80 acres of land that he bought Dec. 23, 1847 in Monroe Township, near New London. He was born Nov. 27, 1822 in North Carolina, son of William and Ruth Cox Newby. He married in Hendricks County Nov. 27, 1844 to Rebecca Compton (born April 25, 1824 in Wayne County, IN), daughter of Joshua and Olive Kenworthy Compton. Thomas died Oct. 24, 1862 in New London, Howard County; he was buried in the Old Pioneer New London Cemetery. Rebecca remarried Gideon Small, two children; she died Aug. 6, 1897, buried in the New London Friends Cemetery, Section 4 Lot 38 Graves 2; these two cemeteries are very close together. Thomas and Rebecca were the parents of four known children: (1) Mary Newby, April 30, 1846-Jan. 21, 1861, never married, buried in the Old Pioneer New London Cemetery; (2) Anna Newby, July 25, 1851-April 14, 1923, married March 22, 1876 in Hendricks County to John Hawkins; (3) Joshua Newby; and (4) Seth B. Newby, Nov. 7, 1858-September 1937, wife Lucella Johnson (1866-Oct. 5, 1920), both buried in the New London Friends Cemetery, Section 3 Lot 28.

(3) Joshua Newby, born Sept. 8, 1855 in Howard County, married Dec. 16, 1880 to Luella Augusta Neal (Jan. 5, 1855-June 1, 1936), daughter of Henry and Eliza Jane Beard Neal. Joshua died Sept. 26, 1930; both are buried in the New London Friends Cemetery. They were the parents of five known children: Orluf Cecil/Cecil Orlif Newby, Feb. 17, 1882-Sept. 19, 1882, New London Friends Cemetery, Section 2 Lot 4 Grave 39; Dorothy Newby, July 10, 1883-Sept. 2, 1969, New London Friends Cemetery, never married; Merrill Newby; Henry Clay Newby, May 4, 1890-Dec. 26, 1909, New London Friends Cemetery; and Thomas F. Newby, born June 29, 1897, married Jan. 15, 1920 to Opal L. Small.

275

Newby Family. Shandra, Dustin, Jim and Patti.

Merrill Newby, born Feb. 22, 1885 in New London, Howard County, IN, married April 15, 1908 in Howard County to Amel E. Long (May 20, 1889-Feb. 14, 1972), daughter of James Thomas and Eliza Hamilton Long. Merrill died March 30, 1969 in Howard County; both are buried in New London Friends Cemetery. Parents of eight children: (1) Hellen Fennetta Newby, April 3, 1909-July 28, 1939, New London Friends Cemetery, never married; (2) Leonard Ralph Newby, Dec. 26, 1910-Feb. 27, 1984, married Nov. 28, 1931 to Emma Carver; (3) Loren Elbert Newby, born Sept. 1, 1914, married Nov. 26, 1937 to Miriam Ruth Hamilton (born Feb. 4, 1917); (4) a child buried in New London Friends Cemetery April 28, 1919; (5) Lemuel E. Newby, born and died June 20, 1920, New London Friends Cemetery; (6) Ermal Jane Newby, born Aug. 29, 1921, married Feb. 18, 1952 to Roger Gibson; (7) Mary Elizabeth Newby, born and died July 20, 1924; and (8) Hanley Lester Newby.

(8) Hanley Lester Newby, born May 3, 1927, married Feb. 28, 1948 in Logansport, Cass County, IN to Louise Ozenbaugh, born Aug. 8, 1928, both still living. Parents of five children: (1) Terry Newby, born Oct. 26, 1948, married Sept. 1, 1972 to Kathy Morgan (born Oct. 24, 1953); (2) Mark Newby, born June 18, 1950, married Aug. 2, 1972 to Linda Timmons (born May 7, 1953); (3) Jennifer Newby, born Jan. 10, 1952, married June 6, 1970 to Philip Frazier (born March 24, 1948); (4) James Lee Newby, born Dec. 5, 1956, married July 2, 1983 to Patricia Loraine Myers Eakin, born April 28, 1957, one son Dustin Lee Newby, born March 26, 1987 in Howard County and a stepdaughter, Shanda Renea Eakin; and (5) Sally Anne Newby, Feb. 28, 1959-July 20, 1961, buried in the New London Friends Cemetery. *Submitted by James Lee Newby*

NEWCOMB - Matthew Newcomb Sr. (1801-1880) and Mary (Carey) Newcomb (1810-1880) were early pioneers in western Howard County. He was born in Pennsylvania and she in Ohio. They came west from Ohio and settled in Delaware County, IN. They reared seven children, William, John, James, Matthew Jr., Harriett, Rebecca, and Mary Jane.

Their three daughters were all married in Delaware County, IN. Matthew Sr. and sons bought farmland in western Howard County, along the New London Road. There is a bridge which still crosses the Wildcat Creek near the old homestead on the New London Road that bears a bronze plaque that reads "Newcom Bridge". The first bridge was wooden, the second was iron and the present one is cement.

The family were Quakers and were members of the New London Friends Church.

Matthew Sr.'s son John was the father of Robert Newcom who was a Kokomo police officer for 38 years, towered 6 feet 5 inches tall. All of the Newcom men were tall and handsome. It was no surprise that Robert was also known as "Big Bob". He was a very familiar face in the city. He wore the proud and prominent Badge #1 and was highly respected by all. His daughter, Margaret, lives in Kokomo.

Great-grandfather William Newcom (1833-1902) son of Matthew Sr. and brother to John was married to Frances Ann Gates (1842-1880). Their farm included land on the east and west side of the New London Road and Wildcat Creek in western Howard County.

Liston Newcom (1869-1955), son of William, as a child remembered playing around the area where the great "Sycamore Stump" that is now on display in Highland Park was taken from. Liston married Nora Crousore (1851-1961) on Oct. 1, 1892. Her parents were John and Mary Evelyn (Plummer) Crousore. Great-grandfather John Crousore was a Civil War veteran. Liston and Nora had two sons, Loren and Jesse Earl (1897-1982). Loren died as an infant.

Jesse Earl married Margaret Stephens (1904-1984) on July 17, 1921. She was a daughter of Albert and Viola (Snow) Stephens. Great-grandfather Hiram Stephens served in the Civil War and died of typhoid fever on Feb. 21, 1863 in Gallatin, TN. His wife was Malinda Davis.

Jesse Earl and Margaret had seven children, Clarice Eileen, Earl Jr., Barbara Jean, Patricia Ann, Mary Lou, William Eugene, and Jerry Lee. William Eugene died at age three months on Nov. 11, 1938.

Newcom Bridge, 1959

While a student nurse, Barbara met her future husband. His father was a patient of hers. On Aug. 26, 1950 she married Larry John Indrutz (1922-1981). They had six children. Gregory Paul died Oct. 21, 1984. Barbara has five grandchildren: Matthew Christopher, Alexander John, and Katherine Elaine Indrutz; Julie Renee and Brian Joel Magnett.

Larry was a son of John (1885-1949) and Lena (Hangu) (1884-1959) Indrutz. His parents immigrated to the United States in 1910 from Romania. He was a letter carrier for the U.S. Postal Service, a member of the Indiana Real Estate Commission, St. Joan of Arc Church and served in the U.S. Army in WWII.

Barbara is a registered nurse, a member of the Good Samaritan School of Nursing Alumnae, Daughters of Union Veterans, Howard County Genealogical Society, and St. Joan of Arc Church.

In Grandmother Nora's McGuffie spelling book a friend wrote: Tis sweet, tis sweet, but oh how bitter, to kiss a young tobacco spitter'. Grandfather Liston chewed tobacco and what a spitter was he. *Submitted by Barbara Jean Newcom Indrutz*

ALLEN T. NEWLIN - Allen T. Newlin came to Howard County from Iroquois County, IL in 1897. Part of the family, including the bird in a cage, made the trip by train, and the rest of the family and the hired man brought their belongings in a wagon. There were five children. Mary, the oldest was 20. She later married "Cappy" Hollingsworth and lived in Russiaville. Addie married Rutherford Scherer and lived in Kokomo. William married Eva Mae Jordan and lived west of Russiaville. Katie married Manville "Jack" Rayl and lived south of Russiaville until she moved to her father's home to care for him. Murrel, who was only three when the family arrived in Honey Creek Township, married Hilda Newlin. He died in the flu epidemic of 1918.

Allen Newlin was born Jan. 14, 1847. He was a great-great-grandson of John and Mary Pyle Newlin of Orange County, NC. His grandfather, Joshua Newlin, moved from North Carolina to Parke County, IN in 1827 when Allen's father, Calvin, was about 12 years old. In 1864 Calvin and his family moved to Iroquois County in Illinois. There Allen married Rebecca Ann Whitted Feb. 24, 1870. They had a son, Andrew Melvin, and a daughter, Clara Arminda, before Rebecca died in 1874.

Allen married Sarah Ann Robbins, daughter of Lindley and Mary (Carter) Robbins in 1876. He developed a fine farm in Iroquois County, IL. In Howard County, he had 120 acres on Highway 26 west of Russiaville.

Sarah died Dec. 21, 1925. She was buried in New London Friends Cemetery near her son Murrel. Allen was buried beside her six years later.

Allen Newlin drove a horse and buggy long after most people were driving cars. One summer day in about 1930 when three of his granddaughters were spending the day with him, he left them with his housekeeper while he went to Russiaville. On the way a car hit his horse. He was not hurt, but the horse had to be destroyed. He did not use his buggy again.

When the tornado of 1965 destroyed much of Russiaville, Mary Hollingsworth survived the storm in her home in Russiaville. Katie Rayl saw Allen Newlin's old home blow away from around her. Eva Newlin, a sister-in-law, was trapped in the debris of her house west of Russiaville. Calvin Newlin's family Bible was found in a field and returned to the family.

Descendants of Allen T. (1847-1931) and Sarah A. Newlin (1850-1925):

Mary Iona Newlin Hollingsworth (1877-1967). Frank Hanley Hollingsworth (1905-1991) married Dora Oliver; they had Emily Jane Hollingsworth Smith and William Penn Hollingsworth. Clyde Carlton Hollingsworth (1908-1930). Alma Melissa Hollingsworth (1911-1915). Isaac Allen Hollingsworth married Helen L. Butler; they had Peggy Ann Hollingsworth and Alma Sue Hollingsworth Pierce.

Addie Ellen Newlin Scherer (1880-1942). Hazel Marie Scherer married Stanley Prevo (1898-1987); they had Ruth Ellen Prevo Stone and Martha Ann Prevo Wenrick. George Allen Scherer married Lucile Tauer; they had James Tauer Scherer, Mary Sue Scherer Slabaugh and Carolyn Ann Scherer Bogott.

William Allen Newlin (1887-1953). Leo Max Newlin (1911-1990) married Fleta Pierce; they had Leo Max Newlin II and Mary Etienne Newlin Mullen. Edna Emogene Newlin (1920-1982) married Floyd Fillenwarth, second marriage Charles Wood; had Vernon Eugene Fillenwarth, Thelma Wood Tulley, and infant son Wood (1958).

Emily Katie Newlin Rayl (1889-1985). Mildred Irene Rayl married Harold Waters; they had Sharon Kay Waters Delery. Rheba Faye Rayl married Guy Everett Shockley; they had Marc Rayl Shockley and Jane Ann Shockley Hoyle. Pheba Maye Rayl (1920-1964) married Marshall Morris (1917-1970); they had Matilda Ann Morris (1951) and Marlin Ray Morris.

Murrel Lindley Newlin (1894-1918) and wife Hilda had Robert M. Newlin (1918), and Mary Lou Newlin. She married Roderick Spindt; they had Katherine Mary Spindt Csellar and Susan Jane Spindt Zano.

Many of the above descendants were born in Howard County and some still reside here in 1993. *Submitted by F.A. Hollingsworth*

REVEREND THOMAS E. NEWLIN - Thomas E. Newlin was born just north of New London Oct. 20, 1868. He was the son of James and Rhoda (Jones) Newlin, and he was the grandson of Thomas Newlin who came with his family to Howard County in 1852 from Orange County, NC by way of Orange County, IN. This elder Thomas

Newlin was the son of John and Mary Pyle Newlin, and John was a descendant of Nicholas Newlin who came to this country from Ireland in 1682. All of these Newlins were Quakers.

Thomas E. Newlin's father was a farmer and a preacher. His son tried farming and teaching before he became a storekeeper and finally a preacher. Both father and son were preachers at Bethel Quaker Meeting.

Reverend Thomas E. Newlin

Thomas was active in the New London Friends Church. When Russiaville Friends Church was established in 1911, he was the first clerk. After he was recorded as a minister in 1921, Thomas preached often at Russiaville Friends Church, Lynn, Reserve, Kempton, and in other nearby Quaker Meetings. He was affectionately known as Uncle Tommy. He was partner in the Newlin and Long Hardware Store in Russiaville, and for a time he had a store in Windfall, later in Sharpsville.

In 1890 he married Callie Hoover. They had two children. Russell was born in 1891 and Hilda in 1897. Russell married Clara Dametz and after their first child was born they moved to Kansas. Hilda married Murrel Newlin and they lived with his parents on a farm west of Russiaville until Murrel died in the influenza epidemic of 1918. Hilda returned to her parents' home in Russiaville for the birth of their daughter, Mary Lou.

In 1921 Thomas and Callie purchased a house from Leslie and Elma Hudson, and with Hilda and Mary Lou they moved from Russiaville to Shirley Corner. Hilda remarried a few years later and went to live in the Chicago area. Thomas and Callie continued to live in the Shirley Corner home until Callie died in 1947. She was blind for the last 10 years of her life. Thomas read to her every day, usually from the Bible.

Thomas continued to live at Shirley Corner a few years more. He spent some time each year with his son Russell in Kansas, with his granddaughter Mary Lou in Pennsylvania and with his daughter Hilda in Wisconsin.

About 1952 he made his final home with his daughter Hilda who then lived beside a lake in Wisconsin. For several years he enjoyed working in the garden and tending the flower beds. Just after his 90th birthday, he had a stroke, and on Feb. 7, 1959 he died. He was buried beside his wife in New London Friends Cemetery.

EMMA (TINDER) THOMPSON COATS NICKERSON -
My great-grandmother was born Emily A. Tinder in 1867 in Tipton County. She married John J. Thompson in 1883 in Hamilton County. John and 'Emma' had five children: Sarah Elizabeth 'Lizzie' born 1884; unnamed female born and died in 1885; my grandmother, Carrie Adeline, born in 1887; Maude Teresa born in 1888; and Harvey born in 1891. Lizzie was born in Hamilton County, the next three in Tipton County, and Harvey in Cass County.

John deserted the family in 1896 and in 1898, in Cass County, Emma married Isaac T. Coats by whom she had Sylvia in 1900 and Goldie in 1904. In the 1900 census Emma and Ike were in Grant County but they were in Howard County by the time they divorced in 1908; so Sylvia and Goldie may have been born either place.

Emma remained in Howard County the rest of her days. She married Aaron Nickerson in 1909 and died of typhoid fever in 1912. She is buried in Crown Point Cemetery along with son, Harvey, who predeceased her

by a few months; and daughter, Goldie, who died in 1921. None of the three have tombstones.

In her will, Emma left to Maude "the restaurant and fixtures belonging to me" and located at 918 S. Main St. in Kokomo, with a lien on the restaurant to enforce payments on debts including Harvey's burial expense. I have found no record to indicate what happened regarding the restaurant and its lien, but there was a baseball card shop at that location when I visited in 1991. I would be interested in acquiring a picture of the restaurant if one exists.

Emma and Aaron lived at 1801 S. Courtland, and Harvey's house at 1809 S. Courtland went to his mother on his death. Emma's probate eventually divided her small estate amongst her five living daughters. The present day residents of 1801 S. Courtland told me that the house has been modernized and no longer looks as it did when Emma lived there.

I am interested in finding Lizzie's and Sylvia's descendants (I am in contact with Maude's sole living daughter). Lizzie married first Fred Coppock and second Fred Salyer. I do not believe she had children by Salyer but by Coppock had son Laurel (1905-1969) who married Frances Howdyshell; and son Warren (1907-?). Laurel and Frances Coppock had daughter Betty who married Robert Jenkins and they had Robert Jenkins Jr. I do not know their locations. I know almost nothing about Sylvia Coats. She visited with her half sister Carrie (and husband Lonnie Rhinehart) in Covina, CA in the 40s or 50s but that's all anyone can remember.

Anyone connected with any of the above families please contact Kathryn Rhinehart Bassett, 1080 N. Holliston Ave., Pasadena, CA 91104-3014. My phone is 818-794-7973. I'm 45 years old so should be around for a long time. If you see this book many years from now, I will probably have the same phone number, but if I don't, I will always maintain my phone listing under my maiden name of Rhinehart.

JOSEPH P. NIELANDER -
Joseph P. Nielander was born Dec. 11, 1866 in Gelsenkirchen, Germany. His father was John Liese Nielander and his mother was Katherine Dreier. His father served in the military and was killed in 1871 when a cannon backfired while celebrating the victory over the French in the town square. His mother studied to be a nurse.

When John died Katherine remarried a man named Miller. She didn't want her sons to serve in the Kaiser's army so she came to America. Her husband didn't want to come to America so they came without him. They left Germany in 1880 and arrived in New York and then from there they travelled to Covington, KY.

Joseph married Katherine Macke on July 23, 1893. They had six daughters and two sons. They were Helen, Lucy, Winifred, Anna, Dorothy, Camille, Paul, and William. Helen Kathleen was my grandmother. Joseph and Katherine first moved to Sterling, IL where their first child was born.

Wedding day - Joseph Nielander and Katherine Macke

By 1895 Joseph and Katherine had moved to Indiana. For a short time they lived in Muncie but they lived in Kokomo most of their life. Joseph was employed as a tool and die maker for the Kokomo Spring Works where he worked on the first nail machine. He also got a patent on an adjustable wrench. He also was a director for The

People's Cooperative Grocery Store Co. Joseph also worked for the Walton-Macke Nail Co. located on the northwest corner of Madison and Armstrong. His brother-in-law, Fred Macke, was co-owner of the company. They were machinists and inventors and designed tools. They improved methods of manufacturing nails from steel wire. They invented wrenches and a mouse trap.

Katherine Macke died Dec. 28, 1928. Joseph then married a cousin to Katherine Macke; her name is Katherine Reisiger. Joseph married her sometime around 1933. Kate died sometime around 1941 or 1942.

Joseph died March 12, 1964 in Oaklandon, IN.

My grandmother, Helen, was born Sept. 2, 1894 in Sterling, IL. She married William Martin on Feb. 16, 1915. February 2, 1936 William died leaving her with nine children: Kenny, Joe, William, Lucille, Virginia, Reba, Mary, Catherine, and Gloria.

My mother, Catherine, was born Sept. 25, 1927. She was married to David Swing March 15, 1947 and they had two children, Richard and Barbara. David worked for Mohr Construction. Catherine worked for Delco Electronics. They were divorced Sept. 30, 1975. David died Feb. 13, 1990 from throat cancer.

Richard was born Aug. 2, 1948. He works at Delco. He married Vicky Boles Jan. 1, 1972. Richard has three children: Michael Swing, Lori Swing and Kimberly Swing. They also have four grandchildren and one on the way.

I, Barbara, was born Aug. 14, 1952 and married Richard Beach Jr. on March 11, 1978. Barbara works at Delco Electronics and Richard is a local barber. They have no children.

NORTHCUTT -
Richard and Mildred (Byrd) Northcutt came to Howard County in 1956, when Richard started working at the Chrysler Transmission plant. They are both natives of Delaware County, IN.

They thought it was a long ride, the first time they came to Kokomo from Muncie, but, in reality, it is a short ride compared to the long distance traveled by their ancestors. Most of their ancestors, on both sides, came from England to Virginia, then to Ohio or Tennessee.

Richard's parents, Charles Leo Northcutt and Helen Irene (Davis) Northcutt, lived in Muncie, IN. Richard's mother, H. Irene, was born in Warren County, TN, as were her parents, Will and Octa (Stroud) Davis, and grandparents, John and Jane (Bennett) Davis and James R. and Millie Jane (Brown) Stroud.

Richard's father, Charles Leo, was born in Muncie. His parents, Roy and Cleo (Morrow) Northcutt were both born in Warren County, TN as were their parents: Joiner and Mary (Mann) Northcutt and Robert and Edna (Huntley) Morrow.

Roy and Cleo moved to Muncie about 1910 and the Morrows and Joiner Northcutt and the rest of his family came to Muncie about 1920, as did Will and Octa Davis. Their ancestors had come from England to Virginia in the era of the 1600s, and then to Tennessee in the 1800s.

Mildred's parents, Earl H. and Nellie (Austin) Byrd were both born in Delaware County, IN. Earl's parents, William L. Byrd, born in Ohio, and Mary M. Brown Feirrell Byrd, born in Indiana, lived in Delaware County, IN for most of their married lives. William's father, Abraham, was born in Virginia and his mother, Rebecca (Myers) Byrd was born in Ohio.

Nellie's parents, Ray and Iva (Gibson) Austin, were both born in Delaware County, IN. Ray's parents, Harmon and Leann (Jacobs) Austin, were born in West Virginia, as were their parents. The Austins came to Delaware County in 1865. Iva's parents, Thomas and Alice (Collins), were from Delaware County, IN, and their parents, Virginia and then Ohio.

Richard and Mildred met in high school in Randolph County, IN. They were married in June 1951, at Albany, IN. Richard worked at Warner Gear, in Muncie, until they moved to Kokomo, in 1956. While living in Muncie, they had two children; Joe, married to Linda Laudeman, of Griffith, IN. They have three children; Nancy, David and Julie. Their second child, Susan, is married to Greg Cox, a native of Howard County, and they have two daughters; Summer and Sarah. Joe and Susan both live in the Greentown area. After moving to Kokomo, Richard and

Mildred had another son, Gene, who is married to JoEllen Davin, born in New Jersey, but coming to Howard County with her parents, when she was young. Gene's two daughters, Amy and Emily, live in Lebanon, IN.

Richard and Mildred Northcutt, taken about 1986.

Richard worked at the Chrysler Transmission Plant for 31 years as an inspector and retired on Dec. 31, 1987. Mildred went back to school at Indiana University-Kokomo in 1970 and taught second grade at Eastern Elementary, in Greentown, for 15 years, retiring in 1988.

They have lived in the Greentown area since 1964 and consider Howard County as their home, even though they were born in Delaware County, IN and their family roots are elsewhere. *Submitted by Mrs. R.J. Northcutt*

HENRY AND MATILDA (BULK) OBERMEYER - Henry Obermeyer was born Jan. 18, 1876 in Westphalia, Germany to German parents, Henry and Anna Maria (Bulk) Obermeyer. Henry's father was robbed and thrown overboard on his immigration voyage to this country. Anna Maria Obermeyer (1856-1922) then married Peter Thinker (1857-1932). Henry's known siblings are as follows:

Charles F. Obermeyer (1881-1953), who in 1904 married Maggie Schmitt (1886-1953), daughter of John and Mary (Zoller) Schmitt; Paul Thinker (1884-1963), who married Ethel (?) (1888-1950); and Augusta Thinker, who married John Rosenbrock.

Henry came to this country in 1890. Upon his arrival in Kokomo, he was employed by Pittsburgh Plate Glass for 11 years. He took up farming, a trade at which he became very successful. The Obermeyer farm remains in the family five generations later.

On Jan. 2, 1898 Henry married Matilda Bulk, daughter of Fred C. and Dora (Pohlman) Bulk, born Sept. 5, 1876 in Howard County. Nine children were born, all in Howard County, as follows:

Dorothy Marie Obermeyer, born July 20, 1899, died Jan. 25, 1962, and who in November 1921 married Clifford Irwin Prifogle, son of Michael John and Louisa (Bossert) Prifogle, born Oct. 31, 1899 in Tipton County, and died July 22, 1979.

Rudolph Fred Obermeyer, born Nov. 23, 1900, died Nov. 27, 1988, and who on June 2, 1929 married Wilma Bernadine Flora, daughter of Orion and Bertha (Bock) Flora, born May 24, 1900, and died Sept. 26, 1956.

Lorena Claire Obermeyer, born Dec. 25, 1902, died Feb. 12, 1990, and who on Nov. 1, 1931 married George Lee Whitehead, son of William H. and Ida (Gehlert) Whitehead, born Nov. 1, 1905, and who survives.

Edward George Obermeyer, born Aug. 4, 1904, died Feb. 5, 1981, and who on Aug. 4, 1931 married Viola Marie Herron, daughter of Jerry and Mildred (Roberts) Herron, born Nov. 24, 1913, and who survives.

Florence Margaret Obermeyer, born May 5, 1907, who married (1) Aug. 11, 1929 Veaux H. Bowman; (2) May 1, 1937 Walter K. Pring, son of George and Aletha (Albright) Pring, born July 17, 1900, died Jan. 7, 1972; and (3) H. Paul Crouch. Florence survives.

Clarence Charles Obermeyer, born Dec. 14, 1909, died Sept. 7, 1972, and who on Dec. 24, 1933 married Mildred Ethel Chism, daughter of William and Evalene (Peck) Chism, born Nov. 15, 1910, died May 20, 1978.

Ruth Rose Obermeyer, born April 24, 1913, died May 6, 1983, and who married (1) Charles Brumfield; (2) Forrest Addington; and (3) Nov. 15, 1949 Claude Harvey Shepherd, born Aug. 24, 1908, died Jan. 3, 1972.

Eleanor Lena Obermeyer, born May 21, 1916, died Dec. 29, 1981, and who on July 30, 1933 married Walter J. Summers, son of James and Margaret Summers, born Aug. 20, 1909, died Dec. 18, 1983.

An infant daughter, who died at birth Jan. 27, 1921.

Henry and Matilda were charter members of St. John's Lutheran Church, Henry being looked upon by other members as the "father" of the congregation. Henry died of heart failure May 20, 1942. Matilda died Aug. 27, 1964. Both are buried in Kokomo Memorial Park. *Submitted by Carl Edward Prifogle*

O'DONNELL - Lida Laura Wilson (July 7, 1873; Aug. 30, 1962) was the fourth child of Ambrose and Phoebe Griffith Wilson. She married (Sept. 10, 1906) Patrick Warren O'Donnell (Jan. 10, 1876; Aug. 30, 1942), the son of Thomas and Harriet Curren O'Donnell, who came from Ireland in 1860. They first lived in Ervin Township and later moved to Clay Township.

Patrick was a farmer. He also helped build the Kappa Post Office and store.

The children of Lida and Patrick are Glen Wilson O'Donnell (Nov. 9, 1907; July 19, 1908); Pearl Pauline 'Pat' (Dec. 17, 1909) who married July 8, 1931, Joseph McGowan (Aug. 22, 1906; July 22, 1973) the son of Michael and Mary McGowan. He joined the Army in 1943, was stationed at Ft. Mead where Pat worked in the Post Exchange in Payroll. Joe worked for Dietzen's Bakery and was in politics and Pat worked at S.S. Kresge.

Dean Cora (July 12, 1912) married Oct. 12, 1941, Homer Ousley (Feb. 26, 1914; Aug. 23, 1977), the son of John and Laura Ousley. He worked at Haynes Stellite, served in the Army 1942-1945, in Europe. After he came home he opened a launderette and recreation room. Their children are: Marchita Kay, March 7, 1944. She received her R.N. at St. Elizabeth's Danville, IL, and became Director of Nursing at Howard Community at Kokomo. She married Sept. 13, 1975, Kenneth Russell Humphrey (June 13, 1947), son of Russell and Alberdeen Humphrey. Kenneth graduated from Purdue and Indiana University, and is president of Humphrey Printing. They have twins, Kay Lynn and Jayne Aynn born Nov. 24, 1977, and Patrick Joseph born June 30, 1982. Kay is on the school golf team and Jayne is on the school tennis team. Patrick J. plays tennis and golf. They attend Kokomo schools.

Larry Dean Ousley born Sept. 28, 1946, attended Purdue, and was in the Air Force 1965-1969, with two and one-half years in Vietnam. He married June 14, 1974, Kathryn Cutress. They divorced in 1986. He is an electrician at Delco and a ham operator. Their children are Andrea Chree born May 29, 1975. She played clarinet in the Western School Band. Her son is Korey Keith Jones born Sept. 18, 1993. Benjamin Patrick born June 18, 1976, plays tennis on the Western School team, and Isaac Christopher born June 8, 1980 attends Bona Vista School.

Byrl Frank O'Donnell born March 25, 1914, married April 28, 1937, Mabel Hunt daughter of Sherman and Carrie Hunt. Byrl retired from Chrysler Corp. Their children are Sharon Kay born Nov. 19, 1937, who worked in Civil Service and retired from P S I in Kokomo; married Oct. 12, 1965, Charles Nace born Nov. 30, 1920, son of Charles and Evaleen Nace, and retired from Conrail.

John Patrick born Nov. 29, 1948, played baseball and basketball at Northwestern School, and graduated from Indiana University and is vice president at First National Bank. He married June 8, 1969, Patti Bostic born Aug. 10, 1948, the daughter of Raymond and Maxine Bostic. They have Ann Marie born Aug. 5, 1973, and attends Butler University; Laura Ann born March 30, 1979, and plays tennis and basketball at Northwestern School.

Matthew born May 18, 1982, plays on the softball team at Northwestern School. *Submitted by Dean Ousley*

OGLE - James Ogle, son of James and Hannah Sarah (Brown) came from Virginia to Indiana in 1829 where he met and married Lucinda Gibson, daughter of William and Sarah Rachel (Dewitt).

James spent his life tilling the soil. He bought land in Delaware County in 1830, but moved his family on to Grant County and into Howard County by 1870. He and Lucinda are both buried at the Forks of the Creek Cemetery in Union Township.

They became the parents of 10 children: Nancy, Rebecca, Elisha, William, Valentine, Nelly, Abigail, Elijah, Patsy, and Phebe.

Valentine was killed in the Civil War at the battle of Yazoo River in Mississippi and is buried at the Forks of the Creek Cemetery.

Valentine's brother, Elijah, born in 1851 married three times: first to Eunice Wilson, then to Mary Crab, and finally to Sarah Lightfoot. They lived in Liberty Township.

Elijah was the father of 14 children: Lucinda and Alice born to Eunice; James, Elisha, Elizabeth, Frank, and Amanda born to Mary; Valentine (known as Vollie) Charles, Bertie, Anna, Burl, Johnie, and Nellie born to Sarah. Nellie, who resides in California, is the only one still living.

Sarah and Elijah Ogle

Vollie married Mary (Jones) and lived his entire adult life in and near Greentown. His occupation was a builder contractor. He was the pioneer who laid the water and sewage lines in Greentown. He owned several properties in Greentown and resided on the property adjacent to the Greentown Glass Factory. This property is now owned by his great-grandchildren.

His wife Mary was well loved in the community as a midwife. She delivered many babies when Dr. Miller was unable to get to the residence. She was often called on to nurse the elderly or those suffering from the smallpox.

She and Vollie were the parents of: Monroe, Delbert, Cleo, Dora, Dorothy, Dwane, and Ruby. All lived in or near Greentown. Dorothy and her husband, Paul Metz owned and operated the Metz Hatchery in Greentown.

Monroe was a quiet-spoken man who had a strong faith in God. This faith led him to pastor a Methodist church for 23 years.

As a young man he helped in the building of the Greentown City Building. He placed a nickel in the cornerstone when it was laid in 1928.

He and Ralph Lamb began a dry cleaning business in Greentown, but his dream was to become a farmer. He eventually obtained this dream by owning and operating two farms in Jackson Township. In addition to this he did custom butchering for the neighbors. In 1950 he went to work for Haynes Stellite where he was noted for various inventions.

Monroe married Audra (Sprong) in 1933, and they became the parents of Wilda, Charlotte, Janice, and Linda. His life was characterized by his love for others and his faith in God. His life's motto was "Only one life will soon be past - Only what's done for Christ shall last." *Submitted by his daughter, Charlotte (Ogle) Nulf.*

OILAR - It was a time when restless American pioneers were making the hazardous trek westward, when the ravages of war and disease had already taken their toll, that a young doctor from Ohio, and his wife, a nurse, came to homestead on land that lies on the present boundary of Howard and Clinton counties.

The eighth of fourteen children, Dr. Levi Oilar, a primitive Baptist, was born in Clark County, OH in 1812.

278

Catharine, a Quaker, was also born in 1812, in Beverly, NJ. It was not until after their marriage in Ohio in 1840 that young Oilar received his degree in Cincinnati. His young wife pursued studies in nursing at the same time.

In the fall of 1845, Dr. Oilar came to Clinton County on horseback to stake his land on what is now Indiana 26, just west of Russiaville. He purchased 120 acres and before departing to join his family in Dark City, OH (adjacent to Richmond, IN) he traded his horse for 40 additional acres and returned home on foot.

In the spring of 1846 with his wife and three children, Ben Franklin, Sara Margaret and Mary Jane, Dr. Oilar moved to his new home traveling by covered wagon. Soon after settling, he opened his office there.

Dr. Levi and Catherine Van Brundt Oilar

Louisa May, their third daughter, was born the first year in the new home and she was to be followed by John McClain in 1848, Henry Clay in 1850, Martin Luther in 1852 and Belsora Catharine in 1855.

Dr. Oilar dispensed much of the medication he gave to his patients and when travel by wheeled conveyances were impossible, he was known to have filled his saddle bags with the necessary medicine and equipment to make his rounds on horseback. Many times Mrs. Oilar went with him to help, and together they treated the early settlers for the then deadly typhoid, malaria, tuberculosis and diphtheria.

One incident is told of how a man on foot suffering the torture of a neglected infected tooth came alongside Dr. Oilar who was on his horse and asked for help. The doctor instructed the man to come still closer and with the appropriate instrument and great dexterity, reached down and extracted the troublesome tooth.

In many cases Dr. Oilar was given a pig, calf or cow in exchange for services.

Russiaville was a very small village and those who could attend went to church service at New London Friends or Union Baptist. Dr. Oilar with some of the children attended Union Baptist and Mrs. Oilar and the remainder of the family went to New London. A wagon was used for transportation and a picnic lunch was often taken to be eaten following services.

There were many hardships for the early doctor and his wife in those days when the Miami Indians were on the Old Michigan Road just west of their home; the winters were an enemy to be reckoned with, and transportation was anything but convenient, yet this couple, with their large family, managed to conquer the obstacles and battle disease in this rugged area.

Dr. Oilar died at the age of 85 in 1897. Mrs. Oilar died at the age of 62 in 1875. It is probable that Dr. Oilar inherited his longevity from his father, Henry, who reached an age over 100, and his grandmother, Elizabeth Montgomery McGlamery, an aunt to Nancy Hanks Lincoln, who lived to be 115 years of age. *Submitted by Josephine Pollock Mason, great-granddaughter of Levi and Catharine Oilar.*

OLD BOB - In July 1861, 47-year-old Pollard Jackson Brown enlisted in Co. F, 3rd Indiana Volunteer Cavalry, 45th Regular Indiana Volunteers. He reported for duty with his nine-year-old greyish-brown Packolett horse Bob, and they were assigned to the Army of the Potomac in Virginia. During much of the war Mr. Brown and Bob delivered dispatches for Gen. Phil Sheridan. At the Battle of Antietam, Maryland (Sept. 17, 1862), Bob was wounded by a shell. Another time when rebel horsemen were pursuing them, Bob jumped a stake and rider fence to carry Pollard to safety as the bullets whizzed by. Later he was shot in the shoulder by a minnie ball at the Battle of the Wilderness, Virginia (May 5-6, 1864). It was reported that Bob ran two and one-half miles with a crippled leg carrying Pollard to safety. He survived this wound and was hit again in the shoulder before the war ended.

Pollard Brown received an honorable discharge on Sept. 16, 1864, after serving three years, one month, and twenty-one days without a furlough. After leaving the military he proudly rode Old Bob back to his home in Lawrence Township, Marion County, IN.

Soon after his return, Brown moved with his family and Old Bob to a farm in Howard Township, Howard County, about four miles east of Kokomo on the Waterworks Road (County Road 50 N). Old Bob quickly became the pride and pet of the local veterans, and no reunion of Civil War soldiers was complete without his presence.

Old Bob escaped death again in November 1874. Pollard Brown, Jr. was driving an extra long straw wagon pulled by Old Bob and another horse in downtown Kokomo. As they crossed the railroad at the southwest corner of the square, a train hit the wagon. The impact threw the driver onto the engine's cowcatcher from which he rolled to safety without any wounds. The horses and wagon were tumbled ahead of the engine with the horses rolling over each other for half a block. The wagon was totally destroyed, but the horses walked away with minor scratches.

In October 1883, Pollard rode Old Bob from Tipton to Indianapolis to attend a reunion of the 3rd Indiana Cavalry. At that time he was 69, and Old Bob was 31.

Brown's devotion to Old Bob is illustrated by an interesting incident. It seems that Brown fell upon hard times and was unable to pay his debts. The Howard County Sheriff went out to Brown's farm to take some of his livestock for payment. Brown met the sheriff and said, "Here's my farm, my cattle and horses, and all my personal property; you can have that; but if you touch Old Bob, you are a dead man." Happily Brown's property was not sacrificed, and Old Bob lived out his remaining days in the care of his owner.

On Sunday, Aug. 14, 1887, Old Bob showed signs of illness so Brown sent for W.H. Thompson, a Kokomo veterinarian. By the time Thompson arrived, Old Bob had died at age 35 years. He was buried under a walnut tree on the Brown farm on Monday, Aug. 15, 1887. Members of the Thomas J. Harrison Post #31, Grand Army of the Republic attended the burial and gave Old Bob full military honors according the ceremonies of their order.

Later Pollard Brown sold most of his farm to William M. Robbins and moved with his wife Nancy to Kokomo. Mr. Robbins placed a picket fence around the grave of Old Bob. It is believed that this burial site was near the road on the south side of County Road 50 N about three-tenths of a mile west of County Road 400 E in what is now an open field.

Pollard Brown was blind the last five years of his life. He was living with his daughter Annie in Nashville, TN, when he died on Feb. 1, 1899, at age 85. His wife Nancy died in Indianapolis on April 23, 1914, at age 88. They are buried in Crown Point Cemetery in Kokomo. *Submitted by Ed Riley*

ORTMAN - John Ortman (1844-1924) was an only son and came over from Germany with his mother and stepfather. He married Mary Rizzleman (1853-1934) and settled near Brookville in Johnson County, IN.

Ten children were born to them. Two died in infancy. These are the other children:

Henry (1874-1940) ran a threshing machine and clover huller.

Edward (1878-1955) well driller.

Anna Ortman Vonderahe ran a boarding house in Kokomo and later operated a hotel in California.

William (1883-1953).

Rosa (1884-1970) ran a boarding house.

Mary Catherine (1886-1972) ran a boarding house with her sister in Torrance, CA.

John Bernard (J.B.) (1880-1969) farmed, threshed, and drilled water wells.

Frank (Buss) (1894-1971) school bus driver and dairyman.

The Ortman boys and their father built a shop on the farm west of Kokomo which their father and mother had bought in 1888. They fixed machinery for neighbors as well as themselves. They also did threshing and clover hulling.

Grandpa Ortman

Frank (Buss) bought a farm south of Kokomo. He married Ella Lantz of Peru, IN. They had one son, Verlin.

John (J.B.) married Josephine Kerby (1892-1940) April 19, 1915. Six children were born to them: Emma, John Bernard II, Robert, Richard, Ned, and Raymond (Mick).

John (J.B.) built his first wooden well drilling machine in 1922. From his first machine grew a business that became one of the success stories of the community. He made a success of the business because he knew it thoroughly, and he worked long and hard at it. It is now operated by the founder's sons and grandsons.

Earlier in life J.B. Ortman was a farmer and operator of threshing machines and clover hullers. Those were the days when the annual threshing day on the farm was the big event of the year. Dinner for threshing crews was a fabulous feast of such size and variety that only farm wives could cook.

J.B. Ortman served on the Howard County Council two terms, eight years altogether. He was one of the most popular members of that governmental body. He took on the job largely because friends suggested that he be a candidate. He became a councilman respected for his fairness, good judgment, and straightforward personality.

He was always modest and had the great ability to make friends, and more importantly, to keep them. People remembered him for his genial qualities, his generous and helpful nature, and his good record as a fine citizen.

Five generations later most of the descendants of John and Mary Rizzleman Ortman live in Howard County.

ROBERT EDWARD AND EVA JANE ORTMAN - Bob was born Aug. 13, 1920 in Clay Township to John B. and Josephine Kerby Ortman. Eva was born May 4, 1923 near Burlington to Ralph V. and Shirley D. Fisher Payne. Bob graduated from Clay Township High School in 1937 and from Purdue University in 1944 in Ag. Econ. Eva graduated from Burlington High School.

They were married Oct. 8, 1941 and began crop farming raising peas, lima beans, tomatoes, corn, soybeans, wheat, oats and hay. They also raised livestock feeding cattle, hogs, sheep and chickens.

Bob was one of the founders of Kokomo Grain and Feed, an active member of many farm organizations and Kokomo Kiwanis Club, and also a former county council member. Eva is a member of Clay 49ers Homemakers, Clay Alpha Study group, and volunteers for charities. They are members of St. Patrick's Church.

Their children: Roberta Jeanne Hickman, born Nov. 22, 1944 married Gary Hickman, a son Ryan Blair Oct. 10, 1972. She is a Purdue graduate living near Carlsbad, CA. Carolyn Joan was born June 18, 1946 and died Aug. 29, 1962. Stanley E. born Sept. 23, 1949 married Jovita Frazier Dec. 22, 1973. Their two daughters are Julie Rose born Oct. 29, 1989 and Amy Joan born Oct. 25, 1981. He is a Purdue graduate in Ag. Econ., and Jovita is an Indiana University graduate with a medical technician degree. Brian V. Ortman born Feb. 12, 1955 married Cynthia M. Clark on May 26, 1979. They have two daughters Erika Jayne born May 20, 1990 and Kathryn Grace born Jan. 6, 1994. Brian is a Purdue graduate of the School of Veterinary Medicine and Cynthia is a Purdue graduate in pharmacy. He is now a captain in the Air Force and they live in Goldsboro, NC.

ALBERT AND LILLIAN OSBORN

Albert was born in Howard County Feb. 15, 1894 and died in August 1986. He married Lillian Thompson Sept. 22, 1917. Lillian was born July 20, 1891 and died Feb. 19, 1961. Albert and Lillian had three sons: Jesse G. born Dec. 9, 1918; Warren Frances born July 5, 1920 and Clyde Leland born Aug. 8, 1925. Jesse married Anna N. Fellow July 24, 1943 and they had four children: Larry, Linda, Judy and Devonna. Warren married Betty Winniger May 5, 1944 and had two children: Patricia, who married Bill Beeler, and Robert. Clyde married Virginia Moore and had two children: Thomas Leland born June 16, 1943 and Roberta Jean born Jan. 1, 1945. Clyde married Virginia Vinyard Dec. 4, 1948. They had two children: Jeffrey Allen born Aug. 8, 1950 and Penelope Susan born Sept. 24, 1952.

Lillian was the daughter of Thornberg Baldwin and Della Uba (Davis) Thompson. Thornberg was born April 18, 1861 and died in 1935. Della was born June 3, 1873 and died Nov. 11, 1962. Both Thornberg and Della are buried in the Friends Cemetery in New London.

Albert's parents were Jesse Albert and Laura Francis (Fleming) Osborn. Jesse was born in Howard County on March 19, 1870 and died Jan. 11, 1957. Laura was born near Phlox, IN on May 26, 1874 and died Jan. 26, 1955. Albert and Laura had four children, all born in Greentown: Albert D., Glenn Eastburn, Leila and Maxine.

Glenn was born June 30, 1897 and died Jan. 10, 1976. He married Flora Thompson Dec. 23, 1917 and adopted Anna Lee who married Jack Dowden.

Leila was born Aug. 8, 1892 and died Nov. 20, 1971. She married Clifford Colvin July 6, 1912 and had four children: Clifford Jr. died at birth; Wendel was born July 16, 1914; Mary Josephine died at birth and William was born Oct. 1, 1920.

Maxine was born March 13, 1907 and married Wayne Dutton April 19, 1930. They had one son, Richard.

The Osborn Family line can be traced back to Queen Victoria in England.

ANNA AND JESSE OSBORN

Jesse Garland Osborn was born Dec. 9, 1918 in Howard County. He attended Wallace Grade School and graduated from Kokomo High School. As a boy, he worked on various farms and joined the Army in 1941, where he served in the European Campaign until October 1945. Upon coming home from the service, he was a trucker until his retirement in 1980. On July 24, 1943, he married Anna N. Fellow. Anna was born in Kokomo on Dec. 28, 1925. Jesse and Anna had four children: Larry C. born Aug. 26, 1944; Linda K. born Jan. 15, 1947; Judy A. born Jan. 1, 1948 and died Sept. 19, 1985; and Devonna J. born Oct. 27, 1949.

Anna was the daughter of Walter E. and Ercie O. (Mendenhall) Fellow. Walter was born in Burr Oak, KS on May 23, 1885 and died Feb. 26, 1973. Ercie was born Aug. 23, 1892 and died April 1, 1962. They are both buried in Greenlawn Cemetery in Greentown.

Walter Fellow was the son of Alphanso L. and Orpha Elizabeth (Cox) Fellow. Alphanso was born July 28, 1858 and Orpha was born April 2, 1859 and died May 14, 1944 and both are buried in the Friends cemetery in Amboy. They were married on July 28, 1879 in Spiceland, IN. Both Orpha and Alphanso were of Quaker background. They moved to Kansas in a covered wagon. Al was a farmer until they moved back to Indiana. They had five children: Anna Elizabeth and Mary E. (twins) born Jan. 11, 1880 in Spiceland (Mary E. died Jan. 11, 1880); Walter E.; Mary Beeson born Oct. 27, 1886 and died in 1938; and Robert William born July 11, 1894.

Anna and Jesse Osborn

Alphanso's parents were Elisha P. and Ann Eliza (Beeman) Fellow. Elisha was born Jan. 3, 1836 and died around 1859. Ann was born April 12, 1838 and died in 1922.

Elisha's parents were John and Abigail (Coleman) Fellow Sr. John was born in North Carolina on Sept. 13, 1793 and died March 24, 1864. Abigail was born March 27, 1809 in Randolph County, IN and died in 1891. John and Abigail were Quakers and Anti-Slavery people. They helped many Negroes escape to the North during the Civil War era. The Fellow family can be traced back to William born June 3, 1635 in England, where the family name was spelled Follow. The Fellow family migrated from North Carolina to Indiana and were farmers and of the Quaker religion.

OTEHAM

Wayne Franklin and Willa Rose (Oland) Oteham moved to Howard County, IN in 1954. They both were born in Attica, Fountain County, IN. Wayne was born March 14, 1918, son of Edmund and Iva Mae (Kellam) Oteham. Willa Rose was born March 19, 1920, daughter of James Roy and Arletta (Ritenour) Oland. Willa Rose is known as Rosie.

Wayne and Willa Rose are the parents of two children: Sharlene Kay Oteham, born Sept. 19, 1941 in Attica, Fountain County, IN, and Ronald Jay Oteham, born Jan. 3, 1946 in Lafayette, Tippecanoe County, IN. Sharlene Kay is known as Kay.

Wayne and Willa Rose built a home near 350 W and 200 S in 1956; they lived there for about 15 years. They then moved to Kokomo, Howard County, IN, until they retired in 1980.

Willa Rose (Oland) Oteham and Wayne Franklin Oteham

Wayne worked for Local 330 Plumbers and Pipefitters in Kokomo, and then Local 440 Plumbers and Pipefitters of Indianapolis after Local 330 consolidated. He also was maintenance supervisor at St. Joseph Hospital for seven years. Willa Rose worked for Delco Electronics in Kokomo, IN for 20 years. When they retired in 1980 they moved to the Lake Freeman area, White County, IN, for the summer months, and Ruskin, FL for the winter months.

Sharlene Kay Oteham graduated from Western High School in 1959. She married Gary Lautenschlager, son of Glen and Erma Lautenschlager, on Dec. 16, 1961, in Kokomo, Howard County, IN. They are the parents of four children: Tracy Carol Lautenschlager, born Oct. 2, 1962; Jon Bryan Lautenschlager born Sept. 24, 1964; Daniel Jay Lautenschlager, born Sept. 22, 1965; and Matthew Gary Lautenschlager, born Feb. 5, 1971. All four children were born in Kokomo, Howard County, IN. Sharlene Kay and Gary Lautenschlager were divorced in 1974. Sharlene Kay married Raymond Middleton on Feb. 4, 1977, in Kokomo, Howard County, IN. Sharlene Kay, Ray and her children moved to Phoenix, AZ in 1979.

Ronald Jay Oteham graduated from Western High School in 1964. Ronald served in the U.S. Navy from May of 1966 to May of 1970. He married Linda Marie Van Houten, daughter of Alva Lee and Evelyn (Elly) Van Houten, on Dec. 12, 1970, in Turtle Lake, Barron County, WI. They are the parents of two children: Ryan James Oteham, born July 1, 1975 and Ashley Marie Oteham, born Feb. 9, 1977. Both children were born in Kokomo, Howard County, IN.

Ron works for Local 440 Plumbers and Pipefitters of Indianapolis, IN. Linda works for Delco Electronics in Kokomo, Howard County, IN. They lived on S. Dixon Rd. in Kokomo, IN from 1972 to 1984. In 1984 they moved to the Tipton-Howard County Line Rd. and 450 W where they built a home.

DANIEL GOSSARD OVERHOLSER

Daniel Gossard Overholser was born on June 23, 1801, in Franklin County, VA, the eldest son of Abraham and Catherine Gossett Overholser. After Catherine's death, Abraham married Barbary Prupecker and moved the family to Preble County, OH in 1815 and farmed until his death in 1826.

Daniel met and married Mary Magdaline Brubaker on Oct. 23, 1823 in Preble County, OH. They had nine children while living in Ohio. In 1838, he moved to Howard County where he owned and operated a grist mill on the Wildcat Creek just east of Burlington. They had four more children all born in Indiana: Martha, Tobias, Daniel, and Rebecca. Several streets in Flora were named after Daniel's daughters and remain so today. Daniel died on Sept. 1, 1871; Mary died in April of 1889. Both are buried at Moss Hill Cemetery near Flora.

Obediah Everett Overholser; Charles Augustus Overholser

The family returned to Flora sometime in the early 1860s. At the outbreak of the Civil War, Tobias and young Daniel, although "Old Order Dunkards," left home without their father's consent and enlisted in Co. "G" of the 63rd Regt. at Norway, IN. Tobias fell at the Battle of Champion Hill, near Jackson, MS. Upon discharge Daniel returned home where he met and married Eliza Ann Seawright. They began farming 15 acres near Darwin (Carrollton) in the spring of 1868. They had 10 children. One of their sons, Obediah married Rosetta Bausom on Sept. 27, 1893, and moved back to Howard County. Obediah and Rosetta had two children, Charles Augustus and Bethel.

Charles Augustus Overholser married Mona Lee Kirkpatrick on Feb. 26, 1921 in Sharpsville, IN. He served in the army during WWI and after his medical discharge settled in Howard County, later moving into Kokomo. There he purchased five acres of land with an existing large red barn which he renovated into a four-bedroom home to accommodate his large family (they raised sixteen children). Although the land was parceled off through the years, the house still stands at 609 North Korby Street. Charles died on June 6, 1954, and Mona followed him on Feb. 18, 1967. They are buried at Crown

Point Cemetery alongside Obediah and Rosetta. Those descendants still living in Kokomo are: Mrs. Robert (Marilyn) Thompson, Mikki Wolf, Rita Rittenhouse, Sharon Overholser, Mrs. Donn (Linda) Sullivan, and Mrs. Michael (Myrna) Mayfield. *Submitted by Linda Overholser Sullivan*

HENRY AND CATHERINE OYLER -

Ten years before the start of the Civil War, Henry Oyler (1822-1893) and his wife Catherine (1823-1923), daughter of John and Hannah (Isley) Woodring, came to Howard County. Henry was the son of Jacob and Susannah (Crowell) Oyler from Franklin County, VA.

They came by covered wagon from their home near Eaton, OH to near Burlington, IN, starting Sunday morning and arriving late Friday evening. During the entire journey Catherine sat on a bureau with her feet on a box packed with bedding, holding her baby girl in her lap, while Henry followed in a wagon behind with a cow and calf completing the caravan.

They passed through Kokomo, then a "town" of three houses. They settled in what is now Monroe Township, first clearing the land and starting their life in Indiana in a little log cabin on the banks of the Wildcat Creek.

Life was hard in those days but filled with tasks that they both enjoyed. There were gardens to tend, chickens to feed and cows to milk. Many a time Catherine would help rake hay and wheat and help bind the flax. She would also spin the wool and weave the jeans worn by the family.

Standing, l to r: Joe Bart Oyler, John Oyler and Calvin Oyler. Seated, l to r: Catherine (Woodring) Oyler and Mary Frances (Oyler) Bell.

Catherine and Henry were members of the Dunkard Church and adhered faithfully to the teachings of their Master.

Catherine and Henry were the parents of five children, four of whom made their homes in Howard County.

Mary Frances (1851-1937) was married to Isaac Bell. Their children were Charles Milroy, Calvin L., Catherine, Roy, and Andrew.

Calvin (1853-1948) made his home in Indianapolis with his wife Lottie Rodkey. They had no children.

John Henry (1857-1945) married Mary Elizabeth Rodkey and were the parents of two, Goldie and Fred.

Joseph Barton (1860-1955) lived in western Howard County with his wife, the former Mary Syrena Ritchey, and were the parents of three children: Juanita Grace, Robert Henry and Lena Leota.

Louisa (1864-1918) married Amos Brubaker. There were no children from this union.

Catherine passed away just three weeks before her 100th birthday and is buried next to Henry in the South Union Cemetery.

Many descendants of these two fine people still live in the Howard County area.

Two sisters and one brother of Henry also settled in Howard County:

Abrilla (1824-1886) was married to Henry Huddleston. There were seven children born to this couple; Elizabeth (1832-1910) who was married to Ephriam Woods; and Albert, who was unmarried.

These three were also members of the Dunkard Church and they are all buried in Pete's Run Cemetery in western Howard County.

PARKS - Walter Miller Parks (March 9, 1878-Sept. 15, 1937) married Clara Montgomery (March 10, 1883-Dec. 26, 1963) on 25th of December 1901 in Scott County, IN. They were the parents of 10 children. Four of the 10 came to Kokomo Howard County in the 1930s. One died as a child and two were casualties of WWII.

Their children were Flora Opal (Dec. 5, 1902-March 27, 1983) married Edgard Colwell Dec. 12, 1922. They had one son, Vincent. They came to Kokomo in 1930. They had two restaurants in Kokomo, The Point where S. Lafountain and S. Washington merge and Colwell Cafe on S. Lindsay by Stellite. They also with help from Flora's brother Valoris made and put up the Christmas decorations in downtown Kokomo for 30 years.

Valoris Parks with Christmas wreath for downtown Kokomo

Valoris (July 7, 1904-Oct. 18, 1953) married Goldie Kallenbach July 22, 1925. They came to Kokomo in 1933. They had five sons and three daughters: Edward, Walter, Helen, Marietta, Barbara, Arnold, James and Robert. Valoris owned a filling station at Leeds and Markland Ave.

Morris (Feb. 5, 1906-October 1968) married Thelma Waisner. They came to Kokomo in 1932. They had one daughter and two sons: Clara, Richard and Morris.

Horace (March 28, 1908-Sept. 4, 1920) is buried with his father at Lexington Cemetery, Scott County, IN.

Cora Mae (May 2 1910-) married Raymond Boyd. They had no children. They have homes in Jackson, MI and Naples, FL.

Walter Jr. (July 25, 1912-) married Evaleen Hostetteler Jan. 28, 1933. They came to Kokomo in 1934. They had one son and two daughters: Walter Ray, Shirley Jane and Della. Walter had a motorcycle race track on his property and his wife was a teacher at Darrough Chapel School. They moved to Hanover, Jefferson County, IN in 1934.

Rolland (Dec. 5, 1915-Feb. 25, 1943) was never married. He died in Italy during WWII.

Muriel Helena (April 25, 1917 -) married Henry Cochran Sept. 12, 1939. They had one son, Larry. They lived at Indianapolis, IN.

Mary Katherine (Sept. 10, 1919-) married William Foster Sept. 29, 1938. They had one daughter, Rebecca Diann. They lived at Indianapolis and now Lehigh Acres, FL.

Robert Leon (May 30, 1922-May 8, 1943) married Lucy Knick. They had one daughter: Mary Lou. Robert died in Italy during WWII and is buried with his brother Rolland at Scottsburg Cemetery, Scott County, IN.

All the issue of Walter Miller and Clara were born in Scott County, IN. The family was brought to Indiana by Walter's great-grandfather Hugh, a veteran of the Revolutionary War. He was born in Orange County, NC and lived in Greenville County, SC and Shelby County, KY before coming to Indiana. Hugh's father Samuel immigrated from England.

My parents are Edward and Erma (Hadlock). They had two children: Paul Edward and Doris Lorrine (Bryant). *Submitted by Paul E. Parks*

ARTHUR E. "GENE" AND WILMA MAE (SMALL) PARKS -

Gene Parks was born Aug. 30, 1926 at 255 South Liberty Street in Russiaville, IN. He was the only son of Blanche (Morrison) and William Heber Parks. (See their biography elsewhere in this book.)

Gene and Wilma Mae Small were married July 18, 1970 at the East Union Christian Church near Ekin, IN in Tipton County. Wilma was born and raised near Ekin where her grandparents were among the early pioneers of the area. She still owns her homeplace near Ekin. Wilma was born on June 1, 1929, and she was one of two children born to C. Otis "Ote" and Fairy (Sturdevant) Small. Wilma graduated from Jefferson Twp. High School (Tipton County) as valedictorian of her class, and later graduated from the Indiana Business College in Kokomo where she also served as a teacher. She was a secretary at Delco Radio and Haynes Stellite in Kokomo prior to holding the position of Executive Secretary at Public Service Indiana for about 12 years.

Gene and Wilma moved into their newly-completed home at 201 South West Street, Russiaville, IN on their wedding day. They had previously designed their home and Herb Farlow had built it for them. They transferred their church memberships to the Main Street Christian Church in Russiaville on Nov. 14, 1987.

Gene and Wilma Parks

Gene's maternal grandparents were Caswell and Emily (Vickers) Morrison. (See Caswell's biography elsewhere in this book.) His paternal grandparents were John and Ida (Nash) Parks. They lived in Tipton County where he was a farmer and a schoolteacher in the area one-room public schools for several years. Ida died of typhoid fever at age 33 and John died of illness at age 55. Gene had one half-brother, James Robert Hodshire.

Gene graduated from Russiaville High School in 1945. He participated as a member of the school's softball, baseball, and basketball teams. He served in the U.S. Navy from Aug. 10, 1945 to Aug. 20, 1946. He took boot camp at Sampson Naval Training Center near Buffalo, NY and then was stationed at Brooklyn, NY until his discharge.

Entering Purdue University in the fall of 1946, Gene lived at Cary Hall for four years prior to graduating in 1950 with the degree of BPE and state licenses to teach physical education, mathematics, general science and health. He earned the degree of MPE in 1955 with a principal's license. Later, he completed additional graduate courses at Purdue and earned a Supervisor of Guidance license and a Superintendent of Schools license.

Gene's professional career of 38 years was as follows:

1950-51: New Waverly High School, Cass County, math teacher and coach.

1951-53: Camden High School, Carroll County, math teacher and assistant coach.

1953-57: Western High School, Howard County, math teacher and freshmen/assistant coach.

1957-58: Gilead High School, Miami County, principal.

1958-64: Western High School, Howard County, athletic director and assistant principal.

1964-66: Maple Crest School, Kokomo, math teacher and coach.

1966-68: Kokomo School System, Director of Project Open Doors.

1968-84: Kokomo High School (Downtown Campus), assistant principal (curriculum).

1984-88: Kokomo High School (Downtown Campus and South Campus), vice principal (curriculum).

A few of Gene's career highlights include the following:

A. Beginning his teaching career at New Waverly High School where the total enrollment in grades 9-12 was 26 students!

B. Serving as assistant principal and as vice principal in charge of the curriculum at Kokomo High School for 20 years. (He vowed to his parents while a 7th grader that he would someday be part of K.H.S.)!

C. He was the first athletic director of Western High School. In this position, he guided the beginning of football at the school, planned the athletic budget, started and coached the school's first cross-country and golf teams, and coached the 1962 baseball team to a conference championship. He was chosen by the Class of 1954 as one of their two class sponsors in his first year at the school. He planned the lights and bleachers for the football field.

D. Serving as principal at Gilead High School.

E. He planned and implemented the Academic "K" Award at Kokomo High School.

F. He implemented the GED program in Kokomo as a part of the Project Open Doors program.

H. He coached the Maple Crest School cross-country teams to the city championship in 1966.

I. He was especially proud to have had the opportunity to know and to serve a large number of students over the years.

Gene gave full credit for his personal and professional success to his parents for their guidance and support, to his wife for her unwavering love and understanding, and to God for making it all come true. *Submitted by Gene and Wilma Parks*

WILLIAM HEBER PARKS AND BLANCHE (MORRISON) PARKS - Heber Parks was born March 14, 1883 in Tipton County of Indiana. His father was John Parks (1855-1906), a schoolteacher and farmer, and his mother was Ida Jane (Nash) Parks (1863-1896) who died at age 33 of typhoid fever. He had a sister, Lucy, who died at the age of about 10. After Heber's mother died, his father re-married and Heber's half-brother, Paul Allen Parks, was born.

Heber's education consisted of attending the Evans School (later called the Prairie Twp. School), Lindley School, Beach Grove School, and he completed the 8th grade at West Middleton School. He voluntarily repeated the 8th grade there because there were no higher grades offered; however, a two-year high school was then offered at West Middleton which Heber completed.

From 1901 to 1906, he worked as a hired hand for local farmers, including Tommy Wells. His monthly pay was from $15 to $19 per month. During this time, he played on a talented amateur baseball team for West Middleton.

On March 26, 1906, he and Daisy Franklin were married. They began their housekeeping on a 40 acre farm in Tipton County that Heber had purchased with his savings earned as a hired hand.

Wm. Heber Parks and Blanche (Morrison) Parks

From 1906 to 1919, Heber engaged in farming and he owned and operated two billiard establishments in Russiaville, one in Burlington, and one in Kokomo. He also owned and operated a restaurant in Russiaville.

His wife, Daisy, died in March of 1919. She is buried in the New London Cemetery.

In the spring of 1919, he bought a new Model T Ford which had a maximum speed of 35 mph. In the fall of 1919, he and a friend, Mr. Pike, drove the car to California, a trip that took twenty days. Heber worked in the Los Angeles area during the winter of 1919-1920, and he returned to Russiaville in the spring of 1920.

From 1920 to 1924, he worked in Kokomo at the Haynes Auto Plant and at the Apperson Auto Plant where he cut leather for the upholstery of the new cars for wages of $1.00 per hour.

In March of 1924, Heber and Blanche Morrison were married. (See her biography below.) Their son, Gene, was born Aug. 30, 1926. Heber's step-son was James Robert Hodshire.

In August 1937, Heber and Blanche sold their farm in Tipton County and purchased a farm located at the southwest edge of Russiaville where they lived for the remainder of their lives.

Heber passed away on Nov. 30, 1983 at the age of 100 years and 8 1/2 months. He is buried in the Russiaville Cemetery.

Blanche (Morrison) Parks (1899-1969) was born in Tipton County. Her father was Caswell Morrison (1848-1933), a Civil War veteran, and her mother was Emily (Vickers) Morrison.

Blanche moved with her parents to Russiaville from Tipton County in 1905 where she completed the first eight years of her education. She was afflicted with tetanus which, along with her mother's urging, resulted in her withdrawal from school.

Blanche had three sisters (Cora, Vida, and Gertrude) and two brothers (Earl and William). Two other brothers, Daniel and Freddy, died in infancy.

She worked at a cook and as a waitress in the Russiaville restaurants until March of 1924 when she married Heber Parks. She operated a cream station in Russiaville for several years following her marriage.

She was active in the Russiaville Friends Church and she often played the piano for their services.

Blanche died on May 31, 1969 at the age of 69 years. She is buried in the Russiaville Cemetery.

ORA AND JANICE PARKHURST - Ora and Janice Parkhurst were both long-time residents of Kokomo. Janice was born Oct. 24, 1909, Kokomo, daughter of Tom and Emma (Mason) Freed. Ora was born Aug. 6, 1902 in Alexandria, IN, son of Alonzo and Elsie (Pentecost) Parkhurst. Janice and Ora were married Sept. 11, 1925, in Kokomo. Ora was an electrician at a steel mill in Kokomo and died Aug. 14, 1956. After her husband's death and her retirement from Stellite in Kokomo, Janice moved to Covina, CA, to live with her son, Richard. She traveled in a caravan with her daughter's family, became separated on the way west, but still made it to California before her daughter's car arrived! She later returned to Indiana and died Nov. 12, 1986.

Ora and Janice had six children, all of whom were born in Kokomo, and have many descendants living in central Indiana. Their eldest child, Elsie Purvis, was born April 30, 1926, and married Harold Purvis. (See their history under the Harold and Elsie Purvis family.) Their second daughter, Edith Cook, was born May 6, 1928, and married Bob Cook. (See their history under the Bob and Edith Cook family.)

Richard Arlen Parkhurst, was born Aug. 5, 1929. He was in the U.S. Army, 1948-1953, serving in Alaska and Korea. He moved to California in 1959, living in Covina most of the remainder of his life. After graduation from Ball State University, he was a high school teacher and retired after 28 years (four years as department chairman). He sang barbershop harmony and was a member of "The Country Gentleman" barbershop quartet. He was active in the masonic fraternity, serving in numerous positions. He died Jan. 22, 1922, in California.

Robert Leon Parkhurst, the second son of Ora and Janice Parkhurst, was born April 14,1932. He served in the U.S. Army August 1953 to June 1955. He worked for 19 years as a bus driver with Greyhound. He retired to Arcadia, IN, with his wife, Marinell (Ouzts) Parkhurst, whom he married in 1953 in Kokomo. She was born in Pontotoc County, MS, daughter of Walter and Nell (Holliday) Ouzts. Marinell is retired from Delco Electronics. Leon and Marinell have one son, Roger Dale Parkhurst, who was born Dec. 26, 1954, Tacoma, WA. Roger, a machinist and musician, was married to Karen McCullough, and has one daughter, Rachael Elizabeth Parkhurst, born Feb. 5, 1975, Indianapolis, IN.

Russell Ora Parkhurst, Sr., was born May 21, 1934 and is married to Jean Hounchell. (See their family history under the Russell and Jean Parkhurst family.)

Donal Eugene Parkhurst was born Feb. 20, 1939. He was a truck driver, active with the Masons and lived in Frankfort, IN; he died March 19, 1987. He married C. Louise Easterday in 1959; she was born Dec. 2, 1940, Elkhart, IN, daughter of Lucein and Evelyn (Rose) Easterday. Donal and Louise had three children: (1) Donal Eugene Parkhurst, Jr., was born Oct. 31, 1959, Kokomo. He lives in Frankfort, IN, is a store manager, and is married to Robin Sanders; they have a son, Camden Blake Parkhurst, born Sept. 17, 1983, Kokomo. (2) Dawn Louise (Parkhurst) Lowery, born Sept. 8, 1961, Kokomo, is a nurse's aide and lives in Rossville, IN. Dawn married Gary Lee Lowery and they have one son, Derek Wayne Lowery, born Nov. 2, 1987, Lafayette, IN. (3) Philip Alan Parkhurst, born Dec. 16, 1966, Kokomo, lives in Frankfort, IN, and is a factory worker.

The above history is abstracted (with permission) and modified from *The Mason White Family History,* copyright 1990, by James M. Freed. *Submitted by Roger Dale Parkhurst*

RUSSELL AND JEAN PARKHURST - Russell and Jean Parkhurst have lived most of their lives in Howard County and his roots in the county extend back several generations. Russell Ora Parkhurst, Sr., was born May 21, 1934, Kokomo, son of Ora and Janice (Freed) Parkhurst. Jean (Hounchell) Parkhurst was born July 13, 1939, Kenvir, KY, daughter of Clayton Hounchell and Mary (Collect) Hounchell. Russell has retired from Haynes Stellite and Jean is employed at Delco Electronics G.M.C. They are interested in racing, golf, and music. Russell and Jean live in Kokomo and have three children listed below:

Russell Lee (Parkhurst) Draper (known as Rusty), born March 3, 1957, is the son of Russell and his first wife Donna Murphy, and was later adopted by Donna's second husband. Rusty has a degree in business and law and has a U.S. Army career, stationed at Ft. Polk, LA. Rusty has a daughter, Christina Draper, and a son, James Draper.

David Michael (Huff) Parkhurst (known as Mike) was born Nov. 5, 1958, Kokomo, son of James E. Huff and Jean (Hounchell) (Huff) Parkhurst, and adopted in 1963 by Russell Ora Parkhurst, Sr. He graduated from Haworth High School, is an employee of Cabot Corporation and is married to Angela Marie McQuary. Angela was born May 5, 1962, in Kokomo, daughter of James A. and Bonnie Lou (Miller) McQuary. Mike and Angela have one son, Nicholas Daniel Parkhurst, born Dec. 18, 1982, Kokomo, and one daughter, Jordon Marie Parkhurst, born Oct. 15, 1990, Kokomo.

Russell Ora Parkhurst, Jr. (known as Dusty), was born Nov. 25, 1961, Kokomo, son of Russell, Sr., and Jean Parkhurst. He is a graduate of Haworth High School and had additional training in mechanical engineering at Indiana University, Kokomo. Russell, Jr., lives in Kokomo after having lived in St. Petersburg and Clearwater, FL, and is a sheet metal worker. He married (1) Donna Sue Wilson, daughter of William Wilson, Jr., and Ann Ella (Ford) Wilson. They had one son, Christopher Ora Parkhurst, born March 6, 1984, Kokomo. Russell, Jr., married (2) Lisa Campbell, and they have one daughter, Kay LaEllen Parkhurst, born June 22, 1990, Kokomo.

The above history was abstracted and updated with permission from *The Mason-White Family History,* copyright 1990, by James M. Freed. *Submitted by Russell and Jean Parkhurst*

EPH PARSONS AND ROSE CURLY PARSONS - *Romance In The Park And A Little Bit Of History.* In the early 1900s there was a skating rink in what is now known as Highland Park. There a romance started as two young people met.

Eph Parsons, a native of Kokomo and Rose Curly a native of Trenton, NJ whose Irish father migrated to the United States from Ireland to work in the pottery plant.

The plant was moved to Tiffen, OH and then to our Kokomo Pottery which we had for many years in Kokomo.

Eph and Rose were married in Kokomo March 15, 1908. To this union were born seven children:

Loren, Donald, Maxine, Helen, Ray, Richard, and Virginia.

Six of their children are still living; one son, Loren, is deceased. All but one have lived in Kokomo all of their lives. Don resides in Peru, IN.

Rose and Eph set up housekeeping in a country home on West Jefferson Road where they lived and raised their children.

Rose and Eph had 57 years together-Rose died in 1965 and Eph in 1975.

A little bit in the history of their life:

Eph was in the milk business. When they were married, at that time he had a one horse milk wagon. Milk was taken to the town in ten gallon cans. The milk was poured into pints and quarts at every stop.

A bit of humor - sometimes Eph would look back and the family cat was helping himself to milk. His early route was on the north side of Kokomo. Some of the descendants of those families are still living in Kokomo.

Eph was also a gardener. He would take vegetables to town in the milk wagon in the afternoon to help support his family.

In the early 1920's glass milk bottles were used. After picking up the milk from the farmers, Eph would bottle the milk into quarts and pints. Raw milk was still being used.

Around 1930 raw milk could no longer be used. It had to be pasteurized. Eph was unable to do this, so he started selling milk from the Med-O-Bloom Dairy. The route had grown to both North and South Kokomo.

During the war to save gas you were only allowed to deliver every other day.

Eph was assisted through the years by his four sons. Donald followed in his dad's footsteps. Donald graduated from Purdue and had his own dairy, in Peru, for several years.

Eph retired from the business in the 1940s. Ray and Richard delivered the milk for their dad until the 1960s.

Eph and Rose enjoyed their years of retirement, fishing, hunting, and spending time with their grandchildren.

They were charter members of the Highland Park Church in Kokomo until the time of their deaths.

The milk business has always been a part of Kokomo's heritage.

Our family tree

Fathers side:
Grandfather: Ephraim
Grandmother: Elizabeth Jane

Mothers side:
John Curley-from Ireland
Catherine Curley

John Curley: Pottery worker in Tiffin, OH, later moving to Kokomo.

Children of Ephraim and Rose Parsons:

(1) William "Loren" Parsons: Jan. 1, 1909-July 29, 1985. He married Lucille Barthelemy, Feb. 22, 1912-Dec. 30, 1984. Their children:

Milton Joseph, July 23, 1939. He married Rosie Psauf. Their children: Carrie Parsons, Michael Parsons, Ann Parsons, and Susan Parsons.

Thomas Eldon, April 12, 1942. He married Carolyn Parsons Jan. 23, 1930

Steve Kent, June 20, 1945. He married Toni Lucia July 6, 1953. Their children: Jennifer Lynn, Marie Catherine, Melissa, Brent Anthony Bousum, Christie Michelle Isenor, Illa Nae Mae Isenor.

Mary Ann Parsons, May 27, 1950. She married Denny Fernung, April 1, 1948. Their children: Rachel Ann, July 7, 1974; Andrew Phillip, Jan. 7, 1978; Alisha Christine, Oct. 10, 1980.

Loren retired from Continental Steel in sales. Lucille was a homemaker. Her parents were French immigrants.

(2) Donald Ward Parsons, May 15, 1911. He married Doris Dubois Aug. 15, 1912. Their children:

Judy Ann Parsons, Aug. 16, 1942. She married Herbert Bolinger, Jan. 17, 1943. Their children Jason Daniel Dec. 26, 1972 and Chris Alan Aug. 22, 1975.

Barbara Ellen Parsons, June 1, 1944.

Rebecca Rose Parsons March 24, 1948

David William Parsons, June 2, 1950. He married Marcia Overmyer April 1, 1951. Their children: Sara Elizabeth, Oct. 4, 1976, Rachel Christine, Aug. 30, 1979; Julia Kathleen, May 18, 1983.

Don was the owner of the Golden Hill Dairy in Peru. He has retired. Doris was a homemaker.

(3) Maxine Clair Parsons, Jan. 24, 1913. She married Eugene Cratzer, Jan. 11, 1915.

They are charter members of the Highland Park Church in Kokomo. Gene retired from Continental Steel. Maxine worked at the south Continental office at the switchboard.

(4) Helen Catherine Parsons, Aug. 17, 1917. She married Freddie Eugene Pasley, May 30, 1917-June 4, 1986. Their child:

Marleene Sue Pasley, Sept. 14, 1943. She married Lewis Clyde Dowden Nov. 8, 1940. Their children:

Toni Lynnette Dowden May 8, 1960.

Joni Jeannette Dowden, Feb. 23, 1961. She married Wayne Allen Smith, July 10, 1959. Their child is:

Michael Allen Smith Sept. 9, 1981.

Helen Rose Dowden, July 7, 1962. She married Scott Rouch, July 6, 1962. Their children: Alexandra Rae June 22, 1988 and Jacob Keith, July 22, 1992.

Fredrick Earl Dowden, March 1, 1961. He married Christina Kay Frazier June 10, 1966. Their children: Bradley Lewis March 12, 1986 and Nathaniel Fredrick, July 16, 1990.

Helen is retired from Delco Electronics. Freddie retired from Local 440. Helen is a charter member at Highland Park Church.

(5) Richard Earl Parsons, Aug. 11, 1921. He married Marie Francis Bell, Aug. 7, 1929. Their children

Rick Parsons, Aug. 10, 1955. He married Cathy Byers, July 16, 1957. Their child: Zachery William June 7, 1985.

Sharon Rose Parsons Sept. 24, 1957. She married Lenard Baxter II April 22, 1961.

Gary Eugene Parsons Dec. 1, 1958. He married Jane Farris.

Sandra Kay Parsons Jan. 3, 1961. She married Stanley J. McNulty. Their children: Clayton Richard, June 21, 1988; Brook Marie, July 30, 1991.

Richard retired from Stellite and the Parsons Dairy. Marie worked at the Ford home on Sycamore and the Kokomo School System. Richard has a twin brother named Raymond.

(6) Raymond Lewis Parsons, Aug. 11, 1921. He married Lavonne Wright, Dec. 17, 1927. Their child:

Randall Parsons May 15, 1955.

Raymond retired from Prudential Insurance and Parsons Dairy. He now is working at Beckley Office and Computer Service. Raymond has a twin brother named Richard. Lavonne worked as a legal secretary and was a secretary at IUK.

(7) Virginia Rose Parsons, April 13, 1925. She married James Robert Evans, June 14, 1924. Their children:

David James Evans April 27, 1955. He married Sherril Bagwell, Sept. 10, 1954. Their children: Heather Ann, Aug. 6, 1974; Heath David, Jan. 13, 1977; Haley Crystal, May 6, 1986; Hillary Brook, May 1, 1990.

Jeffrey Robert Evans, July 20, 1957. He married Cathy Faye Gilliam, Nov. 8, 1956.

Virginia worked at Stellite and was also a homemaker. James retired from the postal service and now works part-time at Dave Evans Tires.

JOSEPH AND INA PARSONS - The marriage of Joseph Parsons and Ina Cook wedded members of families who had been in the United States a long time. The Parsons came originally from Sommerset County, England.

Joseph's mother was a Breedlove, a family widely recognized as being "handy" - the word Frederick J. Turner employed to emphasize the skills in using their hands which Europeans acquired in their adaptation to frontier life.

The mother of Allen Cook, Ina's father, was a Gilbert. They were a Welsh family, living in Henry County, who met periodically in the Gilbert family reunion. Our mother, Ina, attended such a reunion in the early 1920s. The older women wore Quaker lace bonnets and addressed other folk as "thee," "thou," and "thine." The mother of Ina was born Elma Stanley in North Carolina in 1851. The Stanleys came from London. Her father was active in the "underground railway," helping slaves escape to freedom. In 1865, the Stanley family moved to Henry County, IN, joining their kinfolk, crossing the Alleghenies at the Cumberland Gap. Joseph and Ina were married in 1900 and settled in Howard County in a house that Joseph built. They lived in Center Twp 30 years, then Liberty Twp and moved to Kokomo in 1946. They had eight children, three daughters and five sons. Ina died in 1963 age 84 and Joseph in 1972 at age 96.

Joseph Henry Parsons; Ina Cook Parsons

The two oldest children and the two youngest children survive in 1993. Of the daughters, Mildred, born 1908, never married, dying in Kokomo in 1977. Edith was born in 1901; she married Dale LaRowe in 1935. He died in 1987. Edith was a long-time church secretary. They had one son, Myron (born 1939). He graduated from University of Wisconsin with a degree in law and has a practice in Reedsburg, WI. He married Rosemary Waeffler in 1963. They have four children: Mark, Matthew, Christopher and Melinda.

The younger daughter Geneva, married Ernest Fawcett in 1940. He operated the Higbee Body Company in Kokomo for 37 years where Geneva served as secretary. They have one child, John. He graduated from School of Optometry at Indiana University and has a practice in Kokomo. He married Lillie Daffron in 1968. They have one child, Patricia.

The third son, Delbert J. born 1911, graduated from Indiana University Medical School in 1939. He was a physician in Springfield, OH. He married Myrle Davis in 1940. He died in 1976. They had three children. Rebecca graduated from Virginia Commonwealth University with a master's degree. She is on the staff of a school for the disabled. In 1964 she married Buell Messer. They have two sons: Charles and Michael. The latter married Penny Gregory in 1990. They have one son Michael. Both sons work in the family landscape business in Staunton, VA. The second child of Delbert and Myrle, Douglas lives at home. Their third child, Charles, married Jade Westfall in 1971. He graduated from Indiana University Medical School in 1974 and has a private practice in Springfield, OH. They have three children: Anne, Chad and Joseph.

The fourth son, Lloyd born 1914, farmed the family farm in Liberty Twp. He married Melba Freeman in 1936. He died in 1956. They had five sons. Melba and Jerry Joe, live on the home farm. James is a farm manager. He married Madonna Griffith in 1965. They have two sons: Donald and Jeffrey. Daniel is an accountant. He married Kathleen Young in 1964. They have four children: Michael, Rick Allen, Fredrick Lloyd and Jennay. Rolla Lee married Karen Hadley in 1978. He is the county agent of Hamilton County. They have three children: Heather, Holly and Jason Howard. The fifth son, Russell graduated from Wilmington College in 1981 and is a minister in the Society of Friends. Russell married Darlene Beck and

283

they have three children: Robert Lloyd, Alan Joseph and Sarah Elizabeth.

L-R: first row: Delbert J., Joseph, Geneva, Ina, Kenneth; back row: Howard, Lloyd, Oswand, Edith and Mildred

Howard, the fifth son, of Joseph and Ina Parsons, was born in 1916. He had a career as a foreign service officer. He married Priscilla White in 1940. They divorced in 1978. Howard married Evelyn Holmes in 1978. They now live in Madison, CT. Howard and Priscilla had two sons William and George. Williams is a security analyst with Keystone Custodian Funds, Inc. He married Margot Palaith in 1966. They have two sons, Jedediah and Zachary. George lives in Washington, DC and is retired on disability from the US Navy. He married Delores Del-Agua in 1975. They have one son, Alan Drew.

Of the sons of Joseph and Ina, two survive in 1993. Kenneth born 1903, now retired, had most of his professional career in the Department of Agricultural Economics of the University of Wisconsin. He married Pauline Livingston in 1931. Pauline died in 1987. They had two daughters: Priscilla born 1937 and Patricia born 1941. Priscilla married Svat Soucek in 1966; they have no children. They live in Princeton, NJ. She is a professor of Art History at the Institute of Fine Arts, New York City. Patricia married Stafford Kay in 1965. They served in Kenya in the Peace Corps. She is a librarian at Australian Embassy in Washington. They have two children: Peter and Laura.

The second son Oswand, had a career in the west. He married Alice Vandercook in 1941. He died in Scottsville, AZ in 1980, Alice in 1992. They had one child Ann. She married Pedro Estay in 1967. They operate an import-export business in Greensboro, NC and Santiago, Chile. They have one child, Susan. She graduated from Arizona State University at Tempe. She married Sean Daniels in 1993. They are stockbrokers in Los Angeles.

WILLIAM JOE PAYNE - William Joe Payne was born in Forest Township of Clinton County, IN on Oct. 4, 1924. His father was John Leonard Wilkinson Payne born, June 27, 1889 in Madison County, NC, died May 27, 1964 Howard County, IN, the son of Joel Jeptha Payne, who was born Aug. 4, 1853 in Madison County, NC and died Dec. 1, 1946 in Delaware County, IN, and Amanda Amerette Henderson, born Jan. 20, 1860 in Hudson Valley, TN and died April 29, 1905 in Hot Springs, NC. Joel Jeptha Payne's father was Daniel A. Payne, born Nov. 8, 1831 in Buncombe County, NC and died May 21, 1891 in Madison County, NC. Joel Jeptha Payne's mother was Senia Ball born July 16, 1833 Buncombe County, NC and died June 28, 1860 in Madison County, NC.

Our subject's mother was Effie Marie Johnson born Oct. 27, 1895 in Forest Township of Clinton County, and died Sept. 9, 1966 in Howard County, IN the daughter of Albert Tell Johnson and Virena Ellen Vennaman. Albert Tell Johnson's father was Robert Cook Johnson from Isle of Wight County, VA and his mother was Elizabeth Dennis of Henry County, IN. Virena Ellen Vennaman's father was Cornelius Vennaman of Ohio and her mother was Lewrana Morgan born Aug. 20, 1824 in Guilford County, NC, and died Jan. 14, 1897 in Howard County, IN. Lewrana Morgan's father was Kitchen Morgan, born April 4, 1797 and died May 13, 1880 in Parke County, IN and her mother was Sarah Johnston, born June 2, 1800 and died June 1, 1883 in Parke County, IN.

Our subject's brothers were John Robert Payne, born March 18, 1917 and married Emma Jean McAninch, born Aug. 25, 1918, and James Albert Payne, born April 20, 1920 and married Arlene LeMaster, born Jan. 15, 1924, and his sisters were Rosemary Ellen (Payne) Carter, born May 1, 1918 and married to Robert Carter, born Nov. 26, 1913 and died Jan. 7, 1954, and Patricia Sue (Payne) Pruett, born April 5, 1936 and married to John Duane Pruett, born Jan. 2, 1934. All but Patricia Sue were born on the Johnson home place in Forest Township, located approximately two miles east of Forest, IN in Clinton County. Patricia Sue was born on the Honey Creek Township farm located one and a quarter mile west and one and quarter mile south of Russiaville, IN. The family moved to the Honey Creek Township farm in February, 1929. William graduated from the Russiaville High School in the spring of 1942. He later took special courses at IUPUI, Indianapolis and IU, Kokomo Campus. He attended special fire training at Ann Arbor, MI and the Indianapolis-Marion County Fire Training Center. He took special management training courses during his employment with Chrysler Corp.

His family were farmers and he followed that profession until 1948. In January 1948 he joined the Shell American Petroleum Company in Kokomo, IN. In October of 1955 he joined Chrysler Corporation as a security officer. At the time he retired on April 30, 1980 he was fire chief of the Chrysler Kokomo Complex. He was called out of retirement in 1986 to train new Chrysler security personnel and stayed on for several years helping with security work and training.

On April 10, 1943 he married Vivian Marie Wheeler. They had three children, Judith Marie, born Oct. 24, 1943 and married to Jimmy Roger Harbin, born Feb. 20, 1943, John William, born Dec. 3, 1945 and married to Dixie Diane Bolen, and Deborah Lee, born Sept. 26, 1958 and married to Gary Keith Fuller, born Sept. 8, 1959.

William was a Methodist and had been at one time, Sunday School teacher, Sunday School superintendent, finance chairman, youth leader, and lay speaker for that faith. He also had been active for some 20 years of his life in the Boy Scout movement and held a Life Scout rank, and held all troop leadership positions including Scoutmaster in Russiaville, IN.

William was a member and past president of the Taylor Township Lions Club at Center, IN, past president of the Indiana Society of Industrial Security, Member of IOOF Lodge 133 of Kokomo, IN, and member of Naphtali Lodge 389. F &AM at Center, IN.

H.W. (HOD) PEABODY AND BARBARA RUCHTI PEABODY - October 18, 1978, was the beginning of the Peabody history in Howard County, when his profession moved them here from Waukesha, WI to the Scout Executive of Sagamore Council, B.S.A. That position was their livelihood until his retirement in 1988 after 38 years in his profession.

Hod, born Sept. 30, 1923 was raised in Milton, WI. His parents, Kendall William Peabody, born 1888 in Johnstown, WI and Florence Eden Mawhinney born 1888 in Lima Center, WI were farmers much of their lives - Hod is the youngest of six children - Elnora, Kendall, Hannah, Charles, Florence. He served in the Marines during World War II and the Korean Conflict.

Front: Alan and Linda Bacock. 2nd Karen and Eric Peabody, Todd and Nancy Peabody. Back Row: Jack, Barbara, Hod and Tom Peabody

Barbara, born July 29, 1929 in Janesville, WI. Her parents Leo A. Ruchti born 1882 and Hazel Stephns born 1894 in Fennimore, WI where they were both raised. After their marriage, they moved to Janesville as farmers, and then sold insurance. Barbara has one brother Stephen.

The Peabody genealogy has been traced to 61AD in England, from a rugged individual name of Broadie, which later came to mean "body" and pea which mean "mountain" where they lived in Wales; the leader of the clan was named "Peabodie" or the mountain man later changed to Peabody. A gap of several generations has not been traced until we can link it to John Peabody who came to America from England in 1635, and carried the genealogy up to date.

Hod and Barbara met at Milton College in Milton, WI and were married on June 25, 1949. The Peabody family became part of the mobile society of the late 20th century, so each of their three children were born in different cities. Jack Gregory was born Sept. 14, 1950 in Edgerton, WI, Thomas Allen born Oct. 28, 1952 in Oak Park, IL and Linda Lee born March 8, 1956 in Evergreen Park, IL. All three of the children were educated and are graduates of the University of Wisconsin system but each from a different campus.

Jack, a chemical engineer working in the environmental field, has been moved from coast to coast with their family of two sons. Tom chose a career in the United States Marine Corps as a supply officer using his business management education, and they are raising two sons and a daughter. Linda is currently a homemaker and preschool teacher busy raising a son and a daughter. Although they started their married life in Kokomo, they have moved a number of times to different locations around the country in the cable television industry.

Hod and Barbara have spent their entire Howard County life in the Green Acres Subdivision located at 8955 West County Road 00 North South. Gardening is a very important part of their lives and retirement has given them ample opportunity to travel and work as volunteers in many organizations, which include - The First Congregational Christian Church, American Red Cross, Boy Scouts of America, Service Corps of Retired Executives, Habitat for Humanity, Rotary Club, Nearly New Shop, Wildcat Creek Guardians, Meals On Wheels and United Way.

JOHN AND MARIE PEACOCK - In May 1950, John and Marie Peacock purchased the business of the Sam Moore Funeral Home at 705 N. Main St. from Geneva Moore. Sam Moore had passed away two years previous and Mrs. Moore was carrying on the business with the help of her embalmer, Joesph Leap. Joe was now taking a position with First National Bank so Mrs. Moore was anxious to sell. Ambulance calls at that time were $3.00 to any part of Howard County.

In the spring of 1952 the Peacocks purchased the old Redman home at 414 W Jefferson St. from Mary Redman. That building converted into a larger funeral home.

Peacock was elected coroner of Howard County in the fall 1952, 1956 and 1964. He lost a race for mayor to John Miller in the fall of 1959. He also lost a race for coroner in the fall of 1968. In the fall of 1971, John was elected Mayor of Kokomo for one term. Some of the accomplishments John felt he helped bring about were . . . the establishing of a bus system for the senior citizens in 1974, the widening of Washington Street to four lanes, encouraging the railroads to repair many railroad crossings, and the replacing of many damaged sidewalks through the CETA program.

The Peacock Funeral Home was sold in March 1977 and is now owned by Toby Hoffman. John's death followed in April 1977.

WAYNE A. AND BERNICE (WILLIAMS) PEARSON - Wayne A. Pearson was born on Dec. 26, 1912, at Wabash County, IN, the son of Harry A. and Nellie (Burkholder) Pearson. Harry and Nellie were married May 11, 1908, and had two other children in addition to Wayne, an older son, Charles, and a younger daughter, Geneva. Harry Pearson operated a farm near Roann, IN, and died on July 31, 1916, at the age of 30 years. Wayne came to Kokomo with his mother and attended school at Kokomo High School, graduating with the class of 1932.

L-R: Back Row: Neal, Phillip, Ross. Front Row: Bernice, Janet, Wayne Pearson

The following summer, on Aug. 29, 1933, Wayne was united in marriage with Bernice Williams and they became the parents of four children: Janet, Ross, Phillip J., and Neal. Wayne Pearson retired in 1976 after 42 years of service with American Standard Pottery Company and passed away on July 12, 1982, at his home near Burlington, IN.

I. Bernice Williams was born at Kokomo, IN, on July 12, 1914, the only daughter of Ross B. an Emma P. (Brown) Williams, and died on Sept. 9, 1990. Her father, Ross Benjamin Williams, was born in Grant County near the town of Herbst, on July 19, 1885. He was one of six children born to Elijah and Melissa (LaForge) Williams. When he was 20 years of age, Ross came to Kokomo to live and began working at Kingston Products Corporation where he remained employed for 37 years. In May of 1913, Ross was married to Emma Pearl Brown, daughter of Matthew and Nancy Ann (Lanning) Brown, and his death occurred on Jan. 7, 1943. His wife, Emma, was born on Aug. 11, 1885, in Franklin County, IN, and died on Nov. 3, 1980, at the age of 95. *Submitted by Kent A. Smith*

HIRAM PENLAND - Hiram Fernandes Penland was born March 22, 1841 around Elkhart County, IN. His parents were John Penland (born c. 1819 Ohio) and Mary A. Abshire (born c. 1822 Ohio). He married Lettica E. Price around 1865. Together they had three daughters: Mary Ellen born 1865-6 Indiana, Ruth "Lorena" born Dec. 14, 1868 Indiana, and Margaret born c. 1871-2 Michigan. Hiram's wife died Aug. 13, 1873 (age 31) and was buried in the Riverview Cemetery in Berrien Springs, MI. After her death Hiram brought his family to Jerome, IN where he purchased farm land to farm and worked as mill operator at the mill in Jerome. The girls attended school in Jerome. Lorena took two years of eighth grade because she was unable to attend high school as none was available.

Hiram F. Penland and second wife Mary Carey

Hiram eventually remarried a widow named Mary Carey (almost 10 years older) on July 10, 1875 in Howard County. They resided in or near Greentown in Liberty Township with his daughters and his new wife's son Grant Cary (born c. 1874-5). Hiram died May 16, 1927 and was buried in the Greenlawn Cemetery in Greentown. His second wife died sometime before he did.

Besides farming and operating the Jerome Mill, Hiram was also known for building several homes within Greentown, still standing today. Hiram had an eye disease that rendered him nearly blind near the age of 60. His granddaughter, Mary Johnson-Ericson remembers him while in the care of her mother, Lorena Penland-Johnson during the last years of his life. *Submitted by Cathie A. Sutterfield*

RUTH LORENA PENLAND - Ruth "Lorena" Penland was born Dec. 14, 1868 in Indiana. She was the daughter of Hiram Fernandes Penland (1841-1927 Indiana) and Lettica E. Price (1842-1873 Missouri). Lorena was one of three daughters. Her sisters were Mary Ellen born 1865-6 Indiana and Margaret born 1871-2 Michigan. Lorena's mother died at age of 31 in Berrien Springs, MI. After her mother's death her father moved to Jerome, IN where he purchased farm land and operated the mill on the Wild Cat River in Jerome. On July 10, 1875 her father remarried a widow named Mary Carey (born c. 1832 d. ?). The new family resided in Liberty Township near Greentown and the girls attended a one-room school house in Jerome. Besides a new mother, Lorena had a step-brother named Grant Carey (born 1874-5). Lorena loved school and learning as much as she could, so she repeated eighth grade because at that time it was the highest grade available.

Ruth Lorena Penland

On Dec. 19, 1889 in Howard County, Lorena married Austin Lincoln Johnson the son of David Johnson and Belinda Davis of Howard County, formerly of Henry County, IN. Austin was born May 12, 1862 near Greentown and was one of ten children. Together they had a total of 13 children: Charles F. (1891-1957), Don (1892-1970), Emor (1894-1977), Glen (1896-1984), Raymond (1899-1957), Wayne Theodore (1900-still living), Virgil (1902-?), Malcolm (Gig) (1904-1970), Leon Strangeman (1906-1972), Robert Edward (1908-1973), David Franklin (1910-1910), Mary Elizabeth (1911-still living), and Roscoe Carmony (1915-1990).

Lorena was very self-educated and widely read and all were amazed at her ability in spelling and math. As quoted by her only daughter, Mary Johnson-Ericson Dec. 17, 1977: "As I think back on those days I remember a woman, wise, capable in all areas, and energetic. I heard her say that at one time she wasn't away from home, even to Greentown, for a period of three years! She did not complain of her lot and she was one that many came to for her counsel. Her sense of humor was, I am sure, one of the things that kept her encouraged and happy. One of the highlights in her life was when she was chosen the Centennial Queen for the Greentown Centennial. As you know to be eligible you had to have lived in the community for 50 years and be past 75 years of age. The Centennial was in 1948 and she was 80 years old. Her last five years were spent with us in our home (Windfall). She was a joy to have and was active up to within three days before her death in (February 8,) 1961."

Lorena is buried in the Greenlawn Cemetery in Greentown next to her husband who died Sept. 21, 1940. Lorena and Austin had a total of 27 grandchildren living in Indiana, Michigan, Illinois and Wisconsin. *Submitted by Cathie A. Sutterfield*

PERKINS - William Albert Perkins (1880-1925) and Grace Ethyl Jetmore Perkins (1888-1927) were married on Dec. 24, 1904 in Delaware County, IN. Sometime after 1910 they moved to Howard County.

The couple had four children: Ted, Leona Pearl, Ernest Leroy, who died as an infant and Lillian. The first three children were born in Grant County. Lillian may also have been born in Grant County but no record has been found.

William died on March 12, 1925 in his home following an extended illness. Grace remarried shortly thereafter. She married a man named Redding and moved back to Delaware County where she died on May 15, 1927. William and Grace are buried side-by-side in IOOF Cemetery in Marion along with their infant son Ernest.

Leona Pearl (1907-1976) married Jerome Benton Weir (1905-1974) of Anderson on July 6, 1926. His parents were Benton William and Mary Frances Weir. Leona was a housewife and Jerome, called Joe, worked for Dirilyte Corporation of America. Joe and Leona lived in Puerto Rico for a time while Joe helped set up a new factory there.

Joe and Leona had six children: Donald Jerome, William David, Earl Eugene, Lilly Joann, Hazel Eileen and Frank Rudy. All six children were born in Kokomo. The family lived at 1032 W. State St. until the children were grown. At that time the property was bought by Continental Steel. Joe and Leona then built a house on Mohr Dr. After a time the couple moved to the Rochester area where they bought a home on the Tippecanoe River.

Joe died on June 24, 1974. Leona remarked at the time that she wanted to be with Joe on their 50th anniversary. Leona died on July 4, 1976. She was reunited with Joe two days before their 50th anniversary.

William David married Betty Jane Beaman on Aug. 25, 1951. Betty is the daughter of Paul William and Artha Ivaah Worthington Beaman. Betty worked as a secretary until 1958. William worked as a terminal manager for trucking companies. At the time of his death in 1967, he worked for Kain's Motor Co. After Bill's death Betty married Meinert Miller.

Bill and Betty had two children: Suzette Lorraine and William Jr. Both children were born in Kokomo. Bill Jr. has a degree in business from IUK and is working at Chrysler. He married Patricia Kim Stark. She is the daughter of Paul and Carmen Stark of Kokomo. Bill and Kim have two children: William David III and Jennifer Leigh.

Suzette, the author of this article, was born on July 13, 1953 and is employed by Delco Electronics. Suzi married John Robert Kuntz on Dec. 30, 1972. John is the son of George Leroy and Barbara B. Miller Kuntz. John is the assistant parts manager at Kokomo Chrysler-Plymouth.

PETRO - James Addison (1844-1901) and Rebecca Rich Petro (1846-1931) came to Howard County from Rush County, IN in 1867 settling in Taylor Township. The couple had seven children: Ellora Cottingham, Walter, James M., Carrie E. Cuthrell Sprinkle, Joseph E., Alma Quick and Bessie Swan. James was a farmer and was a school teacher during the Civil War. Rebecca was one of the charter members of Macedonia Christian Church.

Their son Joseph Ernest (1878-1952) married Florella Belle McDaniel (1879-1920) on Feb. 21, 1901. Florella was the daughter of Christopher Columbus and Mary Ellen Ayres McDaniel of Union Township. The newlyweds moved to the McDaniel homestead and Mr. Petro farmed the land from 1901 until 1937. Joseph, known as Ernie, and Florella had four children, Mary Esco English (1905-), Robert (1908-), Karll (1913-1924), and Charles (1915-1969). Ernie married Blanche Thrawley McDaniel in 1925. Ernie and Blanche were members of Meridian St. Christian Church in Greentown.

Charles married Ethel Poe (1916-) of Grant County, IN on Oct. 9, 1937. Ethel is the daughter of Sandy W. (1878-1966) and Ina Kelley Poe (1884-1969) who lived around Swayzee, IN much of their life. Both Sandy and Ina came from families who had settled in Grant County in the mid 1800's. Charles farmed the family homestead from 1937 until his death in 1969. Ethel is a homemaker. Charles and Ethel had six children, Charles (1940), James (1941), Carole (1945-), Sharon (1947-), Nancy (1950-), and Joseph (1953-1984). Charles and Ethel

285

became members of Meridian St. Christian Church in Greentown in the 1930's.

Carole, Sharon, Nancy and Joe are graduates of Eastern High School. Carole graduated from Ball Memorial School of Nursing in Muncie and has a BSN from Indiana University. She is currently working on a MLS degree from Indiana University. She worked in hospitals in Indianapolis while pursuing her BSN and later worked in VISTA in Cincinnati, OH. After leaving VISTA she worked in public health nursing in Cincinnati for 15 years. She is currently employed at Saint Joseph at Home in Kokomo, IN as a home health care nurse.

Sharon Petro Hahn and Nancy Petro Laurell graduated from Ball State University. Sharon taught home economics in Miami and Tipton County schools. She is currently a self-employed craftsperson. She has two children, Chad (1977-) and Kimberly (1981-). They live north of Amboy in Miami County.

Nancy worked as an elementary school teacher in Georgia, Ohio, and Texas. She married Richard A. Laurell in 1968; they have three sons, David (1983-), Matthew (1984-), and Stephen, (1986-). They currently reside in Batesville, IN.

Joseph, better known as Joe, attended Ivy Tech in Kokomo. He was a soil tester for a construction firm in Covington, KY and resided in Cincinnati, OH.

Howard County has been a good home to the Petros for over 125 years with the hope for many more good years.

PICKERING - On Nov. 1, 1852, a group of wagons left Rheatown, TN, bound for New London, IN. Several years before, in 1847, Phineas Pickering had left Tennessee with his family and eventually they made their way to the New London area of Howard County. In 1852, he went home for a visit and when he returned to Indiana he was accompanied by several members of his family, including his brother Jonathan with his wife Jane, his sister Rebecca, her husband Wesley Grubbs and their three children - Ellis P. (born 1836), Elizabeth Jane (born 1845) and John (born 1849). As they made their way through Tennessee and Kentucky, Jonathan kept a diary telling of the miles traveled each day, unusual sights observed, and crossing the Ohio River at Cincinnati where they counted 30 steamboats docked and saw their first train. They crossed White River at Indianapolis, journeyed northward on Michigan Road, then to Alto and New London. Wesley and his family were Quakers and settled near the little community of West Middleton. The entire trip took 27 days.

Charles and Ora Belle Webb

Rebecca Pickering died on Nov. 27, 1858. Wesley farmed and had a small parcel of land in Monroe Township in 1877. Elizabeth met a neighbor boy, James M. Webb. The Webbs—George, Sarah and their nine children—lived nearby. James enlisted in the Civil War at New London on Aug. 13, 1862 - the same day as his father George. James mustered out of the Army on July 19, 1865, at Mobile, AL, and a few weeks later, on Aug. 22, 1865, he and Elizabeth were married. They became the parents of Wesley J. (1868-1946), Charles E. (1871-1955), George E. (1872-1955), Rebecca E. (1874-1926), Willis A. (1877-?) and Lucy Ellen (1880) who died in infancy. In 1877 James and Elizabeth moved to Moultrie County, IL, where he had brothers and sisters. James died of tuberculosis contracted during the Civil War and is buried in Yarnel (Hampton) Cemetery near Sullivan, IL. Elizabeth returned to New London and died a few months after her husband on April 30, 1881, from complications of measles. She is buried in the Pleasant Hill Friends Cemetery. Elizabeth's brother Ellis P. Grubbs, who had married Eliza Bright, became the guardian of the young children. Rebecca Eunice was taken by Henry Rinehart and his wife and they moved to Kansas. There she met and married George Flory, and in 1912 they moved to Whittier, CA, where they raised a family of six children. Wesley lived in Frankfort, George moved to Dexter, IA, and Willis lived in Kokomo. Ellis Grubbs died June 29, 1917. He and his wife are buried in the New London Cemetery. My grandfather was Charles Ellsworth Webb. He married his cousin Ora Belle Twineham Sept. 20, 1892. Charles and Ora Belle were devout Quakers, and except for seven years in Sullivan, IL, they lived their entire married life in Monroe Township where they were members of the Friends Church and caretakers of the property and cemetery. They raised four sons - Vern E. (1894-1977), Earl M. (1896-1966), Norval E. (1898-1974), and Walter R. (1900-1986). Norval graduated from Earlham College and was a Friends minister, Earl graduated from Earlham and was superintendent of schools in Berne, IN, Walter was employed by the Kokomo public schools. Vern married Sophronia Allena Howe on June 27, 1914, raised a family of 11 children, and was a postal carrier and barber in Kokomo. They were my parents. *Submitted by Carl E. Webb*

PIERCE - Howard County hosts many descendants of Alexander S. and Nancy (Skinner) Pierce. Alex was born May 6, 1809 in Kentucky or Tennessee. He married Nancy March 2, 1834, in Decatur County, IN. Nancy was born Feb. 19, 1814 and died Nov. 23, 1880. They had nine children. Seven of these children lived in and around Howard County. After Nancy's death Alex married in 1883 to Delia A. McFee. He died March 26, 1899, and is buried with Nancy and son Alexander in Michigantown, IN. Their children were: Mariah Louisa born Nov. 10, 1835, she married Thomas M. Thompson, Sept. 28, 1854 in Clinton County. To them were born, Joseph A., Francis P., Lovil F., Lydia, Lulu E., Ida A., John A. and Charles.

Alexander S. Pierce

Ludica J. born Sept. 10, 1837 married Mathias Yerigan, March 21, 1858 in Clinton County. They had two sons, Samuel C. and James Manford. Mathias died April 3, 1861. She then married John R. Pritts (brother of Catherine Pritts Pierce) Nov. 13, 1862. He served in the Civil War, they had no children and he died March 12, 1877. In 1881 she married Francis M. Hill, in Kokomo. They had no children. She died May 15, 1889 and is buried in Crown Point Cemetery.

Samuel C. is featured elsewhere in this publication.

Harriet was born Oct. 26, 1842. She first married Eli T. Michael, Sept. 30, 1861 in Clinton County. They had two sons, Willard Eli and Fredrick. This marriage was doomed from the start and caused the family a great deal of scandal. They divorced after he come home from the Civil War. She then married Herman Horace Uttinger. They moved to Clay Township in Howard County where she died May 28, 1875. They had no children. She is buried in an unmarked grave at the Shiloh Cemetery.

Charles William was born Nov. 2, 1843 and married Oct. 14, 1867 in Kokomo to Mary Anna Horner. They had three children, Nora Bell, Lovell Dewitt and William Oscar. After Mary Anna's death he had two short marriages. He died July 3, 1917 in White County where he and Mary Anna had moved to. They are both buried in White County.

Henry Samuel was born May 23, 1846. He never married, a casualty of the Civil War. He died in the Cumberland Hospital in Nashville, TN. He was first laid to rest at the Nashville City Cemetery, as were many other Union soldiers. When the National Cemetery was established in Nashville, all the Union soldiers were re-interred in the National Cemetery. He died June 8, 1865.

Wesley/Wesley J. was born Aug. 10, 1848 and married Mary C. Gray in Kokomo before 1880, as they appear in the 1880 Howard County Census living with her father, Amos Gray. Another marriage in Howard County was found dated April 24, 1886 to a Alice Smith. In 1899 when his father died he was listed as living in Indianapolis. A complete search was made of the Indianapolis area and the only Wesley Pierce found was married to a Minnie Wright, who had a son Embert Wright. They are buried at the Crown Hill Cemetery. Nothing else is known of this man and his life, except he was a painter and plasterer.

Alexander S. was born July 27, 1851 in Clinton County. He died as a young man April 27, 1870 and is buried in Michigantown with his parents.

Amanda Jane, the youngest, is also featured elsewhere in this publication. *Submitted by Candy Jones*

CHARLES WILLIAM PIERCE - Charles William Pierce was born, the fifth child of Alexander S. and Nancy (Skinner) Pierce, Nov. 2, 1843 in Decatur County, IN. He married Mary Anna Horner, Oct. 14, 1867 in Howard County. Mary Anna was born Sept. 6, 1853, the daughter of Dewitt Clinton and Mariah (Scott) Horner.

Charles William and Mary Anna (Horner) Pierce

Mary Anna died May 13, 1905. Charles William then married Eliza J. McCloud; he later married again to Eliza Osborne. No children were born to the last two marriages. He died July 3, 1917.

The children of Charles William and Mary Anna were: Nora Bell (Feb. 21, 1872-Oct. 9, 1950). Nora married three times, William Downs, George M. "Jake" Amich and Phillip Heutebuch. She had no children.

Lovell Dewitt, who is featured elsewhere in this publication.

William Oscar (Feb. 9, 1876-June 27, 1944). William married Emma R. Shuey. To this union was born one child, a son, William Orthis. William Orthis was born Feb. 20, 1899.

CLARENCE "CECIL" PIERCE - Clarence Cecil was born June 11, 1898 in White County, IN, the son of Lovell DeWitt and Myrtie Bell (Roberts) Pierce. He married Oct. 30, 1918 to Emma Percival, daughter of Harry and Mary Jane (Connor) Percival. Emma was born Aug. 27, 1898 in Kokomo.

They were the parents of three children: James Robert was born Aug. 10, 1919 in Kokomo. He married Marcella Christine Degler, April 21, 1940 in Kokomo. They had three children, Trudy Kay, Rita Marie and Steven Taylor.

Norma Jean was born Aug. 4, 1922 in Kokomo. She married Paul C. Loman, July 2, 1942 in Kokomo. They were the parents of three sons, Gary Davis, Jeffrey Todd and Gregory. On Sept. 1, 1977 Norma died. She is buried at Crown Point Cemetery.

The third child of Cecil and Emma is Virginia Lee. She married E.P. Severns Jr. and is featured elsewhere in this publication.

Cecil died Aug. 30, 1950 and Emma died on the 20th day of July 1975. They are both buried at Crown Point Cemetery. Cecil had worked at Pittsburgh Plate Glass Company, then for the Continental Steel Corp as a guard. Emma had worked at the Jenkins Glass Factory, Delco and retired from the Stellite Corp.

LOVELL DEWITT PIERCE - Lovell DeWitt Pierce was born Feb. 6, 1874 to Charles William and Mary Anna (Horner) Pierce. He married Myrtie Bell Roberts, Dec. 4, 1891 in White County, IN. She was the daughter of George D. and Elva Rosina (Thorp) Roberts. She was born July 15, 1874.

To this union were born eight children.

Their first born, a female was stillborn Aug. 11, 1892.

Elmer Verne, Sept. 20, 1893-Oct. 26, 1979, married Ferne Victoria LaReau, Oct. 15, 1917. They had one daughter, Nedra.

Clarence Cecil, who is featured elsewhere in this publication.

George William, July 9, 1901-Feb. 11, 1904.

Mable Nora, Dec. 28, 1906, she married Noah King, Nov. 16, 1929. They had one son, Jack Allen.

Lovell Alexander, "Tommy", March 14, 1909-March 1, 1925.

Galen Morris, Dec. 9, 1910-Sept. 27, 1971. He married Margaret Baker in November 1945. They had one son, Mark Galen.

Glen Clyde, April 18, 1916-July 5, 1954, married Pearl Hinderlider, Feb. 4, 1940. They had two children, Larry Eugene and Judith Lee.

Clarence "Cecil" married and raised his family in Howard County mostly unaware of the many "Pierce" relatives they had in the area. The bulk of Lovell and Myrtie Bell's family remained in the White County area.

PIERCE - Samuel Clinton Pierce was born Oct. 2, 1839 in Decatur County, IN, the third child and oldest son of Alexander S. and Nancy (Skinner) Pierce.

On Aug. 1, 1867 in Russiaville he married Catherine Pritts, daughter of Levi and Phebe (Pyle/Pile) Pritts. She was born March 4, 1851 in Somerset County, PA.

Sam was a veteran of the Civil War and member of the GAR.

To them were born nine children. Three of these nine died as infants. Their other children were: Loudisa Delcina "Della" (June 24, 1868-Sept. 23, 1954), Maryette (Feb. 22, 1870-June 17, 1949), Harriet Ellen (Nov. 1, 1873-Nov. 11, 1948), Josie Katherine (Oct. 20, 1877-Nov. 22, 1963), Henry Samuel (Dec. 20, 1883-April 3, 1972) and Alexander Clinton, whose twin died at birth, (March 8, 1886-Nov. 24, 1971). All of their children were born and reared in Howard County.

Sam and Kate Pierce

Della married four times and had five children. Her husbands were in order, Charles Messersmith, no issue; Wesley Hankins, issue were, Harriet Leona Aaron and Katherine Milner; Ward Sewell was husband number three and the father of her other three children, Bessie, who never married, Stella Reel and Carl. Walter Williams was her last husband.

Maryette married Nathan Mognett and had six children: Fred H., Henry, Josephine Pansey Cantrell, Kenneth, Gladys Graham and Samuel. She then married Wesley Cullum; they had no children.

Harriet Ellen married Edward L. Bennett. They had no children.

Josie Katherine married Albert Deardorff and had three children, Raymond Arthur, Ivan Glen and Kathryn Louise Weigel. She than married Ross Wilson.

Henry Samuel or Samuel Henry married Laura Eva Imbler and had six children. The youngest son died at birth. The children were Ralph L., Christine B. Cain, Doris May Hurley, Martha Katherine Krauss and Lester Everett. After Laura's death he married Maude Corfman and they had no children.

Alexander Clinton married C. Evalin Fish and had one son, Richard Otis. Evalin died and he married next to Helen Gribler. They had three children, Clarence (who died age 2), Dorothy Wooley and Mildred Baxter.

Sam died Jan. 23, 1920 at his home and was laid to rest in the Crown Point Cemetery. Kate died Jan. 11, 1932 and was laid to rest next to her husband. The last 15 years of her life were devoted to the rearing of a motherless grandson, Richard.

Many of Sam and Kate's descendents still live in this area.

EDWIN L. AND NORMA J. PLANK - The Edwin Plank family resided in Kokomo 42 years from January 1947 until they moved to Lakeland, FL, September 1989.

Edwin Logan Plank was born Nov. 12, 1921 in Deer Creek Twp., Cass County, IN. His parents were Harry Albert Plank (1894-1963) and Eva Veronica (Logan) Plank (1900-1991), both of Cass County. Edwin graduated from Young America High School in 1939. He attended Ball State Teachers College for three years before entering the Army Air Force. He was a first lieutenant who flew 58 missions in a P-47 fighter plane. He was stationed in Italy in WWII and received the Air Medal with two Oak Leaf Clusters. He was a cost estimator and product engineer at Haynes Stellite Company 35 years and was treasurer of the Stellite Credit Union. Organizations: National Management Association, American Legion, Elks, Noon Lion's Club and Stellite Quarter Century Club in Kokomo.

Edwin L. and Norma J. Plank

Edwin married Norma Jean Barber Jan. 12, 1946. She was born Jan. 17, 1926 in Ervin Twp. Her parents were David Ross Barber (1882-1970) and Julia Gladys (Felton) Barber (1900-1992). Norma graduated from Ervin Twp. High School in 1944, attended Ball State Teachers College and after raising four children received a B.A. in Elementary and Music Education from Indiana University in Kokomo in 1974. She taught private piano 37 years, was piano accompanist for dance schools, Tri Kappa Follies and miscellaneous programs. She was a music, recreation and group therapist at the Regional Mental Health Center, Kokomo. Organizations: Child Study Club, Tri Kappa Sorority, Sigma Eta Sorority of Fine Arts, Inc. (charter member), Kokomo Morning Musicale, Indiana Music Teachers Association (vice-president), Indiana Music Therapist (a founder) and presented music therapy seminars at national convention in New Orleans and Boston.

The Planks have been members of the First Christian Church since 1947 with Ed serving as elder, deacon, S.S. superintendent and currently elder emeritus and Norma as teacher and choir member.

Their children are: (1) Edwin Eugene born Oct. 1, 1947, graduate of Kokomo High School 1966, Tri State College 1970, married Cynthia Lorraine Anders, Warren, IN; resides in Flower Mound, TX, supervisor GTE, Irving, TX. Children: Phillip Edwin, David Andrew, Timothy Aaron and Daniel James; (2) Julia Ann, born Jan. 19, 1950, graduate of Kokomo High School 1968, IUK (BA 1972, MA 1975), married Michael Jeffrey Martin, Kokomo, resides in Warsaw, IN, elementary teacher in Warsaw, IN. Children: Bryan Michael, Melinda Ann and Jan Elizabeth; (3) David Alan born July 14, 1955, graduate of Haworth High School 1973, IUK BA, 1979, MSW at IUPUI 1984 and MA in Biblical Counseling, Colorado Christian University, Denver 1991, married Kerin Jayne Nash of Frostproof, FL, resides Boise, ID, minister of Discipleship and Counseling. Children: Christopher Logan and Lauren Elizabeth; (4) Jan Claire born Sept. 24, 1956, graduate of Haworth High School 1975, IUPUI 1979, was 1975 Indiana Junior Miss, formerly married to Gregg Jensen, resides in Chesapeake, VA, vice-president NationsBank Card Services, Norfolk, VA. Children: Nicholas Jon and Zachary David. *Submitted by Mr. and Mrs. Edwin L. Plank*

POHLMAN - Fred Pohlman and his wife Marie Heidorn Pohlman were born in Germany around 1817. They migrated to America and settled in Lawrence County, OH, 1839. They moved to Dearborn County, IN, then to Indianapolis. They first settled on a farm in Ervin Township, Howard County in 1865. Their first home was in a log house adjoining five acres of cleared ground. Tallow candles were used for light.

Later they moved to a farm in Clay Township located on the northeast corner of roads 600 W and 400 N. To be able to farm the land it had to be cleared of trees and drained. One report is that they would walk on top of the rail fence as they went to church to stay out of the mud and water. They ate a lot of wild game and wild berries. The neighbors tell of Marie Pohlman doing more hard work than any team of mules in the county. One story was she carried a log chain around her neck ten miles to Kokomo to be repaired. As she walked, she worked on her knitting.

Three children: Henry (Oct. 8, 1842-Sept. 7, 1908), Fred Jr. (March 30, 1846-Nov. 21, 1936), Dora Bulk (July 19, 1849-June 16, 1931).

After the death of her first husband, Marie married Siemon Erfcamp. Two children: Sophia, John.

Henry Pohlman married, owned a blacksmith shop in Clay Twp. Three daughters: Barbara Jones, Lesie Gordon and Emma Pohlman.

Fred Jr. Pohlman (farmer) married Mary Sander (Tipton County) (Mary's brother was killed in the Civil War and buried in Arlington National Cemetery). Nine children: Henry married Mary Kerkhoff; Charles married Emma Folkening Kerkhoff; Christian married Doshia Conwell Gilbert; William married Lena Doepke; Dora never married; Frank never married; Christina never married; Dena married Otto Shackel, Minnie married Harry Miller.

Dora married Frederick C. Bulk, a farmer. 10 children: Lena married Wm. Hartman, Sophie married George Schakel, Matilda married Henry Obermeyer, Anna married Fred Lutz, Mary married Harvey Sedan, Ida married Carl Welke, Clara married Ross Hobson, Fred married Pauline Waterman, Elsie married Lloyd Hobson, Alma married John Beahrs.

Sophia, third wife of George Hartman. Five stepchildren: William, George, Rosa Bierman, Frank, Fred.

John Erfcamp married Nellie Folkening. Three children: Fred, William "Bill", Dora Remminger.

Henry and Mary Kerkhoff Polhman had seven children: Lillie Jewell of Kokomo, Anna Miller of Kokomo, Herman (Ervin Twp farmer), Grace Thrush of Clay Twp., Nellie Kuntz of Kokomo, Ray (Peru-a home improvement business), Martha Masbaum of Fort Wayne.

Henry operated a thrashing machine ring for about 10 farmers. It was called the Rat Tail Ring. The women of the church would prepare the noon meals. It was a fun time for the children.

287

Charles and Doshia Pohlman had six children: Harry (Clay Twp. farmer), Mary Schroeter of Ervin Twp., Ester Laag of Ervin Twp., Lena Nichols of Ervin Twp., Carl (Ervin Twp farmer), Lucille Rodabough of Ervin Twp.

William and Lena Doepke Pohlman had three children: Hazel McAninich Rayle, Robert "Bob", George "Buck".

We owe a debt of gratitude to the pioneers of this country. They left behind developed countries to move to America. *Submitted by Grace Pohlman Thrush*

RONALD E. AND BECKY J. POHLMAN -
Ronald E. and Becky J. Steenman were both born and raised in Howard County. They were married on Jan. 30, 1966 at Zion Lutheran Church in Howard County.

Ronald was born on May 7, 1941 to Carl and Elizabeth (Kerkhoff) Pohlman. After graduating from Northwestern High School in 1960 he joined the Army Reserves and worked at Continental Steel. After the steel mill closed he worked for Kokomo Grain at the Amboy Terminal. He was killed in an accident at the terminal on July 17, 1993. He was active in church, AAL, vice-president of the North Union Cemetery, girls softball at Northwestern and 4-H.

Front Row - Ron, Becky and Staci. Second Row - Brian, Linda, Michele. Back - Michael

Becky was born on May 18, 1943 to Sherman and Margaret (Greer) Steenman. She graduated from Kokomo High School in 1961 and from Kokomo Business College in 1962. Becky worked at Delco in Kokomo, retiring after the birth of their third child. Becky is now employed as the assistant kitchen supervisor at Northwestern School. She has also been active in church, girls softball at Northwestern, and 4-H.

Ron and Becky have three children. Brian was born May 7, 1967. He graduated from Northwestern in 1985 and is employed by the Huntington County Farm Bureau Co-op. He met his wife, Michele (Pedde) at a church retreat. They were married in April 1987 and live near Marion, IN with their two lovely daughters, Staci, born Aug. 24, 1989 and Autumn born July 25, 1991.

Michael was born May 25, 1970. He graduated from Northwestern in 1988 and served four years in the U.S. Navy aboard a destroyer, the USS *Fletcher*. He is now employed by Speciality Tool and Die in Kokomo.

Linda was born May 3, 1973. She graduated from Northwestern in 1991 and attended Purdue University. She worked at Howard County Children's Center and is now presently employed at Lowe's in Kokomo.

PREBLE -
1. Thomas Preble came from England to Maryland around 1684, and was an indentured servant for four years. He then purchased 100 acres (where Aberdeen Proving Grounds later stood) for farming. He married Mary Buchnell in Annapolis c1688. They had six children, and were Episcopal.

2. His son, John Stephen Pribble, Sr. born 1697 Maryland married Nancy Ann Gallion, and they had eight children, all born in Maryland.

3. John Stephen Prebble, Jr. born 1736 Maryland, died in Pennsylvania, married 1761, Maryland Clemency Bond. They moved to Virginia and Pennsylvania. They were Episcopal and had eight children.

4. Benjamin B. Pribble born 1779 Maryland, died 1837, Ohio, married 1800 in Kentucky to Lucretia Marshall died 1826. They moved to Ohio in 1807, and had seven children. After Lucretia died, Benjamin married 1833 Elizabeth Slippy 2/w and they had two children.

5. Martin Marshall Pribble born 1805 in Kentucky, died 1885 Indiana, married 1823 in Ohio to Hannah Marshall born 1807 in Kentucky, died 1857 Indiana. He was a farmer. They were members of the Christian Church, and they had seven children born in Ohio. Hannah was buried in a pioneer cemetery east of the old KHS, and later moved to Crown Point. Her stone is one of several placed around the Chief Kokomo historical marker.

6. Benjamin Byron Pribble born 1830 in Ohio, died 1904 Indiana, married 1849 in Ohio, Catharine Cline born 1827 Indiana, died 1915 Indiana. They came to Howard County in 1850. His wife rode a mule and carried their first baby, and he drove a team of oxen. It took them over a month to travel from near Cincinnati to west of Kokomo. They were Christian Church members, and he was a Howard County trustee 1851-2.

7. Oscar Byron Prebble born 1858 Indiana, died 1925 Indiana, married 1877 Isadora Adams. They had six children.

8. Oma Preble born 1885 Indiana, died 1914 Indiana, married 1902 Indiana to Clive Claudius Streeter, a farmer. Oma died while her three sons were young. They lived in northwest Howard County just north of where NHS is now. They chopped their heating wood from a forest where the current NHS athletic field is.

The Streeter family is covered in another article in this book. *Submitted by Rachel Benson*

RUSSELL B. AND FLORENCE J. (KENWORTHY) PRICE -
Russell B. Price, son of Marley J. and Grace M. (Embree) Price married Florence J. Kenworthy, daughter of Clarence William and Maude G. (Etherington) Kenworthy at the Kenworthy residence on North Union Street in Kokomo on March 23, 1946.

Russell and "Flossie" have two sons. Jeffery Allen born Nov. 6, 1948 and Jerry Lee born Nov. 29, 1951. Currently, Jeffery is employed as a supervisor of mechanical components - air control engineering for Delco General Motors in Kokomo while Jerry is the union/manager liaison officer at Chrysler Corporation - also in Kokomo.

Russell B. Price served three years in the Navy during World War II. At one time, his squad maintained the P.T. Boats manned by the young John F. Kennedy.

Russell's working career included 32 years at the Continental Steel Corp. while Flossie was the office manager for *The Kokomo Tribune* for 19 years. Before and shortly after retirement, Russell, being an excellent carpenter and mason, built and re-modeled several houses in the Kokomo area, including building their own home in the Breezy Woods addition of Russiaville.

R.B. and Flossie are keenly interested in good music, especially Country Western. Since retiring several years ago, they have traveled frequently to Nashville, IN; Nashville, TN and Branson, MO.

Their home in Russiaville is the center for the caring for Flossie's 94 year-old mother and the hub of children and grandchildren activities. Gary and Austin Jacob Price, sons of Jeffery and Toni (Guy) Price; and April, Kami and Casey, children of Jerry and Connie Jo (Louks) Price are keeping R.B. and Flossie agile in limb and young at heart.

For further information on Kenworthy/Price families, refer to Clarence Kenworthy/Marley Price.

CLIFFORD AND MARIE (OBERMEYER) PRIFOGLE -
Well-known and highly respected Ervin Township farmer Clifford Irvin Prifogle was born Oct. 31, 1899 in Tipton County. He was the seventh of nine children born to Michael John and Louisa M. (Bossert) Prifogle of Tipton County, a grandson of John and Anna Eliza (Huber) Prifogle of Franklin County, and a great-grandson of German-born Franklin County pioneer, Peter Prifogle. Clifford came from a close-knit family with strong Lutheran roots. He was a charter member of St. John's Lutheran Church of Kokomo.

Clifford's brothers and sisters are as follows: Frank John Martin Prifogle (1887-1915), who married Lillian Waltz (1889-1977); twins Edwin Wesley Prifogle (1893-1893) and John Albert Prifogle (1893-1893); Nellie Lavina (Prifogle) Cochran (1893-1966), who married Arbie Glen Cochran (1894-1967); William Jennings Prifogle (1896-1949), who married Zella A. Wynn (1894-1992); Earl Walter Prifogle (1902-1988), who married Allilee Spurgeon (1906-1989); and Winona Elizabeth (Prifogle) Henry (1906-1992), who married George S. Henry (1901-1955).

Clifford Prifogle Family - Front L-R: Carl Edward, Ralph Eugene. Middle L-R: Leona Ruth, Wilma Marie, Clifford Irvin, Jr. Back L-R: Michael John, Louisa M., Clifford Irvin, Dorothy Marie

On Nov. 24, 1921 Clifford married Dorothy Marie Obermeyer, born July 2, 1899 in Howard County, daughter of Henry Matilda (Bulk) Obermeyer. Clifford and Marie rented farmland for a few years before purchasing their own homeplace located eight miles west of Kokomo and which still remains in the Prifogle family.

The following five children were born to Clifford and Marie, all in Howard County:

1. Wilma Marie Prifogle, born Sept. 9, 1922, who on Sept. 14, 1941 married Albert F. Kennedy, born Oct. 3, 1920, died Sept. 29, 1993. They have four children, Marceita Marie (Kennedy) Click-Wolf, Richard Albert Kennedy, Malcolm Dean Kennedy, and Thomas Joe Kennedy.

2. Leona Ruth Prifogle, born June 10, 1924, who on April 25, 1943 married C. Meredith Wilson, born Feb. 27, 1924.

3. Clifford Irvin Prifogle, Jr., born Nov. 12, 1925, died Oct. 20, 1989, who married: (1) Aug. 26, 1943 Mary Margaret Eller; (2) Maxine Ronk; (3) June (?); and (4) March 15, 1980 Mazy B. (Arnett) Snow. Clifford and Mary have two children, Judith Louise (Prifogle) Camden, and Kenneth Edward Prifogle.

4. Carl Edward Prifogle, born Aug. 10, 1927, who on April 6, 1946 married Virginia Lee Rinehart, born April 22, 1928. They have four children, James Stephen Prifogle, Bruce Edward Prifogle, Diana Lu (Prifogle) Curl-Criss, and Cathryn Maxine (Prifogle) Newton.

5. Ralph Eugene Prifogle, born July 23, 1929, who married: (1) February 14, 1947 Martha Jones; and (2) April 1, 1972 Rita Bennett. Ralph and Martha have four children, Clifford Eugene Prifogle, Michael Kent Prifogle, Terrence Lee Prifogle, and Timothy Allen Prifogle. Ralph and Rita have two children, Scott Michael Prifogle, and Chad Tyson Prifogle.

Following Marie's death on Jan. 25, 1962, Clifford married Pauline Vivian (Maholm) Smelser on Dec. 5, 1964. Pauline was born June 8, 1901 in Tipton County, the daughter of Thomas and Harriet (Swift) Maholm, and widow of Frances Smelser. They resided on the Prifogle homestead until Clifford's death on July 22, 1979. Pauline died Jan. 29, 1988 in Tipton County. *Submitted by Jason Thomas Criss*

PRITTS -
Sometime after the death of Levi Joseph Pritts/Pritz, in 1852, his widow, Phebe Pyle/Pile Pritts, came to the Clinton County/Howard County area with their six surviving children. They came from Somerset County, PA.

The children were: Elizabeth, John R., Oliver Marion, Joseph M., Josephine and Catherine.

On Oct. 21, 1856 Phebe Pritts married Peter Smith.

Nothing is known of Elizabeth. John R. was born Jan. 19, 1841 and served in the Civil War. He married

Loudisa J. (Pierce) Yerigan, widow of Mathias Yerigan and sister of Samuel C. Pierce. They had no children; however, she had two sons from her previous marriage. His health was never good and he died March 12, 1877 in Kokomo. He was buried in the Smith Family Cemetery, located on the family farm in Clinton County.

Oliver Marion was born July 20, 1844. On Jan. 24, 1867 in Howard County he married Mahala Webb. They had a family of seven children: James Monroe, Pearl (Bud), Harrison, Raymond A., William, Mattie Marie and Dora. He also served in the Civil War and died Nov. 13, 1884 in Moultrie County, IL.

Joseph M. was born Aug. 18, 1846 and married Lucinda Powell Pyle June 24, 1870 in Clinton County. Their children were Oliver, Florence, Alva Hayes, Perry, Claude, Cecil, Phebe and Owen Marion. Joseph died Sept. 25, 1918 in Hamilton County. Lucinda died Feb. 7, 1933 in Kokomo. They are both buried in Clinton County.

All that is known of Josephine is she married a man named William Smith, Dec. 8, 1865.

Most of Joseph M. Pritts family is still in Howard County.

Catherine and her husband, Samuel C. Pierce, are featured elsewhere in this publication.

PROPES - James Claude "Buck" Propes was born in Illinois and married Pauline (Bess) Henderson on Aug. 10, 1946. Dwayne Harrison Propes was born in Kokomo, Howard County, IN in 1947. He attended Kokomo High School, graduating in 1965. On Aug. 13, 1966 he married classmate Candy Louise Schick in Silva, NC. They had three children: Angelia Ranae, Rachel Leigh, and Jason Cole. Dwayne served in Vietnam as a radio operator with the 298th Signal Bn. from November 1966 to Nov. 7, 1968. On returning home, he worked at Delco Electronics and later joined the IBEW. He has been employed as a planner/estimator at Ft. Benjamin Harrison in Indianapolis since 1975. He has been an avid fisherman and enjoys dart tournaments. He lives in Indianapolis.

L-R: Angie holding Nikolas, Peter, Dwayne, Rachel, Keith, Jason, Pauline

Angelia Ranae was born at Reynold's Army Hospital, Ft. Sill, OK. She attended Taylor Elementary and Taylor High School in Center, IN. She graduated from Purdue University in 1990, where she received a BA in social work. She married Peter Markopoulos of Palos Hills, IL on Aug. 15, 1990. Peter graduated from Purdue University with a degree in aeronautical/astronautical engineering. He is an engineer working on space shuttle systems for the Marshall Space Flight Center. He is currently attending the University of Alabama at Huntsville where he is pursuing a master's degree. Angie is an AFDC/Food Stamp Caseworker for the Madison County, AL Department of Human Resources. They live near Huntsville, AL with their son, Nikolas Cristian, who was born on June 21, 1990.

Rachel Leigh was born at Howard Community Hospital in Kokomo. She attended Taylor Elementary School and spent her freshman year at Taylor High School. At age 15, she left home to attend Culver Girls Academy, a boarding school on Lake Maxinkuckee in northern Indiana. While at Culver she was a student leader and received several awards for academic performance. In her senior year she was editor of the yearbook. She attended Purdue University, graduating in May, 1991 with a BA in organizational communication. While at Purdue, she began dating Keith Heitzman, a Culver classmate from Vernon, IN. Keith graduated from Purdue in May, 1992 with a BS in construction engineering and management. They were married on May 30, 1992 at the Seiberling Mansion. They live in Aiken, SC where Keith is a construction engineer for Bechtel Savannah River, Inc. He works on environmental restoration projects at the Department of Energy's Savannah River Site.

Jason Cole was born in Kokomo at Howard Community Hospital. He attended Taylor Elementary School and graduated from Taylor High School in 1989. He enjoys a variety of sports, having played organized baseball from an early age. After graduating he played Connie Mack baseball in Kokomo. He lives in Oakford and works in Kokomo.

HAROLD AND ELSIE PURVIS - Harold Eugene and Elsie Elizabth (Parkhurst) Purvis have lived in the Howard County area most of their married lives. Harold, son of Harry and Vera Purvis, was born Sept. 13, 1925, Miami County, IN. Elsie was born in Kokomo, April 30, 1926, daughter of Ora and Janice (Freed) Parkhurst. Before retirement Harold was a truck driver and Elsie was a nurse's aide. They enjoy traveling, camping, and grandchildren in their retirement, and now live in Bringhurst, IN. They have five children listed below:

1. Paula Sue (Purvis) Behrens, born Nov. 5, 1946, Kokomo, is an office supply employee and lives in Florida. She married (1) Harvey Mossholder and (2) Fred Behrens. Paula has two children, Melissa, born Feb. 23, 1966, Kokomo, and Harvey G. Mossholder, Jr., born Aug. 22, 1969, Kokomo. Both Melissa and Harvey, Jr. live in Florida. Harvey Jr., and his wife, Carol, have one son, Harvey G. Mossholder, III, born March 1, 1989, Tampa, FL.

2. Jessica Lee (Purvis) Snider, born April 1, 1949, Kokomo, is employed with Pizza King, and lives in Delphi, IN. She is married to Michael Allen Snider who is retired from a career in the U.S. Army. Jessica and Mike have four children: Angela Denise, born Feb. 10, 1972, Longstuhl, Germany, and who is married to Poririo Herrera and they have one son: Elizabeth Joan, born Jan. 7, 1977, San Antonio, TX; Michael A., born Nov. 27, 1977, Kokomo, and Jessica Lynn, born Dec. 18, 1979, Leavenworth, KS.

3. Jeffrey Eugene Purvis, born April 12, 1953, Frankfort, IN. He is an employee of Krogers and lives in Kokomo. Jeff married Dorothy Lee Barlow, who was born June 23, 1953, Kokomo, daughter of Thomas and Phyllis (Addison) Barlow. Dorothy is an assembly worker for Delco; Dorothy and Jeff have one son, Jeffrey Scott Purvis, born Feb. 20, 1971, Kokomo. Scott is married to Stephanie Sue Bitner.

4. Terry Allen Purvis, was born June 18, 1954, Kokomo. He is a store display worker in North Carolina. He was married to Jeannie Myers and they had one son, Terry Bradley Allen Purvis, born Dec. 27, 1978, Kokomo.

5. Theresa (Purvis) Weitzel, was born June 19, 1956, Kokomo. She is a registered nurse and lives in Bringhurst, IN. She is married to Richard Clyde Weitzel and he works at Grissom Air Force Base. Theresa and Richard have four children: Richard Eugene, born Jan. 7, 1974, Kokomo; Jerry James, born Oct. 18, 1976, Germany; Christopher Shawn, born Nov. 18, 1978, Kokomo; and Matthew David, born Aug. 22, 1980, Kokomo.

The above history is abstracted with permission and modified from *The Mason-White Family History*, copyright 1990, by James M. Freed. *Submitted by Elsie (Parkhurst) Purvis*

PYANOWSKI - Phebe Ault was born in Converse, IN, Nov. 12, 1892 to Jesse and Mahala Jane Ault. Her great-great-grandfather was Charles Carroll, signer of the Declaration of Independence. When Phebe was three, her parents separated, and she stayed with her father. At age 10, her parents reunited, and lived at 1122 E. Monroe Street. After her father died in 1910, she had a difficult time completing her education. She graduated from KHS in 1913, and went to Terre Haute Normal for one year, as her mother did not want her to have further schooling. She worked at various jobs until 1917 when she went to Detroit and lived with her half-sister and husband. She worked for Postal Telegraph, delivering messages to various factories in the vicinity. She was introduced to John Pyanowski by Postal Telegraph manager at John's request.

John was born in Poland June 4, 1899, and came to America in 1907 with his mother, two brothers, and a sister. He road-tested Cadillacs until he enlisted in the Army during World War I.

When the war ended, he and Phebe were married, and came to Kokomo where they worked for Kingston Products. Later John went to work in the tire vulcanizing business. By 1928 he had started his own business with gas station and used tires, named Horseshoe Tire Store. Eventually, he added tire recapping, and was in business until 1944. John and Phebe had six children. The first child, Jessamine, died in infancy. George, fourth child, died at age three. Jean born 1920, John Jr. born 1921, Patricia born 1926, Robert born 1929.

John and Phebe Pyanowski

In 1942 John went to California, taking two daughters with him. He wanted a change of climate to get rid of hay fever. He and Jean obtained jobs at Lockheed Aircraft, and in March 1943, Phebe and Robert came to California. John Jr. was in the Air Force.

In 1945 John obtained a tire recapping business and worked there, as well as Lockheed. In 1959 the tire store burned, and he was unable to replace it. He retired in 1968.

In 1947 Patricia married Bill Cockrell and had two boys, Christopher and David. She divorced in 1954, and later married John Cooper, and had two daughters, Lisa and Kim. John Jr. married Mary Lou Giddings in 1949. Three children were born, Samuel, Robin, and Cathy. Jean married John McGowan in 1954. He was born in Paducah, TX and worked at Lockheed. He died in 1968 of Hodgkin's Disease. Jean married again in 1983 to O.R. Scott, born in Joplin, MO, and worked at Lockheed. Jean retired in 1981. He retired in 1987. In 1991, they moved to Kokomo permanently. Robert married Linda in 1960, and they have a son, Douglas. John died Feb. 12, 1974. Phebe died Oct. 3, 1976. *Submitted by Jean A. Scott, daughter.*

QUAKENBUSH - John D. Quakenbush was born March 1825 in North Carolina. He moved to Indiana as a very young child with his parents Thomas and Hannah (Lee) Quakenbush. They settled first in Orange County, IN; John purchased land in Prairie Township, Tipton County around 1850. On Aug. 31, 1856 John married Martha Rebecca Lybrook, daughter of John C. and Elizabeth Lybrook. The young couple lived for a time in Tipton County but moved their family to Honey Creek Township, Howard County about 1864.

John and Martha were the parents of four children: Leora Ann (June 17, 1857-Aug. 25, 1901); William Henry (July 4, 1864-Feb. 13, 1932); Nancy E. (May 22, 1869-Oct. 7, 1894) married Frank Dabe Dec. 15, 1890; and John T. (1874-188?).

On Oct. 4, 1893 William Henry married Ethleen Carter (March 16, 1867-March 16, 1963), the daughter of Levi and Emily (Newlin) Carter. Will and Ethleen were members of the Lynn Friends Church; both were well thought of in the community. Will served as township trustee for eight years and later served as county assessor for eight years. Will and Ethleen were blessed with three children. Martha Marie (Oct. 30, 1894-Feb. 16, 1984)

289

married Chester Waddell on Feb. 2, 1912; Clarice Emily (Aug. 7, 1896-Jan. 30, 1989) married Wesley Peterson on Nov. 26, 1922; and Warren (June 9, 1898-Nov. 26, 1987) married Mary Jane Clark on Aug. 21, 1920.

William H. and Ethleen (Carter) Quakenbush

Warren and Mary (Aug. 30, 1900-Jan. 23, 1985), the daughter of Fred and Naomi (Huffer) Clark, spent their married life on the farm John and Martha had purchased when they moved to Honey Creek Township. They raised seven children, five daughters and two sons, to adulthood on the farm. They were associated with the Lynn Friends Meeting and raised their children in that faith. Mildred Jane (April 6, 1921-April 21, 1992) married in 1941 to Darrell Schuck and later married Clarence Hawn; Richard John (Sept. 6, 1922) married Shirley Kiethley in 1948; William Frederick (Jan. 30, 1924-Nov. 23, 1946); Betty Joan (Nov. 6, 1925) married Marvin Bingaman in 1945; Ruth Eleanor (April 22, 1931) married Eugene Martin in 1953; Mary Helen (June 9, 1933) married James Rubush in 1951; and Barbara Sue (March 28, 1943) married Rex Hendershot in 1962. Both of Warren and Mary's sons answered the call of their country and served in WWII. Eleanor and Eugene Martin presently own and reside on the Quakenbush farm. In addition to their seven children Warren and Mary were blessed with 20 grandchildren, 26 great-grandchildren, and eight great-great grandchildren, many of whom reside in the area.

Betty married Marvin Bingaman (Sept. 29, 1923) on March 9, 1945 in Russiaville. Marvin and Betty are the parents of three children, Sue (Nov. 26, 1946); Jane (Sept. 22, 1947) married Robert Watkins in 1968; and Don (Nov. 8, 1951). They are blessed with six grandchildren: Maleta, Julie, Rachel, Jeremy, Joshua, and Terrianne. Marvin is retired from farming and enjoys woodworking while Betty is busy with many organizations. Both stay busy with their grandchildren.

Sue married Mike Sheagley in 1970 and they divorced in 1990. They are the parents of three daughters Maleta (July 11, 1973), Julie (March 17, 1975), and Rachel (Sept. 13, 1980). Sue is employed as a cataloguer and genealogist librarian at the Kokomo Howard County Public Library. *Submitted by Sue Sheagley.*

EARL QUINN JR. - Earl Quinn Jr.'s great-grandfather, James Quinn, left his home in Belfast, Ireland, in 1818 to come to the United States. He married Nancy ___? from Ohio. They migrated to Carroll County in the early 1820's. Their son, Archibald Quinn, was born in Carrolton, in Carroll County, IN. He was married first to Elizabeth Parker (m1869-d1879), and then to Sarah Francis Douglas in 1880. Their son, Earl, was born in 1895.

Earl Quinn was from the area around Flora, IN. He had one sister, Ethel; three brothers, Jim, Ernest and one that left home while very young to go out west. He never returned. Word came home that he had met up with bandits. One rumor was that he had an ear cut off—another that he was killed. He also had one step-sister.

In his early years, Earl Quinn's father, Earl, worked for the Barnum and Bailey Circus from Peru, IN. He met and married Theresa Olillia Thompson from Russiaville near Kokomo. They lived in Monon for a while, but lost everything they owned during the Depression. Since they had no home, his mother stayed with her folks in Kokomo, while his father worked on construction, building new highways. Some of the highways he remembered included State Road 22 from Burlington to Kokomo, Highway 18 which runs through Delphi, and other roads close by in the Delphi area. Earl Jr. would tell of hiding in safe places while the construction crew would dynamite for new road openings, and of he and his father camping at the construction sites, sleeping in tents, during the summer months while he wasn't in school. Earl Jr. attended a one-room school house near Monon for one year. The rest of his school years were spent at Wallace School and Kokomo High School. He was always interested in drawing cartoons and building models, mostly airplanes and old cars. In high school his main interest was machine shop. After graduation in 1943, he worked at Continental Steel for one year, then during World War II, he joined the Navy. He returned home in 1945 to Continental Steel where he worked for 33 years before retiring. He then worked for Delco Electronics for 10 years.

In 1947, Earl married Grace Christena Fivecoate. She is the daughter of Jesse Ernest and Beulah Marie (Stafford) Fivecoate. (See Jesse Ernest Fivecoate) Grace attended Roosevelt School for eight years, and received a certificate for perfect attendance for those eight years. She attended Kokomo High School and graduated in 1943. Grace and Earl graduated in the same class, but they didn't meet each other until October in 1946. They were engaged in January of 1947, and married Oct. 2, 1947.

Grace worked in Kresge's 5 & 10 Cent Store as a waitress, and also at Reliance Manufacturing. She was a graduate of the Good Samaritan School of Nursing with four months affiliation in St. John's Hospital in Springfield, IL. She was a birthright member of North Buckeye Friends Church. Earl and Grace were active members of New London Friends Church. They both sang in the church choir with Ann Carter as choir director. Earl especially liked those times. They made many new friends during those years.

Earl belonged to the experimental aircraft association and worked with a chapter in West Lafayette. He loved flying and being around aircraft. One of the highlights of his year was his annual trip to the EAA Airshow in Oshkosh, WI. He built a special room over his home, where he worked on building a single seat plane known as a "Teny 2". Earl was a craftsman and whatever he did was accomplished with perfection. The work he completed on his homebuilt airplane was typical of his fine workmanship.

Grace and Earl's three children are Thomas Michael, Susan Jane, and Timothy Mark. They made a home for Grace's brother Benjamin's son, John Craig "Jack" after his father and mother died.

Tom served six years with the Army Reserves, and is a machine repairman for Chrysler Corporation. Tom enjoys woodworking and has made several fine pieces of furniture for his home and for friends and relatives. He married Julie Kay VanHorn of Windfall. Julie was valedictorian of her high school class and graduated from Indiana University. She is a fourth grade teacher at Western School.

Tom and Julie's children are Randall Scott and Christopher Todd. Scott is attending Indiana University and is majoring in education. He is engaged to Janelle Moore and is to be married July 23, 1994. Todd is a graduate of Vincennes University and is a moldmaker for United Technology Automotive in Fort Wayne. He married Mary Mahlke of Lafayette.

Susan is a very gifted artist. Her paintings and artwork are highly prized and sought after. Stacy Annette, Tisha Marie, and Gregory Stephen, are her children from her marriage to David Miller. Susan is married to Jerry Badgett, a senior engineer with Delco Electronics. Susan and Jerry's daughter is Tina Elizabeth, "Libby".

Stacy is a graduate of Western High School and is married to Burt Hawkins. She and Burt are making their home at Yuma, AZ, where Burt is serving with the Marine Corps. Their daughter, Ashley Ruth, was born in Yuma, Feb. 22, 1994. Tisha graduated from Western High School. She enjoys children, and is working at the Children's Discovery Day Center. Tisha is also very interested in animals and would like to work in a capacity where she can look after their welfare. Greg is a junior at Western High School. He is interested in antique automobiles, and is a very good auto mechanic and an auto body repairman. Libby is a preschooler and is learning to read. She enjoys spending time with her Aunt Sue and Uncle Ed Fivecoate. Libby helps her Aunt Sue bake apple pies, and works with her Uncle Ed in his workshop and garden. She also enjoys shopping with her cousin Christy Fivecoate, and also with her sister Tisha, and grandmother, Grace Quinn. She and her brother Greg like to play video games together.

Tim is a graduate of Western High School, and is a moldmaker for Lorentzen's Tool and Die. He married Patricia Bricker on Feb. 10, 1979. Tim and "Trish" have three children. Joshua Allen, Justin Andrew and Jessica Ashley.

Joshua is interested in basketball and art. Justin likes baseball and piano. Jessica is taking classes for ballet and tap dancing. Patricia does volunteer work at Western School.

Jack is an electrician at Chrysler Transmission. He is a fisherman's fisherman. He knows every fish in central Indiana by their first name, and is a good acquaintance of the rest from Nashville to Minneapolis. Jack married Nancy Carter and their children are Marti and Austin. Marti is a very promising young lady, and Austin is a good student and loves the out of doors.

PAMELA RADEMACHER - Pamela June was born Aug. 19, 1943 in Howard County, Kokomo, IN to Russell R. and June Click Harness. Pamela has one son, Martin Walt Rademacher, born March 6, 1966. "Marty" is now in the United States Marine Corps and on the Marine soccer team. After boot training in San Diego, CA, he was first stationed in Kaneohe Bay, HI. Marty was one of the first to land in "Desert Storm" and one of the first troops to land in Somalia.

Pamela has lived in such places as Long Island, NY; Corpus Christi, TX; San Rafael, CA; Michigan, Indiana, Oregon and many other cities and states around this country of ours.

Pamela has attended 13 different grammar schools, six different high schools, graduating from Ulysses S. Grant High School in Portland, OR—the only school where she spent a full year, her senior one. She's seen the country and is ready to see it again.

L-R: Marty Rademacher and Pamela Harness Rademacher

Her mother, June Harness, is a night club singer and performs around the country. June started tap-dancing at the age of three. Now living in Mexico, she shares her singing talent there. Pamela's father, Russell Harness, also did his share of moving around, as he was a traveling salesman, working all around the country, selling Cessna airplanes and delivering them.

Upon graduation, Pamela was the first female parking lot attendant in downtown Indianapolis. Married at age 17, Pamela worked as cashier at Harvey's and later head cashier at Park Tahoe, now Caesar's Tahoe, training other cashiers. She worked three years at the District Attorney's office in South Lake Tahoe, Nevada and was also a gas station attendant while living at Lake Tahoe from 1959 to 1982, when she moved to Carson City to attend beauty college. After becoming a licensed beautician, she applied for a job at the Governor's mansion in Carson City. Interviewed by Governor Richard Bryan's wife, she was chosen for the position of mansion coordinator in 1983. Prior to Pam's arrival, there had been 12 coordinators in the previous two year period. Pam's duties were to supervise a staff of four, coordinating all functions for the governor and his family, even down to the scheduling of dinner and foods to be prepared. When First Lady Bonnie Bryan could not attend receptions or parties, Pamela would become the state's official hostess, meeting many people. President Gerald Ford was a dinner guest, as were many government officials. Pamela boasts that living in the mansion was one of the better, if not the best, chapter in her book of life.

Pamela is the middle child, sandwiched between two brothers, Russell being the eldest, Forrest the youngest.

Upon Governor Richard Bryan's election as a U.S. Senator in Washington, D.C., Pamela was asked to take a position there, although she instead chose to remain in Nevada and marry Alan Rogers, a sports new columnist with the Carson City *Nevada Appeal.* Governor Bryan gave the bride away at a ceremony in the mansion on Oct. 9, 1989. First Lady Bonnie Bryan was matron of honor and Washoe County District Attorney Miles Lane was best man to a host of 125 guests.

DANIEL AND MARTHA RAMSEYER - Daniel was born March, 1799 in Switzerland. He came to Switzerland County, IN along with his parents, Jacob and Mary (Bearfoot) Ramsyere and brother Philip in 1821. Two other brothers died on the ship from Switzerland in 1812. Daniel was the nephew of the celebrated Marshal Murat of France. Daniel was a blacksmith, a farmer and a politician.

Daniel married Martha Hawkins Dec. 26, 1825 in Switzerland County, IN. Martha was the daughter of John and Massa (Truax) Hawkins. Daniel and Martha and 11 children: Frederick, Philip, John Daniel, Lydia V., Obediah, Martha, Eliza, Linda, Vivian Ann, Joseph B. and Peter V.

Frederic, a surveyor of Tipton County, was born in Switzerland County, Nov. 5, 1826. He died Sept. 3, 1904. He served in the 3rd Reg. Indiana Volunteers during the Mexican War. He married Adelia Heaton, daughter of Joseph Heaton. Adelia was born Aug. 17, 1834 and died March 21, 1916. They had eight children: Oscar V., Flora, Philip E., Abigail, Daniel, Ada B., John and Simon P.

Philip was born Dec. 19, 1827 in Switzerland County and died June, 1903. He settled in Howard County in 1853 working as a blacksmith. He manufactured the first breaking plow ever made in Howard County. In 1867, he moved to Tipton County. December 31, 1855, he married Eunice Roby. Philip and Eunice had seven children: Aprecia, John C., James M., Cebern, Laura, Arthur and Eurelean. Philip and Eunice are buried in the Alto Cemetery in Howard County.

John born Nov. 3, 1829 and died 1886, married Eliza Samples. Both John and Eliza are buried in the Liberty Cemetery in Tipton County.

Lydia was born Feb. 12, 1831 and died July 23, 1833.

Obediah was a farmer and blacksmith in Tipton County and was born June 29, 1832 in Switzerland County. On April 22, 1853 he married Susanna Posten, daughter of Livi Posten. Obediah and Susanna had nine children: Emma J., Martha, Daniel, William and Preston (twins), Nancy A., George B., McClellan, Elizabeth and James A. In 1859 Obediah moved to Tipton County. He served one year in the Army during the Civil War and was also postmaster at Groomsville for eight years.

Martha was born Jan. 8, 1834 and died Oct. 18, 1887. She married David Leap, son of Samuel Leap and they had five children.

Eliza was born July 28, 1835 and died in 1874. She married John Adams July 29, 1857 and they had seven children.

Linda was born Feb. 19, 1837 and died in 1927. She married Dudley Leap, son of Alva and Sophia (McCloud) Leap on March 21, 1866.

Vivian was born Dec. 27, 1839 and died Oct. 29, 1840.

Joseph was born Feb. 28, 1842 and died in 1928. He served in Co. E 146th Indiana Infantry, GAR Post in Vevay, IN. He married Catherine Howard Nov. 29, 1871. Catherine was the daughter of John Howard.

Peter was born Feb. 19, 1945 and died in 1924. He married Julia Banta and they had five children.

RAYL - Whether it's spell Rayl, Rayle, Rayles or Rail, the Rayls of Howard and Tipton Counties are the descendants of two brothers from Pennsylvania who settled in Switzerland County, IN. John Rayl, one of the earliest settlers of Switzerland County, was born in 1775. He came down the Ohio River sometime after 1790, settling first in Kentucky and later in what would be known as Vevay, IN in about 1796. With his brother-in-law, Abraham Miller, he built the second log cabin in Switzerland County. His brother, William Rayl, first settled in Kentucky before 1800 (he was married to Lovisa Duskie in Bourbon County, KY in 1793 and appears on the tax lists for Washington County, KY in 1800). William Rayl purchased land in Switzerland County in 1814. The Rayl brothers were farmers and raised large families - John had nine sons and three daughters, and William had at least two sons and three daughters (there are 20 second-generation Rayls by the 1820 Census, Switzerland County, IN). It has been difficult to prove which children belong to which brother, but some can be attributed:

John Rayl and wife ( ) Miller: Thomas, Samuel, Eli, Noble and John R.

William Rayl and wife Lovisa Duskie: Thomas, Elizabeth.

Not attributed yet: David, Jane, Levi, James H., James, William, John, John C., Catherine, Phebe, Hannah and Sarah Ann.

The Rayls were abolitionists before and during the Civil War—there is a plaque outside the Switzerland County courthouse dedicated to the memory of the Rayle and Pickett families for their contributions to the Underground Railroad. The southern border of Indiana was a very important part of moving blacks north to freedom. The active Rayl member in the Underground Railroad was James F. Rayl, son of Noble Rayl (see above).

Elijah Rayl, born 1805 and wife Catherine Cooper, lived in Switzerland County and later settled in Howard County. Their children were Christian, William F., John P., Katherine E. and Thomas. Thomas moved to Reno County, KS in 1873. William F. Rayl's son, James Christopher Rayl, who also moved to Kansas, is the grandfather of Duward LeMar Rayl (deceased), Waneata Rayl Conkle, Charles Eugene (deceased), Betty Jane Rayl (deceased), Hilda Ann Rayl Currens, Geraldine Rayl Smith (deceased) and Mara Lou Rayl Golightly. Duward was the father of Jimmy Rayl, renowned basketball player for Indiana University.

Thomas Rayl (born May 11, 1796) and wife, Elizabeth Miller, moved to Tipton County before 1858. They are the ancestors of most of the Tipton County Rayls and are buried in the Prairieville Cemetery. Their children: Mary Rayl Thatcher, William Harrison Rayl, Anthony John Rayl, Susan Rayl Thatcher, Louise Rayl Gullion, Caroline Rayl Land and Matilda Rayl Heaton. William Harrison Rayl's children were: Greenberry Rayl, Elwood Rayl, Caroline Rayl Smith, Nancy Rayl White, Thomas Jefferson Rayl, Richardson Rayl, Oscar Rayl, Mary Duncan Rayl Lee, Viola Rayl Spaulding and Joseph Booth Rayl. Joseph Booth Rayl's descendents include the sons of Dr. Emil Cortise Rayl and Cora Blanche Barr Rayl: Harold Eugene Rayl of Kokomo, Gerald Paul Rayl of Newport Beach, CA, Dallas Gayle Rayl of Ligonier, PA, Donavon Francis Rayl of Indianapolis and Allen Blaine Rayl of Kokomo (deceased).

Children of this branch of the Rayl family in the area include Eleanor Rayl of Indianapolis, Susan Rayl of Indianapolis, Elizabeth (Libby) Rayl Riesen of Carmel and Stephen Rayl of Fishers.

LEVI RAYL - Levi Rayl, (Dec. 21, 1800-April 16, 1868), is believed to be the son of John Rayl. Levi married in the Switzerland County, IN Sept. 21, 1819 to Susannah Gullion (1803-March 11, 1865), daughter of John "Jack" and Catherine Riffel Tanner Gullion. All are buried in Twin Springs Cemetery, except Catherine.

They were early pioneers of Howard County, left their farm in Rush County, IN and settled in Harrison Township in January of 1848. The Rayl family moved into a log cabin, which was one of 40 similar structures built by the Indians and was situated in what had in reality been an Indian village. The cabin was 30 x 15 and was formed of logs, the material of the day, with mud mortar between the logs. The floor was formed of pounded dirt, while the chimney was formed of sticks laid in mud. Eight feet of the structure had been cut off and used as a storeroom for whiskey and furs. The floor was laid with moss and the roof was constructed of hickory rim bark. Four acres of ground had been cleared surrounding the cabin.

The removal of the family from Rush County was some undertaking. The main wagon, surmounted by a bed four times the size of the present day wagon beds and crooked in the rear, was drawn by four horses. As there was little roadway existing most of the way the men had to cut down trees and brush to make a passageway. The rest of the moving equipment consisted of four other wagons, three drawn by teams and one by a single horse. The livestock was driven ahead and consisted of four cows and 50 sheep.

Levi and Susannah had 10 children, all born in Rush County, IN except Edward, (1) Lavicia; (2) Julia Ann, married Oct. 23, 1849 to James D.C. Reeder; (3) Mary A. (Feb. 6, 1823-May 12, 1880), wife of Jesse W. Campbell; (4) Catharine, 1st married James Reddy, 2nd married Wilson Brooks; (5) Elizabeth A. (1831-1853), married March 13, 1848 to Francis Gullion; (6) John Franklin (Feb. 16, 1833-Jan. 15, 1916), 1st married Aug. 7-8, 1859 to Mary Ann Waldren, 2nd married Feb. 15, 1897 to Angeline Tolley; (7) Phineas (Oct. 17, 1837-April 3, 1925), 1st married Nov. 25, 1858 to Serepta Shepherd, 2nd married April 8, 1875 to Mary Elizabeth C. Young, 3rd married Oct. 17, 1882 to Sarah A. Poff Denman (April 2, 1847-Jan. 24, 1945); (8) Permelia Jane (March 12, 1843-Dec. 3, 1851); (9) Eli, (Jan. 19, 1845-July 15, 1872); and (10) Thomas Edward/Edward Thomas, (born in 1848/1849 Howard County).

Lavicia Rayl (Oct. 16, 1820-Oct. 31, 1906), 1st married Sept. 23, 1853 to Jesse Thomas Shepherd/Shepard (June 3, 1819-April 3, 1865); 2nd married Oct. 19, 1867 to William Bates, no children. Lavicia and Jesse had three children: (1) Benjamin Franklin (Aug. 4, 1855-March 12, 1935), 1st married Nov. 26, 1879 to Flora Alice Hewitt (April 27, 1863-Dec. 4, 1932), daughter of Enoch James and Sarah Elizabeth Enos Hewitt, 2nd married May 23, 1896 to Martha Jane Hayse Rodgers (Jan. 23, 1863-Nov. 6, 1941), daughter of John C. and Sarah Drusetta Reeder Hayse; (2) Isaiah Thomas (Dec. 25, 1860/61-Sept. 23, 1920), married April 26, 1891 to Cora Lavina "Elsie" Byrkett (June 10, 1874-April 24, 1942), daughter of John William and Mary Baxter Byrkett; and (3) Mary Elizabeth Shepherd (July 12, 1864-Feb. 17, 1915), married Aug. 4, 1880 to Otho Dowden (May 26, 1857-July 2, 1937), son of George E. and Hannah Harpold Dowden. *Research done by Bette Hughes*

PAUL J. AND SHIRLEY F. RAVER - Paul J. Raver and his family came to Howard County in April, 1963 when Paul J. was appointed County Extension Director and County Agricultural Agent for the Purdue University Cooperative Extension Service. He had served as an extension agent since June 1, 1952 and came to Howard County from Hendricks County, IN.

Paul J. was born at Batesville, IN Nov. 25, 1926. After some time as a Purdue University student Paul spent two years in the U.S. Army as a military policeman. Following Army service he worked on the home farm before returning to Purdue University where he received a Bachelor's Degree in Agriculture in 1952. He also received a Master's Degree in Education from Purdue in 1961.

Shirley F. (Schultz) Raver was born at South Bend, IN April 16, 1927 but grew up in Kouts, IN. After graduating from high school in 1945 she attended beautician school and worked as a beautician until Paul and Shirley were married. Shirley is a homemaker.

Paul and Shirley were married at Kouts, In on Oct. 25, 1947. They have five children and 13 grandchildren. Barbara Ann and Paul T. were born at Batesville, IN. Rita Joan was born at Lafayette, IN. Mark J. and Beth Anne were born at Indianapolis, IN. Barbara, Paul and Rita each have three sons. Mark and Beth each have a son and a daughter.

Paul J. is very active in government and community activities. He was a member of the Howard County Plan

Commission for over 27 years and served as president for several years. He is a member of the Kokomo Rotary Club and was their president in 1972-73. As a member of the Indiana and Howard County Farm Bureau he served as chairman of the Local Affairs Committee for many years. He represented the Fifth U.S. Congressional District as a member of the Indiana Commission on the Bicentennial of the U.S. Constitution from 1986-1991. He is also a member of American Legion Post #6 in Kokomo.

Paul J. and Shirley F. Raver

Paul J. was also a leader in activities of the Cooperative Extension Service. He was a member and chairman of many important committees of the Indiana Extension Agents Association during his 37+ years as an extension agent. He served as their president in 1970. He was also a member of the Extension Service Honorary, Epsilon Sigma Phi. He was their Indiana president in 1980 and served on the national board for two years (1983-84) as the representative of the 12 northcentral states. He also served as a State Fair assistant for 30 years.

Paul and Shirley have been members of St. Joan of Arc Catholic Church since moving to Kokomo in 1963. They are active participants. Shirley is a member of the Daughters of Isabella and Paul is a member of the Knights of Columbus.

Paul retired on Aug. 31, 1989 from his position as County Extension Director after over 37 years of service. For three years after retirement he worked part-time for the Indiana Soybean Growers Association and as a corn and soybean inspector for the Indiana Crop Improvement Association. He was elected to the Howard County Council in 1992 and started a four year term on Jan. 1, 1993.

Paul and Shirley continue to reside in the same home they purchased in 1963 when they came to Kokomo.

PHILIP AND CATHERINE RAMSEYER -

Philip Ramseyer was born in Borne, Neuchatel, Switzerland November, 1801 and traveled to Switzerland County, IN with his parents, Jacob and Mary (Bearfoot) Ramsyere and brother Daniel. Two brothers died on the ship from Switzerland in 1812. Jacob purchased land in Switzerland County, IN in 1821.

On March 31, 1823 Philip married Catherine Shadday, the daughter of John and Mary (Fogleman) Shaddy in Switzerland County, IN. He applied for citizenship to the United States Oct. 21, 1828 in Switzerland County Circuit Court. Philip came to Howard County in 1848 where he worked as a farmer. He received a deed signed by President James K. Polk, April 20, 1848.

Philip and Catherine had nine children: Mariah Sarah born Feb. 6, 1824; Philip born in 1828; Jacob born March 13, 1928 and married Celia A. Scott Aug. 23, 1849; Daniel, born Feb. 28, 1832 and married Catherine; George M. born June 26, 1837 and married Eliza Ann Lasley June 25, 1860; Polly born March 14, 1825 and died March 3, 1832; Elizabeth born July 19, 1826; Barbara born Feb. 11, 1830 and Edward Patton born Dec. 3, 1835 and died March 17, 1840. Mariah Sarah married Richard William Etherington who settled in Harrison Township. Richard received a sheepskin deed signed by President Zachary Taylor on March 20, 1849.

Richard was the son of John and Francis (Yancey) Etherington and was born Aug. 10, 1818 in Kentucky. Richard and Mariah had seven children: Catherine born in 1844; Philip born March 5, 1845; John Thomas born November, 1847; William born April 14, 1850; Elizabeth born in 1854; Martha born in 1855 and Robert H. born in February, 1862. All but Catherine were born in Howard County.

John Shaddy, Jr. was born Feb. 26, 1754 in Hillsboro, NC the son of John and Elizabeth Shadday and died Feb. 21, 1859 in Switzerland County, IN. He married Mary Fogelman April 20, 1795. Mary was born Dec. 23, 1776 in Orange County, NC; died April 22, 1866 in Switzerland County and is buried in Bennington Slawson Cemetery. John and Mary had 14 children: Catherine, Elizabeth, Polly, Barbara, Lucinda, Emsley born April 13, 1803, George W., Jacob, Jordan, William born in 1823 in Switzerland County, Hardin, John and Turley. Polly married a Mr. Lowe, Barbara married a Mr. Cole, Lucinda married a Mr. Thompson, Emsley married Polly Leaf, George married Louisa Green, William married Francis Dyer in 1847, Turley married Henry Steel and Elizabeth married Martin Nease.

John Shadday Sr. was born Jan. 3, 1738 and died Feb. 9, 1812. Johns' wife, Elizabeth was born Dec. 4, 1747 and died March 3, 1818 and is buried in Alamance County, NC. John and Elizabeth had seven children: Molly married John Fogelman, Sally married John Coole, Caty married George Fogelman, John Jr. married Mary Fogelman, Rachel married George Fogelman and Jacob.

CAROLE MOLINE RECORD -

Carole Moline Record was born Dec. 26, 1945 in Kokomo. The daughter of Robert L. and Elaine (Moline) Record. Attended Palmer Elementary School, Washington Junior High School and graduated from Kokomo High School in 1964. April 30, 1966 she married Ralph Hendershot. They have one son Gregory Ralph. Their marriage was dissolved May 1, 1989. Carole has worked at St. Joseph Hospital since September 1984. She has one sister, Amy Ann of Largo, FL.

Robert Lincoln Record was born Jan. 8, 1914. The son of Lincoln F. and Grace (Kellar) Record. He married Elaine Moline on Aug. 31, 1940. He was employed at Delco Radio as a draftsman and worked there until his death Jan. 31, 1961. He had two brothers Fred William and Paul Linville.

Lincoln Farlow Record was born in 1881, the son of Adam T. and Armilda (Farlow) Record. He married Jane Grace Kellar June 3, 1903. Lincoln was a local contractor, paving many streets and constructing sidewalks in Kokomo. He died in 1944. He had one brother, Blaine, and five sisters, Della, Mary, Theresa, Blanche and Stella.

Adam T. Record was born June 21, 1845 on a farm near Liberty, NC. At the outbreak of the Civil War his family moved north because of disagreement with the southern cause. Adam enlisted in the northern army with 113th Indiana Infantry and fought until the close of the conflict. After the war he moved to Kokomo and married Armilda Farlow Aug. 29, 1878. He died in 1929 while visiting his brother D.M. Record in Johnson City, TN. Adams father was John F. Record born Dec. 16, 1816 and died June 16, 1880.

Jane Grace Kellar was born Jan. 18, 1882 in Anderson, IN. She was the daughter of George and Minerva (Raynes) Kellar. Grace was a homemaker and poet. She wrote of her family, every day life trips that were taken. She had 11 brothers and sisters. She died April 23, 1936.

Elaine Helen Moline was born Jan. 3, 1916 in St. Paul, MN. She was the daughter of Fridolf F. and Ebba (Brandrup) Moline. She worked as a beautician following high school and then for Indiana Bell Telephone as a switchboard operator. She quit work when Carole was born to raise her family. She died May 28, 1961. She had one sister Margaret.

Fridolf Ferdinand Moline was born in March of 1877 in Orebro, Sweden. When he emigrated to the United States he was a carpenter by trade. In 1910 he married Ebba Marie Brandrup. Their girls were born in St. Paul. The family lived for a time in Seattle, WA. After moving to Kokomo he also worked at the Dirilyte Company, on South Main St., making molds for spoons for the Dirilyte table service. His nephew, Carl Molin, was the inventor of the alloy called Dirigold. He died Jan. 15, 1958.

Ebba Marie Brandrup was born Dec. 24, 1892 in Copenhagen, Denmark. When she emigrated to the United States she worked as a maid and nanny. During the Korean Conflict she worked at the Dirilyte inspecting fins for bombs. She died Sept. 8, 1970. *Submitted by Carole Record*

ADDIE REISINGER -

Addie Reisinger was born Jan. 20, 1856 in Indiana. She was the eldest child of Daniel Reisinger and Rosetta Croker Reisinger. The other children in the family (and the year they were born) were: Clinton (1859), Elmer (1862), May (1865), and Lillie (1867).

When she was about the age of 20, Addie married George Wibel. Not much is known about George except that he was a wanderer. He would disappear for months and years at a time. Addie and George had a son Clarence who was born Feb. 9, 1876. George disappeared sometime after Clarence's birth. In the 1880 census for Howard County, Addie and Clarence were living with her parents and siblings in Howard Township. George Wibel returned at some point as he and Addie had another son, Vern, who was born Dec. 23, 1887. George stayed around at least long enough to have the picture made that accompanies this history.

L-R: George Wibel, Vern, Clarence, Addie

Then he disappeared and was not heard from again. This writer has not been able to find anyone who knows where George Wibel came from or where he went. By 1900 Addie had moved to Arcadia (Hamilton County) with Vern and was taking in boarders to help make ends meet. As he grew older, Vern acquired the craft of glass blowing. He was also a factory manager. He was a WW I veteran, a member of an ambulance company. By 1921, Vern was living in Texarkana, TX. It is believed there is where he met and fell in love with Nannie (Nan) Hays. Then Nan moved to Silver, (Montgomery County), AR with her family. Nan was heartbroken that she and Vern were separated. Soon Vern was sent for - to come rescue Nan from her depression. They were married Oct. 9, 1921. They would have four children: Virginia, Essie (the mother of this writer), Marion, and Nancy.

Vern moved his family back to Arcadia, IN. Times were so bad, that during the Depression years they moved in with Addie. Nan was not happy in Indiana, and would go back home to have her babies. All but her youngest were born in her parents' house at Silver. Nancy was born in Arcadia.

Addie Reisinger Wibel died June 11, 1938 never knowing what had happened to her husband, George. She was preceded in death by her oldest son, Clarence. Clarence had been roofing a house in Tipton when he had an acute appendicitis attack and fell off the roof. He died a few days later on Nov. 20, 1911. Vern Wibel lost his battle with lung cancer and died Jan. 7, 1966 in the VA Hospital in Little Rock, AR. He is buried in the Joplin Cemetery, approximately 10 miles east of Mt. Ida, AR. *Submitted by Alvin Black*

RENIE -

The beginning of the "Renie" family in the United States was around 1818. The records show that young "Renie" was the last living male child and at that time the French were trying to preserve family names so he was excused from the military service at the age of approximately 17 years old. After he received this exemption he immediately planned to go to America.

He booked passage on a sailing vessel with the destination port which is now Mobile, AL. The trip took three months plus. During the trip yellow fever broke out and 17 of the 19 passengers and some of the crew succumbed to the fever. Young Renie and the other passengers became ill but did survive the trip.

On landing at Mobile the customs officer could speak no French and Renie could speak no English which could account for the spelling and pronunciation of the name Renie.

Young Renie got a job going up the river with a crew; they would make boards or shakes and raft them down prior to selling. Each time going up the river they would have to walk back carrying supplies and necessary tools. On the third trip north he decided to keep on going living off the land. When he reached Indiana this is where he decided to settle down and begin his life in America.

Young Bartholomew Renie was born in the Alsace Dist. Paris, France around 1800. He married Mary Ann Busch. Together they had six children born in Jennings County, IN: Charles, Edward, Joseph, John, Augustus, and Mary Josephine all being born in the 1830's. He and his wife lived there all their life until their deaths and are buried in the Vernon Cemetery in Vernon, IN.

One of Bartholomew's sons, Augustus Renie, moved to Tipton County in the early 1880's, with his wife Catherine Gasper; they raised seven children. Charles Henry Renie was born Sept. 26, 1863 and married Elizabeth J. Johnson. Cecilia A. Renie was born Aug. 2, 1865 and married Peter H. Holderith. Josephine Renie was born April 5, 1867 and married Fred Mattingley. Joseph William Renie was born Aug. 17, 1869 and married Anna Catherine Tragesser. Edward John Renie was born Dec. 8, 1871 and married Winnie Qualter. Mary A. Renie was born Feb. 27, 1874 and married John Tragasser. Margaret J. Renie was born on March 13, 1876 and married Michael Wunder.

There are many present day descendents in Kokomo and Howard County from the Charles Renie, Cecilia Renie Holderith, Joseph Wm. Renie and Mary Renie Tragesser families. Some descendants in Kokomo are Joseph Renie, (Sharpsville) Robert Renie, Marsha Renie Sanders, Timothy Renie, William A. Renie, Pat Holderith Tracewell. There are still many Tragesser descendents presently living in the Howard County area. *Submitted by Pat Tracewell*

ELWOOD "BERT" REYNOLDS
Bert Reynolds moved to Howard County as a young man, having been born in Villa Grove, IL, May 31, 1917 to Frank and Vianna Stanford Reynolds.

He met and married Mildred Bell Wolford, March 31, 1934. Mildred was born in Howard County May 26, 1917 to Aruther Henry and Ethel Wolford. She remained in Howard County all her life.

Bert and Mildred Reynolds

They had eight children: Joyce Statler, who remains a resident of this county, Roberta Marsh, Mesa, AZ, Berdina Head, Tanya Stewart, Robert Elwood Reynolds, Kent Allen, Toby Michael Reynolds, all residents of Howard County, IN.

Bert worked at the Hoosier Iron Works during WWII. He then owned and operated Ace Motors for several years. He was also a salesman for the new Fritchie Nash Home, selling Nash Ramblers and other automobiles. Mildred was a housewife and was kept very busy raising their large family. She was very active in the small community of Oakford, having moved there in 1953. She was a member of the Taylor Twp. Homemakers and the Ladies Circle for the Fairfield Christian Church, where her family attended.

WILLIAM FRANKLIN AND VIANNA KATHERINE REYNOLDS
Frank Reynolds was born to James L. and Armilda McComas Reynolds Nov. 29, 1884, in Clay County, IL. He married Vianna K. Stanford Jan. 1, 1906 in Bushton, IL. She was born in Long Pine, NE.

They moved their family to Gary, IN during the Depression in the 1920s to work in the steel mills. From there they moved to Howard County where Frank worked as a carpenter.

They had six children: Jessie Pearl Reynolds, born Jan. 8, 1907, Gladys Mildred Reynolds Ritchie, born Aug. 12, 1909, James Edgar Reynolds, born June 19, 1911, Claude Franklyn Reynolds, born Dec. 7, 1914, Bert Monroe Reynolds, later named Percy Elwood Reynolds, born May 31, 1917 (nicknamed "Bert"), and Juanita Zelma Reynolds Harness, born Oct. 28, 1919.

Frank and Vianna are buried in Crown Point Cemetery along with their son, Elwood Reynolds. Jessie, Ed, and Claude (Curly) are buried in the Albright Cemetery. *Submitted by Berdina Head, granddaughter*

RICH
In the early 1800's, Thomas and Betsy Peacock Rich were pioneers in the New London area. They were farmers, leaders in the Friends Church, and were active in the Underground Railroad.

In 1873, their son Levi (1848-1915) married Susan Josephine Heston. Her parents were George and M. Melissa Jackson Heston. Levi helped with the farming and also worked in a broom factory, where he lost his arm in a machinery accident. Unable to continue farming, he came to Kokomo, opening a combined funeral home and furniture store. He became active in community affairs, and was on the commission that built the new city building, now known as City Venture One.

Their son, Kenneth Heston Rich (1883-1932) married Grace Mabel Morgan (1884-1955). Kenneth became a well loved civic leader, and they were co-owners of the Rich Funeral Home.

Robert Heston Rich (1909-1975), their only child, married Winema Brown (1910-1981) June 4, 1933. Her parents, E. Howard and Ruth Pemberton Brown, were co-ministers of Union Street Friends Church. Bob and his parents were very active in that church, also. Bob pursued his love of music through the years by playing in many bands in the state and later in Florida. His big bass saxophone was his trademark. Winema also loved music and sang in church and other choirs. Bob followed his father and grandfather as funeral director, and Winema was a registered nurse. They sold the funeral home building in 1956 and lived in St. Petersburg, FL until their deaths. The old funeral home building, used by three generations, now houses the Kokomo Rescue Mission. They had two children, Phyllis and Kenneth.

Kenneth Howard Rich (1938-) married Mary Colleen McKee in 1960. Ken has been with the *Kokomo Tribune* in advertising for many years. Colleen trained as an operating room tech., but soon was busy raising their family: Rita, Betsy, Michael, Matthew (died at two months), Amy and Heidi. They all call Kokomo their home base, but as the children graduated from college, their jobs have taken them to different cities. Rita married Fred Kuhlman in 1990. Their daughter is Nicole and his children are Kelly and Tyler.

Phyllis Jean Rich (1934-) married Tom A. Driver (1934-) on Aug. 7, 1955. His parents, Wildon and Anna Boles Driver, had moved to Kokomo in the 1940s, to work at Lincoln Finance Co. Phyllis is a registered nurse and Tom served in the Army, Lincoln Finance Co., and Button Motors. They have four children. Cynthia (1959) married Jeff Kemp in 1983. Their children are Kari, Kasey and Kaylee. Michael (1961) married Diane Jackson in 1982. Their children are Keenan, Ciara, and Caleb. Tim (1963) married Dottie Armour in 1989. They have Ryan. Julie (1976) is a senior at KHS. All the Driver families live in Howard County, and enjoy sharing time together. Phyllis has enjoyed tracing their family histories to pass on to the next generations.

RICKARD
When the first land grants in Howard County were issued by William Henry Harrison, Daniel Rickard (1813-1895) seized the opportunity to enter 200 acres in Clay Township. It was 1846 and a new beginning for the Rickards in Howard County. He was 33, married to Catherine Millard (1822-1906) of Maryland, age 24. Their son, William Henry, was a year old, and Little Sarah Ann was age two. A log cabin was built to accommodate the growing family as it increased with the birth of Frances (1848-1925), Benjamin Franklin (1851-1925), Arcemus "Tynt" (1854-1930), Laura B. 1856, Mathilda B. 1859, John Lewis (1860-1948), and Amanda (died at the age of four).

Anthony (Rueckert) Rickard, the father, was a German from Alsace. His wife Easter came from Maryland b. 1771. Daniel's parents first settled in Warren County, OH, then located on the Miami-Howard County line, west of Cassville. Daniel was the oldest child. He had two brothers, Joseph b. 1816, Samuel b. 1820, and a sister Sarah (Mrs. Jacob Aaron), b. 1818. Anthony died in 1846 and was buried in the Waisner-Rickard Cemetery, the same year Daniel moved to Clay Township on the Webster Street Pike.

Rickard brothers and sisters - Back row L-R: John, Ben, Henry. Front row: Frances, Sarah Ann

They were an ambitious, hard working family and eventually managed to clear the land for farming. It was difficult splitting the rails for fences and digging ditches by hand, for drainage of the very wet soil. All the neighbors came in for the "Log Rolling" and burning of excess logs. Progress ensued and a one-room school was established, Rickard School House #6.

As a young man William "Henry" Rickard fought in the Civil War. He served in the Indiana Infantry, Company 118 and was a member of the GAR. In 1922 when Henry and Drucilla (Fisher) (1852-1929) celebrated their 50th Anniversary, she told of doing weaving for other people in order to get her wedding clothes. Drucilla and her parents, James and Nancy Fisher were founders of the First Baptist Church of Kokomo in February 1875. Henry and Drucilla's son, Arthur Rickard (1885-1963), was an ordained minister and served in Cassville during the time the Methodist Church was built. His daughter, Gladys Jackson, has been a life-long resident of Clay Township and has maintained the Rickard pioneer spirit.

Four of Daniel's children, Henry, Ben, John and Francis (Mrs. Anthony Rice) lived on adjoining farms and raised their families in Clay Township. Laura married Walter Shores and moved to Frankfort, IN. Arcemus followed a sister, Sarah (Mrs. George McIlwain) to Oregon in 1903. Uncle Ben's granddaughter, Freida Cotterman Barker, born Nov. 1, 1900, was born in Clay Township but has lived in Kokomo most of her life. She is very remarkable for her age, interested in her church, Parr United Methodist, and outside activities. Frieda is the oldest living descendant. The Rickards are proud of their forefathers and of their Howard County Hoosier heritage.

HENRY HARRISON RILEY - Henry Harrison and Amazetta (Hightower) Riley and their five children came to Howard County in 1891 from Clinton Township in Decatur County, IN. They rented the H.C. Roberts land in the NW quarter of Section 21 of Howard Township and settled down to farm.

Henry Harrison Riley was born Nov. 20, 1840, in Washington County, KY, the eighth child and youngest son of Lewis and Margaret (Dicky) Riley. He was named after President William Henry Harrison who had been elected earlier that month. His siblings were Mary Ann Riley, Thomas H. Riley, William E. Riley, Margaret Riley, John C. Riley, Jackson Smith Riley, Nancy Riley, Martha Riley, and Sarah C. Riley.

In 1851 after the death of his father, Henry and several other family members moved to Greensburg, Decatur County, IN, where they were employed by the railroad. Later Henry quit the railroad to farm for his mother-in-law. Amazetta (Hightower) Riley was born in Decatur County, IN, on March 17, 1853, the fourth of six children of Archibald and Marietta (Christy) Hightower. Her siblings were George W. Hightower, Patsy Hightower, Lucinda Hightower, Arnetta Hightower, and Julietta Hightower.

Henry Harrison Riley and Amazetta Hightower were married Sept. 1, 1870, in Decatur County, IN. They had eight children. Seven were born in Decatur County, two of whom died before reaching maturity. Jesse Marshall Riley was born Aug. 14, 1872, married Lillie Dallas Barnes Nov. 19, 1896, and died Oct. 13, 1970. Holly Van Riley was born July 4, 1876, and died about 1885. Minnie Olive Riley was born Feb. 20, 1878, married John Roscoe Shockney June 15, 1904, and died Jan. 14, 1957. Charles Melvin Riley was born Feb. 12, 1881, married Stella June Swope Nov. 24, 1904, and died April 2, 1949. Milton Irvin Riley was born Oct. 7, 1883, married Bessie Flae Fox Dec. 24, 1906, and died Dec. 16, 1928. Roe Raymond Riley was born Dec. 12, 1886, married Edna Devona Trostel April 20, 1914, and died Feb. 8, 1947. Roland Edwin Riley was born April 18, 1893, in Howard County, married (1) Beulah G. Shepard May 10, 1913, (2) Edith Blanche Webb March 22, 1926, and died Feb. 18, 1968. Another child died in infancy, name and date unknown.

Henry Harrison Riley Family - about 1905 - Sitting, L-R Minnie Olive, Henry Harrison and Amazetta. Standing L-R Charles Melvin, Roe Raymond, Jesse Marshall, Milton Irvin and Roland Edwin

In 1894 Henry H. Riley bought a 60-acre farm in Section 2, Prairie Township, Tipton County, IN, west of Sharpsville near the Mt. Lebanon Friends Church. The family lived there for seven years during which time Henry and Amazetta joined the Mt. Lebanon Church.

In 1901 Henry sold the Tipton County farm and purchased 114 acres west of Phlox in Sections 22 and 27 of Union Township, Howard County. They lived there for 24 years, during which time they celebrated their 50th wedding anniversary Sept. 1, 1920. Henry died at age 84 on March 7, 1925. Amazetta died at age 79, on Aug. 30, 1932. Her funeral was held Sept. 1, 1932, their 62nd wedding anniversary. They were buried at Greenlawn Cemetery at Greentown, IN. *Submitted by Edwin B. Riley, Jr.*

EDWIN B. RILEY, JR. - Edwin B. Riley, Jr., son of Edwin B. Riley and Roberta Klingman, grew up in Howard Township on his grandfather's farm. (Refer to the Jesse Marshall Riley family history.) He attended Howard Elementary and graduated from Northwestern High School in 1956. He majored in history at Ball State Teachers College and graduated in 1960 with a degree in secondary education. He taught two years at the Berne-French Township School Corporation in Berne, IN, and two years with the Department of Defense Schools in England and France. He returned to Kokomo in 1964 and taught one year at Maconaquah Jr. High School. Since then he has been employed with the Kokomo-Center School Corporation, teaching at Elwood Haynes, Maple Crest, and Kokomo High School Downtown Campus. He received his master's degree from Indiana University in 1975.

Edwin B. Riley Jr. Family 1991 - Seated L-R: Ed Riley, Carolyn Riley, Matthew Slaughter, Dawn Slaughter. Standing L-R: Devin Riley, Mark Slaughter

Ed met his wife, the former Carolyn Rae Bailey, when they were both teaching at Berne. She is the daughter of Ray and Gladys (VanSickle) Bailey of Marshall, MI. Carolyn graduated from Marshall High School and Taylor University with a degree in English. After teaching English and Spanish for several years, she received her master's degree in Library Science from Indiana University in 1969.

The Rileys have lived most of their married lives in Taylor Township. Carolyn has been librarian at Oak Hill High School, Maconaquah High School, Tipton's Washington Elementary and Middle School, and Taylor Junior-Senior High School. They are the parents of Dawn Elizabeth, born Feb. 9, 1959, and Devin Barnes Riley, born June 9, 1973.

Dawn was married Aug. 8, 1981, to Mark Alan Slaughter, son of Keith and Bonnie (Yater) Slaughter of Kokomo. They are both 1981 graduates of Taylor University, and Mark has a degree from Trinity Evangelical Divinity School. They live in Fishers, IN, where Mark is employed with InterVarsity Christian Fellowship. The Slaughters have two children: Matthew Alan, born April 27, 1989, and Rebecca Elizabeth, born Oct. 17, 1992.

Devin is a 1991 graduate of Taylor High School and is a student at Ball State University where he is studying psychology and journalism. He is a member of the BSU cycling team, and he works at a local golf course during the summer.

The Rileys are members of Macedonia Christian Church where Ed serves as a deacon. They belong to several educational organizations and are active in the Howard County Genealogical Society and Howard County Historical Society where Ed serves on the board of trustees. He is also Howard County Historian for the Indiana Historical Society. *Submitted by Carolyn R. Riley*

JESSE MARSHALL RILEY - Jesse Marshall Riley was born in a log cabin on Aug. 14, 1872, in Decatur County, IN, the oldest child of Henry Harrison Riley and Amazetta Hightower. (Refer to the Henry Harrison Riley family history.) He came to Howard County when his family moved here in 1891 and rented the H.C. Roberts farm in Section 21, Howard Township. Jesse married Lillie Dallas Barnes, daughter of Stephen Titus Barnes and Rosella Lacey on Nov. 19, 1896. (Refer to the William Wilson Barnes family history.) She was born in Howard County on Jan. 3, 1877.

The Rileys began their married life in Howard Township where Jesse farmed for Lillie's grandfather, William Wilson Barnes. They had three children: Florence Lucille Riley, born Nov. 30, 1900; died July, 1902; Edwin Barnes Riley, (1906-1975); and Harold Henry Riley, born Sept. 24, 1911; died May 31, 1917.

December 24, 1904, Jesse and Lillie purchased 40 acres from Joe Pence in Section 22, Howard Township, a short distance west of their first home. They lived there the rest of their lives and gradually expanded the farm to 140 acres.

Lillie D. and Jesse M. Riley, 50th anniversary, 1946

The Rileys were members of Salem United Brethern Church and later charter members of Hillsdale United Brethern Church, now Hillsdale United Methodist Church. They were active in the Farm Bureau and Home Demonstration Club. Also Jesse served as Howard Township trustee from 1923-1931. They celebrated their 50th wedding anniversary Nov. 19, 1946, and took a trip through the western states with the Farm Bureau.

Lillie died Oct. 8, 1951, at age 74. Jesse lived to be 98 and died Oct. 13, 1970. They were buried in Crown Point Cemetery in Kokomo.

Edwin Barnes Riley, their only surviving child, was born Oct. 10, 1906. He attended Prairie School and graduated from Howard Township School in 1926. He also attended Purdue University and played in the Purdue Band.

On April 20, 1930, he married Roberta Klingman, a high school classmate. (Refer to the William Klingman family history.) They had two children: Ellen Joan Riley, born Jan. 21, 1931, married Russell Morris, Jr. September 16, 1950, and Edwin Barnes Riley, Jr. born June 1, 1938, married Carolyn Rae (Bailey) Liechty June 14, 1969.

Roberta died July 19, 1940, and Edwin married 2) Miriam Elizabeth "Bettie" Tomlinson March 1, 1942. She was the daughter of George Tomlinson and Augusta Jones.

Edwin and Bettie had three children: Cynthia Anne Riley, born April 26, 1943; Marcia Lou Riley, born July 25, 1945; and Robert Dallas Riley, born June 15, 1955. Edwin worked over 25 years at Haynes Stellite and farmed for his father. He was also a substitute rural mail carrier. Bettie sold Avon for many years and worked in the EUB Church camping program. The family was active in Hillsdale EUB Church, now Hillsdale United Methodist Church.

Bettie died Nov. 22, 1965, and Edwin married 3) Gladys (Buchanan) Shenk Dec. 20, 1968. He retired from Stellite and died April 1, 1975. Edwin and his first two wives are buried at Zion Cemetery in Howard Township. *Submitted by Cynthia A. Girton*

SAMUEL AND LUCILLE (MASON) RINEHART

Lifelong residents of Howard County, Samuel Ross Rinehart and Florence Lucille Mason were married Feb. 8, 1918. Ross, son of John and Susanna (Huddleston) Rinehart, was born Oct. 3, 1887, and died May 19, 1960. Lucille, daughter of Omer and Tessie (Marshall) Mason, granddaughter of Andrew Jackson and Amanda (Odell) Mason, and also Newton and Lucinda (Moulder) Marshall, was born May 5, 1899, and died Nov. 29, 1984. Ross and Lucille had seven children as follows: 1. Mason Rinehart, who married Evelyn Hensley; 2. Maxine (Rinehart) Kirby, who married (1) Lilburn Stull (1918-1958) and (2) Joseph Kirby; 3. Paul Rinehart, who married Jo Ann Ingles; 4. Nina Rinehart (1925-1943); 5. Marilyn Rinehart (1926-1934); 6. Virginia (Rinehart) Prifogle (see below); 7. Buddy Rinehart, who married Emma Lou Fultz.

Ross and Lucille Rinehart Family - Back Row: Bud (7th) Lucille, Ross, Eddie (3rd). Front Row: Maxine (2nd) Virginia (6th) Mason (1st). Not shown: Nina - died at age 17 of brain tumor. Marilyn - died at age 7 of sleeping sickness.

The sixth child of Ross and Lucille Rinehart, Virginia Lee, was born April 22, 1928, Ervin Township Howard County. On April 6, 1946, she married Carl Edward Prifogle, who was born Aug. 10, 1927, Ervin Township, son of Clifford and Marie (Obermeyer) Prifogle, grandson of Michael and Louise (Bossert) Prifogle, and also Henry and Matilda (Bulk) Obermeyer. Carl is retired from farming and Stellite Corporation and they live in Ervin Township. Their homestead is still within a square mile of where each was born and reared. Virginia has taught piano since 1953 and is a part-time organist at Judson Baptist Church, which was founded by her great-great grandfather, Rev. Price Odell, and of which they are members. They have four children listed below:

1. James Stephen Prifogle, born April 14, 1947, Howard County. He married (1) in 1967, Sandra DeFabritis, divorced in 1983; (2) in 1983, Rebecca (Dieterly) Alberson (1949-1991); and (3) in 1993, Pamela (Vint) Graham. They live in Howard County and he is in the transportation manufacturing industry in Lafayette, Tippecanoe County, and she is employed by Haynes International, Inc. Steve and Sandra have three children, all born in Howard County: Stephen Todd, born Sept. 14, 1968, employed by the Howard County Sheriff Department; James Trent, born Nov. 14, 1970, residing in Indianapolis; and Thomas Gregory, born Nov. 5, 1973, residing in Indianapolis.

2. Bruce Edward Prifogle, born Nov. 30, 1948, Howard County. He married Alice Jones and they live in Howard County where he is in the fuel distribution industry and she is a homemaker. They have three children, all born in Howard County: Lucas Wayne, born Aug. 2, 1975; Samuel Lee, born Oct. 12, 1978; and Joel Edward, born Oct. 17, 1980.

3. Diana Lu (Prifogle) (Curl) Criss, born March 3, 1950, Howard County. She married (1) in 1970, Thomas Curl, divorced in 1977 and (2) Dean Criss. They live in Howard County where she is a school bus driver and homemaker and he is an insurance claims investigator. They have two children: Stacey Marie, born Nov. 7, 1972, Boone County; and Jason Thomas, born March 14, 1975, Marion County.

4. Cathryn Maxine (Prifogle) Newton, born Oct. 31, 1953, Logansport, IN. She married Bradley Newton and they live in Howard County where she is a school bus driver and employed in the Newton's family business and he is a glass and paint retailer. They have one son, Wesley Ray, born May 13, 1977, Howard County. *Submitted by Cathryn (Prifogle) Newton*

JOHN M. AND SUSANNA (HUDDLESTON) RINEHART

John M. Rinehart, born Feb. 27, 1845 in Preble County, OH, was the first of seven children born to Jacob and Fanny (Barnhart) Rinehart. A farmer of German descent, Jacob was born Dec. 7, 1820 in Virginia, died of typhoid Jan. 3, 1863, and is buried in Pete's Run Cemetery in Howard County. Fanny was born April 7, 1824 in Virginia, also died of typhoid Dec. 1, 1862, and is buried beside Jacob. The following additional children were born to Jacob and Fanny: Samuel (born 1847); Hugh (1848-1862); Henry (1850-1943), who married (1) in 1876 Susanna Trent, who died in 1877, and (2) in 1882 Sarah Landes (1859-1926); Phillip (born 1853); Charles (1855-1863); and Levi (born 1858). Between 1850-1860 Jacob moved his family to Howard County from Ohio.

The John M. Rinehart Family - Seated L-R: John M., Gladys M., Susanna, Charles F. Standing L-R: Samuel Ross and Amos Loren

John's first marriage was to Elizabeth Brubaker, born Aug. 20, 1845 in Ohio, died Sept. 23, 1872, and buried in Pete's Run Cemetery. The following three children were born to John and Elizabeth: Nancy Evaline (Rinehart) Price (1866-1943), who married Levi Alexander Price (1861-1908), Uriah Martin Rinehart (born 1868), who married Tella H. (?) in 1896, and Frances Viola Rinehart (1871-1871).

On Sept. 8, 1878, John married Susanna Huddleston, daughter of Henry and Abarilla (Oyler) Huddleston, born April 17, 1857 in Indiana, died Dec. 21, 1939, and buried in South Union Cemetery. John and Susanna had the following four children: Charles F. Rinehart (1881-1955), who married in 1902 Rebecca A. Patton (1882-1951), Amos Loren Rinehart (1884-1943), who married in 1906 Myrtle E. Mason (1883-1969), Samuel Ross Rinehart (1887-1960), who married (1) on Sept. 20, 1913 Bertha Alice Stetler (1889-1918) and (2) on Feb. 8, 1919 Florence Lucille Mason (1899-1984), Gladys M. (Rinehart) Moss (1891-1975), who married in 1917 L. Rayburn Moss (1891-1963).

John was a respected member of the Dunkard Church, and like his father, became a prominent farmer. The original Rinehart homestead in Ervin Township still remains in the family five generations later. On Dec. 23, 1911, John died of a ruptured aorta and is buried with Susanna in South Union Cemetery. *Submitted by Diana (Prifogle) Criss*

FRANK AND BERTHA RIOTH

Frank and Bertha (Weaver) Rioth were born and raised in Howard County, IN. Frank (1887-1940) and Bertha (1892-1968) were married in Howard County in 1911. They are the maternal grandparents of Rosalea (Farris) Kenworthy, who is listed elsewhere in this book. Frank and Bertha were the parents of six children: Mildred Dorothy Ellerbrook, Maxine Eleanor Rioth, Kathleen Lois Farris, Alma May Ulerick, Martha Rose Becker, and Gretta Joan Smith.

Frank worked at The Pottery in Kokomo and also worked in a copper shop. The Rioth family lived in several locations in Howard County. Kathleen (1919-1992), their daughter, was married in Kokomo on Feb. 24, 1946 to Burl Farris, a native of New Mexico. They had two children: Edward Michael Farris, born Dec. 10, 1946 and Rosalea Kay, born Jan. 2, 1950. Kathleen worked for the Sanitation Department in Kokomo after the untimely death of her husband in 1953.

Frank was one of six children born to Edward M. and Martha Jane (Polk) Rioth. Edward was born in Alsace-Loraine, France. Edward's mother immigrated to this country about 1856 and settled in the Cass County, IN area. Edward (1852-1915) married Martha Polk Sept. 24, 1879 in Howard County. They lived the rest of their lives in Howard County.

Martha's parents were Thomas J. and Sophia (Harness) Polk. Thomas, a native of Botetourt County, VA and Sophia were married in Carroll County, IN on Nov. 28, 1852. They lived in Ervin Township, Howard County for most of their lives. The parents of Thomas were Joseph and Catherine (Beckner) Polk. In 1831 Joseph (1802-1849) and Catherine (1794-1881) moved from Virginia to Carroll County, IN. Joseph and Catherine both died in Howard County, Ervin Township and are buried in Mound Cemetery. Sophia's parents were George W. and Harriett (Sowards) Harness. George (1768-1876) was born in what is now Hampshire County, WV. He married Harriett in Fayette County, OH. His family settled in Cass, Clinton, Carroll and Howard Counties. Many of his descendants were prominent citizens as lawyers, judges, congressman, and farmers.

The parents of Bertha (Weaver) Rioth were Stephen and Rozella (Anstine) Weaver. Stephen (1868-1938) was born in Howard County. He married Rozella in Miami County, but they lived in Howard County most of their lives. Stephen farmed and was engaged in the real estate business in the Kokomo-Howard County area.

Stephen was the third of eight children born to Daniel and Rachel (Troyer) Weaver. Daniel (1833-1914) was born in Holmes County, OH. In 1861 he married Rachel (1839-1908) in Miami County, IN. They both died in Howard County and are buried in Crown Point Cemetery in Kokomo. The parents of Rachel were Joseph C. and Maria (Hostetler) Troyer. Joseph (1799-1873) was born Union County, PA. Maria (1801-1865) was also born in Union County, PA. They were married in 1825 in Holmes County, OH. They moved to the Miami County, IN area and are both buried in the Zion Church Cemetery in Howard County.

295

RITCHEY - John Franklin Ritchey (Sept. 30, 1851-March 7, 1936) the second child of Robert Ellsworth and Lucretia Ann (Harrell) Ritchey was born in Howard County and is buried at the South Union Cemetery in Ervin Twp. Sarah Elizabeth Myers and John were married May 30, 1878; the girl next door was the daughter and sixth child of James M. and Elizabeth (Massena) Myers. She was born Oct. 13, 1859 in Howard County and died Feb. 4, 1936. Sarah is buried in the New London Cemetery with her mother and father in the family plot. The Myers family came to Howard County from Ohio around 1850.

John F. Ritchey and Sara Elizabeth (Myer) Ritchey

The Ritchey family's occupation of farming was carried on by John. It has been said he was very public-spirited and was quite an orator. John used to stand on the Courthouse Square, gather quite an audience and give the current local politicians a hard time. At that period in time the Courthouse Square was the gathering place for everyone in the area when they came to town.

His father, Robert, gave all of his children valuable land before his death. Some have passed the land down to their families.

John and Sarah had the following seven children: The eldest was Anna Mae (April 5, 1880-Aug. 26, 1949) married Willard Douglas White and then Joe Johnson. She died in Springfield, MO and is buried at the Greenlawn Cemetery there; the second child John Edward "Ward" (Dec. 25, 1881-Oct. 25, 1925) married Catherine Coy. He died in a construction accident at Mishawaka, IN while building a bridge and is buried in Crown Point Cemetery, Kokomo, IN; child number three James Roscoe (Jan. 25, 1887-Oct. 8, 1965) married Elizabeth Ely. He died Grant County, IN and is buried at South Union Cemetery in Howard County; the fourth child Julius Floyd (June 16, 1891-Oct. 10, 1947) married Maude Black and died at the veterans' hospital in Marion County. He was also buried at South Union Cemetery in Howard County; the fifth child Bertha Bell (Aug. 20, 1893-April 24, 1979) married Oliver Sexton and died in Kokomo. She is buried at Crown Point Cemetery; Cora Ellen the sixth child (Oct. 20, 1895-Nov. 5, 1975) married Isaac Harvey Creason and died in Porter County and is buried at Shiloh Cemetery in Howard County; the last little one, number seven, Stella Irene died as a baby on Dec. 24, 1908 and is buried at Crown Point Cemetery.

Many generations have come and gone, still some descendants live in the surrounding area. *Submitted by granddaughter Mary Lucille (Ritchey) Hawkins*

JULIUS FLOYD RITCHEY - Julius Floyd Ritchey, known to everyone as "Floyd", was the fourth child of John Franklin and Sarah Elizabeth (Myers) Ritchey. He was born in Ervin Township of Howard County June 16, 1891.

World War I came along and he answered his country's call by joining the U.S. Army and was assigned to Bat. C, Sixth Regiment, F.A.R.D. He served at Camp Zachary Taylor, KY.

Floyd married Maude Black Jan. 2, 1920 in Howard County. He went to work for the Brauer Foundry as an iron-moulder. His job was in the cupola, which was to mix the right formula for the iron to be poured into the moulds. Except for a short time when he lived in Cass City, MI, he spent his life in Howard County. There were no children from this union.

Julius Floyd Ritchey 1918-WWI

His love and interest in children made him endeared by all his nieces and nephews. Whenever he came to visit, there was always time for a little rough-housing before going in the house to talk with all the other relatives. Hunting was one of his favorite hobbies. The men of the family did this very often. Many happy times were spent for all the family.

October 10, 1947, Floyd died of cancer at Billings Veterans Hospital in Indianapolis. He had been admitted for only two weeks. His final resting place is in South Union Cemetery, Ervin Township, Howard County. While Floyd was in Michigan he had been kicked in the stomach by a horse. The family thought this may have been the beginning of his problems.

Floyd is still remembered, after so many years, by his friends and relatives. He had a great sense of humor and love of life.

RITCHEY-SEXTON - Bertha Bell Ritchey was born Aug. 20, 1893, the daughter and fifth child of John Franklin and Sarah Elizabeth (Myers) Ritchey. Most of her early life was spent in Ervin Township, Howard County.

At the age of 17, Bertha married Oliver M. Sexton, the son of Edgar E. and Ida E. (Hanna) Sexton. He was born July 10, 1890 in Howard County near Alto, in Harrison Township, where he spent most of his young life. It is not known just how they happened to meet. They were married on Easter Sunday April 16, 1911.

The young couple never had any children to bless their home. However, they had many nieces and nephews who loved them very much. The family of Howard and Ruth (Hunt) White always looked forward to Aunt Bo and Uncle Ol's, as they were affectionately known, visit on Christmas Eve. They gave the latest report on Santa's whereabouts with Christmas goodies in hand. Their visit was a merry occasion and enjoyed very much by the children. At that time of year, they were as popular as Santa Claus.

"Bo" and "Ol" Sexton

Oliver and Bertha owned an Indian motorcycle on which they enjoyed traveling from place to place. He was an impressive looking young man being tall and slender. Bertha was short and petite. They were a striking young couple, and they had many friends.

Ol was a tool and die maker by trade and employed by Kingston Products until 1936. At this time, he went to work for Delco Radio Division and was there for 19 years. He retired in 1955 as a tool room supervisor. Sports was one of his favorites as a pasttime. Shortly before he died, the White Sox won the Pennant. He could hardly believe it. However he was disappointed when they lost the World Series. His passing came Oct. 24, 1959 at St. Joseph Hospital in Kokomo, and his interment was at Crown Point Cemetery.

Bertha was a homemaker and loved by all who knew her. She and Oliver were long-time members of Beamer Methodist Church. Her death came April 24, 1979, and she was also put to rest by her companion in Crown Point.

The love and caring of this wonderful couple will be remembered for many generations.

JOHN DONALD ROBARDS - My roots run deep in Howard County. Early pioneers of the county were my great-great-grandparents John and Sarah Robards whom this biography is about, and John and Francis Gordon (see Gordon biography).

John Robards was born April 30, 1848 near Franklin, Johnson County, IN. He was the son of Thomas Davis Robards born 1789 Garrard County, KY and Mary Boles born Ireland.

After the death of his parents John, age 16, rented a farm and followed the agricultural pursuits of his forefathers. During the same year 1864 John took it upon himself to again follow his forefathers and entered the Civil War, fighting for the Union and what he believed in. He joined the 26th Indiana Volunteer Infantry. He met up with his regiment at Donaldsonville, LA. John saw hard service and suffered from sickness. Six months after the close of the war John was mustered out at Indianapolis, receiving an honorable discharge in October 1865.

Four generations - John Robards, great-grandfather (seated). Elizabeth Ann Robards Miller, grandmother, Agnes Blanche Miller Gordon, mother, standing right. Roscoe Leroy Gordon (infant son)

John returned to Johnson County and farming. On Oct. 2, 1868 he married Sarah Elizabeth Dirmit born Feb. 28, 1852. She was the daughter of George and Elizabeth Ann (Brown) Dirmit of Ripley County, IN.

In 1869 they arrived in Howard County and purchased land five miles northwest of Kokomo, what is now Judson Road. They lived in the log cabin already on the land, while adding improvements and buying more land. Total acreage of the farm was 280, on which John farmed and raised livestock. Their home was remodeled until it was so changed it became known as the show home of Howard County. It featured painted ceiling murals and a large chandelier in the front hall. My father, Roscoe Gordon, can recall swinging from this as a small child.

Politically, John, like his father, was a strong Democrat. John served as a trustee in Clay Township; at that time it was a Republican township. John was a member of Post No. 30, Grand Army of the Republic of Kokomo.

September 29, 1912 John was stricken by paralysis becoming totally dependent on his wife and daughters. However, in March 1916, one year before his demise, John applied to the SAR as a descendent of the American Revolution. His grandfather (Jesse Robards from Goochland County, VA) served as a sergeant with Colonels Taylor, Fleming and Morris. Jesse was at the burning of Richmond, VA in 1781. By John's application, his descendents can trace their ancestry five generations before him, into Virginia. John departed this life on March 9, 1917.

296

Sarah Robards died in December 1934 after suffering six years from an automobile accident on a return trip from Kokomo.

The children of John and Sarah were: Kate (1869-1947) unmarried; Elizabeth Ann (1871-1955) married Calvin Leroy Miller; Laura (1873-1874); Maudie (1874-1878); Myrtle (1876-1876); Lulu (1879-1966) married Merrill Jackson; Fern (1883-1884); Ruth (1889-1972) unmarried; Pearl married Studebaker. Numerous descendants still live in Howard County. *Submitted by descendant Teena (Gordon) Mills VanBriggle*

ROCKEY - In 1883, Isaac Lyman Rockey (1857-1925), his wife Mary Ellen (Harter) Rockey (1858-1926), and two young sons, Clarence and Bennett, came to Harrison Twp. and settled on farmland on the Howard-Tipton County Line. This move was necessary because their farm in Ohio had been condemned and would soon become a part of Grand Lake Reservoir between St. Mary's and Celina. Their first Howard County home was on a knoll overlooking Little Wildcat Creek. In addition to Clarence and Bennett, they were the parents of Alta C., Floyd and Everett Lee. In 1888, Isaac, a farmer and excellent carpenter, built a large frame house on Park Road; in 1892 he built a bank-barn. This farm is now part of Chippendale Golf Course.

Isaac Rockey Family - Front Alta C. Rockey. Middle Row: Floyd Rockey, Isaac Rockey, Mary Ellen Rockey. Back Row: Bennett Rockey, Clarence Rockey

April 11, 1907, Bennett H. Rockey (Sept. 13, 1881-June 27, 1947) married Lulu Dale Romack (Nov. 6, 1883-April 20, 1973) of Prairie Twp., Tipton County. They resided on a farm about two miles from the Isaac Rockey home. Bennett, a farmer, raised the usual crops, fed "feeder" cattle and raised hogs. Work horses were used until farm tractors came along. Lulu raised chickens, milked cows, and always had a nice garden. They had a "hired hand" who lived in their home. Bennett was an ardent Democrat; in the 1920's he served as a Tipton County councilman; 1934-1936 and 1936-1938 he was elected Joint-Representative for Howard/Tipton Counties; in 1944 he ran for 5th District Congressional Representative but was defeated. Bennett and Lulu were faithful members of Mt. Lebanon Friends Church; after moving to Kokomo in 1944 they attended Union Street Friends Church. They had one son, James Doyle Rockey.

James Doyle Rockey (July 3, 1917) graduated from Prairie Twp. High School (1935); attended Kokomo Business College (1935-1936). He helped his parents with the farm work. He served in the U.S. Army during World War II (1942-1944). April 9, 1944 he married Sarah Catherine Hostetler (Dec. 10, 1917); she graduated from Howard Twp. High School (1936) and attended Kokomo Business College (1936-37).

She worked at Western and Southern Life Insurance Co. (1937-44); later at Cuneo Press of Indiana (1958-65). Both like to travel; have been in all 50 states and parts of Canada and Mexico. They will celebrate their 50th wedding in 1994. They have three grown children and two grandsons.

James Bennett Rockey (July 3, 1945) graduated from Prairie Twp. High School (1963) and has a B.S. degree from Ball State University (1974). He has been employed at Chrysler Corporation since 1964. He served in the U.S. Army Reserves (1963-64).

The Doyle Rockey Family - Back Row: Left to Right: Nicole Rockey, James Rockey, and Kay (Rockey) Silence. Middle Row: Clinton Rockey, Doyle Rockey, Sarah Rockey, Brodrick Silence, Front Row: Christopher Rockey and Clayton Silence.

Clinton Lewis Rockey (March 16, 1947) graduated from Sharpsville-Prairie High School (1965) and has a master's degree from Ball State University (1970). He taught industrial arts at Taylor Twp. Middle School (1970-1974); worked at Continental Steel until "the Mill" closed in 1986; since then he has been employed at Chrysler Corporation. August 8, 1970 he married Nicole Lynn Pritz (March 1, 1947) at 9th St. Christian Church in Logansport. Nicole graduated from Logansport High School (1965); attended Ball State University for two years, then transferred to Indiana University-Kokomo and has a master's degree (1971). She has been a third grade teacher at Indian Heights since 1970. They have one son, Christopher McClain Rockey, a student at Tri-Central High School. They live 1 1/2 miles from the former Isaac Rockey homestead.

Kay Arden (Rockey) Silence (Sept. 28, 1956) graduated from Tri-Central High School (1974). She has worked for several years, full-time and part-time, in the service department at McGonigal's. Recently she has been a substitute school bus driver for Northwestern School Corporation. October 1981 she married Brodrick Clayton Silence (April 3, 1956) in First Christian Church, Kokomo. He graduated from Tipton High School (1975) and attended ITT, Indianapolis. For several years he worked in the parts department of Wiese's Olds; in 1989 he became a semi-truck driver for J.B. Hunt. They reside in Howard Twp. in the house that formerly was Kay's grandparents' home. In 1984 they bought the house and 1 1/2 acres of land. They have one son, Clayton Rockey Silence, a student at Howard Elementary School.

DONALD W. AND V. JEAN WILE RODEMAN - Don moved to Kokomo in June 1964 to join Delco Radio as an electrical engineer following his graduation from Purdue University. Jean joined the data processing department of Delco Radio and moved to Kokomo in 1965. The Palm Sunday Tornado made apartments almost impossible to find. After weeks of searching without success she was introduced to a delightful and gracious couple, Mr. and Mrs. Arthur Reed, who opened their home to her. She resided with them until apartments became more readily available.

Donald Roseman Family - Front: Don, Suzy. Back: Jean, John

Don was born in Terre Haute, IN May 26, 1942, but his roots go back to southern Indiana's early history. His mother's family settled in the Madison, IN area in the early 1800's, having come from Ireland and England through Pennsylvania and Virginia. His father's family came to Evansville, IN from Germany in the mid 1800's. He graduated from Gerstmeyer Technical School in Terre Haute, IN.

Jean was born in Clinton, IN May 3, 1940. Her family came to Indiana from Ohio. They traveled widely as a result of her father's work as a mining engineer, before they settled near Clinton in Vermillion County, IN on the former Governors James Whitcomb's (governor 1843-1849) and Claude Matthews's (governor 1893-1897) Estate. A graduate of Clinton High School, she graduated from Chicago School of Design before earning degrees from Purdue and Indiana Universities.

They were married June 17, 1967 at University Lutheran Church in West Lafayette, IN, where they met while students at Purdue. They have two children. John Dallas was born Dec. 28, 1969 and Suzanne Lee was born Oct. 3, 1973. Both are students at Purdue.

Don is presently employed with Delco Electronics having completed more than 28 years in engineering and operations management. Jean owns an interior design business and is also executive director of the Kokomo Fine Art Center. They have been members of Redeemer Lutheran Church since moving to Kokomo.

GEORGE RODY - George Rody (Rothe - in German) was born in Beiseforth, Kurhessen, Germany, on Aug. 27, 1823. His mother lived in Maulsfield, Germany. He had one sister, Martha Elizabeth Walter, who had had six sons and one daughter.

On Dec. 25, 1850, George married Martha Elizabeth Metz, who was born in Diekershausen, Kurhessen, on April 24, 1828. They lived in Beiseforth Hessen-Cassel Melsung, Germany. Their first daughter, Elizabeth Ann, was born there. George worked as a basketweaver.

Through the urging of his wife's brother, Henry Metz, George and his family came to the United States, through the port of Baltimore, MD, in 1852. They settled in Holmes County, OH, near Millersburg. George was nationalized there on March 23, 1858.

In 1865, George and Henry moved their families to adjoining farms in Howard County, IN, two miles south and one-quarter mile east of Waupecong, in Howard Township. They had 11 children: Elizabeth Ann, born in 1851, in Germany. Married John Metz, Dec. 26, 1876. Had five children. Lived in Caseyville, KY. She died on Feb. 17, 1899. Buried in Owensboro, KY. Adam, born in Ohio. Married Jenette Whelstone. Blacksmith by trade. Moved to Missouri. Died and buried in Salem, Dent County, MO.

George, born Oct. 23, 1855, in Holmes County, OH. Married Catherine Lorenz, Jan. 20, 1878, in Howard County, IN. Had 11 children. Worked as a farmer. Died on Feb. 12, 1929, near Plevna, Liberty Township, Howard County. Buried in Kokomo Zion United Methodist Church Cemetery, Howard Township, Howard County, IN (400 N-500 E).

Margaret, born in Ohio. Married Joseph Mast. Moved to Missouri. Had six children. Moved to Indianapolis, IN. Died May 21, 1929. Buried in Crown Hill Cemetery in Indianapolis.

Barbara Elizabeth, born in Ohio, in 1858. Married George Rhody Oct. 23, 1878 in Howard County, IN. Had three children. Moved to Marceline, Linn County, MO. Died on May 5, 1921. Buried in Mount Olivet Cemetery in Marceline.

John, born Sept. 3, 1865, in Clay Township, Miami County, IN. Married Maggie Dotterer on July 31, 1890. Had nine children. Died Dec. 11, 1924, Clay Township. Buried in Memorial Park Cemetery in Kokomo, Howard County, IN.

Anna Carolina, born in Howard County, IN, on March 30, 1872. First marriage to Jacob Dotterer on July 31, 1890. Had two children. Second marriage to John Metz in 1900. Had one child. Anna died March 5, 1928.

Charles, born in 1860 or 1862 in Howard County, IN. Killed in a farming accident on Oct. 15, 1878. Buried in Kokomo Zion United Methodist Church Cemetery.

Other children of George and Martha Rody were: Miriam, who died at age six in Ohio, Henry, who died at age four in Howard County; and Mary Kay, who died at age four in Howard County, in 1878. The latter two children were buried at the Kokomo Zion United Methodist Church Cemetery.

George died on Feb. 17, 1897, and was buried in the aforementioned Kokomo Zion United Methodist Church Cemetery. Martha died on Sept. 29, 1917, in Ervin Township, Howard County, and was buried beside her husband. *Compiled by Dessie Rody, granddaughter of George Rody, around 1943.*

RODKEY - John Rodkey Jr. (1826-1875) was an early pioneer of Howard County.

He was born in Pennsylvania, a son of John and Esther Christian Rodkey. In 1836 after John's father died, his mother purchased land in Miami County, OH, where John was reared. He learned the tanner's trade and farmed. He married Elizabeth Dohner in 1848. That same year he purchased land in Indiana, located in the southwest corner of Monroe Township in Howard County. John's wife died in 1849 leaving him with a young son, Warren.

In 1853 he married Evaline Fennell and built a log cabin on the land he had purchased in Indiana. There they raised five children: Perry, Laura, Caroline, Joseph and Jessie.

Rodkey House (ca 1910)

John and Evaline Rodkey's daughter Caroline married Henry Clay Oilar. They were parents of a daughter, Nellie (Oilar) Shilling (1885-1982). She was a librarian at the Kokomo Howard County Public Library from (1944-1964). Nellie's grandfather, John Rodkey was elected county commissioner in 1868, and re-elected in 1871. He held that office until his death in 1875. According to his diaries written from 1870 through 1875 he was active in many other county affairs such as planting trees in the Howard County Court House yard. He also wrote about building a bank barn and a kiln in which to make brick for the house that he built on his land. These buildings are still in use.

John's son Joseph Rodkey, lived on the homestead his entire life. He was also county commissioner, serving from 1916 through 1919, when he was re-elected.

Joseph enjoyed recalling the days of his boyhood when canals were important arteries of travel, and the old Michigan Road was made of wooden planks in the low areas.

Joseph Rodkey married Dora Milner in 1894. They had two children, Grace and Dudley.

Grace married Charles Bowman in 1920, and they lived in Carroll County. They were parents of five children: Martha (Bowman) Messerly, Dora Caroline Bowman, Dorothy (Bowman) High, Joe Bowman, and Rosemary (Bowman) Austin.

Joseph and Dora Rodkey's son Dudley married Lucille Coin in 1923. They had a daughter, Julia Ann, and in 1947 she married Leon Orem. They became parents of three children, Ray, Jay and Kay.

After Julia Ann's grandfather, Joseph Rodkey died in 1956 the Orem family moved into the old homestead, where they presently reside.

Julia Ann's father Dudley Rodkey lived nearby in Clinton County throughout his married life. He owned and operated the family farm with his family, until his death in 1991.

The Orem grandchildren are Ronald and Cheryl, children of Ray Orem. They are the sixth generation to have lived on the John Rodkey land which was purchased in 1848. *Submitted by Julia Ann Orem*

ROSS - Nathanial C. Ross and Edith G. Lowry married May 8, 1932, in Delphi, IN. Nathaniel was from Howard County and Edith was from Argos, IN. They lived and raised their family in Kokomo. To them were born six children: Judith, James, Phyllis, William, Sharon, and Robert.

Nathaniel was self-employed as a semi-truck driver, and later on he was a truck mechanic. He was in business with his father, Jesse, and his brothers Joseph, Henry and Richard at Ross Transit.

Nathaniel's parents were Jesse F. Ross and Amanda Crownover. Amanda's parents were William A. Crownover and Amanda Williams. Jesse's parents were Wm. H. Ross and Rachel Berry.

Before her marriage, Edith was a waitress. Afterwards, she was a full-time homemaker. She was the daughter of Walter and Nora (Smith) Lowry. Edith's grandparents were Anthony A. Smith and Marguerite Pontius and John and Elizabeth Lowry.

Nathaniel passed away on April 18, 1971. Edith passed away on April 27, 1986. They are buried in Sunset Memory Gardens at Alto, IN.

Their daughter Judy married Paul McGuire, Oct. 12, 1950. They have three children: Paul Jr., Pamela, and Diana.

Judy has been a homemaker and an active 4-H leader for 26 years. Her husband Paul is a bricklayer.

Jim was the bachelor of the family. He graduated from Kokomo High School in 1953, and served in the Navy for several years. When he got out, he worked at different jobs in Indianapolis and Ft. Wayne, before moving to Orlando, FL, where he worked at the Epcot Center in the Norway Pavilion Bakery. He loved to bake and do photography. Unfortunately, Jim passed away on March 19, 1993. He is buried in Sunset Memory Gardens Mausoleum and will be sadly missed by his family and friends.

Phyllis married George Martin, Jr., on Jan. 7, 1956. They have one son Jeffery.

Phyllis retired in February 1993 from Delco Electronics, and her husband George is close to retirement from Kokomo Ready Mix.

Bill is married to Margarite (Fields) Delano. Bill's children are Mike and Troy.

Bill currently works and lives in the LaPorte area. He drives a semi for the Lewis Bread Company. Margarite retired from Delco Electronics in 1993.

Now we come to the author of the family history, Sharon I. (Ross) Slagle. Sharon, the fifth child of six children, has worked at Delco Electronics since graduation in 1965. She recently started a Longaberger Basket business. She is also a volunteer at the Kokomo Library and attends Clown College.

On Nov. 18, 1967, Sharon married Arnold L. Slagle in the Bible Baptist Church in Kokomo. They had a foster son, Scott A. Campbell, born Aug. 17, 1970. He passed away on Dec. 14, 1990.

On the 4th of July weekend 1973, they received a beautiful baby girl and named her Tamara Kay. She was born June 6, 1973. Tami graduated in 1991 from Lewis Cass High School and attends Ivy Tech in Kokomo.

In April 1979, Arnold and Sharon divorced. A second marriage to Robert Berry ended in 1986. Tami and Sharon are presently residing in Galveston, IN.

Robert Ross is the sixth child born to Nathaniel and Edith Ross. He graduated from Kokomo High School in 1971 and from IU-K in 1975. He married Pamela Davis, May 24, 1975. In 1978, they moved to the Austin, TX, area. He is presently a district manager with NovaCare, overseeing rehabilitation services for occupational and physical therapy and speech pathology.

Rob and Pam have two children, Ryan and Amanda. *Submitted by Sharon (Ross) Slagle*

RUNK - The first Runk to live in Howard County was Samuel Runk (1816-1907), one of the earliest pioneer settlers of Honey Creek Township. Born in Virginia, he moved with his family in 1844. He was the only man in Howard County owning and living on an original United States patent (a grant of 86 acres which cost him 100 dollars). His first wife, Margaret Ratcliffe (1820-1877) bore him the nine children he had. They were members of the Friends Church at New London and are buried in the New London Cemetery.

Loren Runk and family - taken about 1929 - Seated L to R: Loren (holding Dawn), Mabel (holding Maybelle) Standing L to R: Homer, Wayne, Frances, Stanley

Two of Samuel's nine children were known to have lived in Howard County. His son, John, was named after Samuel's father, John, who served in the War of 1812. He studied at schools in Kokomo and later in Lebanon, OH. He returned to Howard County and taught school nine years at Kokomo and Russiaville. He became a compiler of biographical material for a Chicago publishing house and was at one time an editor of the *Kokomo Gazette.*

Another son, Miles Runk (1850-1926), lived in Howard County. He married Sarah A. Orr, daughter of Robert and Jemima (Franchier) Orr also of Howard County. Miles was a soldier in the Spanish-American War. His rifle is preserved in the Miami County Museum in Peru, IN. They are buried in Prairieville Cemetery near Alto.

Miles and Sarah had six children, all of whom lived part of their lives in Howard County.

There was Norman Runk (1874-1951) who married Cona (James) but later moved and raised their large family in Michigan. Louella Runk Forgey was married to William Forgey and lived and farmed in both Howard and Cass Counties. Nancy Caroline Runk married Grover Crull of Howard County. They lived in Kokomo for a time. Nora Valentine Runk married Herschel Williams of Kokomo. They lived in the county most of their lives and are buried in Crown Point Cemetery. Youngest in Miles' family was my father, Loren E. Runk (1889-1963). He married Mabel Elizabeth Whitesides in 1912. He farmed most all of his life but asthma forced him off the farm in 1941 and he moved to Kokomo where he worked first for Standard Oil then Dietzen's Bakery. They are buried in Galveston Cemetery. Several of their nine children have lived in Howard County.

Wayne Everett Runk (1915-1981) moved to Kokomo from Cass County when he married Nina King of Howard County. They had a girl, Patricia Ann, who attended school in Howard County then married Jerome Kasper and now lives in Milwaukee, WI. They have five children. Her brother, Joseph Anthony Runk, attended Kokomo High School but was better known as a football kicker for the Kokomo WildKats, Buffalo Bills and Green Bay Packers. He married a Kokomo girl, Paula Black, and they have two children. They now live near Richmond, VA.

Wayne's brother, Stanley Robert Runk (1919-1982), married Betty Louise Aaron of Bennetts Switch. Before and during World War II they lived in Kokomo. They had two children-Donna (Keller) who now lives near Bennetts Switch and Larry Robert who lives in Oregon.

Homer Meryl Runk (1923-1967) married Sharon Denman of Kokomo where they lived for a while. They had one son, David Lee. Dawn Caroline Runk married Wallace Lee Wright of Peru, IN, but they lived during the war in Kokomo. She now lives in California. Maybelle Runk, Loren's youngest and the writer of this biography, graduated from Kokomo High School in 1946, became a teacher, married Robert Schuett in 1971 and moved to a Chicago suburb. She will be moving back to Howard County in July or August of 1994.

From 1884 to 1944 some "Runk" has lived in Howard County - we have come full circle. *Submitted by Maybelle Runk Schuett*

SAMPLE - Colleen and William Sample journeyed to Howard County in the summer of 1955 from Greenfield, IN. He came to teach in the Western School System after having taught chemistry, physics, and mathematics in the Hancock County School System, east of Indianapolis.

Colleen and Bill were married in Hillham, Dubois County, IN on Nov. 24, 1951. Constance Colleen Crowder was born July 30, 1931 to Everett Dewitt Crowder and Pearl Alice Freeman in French Lick, IN. William Edward Sample was born to Harold Lewis Sample and Helen Lydia Wilcoxon on Aug. 20, 1929 in Greenfield, IN.

William E. Sample family at wedding of Michael and Laura, Nov. 25, 1978. L to R: Jill, Julie, Leanna, Laura, Michael, Colleen, William and Patrick.

After their marriage, Colleen worked in the Printing Department at Purdue while William attended classes. After his graduation in 1952 and teaching in Hancock County for four years, they, with their children, Michael Edward and Leanna Christine, came to Howard County. During the following summer, after teaching the first year in the new building at Western High School, he went to work for General Motors at Delco Electronics in Kokomo, IN. Semiconductors were new products coming into use in General Motors and Delco was hiring people with scientific training and background.

In the fall of 1960, they moved to Orange County, CA where he spent a short time working as an engineer for Hughes Semiconductor Corporation. They returned in the spring of 1961 and he worked for Delco Electronics until his retirement in 1984.

Their family was as follows:

Michael Edward, born Nov. 9, 1952 in Greenfield, IN. He graduated from General Motors Institute and married Laura Koenig Nov. 25, 1978. They reside in Tipton County with their two daughters, Deana and Christy.

Timothy Joe was born Oct. 7, 1954 in Greenfield, IN. He died Dec. 27, 1954 and is interred in the Mount Lebanon Cemetery, Orange County, IN near French Lick.

Leanna Christine was born Sept. 2, 1955 in Greenfield, Hancock County, IN. After graduation from Purdue University, she married David Arthur Lehmann, Sept. 1, 1979. They reside in Logansport with their two sons, Aaron and Jacob.

Patrick Jay was born Aug. 14, 1957 in Saint Joseph Hospital, Kokomo, while they were living on a farm south of Russiaville. He married Catherine Jill Heinrich, Oct. 17, 1981 after they had both graduated from Purdue and now reside in Ellisville, a suburb of Saint Louis, MO.

Julie Dawn was born March 11, 1960 in Kokomo. She attended Ball State University and resides in Indianapolis, IN.

Jill Diane, born March 11, 1960 in Kokomo. She was married to James Robert Ellis, of Kokomo, Aug. 25, 1979. She and Robert live in Winchester, IN with their three children, Lacey, Brittany, and Ryan. *Submitted by William E. Sample.*

PORTER SANDEFUR (1909-1978) - Porter Sandefur brought his family to Howard County in 1951 from Powell Valley, near Tazewell, TN.

The Sandifer family had lived in Powell Valley for over 100 years, and before that had lived in Virginia since the early 1600s. John Sandifer (1637-1700) and his son, James Sandifer (born 1674), were from York County, VA. James Sandifer's son, William Abraham Sandifer (1728-1784) lived in Goochland County, VA, and served in the Revolutionary War. Matthew Sandifur (1768-1840), the son of William Abraham Sandifer, was from Cumberland County, VA, and served in the Virginia militia. Matthew's son and grandson, William Alexander Sandifer (1804-1875) and Robert Sharp Sandifer (1831-1885; Porter's grandfather), left Virginia and moved to Tennessee in the early 1800s. They settled east of Tazewell, near Forge Ridge, in Claiborne County.

Porter was born in 1909, the fourth child of John (1866-1943) and Susie (Lambert) (1881-1976). Sandefur's eight children: Larn, Silas, Maurine, Porter, Roxie, Joseph, Goldie, and Dillard. John Sandefur taught music and instilled a love for singing and playing musical instruments in all of his children. John's grandchildren and great-grandchildren carry on his love for music and the tradition of family singing.

Porter went to live with his uncle, William Henry Sandefur, when he was 13, and took a job carrying water to the men building the L & N Railroad line from Corbin to Harlan, KY. He was a very capable worker and quickly advanced to "laying track" and "driving steel". He also worked on the road between Corbin and Cumberland Falls, and helped build the bridge two miles east of the Falls. He also worked as a logger, a farmer, and as a coal miner.

In 1933, Porter married Ina Mae Bush (born 1917). They became acquainted while Porter worked for Ina Mae's grandfather, Dr. Joseph Grant Surber. They made their home in Powell Valley on the Bull Ridge Farm. When the mines closed, Porter and Ina moved to Indiana where he found work at Reeds Metal Working Factory. Porter and Ina also ran an upholstery shop in Kokomo. Ina is the family genealogist and also does needlework and quilting.

Porter and Ina's children are Henrietta, Leon, Dwayne and Vivian.

Henrietta is the secretary for I.N.A. Insurance Co. of Arlington, TX, and, like her mother, enjoys needlework. She is married to Cal Stargel, and their children are Anthony (born 1958), Thomas (born 1959-died 1990), and Joy Ann (born 1962).

Leon was a pressman at Cuneo. He married Hellen Phillips in 1957. Leon is the song leader for Honey Creek Baptist Church, and is known for his artistry in wood carving. Leon and Helen's children are Ricki (born 1957) and Wayne (born 1961). In 1979 Leon married Kathleen Stine. Kathleen's three daughters are Judith, Alicia, and Rhonda.

Dwayne was a foreman in the bindery at Cuneo Press. He married Linda Songer in 1958. Their children are Kimmy (born 1959) and Kenneth (born 1960). Dwayne married Rickey Farron in 1975 and their daughter is Melissa (born 1976). Dwayne married Denise Morton in 1986 and Denise's sons are Michael and Christopher.

Vivian works in the Central Technology Center for Delco Electronics. She enjoys photography and music and is a member of the Kokomo Camera Club. In 1989, Vivian and her husband, Lewis Anderson (married 1963), hiked the Grand Canyon, and their photographic record of the trip is outstanding. Vivian and Lewis's children are Jeffrey (born 1964), Tracy (born 1966), and Todd (born 1969). *Submitted by J.E. Finecoate.*

JOSEPH GRANT SANDIFUR (1915-1986) - Joseph Grant Sandifur came to Howard County in 1953 from the mountainous region of southeastern Kentucky. He had worked in the coal mines and also operated a restaurant in Pleasant View, KY.

The Sandifer family had lived in Powell Valley, TN for over 100 years, and before that had lived in Virginia since the early 1600s. John Sandifer (1637-1700) and his son, James Sandifer (1674), were from York County, VA. James Sandifer's son, William Abraham Sandifer (1728-1784) lived in Goochland County, VA and served in the Revolutionary War. Matthew Sandifur (1768-1840) the son of William Abraham Sandifer, was from Cumberland County, VA, and served in the Virginia militia. Matthew's son and grandson, William Alexander Sandifer (1804-1875) and Robert Sharp Sandifer (1831-1885) (Joseph's grandfather), left Virginia and moved to Tennessee in the mid 1800s. They settled east of Tazewell, near Forge Ridge, in Claiborne County.

Joe was born in 1915; his boyhood home was in the foot hills southeast of Cumberland Gap, near Forge Ridge, TN. His parents were John (1866-1943) and Susan (Lambert 1881-1976) Sandifur. John Sandifur was a renowned music teacher who had studied under a music master from England. His children were all gifted with musical ability, and he instilled in them a love of singing and playing musical instruments. There was always lots of music whenever the Sandifur family gathered together, and people came from everywhere to enjoy the entertainment.

There were eight children in John and Susan's family: Larn, Silas, Maurine, Porter, Roxie, Joseph, Goldie, and Dillard. They lived on a rural farm, and everyone pitched in to do the work. At an early age, Joe was handling the plow horses and doing many of the adult chores. He was still a young boy when he went to live with his uncle William Henry Sandifur near Williamsburg, KY and took a job working on the construction of the new road between Corbin, KY and Cumberland Falls. His first job was to carry water from a spring fed lake at the bottom of the mountain up to the crews working on the road. Before the road was completed, Joe was driving a mule team pulling out logs, or wagons loaded with construction materials. He also helped build the Dryland Bridge that spans the gap two miles east of the falls.

Joe joined the CCCs (Conservation Corps) to help his family during the Depression years. He became a member of the Corps boxing team and did very well at the sport. He traveled from camp to camp participating in matches. Later, he worked in the coal mines, and was there during the embattled years when the miners were fighting to unionize.

Later, in Cleveland, OH, he worked as a machinist making crankshafts for battleships. Joe also worked at the atomic testing laboratories in Oak Ridge, TN. In Indiana, he worked on the four-laning of the road between Kokomo and Indianapolis (US 31). In the fall of 1953 Joe went to work for Continental Steel where he continued until his retirement in 1983.

Joe loved music and singing. He was blessed with a clear bass voice, and was an excellent guitarist. As a young man his musical talents were already in great demand, and there were times when he would wade through knee-deep snow to get to an event where he had been asked to play and sing. In the 1940s he sang on a weekly radio program broadcast out of Harlan, KY.

In 1937, Joseph married Audrey Moses. They made their home in Pleasant View, KY, for several years before moving to Indiana. They have been consistently active in

299

the Central Church of God where Audrey taught classes and worked with youth groups, and Joe provided a music ministry. They traveled throughout central Indiana putting on gospel programs where Joe would sing, and he and Audrey would both witness for Jesus Christ. A recording company in Anderson, IN made tapes and records of Joe singing his gospel music and they are distributed throughout Indiana and Kentucky. Joe and Audrey's three children are Sondra, Susan, and Gary.

Sondra is married to Fred Wintland and is the corporate secretary for Kokomo Gas and Fuel. Their children are Lisa and Kathi. Lisa is a Purdue graduate, and is the office manager for Dr. Fawcett. She is married to Scott Baird, and their children are Andrew and Erin. Kathi is attending Indiana University and is married to Mark Sanders. Katy, Hannah, and Issac are their children.

Susan is a volunteer worker for the American Red Cross and for the Christian Women's Club. She enjoys singing with the Christian Missionary Alliance Church Choir. She also enjoys sewing and doing needlework. Susan is married to Ed Fivecoate, and their children are Jeff and Christina.

Christina is a senior at Purdue University and enjoys writing and playing the piano. Jeff is a graduate of Purdue's Kranert School of Business with a master's degree in business management. He is self-employed. Jeff is married to Christine McComas, a graduate of Purdue's School of Pharmacology. Their children are Micah and Abigayle.

Gary Sandifur is married to Lorene Smith. He has a master's degree in business management from Indiana Wesleyan University, and is a maintenance supervisor for Delco Electronics. Lorene teaches advanced mathematics for Kokomo High School. Their two sons are Trent and Travis.

Trent is a member of the National Honor Society, Key, and is president of his class. He also plays varsity football for the Kokomo Wildcats. He has been accepted by Harvard University, and plans to attend classes there in the fall of 1994.

Travis is on the track team for Kokomo High School, a member of the National Honor Society, Key, and the Student Council. His interests include history, government and classical guitar. *Submitted by J.E. Fivecoate.*

SAXON - Several descendants of pioneer Fayette County, IN, residents Alexander and Mary (Baldwin) Saxon had connections to Howard County. One of these was John W. Saxon (1824-1895), the son of William and Nancy (Orr) Saxon and grandson of Alexander and Mary. He traded hotel property in Converse, IN, for the Jos. Boswell farm in Howard County in the mid-1870s. John's wife, Frances (Fisher), may have died in Howard County about 1880, according to one source, but no concrete evidence of this has been found. John did not live long in Howard County. In fact, at the time of the 1880 census, he was living near a daughter and son-in-law in Nemaha County, KS. He died in Miami County, IN.

Another grandson of Alexander and Mary, also named John Saxon, was born in 1833 to Alexander Gillespie and Margaret (McCrory) Saxon. He married Nancy T. King in 1854 in Rush County, IN, but soon moved to Howard County, where he lived until his death in 1913. He and Nancy had one child, a daughter, Martha. John, Nancy, and Martha were buried at Crown Point Cemetery in Kokomo.

William Andrew Saxon, a brother of John Saxon (just above), was born in 1837 in Fayette County, IN. He married Angeline Euphenia Ball there in 1860. The couple moved to Miami County before 1870, then on to Fairfield, Howard County, where William died in 1886. He was buried at Albright Cemetery. William's widow, Angeline, married William M. Price in 1858 in Howard County. The children of William and Angeline (Ball) Saxon were: Annetta Jane; Clara May; Laura B.; Ada; Minnie S.; Margaret "Maggie"; and William W. Annetta Jane married Lewis Alexander and moved to Henry County, IN. They had at least four children. Clara May married first Jonathan M. Rail, and second, John A. Hood. One child was mentioned in her obituary, but it is not known which of her husbands was its father. Laura B. married Charles E. Durham and moved to Henry County, IN. Ada married first George B. Pierce, and second, Charles M. Fox. Minnie S. married Oliver P.M. Finley, then Jonathan Carroll. Margaret "Maggie" married and divorced John W. Sarver. They had one child, Bessie M. Maggie married, second, George Hullinger.

Samuel Saxon, also a son of Alexander Gillespie and Margaret (McCrory) Saxon, was born in 1844. He married Caroline Thomas in 1873 in Fayette County, IN. They moved to Howard County before 1882 and lived in Center Township. Samuel died in Kokomo in 1925 and was buried in Crown Point Cemetery. His and Caroline's children were: Nira Mary, born in 1876 and died unmarried in Kokomo in 1951; Louedna Ruth, born in 1879, married Walter Holmes in 1909 and presumably divorced, died using her maiden name in 1974 in Fort Wayne, IN; Emma E., born in 1879, married Leonard D. Armfield in 1898 in Howard County, and had Blanche Dorothy, Paul, and Eunice; and Margaret E. "Maggie", born in 1882, married Pearl Burgan in 1900, had a son, Ralph Burgan, then married C.E. Coon or Moon before 1924. *Submitted by Dawne Slater-Putt.*

SCHAFER - George Franklin Schafer was born in Liberty Township, Howard County, IN, March 21, 1918, the son of Oris DeWitt and Nina Belle (Souter) Schafer. He was one of three children; Marybelle and Margaret were his sisters. He was reared on the farm at 500 E 500 N. Mary Louise Underwood was born June 3, 1919 to Thomas W. Underwood and Matilda (Hawkins) Underwood. In 1911 the Underwoods moved from Towanda, IL to Howard County upon purchasing farm ground just northeast of Kokomo. Mary Louise was the youngest of five children, which included Ruth (Underwood) Walker, Murl Leoma (Underwood) Goyer, Noel Underwood, and Glen Underwood.

George and Mary both attended Howard Township School together for 12 years. In October of 1940, George and Mary were married at Kokomo Zion United Methodist Church (formerly the EUB church). Over the course of their farming lives they have seen many changes. As children with their families they farmed with horses, but to begin their own farm careers they purchased a small International Harvester "B" tractor as a wedding gift to themselves.

In the early farming years they milked cows, had a variety of farm animals, raised corn and other small grains. From 1940-1962 they raised tomatoes for the Libby canning factory of Kokomo which was located at Market St. and Spraker St. Around 1975 a farm decision was made to specialize the farm operation and begin a start-to-finish hog operation, raise corn and soybeans. George and Mary purchased land in southern Miami County and farmed and rented ground in the immediate area of their Howard Township farm at 200 E 300 N. George and Mary have four children: Ronald Lynn Schafer born Oct. 14, 1942, Roger D. Schafer born March 5, 1944, Jocena K. Schafer, born May 6, 1953 and Melinda Jayne (Schafer) Fourez, born March 20, 1956.

Ron married Holly (Wald) Schafer July 28, 1972 at Grace United Methodist Church and had a son Brandon David Schafer, Feb. 19, 1977. Holly died in 1982. Ron and Brandon live in the brick farm house where Mary Louise was born at 3246 North Touby Pike. Ron has been a school teacher in the Kokomo Center Township Corporation at Bon Air School and farms.

Roger D. Schafer has two children: Bret Witman, born Nov. 5, 1969 and Darcey Lorraine Schafer born July 19, 1972. Roger was service manager at John Deere Implement store in the early 70s and since has been a fireman for the Kokomo Fire Department and farms.

Jocena is a registered dietitian and has worked as a health care professional at St. Joseph Memorial Hospital of Kokomo, Larue Carter Memorial Hospital in Indianapolis, Logansport State Hospital, and Tipton County Memorial Hospital. She is a member of St. Luke's United Methodist Church.

Melinda became an art teacher and married Steven William Fourez of Fairmount, IL. The couple now farm in Illinois and have two children Jeremy William born April 23, 1983 and Katelyn Jayne, born June 28, 1990.

The Schafers have been active honorable participants in their churches, businesses, and community. They are proud of Howard Township and Howard County.

BEN AND AUDREY SCHICK - On Sept. 14, 1910 Benjamin Adam Schick married Audrey Monica Woodruff, in Tipton, IN.

He was born the son of Bernard and Mary Ellen (Quinlan) Schick, July 31, 1888 in Tippecanoe County, IN. He died Feb. 15, 1961 in Kokomo.

Only his love for his family exceeded his love for his sports! Northside Little League baseball and Kokomo Wildcat basketball. He hardly ever missed a game.

She was born Jan. 15, 1900, in Hillisburg, Clinton County, IN. The daughter of Rev. Edward Charles "E.C." and Amanda Jane (Pierce) Woodruff. She died March 10, 1973 in Kokomo.

Ben and Audrey Schick's wedding day.

To this union were born five children, two of whom lost their lives early in life. At the time of this writing they have 11 grandchildren, 26 great-grandchildren and 12 great-great-grandchildren, most of whom live in or near this area. Their children were:

Back row: Roger D. Schafer, Steven W. Fourez, George F. Schafer, Ronald L. Schafer, Brandon D. Schafer, Bret Whitman and Darcey L. Schafer. Front row: Jeremy W. Fourez, Melinda Schafer Fourez, Katelyn Fourez, Mary L. Schafer and Jocena K. Schafer.

Wayne Paul, born May 8, 1914. He was killed in a tragic auto accident, enroute home for the funeral of an uncle Feb. 3, 1937. He was a professional musician. A special note should be made here that he was killed with a fellow musician and friend from Kokomo, Huvon "Sug" Meeks. These two young men shared a life style and friendship together, not knowing that they were distant cousins. This was discovered many years later in doing the family genealogy. The accident happened in Grand Rapids, OH.

Majorie I., born June 21, 1918. She married William J. Janner Sr. Dec. 2, 1939 in Kansas City, MO. They had two sons, William J. Jr. and Wayne C. She has lived many places across the country, but has stayed in this area since the establishment of her weekly newspaper, *The Kokomo Herald*. William Jr. lives in Alabama while Wayne lives here. All of Majorie's grandchildren live here.

Donald E., born Oct. 31, 1925. He married Gladyce Marie Rone, June 14, 1946. They had four children, Candy L., Randy E., Donald J. "Joe" and Fredrick (who died at birth). Their surviving children all live in the Kokomo area. Donald retired from Grissom AFB in 1989. He is also a professor at Ivy Tech. He served in the U.S. Navy during WWII.

Joseph Anthony was born April 13, 1931. He also was a noted musician for such a young age. He went to be with his brother at the tender age of 16. June 13, 1947 he died in an Indianapolis hospital after having had surgery for a brain tumor.

Nancy L., was born Sept. 4, 1932, she married Robert E. Harmon, Dec. 27, 1954. Robert had two small children from a previous marriage who made their home with them, Deborah K. and Richard W. Richard who died in 1982. Born to this union were three children, Robert A., who died as an infant, Belinda J. and Barbara L. Nancy is retired from Delco and Robert from Chrysler. Deborah and Belinda live in the area; Barb lives in Washington state. *Submitted by Candy L.P. Jones.*

DONALD E. AND GLADYCE SCHICK - Donald E. Schick son of Benjamin Adam and Audrey Monica (Woodruff) Schick was born and reared in Kokomo. He attended Riley, St. Patrick's and Roosevelt grade schools. His high school education was at Kokomo High School where he was active in sports, especially baseball.

During WWII he served his country in the Navy, aboard the U.S.S. *Endymion*,. participating in the invasions of Peliliu and Anguar in the Palau Group Islands, Tacloban, Leyte in the Philippines and Okinawa in the Ryukyus. After the war he went to Chicago to attend school at Industrial Training Institute. Upon graduation he started his own business and was self-employed for the next 13 years. At this time he went to Bunker Hill Air Force Base in Civil Service. After 28 years of federal service he retired as the supervisor of the air conditioning section. While supervisor he won the "Duke" Wright Award as the best section in the Air Force two years in a row. He taught many classes for the Air Force which led him to his love of education, teaching night classes several years at Ivy Tech. His teaching went full time when he retired from Civil Service.

His spare time was spent on sports, playing for a number of years. Then coaching. He coached many years of Little League and Babe Ruth League Baseball. He also coached parochial school basketball many years, never having a losing season.

He is a lifelong member of St. Patrick's Catholic Church, where he has served in various capacities.

June 15, 1946 in the rectory of St. Patrick's Church Donald married Gladyce Marie Rone. Gladyce was the only child of Johnny Huey and M. Roxie (Browning) Rone. When she was but two years old her parents divorced. She was born in the family home in Napier, Lewis County, TN. She came to Indiana to live with her mother when she was 13, going to school at Washington and Kokomo High School. She went to work at the Delco plant, leaving there to be a full time mother and homemaker. Their family included four children: Candy L., Randy E., Donald Joseph "Joe" and Fredrick. Fredrick died at birth; he is buried in the Memorial Park Cemetery.

Schick family, taken May 9, 1992, St. Patrick's Church. Seated on steps: Matthew, Jacob, Megan and Jessica Schick. Bottom row, standing L-R: Jason Propes, Laura and Joshua Schick. 1st step: Peter and Angelia Markopoulos, Rachel and Keith Heitzman. 3rd step: Marjorie Janner, Nikolas Markopoulos, Candy and Richard Jones. Top row: Randy and Ellen Schick (Jackie is hid behind Marjorie), Joe and Janet Schick, Chandra and Donald Stradling, Gladyce and Don Schick.

Candy is married to Richard L. Jones, and is featured elsewhere in this publication. Randy is married to J. Ellen Stafford and they have two children, Matthew Adam Stafford and Jacqulyn Ann. Randy also has a daughter, Laura Lee, from a previous marriage. Joe is married to Janet Stafford. Janet and Ellen are sisters and the daughters of Gerald and Mona (Jones) Stafford. Joe and Janet's children are Megan Elizabeth, Jessica Jo and Jacob Adam. Joe has two children from a former marriage, Chandra Lynn and Joshua Michael.

Randy and Joe are both employed at Delco. *Submitted by Candy L.P. Jones.*

DOROTHY ANN SCHMITT AND LEONARD KRISE - Dorothy Ann Schmitt, born May 27, 1920; and Leonard William Krise, born May 8, 1918; were united in marriage in 1938 by Rev. Chester Mitchell. Leonard was the son of Bert C. Krise and Clorus D. (Beard) Krise. Dorothy was the daughter of George Schmitt and Frances (Terwishe) Schmitt.

Leonard served with the United States Army Ski Patrol Troops in Italy during WWII as a cook. During this time, Dorothy worked as a seamstress with the Reliance Company in Kokomo, IN. After WWII, Leonard worked at Globe American and Main Supply in Kokomo. He was also player and manager of the Globe softball team.

Leonard and Dorothy had one daughter, Sandra Ann Krise, born Dec. 21, 1943. They resided in Oakford, IN, until Leonard was accidentally electrocuted in July 1949. Dorothy and Sandra then moved to Kokomo where Dorothy worked at Delco Radio until 1964. Dorothy remarried on July 26, 1951 to Virgil Lester Rust of Kokomo, IN.

Sandra married John David Brittain, Jr., born July 17, 1941, on Feb. 17, 1962. They both are employed at Delco Electronics. John and Sandra had two sons, John David III who was born Aug. 29, 1963 and Michael Anthony who was born on Nov. 8, 1969. John III is self-employed and resides in Kokomo.

Michael married Barbara Jean Kelly on Dec. 22, 1990. They reside in Frankfort, IN with their son, Drake Anthony, who was born on Sept. 3, 1992. Michael is employed at Wabash National in Lafayette, IN.

RUSSELL AND GEORGIA SCHMITT - Russell, the second son of George and Frances, was born in Quincy, IL on Nov. 9, 1917. At the age of five, they moved to Kokomo, IN. He attended St. Patrick School and Kokomo High School. He did furnace work for Harry Klotz and Sears. He and Georgia L. McCarter were married in Lafayette, IN on June 30, 1939. Russell worked at Globe Stove Company as a foreman for 22 years. During the war they made lifeboats and life rafts.

Georgia worked at Kingston until their son, Ronald, was born Jan. 3, 1942. Russell and Georgia started building their home at 2147 N. Purdum with help of family and friends. They moved in on Dec. 10, 1947. Russell then went to work at Swartwout as foreman.

Their third son, Norman, was born Sept. 12, 1955, and 15 months later a daughter, Deborah Jo, was born on Jan. 10, 1957. After Swartwout closed, Russell worked at Kokomo Sales until he retired.

December 1984, left to right: Norman, Deborah and Georgia. Back row: Ronald, Russell and Ray.

After graduating from Kokomo High School, Ronald went to work at Delco. He is now maintenance supervisor. He married Joyce Sears. They had twin daughters, Dena and Donna, born on March 2, 1964. Then on July 29, 1966 Monica was born. Dena married Jeff Linn on Sept. 26, 1989. They have a daughter, Carly, who was born Feb. 26, 1991. Donna married Greg Hobbs on Aug. 25, 1990. Their daughter, Kaitlyn, was born June 1, 1993. Monica married Kevin Bogue on July 7, 1990.

After playing golf about two years at Tipton Golf Course, Ronald hit his first hole in one. His second round of golf that week at Meridian Hills Country Club, Indianapolis, IN, is where he hit his second hole in one. He became part of history.

Raymond, our second born child, went into the Army and was in the 101st Airborne, Screaming Eagles. After service, he married Linda Nesbit who had a daughter, Michelle, born Nov. 6, 1969. Raymond adopted her. Their son, Scott, was born Nov. 27, 1971. Ray worked at Delco. On July 6, 1985, he was killed on a motorcycle at the age of 39. Scott, his son, married Becky Walker. They have a son, Cody. Michelle, his daughter, graduated from Purdue and married Michael Peigh on June 26, 1993.

Norman graduated from Haworth High School and works at Chrysler. He married Patricia Ewing on June 10, 1977. A daughter, Erica, was born Dec. 9, 1979, and on Jan. 24, 1984, twin daughters were born named Stephanie and Stacey. They live on a small farm at 950 West where Norman is a volunteer fireman at Russiaville. Patty works at Tri-State.

Deborah also graduated from Haworth High School. She and Roger Massey were married on June 3, 1978. Roger works at Chrysler. Debbie works at Delco. They live on a farm near West Middletown with their daughter,

Tiffney, born Nov. 13, 1984, and their son, Adam, born March 1, 1987. They all go to Western.

Rut and Georgia celebrated their 54th Anniversary on June 30, 1993.

GEORGE "PETE" SCHMITT
Pete was born Jan. 27, 1924 at 1112 North Union St., Kokomo, IN; his parents were George and Frances. I grew up in the north end of Kokomo and attended eight years at St. Patrick's School and Church. In my years at St. Patrick's I was alter boy and Safety Patrol. This program was just started by Sgt. Forrest Roe of Kokomo Police Department.

George and Barbara Schmitt

After graduation from St. Pat's, I attended four years at Kokomo High School on a vocational course. During this time I played baseball and football for Kokomo High School. I also worked at Washburn Manufacturing Company and Kurlow Grocery Store on East Morgan and Market Street. I graduated from high school on June 8, 1943 and entered the Army on June 9, 1943. Most of my training was in California. I spent two years in the South Pacific area on the invasion of different islands, and finally the occupation of Korea. I was discharged on Nov. 12, 1946.

Pete married Barbara Ann Lykins on March 15, 1947 at St. Joan of Arc Catholic Church. I went to work for Indiana Bell Telephone Company and retired in 1984 after serving 35 years.

I have been busy in my span of life serving the Izaak Walton Conservation as their state president four years, Howard County WLA President and was Telephone Pioneers Chapter President of Kokomo. I am now serving as retirees' vice president, working in the Drop Off Center, belong to the American Legion and the Lion's Club. Bobby and I are enjoying our retirement and spend some time in Florida in the winter, but there's no place like our KOKOMO HOME.

GEORGE A. AND FRANCES SCHMITT
On Nov. 23, 1869, Leonard Schmitt was married in Saint Boniface Church to Miss Adelherd Korte, born Sept. 14, 1847, daughter of Henry and Magdalene Frese. In the year 1868, they emigrated to America from Wachtum, Amt Lorringen, Hanover, Germany, and then moved on to Quincy, IL. Leonard and Adelheld had seven children. Their third child, a son, was born Aug. 4, 1886, whose name was George Aloysuis Schmitt.

George lived and worked in Quincy. At the age of 27 in the year 1913, he married Frances Terwishe at St. Mary's Catholic Church. While keeping residency in Quincy, George worked at Excelsion Plant and Jackson Stove Company. George and Frances had six children, four sons and two daughters. The first born son, Wilbert, was born July 18, 1915. Second son, Russell, was born Nov. 9, 1917. Third son, George, Jr., was born Jan. 27, 1924. Their fourth son, Bobbie Lee, was born Nov. 24, 1925 and he died Sept. 24, 1926. Their first born daughter, Mildred, was born Feb. 8, 1919. Their second born daughter, Dorothy, was born May 27, 1920.

Work was slow and George moved his family to Kokomo in the year 1921. He was employed by the Hoosier Iron Foundry located at Morgan and Webster Street. The Schmitts' residence was in the north-end of Kokomo, 1216 N. Union Street. George went to work for Globe American Corporation on East Broadway. The firm was in stove line production. George became a stove mounter by trade. He also became a committeeman for National Stove Mounter Union and did some traveling for the union.

George A. and Francis Schmitt

George and Frances were members of Saint Patrick's Catholic Church. George was a member of the Holy Name Society and also belonged to the Knights of Columbus. Frances was a member of the Rosary Society and helped the Red Cross during WWII.

George's hobbies were fishing and playing euchre with his fellow workers. He, also, raised his family to be good citizens.

George and Frances built a new home at 919 East Havens, Kokomo, IN, when he was ready for retirement. George retired June 5, 1951 after 25 years at Globe American.

Sickness soon took over the life of George who passed away on Feb. 25, 1954. Funeral services were held at St. Patrick's Church by Rev. Leo Breintenbach with burial in Memorial Park Cemetery.

Frances kept residence on Havens Street until she became ill and was placed in Good Samaritan Nursing Home where she passed away on Oct. 15, 1955. Frances lived just about a year after George's death, but as I write this article, I can say my folks lived a full life and were so proud of their family and especially of their grandchildren.

This couple was sure to be pioneers and great citizens of Kokomo, IN and Howard County.

MILDRED E. SCHMITT AND ROBERT J. CLARK
Mildred E. Schmitt, third child of George and Frances (Terwishe) Schmitt, married Robert J. Clark on July 26, 1941 at St. Patrick Church, in Kokomo, IN.

Mildred was employed at Reliance on North Washington Street. Bob was employed at the North End Tin Shop owned by his father, Jess Clark. On March 1, 1943, Bob joined the Navy and served in the South Pacific until Sept. 30, 1945. He came home then and worked at Kolux Sign Company for 16 years. He owned the Shell Station at the corner of North and Washington Street from 1952-1956. He then went to work at Delco and worked 21 years until he retired on Sept. 1, 1982 as a tinsmith.

February 8, 1947, their daughter, Chiquita Marie, was born. She married Stephen Meyers on Feb. 18, 1967. They both work at Delco. They have two children, Stephanie Marie who was born Aug. 24, 1970. Stephanie works for Shephard Poorman Graphics in Indianapolis, IN. Their son, Heath Lunda, was born on Nov. 4, 1975.

Mr. and Mrs. Robert J. Clark

Gregory Allen, their first-born son, was born on Feb. 13, 1951. He married Mary Gentry on Nov. 7, 1970. They have two sons, Jeremiah Allen, born Feb. 13, 1976; and Nathaniel Lee who was born June 10, 1979. Gregory served in the Military Guards from July 14, 1970 until Sept. 1, 1992, when he retired as a first sergeant. He is employed at Delco Electronics as a tinsmith.

Robert Joseph II, second son, was born on April 3, 1952. He married Christy Branch on Oct. 9, 1971. They had three boys. Samuel died at birth. Brandon Joseph was born Sept. 25, 1974, and Adam Christopher was born on Nov. 15, 1978. Bob went to work at Chrysler for 11 years before he moved to Sunrise, FL. He then married Bette Keshan on Feb. 18, 1984. They have one son, Chris, born on Nov. 23, 1974. Bob is now employed as shift sergeant on the police force at Sunrise, FL.

WILBERT (BUD) AND LUCILLE (TAYLOR) SCHMITT
Wilbert (Bud) Schmitt worked at Globe American 23 years as a shipping clerk until the factory closed. He then went to work at Kolux Sign Corporation as a sign builder and retired in 1981. His hobby is fishing.

On Oct. 27, 1937, Wilbert and Lucille (Taylor) Schmitt were married at St. Patrick's Church. Lucille has been employed at Tupperware Home Parties for the last 26 years. Lucille's parents are Raymond and Edith (Floyd) Taylor of Royal Center, IN.

Bud and Lucille Schmitt

Pamela (Schmitt) Maloney, born Jan. 23, 1943, was their first-born daughter. She is self-employed as a real estate broker at Dorothy Edwards Realtors. Pam has held all offices of Beta Sigma Phi and has been a member for 28 years. On March 3, 1962, Pam married Mike Maloney. Mike works at Delco Electronics as general foreman. Pam worked as a bookkeeper/secretary at Alaska Mutual Savings Bank while Mike was stationed in Alaska with the United States Air Force. They both attended the University of Alaska. Pam and Mike's son, Robert Maloney, born on Aug. 11, 1964, graduated from Haworth High School. He played drums in the marching band. Bob works at Chrysler. He is a member of the Knights of Columbus, 3rd degree. He married Lynn Williams with a daughter, Lynsey Danielle, being born to them on Nov. 14, 1989. Bob is divorced. Lynsey enjoys playschool and books. Pam and Mike's daughter, Shala Renee Maloney, born Sept. 22, 1973, graduated from Kokomo High School and is currently at Indiana University-Kokomo. Shala swam for the Kokomo High School swim team for four years. Shala works at a dress shop in the mall.

Robert (Bob) Schmitt, born Sept. 26, 1946, was their first-born son. Bob's hobbies are fishing and hunting. He was a member of the National Guard. Bob graduated from Kokomo High School. He works at Steel Parts in Tipton as plant superintendent. On Nov. 25, 1967, Bob and Carolyn (Small) Schmitt were married at St. Patrick's Church. Carolyn works at Kokomo Rehab Hospital. Brent Schmitt, their first-born son, born June 2, 1968, lives at Frankfort and works at Franks Cigar Factory. Melissa Schmitt, their daughter, was born Aug. 13, 1971 and lives in Greenfield. Melissa is a marketing director. She works for Indianapolis Food Speciality. Ryan Mathew, their second-born son, born Sept. 17, 1984, goes to Western School. Ryan's hobby is fishing.

David Schmitt, second-born son, was born on May 9, 1951. Dave works at Delco Electronics as a pipe fitter.

David and Debbie (McCarter) Schmitt were married on May 16, 1955 at St. Patrick's Church. Dave and Debbie's hobby is snowmobiling. Debbie works at Handy Hardware. They are both members of Izaak Walton League.

Luann (Schmitt) King, second-born daughter, was born on Dec. 31, 1952 and graduated from Kokomo High School. On April 17, 1971, Luann and Paul Edmund King were married at St. Patrick's Church. Paul works at Delco Electronics as a mold maker. Mark Emmerson King, their son, was born on Sept. 19, 1979. Mark is in all sports. Camela Ann King, their daughter, was born Nov. 13, 1983. Camela's hobby is basketball. Mark and Camela go to Clinton Central School. Luann is a homemaker.

Mary Jo Schmitt, their third-born daughter, was born on Feb. 27, 1955. Mary works at St. Patrick's School as a teacher's aide. Her hobby is crafts. She is a member of St. Patrick Rosary and also the Daughters of Isabella.

James (Michael) Schmitt, their third son, was born May 20, 1956. Pete (nickname) graduated from Kokomo High School. Pete works at B & D Manufacturing as a mold maker and also as office clerk. On April 1, 1989, Jim and Marta (Waites) Schmitt were married at St. Patrick's Church. Marta works at United Presidential Life Insurance. Marta's hobby is painting. Pete and Marta like fishing and camping. Both are members of Izaak Walton League.

SCHRADER - Frederick Schrader (1845-1921) was born in Lippe Detwald, Germany. He came to America at the age of 19, settling in Batesville, IN. He later came to Kokomo and embarked in farming and brick manufacturing. Later he also had brick factories at Montpelier, Elwood and Jonesboro, operating them at the same time he was running the one in Kokomo.

On June 23, 1887, during Kokomo's natural gas boom, a well was driven on the Schrader farm, which was located in the southeast part of Kokomo, near the present location of South Plate and Hoffer streets. This was the greatest gusher ever brought into production in any American natural gas field. The fame of the Schrader well spread fast and far. Pilgrimages were made to it by scientists, sight-seers and promoters from all over the country. The well was opened during harvest time and was permitted to burn full force for several weeks. Farmers of the adjacent countryside cut their wheat at night by its light. The well sent a column of flame straight into the sky for approximately 100 feet. Fred drilled the well for the purpose of obtaining fuel for an extensive brickyard, which he was operating on his farm. This yard furnished brick for most of the factories and many of the business structures erected in Kokomo during the gas boom. It was the main source of brick supply for the old Diamond Plate Glass works, predecessor of the Pittsburgh Plate Glass Company.

In 1889, Monroe Seiberling began the structure of his home in Kokomo. The flat bricks in the mansion were supplied by Fred Schrader, free, with the assurance that Mr. Seiberling would buy bricks from him, for the building of Seiberling's Diamond Plate Glass factory. It was said that Mr. Schrader referred to this transaction as "sugaring".

Fred secured some education training in his native land, but when he came to America he was unable to speak a word of intelligible English. He did not let that difficulty stand in his way, and early applied himself to the business of mastering the language. He learned the trade of a brick maker as a young man at home, and when he settled near Kokomo, devoted himself to that work.

In 1871, he was united in marriage to Elizabeth Hoyer (1852-1924). They had five sons, William, Edward, Harry, Fred and Otto and three daughters, Ella, Clara and Anna. Their grandchildren: Harold Schrader, deceased; Anna A. Schrader Wise, Kokomo; Robert Schrader, deceased; Edward Schrader, deceased; Betty Schrader Olofson, deceased; June Ann Schrader Meinershagen, Kansas City, MO; Richard Schrader, Wenatchee, WA; Earl C. Schrader, Indianapolis; Richard E. Young, Kokomo; and Jeanne Schrader Willman, Jonesboro.

SCHROCK-SHROCK - Jacob Schrock (1803-1857), son of Jacob and Anna (Zug) Schrock, was an Amish-Mennonite pioneer. He married Elizabeth Hostedler (1806-1887) in 1826. They were the parents of 12 children: Catherine, Benjamin, Jacob, Susanna, Isaac, Jonas, Elizabeth, Joseph, Eli, Noah, Lydia, and John. Jacob and Elizabeth brought their family to Howard County in 1848 from Holmes County, OH.

Benjamin Schrock (1829-1878), an Amish-Mennonite minister, married Mary Hochstetler (1835-1925). They had 10 children: Jacob B., Barbara, Malinda, Elizabeth, Ananias, Noah D., John M., Mary, Lomanda, and Ezra T. Benjamin and Mary farmed a half-mile south of the Howard-Miami Mennonite Church at 600 N. and 700 E. in Howard County. They are both buried in the Schrock Cemetery near Plevna, IN.

Noah D. Schrock (Shrock) (1867-1948) married India Nora Louise Turner (1874-1948) in 1891. They were the parents of seven children: Guy Otto, Ethel Aldene, Verna Pauline, Estella Mae, Lillian Leona, Elsie Clarice, and Gerald Leon. Noah loved music and played several instruments. Once when John Philip Sousa and his band came to Kokomo he played with them in a parade at a political rally. Noah and Nora are also buried in the Schrock Cemetery.

Guy Otto Shrock (1892-1964) married Gladys Marie Loman (1895-1974) in 1913. They were the parents of five children: Lloyd Ellsworth, Opal Lucile, Olive Genevieve, Lawrence Loman, and Leon Manson. Guy, like his father and grandfather, was a farmer. He was also like his father in that he was quite musically inclined. He played violin, mandolin, piano, and harmonica. By using a wire frame to hold the harmonica he could play it and the piano at the same time. All of Guy's children raised their families in Howard County.

Opal Lucile Shrock married Thomas Eugene Maddox in 1939. They had two children: Towana Kay and Thomas Eugene, Jr. As a young girl, Opal enjoyed shocking her friends by telling them she had spent the night in jail. Actually, she had spent the night with her aunt and uncle, Estella (Shrock) and Clifton Small, who lived in an apartment in the upstairs of the old county jail when Clifton was sheriff of Howard County from 1929-1933.

Towana Kay Maddox married Fredrick Allen Aldridge. They have four children and three grandchildren.

Fredrick Allen Aldridge, Jr. married Julie Ann Christian. They are the parents of Beth Ann and Fredrick Allen, III. Fredrick, Jr. is manager of Harmon Boats.

Marsha Kay Aldridge married Joseph Jerome Santen, Jr. They have one daughter, Gretchen Elizabeth. Marsha was head of Children's Services at the Kokomo Public Library until the birth of her daughter.

Gregory Edward Aldridge married Michaele Kristina Thomas. He is a software engineer at VIA Development.

Douglas Eugene Aldridge is serving a three-year enlistment in the U.S. Army at Fort Hood, TX.

Thomas Eugene Maddox, Jr. married Sandra Kay Fisher. They have five children and one grandchild: Stacey Marie, a student at Purdue University of Kokomo, Thomas Brian, a student at Indiana University of Kokomo, Anthony Joe, Robert Scott, and Daniel Lee, students at Taylor School. Corey Stephen is the son of Thomas Brian. Thomas, Jr. is a pipefitter at Delco Electronics.

Seven generations and 146 years later, the descendants of Jacob and Elizabeth Schrock still live in Howard County. *Submitted by Towana Aldridge.*

SCOTT - Sarah Elfrieda Werbe was born in Howard County on March 12, 1949, the daughter of Bette Harness Werbe and Harry Nelson Werbe, Jr. She was the eldest of two children. She was very proud to have a younger brother, Harry Nelson Werbe III, who was born on March 8, 1950. With the closeness of their births, Sarah was very protective and proud of her younger sibling. She spoke very "dutchy" early on, so therefore when introducing him or "showing him off" she called him her baby "Bo". "Bo" was born on a very blustery, wintry night and was given the name "Stormy", which he is called to this day.

Sarah attended Wallace School and during her later primary years, attended Maple Crest School. Early on, Sarah took tap dance and ballet instruction from Martha Miller Dance Studio. She was among the last freshman class to attend Central School Building and in 1967, graduated from Kokomo High School. A.B.W.A. Sycamore Belles Chapter awarded her their first chapter scholarship, which she used to pursue her secretarial course at Kokomo Business College. She later joined A.B.W.A. and held all chapter offices, later becoming the chapter's "Woman of the Year". In 1968, Sarah worked for Herbert Moore Accounting and in 1969 took employment with Libby, McNeill & Libby. Libby's was a "fresh pack" tomato canning factory also producing concentrated fruit juices. She worked in the personnel department, payroll, cost and yield department, and became executive secretary to the plant manager, prior to the plant closing in 1980. Sarah is a member of the First Congregational Christian Church and a "life member" of the Y.W.C.A.

Sarah met Jan Hulet Scott in 1968. Jan was born May 17, 1944, the son of Max L. and Evelyn I. (Hulet) Scott. Raised on a farm in Howard County, he was eldest of four children. In 1961, he joined the United States Air Force and served as a cook stationed in Tacoma, WA and later in Shreveport, LA. While in the military he obtained his G.E.D. and in July 1965 was honorably discharged. Returning to Kokomo, he joined the Kokomo Fire Department as a first-class firefighter, a profession which his father had also chosen. Jan also worked part-time for Firestone Tire & Rubber Company as a firefighter and during his tenure worked 24-hour shifts. All who know Jan call him "Scotty" or "Sugar Bear", a name he acquired early on. Scotty is an avid rod and custom car enthusiast and collector and owns a 1939 Pontiac coupe which he purchased in 1965. He is currently customizing a 1960 Buick LeSabre. His interest in custom cars was well-known as he organized the annual car show at Doc's Restaurant in Kokomo. This annual event was held rain or shine Fourth of July weekend for over a decade during the Haynes Apperson Festival. His interest in hand crafting wood collectibles led him to open Scott's Collectibles and Crafts in 1989. His wood "perpetual" calendars were much sought after as were the collection of baseball cards and coin collections and many family heirlooms and ancestor treasures.

Scott Family. L-R: Christopher R., Sarah E., and Jan H. Scott.

Jan and Sarah married in 1970 and Christopher Russell Scott was born to this marriage in 1971. Christopher attended Bon Air Elementary School and graduated from Kokomo High School in 1989 and studied automotive technology from Ivy Tech-Kokomo. During his early years, Chris focused his energies to baseball, playing minor and little leagues at Northside Little League. His parents joined his interest in this sport, his father as team manager and league president, his mother as team mother. Chris continued baseball going on to play Babe Ruth and Connie Mack leagues as first baseman and catcher. Chris' employment has been varied; roofer, stockboy, and long distance moving van helper which led him to states as far away as Mexico, Pennsylvania, Arizona, Florida, and New York, in addition to many others. He is now living in Indianapolis and working for Marsh Supermarkets.

In 1975, Jan became manager of Bon Air Mobile Court, where the family was raised. Having retired in 1992 from the Kokomo Fire Department with 25+ years of service, at the young age of 47, he took employment with Flair Design Ltd. Sarah is employed in the office of Richard N. Bowling, M.D.

This family's ancestors date back many generations in Howard County. Sarah's mother, Bette Jane (Harness) Werbe, and father, Harry Nelson Werbe, Jr., Werbe and Sons Sheet Metal, were born and raised in Howard County. Sarah's maternal grandmother, Gladys Eva "Mimi" (Todd) Harness Aughe, was a gracious, loving, Christian woman. Born in 1890, Gladys was the daughter-in-law of George W. Harness, typical pioneer of the period, industrious tiller of the soil. George farmed over 1800 acres of Howard County soil and gained the esteem and confidence of the people with whom he mingled. It is said that he was one of few with whom Indian Chief Kokomoko would trade. George lived a long and strenuous life to age 108 years. His daughter-in-law, Gladys Eva, lived to be 97 years young and died in her own home in 1987.

Esther Elfrieda (Beckman) Werbe, Sarah's paternal grandmother, was a resident of Howard County her lifetime and actively involved herself in the First Congregational Christian Church as a life member. A pioneer of the time, she died at the age of 99 years in the nursing home. Pioneers of the period, this family did much to promote the advancement of the community and Howard County.

SEAGER - William Robert Seager was born near Dayton, IN on July 25, 1878 to Robert Wallace and Margaret (Patton) Seager. He had two brothers, Wilbert and George, two sisters, Ella and Jennie.

William Robert Seager married Julia Ann Leibenguth, Jan. 6, 1904. They lived on a farm in Carroll County, where they had three daughters: Treso Margaret, Lavena Elsie, and Genevieve Agnes.

William Robert moved his family to Russiaville, IN, then to Union Township in Howard County. After the family was raised, William and Julia Ann moved to Greentown, IN.

William was a painter by trade, in Howard County.

William Robert Seager died Dec. 4, 1961. He is buried in Sunset Memory Gardens.

Julia Ann Leibenguth was born to James Monroe Leibenguth and Maria (Wehr) Leibenguth March 11, 1878. Her parents were farmers in Tippecanoe County near Mulberry, IN where they raised eight children.

Julia Ann Leibenguth married William Robert Seager Jan. 6, 1904. Julia died July 19, 1972, and was buried in Sunset Memory Gardens in Kokomo, IN.

Genevieve Agnes Seager was born May 12, 1915 in Carroll County, IN near Rossville, IN. She was the third daughter of William Robert and Julia Ann (Leibenguth) Seager.

Genevieve Agnes graduated from Union Township High School in 1933.

On Feb. 5, 1935 Genevieve Agnes married Robert Edwin Hawkins of Greentown, IN. They had two children, Judith Ann and Robert Edwin Hawkins Jr. Robert Edwin Hawkins Jr. passed away Feb. 22, 1988.

Genevieve Agnes Hawkins lived most of her life in Howard County, IN. Genevieve was very active in the Shiloh United Methodist Church where she held several offices. She was the District Officer of the United Methodist Women. She sang in the church choir and was a Sunday School teacher.

Mrs. Genevieve Agnes Hawkins now makes her home in Kokomo, IN.

SEVERNS - The Severns family arrived in Kokomo in the late 1920s. Edmond P. Severns grew up in Indianapolis and graduated from Shortridge High School in 1914. His parents were Edmond P. Severns Sr. and Leola K. Severns. Edmond P. Severns married Barbara Beeson from Tipton County in the early 1920s. Barbara was born April 21, 1900 in Aroma in Hamilton County. Her parents were Owen Folger Beeson and Carrie Ann Sperry Beeson. They were both born in Hamilton County. They moved to Tipton County in 1902 to a farm several miles west of Elwood. Barbara had a younger brother and a younger sister. Fred was born Dec. 16, 1902 and Doris was born Dec. 15, 1910. Doris was born at the farm and still lives there today. She married Joseph Alva Perkins who was born in Connersville. They built a new home on the site of the old farmhouse. Joe Perkins passed away in 1976. Aunt Doris continues to live in the house, very proud of her Tipton County heritage.

Edmond P. and Barbara Severns had two children. Diane was born Oct. 20, 1928. Edmond Paul was born Aug. 16, 1930. Even as a young boy he was known simply as E.P. Both of the children were raised in the family home at 1403 W. Sycamore. Barbara graduated from DePauw. She came back to Tipton County where she taught in a one-room schoolhouse prior to getting married and moving to Kokomo. Edmond P. came to Kokomo to work as a salesman at Continental Steel Corporation.

He was very successful in the business world. He was rewarded with a series of promotions and eventually became the President of Continental Steel. He later added the title Chairman of the Board, thus becoming the first person to hold those two titles simultaneously.

Diane and E.P. both attended McKinley School and both graduated from Kokomo High. Diane graduated from DePauw in 1950. She married Harold Bryant. They moved to Grand Rapids, MI and had three sons, Scott, Mike, and Skip. She and Harold later divorced. She then married Tony Farage. They continue to live in Grand Rapids.

E.P. married Virginia Lee Pierce Oct. 1, 1950. She grew up at 1132 N. McCann, the youngest child of Cecil and Emma Pierce. Ginnie, as she prefers to be called, was born March 30, 1931. Her brother, Robert, and his wife, Christine, raised three children: Trudy, Rita, and Steve. Robert and Christine still live at 1511 N. Lafountain. Ginnie's sister, Norma, married Paul Loman. They raised three boys: Gary, Jeff, and Greg. Norma passed away in 1977. Paul and Jeff still live in Kokomo, Gary and his family live outside Galveston, and Greg lives in Indianapolis.

After getting married E.P. served a stint in the U.S. Army stationed in Texas and California. He returned from military duty and resumed working in the family Coca-Cola business. His uncles Frank and Roy, along with his father, had purchased a Coca-Cola franchise in 1936. E.P. became President of Coca-Cola Bottling Company of Kokomo in 1959. He still holds that title today and continues to work on a daily basis.

E.P. and Ginnie raised four children. Craig was born Oct. 4, 1952. Betse was born April 1, 1955. Tim was born Sept. 10, 1958, and Susan was born July 7, 1968. All four children graduated from Kokomo High. Craig is a graduate of Indiana University, Betse is a graduate of DePauw, Tim attended Ball State, and Susan is a graduate of Ball State. Craig started full time in the Coca-Cola business June 1975. He now serves as General Manager. He married Kristi Lynn Needham May 7, 1988. She is the daughter of David and Elaine Needham of Kokomo. She has worked the past five years as a paraprofessional in Kokomo Center Schools. She now serves as the librarian at Wallace and Columbian. Tim started working full time at Coca-Cola in the summer of 1981. He was recently promoted to Sales Manager. Susan also works full time for Coca-Cola. She was married Sept. 18, 1993 to Francis Ellert. Susan is in charge of all fountain sales at our Plymouth operation. Francis is the assistant director of admissions at Culver Military Academy. They

Severns Family

reside in Culver. Betse graduated from DePauw in 1977. She moved to Washington, D.C. and worked as an assistant to Congressman Elwood Hillis. While in D.C. she met her husband, Jack McCullough. Also, in D.C. she was in charge of research for a very prominent book on national defense written by Colonel John Collins. She moved to Seattle, WA with Jack when he took a job with a Seattle law firm. Betse was hired by Boeing. Jack and Betse had a son, John Charles McCullough, born Jan. 21, 1987. In late 1988 we got the worst news the Severns family has ever received. Betse was diagnosed with cancer. It was a particularly aggressive and resistant strain. Betse fought a truly heroic battle, but the cancer eventually claimed her life Nov. 30, 1989. We remember her many accomplishments, but mostly we remember her bravery.

The Severns family has so many things to be thankful for. We are thankful for our family, our friends, and our co-workers. We are thankful that Coca-Cola has provided us and many others a good honest living. And we are very proud of our community. Kokomo has been a great place to grow up and form everlasting friendships. No doubt about it, we are "Positively Kokomo".

SHEARER - For more than 55 years Shearer Printing has conducted business in Kokomo, and in that time many changes have been made incorporating new technology in the printing process. Today, along with printing, they sell office supplies and business machines.

The business had its beginning when four Shearer brothers arrived from the Indianapolis area in 1914 with their mother and step-father. Following the death of the boys' father Charles Oliver Shearer (1875-1910), Ella Lamb Shearer (1879-1957) married Charles Pearsey of Rushville and they moved to Kokomo. Charles was employed at Kokomo Steel and Wire, later became affiliated with the New York Central Railroad. The brothers, Charles, John, Roland and Morris grew up and established homes in the Kokomo area.

Jim and Barbara Shearer

John became a pressman working in local print shops. In 1937, he established Shearer Printing, employing his brother Morris. Roland worked at Blue Cross Drug Store and Charles was with Consolidated Coal Company and Star Building Supply.

304

John (1900-1976) married Quatia Jett (1902) daughter of John Porter and Mattie (Chandler) Jett in 1923. They were parents of Patricia Jester (Mrs. Clifford), James K. and David L. The sons learned the trade while young and following college joined their father in the family business at 100 East Broadway. In 1963, Shearer Printing moved to its present location on Markland Avenue. John retired in 1969 and son James became president until he retired in 1992 and the reign was passed to brother David.

James (1929) graduated Kokomo High School and Indiana University. He married Barbara Carr (1929-1993), in Kokomo in 1951. Barbara retired from Indiana Bell Telephone. Although retired, Jim is currently county commissioner and is active in many organizations in the city and county. The Shearers attend Main Street Methodist Church. Children of this union are Brian, Diane and Marcia.

Brian (1955) attended Indiana University before joining the family business. He married Debbie Murphy of Kokomo and they are the parents of Craig (1981) and Michael (1984).

Diane (1958) is employed by Saint Joseph Hospital. She married Brian Huffman of Kokomo and they are the parents of Patrick (1984) and Amy (1987).

Marcia (1959), graduate of Indiana State University, is a teacher in the Kokomo Center Township School Corporation. *Submitted by James K. Shearer.*

EDWARD AND SARAH SHEPHERD

When only 16 years old, Edward Shepherd joined Co. H, 118th Indiana Inf. to fight in the Civil War. He served 11 months, was honorably discharged, and re-enlisted. He served until the close of the war.

Edward was born in Rush County, IN, on Sept. 8, 1846, to Washington and Rachel Shepherd. Little is known about his parents, but apparently they died before the Civil War began as Edward was living with relatives when he enlisted. He had an older brother Jacob (1844-1913) who also fought in the war. It is believed that the boys had an older sister Sarah who married John Cottingham in 1858 in Howard County.

Edward Shepherd

Edward married Sarah Catherine Campbell on Sept. 25, 1867, in Howard County. Sarah was the daughter of John N. and Mary A. (Boyle) Campbell who came here from Kentucky. Sarah had seven siblings. They included Levi (1844-1898) who married Maria J. Tarkington; Sabastian H. (born 1846) who married S.J. Wainwright; William (born 1851); Susan J. (born 1853) who married J. David Lambert; Joshua (born 1856); Benjamin F. (born 1859) who married Laura Prather; and John Fremont (1861-1919) who married Ida Coy.

The Shepherds had 10 children, three of whom died young. One was a baby girl; another was a son Oscar (1885-1900); and the other was Margaret (1891-1897). The other children were Clara Inez (1868-1932) who married William H. Heaton (see Heaton History); Anna, who married David Crownover/Conover; Emma (1872-1922) who married John Woolley; Jacob (1877-1934) who married Dama Hankins; Alice (1881-1913) who married Arthur Hendrickson; Jessie (1887-1963) who first married Charles Stamm and later married Ora Flora; and Josephine who married Charles Kidder and later married Walter McKinney.

Edward was engaged in farming in the Russiaville area until about 15 years before his death. When he quit farming, he moved to Kokomo and lived at 816 West State Street. His wife Sarah, a member of Courtland Avenue Friends Church, died June 29, 1923. Edward passed away Dec. 11, 1924. Both are buried at North Union Cemetery in Ervin Township. *Submitted by Richard Bennett.*

STEPHEN DECATUR SHOCKNEY

Stephen Decatur Shockney was born Feb. 14, 1833 in what is now Carroll County, MD. When he was five, he came with seven brothers and sisters and their parents, John N. and Jerusha Anderson Shockney, to Randolph County, IN. In 1853 he purchased 80 acres of land in Tipton County on the county line between Tipton and Howard counties. In 1857, he married Abigail Fellow, daughter of John and Abigail Coleman Fellow, who lived across the road on a farm in Howard County. Stephen and Abigail had four children—Eliza Jane who married Isaac Thomas (a brother of her step-mother), Oakey Kelsey, Josephine Antionette Captola who married Elbert Legg, and Anna Abigail who married William E. Kepler. Abigail died in 1868 and in 1870 Stephen married Caroline Elliott Thomas, daughter of Henry and Lydia Thomas. In 1876, Stephen and Caroline bought a farm across the road in Howard County (adjacent to the Fellow acreage) and moved there. They lived in a log home until a new, large home was built in 1882 to accommodate their expanding family.

Stephen Decatur and Caroline Thomas Shockney

This home was destroyed by fire in 1908 and was replaced by a smaller structure. Stephen and Caroline had 12 children—Ida Belle who married John C. Summers, Henrietta who married (and divorced) Dan Moorman, Evangeline who married John Patterson, David Jesse who married Grace Howatt, Rachel who married Thomas Landrum, Rollo Homer who married Myrtle Moorman, John Roscoe who married Minnie Olive Riley, Earl who married Luella Stephenson, Orpha Blanche who married Oscar William Silvey, Alice who married William Lee Shrader, Chester Herbert who married Pearl E. Brankle, and an infant son who survived only three weeks. Stephen's farm remained in Shockney hands until his death in 1930. His original farm (on the Tipton County side of the road) as well as the Howard County farm of the Fellow family were purchased by Stephen's son Roscoe and are still owned by descendants of that family. Stephen's children had frequent family gatherings before his death and continued to have at least annual gatherings. This tradition is still being carried on by his numerous descendants. *Submitted by Roseland Shockney, daughter of Roscoe and Minnie Riley Shockney.*

ALECK AND TILLIE SHORT

The first of the Short family to move to Howard County were Joseph Alexander "Aleck" Short (1851-1903) and his wife Matilda Jane "Tillie" Walker (1857-1943). Aleck, born in Garrard County, KY, was the son of Joseph Joel and Elizabeth (Ham) Short, the grandson of Zachariah and Susan "Sukey" (Jones) Short, and a descendant of William Short (1614-1659) who had immigrated to Virginia by 1634. Tillie, born in Jessamine County, KY, was the daughter of William W. Walker (1832-1908) and Mary Ann "Polly" Murphy (1833-1928), and granddaughter of John and Matilda Jennie (Rew) Walker on one side and of John and Susannah (Stinnett) Murphy on the other.

Aleck and Tillie, married in Jessamine County in 1876, already had five children before moving to Indiana—Thomas Owen (1878-1954), Mary Elizabeth (1880-1943), Owen (1882-1954), Beaty (born about 1888), and Joseph (1886-1942). Five more children were born at Kokomo—James E. (1889-1956), Pearl (born 1891), Martha "Mattie" (born 1893), Gladys (born 1898), and Raymond (1901-1950). Originally a farmer, from 1895 on Aleck (or "Alex") worked for an Indiana utility company. Tillie was a member of the Main Street Christian Church for many years and known as "a woman of good Christian character."

Matilda "Tillie" (Walker) Short (1857-1943)

The eldest child, Thomas Owen, married Alice Ellen Gibbs in Kokomo in 1901 and had two children (Mary Elizabeth and John Samuel). Thomas was employed for 30 years by the Kokomo Gas and Fuel Company, but was an invalid for the last 12 years of his life.

The second child, Mary Elizabeth, married Robert Manning in 1903. When Robert died in 1925, she was left with a son, Wayne, and three daughters (who married, respectively, Chester Peck, Bernard Cooper, and Robert Davenport).

Owen was Aleck and Tillie's third child. In 1903 he married another Jessamine County native, Mary M. Osborn; for most of his adult life Owen worked on the open hearth at the Continental Steel Corporation. Mary died in 1973, the mother of three sons—Earl B. (1903-1956), Kenneth Wayne (born 1907), and Harry Lester (born 1914).

Beaty married Jennie B. Walker in Kokomo in 1907 and was employed as a wire drawer at the rod mill. He and Jennie had four children—Kenosha May (1909-1910); Charles Ray (1915-1975); Vera Evelyn (born 1917); and another son who died before 1975.

The fifth child, Joseph, married four times. His first wife, whom he married in 1904, was Katie Brock; their one son, Willie V. (born in 1905), died at the age of 18 months after accidentally drinking concentrated lye. Joseph, employed as a wire drawer at the rod mill about 1910, married a second time the sister of Fred Hurst. He and Fred were arrested in 1920 (during Prohibition) for violating the Volstead Act; in later years, Joseph ran a billiard hall in Plymouth and a pool room in Kokomo. About 1926 he married Josephine Mae Delrymple. His fourth wife was Loretta Pierce.

James E. was the first child born in Indiana. In 1906 he married Eva Evelyn Stahl (1890-1940), daughter of Benjamin Stahl and Louisa Estella Gause. They had 10 children—Richard Marion (1908-1969); William Victor (1909-1910); Wilbur Lewis (born 1910); Artimissia (born 1913); Thelma (born 1914); Mary Lou (born 1916); Joseph Benjamin (1920-1921); Charles; Alfred Leroy (1923-1933); and Jo Maxine (born 1927). Like his brother Joseph, James was convicted of violating Prohibition, but his case brought some comic relief to readers of *The Kokomo Daily Tribune* in 1926: he and Harry Powell had tried to sneak into the county penal farm to avoid being escorted by the sheriff and seen by their neighbors. The guards, however, refused to admit them without commitment papers, and so the two had to return to town to get the sheriff after all.

Pearl may have been born during a brief return to Kentucky. She was married first to Fred McKay in Howard County in 1908; about 1943 she married a man named Hera (or O'Hara) and lived in New Jersey and Florida.

305

Mattie married three times—first Ernest Mumaugh, then George Bayliss Cosner, and finally George Behner. Her sister Gladys married Byron Boyd.

The youngest child was Raymond, whose wife's name was Thelma. Several years before his death he moved to Plymouth. Twice in his life Raymond made a splash in the Kokomo newspapers. The first time was when he was acquitted of manslaughter after a 1928 hit-and-run automobile accident. Within a month of his acquittal, Raymond was back in the press, this time praised as a hero for leaping into a cold and muddy river to rescue four men whose car had plunged through a wooden railing into the icy waters. *Submitted by CDR Michael O. Brown, CHC, USN*

GERALD W. AND PETRONEL SHUCK
A job brought Gerald to Kokomo: in 1950 (with Globe American Corporation, then on Dec. 17, 1956 to Chrysler Corporation Transmission Plant) and Petronel in 1967 (with Kokomo Haworth High School). They met in 1950 while in school at Jefferson Township High School, Tipton County. After a three year courtship, they were married Oct. 25, 1952 and established residency in Howard County. Both graduated from Jefferson Township High School, 1950 and 1953.

Gerald Wayne was born in Prairie Township, Tipton County, IN, May 6, 1931 and moved to the Kempton area in 1936. He joined the Indiana National Guard June 22, 1948 and received an honorable discharge 28 years later. After graduation in 1950 he moved to Kokomo and became a radio and T.V. repairman and is still licensed. He retired Jan. 1, 1988 from Chrysler Corporation after working for 31 years as a computer operator.

Petronel (Davenport) Shuck was born in Jefferson Township in Tipton County on May 27, 1934. She grew up in Goldsmith, IN.

In 1953 they were blessed with the birth of a lovely daughter Deborah Kaye. She graduated from Kokomo Haworth High School in 1971 and received a certificate from the College of Music, B.S. Degree in elementary education and endorsement in kindergarten. It was the first one given at Indiana University-Kokomo in 1974. She received a Master's Degree later. She was married to Mark Steven Scheid on March 10, 1974. They now live in Avon, IN. Debbie taught piano lessons in her home, and also teaches at the Children's Museum in Indianapolis as her schedule permits and occasionally at St. Susanna. Mark is an electrical engineer and computer programmer at PSI Energy.

Through the adoption procedure we were blessed with a beautiful granddaughter. Debbie and Mark flew to Brazil, South America, December 1987 to adopt this bundle of joy after a 33 day stay. Marielle Vanessa Maristella Scheid was born June 26, 1987. She is now a citizen of the United States of America and very proud of it.

Front row, l to r: Petronel (Davenport) Shuck, Marielle Scheid, and Gerald W. Shuck. Back row, l to r: Deborah (Shuck) and Mark S. Scheid.

In May 1955 our son was born, Steven Jay, but died two days later. He is greatly missed.

Gerald's parents are Marvin Otis Shuck and Ora Pauline (Reese) Shuck. Marvin (Ted) died Jan. 2, 1990. Ora P. was born Sept. 7, 1908 and still lives in Tipton County. His grandparents, Frank and Fern (Bouse) Shuck, married Feb. 24, 1904. His grandfather, Samuel Tillden (Till) Reese died May 19, 1969. His grandmother Lillie (Jacobs) Reese died in February 1918. His great-grandparents, James and Elizabeth (Roe) Reese, were also farmers.

Petronel's parents, Dallas Suite and Mary Elizabeth (Bauer) Davenport, were married Feb. 3, 1934. Her grandparents, Frank C. and Golda (Bitner) Bauer, were married Nov. 24, 1909. Her grandparents, George and Florence E. (Suite) Davenport, married in 1889. Florence was born in Howard County. Her great-grandparents were John E. and Mary Jane (Wellington) Bauer. Her great-grandparents were William and Elizabeth Bitner.

Gerald and Petronel have always lived less than 25 miles from their birthplaces. I guess we would not be considered world migrators. We have lived in Howard County for over 41 years at the same address. We like the community and have no plans of leaving in the near future. We attend the First Church of God and have for over 25 years.

THOMAS R. AND JANET L. SILVER
Tom was born in Lebanon, IN to parents Raymond L. and Joanna R. Silver. The family moved to Kokomo in 1962 after Tom's father was employed at Delco Radio Division, GMC.

Janet was born in Kokomo to parents Gerald G. and Mary Ann (Smith) Peterson. After graduating from Taylor High School in 1977, she attended Purdue University.

Tom graduated from Taylor High School in 1976 and attended Purdue University. Janet and Tom were married in 1978 and lived in Purdue married student housing in West Lafayette.

Janet received a Bachelor of Arts degree in education in 1982 and Tom received a BS degree in pharmacy the same year. Janet later obtained a Master's degree in education from Ball State in 1986.

In 1984 Tom and Janet moved to the rural Sharpsville area where they enjoyed country living. Their first son, Michael T. was born in 1987 there, before the family moved to Greentown in 1990.

Tom has been employed at Peoples Drug Store in Marion and Hooks Drug Store in Kokomo. He was store manager at Hooks By-pass store in Kokomo until he accepted a position as pharmacy manager for Kroger's in 1987. He later joined the Pharmacy Staff of the Howard Community Hospital in 1992.

Upon graduation from Purdue, Janet was employed at Eastern Elementary School in Greentown as teacher of the learning disabled. She is presently employed in the same capacity on a half-day status.

In 1991 Tom and Janet's second son, Daniel W., was born.

Tom's parents live in Kokomo in Taylor Township close to the high school. Tom's brother, James L., is also a pharmacist and resides with his family in Greentown. Janet's parents live in Taylor Township and she has three brothers: Gerald M. of Kokomo, Gregory S. of Greentown and Shawn Rowe of Widnes, England.

The Silver ancestors were French Canadian and the family name was originally Sylvain. Tom's great-grandfather, Joseph Sylvain, immigrated from Canada to New York State with his family in 1874 when he was only three years old. The Silver family worked in the saw mills in upper state New York. The family name was changed to Silver sometime after they came to the United States.

The Thompson family (Tom's mother's ancestors) came to Clinton County, IN in 1830 and were Scotch Irish in origin. Emma Kilgore, a Thompson ancestor, was the first white woman in Clinton County.

The Peterson family are from Scott County, VA. The Smith family (Janet's mother's ancestors) are long-time residents of Indiana.

RAYMOND L. AND JOANNA R. SILVER
Ray and Joanna met as students at Purdue University and were married after Ray received a degree in science in 1955. Both were employed by Allison Division, GMC, and they lived in Lebanon, IN. Ray was a test engineer in the Physical Optics Research Laboratory and Joanna was a computer technician in the Jet Engine Specifications and Design Department.

They moved to Kokomo in 1962. Ray was employed in 1960 as a test engineer in the Minuteman Missile Program at Delco Radio Division, GMC. They built a home in Taylor Township in 1964.

Ray was born in Oriskany Falls, NY, in 1928 to parents Raymond J. and Sarah L. Silver. His father was the first son of the first generation of American citizenship born (1896) to French Canadian immigrants with the original family name of Sylvain. The name was changed to Silver in 1874. Ray's mother was born in 1894 to English parents on a farm in central New York State. Among her ancestors was a Mohawk Indian squaw of the Five Nations.

Raymond L. and Joanna R. Silver

Ray graduated from high school in 1946 and immediately enlisted in the Army Air Force. After graduation from RADAR Repairman School, he was assigned to 9th Air Force Headquarters at Greenville, SC. Upon discharge in 1949, he enrolled in Purdue University.

Joanna was born in 1934 to parents Lawrence and Flossie Thompson of Jefferson, IN. The Thompson family was among the first settlers in the region and one of Joanna's relatives was the first white woman in Clinton County.

Joanna graduated from high school in 1952 and attended Purdue to study chemistry and mathematics until their marriage. She worked at Allison Division until their first son, Thomas R., was born in 1958. Later she commuted to Purdue University where she was employed as computer technician in the Chemistry Department. She resigned in 1962 when they moved to Kokomo and soon after they had their second son, James L., in 1965.

After their sons entered public school, Joanna returned to her studies at Indiana University-Kokomo University Extension Campus and obtained BS and MS degrees in education. She is employed by Taylor Elementary School with 20 years experience.

Ray retired from Delco Electronics after 32-1/2 years of service. He obtained a BS degree in general engineering from Purdue in 1968 and taught evening classes (electronics and mathematics) at IVY Tech. He retired as Senior Project Engineer in the Surface Analyses Section of R&D; areas of responsibility were X-ray, Auger, ESCA and Scanning Electron Microscopy.

Both their sons are Eagle Scouts and members of the National Honor Society. They also both graduated from Purdue with BS degrees in pharmacy. Thomas is employed at Howard Community Hospital. James has an additional degree in micro-biology from Ball State and is employed by Hook's Drug Company. Both are married. Thomas and his wife, Janet (Peterson), have two sons, Michael and Daniel. James and his wife, Robin (Childers), have a daughter, Courtney. Both families reside in Greentown.

C. OTHO SIMPSON
For at least half his life or more, C. Otho Simpson was actively involved in helping Kokomo grow. The oldest in a family of nine children, he knew how to lead people and how to make his voice be heard.

He was especially proud of the Kokomo Public Library, built in 1952 while he was president of the board. Working closely with the contractors, he often used his lunch hour to roam about the construction site, making sure that specifications were met in all aspects of the building.

Born in Center, IN, May 24, 1904, he was the son of Arthur Otho and May Miller Simpson. He was graduated from Kokomo High School in 1922, attended Indiana and Purdue Universities, worked for bakeries in both Kokomo and Cincinnati, OH, and in 1935, went to work in the offices of Continental Steel Corporation, where he remained until his retirement 34 years later.

C. Otho Simpson

In July 1936, he married Nellie Duncan. It was a standing joke between them that he could never remember whether they were married on July 9 and it was 110 degrees, or July 10 and it was 109. They had two daughters, Elizabeth Ann and Barbara Jane, and he taught them by example that living honestly and responsibly and treating people fairly were the right things to do. His six grandchildren learned those lessons, as well.

In his dresser, he kept a hand-written list, How To Get Things Done: 1) Start now. 2) Have a plan. 3) Use your spare time (waiting, walking, traveling). 4) Analyze your methods. 5) Do one thing at a time. 6) Follow through. What he accomplished for his family and his community makes it obvious that for him, the list had real validity.

He was a member of the Kokomo Park Board and the Kokomo Plan Commission during the 1940s. In 1952, he was named to the Kokomo Public Library Board and served in a variety of offices during his 14-year membership. In 1956, he was appointed to the Kokomo-Center Township School Board, and held all offices on that board during his six-year tenure. When Barbara graduated in 1959, he presented her with her diploma.

He was also on the Board of Trustees of Albright Cemetery, where many of the Simpson family are buried. In addition, he was a member of Napthali Masonic Lodge at Center, and the York Rite. He belonged to Grace Methodist Church, and was active in the Elks Lodge in Kokomo.

He loved to fish, he loved to read, and he loved all things about the outdoors. During WWII, he had an enormous garden; tending to his yard was one of his great pleasures. He loved the way things worked, especially machines, and could describe how a combine or a car functioned with equal ease. A social being, he and his wife had a wide circle of friends, and he could make conversation with almost anyone.

Surely, Kokomo has grown and changed since Otho Simpson was there. But he left his mark on his community through his service, and that remains unchanged. *Submitted by Elizabeth Simpson Friedman.*

ROBERT SIMPSON - Robert F. Simpson called Howard County home because of the arrival of his grandfather, Francis Marion Simpson, from Fayette County in 1870 to Tipton County, and then to eastern Howard County in 1878. Francis M. settled near the village of West Liberty and in his later years moved to Greentown where he died in 1909.

Bob's father, Jesse F., was born in 1880 in Howard County, and Robert Franklin was born Dec. 9, 1908 in Union Township, Howard County. He attended Union High School and was a member of the Union Cardinals basketball team.

Bob spent many years as a milk truck driver, picking up milk in 10-gallon cans at farms in Howard and Grant counties and delivering it to the Swift and Co. Dairy in Marion, IN. Bob also farmed in Union Township.

After purchasing a home in 1949 at 509 E. Main St. in Greentown, he worked for C.E. Petro Implements and also the Chrysler Corp. He then started his own electrical business which he continued the rest of his life.

The Lion's Club in Greentown was begun in July 1945. Bob was a charter member and did volunteer electrical work at the Howard County 4-H Fair each year for many years.

Bob was a member and "chief handshaker" at the Jerome Christian Church. When the Rainbow Christian Service Camp near Converse was started, Bob did much of the electrical work on the new camp.

His first marriage was to Clara B. (Hill) in 1932. They were the parents of Ronald D. and Susann M. In 1957 Bob married Gwen Rybolt of Fairmount. Bob enjoyed people and also fishing. He made many trips to Minnesota and later fished in Florida where he and Gwen spent the winters the last 20 years of his life. *Submitted by Jean Simpson.*

RONALD SIMPSON - As the Great Depression tightened its grips on the nation and President F.D. Roosevelt was working out the details of the New Deal, two babies were born. Ronald D. Simpson was born Dec. 27, 1933 on a farm in Union Township in Howard County. His parents were Robert F. Simpson and Clara B. (Hill). Jean Downhour was born May 18, 1934 to farming parents in Wabash County. Her parents were Russell E. Downhour and Vesta A. (Childers).

Sixteen years later, their paths crossed when Ron transferred to Swayzee High School in Swayzee, IN for his last two school years. He had been attending Union High School in Union Township, but went to Swayzee when the consolidation of Greentown High School, Jackson High School and Union High School took place in the fall of 1950. They both graduated in May, 1952 and were married in Herbst Methodist Church in Grant County, May 18, 1952.

Ronald Simpson Family - 1967

Ron and Jean began married life in Greentown where they still reside. The home they purchased in 1959 at 323 E. Main Street was built in 1914 and during the early days of Greentown was used as a boarding house. Their children who called this home were Ronda, April 5, 1954; Emily, July 23, 1955; Lisa, July 28, 1956; Stephen, Sept. 27, 1957-Jan. 7, 1994; and John, Sept. 29, 1961.

The Simpson family attended the Jerome Christian Church for 20 years and have now been members of the Macedonia Christian Church 21 years. Ron has served as deacon, elder and Sunday School Superintendent. Jean taught children's Sunday School for many years and is now piano and organ accompanist.

Ron attended Indiana University Extension in Kokomo when it was located in the Seiberling Mansion and Carriage House. He was elected Howard County Democratic Central Committee Chairman in July 1971. He also served 15 years as precinct committeeman in Liberty Township. Former Gov. Matthew Welsh and former U.S. Senator Vance Hartke visited in their home during those years.

Ron has served in the offices of the Masonic Lodge in Greentown and the York Rite in Kokomo. In 1984-85, he was Grand Commander of the Knights Templar of Indiana. Ron retired in 1987 from Delco Electronics in Kokomo, after 33 years of service, and Jean retired in 1991

having worked at Delco for 25 years. They enjoy traveling and Ron has a small business in his home. They also enjoy five grandchildren, Don Ellis, Jason Ellis, Samantha Martin, Alison Eldridge and Russell Martin. *Submitted by Jean Simpson.*

MILTON RENZEL AND VIRGINIA LOY SLOCUM - Milton Renzel Slocum's ancestral tree included General Henry Warner Slocum of the Civil War and Frances Slocum, the young white girl who was kidnapped by a band of Delaware Indians in the late 1700s and later lived as a Miami woman in the Peru, IN area.

Virginia Claire Loy Slocum's lineage was traced back through the Daughters of the American Revolution as early as the *Mayflower*. Notable ancestors included General White of the Revolutionary War.

Milton Renzel Slocum was employed as a superintendent of midwestern paper mills and transferred from the Akron, OH area to Kokomo in the early 1900s. They brought their seven children with them including Allen Slocum (Bertha), a city councilman in Kokomo and veteran of three wars; Mary Slocum Pollard (Otis); Charles Slocum (Lottie); Charlotte Slocum Fellow (Charles); Robert Slocum, local businessman; Marion Edward Slocum (Evelyn Melinda), Indianapolis attorney; and Jeanette Slocum, violinist and music instructor.

Slocum Family 1915 - The Slocum children, ca. 1915, left to right 1st row, Charles, Jeanette, Allen; 2nd row Marion Edward, Mary, Robert and Charlotte.

Marion, affectionately known as "Cud", was a joyful source of verse, stories and family kinship, and was a graduate of Kokomo High School, 1921. In his carefree boyhood days he roamed with this faithful hound, Jasper, and sold popcorn every day at the train station to buy bread for the family, exemplifying the spirit of the times when family loyalty and devotion came first and foremost.

His daughters, Cherrie Slocum and Serita Slocum Borgeas are keeping alive the family traditions with their children, Kassie, Kelly, Heidi and Andre. They are currently engaged in a search to uncover factual data and anecdotal history of the Slocum family since their father has recently passed away.

SMALL - Jonathan Small (1796-1824) and Miriam Bundy Small were the parents of Gideon, Sarah, Elihu and Joseph Small. Gideon Small (1817-1897) and Dinah Marshall Small were early settlers of Howard County. They were the parents of Joseph, Reuben, Silas and Elizabeth Small Kenworthy. Gideon's second marriage was to Rebecca Compton Newby (1824-1897). Their children were Jennie, who was never married, and Eli Milton.

Eli Milton Small (1868-1942) and Jessie Alice Hunt (1871-1923) were married in the New London area. To them were born Esther Small Taylor, Vera Small Kenworthy, and Marion Creston. Milton Small lived on and owned a farm two miles north of New London which still belongs to his grandchildren.

Esther Small (1896-1983) and C. Russell Taylor (1895-1969) were married Aug. 23, 1925 in a Friends ceremony at the close of Sunday meeting. Their children are Ethel Virginia T. Haynes, Helen Naomi T. Kelly, Lewis Milton, and Carolyn T. Carson.

Vera Small (1900-1991) and Clarence Kenworthy (1900-1978) were married June 7, 1924. They also lived in this area their entire lives. To them were born Ruth Jeanette K. Mote and Marvin Joe Kenworthy.

Marion Creston Small (1905-1993) and Bernice Thomas Small (died 1981) were the parents of Thomas M. and Marianne S. Jackson.

This family of early Quaker heritage is proud to be part of Howard County, IN. *Submitted by Helen Taylor Kelly and Mary Frances Taylor.*

ROBERT SMELTZER - Robert Smeltzer was born in Gallia County, OH on April 29, 1839, a son of Adam (1807-1889) and Margaret (Smith) Smeltzer (1817-1907). Adam and Margaret were married April 3, 1834. Adam's parents were John (1779-1836) and Christina (Blazer) Smeltzer (1784-1848) who were married in Rockingham County, VA Jan. 3, 1803. In 1851 Adam moved his family to Shelby County, OH where young Robert grew to manhood on his father's farm.

On March 10, 1861 Robert married Sarah Ann (Zerbe) (1842-1931), daughter of William (1818-1896) and Mary Ann (Butcher) Zerbe (1821-1902).

At the outbreak of the Civil War he answered his country's call as a private in Co. K, 20th Ohio Volunteer Inf. He served for more than three years and was honorably discharged at Goldsboro, NC at the close of the war.

In May of 1865 he joined his wife and two children who had come to Howard County from Ohio with her parents.

Sarah Smeltzer; Robert Smeltzer

He worked for landowners in the neighborhood, cleaning and ditching and in a sawmill owned by Robert Marquis for a part of two years. He was then able to purchase the "home" 40 acres in Liberty Township in the fall of 1868. He established a comfortable home and developed an excellent farm, to which at a later time he added 40 acres that adjoined the original plot on the north.

Robert made money on grain, hogs, etc. He was industrious and economical and was known as one of the good farmers in the area, always ready to help his needy and deserving neighbors. He was a director of the Amboy Bank and belonged to the G.A.R.

Robert and Sarah were the parents of one girl and two boys.

Emma Jane (1862-1941) who married William Henry Kerby in 1881. To this union were born six sons and five daughters: Alda, Charles, Pearl, Nina, Leo, Josephine, Vada, Everett, Homer, Harry, and Bernard. William and Emma resided in Clay Township until 1922 when they moved to Kokomo.

William (1865-1961) married Hannah Saul on Sept. 20, 1887 and were the parents of six children: Sara Lovina, Robert Raymond, Rilda Pearl, Leota Grace, Hazel Neola, and Samuel William. William lived and farmed near Plevna most of his life.

Charles Francis (1869-1957) was married to Elizabeth Shrock on Dec. 25, 1889. Their children were: Homer Lewis, Lawrence Dewey, Ruby Opal and Mildred Lucille. Charles was a carpenter and cabinet maker. He was a member of the Greentown Methodist Church.

In October 1913 Robert and Sarah moved to Greentown where he died Sept. 3, 1915. They are both interred in the I.O.O.F. Cemetery, Greentown.

SMITH - William Charles Smith, born 1802 in Pennsylvania, met and married in 1825, Lucia Lucus of Virginia, born 1807. William became a Wesleyan minister and he and his family moved to Cincinnati, OH to accept a pastoral position. They had five children:

Elizabeth Jane, born 1826 in Charleston, VA. She married in 1847 to David Moore Gray, born 1810. She died in 1904.

John, born July 12, 1827, in Charleston, VA, first married Nancy Jane ? in 1853 and she died in 1855. John remarried in 1857 to Susan Barnes, daughter of John and Permelia (Gray) Barnes.

Dr. Charles William Smith, born 1832 in Charleston, VA, went to Purdy County, MO. Nothing else is known of him.

John Smith settled in Nashville, IN. He had a daughter, Nancy A., born 1854, by his first wife. He had the following nine children by Susan Barnes:

Charles Damon, born 1858; Sarah M., born 1860; Mary Ann, born 1863; Margaret, born March 10, 1864; Laura Etta, born Dec. 31, 1865; William Harry, born 1867; George W., born July 3, 1871; Emma Mary, born 1875.

Richard married Cora Jane Tutterow (April 19, 1879) on May 14, 1893, in Brown County. They moved to Lafayette, IN around 1910. They had five children: Dorothy Lucille, born Oct. 2, 1920; Harry Damon Smith, Jr., born July 22, 1922 and Bernell, born Dec. 19, 1923. Mary Mildred died July 21, 1925.

Harry Sr. then married Mary Mildred's cousin, Hazel Ruth (Murphy) Imbler, (born Oct. 30, 1904) on Nov. 10, 1928. She was a daughter of Harry and Ella Ruth (Pasdach) Murphy of Kokomo, IN. Harry and Hazel moved to Kokomo in the 1930s. They had seven children: Mary Elizabeth, born April 2, 1929; George Crestin, born Oct. 4, 1930; Charles Lee, born and died 1932; Virginia Rose, born Feb. 6, 1934; Juanita May, born Nov. 5, 1936; Galen Richard, born Oct. 13, 1938 and Nancy Carol, born Dec. 18, 1941. Hazel had a daughter, Lois Ruth, by a previous marriage, born Aug. 11, 1928.

Dorothy Lucille married Sept. 24, 1938 to Harold Jesse Galloway. Harry Damon Smith, Jr. married Feb. 28, 1946 to Lola Belle Zimmerman. Bernell married March 1, 1946 to Nora Joan Hawk. Mary Elizabeth married in 1946 to David M. Bolen. George Crestin married in 1951 to Loretta Horn. Virginia Rose was first married to Donald Rohler; she second married around 1960 to Richard Unger. Galen Richard married around 1959 to Rita Murphy. Juanita Mae married Nov. 27, 1952 to Harold C. Henisa. Nancy Carol first married 1959 Clarence Birch; second married April 27, 1962 to Donald Buckles. Lois Ruth Imbler married around 1946 to Charles Cook.

Hazel Ruth Smith died Oct. 13, 1973. Lois Ruth died in 1985. Nancy Carol died Feb. 13, 1988. Harry Damon Smith, Sr. died May 21, 1988. Harry Damon Smith, Jr. died Jan. 23, 1993.

William Charles and Lucia Smith were the third great-grandparents of Rodger Damon Smith. *Submitted by Rodger D. Smith.*

SMITH/SHAFFER/McCOOL - Daniel Fredrick Smith, was born in Tipton Township, Cass County, son of Samuel L. and Elizabeth (Shaffer) Smith, the ninth of eleven children. Samuel and Elizabeth were both born in Pennsylvania. They left their home state, traveling west by team, stopping in Ohio, where they married Dec. 1, 1842 and remained for some time. Traveling on, arriving in Indiana October 1854, locating on the farm in Tipton Township. It was a tract of timber land, trees standing in their native strength, as yet undisturbed by white man. They cleared the land, and the fields soon produced abundant harvests. The first home was a log cabin. Samuel was successful in his operations, becoming a large land owner. In 1862 they built a large barn and in 1863 built a house, which to this day both are in excellent condition. The house is occupied by Beulah Snell, wife of Clark Snell (1901-1992) great-grandson of Samuel and Elizabeth. Clark was born in this house and lived there until his death at St. Joseph Hospital, Kokomo. Clark was also a successful farmer and banker. The farm is a working farm today.

Picture taken 1875-1879, Samuel L. Smith Family. Standing left to right: George L., Sarah A., Alda M., Samuel H., Elizabeth, John Ross, Daniel Fredrick, Mary Catherine (Molly). Seated, left to right: William B., Samuel L. Smith, Elizabeth (Shaffer) Smith, David.

Daniel went to school and farmed until age 25, when he obtained a patent on a fence he developed, then moved to Kokomo, where he sold fences for several years. In 1888 he married Roanna Arminta McCool (1870-1960) and they returned to farming. They had three children, Evert, Ora, and Ernest. As the children grew up they married and moved away. Evert married Naomi Elizabeth Snyder, moved to Kokomo; they had two children, Fredrick and Doris. Ora married Francis (Frank) Rozzel, moved to Kansas City, MO. They had nine children, Russel, Robert, Richard, Marjorie, Harold, Roanna, Francis (Frank), Hugh, and Naomi Jean (Jeanie). Russel and Richard were born at their grandparents' home in Kokomo. Ernest married Janet Benson, moved to Kokomo; they had four children, Ronold, Keith, Vonna Lou and Judith (Judy), all live in Kokomo, except Keith, who lives in Florida.

Daniel and Roanna moved back to Kokomo where they spent the rest of their lives. Daniel worked at the Plate Glass Factory and Kokomo Rubber Plant. Both were active in community and Southside Christian Church, where Daniel was member of Ancient Order of Gleaners. Daniel died Nov. 9, 1942; Roanna died Dec. 18, 1960. Both are buried at Crown Point Cemetery.

Samuel L. Smith and Elizabeth (Shaffer) Smith Homestead

Samuel and Elizabeth remained on the homestead in Walton until shortly before his death 1890, when they moved to Logansport. Elizabeth died July 24, 1906; both are buried Pipe Creek Cemetery, where several other family members are also buried.

Roanna's parents, Jeremiah McCool 1842-1913 and Cynthia (Rickard) McCool (1842-1906), lived most of their lives in Kokomo, were well-known. Jeremiah served in Civil War and a member of the G.A.R. Both buried at Crown Point Cemetery, as are many other family members.

The author of this article is great-granddaughter of Samuel and Elizabeth and Jeremiah and Cynthia McCool, and granddaughter of Daniel and Roanna Smith. She remembers many happy days spent in their home in Kokomo. Many articles on this family can be found in Howard County Historical Library. *Submitted by Marjorie J. Easter.*

GEORGE RAYMOND SMITH, JR. -
George Raymond Smith Jr. was born Aug. 31, 1932. He has two brothers, Richard Lee Smith, born Aug. 16, 1934 and James Robert Smith, born Aug. 19, 1935. He also has one sister, Marilyn Mae Smith, born June 8, 1937. They were all born and presently live in Howard County.

George attended Darrough Chapel, Wallace, Roosevelt, Meridian, Lincoln, Central, and Kokomo High Schools in Howard County. When he was a senior, he went to school half a day and worked at Continental Steel for the extra board half a day. He graduated from Kokomo High School in 1951.

On Dec. 4, 1952, George went into the United States Army. While in the Army, he served 18 months in Germany, from June 1953 to Nov. 10, 1954. When he returned from Germany he went into the Army National Guard.

In 1955, George met Margaret Ann Thieke. They were married Aug. 3, 1956, in Howard County. During their marriage, they had three children, Tamara Ann Smith, born Aug. 15, 1957, Greg Alan Smith, born June 17, 1960, and Amy Michelle Smith, born Jan. 17, 1968. They lived in Bon-Air addition for 20 years.

After 21 years of marriage, George and Margaret were divorced in 1977.

On Nov. 24, 1982, George married Sara Kathrien Lytle and are presently living in Howard County.

George retired from the Indiana National Guard in August 1992 as a Sergeant Major E9. During his years in the National Guard he has received many medals and awards. Some of those are: two Meritorious Service Medals, five Army Commendation Medals, two Army Achievement Medals, one Distinguished Service Medal, one Indiana Commendation Medal, an Eagle Award (for the recruiter with the highest percentage to the team), Letters from President Bush, State of Indiana Council of the Sagamore of the Wabash Award from Governor Bayh, Legion of Hoosier Heroes from the Adjutant General of Indiana, the gymnasium at the National Guard Armory in Howard County named after him (George R. Smith Gymnasium) plus numerous other citations, ribbons and awards.

George Raymond Smith Jr.

George is also a member of Elks, Eagles and the 32nd Degree Mason with Howard Lodge 93.

George's biological Dad was George "Ray" Raymond Smith. He was born in 1905, in Summittville, IN and died April 25, 1938, in Columbus, IN. He was employed by Glove Stove and Range in Howard County and was also a race car driver. It was during a practice run in the opening of dirt track automobile racing season in Indiana when Ray had a fatal accident. In 1929, Ray qualified for the "Indy 500" but later was bumped by a fraction of a second.

George's Mom was Ivah Mae Wood. She was born May 25, 1911, in Watseka, IL. George "Ray" and Ivah were married July 4, 1928. She worked at the Silver Club and Sycamore Inn in Howard County for many years. Ivah married Harold Allen Smith on July 7, 1941 in Howard County. On June 15, 1960, Harold adopted George, Richard, James and Marilyn. Ivah died Feb. 11, 1986, in Howard County.

The summer of 1993, George worked for the Country Club taking care of the golf course. He is now employed part-time at Syndicate Sales. *Submitted by Ryan M. Stevenson.*

HAROLD J. AND MILDRED C. SMITH -
Harold J. Smith was born at Maces Springs, a small community in the hills of Scott County, VA on March 25, 1906. He was the only child of John Wesley (1881-1930) and Cora Ethel (Robinson) Smith (1890-1911), who were married at Bristol, TN, on Jan. 27, 1905.

Fye 1921—Rear: Mildred, Nellie, Mary, Delbert. Front: William, Danny, Oletha, Aurelia.

John W. Smith was the son of William, a southwestern Virginia fruit orchard farmer, and Irene (Head) Smith. William and Irene had two other children in addition to John, an older daughter, Mary Elizabeth and a younger son, James Clifton Smith.

Soon after Harold's birth, his parents divorced. Ethel was united in marriage to J.C. Mann and to this union were born two children, the oldest being Cecil Mann. The youngest child died a few days before his mother. Ethel passed away on Sept. 12, 1911, at the age of 21.

John W. Smith married Susan Farmer and they had six children: Howard, Roy, Frank, Ada, Earnest and Clyde. John worked on the C&O Railroad and in 1920, moved his family to Boston, a small town about five miles south of Richmond, IN. It was here that Harold met his bride-to-be, Mildred Fye.

On Jan. 12, 1929, Harold Smith was united in marriage with Mildred C. Fye by a justice of the peace in Richmond, IN. A few months later, they moved to Kokomo where Harold found a job as a cook at the Francis Hotel and at the beginning of the Depression, began a family. To this union six children were born: John David, the oldest, married Jewel Price, and they have four children, Charlene, David, Kelly and James C.; Robert married Geneil Brown, and their children are Eric and Todd; James D. married Janet Pearson, and their children are Kent, Kirk, Kristie and Kevin; Billy J. married Judy Lynch, and they have two children, named Mike and Lyn; Richard married Jill Soupley, and their children are Jeff and Julie; and Patricia, the youngest of the six, married John Larke, and their one child is named Lisa.

Smith—Back: Bill, Patty, Dave, and Dick. Front: Jim, Mildred, Harold, and Bob.

Mildred Catherine Fye, daughter of William C. and Aurelia (Gunder) Fye, was born on Aug. 9, 1910, at Kokomo, IN. William C. Fye was born at Preble County, OH on Sept. 15, 1875 and came to Kokomo at the turn of the century. He was a veteran of the Spanish-American War and son of Civil War soldier, Benjamin Fye. William married Aurelia, daughter of Henry and Jane (Chase) Gunder, on Oct. 25, 1899, at Darke County, OH. They had seven children: Mary, Nellie, Delbert, Roy, Mildred, Danny, and Oletha. Aurelia died on June 11, 1924, and William died on July 6, 1966.

Harold and Mildred Smith spent the first 35 years of their married lives working and raising their family at Kokomo. Harold retired from Delco Radio and Mildred retired from Haynes Stellite in 1966. They moved to Florida and stayed 25 years before returning and calling Howard County their home once again. *Submitted by Harold J. Smith.*

H.W. SMITH-OLMSTED -
A Conestoga covered wagon brought Henry Washington Smith, his wife Permelia (Garr) Smith and their four children to this farm at 5300 Old Sycamore Road in 1853. The current address is 5300 W. 00 N.S. The Smith family came to Howard County, IN from Kentucky. Four more children would be born to this family after settling in Howard County. Henry and Permelia Smith built their brick house in 1859. It was the first brick house in Clay Township. A brick "milk house" and a "smoke house" still stand behind the Smith farm house. The "smoke house" is lined with Kokomo newspapers from 1864.

Farm as it appeared in the Howard County Atlas of 1877

The 1877 Atlas states, "The first brick house was built in 1859 by Henry Washington Smith, who is an industrious, enterprising man and the largest landholder of the township. He is a friend of all that tends to advance her interests, and especially of the cause of education; for not only is he a supporter of the township and city schools, but also of the State University, where at one time he had three sons." One of the aforementioned sons was Newton B. Smith. Newton built a home at 814 West Mulberry Street in Kokomo in 1883. His youngest child was Carlisle F. Smith. Carlisle is the father of Marjorie Ann (Smith) Olmsted. Marjorie's children are David Carlisle, who lives in the house Newton and Annie (Yager) Smith built; Elizabeth Ann who is a veterinary assistant in Geneseo, IL; Robert Charles, who is a teacher in Knoxville, IL; and Thomas Lee, who is the current resident of Henry and Permelia Smith's brick farm house. Tom is the Smith's great-great-grandson. The H.W. Smiths raised eight children on this farm and lived there from their arrival in 1853 until their deaths. Permelia died Jan. 24, 1884 at age 64, and Henry died Jan. 20, 1898 at age 81. The farm has been owned by heirs of H.W. Smith since his death.

House at Smith Farm 1993

The Conestoga covered wagon which brought the Smith family from Kentucky to Indiana in 1853 was

309

stored in the barn on the farm for over 100 years. It is now at the Indiana State Museum in Indianapolis.

Tom and Kathy Olmsted started their married life in February 1993 in Tom's great-great-grandparents' brick farmhouse. Tom was born and raised in Geneseo, IL, and Kathy was born and raised in LaGrange, MO. Madalynn Rebecca Olmsted is a native of Kokomo. She was born to Tom and Kathy Dec. 18, 1993 making 1993 a most memorable year for this family. *Submitted by Marjorie A. Olmsted.*

JAMES D. AND JANET D. SMITH - Born in Howard County, IN, in the city of Kokomo, on Feb. 24, 1933, James D. Smith is the son of Harold and Mildred (Fye) Smith. His paternal ancestry is of Virginia and is mentioned elsewhere in this volume. Harold and Mildred became the parents of six children whose names are presented in order of birth: John David, who married Jewel Price and died in 1988; Robert C., who married Geneil Brown; James D., of this review; Billy J., who married Judy Lynch and died in 1990; Richard L., who married Jill Soupley; and Patricia K., who married John Larke.

Jim received his education at Kokomo schools and graduated in the spring of 1952. While attending school he worked at Cuneo Press and after graduation he was employed by Haynes Stellite. On Nov. 23, 1952, Jim was married to Janet D. Pearson at the Bible Baptist Church in Kokomo.

Front: Jim and Janet Smith. Back: Kevin, Kristi, Kirk, Kent

Janet was born on Aug. 9, 1934, at Kokomo, IN. She was the oldest of four children born to Wayne A. and Bernice (Williams) Pearson; her three brothers are Ross, Phillip J., and Neal Pearson. Janet graduated from Kokomo High School and attended Indiana University-Kokomo when it was in the Seiberling Mansion. She was employed at Globe American, Stellite, and Delco, before working for 21 years at Western School Corporation from where she retired in 1992. Jim and Janet have four children: Kent A., the oldest, married Janice Schmaltz, and they have three children, Craig, Ryan and Melissa; Kirk B. married Lee Ann Murphy, and their children are Emily and Bradford; Kristie married Kevin Atkinson and their children are Kyle and Nathan; and Kevin Scott married Amy Smith and they have three children, Rachel, Rebecca and Daniel. *Submitted by Kent A. Smith.*

KIRK BRADFORD AND LEE ANN SMITH - Kirk was born in Howard County (St. Joseph Hospital) Nov. 26, 1956 to Jim D. and Janet D. (Pearson) Smith. Lee Ann (Murphy) was born in Greenfield, IN Sept. 23, 1956 to Carey Jr. and Carolyn Jean (Parker) Murphy.

Lee Ann's family moved to Kokomo in 1960 when her father took a job at Delco Electronics. He taught at West Middleton and Western Schools. Lee Ann has a twin, Linda L. Murphy (Kokomo); a brother, Brian L. Murphy (Indianapolis) born Nov. 1, 1952; and a sister Brenda D. Heaton (Kokomo), born Aug. 8, 1954.

Kirk has a brother Kent A. Smith (Russiaville, IN) born Aug. 4, 1953, a sister Kristie A. Atkinson (Bloomington, IN), born Dec. 1, 1960 and a brother Kevin S. Smith (Tipton, IN), born March 21, 1962.

Kirk and Lee Ann met at Western School in 7th grade and married Aug. 14, 1976 at First Baptist Church in Kokomo, IN. They built at 4940 South 920 West (Howard County), moved in Aug. 14, 1986 and have resided at that Russiaville address since.

Emily Renee Smith was born to Kirk and Lee Ann at St. Joseph Hospital on Feb. 21, 1983 and Bradford Kirk Smith was born on April 19, 1989 at St. Joseph Hospital. Both were delivered by Dr. Phil Burgan.

Lee Ann graduated from Western High School in 1975 and from Indiana Vocational Technical College in 1981. She has been employed by General Motors, Delco Electronics, since 1983.

Kirk graduated from Western High School in 1975 and from Indiana University in 1984. He is a fourth generation employee at Haynes International (Kokomo), since 1981.

Lee Ann's parents were raised on farms in Blackford County (Indiana) near Hartford City. Both were school teachers and retired from Northwestern School Corporation in 1988. They now live in Ft. Myers, FL in the winter and Kokomo, IN during the summer. They have six grandchildren.

Kirk's parents were raised in the Kokomo City limits by factory workers. Kirk's grandparents Harold J. and Mildred Smith still reside in Russiaville. Kirk's mother retired from Western School Corporation in 1992 and his father retired from Haynes International in 1992. Both still reside in Russiaville. They have nine grandchildren.

JACOB LIGHT SMITH - Jacob Light Smith was born in Montgomery County, OH in 1839 and was the youngest of seven children born to John H. and Rebecca (Light) Smith. Jacob's father passed away when Jacob was an infant and his mother rented a farm in Miami County, OH in order to keep her children together and with the aid of her sons managed her affairs so as to live in comfortable circumstances and give to each child a good practical education.

Jacob remained with his mother, managing the farm and looking after her interests until he was about 23 years of age.

Jacob and Martha Smith

In 1864 Jacob married Martha Turner, daughter of Andrew and Rachel (Jones) Turner, both natives of North Carolina. Shortly after their marriage they came to Indiana, first settling in Miami County where they lived for four years after which time Jacob purchased a farm in northern Howard County. The family lived on this farm for about 12 years. He then purchased a farm three miles west of Kokomo. Although the farm was run-down and had been neglected, he proceeded to make improvements and soon had the buildings repaired and the land producing again.

Jacob and Martha were the parents of nine children, three of whom died in infancy.

John Vernon was born in 1864 and married Ida May Knight in 1897. He died in 1941 in Menominee, MI.

Ida was born in 1867 and in 1899 was married to Hylas Morris. They had one daughter, June. Ida lived in Kokomo and died in 1945.

Glenn R. was born in 1849. He was a school teacher and for a time resided in Tipton County and was superintendent of schools at Windfall. He later returned to Howard County where he passed away in 1937. His wife was Sarah Hamilton. They married in 1891 and had two children, Blanche and Paul.

Harry was born in 1892. He was a physician in Middletown, OH. In 1914 he married Nell Bunnell. This union was blessed with two children, Nancy and Jacob Edgar. Dr. Smith passed away in Indianapolis in 1920.

Grace was born in 1874 and in 1899 was married to Ward Jacobs. They lived with her father and raised their two children, Hurshel and Dortha, on the "home place". After the death of her husband Grace moved to Kokomo where she lived until her death in 1937.

Dorothy (Dolly) was born in 1882 and was married in 1901 to Edgar Utterback, a farmer from Johnson County, IN. They made their home there and were the parents of four sons; Dale, Glenn, Forest, and Dwight. In 1926 Dolly passed away.

During the Civil War, Jacob served in the Ohio Home Guard and although he saw no active duty outside the state, he was ready to respond to the call of the government in case his services were needed.

Martha died in 1908 and in 1913 Jacob's obituary stated "He stands high in the esteem of those with whom he mingles, has many warm friends and has ever tried to do the right as he sees and understands the right." *Submitted by Ron Woodward.*

KENT AND JANICE SMITH - Kent A. Smith was born at Kokomo, IN, on Aug. 4, 1953. He is the oldest son of James D. and Janet D. (Pearson) Smith. He graduated with the class of 1971 from Western High School and from Indiana University in 1976. Kent has worked in the maintenance department at Haynes International in Kokomo for the past 20 years.

Kent and Janice Smith with Ryan, Craig and Melissa.

Kent was united in marriage to Janice L. Schmaltz on Jan. 21, 1973 at the Main Street Christian Church at Kokomo, IN. They are the parents of three children, Craig A., Ryan B. and Melissa. They make their home near Russiaville.

Janice L. Schmaltz was the daughter of Charles F. and Nancy (Boyd) Schmaltz and was born at Greencastle, IN, the youngest of three daughters. Her sisters are Beth Ann Higgins of Florence, KY, and Debra Sallee of Kokomo. Janice was in the class of 1985 at Western High School and now is employed there as a teacher's aide. *Submitted by Kent A. Smith.*

SMITH-OLMSTED - A pipe organ graces the living room of this house built in 1883 by Newton and Annie (Yager) Smith at 814 West Mulberry Street in Kokomo. The addition on the east side of the house was added in 1912 for the Moeller Pipe Organ. Newton and Annie Smith's oldest child, Agnes Lee, was responsible for the addition to the house and the installation of the pipe organ. There are very few homes that house a pipe organ in excellent condition.

Agnes Lee Smith was born in this house in 1883 and lived her entire 93 years there. Many youngsters learned to play the piano and organ in this house with Agnes Lee Smith as their teacher. Agnes was church organist in several Kokomo churches in addition to teaching piano and organ to her many students.

The Smith children made up a major part of a chamber orchestra that rehearsed and often performed in this house. Agnes played the organ or the piano, H. Wylie played the violin or the viola and Carlisle played cello. There were various other instrumentalists who played

310

with this ensemble. The Kokomo Morning Musicale also had many of their meetings in this home.

Home built by the Newton B. Smiths in 1883 at 814 W. Mulberry St. in Kokomo. It is now the home of the Smiths' great-grandson David Olmsted, his wife Lisa and their daughters Bethany and Sara.

The Smiths' youngest child was Carlisle F. Smith, born in 1897. Carlisle is the father of Marjorie Ann (Smith) Olmsted. Marjorie's children are David Carlisle, Elizabeth Ann, Robert Charles, and Thomas Lee. David and Tom are now Kokomo residents. Elizabeth is a veterinary assistant in Geneseo, IL, and Robert is a teacher in Knoxville, IL. David, his wife Lisa and their daughters Bethany and Sara are the current residents of the Smith home.

David and Lisa came to Kokomo in 1978 from Geneseo, IL where they both grew up. Bethany and Sara are natives of Kokomo. Bethany Ann was born Oct. 18, 1980 and Sara Elizabeth was born Jan. 15, 1983. David is the great-grandson of Newton and Annie Smith.

The Smith home was noted for the music that lived within it and the beautiful yard and flowers that lived outside. Both traditions are still very much alive at 814 West Mulberry Street.

WILLIAM BAKER SMITH - William Baker and Sarah Ann Canine Smith were early settlers of Howard County moving here from Montgomery County, IN on Feb. 18, 1845.

William Baker Smith was born in Ross County, OH on Dec. 1, 1818 and was one of fourteen children of Ephraim and Charity Farnsworth Smith. He was about five years old when his family moved to Montgomery County. His educational opportunities were limited. His father died when William was quite young and his services were needed on the farm. He attended school, off and on, in a log schoolhouse two miles from his home. After marrying, at the age of 18, he attended school again for a few months and then began teaching. He had charge of the first school taught in Clay Township for two years.

He purchased 160 acres of land 3-1/2 miles southwest of Kokomo and in 1859, purchased a farm of 72 acres for $3200.00 that is now a part of the city of Kokomo.

William Baker Smith was married in Montgomery County, IN on Feb. 18, 1836 to Sarah Ann Canine, daughter of Cornelius and Dorothy Van Nuys Canine. (Sarah was born in Shelby County, KY, Aug. 10, 1819.) Eight children were born to them: Mary Ellen who married Robert McClellan; Cornelius C. who married Georgia Kellar; Charity who married David Fawcett; Milton (died at 17); Dr. Richard H. who married Miranda Freeman; Isaac V.N. who married Fannie Dennison; and William Cadid Smith who married Julia A. Gwin.

William Baker Smith was also an auctioneer, Baptist and a staunch Democrat. *Submitted by Julie A. Smith Pyle.*

WILLIAM CADID SMITH - William Cadid Smith, the youngest child of William Baker and Sarah Ann Canine Smith, attended Howard College and read law for a year in the office of John W. Kern. In 1876-77, he attended law school at Indiana University and graduated from the University of Michigan Law School in 1881. His wife, Julia A. Gwin, was the daughter of Pleasant and Hannah Wimmer Gwin. On the day they were married, Jan. 1, 1883, they took a train to Delphi, IN where he practiced law for the next 63 years. They were married for 60 years and had seven children: Ada Jenny who married Arthur Dern; Bessie Kate (died in infancy); Howard Carroll (never married); Dorothy Marie married Forrest Orr; Edna Julia married Robert Shepherd; Gwin married Mary Harper; and William Baker Smith (II) who married Elizabeth Woessner.

William C. Smith

William C. had many interests besides law. He authored several books on farming and even tried writing fiction without success. He was a partner with his brother in a canning factory in Delphi until it burned and he even co-owned a doughnut business in Miami, FL until it was destroyed by the great Hurricane of '26. He was very active in the Delphi Methodist Church and the Democrat Party. He also served as Carroll County Prosecutor and Mayor of Delphi. *Submitted by Julie A. Smith Pyle.*

SNODGRASS - Max Vernon Snodgrass born July 1, 1932, in Ervin Township, Howard County. He was the fourth child of Walter Norman and Christine (Preston) Snodgrass. He married Ruth Joan White on July 28, 1951, at St. Patrick's Church by Rev. Leo Brietenbach. Joan was the sixth child of Howard Edward and Ruth Ella (Hunt) White on Aug. 8, 1932, in Kokomo.

Joan and Max were childhood sweethearts, another case in the White family where they married the boy/girl next door.

Joan graduated from Northwestern High School in 1950. Max attended high school in Converse, IN. For a short time he worked for the Pennsylvania R.R. and then for Kingston Products. He then went on to work for Kokomo Chrysler Transmission Plant where he worked in Dept. 19, Crib Area and retired on April 30, 1986. Joan worked for Kresge's for eight years, Garrison's Orchard for six years, and worked for Western High School in the cafeteria where she retired in 1986 after twenty years.

Max and Joan Snodgrass

Joan and Max have four children. (1) Mark Vernon born April 30, 1952. He married Cynthia L. Hamilton. They have two daughters, Sarah Rebecca and Brooke Erin. (2) Michael Edward born Sept. 24, 1955. He married Vannie Johnson. They have two sons, Jared Michael and Brandon Phillip. (3) Cynthia Joan born Feb. 22, 1957 and lives in Florida. (4) Sandra Ruth born Aug. 19, 1958. She married James W. Mote. They have two sons, James Jason and David Matthew.

Max was a member of U.A.W. Local 685. He was vice-president of Kokomo Bowling Association after retiring from Chrysler. He was employed at Lowry's East and West Bowling Center in the Pro Shop. In 1988 he bowled a perfect 300 game in the City Tournament. He was a very good bowler and won many awards. His name is in the Hall of Fame in St. Louis, MO for the achievement. Max died Aug. 27, 1993 and is buried at Memorial Park Cemetery in Kokomo, IN.

Joan is a good bowler also and was employed at Lowry's East in the snack bar.

This is another generation of descendants of Jefferson and Elizabeth (Alder) White that still live in Howard County.

ORLANDO ALLEN SOMERS - Orlando Allen Somers was born near Middletown, Henry County, IN Jan. 24, 1843. He was the sixth son of Valentine and Mary McClain (Williams) Somers. The family moved to Howard County near Sycamore and Greentown in 1852. He attended Howard College at Kokomo until he enlisted in the Civil War in August of 1861. He was in the Co. D, 39th Indiana Volunteer Inf.

This regiment of infantry became a part of the Army of the Cumberland and served in the historic battles of Shiloh, Perryville and Stone River. He also served in the mounted infantry in the campaigns of Tullahoma and Chickamauga. The 39th Regt. was famed for having fought the first engagement of the Army of the Cumberland at Upton Station, KY Oct. 12, 1861 and the last of Morrisville, NC April 13, 1865.

Orlando returned to his home near Greentown after his discharge. His health was so shattered that he couldn't do manual labor. He went back to college and became a teacher. In the fall of 1870 he moved to Kokomo, where he taught school for three years. In 1874 he was chosen Superintendent of Schools of Howard County.

At the end of his term he went on the road as a commercial traveler for one year. At that time his health had improved, so he entered the hardware and implement business as a salesman and was later deputy sheriff of Howard County for two years. During President Garfield's, Arthur's and part of Cleveland's administrations he was appointed Postmaster at Kokomo. He retired from that Nov. 2, 1885, a period of almost seven years. In the 1890s he served a term as a member of the County Commissioners board and court.

Orlando A. Somers

He was active in the Republican party from the beginning. In 1898 he was elected to the General Assembly, representing Howard, Miami, Grant, Huntington and Wabash counties. In 1890 he was appointed supervisor of the 12th decennial census for the 11th Congressional District.

He took a deep interest and active part in Farmers' Institute work and was a representative of Purdue University covering the greater part of Indiana.

He devoted much time to the G.A.R. In 1909 he was elected Department Commander of Indiana. The year 1917-1918 he was commander-in-chief of the Grand Army of the Republic. From 1905 until 1913 he served first as recording and then as corresponding secretary in the Society of the Army of the Cumberland and was president of that organization from 1913 to 1920.

The monument at the Crown Point Cemetery, Kokomo, IN was erected in his and Sylvester Bell's honor.

311

The present Sons of the Union Veterans Kokomo Camp #1 was named in his honor.

He was married in 1866 to Mahalia Ellen Morris. They had five sons: Charles, Eldon, Edward, Lee and Percy. Mrs. Somers died Feb. 28, 1886 in Kokomo, IN. On March 24, 1887 he married Emma Heaton and they had two daughters Jean Somers and Mrs. Thrope (Gail) Shinn. He died June 8, 1921 at his home (Maplehurst) Kokomo, IN. Emma Somers died Feb. 4, 1940 in Kokomo, IN. His grandchildren are Raymond Somers, Buffalo, NY; Mrs. Kenneth (Frances) Shockley, Kokomo, IN; Virginia (Somers) Sadler, Florida; A.L. (Ted) Somers, Kokomo, IN; Jack Shinn, Bunker Hill, IN; and Mrs. Richard (Emma Lou Shinn) Grizzle, Chatsworth, GA. (see Jackson) *Submitted by Marian Shinn.*

WILLIAM WESLEY SOMSEL - William Wesley Somsel was born May 5, 1853, in Preble County, OH, the eighth child of David and Rebecca Warrenfelts Somsel. William's parents are buried in Castine (Dark County) OH.

William Wesley Somsel was first married in Preble County, OH, to Mary Hannah Smith, who died at the age of 23, leaving him with a four year old son, David Lewis Somsel (1879-1932). Mary Hannah died on Feb. 16, 1883, and is buried in Castine (Dark County), OH, next to William's parents. William Wesley, his son, and an unmarried sister, Mary Ann Somsel (1836-1920), who had moved in with him to care for his young son, moved to Howard County, IN. They moved to a farm in Clay Township near what is now Northwestern School. It is not clear just what year this was, sometime after 1883. William Wesley had an older brother, Jacob Somsel (1844-1914), and a sister, Lavinia R. (Somsel) Laird, living in Cass County, IN, near Galveston. It might be noted here that Lavonna's husband, Alvin C. Laird (1845-1909), fought in the Civil War with the 93rd Ohio Infantry. He and his wife, Lavonna (1846-1909), are buried in Galveston, IN.

On June 8, 1886, William Wesley married Emily Jane Conwell, daughter of Hiram and Rachael (McDaniel) Conwell. Her parents are buried in North Union Cemetery.

To William Wesley and Emily Jane Somsel were born five children, Effie Mae (1887-1930), Emmett C. (1892-1910), John Vern (1895-1978), Lee (1897-1990), Fay (1899-present).

My father, John Vern Somsel, told about his brother, Lee, and his sister, Fay, watching Elwood Haynes drive his new cars past their farm home in Clay Township, Howard County, IN. This was about 1903. Approximately 1904-1905, William Wesley and Emily Jane and family moved to a farm in Cass County, IN, Bethlehem Township, where he died in 1911.

William Wesley and Emily Jane's son, Emmett (1892-1910), was run over by a circus wagon at Foster Park in Kokomo on Sept. 8, 1910. He was attending a circus of Forepaugh and Sells Brothers. He died 21 hours later at his brother's, David Lewis Somsel, home on North Apperson Way. Family legend says that the death of his son, Sept. 10, 1910, might have hastened the death of William Wesley on March 5, 1911. He died of a heart condition.

My grandmother, Emily Jane, was left with three children of whom my father, John Vern Somsel, was the oldest, plus Lee and Fay and the unmarried sister, Mary Ann Somsel, who was still living with them. My father, John Vern, had to quit school and do the farming at the age of 16. William Wesley was buried in the Galveston Cemetery, as was his wife, Emily Jane, when she died in 1942.

My father, John Vern Somsel, was a veteran of World War I. In 1920, he married Edith Marie Arthurholtz of Lucerne, IN. To them were born five children. A son in 1921 who died at birth, buried in Galveston Cemetery; Lois Irene, born 1925; William Lee, born 1929; Betty Jean, born 1933; James Vern, born 1938. John Vern and Edith Marie Somsel are buried at Scottsburg, IN. *Submitted by James V. Somsel, son of John Vern and Edith Marie Somsel*

CHARLES WILLIAM SOSBE JR. - Chuck Sosbe (March 9, 1950) and Karen Beth Crispen (May 30, 1950) met their junior year at Kokomo High School as students. Chuck served four years in the Air Force, including a stint in Germany, and Karen went to Purdue University, graduating in Education. She was Fashion Coordinator for a fabric company after graduation; a short romance followed and they were married Nov. 24, 1973. They have been blessed with two children, Christopher Allen, born Feb. 2, 1977 and Jennifer Marie born Dec. 6, 1980.

Chuck worked at Continental Steel Corporation until he was hired at the Kokomo Fire Department in 1976. He completed a college degree at Indiana University-Kokomo in Liberal Studies. He raced Quarter Midget and Midget race cars as a hobby until the children were old enough to be interested in sports and then devoted his time to them. He coached the Ponderosa Mets minor league baseball team at Southside while the children played on the team. Chuck has been president of Local 396 Firefighters Union since 1988, is Indiana's 2nd District Vice-President on the Executive Board for the Professional Firefighters Union of Indiana and a state representative for the International Association of Firefighters.

Chuck, Karen, Chris and Jennifer Sosbe

Karen pursued her interest in sewing and needlework by entering many local and state competitions. She and Connie Hoover started the first counted cross-stitch shop in Kokomo called The Needleworks. Several years later Karen had her own shop, Hoosier Heirlooms, where she taught English smocking and French heirloom sewing. She was a charter member of the Smocking Arts Guild of America and was the Chicago National Convention Chairperson in 1986. She also served on the national board of SAGA. She was a 10 year member of 4-H as well as a leader. She is currently teaching U.S. History in the Kokomo-Center School Corporation where she has taught for 21 years. She received her Master's Degree in 1979 and her Paralegal Certificate in 1993 from Indiana University-Kokomo.

Chris has enjoyed swimming and playing baseball at Southside Little League diamond. He was awarded the Dave Fisher Mental Attitude Award for Southside Little League baseball as a 12-year-old. He helped coach when he was too old to play. He was in 4-H for five years and won numerous awards. He was in Boy Scouts and won the Pine Wood Derby. Currently he is an avid computer buff and plans to pursue a career in computers when he graduates from Kokomo High School in 1995.

Jennifer has also enjoyed playing baseball at Southside Little League. She received a plaque for Outstanding Student while at Washington Elementary School in the 4th grade. She also won the Presidential Fitness Award and is an honor student. She has been an active member of 4-H for six years. Jennifer became interested in genealogy when she was 10 years old. She has played basketball for PAL, AAU and was a member of Maple Crest Middle School basketball team. She enjoys sewing, needlework and swimming. She would like to be a physical therapist.

CHARLES WILLIAM SOSBE - Charles "Chuck" was born Dec. 4, 1928, in Kokomo, IN, to Beulah Faithie Anderson of Bloomfield, IN, and Clarence Estle Sosbe of Elwood, IN. He married Wilma Lucille Gollner on June 12, 1948, in Kokomo, IN. She was born March 28, 1929, to Gladys Lucille Lillard of Brookville, IN and William Frederick Gollner of Wheeling, WV. Out of this union were born four children: Chuck Jr., born March 9, 1950; Debora Kay born Sept. 29, 1952; Linda Sue born May 12, 1954; and Timothy Ray born March 3, 1956.

Charles W. and Wilma Sosbe

Chuck went to school in Kokomo, and graduated from Kokomo High School in 1947. He was actively involved in various sports, especially football. In his youth he was a skate boy at Skater's Delight. He also worked as an ice man at Leech's Ice Plant, a laborer at Continental Steel, and a lineman at Indiana Bell, all in Kokomo. He then joined the Kokomo Police Department and rose through the ranks from a patrolman to Chief of Police. He retired after 20 years of service. He also worked for Roberts Express as a truck driver in his retirement. He has enjoyed racing quarter midgets and midget race cars with his sons and family. He belonged to USAC, the Moose, and Fraternal Order of Police. He also enjoys fishing now that he is retired.

Wilma also went to school in Kokomo and graduated from Kokomo High School in 1948. While in her teens she played for four years for the "Shrinettes", a semi-professional softball team as catcher. She has worked at Kresge's at the food counter, in the office at Kokomo Sanitary Pottery as a billing clerk, as a grinder at Haynes Stellite, and as a secretary/receptionist for Dr. Shokri Radpour, an Ear, Nose and Throat Specialist for 26 years. She is also retired now and enjoys ceramics and fishing.

Chuck and Wilma have seven grandchildren: Christopher Sosbe, Jennifer Sosbe, Nicole Lauderbaugh, and Nathan Lauderbaugh of Kokomo, and Lindsay Wagoner, Daniel Wagoner, and Stacy Sosbe of Rochester, IN.

Chuck and Wilma have moved to Moore Haven, FL for the winters and spend summers in Indiana with their children.

CLARENCE ESTLE SOSBE - Clarence was born Feb. 15, 1890, in Elwood, IN, the son of Archable Sosbe and Rhoda Jane Bolton. He came to Kokomo in 1920, just after he was married to Beulah Melton. He worked in the glue factory in Elwood before coming to Kokomo. He had worked at Indiana Bell Telephone for 30 years before he retired in 1946. He was employed as a lineman and troubleshooter.

He was a member of Main Street Methodist Church, Moose Lodge (Governor of the Kokomo Moose two different times), Telephone Pioneers of America, and the CIO-CAW Union. He served in the Army with the Signal Corps in France during WWI. He had emphysema later in life and suffered greatly. He died on April 9, 1961, in Kokomo, and is buried at Sunset Memory Gardens. He was first married to Ella Haggard which ended in divorce. They had two children, Leslie Marion born May 3, 1911, in Brown County, IN. Leslie died Oct. 2, 1978, leaving June, his wife, and their family. William Estle was born Jan. 3, 1915 and died on June 12, 1935 at age 20.

Rebuna Faithie Anderson was born Jan. 1, 1894, in Solsberry, Greene County, IN, to James Anderson and Sarah Emeline Laymon. She hated her first name so much that she had it officially changed to Beulah. She was married first to Harry Melton who died in a boating accident. They had a son, Harley, born June 22, 1913, (spouse-Betty). He died Nov. 3, 1991. Beulah then married Clarence. They had four children, only one of whom is still living. Frances Marie was born Feb. 20, 1921, (spouse-Ellis Nelson), and died May 6, 1962. Jimmie Joe was born Nov. 24, 1927 and he died just over a month later on Dec. 31, 1927. Charles William was born Dec. 4, 1928, (spouse-Wilma Lucille Gollner), and is presently living in Moore Haven, FL, enjoying the sun and the leisure life with his wife Wilma. Paul was born Dec. 8, 1931, and was killed on Jan. 25, 1974, on Highway 35 near Greentown, IN, where he was struck by a hit and run driver.

Beulah also was a member of Main Street Methodist Church and the Pocahontas Lodge of the Women of the Moose. She died unexpectedly on March 6, 1968, and is buried at Sunset Memory Gardens in Kokomo.

SPARKS - Richard Dale Sparks was born April 26, 1927, in Jasper County, IL, a son of Charles Mitchell and Bessie Myrtle (Bryan) Sparks. He married Joyce Fern Foster Aug. 19, 1950. Joyce was born March 3, 1932, in Jasper County, IL, a daughter of Benjamin Franklin and Dean Oral (Wetherholt) Foster.

Richard served in the Korean War (Btry. B, 48th Arty. Bn., 7th Inf. Div.), serving 11 months and 27 days in Korea. After he returned home, they came to Kokomo, IN. Richard worked and retired from Haynes Stellite (now Haynes International, Inc.).

Joyce Foster Sparks and Richard Sparks - February 1992

They have two children, Judith Ann and Clarinda Kay. Judith Ann was born May 9, 1951, in Newton, IL. She married Rudiger (Rudy) K. Walter. They have two sons: Eric T., born Dec. 20, 1977 and Kurt Richard, born Jan. 23, 1981. They live near Carefree, AZ.

Clarinda Kay was born July 28, 1955 in Kokomo, IN. She married David Spraker, a son of La Mar and Mary (White) Spraker. They are the parents of two daughters: Jennifer Kay, born Jan. 27, 1984 and Sarah Joyce, born April 8, 1987. They live in Howard County, IN.

Richard, Joyce and their family moved to Oakford, IN in August 1955. Joyce started working part-time for the Oakford Post Office Feb. 1, 1967, and was appointed Postmaster Aug. 13, 1977.

Richard and Joyce are members of the Oakford Baptist Church. She was the church treasurer for 19 years. Presently she is secretary for the Howard County Genealogical Society. *Submitted by Joyce Sparks.*

SPICER - Churchill Harrison Spicer (1852-1928) was born Owen County, KY May 23, 1852, and was the eighth of nine children of William and Lucy Beck (Hawkins) Spicer. Both his parents were natives of Kentucky. Churchill migrated from Hopkins County, KY to Howard County in 1923, with the majority of his children. He worked for Jenkins Glass Company. He first married Martha A. Harris (1872-1896). She was the daughter of James and Jane (Groves) Harris. They had 11 children: James, Norris, Mary Jane, Joseph, Ida, Frank, Robert, John, Charles, Edmund, and Ethel. Churchill second married Margaret Ann Taylor (1867-1946), daughter of James Henry and Martha Caroline (Fuller) Taylor, Feb. 25, 1897, Hopkins County, KY. To them were born four children; Nora, Oliver, Adrian, and Marshall.

Marshall Harrison (1904-1961) born Hopkins County, KY. On Sept. 21, 1923, Marshall married in Hopkins County, KY Florence Charlotte Ashby, (1907-1982) daughter of Roy and Daisy Belle (Bolin) Ashby. From 1923-1928 he worked for Jenkins Glass Company. He then worked for Kokomo Steel and Wire Company which became Continental Steel. At the time of his death he was employed there in the open hearth furnace area as foreman. Marshall, having a deep passion in the arts and crafts, loved working with his hands sculpting picture frames and knickknacks, and once took his love to church when he carved the pulpit for the chapel. To Marshall and Florence were born four children: Rozella, Samuel, Jack, and Marjorie.

Churchill Spicer; Marshall Spicer and Florence Ashby

Jack Wayne was born April 7, 1930 in Kokomo. On Dec. 30, 1947, in Kokomo, married Delores Mae (Kuntz), daughter of Otto Elmer and Jeannette (McNabney) Kuntz. Jack served in the U.S. Army as a cook stationed for Fort Lewis, WA. He worked for Shell Oil Company 15 years, the Dirilyte Corporation for 2 years, and FMC Corporation in Tipton, IN for 12 years until his retirement in 1986. Jack loved to cook and garden. In 1988 they moved to Clearfield, UT. Jack and Delores had five children: Jerry, Christina, Jack, Karen, and Mark.

Jack Wayne Jr., author of this article, was born Aug. 30, 1952 in Kokomo. He married Myra Patricia Wilsted, daughter of Harold and Gertrude (Neal) Wilsted on June 12, 1973 in Manti, UT. He is employed by Thiokol Aerospace in Promontory, UT as Financial Supervisor. Their children are: Patricia, Kimmerly, and Benjamin. *Submitted by Jack W. Spicer Jr.*

STAFFORD - Herbert G. and Juanita R. (Johnson) Stafford, both retiring from Cabot Corporation, had two children: Steven D. (married Mary Lynn Bath of Tipton) and having two children: Kristin Taylor and Amy Jo Cherry step-child. Jorja Jo Peterson married James Peterson (deceased) having one child (Jamie Jo Ripberger) by previous husband.

Front, L-R: Herbert A. (a), Steven D., Herbert G. Back, L-R: Enoch (c) and Jasper Joseph (b).

(a) Herbert Albert Stafford, my father, was born in Mexico, IN on May 22, 1889. He moved to Elmira, WA in 1892 and homesteaded in Alberta, Canada 1908-1912. He enlisted in WWI at Shelbyville, IN in 1917. After the war he moved to Kokomo, IN and worked at Apperson Auto. There he met and married Marian Rubush. He played in an orchestra in Kokomo. He was manager of the Kokomo Furniture Company from 1923 to 1951 when they closed the store. He then worked at Kokomo Wreckage Furniture Company. He was a member of the American Legion State Band and was Chief of Auxiliary Police in 1943. He passed away in 1979. My father had three children - (1) Carol Yvonne who died at age eight (2) Alice L., having two sons: Charles Daniel O'Neal and Ronald Ray Ratcliff. Alice is now married to Wm. Huffman. (3) Herbert Graydon is referenced above.

(b) Jasper Joseph Stafford, my grandfather, had four children: (1) Ralph E. married Lula, (2) Edgar Earl married Lea Emerson; second marriage to Lilias (Madge) Leighton, (3) Herbert Albert married Marian Agness (Rubush) (Faulkner), and (4) C. Beatrice married Van Howard.

(c) Enoch Stafford, my great-grandfather, and his wife Catherine (Mullen) moved to Liberty Township, Shelby County in 1850 from Rush County, Tippecanoe Township in 1858. During the years they had nine children: (1) Elizabeth married William C. Yager 1859, (2) William E. married Lorinda Hoover in 1868, (3) Julia married Homer Bowman, (4) Nancy Catherine who married John Laturner in 1873, (5) Jasper Joseph, my grandfather, married Mary Alveretta Davis, (6) Mary Augusta, (7) Florilla, (8) Oliver Perry who married Mary Etta Hess, and (9) C.B., who died before the age of 10.

(d) My great-great-grandfather, John Stafford, married Elizabeth (Wainscott). They lived in Franklin County, coming from North Carolina or Kentucky around the year 1812. They had 14 children: (1) William (who was killed by Indians in 1814), (2) Sarah who married George Julian, (3) Nancy married John Ladd in 1818, (4) Tyrah married Susannah Loins in 1818, (5) John married Ellen Shaw Dicky, (6) Martha married William Simmon 1814, (7) Loadicia married Richard Irwin in 1824, (8) Mary married Simeon Spurgeon, (9) Judy married Crabtree Grace in 1831, (10) Susan married Jonathan Shaw, (11) Enoch, my great-grandfather, married Catherine Mullens in 1838, (12) Charlotte married John Vance in 1829, (13) Leanor married Andrew Whisman, and (14) William M. married Precilia Jane Ramsay and moved to Oregon in 1852. *Submitted by Herbert Graydon Stafford.*

GEORGE B. McCLELLAND STAFFORD (1864-1944) - Noah Stafford (1796-1873), his wife Sarah (Jackson 1801), and their seven children left Wayne County, NC and moved to a homestead near the town of Richmond in Union County, IN in 1833. John Stafford (1834-1915), their eighth child, was born in Union County. Noah and Sarah's four other children were also born in that same county. They later lived in Hancock, Henry, and Howard counties, and in Cass, and then Fulton counties. They are believed to be buried near Fletcher's Lake in the extreme southern part of Fulton County.

John Stafford married Mary Elizabeth Beaver in 1860. They were living in Hancock County when the third of their seven children, George B. McClelland (1864-1944) was born. John and Mary lived in Howard County in the 1870s when George was growing up, and moved into Cass County in 1879. John and Mary are both buried in the Galveston Cemetery, Cass County.

George B. McClelland Stafford was named after General George B. McClelland of the Union Army. The B. in George B. Stafford's name may also represent his mother's maiden name, Beaver. George grew up on a farm in western Howard County, near Young America. He had a love for reading and learning, and for music. He became an accomplished fiddle player and was always in demand to play at dances and for social get-togethers. George enjoyed sharing what he had learned, and taught school for several years.

Ella Mae Yater (1877-1966) was the daughter of Bill and Phoebe Yater, and was born in the western part of Erwin Township, in western Howard County. At this time, only a little is known about Ella Mae's family, but it is remembered that her grandmother told about having to stand guard with a rifle to keep the Indians from attacking her husband as he plowed the fields. Ella Mae told about seeing a meteor light up the night sky and fall to the earth. She said that it continued to burn and glow for a period of time, and people came from all over the area to see it. Ella Mae enjoyed writing, and wrote several very interesting short stories. She spent a great deal of her younger years with the Charles Weed family. At the age of 15 she left her family to establish her own home as Mrs. George B. McClelland Stafford.

George and Ella Mae made their first home in Erwin Township, Howard County, and continued to live in that vicinity until 1924 when they moved into Kokomo. Eight of their ten children were born in western Howard County,

313

and the other two children were born in the nearby region of southern Cass County. George continued to teach and to farm after they were married, but finally gave up teaching to farm full-time. George and Ella Mae were members of the Friends Church near Poplar Grove, IN.

George and Ella Mae's children are Letitia "Lettie", Theressa M., Essie, Tessie, Ada, Beulah Marie, (William) Russell, Mary Fern, Grace Leona, and Rettamae.

Lettie married Jacob Metz, a native of Kentucky. They had one daughter, Mary.

Theressa married Reuben Ely and their children are William Otto Ely, Helen Orpha Louise, and Reuben McCullen Ely. Reuben and Theressa moved to Florida in the early 1950s. They made a home for Orpha's children when she died, and raised them as their own. William and Reuben Jr. and their families joined their parents in Florida. William is the Stafford family historian and genealogist, and much of what is written here is a result of his efforts.

Essie married Ezra Paul Shrock and their three children are Thelma, Mabel, and Paul.

Beulah married Jesse Ernest Fivecoate and their seven children are George, Benjamin, Lowell, Grace, Dorothy, Raymond, and Jesse Edward. (See Jesse Ernest Fivecoate)

Beulah Marie remembered living in a one-room log cabin with a dirt floor. She said on cold winter nights, when the fire couldn't keep the house warm, they would all go to their beds and do their homework while snuggled under the covers. The girls would ask each other questions about their homework, and when they were stumped they would ask their father—he always knew the answer. She also related that she had been baptized in the little creek that flows just south of Poplar Grove. Beulah took her final exams at the old Erwin Township School. Her graduation exercises were held at the Friends Church on the north side of the road at 400 north and 710 west. The graduating students met at a home about a quarter of a mile south of the church and made a processional march from there to the church.

William Russell Stafford "Bud" married Edna Evelyn Turner. Their son is William "Billy" Stafford. Billy served in Korea, and was also stationed in Alaska. Billy married Viola Smith and their children are David, Michael, and Angela.

Mary Fern married Earl Raymond Smith. Their four children are Lilian, Vivian, Mildred, and Patricia.

Grace Leona married Irl Lloyd Fivecoate. Their eight children are Roy, Joann, Clarence, Lloyd, Leonard, Harry, Clyde, and Eldon. (See Irl Fivecoate)

Retta Mae married Harold Barlow. Pauline, Richard, and Jerry are their three children.

George B. McClelland and Ella Mae Stafford spent their later years together at 1410 N. Leeds, in Kokomo. George passed away at the age of 81, doing what he enjoyed, fishing at his son's pit on the Deer Creek near Camden. Ella Mae maintained her home on Leeds Street up until the 1960s when she went to live with Beulah and Jesse. She is remembered for her considerate ways, her wonderful stories, and her homemade jellies. George is remembered for his quiet ways, his fiddle playing, and his love of fishing. *Submitted by J.E. Fivecoate*

ADAM STAHL - Adam Stahl was born in Bavaria, Germany, March 31, 1839. He was just a young boy when his parents, Jacob and Catherine Greiner Stahl, came to America in 1852 and settled in Ripley County, near Napoleon, IN, on an 80-acre farm.

Adam married Margaret Hessler in Ripley County. She was the daughter of John and Anna M. Niese Hessler.

In 1875 Adam and his brother George bought 30 acres of land in Taylor Township, Howard County, IN, on which they built a tile factory. The factory was successfully run for 14 years. The partnership was then dissolved and the land was equally divided. They both became successful farmers in Taylor Township.

Adam died in 1918 and Margaret in 1909. Their five children were all born in Howard County, IN.

George A., 1868-1943, married Mary Shrader.

Frederick "Fred" E., 1872-1945, married Minnie E. Lahn.

Stahl Homestead

Lewis H., 1877-1953, married Anna Vandenbosch.

Anna Mary Luvina, 1877-1949, married Henry Kinney.

Charles J., 1879-1946, married Elsie E. Jessup.

Frederick "Fred" attended school in Danville, IL and Indiana Normal School in Terre Haute, IN. He taught school in Liberty Township, Howard County for several years and also worked as a railroad clerk. Fred was killed in an auto accident in 1945, at Paris, IL, at the age of 73.

Two of three children, (all born in Paris, IL), grew to maturity, Willard Ernest and Charles Frederick.

Willard Ernest, 1905-1988, married Elnora Lucille Dutton and Lucille Kinney.

Willard came to Howard County in 1924 and was a farmer all of his life. In 1957 he sold 157.7/6 acres of his homestead, on Albright Road, to the Pendiana Improvement Company, Inc. They sold the property to General Motors in 1959. Delco Electronics is now located on this property. Willard then purchased 262 acres in Clinton County. During the construction of Delco, the home was used as offices for the construction crew. *Submitted by Jack E. Stahl.*

JACOB STAHL - There are two different versions of Catherine's (wife of Jacob) maiden name.

In a reply from a professional genealogist, a Mr. Reinhard Mayer of Germany, who sent a birth certificate of Katharina (Catherine) Stahl, written in German, gave this translation: In the year 1846 at February 5th, there appeared at 9:00 A.M., before the Mayor, George Heinrich Kuntz from Lemburg, a Jakob Stahl, 43 years old, farmer in Lemburg, who declared that his wife Katherina nee Griener, 40 years old, today at 1:00 A.M. had borne a girl whom he wanted to give the name of Catharina. Witness: Ludwig Kuffer, 50 years, Secretary and Jakob Birler, 35 years. Signatures, Jakob Stahl, L. Kuffer, Kuntz, Jakob Birler.

Jacob Stahl born April 12, 1802 in Bavaria, Germany and died June 12, 1870 in Ripley County, Napoleon, IN. He married Katharina (Catherine) Griener who died Sept. 8, 1885 in Ripley County, Napoleon, IN.

In Germany, Jacob was a farmer and stone-mason. Jacob and his family boarded the ship *Georgia* at La Harve, Paris, France and arrived in New York on the 17th of July 1852. They settled in Wheeling, WV, for a short time; by 1860 they were living in Ripley County, Napoleon, IN. They spent the rest of their lives on an 80-acre farm.

The ship's passenger list included: Jacob Stahl 50, father; Catherine Stahl age 46 mother; Friedrick age 19; Jacob age 17; Heinrich age 15; George age 9; Catherine age 8; Adam age 6; Ann Marie age 4; Marie age 4 months. This lists eight children that came to America. Marie was probably born on board ship. She was not listed in the 1860 census of Ripley County, IN. Friedrick was married with two children. This was edited and printed February 1993 by the late Ferol Stahl, who died March 18, 1994.

My grandfather, George Stahl, whom I am named after, was born Feb. 3, 1838 in Lemburg, Bavaria, Germany. He came to America in 1852 as stated in the 1900 United States Census.

He worked on his father's 80-acre farm at Napoleon, IN until he was 21 years old. He worked various jobs until his father sold him and his brother Henry his farm. He worked this land for seven years and then sold it. In October 1872 he and his family moved to Howard County, IN, to join his brother Adam, who had lived here for three years. Together they bought 30 acres of land on which they built a tile factory in 1895. They later added another 10 acres. This tile factory operated for 14 years, at which time the partnership was dissolved and the land equally divided. George added this 20 acres to the 40 acres he bought in 1881. About 1887 he bought 80 acres in Taylor Township (part of the homestead).

George married Anna May Hessler June 14, 1886. Anna was born Aug. 11, 1846 at Milhausen, Decatur County, IN, daughter of John Hessler. Her parents came to America from Germany about 1838. They first settled in Cincinnati, OH for a short time before settling in Milhausen, IN.

George F. Stahl and Margaret L. (Elleman) Stahl

They had 10 children. My father Joseph A. Stahl being one, was born Aug. 8, 1884 and died Dec. 14, 1953. He was born in Taylor Township, Howard County, IN and married Gertrude Blanche Lowlett Feb. 2, 1910 in Kokomo, Howard County, IN. Gertrude born May 3, 1884 died May 27, 1959; daughter of Franklin and Katherine Massey Lowlett.

Gertrude's father was born in Italy and came to the United States as a stowaway on a French ship. He took the last name Lowlett from a French sailor, so no one knows the family name. He ran away because his stepmother made him play the violin on the streets for money.

After he came to Howard County, Kokomo, IN he worked in the Jenkins Glass Factory. He was born 1858 and died in 1945. His wife Katherine was born 1858 and died 1934. They are buried in Crown Point Cemetery, Kokomo, IN.

Joseph Stahl and Gertrude Stahl had six children: Joseph Leo born Jan. 11, 1911; Kenneth Paul "Pete" born July 15, 1913; Everet Elma born Aug. 20, 1915, died March 15, 1919; Edward Earl "Ned" born Aug. 13, 1916; George F. "Dick" born Sept. 15, 1918; Theresa Katherine Greathouse born Jan. 15, 1920.

Joseph A. Stahl sang in the St. Patrick's Church choir for 44 years. After leaving the farm, he got into the fruit and vegetable business.

George F. "Dick" Stahl married Margaret Loraine Elleman Sept. 29, 1939. We will celebrate our 55th wedding anniversary Sept. 29, 1994.

We have three children, Mrs. John (Judith Kay) Helm born April 19, 1940; Steven Gary (Dian Kirby) Stahl born Sept. 17, 1942; and Karen Sue Stahl born Jan. 31, 1952. *Submitted by George F. "Dick" Stahl.*

WILLARD E. STAHL - Willard arrived in Howard County in June of 1922, very soon after graduating from high school in Paris, IL. His father Frederick E. Stahl grew up in Howard County in the Greentown area, the son of Adam and Margaret Stahl. Fred left Howard County to work in Paris, IL for the U.S. Postal Service as a railway mail clerk. In August 1897 Fred married Minnie E. Lahn, the daughter of German parents Ernest and Carolyn Lahn. Minnie's family came from Luckenwalda, Germany in 1877 to join a German settlement in the Paris and Brocton, IL area. Fred visited Howard County frequently from 1880-1920 and bought two farms in this county. One of the 160-acre farms was located southeast of Kokomo on Albright Road where currently the north Delco parking area and original building are located.

Willard assumed ownership of the farm on Albright Road and proceeded to improve the house and add other structures as needed for livestock, grain and machinery storage. There was a small rental house on the northeast corner of this farm where the "hired hand" lived with his family. This man worked for Willard and helped with the farming and construction of improvements.

When buying supplies Willard relied on the Hamer Lumber Company in Greentown. The bookkeeper at this business was a very attractive and efficient young lady, Lucille Dutton, daughter of Chloe (Burgan) and Lonzo Dutton of Greentown. Willard and Lucille became friends and this developed into a courtship which continued and on Jan. 28, 1928 Willard and Lucille were married.

Willard Stahl Sr. Home

Together they farmed, raised chickens, livestock, horses, very large garden, churned butter and used a separator to take cream from milk. Children included: Frederick E. (Bud), Betty Lou, Jack E., Marjorie A., Willard E. Jr., Carl E., R. Wayne, and Sheila M.

Farming continued through 20s, 30s, 40s, and 50s but there were incidents along the way. During the 1930s Willard drove a school bus for Howard County that transported children to Darrough Chapel, St. Joan of Arc and Kokomo High School. Some say he did this to "keep an eye on his children". In May 1948 Lucille passed away leaving a one-week-old baby, Sheila M. The Sisters at St. Joseph Hospital cared for Sheila in the Children's Ward for six months because there was no one at home to care for a new baby.

Changes in the adjoining countryside included the 31 Bypass, constructed in 1949-1951 and Chrysler Transmission Plant was constructed in 1955. The presence of industry was a determining factor in selling this farm to Penn-Dixie Corp. In 1956 Willard bought farm land in Clinton County.

In the mid 50s Willard and Lucile Kinney were married. In August 1957 Kimberly Lynn was born and now Willard has five sons and four daughters.

Education was important. Bud, Betty and Jack began elementary school at Darrough Chapel but transferred to St. Joan of Arc. All other children attended St. Joan of Arc except Sheila who lived with Betty. All attended Kokomo High School except Marjorie who attended Northwestern High School. Carl and Wayne started at Kokomo High School but transferred to Clinton Central in Clinton County to complete high school and graduate.

Three sons: Fred (Bud), Jack and Carl remain in Howard County and live on South Goyer Road. Carl is crane operator for Bud who owns Stahl Welding Inc. Jack is retired from Continental Steel and now works for Bud in the machine shop. Marjorie lives near Russiaville. The other children live as follows: Betty Lou, Plainfield, IN; Willard E. Jr., Frankfort, IN; R. Wayne, Fort Wayne, IN, Sheila M., Apache Junction, AZ; and Kimberly L., Palatine, IL.

Howard County and Kokomo will always be home to the Willard E. Stahl Sr. family. Although some have moved away they still return to Howard County for family reunions and other special events.

STEVENS - In the year of 1836 a lady named Catherine White was born in Germany.

She came to the USA, married to John Stevens and wound up in Blanchester County, OH. They moved to Shelby County, IN and started a family of four boys and three girls.

One of the boys being Phillip Stevens born April 16, 1848. He later moved to Taylor Township, IN and married Cynthia Cherry born June 28, 1855. This union produced eight boys and one girl.

Owen and Ferne Stevens

One of the boys was William Franklin Stevens born Feb. 24, 1877 and he married Mary Lida McKay from Switzerland County, IN on April 8, 1900. To this marriage was born a son, Owen Merideth Stevens, on May 14, 1901. O.M. attended school at Hemlock, IN and Kokomo High School until it burned down. Then he went to Greentown High School and graduated in the class of 1918. He then went into the postal service as a mail clerk. He spent 39 years at the Kokomo Post Office on the stamp window and as clerk in charge of the Finance Section.

When he was asked how he first liked his job, coming from the farm, he said "it sure beats shucking corn."

He went to school with and later married Ferne L. Peters on July 24, 1920. She was the daughter of W.D. and Elizabeth Marvin Peters, farmers of Taylor Township.

O.M. and Ferne were married in the parsonage of the Baptist Church in Oakford, IN.

Their first home was 1730 S. Union, Kokomo. Later they bought 707 S. Wabash. Three sons were born in this house. Robert M. Stevens, class of 42 married Betty M. Moor in 1947 after WWII service as B-24 pilot. Their children: Robert M. Stevens II and Dorothy Ann Vores.

Bob II's children, Todd J. Stevens, Marita J. Stevens and Dustin L. Stevens. Bob II married Regina Pearson Stevens with three boys Bruce, Mike and Jeff Pearson.

Dorothy Ann Stevens Vores of Anderson, IN married Charles E. Vores. She has three boys, Eric J. McBee and Jeffrey A. and Hank Owen Vores.

The second son of O.M. and Ferne is James L. Stevens of class of 46 of Ft. Collins, CO, a retired general foreman from Delco Electronics. He is married to Madeline Fisher Stevens. Jim has two children, James Gregory of San Antonio, TX with daughter Alexis Kong and granddaughter Kiana Kong.

Jim's daughter Michele Ann Hampton, husband Jeff and daughter Emily Lovia reside in Ft. Myers, FL.

Madeline's daughter, Deborah Hillis, husband Gary, son Jared, daughter Faith reside in Ft. Collins, CO.

Third son of O.M. and Ferne is Edgar A. Stevens, class of 48, married Garnell Hosier, class of 49. Ed served in Korea and is retired from Cabot as computer operator. Residing in Kokomo he has two sons, Douglas A. and Mark J. Stevens.

Douglas married Diana Pickett and lives in Springfield, OH with daughter Katy and son Bradley. Mark J. resides in Kokomo.

O.M. and Ferne owned and operated "Steve's Trading Post' in Oakford, IN. Ferne celebrated her 91st birthday Dec. 27, 1993 and is the strong influence in the Stevens family. *Submitted by Robert M. Stevens.*

HARRY L. AND M. ELIZABETH (WALLACE) STEVENS - Henderson Browning Stevens (Sept. 22, 1855-Aug. 30, 1882) was the son of Isaac Stevens. He was married to Amelia Olive Cole (Jan. 24, 1861-Dec. 19, 1935) the daughter of William and Martha E. (Chambers) Cole. They had one son Harry Lee on Aug. 13, 1882. Henderson died at the early age of 26 with typhoid fever. This made life very hard for his young family.

Ollie, as his mother was known to one and all, married George Jester Oct. 18, 1884 in Kokomo and they had five children.

Harry attended Columbia Elementary School until he was eight years old then his family moved to Delaware County, IN.

Harry L. and M. Elizabeth (Wallace) Stevens

Margaret Elizabeth Wallace (Aug. 18, 1885-Jan. 2, 1958) was born in Westboro, OH the daughter of James Corwin and Jeanette (Moon) Wallace. She and Harry L. Stevens were married Sept. 27, 1905 in Delaware County. Five boys and one girl came of this union. Melvin Wesley (Sept. 9, 1906-July 11, 1973) married Emma Charlene Reynolds. Hertha Faustine (Sept. 2, 1910-Dec. 29, 1929) married Thomas Orlen Collett on May 11, 1929. John James (July 5, 1914-April 23, 1984) married Lena Arnold Oct. 1, 1940 and served with the Army during WWII in European Theater. Walter Vernon (Dec. 31, 1919-Aug. 31, 1946) married Esther Stanton. He served with the Navy in WWII. Harry Moroni "Bud" Feb. 6, 1924 married Lois Mae Wagner April 27, 1947. He served with the Navy in WWII and is now working at Cape Canaveral on the Space Project. Edward L. (Nov. 5, 1926-Nov. 21, 1991) married Marietta G. Murray Nov. 23, 1946 and served with the Navy in WWII.

Harry Lee Stevens was a night watchman for Durham Manufacturing in Muncie, IN and retired from there. A hobby he was very proud of was playing Santa Claus for about 10 years at Stilhman's Department Store, also in Muncie. One year he became ill during the Christmas season and the local newspaper had headlines that Santa Claus was in the hospital. Another hobby he enjoyed was raising rabbits and terrier dogs.

Elizabeth was a homemaker and devoted mother. She had a lunch wagon during the Depression years and would go to a factory close to their home and sell sandwiches and pies.

Harry was 80 years old when he died and was survived by four sons, twelve grandchildren and eight great-grandchildren. *Submitted by granddaughter, Hertha F. (Collett) White.*

WARREN BRYAN STEVENS - Warren Bryan Stevens, born Jan. 19, 1926, is a direct descendant of Philip Stevens who was born in Shelby County, IN April 16, 1848, son of John and Catherine Stevens, natives of Germany. John Stevens came to America with his parents when a boy, and the family home was established in Shelby County, IN. In 1879, Philip Stevens came to Howard County and purchased a total of 96 acres for the purpose of diversified farming and the raising of livestock. He was married in 1871 to Cynthia Cherry, the daughter of Eli and Mary J. (Tomlinson) Cherry, a pioneer family of Shelby County. Philip and Cynthia Stevens had nine children, four of whom died at a young age. The children who lived were Charles, Warren, Frank, Samuel, and John.

Philip Warren Stevens, son of Philip and Cynthia Stevens, married Edith Ellabarger in 1901. Warren was a farmer in Taylor Township. Warren and Edith had three children: Harold Leslie Stevens, born Nov. 18, 1903 and died Jan. 2, 1981; Mary Katherine Stevens born May 2, 1913; and Malcolm Charles Stevens who died as a young child. In 1924, Warren was the first elected Democrat to the position of Howard County Commissioner. Upon the death of Warren in November 1927, Edith Ellabarger Stevens completed his term as commissioner becoming the first female commissioner in Howard County.

Warren Bryan and Shirley Ann Stevens

Harold Leslie Stevens married Gertrude Katherine Bongartz on Jan. 19, 1925. Harold Stevens was a staunch Democrat and a farmer in Taylor Township. He retired from Chrysler Corporation, Kokomo, IN in 1964. Harold and Gertrude had one son, Warren Bryan Stevens, born Jan. 19, 1926. Mary Katherine Stevens Peerman currently of Franklin, NC had no children.

Warren Bryan Stevens served in the U.S. Navy in WWII. He married Shirley Ann Auten of Ortonville, MI on Feb. 4, 1949. They had two children: Cynthia Ann Stevens, born Aug. 2, 1950 and Phillip Warren Stevens, born Sept. 25, 1951. Warren Stevens, a conservative Democrat, retired from Continental Steel Corporation in 1982 and still resides in Howard County with his wife, Shirley.

Cynthia Ann Stevens currently of Kokomo, IN married Daniel Joseph Dwyer in December 1977 and has a daughter, Meghan Ann Dwyer, born on April 12, 1983. Phillip Warren Stevens currently of Columbus, OH married Jacalyn Lynn in July 1976 and has a daughter, Katherine Lynn Stevens born Oct. 6, 1979.

HARRY L. AND REBECCA M. STEWART - Harry Lewis Stewart (1907-1992) was born and raised in Howard County. He graduated from Ervin Township High School and attended Purdue University. In 1929, he met Rebecca (Becky) Sellers (1908-1950) at the Myers Drug Store and fell deeply in love. They were married in March 1934 at the Christ Church on the Circle (which was a favorite place to get married) in Indianapolis. They had two sons, Thomas Lewis and Stephen Harry. Tom married Cora Bennett in July 1954 and has two sons, Thomas Lewis, Jr. and William Randall. Steve married Tanya Reynolds in July 1961 and has three children, Lisa Rebecca, Stephen Brian and Ralph (Rusty) Russell.

Becky was known for her personality. As a young adult, she was voted Miss Personality of Kokomo. She also did a lot of antiquing with her sister-in-law, Alice Sellers. Harry was on the Kokomo Police Department and associated with Arrow Finance Company. He retired from the Stellite Corporation.

Harry, Becky, Tom and Steve Stewart

Harry was the son of William Lewis (1878-1970) and Effie Harbaugh (1878-1950) Stewart. He was street commissioner for Kokomo and served as sheriff from 1938-1940 and again from 1942-1946. Effie was the jail cook and loved it. They had three sons, Harry, Glenn and Ralph. Ralph started the Ralph I. Stewart Insurance Agency in 1946 in the old First Federal Building with Thomas J. Sellers (brother of Becky) as a realtor. The business is now owned by his nephew, Stephen H. Stewart. "Lew" owned and operated Stewart Sewer Service, later turning the business over to his son, Harry. Harry operated the business until 77 years of age. "Lew" and his brother were also responsible for the stone quarry on Washington Street.

Lew's parents, Harry Harrison and Jenny Hillis Stewart, were pioneer settlers, erecting the 13th log cabin in Howard County. Harry was friends of David Foster, founder of Kokomo. He was a deputy sheriff and state representative for Kokomo and captain in the Civil War.

Becky's parents were Thomas N. (1875-1941) and Lora Barrows (1879-1954) Sellers. They came from Windfall and raised four children, Deana, Thomas, Donald and Rebecca. Thomas was active in politics, being Recorder of Howard County. He had a fatal heart attack while carrying his grandson, Stephen, down steps at the Katherine Apartments. After his death, his son, Donald R. Sellers, took over his political position and ran for other Howard County offices. Tom J. and Don were also owners of the Victory Bike Shop and Tom dealt in antique bikes and cars.

Becky was active in Phi Chi Epsilon Sorority and both were active members of Grace Methodist Church. Harry was a member of the Howard Masonic Lodge 93 for 58 years, receiving his 32nd degree ring.

In February 1961, Harry married Mary Clevenger Snyder (1913-1988) at Grace Methodist Church. She was a gracious, fun-loving Christian lady and liked by all who knew her. Mary was a beautician for many years before her retirement. *Submitted by Tanya Stewart.*

STEVE AND TANYA STEWART - Stephen Harry Stewart and Tanya Claudine Reynolds were both born and raised in the Kokomo area. They graduated from Kokomo High School, met in high school and were united in marriage on July 14, 1961 at the Fairfield Christian Church in Oakford, IN and are still active members since their marriage.

Steve joined his Uncle Ralph as an insurance agent of Ralph I. Stewart Insurance Agency which was started in 1949 and now owns and operates the business.

They gave birth to Lisa Rebecca on Nov. 24, 1962, Stephen Brian on Nov. 7, 1963 and Ralph Russell on Dec. 20, 1968. Lisa married Michael Chilton of Monticello, IN on June 27, 1987, and they now live in Houston, TX. They have two children, Christopher James, born on Nov. 21, 1989 and Alyssa Michele, born on May 28, 1992. Stephen married Paula Marie Coffman who was also born in Kokomo. They live in Chrisney, IN and have two children, Susan Tanya, born on Aug. 21, 1987 and James Stephen, born on Feb. 16, 1990. Ralph (Rusty) married Danna Maria Gilbert of Columbus, OH. He met her in Florida where he was a professional water skier and also skied for Sea World of Orlando, FL. They were married on Sept. 11, 1993 and have made their home in Florida. They are expecting their first child in July of 1994. Rusty was number three seed on the water ski tour for Freestyle Skiing in the world, appearing on ESPN television.

Steve, Tanya, Steve, Lisa and Rusty

Tanya's father was Percey Elwood (better known as Bert) Reynolds (1919-1981). His parents, Wm. Franklin and Vianna came to Kokomo from Charleston, IL. Frank was known for his carpentry work. Bert worked at the Hoosier Iron and sold cars for Nash Motors. He later owned and operated his own car lot known as Ace Motors.

Tanya's mother is Mildred Bell Wolford, born and raised in the Howard County area by her parents, Arthur and Ethel Bowen Wolford who were both very active in community work and politics. Mildred is a housewife and active in her church. She and Bert raised eight children.

Steve's father was Harry Lewis Stewart (1907-1992), son of Wm. Lewis and Effie (Harbaugh). They were born and raised in the Howard County area. "Lew" was sheriff of Howard County for three terms and Effie was the jail cook. His family was one of the original settlers, having the 13th log cabin in Howard County. Harry took over Stewart's Sewer Service from his father, operating the business until the age of 75 years old. He retired from Stellite Corporation.

Steve's mother, Rebecca (Becky) Margaret Sellers (1908-1950), was the daughter of Thomas N. and Lora Barrows Sellers. They came to this area from Windfall, IN and were quite prominent in politics. Becky was known for her personality and even won the Miss Personality Contest of Kokomo. Becky was an active member of Phi Chi Epsilon Sorority and was known for her antique dealings. Becky and Harry were both active members of Grace Methodist Church.

Steve and Tanya are always involved in the community. Steve is on the Board of the Crisis Center and is active in the Kokomo Noon Kiwanis. He was president of South Side Little League for three years and helped with the American Heart Association. Tanya helped organize girl scouts at Washington School. In 1976, she started Photos by Tanya, touching many lives with her work. She is active in Tri Kappa and Cheer Guild. They are both involved with Kokomo High School and the Wildkat Club. *Submitted by Tanya Stewart.*

STOUT - Penelope Van Princes, an early American settler who was the subject of a recent "Believe it or Not" article, has been linked through family record books to several local residents.

Descendants of John Stout have been traced to the pioneer woman who reportedly survived an Indian attack and lived to be 110 years old.

The nationally syndicated cartoon "Believe it or Not" reported Penelope Van Princes (1602-1712) after journeying to America from Amsterdam at the age of 18, was attacked by Indians who killed her husband, fractured her skull, shoved a spear through her body and left her for dead. She spent seven days in a hollow tree and lived another 92 years and had 502 descendants when she died at 110 years.

The Stout family history reports "the family originated in Amsterdam with Penelope Van Princes of Amsterdam, Holland who married Richard Stout of Nottingham, England. The Dutch ship on which Penelope Van Princes came to America was wrecked off Sandy Hook and she, with some other passengers, landed on the Jersey shore. The Indians fell upon the helpless immigrants and Penelope Van Princes was scalped and badly wounded by a knife in her side. She was left for dead but fortunately was discovered and nursed back to health by a friendly Indian. The wounds on her body were stitched by wither of a tree. A fish bone was used for a needle.

At the age of 85 Penelope asked a grandson "to feel the seams the Indians made then you can tell your grandchildren you know it is true and they can tell their grandchildren".

The records show Penelope met and married Richard Stout in New Amsterdam after recovering from the attack.

After the Dutch surrendered New Amsterdam to the English in 1664, Stout and five other men received a grant of land in New Jersey and founded the village of Middletown. Stout and his family are believed to be the first white settlers in New Jersey, and their descendants have been prominent in the history of the state for 300 years. In 1950 it was estimated there were at least 50,000 descendants of Richard and Penelope in this country.

Richard's great-grandson, Peter, emigrated to North Carolina where he was one of the founders of the Cane Creek Quaker Meeting in 1746. Many of her descendants live in Howard County, IN. *Submitted by Nancy Young Mason, daughter of Clarice Stout Young.*

STOUT - William Stout was born in Orange County, IN Feb. 22, 1818. He was the son of John (Aug. 8, 1789-March 30, 1866) and Elizabeth Moon (April 14, 1789-April 3, 1846) Stout who had come from Orange County, NC to become pioneer settlers in Orange County, IN in 1814. John's roots are traced to John and Elizabeth Bee Stout of Nottingham, England. Their son Richard came to the New World in the mid 1600s. He married Penelope Van Princess, who had been brought to his village by friendly Indians.

1st Row, L-R: Amy, Tyler and Kimberly Ratcliff. 2nd Row, L-R: Tim, Mike and Gloria Ratcliff.

Penelope was a Hollander whose ship had been wrecked on the shore of Sandy Hook near what later became New Jersey. The party reached shore and started for New Amsterdam, leaving Penelope and her sick husband on the beach. Later a band of Indians found them, killed her husband and left her for dead. Penelope was scalped, stomach cut so that her bowels were exposed and her arm was hacked. She managed to crawl to a hollow log and kept alive by eating bark and berries. In time, two Indians found Penelope and took her to their camp where she was nursed back to health. Later she was taken to New Amsterdam where she met and married Richard Stout around 1644. Richard and Penelope were the fourth great-grandparents of William Stout, pioneer to Howard County.

On Dec. 23, 1846, William married Elizabeth Lindley (April 9, 1821-Nov. 22, 1893), the daughter of Thomas (Feb. 2, 1793-Sept. 10, 1850) and Margaret Hollowell (Dec. 12, 1800-Jan. 18, 1852) Lindley who were also pioneer settlers in Orange County, IN. Margaret's uncle, John Hollowell, was the first white settler in Orange County, IN and lived in a cave until he could build his cabin. The first Hollowells came to America from England in 1649 and settled in the Virginia colony. The Lindley family came from Ireland in 1731 and made their home in Pennsylvania. Immigrant Lindley's great-grandfather became a Christian martyr and was beheaded around 1641 in England.

Mary and Carrol Stout

About 1861, William, Elizabeth and their five children: Milton, Lydia, Elmira, Mary Ellen and Sarah Ann came north on the Michigan Road (SR29) from Orange County and settled in Monroe Township, Howard County. The next year their last child was born, Charles Lindley Stout.

Charles (April 1, 1862-Dec. 4, 1942) married Mary Frances Eikenberry (Oct. 20, 1862-July 7, 1940) also a native of Howard County. She was the daughter of Abraham (March 8, 1830-Aug. 30, 1870) and Rhoda Lybrook (Oct. 26, 1836-Dec. 1, 1862) Eikenberry. Charles and Mary Frances had four children: Earl, Ethel, Lena and Clarence Leonard (April 29, 1888-April 20, 1948). Clarence married Mabel Marie Polk (May 10, 1891-May 15, 1974), daughter of Willis (Jan. 9, 1861-Dec. 1, 1940) and Eliza Hendrix (March 24, 1863-Dec. 21, 1948) Polk. They had two sons Loris Polk and Carrol Lavain Stout.

Carrol (May 4, 1928-) married June 13, 1948 to Mary Ratcliff (April 5, 1929-) daughter of Russell (Aug. 19, 1894-April 8, 1961) and Bethel Barber (Aug. 24, 1900-Dec. 26, 1991) Ratcliff. Carrol and Mary are retired from the insurance business and are presently engaged in real estate appraising.

Carrol and Mary have a daughter, Gloria Jeane (May 17, 1952) who married Mike Ratcliff (Jan. 30, 1951). They reside at Fort Wayne, IN with their children: Timothy Michael (March 26, 1976), Kimberly Beth (March 8, 1978), Amy Marie (Jan. 22, 1982), and Tyler Matthew (Nov. 22, 1983). Gloria and Mike graduated from Ashland College in Ohio. Gloria is a teacher and Mike is a nurse.

STOUT-COX-MILLER - John Benton (March 8, 1788-Sept. 9, 1863) and Ann Walker Miller (Feb. 16, 1788-Dec. 3, 1862), both born in North Carolina, came from east Tennessee to the area now known as Monroe Township, Howard County in 1839. They are recorded as Indiana Pioneers for Howard County. John built the first two-story log cabin in the township. He was a surveyor, photographer, and the first harness maker in the county. It is said that he would make the peg holes deeper than needed and it was here that he hid his money. The first cemetery in Howard County, Miller Cemetery, is located near where their home stood. They are both buried there along with other early residents.

Dorcus (June 28, 1810-Sept. 24, 1885) the oldest of John and Ann's 12 children and her husband Er C. Cox (May 20, 1813-May 16, 1861) came to this area about the same time as her parents and settled near them. In 1848, Dr. Wickersham of New London hired a man to bring a hand printing press from Westfield, Hamilton County to Howard County. The press was brought by wagon up the Michigan Road (SR29). At this time, slavery was a hot issue and people felt strongly whichever side they took. It was Wickersham's intention to use his newspaper in support of the abolishment of slavery and this fact was well-known throughout the community. Somewhere between Michigantown and Middlefork the wagon was stopped by five men who tried unsuccessfully to prevent the press from reaching its destination. Er Cox was one of these five men.

Seated, l-r: Joyce Webb holding Lauren Webb, Esther and Loris Stout, Gayle Stout. Standing, l-r: Bob Webb, Connie, Scott, Suzanne, Diane, Jenniffer Stout.

Dorcus and Er had seven children. Their oldest child, Sarah Elizabeth (Feb. 19, 1835-Sept. 22, 1904) married Henry Franklin Bryson (Jan. 8, 1834-Aug. 3, 1875). Henry was killed near Sugar Grove, Monroe Township, by the bursting of a threshing machine pulley and was buried at Miller Cemetery. Along with farming he was also a master carpenter. Sarah and Henry had eight children.

Elizabeth Dorcus Bryson (Feb. 11, 1854-June 18, 1898), second child of Sarah and Henry, married Franklin Pierce Unger (June 30, 1853-March 10, 1927). Franklin was the son of Thomas (Nov. 13, 1826-Jan. 22, 1864) and Martha Lennon Unger (March 28, 1834-March 6, 1889). Thomas died at Chattanooga, TN while serving in the Civil War.

Sarah Irene Leota Bell (Jan. 26, 1880-Oct. 7, 1976) was one of four children born to Franklin and Elizabeth Bryson Unger. She married on Oct. 11, 1905 to Jacob Huffer (Dec. 4, 1877-Feb. 15, 1968) of Carroll County. The couple had six daughters: Mae, Bernice, Hazel, Gladys, Esther, and Pauline.

Esther Irene Huffer (Nov. 23, 1916-) married on March 7, 1937 to Loris Polk Stout (March 23, 1915-). They raised their four children on the farm in Carroll County which has been in the Stout family for over 150 years. They are now retired and living in Burlington, IN. Loris and Esther have four children, eleven grandchildren and three great-grandchildren.

Son Allen Lewis married Cindi Thompson. Grandchildren: Kathy, Katrina and Kurt, and great-grandchildren Cassandra, Kelly Ann and John Carter. Son Richard Leon married Marlene Todd. Grandchildren: Todd, Summer and Andrew. Son Gayle Edward married Diane Bruck. Grandchildren: Jenniffer, Connie, Suzanne and Scott. Daughter Joyce Ellen married Bob Webb. Granddaughter, Lauren. (See Stout-Polk and Stout-Eikenberry also in this publication.)

STOUT-EIKENBERRY-LYBROOK - Daniel Eikenberry (Jan. 16, 1799-Oct. 21, 1859) was the great-great-grandson of Heinrich and Elizabeth Naas Landes whose home was used by General George Washington as a headquarters during the Revolutionary War. British prisoners were kept in the basement of their home. Another of Daniel's ancestors was beheaded in 1614 for his Anabaptist beliefs.

Daniel Eikenberry and Sarah Kingery (Jan. 8, 1805-Nov. 8, 1862) were residents of Union County, IN. They had 13 sons and 1 daughter. When land became available in Howard County Daniel purchased land for some of his sons. After the death of her husband, Sarah brought her younger children and joined her sons in Howard County. She died here and is buried at Pete's Run Cemetery.

One of these sons who came to Ervin Township was Abraham (March 8, 1830-Aug. 30, 1870) and his wife Rhoda Lybrook (Oct. 26, 1836-Dec. 1, 1862) Eikenberry. Both the Lybrook and Eikenberry clans had strong roots in the German Baptist faith. Abraham worshiped at the Howard German Baptist Church, built in 1865, located on a hill west of Stonebraker Bridge in Monroe Township. Rhoda's great-grandfather, Elder Jacob Miller, was the first German Baptist Elder in Virginia, Ohio and Indiana.

Seated, l-r: Allen Stout holding John Carter, Cindi Stout holding Kelly Ann Carter. Standing, l-r: Kathy and Jeff Carter, Heidi and Kurt Stout, Cassandra Carter, Joel and Katrina Rathbun.

Rhoda died about six weeks after the birth of her daughter, Mary Frances Eikenberry (Oct. 20, 1862-July 7, 1940). After the death of her father Abraham eight years

317

later, Mary went to live with Rhoda McCoy. Mary married Charles Lindley Stout (April 1, 1862-Dec. 4, 1942). They became faithful members of the New London Friends Church, Monroe Township.

Mary Frances and Charles Stout raised their four children on a farm west of New London. Son, Clarence (April 29, 1888-April 20, 1948), married Mabel Polk (May 10, 1891-May 15, 1974), daughter of Willis (Jan. 9, 1861-Dec. 1, 1940) and Eliza Hendrix (March 24, 1863-December 1948) Polk.

Loris (March 23, 1915-), son of Clarence and Mabel, married Esther Huffer (Nov. 23, 1916-). Their offspring are Allen, Richard, Gayle and Joyce.

Allen (June 7, 1939-) was raised on the farm which has been in the family for over 150 years. He graduated from Burlington School in 1957 and began working at Union Stellite in Kokomo. Allen joined the Army Reserves and while stationed at Aberdeen, MD, he met Kathryn Cynthia "Cindi" Thompson (Sept. 3, 1942-), daughter of Morton Thompson (Feb. 17, 1915-) and Kathryn Weil Idler (Jan. 31, 1920-). Cindi was born in and raised near Philadelphia, PA. Allen and Cindi were married March 2, 1963. They have three children: Kathryn Cheryl (March 18, 1964) married Jeffrey Carter and lives on the family farm with their children Kathryn Cassandra, Kelly Ann, and John Robert; Katrina Lynn (Nov. 10, 1966) married Joel Rathbun director of a YMCA Camp in Missouri; Kurtis Allen (Aug. 28, 1969) married Heidi Fruitt and lives in Ohio where he attends Ashland Theological Seminary preparing for pastoral ministry. Kathy, Katrina and Kurt are all alumni of Taylor University in Upland.

Allen and Cindi are active at the First Brethren Church in Burlington where they serve as Deacons. Allen is a grain, hog and dairy farmer and Cindi keeps busy with family, church activities, genealogy, writing a church history book and lineage societies. *Submitted by Allen and Cindi Stout.*

STOUT-POLK - Joseph Polk was born Feb. 11, 1802, Botetourt County, VA. On Feb. 3, 1827 he married Catharine Beckner born 1794. The couple and two children, Mary and William, came to some place in Indiana where Thomas was born in 1830. They purchased land in Carrollton Township, Carroll County, in May 1833. By 1844, Joseph had acquired land in Ervin Township, Howard County and lived there with his family which now included Adoline and Joseph. Five years after settling in Howard County, Joseph died Jan. 28, 1849 and was buried in Mound Cemetery, Howard County. Catharine, who was blind in her later years, died April 21, 1881 and is buried next to her husband.

William Lockard Polk (April 8, 1827-Feb. 20, 1908) son of Joseph and Catharine, was born in Virginia. He was married March 19, 1852 to Mariah Kirkpatrick (July 28, 1832-June 2, 1869) the daughter of Benjamin (Aug. 30, 1803-Sept. 30, 1880) and Hannah McCain (July 22, 1812-Dec. 12, 1894) Kirkpatrick. Benjamin was the fourth adult white male settler in Carrollton Township, Carroll County, arriving in October 1833. His brother and two other men arrived a year before.

The Richard Stout Family. L-R: Richard, Marlene, Todd. L-R: Andrew and Summer.

William and Mariah lived in Howard County where their four children, Benjamin, William, Willis, and Mary Alice, were born. After Mariah died at the age of 36, William married Nancy Davis and had three more sons and another daughter.

Willis Veletice (Jan. 9, 1861-Dec. 1, 1940) son of William and Mariah, married Eliza Annis Hendrix (March 24, 1863-Dec. 21, 1948). She was the daughter of Zedock (Dec. 1, 1881-July 27, 1888) and Mary Cromwell Hendrix (April 16, 1820-Sept. 11, 1898). Mary is the daughter of John Cromwell who operated a mill in Carroll County in 1837. Her brother Moses operated an early mill in Howard County.

Willis and Eliza had four children: Earl, Orrel, Mabel, and Edna. Mabel Marie (May 10, 1891-May 15, 1974) married Clarence Stout (April 29, 1888-April 20, 1948), of Monroe Township. They had two sons Loris Polk and Carrol Lavain. Loris (March 23, 1915-) married Esther Irene Huffer (Nov. 23, 1916-) and they had four children: Allen, Richard, Gayle and Joyce.

Richard Leon (Jan. 23, 1943-) married on Aug. 20, 1967 to Marlene Todd (Nov. 2, 1945-March 1, 1986) daughter of John Harvey (Feb. 20, 1912-March 19, 1977) and Martell Swartzkoff (Feb. 28, 1919-March 19, 1987) Todd. John Todd was the founder of Todd Hybrid Seed Corn Company, which was established in 1936. His first seed structure was built on the site where Richard and Marlene live today.

Richard and Marlene have three children: Todd Andrew (Nov. 6, 1970) a graduate of Ball State University, Summer Todd (Oct. 30, 1979) and Andrew Richard (April 27, 1982) both students at Carroll Consolidated School Corporation.

Richard is engaged in farming and Marlene is employed at Kokomo High School as a teacher and Curriculum Supervisor for Business Education. They live in the house which was owned by Marlene's great-grandfather and dates back to Civil War times. Their children are the fifth generation to attend the Sharon Baptist Church where their great-great-grandfather was a minister. *Submitted by Richard Stout.*

MAPLE SUGAR TIME - In the year 1904 Bertha Floyd and William Earl Stout in western Howard County were married. They went to housekeeping in a small house on my Grandfather Stout's farm west of New London in a wooded area, with trees on the south and west and our home in the center of a poplar grove of trees. To them three girls were born, Beulah Lindley, Reba Lewis, and Mary Lou Matlock, and of course our playground was under the poplar trees where we had swings and made mud pies; we didn't know what big toys were, except our little red wagon.

We walked about a half mile to meet the hack for our ride to New London School. The hack was pulled by a team of horses. Our driver was John Hadley and his daughter, Carrie Mae Hadley Gilbert, was our teacher. We wore long underwear and high top shoes to help us keep warm; of course the hack was cold too. We had a buggy, a Casey Cab enclosed with glass, a carriage with fringe on top and a sleigh with bells on the horses.

(L to R) Earl Stout, Edwin Matlock, Judy Lindley Ploughe, Susanne Matlock Gooding, MaryLou Stout Matlock, Barbara Lindley Moore, Bertha Stout, Beulah Stout Lindley, Stewart Matlock and Ronald Lindley in 1941 at the Maple Sugar Camp.

Later my father bought a larger house on the Stout farm, so we didn't have to walk so far to get to the hack.

Almost every spring my family would open the Maple Sugar Camp, as they called it, tapping the maple trees in the woods south of our little house where we girls were born. There was an old log cabin in this woods and they fixed it with a furnace and vaporator to boil the water down to a syrup. Holes were drilled in the maple trees and wooden buckets hung on the spickets. A bob-sled with a team of horses and wooden barrels were used to gather up the water. Wood had to be cut to keep the fire going under the maple syrup. Later when we girls were all married and had families, we would all go and help Mother and Dad. Our children loved helping and playing in the woods.

The smell was wonderful from the syrup boiling down to molasses. Then of course the good part was making taffy and maple sugar and sometimes using black walnuts that we had gathered in the fall from the walnut trees on the farm. My mother always canned the syrup; it would keep for years.

The Stout family is one of the oldest families in western Howard County, dating back to 1859 when William Stout brought his family of five children in wagons to Howard County to a farm near New London. My grandfather Charles was born in Monroe Township three years after they moved to Howard County. Charles made their sixth child, it was his farm that my father and mother, Earl and Bertha Stout and we girls lived on when we were small. *Submitted by Beulah Stout Lindley.*

STREETER - Steven Streeter born 1600 England, died 1652 Massachusetts, married 1640 Massachusetts, Ursula Adams, born 1619 England, died 1679. Steven was a shoemaker and took his "Freeman's Oath" in 1644. They had seven children; the last was born after his death.

Stephen Streeter born 1641 Massachusetts, died 1689 Massachusetts, married 1666 Deborah Smith. They had eight children; the last was born after his death.

Samuel Streeter, yeoman, born 1671 Massachusetts, died 1751 Massachusetts, married Deborah. They had nine children.

Stephen Streeter, yeoman, born 1689 Massachusetts, died 1756 Massachusetts, married 1723 Connecticut, Catherine Adams. They had 11 children.

Dr. John Streeter, born 1731 Massachusetts, died 1810 New York, married 1757 Connecticut, Margaret Hemingway, born 1739 Connecticut, died 1775 Massachusetts. He served in the American Revolution and the French/Indian Wars. They had 10 children. He married 1777 second wife Elizabeth Rowler, and they had four children.

Nathan Streeter born 1763 Massachusetts, died 1830 New York, married 1787 Connecticut, Naomi Alderman. He was a Revolutionary War Vet. They had 12 children.

Benjamin J. Streeter born 1802 New York, died 1886 New York, married Arvilla Adams born 1807 Vermont, died 1864 New York. He was a Baptist preacher. They had 13 children.

Edgar Edward Streeter born 1825 New York, died 1911 New York, married 1849 New York, Mary Maria Curtis, born 1828 Canada, died 1901 New York. He was a farmer and a Civil War Vet. They had six children.

Fredrich Cladius Streeter (farmer) born 1857 New York, died 1931 Indiana, married 1881 Viola Theodosia Campbell. They were members of the Methodist Episcopal Church and had eight children. They lived in North Dakota from 1909 to 1918. Fred came to Indiana on a circus train.

Clive Claudius Streeter (farmer) born 1882 Indiana, died 1951 Indiana, married 1902 Indiana, Oma Preble born 1885 Indiana, died 1914 Indiana. Oma died while her three sons were young: Claude Clive; Wayne Byrum born 1906 Indiana, died 1987 Indiana, married 1936 Indiana, Blanche Wauneta Sellers born 1910 Indiana, died 1981 Indiana; Paul Robert born 1909 Indiana, married 1934 Indiana, Ferol Josephine Garbert born 1911 Indiana, died 1991 Indiana.

Claude Clive Streeter (salesman and farmer) born 1904 Indiana, died 1992 Florida, married 1934 Indiana, Zoe Alberta Blossey. They had four children, all born in Kokomo: Rebecca Jane born 1936; Rachel Ann born 1938; Thomas Wayne born 1943; David Allen born 1946.

Rebecca, an RN, married 1958 Steven Fischer born 1938 Illinois, died 1991 Indiana, a teacher. They had two daughters: Kelly Ann born 1959 Indiana, and Andrea Elaine born 1961 Indiana.

(Rachel) Ann, a clerical worker, married 1960 Donald Nichols born 1938 Tennessee, Air Force. They had two children: James Joel born 1961 Tennessee and Mary Katheryn born 1962 New Jersey.

Thomas, a college professor, married 1968 Christine Pfeiffer born 1946 New York a housewife. They had six children: Carrie Elizabeth born 1970 Virginia; Bradley Thomas born 1973 Illinois; Geoffrey Scott born 1975 Illinois; Troy David born 1977 Illinois; Tiffany Leigh born 1979 Illinois; Cynthia Dawn born 1982 Illinois.

David, an Air Force officer, married 1969 Francoise Delfosse born 1945 Belgium, a housewife. They had five children: Suzanne Marie born 1970 Belgium; Robert Allen born 1973 Belgium; Michelle Alberta born 1974 Belgium; Kimberly Ann born 1978 Belgium; Karen Maria born 1980 Italy. *Submitted by Zoe Streeter.*

JAMES B. AND KATHLEEN M. (BRUMBAUGH) SWARTZ - In 1960, James B. Swartz and Kathleen M. Swartz (Brumbaugh) moved to Kokomo from Canton, OH. Joseph was born in 1960, Laura in 1962, Gregory in 1963 and Julie in 1965. For 26 years, James worked at Delco Electronics. He held positions of Senior Physicist, Senior Product Engineer, Engineering Product Manager, Product Assurance Manager, and Program Manager.

Bottom row l-r: Kathleen, James. Top row l-r: Gregory, Julie, Laura, Joe.

In 1976, James, while Manufacturing Plant Manager at Delco Electronics, invented the technology which produced Computer Portraits. The resulting manufacturing business started as a family operation out of the basement, and grew into a corporation called Cygnus Systems. It went from a black and white alphanumeric image to a color, photographic-like image with sales worldwide. Cygnus Systems, Inc. is now operated by Greg Swartz from a newly constructed site at 3416 S. Dixon Road in Kokomo. After retiring from Delco in 1988, James started another corporation, called Competitive Action. He conducts training workshops nationwide in his Non-linear change process for the restructuring of companies. Joe has an MS degree from Purdue. He has his own business in Computer Programming called Josoft, out of Indianapolis. He married Julia Heflin, from Kokomo, and they have a daughter, Jordan.

Laura has an MS degree from Purdue and now lives in Boise, ID. She is a supervisor at Beacon Light Co. She married Mike Louis from Dayton, OH.

Greg has an electrical engineering degree from the University of Evansville and lives in Kokomo.

Julie has a degree in Computer Science from Indiana State University. She married Ralph Thorpe from Madison and they reside in Ft. Wayne. They have a son, Brendan and a daughter, Kylie.

Kathleen is involved in the businesses as secretary and bookkeeper. *Submitted by Kathleen M. Swartz.*

SWIHART - Mary Loretta (White) Swihart was born March 27, 1923 in Springfield, MO. Her parents were Howard Edward and Ruth Ella (Hunt) White. Shortly after her birth the Whites came to Kokomo, IN.

As a child, Mary attended St. Patrick School and then on to St. Joseph Academy at Tipton for her high school years.

Keith Lamar Swihart was born June 12, 1933 at Pleasant Lake, Steuben County, IN. He was the son of Avinal Bertrude and Mary Pauline (Ling) Swihart. He spent his younger life in this area. Keith and Mary were married May 24, 1952 at St. Patrick Church in Kokomo by Rev. Leo Brietenbach. The young couple moved to Kokomo shortly after their wedding and he went to work for Kingston Products. Later, employment was with Colonial Bread and then with Schembre Beverage Company, Inc. as a driver when he suffered a heart attack on May 6, 1971. Keith is buried at Greenlawn Cemetery in Greentown, IN.

Mary Loretta (White) Swihart

Mary worked for Kingston Products during WWII. After Keith's death, she went to work at Bon Air School in the cafeteria and retired from there. Some of Mary's hobbies have been knitting, crocheting and enjoying her family now that she has 12 grandchildren and 2 great-grandchildren.

The Swihart family consists of the following six children all born in Kokomo: (1) Clare Marie born Feb. 20, 1953. She served four years in the U.S. Army and went to Korea; (2) David Keith born Feb. 20, 1954, received a degree in Business from Butler University of Indianapolis. He now lives in Portland, OR; (3) Mary Ann born July 7, 1955 and lives in Hawaii; (4) Timothy Joseph born Dec. 5, 1958. He served four years in the U.S. Army and went to Germany; (5) Jacqueline Jane born Sept. 29, 1962. She received a degree in teaching from Marian College of Indianapolis and lives there; (6) John Fitzgerald born Aug. 29, 1964, attended Purdue University and studied Forestry. He joined the U.S. Air Force before his death March 2, 1988 in Dayton, OH and is buried at Memorial Park Cemetery in Kokomo. All six children graduated from Haworth High School.

See additional information for the White family in this publication.

TATE - William A. Tate, Jr. was the son of John F. Tate of Howard Township and was born Aug. 10, 1849. When he was 17, he enlisted in the regular army and served for three years. At the age of 20, William married Zenobia Oliver of Phillips County, AR. While living in Arkansas, they had two sons: Frank, born 1874 and Fredric A., born 1875.

Around 1877, Wm. and Zenobia, with their two sons, returned to Howard County. They settled one and one-half miles east of Kokomo, and he became a vegetable farmer. Six more children were born: sons Benjamin, John B. and Berne, and three daughters, Jessie, Ruth and Iva.

William Tate, Jr. was among the first citizens of Howard County to support the dry cause, and rejoiced to see Indiana abolish the legalized liquor traffic.

The National Mitten Works, which was located at 212-216 E. Superior, was started by William around 1914.

In 1916, John B. Tate, William's son, built the Tate Block Building at the corner of Markland and Main Sts. in Kokomo.

Fredric A. Tate, William's next to oldest son, and Clara Melissa Hayes were wed in 1899 in Muncie, IN. Around 1901 they moved to Kokomo. They had two daughters, Lela E., born 1903, and Jeanette E. born 1912,

and two sons, Afton F., born 1918 and Karl E., born 1923. Fredric was a carpenter by trade.

William A. Tate Jr. Family. L-R, Back Row: John, Fred and Frank. Middle Row: Ben, Berne and Jessie. Front Row: Ruth, (mother) Zenobia, Iva and (father) William.

December 1940, Karl E. wed Dorothy L. Boles of Corryton, TN. They lived in Kokomo, and March 1942, had a son, Richard Eldon.

Karl was drafted February 1943. He served in the army during WWII and was in the European Theatre of operations.

Two years after Karl returned from the war, they had a daughter, Shelah Kay, born April 1947.

About 1951, Karl and his best friend, John Harper, opened a used car lot on the southeast corner of Main and Deffenbaugh. Karl retired from Delco in 1983, and he and Dorothy moved to Spring City, TN.

Richard E. Tate and his wife Linda, live in Russiaville. Richard's oldest son, Richard E. Tate, Jr. lives in Seymour, IN. Jim Tate, Richard's youngest son, and his family live in Frankfort, IN. Richard's daughter Julie and her family also live in Frankfort.

Shelah K. Tate-Worthman and her husband Raymond E., who was born in Chicago, live in Kokomo. Shelah has a daughter, Stephanie Kay Taylor, born Nov. 9, 1974. Stephanie and her husband Darwin also live in Kokomo. She has a daughter, Kylie Brooks Wyant, born Dec. 2, 1992.

TAYLOR - Joseph C. Taylor (1782-1861) and Frances Reynolds Taylor (1783-1857), were some of the first settlers in the Howard County area. They came from Virginia and first settled on the banks of the Wabash near Peru, IN in 1832. In 1838 Joseph Taylor, with his son George, came to a point near the old Stonebraker Mill on Wildcat Creek, between what is presently known as Kokomo and Burlington, in Monroe Township, Howard County, where they built a cabin. They then returned to the Wabash River home and moved the family here. They were the parents of 12 children—Anna T. Bell, Henrietta T. DePoy, Betsy T. Givens, John, Polly T. Newman, Jane T. Horner, George (buried in Price Cemetery, Howard County), Jackson, Susan T. Anderson, Catherine T. Jones, Arminda T. Wright, and Joseph, Jr. All these children were born in Virginia except the last three. While on their journey from Virginia, which was a long and tedious one, they were compelled to stop for several weeks in Ohio, where Catherine was born. During the mother's confinement and for sometime afterward Mr. Taylor raised vegetables and some corn. When leaving Ohio, they proceeded to Indiana. Mr. Taylor and family, Isaac Price and Robert Walker were the first white people to inhabit Howard County. The Taylor home near the Stonebraker mill was not to be, as it was found they had built their home on lands belonging to the Miami Indians. Then they came to what is now called Russiaville, IN, and built a log cabin on the north banks of Squirrel Creek, a little stream that crosses the present site of Russiaville, where for two years their only neighbors were the Miamis with whom they were entirely friendly. The log cabin built on Squirrel Creek was very primitive in character, having only one room, the floors consisting of hewed puncheons, the door of very crude patter, with wooden hinges and a latch. A window was in one side of the cabin where greased paper was used to admit light. The roof was of clapboards held by long poles. Joseph entered his 160 acres of land here, getting his deed from the government, paying $1.25 per acre. His first taxes on record show him having paid $3.29 on the land and $2.52 on personal property. Until 1842 there were no trading posts nearer than Burlington, 10 miles distance, and trading was done on foot or by horseback.

Joseph C. Taylor was a slave owner while he lived in Virginia but before leaving the state he gave them all their "Free Papers".

Our family line are the direct descendents of Joseph's son George Taylor (1800-1856) and Margaret Lugar Taylor (1800-1879). Their nine children were Joseph Wesley, Emanuel, John Alexander, Adam, Margaret Frances T. White, Enoch, George, Ralph and Franklin.

John Alexander Taylor (1830-1895) and Helen Barnett Taylor (1855-1880) were the parents of 11 children—James Harvey, George F., William Adam Roland, Nettie Valeda, David Ralph, John Matilla, Murta Jane, Cary Grant, Lewis Lewellyn, Charley and Ramey Delaska. After the death of Helen, John A. married Rebecca Hart and to this union Curtis (1887-1962) was born.

Lewis Lewellyn Taylor (1872-1950) and Rachel Kenworthy Taylor were married in 1893. They lived in the Howard County area most of their lives except a short time in Texas and Oklahoma. They were the parents of Lowell W., Charles Russell, and Wayne W. Lowell and Wayne died at a young age.

Charles Russell Taylor (1895-1969) and Esther Small Taylor (1896-1983) were married at the New London Friends Church in a typical Quaker ceremony after Sunday meeting Aug. 25, 1925. To them were born Ethel Virginia T. Haynes, Helen Naomi T. Kelly, Lewis Milton and Carolyn T. Carson who are all living at this time as Howard County prepares to celebrate 150 years.

Virginia Taylor is married to John E. Haynes. They are the parents of two children, Thomas Ward and Janet Esther H. Bentley. Thomas is married to Linda Kay Roberts Haynes. They are the parents of Christina Marie and Carrie Lee. Janet was married to Kevin Gordon Bentley. They are the parents of Michael John and Scott Gordon.

Helen Taylor is married to Ralph Kelly. They are the parents of Marjorie Kay K. Sullivan, David Wayne, Robert Joe, and Marlita Ann. Marjorie is married to Larry D. Sullivan. They are the parents of Gregory Lyn and Scott Daniel. David is married to Michele D. Dyar Kelly. They are the parents of Brad Aaron and Kyle Richard. Joe is married to Vickie L. Kring Kelly. They are the parents of Jason Andrew and Jeremy Lee.

Lewis is married to Mary Frances Carter Taylor. They are the parents of William Lewis, Richard Allen, Karen Lynn T. Sword and Kathy Joann who died at birth. William is married to Pamela Sue Graham Taylor. They are the parents of Sarah Jo. Richard is married to Linda Gail Canady Taylor. They are the parents of Richard Scott, Christopher Ryan, and Blake Anthony. Karen is married to Donald L. Sword. They are the parents of Amanda Kay, Joseph Tyler, and Jennifer Leighann.

Carolyn Taylor is married to Donald R. Carson. They are the parents of Russell Gage and Linda Marie C. Tones. Russell is married to Li Chan. Linda was married to Darrell Tones. They are the parents of Allison Nicole.

Our family, eight generations later, are proud to be a part of Howard County, IN.

WILLIAM TAYLOR - William Taylor (died June 13, 1872 age 73 years, 4 months, 3 days) married Mary Jenetta Huntley of Ohio (April 14, 1893-April 23, 1893). They lived south of Slick Pole School, east of Russiaville. William and Mary were the parents of two daughters: Mary Ellen and Laurie, and possibly other children.

Mary Ellen married Soloman Hensley on March 9, 1887. They moved to the Bloomington area and were the parents of: Atta, Ethel, Jeff, Blanche, Clara, Elma and Everett. Only Blanche survives at age 98. Their cabin was located on what is now the banks of Lake Monroe.

Laurie married Lorenzo B. Ostler on Aug. 21, 1892. He was a widower. His first wife is interred at Hopewell Cemetery. Laurie died on March 7, 1901 at age 28 years, 11 months and 5 days.

William Taylor; Mary Jenetta Huntley

William, Mary J. and Laurie are interred at Old Liberty Cemetery.

Any further information on this branch of our family would be greatly appreciated. *Submitted by Nancy (Hogan) Reed, great-great-granddaughter of William and Mary J.*

LEWIS SHERMAN TETER - Lewis Sherman Teter was born in Goldsmith, IN Oct. 13, 1908. He was the son of Linville and Etta (Foster) Teter. On Jan. 24, 1936 Lewis married Hazel Blanche Dickey (born Jan. 14, 1914 in Chicago, IL). Hazel was the only child of Arthur E. and Grace (Gardener) Dickey. The children born of this marriage are Dorothy Lee Teter (born Jan. 18, 1937) and Linda Ellen Teter (born Aug. 10, 1938).

Lewis Sherman and Hazel (Dickey) Teter

Lewis graduated from Goldsmith High School in 1926 and attended Purdue University on an agriculture scholarship. After marrying Hazel he worked at Kokomo Sanitary Pottery in the shipping room. He worked at Curtis Wright Corp. in Indianapolis, doing defense work, during WWII. After that he managed the Brennan Farm in Hamilton County from 1943 to 1946. Upon leaving the Brennan Farm, he was Superintendent of Farms at Mt. Ararat Farms in Port Deposit, MD. Upon returning to Indiana in 1949 he became foreman of the slip house at the Kokomo Sanitary Pottery until his death in 1970. He had a fatal heart attack Sept. 30, 1970 in the orchard of his farm at 400 West 250 South in Harrison Township, Howard County.

Hazel was employed at Delco Electronics from 1952 to 1976. She was very active in many civic organizations and was the Senior Intern in Washington D.C., serving with Representative Elwood Hillis in 1979. She was the Indiana State Senior Queen in 1985 and was honored as a Sagamore of the Wabash by Gov. Evan Bayh in 1994. She still currently resides in Howard County.

RONALD L. AND CANDACE K. TETRICK - Ronald Lee Tetrick was born in Marion, IN, Jan. 9, 1945, the son of Everett William Tetrick (1911-1987) and Mary Wilma Hix (1918-living), both natives of Grant County, who were married there on Dec. 12, 1936. Following graduation from Mississinewa High School in 1963, he attended Ball State University in Muncie, IN, finishing all but one class of his Master's Degree in Latin and English in 1968. That August he began teaching Latin at the newly-opened Haworth High School. He returned to Ball State in the summer of 1969 and completed his degree. He now teaches at Kokomo High School South Campus. In 1981 he also became an adjunct faculty member at Indiana University Kokomo, teaching Medical Terminology. He has toured Europe with students on four occasions, and was designated Indiana Latin Teacher of the Year in 1991.

Candace Kay Wintrode was born in Kokomo, IN, on Jan. 8, 1956. After graduating from Haworth High School in 1974, she attended Indiana University Kokomo and Indiana University/Purdue University Indianapolis, completing her Bachelor's degree in 1979, and her Master's degree in 1982, in Social Studies. Ron and Candy were married in Courtland Avenue Friends Church on June 21, 1975, where they are active members.

Ron and Candy Tetrick

After three years of substitute teaching, Candy began working at Volunteers in Community Service, and finished seven years as the agency's Director. She has been employed by the City of Firsts Federal Credit Union since 1989.

Ron and Candy enjoy interests in genealogy, family photography, traveling and collecting Depression glass and other treasures. They moved into their present home in 1978, at 2300 Canterbury Drive, Kokomo, IN.

Although Ron is a transplant to the Howard County area, Candy's maternal roots are a little deeper. Her parents are Herbert Dale Wintrode (1922-living) and Thelma Arretha Edwards (1923-living), who were married in Kokomo on Sept. 28, 1947, in the home of Thelma's parents, Clifford Carl (1897-1976) and Golda May (Stewart) (1901-1990) Edwards. Thelma has spent her whole life in Kokomo, graduating from Kokomo High School in 1941. Except for Candy's early years, her mother worked for Indiana Bell until 1967. Herbert was born near Andrews in Huntington County, and entered the armed service in January 1941, serving in the 1st Armored Div. in North Africa, where he was wounded and received a Purple Heart. He was also in charge of an Italian prisoner of war camp before returning to the United States. After his discharge, he worked in Long Beach, CA and near Houston, TX before returning to Huntington County. Short stays at Delco and Armstrong Lumber Company preceded 34 years as a journeyman machinist for Stellite (later Union Carbide, Cabot and Haynes International), from which he retired in 1985. Several years were spent caring for Golda in their home. They, too, are active members of Courtland Avenue Friends Church, and now spend several winter months each year as "Winter Texans" in Harlingen. Thelma's parents were married in 1918 in Danville, IL. They were soon, however, back in Tipton County, and moved to Kokomo in 1920 when Carl went to work for Haynes-Apperson. He was employed by Kokomo Gas and Fuel Company for 43 years as a serviceman. They, too, attended Courtland Avenue Friends Church, after moving their membership from Liberty Baptist in Tipton County in 1932. Golda worked for a few years as a matron for Indiana Bell, but spent most of her adult years as a housewife.

Howard County holds the limelight now for Ron and Candy, and provides all the qualities and accommodations necessary for a fulfilling life. Whether by adoption or birth, Kokomo is now their home, and they plan to remain here for many years to come. *Submitted by Ronald L. Tetrick.*

CLINE DENZIL AND ADDIE (TEMPLES) THIEKE - Cline Denzil Thieke, who was born Jan. 16, 1908 in Benton, MO and Addie (Temples) Thieke, who was born Sept. 19, 1907 in Dexter, MO were married Aug. 25, 1934.

On Dec. 29, 1935, with the hopes of finding a job, Cline and Addie moved to Howard County where four of Cline's brothers (Wes, Bill, Osby and Thilburn) were already working. Shortly after arriving, Cline found a job farming for Fred Warrick for $1.00 a day. Also included was a one-room, rent-free house, wood for cooking and heating, chickens and a milking cow.

During the next four years, Cline and Addie worked on three other farms for Albert Riffe, Earl Foster and Walter Young.

In 1939, Cline and Addie moved to Tipton where Cline worked for Oaks Manufacturing Company. They lived there approximately one year and then moved back to Howard County where Cline went to work for the Steel Mill. He started working at the Mill for $72.00-$75.00 every two weeks and kept this job for twenty-nine years until he retired.

Addie went to work at Delco in 1946 during the months their children were in school. She would quit when school was out and return to work when school started. Addie was making $17.00 a week when she started work. In 1949, Addie worked full-time for Delco and remained until she retired 20 years later in 1969.

In 1943, Cline and Addie bought their house for $24.00 a month that was located where is now the intersection of Gano Street and between the lanes of the 31 Bypass. In 1949, when their land was bought to make plans for the bypass, Cline and Addie's house was moved to the corner of Gano and Ohio Street.

Thieke Family. L-R, front row: Tom. L-R, middle row: Sharon, Addie, Cline and Margaret. L-R, back row: Marilyn.

Cline and Addie had six children who are: William Lee Temples, who was born Sept. 10, 1925 in Dexter, MO and died on June 12, 1985 in Lafayette, IN. Marilyn Irene Thieke, who was born July 6, 1935 in Dexter, MO and died on March 22, 1991 in Springhill, FL, five years after a heart transplant. Sharon Louise Thieke, who was born April 10, 1937 in Howard County and now lives in Sorrento, FL. Margaret Ann Thieke, who was born July 10, 1939 in Tipton, IN and now lives in Muncie, IN. Thomas Evan Thieke, who was born April 21, 1941 in Howard County and now lives in Greentown, IN. David Wayne Thieke, who was born May 19, 1949 only lived eight hours due to under-developed heart, liver and stomach.

Cline's parents were Edward Thieke who was born Jan. 18, 1873 in Gabtown, IL, and Laura Jane (Blackburn) Thieke.

Addie's parents were, Charles Temples, who was born Dec. 25, 1874 in Dexter, MO and died February 1956 also in Dexter, MO. Mary Ann (McClard) Temples who was born May 24, 1877 in Stoddard County, MO and died Aug. 26, 1958 also in Stoddard County.

In 1984 Cline and Addie renewed their wedding vows for their 50th wedding anniversary.

Cline died Oct. 20, 1985 from cancer in Howard County. Addie presently lives in the same house that was moved 50 years ago. She has 12 grandchildren and 19 great-grandchildren. *Submitted by Tammy Aaron.*

MARGARET ANN THIEKE -
Margaret Ann Thieke was born July 10, 1939, in Tipton, IN. She moved to Howard County in 1940 when her parents, Cline Denzil Thieke, born Jan. 16, 1908, in Benton, MO and Addie (Temples) Thieke, born Sept. 19, 1907, in Dexter, MO returned to Kokomo when Cline received a job at the Continental Steel Mill. (See Cline Denzil and Addie (Temples) Thieke for more complete biography.)

Margaret was the fourth-born of six children. Her brothers and sisters are: William Lee Temples, born Sept. 10, 1925, in Dexter, MO and died June 12, 1985, in Lafayette, IN. Marilyn Irene Thieke, born July 6, 1935, in Dexter, MO and died March 22, 1991 after complications from a heart transplant she had almost five years prior to her death. Sharon Louise Thieke, born April 10, 1937, in Howard County. Sharon presently lives in Sorrento, FL. Thomas Evan Thieke, born April 21, 1941, in Howard County. Tom presently lives in Greentown, IN. David Wayne Thieke, born May 19, 1949 in Howard County. He only lived eight hours due to under-developed liver, stomach and heart.

Margaret Ann Thieke

Margaret met George Raymond Smith Jr. (See George Raymond Smith Jr. for complete biography.) in 1955; they were married Aug. 3, 1956 at Calvary Baptist Church in Howard County.

Margaret was a wife, mother and homemaker until 1973 when she went to work at the Credit Union. She later worked at Engel Jewelers and Erik's Chevrolet in Howard County.

George and Margaret had three children who were all born and presently live in Howard County. They are Tamara Ann Smith, Greg Alan Smith, and Amy Michelle Smith.

Tamara was born Aug. 15, 1957. She married Lance E. Aaron April 7, 1990, in Howard County and has two children, Ryan Michael Stevenson born Oct. 27, 1975 who is presently a senior at Kokomo High School. He joined the Army National Guard March 1993. Ashley Nicole Rietveld, born Feb. 16, 1979 who is presently a freshman at Kokomo High School. Ryan and Ashley were both born in Howard County.

Greg was born June 17, 1960. He married Lisa Ann Field July 20, 1991, in Muncie, IN. They have one son, Matthew Jacob Smith, born Nov. 9, 1992, in Howard County.

Amy was born Jan. 17, 1968. She married Rafael P. Rodriguez Nov. 13, 1991 in Howard County and divorced August 1992. She has two children, Amber Michelle Smith, born Nov. 23, 1987, in Howard County and is in the first grade at Maple Crest School and Rafael Noe Rodriguez, born June 19, 1990 in Akron, OH.

Tamara and Greg attended Bon Air and Haworth High Schools. Amy attended Bon Air, Zionsville Middle School (in Zionsville, IN), Delta Middle School (in Muncie, IN), and Kokomo High School. Tamara and Greg graduated from Haworth High School and Amy graduated from Kokomo High School.

George and Margaret lived in Bon Air addition for 20 years when they divorced Dec. 13, 1977.

In 1979, Margaret left Howard County to work in Zionsville, IN at Bill Estes Chevrolet.

On April 9, 1979, Margaret married Stanley T. Zimmerman, in Reno, NV. They left Zionsville January 1980 and moved to Muncie, IN where Margaret worked for Bill McCoy Ford and Bradburn Oldsmobile. She started working for Weidner Chevrolet in Anderson, IN April 1994.

Margaret and Stan presently live in Muncie, IN. *Submitted by Ashley N. Rietveld.*

LUKE THOMAS -
The Luke Thomas Homestead is located in western Howard County in Monroe Township.

Luke Thomas was born May 9, 1846 in Howard County, the son of Snead Thomas (1815-1876) and Miriam (Lamb) Thomas (1818-1869). Snead Thomas was one of the early settlers in western Howard County. He was a farmer.

Luke Thomas was a Civil War veteran. He enlisted in February 1864 in Co. G, 13th Regt., Indiana Voluntary Calvary. He was stationed in Huntsville and Decatur, AL; Nashville, TN; St. Louis, MO; Louisville, KY; and Vicksburg, MS.

Grandpa and old log cabin where dad was born.

Luke married Lydia Stout on March 31, 1868. They settled on the farm in western Howard County. Lydia was born in Orange County, IN, and came with her parents at the age of 10 by covered wagon to Howard County. It was election day and they waited for the polls to open to vote for Abraham Lincoln before they left. It took them two weeks to make the trip. They tied their cow behind the covered wagon.

Luke and Lydia Thomas had two children, Charles Hillis Thomas, born March 5, 1870-1952, and Elizabeth May Thomas, born Oct. 30, 1873-1974. Elizabeth lived to be 100 years old. Their first home on the farm was a log cabin where their son, Charles, was born. A new house was built later by Luke Thomas from native lumber, which still stands and has since been remodeled. A sugar camp was established on the farm where maple syrup was made by Luke Thomas, Charles Thomas, and his son-in-law Carl Hobson.

Charles Thomas married Olive Austin on June 21, 1899. She was born April 27, 1871-1957 in Henry County, IN. They had three children, Lowell Austin Thomas, born July 28, 1901-1986, Alma Thomas Unger, born June 4, 1904-1981, and Velma Thomas Hobson, born Dec. 3, 1909.

Elizabeth Thomas married Howard Brubaker. They had one daughter, Irene, who married Dr. Robert Evans. They had two sons, Charles Marcus Evans and William Thomas Evans.

Hobson Family. Wayne and Charles. Theresa and Amanda. Carl, Velma and Dawn. Tom, Ann and Jasen.

Velma Thomas married Carl Hobson on Dec. 24, 1932. They had two sons, Charles Alfred Hobson, born July 12, 1937, and Wayne Thomas Hobson, born April 10,

1943. Charles Hobson married Theresa Marie Taylor on May 25, 1963. They had five children, Thomas Anthony Hobson, born May 7, 1964, James Matthew Hobson, born Jan. 12, 1966, Ann Marie Hobson, born Nov. 22, 1968, Dawn Renee Hobson, born May 9, 1978, and Amanda Taylor Hobson, born July 30, 1979. Matthew Hobson died June 24, 1990.

Wayne Hobson married Carolyn Sue (Besser) Myers April 27, 1969-1989. They had one son, Jasen Carl Hobson, born July 11, 1972. Wayne had one step-son, Bradley Scott Myers, born Sept. 21, 1964.

Three generations of the Luke Thomas family have owned this farm—Luke Thomas, Charles Thomas, and Carl and Velma Hobson, the present owners. *Submitted by Velma Thomas Hobson.*

THOMPSON - CLEVENGER

Leslie Blaine Thompson, son of James Howard and Pearl Lilia (Powell) Thompson, was born on Feb. 7, 1887 in Clinton County. Minnie May (Heflin) Thompson was his first wife and they had two sons, Jack Heflin and Ted Richard Thompson.

Jeannette Adeline Clevenger, daughter of Frederick Guy and Hazel Lulu (Keck) Clevenger, was born on Feb. 7, 1907.

Jeannette and Leslie were married in 1936 and had one son, Larry Lee Thompson. They resided at 2124 Apperson Way North. Leslie died on Aug. 6, 1957 and Jeannette lived there for another 25 years before her death on Sept. 7, 1982. They are buried in Crown Point Cemetery, in Kokomo, IN. *Submitted by Marty and Larry Thompson.*

THOMPSON-LUDWIG

Larry was born near Sims, IN March 5, 1937 to Leslie Blaine and Jeannette Adeline (Clevenger) Thompson. Larry is a 1954 graduate of Kokomo High School. He served in the Army Reserve with the 199th Ordinance Co. and was honorably discharged as a staff sergeant.

Larry worked part-time at Smith Brothers Electric until graduation when he became a full-time employee there.

In 1956 Larry married Ethel Louise Kelly, daughter of Kenneth and Martha (Baer) Kelly. They had a son, Michael David Thompson, born July 15, 1957.

Larry and Marty Thompson and Amy Ludwig.

Larry worked at Perfect Circle, in Tipton, for about two years before he tried, unsuccessfully, to become an insurance salesman. He brought his family back to Kokomo, lived at 2135 North Ohio Avenue, and worked again at Smith Brothers Electric. On Aug. 4, 1964 he was hired by Delco Radio, now Delco Electronics, as an electrician.

Larry moved to 2012 North Bell Street on Jan. 1, 1970. His son Michael graduated from Purdue University in 1979 and married Lynda Clare Robinson on June 20, 1981. They reside in Denver, CO.

Martha Colleen 'Marty' Ludwig was born on Oct. 22, 1954 to Donald William and Mildred Marie (Ryan) Ludwig. Marty's family moved from Kokomo to Amboy, IN in 1959. Marty is a 1973 graduate of Oak Hill High School. Marty has a daughter, Amy Jo Ludwig, born Sept. 20, 1974, also a graduate of Oak Hill High School, class of 1993. Marty works at Delco Electronics, where she met Larry.

Larry and Marty were married on Dec. 26, 1990 in Kokomo.

Larry enjoys music, model trains, and is involved with Delco Toastmasters.

Marty collects old milk bottles, milk caps and novelty watches.

Marty and Larry enjoy movies, eating out and genealogy together. They currently reside at 2012 North Bell Street, Kokomo, IN. *Submitted by Marty and Larry Thompson.*

THOMPSON-POWELL

James Howard Thompson (1842-1894), son of Richard and Abigail (Lay) Thompson was born in Darke County, OH. He served in Ohio's Volunteer Inf. during the Civil War. After the war he moved to Texas and was a Texas Ranger for several years.

Pearl Lilia Powell (1867-1941) was the daughter of Elcanah and Mary Ann (McCool) Powell.

In the mid-1880s, James Howard Thompson moved to Kokomo, IN and met and married Pearl Lilia Powell. They had two sons, Leslie Blaine and Leonard Thompson. James and Pearl are buried in Crown Point Cemetery, in Kokomo, IN. *Submitted by Marty and Larry Thompson.*

GENE AND RUTH MAE THOMPSON

Gene Gordon was born Aug. 16, 1934 in Frankfort, IN. He graduated in 1952. He worked for Nickel Plate Railroad, then joined the army in 1957 and served two years in Germany in the 11th Airborne Unit. He joined Delco Electronics in Kokomo August 1961 as a tinsmith.

Ruth Mae Delrymple Thompson was born in Prairie Township, Tipton County Aug. 6, 1929. She moved to Middlefork, IN in 1945, then to Burlington, IN in 1946, graduating from Burlington in 1947. She joined Delco Electronics in 1953, moving to Howard County in 1954 and retiring in 1988.

Gene and Ruth met at Delco in 1963 and married May 31, 1969. They have four children, Robert Gene Achor born Aug. 3, 1950 and died Nov. 27, 1988; Debra Elizabeth Cottingham Pullen born Dec. 10, 1957; Darlene Kay Cottingham Williams born June 17, 1960; and Michael Gene Thompson born Jan. 20, 1974 who is now in the 82nd Airborne, Fort Bragg, NC.

Gene's parents are Fay (deceased) and Mildred Woods Thompson of Frankfort, IN. His paternal grandparents were W. Ira and Grace Schoff Thompson. His maternal grandparents were Mary Pearl Heatherington and Hubert Woods. His maternal great-grandparents were John and Ann Overstreet Woods and William and Mary Jo Heatherington.

Ruth's parents were George and Pauline Elizabeth Hatt Delrymple of Burlington, IN. Her paternal grandparents were David and Joan Emery Delrymple from Windfall, IN. Her maternal grandparents were Prince A. and Gertie Mae Parkey Hatt of Kokomo, IN. Her great-grandparents were William and Susanna Hollingsworth Hatt and William and Sarah Hughes; great-great-grandparents were Joseph and Cynthia McKinney Hatt and Alfred and Mary E. Parkey.

They have seven grandchildren: Robert and Scott Achor of Kokomo, IN; Ryan Pullen, Shanna and Leena Williams of Burlington, IN; and Windy and Elizabeth Achor of Vacaville, CA.

HEADLEY THOMPSON

David Headley (Headley) Thompson, Sr. was born in Kendallville, IN in 1876. He married Emma Gertrude Crawford of Castleton in 1905 and moved to Kokomo in 1917. They had three children, Ralph, Elizabeth and David Jr. Headley was secretary/treasurer of Sailors Brothers Furniture Store for 35 years. He owned land in Florida but lost it after the stock market crash in 1929. As a young man he was middleweight boxing champion, strung guitars and played with a band throughout northern Indiana. He was a member of Kokomo's Main Street Christian Church and sang in their choir. He must have inherited some of his mother's talents as she was a singer and performer on the old Chautauqua circuit that traveled around the Midwest in the 1860s. Headley was well-known for his unusual sense of humor which he often displayed by writing and telling funny stories and poems. Many writings are now in the possession of his grandchildren who still live in Kokomo.

Ralph was also an amateur musician. He played the piano and mandolin in the family band and violin in the high school orchestra. He married Esther Wanita Duncan in 1928. He was traffic manager for the Nickel Plate Railroad in Kokomo, Tipton and Michigan City, IN. He worked for the Grand Union Tea Company and in 1935 began his career at the Kokomo Chrysler Transmission Plant where he was supervisor in Production Control. He and Esther began their family in a five room bungalow on South Indiana which he had purchased while still in high school with money he earned passing papers. The family soon outgrew the bungalow so he moved his family to a larger house at 709 South Main. He had five children, Beverly, Keith, Lewis, Martha and Charles (Chuck), all born in Kokomo. Ralph died in 1968. Esther married Howard Woodward in 1979. She died in 1990.

Elizabeth graduated from Kokomo High School and the University of Wisconsin. She taught school in New Orleans where she married Milton Adler. Elizabeth had many credits to her name. She was listed in "Who's Who of American Women," was a free lance writer and decided to become a photographer at the age of 65. She published calendars featuring pictures of Florida wildlife and wrote stories concerning the environment to accompany her pictures published in the "Florida Wildlife" magazine. She also wrote and took pictures for tourist brochures at various Florida resorts. She divorced Adler in the 1960s and lived in Florida until she died in January 1986. She had two children, Ruth and Coleman.

David Jr. also played in the family band and graduated from Kokomo High School. In 1932 he married Regina May Peek of Indianapolis. He served in the Army during WWII in the Philippines. He worked for Wembley Tire Company in New Orleans, but returned to Kokomo and worked for Chrysler until he retired and moved to Florida. He had three sons, Sherman, Raymond and Mark (stillborn) all born in Kokomo. He and Regina have three grandchildren and four great-grandchildren all living in Kokomo and Howard County. David died in 1986 and Regina lives in Inverness, FL. *Submitted by Raymond Thompson.*

RALPH WESLEY THOMPSON

All five children of Ralph and Esther (Duncan) Thompson were born in Kokomo. Beverly married Donald Wheeler and their story is noted under the James H. Wheeler family.

Keith (deceased in 1986) played basketball for Northwestern High School. He married Johanna (Jo) Powers in 1952 and served in the occupational army in Japan from 1952 until 1954. He came home and started his family while farming the land that had once belonged to his maternal grandfather at Center, IN. He worked for Stellite, Dietzen's Bakery and Chrysler. He and Jo had seven children, Julia (Henry), Keith Patrick, Jay, David, Elizabeth (Pitcher), Charles and Richard. Julia lives in Geneva, IN, Jay lives in Leiters Ford, IN, David lives in Holiday, FL and the rest of the children reside in the Kokomo area. Jo has 12 grandchildren and 2 step-grandchildren.

Keith may be remembered for his free-lance writing contributions to the "Sports Page" newspaper published in Kokomo in the early 1980s. He wrote in dialect with a flair for depicting humorous situations that happened or could have happened to him and his family. One partially true story tells how his son-in-law pulled him into the Tippecanoe River after standing up in their fishing boat; another tells of his grandfather teaching him to make a kite. Only those who knew him well could tell fact from fiction.

Lewis and Keith graduated in the same class at Northwestern High School. Lewis went on to graduate from Indiana Central College where he met Carlotta (Carla) Martinez. They now reside in Concord, CA where they are both teaching in area high schools. They had three children, Brent, born in Indianapolis, IN, Teresa and John both born in Concord, CA. Brent lives in Concord, Teresa in Dallas, TX and John in Sacramento, CA. They have three grandsons all living in Concord.

Martha (Marty) married Mike Cardwell Sr. of Kokomo. Mike worked at Cabot. They were divorced in 1975. Marty worked in payroll at Kingston Products in

Kokomo. She later worked for Howard Johnson and Shenanigans, and currently works at Delco Electronics. She and Mike had four children, Karen (deceased in 1958), Cynthia (Pounds), Michael II and Michelle. Cynthia lives in Chicago, Michael II lives in Kokomo and Michelle is in college in Orlando, FL. Marty has six grandchildren, three living in Howard County.

Charles (Chuck), who played basketball for Northwestern High School and Wabash College, moved to New Orleans to learn the jewelry business. He attended Tulane but soon decided he did not want to pursue a career as a jeweler, so transferred to Louisiana State in Lafayette, LA to complete his education. He is a stock broker for Prudential. At Louisiana State University he met and married Louise Mouton. They had five children: Charles David Jr., Peter, Sean, Eric and Catherine. He was divorced in 1983 and in 1985 married Donna Thomas. He has two step-sons, Stephen and Kevin. His son Charles (David) is finishing law school in Massachusetts; Peter is teaching school in New Orleans. The other children are attending high school and/or college. *Submitted by Johanna Thompson.*

THORNE - In 1847, Jacob Thorne and his wife, Nancy "Lucy", arrived in Howard County from Lauramie Township in Tippecanoe County, IN. They were first settlers there in 1827. Jacob bought 185 acres in Harrison Township. It was noted that he paid cash silver. The land included a cleared area and a primitive log cabin. His farm was located on West Defenbaugh, in the area known as Twin Springs. It was so named because of the flowing of two natural springs from opposite banks of a pair of hills located near Twin Springs Cemetery. Part of that land is now known as Sugar Mill Homesites.

Three sons and three daughters were to survive and marry. Charles, born in 1823, married Sophornia Long, died in 1871, leaving nine children. One, Dr. J.T. Thorne, was an early mayor of Kokomo. James, the second son, died at twenty-one, leaving one child who died in infancy. Daughters: Mary Jane, married Robert Long; Elizabeth, married C. Salenbarger; and Hester married Richard Dimitt.

Walker (1834-1919); Thomas (1855-1929)

Walker Manwarring Thorne, Jacob's third son, born in 1834, walked with his parents to Howard County at age 12 years. In 1854, he married America Long, daughter of T.A. Long, Circuit Judge. He continued the task of transforming the farm, which was forest, into one of the most fertile farms in the county. Walker's only child, Thomas, lived all his life on the family farm. He played an active part in the Twin Springs community, and served on the County Council. He married Mary Bowen, daughter of William Bowen. Two children, Ned and Paul were born in the 1880s. Paul left the farm, moving his family to Kokomo. One of two daughters, Miriam Thorne Fell lives in Kokomo.

Ned Bowen Thorne married E. Blanch Stout on Jan. 1, 1904. They continued to farm the original acres until 1929. The death of Thomas, taxes, and the Great Depression took a steep toll and the land was sold at auction. With the proceeds, after taxes and debts, a smaller homestead at the north edge of West Middleton, also Harrison Township, was purchased at tax auction. Ned helped introduce soybeans to the county and was an agent for the DeLaval Milking machine. Although he never returned to extensive farming, he continued in agro-business.

Ned (1884-1964); John (1907)

Ned's son, John T. Thorne, grew up on the original acreage, graduating from West Middleton High School in 1925. He graduated from Purdue University School of Agriculture in 1929. He went to work for DeLaval Separator Company. In 1972, after 43 years, he retired to the banks of the Little Wildcat on the north side of West Middleton.

John Thorne's daughter and grandson, "J.T.", live on the acreage. Another grandson owns a small farm, less than five miles from Jacob's land. He, with his son, work the same soil as Jacob did 147 years ago, not by hand or by team as Walker, Thomas, Ned and John, but with a John Deere.

Jacob, Nancy, their sons and daughters and their families and many descendants, rest together in Twin Springs Cemetery, very close to the site of the first log cabin. *Submitted by Joanna Thorne Keller*

JOHN AND MARY FRANCIS TOBIAS - John was born Nov. 24, 1909 to Oliver and Nora Wilson Tobias, in Howard County, IN. He spent his entire life here except for his service time. John served with the United States Army during WWII and was stationed overseas in France, Germany, and Italy as well as Key West, FL where he met and married Mary Francis Beasley. They were married in Coral Gables, March 11, 1944. Mary Francis was born in Beckley, WV to John T. and Erma I. Johnson Beasley April 28, 1920.

John and Mary Francis Tobias

John has four sisters, Anna Bell, Mary, Doris and Bernice, and one brother, George. George Tobias was a Kokomo attorney until his death.

John graduated from Kokomo High School in 1928 and from Indiana University in 1933, with a degree in accounting. He worked for Continental Steel before going to the service, then with Cuneo Press for two years, retiring from Delco Radio with twenty-one years service.

He was active in the Elks and a member of Grace Methodist Church. After he retired, he donated his time to the county courthouse in helping to complete their bookkeeping system. He was also appointed to act as city comptroller for a short time.

Mary Francis worked in downtown Kokomo for Lord's Jewelers and the K & S Department Store for several years after coming to live in Kokomo when John was discharged from the service. She retired from Chrysler Casting Plant after 27 years service.

GLADYS EVA TODD - Gladys Eva was born July 11, 1890 in Noblesville, IN, the daughter of Joseph and Anna Watson (Calloway) Kelly. Her adoptive parents were Henry and Harriett Sophronia (Tharp) Todd.

She was a graduate of Maplewood Classical School and attended Purdue University in West Lafayette, IN and the University of Michigan in Ann Arbor. She was employed as one of the first telephone operators in Kokomo. She retired from J.C. Penney's in 1954. She was a member of the First United Brethren Church, at the northeast corner of West Monroe and North Washington streets, Kokomo. Gladys Eva sang in the church choir for over 50 years and was a member of the Progressive Sunday School class.

Gladys Eva Todd

She was an honorary member of the Kokomo Woman's Dept. Club, the American Legion auxiliary, and the Kokomo Art Association. Her hobby was china painting and she took classes while attending Purdue University, West Lafayette, IN. She enjoyed baking and needlepoint and gardening. She had over 90 roses at one time and George Yeagy and Cliffie Gates started her first roses and Japonica hedge, intertwined with purple wisteria, in the mid 1930s.

In 1943, she married Phaon Aughe, a childhood sweetheart, on his part. Phaon died in 1954 at the age of 63. Gladys Eva died Nov. 30, 1987 at the age of 97.

TOLLE - Nancy Applegate Tolle was born 1808, daughter of Jacob and Hannah Rummnes Applegate. Married Benham Tolle Dec. 23, 1823. They lived in Kentucky and moved to Rush County, IN in 1835. They had 13 children. Benham Tolle died Dec. 23, 1853 and is buried in Hannegan Cemetery, Rush County, IN. Nancy moved to Howard County ca 1870. She died Jan. 2, 1878 and is buried in Albright Cemetery, Howard County. Their children were: William, born 1824, died 1901, lived in Howard County; Levi, born 1826, died 1868, married Nancy Moke; James, born 1827; Strather, born 1826 died 1856, married Mary Johns, lived in Tipton and Grant counties; Caroline, born 1831, died in 1908 buried in Albright Cemetery; Elvira, born 1833, married Jacob Sutton; Jonathan, born 1835, died 1912. Served in the Civil War. Lived in Illinois before moving back to Howard County; Lucretta, born 1837; John Sutton died 1922, lived in Tipton County; Henry, born 1839, married, first Sarah Witson, second Minervia Witson, died in 1913. Lived in Howard County; Robert, born 1842, died 1853, buried in Hannegan Cemetery next to father Benham; Minervia, born 1844, married Ben Osborne, died in 1915, lived in Windfall, IN; Permilla, born 1847, married George W. Leisure, died in 1908, lived in Elwood, Madison County, IN; and Nancy Jane, born 1851, married William Fleenor.

Nancy Applegate Tolle

323

The 12th child born to Benham and Nancy Tolle, Permilla, married George W. Leisure. They had eight children. Their second child, Effie, born 1870, in Grant County, married Theodore Wardwell in 1886. They lived in Madison County, Elwood, IN. She died in 1960 and is buried in Elwood City Cemetery. Effie and Theodore Wardwell had four children. Their second child, born 1893, Armelia, married Kay Bradley from Scottsville, KY in 1914. Armelia and Kay Bradley had five children. All born in Elwood, Madison County. Their eldest son, Theodore, born in 1915, married Mina Sprong in 1936. They had six children, all born in Madison County. They lived in Elwood, Muncie and Anderson, IN. Theodore Bradley died in 1987 and is buried in Anderson. He worked for Grand Laundry and Anderson Laundry for about 40 years, retiring from Anderson Laundry in 1986. Their second child, Janice, born in 1940, married Laurence Blanchard in 1962 in Anderson, IN. They have four children: Patricia, born 1962; George, born 1965; Norman, born 1966, all in Muncie, IN; and Eveline, born 1972 in Kokomo, IN. This being the seventh generation from the original ancestor in Howard County, Nancy Tolle.

Laurence and Janice Blanchard moved to Kokomo from Muncie in 1967. Laurence is a watchmaker and Janice is a homemaker. She also is a volunteer and substitute in the Howard County Room at the Kokomo Public Library.

TOUBY - The history of Howard County would not be complete without the Touby family. John Peter Touby was an early Howard County pioneer. He, along with his wife and young son, first settled in Howard County in 1853. The Touby name is now extinct in Howard County, but many Touby descendants remain here under numerous other family names. This biography is only one branch of the Touby family tree.

John Peter Touby was born on Jan. 20, 1824 in Selters, Germany, the second son of John Martin (1795-1872) and Anna Marie (1802-1877) Touby. He was one of ten children. The Touby family left Germany on April 20, 1844 to escape military training and to pursue religious and political freedom. They arrived in New York City on June 30, 1844 and settled near Mansfield, OH.

While their parents remained and were later buried near their Ohio home, John Peter moved to Bentenville, IN in 1850. There he married Jane D. Colville on March 8, 1851. Their first child, Albert Colon, was born on Nov. 21, 1851.

The next move was to Howard Township, Howard County in September 1853. In May of 1854, they moved a short distance to what was later called the Touby homestead where two daughters were born.

Until his death on Oct. 27, 1888, Peter Touby devoted his attention to farming and his Christian beliefs. He was a prominent member of the community, and he and his family were featured in the 1877 Howard County Atlas. A gravel road, built in 1882, was named in his honor and is known to this day as Touby Pike on which the Touby homestead was located.

Albert C. Touby was married to Kate Willits on Oct. 2, 1883. They had six children named Alice, Grace, Emmett, Jennie, Mary and Bessie. Albert and his family were members of the Rich Valley Christian Church. Albert was a successful farmer and acquired 240 acres six miles northeast of Kokomo in Howard Township. He died Oct. 21, 1931. Kate died Sept. 12, 1941.

Bessie Touby, Albert's and Kate's youngest child, was born Sept. 26, 1896. On Feb. 19, 1920, she was married to William Shell Lovejoy soon after his return from WWI. They made their home in Taylor Township, Howard County and became members of the Macedonia Christian Church. Bessie and Shell raised four children, Kathleen, Charlotte, Peter and Miriam.

Shell was a farmer and died Aug. 19, 1975. Bessie lived to be 96 years old and devoted her life to God, her family and her needlework. She was an inspiration to everyone, and it is to her memory that this biography is dedicated. She was very proud of her heritage. She died May 7, 1993.

Kathleen Lovejoy, oldest child of Bessie and Shell, was born May 10, 1921. She married F. Wayne Cannon on Jan. 11, 1942. Soon after they were married, Wayne served in Germany in WWII. After the war, they raised three children in Taylor Township, Howard County. Both are retired, Wayne from Continental Steel and Kathleen from Taylor School Corporation. However, they stay active in Macedonia Christian Church and attending grandchildren activities. Kathleen also keeps the sewing machine very busy. Their family includes: Richard and Linda (Fennell) Cannon and their children, Matthew and Jennifer; Sue and Hugh Wyrick and their children, Corey and Carissa; and Beth and Ed Snavely and their son, Brandon.

Kathleen and Wayne Cannon, Richard Cannon and his family and Sue Wyrick and her family still reside in Howard County 140 years after Peter Touby first settled here. *Submitted by Sue Wyrick.*

TRABUE-SIMPSON - Ephraim Trabue was born Dec. 13, 1796 in what is now Pohatan County, VA to David and Elizabeth Sallee Trabue. The family migrated to Jessamine County, KY and eventually settled on a farm about 15 miles southwest of Lexington. Ephraim helped with his father's farm and mill, and attended school every winter. On Nov. 19, 1820 Ephraim married Elizabeth Long. They came to Lawrence County, IN in 1832 but after farming there decided to find more level land to farm. In 1842 they moved to Taylor Township, Howard County, IN. Ephraim entered 160 acres of land from the government and was successful enough in farming to buy another 160 acres in his later years. Part of his acreage was laid out in lots to develop the town of Tampico, now known as Center, IN. The original plat was in 1852. An additional part of the town was made by Elizabeth Trabue in later years. Children of Ephraim and Elizabeth were William David Trabue, April 2, 1828-Nov. 13, 1897; Massa Malissa Trabue May 21, 1831-Feb. 28, 1920; Marion Minter Trabue March 26, 1834-Jan. 25, 1884; Louise Elizabeth Trabue Dec. 24, 1836-June 24, 1914.

Back row: Eugene Simpson, Orin, Lawrence, Carrie and Norman. Front row: Rev. Denton Simpson, Elsie, Massa Malissa and Bertha ca. 1885.

Ephraim and Elizabeth Long Trabue are both buried in the Albright Cemetery near Kokomo, IN. Other Trabues are also buried there.

William David Trabue later changed his name to William H. Tribette. That in itself is an interesting story.

On Oct. 7, 1849 Malissa Trabue married Denton Simpson who had come to the area after being educated at Franklin College and Indiana University. He was born Dec. 15, 1823, near Bono in Lawrence County. His parents were Elisha and Mary Davis Simpson - Elisha from South Carolina and Mary from Virginia. Elisha and his wife's family were prosperous as farmers and land speculators. The Trabues must certainly have known the Simpson family well in southern Indiana.

Denton Simpson taught one of the first subscription schools in the area. Soon he and Malissa bought a farm east and north of Tampico. Denton became affiliated with the Baptist Church and was ordained a minister in the church on March 13, 1854 and served until the fall of 1906. During that time he continued farming, moving to land he purchased east of Tampico. Children of Denton and Malissa were: Eugene, Lawrence, Orin, Elsie, Carrie and Norman. Ava and Elizabeth died very early. Bertha died at age 18. Eugene joined an uncle in business in Mississippi. Orin who attended Indiana and Valporaiso Universities became a teacher. Lawrence also taught school. Elsie married and moved to California and Carrie graduated from the University with an M.D. degree. Norman became a dentist and practiced in Kokomo.

Children of Denton and Malissa Simpson were: Eugene born Sept. 19, 1852, died March 19, 1917; Orin born June 13, 1854, died July 11, 1936; Lawrence born Feb. 22, 1856; Elsie born July 27, 1861; Carrie born Nov. 27, 1867; and Norman born Dec. 27, 1871.

Orin is buried in Crown Point Cemetery, Kokomo, IN. Carrie is buried in Albright Cemetery southeast of Kokomo, IN.

TRACEWELL - Corwin D. Tracewell was born June 7, 1940 in Wellington Hospital, Wellington, KS to Donald Dailey Tracewell (1912-1985) and Goldie Genieve (Reeves) Tracewell (1918-1985), living in Kansas all of his life and graduating from Wellington High School in 1958. He worked for the *Wellington Times* until joining the Air Force in 1961. After basic training he was stationed at Bunker Hill Air Force Base through 1965.

Patricia L. (Holderith) Tracewell was born July 2, 1943 to Clarence Patrick Holderith (1906-1968) and Nollie Genieve (Smith) Holderith (1907-1990) at St. Joseph Hospital in Kokomo. She made her home with her parents at 1000 North Webster St., attending St. Patrick's Elementary School and graduating from Kokomo High School in 1961. She then attended Kokomo Business College for one year and worked for five years as secretary-receptionist at Kokomo Sanitary Pottery.

Corwin was employed at the T-Way, Montgomery Wards, Hoosier Rack and Engineering Company and Chrysler Transmission Corp. where he has worked for the past 25 years.

On Aug. 19, 1967 Corwin and Pat were married at St. Patrick's Catholic Church. After their marriage they made their home at 1317 West Taylor for five years. In 1972 they moved to 4401 Parkwood Dr. (West Point Addn.) and lived there for 18 years. In 1990 they moved to 400 West 1088 North where they now presently reside.

On Nov. 5, 1968 their first child, Corwin Patrick, was born. Corwin P. attended Northwestern Elementary, Junior High and graduated from Northwestern High School in 1988.

On July 30, 1972 their second child, Christine Marie, was born. Christine M. attended Northwestern Elementary, Junior High and graduated from Northwestern High School in 1991. On May 23, 1993 she became the mother of Caleb James born at St. Joseph Hospital in Kokomo.

On Sept. 23, 1974 Cara Ann was born. She attended Northwestern Elementary, Junior High and her first two years of high school at Northwestern. Her last two years of high school she attended the Indiana Academy of Science Mathematics and Humanities at Muncie, IN, graduating in the second class to ever graduate from this new school in Indiana.

Corwin's paternal grandparents were Jesse Hugh Tracewell (1882-1957) and Martha Pearl (Dailey) Tracewell (1888-1962) of Dalton, KS. His maternal grandparents were William Madison Reeves and Emma Elmira (Seckenger) Reeves of Ord, NE.

Patricia's paternal grandparents were Peter H. Holderith (1849-1922) and Cecilia Ann (Renie) Holderith (1865-1948) of Tipton and Jennings Counties, IN. Her maternal grandparents were Samuel J. Smith (1865-1930) and Cora (Curry) Smith (1867-1949) of Tipton and Franklin Counties, IN.

Corwin's paternal great-grandparents were Thomas Tracewell (1841-1911 and Sara J. Hill (1851-1911) Wellington, KS.

Patricia's paternal great-grandparents were Francis Holderith (1816-1882) and Mary Holderith (1825-1887) Jennings County, IN and Augustus Renie (1838-1917) and Catherine Gasper (1843-1916) Tipton County, IN.

Patricia's maternal great-grandparents were Wm. Smith and Mary Stevens of Tipton County, IN and Wm. A. Curry and Lucinda Stant of Franklin and Tipton Counties, IN. *Submitted by Patricia (Holderith) Tracewell.*

TRAYERS - James Trayers (1876-1957) was born in Detroit, MI, the son of Thomas Trayers and Margaret Waldron. His mother died when he was 12, and he was raised by his Aunt Mary "Minnie" and Uncle John Waldron; his father went to California. James learned the pattern fitter trade at the Michigan Stove Works in Detroit, MI, at the age of 14. On his way home from work, before his 17th birthday, he took out $0.25 from his pay envelope to play pool with friends. When he returned home his Aunt Minnie said, "You know what Uncle John will say when he gets home and finds you took out $0.25." Thus, he left home and went to Piqua, OH. It was in Piqua that he met and married Louise Meiring, the daughter of Frank Meiring and Katherine Sauer. In 1904 "Jimmy" was pursued by three stove companies. One offered $2.75/day and raised it to $3/day, but the Globe Stove and Range Corp. won out. With the move to Kokomo in 1904 Jimmy worked as a pattern fitter for the Globe and became the Superintendent in 1932. During the Depression he worked at a gas station and later the Anderson Stove Company. He returned to the Globe (1939) as Superintendent and continued in that position until he retired (1955). Jimmy enjoyed fishing and baseball. At one time he was treasurer and a fourth owner of the Kokomo Red Sox. He also liked the cherry pies his wife Louise would make. They had two children, William and Mary Katherine.

Trayers Family. Back row, l-r: James Commodore, Mary Louise (Trayers) Commodore, Dolores (Kulow) Trayers. Middle: Bill Trayers Jr., Jim Hall, Arol "Brownie" Hall, Kathryn Trayers, Dee Trayers. Sitting on arm of couch left: Joanna Hall. Sitting: Mary K. (Trayers) Hall, Louise Trayers, James Trayers, Bill Trayers. Child: (sitting on lap between James Trayers and Bill Trayers) Marsha Commodore. Sitting on arm of couch, right: Louisa Hall. 50th anniversary - James and Louisa Trayers, Sept. 23, 1946.

William (1897-1957), was born in Piqua, OH, married Dolores (Kulow) (1898-1971) and they had five children. Mary Louise (James Commodore), children: Marsha (Bruce Dodd) and Marie (David Becker); James, died at birth; Kathryn (Wayne Clark), children: Mark (Carrie Hoy) all above from Kokomo, Mary (Mike Magiera) Sharpsville, and Michael (Darla Long) Walton; Doloris (Louie Kurtz), Florida, children: Linda, Sandra, Doloris and William; and William (Martha), Michigan, children: William "Jim", Susan, Diane, Robert and John.

Mary Katherine (1905-1986) was born in Kokomo. After high school (1924) Mary K. was a bookkeeper at the Kokomo Stamped Metal Company. Her religion was a very important part of her life which she lived by helping others. When someone wanted to repay her kindness, she requested they help someone else and that would be payment for her. June 9, 1930 Mary K. married her high school sweetheart of seven years, Arol "Brownie" Hall (see Hall). They and Mary's parents built 1007 and 1009 N. Webster; this remained the family home until Brownie's death in 1989. When James Trayers retired as Superintendent of the Globe, Brownie became the Superintendent.

Brownie and Mary K. had three children: James (Alice Harris), a dentist in Indianapolis, children: Tom and Kathleen (Bruce Bernard). Louise (Andrew Miller), a nurse Health Services Consultant in Arlington Heights, IL, children: Joe, Mary (Don Prechodko), John, Paul (Karen Artus), Jean (Kent Pharr) and Jim. Joanna (Robert Edgerly) a nurse, lives and works in Denver, CO. *Submitted by Louise (Hall) Miller.*

TROYER - Michael Troyer (1730-1807) migrated to this country about 1745 with his mother. He married Magdalena Mast (1736-1827). Their children were John, Michael, Christian, Barbara, Magdalena, Anna, Jacob, Henry, Mary, Joseph, Andrew, David, Veronica and Elizabeth. They lived in Pennsylvania.

This son, Michael, married Anna Rickenbach and their children were Magdalena, Anna, John, and Abraham. Anna died and Michael married Magdalena Rickenbach, a cousin to the first wife. The children of the second marriage were Jacob, Daniel and Joseph. This family lived in Pennsylvania.

This son, John (1777-1813), married Magadelena Miller (1781-1820). Their children were Samuel, Mary, Abraham, Michael, John and Sarah.

This Michael (1810-1855) married Barbara Miller (1810-1889). This family lived in Ohio. Their children were Jonathan, John, Magdalena, Catherine, Anna, Veronica, Mary, Gertrude, Jeremiah, Barbara, Michael, and Jacob.

This John (1835-1912) in 1852 married Catherine Schrock (1835-1874), daughter of Henry and Barbara (Miller) Schrock. They lived north of Walnut Creek, OH. Their children were Henry, Barbara, Benjamin, John died young, Lizzie Ann, Amanda, Lucinda, Katie, Michael, Eli and Noah. In March 1873 they moved to 550 E 400 N Howard County, IN. In May 1874 they had Mary June and in a few days both mother and daughter died. On Dec. 11, 1874 John married Caroline (Schrock) Kendall (1848-1925), a cousin to Catherine. Caroline's first husband was Simon Kendall. He was a blacksmith who died in an explosion at his shop. Caroline brought two children to this marriage - Emma and Simon Kendall. The children of this marriage were Harve, Sarah, died young, Edward, Ellsworth, Mattie and Joseph. Then in 1881 they moved one-half mile east to the southwest corner of 400 N 600 E. The next born was infant died young, Nathaniel, Emanuel, Nora, infant died young, infant died young, Callie, infant died young, George, infant died young, infant died young. So John fathered 29 children by two wives in a span of 38 years. When the last child was born in 1892, John was 62 and Caroline was 44. This was one of the largest families around. For many years there were 15 or more at each meal besides friends and relatives. The raising of this family was surely an enormous job. Besides being a farmer, John operated a sawmill across the road from his house with a neighbor John Miller. Caroline had an outside bake oven where they would bake 15 pies for the weekend.

Benjamin (1857-1940) in 1881 married Elizabeth Shrock (1861-1905). Their children were Laird, Jennie, Glen, Percy and Carrie. In 1908 Ben married Melissa Lantz and Orval was born.

Laird was to be the mayor of Lansing, MI for two terms.

Jennie lived to be 101.

Glen was a school teacher.

In 1922 Carrie (1900-1968) married the boy next door, Joseph Marner (1899-1978). Their children are Gene, Beulah, Kenny, Wayne, Wilbur and the writer, Larry. Four of these lived in Howard Township. *Submitted by Larry Marner.*

TURNER - The Turners were early pioneers of Kokomo, Howard County, IN.

John Turner was born about 1825 in North Carolina. He married Feb. 17, 1846 Louisa Jackson in Orange County, NC. They settled in Jackson Township, Howard County, IN where they planted their roots. They had three children, Mary was born (1846), Nancy (1850) and Andrew Jackson Turner (March 4, 1854-Dec. 21, 1935). John Turner, a laborer, enlisted Aug. 9, 1862 in Co. D, 89th Regt., Indiana Inf. for three years. At age 37, he received an honorable discharge July 19, 1865 in Mobile, AL. It is believed that he died around 1881 in Madison County, IN.

Andrew Jackson Turner married Oct. 19, 1882 Sarah Ruanna Gustin (Nov. 13, 1866-Dec. 3, 1918). She was the daughter of John W. Gustin (May 24, 1840-Feb. 8, 1929) and Francena Ellis (Aug. 14, 1846-Jan. 1, 1925). Both Andrew and Ruanna are buried in Pendleton. Andrew and Ruanna had seven children. The first three children died in infancy: Albert (1883), Carrie (1884), Verna (1885), Roy Ray (July 10, 1886-Sept. 8, 1964), Mrs. Harry (Valeria Blanch) Moore (March 31, 1893-Jan. 22, 1966), twins born in Pendleton, Mrs. Lloyd (Bessie Francena) Miller (Jan. 24, 1897-June 3, 1918) and Burrell Fredrick (Jan. 24, 1897-Jan. 27, 1974).

Burrell Fredrick and Nancy Stanley Turner

In Anderson, IN, Burrell married March 8, 1919 Nancy Marie Stanley. She was born Jan. 7, 1902 in Lagro, IN, daughter of James Alexandria Stanley born in Wellington, MO (Jan. 28, 1876-July 23, 1954) and Anna Isabelle Stroud born in Elwood, IN (Feb. 18, 1872-June 22, 1952). Burrell and Nancy had eight children: Horace Edward (Oct. 14, 1919-March 30, 1920), Paul Leon (March 5, 1921), Mrs. Ronald (Janet Isabelle) Wigent (March 9, 1924), Joseph Henry (Aug. 20, 1926), Mrs. Edgar (Barbara Mae) Miller (June 29, 1929), Fredrick Neil (February 1934-May 9, 1934), Jack Dean (Oct. 16, 1935), and Daniel Kent (April 5, 1943).

Burrell and Nancy owned a sporting goods store in Anderson before moving their family to Michigan in 1930. They settled in Riverside, MI where they operated a grocery store. Burrell had described those years as the time of the ten-cents-a-dozen eggs and twelve-cents-a-pound bacon and when a grocer had to split coffee into three-cent daily portions so the people could afford some. The Turners moved again in 1934 to Coloma, MI. A tool and die maker by trade, Burrell worked for Felix Sawatzki Welding Shop and a number of shops in the Benton Harbor area before opening his own business, Turners Machine Shop, at his home in 1946. He retired in 1963 turning his business over to his sons. Burrell and Nancy traveled and enjoyed collecting antiques in his retirement. Burrell died at the age of 77 in Benton Harbor, MI of cancer. He is buried in Maple Hill Cemetery, Hartford, MI. Nancy (Stanley) Turner is 91 years old and still lives in Coloma. Burrell shared many fond memories of his youth in Indiana and it will be passed down for many generations.

TURNER - A long time ago there were three brothers, Shadrach, Meshack, and Abednago Turner, living in Virginia; actually it was prior to 1748. Shadrach was the owner of 4400 acres of land in Halifax County, VA. His will, made in 1783, stated that he lived in Henry County, VA and that his wife was Ann. One of their sons was William Turner (Jan. 19, 1753-Dec. 11, 1845) who married Jane Hunter (June 7, 1759?-May 20, 1851) in 1775. Their youngest child was Elkanah Benjamin Turner (Aug. 14, 1801-?). He was a Separate Baptist preacher and married Elizabeth Wingfield. One of their sons was James Copland Turner (April 17, 1849-July 15, 1929). He married Mary Elizabeth Davis (Nov. 30, 1848-Sept. 20, 1924) who was his schoolmate and neighbor in Henry County, VA in 1868.

In the late 1880s James Copland and Mary Elizabeth Turner packed up their wagon and eight children and headed west. A cousin who remembered waving goodbye from her porch said that they never came back. They came first to Bunker Hill, Miami County, IN and within a year to Kokomo, Howard County, IN. James Copland Turner was a carpenter and took part in much of the building of Kokomo. Their fourth child, Lewis Whetzel Turner (Aug. 25, 1874-Nov. 13, 1956) married Lelah Loucinda Wilson (April 28, 1881-Sept. 4, 1912) on Nov. 13, 1901. Lelah L. was the daughter of William (March 13/19, 1838-Aug. 7,

325

1914) and Ellen Jane Longfellow Wilson (July 8, 1848/ July 6, 1849-March 14, 1926). William and Ellen Jane Longfellow were married on Sept. 6/8, 1869. Ellen Jane was the daughter of John (July 8, 1821-May 25, 1908) and Elizabeth Ellis Longfellow (January 1834-April 6, 1901).

Lewis Whetzel and Lelah Loucinda Turner had two daughters, Helen and Adlove Marie (Feb. 23, 1905-April 1, 1983). Lewis Whetzel worked for the power company and retired from there in the early 1950s. Adlove Marie Turner married Ralph M. Cardwell (1902-Oct. 8, 1948) on Oct. 19, 1923 in South Bend, St. Joseph County, IN. Ralph M. Cardwell was the son of Sylvester (1870-1956) and Lena L. Harris Cardwell (1875-1956). Ralph and Adlove had two children, Adlove Joann and Ralph Lewis (July 1, 1933-).

Ralph Lewis Cardwell has spent most of his adult life as the manager and owner of the Toy Mart. On Feb. 16, 1978 he married Margaret Delores Petter Tolan (May 18, 1937-) and became the stepfather of Robert Warren Tolan Jr. (Nov. 20, 1960-), Patrick Allan Tolan (Nov. 7, 1961-) and Andrew Craig Tolan (Oct. 16, 1962-). Margaret is the daughter of William James Havergal and Miriam Lucille Tritsch Petter. She is a librarian. *Submitted by Margaret D. Cardwell.*

SAMUEL AND MARGARET (JOHNSON) TURNER
Samuel Edward Turner was born Oct. 18, 1868 in Tonganoxie, KS to Rev. Jesse T. and Avis (Paddock) Turner. Samuel had two sisters, Mary Frances (Turner) Sturdivant, wife of dentist J.S. Sturdivant, and Eva (Turner) Kaufman, wife of Dan Kaufman.

On Oct. 16, 1892 Samuel married Ora Ellen Moulder, born Aug. 27, 1866 in Orange County, IN, daughter of William and Margaret (Harned) Moulder. Two sons were born to Samuel and Ora but both died in infancy. Ora died of typhoid on Dec. 4, 1899.

On Dec. 20, 1906 Samuel married Margaret Elizabeth Johnson, born Jan. 6, 1875 in Howard County, daughter of Fleming and Rachel (Bundy) Johnson. Samuel was a graduate of William Pinkham School of Theology, Cleveland, OH, and owned a small farm in the Russiaville area. Samuel and Margaret enjoyed nearly 56 years together as husband and wife, were greatly respected in their community, and were active members of the Russiaville Friends Church. Margaret died Nov. 3, 1962. Samuel died Dec. 23, 1964. Both are buried in New London Cemetery.

The Samuel and Margaret (Johnson) Turner Family. (seated L-R) Samuel Edward Turner, Margaret Elizabeth (Johnson) Turner, Avis Rachel (Turner) Criss. (standing L-R) Fred Lewis Turner, Milley Frances (Turner) Merrill, Iryl Jesse Turner, Edith Marie (Turner) Johnston.

The following seven children were born to Samuel and Margaret, all in Howard County:

1. Avis Rachel (Turner) Criss, a former missionary and retired teacher, born Dec. 2, 1907, died March 25, 1992, and who on June 6, 1950 married Ralph Henry Criss, a retired minister, born July 12, 1909, son of Herschel and Virginia (Smith) Criss, and who survives. They have one son, Jonathan Dean Criss.

2. Harriet Esther Turner, born April 20, 1910 and died June 14, 1920.

3. Iryl Jesse Turner, a retired Delco employee, born May 19, 1911, and who married (1) on Aug. 22, 1939 Wava Mae Maurer, a retired teacher, born Sept. 8, 1911, died May 5, 1989, daughter of Samuel and Matilda (Dahl) Maurer; and (2) on April 19, 1991 Mary Verna (Stark) Givens, born Jan. 18, 1946, daughter of Ernest and Alice (Baxter) Stark. Iryl and Wava have one son, Jesse Maurer Turner. Mary has three children from a previous marriage, Elizabeth Marie (Givens) Douglas, Carol Ann Givens, and Paul Ernest Givens.

4. Stanley Ward Turner, born and died Feb. 13, 1913.

5. Milley Frances (Turner) Merrill, born Sept. 18, 1914, died March 20, 1983, and who on Aug. 20, 1938 married Rev. Elmer Granville Merrill, born March 20, 1912, died Dec. 23, 1986, son of James and Flora May (Parr) Merrill. They have two children, Elizabeth May (Merrill) Moorman Cox Nielander, and Joseph Stephen Merrill.

6. Fred Lewis Turner, a retired teacher, born Nov. 6, 1916, died Nov. 15, 1990, and who on June 10, 1942 married Sarah Evalyn Park, a retired teacher, born Sept. 10, 1918, daughter of Rev. and Mrs. James D. Park, and who survives. They have four children, James Edward Turner, Ruth Ardella (Turner) Cosand, David Lewis Turner, and Paul Eugene Turner.

7. Edith Marie (Turner) Johnston, born June 14, 1918, who on Sept. 12, 1947 married Frank W. Johnston, a retired businessman, born June 4, 1909, son of Edwin and Mary (Danfield) Johnston. Frank has two children from a previous marriage, Earl Johnston and Louise (Johnston) Ewing. *Submitted by Stacey Marie Criss.*

TYLER
Three brothers—John, David and Joseph—were born in Tennessee and lived there until about 1825 when they moved to Ohio.

John was born circa 1800. He married Mary M. Tyler in Indiana. They had two daughters, Ella and Rhoda. Ella married William James in 1882 in Howard County. Rhoda married Walter Vanmeter in 1891 in Howard County.

David Tyler was born in Tennessee in 1801. He married Mary Odem (born Tennessee 1802), and they had nine children. Martin (1829), James (1830), David (1833), John (1834), and Samuel (1836) were born in Ohio; born in Howard County, IN, were Nathan (1838), Charles L. (1840), Mary (1842), and George (1844).

Joseph Tyler was born in 1810 in Tennessee and was married in Howard County on Jan. 31, 1845, to Lucy Hutton (born Ohio, 1824). They had six children including David, James, Eyppa, Thomas, Bosewell, and Phebe A. They were all born in Ohio. Joseph's family came to Indiana circa 1836; they moved to Howard County in 1850, settling northeast of Greentown.

My great-grandfather was James J. Tyler (1830-1881), son of David (1801). James married Nancy Leffler (born Ohio 1835) on Jan. 25, 1854, in Howard County, IN. They had David (1856), Susan (1858), Louisa (1860), Barbara (1861), John (1862), Amos (1864), and Sarah J. (1867).

Sarah J. Tyler married Jesse L. Osborn on Oct. 3, 1885. They had five children: Clarence, Mertle, Virgil, Paul, and Charles F. Osborn, all born in Howard County, IN.

Charles F. Osborn, my father, married Violet J. Cobbs in 1938 at Huntington, IN. They had five children, all born at Fort Wayne, IN. They included Kenneth (1938), Charlotte (1939), myself—Richard (1942), Virgil (1949), and Mary (1951).

In the summer of 1993 I located the farm where my Tylers lived. The Tylers were some of the first settlers and builders in Howard County. My Grandmother Tyler used to say she was related to President John W. Tyler, but I have never proved it. My grandmother died in 1952. She and my grandfather are buried at Roanoke, IN. *Submitted by Richard H. Osborn.*

RAWSON VAILE
Rawson Vaile was an out-spoken Abolitionist, dedicated educator and reputable lawyer, who spent the last 31 years of his life in Kokomo. He became a strong influence in the establishment of the Free School system in the city and county.

Born in Bennington County, VT, he graduated with honors, from Amherst College in 1839. While teaching in Spencer, MA in 1840, he fell in love with a graduating student, Anna Pope, daughter of a distinguished Congregational minister. They were married that same year and immediately set to follow his brother, Dr. Joel Vaile, to the 'wilds' of Indiana, namely Richmond.

Settling near his brother, Rawson built a house in Centerville and became Head Master at Whitewater Seminary. During the summer months, he carried the mail via Pony Express between Richmond and Indianapolis. He also studied law and was admitted to the bar in 1844. While in Centerville, he published an anti-slavery newspaper. He frequently debated the issue with influential politicians, in an effort to persuade them to adapt appropriate legislation.

The Vaile House - 320 Vaile Ave. Joseph E. and Isabelle Vaile, children: Anna Pope and Rawson (twins), Victor E. and Theodore U.

After Rawson's wife died leaving him with five young children, he moved to Indianapolis to become editor of the *Free Democrat*, which later merged with the *Indianapolis Journal*. While living there, he married Rebecca Robinson. They had two children, Emma and George. He gave up journalism when he moved to Kokomo in 1857, and opened a law office on the northeast corner of the square.

Purchasing a large parcel of land on the southside of Wildcat Creek, he built an impressive two-story, red brick house near the center of his land. When a new street was plotted which bisected his property, it was appropriately named Vaile Avenue. For many years, the Good Samaritan Hospital stood just east of the house. During that time, the house served as a residence for nurses. The Senior Citizen High-Rise presently stands where the house once stood.

Rawson later built a two-story frame house at 320 Vaile Ave. Various descendants of Rawson occupied the house until 1952, when it was sold outside the family. Rawson died in this house on Dec. 30, 1888. At that time it was listed as the residence of his son, Joseph. Rawson was buried in Crown Point Cemetery, with all three of his wives.

The house he built in Centerville is listed in the National Registry of Historic Places; a marker in front of the house attests to this. Some of his personal possessions are in the Howard County Museum. *Prepared by Ted and Betty Vaile.*

VAILE
Many of Rawson Vaile's descendants left Howard County to become leaders in communities from Virginia to California. Those who remained were a vital and active part of the Kokomo community for 102 years.

His son, Joel Fredrick, was principal of the first Kokomo High School. Joel was also an attorney, practicing law from his father's office for eight years. He was County Attorney at one time. In 1880, he was chosen as delegate to the historic Republican Convention, in Chicago. Two years later he moved to Denver, CO, where he established himself as a famous lawyer by serving as general council for the Denver Rio Grande Railroad, winning their famous litigation against the Rock Island Line.

One son, Joseph, remained in Kokomo, serving as teacher, bookkeeper, County Recorder, and finally, as a popular Justice of the Peace, performing over 300 marriages. Joseph and his wife, Isabelle Voiles Vaile, had four children: Victor, Theodore, and twins, Rawson and Anna.

Joseph died May 24, 1917, at his home, 320 Vaile Ave.; burial was in Crown Point Cemetery.

Victor (Vic), married Edna Wilson. As a merchant, he operated the Vaile Shoe Store, in downtown Kokomo for many years. Later, he was a realtor and co-owner with Bob Finch in the Vaile & Finch Insurance agency. He and Edna were life-long residents of Kokomo; they are buried in Crown Point Cemetery. Their children were: Victor Edward II, Joseph and Wilson, all of whom left the area as adults.

Rawson built this two-story home (corner Vaile Ave. and Apperson). When a road was built bisecting his property (bordered by streets Union, Markland, Ohio and Wildcat Creek) it was named Vaile Avenue.

Theodore (Peany) married Juva Bell. As a youth, he delivered the *Kokomo Tribune* to the Seiberling Mansion. He served as Superintendent of the Continental Steel's Fence Plant, remaining a consultant for several years after his retirement. He and Juva raised two children at 320 Vaile Ave. They were Elizabeth and Theodore Jr. When Juva died in 1941, Theodore married her widowed sister, Edna Bell Lindsay Noggle. All three are buried in Albright Cemetery.

Elizabeth Vaile, a public librarian, married John Pickett, of Kokomo. They had one child, Patricia (Elizabeth died 10 weeks following her birth). Patricia married a Kokomo resident, Phillip Craig. They lived in Kokomo until 1968, when they moved to the Chicago area, with their three children, Desiree, Michelle and Stephen.

Theodore Jr. (Ted), married Betty McCauley, of Clay Township. Ted was an employee of Delco Electronics, Kokomo, for 40 years. He retired in 1987, as Supervisor of Material Services for the Engineering Dept. Ted also became a well-known caller and instructor of Western Square Dancing in Indiana and surrounding states. He was the last of Rawson's descendants to leave Howard County when he moved his wife and three children, Charles, Teresa and Bonita, to Miami County in 1959.

The twins of Joseph Vaile, Rawson and Anna, left Kokomo when they were grown. Rawson became Executive Vice-President with American Blower. Anna married Wilde Ingalls, of Muncie; they migrated to Richmond, VA where they established the Dominion Signal Company. *Submitted by Ted and Betty Vaile.*

VAN BRIGGLE-LAWLESS - Chester Allen Van Briggle was born Jan. 28, 1912 in Tipton County, IN. He was the second son of Walter and Huldham (James), who was of Cherokee descent.

At the age of 18 Chester enlisted in the Tipton County National Guard. He served four years in Co. E, 152nd Inf., as a marksman.

Shortly after leaving the Guards in May 1934, he married Inez Straley. The only child of the couple was Phyliss Joan, born October 1936. Inez died within two months of her birth. With no way of caring for the baby girl, Chester let her mother's family rear her.

March 1937 Chester enlisted for three more years with the Tipton County National Guards. He left on March 1940 as a sergeant.

January 17, 1941 Chester joined the Army. With his rank of sergeant he was stationed at Camp Shelby, MS. He was in leadership of teaching our young men the talents of riflery marksmanship. He left in November 1941.

During his stay in Mississippi, Chester met his second wife. On July 4, 1941 he married Mary Ruth Lawless, born April 5, 1922 in Laurel, MS. She was the daughter of James Bernard and Elizabeth (Graves) Lawless. Her father, James, was Irish, both his maternal and paternal grandparents were immigrants from Ireland.

Van Briggles—L-R: Mary, Joan, Grady and Chester.

After leaving the Army Chester and his new bride returned to Indiana. Here he felt his country still needed him, so on Jan. 24, 1942 (less than three months out) Chester joined the Army. He became a member of the 241st Replacement Co., 74th Replacement Bn. He was sent to the Western Pacific Island of Ryukyus, between Japan and the Philippines. He saw overseas action for the period of one year and nine months. He was mustered out on Oct. 12, 1945 at Camp Atterbury. Chester received the "Asiatic Pacific Theater Ribbon" with two bronze stars for bravery above and beyond the call of duty.

While Chester served, his wife Mary remained in Laurel, MS with her family. On April 28, 1942 their only child was born, Grady Bernard (G.B., Jeep) Van Briggle.

When Chester left the Army, he brought his family to Indiana. Later came two brothers-in-law, Charles and Grady Lawless. All settled in Howard County and worked at Northern Indiana Supply Company. Chester's untimely death came at age 52. Mary worked for Delco until 1975. She still resides in Kokomo.

Their son Grady worked for Delco and retired after 26 years. Much of Grady's past time is spent in the field of art, drawing posters, banners, and woodcarving, some for pleasure, others for customers.

Grady married first to Connie Glass in 1963. Children were: Randy 1964/1964; Kimberly 1965 married first David Fritz, children, David, James, Heather, married second Mathew Carpenter; Lori 1967, children, Jessica, Katelin, Briley; Robin 1969, married Michael Beard, children John, Justin, Joshua (Justin adopted by grandparents Connie and Donald Beatty); Anthony 1970, child Anthony (Jamie); Misty 1972 (last name changed to Beatty 1990).

Grady married Teena (Gordon) Mills in August 1975. She had two sons from a previous marriage; they were: Greyson 1969; David 1972. From this marriage one child was born, March 24, 1982, Chester Allen Van Briggle (named after his grandfather, whom this sketch is about).

Teena wrote "The Van Briggle Family History" in 1988 (a copy is in the Howard County Library genealogy room) showing 15 generations of Van Briggles, from Holland's famous painter Pieter Bruegel to their coming to America, where the name was changed.

Grady's third great-grandfather, Peter Van Briggle of Vevay, Switzerland County, IN, was enrolled as one of the founding families of Indiana during its year of statehood in 1816. His name was honored by being placed on a plaque in the "State House" in Indianapolis. *Submitted by Grady Van Briggle.*

VANDERGRIFF - Clyde Steven "Steve" and Teresa Diana Barnett Vandergriff met and married in Howard County, IN, April 21, 1979. They are the parents of two boys, Jeremy Steven (March 2, 1980 in Kokomo, Howard County, IN) and Joshua Ryan Vandergriff (March 18, 1983 in Knox County, Knoxville, TN).

Steve born June 27, 1955 in Howard County is the son of Clyde Horace (May 17, 1929 in Grainger County, TN-Feb. 12, 1988) and Shirley Marie Caldwell (Dec. 25, 1935 in Knox County, TN-Oct. 16, 1967) Vandergriff. Clyde and Shirley married April 8, 1950 in Knox County, TN. Clyde is buried in the Philldelphea Cemetery in Franklin County, Russelville, AL and Shirley is buried in the Memorial Park Cemetery here in Howard County; they were the parents of three children: (1) Kathy Gail; (2) Jewell Ann and (3) Clyde Steven Vandergriff.

Shirley is the daughter of Filo and Mary Miller Caldwell. Clyde Horace is the son of Oscar DeVaughn Vandergriff (April 10, 1893-April 13, 1965 in Tazwell, Claireborne County, TN), Oscar and his wife, Naomi Laura M. Williams (April 18, 1888-May 23, 1940) are buried in Dyer Cemetery. They were the parents of seven known children: (1) Mossie Ray (April 8, 1917), married Aug. 14, 1943 in Knox County, TN to Roscoe Collins; (2) Zola/Zora G. (July 23, 1919-Jan. 29, 1978), wife of Murl L. Johnson, Dyer Cemetery; (3) Susie Edna (Aug. 30, 1922-Oct. 10, 1972), married Aug. 23, 1943 in Knox County, TN to Fred Austin Bailey, both buried in Memorial Park Cemetery here in Howard County; (4) Estel Lee (May 6, 1924-June 21, 1973), wife Myrtle Clarice Haun, Dyer Cemetery; (5) Lester Carnell (June 26, 1926), wife Bessie Alice Lewelling; (6) Clyde Horace; and (7) Ronnie Vandergriff.

Oscar was the son of Alvis L. (July 1852 in Union County, TN) and Louisa M. Kirby (April 1854) Vandergriff; married Nov. 26, 1873 in Union County, TN. Alvis was a twin son born to James and Mary "Polly" Beeler Vandergriff. It is believed that Alvis and Louisa are buried in Dyer/Atkins Cemetery in Union County, TN, but no proof has been found yet; there is no marker to mark their grave and no record of death has been found as of now. They were in Grainger County, TN in the 1920 Census. They were the parents of seven known children: (1) Martha A.; (2) Jerry Lee (July 7, 1875-Oct. 13, 1945), Dyer Cemetery; (3) Mandy L.; (4) Charles Asroe; (5) Lula Isabell; (6) Oscar DeVaughn and (7) Pryor L. Vandergriff, believe there to be more children.

James Vandergriff (May 19, 1815-Feb. 23, 1898) and Mary "Polly" Beeler (1819-before 1878), were the parents of a large family, 10 known children: (1) Elizabeth "Betsy"; (2) Lindsay (June 15, 1840-Dec. 30, 1904), wife Rachel M. Shelton, McKinney Cemetery; (3) William; (4) Emeline; (5) David; (6) Gilbert; (7) James; (8) Enoch; (9) Mary Ann (July 1952), twin to (10) Alvis L.; ? (11) Charles S. (died Aug. 28, 1898). James married a second time Feb. 24, 1878 to a Nancy Baker. Charles S. could be their son; for James, Nancy and Charles are all buried in Atkins Cemetery, right beside of Dyer Cemetery in Union County. James was the son of Gilbert and Dicy Brock Vandergriff; Gilbert was the son of Jacob and Jane Vandergriff.

Steve, Teresa, Jeremy and Joshua Vandergriff.

Teresa Diana Barnett Vandergriff born Feb. 28, 1960 in Johnson City, Washington County, TN, daughter of Kenneth Wayne and Barbara Ann McInturff Barnett. *Submitted by Steve and Teresa Vandergriff.*

ELEANOR HARNESS VICTORSON - Eleanor Louise Harness was born on Dec. 8, 1912 on the Purdue University campus in West Lafayette, IN, to Russell R. Harness and Gladys Eva (Todd) Harness, as both were attending the university.

Eleanor Louise graduated from Kokomo High School in 1929, at the age of 16. She went to work as manager of the Natalie Hosiery and Lingerie Shop located on North Main Street in Kokomo in the building owned by Judge B.F. Harness.

In the early 1940s, she married Raymond Hughes Howard and they had one son, James Hughes Howard.

Eleanor owned and operated the Yarn Barn at 333 North Indiana, Kokomo, and gave knitting instructions. She was a pattern proof reader for the yarn distributor.

Bowling Friends - Third person from left is Eleanor Harness Victorson.

In July 1957 in the chapel of the First Congregational Church she was married to Martin Von Fredenhagen. The Reverend Garth Shepherd officiated. She was associated with the William H. Turner Company shoe salon. Martin Von Fredenhagen was news director of W.I.O.U. He was educated in the Middle West and helped pioneer the air traffic control system for the Civil Aeronautics Administration. He was head of the Army's Air Operations Research and Development Program. He served in the Army Air Forces throughout WWII, rising to the rank of lieutenant colonel. In 1945 and 1946 he was senior military government officer in the Kobe-Osaka region of Japan. Hagen was recalled to active service during the Korean Campaign. Mr. Hagen was world traveled and well-known in political-diplomatic-governmental-military circles in Washington, D.C.

Eleanor Louise rode horses, enjoyed oil painting and pastels, as well as needlepoint. She was a gourmet cook and collected cookbooks. Her main recreation was bowling.

Ellie, as most folks called her, organized the Civic Theatre group, at her yarn barn, and starred in the Daphne du Maurier play, "Rebecca", taken to the stage at the Sipe Theatre.

Eleanor married Charles A. Victorson in 1949 and moved to Terre Haute, IN.

Both Eleanor and husband died in 1981. Eleanor Louise is buried in Crown Point Cemetery, Kokomo, IN and Vic is buried in his hometown of Minneapolis, MN.

LESLIE W. AND FAY L. WAGNER -
Leslie William and Fay Lois (Kell) Wagner along with their two daughters, Lori Anne and Katherine Mary, relocated to Kokomo from the Milwaukee, WI, area in December 1971. Les' return to employment with Delco Electronics was the impetus for the move.

Les was born on Aug. 14, 1935 in Outagamie County, WI, where his parents, Raymond Frederick and Hazel Mary (Randerson) Wagner, farmed and raised their four children. His grandparents, William and Emma (Schucknecht) Wagner, and Christopher and Bridget (McCormick) Randerson were also farmers. Les graduated from Seymour, WI High School (1953), earned a BSEE degree from the University of Wisconsin-Madison (1958) and a MSEE degree from University of Wisconsin-Milwaukee (1971).

Fay was born on June 30, 1938 in St. Joseph Hospital, Milwaukee, WI, the daughter of Harvey Kell and Loraine (Mohr) Kell. Born of Albert and Anna (Fischer) Luedtke, Harvey was adopted (when his mother died of consumption) by George and Elise (Fenske) Kell. Fay's maternal grandparents were August and Mary (Roden) Mohr. She has one brother Larry. Her father was a railway mailclerk. Fay graduated from Rufus King High School in Milwaukee, WI (1956), and earned a BSCE degree from the University of Wisconsin-Madison (1960). She was hired as the first woman engineer of the City of Milwaukee.

Les and Fay were married on June 15, 1963 in Seymour, WI.

Les joined General Motors Corporation, AC Spark Plug Division in Milwaukee in February 1958. While employed with GM, for now 36 years, he has had diversions which included three months of Air Force Basic Training in San Antonio (1959) and assignment of one year (1964-65) to work on gyroscope development at the Massachusetts Institute of Technology, Instrumentation Laboratory in the Boston area.

Their older daughter Lori, born on March 12, 1965 in Boston, MA, was six years old upon the family move to Kokomo. She graduated from St. Joan of Arc Elementary School (1979), Taylor High School (Valedictorian - 1983), and Purdue University with a BSEE degree (1988). Four sessions of co-oping with IBM Corporation in Research Triangle Park, NC, better prepared her for industrial work experiences. While on a co-op session Lori met her future husband, Michael Richard Kosek of Naperville, IL, who also was an engineering co-op. They were married on Aug. 15, 1987 at St. Joan of Arc Church. Both began work as electrical engineers with Harris Corporation in the Melbourne, FL area in 1988. They now have three children, David Matthew (4), Krista Marie (2) and Cheryl Elizabeth (1). They have moved (Fall 1992) to Ann Arbor, MI, where Mike is employed by ERIM.

March 1992 photo, l to r: David Kosek, Michael Kosek, Lori Kosek, Krista Kosek, Kathy Wagner, Fay Wagner and Les Wagner.

Their younger daughter, Katherine, born on Dec. 15, 1970 in St. Joseph Hospital, Milwaukee, WI, was one year old when the family came to Kokomo. She also graduated from St. Joan of Arc School (1985), Taylor High School (Valedictorian - 1989) and Purdue University with a BSEE degree (1994). Kathy co-oped four sessions with IBM in Lexington, KY, and Endicott, NY. She is employed this summer with Hewlett Packard Corporation in Fort Collins, CO, but has re-enrolled at Purdue for the fall in the graduate engineering program with plans to earn a MSEE degree while being employed as a Teaching Assistant.

CLAUDE CLAY SR. AND MARIE WALL -
Claude and Marie Wall came to Kokomo in 1929 for a job at a new plant constructed by Continental Steel Corporation. Claude was working for a subsidiary of Continental Steel, Chapman Price Steel Company of Indianapolis.

Claude Sr. was born Aug. 30, 1890 in Franklin County, MO. His parents were Isaiah (1840-1916) and Amanda Caroline Hogan (1865-1948) Wall. Prior to World War I, Claude Sr. worked many jobs including the streetcar conductor in St. Louis, farm hand in Montana, Colorado and North Dakota. A job with the telephone company took him to Cuyahoga, OH in 1917. He was working for the Youngstown Sheet and Tool in October 1917 when he received his draft notice. In May 1918, he went to Europe with the American Expeditionary Force as a member of Company B, 319th Field Signal Battalion, 1st Division. He participated in the battles of Toul, 2nd Marne, St. Mihiel, Verdun, and the Argonne. He was honorably discharged in June 1919 and returned to Youngstown, OH. In 1921, he came to Indianapolis to work for Chapman Price Steel Company. While in Indianapolis, he met Marie Caplinger-Wiseman and married her in Franklin, IN, on May 24, 1923.

Clara Anna Marie Caplinger Wiseman-Wall and Claude Clay Wall

Clara Anna Marie Caplinger was born June 30, 1901 in Acton, IN, to Vernon Edgar Caplinger (1881-1944) and Gertrude May Edwards (1882-1942). In 1918 Marie met and married Harold Victor Wiseman (born 1896). They had a child, Raymond Victor, born September 15, 1919. Harold died of pneumonia on Jan. 8, 1920 and Raymond followed him, Jan. 29, 1920, of the same cause. Marie took a job with the phone company and through mutual friends met Claude Wall.

Claude and Marie were living in Indianapolis when Claude Clay Jr. was born on June 12, 1924. Claude Jr. married Janan Crume of Kokomo. Claude Sr. moved his family to Elkhart, IN, to work for Elkhart Paint and Enamel. While living there, Robert Earl was born on May 27, 1927. Robert married Marilyn Grace Barr of Tipton County. After moving to Kokomo in 1929, Patricia Louise was born on Feb. 11, 1931. Patricia married Conrad Eugene Shirar of Kokomo. Claude Sr. continued to work at various jobs with Continental Steel until his retirement in 1955. Marie lived an active life in Kokomo. She was a member of various organizations: The First Baptist Church, founding member of Mothers of World War II, held various offices in the Moriah Rebekah Lodge 109, Loyal Birthday Club, Mothers of Demolay, National Federation of Grandmothers Club, Veterans of World War I Auxiliary, Howard County Women Democrats, and Howard County Senior Citizens Club. She was a precinct committee woman and served on the Election Board. Marie died of heart failure in her home on April 27, 1969. Except for a short stay in Wabash, IN, Claude Sr. continued to live in Kokomo until his death at the age of 99 on Jan. 6, 1990.

Claude Sr. and Marie are buried in Sunset Memory Gardens south of Kokomo. *Submitted by Greg A. Wall.*

ROBERT E. AND MARILYN G. WALL -
Robert Earl Wall and Marilyn Grace Barr met each other while employed by the then called Delco Radio. He was a draftsman and she was the boss's secretary. They fell in love and married on July 10, 1949 in the Hopewell Methodist Church which is located in northern Tipton County on U.S. Highway 31. They took up residence in Kokomo and have lived there ever since.

Robert was born to Claude Clay Wall Sr. and Clara Anna Marie Caplinger on May 27, 1927 in Elkhart, IN. Bob's father was originally from Franklin County, MO, where his family had lived since 1815. After a brief residence in Indianapolis, Bob and his family moved to Kokomo in 1929. Bob's father had taken a job in a new plant at the newly established Continental Steel Corporation. Other members of Bob's family were his brother, Claude, Jr. born June 12, 1924 in Indianapolis, and his sister, Patricia Louise, born Feb. 11, 1931 in Kokomo. Bob started work at Delco Radio in 1945 while a student attending Kokomo High School. Later the same year he became a midterm graduate. By September of that year, Bob was drafted into the Army. Bob escorted German POW's back to Europe where he became a part of the Occupation Forces. He was discharged from the Army in February 1947 and returned to Delco Radio. Bob started out his career touching up old radio drawings and developed his artistic talent over the years to become a nationally recognized leader in the marketing art field. Under his leadership, his group produced corporate presentations and advertising artwork which garnered his group prestigious advertising awards. Bob also created the annual Delco Christmas card using his paintings of local scenes. On June 1, 1992 after 47 years of service, Bob retired from Delco Electronics as manager of Marketing Art.

Robert E. Wall and Marilyn G. Wall

Marilyn was born to Claude Elnor Barr and Ida Bertha Michel on April 25, 1927 in Tipton County. She attended Prairie High School and graduated in May 1945. While at P.H.S., Marilyn was a cheerleader for the "Aces" sports team. After graduation she went to work at Delco Radio until her marriage to Bob. After her children reached school age, Marilyn went to work as a secretary for Tribal Trails District of the Girl Scouts of America. She retired in 1978 after 20 years of service.

Bob and Marilyn had four children, all of which were born in St. Joseph Hospital and delivered by Dr. Thomas Conley.

1) Gregory Alan born Feb. 6, 1950. He married Janet Ann Altic on June 10, 1972. They have two children, Adriene Elizabeth, born Aug. 11, 1977, and Kathryn Marie, born May 21, 1986.

2) Marcia Elaine born Jan. 5, 1952. She married Walter John Vetter May 19, 1973 and had one child, Liberty Tasha Vetter, born Dec. 18, 1976. After a divorce, she married James Swisshelm, Aug. 12, 1978. After another divorce, she married Thomas Breithaupt on July 27, 1985.

3) Brent Lee born June 11, 1953. He married Susan Lee Crume of Tipton County on June 26, 1977.

4) Larry Earl born Aug. 30, 1955. He married Debra Ann Smith of Kokomo on June 18, 1977. They have two sons, Nathan Isaiah born June 20, 1983, and Andrew Michael born June 14, 1985. *Submitted by Robert E. Wall*

WARD - Beverly Randolph Ward, Sr. married Eleanor (nickname Nettie) Glore in 1799 in Kentucky. They became the parents of 13 children including the youngest, Beverly Randolph Ward, Jr. who was born in Rush County, IN in 1824. The senior Beverly Ward died in 1829. In 1838 the younger Beverly Ward accompanied his older brother, James, to Clinton County, IN where James entered 80 acres of land. In 1840 Beverly Ward, Jr. married Nancy Lett, and the next year he took a claim on what was known as the Seven Mile Strip or canal land. The government ceded land seven miles on either side of a canal for agricultural purposes. The Ward family grew with the births of Williamson, James, Sampson, John, Carey, and Preston.

In 1847 the Ward family moved to Alto, IN where Beverly engaged in the cabinet business. Three years later he sold the business and entered Franklin Theological College, Franklin, IN. He was ordained a Baptist minister in the Franklin Baptist Church in 1852. He then held pastorates, sometimes as many as four small churches at a time, in Sharon, Middlefork, Michigantown, Lauramie, Antioch, Deer Creek, Bunker Hill, Thorntown, Young America and others.

At least three, and possibly four, of Beverly Ward's sons served in Indiana military units in the Civil War. Williamson, the oldest, kept a diary from his enlistment in 1861 to his mustering out in 1865. In it he describes being captured by Rebels at the Battle of Stone's River in Tennessee, and of his release when a company of Yankee cavalry charged his captors and the Rebels ran. He also described his sorrow upon learning of the untimely death of his mother in January, 1864. Williamson also wrote about his brother Sampson being hit in the face with a bullet which nearly severed his tongue. He survived that injury, and, after he returned from the war, he moved to a citrus farm near San Diego where he died in 1924.

Rev. Ward married Rebecca (maiden name Campbell) Oakson later the same year that his first wife Nancy died. The second Ward family consisted of Luella, Nellie, Mary, Elizabeth and two others that died in infancy. Elizabeth served as a missionary to Japan for many years, and she married Rev. Frank Stoddard late in life. They had no children. Nellie married Frank Haynes.

(See Haynes)

Williamson Ward, known as "Will, married Rachel Ann Greeson after returning from the war. Their union was blessed with the births of Ida, Flora, Fannie, Harriett, Ola, Oma, and Mary Jane. Ida became a secretary in the Kokomo School System, and Flora was a teacher there; neither of them ever married. Harriett married Lawrence McTurnan, an insurance man from Indianapolis. They had a son, Robert, who became a physician, and a daughter, Judith, who married Bill Dunn and lived at Martinsville, IN. Ola Ward also became a teacher in Kokomo, and she married Albert Blossey. Their children were: Carl, who was an engineer, and daughters Rachel and Zoe. (See Blossey and Haynes) *Submitted by Louis H. Haynes, great grandson of W.D. Ward*

WATTS-WILKINSON - According to the birth certificate of his children, George Washington Watts (BD1825) was born in the state of Maine but sometime later settled in Howard County. At the time of his death on Dec. 29, 1892, George was living at 401 Kentucky Street in Kokomo. George W. Watts is buried at Crown Point Cemetery in Kokomo.

George Washington Watts married Jane (Smith) Watts (BD Feb. 18, 1836). The greater part of Jane's life was spent in Kokomo and the Groomsville neighborhood until her death Jan. 3, 1920. Jane was a member of the Liberty Baptist Church. She had a brother, William (Bill) Smith, who family members say drove the first car on the streets of Kokomo. Another brother, known by the name of Lon Smith, died in Kokomo while mowing along a fence row in the summer of 1934, but his burial site is unknown.

George and Jane Watts were the parents of five living children who lived in or near Kokomo: Mary (Purvis) buried at Greentown Cemetery, Sarah Frances (Butcher) buried at Crown Point Cemetery, James Arthur, Anna Eliza (Kirtley) and William Milton Watts.

My grandfather, James Arthur Watts (BD Feb. 20, 1879), was born in Howard County. James died Aug. 31, 1936 and is buried in Greentown Cemetery. James Arthur married Minnie Mae Wilkinson (BD Oct. 12, 1880) in Kokomo on June 21, 1902. James and Minnie had 12 children.

Minnie Mae (Wilkinson) Watts also had roots in Howard County. She was one of seven children of Benjamin Franklin Wilkinson (BD Nov. 17, 1843) and Bulah (Hilton) Wilkinson (BD May 13, 1845). Benjamin and Bulah were married in Howard County Dec. 12, 1868. Benjamin was also married to Anna Joh (Howard County 1904) and Emma V. Haynes Adair (Howard County 1907). Benjamin died May 13, 1922 and was buried in Greentown Cemetery.

Unfortunately the Wilkinson family became well known in Howard County because of a Sept. 27, 1913 headline in *The Kokomo Dispatch:* "Body of Missing Anna Wilkinson Found in Unmarked Grave".

Anna Matilda (Rudy) Wilkinson, daughter of Samuel Rudy of Kokomo and granddaughter of the Rev. D.J. Rudy of Hemlock, married William Clinton (Clint) Wilkinson (son of Benjamin and Bulah) on July 13, 1902. It was a stormy marriage and by Aug. 29, 1913, Clint's jealousy over Anna's job at the McGuire Restaurant on the west side of Buckeye Street in Kokomo erupted into a violent argument. When Anna tried to leave, Clint, in a jealous rage, hit her with a hammer which resulted in her death. Clint then panicked and buried her body in a cornfield near their farm home.

When the shallow grave was discovered by a neighbor, the Kokomo Police Department was called to investigate, and Anna's body was taken to the Rich and Dimmitt Funeral Home in Kokomo. Later it was determined that the Wilkinson's farm house near Cassville was actually within the boundaries of Miami County. However, because of Anna's family ties in Kokomo, *The Kokomo Dispatch* continued daily news articles of the trial until William Clinton Wilkinson was sentenced to the Indiana State Prison, Oct. 13, 1913. *Submitted by Shirley Watts Perry*

HARNESS-MCCORMACK-WERBE - Bette Jane was born Sept. 29, 1916 in Kokomo, IN to Russell R. Harness and Gladys Eva (Todd) Harness. She is a birthright member of the First United Church. Her first seven years of grammar school were at Wallace School. Her 8th grade year, she was transferred into the city to Central School. However, being "over-crowded", she enrolled in Roosevelt School.

Bette Jane graduated with the class of 1934, a member of Glee Club and Bird Club.

She joined the Y.W.C.A. and was initiated into Delta Theta Omega, where she held all offices. Upon graduation, she went to work for Crosley in 1934, later known as Delco-General Motors Corporation, and was a member of the Delco "35" Club.

Bette Jane attended the Kokomo Business College. She studied Spanish at Kokomo Junior College. She spent several vacations in Clearwater, FL where she modeled clothes and jewelry on "Treasure Island" and the Yacht Club, later moving to Lakeworth and Palm Beach. She attended the "Bethesda-by-the Sea" on the ocean. She married Aristede de Rocha, Italian sculptor. Bette Jane played tennis daily.

In junior high school, she took piano and "elocution" of Mrs. C.H. Brown.

L-R: Sarah Elfrieda Werbe, "Stormy" Werbe, and Bette Harness Werbe

During World War II in 1941, she was sponsored for the Civil Air Patrol and was their National Rifle Association instructor, teaching both rifle and pistol. While a member of the C.A.P., she took flying lessons from John and Verona Ruzicka.

Bette left General Motors employment to pursue x-rays and lab work with Dr. Frank O. Clifford, orthodontist. She organized the first dental assistants organization and was their first president. While working, she married Charles Asa McCormack in Corpus Christi, TX. On their return to Indiana, they settled on a farm in Middletown, and lived in a "log house" with a seven ton stone fireplace. Wonderful experience - "The Good Earth".

Moved back to Kokomo; volunteered as St. Joseph Memorial Hospital as a nurse's aide.

Bette Jane and Charles moved to Los Angeles, CA, where she worked for the Southern California Telephone Company. Bette Jane transferred back to the Kokomo Telephone Company and married Harry N. Werbe, Jr. of Werbe and Sons Sheet Metal, in Covington, KY. To this union were born two children: Sarah Elfrieda Werbe, born March 12, 1949; and Harry Nelson Werbe, III "Stormy" born March 8, 1950. Bette Jane and Harry built a "year-round" home on Lake Bruce, Kewanna, IN where they entertained extensively. They enjoyed the hospitality at the "Rest-A-While". Back in Kokomo, they bought the VanMeter home on South Webster Road.

She joined the Kokomo Jr. Department Club, Kokomo Art Association, the Sculptors Guild and Brown County Arts. Bette Jane took oil painting classes in Florida and California. Her special hobby is "collages" and "dolls".

In 1960, she moved back to 333 North Indiana Avenue, where she now resides. In 1961, she went to work in the offices of St. Joseph Memorial Hospital, as admissions clerk and registrar, weekends workings as cashier, then, transferring to switchboard, all over a period of 22 years. Bette Jane was working as PBX operator during the deadly tornado of Palm Sunday 1965.

During the years, she received several "awards" but most outstanding:

#1 Named the first St. Joseph Hospital newsletter "The Family" and received a monetary award which she used to buy her son "Stormy" his first school drum.

#2 A.B.W.A. statue for "Woman of the Year" of Sycamore Belles Chapter, of which she is a charter member.

#3 Named the Seiberling Mansion museum newsletter "Hi-Lites" and was awarded silver spoons.

Bette Jane is a "life member" of the Howard County Historical Society Museum. She retired from St. Joseph Hospital in 1981.

WELCH-CLARK - Dale Welch moved his family to Kokomo in 1984 to be closer to Chrysler where he is a toolmaker. Dale wed Linda D. Clark in Muncie, IN in 1972. Michael Lewis born 1973 and James Lee born 1976 born in Delaware County. James is a senior at Western School.

Michael wed Jolana Donnita Paul in Kokomo during 1993. On Dec. 8, 1993 Ashley Nicole Welch was born here. Michael is a roofer and lives in West Middleton, IN.

Dale Lewis was born Feb. 4, 1955 to Truman and Clara Welch in Muncie. He has a brother Terry Lee born 1957, who lives in Muncie. Terry and wife Tammi (Green) Welch are the parents of sons Tyler Lee born 1988 and Todd Lynn born 1990.

Truman Dale born 1934 in Marion, IN to Paul and Mildred Welch. He has two brothers Don Irvin and Curtis Dee. Don lives in Marion and Curtis lives here in Kokomo.

Clara Sue (Harless) 1934-1973 was born in Delaware County to Calvin Edward and Nellie Jane (Laughlin) Harless. She was raised from age nine by Louis and Florence (Trueblood) Quimby in Muncie. She worked as a receptionist for Dr. Bumbleburgh many years before she died of cancer. She was a great mother-in-law.

Paul Hillis Welch 1905-1960 born in Van Buren to William and Elizabeth. He is buried there with second wife Mary Jane (Feltt), who first wed Robert Dilliday. William Welch 1854-1952 was born in Grant County to Curtis Welch. Elizabeth Ellen (Thompson) 1859-1952 was born in Van Buren to Nathan 1822-1885 and Rachael (Bevard) 1833-1912.

Mildred Daisy (Collins) Welch born 1915 in Grant County to Nelson and Flossie Collins. After her mother died of T.B. when she was five her father wed Leah Ethelene Nusbaumer born 1901 who still lives on the farm she and Nelson Todd Collins 1891-1979 shared 58 years together, near Van Buren. Leah cared for Nelson Todd and Flossie Collins children; Mildred Daisy, Richard Raymond 1919-1977 and Nelson Kenneth Collins 1917-1979. The sons' families are now living in Van Buren. Leah and Nelson (called Todd) added to their family with; Elizabeth, Emily Caroline, Leah Corrine, Franklin Marion, Benny, Fredrick Eugene, Marvin, and Michael. Of these children Franklin and Fredrick are deceased.

Luther Basel 1845-1914 and Emily Caroline 1859-1952 (Lee) Collins were the parents of Nelson T. They lived most of their lives in and are buried near Poneto, in Wells County, IN. Luther was born in Delaware County and Emily was born in Wells County. Descendants of theirs can be found in the families of Sutton, Ober, and Ogle in Grant and Delaware Counties. Luther co-owned a farm and blacksmith business on 180 acres in Delaware County near the town of Royerton in 1870 with his grandparents, Hannah and Henderson Collins. Luther's father Robert 1828 lived near Royerton, IN and was a farmer, and wed Susan 1830-1873; their children were: Gardner 1844-1929; Gilbert F., Samuel 1852, Emma M., William H. 1859, John Francis 1866, Effie Sue, Andrew (1845-1862; Andrew was killed during the Civil War) and Luther Basel.

WELCH-PAUL - Michael Lewis Welch born April 27, 1973 in Muncie, Delaware County moved with his parents Dale Lewis and Linda Dianna (Clark) Welch in 1984 to Kokomo. He wed Jolana Donnita Traza Shalu Paul on May 8, 1993 in Kokomo. Their daughter Ashley Nicole Welch was born at St. Joseph Hospital here on Dec. 8, 1993.

Michael graduated from Western High School and is a roofer. Jolana was born Jan. 15, 1976 in Kokomo to Sam Jr. and Aileen Delmay (Suttles) Paul. Sam Jr. Paul 1934 was born in Clairborn County, TN to Samuel Robert and Gertrude (Paul) Paul. Aileen was born 1947 in Harlan County, KY to Herman Lee and Margret Gladys (Adkins) Suttles.

Michael's mother Linda Dianna (Clark) Welch was born Nov. 22, 1955 in Delaware County, IN to Ralph Doyle and Wilma Louise (Rollen) Clark. Also born to them were Mickie Jo 1950, wed Paul Vannatter; their children are Kimberly Jo 1972 and Scott Matthew 1975; Debra Elaine 1957 wed Jeff D. Fisher; their children Amber Danielle 1982 Andrea Marie 1984; Martha Jean 1959 wed Clark Meece; their child is Christina Lynn 1976.

Ralph was born in Stearns, KY in 1931 near coal mine area to William Henry and Mattie Mae (Davis) Clark. William was born in Wayne County, KY 1894-1959 to Thomas Henry and Eliza Ann (Correll) Clark. Thomas 1872-1936 was born in Denny Wayne County, KY to Henry 1846-1942 and Rebecca Rose (Morrow) Clark. Henry served with the Union during the Civil War as a scout. Mattie Mae (Davis) Clark was born 1901-1976 to Lemuel Quency and Mary Alice (Davis) Davis in Parmelysville, Wayne County, KY. L.Q. Davis 1852-1936 was born in Warren County, KY to George and Martha Oma Thompson. L.Q., Mary Alice and her mother Katherine 1843-1930 are buried at Parmleysville Baptist Church on the land he donated and built the church, which is still in use today.

Wilma Louise (Rollen) Clark born 1929 to Edwin and Lula Elizabeth (Barnhouse) Rollen in Muncie. Edwin 1876-1962 was born in Chillcothe Ross County, OH to Patrick Henry 1841-1876 and Rachael (Napp) Rollen. Lula 1890-1977 was born in West Virginia to Solomon and Ellen (Sturgeon) Barnhouse. Edwin moved his family from Ohio to Muncie, IN by covered wagon in 1920. This is all the verified information on these family lines.

WELSH - Amanda Caroline (Foster) Welsh was born in Kokomo May 6, 1849. In 1876 she was married to George H. Welsh and went to Sandusky, OH to live. A few years later Mr. Welsh died and his young widow returned to Kokomo with her small daughter, Emma, moving later to Indianapolis where Emma was married to Dr. Thomas Gaddes, a Canadian.

In 1900 the young couple and Amanda established their residence in central and later in western Canada.

Amanda returned to Kokomo in 1926 where she spent her remaining years.

Amanda was one of the 11 children of David and Elizabeth Matilda (Grant) Foster, founders of Kokomo.

David was born July 30, 1808 in Albemarle County, VA to William and Margaret (Buster) Foster. While still a lad his family emigrated to Kentucky. From Kentucky the family moved to Johnson County, IN and on Jan. 17, 1832 David was married to Elizabeth. In 1835 David and Elizabeth settled in Burlington.

After moving in 1840 to Ervin Township in Howard County, David sought a suitable place on Wildcat Creek for a trading post. He purchased land and erected a two-room cabin on the north bank of the Wildcat, near what is now the intersection of Main and Superior Streets. Into one room he moved his family and in the other installed a stock of goods thus becoming the community's first merchant. This small beginning later became the nucleus of the village of Kokomo. Foster Park near the center of the city and a street were named for the founders.

Amanda (Foster) Welsh in center

In the cabin of the Fosters was held the first meeting of the Methodists, which in time grew into the church now known as Grace Methodist Church.

David died in 1877.

Amanda passed away on July 6, 1946 at the age of 97. Even though advanced in years, she remained vigorous in body and intellect. She was always able to describe in detail the events relating to the founding and early history of Kokomo. It was with considerable pride and enjoyment that she rode in an automobile in the parade of July 4, 1944, which was a feature of Kokomo's centennial celebration.

Amanda is buried in the Foster lot in Crown Point Cemetery.

HARRY NELSON WERBE, JR. - Representing one of the oldest and best known families of Howard County, and a man of enterprise and sterling worth:—Is well entitled to notice among the substantial businessmen of Kokomo, and it is with much satisfaction that this story of Harry Nelson Werbe, Jr. is accorded a place in this book. His high standing as a neighbor and a citizen won for him the confidence and esteem of all with whom he associated. A member of First Congregational Church and helped with roof and church repairs. His fraternal relatives are with the Masonic order attaining the 32nd degree honour. He was an avid supporter of the K.H.S. SPORTS and never missed a basketball team game!

The U.S. Navy office gave Harry a very cordial letter, certifying in the most positive terms to his activity, correctness, and faithfulness, in the position stating without equivocation that he was the best inspector the General had ever known in the Navy. "There was not an officer on his staff held in higher esteem, nor on one whose service he relied on more in his field of duty." In fact, words could not frame a stronger or more flattering testimonial.

Before and after the World War II, Harry was active in the Democratic political party. His political activity and enthusiasm were remarkable. Harry was a regular blood donor and had several gallon pins to his credit.

Harry N. Werbe, Jr. owner of Werbe Sheet Metal Shop

Harry was a proud of two children: a daughter, Sarah Elfrieda Werbe, born in Kokomo on March 12, 1949, and a son, Harry Nelson Werbe III, born March 8, 1950 in Kokomo. Harry's leisure time was spent fishing with his family on Bruce Lake-Kewanna, IN, where his wife Bette

Jane (Harness) built a comfortable cottage with fireplace-livable year around. They enjoyed entertaining all family and friends - Everyone was welcome!

Harry and Betty Jane had an airplane in partnership with two other families and took turns in flying.

Harry was considered a sharp dresser with a Barrymore profile. Born Sept. 7, 1903. Death: May 31, 1976; buried at Crown Point Cemetery.

HARRY NELSON "STORMY" WERBE, III -

"Stormy" was born March 8, 1950, the son of Bette Jane (Harness) Werbe and Harry Nelson Werbe, Jr. He attended Maple Crest, Lincoln, and Lafayette Park schools, and graduated in 1968 from Kokomo High School.

Stormy was a member of Cub Scout Pack #41 and Boy Scout Troop #41, George Hiatt, Scoutmaster, and Dr. Ernest Murray, President, Meshingomesia Council, Boy Scouts of America, 1960-1961.

As student manager of basketball, Stormy earned his "K" letter from K.H.S. in 1965, under the direction of Russell Bratton and Coach Joe Platt. His fondness for painting with pasche' airbrush led to his art talent of designing and painting "senior cords" for graduating seniors. After school and on weekends, he worked with his father in the family owned business, Harry Werbe and Sons Sheet Metal, started by his grandfather.

Stormy played basketball at the Y.M.C.A. leagues, receiving "best attitude" trophy in 1961. An avid fisherman and golfer, Stormy continues to golf using a few of his father's clubs.

He attended Ivy Tech-Kokomo, graduating with honors in engineering and industrial drafting.

L-R: Harry Nelson "Stormy" Werbe III and Heidi

Athletically inclined, his major interest is weightlifting, having been a partner in the ownership of Body Unlimited. He continues to weightlift three times weekly and is regimented to healthy eating and fitness, a very honorable trait.

A great animal lover and caregiver, Stormy's longtime friend and companion, a shepherd-labrador dog named Heidi, was in the cancer research program at Purdue University until her cancer battle was lost.

Stormy is the great-great grandson of George W. Harness, a prominent Howard County pioneer.

Stormy presently lives in Indianapolis and works for Beam, Longest & Neff.

MORRIS L. AND ELEANOR JANE WEYAND

- Morris L. (Mory) and Eleanor Jane met shortly after graduation from Indiana University and Purdue University. They were married on Nov. 8, 1957. Jobs kept them in Kokomo. Mory started his career at Continental Steel Corporation as a salesman and became a sales manger. In 1986 he formed Weyand and Associates, Inc., a manufacturers representative agency, with his daughter. Eleanor's career included teaching home economics and general science for Kokomo Center Township School Corporation and the Northern Community School Corporation of Tipton County.

Mory was born in Watseka, IL, July 18, 1932 to Morris A. and Alice Bliss Weyand. Morris A. was born in Royal Center, IN in 1873 and Alice Bliss was born in Royal Center, IN in 1890. Morris A. was a funeral director owning a mortuary in Royal Center and Milford, IL. Morris A. held the number six embalmer's license in Indiana. Alice taught school in Royal Center. They had three children: Morris L., Sara Weyand Lockhart, and Melvin (deceased). Melvin was an attorney and an Illinois state legislator. Sara was a housewife with a love for antiques.

Mory graduated from Onarga Military Academy in 1946 and Milford, Illinois High School in 1950. In 1954 he graduated from Indiana University with a BS in business. He was a member of Lambda Chi Alpha social fraternity. He served in the Korean War with the Army. Mory was active in the YMCA serving as a board of director president and president of the Y-Men Club. He also held membership in Masonic Lodge, Rotary International, and Scottish Rite Lodge.

Eleanor was born in Kokomo, IN, March 20, 1935, to Arthur (Art) and Genevieve (Gene) Elvin Miller. Arthur was born in Kokomo September 26, 1909 (deceased 1985) to John E. and Cora Emma Coppock Miller. They resided in Plevna and Kokomo. Arthur had three brothers: Robert, Max, and Paul (all deceased). Arthur graduated from Kokomo High School in 1927 and graduated from Purdue University in 1931 with a BS in mechanical engineering. After graduation he worked at Bendix in South Bend before beginning his career at Continental Steel Corporation in 1933. He began as a bar mill recorder and progressed to president of Continental Steel Corporation. He was very active in local civic affairs. He served on the board of directors of the Union Bank and Trust Co. He belonged to Theta Chi social fraternity. Arthur was an avid Kokomo High School and Purdue University sports fan and alumni.

Genevieve (Gene) was born in Kokomo, IN, June 4, 1912 (deceased 1990) to Ernest and Myrtle Powell Elvin. Ernest came to Kokomo from Kent County, England. He worked for Continental Steel Corporation. Gene had three sisters Cinga, Marthaellen Elvin Samsel (both deceased), and Lois Elvin Carter of Daytona Beach, FL. She also had a brother Ernest (Bud) (deceased). Gene graduated from Kokomo High School in 1930 and Kokomo Business College in 1931. She was active in the Episcopal Church, Eastern Star, and the American Red Cross. Art and Gene had three daughters who were public school teachers.

Sarah Elizabeth Miller Flowers was born in Kokomo Aug. 30, 1939. She married Warren P. Flowers of Paducah, KY in 1961. They reside in Vidalia, GA. They were the parents of three children: Michael, Melissa Flowers Stiner, and Matthew. Sarah graduated from Kokomo High School in 1957.

Marjorie Dianne Miller Winslow was born in Kokomo, April 13, 1945. Marjorie married James Frederick Winslow of Kokomo in 1966. They reside in Columbus, IN. She graduated from Kokomo High School in 1962. They were parents of two children: Michelle Winslow Rhodes and Dustin.

Eleanor Jane graduated from Kokomo High School in 1953, Purdue University in 1957 with a BS in Home Economics and Physical Education, and in 1968 graduated from Ball State University with a MA in Home Economics and General Science. She was a member of various educational organizations. She was regional board of trustees member for Indiana Vocational College. She was a member of Greek Club.

Eleanor and Mory were parents of two children: Morris Arthur (Marty) born Aug. 10, 1958 in Kokomo and Jane Amelia Hizer Weyand born Oct. 26, 1962. Marty graduated from Kokomo High School in 1976 and Indiana University in 1990 with a BS in Education. He is a social studies teacher. Marty married 'Judy Blaske of Muskegon, MI in 1989. She is a department manager for an Indianapolis retailer. Jane graduated from Kokomo High School in 1981 and Indiana University in 1985. She also studied at Erasasum University in Rotterdam, Netherlands. She has a BS degree in Public and Environmental Affairs. She is a partner with her dad in Weyand and Associates, Inc. Jane married James N. Hizer of Frankfort, IN in 1989. James is CEO of the Clinton County Chamber of Commerce.

During the 1990's the society has become very mobile and most of the family no longer lives in Howard County, but the county still holds many fond and loving memories for the family.

WHEELER/SANFORD -

James (Red or Jim) Henry Wheeler, was born in Illinois. His parents were Robert Clary and Julia Cooper Wheeler. He worked clearing lumber and was a carpenter. He served overseas in the Army in WWI. As a young man clearing lumber, he was struck in the knee with an ax and thereafter walked with a limp. In 1922 he and Edna Margaret Sanford eloped and were married in Dyersburg, TN.

Edna remembered traveling from Prairie Township in Indiana to Missouri in a covered wagon with her father, Jessee Sanford, her brother, Louis, her stepmother and her stepmother's three children. One of the most memorable events was when they were fording a river and the water was too deep. The horses were unable to keep the wagon upright and it turned over causing the family to lose many of their belongings, but they were thankful because they were all okay and as Papa put it, they didn't lose their most prized possession, their horses.

Jim and Edna had a son, Robert James, while living in Missouri, but life was difficult there so they moved to Indiana and settled in Kokomo. There they had three more sons: John Lewis, Donald Eugene and William Thomas. Jim worked for many years at Continental Steel. He was a member of the VFW and was well known for his card playing ability and instant "red head" temper. He often took his boys hunting and was an avid fisherman. He owned a cottage on the Monon River and later purchased one at Nyona Lake which was his pride and joy.

Edna loved to sew and worked during the WWII years at Reliance making parachutes. Around 1946 she went to work at Delco Radio where she became a utility operator. She liked to work and always thought she contributed something to the team as they learned to put the new models of radios together each year. As a young woman she belonged to several lodges where she went through the chairs and took an active part in their meetings. She made all her own formals for these occasions.

She also enjoyed playing cards and always had funny stories to tell of the jokes their friends played on each other when they got together. She retired after Jim died in 1968. She often traveled to Mississippi to see her son Tom but by the late 1970's she was unable to go because of her short term memory loss which caused her to get lost. After that she stayed at home much of the time. She lived to be 84 and died in 1991. *Submitted by Bob Wheeler*

CHARLES AND CAROLYN WHEELER -

Charles J. Wheeler was born Oct. 3, 1935, in Kokomo, IN, to Charles Lee and Lucy (Lawrence) Wheeler. The family lived in and around Kokomo for the first few years but settled in Howard Township where Charles Jr. attended grade school. He then went to high school at Northwestern. Charles joined the Air Force in the fall of 1954 and served in France. On his return, he was employed by Haynes Stellite where he worked for 34 years. By the time of Charles' retirement in April 1993, the factory had been renamed Haynes International.

Charles married Carolyn Sue Bennett on July 10, 1960, at New London Friends Church. Carolyn is the daughter of Dwight and Lillian (Heaton) Bennett (see Bennett History), and was born in Ervin Township, Howard County, IN, on Nov. 6, 1938. She was raised in Monroe Township and attended grade school at New London, junior high at West Middleton, and graduated from Western High School in 1956. She continued her education at Taylor University at Upland, IN, where she received a B.S. degree in education in 1960. She obtained an M.A. from Ball State University at Muncie, IN, in 1966. Carolyn's teaching career began at Clay Township School in Miami County where she taught English and social studies for two years. She then taught at Western School Corporation for 31 years and retired from teaching in June 1994.

Charles and Carolyn are active in their church, Courtland Avenue Friends Meeting, where they serve on various committees. Both have taught Sunday School and have helped with Vacation Bible School. One highlight of their Christian life came in 1974 when they went to Colombia and Ecuador on a witnessing crusade with Men for Missions. They have had a life-long interest in missionary endeavors.

Top: Steve Wheeler; L: Charles and Carolyn Wheeler; R: Cheryl and Todd Hostetler

The Wheelers have been blessed with two children, Stephen Charles and Cheryl Lynn.

Steve was born July 16, 1963, in Kokomo, IN. He graduated from Western High School in 1981 and then went to Ball State University, receiving a B.S. degree in 1985. Steve was interested in a law career and chose to attend the Washington College of Law at American University in Washington, D.C. He graduated with honors in 1989. After passing the bar exam, Steve was hired by Jennings & Associates, a law firm in Carmel, IN, where he has worked since 1989. He is single and has a home in Carmel which he shares with his German shepherd Gracie.

Cheryl Lynn was born Jan. 6, 1967, in Kokomo, IN, and she, too, is a product of Western Schools. She graduated in 1985. She attended IU-K for a semester and went to Ivy Tech for two years, which prepared her for a career as a medical secretary. She worked at Kokomo Family Care until 1992 when she moved to Columbus, IN.

Cheryl married Todd Aaron Hostetler on Dec. 30, 1988. Todd is a 1986 graduate of Northwestern High School, a 1990 graduate of Anderson University, and is working on a Master's degree from Ball State University. He is a certified athletic trainer with SPORTMED in Columbus. Cheryl is employed at Indiana Heart Physicians—Columbus. Cheryl, along with her mother, is a member of the Happy Homemakers Extension Club. *Submitted by Carolyn Wheeler*

CHARLES L. AND LUCY (LAWRENCE) WHEELER - Charles Lee Wheeler was born in Pope County, IL, (near Brownfield), on Aug. 19, 1905, to Robert C. and Julia (Cooper) Wheeler. Charles was the fourth of seven children. His siblings included Ella, Jim, Bessie, Anna, Lucille, and Eula May. The Wheelers moved around a lot in the early 1900's. They lived in Oklahoma, Arkansas, and Missouri before permanently settling in Indiana, first in Tipton County and then in Kokomo, IN.

On Aug. 22, 1925, Charles married Lucy May Lawrence of Parma, MO. She was born there on March 22, 1905, to Fred and Hannah Jane (Orr) Lawrence. Lucy was the oldest of ten children. The others included Delia, Lela, Charles, Chesley, Lester, Junior, Alvester, Edward, and Everett.

Charles started working at Continental Steel Corporation in 1927 and worked there for 34 years. He retired in 1961. Lucy was a devoted mother and dedicated her life to raising her children, but she did work briefly at Delco. To their union were born five children: Floyd, Eddie, Fred, Mildred, and Charles Jr.

Floyd was born May 8, 1926, in Missouri. He attended schools in Kokomo and served in the Navy during World War II. He met Margaret (Peggy) Lemmo of Brooklyn, NY, and they married on Feb. 9, 1946. They had six children: Ronnie, Dian, Billy, Ruth, Barry (who died in 1969), and Charlene. Floyd retired from Cabot Corporation in 1977. He died Feb. 9, 1982, and is buried at Memorial Park Cemetery in Kokomo.

Eddie was born June 13, 1928, in Kokomo, IN. He married Virginia Miller in June 1950, and they had three sons: Mike, David, and Mark. Eddie worked several years at Delco before moving to Florida where he died on Feb. 2, 1976. He is also buried at Memorial Park Cemetery.

Charles L. and Lucy Wheeler

Fred was born Nov. 6, 1930, in Kokomo. He graduated at Northwestern School in 1950 and married Joan Andrews on Dec. 5, 1951. Fred worked at Crescent Dairy for a while and later was employed at Haynes Stellite (now Haynes International) from which he retired in 1991. Fred served in the Army during the Korean War. Fred and Joan have three children: Debbie, Kevin, and Jeff.

Mildred was born on Feb. 26, 1933, in Kokomo. She married Junior Preston on March 25, 1950, and they had three children: Karen, Christine, and Terry. On Feb. 16, 1968, she married Ernest Ferency and they have a son Michael. Mildred worked 30 years at Delco before retiring.

The last of the children, Charles Jr., was born Oct. 3, 1935, in Kokomo. He served four years in the Air Force in France. His marriage to Carolyn Bennett took place July 10, 1960, at New London, IN. They have two children: Stephen Charles and Cheryl Lynn. Charles retired from Haynes International in 1993 after working there 34 years.

Charles Lee and Lucy were members of First Assembly of God Church on North Apperson Street. He and his wife were baptized on May 28, 1944, at Learner's Woods northeast of Kokomo. Charles died on July 8, 1966.

In 1975 Lucy married Harry Marshall. They lived at Gateway Gardens until poor health forced them into nursing homes. Lucy died on Nov. 18, 1981, and Harry died on Feb. 15, 1982. Harry is buried at Crown Point Cemetery in Kokomo, and Charles and Lucy are buried at Memorial Park Cemetery. *Submitted by Steve Wheeler*

JAMES HENRY WHEELER - Jim and Edna (Sanford) Wheeler raised their four sons in Kokomo. Their son, Robert, still lives in Kokomo. He married Ethel Plummer from Tipton (deceased in 1983). One son Robert E., lives in Kokomo; another, Mike, lives near Peru and their daughter, Judy (Welcher), lives in Russiaville. Robert has four grandchildren living in the Howard County area and one step-granddaughter near Peru.

Robert and Ethel both worked for Delco Electronics. He worked in automatic screw machines for 20 years and retired from the skilled trades department. Ethel worked on circuit boards at the main plant. They were very active in their church, the Lutheran Church of Our Redeemer. After Ethel's death, Robert married Janet McDowell and later married Naomi Miller. Robert was a gold wing biker and loved to take long trips on his bike until ill health caused him to consider it unsafe to ride. He enjoyed hunting and fishing and bought his father's cottage at Nyona Lake for his family to enjoy.

John married Naomi Tilley and together they had a daughter, Sue, who now lives in Michigan, and a son, Dennis. He later married Phyllis Bevington and had two girls, Linda and Margaret, who now live in Fulton, MO. He also has a son, John II, who lives in Terre Haute, IN.

John and Bob were charter members of the Indian Heights Volunteer Fire Department. John and Phyllis taught First Aid and were EMT's with that department for many years, but John was forced to leave Kokomo to seek work in his field as a pressman when Cuneo discontinued operations. It was a tough move. John was 52 when they moved to Fulton, MO and they live there today.

Donald (deceased in 1982) married Beverly Thompson of Kokomo and they had a daughter, Marjorie, who now lives in Thousand Oaks, CA and a son, Don II, who lives in Cary, NC. Don and Beverly worked at Delco Electronics, Don as traffic manager and Beverly in accounting and sales. Don played basketball for the YMCA and in the industrial league. He also played softball with the local teams and enjoyed all kinds of sports. His son Don played basketball for Haworth and the University of Evansville.

Tom played football at Kokomo High School, graduating in 1952. He played also at Butler University and Mississippi Southern. He married Darlene Whitecotton and they had three sons, Scott, Greg, and Chris, all living in Hattiesburg, MS. Tom worked for Sears for many years in Mississippi, Florida, Alabama and Louisiana, then returned to Hattiesburg to work for Chain Lighting. He retired in 1992 and enjoys playing golf, fishing and attending Southern football games. His wife Darlene has her doctorate degree in education and is a professor at Cary College where she likes to say she "teaches teachers how to teach." *Submitted by Tom Wheeler*

ROBERT CLARY WHEELER - Robert and Julia Wheeler were married in Pope County, IL in 1893. Robert was a farmer and share-cropped all his life so he moved his family many times during their 44-year marriage. From Illinois they went to Oklahoma, then to Arkansas and Missouri and in 1928 settled in Kokomo, IN. They had seven children: Ella, James, Bessie, Charles, Anna, Lucille and Eula Mae.

They were living in Oklahoma around 1910. Anna was less than a year old and only five of the children were born when Julia developed a severe swelling of the feet and legs commonly called dropsy. They went back to her mother's in Pope County, IL presuming she would die. On their way they stopped in Sara, OK to see some "holiness people". There was a man in the fields working crops. He stopped and had prayer for Julia. The next morning her knees were better. By the time she arrived at her mama's house the swelling had gone down and her feet were so small she had to buy new shoes. Her five children had been exposed to and came down with whooping cough, but she was able to care for all of them. She never had dropsy again. She lived to be 85 years old.

Ella married Dan Hall and they raised their seven children in Ohio. James and Charles raised their children in the Kokomo area. Their stories are being told by their children elsewhere in this book.

Bessie married Orville White. They lived in Colorado for 21 years, but came to Indiana to settle near the rest of her family. Orville worked for the railroad and Bessie worked for many years for the Wm. H. Turner Company. When Turners went out of business, she began working for J.C. Penney Company in the yard goods department. She retired from Penneys in 1968. She and Orville had no children, but to this day at 90, she is the backbone of the many Wheeler nieces and nephews living in the Kokomo area.

Anna married William Thieke and they raised five girls in Kokomo; Marie, Jean, Dorothy, Betty, and Mary. After Bill died, Anna married Emerson Stanton for a short time, but was truly happy later in life when she married Newton Oaks.

Lucille worked at Delco Electronics and married Harold Helton, Cecil Johnson and Robert Hodson (all deceased). They had no children.

Eula Mae had two children, Julia and Bobby (deceased) when she was married to Bill Norris and three children while she was married to Van Emery. Van's children are Sandy, Sharon and Van Jr., all raised in Greentown. Van worked at Continental Steel 42 years and died in 1991. *Submitted by Lucille Hodson*

VIVIAN MARIE WHEELER - Vivian Marie Wheeler was the eldest daughter of Manford Lincoln Wheeler, who was born Oct. 5, 1904 in Carroll County, IN and died July 22, 1940 in Howard County, IN, the son of Charles W. Wheeler, who was born Oct. 27, 1868 in Decatur County, IN and died April 20, 1946 in Russiaville, IN and Lucinda Harrison who was born Oct. 18, 1869 in Franklin County, IN and died Feb. 26, 1937 in Carroll County, IN. Vivian's mother was Josephine Lee, who was born Feb. 26, 1908 in Russiaville, IN and died June, 9, 1992 in Kokomo, IN and was the daughter of Manford L.

332

Lee who was born March 3, 1872 in Clinton County, IN and died May 30, 1957 in Howard County, IN and Lola Nay who was born Aug. 18, 1878 and died May 26, 1917 in Russiaville, IN. Charles W. Wheeler was the son of George W. Wheeler who was born Dec. 29, 1841 in Decatur County, IN and died Dec. 20, 1917 in Howard County, IN, and Nancy Jane Banta, who was the widow of Michael Earlywine prior to marrying George W. Wheeler, was born in 1838 in Switzerland County, IN and died in 1877 in Howard County, IN. George W. Wheeler was the son of Josephus C. Wheeler who was born in 1814 in Kentucky and died Sept. 3, 1886 in Hancock County, IN, and Rebecca Lock who was born in 1816 and died June 19, 1888 in Howard County, IN. Josephus C. Wheeler was the son of Thomas Wheeler who was born in 1785 in Virginia and Edith Gosnell who was born in 1790 in Virginia and died in Indiana. Manford Lee was the son of Cyrus Lee who was born in 1846 in Orange County, IN to Benjamin Lee who was born Aug. 7, 1887 and Queen Amy Lindley who was born March 2, 1809 both in Chatham County, NC, and his mother was Caroline Spray who was born Sept. 20, 1846 in Wayne County, IN and died Dec. 22, 1928 in Russiaville, IN daughter of Thomas Moses Spray who was born Aug. 21, 1819 in Wayne County, IN and died Aug. 9, 1887 in Wabash, IN, and Mary Tamar Huff who was born Feb. 7, 1821 in Wayne County, IN and died Jan. 17, 1869 in Russiaville, IN.

Vivian Marie Wheeler Payne

Vivian's sisters were Mary Jo (Wheeler) Ogle, married to N. Howard Ogle, and Betty Lou (Wheeler) Raney, divorced from Nelson Raney. Vivian was born in Jasper County, IN on Nov. 19, 1927. She received her schooling at Russiaville, IN where she was an above average student. She also taught herself typing and bookkeeping and learned dental assistance and laboratory skills while working in the dental office of Dr. Glenn Bollinger.

On April 10, 1943 she married William Joe Payne. They had three children, Judith Marie (Payne) (Harbin) Tubach, John William Payne, and Deborah Lee (Payne) Fuller. Vivian was a woman pioneer in the work force. She helped with farm work between raising children and keeping a well-maintained home. She and William purchased a home in Russiaville in 1947. She worked at Robert McMinn's appliance store as bookkeeper and saleslady and "Happy" White's and Blanche Bowman's restaurant in Russiaville as a waitress, then spent several years with Dr. Glenn Bollinger as an assistant. She and William built a new home at 3806 East and 100 South in Howard County in 1966. She returned to the dental profession as an assistant of Dr. Richard Rudicel and managed his office until her retirement.

Vivian attended the Quaker Church in Russiaville, IN. Many of her ancestors, on her mother's side, were Quakers who had come from Ireland. After marriage she joined the Methodist Church and raised her children in that church. Her father's family had been active in various churches with Nancy Jane Banta's grandfather Henry D. and her father Daniel H. Banta being ministers in churches in Switzerland County, Decatur County and Rush County, IN.

Grandchildren were Martin Todd, Patty Ann, and Scott Allen, children of Judith Marie (Payne) Harbin and Jim Harbin; Diane Louise, child of John William Payne and Dixie (Bowen) Payne; Keith Allen, son of Deborah Lee (Payne) Fuller and Gary Fuller.

Great-grandchildren were Chad Everett Payne, son of Diane Louise Payne and Kristen Ricque Edwards, daughter of Diane Louise (Payne) Edwards and Gary Wayne Edwards; Christopher Matthew, son of Martin Todd and Sharon (Thayer) Harbin.

L.J. WHITACRE - A wedding! An interurban trip to Kokomo, IN! That was the start of the Whitacre family in the Howard County area. Leonard John Whitacre (Nov. 9, 1894-Sept. 15, 1990) married Ruth Cleo Howenstine (Feb. 26, 1892-Oct. 25, 1970) on April 16, 1916. L.J. was born in Huntington, IN, the son of Scott and Mary Louise (Bradley) Whitacre. Ruth was born in Bippus, IN, the daughter of Bradley and Caroline (Nie) Howenstine. Leonard, employed at the Haynes Apperson Automobile Company, opened his first grocery at 1108 West Monroe on Sept. 13, 1919. L.J. and Ruth purchased their home at 215 South Phillips Street in 1926 for $2,000. After Ruth's death, Leonard married Mae (Alexander) Carr (Sept. 5, 1904-April 5, 1992), daughter of Earl and Leora (Johnson) Alexander, on May 6, 1973.

The oldest of L.J. and Ruth's children was Kathryn Jane (April 22, 1917-July 29, 1987) who married Donald Earl Woolley (Aug. 26, 1916), from Galveston, on April 13, 1941. Kathryn was a floral designer and Don was one of the first employees of Chrysler Corporation in Kokomo. Don and Katy had two sons. Stephen Craig Woolley (Aug. 10, 1942) lives in Brownsville, TX. He married Melody Lea Phillips on June 21, 1969 and they were the parents of one daughter, Camela Lynn Woolley (May 1, 1972-June 26, 1974). Their second son, Gary Kent Woolley (Dec. 1, 1950) married Donna Ruth Almand on Sept. 6, 1975 and have two children, Matthew Kent (Jan. 10, 1980) and Elizabeth Jane (Jan. 23, 1984).

L.J. Whitacre

Wayne L. "Bud" (May 13, 1919) was the second child of Leonard and Ruth's. Bud went into the grocery business with L.J. after returning from World War II. On June 18, 1948, Bud married Jeanette Frances Chapman (Sept. 21, 1919-June 9, 1992). They purchased Leonard's Grocery on Park Avenue, built a new grocery at 1303 East Morgan in 1975 and retired in 1983. Bud and Jeannette had one daughter, Susan Kay (Feb. 2, 1950) who married Larry Bergman on June 6, 1969. They live in Olympia, WA and have four children: Dane Ian (Dec. 24, 1970), Kristina Elke (Feb. 17, 1975), Martin Luther (Oct. 7, 1976) and Victoria (April 2, 1982).

Robert J. (Feb. 12, 1927), the third child, married Margaret Ann Fortner (Aug. 5, 1929), daughter of Dayton and Frances Fortner, on Oct. 8, 1948. Bob, a retired fireman, now resides at the Indiana Veteran's Home in West Lafayette. Bob and Margaret have one son, Bradley Jay (Nov. 26, 1964) who works at Bob Evans Restaurant.

The youngest child, Marilyn Sue (Jan. 1, 1933), became a teacher and married Edwin L. Wagoner (May 13, 1927-Sept. 23, 1962). Ed worked as an engineer at Stellite Corporation.

Marilyn's second marriage on July 12, 1964 was to James Robert McFadden (March 18, 1929-Aug. 3, 1982), also a teacher. Jim was born in Edinburgh, IN, the son of William and Lenora (Gray) McFadden.

Marilyn and Jim have two sons: Scott Robert (April 8, 1967), a librarian, is presently employed at the Butler University Library in Indianapolis, IN and Kent Leonard (Sept. 1, 1969), a part-time college student, is employed by Marsh Groceries; thus, bringing back the grocery tradition in the Whitacre Family.

WHITE - Everett Kenneth White, the second of son of Willard Douglas and Anna Mae (Ritchey) White, was born Sept. 30, 1906 in Benton County, IN. He married Daisy Mae Lincoln on April 22, 1924 in Marshall County, TN. She was the daughter of John and Fannie Mae (Tanner) Lincoln. As a child he moved quite often. His sister Eva was born at Union City, OH in 1908. The family moved back to Kokomo and then to Springfield, MO where they lived for a few years. His mother had a boarding house that did quite well. Everett, his brother Howard and family, along with their father Doug, moved back to Kokomo, IN in 1923.

He worked as an iron moulder for Hoosier Iron and Globe American among others. At one point in time Everett did glass blowing in the making of neon signs. Bowling and hunting were two of his hobbies.

Everett K. White, 1944

Mae and Everett had eight children which were all born in Kokomo. The first Frances Lois, known as Judy, born March 1, 1925. She married Earl Thomas in California; the second child was Margaret Virginia born March 19, 1927. William H. Kromberg became her husband May 15, 1957 in Reno, NV. She died May 30, 1987 in an auto accident; Ceclia Mae the third child was born March 22, 1929 and she married Murray Johnston Nov. 19, 1949 at Manchester, CT; on Feb. 28, 1931 they had their first son and fourth child Joseph Edward. He married Terry Martinez Feb. 28, 1976; the fourth child and second son was Paul Eugene that died at birth Feb. 21, 1933; James Thomas the sixth child was born April 10, 1934. He married Sondra Lee Pope March 12, 1960 in Stockton, CA; number seven was Catherine Rose born Dec. 29, 1935. She married Alexander Mastoras Oct. 26, 1956 in Fresno, CA; the last child and eighth was Theodore Phillip born April 27, 1941. He married Charlene Cummings Sept. 11, 1964 in California.

During WW II, Everett served in the U.S. Navy and was a shop supervisor stationed at Treasure Island, CA. He loved the area so much, after the war Everett came home, gathered his family, sold his house and moved back to Fresno, CA in April 1946. He went to work for the Southern Pacific Railroad until shortly before his death.

Everett died Jan. 1, 1969 in San Francisco, CA of cancer and is buried in the Holy Cross Cemetery at Fresno. Mae died June 29, 1964 in Fresno and is also buried in the Holy Cross Cemetery. *Submitted by Cecelia (White) Johnston*

HOWARD E. AND RUTH E. WHITE - Howard Edward White born Feb. 21, 1899 Ervin Twp., Howard County in the old Isaac Hauck home which stood where the entrance to Green Acres Subdivision is now (890 W.) on old Sycamore Road. He was the son of Willard Douglas and Anna Mae (Ritchey) White. By trade Howard was a mechanic and iron molder and had worked for Hoosier Iron, Malleable Steel Foundry, and Globe American. He was also a master carpenter and built several homes in the Howard County area. January of 1966, after 15 years service, Howard retired from Kingston Products in the heat-treat department. As a young man during the Depression years he played baseball with the Industrial League at Foster Park. Later in the 1950's he played with the Kokomo Dart Ball League. In 1957 he was runner-up for the Kokomo Father of the Year Award.

Howard Edward White and Ruth Ella (Hunt) White

Howard married Ruth Ella Hunt Feb. 18, 1920 in Springfield, MO. She was born Oct. 18, 1897, the daughter of Mark Lafayette and Casandra "Cassie" (Becknell) Hunt in Buffalo, Dallas County, MO. Her father died when she was four and her mother passed away when she was 14, leaving Ruth and her two brothers orphaned with no one to take care of them in Weiser, ID. Ruth was sent to a private school in St. Louis, MO by her father's family. She left school when she was 18 and moved to Springfield, MO. There she lived in a boarding house which was owned by Howard's mother.

The young couple lost their first son at the age of six days in December of 1920. A daughter was born at Springfield in March of 1923. They, along with Howard's brother Everett and his father, moved to Kokomo, IN shortly after.

Ruth and Howard had nine children. All but the first two were born in Howard County. (1) John who died at six days, (2) Mary Loretta married Keith Swihart, (3) Robert Joseph married Hertha (Collett) Little, (4) Richard Lawrence married Vivian Achor, (5) Elizabeth "Betty" Marie, (6) Ruth Joan married Max Snodgrass, (7) William Paul married Sharon Masters, (8) Thomas Mark married Nancy Thomas and (9) Carole Ann married Bruce Johnson. The last eight are still living and all but the last two live in Howard County.

Howard passed away Aug. 14, 1966 and Ruth died Aug. 21, 1978. Both are buried at Memorial Park Cemetery in Kokomo. At this time they have 26 grandchildren, 39 great-grandchildren and two great-great grandchildren.

There could not have been more loving parents and grandparents. They had enough love left over to give to many other children who from time to time made their home with them. *Submitted by granddaughter Patricia Ann (White) McClellan*

JACOB AND LOUISA (MASON) WHITE -

Jacob White was born April 26, 1844 the eighth child of Jefferson and Elizabeth (Alder) White. The family came to Howard County shortly after his birth in Johnson County, IN and he grew to manhood by helping his father on the farm and learning the trade.

The country was engulfed in the Civil War and was touching everyone's lives. Jacob joined Co. "G" of the 147th Regiment of Indiana Infantry on March 9, 1865. During his enlistment he served in his parents' home state of Virginia and became ill, an illness which plagued him the balance of his days. Time to time he was in the Veterans Hospital, Marion, IN. At the end of the conflict, the 147th was sent back to Indianapolis to participate in a big victory parade. The celebration finally over, Jacob's regiment was discharged, and he and his buddies walked home to Howard County, over 60 miles, by way of the Old Michigan Road and through Burlington. He was a life member of the Howard County GAR. Jacob was always known as the "Old Soldier" to his family and friends in his later years.

Louisa Mason born Nov. 29, 1851 was the seventh child of Jacob Daniel and Rebecca (Showalter) Mason born in Howard County. Being the girl next door she soon caught Jacob's eye and they were married Jan. 9, 1868.

Four children were born to Jacob and Louisa. Viola married Oscar Miller, Dora Etta married Charles Gibson, Willard Douglas married Anna Mae Ritchey, and Howard married Stella Almedia Fuller in Portland, OR. At the young age of 34 Louisa died from complications of pregnancy Jan. 23, 1886 and was buried in the Barnett Cemetery. Jacob never married again and always mourned the loss of his young wife. The eldest daughter (Viola "Vi"), who was only 16, took over the duties as mother for her sister and two brothers.

Louisa (Mason) White buried Barnett Cemetery; Jacob White buried Crown Point Cemetery, Civil War Circle

Lobar pneumonia took Jacob on Jan. 24, 1919 at the age of 74 and he was buried in the Civil War Circle of Crown Point Cemetery. For many years his grave was unmarked. However, it is now marked with a military stone of which he is deserving.

Eleanor Miller, the youngest daughter of Viola, said she was just a little girl when her grandfather departed this life. She does remember he had a long white beard which was always on top of the blankets when he was sleeping. *Submitted by great-great-granddaughter Ruth Ann (White) Chambers*

JEFFERSON AND ELIZABETH (ALDER) WHITE -
Jefferson (1805-1866) and Elizabeth (Alder) White (1810-1878) were early pioneers of Indiana and Howard County.

The young family, Elizabeth 20 years of age and Jefferson 22, embarked with a caravan on a long and hazardous journey to Indiana from Wythe County, VA in 1830. Their first child William had just been born.

Jefferson was looking for his "promised land". This phrase became the family saying whenever he had a desire to move.

They traveled west with a two-wheel cart pulled by oxen carrying all of their worldly possessions. There was only room in the cart for the baby to ride. Jefferson and Elizabeth walked to Indiana.

Guards were posted at night to protect them from Indians and scavengers. Each man had to take his turn at watch. Those who slept did so with one eye open.

The caravan made its way over the mountains through Boone's Gap (Cumberland Gap) and north across Kentucky to Ft. Washington (Cincinnati) at the Ohio River. Here carts, animals and people were loaded on huge toll flatboats for the three day trip down the Ohio to Madison, IN.

It was up the Old State Road from Madison to Indianapolis and Hendricks County. At long last there was the reunion with friends and relatives. The family lived for several years in Hendricks and Johnson counties.

Land was opened for settlement in the Miami Reserve and this brought them to Howard County by the Old Michigan Road to Burlington. When Jefferson and Elizabeth came to Howard County, in 1844, it was wilderness, swamps, snakes, mosquitos, wolves and a few homesteads in the early stages of clearing.

They purchased a quarter section of land which today would be located at the north west corner of roads 750 W. and 00 NS. Each year land was cleared for farming and the wilderness began to disappear.

Jefferson bought more land about two miles west of the farm. Here he built Elizabeth's home. Not a cabin but a real house. He continued to improve the farm until his death from lung fever in 1866. The family buried him near the Wildcat River on a hill. He is on his "promised land".

Elizabeth lived another decade and also died of lung fever in 1878. She is buried at the South Union Cemetery.

Grave of Elizabeth (Alder) White; Stone of Jefferson White

Two of their sons enlisted in the Union Army when the Civil War came to Howard County. Andrew was sent to Tennessee and Jacob to his parents' home state of Virginia.

They had twelve children: William, James, Elizabeth, George, Harvey, Jessee, Andrew, Jacob, Mary, Thomas, Malinda and Susan. The last four were born in Howard County. All of them grew to adulthood and went on to live full and productive lives.

Information taken from The Mason-White Family History by James M. Freed. *Submitted by great-great-grandson Robert Joseph White*

ROBERT JOSEPH WHITE AND HERTHA F. (COLLETT) (LITTLE) WHITE -
Robert Joseph was born in Kokomo, IN Nov. 27, 1925. He was the son of Howard Edward and Ruth Ella (Hunt) White. Bob attended Kokomo High School.

Robert and Hertha White

December of 1942 Robert joined the Navy and went through basic training at Great Lakes Naval Training Station. He went to Memphis, TN to ordnance school and then to Hollywood, FL for gunnery school. His active duty time was spent in the South Pacific. Some of the places were the Hawaiian Islands, Guadalcanal in the Solomon Islands, New Guinea, Admiralty Islands, Ulithi, Angaur and Peleliu in the Palau Islands and Guam. He took part in the Philippines Liberation campaign. At Manus, in the Admiralty Islands, Bob witnessed the largest TNT explosion in WWII when the USS *Mt. Hood* blew up, taking 500 lives on Nov. 10, 1944. Bob returned home, completed his high school education and joined the Army being stationed in several places, then remained in the USAR 199th Ordnance Co. and retired in 1965 from the military with the rank of 1st Sergeant (E8).

Bob played baseball in the service. His love for the game came from early days in Kokomo when he played ball with Circus John's teams. This was the closest thing Kokomo had to a little league in the 1930's.

Bob worked for the U.S. Post Office in 1950 and Delco Electronics was his next employer in 1953. He was in plant security and retired after 34 years service in 1987.

McClellan family (l. to r.) Back: Rick and Patty. Front: Aaron, Cynthia and Jim

The year of 1951 was a great one for Bob and Hertha. She was transferred from the Anderson store of Lawson Jewelers to Kokomo as credit manager. It was here they met. Bob was buying rings for another girl. Eventually he broke up with the other girl and the two started seeing each other. They were married in Kokomo on April 12, 1952 and are still going strong.

Ruth and Mark Chambers

Hertha Faustine Collett was born in Muncie, IN on Dec. 29, 1929. She was the daughter of Thomas Orlen and Hertha (Stevens) Collett. Her mother died the same day of complications. The baby was given to Ira P. and Mariah Christine (Sylvester) Little for adoption. They took Hertha home to Anderson at the age of five weeks.

The young life of Hertha was spent in Anderson. Her family moved to Everett, WA in 1943. She went to Everett High School, graduating in the spring of 1948. Hertha also attended Everett Junior College and returned to Indiana in 1949.

Front: Stephanie Middle: Amanda and Anastacia. Back: John and Nicole White; Robert Joseph White.

Bob and Hertha have three children: Patricia is a certified gastrointestinal nurse and is married to Richard McClellan, Jr. They have three children: Aaron Christopher, Cynthia Faye, and James Robert. The family lives in Indianapolis. Ruth Ann is married to Mark Chambers and lives in Greensboro, NC. She is a graduate of IUPUI in Indianapolis and holds a Master's degree from Northwestern University at Chicago. Her chosen profession is a business consultant and has her own company. John Fitzgerald is in the U.S. Army serving in Korea. His family lives at Ft. Eustis, VA. John married Nichole Harless and they have four children: Anastasia Marie, Stephanie Nichole, Amanda Elaine and Robert Joseph.

You might say Bob and Hertha are survivors. They were in the 1965 Palm Sunday tornado and suffered a total loss of their home. They again had a total loss in April 1982 from another tornado. The odds are great that they will never have another; at least let's hope so! *Submitted by John F. White*

WILLARD DOUGLAS AND ANNA MAE (RITCHEY) WHITE - Willard Douglas, known as "Doug," was the third child of Jacob and Louisa (Mason) White. He was born Sept. 1, 1875 in Howard County and grew up in Ervin Twp. as his father and mother had done before him. Doug carried on the tradition of farming and was really quite good at it as well as having a way with animals. It was said Doug really had a good sense of humor and was always playing jokes on everyone around him. He would rather play a joke on someone than eat.

Another early pioneer family to Howard County was the Ritcheys. Doug carried on still one more tradition of the White family by marrying the girl next door, Anna Mae Ritchey, on Nov. 25, 1897. "Annie" was the eldest daughter of John Franklin and Sarah Elizabeth (Myers) Ritchey. They had three children (1) Howard Edward (2) Everett Kenneth and (3) Eva Lucile.

Doug White and granddaughter Mary Loretta (White) Swihart

Doug and Annie moved around quite often. They moved in 1906 to Benton County, IN where Everett was born on September 30. He married Daisy Mae Lincoln and had eight children. He died Jan. 1, 1976 in San Francisco, CA. Eva was born in Union County, OH on Nov. 14, 1908. She married Percy French. They had one son. Death came to her at Douglas, KS Oct. 17, 1927.

One point in time Doug went to follow the wheat harvest in Kansas with the threshing ring and took his oldest son, Howard, with him. They did this for awhile. Annie and Doug along with the children, moved to Springfield, MO where they started a boarding house. This seems to have been a nice place so they settled down here for a few years. Howard married Ruth Ella Hunt, a girl from the area. Doug went back in 1923 to Kokomo, IN. Howard, Ruth and Everett soon followed.

Doug departed this life Dec. 18, 1928 with cancer at the home of his son Howard and is buried at Crown Point Cemetery.

For many years after his death all of his old friends could only say what a good man he was and would laugh about all the jokes he used to pull on everyone. *Submitted by granddaughter Mary Loretta (White) Swihart*

WILLIAM PAUL WHITE - William Paul White, the seventh child of Howard Edward and Ruth Ella (Hunt) White, was born Sept. 13, 1934 in Kokomo, IN. As a child, the family lived in western Howard County. He attended New London School, Ervin Township School and Northwestern High School. Kingston Products was his first full-time employment and then he joined the U.S. Air Force in 1954 and served in Japan. Bill was married to Sharon Sue Masters June 22, 1957 at St. Joan of Arc Church by Rev. Robert Melvin in Kokomo. At the time of their marriage Bill was stationed at Ellington Air Force Base in Houston, TX. The young couple lived there until Bill's discharge in 1958. They returned to Kokomo shortly before their first child was born, and Bill went to work for the Kokomo Fire Department as an electrician on the city fire alarm system. He went to work for Delco Electronics in 1964 with the maintenance department as an electrician. Bill retired Oct. 1, 1994 after 30 years of service.

The White Family - Back L-R: Sharon, Bill, Karen, Jim, Sara Britton, Kathy Britton, Billy, Steve holding Brendon, Joan holding Elizabeth, Stephanie Britton, Samantha Britton

Bill is a very good carpenter and built their beautiful home in Monroe Township. He is a member of UAW Local 292 and is a Past Grand Knight of the Knights of Columbus #656, Kokomo, IN. When time permits, Bill likes to play golf.

Sharon Sue Masters, the second child of William T. and Violet (Clubbs) Masters, was born Dec. 21, 1938 in Kokomo. She graduated from Kokomo High School and went to work for Marsh Supermarket. Collecting Country Crafts for her home is one of Sharons favorite hobbies. She also enjoys gardening and spoiling her six grandchildren.

Bill and Sharon have four children, all born in Kokomo. Kathryn Jo born April 1, 1958 is employed by Society Bank. Dennis Britton and Kathy were married Aug. 25, 1979 and they have three daughters, (1) Sara Christine, (2) Stephanie Marie and (3) Samantha Kate; Karen Sue, the second child, born May 15, 1959 graduated from Clark's Beauty Academy and now is in partnership with Kenlyn Watson. They have a shop called The Mane Attraction. The third child is Steven Paul born Nov. 26, 1960 graduated from Purdue University in Lafayette, IN with a degree in engineering. He also has a Master's from the University of Wichita, KS. After graduating from Purdue, he went to work for Boeing Aircraft at Wichita. Steve met and married Joan Catherine Bonanni June 10, 1989. They moved to Kokomo in 1991 and Steve went to work for Delco Electronics where he is now employed. Steve and Joan have three children (1) William Douglas, (2) Brendon James and (3) Elizabeth Irene. The fourth child of Bill and Sharon is James Michael born Feb. 2, 1963 graduated from Purdue with a degree in engineering then went to work for Delco Electronics in Kokomo. He received his Master's from GMI in 1994. All of the children graduated from Kokomo High School.

More information on the White family is found elsewhere in this publication.

WHITEMAN - Ralph Vernon Whiteman and Roberta Louise Suter were married July 15, 1953 in Meridan Street Christian Church Greentown, IN.

Ralph is the son of Mabel (Helton) and Ray Whiteman. He had two brothers Dale and Russell.

Roberta is the daughter of Gerald and Elpha (Abney) Suter. She had two sisters Mary (Suter) Gang and Harriet (Suter) Godwin, and one brother Gerald F. Suter.

Ralph and Roberta are the parents of three daughters. Vicky Lynn born March 23, 1957 married Kimberlyn Odel Lawson Jan. 8, 1977. They are the parents of Darr Kimberlyn, born Sept. 12, 1979, and Courtney Brooke born Jan. 15, 1982. They live in Greentown.

Karen Jo born Jan. 17, 1959 married William Gordon Nester Feb. 19, 1977. They are parents of Ashley Jo born Aug. 31, 1984 and Samantha Nicole born April 18, 1987. They live in Grant County.

Lisa Kay born Sept. 24, 1961 married Brian Douglas Corder, July 18, 1981. They are the parents of Amanda Brianne born Dec. 3, 1987 and Nathan Allen born March 1, 1991. They live in Greentown, IN, RR.

Whitemans have lived in the same house for over 30 years. Ralph is a Korean veteran. They have two children deceased. They are both retired, Ralph from Chrysler and Roberta from Delco.

WILLIAMS - First Generational Link: Roger Williams, born Wales, England 1601 and died 1683. Married Dec. 15, 1629 to Mary who died 1676. Boarding the ship *"Lyon"* on Dec. 1, 1630 and sailed to the colonies, arriving at Boston Harbor Feb. 5, 1631. After years of unsuccessful resolution they fled Massachusetts and founded Rhode Island. Occupation - minister of Baptist church. They had six children: Mary, Freeborn, Mercy, Providence, Joseph and Daniel.

Second Generational Link: Daniel William, born Providence, RI Feb. 15, 1641 and died May 14, 1712. Married Dec. 7, 1676 to Rebecca Rhodes Powers who died 1727. Occupation unknown. They had three children: Patience, Roger Jr. and Peleg.

Third and Fourth Generational Links: These are in bits and pieces and incomplete. The family born or migrated from Rhode Island to Augusta County, VA, with occupations unknown.

Fifth Generational Link: William Williams, occupation of a farmer, migrated from Virginia to Kentucky in 1801, thereby purchasing land in Lincoln, Knox and Pulaski counties. He died in 1810, leaving several children. His widow Jenny, remarried in 1811 to a widower, Daniel Lewis.

Sixth Generational Link: John Williams, born May 13, 1766 and died Dec. 7, 1838. He married Sarah "Bryant" Williams. John and his family migrated to Kentucky in 1800 with the occupation of a farmer. They left Kentucky in 1812 and migrated to a village near New Castle, IN and remained there until 1816, when they moved on to Everton, IN where he was also a stockman as well as a farmer, remaining there until his death.

Seventh Generational Link: William H. Williams, born Feb. 28, 1819 and died March 15, 1893. On Oct. 4, 1837 he married Susan "Fox" Williams, born Aug. 27, 1822 and died Aug. 21, 1911. They migrated, after studying medicine, to Lincoln Township in Huntington County. They had eight children: Sarah A., Loretty, Orlando B., H. Jerome, John L., William G., Arnold A. and Napoleon B.

Eight Generational Link: Napoleon Bonapart Williams, born Nov. 30, 1845 and died Sept. 20, 1901. He married April 18, 1866 to Martha Elizabeth "Edgar" Williams, born Aug. 30, 1846 and died Feb. 27, 1905. Occupation that of a farmer. They had six children: Florence, Loretta, Gertrude, William A., Arnold Orlando and John N.

Dick, Cecil, Madge Williams

Digressing briefly—

Seventh Generation: William H. and two of his sons were all in the Civil War in the Union Army.

William H. entered as a private and served as a doctor on June 19, 1861 in F Company, 13th Regiment. Mustering out Dec. 20, 1863 in Folley Island, SC.

His son, Arnold Orlando, known in the family as "Uncle Doc." entered as a private and served as a doctor on Feb. 7, 1864 in the F Company, 130th Regiment. Mustering out Dec. 12, 1865 in Charlotte, NC.

The other son, Napoleon B., lied about his age and entered as a bugler in the 23rd Light Artillery. Mustering out July 2, 1865 in Indianapolis, IN.

Ninth Generational Link: John N. Williams, born in Huntington County, Feb. 7, 1878 and died Aug. 23, 1947. He married Sept. 18, 1903 to Ethel S. "Hall" Williams. Born Oct. 25, 1885 and died Sept. 23, 1953. Occupation of a crane operator and hoisting engineer. John and Ethel had three sons, Vergil, Cecil and Earl.

Tenth Generational Link: Cecil W. Williams, born Jan. 4, 1906 in Andrews, IN and died Jan. 24, 1983. Occupation, structural iron worker. He married Nov. 6, 1927 to Madge L. "Decker" Williams, born April 20, 1912 in Elkhart, IN and died Oct. 13, 1993. They had one son, Richard W. Williams.

Eleventh Generational Link: Richard W. Williams, born June 27, 1937 in Kokomo, IN. Unmarried and occupation, office worker for Chrysler Corporation. After 32 1/2 years of service he retired in 1991 having also served for six years as president of Local 1302 UAW. *Submitted by Dick Williams*

ROBERT H. WILLIAMS - Robert was born in Cordon, KY, on March 11, 1920. He is the son of John Robert (born Sept. 3, 1899, died Nov. 18, 1985), and Stella Bell Herron Williams, (April 17, 1900 died Sept. 27, 1988). His family moved to Evansville in 1928.

On Jan. 10, 1942, Robert married Arletta A. Harris in St. Louis, MO. Robert worked in a defense plant until he enlisted in the Army Engineers in June, 1943.

Arletta was born in Lingo, WY, on Jan. 1, 1924. The daughter of William (Henry) and Selma Ring Harris, Arletta became a Hoosier in 1929. She has two brothers, Verl and Herschel Harris. Verl has lived in Greentown since 1959 and retired from Delco in 1983. He has five children, Martha, Alan, Ruth, Mark, and Sarah. Arletta's parents moved from Evansville to Greentown in 1973. Mr. Harris died in 1976 and Mrs. Harris died in 1982. They are buried in the Greenlawn Cemetery.

Robert and Arletta came to Kokomo in October, 1955. Arriving with them were three daughters, Roberta Ann, Carol Diana, and Arleen Mae. Two more children were born after their arrival in Kokomo, Russell Bruce and Constance Sue.

Roberta Ann was born Nov. 15, 1943. She attended Central Junior High School and graduated in 1961 from Kokomo High School. Birdie married Phil Corwin on Nov. 19, 1966. Now residing in Ohio, they have three daughters, Kelly Renee, Kristi Lynn, and Kara Ann. They have one grandchild, Kayla.

Born on Nov. 5, 1946, Carol Diana graduated from Kokomo High School in 1964. She married Brian T. Runyon, Sept. 19, 1964, and has two children, Brian T., Jr. and Kimberly Michelle. In July, 1974, Carol married Tim Damon. Tim has a daughter, Dawn, and on Feb. 25, 1977, Robert Keith was born to Carol and Tim.

Robert and Arletta Williams

Arleen Mae was born April 25, 1952. She graduated from Taylor High School, Center, in 1970. On Dec. 22, 1970, she married Everett W. Miller, Jr. They have two children, Christina Noelle and Brent William. Later, on July 30, 1983, Arleen married Mark Cochran of Forest, IN. Mark has two children, Phillip Martin and Lacee Marie. Arleen works for Haynes International, Inc.

A New Year's Eve baby, Russell Bruce was born at St. Joseph Hospital on Dec. 31, 1957. A graduate of Western High School in 1976, he then attended Ivy Tech. In June, 1983, he married Cindy Pickett. They have two children, Dean Russell and Dustina Ann. Russell is the Williams in Colvin and Williams Construction, Inc.

Constance Sue was born on Feb. 27, 1960 in St. Joseph Hospital. A 1978 Western High School graduate, she married Randy Parks on March 18, 1978. They live in Clinton County with their three children, Jennifer Nichole, Kenneth Randall, and Troy Herron.

While living in southwestern Howard County, Robert retired from Chrysler Corporation in 1979. Robert enjoys Wednesdays with the Noon Lions Club. Arletta volunteers at the Kokomo Public Library. Both enjoy the out-of-doors and gardening. Robert and Arletta are active members of Chapel Hill Christian Church in Alto, IN. *Submitted by Arletta Williams*

WILSON - The Wilsons of Baniffshire and some families around Edinburgh are cadets of the Innes of Aberchider.

The Wilsons of Caithiness and Sutherland descend from William, son of that George, who was chief of clan Gunn in mid-15th Century.

For long among the best known of the name were the Wilsons of Bannockburn.

It is unknown when the Wilsons migrated to America, but when they came they settled in eastern Kentucky. From there the family divided, some stayed in Kentucky and others came north to Indiana. There were Wilsons in both Confederate and Union armies. John C. Wilson is buried in South Union Cemetery in Ervin Township.

Ambrose Wilson, son of John C. and Polly (McDowell) Wilson, was born in Ripley County, IN, Aug. 25, 1839; died April 17, 1936, aged 96 years, 7 months and 22 days. He was of a family of seven children, all of whom have preceded him in death. In 1853 he, with his father, mother and brothers and sisters, came to Ervin Township and settled upon the southeast quarter of Section 15.

They came from Ripley County by train to Sharpsville, then the terminus of the L.E.&W. Railroad. They were met there by his uncle, "Muck" McDowell, and taken to Ervin Township where he resided until death. He attended one of the first schools in Ervin Township and was its oldest surviving pupil. "Billy" King was his teacher, long since deceased.

In 1864 he was married to Phoebe Griffith, daughter of George Griffith, who then resided in the same house where he died. To this union seven children were born, Sylvester, Cora Ridgeway, Pearl Byrum and McDonald "Mack," all of Ervin Township, and Lida O'Donnell of Clay Township. A daughter Florence, and son Frank preceded him in death. The wife died Feb. 2, 1894, since which he made his home with his children.

Ambrose Wilson and Phoebe Wilson

McDonald George Wilson (1878-1955) and Maude Huddleston (1880-1979) had six children: Guy (1904) who married Madge Freeland (1905-1987). Their son Lyndal married Ann Wood and they have Michelle, who married Paul Worthington; Lisa who married Michael Kelly and has Ann and Jackson; and Guy and Stephen. Their daughter Sharon married William Watson and has,

Celia who married Luigi Perilla, and they have Stephen, Jennifer and Michelle; David married Angela Capitani, and they have Diana; and Rosemary Watson.

Earl Wilson (1907 -) married Marjorie Rice (1906-1967). Their son Max married Maryanna Saunders; their children are, Thomas who married Bridgette Harris and has Lauren, Marjorie and Olivia; Elizabeth; and Amelia who married James Bouson, and has Autumn and Christy. Earl married second Elizabeth Kelly Redding.

John Wilson (1909 -) married Henrietta Sence. Their daughter Lois married Joe Patty, and they have Douglas, and Delene who married Robert Linzey and have Joel and Cecilia. Their son Glen married Carolyn Lantz, and had Kent who married Cynthia Hicks and has, Tyler, Travis and Kylee; a son Kris (1964-1982). Glen married second Deloris Kling Miller. Their son William married Jane Tucker and has Stephanie, Shaun and Scanlon.

Mary Wilson (1912 -) married Lester Kelly (1910-1959). Their daughter Kay married Dirk Young, dec'd; 2nd David Knoll; 3rd Joseph Noel. Her children are Eric Young Knoll and Kelly Knoll, and Katherine and Karen Noel. Their son Joseph married Ann Miller, and has Sarah and Jennifer. Joseph married second, Eleanore Kelly.

Mildred Wilson (1914 -) married Scott Jones, dec'd.

Wayne Wilson (1918-1988) married Jane Turner. They had Constance, who married Steve Little and has a son, Seth. She married second, Kevin Anderson; Cheryl married Thomas Smith, Robert Kress and Eric DeWitt. *Submitted by Mary Wilson Scott*

CHESTER W. AND MARJORY L. WILSON -
Chester and Marjory are both natives of Howard County. The migrations during and after the Civil War brought their families to Howard County. Chester's forefathers were: Wilson, Johnson, Bryan, and Grau. Marjory's parents names were Newlan and Hand.

The census of Sussex County Delaware 1860 showed Asa J. Wilson born 1826 and Elizabeth born 1830. They were the parents of Mary, Bashie, William C. and Callie. Following the death of Asa Jr., Elizabeth's brother, who had settled in Jackson Township, Howard County, went to Delaware and brought Elizabeth and the four children to his home.

The Johnsons' lineage can be traced to England, coming to the colonies by the ship *Godspeed,* in the year 1610. The families established in Virginia and then came to Henry County, IN. In 1848 David and Belinda Johnson came to Howard County. They laid claim to land two miles northwest of Greentown. David went by foot to Ft. Wayne where he received a "deed" signed by President Zachary Taylor. The Johnson built a lean-to shanty northwest of Greentown. In the fall they built a cabin, where over the years they raised a family of ten children.

David and Belinda's eldest son, John, was the father of nine. The third of the nine children was "Melissa". She united with William C. Wilson in marriage. They became the parents of seven children; three died in infancy. Those living were: Gale, father of (Ardee, Avonnelle and Mary Helen) Glen L. father of (Dorothy, Mildred, Chester and Inis) Loren D. father of (Jessie, Shirlee and Amaryllis) Laird E. father of (Janet P.).

Chester and Marjory Wilson

In the year of 1873, the family of Daniel and Mary Bryan came to Howard County from Darke County, OH. They established their home in Ervin Township. There were seven children. The Bryans were involved in education, politics and farming. Later they moved to East Sycamore Road.

The Graus originated in Germany. They came to America in 1849 settling in Ohio. Then coming to Howard County in 1875 and buying ground at 400 N. 450 E. Their family consisted of 11 children. The 11th child "Sarah" became the wife of James J. Bryan. James and Sarah had two daughters, Opal (Bryan) Smeltzer and Arbutus (Bryan) Wilson.

Arbutus Bryan and Glen Wilson were married Oct. 30, 1915.

On April 9, 1941 Chester was attending a youth fellowship roller skating party at the Aragon Roller Rink on the northwest corner of the Court House Square in Kokomo. He became acquainted with Marjory L. Newlan.

Marjory's family had come to Howard County in the year of 1917. The family operated a dairy business for several years northeast of and in Kokomo. Her parents were Earl and Ethel (Hand) Newlan.

Chester graduated from Greentown High School and entered the Army Air Force in May of 1943. In October of 1944 Marjory went by train to Denver, CO. At the Lowry Air Force Base Chapel on Oct. 16, 1944 at 5:00 p.m. they were married by the base chaplain Alvin Nygaard.

In their early married years, because of the service, they lived in Denver, Fresno, Boise, Salt Lake City, and Vallejo. They returned to Howard County in 1947.

They were employed on the farm for two years, then went to work at the Studebaker Plant in South Bend. After working, going to school and raising a family Chester graduated from Bethel College in Mishawaka, IN. Following graduation they, with their four children: Ronald, Gary, Dee Ann and Gregory, moved to their first pastorate at Decatur, IN.

The Wilsons' ministry was pastoral, evangelistic and musical. Marjory was a graduate of Sherwood School of Music in Chicago. She was an accomplished pianist and organist. She taught both instruments for several years. In the first year of their second pastorate on Nov. 4, 1961, because of a tragic accident their youngest son Gregory was taken from them.

Chester, Marjory and two of their children Ronald and Dee Ann formed a quartet which sang together for several years. Their other son, Gary, became a minister to the deaf and has served in several states in this capacity.

Due to poor health, in the spring of 1990, they decided to retire from the ministry. They had completed 40 years and had traveled and ministered in 47 of the 50 states.

The heritage of Chester and Marjory was rich and very fruitful. Today they reside at their home 800 E. 1739 N. They have three children, seven grandchildren, three step-grandchildren, three great-grandchildren and five step-great grandchildren.

ARTHUR HENRY AND ETHEL BELL BOWEN WOLFORD -
Arthur H. Wolford was born April 3, 1876 in Tipton County. He died in an automobile accident Dec. 31, 1925 as a result of suffering a coronary failure. He was born in Goldsmith to Solmon Wolford.

He was married to Ethel Bell Bowen in 1903 in Howard County and resided in Howard County the remainder of his life. Ethel Bowen was born in Howard County July 27, 1888 and died Oct. 5, 1949. They are both buried in Crown Point Cemetery.

They had four children: Hazel Wolford Lytle who died in 1950 of cancer; Roy Thomas Wolford, May 14, 1908, died September 1990; Harold L. Wolford, Oct. 14, 1911 died Feb. 1917; and Mildred Bell Wolford Reynolds, born May 26, 1917.

Ethel was very active in the Friends Church on North Buckeye Street and worked very hard for the Republicans. She was a good seamstress. She raised her daughter Mildred alone, after losing her husband in the auto accident. *Submitted by Berdina Head, granddaughter*

DAVID MILTON WOLFORD AND GERTRUDE PEARL (GOINS) WOLFORD -
David was the second child born into a family of seven on June 4, 1869 in Hagerstown, IN. His father was John Michael Wolford born Oct. 27, 1846 in Henry County, IN. John was the son of Daniel Wolford born in Hagerstown, MD Sept. 22, 1821 and Deborah (Carroll) Wolford born Sept. 16, 1828 in New Castle, IN. David's father John and also his grandfather Daniel served in the Civil War. John was in Company C, 9th Indiana Calvary and Daniel was in Company E Indiana Volunteers.

David Melton Wolford and Gertrude Pearl (Goins) Wolford

They both survived the war but had many medical complications from that day forward until their death, Daniel on April 15, 1889 and his son soon after, Sept. 20, 1890. David's mother was Asenath C. Baldwin who was born June 29, 1849 into a large family of 12 children including herself. Asenath's father David Baldwin was born Jan. 18, 1822 in North Carolina and her mother Ruth Howell was born March 26, 1823 also in North Carolina. David had three brothers, Nathan Emery, John H., and Edward E. Wolford and three sisters, Sarrah Etta, Della May, and Dollie E. Wolford. Gertrude Pearl Goins became the wife of David Wolford Nov. 30, 1899 in Hamilton County, IN and moved to Howard County between 1912 and 1915. Gertrude was born Oct. 29, 1883 in Hamilton County, IN and was the daughter of Silas Goins born February 1855 in Indiana and Anna (Martin) Goins born Jan. 10, 1856 in Ohio. Gertrude had two sisters, Laura Alice and Ethel Goldie Goins, and two brothers Jasper Oliver and George Raymond Goins.

David was park superintendent for the city of Kokomo, IN from the early 1920s until the early 1930s. A picture of him standing along side of Ben, the large steer, is on display at the Pavilion that was built for Ben at Highland Park in Kokomo, IN. David and Gertrude gave life to 13 children: Goldie Effie May, Oliver Burdett, Chester Arther, Myrtle Lavana, Everett Arlow, Jesse Melton, Earnest Harold, Walter Kenneth, Della Marie, Robert James, Edna Pearl, William Raymond and Ralph Eugene Wolford. David and Gertrude lived and worked in Howard County, IN until their death, David on Nov. 19, 1951 and Gertrude on May 23, 1955.

The lives of David Melton and Gertrude Pearl (Goins) Wolford may seem to have played but a small part in the history of Howard County until you think of the ones they left behind. Then you realize that even after death, people like David and Gertrude continue to give life itself to Howard County. *Submitted by Walter L. Wolford*

WOOD/DRINKWATER -
Charles Raymond "Ray" Wood was born in Indianapolis, IN, June 4, 1878. He was one of six children born to George Philip and Mary Elizabeth Hine Wood.

The Wood family came to Kokomo in 1888, when Ray's father assumed part-ownership of the newly-established Wood-Miller Pulp and Paper Mill. Ray attended the Maplewood Classical School as a teenager. He later fought in the Spanish-American War and the Spanish Insurrection and was discharged as a first lieutenant, Co. I, 39th United States Volunteer Infantry, May 6, 1901. He then became a junior partner in his father's paper mill company.

Mazy Belle Drinkwater was born May 9, 1882, in Kokomo, the only daughter of William Worley and Emily Mills Drinkwater. Mazy had three brothers. She graduated from Maplewood Classical School, Class of 1900, and successfully passed her teacher's examination.

Ray and Mazy were married Aug. 22, 1906. In the next six years, the couple produced a family of five fine boys - George William, Charles Raymond, Jr., John Richard, Worley Drinkwater, and Robert Mills.

The family moved away from Kokomo in 1910, and eventually settled in Webster Groves, MO around 1915. Ray became the midwestern sales representative for the River Raisin Paper Company of Monroe, MI, owned by his brother George Harley Wood. Ray and Mazy remained in Webster Groves until the time of their deaths in 1945.

Ray and Mazy's parents were all born in Ohio.

George Phillip Wood was born in Piqua, OH, March 3, 1845, the son of Charles A. and Hannah French Washer Wood. George fought in the Civil War, then traveled from Ohio to Indianapolis, IN in 1865.

Ray and Mazy Wood with sons l-r, Richard, Worley, and George Jan. 23, 1942

Mary Elizabeth Hine was also born in Piqua, OH, Dec. 15, 1849, the daughter of Charles Henry and Elizabeth Apgar Hine.

George and Mary were married Feb. 27, 1868, in Marion County, IN. After moving to Kokomo in 1888, the couple remained there the rest of their lives. George died in 1908, and Mary followed in 1925. Their daughter "Mayme" Wood owned and operated the Wood Movie Theater in Kokomo.

William Worley Drinkwater was born in Darke County, OH, April 30, 1855, the son of Thompson (a farmer) and Rebecca Murphy Drinkwater. Their family came to Howard County in 1865, and settled on a farm five miles east of Kokomo.

When Thompson Drinkwater died in 1875, William assumed responsibility for running the farm and supporting his mother and sisters. He simultaneously completed his education.

Emily Mills, daughter of William (a farmer) and Margery Adams Mills, was born in Preble County, OH, Feb. 8, 1860. Her family came to the Galveston community in 1865.

William and Emily were married in Howard County, March 3, 1881. They began their married life on a farm in Miami County and moved to Kokomo in 1889.

William entered the insurance and real estate fields. In 1930, he and his son J.O. Drinkwater organized the realty firm of W.W. Drinkwater and Son. Emily and William died in Kokomo in 1930 and 1935, respectively.

Both the Wood and Drinkwater couples were regular members of the Grace ME Church and participated in a variety of business, civic, and social organizations. They were deeply and actively committed to their families, church, and community. *Submitted by Mrs. Ellen Wood Kubica*

WOODRUFF - Edward Charles Woodruff was born July 23, 1851 in London, England. As a small child he came to America with his mother, Honora McQuinlin. Before he was 16 he came to to Indiana on the train. He began his railroad employment at the age of 13, working his way up from the bottom to become crew chief. He supervised the laying of the tracks from Frankfort to Anderson.

While in Clinton County he met and married Amanda Jane Pierce, the youngest daughter of Alexander S. and Nancy (Skinner) Pierce, Jan. 1, 1873. Amanda was born July 13, 1854 in Clinton County, IN.

They were the parents of six children, all born in Hillisburg, Clinton County, IN.

Their children were:

Nancy Ellen "Nell" was born Dec. 31, 1873. She married Herbert J. Spencer. They lived in Indianapolis and had no children. She died Aug. 6, 1949.

Ludica Lucille, she went by "Lucille", was born 1876. She married Wm. Oliver Dudley, Nov. 23, 1897 in Anderson, IN. They lived in Brooklyn, NY near E.C.'s mother and half siblings. They had one daughter, Fleeta.

E.C. and Amanda Woodruff

Edward Charles Jr. "Ed" was born Dec. 4, 1878. He married first to Hattie Gardner (of Grant Co., IN) April 15, 1899 in Madison County, IN. They had four sons, James Paul, Gordon, Mayne and Paul. James Paul died age 10 from pneumonia. Mayne died age two and Paul a few days after birth. Hattie died Sept. 10, 1905 after a gasoline explosion. He then married Ethel Woodring, May 12, 1906. They had one daughter, Helen Jane. Ed & Ethel settled in California where he died Dec. 31, 1959.

Le Roy was born Nov. 16, 1880. He married Ida Frances Robinson Jan. 19, 1903 in Madison County, IN. They had three sons: Paul, who died a few days after birth; Raymond Charles, who drowned at the age of 25; and Garland. He then married Mary Louise Engle. They had no children; however, she raised Raymond and Garland. They lived in Kokomo and LaPorte. He died Feb. 17, 1940 in LaPorte, IN.

Audrey Monica was born Jan. 15, 1890. She married Benjamin A. Schick. This family is featured elsewhere in this publication.

Herbert R. was born May 5, 1894. He was married to Nannie Catherine Nelson in 1911. They had three children: Charles Herbert, Juanita and Robert, who was a WWII POW. They lived mostly in Anderson, IN, where Herbert died Sept. 27, 1958. He had at least one marriage after Nannie's death, but no other children.

Edward Charles "E.C." became a Methodist minister later in his life. He died Oct. 3, 1934 in Kokomo. Amanda died Dec. 15, 1923 in Tipton. They are both buried at the Fairview Cemetery in Tipton.

It should be noted here that E.C. and Amanda had a total of 17 grandchildren, twelve of these being grandsons. Seven of the 12 grandsons died at young ages as the result of tragedy striking this family over and over again. One of their surviving grandsons was a POW during WWII. It was this family's strong faith in God that sustained them during these tragic events.

E.C. and Amanda were the great-grandparents of this writer. *Submitted by Candy Jones*

WOOLLEY- On July 6, 1797, near Tom's River, NJ, was born James W. Woolley. Nothing is known of his family. In 1819, he moved to Hamilton County, OH, near Cincinnati. There, in 1820, he married Rachel Guthrie of Virginia.

In 1822, James and Rachel moved to Orange County, IN near Chambersburg, where he established a wagon-making business. Over the next 22 years, they birthed 14 children. Of these, three died in childbirth or infancy. A remarkable 11 lived to adulthood, ten to go on to marry and raise children.

In the 1850's, much of the family moved to Cass and Howard counties. A few of the family settled in Taylor Township, near the residence and church of Rev. William A. Albright. There the youngest Woolley child, James Madison, married the youngest of the Albright's 13, Margaret Olive. In 1871, James W. succumbed to pneumonia at his residence. His obituary appeared in *The Kokomo Democrat*. Nine years later, Rachel passed away. Both are buried in Section 1 of Albright Cemetery.

Charles Claborn resided in New London. He first married Martha Ellen Lee, and they birthed three children. Only one, Ostin Lee, lived beyond infancy. Seven years later, he married Susan Jackson, and sired two more, Martha Jane and Ardra Charles. It is interesting to note that both sons chose teaching as their profession. Ostin had an only daughter by his second wife. They named this child Laura Lee, after his first wife who died young. Ostin lived out his years on a farm in Taylor Township. Ardra lived on a farm near Alexandria in his later years, near his three sons and daughter.

From Left: Catharine Dorcas Woolley Hercules, Milford Franklin Woolley, James Madison Woolley, Martin Newell Woolley, Hubbard Allen Woolley, Sarah Ellene Woolley Maker

Hubbard Allen married his first wife, Elizabeth E. Lee, in Parke County. They had four daughters and two sons, one of whom died in childhood. Later, in Howard County, he married Mary A. Peters, and sired four more daughters. He was a farmer, operating a nursery and raising sweet potatoes. Hubbard moved to Cass County, and died in Galveston. Today, two of his great-grandchildren, Donald and Mary Dunkin, live in Kokomo and Galveston.

Catharine Dorcas Woolley married John Taylor Hercules. See Hercules in this book.

James Madison lived out his life in Taylor Township and Kokomo. In the 1870's he began operating the toll gate on Jefferson at Phillips. In 1880, he added a grocery store in the building, and in 1892 a Sunday School. The building burned in 1939, the last remaining structure of its kind. In 1905, James made an unsuccessful bid for City Judge on the Socialist ticket. James and Margaret had two sons and two daughters who lived to adulthood. Clora Alice married James Harvey Garritson, who was in the grocery business. Clora, known as Alice, became a renowned teacher in Kokomo, where her daughter, Frances Camille Garritson Anderson, and two grandsons, C. Thomas and Jerry, live. Ora Ashton married Mabel H. Hayworth, who died less than five months later. Ora later moved to Florida and became a farmer, dying at age 38 of malaria. Anna Francis married Otis "Ote" Howard, of insurance and real estate fame in Kokomo. They had two sons and a daughter. Ote lived to a few days shy of 98 years old. The *Kokomo Tribune* featured him in a couple of articles in his later years. Charles Claborn, named after his uncle, married Jessie May Smith and raised two sons and a daughter. It is interesting that for three consecutive generations, the oldest son sired two sons as his first two children. Charles was supervisor of the trolley and bus drivers in Kokomo in the 1930's. One grandson, Charles Edgar, a daughter, Lillian Bernice Arthur, and a daughter-in-law, Mabel Irene Oakes Woolley, live in Kokomo.

Martin Newell lived for a while in Miami County, where he became associated with a cousin who practiced medicine. Martin, something of a gypsy in the family, moved to Kansas, Texas, California, and finally Oklahoma. It is interesting to note that his grandson and great-grandson followed in the medical profession.

Milford Franklin lived near Kokomo briefly, marrying in Cass County in 1870. He then moved to the

Crawfordsville area, and is buried in Wallace. Milford (Frank) served in the Civil War.

In 1993, through an article in *The Tribune*, four descendants of the children of James W. and Rachel met and found they shared an interest in researching family history. *Submitted by James Lee Woolley-Michigan, Dr. Paul Vincent Woolley III-Pennsylvania, James Newman-Michigan, and Beverly Joan Thompson Wheeler-Kokomo*

JOHN WRIGHT - We trace the Wright Family back to John Wright who was born in 1829 in Indiana. The 1860 census shows him living in Harrison County, Franklin Township with his wife Rebecca Thomas, whom he married Jan. 5, 1854. Rebecca's family were farmers in Harrison County. Her parents were both born in North Carolina. She was born in Indiana. John's mother was born in North Carolina, and his father in Virginia.

The 1880 census shows John and Rebecca having a family. The names of their children were John O., Thomas J. and George B.M. George Brinton McCelland was named after the famous general and is the ancestor the Kokomo line originated from. George, who went by the name of Mack was born Jan. 21, 1864. He married Alda Isabelle Brown on Nov. 24, 1889 and had Clifford T., Ethel G., Ella G., Pearl, and George Dewey. Mack was in 1900 a farm laborer. They in 1900 were living in Morgan Township, Harrison County. In 1910, Mack worked as a sawyer in a hub factory. Mack moved to Kokomo shortly after his wife died in 1913. Mack was foreman of construction work at the Pittsburgh Plate Glass Company's plant in Kokomo. He married Winifred Broadlick of Kokomo. Mack died Feb. 26, 1930 and is buried at Crown Point Cemetery. His son, George Dewey, went by the name of Bill. He was born November, 1898 in Harrison County. Bill married Lela Ann Stewart and had Dewey Charles, Isabelle, and Betty. Bill worked in Kokomo for General Electric. Lela Ann died at the age of 32 in 1929. Bill later married Frances Webb who is related to David Foster. Bill died May 9, 1950 and is buried at Crown Point. Frances Webb Wright died January 1992.

The Wright Family 1986 - Back Row: L to R: Danny Wright, Larry Wright, Lorrie Wright, Ann Wright. Front row: Curtis Wright, Dewey Charles Wright

Bill's son, Dewey Charles, was born Dec. 24, 1922 in Kokomo. He married Ruth Tull whose parents were Hazel Gibson and Levi Thomas Tull. Hazel's grandmother was 100% Indian and lived in Jessamine County, KY. Levi's family came from Clark County. Levi served in the Rainbow Division during WWI and received the Purple Heart Medal. Dewey Charles and Ruth had five children: Daniel, Larry Edward, Ann, Curtis and Lorrie. Dewey Charles worked as a construction worker. He died Oct. 31, 1986 and is buried with his wife Ruth who died (Nov. 20, 1982) at Albright Cemetery.

Daniel is married to the former Mary Rocchio and is employed at Rocchio Sports in Kokomo. They have one son Daniel. Larry Edward lives in Boca Raton, FL and is president of MIG Realty Advisors, Inc. Larry married the former Carol Medina in 1987. Ann is married to Michael White and their children are Brian Alan and Carrie Anne. Ann is employed at Magnetech and Michael is employed at Delco Electronics in Kokomo.

Lorrie is married to Andrew Mittower. Andrew is a lawyer and both he and Lorrie work and reside in Indianapolis. Curtis is employed in manufacturing and resides in Kokomo. The Wrights have called Kokomo their home for many years and consider it a wonderful place to raise a family.

WRIGHT - Arriving from Henry County in 1868, Amos Wright and his wife Vashti bought 40 acres on Dec. 25, 1868 for $1800.00. The land is located southwest of the Wildcat Creek about two miles south of Greentown.

Four children, Clifton, Curtis, Emma and Chester G., were born and raised on this homestead. Chester G. was only 14 months old when his mother died in 1882. The women of the neighborhood took care of him. During the next 14 years Amos and Chester lived alone.

Chester went to school at Richville nearby. They were of Quaker faith where both church and school are combined. As time passed more Quaker families established homes south of the Wildcat. A new worship place was needed so Amos donated ground 1/4 mile from his home. Building started in 1874 with bricks fired in a kiln and burned on the church ground. The foundation was hauled by oxen from Kokomo. Donated labor and materials held the cost to $1,827.27. The meeting house was completed in 1875. Amos served as trustee; later on, Chester G. continued and both taught Sunday School.

Chester G. met Eva Murphy and married Dec. 6, 1911. Together they lived and farmed with Amos until his death in 1913.

Chester G. inherited the homeplace. Time passed—some bad, some good. They were able to buy more land. Six years later their only child Chester G. Wright Jr. was delivered by a Chicago doctor on a makeshift dining room operating table. Chet's birth was the first caesarean baby born at home in Howard County.

November of 1936 disaster struck; a spark from the woodstove ignited the roof burning the homestead. With the help of their neighbors and a mortgage debt, another house was built on this same site in 1938. One year later Chester G. had a heart attack. He continued to farm with his son's help.

L-R: Chester G., Eva, Conrad, Phyllis and Chester Jr.

Chester Jr. met and later married Phyllis Hill Nov. 28, 1942. Working together they bought farmland and set up housekeeping on Road 200. In 1949 they bought a farm in Union Township and moved in Feb. 2, 1950. Three years later on Aug. 5, 1953 their son Conrad C. Wright was born.

In 1955 the New Salem Friends Church was enlarged and modernized. The dedication was June 24, 1956. Chet Jr. continued as a trustee and served on the building committee.

Chester G. and Chester Jr. farmed together until Chester G.'s death on June 1, 1959. Eva remained on the farm four more years until her death on Dec. 3, 1963.

As Conrad became older, he too followed the Wright farming tradition.

On June 1, 1977 Chet Jr. had open heart surgery. Unable to continue the daily farming operation, Conrad took over his father's duties.

The old homestead was later sold to Tim and Susan Cheek in 1982 and they remodeled in 1992.

With Chet's Quaker Christian belief in death as a beginning of life, he passed away June 2, 1984 after a blood clot hit his brain cutting off its supply of oxygen.

Phyllis continued living on the farm until Sept. 28, 1990 when it was sold to Dave and Ethel Parrish. She is remarried to Robert Miller and resides in Kissimmee, FL.

Today, the third C. Wright Farm tradition carries on. Conrad C. and Jan now farm 400 acres. The homeplace is located at 9250 East 200 South, Greentown.

JOHN PRIOR AND HEPSIBAH COATS WRIGHT - The story of the Wright family, preceding their pioneer settlement in Howard County, is identical to that of vast numbers of Quakers who pushed frontier lines from Pennsylvania into Virginia, the Carolinas, Tennessee, Indiana and Illinois. James Wright, born 1671/1677, whom Quakers records name as a "distinguished minister of the Society of Friends", lived in Chester County, PA and the Shenandoah Valley of Virginia. He married Mary (possibly Davis) around 1707. His son, John Wright, born 1716, married Rachel Wells, who in her Quaker ministry, rode horseback 200 miles through North Carolina wilderness to gain permission to set up Cane Creek Friends Meeting in 1751. Their 16th child, Isaac Wright born 1764, married Susannah Haworth born 1766, daughter of Richard and Ann Dillon Haworth. Susannah's Haworth ancestry is the same as that of Pres. Herbert Hoover. Isaac and Susannah and their son, John Prior Wright, figured prominently in the pioneer history of Howard County.

John Prior Wright and Hepsibah Coats Wright

John Prior Wright had lived with his parents and seven sisters in Tennessee, Union and Randolph County, IN, and Vermillion County, IL prior to coming to Howard County. Children of Isaac and Susannah were: Nancy Ann 1785, Mary, 1793, Sarah 1796, Charity 1799, John Prior March 16, 1802, Elizabeth 1804, Naomi 1807, Susannah 1810. John Prior was born in Tennessee and married Hepsibah Coats born 1803 in South Carolina, daughter of William and Mary Jay Coats, in Bartholomew County, IN in 1822. After their marriage they lived in Vermillion County, IL where nine of their 12 children were born, Wm 1823, Isaac 1826 (died inf.), Mary 1824, Sarah 1827, Rhoda 1829, Richard 1833, David 1837, Rachel 1841, Leroy 1845, Charity, 1847. The family was in Vermillion County, IL at least by 1823 and owned land in Section 26 until 1842. They were millers.

When Howard County opened for land purchases, John P. Wright rode horseback to Indiana with only a blazed trail to guide him in 1840 as told in the County 1877 Atlas. He returned the following spring with his family and parents. Their first farm was west of New London, known as Dugan Jones farm. It was here that Isaac and Susannah died in 1844 and were buried in the old Quaker Cemetery at New London. John P. and family moved to what was the homestead 3/4 mile northwest of Russiaville.

The first meeting for the Society of Friends at New London "was held in the woods . . . the next being held house to house . . ." Six people were present and John P. and Hepsibah were among the leading promoters. Through the years they held responsible positions; John P. "sat at the head of the Meeting" (as Friends say) for 20 years. He attended Meeting twice a week until the end of his life, nearly always on foot. He played a major role in activities of the Underground Railroad and engaged in much active poor relief. When the Civil War ended, a former slave was residing with the Wright family for whom John P. took over the care and education.

339

John P. and Hepsibah Wright remained well and active until 1882 when he fell from his haymow and broke a hip. He was 80 years old at the time. After a short illness he passed away 2nd day 4th mo. 1882. Hepsibah outlived him until 1892. They were both laid to rest in the newer New London Cemetery in the northeast part close to a deep ravine. Their stones are separate, simple, and show clasped hands. A stately, tall, beautiful blue spruce stands sentinel nearby. *Submitted by Mary Wright Dennis*

SAMUEL LUKE WYANT - Samuel Luke Wyant moved to Kokomo at the age of five years. Luke, the son of Donald R. and Kym Coomler Wyant, moved back to Howard county in January of 1990. They had lived in Tulsa, OK for eight years, where Luke was born in 1984. Although Luke and his parents knew they would miss the rich spiritual lifestyle of Tulsa, new business opportunities awaited them in Kokomo.

Luke's mother, Kym, had two sisters, Ange Fletcher and Joan Lee. She was the youngest daughter of Paul and Willie Johnston Coomler. Paul worked at the downtown Firestone for over 30 years as service manager. Paul, the only son of Floyd and Faye Howell Coomler, was a World War II veteran who grew up in Lagro, IN, with his sister Helen. The Coomler family came to America from Switzerland, landing at the Port of Philadelphia on Aug. 30, 1749. They left Lancaster County, PA in the 1800's, and settled in Wabash County. Luke's grandmother, Willie Johnston Coomler, was born in Estill, SC, where her family came to America from England.

The Willis Kenworthy Family

Luke's father, Don, had three brothers, Charles, Wm. Thomas, and Ernest, and one sister Elouise Zeck. He was the youngest son of Clay and Catherine Kenworthy Wyant. They farmed in western Howard County. Clay retired from the bridge and construction business. The Wyants came to Montgomery County from Virginia in 1796. Many of the nine children of that family settled in Boone and Clinton Counties. Later generations settled in Carroll and Howard Counties.

Luke's Howard County ancestry is linked with the Kenworthy and Stouts, through his grandmother, Catherine Kenworthy Wyant. She was the daughter of Earl Kenworthy whose mother was Hanna Stout Kenworthy.

The Stouts came from Nottinghamshire, England to New Jersey in the mid 1600's. By the early 1800's, the Stouts had moved into Indiana. There are many Stouts in Howard County, but over 50,000 cousins throughout America.

The Kenworthys came from Warwickshire, near the Kenilworth Castle, in the west part England. They came to the New World in colonial times. Some of them came shortly after the arrival of William Penn and those early Friends (Quakers) who came from England on the ship named *WELCOME*. The ship landed at Delaware, in 1682. The first to arrive in Howard County was Willis Kenworthy, who is in the picture. Apparently New London was settled about 1840. By 1845, enough Quakers had settled to start a Quaker Meeting known as Honey Creek. Then another meeting started in 1846 at Poplar Grove. They met together in alternating locations until 1849, when they only met at Honey Creek, which later became known as New London in 1852. Willis's son, Milton, married Hanna Stout and they became the parents of Earl and Murray who kept the Howard County Quaker tradition going.

Today, Luke is one of many cousins with a great Howard County American Heritage.

YOUNG - John Emmett Young was born March 24, 1895 in Silverwood, IN, and died May 19, 1987 in Howard County, IN. John's parents were Josephus and Sarah Saparona (Stewart) Young. Josephus was born June 6, 1845; his place of birth is unknown. He died June 17, 1897 in Silverwood, IN. He married Sarah Stewart on Dec. 26, 1869 in Brazil, IN. Sarah was born July 22, 1850 in Brazil, IN. Josephus and Sarah had 11 children: Rosalene, Leonard Fountain, Marvin Edgar, Charles Coleman, Harriet May, Marvin, Daisy, Joseph Wesley, Eli Hendrick, Melvin Elmer, and John Emmett Young.

John's paternal grandparents were James and Eliza (Weaver) Young. James was born in 1815 in Clemont County, OH, and died there in 1862. James married Eliza Weaver on Aug. 5, 1839 in Bethel, OH. They had six children, Spencer, Josephus, Mary Ellen, Samuel, James M. and Lafayette E. Young.

John's maternal grandparents were John and Lucinda (Hall) Stewart. They were married on Aug. 29, 1850 in Clay County, IN. They had seven children, Sarah, John, Charles, Marvin, Robert, Harriet, and Naomi Stewart. John Stewart's parents were Robert S. and Sarah (Myers) Stewart. Lucinda's father was Marom C. Hall.

John Emmett was married twice, first to Nellie Gay (Brewer) on Sept. 26, 1919 in Rockville, IN. She was born March 16, 1897, and died Aug. 29, 1930 in Phoenix, AZ. Nellie developed tuberculosis so John took her to Arizona in hope that her health would improve, but she never recovered. John and Nellie had three children, Charles Joseph, Harold Raymond and Margaret Josephine Young. All three children were born in Howard County, IN. Nellie's parents were Charles and Jane (Evans) Brewer.

Charles Joseph married Betty Jane (Massey) Young on Oct. 9, 1941 in Howard County, IN. They had four children, Joseph Le Roy, Steven Michael, Max Lee, and Susan Gay Young. Harold Raymond married Virginia Moore on Oct. 26, 1968; they did not have any children. Josephine was born Oct. 26, 1922, and died Dec. 21, 1971 in Kokomo, IN. She had one daughter, Sarah.

John's second wife was Maimie Lunger (McMurtrey); she was born April 26, 1909 in Clinton County, IN. John and Maimie had two children, Helen Louise and Donald Richard Young. Helen Louise married Stanley Parks Snow on July 21, 1950. They had one daughter, Deborah Lynn Snow. Donald married Mary Ellen (Bush) Young on Nov. 29, 1958. They had two children, Kathy Jo, and Douglas DeWayne Young.

Maimie's first husband was Mark McMurtrey. Mark died Feb. 28, 1929 they had one child Thelma McMurtrey. Thelma married David Tomlinson. Their children are Linda Lucille, Mark Allen, David Keith and Kelly Rae Tomlinson.

John was employed at Satelite from which he retired. John lived a good life and he died at age 92. This history was written by Joseph Le Roy Young. *Submitted by Joseph Young*

YOUNG - John Young was a founder of Butler College in Indianapolis with his friends John C. New and Ovid Butler; he served as Butler's first president in 1855-57.

President Abraham Lincoln appointed John Young consul to Ireland; there, on Jan. 30, 1862, Robert L. Young was born. At the birth, letters of congratulations were sent by Queen Victoria and President Lincoln; these letters became treasured possessions of Robert Young.

The family returned to Indianapolis, and Robert Young attended city schools and Butler College. He also attended the University of Illinois at Urbana, graduating in 1883. Artistically gifted, he decided on a career as an architect, and moved to California to work as a draftsman.

About 1890 he came to Kokomo and took a position as architect with Armstrong-Landon and Company. He designed the Kokomo High School building that served from 1898 until it burned in 1914. The design for the new Grace United Methodist Church building still standing at Washington and Mulberry streets was his.

He met Clara White Kitchen, young widow of Kokomo furniture dealer Manson C. Kitchen (1853-93), and they were married in 1897. Young became step-father to Clara White's daughters, Miriam and Gracie.

Cousin Ida, R.L. Young and Clara Kitchen Young

The family moved to Newton, MA, where Young worked for John Randolph Coolidge, a nephew of future President, Calvin Coolidge; he built a house for his family that increased by two sons, J. Russell (born in 1901), and Arthur (born in 1902).

In 1903 Young moved back to Kokomo and opened an office. Known as R.L. Young, he designed many business buildings for Kokomo's growing industries, and he designed many private residences for the city's burgeoning population. In 1908 he built a low-slung house for himself at 1223 E. Jefferson Street. He designed inventor Elwood Haynes' tile-roofed home on South Webster, now the Elwood Haynes Museum.

Clara Young had been supervisor of music in Kokomo's schools; in 1920 Robert and Clara Young retired and moved to Florida. Six years later they returned to Kokomo, and R.L. tried in vain to keep his Jefferson Street house during the Depression years.

Clara Young died in 1935 and was buried beside her first husband in Rushville. R.L. Young declined mentally in his final years; his son Russell cared for him until he died at Indianapolis on Nov. 17, 1944. He was buried in his father's plot in Crown Hill Cemetery.

Lincoln Coles, son of Kokomo florist W.W. Coles, married Miriam Kitchen; their children were sons Lawrence, Weldon, Manson, and Walter Coles, and daughter Alice Coles.

Arthur Young, now deceased, was president of Kokomo's Midwest Plating; his sons are David H. Young of Kokomo, and Phillip Young, now deceased. *Submitted by Jeff Halton*

DONALD AND MARYELLEN YOUNG - Donald R. and Maryellen Bush Young are both native to Kokomo and Howard County. Donald was born on July 20, 1934, in Center Township, Howard County. Maryellen was born in Kokomo on April 19, 1939.

Donald was born and raised in Darrough Chapel. He attended Darrough School and graduated from Kokomo High School in 1952. He worked on Dale Duncan's farm before going to Haynes Stellite Company previous to enlisting in the U.S. Army. He served in the 11th Airborne Division from 1954 to 1957.

In 1958, he resigned from Haynes Stellite to go to barber school. He worked at Tom's Barber Shop and Dick Goodknight's Barber Shop, both in Kokomo. In 1963, Donald began employment at Continental Steel in the plant security department. He was employed there until the plant closed in 1986. He presently is again engaged in barbering, having a shop in Darrough Chapel.

Maryellen was born and raised in Kokomo, living on South Locke Street. She attended Meridian School and graduated from Kokomo High School in 1957.

Donald and Maryellen were married in Hemlock, IN, at the Mt. Gilead Baptist Church on Nov. 29, 1958. They lived on South Main Street in Kokomo for a short while before moving to Darrough Chapel, where they currently reside.

They both were members of Darrough Chapel Congregational Christian Church for many years, both being active in church and community affairs. Maryellen held Good News Club and Girl's Club meetings at her home and taught Sunday School classes at church. She also was involved in Ladies Aid Society missions. Donald was a deacon at Darrough Church and Foursquare Gospel Church and supported the Boy Scouts in the community.

They raised two children, Kathy Jo and Douglas Wayne, in the Kokomo and Howard County area and have enjoyed living here, and found it a good place to live and raise their children.

Although Donald and Maryellen are both native to Kokomo, their parents are from southern Indiana. Donald's parents, John and Mamie Lunger Young, are from Fountain County. Maryellen's father, Rolly Bush, is from Brown County. Her mother, Iva Kimbel Bush is from Howard County. *Submitted by Kathy Jo Cranor*

JOHN EMMETT YOUNG - John Emmett Young was born in Silverwood, IN, in 1895. He left Fountain County and came to Howard County in 1918 or 1919. He wanted to get out of the coal mines and had heard about the gas discovery that was making Kokomo a boom town.

His first days in Kokomo were an experience as he had no job and only a little money. At that time, the police would let men sleep overnight in the jail. They could stay one night and had to stay elsewhere the next night, so they would go to Opalescent Glass Company and sleep behind the furnaces to keep warm. This continued until John got a job at Pittsburgh Plate Glass. After getting a job, he boarded at "Ma Teen's" boarding house on Vaile Avenue, just east of the old Pennsylvania Railroad.

On Sept. 26, 1919, John married Nellie Gay Brewer. They lived on South Plate Street before moving to Darrough Chapel in 1920. In 1929, John and Nellie moved to California and Arizona in an attempt to prolong Nellie's life, as she had contracted tuberculosis. Nellie died in Phoenix, AZ, on Aug. 29, 1930. They had three children, Charles Joseph, Harold Raymond and Margaret Josephine.

John E. Young, Mamie Lunger Young

John and the children returned to Kokomo and sometime later, John went to work for Haynes Stellite Corporation.

In 1931, John heard that Mamie Lunger McMurtrey had become a widow with one daughter, Thelma Lucile, to raise. He asked Mamie to come to Kokomo to live and to tend his children so he could work and also provide a place for her and her daughter.

On Nov. 10, 1931, John and Mamie were married in Kokomo. They bought property in Darrough Chapel and had a house moved on to it. The house originally stood on ground north of Wildcat Creek and south of Kokomo High School. They couldn't afford to pay the power company to drop lines all this distance, so a man stood on the roof of the house and raised the lines with a pole.

They lived at this location for over 50 years, attending and having membership in Darrough Chapel Congregational Christian Church and being active in the Parent Teacher Association and school lunch programs. John was a 50 year member of Howard Masonic Lodge and Mamie is a member of the Order of Eastern Star.

John and Mamie had two children, Helen Louise and Donald Richard.

RHODA AND PETER YOUNG - (Taken from the files of the *Kokomo Tribune - July 1928*) - Hard work, abstinence from tobacco and such narcotics as coffee are the beautitudes to which Peter B. Young, 92, one of the oldest of Ervin Township's residents, attributes his ripe age and Mrs. Young, his partner since pioneer days in Howard County believes in the same formula. She is 85.

Recently Mr. and Mrs. Young celebrated their 68th anniversary of their wedding. At that time, Mr. Young, who is an accomplished violinist, played an entire program of number for the guests who called on him and his wife.

Mr. Young is greatly interested in politics and the other news of the day. He is a staunch Democrat and believes that Al Smith would make a good President. He served six months in the Union Army during the Civil War and was a great admirer of General George B. McClellan, who was the first commander of the Army of the Potomac and who later was the Democratic presidential nominee.

Rhoda and Peter Young

The Ervin Township pioneer is active on his farm, having dug two bushels of potatoes only last week. He and Mrs. Young are kept busy raising chickens and tending their garden and Mrs. Young is an active housekeeper.

Mr. Young came to Howard County from Ripley County when he was 18 years old, and Mrs. Young migrated from Ripley County at the age of 11. They were married in 1860 and have lived on Route 1 in Ervin Township all their lives with the exception of a few years that were spent in Burlington.

To this union of pioneer folk were born five children, three of whom are living. They are Mrs. Charles Amos, of 715 North Morrison Street, Benjamin B. Young, of Kokomo, and William Young, who lives on the homestead. The children who have passed on were Mrs. C.B. Hite of Kokomo, and Charles Young, also of Kokomo.

Mr. Young used to be a zealous pipe smoker, but gave up the habit about 20 years ago, contending that tobacco was an impediment to long life. A short time afterward he put coffee on the black list.

This sturdy old couple are looking ahead now to celebrating their 69th and 70th anniversaries of married life. *Submitted by Mona Lewe, great great granddaughter of Rhoda and Peter Young*

FRED YOUNGMAN - Few Howard County people made a greater impact on their times than did Fred Youngman. Born Feb. 18, 1845, in Bavaria, Germany, his grandfather owned a tavern where his father, Michael Youngman, once held the reigns of the Emperor Napoleon's horse when his party stopped for refreshments.

In 1854 the Youngmans came to America, settling in Ripley County, IN. Fred Youngman continued the scant education he had started in Germany; a few months before his 13th birthday he began working for a Decatur County man for eight dollars a month, learning the tile making business. They turned out the first machine-made tile in Indiana.

In the early 1860's Fred Youngman came to Taylor Township, Howard County, to operate a tile factory. After the season he went to Louisville, KY, and worked in a meat packing plant. He moved on to Boone County, where he started a tile factory with another man; he sold this successful business and returned to Howard County, purchasing the tile factory he had formerly operated. Here he made most of the tile that drained southern Howard and northern Tipton counties.

He acquired 385 acres of land around the tile mill and took up farming. He raised corn that he fed to sheep and hogs; he also was a successful thresherman; and he made many local investments that prospered.

In 1870 he married Eva Hoyer, also from Bavaria. Their children were: Luna (Becker, born in late 1870), Rosa (Becker, born in 1874), and Nellie (Grishaw, born in 1880).

Fred Youngman built his showpiece brick Italianate-style house in 1876; at one time it was known as the finest country home between Kokomo and Indianapolis. This grand house was struck by lightning in June, 1992, and was destroyed. In 1891 he built the large 'bank' barn that still stands, one of the largest structures of its kind in Howard County.

In his final years Fred Youngman retired to a two-story frame house he had built across the road from his brick house. His wife, Eva, died in 1912, and he lived with his daughter Nellie Grishaw. He lived to be 88 years of age, but grew lonely toward the end, having outlived all the heads of families in the area. He died on Jan. 18, 1934, and was buried beside his wife beneath a huge tombstone in Albright Cemetery.

Today, though the name Youngman is no longer connected with the Fred Youngman farm, relatives still own all the land; and four large evergreens mark the spot where "the finest country home between Kokomo and Indianapolis" once stood. *Submitted by Jeff Hatton*

JOHN M. YORK - John York (1884-1962) was from Brocton, IL and married Blanche Gibbs (1888-1951) in 1904, Daleville, IN. In Daleville John worked as a horseman at a horse barn breaking horses and mules to a harness or saddle. John could break any horse or mule given to him without falling out of the saddle. Later he worked at the Muncie Nut and Bolt Co. making 12 1/2 cents per hour which was not enough to support Blanche and their two children: Edna (1905-1989) and John E. "Bud" (1907) presently living in Kokomo.

John came to Kokomo in December 1907 and landed a job as a millwright at the Kokomo Fence and Machine Co. (later Continental Steel). Blanche. Edna and Bud arrived on the train in February, 1908.

Living in Kokomo for the next 54 years, John and Blanche moved 13 times and had three more children delivered by Dr. William Harrison: Woodrow (1913) born in the Beamer Methodist Church parsonage which the Yorks were renting; Mary Louise (1916); Robert (1921-1987).

John and Blanche York 1943

It was not easy for John and Blanche to raise five children. Blanche, a wonderful cook and meticulous housekeeper, canned produce from John's garden each summer and cooked huge quantities of food without waste on a kerosene stove (her first gas stove was in the early 1940's). Laundry each Monday required John to get up early and heat gallons of water on the kerosene stove for the family laundry. A pot of beans cooked on the stove all day every Monday for the family supper that night. A favorite meal during the week consisted of fried potatoes, and home-canned corn and tomatoes. Blanche's children and grandchildren were especially fond of her specialties: homemade noodles, desserts, and candy - candy made with

341

black walnuts which the Yorks dried every fall on the tin roof of their house at 1314 N. Lafountain (house still stands today). Her famous "nothing" pie recipe has remained in the family for years:

Blanche's Nothing Pie

1 cup sugar (1 1/2 cups for a deep pie)
4 Tbs. flour (rounded)
2 cups water
1 Tbs. vanilla
2 Tbs. melted butter
pinch of salt

Mix all ingredients in a bowl and pour in an unbaked pie shell; sprinkle the top generously with cinnamon; bake at 350 degrees for 1 hour 15 minutes to 1 hour 30 minutes.

Blanche had a stroke in 1940 which affected her speech and paralyzed her right arm, but she continued to keep house at 1318 N Wabash where she and John lived when she died in 1951.

John's favorites from his garden were huge white radishes, popcorn, and yellow tomatoes. His garage where he repaired Model T and Model A Fords for extra money was a wonderful place for his grandchildren to play because he saved everything in empty jars and in Koweba or Monarch brand cans that had contained food which John purchased on payday every Friday evening at the Whitacre Grocery at the corner of Broadway and Lafountain. John was working at the Kokomo Fence when it caught fire in 1921. He barely had time to retrieve his tool box before the roof fell in. He retired from the company in 1952 after 44 years of service.

JON DEAN AND PATRICIA ZECK - Jon (born Jan. 7, 1942) met Patty (born Jan. 15, 1946) "by accident" when he was a deputy sheriff and worked the accident she had enroute to her teaching job at Northwestern High School. They were married on Aug. 8, 1970, in Terre Haute, IN, and had two children: Melanie (Aug. 30, 1977) and Jon (April 16, 1980). The faithful dog Stormy joined the family right after Desert Storm and the 1991 Ice Storm.

The Zeck family began in Germany around the 1650's starting with Johann Jakob Zech and his wife. Their son Hans Nickle (1657-1717) and his wife Sara had a son Andreas (b. 1685) who married Suzanne (1680-1720). Their son Johan Jacob (1713-1798) came to America on the ship *Duke of Wurtenberg,* which landed in Philadelphia in October 1751. While on board ship, he married Anna Maria Kohlerin (17_-1779). They lived in York County, PA, and had five sons: Johan Michael, Johan Daniel, Johan Dietrich, Johan George, and Johan Jacob, Jr. Our direct lineage is through Johan George Zech (1757-1820.)

Jon Dean Zeck

Johan George's wife was Margaret Walther (born 1760). He served as a guard in the Revolutionary War in the 5th Regiment of the York County Militia from Jan. 7, 1777, to 1783. Dietrich died at age 17. The other four boys received land from the government for their part in serving in the war. Jacob Jr. lived long enough to draw a pension from 1832 to 1842, when he died. In approximately 1810, he and his family moved from Pennsylvania to Preble County, OH, in Grattis Township.

Their son Daniel, who was born in 1801, married Susanna Izor in 1825. They left Preble County in approximately 1833 for Carroll County, IN. Their son Daniel (1837-1900) married Caroline Poundstone (1847-1916) and settled in Deer Creek Township, Cass County, IN, where he was a carpenter and a farmer. Their son Everett (1874-1948) married Stella Wilson (1876-1959). They also lived in Deer Creek Township where he was a farmer. They had three children: Daniel (1904-1978), Catherine (1903-1980), and Clarke (July 5, 1908-still living).

Zeck-Fouts Cabin built 1838-39

Daniel and his wife Ora had three children: Daniel, Donald, and Deborah. Daniel and his wife Patty had two children, Brad and Brenda. Donald and his wife Bessie had three children: Rod, Dawn, and Ryan. Deborah and her husband P.D. Gunther had two children: Patrick and Danielle. Catherine and her husband had two children: Imogene and Joe Zeck Hale. Imogene's children were Kent and Christy Fissel. Joe's children were Norman and Charlotte.

Clarke came to Kokomo in 1929 and married Emily Louise Sims (born June 30, 1912) on July 22, 1931. He owned and operated a Shell Station at Markland and Washington for 37 years before working at Ledford Ford for another 13 years. They had two children: Joellen Zeck Martin Buckhout and Jon Dean Zeck. Joellen and her husband Steve had three children: Michael, Kathryn, and Lori.

JOSEPH A. ZEIGLER - Joseph was born Sept. 12, 1835, in Cumberland County, PA, the son of Christian Zeigler and Mary Adams. Not much is known about his early life. He went to Fountain County, IN, just prior to the Civil War and enlisted in the 63rd Indiana Infantry Company "C". He saw action at Second Manassas (Bull Run) and was taken prisoner there. He was released and taken prisoner again at Centreville, VA, a short time later. He suffered from "camp diarrhea" and rheumatism which affected him the rest of his life. After his discharge, he married Julia Ann Martin of Fountain County. They moved to Shelby County, IL, for a short time and then to Tippecanoe County, IN. They stayed there only a short time and then went to Clinton County until 1890 when they went to Howard County to live out their lives. He was a member of the G.A.R. He died on Oct. 15, 1921, in Kokomo, and is buried in Crown Point Cemetery there.

Julia Ann was born Dec. 12, 1839, in Fountain County, IN, the daughter of James M. Martin and Loisa Johnson, both natives of that county. She married Joseph Oct. 14, 1865, and they had five children. Their children were: James C., born Aug. 24, 1866, (spouse-Dora B. Gipe); Mary Louise, born March 13, 1868, (spouse-Prichard); Adaline Lavina, born Sept. 24, 1870, died in infancy; William Joseph born Dec. 14, 1873, (spouse-Claudia Evelina Redden); and Oscar Clayton, born Oct. 15, 1878, who never married.

Julia was a member of the Christian Church and when she came to Kokomo, she joined the First United Brethren Church, being among its charter members. She suffered greatly during her last years. She died May 27, 1915, and is buried in Crown Point Cemetery next to Joseph.

WILLIAM JOSEPH ZEIGLER - William, born Dec. 14, 1873, in Clinton County, IN, was the son of Joseph A. Zeigler, a Civil War Veteran and POW, and Julia Ann Martin. He came to Kokomo from Clinton County when he was 17 years old. After high school he worked a short time at the Paper Mill in Kokomo, where his brother Clayton also worked. He married Claudia Evelina Reddin (Clinton County) on Nov. 17, 1892, in Howard County. After the marriage he worked at the Globe Stove and Range Company and became a foreman. At Globe, a superintendent wanted William to fire a couple of men, including his brother Oscar Clayton.

William and Claudia Zeigler.

He refused to fire the men, so he was fired. While he was a foreman he helped other workers and was known for his kindness. It was believed that this kindness led to his firing. He then worked at Haynes-Apperson as an electrician. In his early 50's, he worked at an automotive company on Park Avenue near the Steel Mill. It closed due to the Depression and he was out of a job. During the Depression, he didn't work. To help his family get through the Depression, he and his family made ice box cookies and donuts and sold them in Kokomo. At Thanksgiving, they made mince meat to sell.

Ray and Roxie Zeigler.

After the Depression, he and Claudia went to South Bend for two to three summers because she had severe asthma and the climate seemed to help her. He worked at a body shop there.

After Claudia died, he worked a a grocery store on North Washington where the Factory Connection is now. He also did part-time jobs such as painting and mowing in a lawyer's yard. He died on Dec. 13, 1951, and is buried in Crown Point Cemetery in Kokomo.

Claudia was born March 1, 1875, in Clinton County, IN, the daughter of William Reddin and Artmesia Knickerbocker. Her father died when she was very young

Four generations: L-R: Artmesia (Knickerbocker) Redden Harness, Claudia (Redden) Zeigler, Maude (Zeigler) Crispen, Loren Crispen

and her mother then married Jacob Harness. Claudia came to Howard County with her parents when she was 16 and married William two years later. They had three children- Maude Marie, born Sept. 18, 1894, (spouse Homer Boyd Crispen); Raymond George born Aug. 24, 1899, (spouse Roxie Fulwider); and Dorothy May born May 24, 1916, who died in infancy on Sept. 19, 1916. She was housewife and a devoted wife and mother. She was a member of North Street Baptist Church. Claudia died on July 8, 1936, as a result of failure to recover from a mastoid operation. She is buried next to her husband in Crown Point Cemetery in Kokomo.

WILLIAM ZERBE

In 1866 the Zerbe name was added to the early settlers of Howard County. Today there are many descendants of that early family, but only two families are now living in Kokomo carrying on the name.

My great-grandfather, William (1818-1896), was the pioneer who came to Howard County in 1866. He was born in Schuykill County, PA, Oct. 25, 1818, the eldest son of David (1792-1857) and Elizabeth Koller (ca1800-1859). William was the fifth generation from the first immigrants, John Phillip, Mardin and Lorentz Zerbe, three brothers that migrated to the English colonies of North America from the territory of Alsace-Lorraine between France and Germany.

David Zerbe was a descendant of Lorentz who sailed from Rotterdam, Dec. 24, 1709, landing in New York, June 1710. In the early 1700's he traveled east into Pennsylvania, where William was born. In 1839 he moved his family to Shelby County, OH. There William married Mary A. Butcher (1821-1902) on Oct. 10, 1839.

At 17, William learned the trade of millwright from his father and pursued it for two years, after which he worked in a shipyard, then on the canal for a season. For two years he worked on a farm for a man at $75 per year. Working as a farm hand he was able to buy a team, rent farm land and make a living. He purchased 30 acres and two lots in Sidney, OH and continued working on a farm, except one summer, which was spent working with an engineer in locating the Bellefontaine-Indianapolis Railroad. In the spring of 1866 he moved with his family to this county.

William A. Zerbe, Mary A. Butcher Zerbe

My grandfather Charles Zerbe (1848-1894) was one of eight children moving from Ohio. They settled in Liberty Twp. west of Plevna, known as Pleasantville.

The other seven children were: Sarah Ann (1842-1931) married Robert Smeltzer (1839-1915); George Washington (1844-1923) married Anna Marrs (1843-1886) married Sarah Brenneman Nichols; Mary Elizabeth (1847-1937) married Charlton Bull (1847-); Robert David (1851-1900) married Philaphen Spohn; John L. (1853-1938) married Margaret Dick (-1935); William H. (1860-1931) married Lillie Nuner (1866-1922).

Charles Conrad Zerbe married Louisa Lindley Dec. 31, 1871. Knowing farming from his ancestors, he purchased land and farmed, raising six children. The eldest, John Wesley (1873-1956), was a minister in the Methodist Church and a speaker in demand for commencement and baccalaureate services in this area for years. He never owned a car and on June 13, 1937 "Ripley's Believe It Or Not" recorded that he had attended every Sunday for 1853 consecutive Sundays. In an eight-year period he walked 21,300 miles to take care of the Lord's work. Laura Etta (1847-1940) married William Hensler; Clara T. (1878-1906) married Joseph Rogers (1873-1933); Nora (1882-1964) married Seth King (1882-1947); Maude (1886-1970) married Riley Kendall (1884-1970); Roscoe (1892-1975) married Francis I. Wolf (1891-1962). Grandfather died at 45 years, was well-known and it was said that the funeral was largely attended being followed to the cemetery by the largest concourse of relatives and citizens ever witnessed in this community.

My father Roscoe, the youngest of the family, was only two years old when his father died. His mother struggled and kept the family together with the help of the other children. His Uncle Joseph Rogers had a great influence upon his early years and encouraged him to get an education, going to Manchester College. On Sept. 2, 1911 he was married to Frances I. Wolf of Miami County, where he moved the same year.

Finding in my background a strong belief in God and the intense desire to persevere has been rewarding and proved to be a good example for this descendant of William Zerbe, Joan Zerbe Bargerhuff. *Submitted by Joan Bargerhuff.*

ZERBE, SMELTZER, SAUL FAMILIES

William (born Oct. 25, 1818) died April 2, 1896 and Mary Ann (Butcher) Zerbe (born Feb. 22, 1821 died Sept. 4, 1902) both natives of Pennsylvania and of German-Swiss descent came to Howard County in the spring of 1866 from Shelby County, OH. They located on a farm of 160 acres on Touby Pike near Plevna. Their family consisted of Sarah Ann, George, Mary E., Charles C., Robert D., John L., William H. A daughter, Clara, died in Ohio.

Sarah Ann (Zerbe) Smeltzer and Robert Smeltzer moved to Liberty Township, Howard County, IN, shortly after the Civil War ended. They came with her parents. Sarah Ann born April 21, 1842 in Sidney, OH and Robert born April 29, 1839, Gallia County, OH. His parents were Adam and Margaret (Smith) Smeltzer. Sarah Ann and Robert were married in Sidney, OH on March 10, 1861. Two children were born to them in Ohio; Emma Jane on April 28, 1862 and William Henry on Jan. 5, 1865. Another son, Charles, was born in Howard County, Sept. 3, 1869. They lived on a farm 2 1/2 miles east of Plevna and in Greentown.

Robert and two of his brothers, Thomas and Reuben, served in the Union Army during the Civil War with Co. K, 20th Regt., Ohio Vol. Inf. Thomas served in the Cavalry also and was taken prisoner to the famous Andersonville Prison.

Robert was a farmer and carpenter. Sarah Ann was an accomplished seamstress and handmade quilts for each of her grandchildren. A great-granddaughter in Kokomo is a proud possessor of a candlewick spread embossed with Sarah Ann's name and the date of 1874.

Sarah Ann (Zerbe) Smeltzer died April 19, 1931 and Robert Smeltzer died Sept. 3, 1915.

My grandfather, William Henry Smeltzer, farmed land on Touby Pike, 1/2 mile west of Plevna that belonged to his Grandfather Zerbe, which he later purchased, and also adjacent land he bought from his wife's family.

Wm. Henry and Hannah (Saul) Smeltzer and their six children on homeplace west of Plevna. ca 1905

Hannah Louella Saul, born April 26, 1869, in Seneca County, Bloom Township, OH, married William Henry Smeltzer on Sept. 20, 1887. They walked to Kokomo from Plevna for the ceremony as there was no other form of transportation. Her parents were Edward and Lovina (Kagy) Saul of Seneca County, OH. Hannah had been sent by her mother to Indiana to keep house for her brother, John Kagy Saul, who was proving land. This task was cut short by Hannah's marriage. Since he had lost several sisters by marriage, John Kagy Saul decided to get married himself, and he married Suzanne Smiley Sept. 20, 1888.

William and Hannah (Saul) Smeltzer had six children who grew up in Howard County. Sarah Lovina born May 20, 1888, died April 1978, married Harry Barnes; Robert Raymond born Sept. 9, 1891, died 1987, married Opal Bryan; Rilda born May 4, 1893, died May 29, 1921, married Roy Troyer; Leota Grace born June 28, 1896, married Louis John Pfefferle; Hazel Neola born Jan. 31, 1900, married Clarence Henry (divorced), married H. Gayle Curlee; and Samuel William born April 6, 1902, died 1988, married Rosella Pratt.

Hannah and William Smeltzer had one son, Samuel William, who served in the U.S. Army during WWII in Africa and Europe. Robert Raymond had one son, Russell, who served in WWII. Leota's daughter, Georgianna, was with the Navy Waves during WWII in Washington, DC; a son Robert was in the Navy on the battleship *Tennessee* in the South Pacific; and a son William was in the Army in South Carolina. Hazel's son Harry Henry was also in the Army during WWII.

Hannah Smeltzer loved gardening, crafts, family and friends. Her flowers were beautiful and prolific. Passers-by on Touby Pike often stopped and commented on their beauty and were often rewarded with an armful of blooms. During WWII, the U.S. Navy took William and Hannah's virgin woodlot and made an emergency landing field for Bunker Hill Navy Air Station, now called Grissom. Hannah died Dec. 12, 1943 and William Henry July 22, 1961. They are buried at Greenlawn Cemetery along with Sarah Ann and Robert Smeltzer and others of the family.

Leota Smeltzer Pfefferle attended the local school and Greentown High. She also attended Marion Normal and Ball State from which she received her teaching certificates. She then taught at White School (now torn down) until her marriage in 1920. She and her sister Hazel are enjoying their 90's at this writing.

Emma Jane Smeltzer Kerby and her husband William Henry Kerby with their family are covered in another's family history.

Charles Smeltzer died Nov. 27, 1957 married Elizabeth Shrock on Dec. 25, 1889. She was born July 12, 1870 and died Dec. 11, 1937. They had these children: Homer L. born Dec. 30, 1890, died June 3, 1964, married Anna Boyer; Lawrence born May 29, 1897, died Feb. 20, 1980, married Mary Harper; Ruby born March 23, 1900, married Ralph Lamb; Mildred born Nov. 11, 1905, married A. Lee Shoemaker (divorced). *Submitted by Georgianna Pfefferle Rutherford*

JACOB AND DAMARIS JANE GARRISON

Jacob was born around 1835 in Preble County, Ohio. He married Damaris Jane Shinn November 28, 1860 in Howard County. Damaris was born January 17, 1844 in Burlington the daughter of Mahlon and Mary (Edwards) Shinn. Damaris died on April 19, in Selah, Washington.

Jacob and Damaris Jane Garrison

Jacob and Damaris had 5 children: Mary Lela, Clara Evaline, Sarah Orpha 'Rose', Fannie Dora and Mahlon Wilson. Mary Lela was born September 27, 1863 in Carroll County and died January 26, 1920 in Howard County. She married Robert H. Etherington September 16, 1886 in Howard County and they had seven children. Clara was born January 18, 1862 in Carroll County and married Godfrey Steinhagen January 8, 1898. They had one son, David. Sarah was born May 4, 1865 and married Will Burnsworth in 1901. Fannie was born August 15, 1867 and married Almond Banta June 1, 1890 in Howard County. Mahlon was born January 27, 1869.

John Garrison was born around 1781 in Virginia and died in 1869. He married Sarah Eikenberry in Virginia. She was born around 1794. John and Sarah had seven children: Joel Kenton born in March, 1826 in Rockinham County, Virginia and married Margaret; Peter born around 1827 in Virginia; Edah 'Edi' born around 1828 in Virginia and died May 14, 1911 in Monroe Township, Howard County; Jeremiah born November 18, 1829 and married Sarah Clingenpeel October 4, 1859; John born around 1831 in Preble County, Ohio, married January 12, 1862 to Huldah who was born in September 1844, in Miami County, Ohio; Francis born around 1833 in Preble County, Ohio and married George Fellows; and Jacob born around 1835 in Preble County, Ohio.

The Shinn (Sheene) ancestry has been traced back to the 1520s to Freckingham Parish, Hartford County, England. Mahlon Shinn, the son of Clement and Mary (Thompson) Shinn, was born in Harrison County, West Virginia, September 15, 1798, and died March 5, 1871. He was Justice of the Peace, Postmaster, farmer, and ran a sawmill in Burlington. He was married to Mary Edwards in 1825. Mary was born January 4, 1805, in West Virginia and died August 11, 1892 in Burlington. Mary's parents were Jesse and Sarah (Thompson) Edwards. Jesse was born September 2, 1773 and died March 30, 1823. He married Sarah August 23, 1796. Sarah was the daughter of Robert and Elizabeth (Ross) Thompson. Jesse's father was David and he married Sarah Parks around 1770.

Clement Shinn was born in 1773 in New Jersey and died in Shinnston, West Virginia. He married Mary Thompson in 1794 in Shinnston. Clement and Mary had eight children: Rhoda, Orpha, Mahlon, Josiah, Seth, Sarah, Olive, and Moses. Clement's father, Levi, settled Shinnston, West Virginia in 1778. He was born in 1748, died in 1807, and married Elizabeth Smith in 1772. Elizabeth was born in 1755 and died in 1813. Levi's parents were Clement and Elizabeth (Webb) Shinn.

DANIEL C. MILLER (See story on page 264)

Eli Kaser Barn

Index

Despite checking and re-checking there will be errors in this index. Where more than one history was turned in on a family the spelling may vary as to given names and surnames. It was not possible for the compilers to get in touch with everyone where the spelling seemed suspect.

A

AARON, Ashley Nicole Rietveld 321, Betty Louise 299, Harriet Leona 287, Jacob 293, Lance E. 321, Ryan Michael Stevenson 321
ABBOTT, 40
ABEL, David 96
ABNEY, Dick 138, Edna (York) 138, Howard 138, Judy 138, Karyn 138, Katie 138, Kent 138, Kevin 138, Kim 138, Kriss 138, Kristopher 138, Mary Beymer 138, Maude (Stephenson) 138, Nancy 138, Nona 138, Peg 138, Raymond 138, William H. 138
ABRAMS, William R. 66
ABSHIRE, Mary A. 285
ACHOR, Anna Blanche Harper 138, Daniel 138, Dean 138, Doloris 138, Donald 138, Earl 138, Elizabeth 322, Ethel Lillian 138, Florence Catherine 138, Gilbert 138, Michael 138, Noah 138, Orange 138, 211, Pamela 138, Patrica 138, Peggy Jo 138, Rebecca 138, Robert 138, 322, Robert Gene 138, Vivian 334, Vivian Christina 138, Wayne 138, Windy 322
ACHORS, Beverly Jeanine 138, Christie (Robinson) 138, Emma 138, Gregory 138, Herman Delbert 138, Herman Kent 138, Jeffrey 138, Judith Kay 138, Kitty (Shaw) 138, Konner 138, Kyle 138, Orval 138, Sherri Janae 138, Will 138
ACKLEY, Lola G. 220
ADAIR 34, Brian K. 48, David Francis 139, Emma V. Haynes 329, Francis Edmond 139, Hilda (Thompson) 139, James Donald 139, Joseph Edmund 139, Maude (Waymire) 139, Robert L. 48, Robert Lawrence 139, Russell W. Jr. 48, Russell Waymire 139, Russell Waymire Jr. 139, Ruth Ellen 139
ADAMS, Annette Lynn 223, Arvilla 318, Brian 25, Cherie Renee 275, Daniel 145, E.C. 55, Hondel 85, Isadora 288, Joel 54, John 291, Mary 342, Paul 185, Ralph 75, Robert 78, Thomas F. 223, Ursula 318
ADAMSON, Karla Sue 238, Ruth A. 244
ADDINGS, Matilda 194
ADDINGTON, Forrest 278, Luther 62, 64, Thomas 35
ADLER, Coleman 322, Milton 322, Ruth 322
ADMELL, Josephine 269
AESCHLIMAN, Lewis 201
AGAL, Steve 23
AHLBRAND, Carl 84, Dorthea 107
ALBAUGH, Aaron 228, Clara Alien 139, Clara C. 228, 232, Estella "Stella" (Hall) 207, Lee 139
ALBERSON, Gene 100, Rebecca (Dieterly) 295
ALBERTIRESON, Penninah 142
ALBRECHT, Anna Barbara 139, Barbara 139, Christian 139, Jacob 139, Johnannes (John) 139, Judith 139, Ludwig 139, Magdalen 139
ALBRIGHT, Adolphus 139, Alexander 139, Alvis 139, Belinda 140, Bertha 139, 'Bird' 140, Birdie Ellen 140, 269, Carol 139, Catherine 139, 156, Claude Lewis 140, Dallas 140, Daniel 139, Decie 139, Decie (Sarah) 139, Dora Eunice 140, Durant 139, Edmund Ephraim 140, Edward C. 48, Eleanor 139, Elizabeth 139, Elizabeth Ann 140, Elizabeth Snoderly 140, Emily 139, Fon 139, Frank 139, Fredrick Arthur 140, Gary 140, George 139, George Nelson 140, Glen 139, 140, Hannah 139, Harvey 'Vern' 140, Henry 139, Henry J. Lacy 269, Henry J. 'Lacy' 140, Henry J. Lacy 140, Hester Ann 140, Jacob 27, 139, Jacob Jr. 139, James 139, James Newton 'Newt' 140, Jerry 139, Jessie 269, Jessie Irene 140, John 48, 98, 139, 140, Joseph 139, Joseph Skeen 140, Julia 139, Kenneth 261, Kenneth Lacy 140, Lacy 98, Lattie 139, Loretta 139, Louise 139, Margaret 139, 269, Margaret Elizabeth 140, Margaret Hodge 140, Margaret Olive 338, Martha 139, Mary 139, Mary (Polly) 139, Mattie E. Smiley 269, Maude 139, 269, Maude Eunice 140, Michael 139, Mona Belle 140, Nellie 139, Newton A. 140, Oliver 87, Paul Robert 140, Pauline 269, Pauline Lucille 140, Perle 140, Perry 175, Robert 139, Rowena 140, Rowena (Doran) 259, Ruth 140, Sallie 139, Sophia 139, Susan 140, Tamar 139, Tamer 139, Terry (Jay) 139, Walter 139, William 139, William A. 338, William 'Billy' 140, William Burgess 140, William Burgess 'Bird' 98, 140, William Luther 140
ALDERMAN, Naomi 318
ALDRIDGE, Beth Ann 140, 252, 303, Darlington 140, Douglas Eugene 140, 252, 303, Edna 225, Edward Ralph 140, Frank 140, Fredrick Allen 140, 252, 303, Fredrick Allen III 140, 303, Fredrick Allen Jr. 140, 252, Fredrick Allen, Jr. 303, Fredrick III 252, Gregory Edward 140, 252, 303, Gretchen Elizabeth 303, Harvey 140, James 140, Jeremiah 140, John 140, Judith Diane 140, Lela Vivian 140, Leona Mae 140, Lucinda 140, Luella Ruth 140, Marjorie Jane 140, Marsha Kay 140, 252, Marsha Kay 303, Michael Edward 140, Newton Rutherford 140, Porter 140, William Clurid 140, William Edward 140
ALEXANDER, Don 234, Earl 333, Gene 211, J.C. 34, John C. 234, John, Sr. 48, Leora (Johnson) 333, Lewis 300, Lowell 153, Lucinda 212, Paul 257
ALFLORETTA, Edna 197
ALFORD 86, Grant 80
ALLEN 52, 54, 273, Brian 96, Carrie (Emery) 170, Donald Wayne 147, James G. 273, James Milton 151, Jane Ann 170, Jeanne 96, John 96, 273, Louis E. (Bill) 226, Lydia (Eickenberry) 273, Margaret 96, Muriel 96, Nancy 273, Oscar 59, Sarah E. 147, Sarah Jane (Jenny) 273, Wayne E. 147, Wilbert 170, William 96
ALLEY, Idella 224, June 19, Leota Mae 180, Margaret Louisa Balser 180, Noah H. 180
ALLISON, Ava 200, George 38, James D. 211, William 84
ALMAND, Donna Ruth 333
ALMON, Ruth 212
ALSPAUGH, Rodney E. 187
ALTIC, Janet Ann 329
ALTMAN, Abby Rose 228, Eric Michael 228, Michael P. 228
ALVEREZ, Estell 235
ALVEY, Betty 141, Charley 141, Emma 141, Glen 141, Harold 141, Howard 141, Louise Fernung 141, Morris 141
ALVORD, Lorenzo D. 173
AMICH, George M. "Jake" 286
AMMERMAN, Albert 168, Dennis 243, Elisha 168, Rachel Burke 168, Susan Marie Bond 143, Walter 243, Wayne 243, William 168
AMMON, Margarate 248
AMONS, G.W. Jr. 19, Jane 19, Bessie 141, 256
AMOS, Beulah 141, Charles 341, Ethel 225, Eva 141, Fred 269, James W. 141, Lacie 140, Lon 140, Mary Lorraine 140, Nicholas Day 141, Ray 141, Thelma 141, Thomas 141, William 141, William Cook 141
ANDERS, Cynthia Lorraine 287
ANDERSON 95, Aaron Matthew 141, Andrew William Joseph 141, Andy Jr. 246, Arnold 202, Ashley Brooke 141, Austin Michael 148, Beulah 312, Beulah Faithie 312, C. Thomas 338, Cami 246, Carlie 246, Cecil 175, Chad Patrick 141, Charles Edward "Ed" 197, Charles Thomas "Tom" 197, Cory 246, David William 141, E.R. 114, Frances Camille Garritson 338, Francis B. 141,

344

Isaac Henry 141, James 312, Jeffery Michael 148, Jeffrey 299, Jerry 338, Jerry Edward 197, Joshua David 141, Kevin 337, Krista Nicole 141, Laura Virginia 262, Lewis 68, 299, Martha (Noel) 141, Mary (Henry) 148, Matthew 177, Maud A. 232, Nannie (Martin) 141, Patricia A. (Lindley) 246, Perry 148, Raymond 141, Rebuna Faithie 312, Sarah Elizabeth 142, Stephen Patrick 141, Steven Charles 148, Susan T. 319, Teresa 246, Tiffany Lynn 141, Todd 299, Tracy 299, Tray 246, W.C. 74, William 141, William Caywood 141, William Patrick 141
ANDICH, Esther 76, Irv 76
ANDREWS 145, Crispin 225, Donald 225, Joan 332, Leah 225, Louise 114, M.R. 79, Ollie 269, Rachel 225, Silas 48
ANGRICK, Anna 148
ANSPACH, Elizabeth 183, John Adam 183
ANSTETT, Christina 142, Christiphor 142, Christy 142, Joe 142, Joene 142, John 142, Josephine 142, Lou Ann 142, Lulu 142
ANTHONY, Teresa 148
ANTL, Hugo 151
ANTRIM, William 33
ANWEILER, Betty (Whited) 198, Betty J. 142, Catherine 142, Edna May (Nicholson) 142, John 198, John Otto 142, John V. 142, Mae (Nicholson) 198, Martha (Young) 142, Nancy 198, Nancy Kathryn 142, Otto 198, Otto Oliver 142
APPERSON, E.S. 48, Edgar 10, 113, Elmer 10, 113
APPLEGATE, B.W. 48, H.C. 38, Hannah Rummnes 323, Jacob 48, 323, James Harvey 196
ARCHER, Edgar 176, Harrison 27, James 176, John 176, Mary Lee 176, Washington 33
ARCHIBALD, Alan 213, Becky 213, Delaney 213, Taylor 213
ARMFIELD, Blanche Dorothy 300, Calvin C. 142, Dale R. 143, Eunice 300, Grace (Davis) 143, Herman 143, John 142, Joseph W. 143, Lawrence W. 143, Lele Pearl 143, Leo 143, Leonard D. 143, Leonard D. 300, Lida 273, Logan 143, Lorina C. 143, Lucy 143, Lydia B. 143, Merrill 143, Paul 300, Roger Dale 143, Russell J. 143, Solomon 142, Thankful (Cimmons) 142, Walter M. 143, William 142
ARMOUR, Dottie 293
ARMSTRONG, A.F. 131, Addison F. 226, Edward A. 69, H.A. 226, Horace 131, Margret 229, Thomas 31
ARNETT, Asbury 143, Benjamin 143, Charlotte 143, Edward 143, Edward A. 143, Elbert L. 143, Elizabeth 143, Eunice 143, Grant 141, Hannah 143, Harold Anderson 141, Imogene 179, Jacob Allen 141, James Henry 143, Jane 143, Jesse 143, John 143, Lemuel Ernest 141, Mary (Cramblet) 141, Rachel 143, Rebecca 143, Sarah 143, Sarah Ann 143, 178, Thomas 143, Tommy 143, Valentine B. 143, Valentine M. 143, Waldo 143, William Edward 141, William H. 141, Willis 143, Winifred 143
ARNEY, Jane (Beatty) 147
ARNOLD, Catherine 159, 160, John 159, Lena 315, Louise Klensch 159, Martha 229, William T. 70
ARPH, Catherine 143
ARRASMITH, Charles 247
ARTHUR, J. Franklin 83, John J. 83, Lillian Bernice 338, Will 83, William J. 83
ARTHURHOLTZ, Edith Marie 312
ARTIS, Bart 143, Burt 143, Duff 143, Eva 143, John 143, Sarah 143, Sarah Hartwood 143, Thomas 15, Victoria 143
ARTUS, Karen 325
ASBELL, Minnie B. 208
ASCHENBERG, Barbara 267, James 267, John 267, Michael 267, Thomas 267, William 267
ASHBURN, Bill 97, Rosella 107
ASHBY, Daisy Belle (Bolin) 313, Florence Charlotte 313, Ida May (Lutz) 191, Jerimiah 191, Nellie Victoria 191, Roy 313
ASHCRAFT, Boyd 139, Darin 139, Darla 139, Stacey 139
ASHENFELTER, Betty 124, Duaine L. (Bucky) 124, Jack 124, Linda 124, Viola 124
ASHLEY, Charles 125, Harvey Lee 269, Howard 269, Laomi 28, 48, Maurice 14, Rebecca Thomas 217
ATKINS, Chet 154, Lowell 154
ATKINSON, Kevin 310, Kristie A. 310, Kyle 310, Nathan 310
ATKISSON, Bonnie 143, Catherine 143, Chris 143, Chrissi 143, Clara 143, Edgar 143, Ellen 143, Ethel 143, James 143, John Elbert 143, John Ellison 143, John Jr. 143, Mable 143, Michael 143, Mickey 143, Nikki 143, Steve 143
ATWOOD, Kiturah 185
AUGHE, Gladys Eva "Mimi" (Todd) Harness 304, Phaon 323
AULT, Aaron Lee 217, Austin Matthew 217, Carrie Ann 217, Christopher 143, David Lawrence 217, Emery 219, Hannah Eileen 242, Jacob 145, Jesse 13, 143, 289, Mahala Jane 289, Margaret Lily 143, Phebe 143, 289, Phoebe (Sparks) 143, Richard Gregory 217, Sylvester E. 143, Todd 242, Zachary Jacob 217
AUSTIN, Alice (Collins) 277, Ann 60, Harmon 277, Iva (Gibson) 277, Leann (Jacobs) 277, Olive 321, Ray 277, Rosemary (Bowman) 298, Sara Ann Merrick 143, Thomas 277
AUTEN, Adriaen Hendrickse 143, Shirley Ann 316
AUTER, Abram 144, Abram Terry 144, Abram Terry 144, 226, Caroline Atlanta 144, Caroline Matilda 144, Edith Jane 144, Edith Minerva 144, John VanTine 144, Junaneta 144, Junieta 144, Lella Carolina 144, Mabel Irine 144, Mary Helen ("Ella") Mathews 144, Robert Leroy 144, Sarah Sidella 144, Thomas 144, Thomas Atkins 144
AUVIL, Ruth Joyce Prather 200
AVERY, Dorcas 86, Eli 86, Enoch 86, Perry 79
AWE, Susan 251

B

BABB, Jaime 157, 200, 255, Larry 157, 200, 255, Scott 157, 200, 255
BABYLON, E. 34
BACHARACH, Karen 138
BACHELOR, Floyd B. 250
BACON, Deborah (Smith) 158, Nancy 158, Nellie 264, William 34, 158
BADGETT, Jerry 290, Tina Elizabeth "Libby" 290
BAER, Kim (Mickelson) 86, Sarah 176
BAGWELL 271, Annis Belle (Cohee) 168, Archie Ray 168, Carol Ann 168, Delbert Ray 168, Doris Aggeleze 168, Dude 42, Frank 42, Gene 271, George 96, Joan 168, Milton Arthur "Archie" 168, Nancy Kay 168, Peck 42, Richard Gene 168, Sherril 283, Sue 168, Wilford "Gene" 168
BAILEY 208, Abraham 159, Carolyn Rae 294, David 51, Donald E. 70, Fred Austin 327, Gladys (Van Sickle) 294, Henry 52, Levi 52, Malisse Ellen 159, Marji 26, Mary 159, Ray 294
BAIRD, Andrew 300, Esther 156, Scott 300
BAKER, Ada A. 208, Alice 144, Andrew 192, Arnold 218, Arthur Lindsay 144, Aura Belle 144, Betty 218, Betty Jane 141, Bradley Scott 145, Carl 141, Cassie Johana 145, Charles 218, Clinton Edgar 217, Cora E. 144, Cyrus 212, Earnest 144, Elizabeth Jane 144, Florence 144, Florence Bowman 141, Ginger Roselean 145, Harvey 141, Harvey 'Ted' 144, Helen 218, Isabel 144, 151, Ivan Lawrence 144, James 218, Jessie Pearl 217, Joseph 144, Kimberly Lynn 145, Lauren Renee 145, Leslie Camerson 145, Levi Ivan 145, Lindsay Michelle 145, Lisa Nicole 145, Loren D. 145, Lucy 218, Lucy Ann 144, Luke Bradley 145, Luther Watson 144, Margaret 287, Martha 234, Martha Frances 144, Mary 144, Mary Adelaide 144, Maude 141, 144, Maurice 144, Melvina 'Bine' 144, Nancy 327, Nancy Belle 144, Nancy Jane (Laughner) 192, Orville Mills 144, Paul Robert 145, Perry 218, Peter Lawrence 145, Phebe (Pease) 192, Ruth 218, 230, Samuel Maurice 144, Virginia 218, Watson 144, 151, William 192, William Harrison 144, William Oscar 144, Zephaniah W. 27, 33
BALDWIN, Abigail J. 145, Albert Benton 145, Ann 190, Asenath C. 337, C.P. 51, 52, Charles A. 145, Charles P. 52, 54, Cynthia 163, David 337, Elias Jackson 'Lucky' 145, Elizabeth 145, Francis M. 145, Henry J. 145, Indiana 145, Indiana Ann 145, John 163, Kimberly 225, Laura Annis 145, Nancy 163, Orpha 145, Phebe 143, Rachel 52, 145, Ralph'145, Samantha A. 145, Sarah 226, Silas 15, Silas S. 60, 145, 151, 197, Susan 107, Susan (French) 151, Susan (Stull) 151, Susan Stull 145, Theresa (Teddi) 215, Thomas 151, Thomas L. 145
BALKER, Cecile A. (Hendricks) 216
BALL, Amos 211, Angeline Euphenia 300, Audra Mae 172, Audra May 172, Beatrice 145, Devella (Dee) 145, Elva Grace 211, Frank 172, Frank W. 145, George 35, Isadore (Whiteley) 211, Lemoine 145, Martha 216, Neoshia 145, Rebecca Ann 145, Robert 223, Sarah (Wilson) 211, Senia 284, Solomon 211, Veneda 145, Wesley 14, Willard 223
BALLARD, Addie 220, Jane 149
BALLENGER, LaWana R. (Pinky) 153, Ralph Armstrong 153, Steven Paul 153, William R. (Bill) 153
BALSEY, Henry 184
BALYO, John 75
BANKS, Thomas 52
BANNON, Bette 48
BANTA, Almond 344, Daniel H. 333, Henry D. 333, Julia 291, Nancy Jane 333
BARBARA, Martha 187
BARBER, Abner Ratcliff 145, Adelia 199, Alpheus Clifford 145, Charles Henry 145, Clara 199, David 145, David Ross 145, David Ross 146, 287, Earl 145, Edward 199, Eva 199, Glee 152, Harriet 199, Joseph H. 145, Julia Gladys (Felton) 287, Mark 145, 146, Mark Allen 145, Martha Ellen 145, Mary 199, Mary Charlotte 145, Mary Sadona 145, Mary Terrell 145, Nancy Jane 145, Norma Jean 287, Reuben 199, Robert Terrell 145, Roy 199, Susan 199, Walter Harold 145, William 199, William Lester 145, Wilson 199
BARGERHUFF, Joan Zerbe 343
BARGERSTOCK, Randy 80
BARKDULL, Albert 52, Phillip 51, 52
BARKER, Abigail 259, Fanny (Low) 259, Freida Cotterman 294, John 259, Nicholas 259, William 3
BARKHAUS, Linda Sue 271
BARKLEY, John R. 125, Milton 23, 26
BARLOW, Billy 248, Dorothy Lee 289, Harold 314, Jerry 314, Pauline 314, Phyllis (Addison) 289, Richard 314, Thomas 289
BARNARD, Donald 146, George 146, Harold 146, Hobert 146, Mary Jane 146, Robert Joe 146, Ross 146
BARNES, Andrew 146, Betsy 146, Cassius Lamantine 146, Charles 146, Della Beale 148, Donald 70, Earl 228, Elizabeth 146, Elizabeth Barlow 146, Garrett 146, George M. Dallas 146, Harry 343, Harry Roper 146, Hazel 211, Jefferson 146, John 308, John W. 228, John William 146, Lillie Dallas 146, 294, Lybarthus 146, Mable Marie 146, Morris 146, Permelia (Gray) 308, Rosa 146, Sally 146, Stephen 146, Stephen Titus 146, 294, Susan 308, William W. 34, William Wilson 146, 294, William Wilson Jr. 146
BARNETT, Barbara 254, Barbara Ann McInturff 146, 185, 275, 327, Brandi Michelle 146, 185, Caroline 147, Charles 254, Christopher Keith 146, 181, 185, David Conner 147, Earl 181, Edward 147, Elnora (Wilson) 254, Frank 147, Fred 147, Harry 147, Helen Pauline White 181, James 15, 147, James C. 147, Jesse 15, Jesse C. 16, John Franklin 147, John W. 147, Joshua 15, 16, 44, Kenneth Wayne 146, 185, 327, Kenneth Wayne 181, 275, Logan Keith 146, 185, Rebecca 147, Rhoda 231, Robert W. 254, Teresa 254, Teresa Diana 181, Thomas 254, Tressie 163, Vicki 254, William Joshua 147
BARNHART, Bessie Glee 205
BARNHOUSE, Ellen (Sturgeon) 330, Solomon 330
BARR, Claude Elnor 329, John 52, Marilyn Grace 328
BARRETT 48, Annette (Schoenhaus) 261, Edward Allen 260, 261, Edward M. 261, Elizabeth A. 261, Julia 103, M. Scott 261, Morris 261, William W. 261, Wm Paul 89
BARRICK, Eleanor 107, Elsie Mae (Teel) 145
BARRINGTON, Richard 15
BARROW, Barbara 183
BARTHELEMY, Lucille 283, Marcia 202
BARTLETT, Clara 107
BARTLEY, Mary Lou 149
BARTON, Doris 218, Earl 218, Kathleen Annette 218
BARTRUM, Bernard 209, Diane 209
BASKETT, Phil 74
BASS, Tom 183
BASSETT, Dulcinea 263, Henry P. 16, Jeremiah 48, Kathryn Rhinehart 277, Richard 15, Zachariah 15
BATCHELOR, Inez 64
BATES 28, Amos 15, Andrew 35, Beth Ann 223, Catherine 28, Charles Larry 223, David 16, 18, Ephraim 27, Ephriam 33, Isaac 45, John 33, Joseph 35, Katherine Lee 223, Sally Jane 223, William 291
BATEY, Leslie 96, Mary A. 274, Sarah 274, Thomas 254, W.H. 274
BATH, Mary Lynn 313, Tim 125
BATSON, Emily 28, Jane 28, Nathaniel 33, Thomas 33
BATY/BATEY, Mary Adaline 275
BAUER, Frank C. 306, Golda (Bitner) 306, John E. 306, Malissa "Mame" 155, Mary Jane (Wellington) 306
BAUMGARDNER, G.W. 50, Jacob 48, 50, 96, Majesta 247, Washington 48
BAUMGARTNER, Jacob 53
BAUR, Catherine 239
BAUSOM, Rosetta 280
BAXTER, Hannah 215, Lenard II 283, Mildred 287, Thaddeus 18, Wayne 23
BAYER, Alean 258
BAYLESS, Betty (Mason) 255
BEACH, Richard Jr. 277
BEACHY 42, Marlin 29, Marvin 29
BEAHRS 161
BEAHRS, John 161, 287
BEAKS, William 268
BEALE, Susannah 163
BEALS, Arthur Edwin 260, Colonzo Chelcie 260, Jesse Franklin 260, Mary Esther 260, Nathan C. 48, 49, Oliver C. 259, Oliver Cromwell 260, Richard 260, Richard Henry 260, Sarah Eliza May 260, Sarah Jane (Symons) 260
BEAMAN, Artha Ivaah Worthington 285, Betty 147, Betty Jane 285, Bruce Tyler 147, Chester 147, Claud 147, Court 147, Dale 147, Garnettie 147, Gladys 147, Judith 147, Lorenzo 147, Marlene 147, Mary Anina Ruth 147, Paul 147, Paul Jr. 147, Paul William 285, Samuel 147, Wright 147
BEAMER, Lula M. 175
BEANE, Thomas 208
BEAR, Ann 220
BEARD, A.M. 86, Carol 100, John 327, Joshua 327, Justin 327, Michael 327, Myron 48, Thomas 48

BEASLEY, Cindy 180, Erma I. Johnson 323, John T. 323, Mary Francis 323, Robert 180, 225
BEATIE, Mary 143
BEATLEY, Grace 224, Martin 224
BEATTY, C. Paul 148, Connie 327, David 147, Donald 327, Dora (Anderson) 148, Helen Edith (Huston) 148, John 148, Joseph David 147, Joseph David Jr. 148, Michael Wayne 147, Misty 327, Natalie Rochelle 148, Samuel Todd 147, Sanford 148, Sarah (Purvis) 148, Sarah Jayne 148
BEATY, Dorothy Ellen 147, Jane Elizabeth 147, Joseph 147, Rachael Downs 147, Rachael Louise 147, Ralph Downs 147
BEAVER 148, Mary Elizabeth 313
BECHDOLT, Burl 269
BECK, Agnes 157, 255, Bill 207, Darlene 283, Drusilla 210, Frances 176, Geneva (Torrence) 18, Grace Jane 177, Laurel J. 51, Mike 207, Rena 275, W.E. 34, Whitney 145
BECK-LUSHIN, Sandra 145
BECKER, Barbara Ellen 271, David 325, Leona Irene (Studebaker) 271, Luna Youngman 341, Martha Rose 295, Ralph Thomas 271, Rosa Youngman 341
BECKETT 52
BECKNER, Catharine 318, Levi 15, Mary 145
BECKOM, Barbara Mae 148, Donald Ray 148, Harold Wayne 148, Jan William 148, Jay Donald 148, Mary Louise 148, Monique Marie 148, Teresa 148, Teresa Rae 148, William A. 148
BEECHING, Charles 139, Todd 139
BEEDE, Cynthia 273, Jordan 273, Nathan 273
BEELER, Bill 280, Elizabeth (Emrich) 184, George 184, Margaret 184
BEESON, Barbara 304, Carrie Ann Sperry 304, Josiah 18, Martha Mason Caldwell 164, Owen Folger 304
BEEVER, Carl Henry 148, Louise 148, Skippy 148, Yvonne Jeannette 148
BEHAM, Nettie 167
BEHELER, Joan Smith 43
BEHNER, George 306
BEHR, Frank 156
BEHRENS, Fred 289, Paula Sue (Purvis) 289
BEIHOLD, Marjorie Johnson 163, Paul Duane 163, Thomas Edison 163
BEITER, Robert 119
BELCHER, George Wheaton 148, Sherri (Richmond) 148, Shon 148, Steve 148
BELL, Andrew 281, Anna T. 319, Burrell 15, Calvin L. 281, Catherine 281, Charles Milroy 281, Dena 96, Helen 184, Isaac 281, James 27, 33, Juva 327, Marie Francis 283, Roy 281, Sarah Irene Leota 317
BELSAM, Marie 169
BELT, Anna Bortsfield 256, Charles 256, Ida 256, J. 34, Joshua 33, Robert W. 75
BENCE, Jesse Mary 182
BENDER, Floyd Harry 219, Roy 219, Wm. Troy 219
BENGE, A. 46, A.E. 100, Benjamin Harrison 149, Bessie Elizabeth 149, Buldah 149, Charles Vernon 149, Charlotte 107, Dorighert 148, Dorothy Helen 149, Effie May 149, Elma 149, Geneva 148, George Huffer 149, George Huffer 149, Georgia Arlene 149, Harold Vance 181, Harriet 149, Henry 149, Howard Clayton 149, Irma 149, James T. 149, Jennie Alice 149, John J. 149, John Marvin 149, Lillian 149, Luther Robert 149, Luther Wayne 149, Margaret Elizabeth Harpold 181, Martha 148, 149, Obediah 148, Pearl 149, Phebe 149, Richard Donald 149, Robert 148, Robert Luther 149, Roy Dean 149, Samuel 148, Stanley Russel 149, Thomas 148, William A. 148, William Henry 149, 181, William Martin 149, Wilma Jean 149
BENNETT, Agnes 149, Barbara 149, Becky 149, Betty Jo 150, Bill 149, 150, 215, Bill Jr. 149, Buell 149, Buell Everett 150, Carolyn 149, 150, 215, 332, Carolyn Sue 331, Carrie Catherine 193, Catherine (Kunkle) 193, Catherine Victoria 149, Connie 149, Cora 316, Cyndy 149, Dale E. 150, David 149, Debbie 149, Dick 149, 150, 215, Don 150, Dora Ellen 149, Dwight 48, 149, 215, 331, Edward L. 287, Edwin Murviel 149, Eliza (Mow) 149, Everett Nathaniel 149, Glenda 149, Harriet J. 180, Jackie 149, James H. 180, Jeff 149, Jennie Maude 149, Jimmy 149, Joan (Richardson) 149, John 149, 150, 215, John Jr. 149, John Nathanial 149, Judith Ann 149, Judy 149, 150, 215, Julia M. 169, Kenneth 150, Kenny 150, L.L. 48, Laura 149, Lawrence C. 180, Lawrence William 180, Lillian 48, Lillian (Heaton) 331, Lou Ann 149, Lucius L. 51, Major 149, Malinda Catherine (Hagey) 149, Malinda Evaline 149, Mary Catherine 150, Maxine 149, 150, 215, Melvin 92, Minnie Bell 149, Minnie Bell (Hamilton) 149, Nellie 149, 273, Nicole Laraine 249, Pam 149, Paul 99, 149, 150, 215, Paul D. 218, Paul Wayne 149, Ramona Mae 150, Ray 257, Rick 149, Rita 288, Roland 149, Roland Jr. 150, Ruth Ellen 180, Samuel 193, Sandy 150, Stephanie Christine 249, Tami 149, Ted 149, 150, 215, Thelma Ruth 180, Vickie 149, Walter 122, William E. 149
BENSON, Dove 223, Janet 308, Marilyn Sue 152, Nancy Lee 152, William Henry 152
BENTLEY, Janet Esther H. 320, Kevin 214, Kevin Gordon 320, Michael 214, Michael John 320, Scott 214, Scott Gordon 320
BERGAY, Janice Carol 267
BERGERON, Alexandra 177, Stephanie Jane 177
BERGMAN, Brian Anthony 153, Cindy Ann 153, Dane Ian 333, David Lee 153, George 84, Gina Nicole 153, Kay Tiffany 153, Kelly Sue 153, Kimberly Diane 153, Kristina Elke 333, Larry 333, Lydia 84, Martin Luther 333, Myrtle 84, Otto 203, Richard D. 153, Richard Dean 153, Sharon 215, Troy D. Keith Allen 153, Victoria 333
BERJAME, Alma Babago 179
BERNARD, Bruce 325, Debra Kay 150, Edward Charles 150, Fern Olive (Hutchins) 150, Henry 150, Jason Edward 227, Jennifer Lynn 227, John Ernest 227, Leon 150, Matilda (Romer) 150
BERNDT, Ed 73
BERNE, Jessie 319
BERREHSEM, Wilhelmina "Minnie" Charlotte 201
BERRY 273, Aaron L. 150, Aaron Leander 150, Chester 78, Eliza (Ellison) 186, Henry 186, Myrtle 150, Rachel 298
BERRYMAN, George Albert "Al" 150, Heather Nicole 150, Kenneth Allen 150, Linda Kay 150, Ryan Matthew 150, Scott Wesley 150
BESS, Alma Ruth 202
BESSLER, James George 275, Justin Edward 275
BETHEA, Eddie 148
BETZNER, Carrie 247
BEUCUS, Iva 151, William 151
BEVELHYMER, Nora May 144
BEVER, Henry S. 148, Luke 148
BEVERIDGE, Albert 55
BEVINGTON, Ann Rebecca 151, Charles 151, Donna 208, Phyllis 332, Sarah 151
BEYER, Elisabeth 193
BICKEL, Kasey Allen 225, Kent Richard 225, Kent Scott 225
BICKLE, Aaron 33
BIDDLE, Grover 208, Helen 208, Leatha Robinson 208
BIDDLECUM, Homer 62, Homer G. 66
BIEDENHARN, Joseph 119
BIERMAN, Rosa 287
BIGLER, Cleon E. 91
BILLINGSLEY, Etty 184
BILLITER, Wayne 25
BINCKLEY, Christian 183, Elizabeth 183
BINGAMAN, Don 290, Jane 290, Marvin 290, Sue 290
BION, Rella Jacoby 254
BIRCH, Clarence 308
BIRDEN, Charles E. 149
BIRDSONG, Lori 231
BIRELAY, Audrey 253
BIRLER, Jakob 314
BIRNELL, Nancy L. 173
BISHOP 39, Frank 104
BISSONNETTE, Jackie (Mason) 256
BITNER, Alton Leroy (Roy), 150, Anthony Shane 151, Betty Lou 150, Brian Michael 151, 204, Charles 150, Charlotte Diane 151, Connie Sue 150, Dawn Diane 151, Elizabeth 306, Erica Jane 151, 204, Franie 197, James Eric (Jamie) 150, Jane Ann (Clark) 204, Janet Leigh 151, Jean Elizabeth (Sis) 150, Jeffry Eugene Sr. 151, Jennifer Jean 151, Jocelyn Leigh 151, Judy Kay 151, Kevin Michael 204, Kevin Michael (Mike) 150, Lula (Dietz) 150, Mark Leslie 151, Marsha Ann 150, Mary Jane 140, Mavis Irene 151, Otho Ervin 150, Patty Ann 150, Paul Ervin Jr. 150, Paul Ervin Sr. 150, 204, Ralph Eugene 150, Robert Clayton 150, Sheila Lynn 151, Stacy Marie 151, 204, Stephanie Sue 151, 289, Steven Leroy 151, Tina Louise 151, Todd Allen 151, Wesley Scott 151, William 306, William Rodrick 151
BIZJAK 207
BLACK, Edna Martha 143, Frank H. 143, Maude 296, Paula 299
BLACKBURN, Jeffery D. 66
BLACKLIDGE 13, Kent H. 125, Richard H. 125
BLACKWELDER, Boyce W. 80
BLACKWOOD, Grant 217
BLAIR, Peter Y. 60
BLAKE, Miriam Tharp 133
BLANCHARD 37, 38, 48, Charles 27, 151, Eveline 151, 324, Eveline Shepherd 151, George 151, 324, Janice 151, 187, Laurence 151, 324, Leslie 151, Neil 151, Neil Jr. 151, Norman 151, 324, Patricia 151, 324, Richard 151
BLANGY, Jere 151, Jerry Benjamin 151, Mary 16, 61, Mary (Frazee) 151, Mary Elizabeth 151, Pearl 162, 174, Ray Charles 151, Rebecca Ann (Kellis) 151, Richard Ray 151
BLANKENSHIP, Benjamin 206, Linnie Mae (Crowe) 206
BLASKE, Judy 331
BLAZER, David 48, Richard 48
BLEDSOE, Dave 20
BLEVINS, Susan 250
BLISS, Carlyn 179, Mara 179, Neal 179, Sarah 162, Steven 179, Walter 85
BLODGETT, Lucy 104
BLOOD, Mary Merrill 159
BLOOMER, Allen Trimble 144, Bertie 151, Blanche 151, Bonnie 151, Charles Edwin 151, Edith 151, Emerson 151, Emma Rosetta 151, Ernest 151, Fannie 151, James 151, Jennie Bell 151, Jesse 151, Joseph B. 151, Joseph Bevington 144, 151, Lelia 151, Linnie 151, Lloyd 151, Phoebe Ann 151, Rebecca Alma 151, Samuel Watson 151, Solon 151, William Allen 151
BLOSE, Viola R. 153
BLOSSEY, Albert 329, Albert Frederich 151, 204, Albert Frederick 151, Carl 329, Carl Ward 151, Christian Albert 151, Clara 151, Clara Agusta 151, Cole Barber 152, Daniel Fahnestock 152, Douglas Field 152, Elizabeth 152, Emma Ann 151, Ernest Carl 151, Ernest Daniel 151, Ida Antonio 151, Jean Elizabeth 152, Mary 151, Mary Robert 151, Mildred E. 151, Peter North 152, Rachel 329, Rachel Louise 151, Robert Gates 152, Ryan Fahnestock 152, Zoe 329, Zoe Alberta 151, Zoe Alberta 318
BLOUNT, Brazilia M. 85, Marietta (Addie) 181, Nellie (Rayl) 98
BLYSTONE, Louisa 214
BOCK, Bertha May 152, Blanche 152, Clarence 152, Daniel 59, 152, Daniel Hobson 152, 220, Daniel Lawrence 152, Eliza Ann Eikenberry 199, Frances 152, Grace Mable 152, Lizzie (Gable) 152, Martha 152, Samuel 59, 199, Samuel Abraham 152, Samuel E. 152, Susanna 152, Susanna (Erbaugh) 152
BODE, David Wayne 238, Klarissa Ann 238, Kyle David 238
BOES, Richard Charles 183
BOGAN, George Alfred 234, James Ragene 234, Jo Kanable 234, Josephine 234, Josephine (Alexander) 234, Patty Arline 234, Roy C. 234
BOGARD, Ritta Dean 181
BOGART, Robert 180
BOGLE, Victor 102
BOGOTT, Carolyn Ann Scherer 276
BOGUE, Bradley 152, 223, Brandon 152, 223, Brian 152, 223, Charles 152, Christina A. 51, Debra (Turner) 152, Ellen Sue 152, 223, Harry 152, 223, Kevin 301, Kimberly 152, 223, Lannie L. 48, Philip Wayne 152, 223, Ralph 41, Russell 147, Samuel 33, Scott 48, Stella LaRowe 152
BOHAN, John 103, 125
BOICE, Eleanor 220, George 220
BOLEN, Brent 152, Burnell James (Jim) 152, David M. 308, Dixie Diane 284, Harry Douglas 152, James Jr. 152, Leanna Ade 152, Margaret Elaine 152, Michael 152, Mitchell 152, Vera Louise 152
BOLES, Dorothy L. 319, Mary 296, Vicky 277
BOLIN, Laura 234
BOLIN, Lily M. 224
BOLINGER, Benjamin 153, Betty 153, Chris Alan 283, Christopher 153, Clifford M. 153, Cornelius M. 153, Cornelius Mark 153, Deloris Marie 153, Donald John 153, Donald John II 153, Eleanor 153, Ethel 215, Etta Louise 153, Gregory Howard 53, Helen Louise 153, Herbert 283, Howard 153, Jason Daniel 283, Jeffery Allen 153, Jody Lynn 153, Karen Kay 153, Keith 153, L. Owen 153, Linda 153, Lisa Ann 153, Marcia Ellen 153, Marie 14, 153, Matthew 153, Matthew August 153, Michael 153, Michael Owen 153, Mildred Ann 153, Nina Mae 153, Peggy Lee 153, Phyllis Ann 153, R. Wayne 153, Ralph Wayne 153, Roy W. 153, Ruth 153, Sharon Sue 153, Sherman 153, Stella Mae 153, Stephen Wayne 153, Stephenie Joan 153, Susan 153, Terry Loy 153, Victor C. 153, Walter M. 153, Zella Izola 153
BOLINGERS, Fern 14, Sherman 14, Viola 14
BOLLINGER, Glenn 25, 26, 333, Mary Ellen 153
BOLTON, Bertha 154, Conlas 154, David 154, Delphine 154, Graylon 154, Jack 154, Jasper 154, Jeremiah 154, Josie 154, Rhoda Jane 312, Rose 154, Thomas 154, Willard 154
BONANNI, Joan Catherine 335
BOND, John 66, Maryland Clemency 288, Melinda Sue 143, Ray 35
BONE, 28
BONGARTZ, Gertrude Katherine, 316
BONTENBALL, Henry 208
BONTRAGER, 29
BOOERHOLSER, Daniel 16
BOOHER, Marie 107
BOONE, Daniel 224, Jessamine 190
BORGEAS, Serita Slocum 307
BORTSFIELD, Samuel 15
BORUFF, Hazel C. 155
BOSLAUG, Zola 274
BOSTIC, Maxine 278, Patti 278, Raymond 99, 278
BOSTON, George 204
BOSWELL, Harriett 145
BOTTS, Edgar 100
BOUCHER, Joseph 204
BOUGHER, Jill 163
BOUGHMAN, Joe 97
BOUGHTON, Bill 154, 212, D. Scott 154, David 154, Helen Stearns 154, Jesse 154, Nancy 154, 212, Nancy Luella Harris 154, Robert Scott 154, Sibyl 154, Stuart 154, William Stearns 154
BOURNE, Carl 200
BOUSON, Autumn 337, Christy 337, James 337
BOUSUM, Brent Anthony 283
BOWEN 59, Elmer 19, Ethel Bell 337, Francis Alice 270, Guy W. 19, Mary 323, S.N. 19, Sarah Jane 241, William 323

BOWERMAN, David E. 80
BOWERS, Bob 154, Cliff 154, Colin K. 154, Dan D. 154, Frances 238, Harlan V. 154, Harlan V. Jr 154, John 66, 231, Linda 202, Maude A. (Frazier) 154, Ronnie D. 154, Tom 154, Ulysses 154
BOWLAND, Dan 43
BOWLES, E.W. 83
BOWMAN 248, Ann Eliza 190, Ashton Daniel 249, Blanche 333, Brandon Michael 244, Brian Christopher 244, Charles 298, David Cameron 249, Dora Caroline 298, Edith 268, George William 244, Homer 313, Jane 195, Joe 298, Lisa Ann 249, Mark Douglas 249, Paul Gene 249, Paul Keith 249, Polly Couch 65, Sheryl Lynn 249, Tiffeny Diane 249, Veaux H. 278
BOWSER, Danielle Grace 239, Kristina Marie 238, Timothy 238
BOYCE, Carla 153, Carolyn 153, Edward 153, Jennifer Ann 153, Nathan Edward 153
BOYD 59, Lenore Hunt 154, Bob 97, Byron 306, Henry 51, Lemuel E. 51, Raymond 281, Sarah 234
BOYER, Anna 343, Blanche 234
BRABAY, Joseph A. 68
BRACKEN, Robert 48
BRACKETT, Phebe 190
BRADBURY, William 27, 33
BRADEN, W.W. 35, William 36
BRADLEY, Armelia Wardwell 151, Barbara Ann 155, Billy 23, 155, Carolyn 155, Clarence Hiram (Bo-Dad) 155, Freda Juanita 155, 223, 233, Gladys Irene 155, Glanda 155, Helen Marie 155, Henry 58, Inez 155, Janette 155, Janice 324, John Henry (Poppy) 155, Kay 151, 324, Lloyd 155, Lois 155, Martha Lorain 155, Mary Edna Mae Bell 155 Mina Sprong 151, Richard 155, Rita Ann 155, Talmadge 155, Ted 151, Theodore 324
BRADSHAW, Donna Cordelia 195, John Martin 195, Lowell Ray 195, Mary Emma (Freed) 195, Phillip Curwood 195, Raymond 195 Thomas L. 195
BRAGG, George 64, 65
BRANCH, Christy 302, Jacob Andrew 151, James 151, Joseph LaVerne I 151, Joseph LaVerne II 151, Kathleen Anne 151, Kimmie Elaine 151
BRANDENBURG, Elizabeth 146, Lucinda 274
BRANDON, Mary 197, Wyoma A. 146
BRANDRUP, Ebba Marie 292
BRANDT, Marjorie 243
BRANKLE, Gladys Jane (Cowgill) 171, Melinda 171, Michael 171, Pearl E. 305, Robert 171
BRANSON, Joseph 33, Lola Grace 200, Michael 27, 33
BRANSTETTER, Gerline 215, Helen 215, Morris 215, Owen 215
BRANT, Maude Mae 254, Tom 25
BRANTLEY, Augustus 155, Benjamin 155, Bessie 155, Carlie Ann 155, Chester 155, Daniel Milton 155, Easter 155, Elisha 155, Floyd 155, Freeman 155, Hazel Catherine 155, Iva Fern (Crousore) 155, James 155, James Harvey 155, John 155, John Robert 155, Joseph 155, Louisa 155, Martha 155, Martha Ann 155, Nancy 155, Parlena 155, Prior Lee 155, Rebecca (Nichols) 155, Rhonda 155, Robert 155, Sarah 155, Sarah Jane 155, Silas 155, Thomas 155, William 155, William Harvey 155, Winifred 155
BRASHEAR, Phyllis (Kabrick) 207
BRATTON, Russell 331
BRAUER, Robert 106
BRAXTON, Hannah 176, Tom 176
BRAY, Andrew 27
BREEDLOVE 283, Alfred "Jack" 155, Charles 155, Dick 155, Earl (Jiggs) 155, Emma 155, Fred 155, George Washington 156, Henry 155, Ira Ambrose 155, James 155, 156, 179, James Madison 156, James Madison 155, Jan (Sutton) 155, Jayne 155, Jeramiah 156, John Luther 155, Josephine (Cross) 155, Julie 155, Laura B. (England) 179, Nancy Agnus (Medsker) 155, Naomi M. 179, William F. 155
BREINTENBACH, Leo 302
BREITENBACH, Leo A. 94
BREITHAUPT, Thomas 329
BRENNADON, Mary E. 260
BRENNEDON, Mary E. 260
BRENT 208
BRENTON, Amanda 156, Callie O. 156, Charles Cholafax 156, Dale 25, Elizabeth 156, Hannah (Hubble) 156, 268, Henry 156, Isaac Newton 268, James 156, John 156, Joseph 156, Kizzie Jane 156, 268, Mallie 156, Mary 156, Mary (Woodfield) 156, Nancy 156, Nancy C. 156, Oliver 156, Phoebe 156, Rebecca 156, Robert 156, Sadie 156, Samuel 156, Samuel P. 156, Sarah 156, Washington 156, William 156, William D. 156, William McClain 156
BRETHEN, Linda Rae 238
BREWER 86, Charles 340, Henry 33, James 28, Jane (Evans) 340, Lorenzo 33, Mahlon 196, Nellie Gay 341, W.J. 27, Wilson 33
BREWSTER, Kim 108, Mary 108
BRICKER, Patricia 290
BRIDGEWATER, Aaron Jacob 238, Amanda Lynn 238, Marcia Ann 238, Marvin Gordon 238, Randall Lee 238
BRIETENBACH, Leo 228, 311, 319
BRIGGS, Agness 241
BRIGHT, Eliza 286, Elizabeth 208, Joseph 15
BRIMEY, J. 34
BRINCEFIELD, Gary 223, Gary Cash 223, Jill Elaine 223, Sharen S. (Tyner) 183
BRINK, Carleen (Cox) 170, Dick 170, Dixie 170
BRISCOE, Judy 187
BRISEY, S.A.J. 27
BRITTAIN, Drake Anthony 301, John David III 301, John David, Jr. 301, Michael Anthony 301
BRITTIAN, Anna 234
BRITTON, Charles 219, Dennis 335, Mabel 218, Samantha Kate 335, Sara Christine 335, Stephanie Marie 335
BROADIE 284
BROADLICK, Winifred 339
BROBST, Alberta 159
BROBST, Nora 160
BROCK, Daniel Lee 150, Douglas Lee 150, Jeffery Allen 150, Kate 163, Katie 305, Marie Elaine (Adair) 139, Mary Kay 163, William 163
BROCKMAN, Anna M. (Mitchell) 250, Audrey V. (McIntosh) 250, Ira T. 250, Kathy 108, William T. 250
BROCKWELL, Alicia Buckley 160
BRODESSER, Annah (Birkhauser) 182, Isabelle (Hunt) 182, Theodore 182
BROMLEY, Alexander Thomas 156, Bruce 156, Daniel 156, Elizabeth 156, Esther 156, Genevieve 156, James 156, Janice 156, Jay Myron 156, Jay Thomas 156, Joel 156, John William 241, 156, Lee 3, Lee Myron 156, 241, Lillian Smith 156, Linda 156, Luman William 156, Matthew 156, Nancy Ann 156, Susanna Kidd 156, Thomas Lee 156, 241, Virginia 3
BROO, Carl 31
BROOKBANK, William 27
BROOKE, Beth (Millard) 157, Charles 157, Correll (Lutz) 157, Gertrude 248, Isaiah 157, James 157, Lindsey 157, Matilda (Heiser) 157, Reginald 157, Susan 157
BROOKS, Alberta, James 18, Lavinna 19, Stephen 18, Wilson 291
BROOKSHIRE, Emsley 37
BROUSE 98, Andrew 226
BROWER, Alfred 157, Ansel 157, 255, Barbara 157, Betty 157, Dale 157, 199, 255, Daniel 157, Eldon 157, 255, Ethie 223, Florence 157, Frank 157, Jacob 157, Janet 157, 199, 255, Joel 15, 59, 157, John 157, Jonas 157, Jonithan 157, Katie 157, Leonidas 157, 255, Leroy 256, Linda 157, 199, 255, Lyda 157, Marion 97, Marjorie 157, 255, Minnie 157, Nancy 157, 199, 255, Nelda 157, 255, Phyllis 157, 255, Robert 157, 255, Ruth 96, Sarah 157
BROWN 86, A.W. 34, Agnes 157, Albert Wendell III 158, Albert Wendell Sr. 158, Alberta Wendell Jr. 158, Alda Isabelle 339, Annie 279 C.H. 87, 329, Carey 27, 33, Carlos, Guy 158, Charles 158, Clark Matson 217, Dewey 235, E. Howard 66, 293, Edith 158, Elias 53, 157, Elizabeth 158, Elza F. 80, Emily 158, Emma 158, Emma Pearl 285, Erie 157, Eugene 35, Gary 226, Geneil 309, 310, George 246, George W. 15, Gloria, Ann 158, Gloria Ann 273, Grant 56, Hampton 52, 53, 157, Herman 141, Howard L. 158, Ida Bell 233, Jacqueline 217, James 158, James Eugene 158, Jerome 157, Jonah 157, Joseph 51, 53, 157, Kyle, Montgomery 158, Laura, Frances 158, Lesta Ruth Kelly 235, Lizzie 158, Louie 158, Mandy (Glaspie) 158, Manny 56, Mary 157, Mary (Spillman) 156, Mary Elizabeth (Lyle) 158, Mary L. 158, Matthew 285, Mercer 63, Nancy 158, 279, Nancy Ann 158, Nancy Ann (Lanning) 285, O.H. 34, Patrick 158, Pollard 58, Pollard J. Jr. 158, Pollard Jackson 158, 279, Quentin Terrell 158, Reta 273, Richard Henry 217, Robert Coleman 158, Robert Leon 158, Rosy 158, Ruth Pemberton 293, Sarah 246, 247, Sarah A. 248 Tarita Ann (Wilson) 158, Tempa 82, Tempey Patsey 148, Theron 157, Thomas 61, W.M. 34, Waldo 157, Walter 66, William 156, 158, 273, William Bacon 158, William H., Jr. 70, William Horton 158, Winema 293
BROWN-ELLIOTT 102
BROWNESS, Ann 241
BROWNING, Alford McKinley, "Mac" 159, Charles Henry Smart 159, Cherie 159, Daris Wayne 158, Dorsey Pearl 80, E.P. Jr. 158, Elzie Parker 158, Esther Lee 158, Fannie Mae 159, James 158, Joyce 158, Judy 158, Louie Netherland 158, Louis A. 158, Martha Celine 158, Mary Roxie 158 Peggy I. 158, Ruth 158, S. Sue 158, Sylvia Pear (Cunningham) 80, William 158, William Allen 158, William Tait 159, Wm. Howard 158
BROWNLEE, John H. 85
BROWNLOW, Doris E. (Black) 203
BROWNLOW, Erika Lynn 203, Evan Keith 203, Ivan 203, Richard L. 203, Rosann (Grady) 203
BRUBAKER, Abraham 15, Abram 15, Amos 281, Charles 96, Elizabeth 295, Emma (Harter) 186, Faye Marie 186, Harley E. 159, Hester 159, Howard 25, 321, Irene 321, Jennifer, Lynn 159, Jonas 46, 59, Louis 159, Mary 218, Mary Jo 159, Mary Magdaline 280, Melissa Ellen 159, Phenny A. 216, R. Alan 15, 159, Roy A. 159, Uriah S. 186,
BRUCE, Charles W. 206, Clara Grinslade 90, Ernest 140
BRUCK, Diane 317
BRUEGEL, Pieter 327
BRUFF, Charles 159, James F. 159, John R. 159
BRUMBAUGH, Hester 247, Martha 234
BRUMFIELD, Charles 278
BRUMMETT, Arthur 164, Beatrice 164, John 48
BRUNK 35 Inez G. 175, Jacob 27, 28, 32, 34, L. 36, Mary Kathryn (Zahn), 175, Nathan 175
BRUNNENMILLER, Aletha 159, Barbara 159
BRUNNENMILLER, Bruno 159, 160, Charles 159, Effie May 159, Frank 159, George 159, Grace 159, John A. 159, Joseph 159, Karolina Gross 159, Kaspar 159, Louise 159, Mary 159, Mary Etta 159, Pearl 159, Phillip 159 Sam 159, Terrence 159
BRUNOMILLER, B. 34
BRUNSON, Sylvester 33
BRUST, Lynn 74
BRYAN, Daniel 337, Daniel E. 241, James J. 337, Mary 337, Maude (Sale) 180, Opal 343, Richard 210, Rosa H. 197, Samuel 180
BRYANT, Carl 175, Ethel Ita 220, Graner 35, Harold 304, James 220, Janice 175, John 8, June (Fox) 175, Mike 304, Olive (Ladd) 220, Scott 304, Skip 304
BRYSON, Elizabeth Dorcus 317, Henry Franklin 317
BUCHANAN, Cora 90, Eva 90, Helen 226, James 40, Mary 90, Rita 25, T.M. 90, Wm. 90
BUCHHOLZ, Caroline (Sonnemaker) 160, David, Frederick 160, Heinrich Friedrich 160, Henry Percell 160, James Richard 160, June Marie 160, Laura Marie 160, Magdilena (Felton) 160, Mary Elizabeth 160, Robert Henry 160
BUCHMAN, Balser 223, Henry 223, Jacob 223, Obluna 223
BUCHNELL, Mary 288
BUCK, O.H 106
BUCKLES, Donald 308
BUCKLEY, Fred 160, Gary 160, Karen (Felt) 160, Matt 160, Robert 160, Terry 85
BUCKNER, A.N. 161, Albert 160, 161, August Newton, Jr. 161, August Newton, Sr. 161, Augustus Newton 160, Augustus Newton Jr. 160, Beverly Ruth 161, Carl Richard (Dick) 161, Elizabeth Jill 161, Esther 105, 161, Esther Lily (Heisel) 160, Isaac Newton 160, 161, Kenneth Craig 161, Lois 160, 161, Noel 160, 161, Omar 160, 161, Rebecca 160, 161, Richard 160, 161, Robert 160, Robert Lee 161, Ronald Joseph 161, Ruth 160, Ruth Ann 161, William 160
BUELL, Clydia Belle 168
BUERSMEYER, Tom 121, Tracey 121
BUGHER, Clarence 241, Frank 241
BULCK, Frederick C. 161
BULK, Alma 287, Alma "Moose" 161, Anna 287, Anna "Mudder" 161, Arian 141, 256, Caroline "Lena" 161, Clara 287, Clara "Hale" 161, Dora 287, Dora (Pohlman) 278, Elsie 287, Elsie "Shurp" 161, Fred 287, Fred C. 278, Fred "Fritzen" 161, Frederick C. 287, Ida 161, 287, Lena 287, Mary 161, 287, Matilda 278, 287, Matilda "Tillie" 161, Sophia "Soaf" 161, Sophie 287
BULLOCK, Delia (Patterson) 231, Helen 231, Nora Ireno 164, Perry 231
BUNCH, Jane 207
BUNDY, Mary 178, Omar 186, Priscilla 231 Rachel 231, Samuel 231
BUNNELL, Blanche Tabitha (Kellenburger) 238, Nancy Ellen (Shields) 238, Nathaniel 238, Nell 310, Stephen 238, Stephen Nelson 238
BUNTZ, Fredrick 23
BURCHFIELD, Alma (Mason) 256, Clarence 256, Elizabeth (Rider) 256, Samuel 256, 257, Sarah Ellen 257
BURDEN, Johnathan 95, Johnson 95
BURDING, William H. 13
BURGAN, Pearl 300, Phil 310, Ralph 300
BURGER, Ray 50, Truman 80, Wilbur 50
BURGETT, Anna Mae 162, 225, 235, 251, Beulah 235, 251, Beulah Alice 162, 225 Dick 21, Elsie Lenore 161 Homer 225, Homer "Dick" 166, Homer E. 170, Homer E. "Dick" 184, 235, Homer Emanuel 161, Homer Emanuel "Dick" 251, James Henry 161, Kate 235, 251, Kathryn 225, Lelah 21, 225, 251, Lelah Evalyn 162, 235, Mary Kathryn 162, 169 Nora 225, 235, 251, Nora Pearl 162, 184, Sophia (Rader) 161, Stella 166, Stella (Stafford) 170, 184, 225, 235, 251, William Jacob 161
BURKE, Florence Elma 202, William 177
BURKHALTER, Andrea 246, Audrey L. (Lindley) 246, Mark 246, Sheri 246
BURKHART, Elizabeth Jane 213
BURKHOLDER, J. 34, Jacob 28, Salome 28
BURNELL 149
BURNS 58, Celia 208, Hugh 33, James 82
BURNSWORTH, Will 344
BUROKER, Mary Moorman 36
BUROUGHS, Drusilla 234 Emma 234

BURRIS, Solomon 35
BURRUS 89
BURT, Lowell 211
BURTON, Lillian 197, Marsha 141, Martin 20, Pat 78, Sarah 214, W.R. 34, Walter Sr. 275
BUSBY, Captain B. 18, Janice (Fawcett) 139, Paul 139, Susan Kay 139
BUSCH, Mary Ann 293
BUSH, Ina Mae 299, Iva Kimbel 341, Mary Agnes 151, Maryellen 162, Rolly 341, Rolly Franklin 162, Rolly Jr. 162 Viola Elizabeth (Conard) 162, Viola Jean 162, William 162
BUSHON, Harriett 199
BUSHONG, J.A. 53
BUSTAMANTE, Caroline 162, 179, Laura 162 Luis 162, Paul 162
BUTCHER 171, A.P. 177, Angie Monette 178 George 177, Ida Hazel 171, Isaac N. 177, John 177, John B. 15, John Bryant 177, John Orville 177, Mary A. 343, Monette 177, Myrtle 177, Orville 177, Sadona (Brown) 177 Saloma 15, Sarah 177 Sarah (Thomas) 177, Sarah Frances Watts 329, Solomon T. 177, William 15, 177
BUTLER 34, Anna 163, 200, 219, Anthony 179, Avan 163, 200, Betty 163, Beverly 197, Bonnie K. (Lindley) 246, Carol 163, Christopher 163, Clarence 163, 200, Clarence Ora 162, Claude 163, 200, Dallas 163, 200, Dan 179, Danny 163 Deloris 163, Denise 197, Denney 163, Don 163, Donal 163, Donald 200, Dorothy 174, Dorsel 163, Earl J. 162, 221, Earl L. 197, Edith 163, Edward 163, Eli 163, Eliza Patterson 162, Elizabeth 163, Ersalee 163, Esther Lorene 163, Eva 162 Fred Otis 162, Frieda 163, George 163, Glen 163, Glenn 200, Hazel Oveda (Miller) 221, Helen L. 276 Helen Lucile 163, 221, Isabel 163, Jack 163, Jared 197, Jared Patterson 162, Jared William 163, Jenny 197, Jenny Michelle 163 Jesse 163 Jessie 140, John 163, 218, 219, 229 John Anderson 163, 200 Joseph J. 162, Joyce 163, Julia 197, Julia Denise 163, Karen 163 Kenneth 163, Kim 153, Loura 162, Marion 163, Marita 163, Mary 163, 200, Morris 163, Myrtle Ethel 162, Noble 163, Obadiah 200, Obediah 163, Odel 197, Odel Ann 163, Ora 21, 25, Ovid 340, Patsy 163 , Peter 197, Peter Eric 163, Phebe 163, Phoebe 163, Rachel Elsie 162, Ralph M. 163, Ralph M. 163, Robert 163, Rosalyn 163, Sallie 163, Sarah 163, Sarah (Dillner) 163, Sarah Ann (Overman) 200, Smith 163, Stephanie Leigh 163, Susan 163, Susannah 163, Sylvanus 163, Thelma 163, 200, Tina 246, Virginia 163, Wills 163, Wilma 163
BUTTERS, Edwin 248
BUTTERWORTH, Walter 165
BUTZ, Amanda Mae 234
BUZAN, Jane 163
BYERS, Bethany 176, Bryan 176, Cathy 283, Fred J. 106, John Wesley 11, Joseph Robert 163, Joseph Robert Jr. 163, Julie Lynn 163, Laura Lillian (Woodard) 163, Linda Ellen Teter 163, Lori Lee 163, William C. 163
BYES, Stephen 80
BYMASTER, Rosa Mae 256

BYRAM, Ronald 235
BYRD, Abraham 277, Claude 31, Earl H. 277, Elizabeth 209, Mary M. Brown Feirrell 277, Nellie (Austin) 277, Rebecca (Myers) 277, William L. 277
BYRKETT, Cora Lavina "Elsie" 291, John William 291, Mary Baxter 291
BYRUM, Caleb Parker 164, Charles 257, Everett 80, Exum 164, Jean 257, John 164, Lela Pearl (Rice) 256, Levina 164, Pearl 336

C

CABLE, Jane 268
CAGE, Everett 164, Lilia Dale (Fisher) 164, Margaret Josephine Mason 164, Ray E. 232, Ray Edward 164, Ray Everett 164, Rebecca Lee 164, Rhonda Ellen 164, Royce Leon 164, Rozella Lynn 164
CAGLEY, John 212
CAIN, Christine B. 287 Mary H. 220
CALAWAY, James Cecil 138
CALDWELL 28, A. 34 Andrew 27, Andrew P. 33, Andrew W. 51, Douglas Daves 164, Elizabeth 49, Erin Anne 164, Filo 327, J.S. 34, James 27, 32, 33, John 28, John Martin 164, Mary Daves Mason 164, Mary Miller 327, Paul "Spid" 174, Peggy Anne Herron 164, Shirley Marie 327, Wanda (Currens) 174, William Courette 164, William Courette Jr. 164, William Stanton 164
CALHOON, James 226, Sarah 226, William 226
CALHOUN, William 169
CALLIEN, Katie 219
CALOWAY 86
CALQUHOUN, Alexander 226
CALVERT, Cathy Elaine 164, Chad 164, Connie Jo 164, Gary Lee 164, George 165, Janet Kay 164, Janet Kay (Brummett) 164, John Oscar 164, Owen 164, Randy Dennis 164, Raymond B. 164, Sarah 275, Tina Melvina (Stephens) 164
CALVIN, Hiram 33
CAMACHO, Rachel E. 153
CAMDEN, Judith Louise (Prifogle) 288
CAMERON, Dave 23, William 14
CAMPBELL, A.C. 14, Alexander 68, Alfred "Pee-Dad" 257, Alice, (Johnson) 222, Benjamin F. 305, Jesse W. 291, John Fremont 305, John N. 305, Joshua 305, Leona Ruth 222, Levi 305, Lisa 282, Mary A. (Boyle) 305, Perl 222, S.N. 58, Sabastian H. 305, Sarah Catherine 305, Scott A. 298, Susan J. 305, Viola Theodosia 318, William 180, 305
CANARD, Edna May 192
CANDLER, Asa 119
CANDLISH, Carol (Getz) 198
CANINE, Cornelius 311, Dorothy Van Nuys 311, Margaret Isabel 189, Sarah Ann 311
CANNON, F. Wayne 324, Jennifer 324, Karla Kay 238, Linda (Fennell) 324, Matthew 324, Richard 48, 324, Robert 238, Wayne 85
CANTRELL, Josephine Pansey 287
CAPITANI, Angela 337
CAPLINGER, Vernon Edgar 328

CAPPS, Glen 86, Sherri 86
CAPTOLA 305
CARBERRY, Mary 144, Phyllis K. (Huffer) 234
CARDOVIA, Thracy 180
CARDWELL, Adlove Joann 326, Angela Marie 151, Artie 188, Cynthia 323, Dora I. 187, Evan C.188, Evan Cooper 188, Jack Lee 151, Joan Margarette 182, June 187, Karen 323, Lena L. Harris 326, Margaret Tolan 3, Michael II 323, Michelle 323, Mike Sr. 322, Ralph Lewis 326, Ralph M. 326, Sylvester 326
CAREY, Cecile May 152, Georgianna 172, Grant 285, Helen 265, Mary 268, 285
CARICO, Mary Helen 235
CARLISLE, Anne Elizabeth 175, John M. 175, Margaret A. 175
CARLSON, Phillip John 149
CARNEGIE, Andrew 87
CARNEY, Bessie Marie 153, Mary 141
CARPENTER, Gary 72, 73, L.L. 90, Linda 72, Mathew 327, Sid 261
CARR, Ada 247, Barbara 305, Eugene LeRoy 226, Mae (Alexander) 333, Myrtle 183, Rachel 65, Thomas 183
CARROLL, Charles 289, Jack 197, John Garritson 197, Jonathan 300, Margaret 170
CARRUTH, Samuel E. 70
CARSON, Carolyn T. 307, 320, Donald R. 320, J.K. 83, Michael 95, Russell Gage 320, Sally 216, Wanita 220
CARTER, Adam 33, Ann 47, Arvilla 165, Bob 179, Brandon 142, Buck 25, Burton Calvin 165, Cassandra 317, Charles E. 66, 231, Charles Eli 165, Clarence C. 165 Dan 165, 179, Dane 165, Dorothy 21, Doug 179, Eli 46, Emily (Newlin) 289, Enoch Lindley 165, Ethleen 165, 289, Florence Elsie 165, Fredric 64, Gene 165, George 165, Glen 180, Helen 21, J. 34, James David 165, Jeanette 21, Jeffrey 318, Jessica 190, John 317, John Braxton 274, John Robert 318, Kathryn Cassandra 318, Kelly Ann 317, 318, Kenneth 142, L. 34, Laura Ann 165, Laurel 165, Lee Edwin 66, Leota Delphine 274, Levi 165, 289, Lissa 165, Lloyd 46, Lois Elvin 331, Lota Delphina 274, Maia 165 Mary Alice 165 Mary Ann 165 Max 165, N.U. 34, Nancy 290, Nathan 165, Nicholas 165, Noah 27, 33, 34, Norma Lieutal 187, Oakley 66, Oliver Bales 165, Pamela Jane (Anderson) 141, Reba 46, Rosemary 165, Rosemary Ellen (Payne) 284, Sarah Catherine (Fix) 274, Sarah Rozella 165, Seth 165, Steve 179, Tim 165, Tyson 165, Walter 66, Will 165, William 66, 179, William Andrew 165
CARTMELL, Shirley (Brown) 157
CARTWRIGHT, Fred 180, Joseph 180, Sallie 180, Viola 180, William Henry 180
CARVER, Adeline (Vaught) 148, Emma 276, Frances (White) 148, Herbert 233, Janice I. 233, John W. 148, Mathew 148, Ronald D. 233
CARY, Grant 285
CARYL, Frank 214, Lisa 214
CASHNER, Elizabeth 216

CASKY 35
CASS, Evert 245, Lewis 29
CASTER 28, L. 34
CASTERLINE, Ira 184
CASTLE 53, Ruth 107
CATE, Clarkson 38, Daniel 35, John 38, Priscilla 211, Rachel (Pierce) 38
CATES, Priscella 211
CATRON, Charles 23, Marda Gene (Towe) 224, Mary Emily (Teel) 145
CATT, Clarence M. 218, Harold L. 218, James M. 218, Ralph J. 218, Russell L. 218, William L. 218
CAUDILL, J. Herschel 80
CAUDLE, Buckner 216, Mary Ann 216
CAUTHORN, Martha 229
CAYLOR, Gladys 107, Johnnie 41, Walter 41
CECILE, Emma 234
CEDARS, Helen 148, Mary E. 107
CEMER, A .34
CEPEDA, Orlando 11
CHAFFEE, Steve 25
CHALFANT, Martha 226
CHALLIS, Bradley 263, Kristen 263, Marvin 263, Pam (Middleton) 263
CHALMERS, Allis 164
CHAMBERS, Charles 208, Elinor 176, Elizabeth 177, Grace 177, Hannah 177, James 177, Luella 14, Mark 335, Mary 177, Mary Lindley 177, May 177, Mildred 197, Richard 177, Samuel 177, Samuel Jr. 176,177, Sarah 177, Smith 27, Vera 199
CHAMNESS, Abigail 219, Elmer 219, Lenna 64
CHAMP, E. 34
CHAN, Li 320
CHANDLER, Bennett H. 48, Bill 25, Elizabeth (Hiott) 143, John 143, Maria 272, Phoebe 234, Ray 25, 26, Samantha O. 143, Virgil 26, Virginia Mae 275, Wolford 229
CHANEY, Amy 234, Mary Catherine 174, Vaughn 174, Vaughn Jr. 174
CHAPLIN, Dick 25
CHAPMAN, Jeanett Frances 333 Lester 264
CHARLES, G.W. 10, Harry William II 163, Matt Edward 163, Scott Allen 163, William 197
CHASE, Robert 187, Seth W. 51
CHASTEEN, Barbara Eloise165, Charlotte Gladys (Davenport) 165, Clarence "Jack" Wilson 165, Dede 251, Deidra (Dede) Beth 166, Don 25, Don Fredric 165, Holly 251, Holly Anne 166, Jack Wilson 165, Stacy 251, Stacy Jane 166
CHAVEZ, Marilyn 92
CHEECK, Cynthia 138, Ervin 138, James R. "Pete 138, Marin E. 138, Oliver Earl 138, Bruce 166, Catherine 211, Charles H. 166, Charles Hershey 166, Cynthia 211, D. Kay 166, Edwin W. 166, Eva (Hullinger) 166, Fred 166, Gerald 3, 166, Jason 211, John 166, John W. 166, John Walter III 166, Paul 42, Paul W. 166, Sarah Eva (Ronk) 166, Stacy Jo 166, Stephanie Kay 166, Susan 339, Theo Docia 166, Tim 339, Wilbur (Bill) 166
CHELF, Charles W. 151
CHENOWITH, Laura 160
CHENY, Ann 266
CHERRY, Amy Jo 313, Cynthia 315, Eli 315, Mary J. (Tomlinson) 315

CHEW, Charles 25, Clifford 25, Sarah (Sadie) 219
CHIEF Richardville 32
CHILES, Deborah Sue 217
CHILTON, Alyssa Michele 316, Christopher James 316, Michael 316
CHISM, Evalene (Peck) 278, Mildred Ethel 278, William 278
CHITWOOD, Barbara Carlier 245, John 245, Margaret Jane 245, Martha 245
CHOATE, Calvin 62
CHRISTENSON, John 32, Christian, Julie Ann 140, 252, 303
CHRISTNER, P. 34
CLARE, Mildred 274
CLARK, Adam 103, Adam Christopher 302, Albert 166, 167, 270, Alex 167, Alexander 176, Almira 167, Anthony Michael 182, Benjamin Rian 182, Bertha Jewel 166, 270, Betha J. 257, Betsy 167, Brandon Joseph 302, C.B.F. 53, 54, Calvin 167, Charles 166, Charles Benjamin Franklin (C.B.F.) 167, Chiquita Marie 302, Chris 302, Cynthia M. 280, Debra Elaine 330, Don R. 167, Edith 167, Edward 167, Elisha 166, 167, Eliza Ann (Correll) 330, Eliza Winston 270, Ernest 167, Eva Clark 166, Fred 290, Gregory Allen 302, Henry 330, Horace 166, Horace G. 166, Ida Belle 166, Ira G. 13, J.S. 34, J.W. 100, James 167, Jane Ann 150, Jemina 167, Jeremiah Allen 302, Jess 302, Jessica Leigh 182, John C. 251, John P. 64, Joseph 166, Joseph Wilson 151, Lettice 167, Lewis 166, Linda D. 330, Louisa Aldine 246, Lulu 167, Manuel 166, Mariam 167, Mark 325 , Martha Jean 330, Marvin Ronald 182, Mary 325, Mary Jane 290, Mattie Mae (Davis) 330, Merrilla 166, Michael 325, Mickie Jo 330, Minnie 166, Nancy 167, Naomi (Huffer) 290, Nathan 167, Nathan Jr. 167, Nathaniel Lee 302, Oran A 167, Phynis Rhodema "Judy" Hendricks 216, Queen Esther 176, Ralph Doyle 330, Ranson 166, Rebecca 167, Rebecca (Fadley) 167, Rebecca Rose (Morrow) 330, Rhoda 167, Robert J. 302, Robert Joseph II 302, Roy 23, Ryan Joseph 251, Samuel 302, Shelby Jean 198, Susan (Daggett) 166, Thomas Henry 330, Wayne 325, William 166, 167, William Henry 330, Wilma Louise (Rollen) 330, Winston 167, Wm. M. 151
CLARKE, Gordon 62
CLATTABUCK, Louisa 177
CLAWSON, Melinda 273, Raymond 273
CLAY, Henry 13
CLAYTON, Earl 23
CLELLAN, John 35
CLELLAND, Jewell Aldine 241
CLEM, Fred 142, Mary (Sandifur) 142
CLEMENT, Catherine 231
CLEMENTS, John W. 27
CLEVANGER, Mildred Middlesworth 36, Amos Blaine 167, Arlie Isaac 167, Arlie Unger 167, Cecile Ann 167, Charles Henry 167, Dollie Alice 167, Frederick Guy 322, Frederick Guy 167, Frederick Guy 167, Gilbert Ross 167, Hazel Lulu (Keck) 322, Jeannette Adeline 167, 322,

John William 167, Joseph E. 167, Leota Elmire 167, Michael Joseph 167, Mildred Louise 167, Naomi Ruth 167, Neva 273, Samuel Guy 167, Sarah (Gosset) 167, Sarah Elizabeth 167, Squire 35, 167, Vern Ray 167, Walter Amos 167

CLICK, Carmen 210, 211, Dick 210, 211, June Eileen 210, 211
CLICK-WOLF, Marceita Marie (Kennedy) 288
CLIFFORD 305, Frank O. 329
CLIFTON, Alva 149
CLINE, Bob 200, Catharine 288, David 16, George 164, Lenora 21, Susan 164, Thomas 144
CLINGENPEAL, Arthur 43
CLINGENPEEL, Sarah 344
CLORE, Andrew 235
CLOSE, Mary 13
CLOUSE, Della 80
CLOUSER, Benjamin 168, Benjamin F. 167, Lamoine 167, Leo 167, Matthew 168, Rodney 168, Sadie Belle (Mitchell) 167, Sidney 168
CLUBBS, A. Charles 258, Addie 258, Blanche 258, Charles 258, Rosalie 258, Rozelma (Meade) 258, Viola 258, Violet 258
CLUTICK, Mable Joan 149
CLYMER, David 171, Jeffery Lynn 171, Pamela Gale 171
COAN, Arthur 247, Charles 247 David 247, Elizabeth 247, Eugene 247, George W. 247, Jane 247, Jason 247, Nancy 247, Patricia 247, Robert 247, Virginia 32
COAPSTICK, John 171
COATE, Clarence 225, Irene 225, Raymond 225, Robert 15, 16, 60, Roland 225, Thelma 225
COATES, Lula Ewing 213
COATS, Goldie 277, Hepsibah 339, Isaac T. 219, John 219, Mary Jay 339, Sally (Wright) 219, Sylvia 277, William 18, 339
COBB, Clarence 253, Henry 20, John T. 48, Michael 48, R. 18, R.C. 48
COBBS, Violet J. 326
COBURN, Charlotte 247, Edver W. 247, Jonathon 247, Lesley 247, Marcia 247, Philip 247, Walter H. 247
COCHRAN, Arbie Glen 288, Arda Berle 116, Henry 281, Lacee Marie 336, Larry 281, Mark 336, Nellie Lavina (Prifogle) 288, Phillip Martin 336
COCKRELL, Bill 289, Christopher 289, David 289, Edwin 23
CODER, Melissa 145
COE, Andrew J. 168, Francis Marion 168, Freida 187, John 168, John Wesley 168, Marion 19, Orpha Ellen 168, Rachel Ann 168
COFFELL, Ezra 106
COFFIN, Levi 61
COFFMAN, Brenda Sue 183, James 23, 86, Paula Marie 316, Samuel 27
COGHILL, Hilda Lucille (Adair) 139
COHEE, Annis Belle 168, 169, Delite 168, 169, Eva Pearl 168, 169, Flora J. 168, 169, Frank 232, Frank E. 168, 271, Frank Edgar 169, , Frank Edgar 168, 271, George 168, 169, Hinson 169, Ida 169, John Elmer 169, John Elmer B. 168, Laura 168, 169, Roxey 169, Vesta (McGraw) 232, William Burt 168, 169, William L. 168, 169, 271

COHEE-SHESTECK, Roxey 230, 231, 232
COIN, Lucille 298
COLBURN, John 140
COLDAZER, Jacob 70
COLE 292, Albert Clayton 169, Amelia Olive 315, Andrew J. 51, Clayton 214, Elbert 85, Elizabeth (Mason) 255, Elva 214, 225, Enid (Roler) 169, Estella (O'Bryant) 225, Henry C. 112, Mark 169, Martha E. (Chambers) 315, Mary (Leap) 169, Max 48, 169, Perry 225, Rhoda 64, Tracy 48, William 315
COLEMAN, Abigail 190, B.J. 95, Daniel 191, Elijah 190, Mary Parker 190, Tiny 208
COLES, Alice 340, Lawrence 340, Lincoln 340, Manson 340, Walter 340, Weldon 340
COLESCOTT 28, 39, 40, Beatrix 159, Celia Wooters 159, John 29, John W. 159, Olive 231, Rebecca Crabtree 159, Steve 39, Wesley 159
COLINS, Richard Raymond 330
COLLETT, Hertha (Stevens) 335, Hertha Faustine 335, Thomas Orlen 315, 335
COLLEY, Thomas 84
COLLIER, Katie Lee 29
COLLINS, Alta 263, Andrew 330, Benny 330, Christopher 177, Edna 218, Elizabeth 330, Emily Caroline 330, Emily Caroline (Lee) 330, Emma M. 330, Flossie 330, Frances 201, 202, Francis 218, Franklin Marion 330, Fredrick Eugene 330, Gardner 330, Gilbert F. 330, Hannah 330, Henderson 330, Jane Duke 177, Jeffrey 177, John Francis 330, Leah Corrine 330, Luther Basel 330, Marvin 330, Mary (Young) 202, Mary Jane 78, Michael 330, Monette Weaver 177, Nelson 330, Nelson Kenneth 330, Ott 250, Robert 330, Ronald 177, Ronald Wayne 177, Roscoe 327, Samuel 330, Susan 330, Thomas 202, 218, William H. 330
COLSCOTT, W. 34
COLTON, Robert 232
COLVILLE, James S. 90, Jane D. 324
COLVIN, Clifford 280, Clifford Jr. 280, Mary Josephine 280, Wendel 280, William 280
COLWELL, Edgard 281, Vincent 281
COLYAR, Naaman 65
COMBS, Allan D. 80 , "Chris" 13
COMER, Elizabeth 194, Jan B. 194, Kevin M. 194, Max 194, Nathan 18, Ray 69, Sylvia 220, Wilma Maxine 200
COMMODORE, James 325, Marie 325, Marsha 325
COMMONS, David 62
COMPTON, John 66, 221, Joshua 275, Olive Kenworthy 275, Rebecca 275
CONES, Matilda 183
CONGRESS, Frances 133, William 195
CONKLE, Charles 117, G.S. 34, Waneata 117, Waneata Rayl 291
CONN, Mary Jane 268
CONNAWAY, Mitilda 234
CONNELL, Bertha (Hughes) 98
CONNELLY, George 46
CONNER 245, Beulah 169, Clementine 234, Clotelle 169, Elva Louise (East) 169, Howard Claude 169, Kurt Victor 170, Leo Claude "Bud" 169, Sean O.

170, Stella Evelyn 169, Theresa Brook 170, Vickie Mavis 170, Victor Dee 169, Kathryn 162
CONNOR, Hannorah 237
CONOVER 305
CONRAD, Adam 86, Catherine 86
CONWAY, Anderson 55, Benjamin F. 167, Carolyn Sue 167, Everett 167, Everett G. 167, Frank 175, James 274, Manville E. 167, Mazy (Keever) 167, Pauline 21, Sarah 271, Trell 200
CONWELL, Addie L. 275, Albert 237, Albert Frank 218, Bob 117, Emily Jane 312, Emma 237, Hiram 312, Howard 237, Katie Pearl (Kerby) 237, Levi 237, Mildred 237, Onas 237, Rachael (McDaniel) 312
COOK, Ahaz 246, Alazo 245, Allen 283, Alta (Milburn) 170, Amanda Thompson 246, Amana Jane 65, Barbara Lynn (Hunter) 224, Bernie 66, Bill 53, Blaine C. 170, Bob 170, 282, Bryan J. 170, Burns 145, Cecil 170, 175, Charles 308, Charles Robert 170, Chelsea Elizabeth 170, Edith 170, 282, Edith Joann (Parkhurst) 170, Emily (Ratcliff) 235, Emily Ann 170, Esther May Cowgill 171, H.C. 34, Helen 107, Ilona 224, Ina 283, James 235, James Russell 235, Jerry 83, John 35, Josephine 246, Kathy 165, Kevin Thorton 170, Lawrence Franklin 144, Lelah 25, 170, 184, Lillis B. 246, Lillis B. (Wilkerson) 246, Loretta 171, Martin Seth 170, Maude (Brown) 233, Maudie Louise Buslong 149, Merle Mae (Shuck) 170, Michael 175, Michael Warren 170, Nick Joseph 53, Otis 224, R. 201, Rodger 175, Rodger Wayne 170, Ron 224, Ross C. 170, Russell 25, Russell Lowell 235, Sarah 246, Tia Alyssa 171, Troy Andrew 171, Zachary Michael 170
COOKSEY, Mary (Case) 180, Matilda 180, Zacheriah Jr. 180
COOL 197
COOLE, John 292
COOLIDGE, Calvin 340, John Randolph 340
COOMER, Ange Fletcher 340, Faye Howell 340, Floyd 340, Helen 340, Joan Lee 340, Paul 340, Roscoe C. 269, Willie Johnston 340
COON, C.E. 300
COONS, Wm. 48
COOPER, Bernard 305, Catherine 291, Eva 157, Fern 157, Goldie 157, Hazel 157, John 289, Kim 289, Lewis Cass 212, Lisa 289, Nona 158, Richard 91, T.A. 85, W.B. 34, William 157
COPELAND, Bill 25
COPLAN, Davy 190
COPLEN, James P. 116
COPP, Albert 170, Anna Emoline 170, Harrison 170, Jesse 170, John 170, John Paul 170, Martha (Henry) 170
COPPAGE, Joseph 159
COPPOCK, Aaron 51, 170, Betty 277, David Grant 170, Dorcas 170, 267, Esther 185, Fred 277, Jane 170, John 170, 267, Laurel 277, Margaret 170, Margaret (Tucker) 170, Martha Patricia (Williams) 170, 267, Cora Emma 331, Rachel 170, Sarah 170, Warren 277
CORBIN, Lydia Ann 170

CORDER, Amanda Brianne 336, Brian Douglas 336, Nathan Allen 336
CORFMAN, Maude 287
CORMANY, Catherine 254
CORN, Minerva (Ambrose) 203, Nora (Hunley) 203, Sylvester 203, William Pleasant 203
CORNSTALK, Peter 147, 249
CORRIGAN, Joyce G. 179
CORWIN, Kara Ann 336, Kelly Renee 336, Kristi Lynn 336, Phil 336
CORY, Martha 59, Norman 59
COSAND, Abram T. 175, Gurney 197, Nathan 46, Nigel 197, Peninah 222, Ruth Ardella (Turner) 326, Vern 197
COSNER, George Bayliss 306
COSTLOW, Hazel 265 Henrietta 171, J.P. 14, Martha 265, P. 34, Patrick 27, 171, William 265
COTNER, John Pierce 182
COTTERMAN, 28, Alice (Richard) 257, Brian 267, Charles 257, David 267, Julia Betty 257, Sandy 267, William 267
COTTEY, Reuben 119
COTTINGHAM, Ellora 285, John 305
COUCH, Fred 86, Mary V. (Polly) 64
COUGHLIN, Agness Ellen 175, Barbara Ann 176, Catherine Dolores 175, Catherine Dolores 170, Cecil 175, Cornelius 175, Daniel 176, Dolores 176, Edward 175, 176, Ella (Hooley) 175, Ella (Hooley) 170, Frederick 176, Frederick Timothy 175, George 175, George Edward 175, James 175, James Harold 170, 175, Janet 176, John 170, 175, John Horace 175, Joseph Michael 176, Kathie 176, Kathleen 175, Lelah (Davis) 170, Madaline Florence 175, Marie 175, Martha 176, Mary Carlisle 175, Patricia Elizabeth 175, Rebecca Edna 175, Robert 176, Robert Patrick 175, Rosemary Wanda May 175, Tim 170, 175, Timothy 175, Viola 170, Virginia 175, Wanita 170
COULTER, Corrine 153, Eric 157, Lucinda (Hill) 157, Philip 157, Ron 275
COURTER 86
COURTLAND, James 13
COURTS, Karen 96
COVALT, C.D. 53, Elizabeth Harriet 231, Jonathan 231, Rachel 231, Wanita Durr 204
COWAN, James 196, John 196
COWELS, J.G. 129
COWGILL, Fred 171, Orval Aaron 171, Orval Farl 171, Othella Frances 171, Stephen Corder 171, Susan Dawn 171
COX, Edgar 128, Elisha Aaron 216, Elizabeth Snethem 216, Er C. 317, Greg 277, Hildreth Anita 168, Jeremiah 19, Johnathon 216, Lucinda 224, Lydia 19, Marion 232, Mary Beth 23, Milton 65, Rachel 252, Rosetta 216, Sarah 277, Sarah Elizabeth 317, Sheridan 103, Summer 277, Susanna 216
COY 218, Alexander 171, 180, Catherine 296, Clara 257, Clara Durfella 256, Edward M. 156, Hazel 59, Ida 305, James H. 257, James Henry 171, John 171, Mary (Smith) 171, Mary Ellen (Breedlove) 155, Mary Jane 257, W. Oscar 171
CRAB, Mary 278

CRABTREE 28, E. 34, Edward 159, Lurenna Goyer 159
CRAIG, Carol 232, Desiree 327, Donna M. 226, Erma G. (Crews) 226, Eva L. (White) 171, Louie E. 226, Louie E. 171, Martha 107, 108, Mary 167, Mary Catherine 234, Michelle 327, Phillip 327, Reuben 184, Stephen 327, Will Clark 171
CRAMER, Carl Collins 172, Edgar L. 194, Edgar L. 172, Edna Maude (Helmer) 194, Eliza (Pierce) 172, Ethel Pearl 172, 194, Henry 172, Roy Edgar 172,
CRANDALL, Axie 169, Lydia 14, 237
CRANE, Mary 229
CRANMER, Irene 225
CRANOR, Arthur, 35, Cecil (Elliott) 175, Dan 36, Della 237, Elsworth 38, Frank 175
CRATZER, Eugene 283
CRAWFORD, Bryant 151, Emma Gertrude 322, Frank 151, Goldie Marie 254, James 260, James Preston 254, John 151, Maida 151, Martha Ann (LaDow) 260, Neaty M. 259, Neaty Marie 260, Nellie 151, Preston 47
CREASON, Anna 188, Isaac Harvey 296
CREIGHTON, Aaron Michael Joseph 163, Cameron Lee 164, Kayla Ellen 163, Michael Karl 163, Phyllis 163, Robert 163
CREWS, Erma Gladys 171, Walter Barry 171, Willie Mae (Pennington) 171
CRIBB, Barbara Angeline Slade 178, Barbara Slade 177
CRIBB-DAYHUFF, Martha 177, Richard Edward 177
CRIDER, E.C. 46, Gussie 99
CRIETZ, Sarah Keck 173, Valentine 173
CRILLEY, M. 34
CRIP, Charlotte 222
CRIPE, Anna Louise (Ann) 222, Henry J. 222, Jeanette 222, Mary 145, Samuel 222, Susan (Wise) 222
CRISPEN, Betty Jane 172, Doris Eileen 172, Helen Louise 172, Homer Boyd 172, 343, James A. 172, Karen Beth 172, 312, Lawrence Wayne 172, Loren Kenneth 172, Norma Lucille 172, Omer 172, Rosemary Jean 172
CRISS, Avis Rachel (Turner) 326, Clark Augustus 172, Clark Wayne 173, Dan Maurice 173, Dana Bryll 173, Daryll Kaye 173, Dean 295, Diana Lu (Prifogle) (Curl) 295, Donald 75, Earl Bryan 172, Eva Irene 172, Herschel 326, Herschel W. 231, Herschel William 172, Jason Thomas 231, Jonathan Dean 173, 231, 326, Kenneth William 173, Mary Magdalene (Traxler) 172, Millard Harrison 172, Orville Dewey 172, Oscar David 172, Ralph Henry 173, 231, 326, Rayman Herbert 172, Stacey Marie 231, Virginia (Smith) 231, 326
CRIST, Martin 18
CRITCHLEY, Albert 11, Edward 11, Ellen 11, Ellen (Gerrard) 173, George 11, 200, James 11, John 11, Robert 11, Thomas 11, Aurora (Scoven) 98
CRITCHLY, James 173, James Jr. 173, John 173, Lambert 173, Lily 173, William 173

349

CRITES, Benjamin 173, Benjamin F. 173, 267, Caroline (Foy) (DeMoss) 151, Charles 173, Charles Leonard 267, Dale 173, Dean 173, Duane 173, Edward Louis 174, Elizabeth 173, Elroy D. 267, Fietta 173, Frankie 173, George Washington 174, Harold 173, Henry 151, 173, Jacob Elsworth 173, John K. 173, Laramie 173, Laura 162, Laura Ann 174, LeeRoy 173, Lucenia 173, Mary 173, Mary Ann 173, Mary 'Polly' 173, Michael 173, Oscar 173, Phyllis 199, Rachel Mote 173, Raymond 199, Rick 173, Rosabelle 199, Roy 173, Sarah Ann Keck 173, Sarah 'Sallie Ann' 173, Tobias 173, Valentine 173
CROCKETT, Leonard 243
CRODDY, Jane 180, Wayne D. 114, William A. 51
CROMWELL, John 318, Mary 318, Moses 318
CRONE, Elizabeth 175, Fred 175, Wanda Mae 175, Winifred 175
CROOKTON, Mary Eileen (Dailey) 150, Richard Leo 150
CROSS, Arthur 148, Clyde 266, Cody Christopher 148, Tayler Marie 148
CROSSMAN, A.B. 180
CROUCH, H. Paul 278
CROUSORE, F.M. 219, J. 34, John 276, Leo Everett 270, Mary (Polly) 244, Mary Evelyn (Plummer) 276, Maude 225, Nora 276, Pauline Elizabeth 202, Pete 202, Robert 249
CROUSSORE, John N. 51
CROW, Justin Adam 226, Shane Michael 226
CROWDER, Charles F. 228, Constance Colleen 299, Everett Dewitt 299
CROWNOVER, Amanda 298, David 305, William A. 298
CROXFORD, Carolyn Lee 151
CRUCIANI, Mary 179
CRULL, Betty 147, Franklin 147, Grover 298, Robert 147, Thomas 147
CRUME, Anna Breckinridge 249, Helen 185, Janan 328, Susan Lee 329
CRUMLEY, Aaron 90, J.C. 34
CRUMP, Ronald E. 80
CRUMPACKER, Ben 218, Clealia 218, Donald 218
CRUTHIRD, George 35
CSELLAR, Katherine Mary Spindt 276
CUBEL, Harry 83
CULBERTSON, David 174, Davidson 174, John 174, John Frederick 174, Morton Colfax 174, Russel Phillip 174, William 174
CULLINS, Cornelius 53, Fay 56, Howard 56
CULLUM, Wesley 287
CULP, Teresa 238
CUMBERLAND, Martin 196
CUMMINGS, Charlene 333, Joseph 143 Mary Polly (Arnett) 143, Patrick L. 252
CUMMINS, Clessie 222, Robert 96
CUNNINGHAM, 28, Adria Nellie Kissinger 182, Delano 66, Dick 44, 46, Ella 273, J. 34, Melissa Ann (Missy) 239, Susan (Suzy) Tennille 239, Todd Leon 239
CURL, Diana L. (Prifogle) 231, Diana Lu (Prifogle) 173, Jason Thomas 295, Stacey Marie 295, Thomas 295

CURL-CRISS, Diana Lu (Prifogle) 288
CURLEE, Abraham 85, H. Gayle 343, J.R. 34, Margaret 85
CURLESS, Ada 220, Elsie 174, Frank 174, James Merrill 174, Jennie 218, Jennie E. 174, John 174, 218, Nettie 174, Roanna (Zentmeyer) 218, Ruby 174
CURLEY, Catherine 283, John 283
CURLY, Rose 282
CURRENS, C.C. 36, Clarence C. 174, Diana 174, Douglas 174, Eliza Rose (Fehrle) 174, Glen 174, Hilda Ann Rayl 291, Jack Elliott 174, Nancy Ann 174, Robert J. 174, Rufus 174, Wm. 48
CURREY, Melba 220
CURRY, C.H. 95, William 74, Wm. A. 324
CURTIS, Mary Maria 318, Richard 23
CUSICK, Steve 85
CUSTER, John 274, Mark Stephen 193
CUTRESS, Kathryn 278
CUTTRISS, Allen 99, Kathryn 259
CYPHERS, Betsy 220

D

DAFFRON, Lillie 283, Lillie Elizabeth 189
DAGGETT, Cody Ryan 214, Kari Lenae 214, Michael Drew 214
DAILEY, Larry 80, Mahala Jane 143, Mark 107
DAILY, Nettie Jane 254, Wiley 254
DAIN, Karla D. (Helms) 215
DALE, Jennie 199, William 123
DALEY, Patrick Joe 190
DALTON, Linda 141
DALY, Cameron 190, Carah 190, Pat 190
DAMETZ, Clara 277
DAMON, Dawn 336, Robert Keith 336, Tim 336
DANDO, James 74
DANIEL, John William 182
DANIELS, Margaret 234, Peter 48, Sean 284
DAPP, John 92
DARBY, Arline 66, Samuel 35, Thomas 35
DARLING, Wesley A. 194
DARNELL, Carl 62, Cassie 154, J.M. 13, Jessica N. 234, Joyce Ann (Huffer) 234, Lenore Ellen 154, Simpson 154
DARROUGH, W. 48
DAUGHERTY, Alice 265, Arthur 237, Ellen 237, John 237, John Joseph 265, Mary Leona 237, Sarah M. 265, Margaret 237
DAVENPORT, Dallas Suite 306, Florence E. (Suite) 306, George 306, Mary Elizabeth (Bauer) 306, Robert 305
DAVID, Andrew Carlton 175, Angeline 175, Clifford 175, Doyle Edward 175, Edward E. 175, Elizabeth 168, 169, 271, Fred 48, George 175, George W. 175, Ivy A. 175, Jacob 169, Jacob E. 175, Jan Edward 175, John W. 175, Madonna Jean 175, Myrtle 175, Nicholas Edward 175, Priscilla 187, Rocky Joseph 175, Stephen Bryant 175, Stephen Bryant Jr. 175, Theodore E. 175, William 175, Zachary Edward 175

DAVIDSON, Burchard 15, Esther 143, Esther Black Tuggle 143, James 27, 33, Jeff 25, Reed W. 143
DAVIES, Donald 147, Janet Lyn (Beatty) 147, Marc Gregory 148
DAVIN, JoEllen 278
DAVIS, 28, 273, A. 34, Abraham 35, Acenith 256, Anna (Lydia Ann) 190, Anna Cora 151, Annabelle 176, B. 34, Barbara 197, Barbara Jane 163, Belinda 231, 285, Benjamin 273, Beverly Jean 163, Bradley James 239, Carol 176, Cynthia 176, D.F. 12, D.J. 80, David 27, Dorothy Irene 243, Elizabeth 79, Elizabeth Jane (Watts) 273, Ellen L. 175, Ernest 97, Evan 176, Frank "Frankie" 176, George 100, 330, George C. 106, George M. 91, George W. 175, H.C. 34, H.H. 34, Harold 176, Harry O. 114, 116, Henrietta 175, Herbert Jr. 193, Herbert Lester 193, Horace, Walter 175, Isaac 190, Jack 257, Jacob 231, Jane (Bennett) 277, Jeremiah 175, John 277, John N. 176, Joseph Odessa "Dessie" 176, Josephine, (Stone) 193, Katherine 330, Kimberly Brooke 239, L. 34, Laura Bell 175, Leanna Marie 179, Lelah Elizabeth 175, Lemuel Quency 330, Lloyd 193, Luella 208 Luella Merle 176, Malinda 276, Martha Jane 273, Martha Oma Thompson 330, Marvin 238, Mary 267, Mary (Fye) 198, Mary Alice (Davis) 180, Mary Alveretta 313, Mary Elizabeth 325, Mary Lane 273, Mary Susan 175, Monell Olive 175 Morris 193, Myrle 283, Nancy 318, Nathan James 175, Nellie Adessa (Trittle) 170, Nellie Edna 175, Norman 65, Octa (Stroud) 277, Orian N. 175, Pamela 176, 298, Paul 179, Rachel 273, Ralph 197, Ralph Wayne 163, Robert 176, 193, Robin Michelle 239, Rosina Jane 175, Ross 53, Samuel Harvey 212, Sarah 176, Sarah Elizabeth 175, Shelby Rose 171, Stacy 14, 75, 198, Tabitha Ann 242, Tanya 171, Timothy Jon 239, Tom 171, Walter Horace 170, Wheeler 96, Will 277, William 212, Wilma 53
DAWSON, 39, Bill 42, Ethel 223, Michal Elaine Sallee 198, Richard Craig 198, Robert 198, Rolla 42, Rosa 160
DAY, Elizabeth 141, Estella 140
DAYHOFF, A.F. 226
DAYHUFF, A.F. 178, Andrew F. 177, Ann 177, Catharine 177, Catherine A. 177, Charles 176, 178, Charles Bradford 177, Charles Hal 177, Charles Hal 178, Charles Hal III 177, Charles Hal IV 177, Charles Hal Jr. 176, 177, Charles Hal Jr. 178, Daniel 177, 178, Daniel F. 177, Ellen 177, Hannah 177, Hannah C. 177, Heather 177, Jason 177, Jessie T. 177, Ladie 177, Lilly 177, Lilly C.J. 177, Mariah R. 178, Marian Alicia 178, Marian Perry 178, Marietta 177, Martha 177, 178, Mollie P. 177, Monette 176, Richard 177, Samuel 177, 178, Sarah (Sallie) 177, William Duke 177
DE GAULLE, Charles 195
DE GROFF, Magdalena 143
DE LON, Alice 99
DE ROCHA, Aristede 329

DE VORE, Freda 99
DE WITT, C.R. (Bob) 179, Chad Edward 179, Clarence Elmer 179, Clarence Jeffrey 179, Doris 179, Earl Edison 179, George W. 179, Hazel G. 179, Henry 179, Henry F. 179, Jim 179, Joe 179, John W. 179, Joseph F. 179, Lucy 179, Mark 179, Mark Allen 179, Parthena A. 179, Ruby D. 179, Sarah (Youngman) 179
DEAM, Hannah 196
DEAN, Aaron 178, Caleb 178, Dorothy 253, Eli 178, Jack 135, 178, James 56, Jeff 178, Jennifer 178, John 178, Judy 135, 178, Lamaar 56, Letha M. 236, Margaret K. 64
DEARDORFF, Aaron 245, Albert 287, Ivan Glen 287, Michael 26, Ralph 14, Raymond Arthur 287
DEARINGER, Anielisa 216, John Omer 256, Omer 255
DEATON, Ronnie 148, Sandra 148
DEBARD, Kevin 190, Peggy Denice 190, Robert 190, Ronald 190
DEBARDELEBEN, Joan 182
DEBERD, Sarah 219
DEBOO, James 261
DECROES, 106, Leon C. 106
DEFABRITIS, Kara 199, Laura 199, Sandra 295, Scott 199, Stephanie 199
DEFFENBAUGH, Catharine 273, George 273, Maria 273
DEFORD, Calvin 180, Gracie ("Grace") Frances 180, Harriett (Stuart) 180, Minnie 234
DEGASTYNE, Yolande 190
DEGLER, Marcella Christine 286
DEGRAAFF, Ronald 23
DEGRAFFENREID, Cynthia (Cindy) 215, Karen Elaine Dowden 147, Marty Lane 147, 181, Norma Jean 147, Stella 255, William Hale 147
DEHART, Catherine Boone 224
DEHAVEN, J.W. 34, Margaret 199
DEHNER, Paul W. 94
DEICHLER, Jane 165
DEIS, Jane (Host) 176
DEISCH, Roscoe 179
DEL-AGUA, Delores 284
DELANO, Margarite (Fields) 298
DELERY, Sharon Kay Waters 276
DELFOSSE, Francoise 319
DELL, Dianna 32, Gordon 32
DELON, Alice Loren 178, Alice Lorene 143, 197, Ann 178, Aubrey Flint 143, 178, Austin J. 178, Benjamin 178, Charles 178, David 178, Emma Lenora 143, 178, Francis 178, Fred K. Jr. 197, Fred K. Sr. 197, Fred King 178, Fred King Jr. 143, 178, Fred King Sr. 143, Gailen Louese 143, 178, 197, 212, Hannah 178, Hannah Lenora 178, Harry Everett 143, 178, Henry 178, Horace J. 143, 178, Jesse 178, John Anthony 178, Johnathon 178, Joseph 178, Josiah 178, Julia Emmagene 178, Margaret 178, Mark 178, Mark Anthony 178, Mary 178, Miriam 178, Nancy 178, Nathan 178, Penelope 178, Penina 178, Rheuben 178, Samuel 178, Sarah 178, Simon 178, Walter 178, Walter V. 143, William 178, William Homer 178, William Pearl 143, 178
DELONG, Claude 154
DELRYMPLE, David 322, George 322, Joan Emery 322, Josephine Mae 305, Pauline Elizabeth Hatt 322, Ruth 138
DELVECCHIO, Anthony 179, David 179, Dominic 179, Eryn 179, Felice 178, James 179, Jeanette 179, John 179, Kristin 179, Mark 179, Mary 179, Nicholas 179, Nick 162, Philip 162, Phillip 179, Richard 179, Robert 179, Sara 179, Serafina (Zeppetella) 179, Steve 179, Thomas 179, Victoria 179
DEMMING, Emma 246
DEMOSS, Bertha 174 Caroline (Foy) 173, Ellen 234, Frank 174, Grace 248, Grace P. 174, Grethel 174, William Harvey 174, William Riley 174, William Riley Jr. 174
DENMAN, Sarah A. Poff 291, Sharon 299
DENNIS, 250, Elizabeth 284, Jesse 51, Judy 62, Peter 91, Rod 62
DENNISON, Fannie 311
DENSMORE, Peggy (Crites) 173
DEPOY, Henrietta T. 319
DERMOND, Philip 65
DERN, Arthur 311
DEROLF, Chuck 83
DESANTO 227
DESHON, James 272, Levina (Bright) 272, Mary Jane 272
DESTOCKI, Andrew James (Drew) 239, Walter Andrew (Andy) Jr. 239
DETAMORE, William 35
DEVORE, Catherine 141, Frank 14, John Wm. 271 Loretta I. 180
DEWEESE, Edith 21
DEWITT, Alvin 148, Anita (French) 255, Darbin Munson 153, Darrick Leigh 153, Diedra Ann 153, Dustin Bryce 153, Eric 337, Jack Richard 153, Zella (Wilson) 148
DEWITTE, David 100
DHONT, Edward 92
DIAZ, Benjamin Augustine 275, David Leonard 146, 275, Jesus 275, Marcia Lynn Ann Miller 275, Michael David 146, 275, Nikki Chantal Johnson 275, Socorra Esquivel 275
DICE, Cecelia Ray 217, James H. 217
DICK 39, A.R. 245, Clarol 21, Frances (Brand) 251, Jacob 251, Margaret 343
DICKENSHEETS, Richard 265
DICKEY, Andrew 138, Arthur E. 320 Christian 186, Cyril 138, Emma Mae 138, Grace (Gardener), Hazel Blanche 320, Marie 138
DICKINSON, Martha 206
DICKISON, Abraham 179, 180, Alma 180, Amos 179, Daniel 180, Daniel David 179, David G. 225, David Grandville 179, David Granville 180, Dawn Darlena 179, Ella 180, Elvina Jane 180, Esta 180, Ethel Ivy (Washington) 179, Flora 180, Glen 180, Griffy 179, Hannah 179, Hannah (Kiger) 179, 180, Harvey 180, Iva Ethel (Washington) 225, James 179, 180, John 180, Joseph E. 179, Lavina Jane 179, Lowell 180, Lucille 180, Lucy 180, Marietta 180, Martha 180, Mary Catherine 180, 225, Mary Catherine (Ellis) 179, Ned 180, Omer 180, Raymond 180, Robert 180, 186, Robert Abram 179, Russel 180, Russell 180, Sharon Romain 179, 186, Virden 179, Vonda Lou 179, 186, Wanda Sue 179, 186, William 180, William Abrum 179, 186
DICKS, Anna (Fisher) 176, Deborah 176, Peter 176, Zachariah 176
DICKY, Ellen Shaw 313
DILLER, Walter 61
DILLIDAY, Robert 330
DILLIDAY, John 112
DILLINGER, John 112

DILLMAN, Carol 78, David 19, John 48, Ruth 107
DILLNER, Augustine 163
DILLON, Dorcas 191, George 138, Isabella 234, John 191, Mary "Polly" 191, Sarah (Ward) 138
DIMITT 59, Richard 323
DIRMIT, Elizabeth Ann (Brown) 296, Sarah Elizabeth 296
DISHON, Donna Kay 186, Harry 186
DISINGER, Clarence 157, Frank 157
DISNEY, Jerry Neil 173, Kathryn Ann (Spence) 173
DITORE, Carmen 177
DITTO, Christiana 141
DIX, Martha 27
DIXON, Carolyn 197, Evelyn 197, Jonathan 66, Joseph 31, Lee 197, M.R. 95, Mary 176, Nathan 63, Silas 176
DODD, Bruce 325
DOEPKE, Lena 287
DOHNER, Elizabeth 298
DONAHUE, Mary 14
DONELSON, Artie Mesa Gullion 214, Jessie Waters 214, Lawrence Arthur 214, Loren 214, Phyllis June 214
DONNELL, Alexander 180, Alman "Everett" 180, Edward Everett 180, Helen 243, Jane (Cox) 180, Laura Evelyn 180, Lloyd Alman 180, Mark Edward 180
DONSON, Edward 180, Esther (Bryan) 180, Harry 180, Jeffrey Alan 180, Linda LeAnne 180, Nancy Jane (Colbert) 180, William Harry 180
DOOLITTLE, Martha Florence (Arnett) 141, Miles 141
DORAN, Barbara June 261, Charles Edwin 261, Dee William 261, Edna Rowena 261, Martha Roberta "Bobbie" 261, Max J. 261, Virginia Edith 261, William Dee 260, 261
DORISSE, Fred. W., Sr. 69
DORMAN, L.V. 34, M. 34, Mahale 27
DORRELL, Daniel 212
DORSEY, J. 34, Jill 213
DORTON, Bertha (Rooney) 274, Betty (Wright) 274, Howard 274, John 274, Thomas 274
DOSSETT, James 186k Matthew 186 Phebe (Lynch) 186 Sarah (Berry) 186
DOTTER, J. 34
DOTTERER 39, Ben 43, Jacob 298, Maggie 298, Manny 41, Willie 42
DOTY, Mary Louise 249, Samuel 212
DOUCET, Lyell 125
DOUGLAS, Elizabeth Marie (Givens) 326, Fleeta Mae 145 Robert W. 63 Sarah Francis 270, 290
DOUGLASS, Daniel P. 23, Dorothy 228
DOW, Jane 186
DOWDEN, Barbara Ann 149, Barbara Ann McInturff 147, Barbara Dean 181, Bertha May 181, Betty Jo 181, Beulah Jeane 180, Bradley Lewis 283, Caroline Josephine Wilcox 146, Clyde Morris 180, Donald Ray 180, Doris Jeanette 180, Dorthea Ruth 180, Earl Dewayne 180, Edith Cora 181, Erma Bernice 180, Esther Eileen 181, Eva Blanche 181, Everett Darrell 181, Fredrick Earl 283, George E. 180, 291, George Ronald 181, Hannah Harpold 180, 291, Helen Rose 283, Jack 280, Jackie Wayne 181, Jesse Curtis 181, Joni Jeannette 283, Karen Elaine 181, Kevin Wayne 146, 181, Kevin Wayne Jr. 146, Kyle Robert 146, Lewis Clyde 283, Lila Mae 180, Lois Fay 180, Lula Ethel 181, Mae 180, Maria Rosena 181, Marjorie Laverne Dunn 181, Mary Catherine 181, Mary Elizabeth 180, Nathaniel Fredrick 283, Otha 180, Otho 149, 291, Otis "Bud" Wayne 181, Otis Wayne 181, Pearl 180, Robert "Bob" Joe 181, Robert J. 149, Robert Joe 146, 147, 181, Robert Scott 146, 181, Toni Lynnette 283, Virginia Barbara Leonard 146, 147, Walter 25, Walter William 181, Wilbur Raymond 181, William Clarence 181
DOWNEY, Beverly 107, Beverly (Grinslade) 205, Essie Mae 150, Linda 26, Linda Vary 22
DOWNHOUR, Albert 181, Andrew 181, Charles 181, 248, Edith Jean 181, Eliza 181, Elizabeth 181, Ellen Jane 181, Eremel 248, Esther 248, Eva (Swisher) 181, Florence 181, Floyd 248, Frank 181, George 181, Henry 181, 248, Jean 307, John 96, 181, Mary 96, Mary Jane 248, Minnie 181, Perry 181, Russell E. 181, 307, Russell Jr. 181, Susie 248, Vesta A. (Childers) 181
DOWNING, Melbadean (Foland) 193
DOWNS, William 286
DOYLE 94, J.W. 82
DRABENSTOT, Arliss Jean 218, Fred 160, Martha 160
DRAEGER, Arden A. 125
DRAKE, Aubrey 190, Kim E. 190, Matilda C. 195, Nancy Sue 190, Summer 190
DRAPER, Cela 86, Christina 282, Fern Alice (Grinslade) 205, James 282, Nancy 86, Russell Lee (Parkhurst) 282, William 86
DRAYER, Matilda 225
DREAR, Mary 212
DREIER, Katherine 277
DREYER, Bill 39, John 39, Sam 39
DRINKWATER, Ed 40, Emily Mills 337, J.O. 338, Mazy Belle 337, Rebecca Murphy 338, Thompson 338, W.W. 34, William Worley 337, 338
DRIVER, Anna Boles 293, Caleb 293, Ciara 293, Cynthia 293, Julie 293, Keenan 293, Michael 293, Ryan 293, Tim 293, Tom A. 293, Wildon 293
DROLL, Andrew 182, Charles Malcom 181, Laren Charles 182, Larisa 182, Michele Lynn 182, Randall Bogard 182
DRUECKER, Grace 182, Harold Joseph 182, Joseph 182
DRUSHEL, Elizabeth 235
DUBOIS, Doris 283
DUBOSE, Richard, 85
DUCKWULER, Mary 239
DUDDY, Mary Jane 200
DUDLEY, Fleeta 338, Oliver 338
DUECKER, Sheldon 70
DUFFITT, Consuella (Connie) 148
DUFRAME, Elma Leona (Hellman) 256
DUINETTE, George 48
DUKE 85, A.J. 48, Alexander 177, Bob 208, Charles 177, David 177, David D. 178, George 177, Georgia 177, Hattie 177, Jane 178, Ladie 177, 178, May 177, Nannie 177, Nannie (Littler) 177, William 177
DUMOULIN, Alice Victoria 182, Daniel Lynn 182, David Dean 182, Deborah Ann 182, Donald Dwaine 182, Donald Dwaine II 182, Edward John 182, Ernest Fredrick 182, Frederick Ferdinand 182, Jayne Faye 182, Jean-Baptiste Marie 182, Leslie Allan 182, Linda Kay 182, Mark Alan 182, Mary Ellen 182, Mary Ellen 182, Michael Kent 182, Patrick Keith 182, Ralph Leslie 182, Regina Louise 182, Robert Eugene 182, Rosemary 182
DUNCAN, Amanda 183, Betty 172, Betty Jean 183, Bill 183, Bradley Kent 183, Charles 217, Charles E. 183, Charles Leslie 183, Clarence Carl 183, Dale 340, Dale Edward 183, Donald Eugene 183, Doris Eileen 183, Dwain L. 183, Elise 183, Ermie Ruth 183, Estel G. 183, Esther 237, Esther Wanita 217, 322, Fred L. 183, Fredrick Carl 183, George 183, George Armor 183, George Lee 183, Henry Carlton 183, Howard 51, Howard (Beanie) 183, Howard Edward 183, J.J. 48, Jacob A. 183, James 183, Jesse Earl 183, John 183, John Eberly 183, John Francis 183, John James 183, John Pearl 183, Julie E. 183, Junior 97, Larry Wayne 183, Lauren 183, Lisa 183, Lisa A. 183, Margaret 183, Margaret (Baldridge) 183, Marion 25, Marlea 183, Mary 99, Mary Elizabeth 183, Mary Matilda 183, Mildred S. 183, Nancy (Sergeant) 183, Nellie 307, Nellie Lee 183, Nila Josephine 202, 217, Omer C. 183, Orange Lester 183, Robert H. 183, Roscoe Kern 183, Sandra Sue 183, Simon Von 217, Stephen Kent 183, 223, Virgil G. 183, William 183, William Dale 183
DUNDAS, Irena 201, Robert 201
DUNGAN, Steve 25, Wayne 83
DUNKIN, Carrie (Barnett) 147, Donald 338, Mary 338
DUNKLE, Fayfern 236
DUNLAP, Elmer E. 54, 56, 100, George 197, Miriam 204, Ruth 230
DUNMOYER, Angie 238, Dwight 238
DUNN, Bill 329, Clinton 193, Daisy Dean Havens 181, Eileen May 180, Emily 202, Forest 180, Georgia 195, Jackson 181, Janet Sue 193, Katherine 50, Marjorie Laverne 181, Mary 180, Sarah Elizabeth (Lizzie) 155
DUPLER, Charlotte 184, Clarissa 183, Clyde 183, Darrell 184, Delilah Deakyne 184, Della 183, Edward 183, Elizabeth 183, Emma 183, Emmanuel 183, Frank 183, Frederick 183, Georgia Arnold 184, Harley 184, Harry 183, Henry 183, Jacob 183, Jonathan 183, Margaret 184, Marilyn 183, Minnie 183, Perlina 184, Phil 184, Philip 183, Plennie 184, Reuben 183, Serelda 184, Solomon 183, Woody 183
DUPPENGEISER, Martha C. 208
DURBIN, Lila 270
DURFEY, David 182, Grace Marie 182, James 182
DURHAM, Charles E. 300, Danny 167, David 167, Richard 167
DURKES, Chester Lewis 189, Cleo Eva Antrim 189, Earlene Agnes 189

DURR, Eugene 204, Harry 204, John S. 204, Larry 197, Paul 204, Russell 25, Wilford 204
DUSKIE, Lovisa 291
DUTRO, Sarah A. 202
DUTTON, Alice C. 213, Anna Emoline (Copp) 170, Boyd R. 53, 170, Bud 59, Chloe (Burgan) 315, Elnora Lucille 314, Floyd 170, John Edgar 'Bud' 170, Kelta 170, Lonzo 315, Lucille 315, Phyllis 59, Richard 280, Wayne 280
DWIGANS, Ethlyn 78
DWYER, Cynthia Stevens 214, Daniel Joseph 316, Meghan Ann 214, 316
DYAR, J.T. 48
DYE, Gene 23, 86, Helen 269, Willis B. 106
DYER, Charles DeVoe 187, Francis 292, Susan Elizabeth Strawbridge 221, Verla 107

E

EADES, Catherine 213, Ellen Dora 156, John 180, 225
EADS, Isaac 48, Lora 96
EAKIN, Patricia Loraine Myers 276, Shanda Renea 276
EARLY, Alice 257, Alice (Mason) 195, Catharine (Burchfield) 195, 256, George Clinton 212, Jacob 195, John 256, John B. 15, Joseph B. 212, Joseph Sr. 15, Madora Alice 256, Margaret 256, William 195, 256
EARLYWINE, Byron 25, 251, Byron "Si" 184, Charles William 184, Dawn Joy 184, Michael 333, Nora 25, 162, 170, 251, Osa Bell (Harter) 184, Rodney Byron 184, Rodney Lee 184
EASH, Susanna 253
EASTERDAY, C. Louise 282, Evelyn (Rose) 282, Lucein 282
EASTERLING, Thomas 45
EBERSOLE, Roy 41
EBRIGHT, William 35
ECHELBARGER, Brandon 231, Bret 231, Brian 231, Brianne 231, Conde 231, James C. 231, Jarret 56, Kristen 231, Lisa 231, Tyler 231
ECKERT, Lee 26
ECKLES, Nancy 108
ECKLUND, John Milton 182
ECKMAN, Karen 214
EDGERLY, Robert 325
EDGERTON, Reuben 44, 207
EDISON, Thomas 127
EDMONDS, Clarrissa 33
EDMONDSON, Clarence 11
EDRINGTON, A. 83
EDWARDS 86, Alvin Harold 267, Brooke Renee 214, Clifford Carl 320, David 344, Elmer (Doc) 184, Esther 184, Ethel Marie (Weidert) 267, Etta 184, Forrest 19, 25, Gary Wayne 333, Gertrude May 328, Ginger 190, Golda May (Stewart) 320, Henry 13, James 97, 184, Jesse 344, John 250, Judy 192, Kathleen 267, Kristen Ricque 333, Linnie T. 13, M. Glen 184, Mary 184, 344, Mildred (Pat) 184, Opal 19, Roscoe 184, Sarah (Thompson) 344, Thelma Arretha 320
EHRHARD, Anna Catherine 268, Catherine 268, Charles 268, Frederick 268, John 268

EHRMAN, Bob 209, George 184, George Loren 184, George Parker 184, George W. 184, J. Frank 184, 266, John 184, John Frank 184, Lester Ray 184, Lillie 184, Marion J. 184, Mary 184, Nellie 184, Prainey (Eshelman) 184, Rosemary 184, Sarah C. 184, Thomas Ray 184, Vina Alta 184, William A. 184
EICHOLTZ, Grace 177
EICKENBERRY 273, Isaac 273, Sarah (Mellinger) 273
EIKENBERGER, Kenneth 64
EIKENBERRY, Abraham 317, Alvin 59, Clifford 149, Daniel 317, Eliza Ann 152, Judith 256, Kayla 196, Kevin 196, Mary Frances 317, Michael 196, Nancy Ann Gregory 59, Rhoda Lybrook 317, Samuel 59, Sarah 344, Sharon 243, Willis Andrew 245
EINSTEIN, Albert 159
EISEN, Donna June 194
EISENHOWER, Dwight David 151
EISENSTEIN, Alyssa 195, Leah 195, Mara 195, Stan 195
EKLEM, Alexander 224, John 224, David 224, Domenica 224, Katherine 224, Philip 224
EL WARNOCK 37
ELDER, Richard 171
ELDRIDGE, Alison 185, 307, James 185, John 202, Matilda Alice 202, Polly Ann (Morris) 202, Ronda (Simpson) 185, William (Bill) 185
ELLABARGER, Arthur H. 185, Barbara Lee 185, Carl Edward 146, 185, Carl Lester 185, Edith 315, Edith L. 185, Ephraim 185, Ephraim Frank 185, Eva E. 185, Gina Michelle 146, 185, Gladys Irene Minglin Harrell 146, Jacob 185, Lisa Darlene 185, Lowell Wayne 185, Mary Hoover Kolb 185, Mary Lois 185, Orin Albert 185, Wayne Orin 185
ELLEMAN, Charles Elmer 185, Crystal 162, Crystal (Wilson) 185, Elmer Ellis 185, 209, Enos 185, H. Ralph 185, Harold Burdette 185, Harold Ralph 209, John H. 185, Margaret Loraine 185, 314, Ray Burdette 185, 209
ELLEMEN, William 185
ELLER, Abraham 185, Alan 186, Catherine 186, Charles 185, 186, Charles Abraham 186, David 186, Elias 185, Esther 185, Flora 185, Flora Saloma 216, Gary 186, Gregory 186, Harold 59, 186, Howard 186, Jacob 185, Josiah 185, 216, Judith 186, Kym 186, Larry 186, Lena 185, Lynn 186, Magdalene 185, Marjorie 59, Mary 186, Mary Margaret 288, Melvin 23, Michael 186, Nancy 185, Orpha 185, Ortha (Brubaker) 216, Pauline 59, 186, Richard 186, Robert 186, Ruby 186, Ruthadele 152, Sherry (Kasey) 186, Stephanie 186
ELLERBROOK, Mildred Dorothy 295
ELLERS, Mildred 107
ELLERT, Francis 304, Susan Severns 119
ELLIOT 245, Bob 215, A.M. 34, Charles 27, Glenna (Woolen) 222, Hammer "Mick" 175, James P. 33, John 174, Mary Lucy 222, Naomi 174, Pinniah 212, Rosa (Elliott) 174, Roscoe 175, W.G. 48, Wilson 222
ELLIS, Ann Moulder 268, Arthur 171, Bob 97, Brittany 299,

351

Catharine (Jones) 171, Chester 21, Claude 36, Don 307, Effie (Hightchew) 191, Emma 171, Flurry 191, Francena 325, George Washington 186, Gerna Jeanette 191, Isaac 171, J. Hammer 38, 64, Jack Eugene 186, James 65, James A. 53, 54, 64, James H. 177, James Robert 299, Jason 307, Jesse 53, 64, Jesse Hammer 190, Joseph 180, Lacey 299, Madge Elizabeth (Bassett) 186, Maggie 275, Marvin 191, Mary Catherine 180, Nancy Violetta (Noble) 191, Nehushta (Miles) 180, R.B. 34, Rebecca Ruth 64, Robert George 186, Ryan 299, Stephen Jay 186, William 15, William Gale 171

ELLISON, Annie 186, Authur Swain 186, Bessie Arminda 186, Bradley 186, Charley 29, Dessie Mae 155, 179, 186, Dina 186, Edith Irene 186, Elizabeth 186, Ellen Lee 186, Emerson 186, Esther 186, Finna Esther 186, Hazel 193, Hazel Louisa 186, Hazel Louise 155, James 186, Jefferson 186, Joseph Lafayette Jr. 186, Joseph Lafayette Sr. 186, Joseph Ulyess 186, Louisa (Dossett) 186, Margaret Melinda (Lyke) 186, Marley 186, Marylin Louise 155, 186, Millie Maxine 155, 186, Robert 186, Sarah 186, Sarah Melinda 186, Tilda 155, Uyless 186, William Matthew 155, 186, Zettie Marie 155, 186

ELSEA, Ethel Mae 223

ELVIN, Cinga 331, Ernest 331, Ernest (Bud) 331, Lily Eliza 270, Myrtle Powell 331

ELY, Elizabeth 296, Reuben 314, Reuben McCullen 314, William Otto 314

EMERSON, Lea 313, Leland 85

EMERY, Sandy 332, Sharon 332, Van 332, Van Jr. 332

EMLER, Ronald 273

ENDECOTT, Ann Mariah 270, John 270, Thomas Jr. 270

ENDERS, Anna (Cline) 248, Katie 248, William E. 248

ENDICOTT, Antonette 141

ENDLICH, Rosine Christine 241

ENDRUES, W. 34

ENGELMAN, Cecelia 264, Christian 264

ENGLAND, Don 85, Harry Eugene 186, Laura Belle 156, Luwanna Kay 186, Shannon Mae 186, Virginia (Winslow) 186

ENGLE, Mary Louise 338

ENGLISH, Mary Esco 285

ENOS, George 234, Magdalena 233

ENRIGHT, James 180

ENYART, Frank 119

EPPERSON, Locky 78

EPPLEY, Anthony Wayne 163, Christopher Davis 163, Wayne Allen 163

ERFCAMP, Fred 287, John 287, Siemon 287, Sophia 287, William "Bill" 287

ERICSON, Harold 230, Mary 230, Mary Ann 153

ERLEWINE, Susan 123

ERNNEZ, Armina 270

ERTEL, Charles 187, Charles Delbert 187, Elizabeth 151, 187, George 18, George Franklin 187, Harvine 187, Ida May 187, John Perry 187, Joseph Benjamine 187, Lewis 187, Lucy Almeda 187, Mary Leota 187, Mary Ludy 187, Nettie Estella 187, Peninnah Elizabeth 187, Philip 187, Rowena Houston 187, Silas Marion 187

ERVIN, Robert 15, 249, Walter E. 98

ERWIN, Edna 180

ESTAY, Pedro 284 , Susan 284

ESTES, Joseph 241, Mark Max 171, Max 171, Nathan 171, Tanya 171

ETHERINGTON, Adeline (Lincoln) 188, Amanda E. 187, Ann 188, Arthur B. 187, Artie (Cardwell) 187, Becky 188, Berniece 187, Bertha Frier 236, Beryl Dean 187, Bobby 187, Catherine 188, 292, Chad 188, Conrad Dewaine 187, Crystal 187, Dale 20, Dale Edward 187, Damaris Jane 188, Damaris June 188, Daniel Dean 187, David 188, Dawn Elaine 187, Donald B. 187, E. Elaine 187, Edith 187, Elizabeth 187, 188, 292, Everett Merrill 187, Francis 187, Francis (Yancey) 188, 292, Francis Willard 187, G. Sue 187, George 188, George Earl Jr. 187, Glen 20, Glenn Thomas 187, Gloria 187, Harry 187, 188, Irene (Terhune) 187, Jack 187, James Glenn 187, Jessie Florence 188, John 187, 188, 292, John Lincoln 187, John Mark 188, 201, John Mark Sr. 269, John Murphy Jr. 187, 201, John Thomas 187, 188, 292, Joseph Mark 187, Larry 187, Leroy A. 187, LeRoy Anson 188, Lewis C. 187, Linda 187, Linda Lou 187, Mariah (Ramseyer) 187, 188, 201, Mariah Sarah (Ramseyer) 188, Marjorie 187, Marsha 187, Martha 188, 292, Mary Jane 187, Mary Lela (Garrison) 187, 201, Mary Lou 187, Maude Geneva 236 Maxine 187, Mindy 188 Oliver 236, Paul 19, Paul Eugene 187, Philip 188, 292, Phillip 187, Ralph 187, Rebecca (Moore) 187, Richard 187, Richard William 187, 188, 292, Richard Wm. 201, Robert A. 187, Robert H. 187, 188, 201, 292, Robert H. 344, Roberta A. 187, Rosemary 225, Russell Howard 187, Ruth Ellen 187, Samuel P. 187, Sandra K. 187, Sheila 187, Suzie 188, Thomas 187, Vergie 188 Vergie (Murphy) 201, Vonna 220, Vonna (Hite) 201, Ward 187, William 187, 188, 292

ETNIRE, Frank 119

ETTA, Mary 189

EVANS 28, Abby Lynn 240, Amy Marie 240, Charles E. 65, Charles Marcus 321, David 31, 33, David James 283, Edna Elizabeth 154, Eliza Eleanor Moulder 268, Haley Crystal 283, Heath David 283, Heather Ann 283, Hillary Brook 283, James Robert 283, Jeffrey Robert 283, John 27, 33, 51, 268, Kent 240, Laura 65, Lewis Ancil 154, Mary Jane 154, Minnie 274, O.L. 60, Robert 321 Robert M. 25, William Thomas 321

EVERHART, Contina 186, Gloria Jean 186, Laura Jean 186, Ralph 186, Ronda 187, William Matthew 186

EVERLING, Danny L. 188, Joan Stone 188, John Adam 188, Lewis Allen 188, Mildred (Foland) 193, Traci 193

EVERS, Christina 255, Jerry Lee 275

EVRARD, Elizabeth Justine (Peters) 182, John Joseph 182, Mary C. 182

EWAN, Esther 193

EWING, Keith 166, 257, Louise (Johnston) 326, Melody Sue 166, 257, Patricia 301, Timmothy Kent 257, 166, William 153

F

FAGAN, Frank 55

FAGUE, Robert 85

FAHEY, Catherine 237

FAHL, J. 34, Joseph 90

FAHNESTOCK, Sarah 152

FAIR, Austin 152, Sandra Joyce 152, Victoria Louise 152

FAIRBANKS, Nina 13

FALK, Frank 90

FANSLER, Margaret Ann 225

FARAGE, Tony 304

FARLEY, D.S. 34, David S. 27, 32, Mary Anne 233

FARLOW 45, Alfred 27, 33, Armilda 292, Herb 281, Joseph 176, Lilith M. 63, Ruth 176

FARMER, Benjamin F. 51, Susan 309

FARMWALD, Barbara 264

FARR, Iris 157, R.L. 96

FARRINGTON, Albert 189, Alfred 189, Arlie Monroe 189, Clytice 189, Delight 189, Eliza Anne 189, Ellen 189, Emesly 189, Eugene 189, Flora B. 189, Jabez 189, Jabez L. 189, John A. 188, John W. 189, Laura L. 189, Lloyd 189, Mary E. 189, Maxine 189, Melville 189, Sarah 189, Stephen Joseph 182, Velma 189, Victoria 189

FARRIS, Burl 295, Edward Michael 295, Jane 283, Kathleen Lois 295, Rosalea 236, Rosalea Kay 295

FARRON, Rickey 299

FARTHING, Jeffery Scott 257, Jeffery Scott 166, John 166, 257, Penny Jolene 166, 257

FAULKINRAUGH, George 33

FAULKNER, George 246, Rachel 143

FAWCETT, Albert E. 189, Albert Ellsworth 189, Benjamin 189, Charles B. 189, Charles W. 189, Charles Warren 189, Crawford 189, D. 34, Dale 48, 230, David 27, 189, 311, David Alan 190, Ernest 230, 283, Ernest W. 189, Ernest William 189, Ester Hinton 189, Eva Merle 189, Frank Omar 189, Glen 230, Glen Dale 189, Glen David 189, Gregory 230, Gregory Bruce 189, Harry 25, Harry R. 123, Henrietta 189, Henrietta Gay 189, James 189, Jason Aaron 189, John 230, 283, John Edwin 189, John M. 189, John Marshall 189, John P. 189, Jordan Conner 190 Kent Evan 190 Levi "Lee" 189, Lillian 189, Martha H. 189, Martha Jackson 189, Mary 189, Mary Fawcett 189, Melinda Piper 189, Nellie 189, Patricia 283, Patricia Ann 189, Peggy 230, Peggy Jane 189, Ralph Owen 189, Richard 189, Ruby 230, Russell 189, Silas H. 189, Silas Henton 189, Susan E. 189, Will 159, William Benjamin 189, William E. 189, David 189, Edna 189

FAY 39, Wm. 42

FEATHERER, Reena (Smith) 201, Walter 201

FEGLEY, Mary C. 164

FELKER, Agnes 224

FELL, John E. 116, Kathryn 107, Miriam Thorne 323

FELLOW, Abigail 55, 190, 305, Abigail (Coleman) Sr. 280, Abigail Coleman 305, Alphanso L. 280, Alvin 261, Ann Eliza (Beeman) 280, Anna Elizabeth 280, Anna N. 280, Bennett 190, Charlotte Slocum 307, Elijah 190, Elisha 190, Elisha P. 280, Ercie O. (Mendenhall) 280, Jane 190, John 54, 55, 190, 280, 305, Mary 190, 280 Mary E. 280, Orpha Elizabeth (Cox) 280, Rachel 190, Rachel Peelle 190, Robert 190, Robert William 280, Walter 280 Walter E. 280

FELLOWS, Celestia 184, George 344, 'Rene' Doran 140, Samuel W. 184

FELTON, Barbara (Christman) 160, Eliza 82, John 160, Julia Gladys 145 Robert 51

FENN, David 268, Dora (Keeler) 268, Dora (Meranda) Mugg 143, Edward 143, Ella C. 143, Eugene 48, Nellie M. 268

FENNELL, Evaline 298

FERENCY, Ernest 332, Michael 332

FERGUSON, Faye 19, Helen 20, James 95

FERNUNG, Alisha Christine 283, Andrew Phillip 283, Denny 283, Madella 10, Rachel Ann 283

FEWELL, George T. 145

FIC, Catherine 223

FICKLE, Bessie Lee 174

FIELD, Lisa Ann 321, W.F. 159

FIESS, Fred 84

FILLENWARTH, Floyd 276, Gene 25, Vernon Eugene 276

FINCH, Bob 327, Lisa 25

FINEBERG, Harvey 245

FINLAY, Otheniel 23

FINLEY, Claude 262, Oliver P.M. 300

FINNEY, David A. 149, Mary Alice Ford 149, Mary Christina 149, Susan Josephine 157, Walter 157

FIPPS, Ernest J. 231, Ernest Joseph IV 231, Kiersten 231 Lisa D. 96

FIRST, Golda Irene 263

FISCHER, Andrea Elaine 319, Jacquetta 263, Kelly Ann 319, Paula Lynn 263, Steven 319, Theodore 263

FISH, C. Evalin 287

FISHER 39, Aaron 190 Abigail Eliza 191 Amber Danielle 330, Amos 191 Andrea Marie 330, Ann 145, Anna 191, Bud 43, Catherine (Strome) 20 Charlotte Sue 190, Cierra 190, Clarence 190, Clayton 190 Cynthia Diane 190, Daniel 191, David 191, Delia 191, Dora Sylvia 191, Eli C. 190, Eliza Ann 190, Eliza Ann 197, Estella 190, Frederick D. 190, Glenn 22, Hannah (Berriner) 190, Harvey Allen 191, Haskett 191, Henry 191, Isaac 52, 204, James 190, 294, James Blaine 190, James Montgomery 191, James Owen 190, 197, Jean 191, Jeff D. 330, Joe 190, John 190, John Benford 190, 191, John D. 191, John Elias 191, John Matthew 190, Jonathan 190, Juanita Mae 19, Katherine (Harness) 190, Kyle 190, L. 34 Lucy 183, Lydia 191, Mabelle 190, Martha Catherine 191, Martha Jane 191, 267, Mary 60, 191, Mary E. 204, Nancy 294, Nathan 190, Noah 191, Ollie (Purvis) 190, Omer 190, Ora 217, Patsy Jean 190, Ralph Thomas 191, Reece 191, Reese 25, Robert 190, Roy 190, Samuel 196, Sandra Kay 190 252, 303, Sarah 191, Solathiel 191, Solomon 183, Stacy Rene (Duncan) 183 Susan 190, Walter Joe 190, William 191, William Montgomery 190, Zachariah 190, Calvin 190, Louisa 190, Marilla 190, Mary A. 190, William 190

FISSE, Henry, Jr. 128

FISSEL, Christy 342, Kent 342

FITE, Elizabeth (Rhuddy) 191, John 191, John Frederick Jr. 191, John Frederick Sr. 191, John Perry 191, Linda Gail 191 Marsha Kay 191, Michael Eugene 191, Nellie (Ashby) 191, Sandra Jeanne 191

FITZGERALD, Eva M. 123, Charles 140, Charles Albright 140, Phyllis 140

FIVECOAT, Michael 192

FIVECOATE, Abigayle 192, 300, Allen Ray 192, Angie 131, Bart 192, Benjamin 192, 290, 314, Benjamin Thomas 192, Beulah Marie (Stafford) 290, Brad 192, Brent 192, Carl 191, Catherine Joan 192, 242, Chad 192, Charles 192, Christenna (Kessler) 191, Christina 192, 300, Christy 290 Clarence 314, Clarence Edward 192, Clyde 314, Clyde Allen 192, Cynthia Lynn "Cindy" 192, Dennis 192, Donald 192, Dorothy 192, 314, Ed 290, 300, Edith 192, Eldon 314, Eldon Dallas 192, Emmaline 191, Florence 192, George 192, 314, George (Bud) 192, Gerald 191, 192, Glen 191, Grace 192, 314, Grace (Stafford) 242, Grace Christena 290, Harold 191, Harry 314, Harry Ray 192, Ira 191, 192, Irene 191, Irl 242, Irl Lloyd 191, 314, James Almon 192, Jane 192, Janice 192, Jeff 300, Jeffrey 192 Jesse 191, 192, Jesse Edward 192, 314, Jesse Ernest 191, 192, 290, 314, Joann 314, Joe 131, John Craig "Jack" 192, 290, Joseph 192, Josh 192, Kenneth 191, Kim 192, Leona 191, Leonard 314, Leonard Max 192, Lloyd 314, Lloyd Wayne 192, Loren 191, Lowell 192, 314 Lulu, 192, Malinda 192, Marie 191, Mark 192, May 192, Maude (Miller) 191, Micah 192, 300, Mike 192, Nellie 192, Nora 192, Pearl 192, Raymond 191, 192, 314, Robert 192 Roy 314, Roy Almon 192, Russell 191, Sarah 192, Sharon 192, Sheryl 192, Shirley 192, Steve 192, Susannah 192, Thomas 192, Todd 192, Troy 192

FLEEK 35

FLEENOR, Mabel 107, Vergil 138, William 323

FLEMING, Joe 225, John 55, Joseph 79, June 107, Mary (McNew) 243, Mary Helen 225, Richard 225, Ruth Ann 225, Samuel 243, Theresa Margaret 243, William 55

FLETCHER, A.A. 96, Anna Mae 172, Dove (Adair) 192, Edith L. 233, Harold Eugene 192, Iva Baker 192, James 192, Thomas Benton 192, Thomas Dayton 192, Thomas Doyle 192

FLORA, Amos K. 59, Bertha (Bock) 278, Bertha May Bock 199, Carl Lawrence 152, 199, Cecile Carey 199, Daniel 16, Elizabeth Huff 199, Fred 199, Fred Carlyle 152, Joel Amos 199, Mildred Tomlin

199, Ora 305, Orion 278, Orion S. (Ora) 199, Patricia Irene 199, Rhonda 238, Wilma Bernadine 278, Wilma Obermeyer 199
FLOREA, Mary Helen 223, Ray 223
FLORER, David P. 226
FLORES, Abram 15
FLORY, George 286
FLOWERS, Matthew 331 Michael 331, Sarah Elizabeth Miller 331, Warren P. 331
FLOYD, Bertha 318, Elizabeth Augustia "Gustin" 149, Elizabeth Huffer 149, John 149, Morgan C. 162, Neva Catherine 198
FLOYS, Mary 99
FLUHART, Catherine Marie 193, Daniel Herberg 193, Daniel Odford 193, 265, Danny Morris 193, Elizabeth Ann 193, John August 193, Margaret Elizabeth 193, Mary Patricia 193, Sarah Ellen 193, Thomas 193, Thomas Edward 193
FLYNT, John 243, Josephine Jackson 243
FOGELMAN, George 292, John 292, Mary 292
FOLAND, Bradley 53, 193, Craig 56, Craig A. 193, Curtis 193, Fletcher 193, Forrest 193, Franklin 53, 193, Frederick 193, Sherwood 193
FOLEY, Maurice D. 94
FOLKENING, James H. 183, Nellie 287, Rodney Bryce 183, Ryan James 183
FOLKERS, Carl H. 254, Helen (Warren) 254
FOMOUS, Loretta (Mason) 256
FOOR, Robert C. 51
FORBAR, Roseanna Sweet 183
FORBES, Earl 66, Eugene Franklin Jr. 150, Eugene Franklin Sr. 150, Pauline 78, Richard 78, Saundra Lou 150, Sharon Sue 150
FORD, Amanda E. (Nelson) 193, Ambrose 254, Arnold 254, Brutus 193, Cathryn 157, Charles 186, Charles F. 193, Charles Lee 193, Dellie 193, Donald 193, 254, Edward 99, Eliza (Walters) 254 Elizabeth 193, Emily Lucreen 193, Emma Alice 123, Florence 254, Floyd 193, 257, Goldie 193, Hattie 193, Ida J. 193, Isabelle 123, Jamakie Ann 186, 193, James B. 193, James Parlon 193, Jerry Allen, 186, 193, Johnson 254, Lafayette 254, Lee 193, Lloyd Edgar 193, Lucretia (Engle) 193, Mannie 193, Marvin 193, Mary Josephine 254, Milas 193, Nora 193, Olive 254, Oscar 254, Osco 193, Parley 193, Pauline 193, Ralph 254, Reeve 193, Rufus 193, Stellie 193, Theodore Roosvelt 193, Thomas A. 193, William 254, William Robert 193, Willie 193
FORDING 218, Bobby Russell 193, Catharine 193, Christina 193, Christopher 193, Clyde Elmer 193 David Frank 193, Ernest William (Bill) 193, Esther Ann 193, Ewan 193, Ida Viola 193, Imajean Marie 193, Jack Richard 193, Jacob 193, Jesse J. 193, John 193, John W. Jr. 193, John Wesley 193, Lillian 96, Mabel Mary 193, 202, Margaret 193, Margaret E. 193, Mary Catherine 193, Mary Elizabeth 193, Minnie L. 193, Nellie D. 193, Ocal (Doc) 193, Pearl 193, Priscilla 193, Rosa 193 Russell 193, Thelma A. 193, Thomas 193, William Henry Harrison 193
FORDYCE, Catherine 193, Cecil Hubbard 195, Charles 195, Clifford 195, Diane Elaine 194, Elsie Lucinda 195, Glenn 195, Jacob Henry 195, James 195, Jeffrey Lewis 194, Lester Martin 195, Murrel 193, Zed Lewis 193
FOREMAN, William H. 220
FORGEY, Andrew 173 Louella Runk 298, William 298
FORGY, Alexander 15
FORSYTHE, Bill 169, L. 34
FORT, Dorothy M. 250, Edward 250, Emma 202, Emma Rene 202, Harriet (Hatcher) 202, Julia (Moran) 250, Wilson 202
FORTNER, Bradley Jay 333, Dayton 333, Frances 333, James 45, Margaret Ann 333 Martha 269
FORTNEY, Ed 200
FOSGATE, Orville 25, Russell 25
FOSTER, Benjamin Franklin 313, Benjamin L. 267 David 8, 48, 70, 112, 145, 209, 227, 249, 268, 316, 330, 339, Dean Oral (Wetherholt) 313, Earl 321, Elizabeth 70, Elizabeth Matilda (Grant) 330, Joyce Fern 313, Louisa Catherine 254, Margaret (Buster) 330, Martha Jane 220 Rebecca Diann 281, Sarah 220, Vincent 220, William 281, 330
FOTOVICH, Benjamin 214, Emily 214, Thomas 214
FOUCH, Brandon Scott 249, Cecil 143, Curran Allen 249, Gene 143, Irene (Miles) 143, Jack 249, James 143, John 143, Lilly (Van Ness) 143, Mariruth 143, Scott Ashley 249, Vera Juanita 143
FOUDY, Lawrence E. 80
FOUREZ, Jeremy William 300, Katelyn Jayne 300, Melinda Jayne (Schafer) 300, Steven William 300
FOUST 40, Adam Michael 194, Delena 273, Floyd 194, Jeffrey Scott 194, Justin Thomas 194, Karen Elizabeth 194, Marvin 194, Patti 194, Stella 194
FOUTS, Clara Alvina 270, Lewis 100, Margaret Ann 255
FOWLER, Pauline 192, Susannah 146
FOX, Bessie Flae 294, Carly 175, Charles M. 300, George 60, James 175, Jane 175, Jesse W. 70, Louise 86, Mary (Cox) 64
FOY, Elizabeth 183, Harriet 173, Jacob 173, 183, Margaret 183, Margaret Russell 183, Nancy Shunk 173
FRAKES, Sarah 249, T. 34
FRANCAR, Elsie Leota 195
FRANCIS 145, Matilda Alice 198
FRANK, Marian Alicia Dayhuff 176, Thomas Paul 177
FRANKLIN, Benjamin W. 268, Charles William 3, Daisy 282
FRANZ 92
FRAWLEY, Francis 94
FRAZEE, Angeline 194, Anna Mariah 194, Clara 194, Clark 194, Frank 194, George E. 194, George Oscar 267, John N. 194, Jonas Joseph 194, Joseph G. 194, Laura 194, Louis 151, Marvin E. 194, Mary Ann (Tevis) 151, Nellie 194, 267, Theodore F. 194, W.S. 34, William David 194, 267, William Samuel 194
FRAZIER 48, Adeline 177, Christina Kay 283, Delores 194, Eric Michael 194, Frank 171 Gregory Wayne 194, Helen 171, J. 34, James 51, Jennie Pearl (Clarston) 194, Jovita 279, Kimberly Annette 194, Leslie Dwight 194, Melissa Erin 194, Philip 276, Richard L. 12, Richard "Rusty" 194
FREDERICK, J.E. 132
FREDRICK 79, Deborah 230
FREED, Alexca A. 195, B. Leon 196, Bertha Dell 195, Charlotte 196, Clarence Franklin 195, Dee Leo 196, Doris (Webster) 195, Elizabeth (Ramsayer) 195, Emma (Mason) 256, 282, Emma Elizabeth (Mason) 195, Fernandes 195, Frances Congress 195, Frances Morton 195, Hubert Howard 195, Ida Amarsky 195, James 196, James M. 170, 171, 196, James Martin 195, Jeffrey L. 195, John 195, John Lovell Linley 196, John Milton 195, John Wesley 196, Joseph 195, Joseph Gerald 195, Joseph Howard 195, Joseph Martin 195, Judith 195, Leo Darwin 195, Leslie 196, Mabel (Ketchum) 195, Marilyn 195 Mary (Webb) 195, Mary Dee 196, Matilda (Willis) 195, Merlin 196, Michael 195, Morris 195, Noah 195, Oscar L. 195, Regina (Rife) 195, Robert 133, 195, 196, Ronald 196, Shannon Dee 196 Sharon (Cooke) 196, Sol 133, Susan 195, Tom 195, 256, 282, Vera (Hadley) 195, Zelma Ruth 196
FREELAND, Alexander H. 196, Clark 196, Edward 196, Hannah 196, Harry 196, Isaac 196, Kenneth 83, 196, Linda 196, Lora 196, Madge 336, Mark 196 Myrtle 196, Owen 3, 16, 196, Richard 196, W.B. 70
FREELS, Luke 23
FREEMAN, Brian 186, D.O. 12, Daniel 65, David 196, Emil 96, Harriett 196, James 186, Jeffery 186, Joshua 196, Lindsey 196, Louisa Jane 196, Mary 196, Mary Buckingham 196, Mary Jane 196, Melba 283, Michael 186, Miranda 311, Nancy 183, Nathan 65, 196, Nathan Jr. 196, Nathan, Jr. 65, Oliver 196, Oliver Winifred 196, Pearl Alice 299, Rachel 196, Richard 196, Rose 96, Ruth 3, Sarah 196, W.A. 65, Wesley Lytle 196, William 196, Winnie Olivette 196
FRENCH, Abigail (McGilliard) 145, 151, 191, Adam Miller 196, Alfloretta 197, Alfred 145, 196, Alonzo Lewis 197, Andrew 197, Ann 191, 196, 197, Benjamin 196, Charles Basil 197, Charlotte 196, Daniel 196, Edna Alfloretta 143, 178, Elizabeth 196, Elizabeth 'Betsey' 196, Elsie Odessa 197, Eunice Ann 197, Evert Thomas 197, Francis 145, 196, Helen (Mason) 255, Hewitt 197, James 145, 151, 191, 196, James Diller 197, Jane 196, Jeremiah 196, John 197, Laura 197, Levina 14, Lot 196, Martha J. 196, Mary 196, Mary 'Polly' 196, Myron Andrew 197, O. Dale 255, Percy 335, Pheamy 'Amy' 196, Ralph 15, 145, 191, 196, Sarah 196, Susan 145, 197, Susan (Striebel) 182, Sylvia 197
FRESE, Magdalene 302
FREY, John 264, Magdalena 264
FRIEND, AnnaBelle 218, Benjamin Harrison 197, Bud 197, Mary Lou 197, San 197
FRIER, Bertha Jane Gillam 208, Inez 208, John H. 208
FRISTOE, William 180
FRITZ, Alice Vilola 197, Benny 197 Carl 197, Chancy 197, 234, Christian 197, 234, Christian W. 234, Cleo 197, David 327, Elizabeth 197, Ettie Lee 197, Evelyn 197, Frank 197, Heather 327, Hiram 162, 197, 234, Howard Monroe 197, James 197, 327, John 197, 234, Josiah 197, 234, Kenneth 197, Leota 197, Lessie 197, Lillie 197, Lottie 197, Lou 197, Margaret 197, Mary Catherine 234, Mary Catherine (Polly) 234, Mary Catherine (Shultz) 234, Mary Catherine Polly 197, Maude 197, Minerva 197, Oscar 162, Susan 197, Valentine 197, Virginia 197, Walter 197, Walter O. 197, William 197, 234
FRUITT, Heidi 318
FRY, C.O. 51, Charles 82, Charles O. 53, 54, Marie Vaughn 172
FRYBACK, John 243, Kenneth 243
FUHRMAN, Kay 179
FULFER 273
FULKERSON, Eugenia 125
FULLER, Deborah Lee (Payne) 333, Gary 333, Gary Keith 284, Keith Allen 333, Stella Almedia 334
FULMER, Sandra Ann 244
FULTZ, Emma Lou 257, 295
FULWIDER, Roxie 343
FUNK, Bryan Christopher 179, C. Alan 94, Donald 179, Melinda Sue 179, W. 34
FUREDY, Frances 265
FYE 28, Aurelia (Gunder) 309, Benjamin 309, Danny 309, Delbert 309, George H. 273, Hazel 273, Mary 309, Mildred 309, Mildred Catherine 309, Nellie 309, Oletha 309, Roy 309, William C. 309
FYFFE, Lennie (Mason) 256 William 256

G

GABLE, Cathy 187, Edwin 187, Helen 187, James 187, Marilyn 187, Mark 187, Miriam 187, Richard 187, Sara 187
GABRIEL, Elijah 245
GADDES, Thomas 330
GADOMSKI, Andrew 195, Elizabeth 195, Robert 195
GALBREATH, Shannon 193
GALLAGHER, Raymond 92, Robert A. 127
GALLION, Dorothy 171, Nancy Ann 288
GALLISON, J. 34
GALLOWAY, Bruce 140, Harold Jesse 308, Joshua 29, Richard 140, Francis 52
GANDER, Etta (Mason) 256, George 256
GANG, Mary (Suter) 335
GANNON, Myron E. 174, 19, Myron Edward 60
GARBER, J. 34
GARBERT, Clara 184, Elizabeth Ann 165, Ferol 184, Ferol Josephine 318, Fred 184, Hazel Marie 212, Lorain 99
GARDNER 248, Alma Lee 181, Hattie 338, Helen Irene 181, Janet 181, Phyllis 181, Robert 181, Rosemary 181, Russell Lee 181, Ruth 181
GARINGER, Absolum 33, Alexander 33, David 33, Elizabeth 33, Isaac 33, John 33
GARNER, Edom 20, 244, Henry 48, Job 46, 48, Rebecca 46
GARR, Jesse D. 19, John 43, Mabel 14
GARRA, Robert 64
GARRELL, Washington 27
GARRETT, Leander 212, Leander P. 184, Lulu B. 184, Mary Harrell Early 184
GARRIGUES, Arnald 174, David 174, Jean 174, Matthew 174 Milton 174, Timothy 174
GARRIGUS, Allen O. 98, Alma (Lovett) 98, Bathsheba Losey 174, Calvin 174, Jacob 174, John S. 35, M.L. 28, Timothy 51
GARRINGER 28, Abner 27, Alexander 27, David 27, 28, Isaac 27, J. 34, Sarah 201
GARRISON, Clara Evaline 344, Damaris Jane (Shinn) 188, 201, 344, Edah 'Edi' 344, Fannie Dora 344, Francis 344, Huldah 344, Jacob 188, 201, 344, Jeremiah 344, Joel Kenton 344, John 344, Mahlon Wilson 344, Margaret 344, Mary 188, Mary Lela 188, 344, Paul 238, Peter 344, Sarah Orpha 'Rose' 344
GARRITSON, Dorothy Jane 197, Frances Camille 197, James Harvey 197, 338, Margaret Ellen 197, Martha Josephine 197, Mary Bess 197, Mayme 197, Reed 197
GARROD, Barbra Sue (Brummett) 164
GARSHWILER, Angeline Mary Utterback 185, Ara K. 185, Lulu 185
GARTON, Leslie 184
GASHO, Claude 189
GASPER, Catherine 293, 324
GASTON, E.H. 95
GATES, Cliffie 323, Delores 197, Edward 198, Frances Ann 268, 276, Gusta 198, Jerry 48, 197, Leann 197, Myron 14, Rebecca 145, Robert 197, Roy 29, Scott 197, Todd 197
GAUSE, Louisa Estella 305
GEARHART, Gerald 86, Mamie E. 197, Samuel 83, Sara 83
GEARHEART, Martha 257
GEBHART, Harold 232
GENNEBECK, Alice P. 189, John 189, Lucinda C. Ozer 189
GENTRY, Barbara Ellen 187, Charles 64, Elisha 38, Fanny 64, 65, Mary 302, Mary Alice 38
GEORGE, Bob 97, Enos 216, Ruth 216
GERBER, Lottie 76, Max 31, 32, 76
GERHARD, Charles John 213, Charles L. 213, Daniel 213, Gretchen Florine 213, Paul D. 213, Richard P. 213
GERHART, Clara 242, Dick 97, George 208, Martha 236
GESSE, Brad 240, Duane 240
GETTINGER, Anna E. Catheart 208, Charles C. 208, Dortha L. 208
GETZ, Amelia (Dehne) 198, James 198, Larry 142, Larry G. 198, Robert 198, Ruth (Davis) 198, Staci 198, Staci Leigh 142, Vickie S. 198, Vickie Sue (Anweiler) 142
GEVIRTZ, Palmer 133, 195
GHENT, Minnie Mae 217
GIBBONS, Annie Laura 151
GIBBS, Alice Ellen 305, Carol 140, Mary 140, Robert 219, Teresa 140, William 140
GIBSON, Betty 198, Bobby 198, 213, Charles 334, Elizabeth Ann 198,

George Stewart 198, Hazel 339, Lucinda 278, Mattie Francis (Bell) 198, Nancy Ellen 198, Roger 276, Sarah Rachel (Dewitt) 278, Susan Glenn 198, Will 193, William 278
GICH, Tina Louise 228
GIDDINGS, Jay 226, Mary Lou 289, Minerva Ann 226
GIDEON, Frank 171, Susan 171
GIFFORD, Arthur Floyd 198, Arthur William 198, Esther 44, Hannah 253, Harry Hendricks Franklin 198, Irene Esther 198, Mark 25, T. Volney 48, Theida 99, Thomas 198, Tom 21, William 44
GILBERT 283, Adda E. 198, Betsy Gwinn 198, Carrie Mae Hadley 318, Danna Maria 316, Doshia Conwell 287, Ell 199, Ella 199, Ella (Gannon) 257, Elvadore 257, Ernest 199, Harold D. 198, Harold Deo 199, Harold W. 198, 199, Henry 199, Henry W. 198 Howard 15, Howard (Gib) 199, John 213, Luella (Addler) 199, Marjorie 186, Mary P. 257, Patricia Irene 152, Patricia Louise 199, Paul Stuart 199, Philip Alan 19, Raymon 174, 199, Raymond 15, Richard Deo 199, Ron 31, Ronnie 96, Rosemary 199, "Splint" 191, William Addison 198
GILES, W.H. 95
GILL, Barbara Joyce 205, Bob 205, Carl 205, James Manor 205, Jim 205, Linda A. 205, Nancy Jane 183, Rebecca 156
GILLAM, Albert 199, Andy 199, Bertha 199, Chester 199, Clarence 199, Elmer 199, Ethel 199, Everett 199, Harrison 15, 199, Hattie 199, Hazel 199, Henry 15, Henry Harrison 199, Jacob 199, James 199, John 199, Jonathan 199, Lois 199, Mabel 199, Mary 199, Mary Jane 199, Milton 199, Morton 199, Otto 199, Ova 199, Rebecca 199, Robert 199, Russell 153, 199, Ruth 157, 199, 255, Sarah 199, Vera 96, 199, Wardie 199, William Pearl 199
GILLARD, Marguerite 263
GILLETT, Judith 251
GILLIAM, Cathy Faye 283
GILLOGLY, Alan 85
GILSON, Arch 48, Ivy 175, William 175
GINGERICH 29, Carolyn 183, Fenton 134, Ivan 134, Rex 134
GIPE, Dora B. 342
GIRTON, Estel 204
GIST, Deborah 196
GIVENS, Addison 200, Bertha 200, Betsy T. 319, Betty, 214, Carol Ann 326, Charles 200, Edward 200, Elizabeth 200 George Clifford 200, Harry Melvin 200, James 200, James Jerry 200, Kenneth Earl 200, Lora Belle 200, Mary (Stark) 231, Mary Verna (Stark) 326, Nancy 200, Otto 200, Paul Ernest 326, William E. 203, William Eugene 200
GLASCO, Elizabeth 212
GLASS, Charlotte 163, Charlotte Rose 200, Claude 163, Claude Sherman 200, Cloid Arthur 200, Clyde 163, Clyde Eugene 200, Connie 327, Deborah J. 100, Duane 163, Duane Alan 200, Francis 163, Francis Leroy "Frank" 200, Johanna 177, Othel 200, Raymond 200, Sarah Amanda (Ogle) 200, Sharon 163, Sharon Kathleen 200, Shirley 163, Shirley Lynne 200, Ulyssis Eubirda "Bird" 200, Wilda Clare 200, Wilma Inez Pearl (Butler) 200
GLASSBURN, Clyde 267, Diana 267, Dixie 267, Donna 267, Jack 267, Joanne 243, Julia 267, Roger V. 180
GLIDDEN, J.W. 34
GLOVER, Allison G. 267, Jeanetta May (McCartney) Cowgill 171, Ortho D. 267
GLUNT, Joanna 50
GODDARD, Elinor 201, Sarah 201, William 201
GODFREY, Diane 23
GODWIN, Harriet (Suter) 335
GOETZEN, Barbarella 201, Ethel (Featherer) 201, George Sr. 201, George William III 200, George William Jr. 201, Jason 200, Mary (Brohan) 201 Nancy (Etherington) 200, 220, William 201
GOFF 52
GOINS, Anna (Martin) 337, Ethel Goldie 337, George Raymond 337, Gertrude Pearl 337, Jasper Oliver 337, Kermit 23, Laura Alice 337, Silas 337
GOLDEN, Glennie (York) 228, Harry Scott 228
GOLDING, Della (Bradshaw) 263, Eleanor 268, Frank 245, Hannah 268, Mable 263, Thomas 251, William 35, 263
GOLDKETT 248
GOLIGHTLY, Elnora 214, Mara Lou Rayl 291, Sid 134
GOLLNER, Catherine Louise 201, Frederich "Fred" William 201, Helen Lorraine 201, Mary Elizabeth 201, William "Bill" 201, William Frederick 312, William Frederick Jr 201, Wilma Lucille 20, Wilma Lucille 312, 313
GOMEZ, James 171, James Andrew 171, Royce Ann Cook 171
GOOCH, Dessie Mildred (Brown) 80, Frances 187, George A. 80
GOOD, Catherine 201, Delila 201, Drucilla 201, Emma 201, Eulila 201, Eunice 201, Harriet 20, Jacob 27, 32, 33, 59, 201, Jesse 201, Joseph 201, Lucinda 201, Mary 201, Mary "Polly" 201, Oliver 201, Philip Starr 201, Salathiel 27, 31, 33, 58, 59, 201, Sarah 201, Sarah Goddard 201, Ulilah 58, Virginia 201, William 201
GOODE, Rodney 148
GOODKNIGHT, Dick 340
GOODMAN, Jennifer 217, Ray 219
GOODNIGHT, Ethel 234, Kenneth 25, Lincoln 25, Mary Inez 25, Phoebe 23
GOODWIN, Eliza Jennie 148, J. 34
GOODWINE 28, C.P. 34, Mary 159
GORDON 40, Albert 201, 202, Albert Milton 202, Alberta Wilson Bone 273, Anna 31, Anna Lee 202, Anne Elizabeth 202, Betty (Smiley) 202, Cindy 202, Claude 197, Della 156, Erick 20, Flossie Blanche 202, Frances 107, Francis 296, Frederick Milton 202, George 201, George A. 103, George Grant 202, Gregory 202, Henry Clay 202, Holly 202, Ida 201, James William 202, Janice 202, Jeffrey 202, Jerry 202, John 201, 202, 218, 296, John Taylor 202, Kathy 202, Kenneth 202, Lewis (Chet) 202, Lucille 202, Mary 201, Mary Frances 202, May Pauline 202, Milton Grant 20, Morton 201, Nellie 238, Nellie (Young) 233, Olive Lou 202, Paul Elsworth 193, 202, Peter 201, Peter Elsworth 202, Pheba Ann 202, Robert 201, 202, Robert Morton 202, Roscoe 202, 296, Roy 201, 202, Sarah 201, Sarah Ann (Reed) 202, Sarah E. 202, Sarah Jemima Jane 202, 218, Simion 201, Sondra 202, Stephen 202, Sylvia Ossie 202, Teena 202, Thomas 202, Thomas Randolph 202, William 201, 202, 218
GORE, Ann (Druecker) 182
GORMAN, James 28, James L. 37
GORTON, Abigail Suzanne 202, Alfred Edwin 202, Ashton Earl 202, 217, Ashton Ellison 202, Ashton Samuel 202, Benjamin Lewis 202, Charles Edwin 202, Clayton Charles 202 Frances Ione 202, Joseph II 202, Mary (Maplet) 20, Michael Gamble 202, Samuel 202
GOSHERN, Norman 192
GOSNELL, Edith 333
GOSNOL (Garrell), Washington 33
GOSSETT 39, Asa 35, J.D. 38, P.W. 35
GOTHARD, Janet E. (Eads) 179
GOTT, Neva 197
GOULD, Andrew Clark 257, Andrew Clark 166, Larry 166, 257, Matthew J. 257, Matthew Jay 166 Walter 13
GOYER 28, C. 34, Claudius 58, Harry Elwood 202, J.G. 34, John 48, John G. 27, Murl Leona (Underwood) 202, 300, V. 34, Vespasian 27, Ernest 29, Ronald 29, Crabtree 313
GRADY, Barbara J. (Greer) 203, Bernice Lily (Johnson) 203, Esterline 203, George 202, George Cornelius (Duke) 202, George Edward 203, Isham 202, Isham Jr. 202, Jeannie 203, Josephus 202, 203, Katherine "Kay" Marie 150, Louis 202, Margret (Lani) 203, Robert (Bobby) 203, Rosann 203, Stephen 203, William 203, William E. (Shake) 202, William Henry (Bill) 202, William R. 203, William R. (Billy) 203
GRAF 39, Anna (Schudel) 203, August 203, Carol June (Corn) 203, Doyle Herbert 203, Fern (Berry) 203, Frank 42, Gary Lee 203, Herbert 203, Kyle Patrick 203, Settie 247
GRAGG, Jerry 86
GRAHAM, Caroline Matilda 144, Carolyn Sue 203, Charles 14, Charles Norman 203, Chester 21, D.A. 95, Edna Grace 203, Elizabeth (Lehman) 203, Esther Eileen, 200, Gladys 287, James Adair 203, John Richard 203, Lavada Ellen 203, Martha 234, Mary Elizabeth 203, Maude Belle 203, Minardean (Foland) 193, Norma Louise 203, Pamela (Vint) 295, Paul Edward 203, Robert Lee 203, Ruth Helen 203, Susanna 143, Thomas Bell 203, Violet Annabelle 205, William Thomas 203
GRAMMER, Nora (Harper) 203, Rhonda Jean 151, 204, Sarah Jeanette 204, Thomas Edward 204, Troy Edward 204, William Earl 203, William Edward 203

GRANGER, Ella Emma 141, George W. 141, Jama 253, Margaret Lousaina (Wilson) 141
GRANSON, Alfred 224, David 224, Elaine 224, Fred 224 Frederick Jules 224, Joseph 224, Richard 224
GRANT, Ulysses S. 228, Virginia Lee 185
GRASS, Betty Jean 195, Cordelia Isabelle (Freed) 195, James 195
GRAU 28, Albert 204, Alberta 204, Charles 204, Charles W. 204, David 204, Elizabeth 243, Gladys 204, J.A. 34, Jerry 204, John 245, John A. 204, John A. 204, Kathryn 107, 204, Mae 204, Merle 204, Miriam 204, Oaroe 204, Richard 204, Rosina Kauffman 243, 245, "Sarah" 337, Theodore 204
GRAVES, Ila 158, Otis 238, Roy Wayne 238
GRAWCOCK, Amy Lynn 234, John 234, Linda Bugher 235
GRAY, Amos 286, Bell (Stephenson) 138, Clinton 18, Dan 138, David Moore 308, Harry 14, Helen 265, James 16, Mary C. 286, Sarah 234
GREATHOUSE, Theresa Katherine 314
GREEN, Celestine 12, Louisa 292
GREENE 142
GREENLEE, Howard 25, 26
GREENO, Carl 131, Carl Jr. 131, Kent 131, Patty 131
GREER, Barbara Jean 204, Bessie Berneice 140, Charles Edwin 204, Elva (Mason) 255, Emma A. (Tanner) 203, Florence 204, Howard E. 255, Howard Jasper 204, James Alvin 204, Jasper 204, Jeanette Iona 204, Joe 23, John Richard 204, Maggie 204, Myrle Eugene 204, Paul Arthur 204, Peggy Louise 204, Ralph Louis 204, Rosa 252, Rosemary 204, Shirley Ann 204, William Irving 204, William Irving 204, Wm I. 203
GREESON, David 183, 204, 218, David Alan 141, David Matthew 141, Elizabeth 204, Isaac 204, Jacob 204, Jacob (Isaac) 204, Miriam 141, Oscar 220, Rachel Ann 204, 329, Roberta 223
GREGORY, E.E. 95, Lenora Miller 59, Luke 59, Penny 283
GRESSMAN, Gay Ann 174, William 174
GRIBBLE, Rebecca 234
GRIBLER, Helen 287
GRICE, Gary 26
GRIFFIN, Mary 139
GRIFFITH, Catherine 60, Edith 255, 256, George 60, 336, Jay 187, Madonna 283, Phoebe 336, Susan 19, Tatman T. 60, William T. 60
GRIGGS, Reuben 15
GRIGGSBY, William 68
GRIM, Catherine Elizabeth 204, Henry L. 204, John Samuel 204, Joseph L. 204, Levi 204, Luther D. 204, Margaret V. "Rett" 204, Nicholas 204, Samuel 204, Susannah Jones 204, Tilla 204, Willie O. 204
GRINER, Alice Cornthwaite 172
GRINNELL, Edna 159
GRINSLADE 27, 28, Beulah 205, Charles Luther 205, Elizabeth Frances 205, John 205, John II 205, John III 48, John W. 205, John William 205, John Wilson III 205, Josiah 205, M.E. 90, Rosa 222, Samuel M. 205, Sarah Jane 205, T. 34, Thomas 205, Thomas Schuyler 205, Timothy Joe 205, W.E. 100, Wilson 222, Wilson Elmer 205
GRISHAW, Nellie Youngman 341
GRISSO 86
GRISSOM, William Levi 149
GRISSUM, Goldie 274
GROGAN, John 94
GRONDALSKI, Elizabeth 189
GROSE, Betty 215, Herschel 215, Herschel Jr. 215
GROSS, Arthur 40, Arthur E. 233, Bon E. 233, Burl W. 233, Dallas B. 233, James B. 233
GROVE, Earl 219, Emily 205, Jennifer 205, Kenneth L. 205
GROVES, Amy (Forest) 217
GRUBB, Bonnie 263, Russell 263
GRUBBS, Elizabeth Jane 286, Ellis P. 286, John 286, John R. 19, Mildred 270, Wesley 286
GRUNDON, Nancy 254
GUGE, Alice (Smith) 206, Ananias 206, Archie Carl 206, Barbara Mae 206, Charles 206, Charles Robert 205, Charles Russell 205, David Wesley 206, David Wesley 206, Donald Gene 205, Donald Glenn 205, Francis 206, James V. 206, Jesse 206, John 206, Judith Ray 205, Loren Oris 206, Margaret 206, Martha 206, Mary Louise 205, Nicholas 206, Oliver Franklin 205, Oliver Franklin "Frank" 206, Orla Rex "Pat" 205, Patricia Ann 205, Rex Loren 205, Richard Lee 205, Samuel 206, Sarah 206, William 206
GUILINGER, James 170
GUIN, Ann 234
GUIOT, Ernistine 224
GULLION, Catherine Riffel Tanner 291, Francis 291, Ida Belle 189, John "Jack" 291, Louise Rayl 291, Pam 25, Sarah 273, Susannah 291
GUNDER, Henry 309, Jane (Chase) 309
GUNNELL, Mary 107
GUNTHE, Joe Zeck Hale 342
GUNTHER, Charlotte 342, Imogene 342, Norman 342, P.D. 342
GUSHWA, Floyd 248
GUSTAFSON, Cathleen Joyce 183
GUSTIN, John W. 325, Sarah Ruanna 325
GUTHRIE, Rachel 338
GUY, Arvelee 218
GUYER, Elizabeth Ann 222, Rachel 222
GWIN, Hannah Wimmer 311, Julia A. 311, Pleasant 311
GWINN, Charles 264, Francis 264, Washington 60

H

HAAK, J.W. 83
HAARER, Mary Ellen 253
HAAS, David 33, John 27, 33
HABNE, George W. 210
HACKENBRACHT, Carl 206, Dennis 206, Francis 206, Frank William 206, George Daniel 206, Howard 206, Jo Ellen 206, Joyce 206, Kenneth 206, 268, Lillian 206, Mary Ellen 206, Miriam 3, Nancy 206, Sherrill 206, Velma 206
HACKENBRAUGH, Vohann Heinrich 206
HACKERD, Floyd 184

HACKSON, C.H. 95
HADLEY, Amelia (Wolf) 195, David 66, Homer 195, John 318, Karen 283, Lewis I. 66, Marie 107, Marie S. 63, Milton 29, 33
HAGAN, Nora Helen 237
HAGEMAN, Theresa 179
HAGEN 328, Mary 197
HAGERTY, James 217, Mary (Corwin) 217
HAGGARD, Ella 312
HAHN, Chad 286, Kimberly 286
HAINES, Maranda Alice 149
HAINES/HAYNES, James M. 149, Maranda Parish 149
HAINLEN, A.C. 38, 207, Alta 207, Bert 36, Brandon 207, Carolyn 38, Earl 38, 207, Elizabeth 207, Eloise 207, Eric 207, Gene 38, Jackie 38, Karen 38, Kyra 207, Len 38, 207, Lloyd 38, 207, Lousetta 207, Lyle 207, Mike 38, 207, Mya 207, Paul 38, 207, Paul Jr. 38, Paul, Jr. 36, Pauline Crandall 207, Randy 207, Travis 207, Trent 207, Yonda 207
HALE, Andrea Lynn 182, Charles William 182, Christine Renee 182, Cleo 25, Donald 152, Donna Annette 152, Kathryn Ann 152, Nora 51
HALEY, Ida Belle (Clark) 238, John H. 238, Sarah 176, William 176
HALL, Alexander 207, Anthony 207, Arol 207, Arol "Brownie" 207, 325, Betty (McCoy) 158, Catherine (Maddox) 207, Dan 332, Gladys 107, Helen (Beck) 207, Ira 207, James 325, Janetta "Nettie" 207, Joan (Mason) 255, Joanna 325, Kathleen 325, Lawrence 207, Lewis 158, Louise 325, Luther 48, Marom C. 340, Mary C. 257, Meda (Dillman) 207, Milton L. 158, Opal (Crume) 207, Sarah 163, Thomas 15, Tom 325
HALLIBURTON, Diana (Smith) 182
HALLOWELL, Grace Belle 264
HALPIN, Robert 94
HALVIE, Mary 230
HAM, Richard Dean Jr. 183
HAMILTON 53, 94, Anna May 107, 268, Anna Ruth 208, Archibald 208, Archibald S. 208, Benjamin 191, Beulah Alice 208, Brian Lee 208, Charles 208, Charles Monroe 208, Clarence F. 208, Cy 208, Cynthia "Cyndi" Louise 208, Cynthia L. 311, Doris Bernice 208, Dorthy 208, Elsie Gertrude 208, Ernest Dale 208, Eva 208, Florence (Middleton) 18, Florence Middleton 207, Floyd 25, Francina (Smith) 149, Frank 208, Fred 208, Harriett 263, Harry Leroy 208, Harvey 208, Heil 59, Henry 208, Henry Seymor 208, Hile 15, Ila Otto 208, Jacob 59, James 18, 96, 148, 191, 208, Jason 191, Jeffery Dale 208, Jerry 25, 26, Joel 208, John 207, Justin 191, Lavina C. 208, Lex 207, 208, Margery "Madge" L. 208, Martha 208, Mary 142, 208, Mary (Stuck) 148, Mattie Wilson 207, Maude 208, Miriam Ruth 276, Nat 97, Nellie B. 208, Pamela Sue 208, Phil 154, Philip T. 123, R.R. 14, Rebecca "Becky" Sue 208, Richard Lee 208, Rile 208, Robert 208, Sally Ann 208, Samuel 208, Sarah 208, 310, Sylvester 25, Thomas Dale 208, William 149, 208
HAMLER, Clarence 43
HAMMANN, Kay 211, Martha 211, Mary Catherine 211
HAMMER, Jess 141
HAMMOND, Bob 83
HAMP, Arthur Jr. 125, Bob 97, David 125, Robert J. Sr. 125, Robert Jr. 125
HAMPTON, Emily Lovia 315, Jeff 315, Michele Ann 315
HANCOCK, Betty 50, Celia 143, Franklin 51, Jehu 51, Lee Ann 244, Maxine (Renshaw) 168
HANGER 248
HANKINS, Amy 208, Carolyn 208, Dale 208, Dama 305, Elizabeth J. 208, Garfield 208, Helen 208, Iola Mae 249, John R. 208, Kevin 208, Robert 208, Wesley 287
HANNA, Belle Sherfy 123, Chester L. 208, G. Bright 208, G. Bright 176, Geneva 208, Glenn 208, Guy 208, J.L.D. 15, Joseph Lorenzo Dow 208, Josephine 208, O.H. 83, Palestine 208, Winifred 208
HANSON, Barbara 155, Francis 54, Robert 54, Benjamin Franklin 252, Borden 252, Denzel 25, Edwin 252, Elijah 252, Esther Jane 252, Florence 252, Levi 252, Maggie 22, Martha 252, Newton 252, T.A. 21, Thomas 252
HARBAUGH, Margaret 141
HARBIN, Christopher Matthew 333, J. Dereck 91, Jim 333, Jimmy Roger 284, Martin Todd 333, Patty Ann 333, Scott Allen 333, Sharon (Thayer) 333
HARDEBECK, Irene 99
HARDEMON, William 15
HARDIN, E.A. 34, T. 34
HARDING, Anna 25, Logan 25
HARDY, Alice 176, Colleen 207, Lela 63
HARGISS, Abraham 206, 207, Bessie Lou (Blankenship) 206, Cheri Sue 206, David K. 206, Jeffrey 207, Jeffrey David 206, Martha Jane (Culpepper) 206, Nancy Sue Reynolds 206, William David 206
HARGRAVE, Doramae 25
HARL, Yvonne Carol 182
HARLAN, Amy Nichole 142, Brian John 142, Francis Eugene 142, Mark Allen 142, Martha 214, Mary Elizabeth 142, Roberta 142, Roberta (Clem) 142
HARLAND, Emma Jane 234, Jemima 189
HARLESS, Calvin Edward 330, Nellie Jane (Laughlin) 330, Nichole 335
HARLEY, Angelina 33, Joshua 33, Maggie 263
HARLOW, Clyde G. 209, Cora A. 209, Doris Carolyn 209, Elizabeth Ann 238, Elizabeth Evans 209, Erasmus V. 209, Gary 238, George Albert 209, Grace 209, Jeff 96, Joey Bruce 209, John 209, John Blout 209, Katherine Minerva 209, Lawrence A. 209, Lester 209, Lester Gerry 209, Melinda 238, Minerva Tyner 209, Nancy Coleman 209, Orlando 209, Tom 238, Ulla A. 209, Zenas L. 209
HARMER, Ruth 224
HARMON, Barbara L. 301, Belinda J. 301, Charles 15, 18, 48, 50, 96, 209, Charles M. 209, Deborah K. 301, Elizabeth 209, Ethel 258, Frank 74, Hiram 209, James 209, James R. 209, John 209, John B. 209, John T. 209, Mabel Cassandra 266, Martha 207, Mary 209, Mary Ann 209, Mildred 209, Moses 266, Nancy Jane 209, Richard 209, Richard W. 301, Robert A. 301, Robert E. 301, Samuel Roy 266, Stephen 266, William 209, William M. 209
HARNESS, Agnes Smith 219, Alice Smith 211, B.F. 13, 328, Bette Jane 329, Betty 99, Daisy 173, Donna 210, Eleanor Louise 211, Eleanor Louise 327, Elizabeth Tepebo 209, Forest A. 209, Forrest 210, 291, Forrest Bruce 211, Forrest Bruce 210, George 210, George Sr. 173, George W. 211, 295, George W. 304, George W. Jr 210, Gladys Eva (Todd) 211, 327, 329, Harriat 210, Harriett (Sowards) 295, Ida Florence 210, Jacob 343, John 209, Juanita Zelma Reynolds 293, June Click 290, Minnie Augusta 185, 209, Pamela 210, Pamela June 211, Peter Michael 209, Russ 210, Russell 210, Russell Marvin 210, 211, Russell R. 290, Russell R. 210, 211, 327, 329, Russell Robert 211, Summer 210, Susan 173, William Lewis 209
HARPER, A.W. 38, Anna Blanche 211, Betty Charlotte 211, Candace 211, Carl 211, Charles M. 211, Clarence Ervin 211, Claud 211, Cora 211, Dale 211, David L. 211, Edna 211, Frances 211, Garnet 211, George 211, Gerald 211, Glen 35, 211, Glendel Marshall 211, Harold 211, Howard, 35, Howard Samuel 211, Ida B. 238, Ida Gilliland 238, James 211, James Henry 238, James Omer 211, James Robert "Pete" 211, John 319, John L. 211, Josie 211, Kenneth "Bill" 211, Leona 211, Lydia Mae 211, Marion Scott 211, Mary 211, 311, 343, Mary (Loughery) 211, Mary M. 271, Matthew Jay 211, Mildred 211, Oliver Earl 211, Paul Howard 211, Rachel Anna 275, Richard 138, 211, Richard Clem 211, Sue 211, Tom 36, 211, Victor 211, William Andrew 211, William C. 211
HARPOLD, Margaret Elizabeth 149
HARRELL, Alfred 185, Arthur Garland 212, Brad Harrell 185, Clara Josephine 212, Comfort 212, Comfort Emaline 212, Effie 198, Eliza Jane 212, Elizabeth 15, Frank 197, Frank E. 198, Gladys Irene Minglin 185, Gregory Lee 185, Henry G. 212, James Edward 212, James Murray 212, Jane 212, Jemima 212, Jeremiah 15, 211, 212, Jeremiah R. 212, John Fullen 212, Jonathan 212, Linda 212, Lucretia Ann 212, Lute 198, Margaret 212, Margaret Evelyn Weinle 212, Martin Van Buren 212, Mary Elizabeth 212, Mary Jemima 212, Mary Lou 189, Minnie Jane Beatty 185, Moses 212, Ray Duncan 212, Richard E. 185, Sara Jane 212, Sarah 212, Sarah (Osborn/Osborne) 211, Sarah Osborne 212, Shelby Moses 212, Stephen 212, Susan 212, Tighlman A. 16, Tighlman "Ted" Ashley Howard 212, Tracy 212, Vivian 197, William 212, William Madison 212, William Wesley 212
HARRIMAN, Mattie (Gentry) 256
HARRINGTON, Carolyn 179
HARRIS, Alan 336, Alice 325, Arletta A. 336, Bartlett 212, Bob 154, Bridgette 337, Charles 212, Charles Arnel 212, Christine 212, Christopher 212, Don 154, Donald Lawrence 212, Elmira Melissa 212, Elsie Drahosh 154, Elsie Ethel Drahosh 212, Everett Neil 178, 197, 212, Fannie Elizabeth Shepard 181, Henry 212, Herschel 336, Homer 212, Hyldred Glorene 212, Ida B. 212, James 313, James Henry 154, James Henry 212, Jane (Groves) 313, John 212, John Franklin 212, Jonathan Pritlow 212, Joseph 212, Lois 154, Mark 336, Martha 197, 336, Martha A. 313, Martha Jane 163, Mary 212, Mary Grace 212, Mary Samantha 212, Minnie Myrtle 181, Nathaniel 212, Neil Thomas 212, Neil Thomas 178, 197, Nellie 140, Rachel 212, Rebecca 239, Robert Alan 212, Ross 212, Ruth 336, Sarah 336, Sarah Ester 212, Selma Ring 336, Thomas H. 181, Thomas Paul 178, 197, Thomas Paul 212, Velma May 212, Verl 336, Victoria 212, W.H. 83, Walter Lee 212, William 212, William (Henry) 336, William King 212, William Paul 212
HARRISON, Charlotte Elizabeth 212, Eli 251, Eliza Ann (Mason) 251, John 15, 16, 18, 251, John Wesley 251, Laura Jane 218, Lucinda 332, Norma Jane 141, Rachael 215, Rachel (Cruse) 251, Richard V. 201, T.J. 103, William 257, 341, William Henry 176
HARSHBARGER, Carolyn Jean 142
HART 249, Amy (Chaney) 234, Andrew 35, Becky 212, Benjamin B. 234, Bill 212, Delilah 234, Dorothy 212, Francis 234, Georgia 21, Hu Ween Veletta Zellar 212, Jim 212, John 145, 212, John Gilbert 212, John M. 234, John Marcus Sr. 212, Melody 212, Miles 234, Polly 214, Rebecca 320, Terri 212
HARTER, Gladys 171, William G. 116
HARTLEROAD, Jay 213, Ray 213, Ronald J. 213, Ruth Brenton 213, Susie 213, Tim 213
HARTMAN 161, Frank 14, 287, Fred 287, George 287, Henry William 80, Mazie M. 241, William 287, Wm H. 161, Wm. 287
HARTMANN, George 84
HARTSUCK, E.J. 46
HARVEY, Doc 15, Elizabeth 177, Jacob 52, Jessica 177, John 228, Latrelle 177, Opal 228
HASACUSTER, Bernie Taylor 179, John Michael 179, Marcia 179, Michelle 179, Monica 179, Richard 179
HASKETT, Byron 177, Elizabeth (Ralston) 177, Joseph 48, Luvenia (Jones) 177, Thomas 177, Thomas Dayhuff 177, Thomas Linn 177
HASLER, Casper 138, Catherine 138, Louisa 138, Pearl 266
HASTIE, John 48
HATCHER, Frank Roy 89
HATFIELD, William 35
HATHAWAY, Lucinda 79
HATT, Cynthia McKinney 322, Gertie Mae Parkey 322, Joseph 322, Prince A. 322, Susanna Hollingsworth 322, William 322
HATTON, Alice 213, Alice C. (Dutton) 170, Beulah 213, Carrie Jane 213, Francis Marion 213, Gwendolyn 213, Henry S. 52, 54, Henry Simon 213, J.H. 48, James 53, James M. 52, 56, James Madison 213, James Marion 213, Janalyce K. (Kendall) 236, Jeff 56, Jeffrey A. 213, Loraine 213, Mary Elizabeth 172, Ryan Nathaniel 213, Shannon Chere 213
HAUCK, Inez 255
HAUN, Charlotte 222, Earl C. 159, George 222, Martin Gentry 159, Mary Waneta 159, Myrtle Clarice 327
HAUS, Charlotte 78
HAVENS, Aaron W. 85, Bessie 213, Charles H. (Goof) 213, Clara H. 213, Emma 213, George Cedric 213, Henry Bascomb 213, James 213, Robbin 192, William Walton 213
HAVERGAL, William James 326
HAVLIN, Charles 248
HAVNER, Vance 75
HAWK, Nora Joan 308
HAWKINS, Allan 213, Ashley Ruth 290, Beulah 213, Burt 290, Doris 213, Ebenezer 213, Edra 163, Fred 213, Genevieve Agnes 213, Henry 83, James 213, James Perry 213, John 275, John Bluford 15, Judith Ann 214, 304, Judith Ann 213, Kenneth 213, Lavon 106, Martha 291, Massa (Truax) 291, Mildred 213, Reuben 51, 52, 82, Robert 213, Robert Edwin 213, Robert Edwin 304 Robert Edwin Jr. 214, Robert Edwin Jr. 304, Susan Elizabeth 213, Theodore 213
HAWN, Clarence 290, Frances 268, Sarah A. 220
HAWORTH 245, Ann Dillon 339, Arthur 62, 64, C.V. 11, 103, 167, 222, Gloria Jean 218, Isaac 16, Jonathan 44, Mabel 262, Martha Esther 262, Mary Ellen (Robbins) 262, Richard 339, Ruby Dee 262, Stephen 262, Susannah 339, Theodore 262, Theodore R. 259, Theodore Robbins 262
HAYDEN, Ella Lounetta 148, John 148
HAYEN, Aaron Matthew 214, Lawrence Brad 214, Lawrence Brad 214, Warren Henry 214
HAYES 49, Clara Melissa 319, Mary Ann "Molly" (Breedlove) 156
HAYNES, Andrew 214, Anthony 214, Asa 214, Beverley 214, Bobby 214, Caitlin 214, Carrie 214, Carrie Lee 320, Charles 214, Christina 214, Christina Marie 320, Content 214, David 214, 225, Deborah 214, Dorothy 107, 214, Eliza 214, Elizabeth 214, Elwood 10, 103, 113, 120, 197, 222, 312, 340, Enoch 214, Esther 214, Ethel Virginia T. 307, 320, Frank 14, 214, 329, Franklin 214, Jacob 214, James 214, Janet 214, John 214, 225, John E. 14, Joseph Wilbur 214, Lawrence 214, 225, Linda Kay Roberts 320, Louis 200, 214, 225, Lydia 214, Malinda 214, Marilyn 214, Martha 214, Mary Edyth 200, 214, Milton 214, Mitchell 214, Paul 214, Peter 214, Samuel 214, Sarah 214, Stephen 214, Thomas 214, Thomas Ward 320, Tyler 214, Ward 14, 214, 225, Warren 214, Wesley 214, Wright 214, Zechariah 214, John E. 320

HAYS 58, Nannie (Nan) 292
HAYSE, John C. 291, Sarah Drusetta Reeder 291
HAYWORTH, Jonathan 147, Mabel H. 338
HAZELTINE, Lora (McLaughlin) 98
HAZLETT, John 266, Margaret 266
HEA, Berdina 293, Bob 214, Bobette Lenae 214, Kelly Lynn 214
HEADLEY, E. 34, W.B. 34
HEAGY, H. 34
HEALTON, John 65, Jonathan 65, William 65
HEALY, Tom 263
HEART 13
HEATHERINGTON, Mary Jo 322, Mary Pearl 322, William 322
HEATON, Adelia 291, Adolphus 215, Alice 215, Amelia 214, Andrew 214, Anna 215, Beverly 215, Bob 215, Brenda D. 310, Carl 215, Carl "Buck" 25, Catherine 234, Charles 215, Charles Eli 215, Clara 215, Clara Inez (Shepherd) 149, Cornelius 19, 215, Daniel 214, 215, Daniel M. 215, David C. 215, Delia 215, Don 215, Ed 215, Eli 215, Elizabeth 214, Emma 215, 312, Fannie 19, Flora 215, Frank K. 215, Freddy 215, Garnet 25, Hannah 215, Henry 214, Henry C. 215, James 214, John O. 103, 225, John Osborne 214, Joseph 215, 291, Joseph W. 18, 251, Leonidas V. 149, Lillian Irene 215, Lillian Irene 149, 150, Linda 215, Louisa 214, Lucille 215, 253, Lucinda 214, 225, Lucinda Mary 215, Lula Alice 215, Matilda Rayl 291, Nathaniel McKinley 215, Pearl 215, Peggy 215, Roy 215, Sarah 215, Thaddeus Baxter 215, Vanburen 214, William 214, William H. 149, 215, William H. 305, William Robert 214
HEAVILIN, Robert E. Sr. 66
HECKMAN, Tom 257
HEFLIN, Bailey Louise 182, Cory David 182, Cynthia Louise 182, David Albert 182, Donna D. 182, Julia 319, Robin Lee 182, Sandy 182, Sean Thomas 182, Sharon Kay 182, Susan Elaine 182, Theresa Ann 182, Thomas David 182, Travis David 182, Troy William 182, Tyler Lee 182, William Robert 182
HEINBAUGH, Dale 83
HEINEMAN, Julia 224
HEINMILLER, Anna 198, Anna Elizabeth 191, Johannes 191, Scott 191
HEINRICH, Catherine Jill 299
HEINZMAN, Alexander (Alex) 215, Ariana 215, Derek 215, Harry 215, James 215, Jamey 215, Jordan 215, Katherine (Katie) 215, Luther (Boots) 215, Rachel 215, Shirley 215, Stephen 215, William 215
HEISEL, Esther Lilly 161, John 160, Lenhard 160, Rudolph Herman 160
HEITZMAN, Keith 289, Keith Stewart 232
HELLMANN, David 92
HELM, Bert 262, John 185, Judith Kay (Stahl) 314
HELMER, Dora LaFrances (Collins) 172, Edna Maude 172, Martin Henry 172
HELMS 85, Aire 215, Arie 215, George F. 216, H. Brent 215, Herb 272, Howard F. 215, 216, Howard Foster 215, 216, Howard Frank 215, Jeffry S. 215, John 215, John Jr. 215, Lela Mildred (Walker) 215, 216, Lucile 215, 216, Marion Francis (Morrison) 215, Mary E. (Kellie) 216, R.L. Jr. 216, Ralph 215, Ralph L. 216, Roy 23, 166, 251, William 48, 215
HELMUTH, Dewey 32, Joseph J. 32, Mildred 32
HELTON, Harold 332, Harriet Rosetta Martin 235, John Robert 235, Ruth 235
HELTZEL 18, Evelyn 243, Robert 197, Robert J. 132
HELVIE 22
HEMERLEY, Julia 140
HEMINGWAY, Margaret 318
HEMMEGER 59
HEMMEGER, Earl 216, Elmer 216, Fred 216, Virginia 216
HEMPER, Henry 33, Henry G. 27
HEMPSTER, H.G. 34
HENDERSHOT, Bob 208, Gregory Ralph 292, Jeff 23, Ralph 292, Rex 290
HENDERSON, Amanda Amerette 284, J.F. 48, Lowell 97, Mary Belle 274, Mary Iris 234, Pauline (Bess) 289, W. 34, William 33
HENDRICKS, David 216, Edd B. 216, Elijah 216, James Emerson 216, James M. 216, John E. 216, John L. 216, John Levi II 216, L. June 216, Nancy A. 218, R. Rex 216, Robert T. 216, Thomas Payne 216, William D. 216, William David 216
HENDRICKSON, Arthur 305, Junie 21
HENDRIX, Auda 273, Eliza 318, Eliza Annis 318, Zedock 318
HENISA, Harold C. 308
HENLEY, Dorothy 237, Martha 176
HENNESSEE, John Robert 238, Joseph Wesley 238, Samuel Dennis 238, Samuel Dennis II 238
HENNINGER, Christina 204
HENRY, (Esther) Agnes (Hagerty) 217, (Mary) Virginia 217, Abraham 216, Catherine 216, Charles 157, 255, Cheryl 157, 255, Clarence 343, Cora Omega 216, David 217, Everett Ehrman 216, Fred 157, 255, Fred B. 217, George S. 288, Glenn 216, Goldie 216, Harry 343, Isaac F. 217, James 196, John Short 217, Mark Eugene 217, Martha (Barrett) 217, Mary Jane 157, Mary Jayne 255, Mary Lucille 216, Michael William 216, Patrick 75, Russell 216, Vada 216, Winona Elizabeth (Prifogle) 288
HENSELL, Estella 191
HENSLER 39, Ananias 258, Dallas 23, Larry 258, Lucius 258, Vera 258, William A. 258
HENSLEY, Atta 320, Blanche 320, C.P. 125, Cathy S. 179, Clara 320, Elma 320, Ethel 320, Evelyn 257, 295, Everett 320, Jeff 320, Soloman 320
HENTON, Esther 189
HERA 305
HERBERG, Elizabeth 193, Richard 193
HERCHENROEDER, Eunice 73, Mike 73
HERCULES, Arrah Cornelius (Neil) 217, Catherine 217, Esther 217, Ivy Pearl 217, James 217, Jane 217, John Taylor 217, 338, Lewis (Lute) 217, Mary 217, Otis Welby 217, Samuel 217, Sarah 217, William 217
HERITIER, Marie-Victorie 182
HERR, Sue 26, Winona 139
HERRBACH, R. Wynne 163
HERRELL, Bobby Joe 217, Cecelia Marie 217, Daniel Joe 217, Dennis Jay 217, Dennis Jay 155, 223, 233, Derek Daniel 217, Floyd Eldon 217, Jason Kyle 217, Jeffrey Lee 217, Jennifer Marie 217, Joe 217, Kevin Kyle 217, Rachael Dawn 217, 223, 233, Rachael Dawn 155, Rebekah DeeAnn 155, Rebekah Deeann 223, 233, Rebekah Deeann 217, William (Bill) Jefferson 217, William Jefferson 217
HERREN, Pat 192, Thomas W. 218, William 218, William Marion 218
HERRERA, Poririo 289, Rose Emma 225
HERRINGTON, Will 45
HERRON, Belle 183, Daisy 218, Daisy Marie 193, Esther Charlotte 218, Frances Bell 149, Fred 218, George 218, Grace Martin 164, Jerron "Jerry" Isaiah 218, Jerry 278, Jesse 218, Joseph 183, Lela E. 218, Louisa 218, Mildred (Roberts) 278, Mildred May 218, Minnie 218, Thomas 183, Thomas W. Jr. 218, Viola 218, Viola Marie 278, William Aaron 164
HERSCHBERGER 29, Catherine 236, Matilda 241
HESS, Mary Etta 313
HESSLER, Anna M. Niese 314, Anna May 314, John 314, Margaret 314
HESTON, M. Melissa Jackson 293, Susan Josephine 293
HETHCOAT, Charles 218, Eli 218, Etta 218, Hester 218, James Edmund 218, Lucinda 218, Mary 218, Anna (Butler) 200, Anna Belle 163, 174, Bessie 218, Claude 218, Claude D. 163, 218, Clyde 218, Elizabeth Betty 202, Elsie 218, Everett 218, Hazel 218, Hurshel 163, 200, 218, 219, Hurshel B. 174, Hurshel Curless 174, Janice 163, Jennie 218, Jim 202, Marie 218, Max 163, 218, Melba 163, Merrill 163, 218, Merrill LaMarr 174, Merritt 163, 218, Myrel 218, Sarah 218
HEUSER, Dorthy 138
HEUTEBUCH, Phillip 286
HEWITT, Carolyn Joan (Bender) 218, Enoch James 291, Flora Alice 291, Heather 218, James Lindley Marshall 218, Mark 218, Mary (Guy) 218, Megan 218, Sarah Elizabeth Enos 291, Troy 218
HEXIMER, Gabriel 203, Idella (Schweitzer) 203
HIATT, Anna (Butler) 218, Arliss 163, Arliss Jean 219, Blanche 219, Catherine Good 219, Charley 219, Charlotte 219, Charlotte (Coats) 219, Clinton 219, Cordelia 219, Dillon 219, Effa 219, Elsie 219, Everett 219, Gladys 219, Helen Swisher 219, Ida 219, Inez 219, John 176, Jonathon 219, Kenneth 219, Leslie 219, Levi 201, 219, Lindley 64, 218, 219, Lovella 219, Mable 219, Mahala 219, Martha 176, Mary 62, 66, 219, Matilda 219, Maude (McCoy) 218, Morton 219, Omer 219, Orla 219, Pauline 219, Richard 219, Russell 219, Salathiel 219, Sirena 219, Sophrana 219, Stella Effie 156, Virgil 219, 18, Warren J. 219, William 219, Wilson 219, Wilson J. 219, Zella 219
HIBBARD, Susanna 202
HICKAM, Horace 241, Morna Mahala 241, 270, Gary 279, Helen 108, Ira 19, Roberta Jeanne 279, Ryan Blair 279
HICKS, Bob 86, Cynthia 337, Delores J. 198 , Fanny Grace (Kemper) 219, Frank 219, Joan Lee 182, John Ralph 219, John Wayne 182, Marilyn Agnes 219, Paul 66, Rita Ellen 182, Robert Edward 182
HIGGINS, Beth Ann 310, Jonathan 201, Magnolia (Stephenson) (Kitley) 138, Martha 271, Smith 102
HIGH, Dorothy (Bowman) 298, Marinell 92
HIGHT, Alta Marie 193, Betty 174
HIGHTOWER, Amazetta 294, Archibald 294, Arnetta 294, Eva 192, George W. 294, Julietta 294, Lucinda 294, Marietta (Christy) 294, Patsy 294
HILBORN, Amos 160, Caroline (Witmer) 160, Jacob 160, Laura (Reichard) 160, Nellie Norene 160
HILE, Joyce Hester 235
HILGERS, Dean 184
HILL, Albert 25, Betty J. 220, Brandon 157, Charles 64, Charles G. 220, Clara B. 220, Connie 157, Edith May (George) 212, Edward John 182, Emita B. 102, Francis M. 286, Gail 157, George 220, Gilbert Henry 212, J.L. 34, James F. 220, John 182, June (Brown) 157, Kenny 86, Lindan 157, Lindan Jerome 157, Louetta Davis 212, Mabel 107, Phyllis 339, Phyllis J. 220, Ralph 174, Raymond 157, Raymond Isaac 220, Robert 157, 174, Robert E. 220, Sara J. 324, Thomas 27
HILLARD, Frank Leslie 141, Renna Bernice (Arnett) 141
HILLIS, Deborah 315, Faith 315, Gary 315, Glen 10, Glen R. 132, Jared 315, V.S. 98
HILTON, Carlton 200
HIMES 85
HINDERLIDER, Pearl 287
HINE, Charles Henry 338, Elizabeth Apgar 338, Mary Elizabeth 338
HINES, Bernard 237
HINKLE, Esther (Brock) 167, Henry 167, John 85, Margaret Ann 167, Mary 85
HINSHAW, Bertha 259
HINTON, Dr. W.W. 18
HINTZ, Jami 190, Jim 190, Teresa Ann 190, Tiffany 190, Victoria 190
HIRONS, Cinthia Kay 275, Richard 275
HIRST, Joan Elizabeth 272, Marie Katherine (Schmidt) 272, Raymond M. 272
HITE, Abraham 220, Andrew 220, Ann 220, Appolonia (Keller) 220, Arminda 220, C.B. 341, Carolyn Sue 239, Cassius Clay 220, Daniel 220, David 220, Elizabeth (Boice) 220, Gene 239, Gerald 220, Ida 220, Jack 97, John 220, Joseph 220, Julius 220, Julius Sheridan 220, Lewis 220, Lydia (Maple) 220, Magdaline (Rosenberger) 220, Mildred Powell 239, Nancy J. (Wills) 220, Noah 220, Onda 220, Raymond Vernon 220, Rebecca 220, Robert 220, Samuel Bell 220, Vonna Lou 187, Wayne 220, William Harvey 220
HIX, Mary Wilma 320
HIXON 226
HIZER, James N. 331
HOAGLAND, Mary Elizabeth 254
HOBBS, Greg 301, Kaitlyn 301
HOBSON 161, Abe 221, Absolon N. 220, Alfred 221, Amanda Taylor 322, Ann Marie 322, Anna E 220, Barbara 221, Carl 321, Charles Alfred 321, David 220, Dawn Renee 322, Elihu 221, 259, Elizabeth Sarah 220, Ella Blanche 152, 220, Elsie Marie 252, Enos 259, Enos Kaye 259, Fannie Candice 259, Florence 220, George William 220, Georgia 220, Grace 259, Howard 259, Ida 221, James 220, James Matthew 322, Jasen Carl 322, Jesse 220, 221, Lloyd 161, 287, Mark 221, Martha J. 220, Mary Ann 220, Mat 221, Matilda (Tillie) 220, Nancy 220, Ossian 259, Paul 221, Peggy Ragland 221, Richard C. 220, Robert 220, Robert P. 220, Ross 161, 287, Sarah 259, Sarah Milburn 220, Thomas Anthony 322, Velma Thomas 321, Vincent 220, Wayne Thomas 321, William 14, 220, William F. 220, William Penn 252
HOCHSTEDLER, 28, 29, Billy 36, Emanuel 29, Lester 29, Mattie 253, Orem 28, Zach 34
HOCHSTETLER 28, 29, 303
HOCKER, G.W. 34
HOCKETT, Abigail 65, J.G. 13, Jake 228, Joseph 35, 37, Josephine 62, 64, 65
HODGE, Margaret 140
HODGES, Mary (Polly) 204, Nancy 245
HODGIN, Charles N. 197
HODSHIRE, James Robert 281, 282
HODSON 86, David 234, 248, David Benton 234, David Benton 234, Delilah 234, Emma Cecil 234, George 197, George W. 234, Grace 197, John Luke 234, Lenora Catherine (Pixler) 234, Marble 248, Mary 234, Mary Ann 248, Miles Jefferson 234, Nathan 65, Nellie 223, Ora O. 197, Robert 332, Robert W. 269, William Eli 234, Winifred 248, Zarchiriah 65
HOFFMAN, Edna 253, 262, Toby 284
HOFSTROM, Dana 213, Kirk 213, Mark 213, Terri 213
HOGLAND, James 35
HOGUE, Joel A. 250, Lola M. (Brown) 250
HOLBERT, Minerva 177
HOLDER, Bonnie 121, Charlotte 176, Lisa 121, Lyle 121, Stephen 121, Wayne 121
HOLDERITH, Catherine 221, Cecilia Ann (Renie) 324, Cecilia Renie 293, Clarence P. 221, Clarence Patrick 324, Frances 221, Francis 324, Frank A. 221, George L. 221, Joseph 221, Joseph D. 221, Martha 221, Mary 221, 324, Mayme M. 221, Nollie Genieve (Smith) 324, Patricia Louise 221, Peter H. 221, 293, 324
HOLIDAY, Alice 66
HOLLAND, William Franklin 149
HOLLER, Daniel 33
HOLLETT, Clara Delite 262, Cora Elizabeth 262, Dwight Henry Hazard 262, Elma 259, Elma (Mendenhall) 261, James

Bertram 262, John A. 259, John Alexander 262, Lloyd Lester 262, Lucile Abigale 262, Opal Hope 262, Orpha Dean 262
HOLLINDEN, Ann (Beck) 207
HOLLINGSHEAD, James 35
HOLLINGSWORTH, Alma 197, Alma Melissa 276, Alma Sue 163, 221, Arthur 64, Arthur Edward 222, Benjamin 222, C.W. "Cappy" 221, Cale 24, 25, Calvin 222, Cappy 66, "Cappy" 276, Charles 222, Clyde Carlton 276, Darin 25, David E. 222, Frank Hanley 276, I.A. 66, Isaac 26, 221, Isaac Allen 163, 221, 276, Issac A. 197, Izaac 222, Joel 24, 25, Karleen 222, Lauren 222, Lloyd 237, 238, Louisa (Comer) 222, Lucille 222, Lynn 222, Mary Iona (Newlin) 221, 276, Melissa 222, Monte 38, Nelson 25, O.P. 35, Peggy 197, Peggy Ann 163, 276, Robert M. 222, Sam 66, Samuel P. 222, Sherman 38, Spencer 222, Ted 222, Tracy 222, Valentine 222, William Penn 276, Wilson 222
HOLLOWAY, Herman D. 217, Mabel C. 217
HOLLOWELL, John 317, Michel 176
HOLMAN, Dora Dean 174
HOLMES, Catharine (Kitty) 270, Evelyn 284, Walter 300
HOLSTEIN 39
HOLT, Barbara Catherine 139, Connie 224, Dillard M. 247, Jan René 248, Marilyn G. 29, Virgil 247
HONEY 59
HONEYWELL 86
HOOD 52, Hubert Cleveland 193, John A. 300
HOOKER, Linda 239
HOOLEY, Paul 253
HOOPER, Bessie L. 171
HOOVER 52, Aileen 213, Callie 277, Connie 312, Frank T. 35, Herbert 339, Lorinda 313, Mary Catherine 212, William Howard 181
HOPKINS, Jane 55, M.B. 103, Mary 208
HOPPER, J.T. 19
HOPPES, James Jr. 48
HOPWOOD, Magdaline 220
HORINE, J.A. 48, J.N. 52
HORN, Charles 145, Lauretta Ellen 156, Loretta 308
HORNER, Dewitt Clinton 286, Jane T. 319, Mariah (Scott) 286, Mary Anna 286
HORNSTIEN, Karen Kae 183
HORTON, George B. 158, Lindsay Oliver 158, Reta Mae 158, William C. Jr. 212
HOSIER, Garnell 315, Harry "Junior" 235, Kathryn Dee "Kathy" 170, Kit Lee 170, Marsha Leigh 235, Mildred 171, Paul Raymond 170, Ted 171
HOSS, L.C. 125, P.E. 125
HOSTEDLER, Elizabeth 303
HOSTETLER 56, Albert 248, Albert Clinton 248, Albert Clinton 222, Anna 248, Carrie 248, Cathy (Getz) 198, Elmer 248, Fern Locke 223, Ivory 248, Jacob L. 222, 248, Kate Locke 248, Katie (Enders) 222, Lizzie 235, Maude 248, Sarah Catherine 223, Sarah Catherine 297, Todd Aaron 332, Willard 248, Zacharia 248
HOSTETTELER, Evaleen 281
HOTALING 86
HOUGHMAN 229

HOUNCHELL, Clayton 282, Jean 282, Mary (Collect) 282
HOUSE 28
HOUSEHOLDER, Betty 243, Mary M. 236
HOUSER, C. Raymond 80, Jacob 190, Louviana 212
HOUSTON, Anderson 52, John 187, Rowena 187, Susan 187
HOWARD, Arley Mae (Freed) 196, Bertha 196, Catherine 291, Ernest 196, Ethel 219, James Hughes 328, John 291, Otis "Ote" 338, Raymond Hughes 328, Thomas 196, Thomas, Jr. 196, Tilghman A. 77, Tilman A. 51, Van 313, William Eugene 196, William N. 241
HOWATT, Grace 305
HOWDYSHELL, Frances 277
HOWE, Osa Mae 242, Sophronia Allena 286
HOWELL 39, 41, 245, Blanche 213, Larry 85, Matthew G. 268, Rachel 190, Ruth 337, Tense 268, Wm. 42, Zelma 268
HOWENSTINE, Bradley 333, Caroline (Nie) 333, Ruth Cleo 333
HOY, Carrie 325
HOYER, Elizabeth 303, Eva 341
HOYLE, Jane Ann Shockley 276
HOYT, Minnie 208
HUBBARD, Elizabeth 190, Jeremiah 45, 47, Melvin 269
HUDDLESTON, Abarilla (Oyler) 295, Henry 281, 295, Maude 336, Susanna 295
HUDELSON, David 178, Ellen 178, Hannah 178, Marietta 178
HUDKINS, Deborah (Pickett) 246
HUDSON, Elma 277, Hannah 143, Henry 245, Kelsea Nicol 249, Leslie 277
HUEMMER 92
HUESTON, Phil 56
HUFF, James E. 282, Mary Tamar 333
HUFFER, Anna 149, Bernice 317, Cecil 215, Earl E. 234, Esther 318, Esther Irene 317, 318, Genevieve 234, Genevieve Kanable 234, Gladys 317, Harold W. 234, Hazel 317, Jacob 317, John 149, Mae 317, Pauline 317, Susie Mae (Weaver) 234
HUFFMAN, Amy 305, Brian 305, Nancy J. 33, Patrick 305, Wm. 313
HUGGINS, Mary 220
HUGHES, Alexander 223, Bette 3, Betty Louise 223, Betty Richards 234, Carl Leroy 223, Carl Verlion 151, Cleo Edward 223, David 223, David Carl 151, Dorothy Opal 223, Edna Irene 223, Edna Irene 275, Elsie 223, Frances Fern 223, Francis 223, Frank G. 106, Hamilton 223, James 223, Joseph 223, Linda Kay 234, Mabel 26, Mildred Pauline 223, Morris Edward 223, Noah 41, Noley 96, Raymond 234, Richard 223, S.D. 95, Samuel 223, Sarah 322, Stewart 223, Thelma Mae 223,233, Thompson 223, William 48, 223, 322, William Jr. 223, Wilma Pearl 223
HUGUENOT 143
HULLINGER, Bart 230, Carrie 230, Clyde Eli 166, George 300, Joan 32, Keith 230, Kent 230, L. 34, Mary Ilo (Trott) 166, Ned 32, 230, Pamela 230, Scott 230, Stephanie 230

HUMBARGER, Dora 140
HUMBER, Joe 197
HUMBERT, Eliza 197, Elizabeth 234, Frank 197, Harrison 197, Sam 197
HUMPHREY, Alberdeen 278, Jayne Aynn 278, Kay Lynn 278, Kenneth Russell 278, Patrick Joseph 278, Russell 278
HUMPHRISS, Andrew Arthur 153, Charles Jr. 153, Charlie 153
HUNDLEY, Dora 171
HUNER, John 42
HUNICUTT, William 64
HUNKLER, Joanne 235
HUNLEY, Carson 150, Celia Jane (Fairchild) 203, David Lee 150, John Thomas 203
HUNNICUTT, Wanda 218
HUNSICKER, Clinton 223, Harry 223, Homer 223, Laura 223, Montie 223, Myrtle 223, Ora 223, Peter 223
HUNSINGER, Clint 152, Clyde 152, Clyde Sylvester 223, David 223, Dove Benson 152, Lois 152, 223, Pamela 223, Wayne 223
HUNT, A.W. 14, Almon 171, Anita 62, Carrie 278, Casandra "Cassie" (Becknell) 334, Dorothy Jean 241, E.S. 131, Ernest 155, Ernest Martin 155, Ferne 251, Henry 131, Howard 219, Jennetta 219, Jessie Alice 307, John 171, John Thomas 171, Levi 168, Mabel 278, Margaret (Cline) 168, Margaret Lines 197, Mark Lafayette 334, Minnie B. 168, Nathan 44, Ruth Ella 334, 335, Sandra 171, Sheila 171, Sherman 278, Virgil 102
HUNTER 27, Clarion Elijah 234, Emma Majesca (Thompson) 234, Jane 325, Jerri 223, Robert (Bob) Wilson 223, William C. 223
HUNTLEY, Mary Jenetta 320
HUNTLY, Harold 207, William 207
HUNTSINGER, John C. 51
HURLEY, Doris May 287, Nancy 197, Rebecca Margaret (Breedlove) 156
HURLOCK, Bea 206, Duane 180, 225
HURST, Fred 305
HURT, Mary Beth 145
HUSKINS, Barbara Michelle Johnson 146, Florence Johnson Walker 146, 229, Harry Leonard 146, 229, Jason Allen 146, 229, Ricky Allen 146, 181, 229
HUSTON, Charles 196, Foreman 148, Jennifer Jo (Hunter) 224, Leroy 148, Lola (DeWitt) 148, Magnolia (Ash) 148, Thomas 13
HUTCHINS, Charles 150, Edwin 150, Olive Marie (Smith) 150, Orin 62
HUTCHINSON, Marvin 153, Scott 29
HUTSON 28, Albert F. 100, W. 34, William 27, 28
HUTTINGER, Harry 23, 25
HUTTON, Lucy 326
HYMAN, Annette Grau 204
HYNDS, Bridget 224, Carl Jr. 224, Carl Sr. 224, Carol 224, Elaine 224, Grant 224, Jane 224, John Perry 224, Joseph 224, Mary Grace 224, Monica 224, Patrick 224, Philip 224, Raymond 224, Robert 224, Russell 224, Sandra 224

I

IDLER, Kathryn Weil 318
IMBLER, Brenda 224, Harvey 224, Hazel Ruth (Murphy) 308, Joseph 48, Laura Eva 287, Maxine 224, Mike 224, Shannon 224, Sherry 224
IMEL, James 201
IMLAY, Helen Mae 205
INDRUTZ, Alexander John 276, Gregory Paul 276, John 276, Katherine Elaine 276, Larry John 276, Lena (Hangu) 276, Matthew Christopher 276
INGALLS, Wilde 327
INGELLS, Ross 42, Abraham 224, Ann 224, Boone 224, Catherine 224, Claude 171, Claude F. 185, Dottie 23, Edith 224, Eleanor 224, Elizabeth 224, Emma 224, Etha Monelle 224, Eva Mae 224, Fredrick 224, George 224, Hale 171, Henry Boone 224, Iva Merle 224, James 171, 224, James Jr. 224, Jean 224, John 48, 171, 224, Joseph 224, Lena 171, Logan 171, Lulu 171, Marion 224, Matthew 224, Nancy Jane Mugg 224, Offa 171, Orval Verne 224, Rachel 224, Rosa 171, 224, Rosa Elizabeth (Lizzie) 183, Rosa Garr 224, Ruth 224, Susannah 224, Thomas 224, Wayne 73, 224
INGLE, Dorothy Turley 204, Frances 261, James D. 106, Mary Ellen 146, Norman David 146, Sharon Sue Kendall 146
INGLES, Abraham 48, G., Sr. 48, Jo Ann 257, 295, John 48, Judith 242, Kathryn 242, Nancy 242
INSULL, Samuel 127, 209
IRBY, Arlie Garnet 200
IRICK, Barbara 138
IRONSIDE, Harry 75
IRVIN 59, W.C. 95
IRWIN, Alice 225, Archie 225, Benjamin F. 180, Benjamin Franklin (Frank) 225, Benjamin Frederick (Ben or Fred) 225, Betty Ann 200, Carolyn 180, Carolyn J. 225, Cindy 225, Daniel 225, Donnie 180, 225, Edna 179, Emily 225, James Edmond (Ed) 225, Jesse C. 225, Joel 225, Joel Thomas 225, Joel Thomas (Tom) 225, Joyce 180, 225, Karen Lynn 227, Lucinda 225, Mary Alice 225, Mose 42, Phyllis 225, Priscilla (Morris) 225, Richard 313, Sam 39, Samuel 225, Samuel J. 225, Sherry 180, 225, Thomas J. 225, Thomas Jefferson (Jeff) 225, Virgile Lee 225
ISAAC, Ashley 238, Benjamin 238, David 238
ISENHOUR, Benjamin 151, Catherine Becker 151, Hans Nickolas 151, Jacob 151, Johannes 151, Rhoda Derry 151
ISENOR, Christie Michelle 283, Illa Nae Mae 283
ISHAM, Richard D. 125
IZOR, Susanna 342

J

JACKMAN, David 48, Minnie 51
JACKSON 59, Alfred "Alf" 180, Alice May 225, Andrew 35, Benjamin 29, 33, Betty 225, C.A. 34, C.S. 34, Carolyn 229, Charles 225, Clara 225, David E. 225, David S. 225, Diane 293, Dr. Paul 23, Dutton H. 189, E. 34, Elda 225, Ellen Louise 225, Ezra 215, 225, Frances 225, Frank 203, Franklin 187, Gideon T. 158, Gladys 294, Glen 225, Harriet 28, 33, Jane 33, Jefferson 53, 64, John W. 27, 33, Julia 225, June 225, Laura 225, Louisa 325, Marianne S. 308, Martha 143, Mary 214, 225, Melvin 225, Merrill 297, Michael 32, 243, Mildred 225, Osee 225, Ralph 225, Rebecca 147, Rebecca Moore 188, Susan 338, Wesley 27, William Thomas "Billy" 180
JACOBS, Catherine 215, Dortha 225, 237, 310, Gene 184, Hurshel 225, 310, Jackson 225, James 225, James Everett 225, Karlene 225, Kenneth 225, Matilda (Robards) 225, Milburn 225, Mildred 143, Samuel 225, Stella 225, Ward 225, 310
JACOBY, Iosa Ill 159, Mary Elizabeth (Haas) 254, William 254
JAMES, Beulah 170, Charles Wilson 225, David 33, Edith Minerva 226, Edith Minerva 144, Frank 225, J.A. 131, James 225, Jesse 225, Jesse (Black) 225, Johnathan Atkins 225, Johnathan Atkins 144, Julia A. 149, Lella 226, Marie 273, Martha 226, Matilda 226, Richard 225, Viola 149, William 326
JANNER, Brant Matthew 226, David Wayne 226, David Wayne 227, Donna Mae (Craig) 172, Karla Ann 226, Marjorie I. (Schick) 226, Melissa Diane 226, Nathaniel Lee 226, Shannon DeLei 226, Shannon DeLei 172, 227, Theresa Lynn 226, Wayne C. 226, 301, William J. 301, William J. III 226, William J. Jr. 226, 301, William J. Sr. 226, Zachariah Joseph 226
JANUSZKIEWICZ, Alexander George 234, Joseph 234, Joseph Kyle 234, Josephine Alexander 234, Rhonda Beth Karns 234, Samantha Jo 234, Walter Kyle 234
JAONS, Milton 33
JARRARD, Danny 206, Heather 206, Shannon 206
JARRETT, Bob 25, Deborah Kay 235, Dick 25, Fred Jr. 246, Heidi 246, Karen S. (Lindley) 246, Kay 25, Kent Allen 235, Richard Merle 235, Richard Merle Jr. 235
JAY, Alexander Thomas 227, Andrew Irwin 227, Austin "Pan" 227, Bathsheba Ellen 227, Charles Augustus 227, Charles Woods 227, Charles Woods 227, Cynthia Louise 227, Flora Alma 227, Gilbert "Gibb" D. 227, Grace 84, 108, Gregory Scott 227, Joseph P. 8, Joseph Powers 227, Joseph Walter 227, Juliellen 227, Kelly Nichole 227, Louise 227, Maude Piles 227, Melissa Ann 227, Naomi "Grace" 227, Nora Alliece 227, Samuel 227, Scott Thomas 227, Thomas 227, Thomas B. 8, Thomas Brush 227, William Oliver 227
JEFFERSON 14
JEFFRIES 248, John 23, 86
JENKINS, Daniel 175, David Howard 228, Elizabeth 144, Elmer 228, Frederick 228, Frederick Howard "Fred" 228, Heather Lynn 228, Howard G. 228, Irene 228, J.L. 79, Lucy H.

357

(Gray) 228, Mark Daniel 228, Milford 149, Rachel 3, 206, Richard 228, Richard Dean "Dick" 228, Robert 277, Robert Jr. 277, Sarah Lucinda 228, Tara Jean 228
JENNINGS, Emma 219, Margaret E. 51, Ruth Alice 108
JENSEN, Gregg 287, Nicholas Jon 287, Zachary David 287
JESIOP, Isaac 35, 37, Thomas 35, Todd 35
JESSUP, Elsie E. 314, John 97, 220, Reuben 45
JESTER, George 315, Patricia 305
JETER, William O. 60
JETT, Gailen 197, John Porter 305, Mattie (Chandler) 305, Paul 171, Quatia 305
JEWELL 91, Jack 180, 225, Lillie 287, Milley 33
JOB, Betty Kay 152
JOH, Anna 329
JOHANNING, Emil 115, Les 115, Teresa 115
JOHNS, Mary 323, Robert 'Bob' 53
JOHNSON 34, Abigail 66, Abram L. 231, Adam 272, Aimee 230, Albert Lincoln "Bert" 232, Albert Tell 284, Alfred Lincoln 232, Alice (Hendricks) 216, Amanda 229, Amy 229, Anderson 231, Andreas 272, Andrew 225, Andrew Jackson 228, Andrew Mark 228, Andrew Neil 228, Anne 229, Anne Nichelle "Shellie" 149, Anthony 229, Arnold Nel 275, Austin Lincoln 231, Austin Lincoln 230, 231, 285, B.B. 125, Barbara 53, Barbara Ann McInturff Barnett 146, 229, Barbara Michelle 181, Barbara Michelle 229, Belinda 230, 337, Belinda (Davis) 230, Ben 42, Benjamin 175, Benjamin Bates 232, Benjamin Bates 228, Bernice 203, Berry 229, Beverly 230, "Billy" 258, Birdie 89, Blanch 230, Bob 36, 232, Bradley 229, Brittany 246, Brooke 229, Bruce 334, Bruce Neil 228, Cale 230, Callie 230, Calvin 173, Cara 230, Caryn Dawn 231, Cathie Ann 231, Cecil 332, Charles 230, Charles F. 230, 285, Charles I. 70, Charles W. 231, Charles W. 231, Charlie 89, Christopher 230, Cindy Lynn 231, Clement 229, Cleo 275, Clyde 230, Comer 275, Courtney 230, Craig Douglas 228, Daniel R. 75, David 225, 230, 231, 285, 337, David Franklin 230, 285, Deborah "Debbie" Lynn 218, Dempsey 231, 232, Denese 131, Dennis 175, Diane 225, 229, Don 230, 285, Donna 175, Dorothy 36, 232, "Duke" Harold James 218, Edith 232, Edna 228, 232, Edward 169, 231, 232, Effie Marie 284, Elizabeth 175, 229, Elizabeth J. 293, Ellen 232, Elva 231, Emor 230, 285, Ernest Eugene "Gene" 232, Ethel 14, Everett 19, 36, Everett Guy 228, Fleming 231, 326, Florence 275, Frances 229, Fred Bates 232, Fred Bates 228, Gary Glenb 231, Gary Michael 230, Gary Wayne 218, George 228, Gertrude 228, Giles 229, Glen 169, 230, 231, 285, Glen Richard "Dick" 218, Gregory 229, Gregory Alan 218, Guy 36, H.K. 90, H.L. 95, Hannah Jane 231, Hansel 230, Hattie 239, Helen Ruth (Phillips) 228, Henry Clay 229, Hiram 233, Homer 75, 134, Horace 89, Hugh B. 158, I.C. 34, Isabelle 231, J. Grant 66, J.D. 133, Jack 230, Jackie 275, James D. 232, James R. 229, James R. 229, James W. 229, Jane 229, Jay C. 230, Jennie 212, Jennifer 230, Jeremiah 228, Jerry 230, Jesse 228, 232, Jim 272, Joan 230, Jody 230, Joe 296, Joel 229, Joel W. 229, John 158, 175, 230, 231, 337, John Butler 232, John Crittenden 232, John D. 228, John L. 7, 230, John W. 231, Joseph Bundy 231, Joseph D. 232, Joseph "Joe" Wayne 218, Justin 230, Katy 108, Kenneth 229, Kevin 229, Kimberly 230, Kristi 229, Kristina Nichole 228, L. Faye 158, Langston 229, Larry 85, 229, Larry D. 48, Laura S. 231, Lelan 229, Lennie S. 229, Leon Strangeman 230, 285, Lillian (Stratton) 231, Lois 22, Loisa 342, Louisa 231, Lowell 25, Lozell 21, Lucella 275, Lucinda 233, Lucy Jane Lewis 181, 229, Lyndon B. 210, Mahale Emmaline 231, Malcolm (Gig) 285, Malcolm "Gig" 230, Margaret 232, Margaret Elizabeth 231, Margaret Elizabeth 326, Maria (Enos) 233, Marian 232, Marilyn 175, 230, Mark 230, Martha 107, 229, Martha (Butler) 228, Martha Butler 232, Martha R. 231, Mary 146, 228, 229 Mary Ann 168, Mary Ann S. (Anna) 229, Mary Ann Waits 218, Mary Elizabeth 230, 285, Mary Johnson 228, Mary M. 231, Mary Mourning 232, Mary Rose 275, Mattie 89, Melissa 229, 231, "Melissa" 337, Michael 231, Michael Douglas 228, Mildred 228, Milley (Stanley) 231, Milley P. 231, Minerva 229, Miriam 153, Mourning 231, 232, Murl L. 327, Nancy 230, Naomi Grace 227, Nichole 229, Nikki Chantal 181, Nikki Chantal Diaz Neal 146, Oliver Morton 231, P. 34, Patricia 89, Paul 85, Penny Jean 218, Philip 229, Phineas W. 27, Rachel (Bundy) 326, Raymond 230, 285 Richard 230, Richard Chandler 230, Richard W. Jr. 225, Robert 175, 228, 231, 232, Robert Barclay 66, 228, Robert Cook 284, Robert Dexter 232, Robert Edward 230, 285, Roger 229, Rosalee 175, Roscoe Carmony 230, 285, Ruby Marie 275, Ruby Olive 189, Ruth (Phillips) 202, Samuel B. 231, Sarah Ann 231, Sarah Jane (Nelson) 173, Sarena 229, Scott Franklin 230, Servina 275, Shirley Ann 218, Stephanie 229, Stephen 225, Sterling 23, 26, Steve 45, Steven 25, Steven R. 186, Strangeman 231, Susan 229, Susan M. (McKillip) 272, Susannah 229, 268, Thelma 205, Thomas 228, 229, Thomas Michael 228, Timothy 229, Vannie 311, Virgil 218, 230, 285, Virginia Ann 275, Von 230, Walter Burton 181, Walter Burton Jr. 146, 275, Walter Burton Jr. 181, 229, 275, Wanda Gaye 275, Waneta 190, Wayne 230, Wayne Eugene 230, Wayne Ted 230, Wayne Theodore 285, Wendell 228, William 158, 205, 228, 229, 231, William "Billy" 113, William Earl 228, William R. 195, William T. 229
JOHNSON-ERICSON, Mary 285
JOHNSTON 86, Earl 326, Edith Marie (Turner) 326, Edwin 326, Frank W. 231, 326, Mary (Danfield) 326, Murray 333, Sarah 284, Stephen 154
JOLLY, Phyllis 264
JONES, Abba 212, Alice 295, Alta Cooper 141, Anthony Edward 232, Anthony Edward II "A.J." 232, Augusta 295, Barbara 287, Barbara Ann 223, 233, Benjamin 86, 253, Benjamin Franklin 233, Bland 18, Bob Jr. 75, Bonnie 140, Candy 3, Carlous 149, Carolyn Sue 149, Catherine T. 319, Christine Opal 185, Clifford D. 232, Daniel R. 46, Deborah 176, Earl 99, Edyth 200, F.B. 95, Flora Edna 155, Freda J. (Bradley) Jr. 109, George Thurman 155, H.H.P. 95, Henry 202, James Lafayette 233, James "Marion" 233, Jane 82, Jennifer 160, John Earl 233, John Earl III 155, 223, 233, John Earl III 109, John Earl Jr. 155, John Earl Jr. 223, 233, John "Earl" Sr. 109, 223, Jonathan 176, Kenneth L. 180, Korey Keith 278, Kristin Marie 232, L. Helen (Roush) 232, Lawrence Arnold James 233, Linda 149, Lori 149, Mabel Jane 253, Margaret (Weimer) 190, Martha 288, Martha Bell 233, Martha Jane 195, Martha Moriah (Breedlove) 156, Mary 86, Mary Ellen 189, Maud D. 183, Merlyn 78, Morris R. 66, Moses 52, Nora Maxine 233, Pamela 270, Patricia 270, Pop" 35, Ray 259, Richard L. 232, 301, Robert L. 55, Robin 109, Robin Jo 155, 217, 223, 233, Rosemary 78, Sandra 270, Scott 337, Stanley 270, Thelma Mae (Hughes) 109, Thomas John 232, Timothy Joel 232, Tina 149, Tom 270, Tom Jr. 270, Verna Hazel 233, Viola (Fair) 253, W.S. 34, William 52, 141, William P. 51
JORAY, Bruce Charles 233, Charles 233, Charles N. 123, Craig Alan 233, Delores (Egly) 233, Elizabeth Erin 233, Molly Kathleen 233, William 233
JORDAN, Alexander 233, Amanda F. 233, Anna M. 233, Bonnie Diane 233, Clara Louisa (Bartley) 228, Clarence Elmer 233, David 228, David E. 233, Donald Joseph 233, Estella May 233, Eva Mae 276, Evelyn 99, George 233, Grace 233, Herbert Leo 233, Janet Elaine 233, Jeffrey D. 233, Jerry 233, John Herman 233, John J. 233, John William 233, Joseph 233,274, Larry Wayne 233, Lee Dwayne 233, Leona Bruce 206, Lewellyn 233, Lyndall 73, Mandie 233, Mary Elizabeth 233, Mona Ione 233, Moses Benjamin 233, Rachel Louisa 228, Ralph L. 233, Richard 275, Rickie Dale 233, Robert G. 233, Ross G. 233. Ross Glen Jr. 233, Sarah (McClain) 233, Steven K. 233, Sumner Leo 233, Velma Iretha 233, Violet Ione 233, Vivian Irene 233, Walter T. 233
JOSEPH Sylvain 306
JOYCE, Joan (Towe) 224, John 97
JOYNER, Mary Lou 202
JUDKIN, W.B. 18
JULIAN, George 313
JULIEN, Susan 273
JULIUS, Amanda Ellen 141, Lois Delong 234, Penny Elaine 234, Philip 234
JULOW 39, Bill 42
JUMP, Catherine 273
JUNGHEN, Johann Henrich 266
JUSTICE, Charles V. 27, Deborah Vasta 229, Fannie 146, Harriett Roberts 229, Jake 229, Millie 201, William 33
JUSTUS, Mary Catherine 217

K

KABRICK, Ralph 207
KAIN, John 33
KAISER, Kaitlyn Elaine 223, William 223
KALLENBACH, Goldie 281
KALSCHEUR, Craig 196, Tracy (Freed) 196
KAMMEYER, Annalissa 139, Randy 139
KANABLE, Anita (Martin) 126, Catherine 234, Cecile 234, Charles 234, Curtis 234, David 234, Edith Josephine 234, Emma Cecile (Hodson) 234, George 234, Ira 234, Jacob 234, Jacob III 234, Jacob Jr. 233, John 25, 234, John E. 234, John Elmer 234, John Elmer 234, John Elmer Jr. 234, John Elmer Sr. 234, Levi 234, Magdalena (Enos) 234, Mickey 23, Milton Shakespeare 234, Robert 25, 234, Salome 234, Samuel E. 197, Samuel Enos 234,
KANDEL, Peter 235
KANE, Grace 27, John 27
KARNS, Anita 253, Anna Dean (Yager) 234, Bonnie (Hunter) 234, Brandon Scott 234, Dustin Gene 234, Earl Jacob 234, Emily Kristine 235, Gregrey Gene 234, Heidi Breanne 235, Jeffrey (Dean) Jr. 234, Jeffrey Dean 234, Joshua Adam 234, Kristopher Todd 234, Lowell Dean 234, Loyle Dean 234, Tyler Brandon 234
KARR, K.A. 34
KARSTEDT, W.M. 93
KASE, George H. 84
KASER, Eli 264, 344, Everett 264, Goldie Magdalena 264, Hollie 264, Richard 264, Toby 264
KASMEYER, Ed 197
KASPER, Jerome 299
KAUFFMAN, Clarence 42, Moses 222, Regina 204
KAUFMAN, Dan 326, Diane 148, Eva (Turner) 326, Jack 148, Johanna 79, Kim 148, Kristy 148, Kyle 148
KAUFMANS 39
KAUTZ, A.J. 103, Blanche 125, John A. 125
KAVANAUGH, Philemon 188
KAY, Anna Mae 203, Cheryl 183, Laura 284, Peter 284, Stafford 284
KAYLER, Bonnie 261
KAYLOR, Barbara Ann (McInturff) 181, David Waylon 181
KEARNEY, Caroline 247, Fred 247, Mark 247, Matt 247, Pauline 247
KECK, Catherine Ann (Poe) 167, Hazel Lulu 167, J. 48, Michael U. 167, Randy 85
KEELER, Ezra 268, Mariah 268, Nellie 268
KEENAN, Henry 13
KEESLING, Edith 275
KEIL, Margaret "Peggy" 233, Paul 233, Rosemary (O'Brien) 233
KEIM 42, A.L. 41, 180, 215, Abe 180, Carolyn Joan 180, M. Marjorie (Shrock) 180, Suzanne (Troyer) 180
KEISLING, L.M. 14, Lloyd 46
KEITER, Russell 225, Walter 140, 225
KEITH, Becky 230, Christie 230, Jeffrey Lynn 273, Jonathan Lynn 273, Robert S. 230, Susan 230
KELL, Elise (Fenske) 328, George 328, Harvey 328, Larry 328, Loraine (Mohr) 328
KELLAM, Harry M. 91, Janice 218
KELLAR, Abraham 235, Alton Eugene 266, Anna Lee 235, Catherine 235, Charles Frederick 235, Charles Richard 235, Claude Earl 235, David Wayne 235, Edward Bryant 235, Elizabeth Kuykendall 235, George 292, Georgia 311, Georgie Ann 235, Grace Maud 235, Isaac 235, Isaac Hite 235, Jane 235, Jane Grace 292, John Homer 235, Kathryn Elaine 235, Katie 13, Katie Adella 235, Leslie D. 235, Lewis Cass 235, Lewis R. 235, Lewis Ralph 270, Martha 235, Mary Ann 235, Mary Elizabeth 235, Michael 235, Minerva (Raynes) 292, Moses 235, Paul D. 235, Paul D. Jr. 235, Pearl 235, Phyllis Jean 145, Raymond L. 235, Rebecca Ellen 235, Sarah Kate 235, Susan 235, Susan Garr 235, William Agun 235, William Lloyd 235
KELLENBURGER, Ellen (Hines) 238, Harrison 238
KELLER, Anna Maria (Appolonia) 220, Armour 23, John 220
KELLETT, Patricia Jo (Maish) 252
KELLEY, Bob 143, Donald 143, E.W. 102, Ethel (Freeland) 143, Gary 143, Howard 143, John 143, Leona 50, 143, Leona Mae 143, Loren 143, Marjorie 143, Marlene 143, Mary C. 143, Oleta 50, 143, Richard 143, Shirley 143, Wilma 50, 143
KELLIE, Truman 97
KELLY, Robert Joe 320, Ann 336, Anna Watson (Calloway) 323, Barbara Jean 301, Brad Aaron 320 Connie 235, Daniel 235, David Wayne 320, Dessie (Rollins) 235, Dorothy 171, Edward 235, Eleanore 337, Elizabeth Tracy 235, Ethel Louise 322, Harriet Keiver 235, Helen Naomi T. 307, 320, Homer Edward "Dick" 235, Jackson 336, Jason Andrew 320, Jennifer 337, Jeremy Lee 320, Jesse Holman 235, Jesse Marion 235, John 235, Joseph 323, 337, Joyce Goodman 219, Julia Elaine 235, Kathryn Eloise 235, Kay 337, Kenneth 322, Kimila Ann 235, Kyle Richard 320, Lester 337, Lora Jane 235, Lowell Fredrick 235, Lucille 230, Lucinda Belle Monroe 235, Marilyn Jean 235, Marion Orval 235, Marjorie Joan 235, Marlita Ann 320, Martha (Baer) 322, Martha Alice Name 235, Mary 183, Max Allen 235, Michael 336, Michele D. Dyar 320, Oneda 235, Paul 171, Phillip Wayne 235, Ralph 320, Reba 235, Richard 235, Roy Ernest 235, Russell E. 235, Samuel Edward 235, Sarah 337, Sherrie Algeria 235, Shirley Jane 235, Vickie L. Kring 320, Walter 23, 86, Zena 25

KELSEY, Paul 46
KELSO, H.L. 79
KELVIE, Kathryn 139, Mary Jane Baskett 139, Patricia "Patsy" Albaugh 139, Russell 139, William 139
KEMP 113, Clarence 25, Jeff 293, Kari 293, Kasey 293, Kaylee 293
KEMPE, Carolyn 107
KEMPER, Alonco 220, F.S. 89, Franklin S. 203, John E. 219, LeRoy W. 70, Lon 223, Marion R. 220, Mary E. 219, Nada 223
KENDALL 41, Anna (Yoder) 236, Carl 203, Caroline (Schrock) 325, Christian J. 236, Elsie Fern 236, Emma 325, Eugene L. 236, Fred Earl 236, G.A. 90, Harold Richard 236, Henderson 267, Janalyce K. 213, Joanne E. 236, John "Big John" 235, John William 236, Joseph 235, 236, Joseph Terry 267, Lena Mae 203, Lewis Ren 236, "Little John" 236, Martha Anna 236, Mary Florence 236, Merle Marie 236, Monroe 42 Nathaniel 236, Paul 36, 38, Pauline (Booth) 203, Philip 236, Riley 343, Sherman 37, Simon 41, 325, Spike 42, Terry 236, Velma 36, 38, Vern E. 236, William Harvey 236
KENDALLS 39
KENDRICK, Bess 147
KENNARD, Susannah 212
KENNEDY 28, Albert F. 288, Claud 207, Dorothy 107, 207, James Wesley 144, John 207, Malcolm Dean 288, Mary Louise 225, Richard Albert 288, Thomas Joe 288, Willie 40
KENNEDYS 39
KENNER, Regina 33
KENT, Gary Woolley 333
KENWORTHY, Allen 19, Amos 65, Benjamin 236, Bertha Estella 257, Carrie 14, Clarence 308, Clarence W. 257, Clarence William 288, Clarence William "Willie" 236, David 237, Donna 23, Earl 340, Elizabeth 19, Elizabeth Small 307, Florence J. 288, Floyd T. 237, Hanna Stout 340, Jennie Colburn 236, Jonathan 237, Lula (Terwilliger) 237, Marsella (Summers) 237, Martha (Layton) 237, Marvin Joe 308, Mary Carter 236, Matilda 19, Maude G. 236, Maude G. (Etherington) 288, Maude G. Etherington 257, Melody 237, Merrell 236, Michelle 237, Milton 340, Murray 65, 340, Naomi (Henderson) 237, Rosalea (Farris) 295, Ted 25, Thomas 237, Uriah 236, Vera Small 307, Wayne 237, William Riley 237, Willis 66, 340
KENYON, Betsey 152
KEPLER, Elden 56, Minnie 64, William 55, 56, William E. 305
KEPNER, Eliza Jane 191
KERBY, Alda 237, 308, Bernard 237, 308, Bill 237, Catherine 237, Catherine (Fahey) 237, Catherine (Kate) 237, Charles 237, 308, Clarence 237, Elsie 237, Emma (Smeltzer) 225, 267, Eugene 237, Eva 237, Everett 237, 308, Fred 237, Gene 237, Hannah 237, Hannorah 237, Harry 225, 237, 308 Helen 237, Homer 308, Homer (Gus) 237, James 237, James Bernard 237, Jeremiah 237, Joseph 237, Josephine 237, 279, 308, Julia 237, Leo 237, 308, Leona 237, Lydia (Crandall) 237, Margaret 237, Marie 237, Mary 237, Mary (Molly) 237, Michael 237, Nina 237, 308, Patrick 237, Paul 237, Pearl 237, 308, Phyllis 225, 237, Robert 237, Timothy 237, Vada 237, 308, William 225, 237, 267, William H. 237, William Henry 237, 308, 343, William T. 237
KERKHOFF, Emma Folkening 287, Mary 287
KERN, J.H. 18, Herman 42, John W. 311, Lewis 220, Ora 238, Susann 263
KESHAN, Bette 302
KESSELL, Geneva 181
KESSLER, Christena Emaline 192, Cora 21, Glenn 240, Oliver 240, Ruby 240
KESSNER, Clarence 35
KETCHUM, R.T. 75
KEYTON, G. 34
KIBLER, Mat 229
KIDD, Susanna Williamson 156, William Henry 156
KIDDER, Charles 305, Mary J. 253, William 245
KIDWELL, Bedford M. 237, Benton M. 237, 238, Beulah 238, Beulah Mae 237, Buford Marion 237, Chris 238, Clio Wilson 237, 238, Cynthia 238, Deborah Louann 238, Derrick 238, Frances (Bowers) 154, James Eric 238, James Kenneth 237, Jason Kenneth 238, Kenneth James 238, Kenneth Randall (Randy) 238, Nora Helen (Hagan) 237, Pam 238, Steven Wilson 238
KIETHLEY, Shirley 290
KIGER, John 179
KILANDER, Francis Marion 251, Letta Ellen (Younce) 251
KILE, J. Frank 61
KILGORE, Emma 306
KILKUSKI, Mary Ann 177
KILLEN, Emma 211
KILTY, David John Patrick 206
KIMBALL 27, Thomas 48
KIMBEL, Charles Western 162, Iva 162, Rosa Ellen (Stewart) 162
KIMBLER, Albert 96
KING 184, "Billy" 336, Camela Ann 303, Charles 42, Darline 239, Don 239, Edna 134, Edward Grant 272, Ellen 239, Emily 138, Florance 239, Frances Andres 272, Frank 42, 240, Franklin Gene 239, Geraldine 239, Ida Ellen (Werst) 272, Indiana 270, Ione 239, Jack Allen 287, James 134, Jay 134, Jerry 134, Joan 239, Joe 42, John G. 48, Leslie 239, Leslie Norman 239, Loeta 239, Luann (Schmitt) 303, Lynn 230, Mark Emmerson 303, Nancy T. 300, Nina 299, Noah 28, Paul Edmund 303, Ray 23, Rebecca 178, Robin 239, 240, Roger 134, Ronald 134, Roy 64, 239, Samuel 27, Sara Jane 65, Seth 343, Shirley (Kitts) 240, Shirley Jean (Kitts) 239, W.E. 161, William 16
KINGERY, Christian 59, Lillian 107, Richard 23, Sarah 317
KINGMAN 34
KINGREY 146
KINGSEED, 39, Afton 43, Afton (Swingley) 240, Albert 41, 240, Albert Christopher 239, Alec 40, Alexander 239, 240, Anthony 239, Anton 239, Beverly Lynn 240, Bob 43, Catherine 239, Charles 239, Charles Edward 239, Christian 239, Elizabeth 239, Emelia 239, Frank 239, Geneva Madge 239, 240, Glen 240, Greg 240, Henry 239, Jane 240, Jean Carolyn 240, Jim 240, John W. 239, Joseph 239, Julie 240, Kelly 239, 240, Kelly Robert 239, 240, Lena Elizabeth 239, Lucinda 239, Margaret 239, Martha (Saul) 240, Martin 239, Mary 228, 239, 240, Mary (Duckwuler) 240, Mary Lovina 239, Max 239, 240, Mildred 107, Mildred (Modak) 240, Milton Peter 239, Nancy Lee 240, Patricia 240, Peter 39, 239, 240, Ralph 41, 42, 240, Ralph Alexander 239, Robert 240, Robert Lee 239, 240, Robert Lee 240, Robin (King) 240, Rosa 239, Rosa May 239, Sophia 239, Terry 239, 240, Terry Lee 240
KINGSLEY, Robert 48, George 113, 224, 258
KINNAMAN, Leroy 92
KINNEY, Althea 187, Henry, 314, Lucile 315 Lucille 314
KINSEY, Lola (Barnett) 147, Robert J. 26, Virginia 267
KIPLINGER, Catharine 169
KIRBY 39, Dian 185, 314, Effie 237, Florence 237, Frank 180, Harley 237, Jim 42, Joseph 237, 257, 295, Maxine (Rinehart) 295, Maxine (Rinehart) (Stull) 257, Michael 237, Tim 42, Walter 237
KIRK, Bertha 151, Chester 151, Dora Isabelle (Jacobs) 238, Elisah E. 238, Ernest 151, George 151, Jeffrey Allen 238, Jesse 151, John Ernest Sr. 238, Kenneth Allen 238, Laura Katherine 238, Maude 151, Mildred Marie (Haley) 238, Phyllis Irene (Bunnell) 238, Richard Dennis 238, Robert Sr. 9, Tori Lynn 238
KIRKEN, Blanche Ann 156
KIRKENDALL, Bob 25, Carolyn Sue 238, Claude James 238, Cynthia Sue 239, Deborah Lynn 239, Donald Winston 238, Edna Moulder 238, Ettis 238, Ettis (Howard) 238, Ettis Henry 238, James 238, James Richard 239, James Vernon 238, Jamie Renee 239, Jane Ann 238, Jean Ellen 238, John Neal 238, John Neil 238, Marianna 238, Marilyn Lue 238, Martha (Lucille) 238, Robert 26, Robert "Choppy" 25, Robert Virgil 238, Sarah Elizabeth 238, Sarah Elizabeth Maish 238, Waldo Jr. 238, Waldo Moulder 238
KIRKER, Thomas 35
KIRKHAM, Rosabelle 96, Vernis 96
KIRKMAN, Jennifer 207, Peter 48, 50, Ramona 183
KIRKPATRICK, Flora 199, Mariah 318, Mona Lee 280, Paul 59, Thomas 174
KIRTLEY 141, Abraham 241, Anna Eliza Watts 329, Frances E. (Bland) 241, Frances Elaine 241, Francis 241, Jessie Agnes (Branson) 241, John 241, Judith (Calloway) 241, Laura Susan 241, Lemuel 241, Lewis 241, Lidea (Underwood) 241, Lucille 241, Lucy Mae 241, Margaret (Roberts) 241, Mary (Lewis) 241, Mary Jane (Covert) 241, Noah Raymond 241, Ottis Franklin 241, Thomas Sr. 241, William Franklin 241,
KISER, Connie 192, O. 27
KISTLER, Bertha 64, Mary 179
KITCHEN, Clara White 340, Gracie 340, Manson C. 340, Miriam 340
KITTS, Fred 239, William 239
KLECKNER, W.A. 83
KLENCK, Marilyn Jean (Spence) 173, William John 173
KLEYLA, Anabel 167, Gladys Doggett 167
KLINE, Roscoe Alva 181, Sarah Gano 181, William 181
KLING, Nellie Leona 241
KLINGELSMITH, Nora 241
KLINGMAN 28, Albert 241, Andrew Elmer 241, Bernice Roberta 241, Christina 241, Cora E. 241, Edna E. 241, Erma E. 241, Frederick 241, Ketric 241, Letta M. 241, Olaus W. (Pete) 241, Roberta 294, 295, Titus Andrew 241, William 241, 295
KLINGMANN, Christian 241, Elisabethe Friedericke 241, Georg Peter 241, Johann Georg 241, Katharine 241, Luise 241, Wilhelm 241, Harry 301
KNABLE 233, Jacob Sr. 233
KNICK, Lucy 281
KNICKERBACKER, David Buel 91
KNICKERBOCKER, Artmesia 342
KNIGHT, Aaron David 143, Diane Ruth 143, Ida May 310, Isaac N. 48, J.V. 83, Traci Lynn 143, Willy 117
KNIPE, Dorothy Hunt 155, Harry George 241, John 241, John Richard 241, Julia Lenore 241, Julie Ann 24, Kathryn Ann 241, Samuel 241, Thomas 241, Thomas Jr. 241, Thomas Landle 241, Virginia 156, 241, Willis Hickam 241, Zora Ethel 241
KNIPE-MILLS, Julia 155
KNOLL, David 337, Eric Young 337, Kelly 337
KNOTE, Emily 189
KNOX 86, L.E. 47
KOCH, Alice 196
KOEHLER, Alma 153
KOENIG, Laura 299, Lulu Belle 78
KOENIGSAMEN, Anton 239
KOFAHL, Harry 141, Maxine 141, Nadine 141
KOHLERIN, Anna Maria 342
KOHN, Misch 76
KOLB, Charles 179, Fred 179, Natalie 179
KOLLATH, Irene 174
KOLLER, Elizabeth 343
KOMITT, Jacob 19
KONG, Alexis 315, Kiana 315
KONK, George 244, Jany 244, Jesse 244, Lucy 244, Luther 244, May 244, Sarah 244
KOON, Clinton Harry 275, Todd 275
KOONTZ, Walter 240
KORBA, Walter 23
KORTE, Adelherd 302, Henry 302
KOSEK, Cheryl Elizabeth 328, David Matthew 328, Krista Marie 328, Michael Richard 328
KOSNOT, Ruth (Tate) 234
KRALL 248
KRAMER, May Caroline "Carrie" 182
KRANER, Augustus G. 242, Beth Ann 242, Charles 192, Charles Allen 158, 242, Charles Allen 242, Charles "Charlie" 242, Connie 242, Edwin Marion 158, Edwin Marion "Liz" 242, Elizabeth Ann 242, Jack 242, Jerry 242, Joan 242, Karen 242, Karen Yvonne 242, Karla 242, Karla Yvette 242, Karol 242, Karol Ann 242, Kathryn Jo 242, Kathy 242, Katlynd Mary Jo 242, Kelli 242, Kelli Lynn 242, Kerri Grace 242, Kerri Kraner 242, Kurt 242, Kurt Allen 242, Mark 242, Mary Roxie (Browning) 242, Michelle 242, Rose Ann (Fravel) 242, Zakary Allen 242
KRATZER, Barry 32, Candace 238, Kenneth 204, Thomas 204
KRAUSS, Martha Katherine 287
KRESS, Henrietta 218, Minervia 220, Robert 337
KRIBBS, Anita 157
KRING 28, Elijah 242, Frank 242, George 242, Howard 243, Johan Jost 242, Roger 243, Susan 243
KRISE, Bert C. 301, Clorus D. (Beard) 301, Constence Sue 151, Leonard William 301, Sandra Ann 301
KRITZER, L. 34
KROEGER 94
KROGH, Lois (Barner) 221
KROMBERG, William H. 333
KRULL, Edwin 106
KRUPP, Wayne 56
KUBLY, Jennifer Ann 226, 227, Melissa Diane (Janner) 227
KUFFER, Ludwig 314
KUHLMAN, Fred 293, Kelly 293, Nicole 293, Tyler 293
KUHNS, D. 34, James 23, Joseph 90, Leroy 104, Thelma 184
KULL, George 172
KUNTZ, Barbara B. Miller 285, Cameron 155, Corbin 155, Delores 243, 272, Elmer 243, George Heinrich 314, George Leroy 285, Harry 243, Jacob Elmer 272, Jacob Elmer 243, Jeannette (McNabney) 313, John Robert 285, Juliana (Woolf) 243, Leo 243, Mark 155, Mary Jane 243, 272, Mary Leona 243, Nellie 28, Otto Elmer 243, 272, 313, Robert 243, Robert Daniel 243, Russell 243, Theresa 243, 272, Theresa Margaret (Fleming) 272, William 243, 272
KURTZ, Arthur 243, Bertha Conkle 244, Catheryn 243, 244, Cathryn 230, Charles 29, 243, 24, Charles E. 230, Christian 244, Christian A. 243, Doloris 325, Dora Hepperly 243, Elizabeth Grau 245, Gretchen 107, Harley 243, Ira 243, John 243, Lester T. 32, Linda 325, Louie 325, Mable 230, 243, Robert 243, Rosa 243, Roscoe 243, Sandra 325, William 325
KWIATT, Tamra Cravens 147
KYGER, George Washington 144

L

LAAG, Ester 288
LABOYTEAUX, Anna 28
LACEY, James 146, LeRoy 122, Rosella 146, 294
LACKEY, Reason 48, 96
LACLUYSE, Debbie 231
LACY, Charles 3, Henry J. 140
LADD, John 313
LADEN, William 53
LADOW, Arthur 216
LAFOUNTAINE, Archangel 264, Catherine Richardville 264, Francis 264
LAGGE, Elaine E. 199
LAHN, Carolyn 314, Ernest 314, Minnie E. 314
LAIRD, Alvin C. 312, Charles 14, Lavinia R. (Somsel) 312
LAKE, J.W. 138
LAMAR, Rosemary 261
LAMB, Absolem 65, Benjamin F. 65, C. Ray 48, Charles 65, Esau 167,

H. 34, Hannah Naomi 167, Henry 167, Hezekiah 167, John 44, 167, 207, Josiah 167, Lydia 167, 207, Ned 48, R. 46, Ralph 278, 343, Sarah 170
LAMBERSON, Daisy 184, Inez 234
LAMBERT, Annis 243, Annis Preble 243, Betty 243, Carol 214, Cassie Ann 153, Catherine 243, Deborah 243, Edna 243, Flora Flynt 243, Helen Virginia 180, J. David 305, Jacob 243, John 243, Kate 243, Lawrence 243, Lawrence Reid 180, Linnie "Joanne" 180, Madge 243, Mary 243, Myrtie 243, Ora 243, Reid 180, 243, Ward 243
LAMM, Michael Aaron 159, Phyllis O. 159, Vivian Audrey 159, William Howard 159
LAMNECK, Forrest 62
LANCASTER, James 51
LAND, Caroline Rayl 291, Christopher Michael 244, Hershel 204, Ira Delere 243, Jerry Lee 243, Jerry Lee, Jr. 243, Kari Leah 244, Kerry Lee 244, Robert Delere 244 Sherry Lee 244
LANDES, Elizabeth Naas 317, Heinrich 317, Sarah 295
LANDIS 273
LANDON, George 131, George W. 13, Hugh McK. 131
LANDRETH 189
LANDRUM, David 44, 240, Elydia A. 212, Mildred 240, Nancy Jane 21, Thomas 15, 44, 305
LANE, Caleb 27, 33, Isaac 196, James 16
LANGLEY, Alice 244, Archie 225, Arminda A. 244, Curtis 244, Dylan 232, Edom 244, Elce 244, Ellen J. 244, Emeline 244, Emmia 244, Hannah (Smith) 244, Jessica 232, John 244, John C. 244, Jonathan 244, Jonathon 244, Louisa Ellen 244, Mary (Swisher) 225, Mary Elizabeth 244, Namomi 244, Rebecca 244, Rhoda 225, 244, Rosa 244, Samual 244, Samual Gidion 244, Samuel Edwin 232, Silas 225, 244, Tence 244, William 244
LANGSCHIED, Jim 125
LANNING 56
LANTZ 41, Barbara 28, Carolyn 337, Chris 39, Ella 279, Floyd 39, Fred 39, 42, George 42, Hamilton 42, Jack 39, 40, 43, John M. 241, Joseph 25, Lowell 43, Lynn 30, Melissa 325, Salome 28, Sidney F. 28, Steve 30
LAPE, Elmira Margaret 234
LAREAU, Ferne Victoria 287
LARKE, John 309, 310, Lisa 309
LAROW, Nancy 196,
LAROWE, Christopher 283, Dale 283, Edith 107, John 24, Mark 283, Matthew 283, Melinda 283, Myron 283
LARSEN, Lloyd 80, Lameta Rose (Smith) 244
LARUE, Bert Ray 244, Dan 244, Delma Jean (Smith) 244, Gary 244, Luna Wicks 244, Mautice E. (Jack) 24, Melvin Spencer 244
LASH, Barbara 201
LASLEY, Eliza Ann 292
LATURNER, John 313
LAUDEMAN, Linda 277
LAUDERBAUGH, Nathan 312, Nathaniel C. 185, Nicole 312
LAUER, Richard 90
LAUGHLIN, Daniel 33
LAUGHNER, Dawn Marie 148, Elizabeth (Ottinger) 192, William 192
LAURELL, David 286, Matthew 286, Richard A. 286, Stephen 286
LAURENCE, Norman T. 193
LAUSCH, Brian 243, 245, Carolyn 245, Edwin 245, Eric 245, Eugene 245, Jonel 245, Joshua 245, Judy 27, 32, 243, 245, Keith 27, 32, 243, 245, Kristen 245, Mary 245, Ralph 230, 243, 244
LAUTENSCHLAGER, Daniel Jay 280, Erma 280, Gary 280, Glen 280, Jon Bryan 280, Matthew Gary 280, Tracy Carol 280
LAVENDUSKIE, Doris M. 213
LAVENGOOD, Martha Jean Pyke 36
LAW, Zien Ellen 274
LAWERENCE, Viola J. 166
LAWLESS, Charles 327, Elizabeth (Graves) 327, Grady 327, James Bernard 327, Mary Ruth 327, Michelle Irene 251, Patrick Van 251, Van 251
LAWRENCE, Alvester 332, Anna Rebecca 245, Charles 332, Chesley 332, Daniel 220, Delia 332, Earnest Basil 245, Edna J. 245, Edward 332, Elizabeth 255, Elsie C. 245 Eva 245, Everett 332, Fred 332, Gordon 149, Hannah Jane (Orr) 332, Jacob 15, Jacob S. 245, John 245, John Frank 245, John Showalter 245, Junior 332, Laura Etta 245, Lela 332, Lester 332, Linda 179, Magdalena Bach 245, Margaret Jane 245, Martha E. 245, Mary Catherine 245, Mary Jane 234, Ralph 62, Sarah 245, Sarah S. Showalter 245, Valentine 245, Waity Belle 245
LAWSON, Courtney Brooke 335, Darr Kimberlyn 335, Kim-berlyn Odel 335, Michelle (Lindley) 246, Nathaniel Wayne Lindley 246, Sarah Ellen 167
LAY, Cory Johnathon 148
LAYMAN, John 96
LAYMON, Sarah Emeline 312
LAYTON, Robert 179, Sarah 33
LEACH 140, Betty Jo 192, John M. 58, Joshua Clinton 123, Mary Florine 213, Pearl 18, Susan E. 167
LEAF, Polly 292
LEAP, Alva 291, David 291, Dudley 291, Joseph 284, Samuel 291, Sophia (Mc- Cloud) 291
LEARNER 28, 162, B. 34, Barnhart 58, Benjamin Franklin 27, Bernhart 18, 27, 31, 33, Carl 97, J.W. 34, Phoebe Bates 58
LEAS, Ina (Abney) 138, Ralph 138
LECKLITNER, Michelle 139
LECKRONE, Helen Iretha 233, Mary 215
LEE, Abraham 37, Benjamin 333, Beverly 253, Cyrus 333, Elizabeth E. 338, Elmer 50, Gurney 62, Henry 144, John 50, Lloyd 52, Manford L. 332, Martha Ellen 338, Mary Duncan Rayl 291, Richard 14, 140, Richard 'Joe' 140
LEEDS, J.M. 125
LEESON, Nancy Ellen 270
LEFFERT, Betty Overton 153
LEFFLER, Beverly A. 179, Nancy 326
LEFFUL, Katricka 204
LEGER, Camela 157, 199, 255, Leo 157, 199, 255
LEGG, Elbert 305
LEHMAN, Franklin William 203
LEHMANN, Aaron 29, David Arthur 299, Jacob 299, Ruth 196
LEHR 248
LEIBENGUTH, James Monroe 304, Julia Ann 304, Maria (Wehr) 304
LEIGHTON, Lilias (Madge) 313
LEISURE, Effie 324, George W. 323
LEITER, Arlene 248, Cloyce 248, Devon 248, Ellen 248, Eric 248, Everett 248, Fred 248, Gale 248, Gerald 248, Shirley 248, Vicki 248
LELLINGTON, John 33
LEMASTER 28, Arlene 284, William 27, 34
LEMASTERS, Aneta 230, Isaac 33, Mary Emma 269
LEMING, Mahala 234
LEMLEY, Brenda Carol 173
LEMMO, Margaret (Peggy) 332
LENEHAN, Jane 245
LENINGTON 28, J.T. 34
LENNINGTON, Mary Priscilla 225, Sarah Jane 246
LENNOX, Mary 214
LENON, Levi 145
LEON Vandivier 116
LEONARD, Eli 191, Horace Charles 181, Joab 191, Margo (Mason) 256, Marie Elizabeth Pohl 181, Relta 247, Sara 108, Virginia Barbara 181
LETT, Balaam 245, Beverly Ward 245, Cynthia 245, Daniel 245, John Osborn(e) 245, Luranna 245, Margaret Serilda 245, Martha R. 245, Nancy 329, Sally 245, Sampson 245, Sarah (Sally) Osborn(e) 245, Sarah Ann 245, Thomas H. 245, Walter Goodhue 245
LEWE, Mona 256
LEWELLEN, David 275
LEWELLING, Bessie Alice 327
LEWELLYN, Melissa 212
LEWIS, Aloma M. 229, Betsy 229, Bill 21, 26, Charles 245, Charles Kimball 254, Charlie 25, Daniel 336, David Adkins 229, 275, David Jr. 229, Deborah Vasta Justice 275, Elbert B. 229, Garrett 229, George 33, Gerald 91, Gilbert 25, Harriet 229, Harriet Adkins 229, Harriet Gerber 76, Ida Belle 208, James Mathew 229, James Willard 229, John W. 27, Julia A. 229, Maisie 220, Marthy J. 229, Massey Mae 229, Melba Elizabeth 254, Myrtle 234, Nancy Jane 229, P.J. 95, P.M. 95, Reba 318, Samuel 27, 33, 229, 275, Sarah E. 229, Servania 229, Susannah 148, Thomas G. 229, Toka May 229, William 229, William T. 229, William Terrell 148
LICHTENWALTER, Daisy 247
LIECHTY, Carolyn Rae (Bailey) 295
LIEPLER, Nancy 33
LIGGETT, Dawson 23
LIGHT, Anthony Bryan 232, Christian 254, Sarah Cormany 254
LIGHTFOOT, Nancy Margaret (Reeder) 150, Newton 15, Rachel Laney 150, Sarah 278
LILLARD, Gladys Lucille 201, 312, Jerry 201
LINCOLN, Abraham 321, 340, Adeline 187, Daisy Mae 333, 335, Fannie Mae (Tanner) 333, John 333, John T. 188, Nancy Hanks 279
LINDLAY, Jonathan 177
LINDLE, Eveline 234
LINDLEY, Albert 231, Alisha 246, Amanda Almeda 246, Ambrose 245, 246, Ambrose Eldon 246, Aron 177, Beulah 318, Charles 29, 33, 245, 246, Clyde 66, Doris Winifred 246, Earnest 246, Elinor 177, Elizabeth 317, Elnora 245, 246, Ernest 246, George 197, Glen 231, Guliema 176, Hannah 245, 246, Harriet 245, 246, Isabella 245, Isabelle 246, J. 34, James 160, 245, 246, James R. Jr. 246, James Robert 246, James Robert Sr. 246, Jenny 245, 246, John 48, 160, 245, 246, John L. 246, John L. 246, John W. 246, Jonathan 176, 177, Jonathon 246, Karen 246, Keith D. 246, Lavina 245, 246, Louisa 245, 246, 34, Lyddia 246, Lydia 245, Margaret Hollowell 317, Marsha 246, Martha 245, 246, Mary 160, 176, 245, 246, Mary Elizabeth 246, Mary Hannah 246, Matt 246, Nancy 245, 246, Nina 219, Norvel 21, Owen 177, Queen Amy 333, Rachel 245, 246, Rowena Corrine 160, Ruth 65, Samuel 160, 245, 246, Samuel Arthur 246, Sarah 245, 246, Simon 245, 246, Susannah 245, 246, Tence 245, 246, Thomas 245, 246, 317, Troy 246, W.W. 21, 104, Walter 160, Wanita 246, William 245, 246, Wilmer 46, 66, Winifred 246, Zachariah 177
LINDSAY, Conrad 23, James 158, John 68, Virginia 158
LINDSEY, Harriet Francis 144, Joseph 144
LINEBACK, Clifford 100, Robert C. 187, Roberta 21
LINES, Rolland 197
LINK, Margaret Elizabeth "Peggy" 249
LINN, Carly 301, Jeff 301, Winifred Joan (Jay) 227
LINSDAY, N.R. 123
LINSICUM, Caleb 35, George 35
LINZEY, Cecilia 337, Joel 337, Robert 337
LIPINSKI, Jim 25, John 25
LISTON, Catherine F. 197
LITTLE, Elizabeth (Mast) 232, Elsie Mae 268, Hertha (Collett) 334, Ira P. 335, Juanita 99, Margaret 230, Margaret Elizabeth 189, Mariah Christine (Sylvester) 335, Sanford 232, Seth 337, Steve 337, Tressie 230, Tressie Irene 232
LITTLER, Eliza Jane 146, John 146, Joseph H. 226
LITTRELL, Wilburt 70
LITWILLER, Christian 160, David 160, Elizabeth (Lichti) 160, Maria (Miller) 160, Peter 160
LIVELY, Danita Lynn 254
LIVELY-MARTIN, Katlyn Marie 254
LIVINGSTON, Lilly 202, Pauline 284
LOBECK, Walter J. 84
LOCK, Abraham 246, 247, Antrim 247, Daniel 246, Edgar 247, Eli 247, Elias 247, George 247, John Abraham 246, Laura 247, Louisa 246, Mary 246, Michael 246, Rebecca 333, Sarah 247, William 247
LOCKE, Abraham 247, 248, Antrum 248, Atrium 140, Charles H. 247, Daniel 248, Diane 247, E. 34, Eli 222, Elias 247, 248, Elsie 247, Frederick Omada 247, George 248, George L. 247, Harry Paul 247, Hazel Lucy 247, Jerry Frederick 247, John 248, John Edgar 248, Kate 222, Kate L. 248, Laura 248, Louis 248, Lucy Marurette (Grinslade) 205, Lula Belle 248, Michael 265, Mike 248, Philip R. 247, Sara Catherine 248, Sarah (Yager) 222, Sarah A. 265, Sarah Brown 247, Sarah M. 90, Susannah (Lyons) 265, Thomas 222, Thomas Jesse 248, William 248, William Frederick 247
LOCKHART, Sara Weyand 331
LOCKRIDGE, Andrew 33, John D. 27, 33
LOCUST, Adaline 15
LOFFER, Christian 27, 31, 33, Daniel 27, Simon 33, Simon L. 27, Solomon 219
LOHRMAN, George 48
LOINS, Susannah 313
LOMAN, Dorothy 262, Edith 253, 262, Gary 304, Gary Davis 286, Gladys Marie 303, Greg 304, Gregory 286, Jeff 304, Jeffrey Todd 286, Paul 304, Paul C. 286
LONG, Alice 153, Amel E. 276, America 248, Blanche 248, 269, Carl 248, 269, Carmon 19, Carolyn 238, Catherine 153, Charles W. 19, Chester Clarence 174, Clarence 248, Dale 248, 269, Darla 325, David 48, 248, Donna 248, Eleanor 248, Eliza (Hamilton) 148, Eliza Hamilton 276, Eliza Jane 248, Elizabeth 324, Ellen 248, Elsie 248, Elsie Mae Krall 174, Esther 248, Everett 248, Grace 248, Gracie 269, Harry 248, Jacob T. 269, Jacob Thomas 248, James 153, 248, James Thomas 148, 276, John 249, John T. 248, John Thomas 248, Lola Mae 248, Madge 248, 269, Margarate 248, Margaret (McClanahan) 148, Martha 248, Mary 248, Mary Ann 248, Mary Ellen 197, Mary Frances 248, Mary J. (Thorn) 269, Maxine 248, Mazie 248, 269, Norma 139, Omar 269, Omer 248, Omer F. 174, Paul Denton 153, Polly 248, Regena 197, Robert 248, 323, Robert M. 248, 269, Robert M. 248, Roscoe 248, 269, Roy 153, Ruth 248, Sally (Helms) 216, Sarah 149, Sophronia 248, 323, T.A. 18, 59, 323, Tanya Cheri 153, Thelma 248, Thomas A. 13, 148, 248, Thomas Ammon 248, 249, William 248, William Harry 174
LONGFELLOW, Ann 169, Elizabeth Ellis 326, John 326, Mary Katherine 50
LOOP 39, Henry 27, 249, James David 249, James Paul 249, John Nicholas 249, Joseph Brice 249, Joseph Marsh 249, Margaret Elizabeth "Maggie" 249, Peter 249, William Lowell 249
LOPEZ, Louis 233
LORD, Ruth 154
LORDEMANN, Francis 94
LORDING, Fred 194
LORENZ, Catherine 297, George 42, 43, Henry 39
LOUCKS, Michelle 165
LOUIS, Mike 319
LOUISE, Helen Orpha 314
LOUKS, Beverly 175, Floyd 175
LOVE, Iva Ruth 239
LOVEGROVE, Rosemary Goyer 202
LOVEJOY, Charlotte 324, Jacque Lynn 147, James L. 147, Kathleen 324, Minnie Mae 249, Miriam 324, Peter 324, William Shell 324
LOVEJOY-SISSON, Janet Lee 147
LOVELACE, Beth Ann 157, 255
LOVELACE, Robert 157, 255
LOW, Celestia 'Lettie' Francis 188
LOWBERT, Martha M. 202
LOWE 86, 292, Ann 265, Ann (Coverdale) 148, Bessie 217, Carl James 217, Dorothy Irene 217, Edith Marie 217, Edward 217, Isaac Corneilous 217, John 59, 148, John C. 217, Lorena 230,

M.A. 95, Mary 217, Patty Lou 217, Voris (Buss) Lee 217
LOWERY, Dawn Louise (Parkhurst) 282, Derek Wayne 282, Donald 223, Eileen Ruth 249, Gary Lee 282, Loyal 249, Nora 249
LOWLETT, Franklin 314, Gertrude Blanche 314, Katherine Massey 314
LOWRY, Christopher 235, David 235, Edith G. 298, Elizabeth 298, Jeffrey 235, John 298, Joseph 48, Matthew 235, Nora (Smith) 298, Samuel A. 51, Walter 298
LOY, Ethel 193, Lois 153
LOZIER, John 256, Lova (Mason) 256, Martha 257
LUCAS, Alice (Walls) 250, Azariah 250, Bill 41, Brian K. 249, Edward 273, Frieda A. 249, George 50, George Charles 273, Gladys Marie (Hogue) 250, James 50, James Edward 273, Kevin A. 249, Lucien Bruce 250, Mary Edna 273, Ruth Elizabeth 273, Stanley A. 249, Carlos Jose 162
LUCIA, Diego Arbelaez 162, Elva 162, Juan Gregorio 162, Toni 283
LUCKEY, James 33
LUCUS, Lucia 308
LUCY Jane Lewis Johnson 275
LUDWIG, Amy Jo 322, Donald William 322, Martha Colleen 'Marty' 322, Mildred Marie (Ryan) 322
LUEDTKE, Albert 328, Anna (Fischer) 328
LUELLEN, Elwood 147
LUERS 94
LUKOVIAK, Eleanor 230
LUNG, Barbara Ann 263
LUNGER, Maimie (McMurtrey) 340
LUNSFORD, Dallas F. Jr. 250, Dallas F. Sr. 250, James Franklin 250, Marilyn Sue 250, Mary R. (Lewis) 250
LUSHER, Nellie 248
LUSHIN, Chad 145, Daniel 250, Jean 12, Jean Paul 145, 250, Kara Nikole 145, Kathryn Diane 250, Paul 145, Paul K. 250, Sally 145, Stephen 250
LUTTRELL, Charles 73, 85
LUTZ, Charles 157, Correll 157, Fred 161, 287, Minnie (Circle) 157
LYBROOK, Elizabeth 289, Elsie 255, Harvey 255, 256, John C. 289, Martha Rebecca 289, Thelma (Roach) 145
LYERLA, Ella C. 160
LYKE, Dicie (Lyons) 186, Michael 186
LYKINS, Barbara Ann 250, 302, Janet Sue 251, John 250, Mary Bell (Richardson) 250, Pearl S. 250
LYLE, Channie (Bobbit) 158, Walter 158
LYNCH, Catherine Isenhour 151, James 237, Judy 309, 310, Mabel B. (Dillon) 251, Paul L. 251, William Edward 251
LYNN, Jacalyn 316
LYONS, Hiram Wesley 168, Mark 23
LYSLO, Kristen Anne 164
LYTLE, Elizabeth 196, Hazel Wolford 337, James 230, Sara Kathrien 309, Wesley 230

M

MACADAM, Simon 221
MACAN, Dean 214
MACDONALD, Mark 243, Teresa Kynne 182
MACFARLANE, Kathleen 180
MACK, Alexander 59
MACKE, Fred 277, Katherine 277
MACY, David 52
MADDOCK, Gail Marie 252, Harry Lee 251, James Cletus 251, Kenton P. 251, 252, Kenton Paul 251, Lezlie Sue 252, Mary Alice (Sloan) 251, Mary Alice (Sloan) 251, 252, Stanley C. 252, Steven H. 251, Todd L. 252
MADDOX, Alta 243, Anthony Joe 190, 252, 303, Charles Courtland 252, Charles Edgar 252, Clarabelle Roselee 252, Cleo 257, Cleo Sherman 252, Corey 190, Corey Stephen 252, 303, Daniel Lee 190, 252, 303, Everett 252, Floyd Harold 252, Garland Solomon 252, Grant 252, Inez 252, James Thomas 252, James Woodrow 252, Joseph Valentine 252, Leo 252, Lewis Fredrick 252, Lonnie 243, Lucy Jane 252, Margot Josephine 197, Marian Louise 252, Minnie 252, Raymond Floyd 197, Robert Scott 190, 252, 303, Stacey Marie 190, 252, 303, Thomas 252, Thomas Brian 190, 252, 303, Thomas Eugene 252, 303, Thomas Eugene Jr. 252, Thomas Eugene, Jr. 303, Thomas, Jr. 190, Towana Kay, 140, 252, 303
MADEN, Jerry 25
MADSEN, Mark 225
MAE, Anna Lynch 170, Edna Chandler 21
MAGGARD, Arnold 83
MAGGART, Alice Vivian 269, Beverly A. (Rose) 252, Christopher Lee 252, Daniel Cliff 252, Gladys 252, Heather Lynn 252, John V. 252, Joshua Seth 252, Joyce Caroleen (Meadors) 252, Monty Cliff 252, Vernon R. 252
MAGIERA, Mike 325
MAGNETT, Brian Joel 276, Julie Renee 276
MAHER, Lawrence 153, Nora 218, T. 34, Tom 269
MAHLKE, Mary 290
MAHOLM, Harriet (Swift) 288, Thomas 288
MAIER, Elinora 148, Josef 148, Louise Katherine 148
MAIN, John M. 241, Mary Jane 241
MAISH, Balford 253, David 252, 253, Donald 253, Enoch 253, Flossie 25, Floyd 253, George 253, James 253, John George 252, Katherine 253, Matt 253, Myron 252, 253, Paul Wade 252, Ralph 50, 253, Ruth 50, 253, Thomas 253, Willard 253, William 253
MALABY, C.A. 147, Carl A. 253, David Carl 253, Ferne 197, Joshua David 253, Linda Frazier 253, Malinda Jo 253, Martha Jane 253, 262, Thomas 253, Thomas Albert 253, Thomas C. 253, W.B. (Mal) 253, William 15, 253
MALLET, Martha 33, Westley 33
MALONEY 94, Joe 25, Lynsey Danielle 302, Mike 302, Pamela (Schmitt) 302, Robert 302, Shala Renee 302
MALOTT, Viola 263
MANFREDI, Gregg 145, Vendala Dawn (Lushin) 145
MANLOVE, Patricia Ann 254
MANN, Cecil 309, Christina 157, J.C. 309, Mary 205, Norma Jean 192
MANNING, Robert 305, Wayne 305
MANONEY, Frank M. 149
MANOR, Alcyon 205, Avis 205, Benjamin 205, Caleb 205, David James "DJ" 205, Elizabeth 205, Samuel 205
MANRING, Cora 159
MANSHIP, Lindsay 191, Polly 191, William 191
MANUEL, Theophilus 48
MAPLE, Elijah Grant 220, Lydia Letitia 220, Meredith 35, Nellie (Chapman) 247, Sarah Elizabeth (Friermood) 220
MARCH, Albert C. 219, Emily Nancy 219
MARCHIONE, Joshua L. 214, Kaylee Lynn 214
MARDOCK, Hubert 66
MARGISON, Linda 125
MARIGAN, Michael 196
MARINE, Asa 35, Ziba 35
MARIS, Aaron 268, Eleanor 268, Martha 108
MARKLAND 32, D. 34, Phoebe 275
MARKLAND-HULLINGER 32
MARKOPOULOS, Nikolas 232, Nikolas Cristian 289, Peter 232, 289
MARKS, Mame (Styer) 98
MARLER, Audrey 78, Lyman 78
MARNER, Abraham Lincoln 253, Beulah 325, Beulah Irene 253, Dena Catherine (Katie) 253, Eugene Francis 253, Gene 325, Jacob 253, Joseph 325, Joseph Elmer (Joe) 253, Kenneth Percy 253, Kenny 325, Larry 325, Larry Paul Dale 253, Thomas Wayne 253, Wayne 325, Wilbur 325, Wilbur Joseph 253
MARONEY, Alice Louise (Teel) 145, Bill 50, Florence 50
MARQUIS, J.G. 34, Robert 308
MARQUOIS 39
MARRS, Anna 343
MARSH, Roberta 293, Ruth 157, 255
MARSHALL, Balsora Josephine 254, Benton 254, Clayton 190, Coty 190, E. 34, Elizabeth (Pitts) 254, Floyd 23, Hannah 288, Harry 332, Hugh 254, J. 34, James 254, Jared 66, Jesse 219, John 219, Laurie 225, Lucinda (Moulder) 256, 295, Lucretia 288, Mary 219, Newton 256, 295, O.G. 116, O.G. (Pud) 23, 25, Oliver 254, Philip 253, Tessa 255, Tom 219
MARSTON, Lester C. 250
MARTIN 28, 245, Adam Joseph 147, Albert 141, Amos Addison 254, Anna Elizabeth 208, Basil Orem 244, Bill 26, Bill Jr. 24, 25, 126, Bill Sr. 24, 25, Brent Jay 153, Brian Kent 147, Brooks 23, 66, Bryan Michael 287, Carl 126, Catherine 277, Cecile 140, Cherie Beth 153, Cory 126, D. 34, Daniel 27, 31, 33, Daniel Allen 147, Daniel W. 51, Derrick 126, Don 3, Douglas Kent 254, Earl Wayne 254, Ed 24, 25, 126, Elizabeth 225, Elizabeth Ann 254, Esther 174, Eugene 290, Eugene V. "Red" 126, Frances Mae (Anderson) 141, Franklin Welsh 193, George, Jr. 298, Glen Warren 254, Gloria 277, Gregory Brant 254, Hannah 28, I.W. 15, 16, Israel Watson 254, J.H. 49, James 196, Jan Elizabeth 287, Jason Robert 249, Jeffery 298, Joe 277, Joellen Zeck 342, John 33, 133, John G. 51, Julia Ann 342, Karen Anne 254, Kate F. 13, Kathryn 342, Kenny 277, Kevin 242, Kyle William 249, Leon C. 197, Leslie 153, Loren Ross 254, Lori 342, Lucille 277, Luke 88, M. 34, Marjorie W. (Folkers) 254, Martha (Hudson) 141, Mary 277, Mary A. (Adams) 254, Mary Elizabeth 147, Matthew Thomas 242, Max 24, 25, 126, Melinda Ann 287, Michael 342, Michael Dean 242, Michael Jeffrey 287, Nichole Yvonne 254, Peter 225, Phyllis 180, Reba 277, "Red" 25, Reuben M. 254, Rosemarie Massoth 258, Russell 307, Sally 148, Samantha 307, Samuel 254, Saralyn 25, Shane Matthew 254, Shepherd 33, Stephen Brant 254, Steve 342, Theresa Maria 254, Tracy Leanne 254, Truman G. 254, Virginia 277, William 33, 277, William A. "Bill" 126, William C. 160, William Shephard 141, William Sr. 23
MARTINDALE, D. 34, J.L. 34, Samuel 33, Thomas 28
MARTINEZ, Carlotta (Carla) 322, Terry 333
MASBAUM, Martha 287
MASH, James 33
MASON 161, Ada 255, 256, Alice 256, Amanda (Odell) 295, Andrew Grover 256, Andrew Jackson 255, 256, 295, Arian 141, Arlene 141, 256, Barbara 255, Becky 256, Benjamin 255, Benjamin Franklin 255, Bessie 141, Bonnie 256, Carl 256, Carla 256, Carlyle 255, Cecil 80, Charles Jefferson 255, Charles Nelson 257, Charles Otto 164, Christena 255, Christina 255, Christina (Everly) 255, Claude 255, Clifford 256, Dan 255, Daniel 255, David 141, 256, Dean 256, Dema Leone 256, Donald 141, 256, Donald G. 83, Earl 255, Earl Marshall 257, Eliza 255, Eliza Ann 251, 255, Elizabeth 255, Elizabeth (White) 171, 195, 256, Elliott 51, Elsie 255, Elsie May 256, Ethie 256, Eva 255, 256, 257, Florence 255, 256, Florence Lucille 257, 295, Flossie P.E. 51, Flossie Phoebe Ellen (Springer) 164, Garman 255, Genevieve 257, George 255, Gerald 255, Glen 255, Grover 255, Harley 256, Howard 255, Izaac 255, Jack 257, Jacob 15, 195, 255, Jacob D. 255, 256, Jacob Daniel 251, 256, 257, 334, Jacob Harvey 256, 257, James Franklin 256, 257, Jean 141, 256, Jefferson 255, Joe 255, John 255, Joseph 141, 256, Joseph Howard 257, Joseph Wesley 255, Josephine 141, Judith 141, 256, Judy 257, Lester 256, Lettie 255, 256, Lillie 256, Lillie Omer 255, Lonzo 256, Louisa 255, 334, Lucille 255, Marcia 141, 256, Marco 256, Mark 255, Martha 195, 255, Martin 255, Martin Van Buren 255, 256, Marvin 256, Mary Jane 171, Mary Rebecca 157, 255, 256, Mona 141, 256, Myrtle 107, Myrtle E. 295, Nicholas 255, Norman D. 256, Omer 255, 295, Omer Otto 256, Orville 255, Oscar Roscoe 256, Philip 255, Phillip Lawrence 255, Ralph L. 255, Rebecca 15, 195, 255, Rebecca Ann (Showalter) 251, 255, 256, 257, 334, Renna 141, 256, Robert 141, 256, Rod 85, Roscoe 255, Sara 141, Sheryl 141, 256, Simon 171, 195, 255, 256, Simon Peter 255, 256, 257, Solomon 255, Stuart 255, Susan 141, 255, 256, Tessie (Marshall) 295, Thomas Jefferson 257, Virgil 255, Virgle 255, Walter 256, Ward 256, Wayne 141, 256, Wendell 255, William 255, William Andrew 257
MASONS, Jacob D. 257
MASSENA, Elizabeth 269
MASSEY, Adam 302, Amanda 257, Belle 257, Betty 257, Betty Jane 166, 270, George F. 257, George W. 257, Gertie B. 257, James M. 166, James Manford 257, 270, James Manford Jr. 257, Martha 257, Mary Elizabeth 257, Maxine 257, Maxine Mae 166, 270, Minnie 257, Nancy 257, Nancy Lee 166, 270, Noah Robert 257, Noah Wesley 257, Pearlie J. 257, Robert O. 257, Roger 301, Sarah Catherine 257, Stephen 257, Tiffney 302, Virginia 257, Virginia Joan 166, 270
MASSOTH, Bertha E. (Kenworthy) 236, Catherine 258, Frank 258, Hazel Isabelle Mitsch 257, John 236, John Francis 258, John Martin 258, John W. 257, Joseph Conrad 258, Martin 257, Mary Ann 236, 257, Mary Becker 258, Paul 200, Paul Edward 258, Robert J. 236, Robert Joseph 257, 258, Thomas 236, Thomas M. 257
MAST 29, Jerry 39, 41, Joseph 298, Magdalena 325, Moses 258, Paul 31, Woodrow 43
MASTERS, Betty 258, Catherine 234, Dawn 259, Dorothy 258, Goldie (Krause) 258, Ira 258, Judith Ann 258, Robert "Bob" 258, Robin 259, Sharon 334, Sharon Sue 258, 335, Violet (Clubbs) 335, William R. "Billy" 258, William T. 335, William Tilford 258
MASTORAS, Alexander 333
MASTS 39
MATCHETTE, Anne 157, Col. 157, Daniel 157, John 157, June 157, Michael 157, Roberta (Hill) 157
MATHERSON, J.S. 95
MATHEWS, Charles Henry 144, Douglas Lee 275, Jane (Rule) 144, Mark William 275, Samuel William 275
MATLOCK, Edwin 191, Elizabeth 147, Mary Lou 318, Sena (Stewart) 14
MATSON, Elizabeth 205
MATTHEWS, Mark 23, 86
MATTOX, Dan 83
MAU, Johan 149
MAUDLIN, Deborah 141
MAURER, Matilda (Dahl) 326, Samuel 32, Wava Mae 231, 326
MAWHINNEY, Florence Eden 284
MAXWELL, Painter S. 35, Riley 35, Stokes 35
MAYER, Norma 253, Walter 70
MAYFIELD, Cordelia 125, Myrna 281
MAZABEL, Carolina 162, Elva Lucia 162
MAZE, John 145
MCANINCH, Emma Jean 284, Mary Esther (Armfield) 143
MCASHLAN, Linda 121, Tim 121
MCBEE, Eric J. 315, Leonard 186, Lorrie 186
MCBETH, Miles R. 13
MCBRIDE 89
MCCAIN, Benjamin 31, Glen 188, Hannah 318, Hope 21, 25, John 197, Susie 187
MCCANN, Mark A. 163, Molly Michelle 163, Willis J. 169
MCCARTER, Georgia L. 301
MCCARTHY, Joseph 210, Timothy 261

MCCAUGHAN, Russell 14
MCCAULEY, Alfred 269, Bertha Blanche 269, Betty 327, Betty Lou 269, Blaine 269, Blanche 269, Burl 269, Burley Cleon 269, Cecil 269, Clarence 140, Clarence Everett 269, Cyrus Edward 269, Elizabeth Edwards 269, Elmer 269, Ernest 269, Everett Lacy 269, Hazel Edith 269, James A. 269, James R. 269, John J. 269, Jon R. 269, Leora 269, Leora Lee 269, Leslie 269, Lola Mabel 269, Lula 269, Lulu Mae 269, Margaret 269, Margaret Louise 269, Milton Hamilton 269, Pearl 269, Perry Morton 269, Robert (Bob) 269, Robert Otis 269, Russell 269, Sarah Pruella Swisher 269, Valerie 269, William Clayton 269, William Jefferson 269, 270
MCCLAIN, Anna Clara (Dottie) 163, Austin 225, Basil 56, Bobby Warren 11, Elizabeth (Mover) 233, Evan 225, Francis 225, Francis E. 48, James 156, John 233, Mary L. 11, Nancy Jean 151, Rex 225, Sharon 225, Terry 225, Tressie 230
MCCLANAHAN, Margaret 200, 248, Margaret McCleur 249
MCCLELLAN, Aaron Christopher 335, Cynthia Faye 335, George B. 341, James Robert 335, Mary Ridgeway 196, Richard, Jr. 335, Robert 311, William 189
MCCLELLAND, Essie 14, Susan E. 189, W. 34
MCCLINTOCK, Virgil 121
MCCLOSKEY, Allen 148
MCCLOUD, Eliza J. 286
MCCLUNG, Fred W. 132
MCCLURE 86, James 226, Martha 226, Nancy 146, Rebecca Grau 204, Samuel 226, Thomas 18, 59, Jeff 23
MCCOMAS, Ann 141, Chris 192, Christine 300
MCCOMBS, Alice 139
MCCONNELL, Grace 172, Sharron 189
MCCOOL, Cynthia (Rickard) 308, Gabriel 103, James 15, Jeremiah 308, Roanna Arminta 308
MCCORMACK, Charles Asa 329, John 35, Robert 26
MCCORMICK, Clarence L. 150, Howard 150, John 35, Ned 150 William 27, 33
MCCOY, Carol Anne 254, Charles 56, Clarence Everett 254, George 21, 86, George Brant 254, Katie 56, Maude 219, Mildred Rosalee 209, Omer 96, Polly Ann 269
MCCRACKEN, Sarah Elizabeth 145
MCCULLOCK, Mary Katherine 217
MCCULLOUGH, Jack 304, John Charles 304, Karen 282
MCCUNE, Elmer 212
MCDANIEL, Blanche Thrawley 285, Christopher Columbus 285, Florella Belle 285, Joyce 149, Mary Ellen Ayres 285, Samuel B. 95
MCDANIELS, Samantha 15, Virgil 193, Walker 193
MCDONALD, James 13, Ora Lee 180
MCDONOUGH, Ann (Del- Vecchio) 179
MCDOWELL, Alvin 15, Amanda Jane 196, Cintha A. 270, Cynthia 270, D.A. 90, Dabo 270, David A. 85, Elizabeth 270, Jackson 15, Jane 270, Jane (Young) 270, Janet 332, John 151, 270, John D. 270, Luther 15, Martha L. 270, Mary (McElroy) 151, McElroy 270, "Muck" 336, Pine 270, Samuel 270
MCELFRESH, Ferris 234 Grace 234
MCELWEE, A.K. 13
MCFADDEN, James Robert 333, Kent Leonard 333, Lenora (Gray) 333, Scott Robert 333, William 333
MCFALL, Gladys 72, Herbert 72, Walter 73
MCFARLAND, Bertha Pearl 270, David 270, David Nelson 270, Flora Jane 270, John 270, Joshua 270, Laura 194, Lilly Bell 270, Lula McFarland 270, Mary 270, Missouri Ann (Woods) 270, Nancy (Moomaw) 270, Nancy Florence 270, Nancy Florence 166, Rachel 270, Robert Erwin 270, Sarah 270, Sarah (Hixon) 270, Sherman Francis 270, Timmothy 270, Timmothy Leonard 270, William 270
MCFATRIDGE, Alfred 270, Andrew Jacob 271, Ann Louise 271, Anna Elizabeth 270, Belva 270, Clarissa 270, Cleona Mae 270, David Alan 271, Douglas Lee 271, Edith 270, Elizabeth 270, Elizabeth Ann 270, Emma 270, Estella Anna 270, Ethel 270, Francis Marion 270, Franklin Pierce 270, George Gabriel 270, George Washington 270, Grace 270, Harry 270, Hazel 270, Holmes 270, Hugh 270, Hugh George 270, Ira Lewis 270, James Charles 271, James Clayton 270, James Robinson 270, James Winfield Scott 270, Jane 270, Jessica Lauren 271, Jo Ann 271, John 270, John Wesley 270, Julie Ann 271, Lewis C. 270, Lewis Cass 270, Lydia Ellen 270, Mabel 270, Malinda Armilda 270, Mary 270, Mary Abigail 270, Mary Ann 270, Mellie 270, Mertie Ann 270, Milo Minton 270, Nancy 270, 271, Pearl William 270, Peter Wilson 270, Thomas Henry Stockton 270, Walter 270, Walter Price 270, Walter Price Jr. 271, William Clancy 270, William Jasper 270, William Orla 270
MCFEE, Delia A. 286
MCFERRIN, William 122
MCGAIL, Lottie Ellen 156
MCGEE, Elizabeth Jane 156
MCGILLIARD, Abigail 196
MCGILVREY, Bill 73
MCGLAMERY, Elizabeth Montgomery 279
MCGLYNN, Michael 30
MCGONIGAL, Harry E. 134
MCGOVERN, Arthur C. 171, Hazel 171, Thomas C. 171
MCGOWAN, George 13, John 289, Joseph 278, Mary 278, Michael 278
MCGRANE, Annah 182
MCGRATH, Emma 66
MCGRAW, Aden 142, Annis Belle 271, Annis M. 271, Carrie D. 271, Cora 271, Delite 271, Eliza 142, Frances 271, Francis 168, 271, J.H. 34, James Harrison (Harry) 271, John W. 271, Laura 271, Louella B. 271, Roxey 271, Vesta Martha 168,169, 271, Waldo J. 271, William 271
MCGUIRE, Diana 298, Floyd 193, John 155, Lilly E. 218, Louisa (Williams) 155, Mary Elizabeth 155, Pamela 298, Patricia Colean 173, Paul 298, Paul Jr. 298, Wanda 192
MCHALE, Sara 141, 256
MCHONE, McHagey 13
MCILHENEY, Nancy Agness 144
MCILWAIN, George 294, Martha 36
MCINDOO, Walter 74
MCINTIRE, Aaron 188, Elizabeth 187
MCINTOSH, Alexander Frances 271, Barbara 3, Frieda M. (Constable) 250, Ira E. 156, James W. 51, John Mark 271, Kathryn 271, Michael 271, Oscar D. 250, Richard 75, Richard II 271, Richard Thornton 271, Ruth Caroline (Gilbert) 271
MCINTURF, James F. 51
MCINTURFF, Connie Ruth 218, Pansy Inez Miller 181, 218, 229, 275, Willard James 181, 218, 229, 275
MCKAY, Delores Faye 21, Fred 305, Irving Leon 212, Iva Verna Athens 212, Mary Lida 315
MCKEE, Mary Colleen 293
MCKENNEY, A.E. 83
MCKENSIE, Frances 222
MCKIBBEN, Ira 142, Mike 130, Phyllis 142, Nellie 142
MCKILLIP, Aaron 272, Alexander 271, Andrew 272, Arthur Dale 272, Brandon 272, Christine 272, Donald Gene 272, Gabriel 272, James 272, Mark J. 272, Matthew A. 272, Michael 272, Michael D. 272, Patrick 272, Rachel 272, Ralph Vernon 272, Wanda 272, Zachary 272
MCKINNEY 56, Charles Elmer 272, George 272, Goldie 272, Horace 14, Lula 14, Matilda Edgar 172, Michael 92, Sylvia Mae 154, Walter 305
MCKINSEY, Cynthia Jo 183, George W. 213, Orpha Dean 213
MCKNIGHT, Mary Jo 202
MCKOWAN, James 86
MCLAY, Rose 19
MCLEAN, J. 13
MCLELLAN 78
MCMAHON 273
MCMANAMA, Lillian 145
MCMANNIS 273
MCMILLEN 245, Mary 212
MCMILLIN, David 86
MCMINN, Gail 25, Robert 116, 333
MCMONIGAL, H.E. 125
MCMULLEN, Mary 246, Phoebe E. 213
MCMURTREY, Mamie Lunger 341, Mark 340, Thelma 340, Thelma Lucile 341
MCNABNEY, Elizabeth 272, James Ross 243, 272, Jean 272, Jeannette 243, 272, Mary 272, Mary Jane (Deshon) 243, Paul 272, Rebecca Catherine (Ladd) 272, Ross 272, Vivian 272, William 272, William James 272
MCNALLY, Arlene 78, Thelma Arlene 192
MCNEAL, Brian 273, Eli 273, Elizabeth (St. Clair) 273, George Lawrence 273, George Lawrence 273, James V. 273, John 273, Marjorie Ellen 273, Paige 273, Raymond Lawrence 273, Steven Lawrence 273
MCNULTY, Brook Marie 283, Clayton Richard 283, Stanley J. 283
MCNUTT, Elizabeth 247
MCQUARY, Angela Marie 282, Bonnie Lou (Miller) 282, James A. 282
MCQUEEN, Uriah 50, 96
MCQUINLIN, Honora 338
MCQUINN, Oren 25, Phyllis 25
MCQUISTAN, George 55, Ida 55, Robert 55
MCQUISTION, Mary 230
MCQUISTON, Alice 273, Annie 273, Barbara 273, Cerena Florence 273, Ernest Ellsworth 273, Everett Andrew 273, Everett C. 273, Gilbert 273, Harrison 273, Isaac 273, Jane 273, Jared Andrew 273, Jerry Lee 273, Jerry Lee 158, Jerry Lee Jr. 273, Jesse John 273, John 273, Loren 273, Lucinda 273, Margaret 273, Naomi 273, Rachel 273, Ralph 160, Robert 273, Simeon 273, Tamara Lynn 273, Tyler Lee 273, Virgil 273, Wesley 273, William 273
MCREYNOLDS, Charles 273, Charles William 274, Clarence Samuel 273, George Martin 273, Hannah 273, James 196, 273, James Robert "Jim Bob" 274, John 273, Julia 274, Mabel Katherine 273, Martin Luther 273, Mary Catherine 274, Mary John 196, Mary Martha 274, Mary "Pollie" Phipps 273, Peter Wesley 273, Rachel 196, Raven 273, Robert 273, Samuel 273, Samuel Wiley "Sammy" 273, Sarah 273, Sarah Catherine 274, Sarah Matilda 274, Thomas Calvin 274, Thomas Calvin 274, Thomas Calvin Jr. 274, Thomas III 274, Thomas Jr. 274, Wesley 274, William H. 273
MCROBERTS, G. 177, Gary 177
MCTURNAN, Judith 329, Lawrence 204, 329, Robert 329
MCVETY, Ombra 206, Ormba 275
MCVEY, Catherine 176, Edward 176
MCWILLIAMS, Stella 230
MEACHAM, Alyce 259, George 179, James Silas 80, Josephine (Mossholder) 80, Lula 80, Wilma 80
MEADORS, Charles E. 236, Edith G. (Bryant) 252, William B. 252
MEADOWS, Edward 148
MEANS, Hugh 35, W.J. 25
MECK, Edward 258, G.E. 13, Harry J. 106
MEDINA, Carol 339
MEDLAN, J. 34
MEDLEY, George 195, Grace Mae 180, Hazel 195, James 180, Jody 195, Kenneth 195, Martin 195, Mary Jane Bailey 180, Ross 195, Sallie Jane (Freed) 195, Thomas Paul 195
MEDLIN, N.A. 34
MEECE, Christina Lynn 330, Clark 330
MEEKS, Huvon "Sug" 301, Thelma 182
MEHLIG, Juliana 125
MEINERSHAGEN, June Ann Schrader 303
MEIRING, Frank 325, Louise 325
MEISTERMAN, Alan 195, Cheryl (Freed) 195, Dan 195, Mollie 195, Sam 195
MELLINGER 273
MELTON, Betty 312, Beulah 312, Harley 312, Harry 312
MELVIN, Robert 335
MENCE, S.W. 34
MENDENHALL, Abigail 259, 260, Abigail (Barker) 259, 262, Abigale 261, Bertha Ann 260, 261, Clara 262, Clara Daisey 259, 262, Delphina 259, Edwin 260, 261, 262, Edwin S. 260, Edwin S. 260, 261, Edwin Stanton 259 260, Elizabeth 143, Elma 259, 262, Franklin 259, Harry Loren 260, 261, Henry 60, 259, 260, 261, 262, Ira J. 259, Jeramiah 259, John Sr. 259, L. Maude (Weaver) 261, Lydia 167, Margaret (Young) 259, Mary 260, Miriam Lucinda 259, Narcissa Ann 259, Nathan 48, Nathan Hobson 259, 262, Neaty 260, 261, Neaty M. 260, Owen F. 261, Owen Fowler 260, Paul Ancil 260, Ruth Eleanor 260, Walter 21, Warren 172
MENDEZ, George 85
MERANDA, Amanda Viola 273, Ida 220, Margaret 85, Mary 241, William F. 85
MERCER, Lenore 152
MEREDITH, Elisha Filmore 260
MERILL, Frank 177
MERIWETHER, Ranita Ellen (Grady) Olive 203
MERREL, Irene 107, Alice B. 'Allie' 253, Allie 262, Anita 3, Clarence 61, Clarence C. 253, Clarence Curtis 'Pat' 262, Ellis 60, Erwin 262, Erwin G. 253, Estelle 162, Harriett (Van Cleave) 253, Joy Delight 197, Orman 262, Orman Benjamin 253, Robert B. 253, Robert Wilson 60, 253, 262, Rodney 253, Ryan 253, Ward 262, Ward C. 253
MERRICK, Myron 197, Myron 'Mike' 143
MERRIFIELD, Gyla Jean 148, Jamie Rae 148, Jana Lynn 148, Janelle Yvonne 148
MERRILL, Anthony (Tony) Lynn 263, C. Ralph 263, Elmer 65, Elmer Granville 231, 326, Eric Jerome 263, Eva 269, Flora May (Parr) 326, Hal 243, James 326, Jim 243, Joseph Stephen 326, Leslie 243, Milley Frances (Turner) 326, Myrtle Belle (Osborn) 263, Roy Stanley (Stan) 263, Ruth 243, William 183
MERRIMAN, C.L. 83
MERSHAD, Anne Caldwell 164, Martin Joseph 164, Mary Grace 164
MESSENGER, Fenton 23, 86
MESSER, Buell 283, Charles 283, Linda Kay 250, Michael 283
MESSERLY, Martha (Bowman) 298
MESSERSMITH, Charles 287
METCHEAR, Charles 13
METZ 28, H. 34, Henry 297, Jacob 314, Jake 191, John 297, 298, Martha Elizabeth 297, Mary 314, Melinda (Foland) 193, Oscar 59, Pat 59, Patricia (Dutton) 170, Paul 278
METZ-SCHAFER 32
METZGER, Dorothy L. (Shanahan) 159, Joe C. 159, Peggy Jo 159
MEYERS 14, Bill 41, Heath Lunda 302, Jim 240, Larkin 27, Stephanie Marie 302, Stephen 302
MICHAEL 39
MICHAEL, Al 86, Eli 42, Eli T. 286, Fredrick 286, Harriet 286, Willard Eli 286
MICHAELS, Myrtle 42
MICHAELSON, Josephine Hollingsworth 222
MICHEL, Ida Bertha 329
MICHNER, Dick 97
MICKELSON, Betty 32, Bob 32
MIDDLESWORTH, Abraham 263, Charlotte 263, Clarence Wm. 263, Denise 263, Denny Lynn 263, Evan Charles 263, Glen 263,

Homer 263, Jana Gae 263, Jason Rae 263, John 263, John Jr. 263, Joseph Earl 263, Joseph Jr. 263, Joseph Sr. 263, Joseph Trent 263, Katie Lynn 263, Kelly Paris 263, Kimberly Ann 263, Lilith 230, Lonnie Rae 263, Martha 263, Mary Doris (Winegardner) 263, Randy Joe 263, Robert G. 263, Rosamond 263, Shawn Marie 263, William 263
MIDDLETON, Allen 216, Alvin 263, Anna 18, Anna Strattan 207, Ascenith 216, Calvin W. 216, Charles 18, Charles E. 19, David 216, Dorothy (Shockley) 263, E. Francis 216, Eli 216, Ervin 263, Howard 263, Hudson (Bud) 216, James L. 216, Jane 18, 19, 216, Jane Moulder 207, 268, John 18, 207, Joseph M. 216, Lemuel 216, Levi 216, Mae (Jackson) 263, Mary 207, May 18, Raymond 280, Rhodema Jane 216, Samantha 263, Steve 263, Tammy (Spotts) 263, William 18, 19, 207, 216, WilliamLevi 207
MIKESELL, Catherine 148
MILAR, Melba 218
MILBURN, Allen 238, Andrew 170, Brent 25, Catherine (Shaffer) 170, Darrell 23, 26
MILES, Charles 143, 230, Ella (Campbell) 143
MILL, Jones 52
MILLARD, Catherine 293, Howard 157, Mary (Brubaker) 157
MILLER 28, 29, 42, 48, 59, 291, A.H. 25, Abner D. 264, Abraham 291, Absolem 33, Ada 37, Agnes Blanche 201, Albert 40, Alice Viola (Fritz) 162, Amanda 264, Ann 337, Ann Walker 317, Anna 287, Arthur 21, Arthur (Art) 331, Arthur Caleb 160, Arthur, Jr. 261, Barbara 263, 325, Bettie (Stewart) 14, Billy Joe 180, Brent William 336, Calvin 35, Calvin Leroy 201, 297, Carl 172, Charles 263, Charley 41, Chauncey 149, Chester 218, Christian 160, Christina Anstett 142, Christina Noelle 336, Cora Emma Coppock 331, Corbin 263, Daniel 264, Daniel C. 264, 344, David 290, Della Mae 187, Deloris Kling 337, Don 40, Dora Esther 176, Dorcus 317, Douglas 190, Douglas R. 160, Edgar 325, Edith Joan 241, Elder Jacob 317, Eleanor 334, Eli 39, Elisabeth 241, Elizabeth 142, 196, 291, Elizabeth (Lizzie) 264, Elizabeth Ann Robards 201, Emma (Suit) 176, Emma Luessa 167, Emma Luessa 167, Enos 29, Everett W., Jr. 336, Flo 266, Frances Ludwig 275, Frank 160, Genevieve (Gene) Elvin 331, George Franklin 160, Georgia Carol 228, Grace 237, Gregory Stephen 290, Ham 35, Harry 14, 287, Harry Van Jr. 263, Harry Vane 263, Hazel O. 197, Hazel Oveda 162, Henry 39, Ida 263, Isaac 48, 263, J. 34, J. Wesley 58, James 28, 29, 32, James Alan 247, Janet 25, Janet (Martin) 126, Jean 325, Jennifer 142, Jessie 263, Jim 325, Joe 325, John 284, 325, John Arthur 263, John B. 44, John Benton 317, John Benton 59, John Corbin 263, John D. 264, John E. 263, 331, John J. 33, Julia Lynn 190, Laura 253, Leah 28, Lee R. 187, Leonard Wilson 275, Lloyd 325, Lora 40, Madonna (Foland) 193, Madonna Bell 263, Magadelena 325, Maggie 163, Maria (Roth) 160, Marion 218, Mark S. 160, Mary 149, 325, Mary Elizabeth 167, Maurice R. 94, Max 331, Maxine 218, Meinert 285, Naomi 332, Neal T. 160, Nolan 47, Oscar 197, 263, 334, Owen 247, Paul 325, 331, Peter 59, 167, Phil 148, Richard Arlen 263, Robert 331, 339, Russell 218, Samuel 28, Sarah 263, Sophia 264, Stacy Annette 290, Stephen Douglas 160, Thomas 48, Thomas P. 176, Tim 211, Tisha Marie 290, Virginia 332, William 14, 35, 45, William Chauncey 263, William H 245, William Robert 263
MILLER-STOCKWELL, Vera Helen (Arnett) 141
MILLIGAN, Clara 252
MILLIKAN, Rebecca Ann 146
MILLIKAN, T. 48
MILLIKEN, Louisa Tate "Ida" 158
MILLS 43, Bernal 21, Charles 14, 265, David 202, 327, Emily 338, Greyson 202, 327, Harrison 224, J.H. 25, James 66, 202, Jenevieve Evelyn 182, Leona 163, Margery Adams 338, Mary 269, Newton 27, Paul J. 106, Teena (Gordon) 327, Ulysses 183, Virginia 155, William 338
MILLSAP, Ed 257, Martha Catherine 257
MILLSPAUGH, Rob 74
MILNER, Dale 23, Dora 298, Katherine 287
MILTON, John 95
MINGLIN, Grace Eden Whaley 185
Minglin, Lester Calvin 185
MINGUS, Catherine 265
MINTON, Marty 80
MISHLER, B. 34
MITCHELL 14, Annette 78, B.D. 107, Charles Cliff 218, Chester 96, 301, Elizabeth 245, Margaret 173, Theodore Commett 200
MITSCH, Hazel Isabelle 258
MITTOWER, Andrew 339
MOAN, Robert 92
MOCK, Kelsie 155, Kylie 155, Mike 155
MODAK, Mildred Ann 240, Paul 240, Stella (Mitrovich) 240
MOE, Kim 86
MOFFATT, Sidney 217
MOFFITT, Brian 264, David 264, Franklin David 264, Harriett (Whybrew) 264, Harry 264, Helen (Ridenour) 264, Homer 264, James 264, Janet 264, Katherine (Harlow) 264, Lawrence Harvey 264, Lena 264, Lucinda 264, Martha 264, Martha O. (Dille) 264, Robert 264, Ronald 264, Suzanne 209, 264, Walter 209, 264, Willodean (Owens) 264
MOGNETT, Fred H. 287, Henry 287, Kenneth 287, Nathan 287, Samuel 287
MOHLAR, John 267, Susannah 267
MOHR, August 328, Barbara 264, Carolyn 264, Daniel 264, Dee Ann 264, Dee S. 264, Doug 264, George William 264, Golda 264, James 264, Joan Goldsmith 264, John D. 264, Mary (Roden) 328, Polly Stephenson 264, Stanton 264, Tonia 264, William 264
MOKE, Nancy 323
MOLDEN, Lori (Lushin) 145, Scott 145
MOLIN, Carl 8, 292
MOLINE, Amy Ann 292, Ebba (Brandrup) 292, Elaine Helen 292, Fridolf F. 292, Fridolf Ferdinand 292, Margaret 292
MONROE, James 44, Olive 237
MONTE, Patricia Ann (Freed) 196
MONTGOMERY, Abigail 190, Anna (Mason) 256, Clara 281, Rhode 256, S.T. 125
MOODY, Cary 180
MOOMAW, Ann (Gray) 270, Henry 270, Nancy 270
MOON 300, Blaine 272, Celeste 272, Charity 272, Cindy 272, Ellen 156, James 33, Jared 272, Jason 272, Jesse 33, Joseph 272, Ruth 228, Solomon 33, Stevan Von 272, Viola (Dixon) 272
MOOR, Betty M. 315
MOORE 28, A.W. 235, Allen W. 265, Allen W. 80, Allen Wayne 265, Allyson 264, Barbara 80, 107, Barbara E. 265, Ed. S. 98
MORRIS, June 310, Mahalia Ellen 312, Margaret Elizabeth 265, Margaret Elizabeth 193, Marian Ruth 265, Marlin Ray 276, Marshall 276, Martha Ann 197, Mary Ann 252, Matilda 265, Matilda Ann 276, Matilda Morris 265, Myer 265, Perry 216, Rebecca 212, Russell, Jr. 295, Stacy 208, T.M. 140, Thurman B. 70, William B. 35
MORRISON, Albert 266, Alice Carol 266, Blanche 266, Caswell 266, 281, 282, Cora 266, 282, Daniel 266, 282, Earl 266, 282, Eliza (Marshall) 266, Emily (Vickers) 281, 282, Enoch 266, Freddy 282, Gerald William 266, Gertrude 266, 282, Hannah 265, Harold H. 266, Homer C. 266, Joe 197, John 266, Lois Catherine 266, Loree 266, Madge Irene 99, Margaret 13, Miles 266, Nina Jean 266, Nina Jean 185, Rachel 13, Robert 48, Russell 266, Susan 252, Velma Ruth 266, Vida 266, 282, William 265, 266, 282, William Alfred 266
MORROW, Brian 267, Charles L. 266, David 267, Diane 266, Dorothy 147, Edith Marie 147, Edna (Huntley) 277, Georgia 213, Helen 266, Jackson 27, 156, Jason 267, Joan 198, Karen 267, Kevin 267, Lum A. 197, Richard 266, Robert 277, Ronald Louis 266, Scott 267, Stephanie 267, Steven 267, Tonya 224
MORTON, Denise 299, Elizabeth 82, Ethel 256, James 82, William F. 36, Wm. 48
MOSES, Audrey 299
MOSLEY, Nancy 15
MOSS, Audrey Lucille (Dawson) 267, Betty 237, Clifford 267, Darlene Marie 267, David Earl 267, Doris 237, 267, Dorothy 237, 267, Edith 237, 267, Elmer 237, Elsie 237, Esther 237, 267, Fred 267, Gayle 267, Gene 237, Gladys M. (Rinehart) 295, Glen David 267, Gordon 237, 267, Gregg 267, Harold 97, Harry Earl 267, Herman 237, Hershel 237, Homer 267, Jesse 237, 267, Jesse Ray 267, John 267, Kathleen Marie 267, Kathy 267, L. Rayburn 295, Mary 237, Mina 267, Moses 267, Nina (Kerby) 237, Nina Julia (Korby) 267, Norma 237, 267, Orville Herman 267, Ray 35, 237, Robert 267, Roma 267, Russell 237, 267, Vada (Kerby) 237, Wayne 237
MOSSBURG 172
MOSSER, Bruce David 168, Dean Bradley 168, Diane 168, Roger R. 168, Susan 168
MOSSHOLDER, Carol 289, Harvey 289, Harvey G., III 289, Harvey G., Jr. 289, Melissa 28
MOTE, Alfred 267, David 251, David Matthew 311, David Matthew 166, Dennis 66, Dorcas (Coppock) 194, Dorcas (Patty) 267, Franklin Earl 267, George Roscoe 267, James 170, James Jason 311, James W. 311, James Wallace 166, Jesse 170, 194, 267, Jesse Lee 267, Levi 267, Rachel 173, 267, Ruth Jeanette K. 308, Sarah A. 267, Verlinda 194, 267
MOULDER, Edna 238, Eleanor Maris 207, 267, Elizabeth Borland 267, Harry L. 131, Harry L. Jr. 131, Harry L. Jr. 268, Harry Louden Sr. 268, Henry 238, Henry Clay 268, J. McLean 268, Jacob 267, 268, Joanne 268, John 48, 207, 267, John C. 131, 268, John Milton 268, Larry 268, Lewis 267, Linda 268, Lucy 13, Margaret (Harned) 326, Martha Catherine 268, Martha Hadley 238, Oliver Lewis 268, Ora Ellen 326, Sally 268, Sharon 268, Thomas M. 60, Thomas Marion 268, Thomas P. 131, Thomas P., Jr. 268, Thomas Penn, Sr. 268, Valentine 267, William 326
MOUTON, Louise 323
MOUTRAY, J.I. 114
MOW, John Adam 149, Margaret (Martin) 149
MOWATT, John Robert 274
MOYERS, Myrtle 196
MUCKERHERN, Charles 10
MUDD, Samuel A. 193
MUGG 48, Edward 224, Simeon 48, William 48
MUHL, A. Herbert 84
MUIR, Mark Douglas 232, Meredeth Ann 232
MULLEN, Agnes (Newcom) 268, Betty Jo 268, Cynthia 268, Daily C. 268, Ellen (Benner) 268, Emery 268, Frank 84, 268, Mary Etienne Newlin 276, Max E. 268, Noble 268, Steven 268
MULLENS, Catherine 313, David 23
MULLER, Timothy 84
MUMAUGH, Clifford R. 254, Ernest 306, Francis R. 254, Jeraldean J. (Fletcher) 254, Joan M. (Slusher) 254, Lillian M. (Spaulding) 254, Merrill R. 254
MUMMERT, Earl Elias 156, Ernest 250, Nellie Louise (Breedlove) 155, Wm. D. 250
MUNCIE, Wm. 40
MUNDY, Carolyn Jeanette 204, Floyd 204, Virginia 204
MUNKRES, James 256, Mertie (Mason) 256
MUNSEL 248
MURAT, Marshal 291
MURPHY 34, 42, 156, Ada Mary 269, America Elizabeth 147, Brian L. 310, Carey Jr. 310, Carolyn Jean (Parker) 310, Charles Raymond 203, Chester 248, Chester Arthur 268, Chester Arthur 269, Clarence 'Bud' 268, David C. 269, Debbie 305, Deva 268, Donna 282, Ella Ruth (Pasdach) 308, Eva 339, Florence 212, Harry 308, Herman E. 268, Isaac 231, John 237, 305, Kizzie Jane (Brenton) 187, Lee Ann 310, Lew 42, Lewis 156, Lewis Ellsworth 187, 268, 269, Linda L. 310, Margaret C. 269, Marie 269, Mary Ann "Polly" 305, Mary Ellen 268, Mike 237, Oka Irene 269, Polly Ann (McCoy) 268, Rita 308, Robert 180, Sarah A. 269, Susan Elizabeth 248, Susannah (Stinnett) 305, Susannah Elizabeth 269, Theodore 'Pete' 268, Vergie 188, Vergie Opal 268, Vergie Opal 187, William L. 269
MURPHYS 39
MURRAY, Charles D. 125, Elmer 270, Geneva Enda 270, J.A. 34, Lula Martha 270, Margaret 79 Marietta G. 315, Roy 270
MUTRAN, Tamara Renee 251, Ted Thomas 2511, Terri Ann 251, Theresa Dawn 251, Thomas S. 251
MUTZ, John 187
MYERS, Bradley Scott 322, Bruce 78, Carolyn Sue (Besser) 322, Charles Agustus 164, David 269, Elizabeth (Massena) 296, Fay 26, Jack 65, James Haworth 269, James M. 296, James M. 269, Jeanne 230, Jeannie 289, John H. 269, Joseph 269, M. 34, Mary Ellen 269, Paul 75, Ralph 75, Roy 149, Sara Elizabeth 296, Sarah Elizabeth 269, Timothy M. 170, Violet Mae 164, William 269, Wm. 42
MYGRANT, Rola 14
MYLER 208

N

NACE, Charles 278, Evaleen 278
NAGLE, Dottie Whorell 261
NAME, Eliza Jane Crockett 235, Hillary C. 235, Noble C. "Skip" 78
NAPHEW, Glen 96, John 180, Marjorie Shrock Keim 204
NASH, Alison 275, Bertha 274, Beth 275, Burnett Marion 274, Charles 274, Charlie 15, Clifton C. 274, Elizabeth (Orr) 275, Ellis 15, 274, Ernest 15, 274, Estaleene 275, Estel 275, Everett 274, Ferdinando 274, Fred 15, 275, Frederick 275, George W. 274, Grace 274, Hannah 274, Herbert 274, Homer 274, James 275, Jane 274, Jane (Barr) 274, Janice 275, Jesse 274, Jesse Jr 15, Jesse Jr. 274, Jesse, Jr. 52, Jessie (Burns) 274, Johanna 275, John 274, Joseph 274, 275, Kerin Jayne 287, Lester 275, Lois 275, Marie 275, Mary (Pike) 274, Mary A. (Batey) 15, 52, Mary Jane 274, May 15, 52, 274, Minta (Burns) 274, Ollie 274, Oscar 275, Penny Susan 275, Raughlia 275, Richard 274, Richard IV 274, Roy 96, 274, Sterrett L. 64, William 274, William G. 223
NATION, Carrie 195, Christopher 268, Enoch 268, John 268, Joseph 268, Lucretia 268, Sampson 268, William 268
NAY, Amy Michelle 275, Angela Sue 275, Chester Ballard 275, Chester Otho 275, Edward Lee 275, Harry Lee 275, Harry Leo 275, Heather Marie 275, Icy 275, John 275, Laura 275, Lola 333, Margaret Rose 275, Martha 275, Melton 275, Melviene 275, Nancy Ellen 275, Pearl 141

NAYLOR, Alta Daisy (Freed) 195, Joseph 195
NEAL, Benjamin 148, Cody Mathew 146, 275, Eliza Jane Beard 275, Elsie (Johnson) 195, Enos 48, Henry 275, Luella Augusta 275, Manford 174, Mary 247, Mathew Franklin 181, Mathew "Matt" Franklin 146, 275, Mellie 200, Susanna (Elleman) 148, Susanne 183
NEALL, F.C. 34
NEASE, Martin 292
NEAVE, James S. 268
NEEDHAM, David 304, Elaine 304, Kristi Lynn 304
NEELY, Henry 91, Henry R. 159
NEER, Dana 75
NEFF, Grace 215
NELSON, Bertha (Mason) 256, Ellis 312, George 256, Karin Johanna 213, Nannie Catherine 338
NESBIT 59, John 13, Linda 301
NESTER, Ashley Jo 335, Samantha Nicole 335, William Gordon 335
NETHERCUTT, Sarah 246
NETTLETON, Dora (Mason) 256
NEUHAUSER, Larry Lee 173, Susan Virginia (Spence) 173
NEVERGALL, H. 34
NEW, John C. 340
NEWBURN, Benjamin Harrison 206, Benjamin Harrison Jr. 206, Doris Maxine 206, Everett Nathaniel 206, Robert Lewis 206
NEWBY, Amel (Long) 148, Anna 275, Cecil Orlif 275, Dorothy 275, Dustin Lee 276, Emma (Carver) 148, Ermal Jane 276, Glen 26, Glendola 107, Hanley Lester 276, Hellen Fennetta 276, Henry Clay 275, James Lee 276, Jennifer 276, Joshua 148, 275, Kenneth 61, Lemuel E. 276, Leonard 148, Leonard Ralph 276, Loren Elbert 276, Lou Ann 147, Louella (Neal) 148, Mark 276, Mary 275, Mary Elizabeth 276, Merrill 148, 275, Rebecca (Compton) 148, 307, Ruth 19, 20, Ruth Cox 275, Sally Anne 276, Seth B. 275, Terry 276, Thomas 148, 275, Thomas F. 275, William 275
NEWCOM, Barbara Jean 276, Charles 268, Charles "Pete" 268, Clarice Eileen 276, Earl Jr. 276, Eva 171, Jerry Lee 276, Jesse Earl 276, Liston 276, Loren 276, Margaret 276, Mary Lou 276, Matthew 268, Patricia Ann 276, Robert 276, William 171, 268, William Eugene 276
NEWCOMB, Harriett 276, James 276, John 276, Mary (Carey) 276, Mary Jane 276, Matthew Sr. 276, Matthew Jr. 276, Rebecca 276, William 276
NEWELL, Elizabeth 125
NEWHERD, George Frederick 266, John Jacob 266, Lorenz 266
NEWHOUSE, Eloise Powell 36, Lola Lodosca 194, Mary Francis 194
NEWKIRK, Francis 19, Frank L. 271, George 19
NEWLAN, Earl 337, Ethel (Hand) 337,
NEWLIN, Addie 276, Allen 66, 221, Allen T. 276, Andrew Melvin 276, Calvin 165, Clara Arminda 276, Edna Emogene 276, Emily Jane 165, Eva 276, Fleta P. 63, Hilda 276, 277, Hiram 18, 45, 125, James 276, John 276, 277, Joshua 276, Katie 276, Leo Max 276, Leo Max II, Mary 276, Mary Francis 138, Mary Lou 277, Mary Lou 276, Mary Pyle 276, 277, Murrel 276, 277, Murrel Lindley 276, Nancy A. 66, Nicholas 277, Rebecca (Hadley) 165, Rhoda (Jones) 276, Robert M. 276, Russell 277, Samera 46, Thomas 151, Thomas E. 66, 276, W.H. 46, 48, William 276, William Allen 276, Zimri 66
NEWLON 138
NEWMAN, Julie Lynn 198, LeRoy 198, Marie 218, Michael Francis 198, Pamela Lynn Sallee 198, Phylora Fern 153, Polly T. 319
NEWPORT, Agnes 183, Virginia 267
NEWSOM, Roy 119
NEWTON, Brad 25, Bradley 295, Cathryn Maxine (Prifogle) 288, 295, Everett 99, Isaac 156, Jeff 29, Norman 45, Virginia 261, Wesley Ray 295
NICE, John E. 16
NICHALSON, J.F. 158
NICHOLS, Donald 319, James Joel 319, Lena 288, Mary Katheryn 319, Sarah Brenneman 343, Sherman 66
NICHOLSON, Benjamin 142, Howard 261, Lowell 65, Lucille 107, Sarah Hannah (Carter) 142
NICKEL, Sandra 189
NIEHAUS, Norman 148
NIELANDER, Anna 277, Camille 277, Dorothy 277, Elizabeth May (Merrill) Moorman Cox 326, Helen 277, Joseph P. 277, Lucy 277, Paul 277, William 277, Winifred 277
NIESEN, Francis 92
NIESSE, Donna 248
NIGHT, Nathan D. 66
NILES, Brenda 178
NILMEIER, Thelma (Mason) 256
NIP-PO-WAH 27
NIVER, Florence 255
NIXON, Don 125, Elizabeth Moulder 268, Joan 125, Joseph Jr. 125, Marian 125, R. 34, Richard 60, 63, 103
NOBLE, Daniel F. 270, Deke 25, Frederick 191, Leafy (Harrison) 191, Osa 270
NOEL, Joseph 337, Karen 337, Katherine 337
NOGGLE, Edna Bell Lindsay 327
NOLTE, Fred Jr. 218
NORDMAN, John 215
NORDYKE, 245, Cilles 208, Daniel 208, James 208, Sarah Lindley 208
NORMAN, Roscoe 97
NORRIS, Bill 200, 332, Bobby 332, Julia 332
NORTH, Austin 11, Elizabeth Delana 183, Elizabeth Saul 85, Larker 27
NORTHCUTT, Amy 278, Charles Leo 277, Cleo (Morrow) 277, David 277, Emily 278, Gene 278, Helen Irene (Davis) 277, Joe 277, Joiner 277, Julie 277, Mary (Mann) 277, Mildred (Byrd) 277, Nancy 277, Richard 277, Roy 277, Susan 277
NORTHUM, Polly 191
NORTON, C.B. 34, Clara 205
NUNER 39, Bob 42, Jim 42, Lillie 343
NUNN, Margaret Jane 219
NUSBAUMER, Leah Ethelene 330
NUTTER, Cynthia Ann 168, Joseph 168, Nancy Ann (Gerhart) 168
NYENHUIS, Ruth 261
NYGAARD, Alvin 337

O

OAKLEY, J.M. 34, John 33, Loren 238, Orville 99
OAKS, Newton 332, Oscar 219
OAKSON, Rebecca (Campbell) 329
OATLEY, Ola S. 64
OBERMEYER 27, 161, Anna Maria (Bulk) 278, Charles F. 278, Clarence Charles 278, Dorothy Marie 278, 288, Edward 218, Edward George 278, Eleanor Lena 278, Elenor 99, Florence Margaret 278, Henry 278, 287, 295
OBERMEYER, Henry Matilda (Bulk) 288, Lorena Claire 278, Matilda (Bulk) 295, Rudolph Fred 278, Ruth Rose 278, Viola 122, Wilma Bernadine 152
OBERMYER, Henry 161
OBORN, J.W. 87
O'BRIEN, J.H. 94
ODELL, Amanda Jane 255, 256, Elizabeth (Cline) 256, Price 255, 256, 295
O'DELL, Price 83
ODEM, Mary 326,
ODEN Gaudeta 237
ODIM, David 33, John 33, W.G. 33
ODOM, Carroll 205, Hannah 268, Lewis 27, 268
ODON, L. 34
O'DONNELL, Ann Marie 278, Byrl Frank 278, Dean Cora 278, Glen Wilson 278, Harriet Curren 278, John Patrick 278, Laura Ann 278, Lida 336, Matthew 278, Patrick Warren 278, Pearl Pauline 'Pat' 278, Sharon Kay 278, Thomas 278
ODUMU 39
OGG, R.A. 103
OGLE, Abigail 278, Alice 278, Amanda 278, Anna 278, Audra (Sprong) 278, Bertie 278, Burl 278, Charlotte 278, Cleo 278, Delbert 278, Dora 278, Dorothy 278, Dwane 278, Elijah 278, Elisha 278, Elizabeth 278, Frank 278, Hannah Sarah (Brown) 278, James 278, Janice 278, Johnie 278, Linda 278, Lucinda 278, Mary (Jones) 278, Mary Jo (Wheeler) 333, Monroe 278L, N. Howard 333, Nancy 278, Nellie 278, Nelly 278, Patsy 278, Phebe 278, Rebecca 278, Ruby 278, Valentine 278, Valentine "Vollie" Charles 278, Wilda 278, William 278
O'GORMAN, Ella Fay 165
O'HARA 305, Mildred 234
OILAR, Belsora Catharine 279, Ben Franklin 279, Catharine 279, E. Joan 186, Harry 21, Henry Clay 279, Henry Clay 298, John McClain 279, Levi 278, Louisa May 279, Lucille 21, Martin Luther 279, Mary Jane 279, Robert 26, Mary Margaret 279
OLAND, Arletta (Ritenour) 280, James Roy 280
OLD BOB 279
OLDFATHER, Albert L. 193
OLIVER, D.C. 224, Dora 276, Zenobia 319
OLMSTED, Bethany Ann 311, David Carlisle 309, 311, Elizabeth Ann 309, 311, Lisa 311, Madalynn Kennedy 310, Marjorie Ann (Smith) 309, 311, Robert Charles 309, 311, Sara Elizabeth 311, Thomas Lee 309, 311
OLOFSON, Betty Schrader 303
OLSON, Anna 264, Ben 174

OLVIN, Pearl 42
OLWIN 39, Dora Belle 168
O'NEAL, Charles Daniel 313
O'NEIL, Mariam E. (Mayme) 167
OOLEY 39, 273
ORCUTT, Vessa "Bessie" (Hall) 207
O'REAIR, Beverly 197, Carroll Lou 197, Henry Garritson "Gary" 197, J. Hugh 197, Robert Hugh 197
OREM, Charles Wayne 26, Cheryl 298, Fern 25, Jay 298, Kay 298, Leon 298, Nancy 273, Nellie 25, Ray 298, Ronald 298
OREN, Sarah 214
ORMAN, Herbert 75
ORR, Audra 255, Clint Allen 183, Cora 255, Estle 255, Florence 255 Forrest 311, Frank 255, 256, Harold 138, Jemima (Franchier) 298, Joseph 144, Lester 255, Matthew 138, Melissa 138, Nancy Rebecca 144, 151, Otis 255, Robert 298, Robert D. 159, Sarah A. 298, William H. 19
ORSBURN, Carolyn 225, Francis 224, Janice 225, Omer 224
ORTEL, Jeanne Mae 184
ORTMAN 14, 36, Amy Joan 280, Bernard 99, Brian V. 280, Carolyn Joan 279, Edward 279, Emma 99, 237, 279, Erika Jayne 280, Eva Jane 279, Frank (Buss) 279, Henry 279, John 237, 279, John B. 279, John Bernard (J.B.) 279, John Bernard II 279, Josephine (Kerby) 237, Josephine Kerby 279, Julie Rose 279, Kathryn Grace 280, Lin 23, Mary Catherine 279, Ned 237, 279, Raymond 237, Raymond (Mick) 279, Richard 237, 279, Robert 237, 279, Robert Edward "Bob" 279, Rosa 279, Stanley E. 279, Verlin 279, William 279
OSBORN 48, 245, Albert 280, Anna Lee 280, Austin 66, Charles F. 326, Charlotte 326, Cindy Diana 275, Clyde Leland 280, David Louis 275, Devonna 280, Devonna J. 280, Glenn Eastburn 280, Herman Kenneth 263, Jeffrey Allen 280, Jesse Albert 280, Jesse G. 280, Jesse Garland 280, Jesse L. 326, Judy 280, Judy A. 280, Kenneth 326, Larry 280, Larry C. 280, Laura Francis (Fleming) 280, Leila 280, Linda 280, Linda K. 280, Mary 326, Mary M. 305, Maxine 280, Patricia 280, Penelope Susan 280, Richard 326, Roberta Jean 280, Sharon (Sherry) June 263, Thomas Leland 280, Virgil 326, Warren Frances 280
OSBORN(E), Elizabeth 245, John 245
OSBORNE, Comfort Langrum 212, Eliza 286, Marcile 236, Meda Froflich 36, Rachel 214, Stephen 212
OSBURN, Francis E. 48
OSTLER, Lorenzo B. 320
OSWALT, Mary 196
OTEHAM, Ashley Marie 280, Edmund 280, Iva Mae (Kellam) 280, Ronald Jay 280, Ryan James 280, Sharlene Kay 280, Willa Rose (Oland) 280
OTT, Rebecca 246
OTTO, Elmer 29, Freeman 29, Marvin 29
OUELLETTE, Pamela Ann 228
OUSLEY, Andrea 278, Benjamin Patrick 278, Homer 278, Isaac Christopher 278, John 278, Larry Dean 278, Laura 278, Marchita Kay 278

OUZTS, Nell (Holliday) 282, Walter 282
OVERHOLSER, Abraham 280, Bethel 280, Catherine Gossett 280, Charles Augustus 280, Daniel 218, 280, Daniel Gossard 280, David 59, Jemima Collins 263, Leona Fidilla 263, Martha 280, Nancy Ann 218, Obediah 280, Rebecca 280, Sharon 281, Tobias 263, 280
OVERMAN, Ben F. 175, Ester 273, Hannah 178, Miriam 54, Mordecai 48, Obediah 163, Price 163, Sarah 219, Sarah Ann 163, 218
OVERMYER, Julia Kathleen 283, Marcia 283, Rachel Christine 283, Sara Elizabeth 283
OVERTON, Grace Sloan 42
OWEN, James 46, William 173
OWENS, Howard 264, Jacob 193, Juanita 264, Rachel 235
OWINGS, N.J. 34
OYLER, Abrilla 281, Albert 281, Calvin 281, Catherine 281, Elizabeth 281, Fred 281, Henry 281, Jacob 281, John Henry 281, Joseph Barton 281, Juanita Grace 281, Lena 150, Lena Leota 281, Mary Frances 281, Robert C. 225, Robert Henry 281, Susannah (Crowell) 281
OZENBAUGH, Louise 276

P

PACK, Leanna 158
PADGETT, Elvina (Barney) 224, J.H. 116, Jake 25, Mary 21, 23, Mary Irene 148
PAGE, Bob 97
PALAITH, Margot 284
PALM, Susan Elizabeth 197
PALMER, Cora Bell 204, Eddie 204, Elmer 204, Emma Sylvia 204, Freddie 204, Jesse Samuel "Jim" 204, Jonathon 204, Karen Denise 182, Leondus M. "Lonzo" 204, Rebecca A. Brandon 204, Robert 33, Robert D. 27, Russell Lee "Pete" 205, T.H. 103
PARK, James D. 326, Sarah Evalyn 231, 326
PARKER, Asa 48, Chester C. 236, Clyde 9, Deliah 157, Elizabeth 290, Esther 23, Esther Grace 184, Ezekiel 48, Henry 35, Kathy 23, Maude 273, Omer 149, Theodoria Jane (Dosha) 233
PARKEY, Alfred 322, Mary E. 322
PARKHURST, Alonzo 282, Camden Blake 282, Christopher Ora 282, David Michael (Huff) 282, Donal Eugene 282, Donal Eugene, Jr. 282, Elsie (Pentecost) 282, Goldie Janice (Freed) 196, Janice 282, Janice (Freed) 170, 282, 289, Jean 282, Jean (Hounchell) 282, Jean (Hounchell) (Huff) 282, Jordon Marie 282, Kay LaEllen 282, Marinell (Ouzts) 282, Nicholas Daniel 282, Ora 170, 196, 282, 289, Philip Alan 282, Rachael Elizabeth 282, Richard Arlen 282, Robert Leon 282, Roger Dale 282, Russell 282, Russell Ora, Jr. 282, Russell Ora, Sr. 282
PARKS, Arnold 281, Barbara 281, Blanche (Morrison) 281, Blanche (Morrison) 282, Clara 281, Cora Mae 281, David 193, Della 281,

Doris Lorrine (Bryant) 281, Edward 281, Erma (Hadlock) 281, Flora Opal 281, Gene 281, Heber 282, Helen 281, Horace 281, Ida (Nash) 281, Ida Jane (Nash) 282, James 281, Jennifer Nichole 336, John 281, 28, Kenneth Randall 336, L.S. 95, Lucy 282, Marietta 281, Mary Katherine 281, Mary Lou 281, Morris 281, Muriel Helena 281, Paul Allen 282, Paul Edward 281, Randy 336, Richard 281, Robert 281, Robert Leon 281, Rolland 281, Sarah 344, Shirley Jane 281, Troy Herron 336, Valoris 281, Walter 281, Walter Jr. 281, Walter Miller 281, Walter Ray 281, William Heber 281
PARR, James A. 66, W.D. 70
PARRISH, Sarah 179
PARSE, Alice 253, Alice Lucille 252, Jesse Hendricks 252, Martha 252, Oliver Howard 252
PARSON, James 19
PARSONS, Alan Drew 284, Alan Joseph 284, Ann 283, 284, Anne 283, Barbara Ellen 283, Carolyn 283, Carrie 283, Chad 283, Charles 283, Daniel 283, David William 283, Delbert J. 283, Don 257, Donald 283, Donald Ward 283, Douglas 283, Edith 283, Eliza Jane (Breedlove) 156, Elizabeth Jane 283, Eph 282, Ephraim 283, Fredrick Lloyd 283, Gary Eugene 283, Geneva 230, 283, Geneva Jane 189, George 284, Heather 283, Helen 99, 283, Helen Catherine 283, Holly 283, Howard 99, 284, James 283, Jason Howard 283, Jedediah 284, Jeffrey 283, Jennay 283, Jennifer Lynn 283, Joseph 283, Judy Ann 283, Kenneth 284, Lloyd 283, Loren 283, Marie Catherine 283, Mary Ann 283, Maxine 283, Maxine Clair 283, Melba 65, Melissa 283, Michael 283, Mildred 283, Milton Joseph 283, Oswand 284, Patricia 284, Priscilla 284, Ray 283, Raymond Lewis 283, Rebecca 283, Rebecca Rose 283, Richard 283, Richard Earl 283, Rick 283, Rick Allen 283, Robert Lloyd 284, Rolla Lee 283, Russell 283, Sandra Kay 283, Sarah Elizabeth 284, Sharon Rose 283, Steve Kent 283, Susan 283, Thomas Eldon 283, Virginia 283, Virginia Rose 283, William 284, Zachary 284, Zachery William 283
PARVIN, Donald 26
PASKELL, Alvera 108
PASLEY, Freddie Eugene 283, Helen 107, Marleene Sue 283
PASQUALE, Lynn 78
PASSONS 248
PASSWATER, Orville 56
PATTEN, M.T. 48, Pennina 189
PATTERSON, Charles A. 13, James M. 79, John 12, 305
PATTON, Arthur C. 85, George 195, John 245, Rebecca A. 295, Rose 96
PATTY, Delene 337, Douglas 337, Joe 337
PAUL, Aileen Delmay (Suttles) 330, Gertrude (Paul) 330, Jolana Donnita 330, Sam Jr. 330, Samuel Robert 330, William 75
PAVEY, Leonard 26, Lorretta 234
PAXTON, Andy 219
PAYNE 86, Chad Everett 333, Daniel A. 284, Deborah Lee 284, Diane Louise 333, Dixie (Bowen) 333, Edna Jones 48, James Albert 284, Joel Jeptha 284, John Leonard Wilkinson 284, John Robert 284, John William 284, 333, Judith Marie 284, Ralph V. 279, Shirley D. Fisher 279, William Joe 284, 333
PEABODY, Barbara Ruchti 284, Charles 284, Elnora 284, Florence 284, H.W. "Hod" 284, Hannah 284, Jack Gregory 284, Kendall 284, Kendall William 284, Linda Lee 284, Thomas Allen 284,
PEACOCK, John 284, Joseph 66, Marie 284
PEARCH, Ira 255, 256, Lovell 255, Pauline 255, Ruth 255
PEARCY, Marjorie Maxine 246
PEARRE, R.E. 68
PEARSEY, Charles 304
PEARSON, Bernice (Williams) 310, Bruce 315, Charles 284, Geneva 284, Harry A. 284, Janet 285, 309, Janet D. 310, Jeff 315, Levi 48, Mike 315, Neal 285, 310, Nellie (Burkholder) 284, Phillip J. 285, 310, Ross 285, 310, Wayne A. 284, 310
PECK, Chester 305, Corum 85, Ray 138, 184
PEEK, Jane Sadie 202, Pearl Findley 147, Regina May 322
PEEL, Max E. 122
PEELE, Edmund 52, 53, 64, Mary J. 53
PEERMAN, Mary Katherine Stevens 316
PEIGH, Michael 301
PELGEN, Cheryl Marie 190, Cody 190, David Gabriel 190, Michael Lee 190, Robert 190, Ronald 190, Virginia 190
PELLETT, Francis 207
PEMBERTON, John 119
PENA, Ethel 156
PENCE, Harold 211, Minnie 217, Rachel 274
PENDERGRASS, Glessie (Parrish) 211, Paul 211, Wilma Jane 211
PENLAND, Hiram Fernandes 230, 231, 285, John 285, Letticia (Price) 230, 231, Lorena 231, Margaret 285, Mary Ellen 285,, Ruth "Lorena" 230, 231, 285
PENLAND-JOHNSON, Lorena 285
PENN, Martha 247, William 60, 176, 209, 222, 340
PENNINGTON, Addelia 269, Andrew 86, Martha 235, Murl 169
PENTECOST, Mary Jane 198
PEPKA 138
PERCELL, Effie Pearl 160, Elizabeth (Drabenstot) 160, James Robert 160, Nancy (Wilson) 160, William 160
PERCIFIELD, Michael 85
PERCIVAL, Emma 286, Harry 286, Mary Jane (Connor) 286
PERILLA, Jennifer 337, Luigi 337, Michelle 337, Stephen 337
PERKINS, Donna 196, Elizabeth 141, Ernest Leroy 285, Grace Ethyl Jetmore 285, Joseph Alva 304, Leona Pearl 285, Lillian 285, Minerva 212, Ted 285, William Albert 285
PERO, Rebecca 85
PERRIGEN, Suzette Rachel (Grady) 203
PERRY, David 95, Emma 189, H.A. 95, H.F. 83, James W. 189, Marian Weaver 176, Mary Jane Hensley 189, Walter 64
PERSIFALL/PURCIFUL, Sina Christina 149
PERVIANCE, B.T. 83
PETER 39
PETERS, Daniel 231, Elizabeth Marvin 315, Ferne L. 315, John 43, Leona (Spanwell) 231, Mary A. 338, Pernell 231, Stephen 35, W.D. 315
PETERSEN, David 64, Denise Renee 163, Jeanine 163, Paul 163
PETERSON, Gerald G. 306, Gerald M. 306, Gregory S. 306, James 313, Jorja Jo 313, Louise 214, Mary Ann (Smith) 306, Russell 96, Shawn Rowe 306, Wesley 290
PETRO, Carole 285, Charles 285, James 285, James Addison 285, James M. 285, Joseph 285, Joseph E. 285, Karll 285, Nancy 285, Rebecca Rich 285, Robert 285, Sharon 285, Walter 285
PETTENGILL, Herbert D. Jr. 66
PETTER, Miriam Lucille Tritsch 326
PETTIJOHN, C. 31
PETTY 39, Malinda 199, Ola 65
PETTYFORD, J.F. 95
PETTYJOHN 48
PFAFF, Suzie 210
PFEFFERLE, Georgianna 343, Louis John 343, Robert 343, William 343
PFEIFFER, Christine 319
PHARR, Kent 325
PHELPS, Alice 187, Tom 117
PHILIPPS, Laura Ann 148
PHILIPS, A.F. 125, C.H. 125, T.C. 125, W.R. 125
PHILLIPS, Bryan David 148, Deborah A. 193, Elizabeth 140, Esther 62, Hellen 299, Homer 202, Isaac 62, Joseph J. 26, Karen Jo (Beatty) 147, Lindsay Marie 148, Mary 206, Melissa Kay 148, Melody Lea 333, T.C. 103, Timothy 232, Winifred 146
PHIPPENNEY, Rosalinda 201
PHIPPS, Clifford 23, Mary Lou 273
PICKARD, Joan (Gordon) 202
PICKERING, Ellis 82, Emily 234, Ernest 75, Jane 286, Jane (White) 219, Jonathan 219, 286, Jonathan R. 51, Lelah 219, Phineas 286, Rebecca 286, Ruth 25
PICKETT, Benjamin D. 16, Chris 246, Christine 246, Cindy 336, Clerwell 27, Diana 315, Everett Carroll 154, Gene 122, Grant 38, Guy 35, Jason 246, John 327, Mary 108, 192, Mary Roach 154, Michelle 249, Nathan 131, Oscar 38, Patricia 327, Richard Oliver 154, Tim 246, Zackery 246
PICKNEY, Vivian 186, William 186
PIERCE, Alexander Clinton 287, Alexander S. 286, 287, 338, Alma Sue Hollingsworth 276, Amanda Jane 286, Amanda Jane 338, Catherine Pritts 286, Cecil 304, Charles Edward 221, Charles William 286, 287, Christine 304, Clarence 287, Clarence Cecil 286, 287, David Allen 163, 221, Dolly Mae (Ringeisen) 221, Elmer Verne 287, Emma 304, Ezra 48, Fleta 276, Galen Morris 287, George B. 300, George William 287, Gladys Ruth 147, Glen Clyde 287, Harriet Ellen 287, Henry Samuel 286, 287, Holly Suzanne 163, 221, James Robert 286, John Edward 163, 221, Jonah 52, Josie Katherine 287, Judith Lee 287, Larry Eugene 287, Lester Everett 287, Loretta 305, Loudisa Delcina "Della" 287, Lovell Alexander 287, Lovell DeWitt 286, 287, Ludica J. 286, Mable Nora 287, Mariah Louisa 286, Mark Galen 287, Mary Anna (Horner) 287, Maryette 287, Myrtie Bell (Roberts) 286, Nancy (Skinner) 286, 287, 338, Nedra 287, Nora Bell 286, Norma 304, Norma Jean 286, Ralph L. 287, Richard Otis 287, Rita 304, Rita Marie 286, Robert 304, Samuel C. 286, 289, Samuel Clinton 287, Steve 304, Steven Taylor 286, Trudy 304, Trudy Kay 286, Virginia Lee 287, Virginia Lee 304, Wesley 286, William Orthis 286, William Oscar 286
PIKE, John 274, Mary 274
PILE 288, Ervin 148, Luanna 148
PINGLETON, Margaret 23
PINKERTON, Frederick K. 197, Ralph 23
PINKHAM, William 47
PIOTROWICZ, Brenda 72, John 72, 85
PITCHER, Amber Cheri 238, Brandon William 238, Scott 238
PITMAN, Dorothy 65, Hiram 249, Maggie 249
PITZER, Jane 107, Mary 209
PIXLER, Charles 234, Hodson 234, Ira 234, Lenora 234, Lenora Catherine 234, Lessie 234, Mahala 234, Rivers 234, Sarah 234, Thomas Van 234, Willard Earl 234
PLANK, Anna Catherine (Heinmiller) 191, Christopher Logan 287, Daniel James 287, David Alan 287, David Andrew 287, Edwin 145, 146, Edwin Eugene 287, Edwin Logan 287, Elias 191, Eva Veronica (Logan) 287, Harry Albert 287, Jan Claire 287, Julia Ann 287, Lauren Elizabeth 287, Lydia Caroline 191, Norma Jean (Barber) 145, 146, Phillip Edwin 287, Timothy Aaron 287
PLANKENSTAVER, George 48, Thomas 48
PLATT, Fay 145, Joe 331, William 212
PLETCHER, Don 268
PLONA, Phyllis 107
PLOSS, Fred 154, Goldie 154, Jennifer 154, Jodi 154, Michael 154
PLOTNER, Harry R. 168, Jody Kay 168
PLOUGH, Debbie 135
PLOUGHE, Isaac Newton 245, Preston Hopkins 245, T.C. 83
PLUMMER, Dale 197, Dwaine 197, Ethel 332, Frances Marie 193, Fred 197, John F. 91, Louise 197
POE, Ethel 285, Ina Kelley 285, Sandy W. 285
POET, L.E. 183
POFF, Matthew 48, Samuel 48, William 48
POHLMAN 161, Autumn 288, Brian 288, Carl 288, Charles 287, 288, Christian 287, Dena 287, Dora 161, 287, Dora Bulk 287, Doshia 288, Elizabeth (Kerkhoff) 288, Frank 287, Fred 287, Fred Jr. 287, George "Buck" 288, Gordon 287, Harry 288, Henry 287, Lena Doepke 288, Lesie 287, Linda 288, Marie Heidorn 287, Michael 288, Michele (Pedde) 288, Minnie 287, Robert "Bob" 288, Ronald E. 288, Staci 288, William 287, 288
POISEL, Abner 33
POLAND, Philip 243, Robert 243, Stephen 243, Thomas 243
POLASKE, Clarence 157
POLHMAN, Henry 287, Herman 287, Mary Kerkhoff 287, Ray 287
POLITZ, Bill 97, William 99
POLK, Adoline 318, Benjamin 145, 318, Catherine (Beckner) 295, Earl 318, Edna 318, Eliza Hendrix 317, Emerson 196, Ernest 255, Ernest R. 256, Ethel 255, Joseph 15, 295, 318, Mabel 318, Mabel Marie 317, Martha 295, Mary 318, Mary Alice 318, Orrel 318, Orville 255, Sarah Alice 212, Sophia (Harness) 295, Thomas 318, Thomas J. 295, William 318, William Lockard 318, Willis 317, 318
POLLARD, Mary Slocum 307
POLLEY, J.W. 10
POLLOCK, James 27, Josephine 141, 256, Ralph 66
POLOCK, James 33
POND, Eleanor Margaret 271
PONDER, Mary 262, N.V. 262, Sally Dee 259, 262
PONTIUS, Marguerite 298
POORE, Mary 14
POPE, Anna 326, Gary Lee 152, James Lawrence 152, Lena 13, Robert 152, Sondra Lee 333
PORTER, Eliza Jane 144, Gene Stratton 242, Judy (Krajewski) 86, Mazie 61
POSTEN, Livi 291, Susanna 291
POSTGATE, Mary 216
POTTENGER, David 23
POTTER, J.W. 70, Marlene 149, Orra Elvira 216, Terrie 195
POTTS, Brenda 138, David 138, Gilbert 138, Karen 138, Marsha 138, Wilma 138
POUND, Faye 238
POUNDSTONE, Caroline 342
POWELL 42, E. 36, Ernest 50, Harry 305, Jerri 166, Jimmy 37, John 35, 113, Kenny 166, Lemuel 35, 37, Lloyd 21, Mary Ann (McCool) 322, Pam 166, Pauline (Fansler) 166, Pauline (Shrock) 166, Pearl Lilia 322, Regina Ann (Grinslade) 205, Robert 86, Ronald "Red" 166, Ronnie 166, Sarah 234, Sarah E. 225, W. 36, Wayne 42, 189, Sarah 37
POWER, Francis M. 15, John Thomas 212
POWERS, Annie E. 227, Iva Pearl 254, Johanna (Jo) 322, Rebecca Rhodes 336
PRAME, Frances M. 173
PRATHER, Laura 305
PRATT, Robert J. 94, Rosella 343, Sarah J. 149, William 149
PREBBLE, John Stephen, Jr. 288, Oscar Byron 288
PREBLE, Oma 288, 318, Thomas 288
PRECHODKO, Don 325
PRESING, Zella 197
PRESTON, Christine 332, Junior 332, Karen 332, Terry 332
PREVO, Stanley 276
PRIBBLE, Benjamin B. 288, Benjamin Byron 288, John Stephen, Sr. 288, Martin Marshall 288
PRICE, Anna 14, 171, April 288, Austin Jacob 288, Casey 288, Charles 13, 152, 171, Connie Jo (Louks) 288, Dennis 171, Elizabeth (Miller) 255, Florence J. (Kenworthy) 236, Gary 288, George 171, Gerald 171, Grace M. Embree 236, 288, Harold 171, Isaac 15, 44, 147, 319, Jacob 15, Jeffery 236, Jeffery Allen 288, Jerry 288, Jerry A. 236, Jerry Lee 288, Jewel 309, 310, Kami 288,

Katharine 44, Lettica E. 285, Levi Alexander 295, Luther 255, Marcheta (French) 255, Marinda (Gorden) 171, Marley J. 236, 288, Mary 262, Mary Catherine 15, Mary Katharine 44, Michael 16, Nancy 44, Nancy Evaline (Rinehart) 295, Oscar 171, Pearl 255, Richard 171, Robert 171, Russell B. 288, Russell B. 236, Sophia 270, Sophia Angelina 270, T. 95, Thomas 231, Toni (Guy) 288, William M. 300
PRICHARD, Mary Louise Zeigler 342
PRICKETT, Phyllis Rogers 36
PRIDAY, Brad 178, Kayla 178, Kelsey 178
PRIEST, Lewis 173
PRIFOGLE 161, Anna Eliza (Huber) 288, Bruce Edward 288, 295, Carl 231, Carl Edward 257, 288, 295, Chad Tyson 288, Clifford 295, Clifford Eugene 288, Clifford Irvin 288, Clifford Irvin, Jr. 288, Clifford Irwin 278, Earl Walter 288, Edwin Wesley 288, Frank John Martin 288, James Stephen 288, 295, James Trent 295, Joel Edward 295, John 288, John Albert 288, June 288, Kenneth Edward 288, Leona Ruth 288, Louisa (Bossert) 278, Louisa M. (Bossert) 288, Louise (Bossert) 295, Lucas Wayne 295, Marie (Obermeyer) 295, Michael 295, Michael John 278, 288, Michael Kent 288, Peter 288, Ralph Eugene 288, Samuel Lee 295, Scott Michael 288, Stephen Todd 295, Terrence Lee 288, Thomas Gregory 295, Timothy Allen 288, Virginia (Rinehart) 231, 295, William Jennings 288, Wilma Marie 288
PRINCE, Jack 222
PRING, Aletha (Albright) 278, George 278, Walter K. 278
PRITCHARD, Mary 178
PRITTS, Alva Hayes 289, Catherine 287, 288, Cecil 289, Claude 289, Dora 289, Elizabeth 288, Florence 289, Harrison 289, James Monroe 289, John R. 286, 288, Joseph M. 288, Josephine 288, Levi 287, Levi Joseph, 288, Mattie Marie 289, Oliver 289, Oliver Marion 288, Owen Marion 289, Pearl (Bud) 289, Perry 289, Phebe 287, 288, 289, Raymond A. 289, William 289
PRITZ 288, Nicole Lynn 223, 297
PRITZKAU, Flossie (Mason) 256
PROPES, Angelia Ranae 232, 289, Dwayne H. 232, Dwayne Harrison 289, James Claude "Buck" 289, Jason Cole 232, 289, Rachel Leigh 232, 289
PROSS, Max 106
PROSSER, Rebecca 207
PROYER, Horace 19
PRUETT, John Duane 284, Patricia Sue (Payne) 284
PRUPECKER, Barbary 280
PSAUF, Rosie 283
PTACIN, Gregory J. 125
PUCKETT 48, Sherry 243
PUGH, Bathsheba 227, William T. 51
PULLEN, Alice 208, Joyce 171, Ryan 322
PURCELL, Margaret 257
PURDUM, Nelson 112
PURDY, Nina Dale 170
PURSLEY, J. 34
PURVIANCE, Levi 144
PURVIS, Elsie 282, Elsie Elizabth (Parkhurst) 289, Harold 282,

Harold Eugene 289, Harry 289, Jeffrey Eugene 289, Jeffrey Scott 289, Mary Watts 329, Maxine 187, Terry Allen 289, Terry Bradley Allen 289, Vera 289
PUSATERI, Aaron James 151, June Arlene (Carlile) 151
PUTNEY, Everett 248
PYANOWSKI, Cathy 289, Douglas 289, George 289, George Vincent 143, Jean 289, Jean Antoinette 143, Jessamine 143, 289, John 143, 289, John Jr. 143, 289, Linda 289, Partricia Eileen 143, Patricia 289, Robert 289, Robert Adrian 143, Robin 289, Samuel 289
PYKE, J.W. 34, Mary 274
PYLE 86, 288, Elizabeth 269, Howard 3, Jane 3, Lucinda Powell 289

Q

QUAINTANCE, Alice D. 13, Eli 13, Lucy 195
QUAKENBUSH, Barbara Sue 290, Betty Joan 290, Clarice Emily 290, Frank Dabe 289, Hannah (Lee) 289, John D. 289, John T. 289, Leora Ann 289, Martha Marie 289, Mary Helen 290, Mildred Jane 290, Nancy E. 289, Richard John 290, Ruth Eleanor 290, Thomas 289, Warren 290, William Frederick 290, William Henry 289
QUALTER, Winnie 293
QUEIN, LaRue 253
QUICK, Alma 285, Gary Jay 153, George 153, Glenda 204, James 19, James Richard 181, Robert Lee 153, Velma 163, Wade 200
QUIMBY, Florence (Trueblood) 330, Louis 330
QUINN 175, 271, 273, 290, Archibald 290, Austin 290, Bernard 97, Christopher Todd 290, Earl Jr. 192, 290, Ernest 290, Ethel 290, James 290, Jessica Ashley 290, Jim 290, Joshua Allen 290, Justin Andrew 290, Marti 290, Nancy 290, Randall Scott 290, Susan Jane 192, 290, Thomas Michael 192, 290, Timothy Mark 192, 290, Timothy R. 187
QUIRING, Marjorie 253

R

RABBE, Patricia 3
RADABAUGH, Dorothy 50, Marion 50
RADCLIFF, Agnes 197, Amy Marie 317, Kimberly Beth 317, Mike 317, Timothy Michael 317, Tyler Matthew 317
RADEMACHER, Martin Walt 290, Pamela June 210, 290
RADER, Edna Mae 248
RADMACHER 94
RAGLAND, Russ 186
RAIL, Jonathan M. 300
RAINES, Harry 183
RAISOR, Ivan 134, Mike 134
RAJALA, Annie 230
RAKESTRAW, Henry E. 49, Malinda (Hendricks) 216
RALPH, Harold 13

RALSTON, Samuel 228, Thomas 27
RAMEY, R. 34
RAMIREZ, Carol 154
RAMSAY, Precilia Jane 313, Alta Mae 195, Isaac 18
RAMSEYER, Abigail 291, Ada B. 291, Aprecia 291, Arthur 291, Barbara 292, Catherine 292, Cebern 291, Daniel 291, 292, Edward Patton 292, Eliza 291, Elizabeth 291, 292, Emma J. 291, Eurelean 291, Flora 291, Frederick 291, George B. 291, George M. 292, Jacob 292, James A. 291, James M. 291, John 291, John C. 291, John Daniel 291, Joseph B. 291, Laura 291, Linda 291, Lydia V. 291, Mariah 187, Mariah Sarah 188, 292, Martha 291, McClellan, 291, Nancy A. 291, Obediah 291, Oscar V. 291, Peter V. 291, Philip 18, 291, 292, Philip E. 291, Phillip 188, Polly 292, Preston 291, Silas D. 19, Simon P. 291, Vivian Ann 291
RAMSYERE, Jacob 291, 292, Mary (Bearfoot) 291,292, Philip 291
RANDALL, Alvin 193, Armanda 19, D. 34, Floyd 193, Leslie 25, Max 23, Opal 25, Shirley 193, Thomas 193, John W. 194, Mariah 194
RANDERSON, Bridget (McCormick) 328, Christopher 328
RANDOLPH, Charles M. 51, Francis M. 150, Jary 53, Jay 96, Josiah 96, Melinda (Baker) 150, Silas F. 51, William 96, 150
RANEY, Betty Lou (Wheeler) 333, Carmen 233, Nelson 333
RANI, Daniel 33
RANKIN 34
RANSDELL 229
RAREY 28, D. 34, Daniel 28, George 27
RATCLIFF, Bethel Barber 317, Blanche E. 172, Clara Lillian 238, Ida 159, Isaac 65, John T. 66, Mary 317, Owen 66, Rebecca 66, Ronald Ray 313, Russell 317
RATCLIFFE, A.C. 19, Elizabeth 19, Jesse 19, John 19, Margaret 298, Martha 19, Rachel 19
RATHBUN, Joel 318
RATLIFF, Earl Robert 159, Francis B. 159, Larry David 159, Mary Frances 159, Ruth Ann 159
RAUTH, Margaret 239
RAVER, Barbara Ann 291, Beth Anne 291, Mark J. 291, Paul J. 291, Paul T. 291, Rita Joan 291, Shirley F. (Schultz) 291
RAWLINGS, Elva 169, Lauretta 183, Mollie 169, William 169
RAY 89, Barbara 192, Chesley 209, David 85, Kitura Bell 217, Lela 223, Mahala 235, Naomi 50, Rachel 256, Robert 246, Thelma 171, Vernon 171
RAYBURN, Hayden 247
RAYL, Allen B. 268, Allen Blaine 291, Anthony John 291, Barbara 19, Betty Jane 291, Catherine 291, Charles 117, Christian 291, Cora Blanche Barr 291, Dallas Gayle 291, David 291, Donavon Francis 291, Durwood 117, Duward LeMar 291, Eleanor 268, 29, Eli 291, Elijah 291, Elizabeth 268, 291, Elizabeth A. 291, Elwood 291, Emil Cortise 291, Emily Katie Newlin 276, Francis E. 198, George A. 198, Gerald Paul 291, Glen 186, Greenberry 291, Hannah 291, Harold Eugene 291, James 291, James Christopher 291, James F. 291, James H. 291, Jane 291, Jimmy 291, John

14, 291, John C. 291, John Franklin 291, John P. 291, John R. 291, Joseph Booth 291, Julia Ann 291, Katherine E. 291, Lavicia 291, Levi 291, Manville 66, Manville "Jack" 276, Mary A. 291, Matilda 215, Mildred Irene 276, Noble 291, Oscar 291, Permelia Jane 291, Pheba Maye 276, Phebe 291, Phineas 291, Rheba Faye 276, Richardson 291, Samuel 291, Sarah Ann 291, Stephen 291, Susan 291, Thomas 291, Thomas Edward 291, Thomas Jefferson 291, Vera 186, William 291, William F. 291, William Harrison 291
RAYLE, Hazel McAninich 288
RAYLS, Bill 135, 178
RAYMOND, Willard 167
REA, Richard 19, Richard R. 104
REABEL, Robert 208
REAGAN, Jehu 47, 61, Laura 140
REAMES, Beatrice 224, William 224, Ethel 155
REAMY, Dorothy 159
RECORD, Adam T. 292, Armilda (Farlow) 292, Bernice 216, Blaine 292, Blanche 292, Carole Moline 292, D.M. 292, Della 292, Elaine (Moline) 292, Fred William 292, Grace (Kellar) 292, John F. 292, Lincoln Farlow 292, Mary 292, Paul Linville 292, Robert Lincoln 292, Stella 292, Theresa 292
REDDICK, Angelo 138, Ella (Stephenson) 138
REDDIN, Claudia Evelina 172, 342, William 342
REDDING, Elizabeth Kelly 337, Esther 14, Gene 23, Rex 222, Sarah 225
REDDY, James 291
REDMAN, Birtha Mae 195, Mary 284
REDMON, Sharon 233
REDMOND, B.F. 13
REE, Rose 219
REECE 190
REED, Abby 190, Arthur 297, Carol 190, Cecil 46, Darrell 163, Deloris 163, Doris 163, Doyle 163, Gary Robert 182, George Vincent 197, Harrison 246, Holly 190, Judy 180, Lillian 163, Mark 25, Mary 44, Matthew 190, Olive 201, Rebecca Alice 197, Robert 163, Russell 46, Sarah 201, Thomas 190, W.H. 10, Wanita (Coughlin) 176
REEDER 245, J.M. 34, James D.C. 291, Jonathan 35
REEL, Cyrena 156, Sallie 171, Stella 287
REEM, J. 34
REESE, Elizabeth (Roe) 306, James 306, Lillie (Jacobs) 306, Samuel Tillden (Till) 306
REEVES, Emma Elmira (Seckenger) 324, Linda 230, William Madison 324
REICHARD, John 160, Mary (Witmer) 160
REICHERT, Mary 221
REID, Ada 229, Elizabeth 183
REIGEL, Linda Johnson 152
REIFF 13
REISH, Paul 62
REISIGER, Katherine 277
REISINGER, Addie 292, Clinton 292, Daniel 292, Elmer 292, Lillie 292, May 292, Rosetta Croker 292
REMINGTON, Pete 39, 40
REMMINGER, Dora 287
REMY, C.A. 138, Walter 138

RENCH, Daisy Bilby 204
RENIE 292, Augustus 221, 293, 324, Bartholomew 293, Catherine (Gasper) 221, Cecilia A. 221, 293, Charles 293, Charles H. 221, Charles Henry 293, Edward 293, Edward John 293, John 293, Joseph 293, Joseph William 293, Joseph Wm. 293, Josephine 293, Margaret J. 293, Mary A. 293, Mary Josephine 293, Robert 293, Timothy 293, William A. 293
RENSHAW, 271, Delite (Cohee) 168, Jerry L. 168, John M. 168, Leo 271, Leo J. 168, Mary Louise (Granson) 224, William J. 168
RESER, David 25, David M. 45, Michael 26
RESLER, H. Dean 104
RETHERFORD, John 62, 66
RETHLAKE, John Bernard 271
REVOLT, Barbara Dianne (Ellis) 186, Christine 186, Debra 186, Jeffrey 186, Robert 186
REX, Wm. 48
REYNOLDS, Allen 66, Armilda McComas 293, Berdina 214, Bert 293, Bert Monroe 293, Elwood 293, Emma Charlene 315, Ezra 35, Frank 293, Henry 213, Iva M. (Jordan) 206, James Edgar 293, James L. 293, Jessie Pearl 293, Kent Allen 293, Martha 213, Mildred Bell Wolford 337, Percey Elwood (Bert) 316, Percy Elwood 293, Robert Elwood 293, Tanya 316, Tanya Claudine 316, Toby Michael 293, Vianna 316, Vianna Stanford 293, Wilbur 206, Wm. Franklin 316
RHEA, Alexander 35
RHINEHART, Lonnie 277
RHOADES, Larry 78
RHODA, G. 34
RHODES, Andrew 177, Dustin 331, Eva May 143, Frank 143, J. 34, Michelle Winslow 331, Riley 177, William 177
RHODY, George 298
RICE, Alfred L. 257, Anthony 294, Bonnie 19, Dixie 257, George 145, Hale 196, Harriett (Young) 256, Ida Mae 257, Isaac 229, James 256, Marjorie 337, Minnie 196, Peter 15, Rae 196
RICH, Amy 293, Anna 65, 196, Betsy 293, Betsy Peacock 293, Heidi 293, John 85, Kenneth C. 106, Kenneth Heston 293, Kenneth Howard 293, Levi 293, Lowell 104, Mary Ann 60, 63, Mary Lou 32, Matthew 293, Michael 293, Moses 52, Moses L. 65, Phyllis Jean 293, Rita 293, Robert Heston 293, Ronald 32, Sarah 219, Thomas 293, William 65
RICHARDS, Andrew 208, B.B. 60, Barbara Ann 208, Bernard 262, Edgar 48, Jewell Ray 149, Thelma Hall 208
RICHARDSON, Dow 125, E.O. 107, Enoch 196
RICHARDVILLE, Jean Baptiste 27, 264
RICHASON, Patricia Elaine 173
RICHER, Nick 41
RICHEY 28, Alice Jane 147, Christina Lynn 147, Mary Durr 204
RICHMOND 94, Corydon 123, Floyd Jonnie 148, N.P. 125
RICKARD, Amanda 293, Anthony (Rueckert) 293, Arcemus "Tynt" 293, Arthur 294, Ben 294, Benjamin Franklin 293, Daniel 293, Drucilla (Fisher) 294, Easter 293, Frances 293, Francis 294, Henry 294, John 294, John Lewis 293,

Joseph 293, Laura B. 293, Mathilda B. 293, Neppie 209, Samuel 293, Sarah 293, Sarah Ann 293, William Henry 293
RICKENBACH, Anna 325, Magdalena 325
RICKETTS, Clem 83, F. 34, M. 34
RICKEY, John 48
RICKLE, Abbie 177
RIDENOUR, Lottie 96, Richard 96
RIDER, Jeremiah 184, John 15
RIDGEWAY, Cora 336, Elsie 260, Fannie Ladoska 216, James 15, Ruth Ann 190
RIDGLEY, Golda 194, 267
RIDNOUR, Ruth 107
RIEBE, Don 23
RIEGER, Marion 186
RIESEN, Christopher 268, Christopher L. 131, Elizabeth (Libby) Rayl 291
RIFFE, Albert 321, Lydia Alice 145, Sheryl 193, Ted 97, William 16
RIFFLE, William 16
RIGGS, B. 36, David Lee 193, Isabelle 234, Pamela La'el 193, Roger 193, Samuel H. 35, W. 34, Wilbert 36, Wilberta 36
RILEY, Amazetta (Hightower) 294, Charles Melvin 294, Cynthia Anne 295, Dawn Elizabeth 294, Devin Barnes 294, Ed 34, 59, 85, Edwin 31, Edwin B. Jr. 294, Edwin Barnes 294, Edwin Barnes, Jr. 295, Edwin Barnes, Sr. 241, Ellen Joan 295, Florence Lucille 294, Harold Henry 294, Henry Harrison 294, Holly Van 294, Jackson Smith 294, James Whitcomb 228, 250, Jesse Marshall 294, Jo 69, John C. 294, Lewis 294, Marcia Lou 295, Margaret (Dicky) 294, Margaret 294, Martha 294, Mary Ann 294, Milton Irvin 294, Minnie Olive 294, 305, Nancy 27, 294, Raymond 23, Robert Dallas 295, Roberta Ruth 201, Roe Raymond 294, Roland Edwin 294, Sarah C. 294, Thomas H. 294, W.H. 34, William E. 294
RIMES, Marilyn V. 161
RINEHART 40, A. Loren 255, Amos Loren 295, Buddy 257, 295, Charles 295, Charles F. 295, Fanny (Barnhart) 295, Frances Viola 295, Henry 286, 295, Hugh 295, Jacob 295, Jeffrey Allen 213, John 31, 59, 257, 295, John M. 295, Judith Ann (Hawkins) 198, Julia Ann 213, Kenneth 255, Kenneth F. 213, L. Keith 255, Lawrence R. (Bud) 255, Levi 295, Marilyn 257, 295, Mason 257, 295, Mertie (Mason) 255, Nina 257, 295, Paul 257, 295, Phillip 295, Russell 25, Samuel 295, Samuel Ross 257, 295, Susan Kay 257, 295, Susanna (Huddleston) 257, 295, Tella H. 295, Uriah Martin 295, Virginia 257, Virginia Lee 288
RING, Mary G. 13, Samuel 33
RIOTH, Bertha (Weaver) 295, Edward M. 295, Frank 295, Martha Jane (Polk) 295, Maxine Eleanor 295
RIPBERGER, Jamie Jo 313
RISHEL, Arthur 197, Claude 197, Elsworth 197, Monsell 197
RITCHEY, Anna Mae 296, 334, 335, Bertha Bell 296, Cora Ellen 296, Glen 15, Harold 15, James Roscoe 296, John Edward "Ward" 296, John F. 269, John Franklin 296, 335, Julius Floyd 296, Lucretia 15, 212, Lucretia Ann (Harrell) 296, Mary Syrena 281, Ray 243, Robert 15, 212, Robert Ellsworth 296, Sarah Elizabeth (Myers) 296, 335, Stella Irene 296,

RITCHIE, Gladys Mildred Reynolds 293, Sarah Olive 225
RITTENHOUSE, Mary Effie 213, Rita 281
RITZ, Rudolph A. 84
RIX, William 83
RIZER, Okey 33
RIZZLEMAN, Mary 279
ROACH, Clarence 145, Dora 145, Dora Jr. 145, Earl 145, Edmond C. 208, Laura Alice (Dunkin, Deane) 145, Minnie Zephel 145, Paul 145, Russell 145, Ruth Moss 36, Wilbur 145
ROADEN, Chester Wayne 182
ROADS, Berton 214, Martin 214, Rachel 214
ROARK, Sammy 78
ROBARDS, Elizabeth Ann 297, Fern 297, Jesse 296, John 225, 296, Kate 297, Laura 297, Lulu 297, Maudie 297, Myrtle 297, Pearl 297, Ruth 297, Sarah 296, Thomas Davis 296
ROBB, Ann Claire 172
ROBBINS, Bethia 268, Betty 20, Lindley 165, 276, Mary (Carter) 276, Sarah Ann 276, William M. 279
ROBERTS, Albert 218, Alice 257, Charles Henry 269, David Russell 139, Donnell Bruce 180, Doris 174, Dorothy 180, Elva Rosina (Thorp) 287, Ezra 68, Fanny 64, George D. 287, Gilbert 139, Grace Mildred 218, H. Andrew Kelvie 139, H.C. 34, 294, Hallie 139, Harriett Poirier 218, Isaiah 31, Josiah M. 33, Lilly 139, Linda 214, Lorine 253, Matthew Paul 139, Myrtie Bell 287, Richard Gilbert 139, Sherri (Milburn) 86, Sue Ann 180, Thomas 47, Thomas Edward 180, Vera Maxine 180, Zack 180, Alexander 83, Butler 248, Dorothy 248, Doug 56, Elizabeth 83, Gene 248, James F. 180, 225, Lois 248, Mary 248, Mary E. 197, Mary Elizabeth 163, Minnie 189, Neil 248, Pete 14, Ross 248, Russell 66, 248, W.H. 95
ROBEY, Robert 25
ROBINSON, Bertha 155, Clayton 155, David 196, Donald 155, Hazel Katherine Brantley 181, Helen Louisa 155, Ida Frances 338, James Robert 155, Kimberly Kaye 183, Lynda Clare 322, Mack 164, Pryor 155, Rebecca 326
ROBY, Eunice 291
ROCCHIO, Mary 339
ROCKEY, Alda (Kerby) 237, Alta C. 297, Andrea 176, Bennett 297, Bessie 236, 237, Blanche (Kerby) 176, Charles David 176, Charles Vernon 176, Christopher McClain 223, Christopher McClain 297, Clarence 176, 237, 297, Clinton Lewis 223, Clinton Lewis 297, Everett Lee 297, Floyd 297, George 237, George Franklin 176, Isaac Lyman 297, James Bennett 223, James Bennett 297, James Doyle 223, 297, Jennifer Ann 176, John C. 176, John Thomas 176, Kay Arden 223, Lesa Lynn 176, Mary Ellen (Harter) 297, Monica Jo 176, Ralph 237, William 237
ROCKWELL, Michael 188
RODABOUGH, Lucille 288
RODEMAN, Donald W. 297, Jean

Wile 297, John Dallas 297, Suzanne Lee 297
RODERICK, Velma A. 204
RODGERS 86, Lloyd Arnold II 250, Martha Jane Hayse 291, Raymond 25
RODKEY, Caroline 298, Dudley 298, Earl 266, Edith 255, Esther Christian 298, Goldie 281, Grace 298, Jessie 298, John 298, John Jr. 298, Joseph 298, Julia Ann 298, Laura 298, Lottie 281, Marilyn 186, Mary Elizabeth 281, Perry 298, Warren 298
RODMAN, Elizabeth 209, William S. 48
RODRIGUEZ, Rafael Noe 321, Rafael P. 321
RODY, Adam 297, Anna Carolina 298, Barbara Elizabeth 298, Charles 298, Elizabeth Ann 297, Fred 42, 43, George 297, Henry 298, John 298, Margaret 298, Mary Kay 298, Miriam 298
ROE 248
ROFELTY, Grace 14
ROGERS, Alan 291, Ben 39, Brenda Jo 143, Golda E. 149, Jessica Jo 143, Joseph 343, Robert Lee 238, Virginia Lee 238
ROHLER, Donald 308
ROHR, Henrietta 213
ROLAND, Phoebe Jane 212
ROLER, Dean 238, Leona 238, Melvin Earl 238
ROLFE, Ron 97
ROLLEN, Edwin 330, Lula Elizabeth (Barnhouse) 330, Patrick Henry 330, Rachael (Napp) 330
ROLLINS, Charles 25, Cooper 21, John 180, Paul 23
ROLSTON, Thomas 33
ROMACK, Lulu Dale 297
ROMER, Henry 150, John Joseph 150
RONE, Gladyce 158, Gladyce M. 242, Gladyce Marie 301, Johnny Huey 301, M. Roxie (Browning) 301, Mary Roxie (Browning) 242
RONK, Cora Ann 173, Mary Darcus 174, Maxine 288
ROOSEVELT, Teddy 182, Theodore 162
ROPER, Sarah Jane 146
ROSE, Charles 194, Irma 194, Margarette 19, Mark Allen 194
ROSENBAUM, Robert 25
ROSENBURGER, Emma E. 231
ROSENBROCK, John 278
ROSENTHAL, Samuel 76
ROSS, Amanda 298, C. 34, Henry 298, James 298, Jesse F. 298, Joseph 298, Judith 298, Mike 298, Nathanial C. 298, Phyllis 298, Richard 298, Robert 298, Ryan 298, Sharon 298, Troy 298, William 298, Wm. H. 298
ROSSMAN 161
ROTH, Alan 253, Cora 253, J. 34
ROTHE 297
ROTHERAM, Anna 258
ROUCH, Alexandra Rae 283, Jacob Keith 283, Scott 283
ROUSH, Roxie 248
ROWLAND, George P. 271, Richard 150, Ruth Marie 193
ROWLER, Elizabeth 318
ROY, Bernard 171, Kathryn 171
ROYALTY, Nancy Jane 196
ROZZEL, Francis (Frank) 308, Harold 308, Hugh 308, Marjorie 308, Naomi Jean (Jeanie) 308, Richard 308, Roanna 308, Robert 308, Russel 308
RUBUSH, James 290, Marian 313
RUCHTI, Leo A. 284, Stephen 284
RUDE, Everett 148

RUDICEL, Richard 333
RUDY, D.J. 329, Samuel 329
RUGG, Samual L. 103
RULON, Neal Alan 239, Nicolas James 239, Roy 239
RUMPLE, Adaline (Lorts) 242, Daniel 242, Edna F. 242
RUND, Donna L. 249
RUNK, Cona (James) 298, David Lee 299, Donna 299, Homer Meryl 299, John 298, Joseph Anthony 299, Larry Robert 299, Loren E. 298, Maybelle 299, Miles 298, Nancy Caroline 298, Nora Valentine 298, Norman 298, Patricia Ann 299, Samuel 298, Stanley Robert 299, Wayne Everett 299
RUNNELL 174
RUNYAN, Susannah 238
RUNYON, Brian T. 336, Brian T., Jr. 336, Kimberly Michelle 336
RUSE, Crystal 149
RUSH, Daniel 15, Esther 190, Jody Kay 189, Merle 95, Stan 48, Stanley 189, Susannah 192, Todd Raymond 189
RUSK, Barbara Ellen 174, Cloyd 248, Elmer 248, Jay 248, Lewis 248, Lloyd 248
RUSSELL 28, 29, Eliza Jervis 212, Euretta 107, Frank H. 250, John F. 27, Nancy 227, Rose 107
RUST, Delores 36, Ina Edith 211, Virgil Lester 301
RUZICKA, John 329, Verona 329
RYAN, Henry 48, Jeanette 25, Phillis Hollingsworth 222, Robert Wayne 149, Roger 25
RYBOLT, Gerald 106, Gwen 307
RYMAN, Alisha Lyn 179, Douglas 179, Matthew Abram 179, Michael Douglas 179
RYSONG, Francis 99, Joe 99

S

SADLER, Neal R. 79, Virginia (Somers) 312
SAGER, Elmer 197, Joanna 207, John 207
SAILORS 86
SALE, W.S. 34, William S. 58, 150
SALENBARGER, C. 323
SALLEE, Debra 310, Francis Marion 198, Theda 107, 108, Theda Elaine Gifford 198
SALMONS, George 15
SALS, Barbara 196
SALSBERY, Ann Clarissa 238, Jefferson Leon 238, Ted 25, Ted L. 238
SALYER, Fred 277
SAMPLE, Christy 299, Colleen 299, Deana 299, Harold Lewis 299, Jill Diane 299, Julie Dawn 299, Leanna Christine 299, Michael Edward 299, Patrick Jay 299, Ray 25, Timothy Joe 299, William Edward 299
SAMPLES, Eliza 291
SAMS, Howard W. 164
SAMSEL, Marthaellen Elvin 331
SANDEFUR, Dillard 299, Dwayne 299, Goldie 299, Henrietta 299, Joseph 299, Kenneth 299, Kimmy 299, Larn 299, Leon 299, Maurine 299, Melissa 299, Porter 299, Ricki 299, Roxie 299, Silas 299, Susie (Lambert) 299, Vivian 299, Wayne 299, William Henry 299

SANDER, Mary 287
SANDERS 197, Benjamin 190, Brandon 190, Diana 190, Gary Allen 190, Hannah 190, 300, Isaac 190, Issac 300, Jacob 190, Kathianne 190, Katy 190, 300, Mark 300, Mark Edward 190, Marsha Renie 293, Milton 274, Monica 190, Nicholas 190, Paul Wesley 190, Robin 282, Ryne 190, Tom 190, Wendy 190
SANDERSON, Mary (Mason) 256
SANDIFER, James 299, John 299, Robert Sharp 299, William Abraham 299, William Alexander 299, Dillard 299, Erin 300, Gary 182, 300, Goldie 299, Joseph 299, Joseph Grant 299, Larn 299, Lorene 182, Lorene (Smith) 182, Matthew 299, Maurine 299, Porter 299, Roxie 299, Silas 299, Sondra 300, Susan 192, 300, Susan (Lambert) 299, Travis 300, Trent 300, William Henry 299
SANFORD, Edna Margaret 331, Jessee 331, Louis 331
SANTEN, Gretchen Elizabeth 140, 252, Joseph Jerome, Jr 140, 252, 303, Marsha 140
SAPARONA (Stewart), Sarah Young 340
SARGEANT, A.J. 193
SARGENT, Robert 113
SARVER, Bessie M. 300, Charles 257, John W. 300
SAUCER, Elva Alice 228
SAUER, Katherine 325
SAUL 85, 169, Abe 39, 40, Amos 43, Delores 48, Dolpha 169, Edward 40, 343, George 39, Hannah 308, Hannah Louella 343, Jessie 187, John 39, 40, John Kagy 343, Lovina (Kagy) 343, Martha 40, 239, Marvin 188, Marvin O. 188, Richard 48, Steve 40
SAUNDERS, Maryanna 337
SAVAGE, T.C. 258
SAWYER, David 48
SAXON, Ada 300, Alexander 300, Alexander Gillespie 300, Annetta Jane 300, Clara May 300, Emma E. 300, Frances (Fisher) 300, John W. 300, Laura B. 300, Louedna Ruth 300, Margaret (McCrory) 300, Margaret "Maggie" 300, Martha 300, Mary (Baldwin) 300, Minnie S. 300, Nancy (Orr) 300, Nira Mary 300, Samuel 300, William 300, William Andrew 300, William W. 300
SAYLES, Tilman 144
SAYRE, John M. 70
SCEARY, E. 34
SCHAAF 39, Audrey 107, Diana June 252, Ed 42, Elsie Smith 207, Eugene 36, Gus 43, Harold 36, 207, L. 36, Louise 107, N. 36, Verna 42
SCHAEFER, Nina Pauline 243
SCHAEFFER, Donna 23
SCHAFER, Annabelle 233, Bernice 249, Brandon David 300, Bret Witman 300, Darcey Lorraine 300, David 28, 32, George Franklin 300, Holly (Wald) 300, Jocena K. 300, Margaret 300, Marybelle 300, Nina Belle (Souter) 300, Oris DeWitt 300, Patricia 249, Roger D. 300, Ronald 32, Ronald Lynn 300
SCHAFER-GINGERICH, Orval 32, Sharon 32
SCHAKEL, George 161, 287
SCHARE, Brenda 50, Jerry 50
SCHARFF, Susanne 234
SCHEID, Marielle Vanessa Maristella 306, Mark Steven 306

367

SCHEIDT, William 84
SCHERER, Addie Ellen Newlin 276, Curt 35, Curtis 211, George Allen 276, Hazel Marie 276, James Tauer 276, Rutherford 276
SCHICK, Audrey Monica (Woodruff) 226, 301, Benjamin A. 338, Benjamin Adam 226, 301, Benjamin Adam 300, Bernard 300, Candy 242, Candy L. 232, 301, Candy Louise 289, Chandra Lynn 301, Donald E. 232, 301, Donald Eugene 226, Donald J. "Joe" 242, 301, Donald Joseph "Joe" 242, 301, Fredrick 301, Fredrick 242, Gladyce M. (Rone) 232, Jacob Adam 301, Jacqulyn Ann 301, Jessica Jo 301, Joseph Anthony 226, 301, Joshua Michael 301, Laura Lee 301, Majorie I. 301, Marjorie Ione 226, Mary Ellen (Quinlan) 300, Matthew Adam Stafford 301, Megan Elizabeth 301, Nancy L. 301, Nancy Loudica 226, Randy 232, 242, Randy E. 301, Wayne Paul 226, 301
SCHINI, Paul 56
SCHIRER, Edward 153
SCHMALTZ, Charles F. 310, Janice 310, Janice L. 310, Nancy (Boyd) 310
SCHMIDT, Bertha Marie 151
SCHMITT, Bobbie Lee 302, Brent 302, Carolyn (Small) 302, Cody 301, David 302, 303, Debbie (McCarter) 303, Deborah Jo 301, Dena 301, Donna 301, Dorothy 302, Dorothy Ann 301, Erica 301, Frances 301, 302, Frances (Terwische) 251, 301, 302, George 251, 301, 302, George Aloysuis 302, George, Jr. 302, George W. 251, James (Michael) 303, John 278, Leonard 302, Lucille (Taylor) 302, Maggie 278, Marta (Waites) 303, Mary (Zoller) 278, Mary Jo 303, Melissa 302, Michelle 301, Mildred 302, Mildred E. 302, Monica 301, Norman 301, Pete 302, Raymond 301, Robert (Bob) 302, Ronald 301, Russell 301, 302, Ryan Mathew 302, Scott 301, Stacey 301, Stephanie 301, Wilbert 302, Wilbert (Bud) 302
SCHMUCKER, John 253, Magdalena 253
SCHNEIDER, Jay Norman 153
SCHONER, Leo F. 266, Rita Carol 266
SCHORE, Marie 208
SCHRADER, Anna 303, Clara 303, Earl C. 303, Edward 303, Ella 303, Fred 303, Frederick 303, Harold 303, Harry 303, Otto 303, Richard 303, Robert 303, William 303
SCHREPFERMAN, Alan 243, Julie 243, Katherine 243, Susan 243, Wayne 243
SCHROCK, Ananias 303, Anna (Zug) 303, Barbara 303, Barbara (Miller) 325, Benjamin 303, Catherine 303, 325, Eli 303, Elizabeth 303, Ezra T. 303, Henry 325, Isaac 303, Jacob 303, Jacob B. 303, John 303, John M. 303, Jonas 303, Joseph 303, Lomanda 303, Lydia 303, Malinda 303, Mary 303, Noah 303, Susanna 303, Wes 42
SCHROEDER, Hugh 84
SCHROETER, Mary 288
SCHUCK, Darrell 290
SCHUELER, Cecila Jane 241
SCHUETT, Robert 299

SCHULER, Bob 97
SCHUYLER, Mary 183, 243, Myrtle 243
SCHWARTZ, Beverly J. 143
SCHWENGER, George 97
SCOTT 86, 273, 274, 322, Celia A. 292, Christopher Russell 303, Elma Mae 212, Evelyn I. (Hulet) 303, Geraldine Armstrong 251, Hannah 273, Harold M. 174, James 18, Jan Hulet 303, Jean (Pyanowski) 143, Jesse D. 48, Joseph A. 193, Leannah 85, Max 174, 303, O.R. 289, Orville 174, Samuel T. 90, Sharlott 64, Wilma D. 144
SCRUGGS, Artie 48
SCUDDER, Glendora 260
SDUNEK, Helen 232
SEAGER, Ella 304, Genevieve Agnes 304, Genevieve Agnes 213, 304, George 304, Jennie 304, Lavena Elsie 304, Margaret (Patton) 304, Robert Wallace 304, Treso Margaret 304, Wilbert 304, William Robert 304
SEAGRAVE, Elsie 107
SEAGRAVES, John 97, Nora 140
SEARS, Joyce 301, Mike 20
SEAVER, D.V. 14
SEAVERS 248
SEAWRIGHT, Eliza Ann 280, John 48
SEDAM, Harvey 161
SEDAN, Harvey 287
SEEKRI 227
SEGO, Arthur A. 94
SEIBERLING, A.G. 227, Monroe 303
SEIBERLING-KINGSTON 102
SEIFERT, Margaret 264
SEITZ, Walter 14
SELL, Sandra 148
SELLARS, Max P. 116, William 19
SELLERS, Addie 235, Alfred Perry 267, Alice 316, Blanche Wauneta 318, Christopher 149, Deana 316, Donald 316, Gene E. 48, George 235, Jane 13, Jerry 48, 149, Lora Barrows 316, Lora Barrows 316, M.S. 12, Mary (Cole) 267, Max 25, Rebecca (Becky) 316, Sarah Elizabeth 267, Tara 149, Thomas 316, Thomas N. 316, W.P. 13
SELPH, Harriet 25
SEMROW, Kevin 242, Kody Garrett 242, Kolby Charles 242, Kolton Theodore 242, Kord Ahron 242
SENCE, Henrietta 337
SEVERNS, Betse 304, Craig 119, 304, Diane 304 E.P. Jr. 287, E.P., Jr. 119, Edmond 119, Edmond P. 304, Edmond P. Sr. 304, Frank 119, Leola K. 304, Roy 119, Susan 304, Tim 119, 304
SEVERS, Ruby Henderson 197
SEWARD, Amasa B. 51, Levi 234, Lisa (Lindley) 246
SEWELL, Bessie 287, Carl 287, Eddie 96, Vernon 85, Ward 287
SEXTON, Edgar E. 296, Ida E. (Hanna) 296, Oliver 296, Oliver M. 296
SHACKEL, Otto 287
SHADDAY, Catherine 292, Elizabeth 292
SHADDOCK, Maud 14
SHADDY, Barbara 292, Catherine 292, Caty 292, Elizabeth 292, Emsley 292, George W. 292, Hardin 292, Jacob 292, John 292, John Jr. 292, Jordan 292, Lucinda 292, Mary (Fogleman) 292, Molly 292, Polly 292, Rachel 292, Sally 292, Turley 292, William 292

SHADEL, B. Frank 19
SHAEF, Ed 90
SHAFF, Linda 249, Sonya 249
SHAFFER, Belle 219, Irene 257, Marian (Bachelor) 250, Marvel 189, Nancy 159
SHALLENBERGER, Keith 224, Kevin 224, Kiel 224, Kohl 224
SHANE, Doug 225, Ted 225, Trey 225
SHANK, Cora Ellen 241, David W. 241
SHANKS, Charles Dewayne 181, George W. 181, Henry F.J. 181, Mary Nicholson 181
SHANNON, W.D. 95
SHAP-PAU-DO-SHO 27
SHARP, Dorothy Mae 99, Laura Alice 211, LuEmma 212, Suzanne Elaine 198
SHARPE, Allen 48, Lewis 52, M. 96
SHAUL 86
SHAW, Beulah Lorea 197, Cecil 157, Christian Monroe Clinton 197, Elzie 197, Howard 197, Irene Virgil 197, James C. 197, Jonathan 313, Letitia 197, Mable Grace 233, Maggie 197, Margaret 234, Sarah 179
SHAWHAN, Emma 185, Enoch H. 185, Malinda Humbert 185
SHEA, Mark Jeffery 182, Matthew Heflin 182
SHEAGLEY, Julie 290, Maleta 290, Mike 290, Rachel 290
SHEARER, Brian 305, Charles 304, Charles Oliver 304, Craig 305, David L. 305, Diane 305, Ella Lamb 304, James K. 305, John 304, Marcia 305, Michael 305, Morris 304, Roland 304
SHEETS, Elvy C. 149, Laura Marie 252, Mary Evelyn 215
SHEFFER, Mary Juanita 23
SHELL, Catherine 183
SHELLENBERGER, Christina 193
SHELLEY, Sarah G. 267
SHELTON, Lydia 208, Rachel M. 327
SHENK, David A. 100, Gladys (Buchanan) 295, Reuben 48
SHENKS, Laura 141
SHEPARD, Beulah G. 294, William Richard 144
SHEPHERD, Alice 305, Anna 305, Benjamin Franklin 291, Beverly 23, Clara Inez 305, Clara Inez 215, Claude Harvey 278, Donald R. 187, Edward 68, 305, Emma 305, Garth 328, George 75, Isaiah Thomas 291, Jacob 305, Jesse Thomas 291, Jessie 305, John 151, Josephine 305, Margaret 305, Mary Elizabeth 180, 291, Opal 46, Oscar 305, Rachel Shepherd 305, Richard 23, Robert 311, Sarah 305, Serepta 291, Thomas 68, Washington 305
SHEPHERD/SHEPARD, Jesse Thomas 180, Lavicia Rayl 180
SHEPLER, Alta 248
SHERON, James Everett 194
SHERRILL, Kenneth 141, Lillie Mae (Arnett) 141
SHERROD, William 177
SHESTECK, Joseph F. 169, Roxey 271
SHESTECK-JOHNSON 271, Roxey (Cohee) 168
SHEWMAN, William 85
SHIELDS, Donald 157, Estella (Ridlen) 157, Joshua J. 238, Lee 157, Lula (Weeks) 157, Ora Elmer 157, Otho 157, Rachel Ann 275
SHIETZE, Melinda Carol 146
SHILLING, Nellie (Oilar) 298

SHINN, Clement 344, Damaris Jane 344, Elizabeth (Webb) 344, Emma Lou 312, Frank 35, Gail (Somers) 312, Jack 312, Josiah 344, Levi 344, Mahlon 344, Mary (Edwards) 344, Mary (Thompson) 344, Moses 344, Olive 344, Orpha 344, P.B. 14, R. 35, Rhoda 344, Sarah 344, Seth 344
SHIPLEY 273, Eric Lowell 182
SHIRAR, Conrad Eugene 328, Gerald 29, Kathleen 138
SHIRK, E.H. 34
SHIRLEY, D.J. 48, Dowell E. 116, Margaret Catherine 248, Max 97
SHOCKEY, Janice 235
SHOCKLEY 31, Charles D. 241, E. 34, Frances 312, Guy Everett 276, L. 36, Marc Rayl 276, Phebe Ellen 213, Roy 263
SHOCKNEY, Alice 305, Anna Abigail 305, Chester Herbert 305, David Jesse 305, Earl 305, Eliza Jane 305, Evangeline 305, Henrietta 305, Ida Belle 305, J. Roscoe 54, Jerusha Anderson 190, 305, John 190, John N. 305, John Roscoe 305, John Roscoe 294, Josephine Antionette 305, Mary Marie 275, Oakey Kelsey 305, Okey 54, Orpha Blanche 305, Rachel 305, Rollo Homer 305, Stephen 54, Stephen Decatur 305, Stephen Decatur 190
SHOEMAKER, A. Lee 343, Calvin 138, Grace (Huffer) 138, Roxie Marie 138
SHOFFNER, Diane 180
SHOLTY, Evelyn Lucile 153
SHOLTZ 86
SHOOK, A.L. 83, A.S. 83, Peter 27
SHORES, Walter 294
SHORM, Frederick 208
SHORT, Alfred Leroy 305, Artimissia 305, Barbara Ann 158, Beaty 305, Charles 305, Charles Ray 305, Earl B. 305, Elizabeth (Ham) 305, Gladys 305, Harry Lester 305, James E. 305, Jo Maxine 305, John Samuel 305, Joseph 305, Joseph Alexander "Aleck" 305, Joseph Benjamin 305, Joseph Joel 305, Kenneth Wayne 305, Kenosha May 305, Leroy T. 198, Marie E. 198, Martha "Mattie" 305, Mary Elizabeth 305, Mary Lou 305, Owen 305, Pearl 305, Raymond 305, Richard Marion 305, Susan "Sukey" (Jones) 305, Thelma 305, 306, Thomas Owen 305, Vera Evelyn 305, Vivian Berniece 198, Wilbur Lewis 305, William 305, William Victor 305, Willie V. 305, Zachariah 305
SHOWALTER, Anna F. Funkhouser 245, Bernard 253, Christian 245, Christiania "Ann" (Funkhouser) 255, Christopher 255, Isacc 100, Rebecca 255, 256
SHRADER, Buell 14
SHRADER, Mary 314, S. 34, William 53, William Lee 305
SHROCK 28, 42, 43, Andy 42, Della (King) 166, E. 34, Eldon 204, Elizabeth 308, 343, Elsie Clarice 303, Emerson 41, 43, Estella Mae 303, Ethel Aldene 303, Ezra Paul 314, Floyd 42, Gerald Leon 303, Guy Otto 303, Harry 41, 42, Harry B. 43, J. 34, Jacob 27, Jim 41, John C. 180, John C. 204, Kenneth 42, Lawrence Loman 303, Leon Manson 303, Lillian Leona 303, Lloyd Ellsworth 303, Mabel 314,

Merle (Grau) 180, Noah D. (Schrock) 303, Olive Genevieve 303, Opal Lucile 303, Opal Lucile 252, Paul 314, Percy 42, 166, Thelma 314, Verna Pauline 303
SHROCKS 39
SHUCK, Deborah Kaye 306, Fern (Bouse) 306, Frank 306, Gerald Wayne 306, Hazel 108, Marvin Otis 306, Mary 234, Ora Pauline (Reese) 306, Petronel (Davenport) 306, Steven Jay 306
SHUEY, Emma R. 286
SHUGART, Constantine 67
SHULTZ, Amy 234, Catherine 197, 234, Christie 13, George 13, 197
SHUMACKER, J. 34
SHUTTERS, Mary 197
SIBERT, Ada 59
SICKAFOOSE, George 96
SIESEL, Harold Joseph 150
SILENCE, Brodrick Clayton 223, 297, Clayton Rockey 223, 297, Kay Arden (Rockey) 297
SILER, Elwood C. 66, Sylvina 139
SILVER, Courtney 306, Daniel 306, Daniel W. 306, James L. 306, Janet (Peterson) 306, Joanna R. 306, Michael 306, Michael T. 306, Raymond J. 306, Raymond L. 306, Robin (Childers) 306, Sarah L. 306, Thomas R. 306
SILVEY, Oscar William 305, Rebecca (Whited) 142
SIMMON, William 313
SIMMONS, Melinda 23, Thompson 27, 33
SIMONS, E.D. 46
SIMONTON, Sarah Jane 194
SIMPSON, Arthur Otho 307, Ava 324, Barbara Jane 307, Bertha 324, C. Otho 306, Carrie 324, Clara 175, Clara B. (Hill) 307, David Lewis 187, Denton 48, 49, 103, 324, Edith 187, Elizabeth 324, Elizabeth 324, Elizabeth Ann 307, Elsie 324, Emily 307, Eugene 324, Eva (Dixon) 187, Francis Marion 307, Jean (Downhour) 185, Jesse F. 307, John 307, Lawrence 324, Lisa 307, Marilda 273, Mary Davis 324, Mary Kathleen (Freed) 196, May Miller 307, Norman 324, Orin 324, Ralph 211, Robert F. 307, Ronald D. 185, 307, Ronda 307, S. 53, Stephen 307, Susann M. 307, Vesta A. (Childers) 307
SIMS, David 214, Emily Louise 342, Paul 219, Sarah 214
SINCOX, Ann Kettering 77
SINGER, Dwight 23, Dwight V. 100, Linda 23
SINKS, Henry A. 19
SIPEE, A. 34
SIPES, Gary 25, Pat 26, Ralph 25
SISTEK, Vincent 169
SITES, Eli 218
SITGREAVES, Richard 267
SITTON, John M. 75
SKEEN, Joseph 48
SKIDMORE, Artie Melissa 158, Isom H. 158
SKILLMAN 27, Elizabeth 272
SKINNER, Alice Baker 144, Marion Collins 144
SKOMP, Roy 74
SLABAUGH, Catherine 253, Lee Roy 200, Mary Sue Scherer 276
SLAGLE, Arnold L. 298, Sharon I. (Ross) 298, Tamara Kay 298
SLANKARD, Jessie 273
SLATER, Nancy Jane 151
SLAUGHTER, Bonnie (Yater) 294, Keith 294, Mark Alan 294, Minnie Belle 271

SLAUGHTERS, Matthew Alan 294, Rebecca Elizabeth 294
SLAYTON, Andrew Charles 275, Charles 275, Luke Edward 275
SLIDER, Jesse 27
SLIPPY, Elizabeth 288
SLOAN, Andrew Jackson 251, Catherine (Whitaker) 251, Charles Whitaker 251, Chas. 42, Julia Anna (Dick) 251, Minnie Faye (Kilander) 251, Virgil Todd 251
SLOCUM, Allen 307, Charles 307, Cherrie 307, Frances 27, 307, Henry Warner 307, Jeanette 307, Marion Edward 307, Milton Renzel 307, Robert 307, Virginia Claire Loy 307
SMALL, Bernice Thomas 308, C. Otis "Ote" 281, Clifton 303, Dinah Marshall 307, Eli Milton 307, Elihu 307, Estella (Shrock) 303, Esther 307, Fairy (Sturdevant) 281, Gideon 275, 307, Hannah 167, Henry Bowen 167, Howard 167, Janet 167, Jennie 307, Jonathan 307, Joseph 307, Marion Creston 308, Mira 66, Miriam Bundy 307, Opal L. 275, Reuben 307, Sarah 307, Silas 307, Thomas M. 308, Vera 308, Wilma Mae 281
SMALLWOOD, James 141, Lois McConnell 141
SMELSER, Frances 288, Pauline Vivian (Maholm) 288
SMELTZER, Adam 308, 343, Charles 343, Charles Francis 308, Christina (Blazer) 308, Emma 237, Emma Jane 308, 343, Hannah Saul 40, Hazel Neola 308, 343, Homer L. 343, Homer Lewis 308, John 308, Lawrence 211, 343, Lawrence Dewey 308, Leota Grace 308, 343, Margaret (Smith) 308, 343, Mildred 343, Mildred Lucille 308, Opal (Bryan) 337, Reuben 343, Rilda 343, Rilda Pearl 308, Robert 237, 308, 343, Robert Raymond 308, 343, Ruby 343, Ruby Opal 308, Russell 343, Samuel William 308, 343, Sara Lovina 308, Sarah (Zerbe) 237, Sarah Ann (Zerbe) 308, Sarah Lovina 343, Thomas 343, William 308, William Henry 343, Wm. 40, 43
SMILEY, Cynthia 218, Everett 48, Mattie 140, Suzanne 343
SMITH 28, 35, 42, 54, 56, 85, Ada 309, Ada Jenny 311, Agnes Lee 310, Alexander 95, Alice 210, 236, 286, Allerd C. 251, Amber Michelle 321, Amy 310, Amy Michelle 309, 321, Andrew James 271, Anna 235, Anna Beatrice (Criss) 172, Annie (Yager) 309, 310, Anthony A. 298, Arthur 274, Asa 265, Ashley 247, Aubrey Meghan 251, Basil 197, Bernard Ray 183, Bernell 308, Bessie Kate 311, Beth Ann (Hunter) 224, Beverly 186, Billy J. 309, 310, Blanche 310, Bradford 310, Bradford Kirk 310, Brady 191, C. 48, Carlisle F. 309, 311, Caroline Rayl 291, Catherine 138, Ceceilia 92, Charity 311, Charity Ann 189, Charity Farnsworth 311, Charlene 309, Charles Damon 308, Charles Lee 308, Charles William 308, Clifford 199, Clyde 309, Cora (Curry) 221, 324, Cora Ethel (Robinson) 309, Cornelius 235, Cornelius C. 311, Craig 310, Craig A. 310, Cynthia 186, Cynthia (Cripe) 219, D. 34, Daniel 310, Daniel Fredrick 308, Daryl 191, David 16, 31, 32, 193, 309, David E. 28, Deborah 318, Debra Ann 329, Debra Lee 182, Delbert H. 13, Delmar Cleveland 244, Don 25, Donald B. 116, Donald B., Jr. 116, Donald P. 203, Doris 308, Dorothy 202, Dorothy (Dolly) 310, Dorothy (Runnels) 176, Dorothy Lucille 308, Dorothy Marie 311, Dwight 66, E. Wesley 48, Earl Raymond 314, Earnest 309, Eddie 75, Edna Julia 311, Elizabeth 205, 344, Elizabeth (Shaffer) 308, Elizabeth B. 13, Elizabeth Jane 308, Emily 310, Emily Jane Hollingsworth 276, Emily Renee 310, Emma Mary 308, Ephraim 311, Eric 193, 309, Ernest 308, Evert 308, F.M. 34, Frank 309, Frank W. 14, Frederick 99, Fredrick 308, Galen Richard 308, George 40, George Crestin 308, George "Ray" Raymond 309, George Raymond Jr. 309, 321, George W. 308, George W. 14, Gerald Warren 194, Geraldine Rayl 291, Gladys 66, Glenn R. 310, Grace 225, 310, Greg Alan 309, 321, Gretta Joan 295, Gwin 311, Hannah 19, Harold 310, Harold Allen 309, Harold J. 309, Harriet 31, Harry 310, Harry Damon, Jr. 194, 308, Harry Damon Sr. 194, Harry Sr. 308, Henry Washington 309, Howard 309, Howard Carroll 311, Hugh Edwin 172, Ida M. 13, Irene (Head) 309, Isaac V.N. 311, Isabelle 176, J.O. 104, Jacob 225, Jacob Edgar 310, Jacob Light 310, James 48, 180, James C. 309, James Clifton 309, James D. 309, 310, James D. 310, James Edward 141, James Robert 183, 309, James W. 210, Janet D. (Pearson) 310, Jeff 309, Jennifer 193, Jessie May 338, Jim D. 310, John 308, John David 309, 310, John H. 310, John Vernon 310, John Wesley 309, Joseph A. 173, Juanita May 308, Judith (Judy) 308, Julie 309, Karen Lynn 183, Keith 308, Kelley Dyan 141, Kelly 309, Kent 309, Kent A . 310, Kent A. 310, Kevin 309, Kevin S. 310, Kevin Scott 310, Kirk 309, Kirk B. 310, Kirk Bradford 310, Kristie 309, 310, Larry 187, Laura Etta 308, Lee Ann (Murphy) 310, Leo David 183, Leonard 55, Lilian 314, Linda Sue 194, Lois 96, Lon 329, Lorene 300, Lucinda 58, Lura Belle 265, Lyn 309, M. 34, Margaret 168, 253, 262, 308, Margret 203, Marianne Louise 183, Marilyn Mae 309, Mark Allen 183, Martha 175, Martha (Turner) 225, Martin 27, 58, Martin Van Buren 201, Mary 210, 234, Mary (Merrifield) 234, Mary (Utz) 173, Mary Ann 308, Mary Elizabeth 308, 309, Mary Ellen 311, Mary Hannah 312, Mary Helen 182, Mary Mildred 308, Mary Mildred (Dexter) 194, Matthew Jacob 321, Melissa 310, Michael Allen 283, Michael Kent 271, Mike 309, Mildred (Fye) 310, Milton 311, Minnie 219, Miriam (Foland) 193, Monica Ellen 183, Myra Bell (Clark) 244, Nancy 310, Nancy A. 308, Nancy Carol 308, Nancy Jane 308, Neil Joseph 251, Nellie 171, Nelson Blaine 182, Newton 310, Newton B. 309, Nollie G. 221, Ora 153, 308, Patricia 309, Patricia Elaine 183, Patricia K. 310, Paul 310, Permelia (Garr) 309, Peter 288, R.H. 226, Rachel 177, 178, 310, Rebecca 310, Rebecca (Light) 310, Rebecca Jean 150, Reuben 33, Richard 14, 230, 308, 309, Richard H. 311, Richard L. 310, Richard Lee 309, Robert 309, Robert C. 310, Rodger 170, 172, 194, 267, Rodger Damon 194, Rodger Damon 308, Ronold 308, Rosie Sara 155, Roy 309, Ryan 310, Ryan B. 310, Samuel 186, 219, 221, Samuel J. 324, Samuel L. 308, Sandy 22, Sarah Ann Canine 189, Sarah Ann Canine 311, Sarah M. 308, Stanley Kent 183, T.C. 83, Tamara Ann 309, 321, Theopolis 275, Thomas 337, Thomas Kevin 183, Thomas W. 48, Tobias 176, Todd 309, Travis 19, Valarie 191, Viola 314, Virgil 228, Virginia Cleveland 173, Virginia Rose 308, Vivian 314, Vonna Lou 308, W.E. 34, Wayne 183, Wayne Allen 283, William 19, 289, William (Bill) 329, William B. 189, William Baker 311, William Baker II 311, William Cadid 311, William Charles 308, William Harry 308, Wm. 324
SMITHERMAN, Charles 147
SMOKER, Jason 157, Jennifer 157, Lindsey 157, Mike 157, Mildred (Allen) 157, Raymond 157, Sarah 157
SMOOT, Cheryl 140, Nathan 140
SMOTHERS, S.M. 95
SNAVELY, Beth 324, Brandon 324, Ed 324
SNELL, Bertha 247, Beulah 308, Clark 308
SNIDER, Angela Denise 289, Barbara 33, Elizabeth Joan 289, Jessica Lee (Purvis) 289, Jessica Lynn 289, Martha (Fordyce) 195, Michael A. 289, Michael Allen 289, Ralph 84
SNIDER/SNYDER 28
SNIPES, Geneva L. 195
SNODERLY, Elizabeth 140
SNODGRASS, Brandon Phillip 311, Brooke Erin 311, Christine (Preston) 311, Cynthia Joan 311, Jared Michael 311, Mark 208, Mark Vernon 311, Max 25, 334, Max Vernon 311, Michael Edward 311, Sandra Ruth 311, Sarah Rebecca 311, Walter Norman 311
SNOW, Deborah Lynn 340, Emily Jane 225, Jesse 65, Jessie 62, 143, John M. 225, Mazy B. (Arnett) 288, Paul 189, Sarah (Bundy) 225, Stanley Parks 340
SNYDER, David 25, Della Mae 260, Henry 25, Iva 51, John Bolivar 220, Lois 179, Mary Clevenger 316, Naomi Elizabeth 308, Steve 268, Susie Glenn 220
SOBLOTNE, Roy 172
SOLENBURGER, Dana 184
SOLLENBERGER, Dana Hollingsworth 123
SOMERS, A.L. (Ted) 312, Charles 312, Edward 312, Eldon 312, Emma 312, Horace 35, Jean 312, Lee 312, Mary McClain (Williams) 311, O.A. 55, Orlando 215, Orlando Allen 311, Percy 312, Raymond 312, Valentine 35, 311
SOMMERS, Albert 31
SOMSEL, Betty Jean 312, David 312, David Lewis 312, Effie Mae 312 Emmett C. 312, Fay 312, Jacob 312, James Vern, 312 , John Vern 312, Lee 312, Lois Irene 312, Mary Ann 312, May 14, Rebecca Warrenfelts 312, William Lee 312, William Wesley 312
SONGER, Linda 299
SOOTS, Andrea 179, Andrew 179, Angela 179, Arthur 179, Austin 179, Carolyn 179, Joseph 179, Mary Lou 179, Patricia 179
SOSBE, Archable 312, Betty Jean 141, Charles "Chuck" 312, Charles William 313, Charles William 201, Chris 172, Christopher 312, Christopher Allen 312, Chuck 312, Chuck Jr. 312, Clarence Estle 312, Clarence Estle 312, Debora Kay 312, Donald 141, Frances Marie 312, Glenn C. 141, Jennifer 172, 312, Jennifer Marie 312, Jimmie Joe 312, June 312, Leslie Marion 312, Linda Sue 312, Paul 313, Stacy 312, Timothy Ray 312, Walter A. 141, William C. 141, William Estle 312, Zora Ellen (Arnett) 141
SOTTONG, Gladys 192
SOUCEK, Svat 284
SOUDER, Ed 222, Ed M. 125
SOUPLEY, Jill 309, 310
SOUVERS, Harrison 188
SOWERS, Harriett 210
SPANGLER 43, Jeannie 22, Mary K. 236, Mary Louisa "Mollie" 247, Molly 247, Norma Jean Durr 204, Peter 247
SPARKS, Bessie Myrtle (Bryan) 313, Charles Mitchell 313, Clarinda Kay 313, Joyce 51, Judith Ann 313, Richard Dale 313, Sally 270
SPARLING 273
SPAULDING, Hugh 66, Mary 196, Viola Rayl 291
SPEALMAN, Jonathan 86, Margaret 86
SPEAR, Robert 33
SPEARS, Grace (Achor) 138
SPENCE, Audrey Leota (Merrill) 173, Frank Merrell 173, Helen Mary (Criss) 173, Joseph Steven 173, Peter Glen 173, Thomas S. 173, Timothy Criss 173
SPENCER, Brenda Lee 205, David Lee 205, Garnet 14, Herbert J. 338, Jennie Rose (Grinslade) 205, Jody Lee 205, John 48, Margaret Elizabeth (Clanorin) 272, Maude 245, 246, Maxine 214, Nora Blanche 272, Square 272, Virgil Lee 205
SPICER, Adrian 313, Benjamin 313, Charles 313, Christina 243, 272, 313, Churchill Harrison 313, Delores 3, Delores Mae (Kuntz) 313, Edmund 313, Ethel 313, Florence Charlotte (Ashby) 243, 272, Frank 313, Ida 313, Jack 78, 243, 272, 313, Jack Wayne 272, Jack Wayne 243, James 313, Jerry 243, 272, 313, John 313, Joseph 313, Karen 243, 272, 313, Kimmerly 313, Lucy Beck (Hawkins) 313, Marjorie 313, Mark 243, 272, 313, Marshall 313, Marshall Harrison 243, 272, Mary Jane 313, Nora 313, Norris 313, Oliver 313, Patricia 313, Robert 313, Rozella 313, Samuel 313, William 313
SPIES, Friederche Marie 206
SPILLMAN, Thomas 156
SPINDT, Roderick 276
SPITZENBERGER, George 27
SPOHN, Philaphen 343
SPOLEDER, Elizabeth (Traurbauch) 243, Henry 243, Mary Magdalena 243
SPRAKER 59, D.C. 113, David 313, DeLos 13, 14, Jennifer Kay 313, La Mar 313, Leora 14, Mary (White) 313, Sarah Joyce 313, Verna (Smith) 14
SPRAY, Caroline 333, Thomas Moses 333
SPRINGER 28, Ed 96, Gary 3, J. Lee 171, Lee 96
SPRINKLE, Carrie E. Cuthrell 285
SPROALS 39
SPRONG, Gustie Lynch 151, Milton 151, Mina 324, William 151
SPROUGH, Johannis 151
SPROWLS, Mary L. 213
SPUNCE, Enoch 33
SPURGEON, Allilee 288, Simeon 313, Tolly, 35
SPURLIN, Wilfred 96
SQUIER, Merle W. 80
ST. CLAIR 273
STADT, Anna 144
STAFFORD, (William) Russell 314, Ada 314, Alice L. 313, Angela 314, Beulah 191, Beulah Marie 314, Beulah Marie 192, C. Beatrice 313, C.B. 313, Carol Yvonne 313, Catherine (Mullen) 313, Charles 33, Charles W., Jr. 162, Charlotte 313, David 314, Edgar Earl 313, Elizabeth 313, Elizabeth (Wainscott) 313, Ella Mae (Yater) 191, Enoch 313, Essie 314, Florilla 313, Frank 65, 66, George B. McClellan 191, George B. McClelland 313, Gerald 301, Grace Leona 314, Grace Leona 191, Herbert Albert 313, Herbert Albert 313, Herbert G. 313, J. Ellen 301, Janet 301, Jasper Joseph 313, Jasper Joseph 313, John 313, Juanita R. (Johnson) 313, Judy 313, Julia 313, Kristin Taylor 313, Leanor 313, Letitia "Lettie" 314, Lettie 191, Loadicia 313, Lula 313, Marian Agness (Rubush) (Faulkner) 313, Martha 313, Mary 313, Mary Augusta 313, Mary Fern 314, Michael 314, Mildred 314, Mona (Jones) 301, Nancy 313, Nancy Catherine 313, Oliver Perry 313, Patricia 314, Ralph E. 313, Rettamae 191, 314, Sarah 313, Senah Ann (Wisehart) 162, Stella Effa 162, Steven D. 313, Susan 313, Tessie 314, Theressa M. 314, Tyrah 313, William 313, William A. 48, William "Billy" 314, William E. 313, William M. 313
STAHL, Adam 314, Ann Marie 314, Anna Mary 237, Anna Mary Luvina 314, Benjamin 305, Betty Lou 315, Carl E. 315, Catherine 314, Catherine Greiner 314, Charles Frederick 314, Charles J. 314, Edward Earl "Ned" 314, Eva Evelyn 305, Everet Elma 314, Ferol 3, 110, 314, Ferol Palmer 204, Frederick E. 314, Frederick E. (Bud) 315, Frederick "Fred" E. 314, Friedrick 314, George 314, George A. 314, George F. "Dick" 314, George F. "Dick" 185, Heinrich 314, Jack E. 315, Jacob 314, Jakob 314, Joseph A. 314, Joseph Leo 314, Judith Kay 185, Karen Sue 185, 314, Katharina (Catherine) 314, Kenneth Paul "Pete" 314, Kimberly Lynn 315, Lewis H. 314, Margaret 314, Marie 314,

Marjorie A. 315, R. Wayne 315, Sheila M. 315, Steven Gary 185, 314, Willard E. 314, Willard E. Jr. 315, Willard Ernest 314
STAMM, Alonzo 208, Charles 305, Effie Nora A. 208, Jacob 208, S. "Letta" C. Eads Dulanty 208
STANFIELD, David 35, 36
STANFORD, Vianna K. 293
STANLEY, Claude 25, Elma 283, George 219, James Alexandria 325, Milley 232, Minerva 201, Nancy Marie 325, Nathan 29, 33, William 27, 29, 33, William A. 13
STANT, Lucinda 324
STANTON, Emerson 332, Esther 315
STARBUCK, Andrew 62, Blaine 64
STARGEL, Anthony 299, Cal 299, Joy Ann 299, Thomas 299
STARK, Alice (Baxter) 326, Carmen 285, Ernest 326, Patricia Kim 285, Paul 285, William M. 27
STARKS, William 33
STARNER, Rose 193
STARR, Jacob 201, William 201
STATLER, Joyce 293
STEEL, Henry 292
STEELE, Arthur 13, Charles J. 13, Jennie C. 13, Marion E. 13
STEENMAN, Becky J. 288, Margaret (Greer) 288, Sherman 288
STEEVER, Ethel 72, Rolland 72
STEINHAGEN, David 344, Godfrey 344
STEPHENS 48, Ada Pearl (Sowers) 195, Albert 276, Harry Leslie 194, Hiram 276, James 33, 201, Margaret 276, Viola (Snow) 276
STEPHENSON, Elaine Davis 264, Jack 264, Joel 82, Leroy 138, Luella 305
STEPHNS, Hazel 284
STERLING, Ada Ion Brinson 149, Ann Nichelle Johnson 147, Ann Nichelle "Shellie" 181, Eric Lee 149, Jordan James 147, 149, Lester Lee 147, Lester Lee 149, Ollie James 149, Richard James 147, 149, Sandra Kay (Benge) 149, Sandra Kay Benge 147, Shellie 149
STETLER, Bertha Alice 295, Daniel 255, Elizabeth (Glaze) 255, Elmer 3, Ethel 3, Nancy 255
STEVENS, Atlanta 248, Bradley 315, Bruce E. 232, Catherine 315, Charles 315, Cynthia Ann 214, Cynthia Ann 316, Douglas A. 315, Dustin L. 315, Edgar A. 315, Edward L. 315, Elijah 189, Frank 315, Gideon 48, Harold 175, Harold Leslie 315, Harry Lee 315, Harry Moroni "Bud" 315, Henderson Browning 315, Hertha Faustine 315, Isaac 315, James 27, James Gregory 315, Jeremiah 242, John 315, John James 315, Katherine Lynn 316, Katy 315, M. Lee Ann 232, Madeline Fisher 315, Malcolm Charles 315, Marita J. 315, Mark J. 315, Mary 324, Mary Katherine 315, Melvin Wesley 315, Owen Merideth 315, Philip 315, Philip Warden 185, Phillip 315, Phillip Warren 316, Regina Pearson 315, Robert M. 315, Robert M. II 315, S. 34, Samuel 315, Shirley Ann Auten 214, Todd J. 315, Walter Vernon 315, Warren 315, Warren Bryan 315, Warren Bryan 214, 316, William Franklin 315
STEVENSON, Betty 186, Edith (Miller) 255, Rebecca 214
STEWARD, Henry 33
STEWART, 340, Alice Marie (Peggy) 149, Charles 340 , Effie (Harbaugh) 316, Effie Harbaugh 316, Elmer 21, G. 34, George 27, Glenn 316, H.H. 13, Harriet 340, Harry 316, Harry Harrison 316, Harry Lewis 316, Harry Lewis 316, Hugh 25, J.C. 34, Jack 172, James Stephen 316, Jenny Hillis 316, John 177, 340, John Phillip 177, June 149, Lela Ann 339, Lisa Rebecca 316, Lucinda (Hall) 340, Marvin 340, Naomi 340, Ralph 316, Ralph (Rusty) Russell 316, Ralph Russell 316, Robert 340, Robert S. 340, Sarah (Myers) 340, Stephen Brian 316, Stephen H. 316, Stephen Harry 316, Susan Tanya 316, Tanya 293, Thomas Lewis 316, Thomas Lewis Jr. 316, William Lewis 316, William Randall 316, Wm. Lewis 316
STIEFENHOEFOR, Harriet Mae 230
STIEMKE, Adolph J. 84
STINE, Esther 236, Kathleen 299, Mary 270
STINER, Melissa Flowers 331, Wayne 48
STIRLING, Marion 226
STITES, Mary 32, Ronald 32
STODDARD, Frank 329, Willard 13
STOLL, Joel 29
STONE, Blanch Ada 202, Dock 245, John H. 202, Mary 202, Ruth Ellen Prevo 276, Sarah Ellen (Brown) 202, Solomon 202
STONEBRAKER, Cecil 257, Donna 257, Gale 257, Horace 257, J.W. 44, Lucy (Allread) 257, Madalyn 257, Sharon 257, Wayne Carlton 257
STONEMAN 48
STORE, Lora 173
STOREY, James 23
STORMS, Dale 72, 73, Henrietta 73, J.H. 83, Ray 73
STOUT, A.B. 130, Albert 25, Allen 318, Allen Lewis 317, Andrew 317, Andrew Richard 318, Bethanne 130, Burrell 25, Carrol Lavain 318, Carrol Lavain 317, Charles 318, Charles Lindley 317, 318, Cindi 59, Clarence 318, Clarence Leonard 317, Connie 317, Darrell 85, David 130, Denny 130, E. Blanch 323, Earl 317, Elizabeth 66, Elizabeth Bee 317, Elizabeth Moon 317, Elmira 317, Ethel 317, Florence 148, Gayle 318, Gayle Edward 317, Gloria Jeane 317, Jeff 23, 25, 130, Jeffrey Kennard 130, Jenniffer 317, John 202, 316, 317, John Edward II 202, Joyce 318, Joyce Ellen 317, Kathryn Cheryl 318, Kathy 317, Katrina 317, Katrina Lynn 318, Kennard 23, 25, 130, Kurt 317, Kurtis Allen 318, Lena 317, Loris Polk 317, 318, Loris Polk 317, Lydia 317, 321, Mary Ellen 317, Megan 130, Milton 317, Morgan 130, Reuben 148, Richard 316, 317, 318, Richard Leon 317, Sarah Alice 170, Sarah Ann 317, Scott 317, Silas 60, Summer 317, Summer Todd 318, Susan 160, Susannah 246, Suzanne 317, Todd 317, Todd Andrew 318, Wallace 25, 130, William 317, 318, William Earl 318
STOVER, Cassondra Louise, "Sandy" 182, Dennis Glenn 182, Flossie 150, Howard 150, Jacob 27, 28, 33, James Maurice 182, Thursia Mae (Lewis) 150
STOWELL, Joseph M. III 75
STRALEY, Inez 327, Mary Angeline 153
STRANGE, Cynthia Ann 163, David 163, 197, Michael Stephen 163
STRATTAN, Jane Thomas 207, Jonathan 207, Joseph 207, Prudence Edgerton 207, Arthur Elvin 162, C.E. 19, Eli B. 162, Florence 19, Hazel 19, Joseph 18, Lillian 231, Rachel Ellen 162, Rebecca Mote 162, Samuel 18, Susan Mira 162
STRAUSS 39, Hugh 25
STRAWBACK, Charles 48
STRAWBRIDGE, Betty Bock 156, Charles Lawrence (Larry) 221, Charles Thomas 221
STRAWBRIDGE-BROMLEY, Anna Elizabeth 152, Anna Elizabeth Bock 220
STREET, I.F. 19, Jack 184, James 184, James Murray 212, John 48, Joseph 184, Margaret Helmich 212, Margaret Murray 212, Marietta 19, Robert 184
STREETER, Benjamin J. 318, Betty (Wolfe) 255, Bradley Thomas 319, Carrie Elizabeth 319, Claude Clive 152, 318, Clive Claudius 288, 318, Cynthia Dawn 319, David Allen 318, Deborah 318, Edgar Edward 318, Fredrich Cladius 318, Geoffrey Scott 319, John 318, Karen Maria 319, Kimberly Ann 319, Michelle Alberta 319, Nathan 318, Paul Robert 318, Rachel Ann 318, Rebecca Jane 318, Robert Allen 319, Samuel 318, Steven 318, Suzanne Marie 319, Thomas Wayne 318, Tiffany Leigh 319, Troy David 319, Wayne Byrum 318
STRIEBEL, Isabel 182, Michael 182, Stephen 182
STRINGER, Bonnie Lee 153, Isabella 207, Shadrach 18, 207, Sherry Lynn 153, Wesley Earl 153, William 153
STROHBEHN, Ben 75
STRONG, Edwin B. 72, Mary 149
STROUD, Anna Isabelle 325, James R. 277, Millie Jane (Brown) 277
STROUP, Winifred 176
STUART, Henry 20
STUBBS, Thomas 19, 45
STUCKY, Obluna 223
STUDABAKER, W. 34, 297
STULL, Lilburn 257, 295
STURDIVANT, J.S. 326
Sturdivant, Mary Frances (Turner) 326
STYER, William 31
STYGLES, Herbert 13
STYLES, Jonathan 86
SUITE, George W. 188
SULLIVAN, Addie 250, Angilina (Bryant) 272, Barbara 264, Charlotte 272, Connie 264, Donn 264, Donna Lynn 264, Dulcenia 264, Edward Howard 264, Gregory Lyn 320, John 35, 264, June Ann 264, Kathy 264, Larry D. 320, Marjorie Kay K. 320, Merl J. 250, Scott Daniel 320, Turner 35, 272
SUMAN, John 275
SUMME, Esther 96, George 96, Rolla 96
SUMMERS, Arthur Clifford 167, Edward 180, Eliza (Copeland) 237, Elizabeth (Wines) 237, Golvin 237, James 278, Jim 36, John 52, John C. 305, John Milt 170, Lema 167, Margaret 278, Mary M. 158, Minerva 193, Simon 167, 237, Simon Jr. 167, Sue Hullinger 36, Walter J. 278, Wesley 41
SUMMERTON, Helga 51
SUMPTION, Jeanness 155, Julia 155, Julia Alberta 155, Julia Cora Cady (Dode) 155, William H. 155
SURBER, Joseph Grant 299
SURFACE, Hugh E. 212
SURRY, James 48
SUTER, Brenda Kay 249, Elpha (Abney) 335, Gerald 335, Gerald F. 335, Harriet 249, James Brian 249, Mandy Mae 249, Pamela Jeanne 249, Robert Elhanan 249, Robert G. 249, Robert James (Jim) 249, Robert Todd 249, Roberta Louise 335, Sandra Kaye 249
SUTHERLIN, Jr. 25
SUTTERFIELD, Paul 78
SUTTLES, Herman Lee 330, Margret Gladys (Adkins) 330
SUTTON, Abe 271, Charles (Tug) 185, Jacob 323, Jan 72, Mary 155, Max (Tony) 155, Nancy "Jane" 168, 271, Rebecca 245, Ruth M. 51, Stan 72, Stanley 85
SWAIM, Elizabeth 268, Josephine 196
SWAIN, Brad 29, Frances Morgan 159
SWAN, Bessie 285, D.S. 52, Paula Lynn 232
SWANSON, Joan 216
SWARTS, Kathleen 230
SWARTZ, Gregory 319, James B. 319, Jordan 319, Julie 319, Kathleen M. 319, Laura 319, S. 34
SWARTZENDRUBER, Stella Beatrice (Heximer) 203
SWARTZKOFF, Martell 318
SWATZ, Joseph 319
SWAVEY, Patricia Ann (Adair) 139
SWAYZEE, Jean 25
SWEENEY, Mary 207
SWEET, Leonard 70
SWIFT, Beth Ann 165, John 27
SWIGERT, Grace B. 206
SWIHART, Avinal Bertrude 319, Clare Marie 319, David Keith 319, Jacqueline Jane 319, John Fitzgerald 319, Keith 334, Keith Lamar 319, Mary Ann 319, Mary Loretta (White) 319, Mary Pauline (Ling) 319, O.M. 11, 103, Timothy Joseph 319
SWINFORD, Shawn Allen 242, Stacey Nicole 242, Steven 242, Steven Ray 242
SWING, Archie 180, 225, Barbara 277, David 277, Kimberly 277, Lori 277, Michael 277, Richard 277, Sarah 158
SWINGLE, Susannah 267
SWINGLEY, Afton 239
SWISHER, Benjamin 244, Elizabeth 244, George 219, James 182, Jane 244, Jascha Droll 182, Louis 244, Lucinda J. 270, Mary 244, Rachel 244, Samual 244, Sarah Pruella 269
SWISSHELM, James 329
SWOPE, Stella June 294
SWORD, Amanda Kay 320, Donald L. 320, Jennifer Leighann 320, Joseph Tyler 320, Karen Lynn T. 320
SYKES, Karen Sue 145
SYLVAIN 306
SYLVESTER Flora, Orion 152
SYMONS, Dora (Martz) 98

T

TABOR, Kenneth C. 80
TAFLINGER, Bruce 187, Dan 31,
TAFT, Robert A. 210
TAIT, Netherland 159
TALBERT, Arvilla 104, Betty 107, Hulda Mae 193, Jack 25, 26, Larry 22, Luther 25, Marsha 25, Mildred 14, 21, Norm 97, Sam 26, Sammie 62, Samuel 65, 66
TALLEY, Gertrude 89, John 89
TANNER, Arcena Iona (Watkins) 204, Emma (Armanda) 204, Joseph Henry 204
TARKINGTON 59, Arthur 270, George 270, Harry 270, John J. 270, Laura 270, Lewis 270, Lydia 270, Maria J. 305, Mattie 270, Oscar 270, Will D. 106
TATE, Afton F. 319, Benjamin 319, Berne 319, Bradley 272, David 80, Frank 319, Fredric A. 319, George D. 34, Iva 319, Jeanette E. 319, Jim 319, John 33, John B. 319, John F. 27, 319, Julie 319, Karl E. 319, Lela E. 319, Linda 319, Mary Helen 250, Richard E., Jr. 319, Richard Eldon 319, Ruth 319, Shelah Kay 319, Sidney 95, Verna Mable (McKinney) 272, William A., Jr. 319
TATE-WORTHMAN, Shelah K. 319
TATEM, William 60
TATMAN, Donna 239
TATONE, James 263
TAUBENSE, Jack 97
TAUER, Lucile 276
TAYLOR 59, Adam 320, Ann 178, Anna Mae 162, Anna Mae (Burgett) 166, Bernice Kay (Grinslade) Reser 205, Beverly Jean 185, Blake Anthony 320, C. Russell 307, C.G. 46, Cary Grant 320, Charles Russell 320, Charley 320, Christopher Ryan 320, Cleo "Jack" Lavon 166, Cleo Lavon "Jack" 251, Craig 23, 86, Curtis 320, David Ralph 320, Edith (Floyd) 302, Emanuel 320, Enoch 320, Esther Small 307, 320, Frances (Reynolds) 148, Frances Reynolds 319, Franklin 320, George 15, 319, 320, George A. 44, George F. 320, Helen Barnett 320, Ira Jr. 25, Irene 234, Jackson 319, Jacqueline Ann 166, 251, James Harvey 320, James Henry 313, John 319, John Alexander 320, John Matilla 320, Joseph 13, 15, 148, Joseph C. 319, Joseph, Jr. 319, Joseph Wesley 320, Kathy Joann 320, Laurie 320, Lewis 26, 66, Lewis Lewellyn 320, Lewis Milton 307, 320, Linda Gail Canady 320, Lowell W. 320, Margaret Ann 313, Margaret Lugar 320, Marianna 23, Martha Caroline (Fuller) 313, Mary Ellen 320, Mary Frances Carter 320, Mike 230, Murta Jane 320, Nettie Valeda 320, Pamela Sue Graham 320, Pat 21, Rachel Kenworthy 320, Ralph 320, Ramey Delaska 320, Raymond 302, Richard Allen 320, Richard Scott 320, Robert 230, Ross 12, Roy 48, Sarah Jo 320, Steve 230, Theresa Marie 322, Virginia 214, W.H. 95, Wayne W. 320, William 35, 320, William Adam Roland 320, William Lewis 320, Zachary 187, 188, 201, 337
TAYLOR-CHASTEEN, Jacqueline 27

TEAGARDIN, A. 34
TEDFORD, I.C. 83, Willard P. 83
TEDLOCK, John, 179, Sally Carol 179, Steven K. 179
TEEL, Joe 145, Josephine (Clark, Haskett) 145
TEMPLE, Bud 45
TEMPLES, Charles 321, Mary Ann (McClard) 321
TEMPLIN 28, 208, Cerena Florence (McQuiston) 236, Christopher 223, Christophor 152, Cora Dell 236, Dale 257, David 152, 223, Delilah 58, Dorothy 152, Eulila 201, Eunice Beals 201, J.G. 34, 48, Jacob G. 27, Jennifer 152, 223, Mary D. 158, Ray 152, Richard 31, Robert 201, T. 34, Timothy 27, 31, 33, 58, 201, William Timothy 236
TENBROOK, Donovan 267, Sharon 267, Shirley 267
TENNESON 43
TERFLINGER, J.V. 96
TERRAL, John 33
TERRELL, Eldon 85, John 27, Richard 18
TERRIS, Bob 212
TERWISHE, Frances 302
TETER, Dorothy Lee 193, 320, Etta (Foster) 320, Hazel 107, Hazel (Dickey) 193, Hazel Dickey 163, Lewis 163, 193, Lewis Sherman 320, Linda Ellen 163, 320, Linville 320
TETRICK, Everett William 320, Ronald L. 60, 62, Ronald Lee 320
THARP, Cora A. 230, Esaes 33, Ira 160, Mina 133
THATCHER, Alexander 48, David 48, Jesse 48, John Wayne 182, Jonnah Whitney 182, Justin Wayne 182, Mary 107, Mary Rayl 291, Susan Rayl 291
THIEKE, Addie (Temples) 320, 321, Anna Elizabeth (Wheeler) 183, Betty 183, 332, Bill 321, Cline Denzil 320, 321, David Wayne 321, Dorothy 332, Edward 321, Jean 332, Laura Jane (Blackburn) 321, Margaret Ann 309, 321, Marie 332, Marilyn Irene 321, Mary 332, Osby 321, Sharon Louise 321, Thilburn 321, Thomas Evan 321, Wes 321, William 332, William Lee Temples 321, Willie Richard 183
THINKER, Augusta 278, Ethel 278, Paul 278, Peter 278
THOMAS 48, 85, 89, Barbara 253, C.B. 59, Caroline 300, Caroline Elliott 305, Charles 27, Charles E. 219, Charles Hillis 321, Donna 323, Earl 333, Edgar Lloyd 166, Eleanor 158, Elizabeth May 321, Guy R. 241, H.T. 48, Isaac 305, James William 166, 257, Jane Shockney 190, John 216, Kathryn Ann 193, Kevin 323, Ladoska 201, Ladoska A. 202, Lloyd Edgar 257, Lowell Austin 321, Luke 321, Lynvall 26, Martha Ann 270, Michaele Kristina 140, 252, 303, Miriam (Lamb) 321, Miriam Lamb 207, Nancy 334, Ora 65, R. 48, Rebecca 339, Rebecca May (Freed) 195, Reuben 48, Richard Marlin 193, Snead 207, 321, Stephen 323, Susan Elizabeth 193, Uriah 245, William 195
THOMISON, Dorothy 173, Lassie (Johnson) 173, William 173
THOMLINSON, David Keith 340, Linda Lucille 340, Mark Allen 340

THOMPSON 86, 292, Abigail (Lay) 322, Amanda C. 246, Benjamin 44, Betty Jean 230, Beverly 322, 332, Bill 139, Bob 139, Brent 322, C. 36, Carmen 174, Carrie Adeline 277, Catherine 323, Charles 286, Charles (Chuck) 322, 323, Charles David Jr. 323, Chester 197, Cindi 317, Darlene Kay Cottingham Williams 322, David 322, David Headley (Headley) Sr. 322, David Holt 217, David Jr. 322, Debra Elizabeth Cottingham Pullen 322, Della Uba (Davis) 280, Edwin 139, Elizabeth 322, Elizabeth (Ross) 344, Ellen 139, 196, Ellen (Simpkins) 139, Ellen (Simpkins) 196, Eric 323, Esther (Duncan) 322, Fay 322, Flora 280, Flossie 306, Francis P. 286, Grace Schoff 322, H.F. 95, H.H. 95, Harvey 277, Hollis Galathia (Freed) 196, Hugh L. 102, Ida A. 286, Jack 139, Jack Heflin 322, James Howard 322, James Howard 322, Jay 322, Jeannette Adeline (Clevenger) 322, Jim 139, Joe 139, John 322, John A. 286, John J. 277, Joseph 139, 196, Joseph A. 286, Julia 322, Kathryn Cynthia "Cindi" 318, Keith 322, Keith Patrick 322, Larry 322, Larry Lee 322, Lawrence 306, Leonard 322, Leslie Blaine 322, Levi 144, Lewis 322, Lillian 280, Lovil F. 286, Lulu E. 286, Lydia E. 286, Marilyn 281, Mark 322, Martha 322, Martha (Marty) 322, Maude Teresa 277, Michael 246, Michael David 322, Michael Gene 322, Mildred Woods 322, Minnie May (Heflin) 322, Morton 318, Nathan 330, Noah 38, Pearl Lilia (Powell) 322, Pete 139, Peter 323, Rachael (Bevard) 330, Ralph 197, 322, Ralph Wesley 217, Raymond 322, Richard 322, Robert 197, 344, Ruth 139, 197, Ruth Mae Delrymple 322, Samuel 44, Sarah 177, Sarah Elizabeth 'Lizzie' 277, Sean 323, Sherman 322, Ted Richard 322, Teresa 322, Theresa Olillia 290, Thomas M. 286, Thornberg Baldwin 280, Tom 139, W. Ira 322, W.H. 279, W.W. 27, William 66, William (Bill) 196
THOMSON, Robert Gene Achor 322, Sophia 268, William H. 51
THORNBURG, F.F. 70
THORNE 59, Anna America 220, Charles 323, Elizabeth 323, George E. 98, Hester 323, J.T. 323, Jacob 323, James 323, John T. 323, Mary Jane 323, Mary Jane 248, Nancy "Lucy" 323, Ned 323, Paul 323, Thomas J. 19, Walker Manwarring 323
THORP, Alfred 37
THORPE, Brendan 319, Kylie 319, Ralph 319
THRAILKILL, Dorsin 33, Mary 33, Polly 58
THRALL, John 144
THRUSH, Grace 287
THUMB, Tom 46
TIBBETS, Joseph 204, Margaret Tully 204, Rachel 204
TIBBETTS, Alfred 196
TICE, Jonathan 75
TICKFER, Bernard J. 172, Mary Ball 172
TIERCE, Christian 33
TIGNOR, Sterling 227
TILEY, Dessie Lovina (Rhodes) 265, James Caleb 265

TILLEY, Naomi 332
TIMMONS, Linda 276
TINDER, Emily A. 277
TINO, Cindy Gay 190
TIPTON, Anna Lee 229, Barbara (Bowers) 154, Bettie Louise Cooper 229, Dock Witt 229, Joe Berry 229
TIREY, G. 27
TITERIKNGTON, Elaine Lines 197
TITUS, Arzell 257
TOBIAS, Anna Bell 323, Bernice 323, Doris 323, George 323, John 323, Mary 323, Nora Wilson 323, Oliver 323
TODD, Charles Thomas 193, David Lee 193, Gladys Eva 323, Gladys Eva 211, Harriett Sophronia (Tharp) 323, Henry 323, John Harvey 318, Marlene 317, 318, R.H. 83, Sarah Elizabeth 193, Smith C. 52
TODHUNTER, Whalen 27
TOLAN, Andrew Craig 326, Margaret Delores Petter 326, Patrick Allan 326, Robert Warren Jr. 326
TOLLE, Ben Osborne 323, Benham 323, Caroline 323, Elvira 323, Henry 323, James 323, John Sutton 323, Jonathan 323, Levi 323, Mary 59, Minervia 323, Nancy Applegate 323, Nancy Jane 323, Robert 323, Strather 323, William 53, 323
TOLLEY, Angeline 291, Ina Belle 174
TOMLIN, Dolly Mildred 152
TOMLINSON, David 340, George 295, Kelly Rae 340, Miriam Elizabeth "Bettie" 295
TOMPKINS, Daniel 182
TOMS, Anderson 232
TONES, Allison Nicole 320, Darrell 320, Linda Marie C. 320
TONEY, Ken 23
TORRENCE, Robert 19, Ross 18, Ruth 18, Sarah 18, 19
TOST, Kenneth 65, 66
TOUBY 32, 39, 43, A.C. 34, 90, Albert C. 32, 247, Albert Colon 324, Alice 247, 324, Anna Marie 324, Bessie 247, 324, Dorothy 247, Emmett 324, Emmett P. 247, Emmett P. 32, 247, Frances 247, Grace 324, Jane C. 247, Jennie 247, 324, Joan 247, John Martin 324, John Peter 324, Leora 247, Louise 247, Mary 247, Max P. 34, Peter 30, 32, 247, Virginia 247
TOW(E), Mary Cozetta 263, William 263
TOWE, Beryle (Metsger) 224, Corwin (Doc) Metsger 224, J.V. 224, Jerrel (Jerri) 224
TOWLES, Don 257
TOWNSEND 28, Almina 23, Lowell 104, Virgil 25
TRABUE, David 324, Elizabeth 48, Elizabeth Sallee 324, Ephraim 48, 324, Louise Elizabeth 324, Marion Minter 324, Massa Malissa 324, Melissa 49, William David 324
TRACEWELL, Cara Ann 324, Christine Marie 324, Corwin D. 324, Corwin Patrick 324, Donald Dailey 324, Goldie Genieve (Reeves) 324, Jesse Hugh 324, Martha Pearl (Dailey) 324, Pat Holderith 293, Patricia L. (Holderith) 324, Thomas 324
TRAGASSER, John 293, Anna Catherine 293, Mary Renie 293
TRAYERS, Diane 325, Dolores (Kulow) 325, Doloris 325, James 325, John 325, Kathryn 325,

Martha 325, Mary K. 207, Mary Katherine 325, Mary Louise 325, Robert 325, Susan 325, Thomas 325, William 325, William "Jim" 325
TREES 28
TRENT, Susanna 295
TRESLER 21
TRESSLER, Jacob 247
TRIBBETT, John 27, William H. 324
TRICK, J.C. 34
TRIMBLE, Edith 123
TRINE, William 48
TRITTLE, Nellie A. 175
TROBAUGH, Nicholas 86
TROSTEL, Edna Devona 294
TROTT, Meredith 178
TROTTER, Nancy 191
TROTTIER, Donna 253
TROUT, Lorena 206
TROWBRIDGE, David Lee 168, Irwin 168
TROXWELL, Jennie 145
TROYER 28, 29, A. 34, A.B. 34, A.E. 34, Abraham 325, Alfred 39, Almeda Lucella 253, Amanda 325, Andrew 325, Andrew J. 28, 241, Anna 325, Barbara 248, 325, Benjamin 325, Callie 325, Carrie 253, 325, Catherine 325, Christian 325, Daniel 325, David 325, E.R. 34, Edward 325, Eli 325, Elizabeth 264, 325, Ellsworth 325, Emanuel 43, 325, George 325, Gertrude 325, Glen 325, Harve 325, Henry 325, J.E. 34, Jacob 325, Jennie 325, Jeremiah 325, Joel Abraham 253, John 31, 325, Jonathan 325, Joseph 325, Joseph C. 295, Katie 325, Laird 42, 325, Lizzie Ann 325, Lucinda 325, Magdalena 325, Maria (Hostetler) 295, Martin J. 253, Mary 325, Mary Ann 241, Mary June 325, Mattie 325, Michael 325, Milt 42, Miriam Caroline 253, N. 34, Naomi 183, Nathaniel 325, Noah 325, Nora 325, Omar Ray 253, Orval 325, Percy 325, Philip Lee 253, Roy 343, Samuel 325, Sarah 325, Sylvia Mae 253, Veronica 325, Willard Allen 253
TROYERS 39, James 8
TRUAX, David 27, 33, 34, Dennis 27, E. 34, James M. 33, Warren 31
TRULLINGER, Gabriel 196
TRYBERGER, William 51
TUBACH, Judith Marie (Payne) (Harbin) 333
TUBBS, Emily 171
TUCKER, Benjamin 15, 60, 61, D.W. 16, Jane 337, June 187, Lincoln 145
TUDOR, Clinton B. 51, Kent 247, Russell E. 51
TUDORS, C.B. 169
TUGGLE, Derek Delon 143, George E. 143, Kelly Marie 143
TULL, Levi Thomas 339, Ruth 339
TULLEY, Thelma Wood 276
TULLIS, William 86
TUNIS, Richard 156, Richard Morris 156, William 156
TURBEVILLE, S.H. 70
TURLEY, Dalton 14, Jennifer M. 234, Julia 256, 257
TURNER, Abednago 325, Adlove Marie 326, Albert 325, Andrew 310, Andrew Jackson 325, Ann 325, Avis (Maddock) 231, Avis (Paddock) 326, Avis Rachel 231, Avis Rachel 173, Barbara Mae 325, Bessie Francena 325, Beverly (Mason) 256, Burrell Fredrick 325, Carrie 191, 325,

Daniel Kent 325, David Lewis 326, Debbie 191, Debra 223, Delilah Elizah (Breedlove) 156, Edith Marie 231, Edna Evelyn 314, Elkanah Benjamin 325, Elnora 231, Fred Lewis 231, Fred Lewis 326, Frederick J. 283, Fredrick Neil 32, George W. 96, Harriet Esther 231, Harriet Esther 326, Helen 326, Hillary 197, Horace Edward 325, India Nora Louise 303, Iryl J. 231, Iryl James 326, Jack Dean 325, James 191, James Copland 325, James Edward 326, Jane 337, Janet Isabelle 325, Jerry 191, Jerry Jr. 191, Jesse 60, Jesse Maurer 326, Jesse T. 231, 326, John 325, Joseph Henry 325, Lewis Whetzel 325, Lois 152, Margaret Elizabeth (Johnson) 173, Martha 310, Mary 325, Meshack 325, Michael 191, Milley Frances 231, N. Berniece (Copp) 170, Nancy 325, Paul Eugene 326, Paul Leon 325, R. 35, Rachel (Jones) 310, Robert 152, Roy Ray 32, Samuel Edward 173, Samuel Edward 231, 326, Shadrach 325, Stanley Ward 231, Stanley Ward 326, Tanya 191, Valeria Blanch 325, Verna 325, William 325, William H. 328
TURNPAUGH, Helen (Bowers) 154
TUSING, Jean (Bowers) 154
TUTTEROW, Cora Jane 308
TWINEHAM, Ora Belle 286, Ruth 190
TYGART, Rosie 166
TYLER, Amos 326, Barbara 326, Bosewell 326, Charles L. 326, Clarence 326, D.A. 34, David 27, 326, Ella 326, Eyppa 326, Frank 27, George 326, J.W. 34, James 27, 326, John 326, John W. 326, Joseph 27, 326, Louella 89, Louisa 326, Martin 326, Mary 326, Mary M. 326, Mary Ruth 147, Mertle 326, Nathan 326, Nathaniel 27, 33, Paul 326, Phebe A. 326, Rhoda 326, S.W. 34, Samuel 326, Sarah J. 326, Susan 326, Thomas 326, Virgil 326
TYNER, Carl 122, Harold Wilburn 223, Jewel Lee 223, Karen Lou 223, Sharen Sue 223
TYRE 41, Elijah 28, John 33, O. 34
TYSON, Daniel 13, Hannah 252

U

UHRIG, John 265, Margaret Eve 193, 265
UITTS, Harley 25, Susan A. 212
ULERICK, Alma May 295
ULLMAN, Walter 84, William 84
ULP, Catharine 252
ULRICH, Frank 84
UMBARGER, Kent 84
UMPHRIES, Ashley 231, Ian 231, Kevin 231
UNDERWOOD, Glen 300, Mary Louise 300, Matilda (Hawkins) 202, 300, Noel 31, 300, Thomas W. 32, 202, 300
UNGER, Alma Thomas 321, Elizabeth Bryson 317, Franklin Pierce 317, Martha 238, Martha Lennon 317, Rhea 157, Richard 308, Thelma Mae 148, Thomas 317
UNGERER, Walter J. 81
UNRUE, Omar 21
UNTHANK, Sarah J. 158

371

UNVERSAW, Ernestine 14
UTTERBACK, Cynthia 270, Dale 310, Daniel 270, David 270, Dwight 310, Edgar 310, Forest 310, Glenn 310, Levern 270, Martha 225, Nancy 270
UTTINGER, Herman Horace 286

V

VAILE, Anna 326, Bonita 327, Charles 327, Elizabeth 327, Emma 326, George 326, Isabelle Voiles 326, Joel 326, Joel Fredrick 326, Joseph 326, 327, Rawson 326, Ted 269, Teresa 327, Theodore 326, Theodore (Peany) 327, Theodore Jr. 327, Theodore Jr. (Ted) 327, Victor 326, 327, Victor Edward II 327, Wilson 327
VALKENBURGH, Karl Van 275
VAN BRIGGLE, Anthony 327, Briley 327, Chester Allen 327, Grady Bernard 327, Huldham (James) 327, Jessica 327, Katelin 327, Kimberly 327, Lori 327, Peter 327, Phyliss Joan 327, Randy 327, Robin 327, Walter 327
VAN DRESEN, Miriam Josephine 144
VAN HORN, Jean 25
VAN HOUTEN, Alva Lee 280, Evelyn (Elly) 280, Linda Marie 280
VAN NEMAN, Ruth 235
VAN PRINCES, Penelope 316, Penelope 317
VAN SICKLE, Franklin 31
VANBIBBER, Lottie 65
VANBIBLER, Dayton 219
VANBRIGGLE, Chester Allen 202, Grady 202
VANCE, John 313, Margaret Edith 147
VANDENBARK, Lillian 166, Mary Moulder 268
VANDENBOSCH, Anna 314
VANDERCOOK, Alice 284
VANDERGRIFF, Alvis L. 327, Charles Asroe 327, Charles S. 327, Clyde Horace 147, 327, Clyde Steven 147, 181, 327, David 327, Dicy Brock 327, Elizabeth "Betsy" 327, Emeline 327, Enoch 327, Estel Lee 327, Gilbert 327, Jacob 327, James 327, Jane 327, Jeremy Steven 147, 327, Jerry Lee 327, Jewell Ann 327, Joshua Ryan 147, Joshua Ryan 327, Kathy Gail 327, Lester Carnell 327, Lindsay 327, Louisa M. Kirby 327, Lula Isabell 327, Mandy L. 327, Martha A. 327, Mary Ann 327, Mary "Polly" Beeler 327, Mossie Ray 327, Oscar DeVaughn 327, Pryor L. 327, Ronnie 327, Shirley Marie Caldwell 147, Susie Edna 327, Teresa Diana Barnett 146, 327, William 327, Zola/Zora G. 327
VANDERKOLK, Diane 160
VANDIVIER, Leon 25, 116
VANDIVIER, Mazie 116
VANDUSEN, Bruce 125
VANHOOK, Aaron 51
VANHORN, Julie Kay 290
VANLUE, W. 34
VANMETER, Betty Jane 138
VANMETER, Walter 326
VANNATTER, Kimberly Jo 330, Paul 330, Scott Matthew 330

VANTINE, Lulu 119
VANTYLE, Richard 65
VARNETTI, Rose Marie 229
VARNEY, Janice 19
VAUGHN, Florence 173, Gertrude 15
VEACH, Nancy 19
VENNAMAN, Cornelius 284, Virena Ellen 284
VERMILION, Charles Marian 216, Edna May 216
VERN, Joseph Williams 48
VERNON, Anna 197, Lydia 197, Martha 197, Mary 197, Maude 197, Ross 197, Susan 234, Tom 197
VETTER, Liberty Tasha 329, Walter John 329
VICKERS, Emily 266
VICKERY, Jerriter 268
VICTORSON, Charles A. 328, Eleanor Louise (Harness) 211
VILLA, Richard T. 94
VINCENT, Rachel 187, Randy L. 251, Tiffany LeeAnn 251
VINYARD, Virginia 280
VOGUS, Betty Jo 197, Dayton 197, Earl 197, Edith 197, Jane Ann 197, Linda L. 197, Russell 197, William M. 197
VOIGT, Cheryl Louise 275
VON FREDENHAGEN, Martin 328
VONDERAHE, Anna Ortman 279, Anthony Mills 182, Deanna Marie 182, Dorothy Irene 183, Ernest Edward "Brub" 182, Jan Ellen 182, John Ernest 183, Lewis 182, Mary Eleanor 182, Michael Lewis 183, Ronnie Lee 182
VOORHEES 144, Jane 147
VOORHIS, Arlene 56, Gary 56, Warren 54, William 53
VORES, Charles E. 315, Dorothy Ann 315, Hank Owen 315, Jeffrey A. 315
VORIS, Carmen Gayle 153, Christin Gae 153, Clayton Gene 153, Curt Gregory 153, David Lee 153
VORNAUF, Maude M. 185
VOSS, JoAnn 175, Marcelle 175, Wayne 175

W

WACHOB, Thomas W. 251
WADDELL, Betty 23, Bob 25, Chester 126, 290, Chet 25, Earl 25, Eugene 25, 26, Gene 26, Helen 116, 234, Jack 25, 26, Jeaneen 66, Myrna 25, Randy 25, Robert 25, Roger 26
WADDLE, M. 34
WADE, John B. 149, Laura 253
WAEFFLER, Rosemary 283
WAGGONER, Ron 86
WAGNER, Emma (Schucknecht) 328, Fay Lois (Kell) 328, Hazel Mary (Randerson) 328, Herman 56, John 248, Katherine Mary 328, Leslie William 328, Lewis 200, Lois Mae 315, Lori Anne 328, Lou 257, Raymond Frederick 328, Robert 248, Sue Ellen 217, Teresa 196, William 328, William A. 66
WAGONER, Daniel 312, Edwin L. 333, Laurel 255, Lindsay 312, Mildred (Wikle) 255, Raymond 255, Ron 23
WAHL, Hannah 164
WAINWRIGHT, S.J. 305
WAISNER 28, S. 34, Thelma 281

WAITER, Danny 217
WAITS, Della Olive 225
WAKEFIELD 14
WAL, Ralph 48
WALDEN, Alice Belle (Freed) 195, George 195, Kathy 23, 86, Rich 86, Rick 23, Tempa 154
WALDEN-HEISCHBERG, Patricia 220
WALDREN, Mary Ann 291
WALDRICK, F. 34
WALDRON, Ellis 259, John 325, Margaret 325, Mary "Minnie" 325
WALKER 86, 273, Ancel 116, Becky 301, Harry 226, Henry 238, Jennie B. 305, John 305, Leonard A. 80, Marie 273, Mary 183, Matilda Jane "Tillie" 305, Matilda Jennie (Rew) 305, Robert 15, 44, 319, Ruth (Underwood) 300, Thomas 183, William 44, William W. 305
WALL, Adriene Elizabeth 329, Amanda Caroline Hogan 328, Andrew Michael 329, Brent Lee 329, Claude Clay Jr. 328, Claude Sr. 328, Gregory Alan 329, Isaiah 328, Kathryn Marie 329, Larry Earl 329, Marcia Elaine 329, Marie 328, Nathan Isaiah 329, Patricia Louise 328, Robert Earl 328
WALLACE, Almary 95, Elizabeth 223, J.P.Q. 95, James Corwin 315, Jeanette (Moon) 315, Margaret Elizabeth 315
WALLS, Richard Thomas 180, Sharon Eileen Donnell 180
WALSH, John 177, Misti Dawn Newman 232
WALTER, Ambrose 33, Eric T. 313, Kurt Richard 313, Martha Elizabeth 297, Rudiger (Rudy) K. 313
WALTERS, Courtney 246, Elizabeth 234, James 62, John 65, Justin 246, Regina 246, Rhonda 246, Rita M. (Lindley) 246, Rodney 246
WALTHER, Margaret 342
WALTZ, Lillian 288
WANCA, David Edward 147, Edward 147, John Christopher 147, Stephen Christopher 147
WANDLE, Bonnie Jean (Pat) 243, Oren Denver 243, Peggy Joy 243, Richard Lee 243
WARD, Beverly Randolph Sr. 329, Carey 329, Dora Pearl (Grinslade) 205, Eleanor Glore 329, Elizabeth 329, Fannie 329, Flora 329, Flora Esta 204, Harriet Rebecca 204, Harriett 329, Ida 329, Ida Izora 204, James 329, John 329, Luella 329, Margaret 185, Mary 329, Mary Jane 329, Nancy 329, Nellie 214, 329, Ola 329, Ola Grace, 151, 204, Oma 329, Preston 329, Sampson 329, Williamson 329, Williamson Dixon 204
WARDEN, Lena Ruth 185, Lowell 25, Lulu Jane Henry 185, William Manford 185
WARDWELL, Armelia 324, Hugh 151, Theodore 151, 324, William 151
WARE, Charles 223, John 25, John R. 48
WARMAN, Chet 97
WARNER, Ann 224, Juanita Bessie 190, Mavilla 145
WARNICK 39
WARNOCK 37, Armem 36, Cletus 183, Delight (Renbarger) 183, Ed 37, Ethel 228, Glenna L. 183, Mary 36

WARREN, Beth 156, Ron 173
WARRICK, Fred 321, Mary 196
WASHBURN, Edward 220, Kenneth 72, 73, Nancy 72
WASHINGTON, Booker T. 68, George 180, George Sr. 180, Iva Ethel 180, Margaret K. 171, Robert 99, Thomas J. 180, Thomas Jefferson 179, Vilena Claravine (Golding) 180, Violena Clara (Golding) 179
WATERMAN, Pauline 287
WATERS, Harold 276
WATKINS 45, 86, 245, Alsa 28, Amanda 33, C.T.H. 95, Hazel Edith 269, Jim 23, Robert 290, Thomas 27, 33, Thomas W. 28
WATSON, Addie (Malicoat) 188, Celia 337, Clyde 65, Dale 26, David 337, Elmer 25, 116, Frank 188, Guy B. 97, Kenlyn 335, Lenna 65, Rosemary 337, William 336
WATTS 273, George Washington 329, James Arthur 329, Jane (Smith) 329, Mary (Polly) 225, William Milton 329
WAVRA, Bob 74
WAY, Nancy 139
WAYNE 208, Jack Jr. 313
WEAKLEY, M.F. 34
WEATHERFORD, Barbara Jean 149
WEATHEROW, Margaret 272
WEAVER 28, 34, 52, Barry 138, Betty 174, Brian Lawrence 138, Daniel 34, 295, Elizabeth Ann 138, Jane Ellen (Hughes) 260, Jemimah 143, Leora Maude 260, May 260, Peter VanNuys 260, Rachel (Troyer) 295, Robert 96, Rosa Alice 205, Rozella (Anstine) 295, Stephen 295
WEBB, Bob 317, Cecil 31, Charles E. 286, Cynthia Pearl 228, Dora 236, Earl M. 286, Edith Blanche 294, Frances 339, George 286, George E. 286, Helen Irene 249, James 33, James M. 286, Jeff 166, Lauren 317, Lucy Ellen 286, Mahala 289, Norval E. 286, Rebecca E. 286, Sarah 286, Vern E. 286, Viola 176, Walter R. 286, Wesley J. 286, William 27, Willis A. 286
WEBBER, Bradley 48, Joetta 48, Jonnie 48, Tom 83
WEBSTER, Brinton 27
WEED, Charles 313, Lucretia 'Lula' Alice 197
WEEDEN, Bernice 261
WEEKS, Amanda (Huckleberry) 157, Emery 38, Joseph 157
WEELER, Bessie 332
WEESNER, Amanda 204
WEGER, Charles George 270, Martha Magdalene 270
WEIDNER, Daniel J. 202, Margaret J. 145
WEIGEL, Kathryn Louise 287
WEIGLE, Mary 234
WEILAND, Aileen Scott 123
WEIR 249, Benton William 285, Donald Jerome 285, Earl Eugene 285, Frank Rudy 285, Hazel Eileen 285, Jennifer Leigh 285, Jerome Benton 285, Lilly Joann 285, Mary Frances 285, Suzette Lorraine 285, William David 285, William David III 285, William Jr. 285
WEISENAUER, Chuck 42, Dick 42, H.J. 39, John Edward 43
WEISENBERGER, G. 34
WEITZEL, Christopher Shawn 289, Jerry James 289, Matthew David 289, Richard Clyde 289, Richard Eugene 289, Theresa (Purvis) 289

WELCH 86, Ashley Nicole 330, Clara 330, Curtis Dee 330, Dale 330, Dale Lewis 330, Don Irvin 330, Elizabeth 330, James Lee 330, Jolana Donnita Traza Shalu Paul 330, Linda Dianna (Clark) 330, Mary Jane (Felt) 330, Michael Lewis 330, Mildred Daisy (Collins) 330, Paul Hillis 330, Tammi (Green) 330, Terry Lee 330, Todd Lynn 330, Truman 330, Tyler Lee 330, William 330
WELCHER, Judy Wheeler 332
WELDER, Sophia 139
WELKE 161, Carl 161, 287
WELKER, John 197
WELLER, Bessie 217, Clinton 217, Frank 72, Tracy 72
WELLINGER 197
WELLS, Allen 194, Kari 107, R. Ruth (Hendricks) 216, Rachel 339, Tommy 282
WELSH, Amanda Caroline (Foster) 330, Elmira 155, Emma 330, Erastus 34, George H. 330
WELTY, Daniel 59, John 48, Susannah 201
WENRICK, Martha Ann Prevo 276
WERBE, Bette Harness 303, Bette Jane (Harness) 330, 331, Bette Jane (Harness) 211, 304, Esther Elfrieda (Beckman) 304, Harry N. III 211, Harry N. Jr. 329, Harry Nelson III 303, 329, 330, Harry Nelson III, "Stormy" 331, Harry Nelson, Jr. 303, 304, 330, 331, Sarah Elfrieda 303, 329, 330
WERMOFF, Elizabeth Kay 230
WERT, Andrew 133, Myrtle (Hall) 207, Phillip B. 133
WESLEY, John 70
WEST 28, Henderson 15, Howard 181, Joel 211, John 274, Mary 211, Phebe 211, Sarah 242, Susan 135
WESTFALL, Charles 156, Jade 283, Joseph 92, Wilma Joan 182
WETHERALD, Kevin Joseph 193
WETTERHOLD, Elizabeth 254
WEYAND, Alice Bliss 331, Eleanor Jane 331, Jane Amelia Hizer 331, Melvin 331, Morris A. 331, Morris Arthur (Marty) 331, Morris L. (Mory) 331
WHEELER, Anna 332, Barry 332, Bessie 332, Billy 332, Carolyn 3, 48, Charlene 332, Charles 332, Charles J. 149, 331, Charles Jr. 331, 332, Charles Lee 331, 332, Charles W. 332, Cheryl 149, Cheryl Lynn 332, Chris 332, David 332, Debbie 332, Dennis 332, Dian 332, Don II 332, Donald 332, Donald Eugene 331, Eddie 332, Edna (Sanford) 332, Ella 332, Eula Mae 332, Floyd 332, Fred 332, George W. 333, Greg 332, Hannah J. 241, James (Red Jim) Henry 331, James 332, Jeff 332, Jim 332, John 332, John II 332, John Lewis 331, Josephine Lee 332, Josephus C. 333, Julia 332, Julia (Cooper) 332, Julia Cooper 331, Kevin 332, Linda 332, Lucille 332, Lucy (Lawrence) 331, 332, Manford Lincoln 332, Margaret 332, Marjorie 332, Mark 332, Mike 332, Mildred 332, Richard 80, Robert 332, Robert C. 332, Robert Clary 331, Robert E. 332, Robert James 331, Ronnie 332, Ruth 332, Scott 332, Stephen Charles 332, Steve 149, Sue 332, Thomas 333, Tom 332, Vivian Marie 284, 332, William Thomas 331

WHELSTONE, Jenette 297
WHINERY, Abigail Paist 144
WHISLER, Samuel, Jr. 85
WHISMAN, Andrew 313
WHITACRE, Jacob Harold 262, Kathryn Jane 333, Leonard John 333, Marilyn Sue 333, Marilyn Sue Buller 153, Mary 231, Mary Louise (Bradley) 333, Robert J. 33, Scott 333, Susan Kay 333, Wayne L. "Bud" 333
WHITAKER, Mary 219, Nancy 225
WHITCAMPER 86
WHITE 86, Alpheus 19, Amanda Elaine 335, Anastasia Marie 335, Andrew 96, 334, Andrew Michael 138, Anna Mae (Ritchey) 333, Benjamin Howard 138, Brendon James 335, Brian Alan 339, Bruce 157, Carole Ann, 228, 334, Carrie Anne 339, Catherine 315, Catherine Rose 333, Ceclia Mae 333, Christina Ann 138, Clayton 157, Cody 157, D.A. 90, Delois 74, Dora Etta 334, Elizabeth 15, 257, 334, Elizabeth (Alder) 148, 256, 257, 311, 334, Elizabeth "Betty" Marie 334, Elizabeth Irene 335, Emma (Newcom) 148, Eva 333, Eva Lucile 335, Everett 334, Everett Kenneth, 333, 335, Everett Kenneth 333, Frances Lois 333, G.H. 95, Gary 48, George 334, "Happy" 333, Harvey 334, Heather (Hill) 157, Hertha 3, 16, Howard 138, 296, 333, 334, Howard E. 228, Howard Edward 311, 319, 333, 335, J.W. 34, Jacob 334, 335, James 334, James Michael 335, James Thomas 333, Jane 223, Jefferson 15, 148, 256, 257, 311, 334, Jerry Lawrence 138, Jessee 334, John 334, John Fitzgerald 335, John Hazen 91, Joseph Edward 138, 333, Joshua Joseph 138, Karen Sue 335, Kathryn Jo 335, Lillian 99, Louisa (Mason) 335, Malinda 334, Margaret Frances T. 320, Margaret Virginia 333, Martha E. 19, Mary 334, Mary (Hendricks) 216, Mary Alice 99, Mary Loretta 334, Michael 339, N.H. 90, Nancy Rayl 291, Orville 332, Patricia 335, Paul Eugene 333, Priscilla 284, Richard Joseph 138, Richard Lawrence 138, 334, Robert Joseph 334, 335, Ruby 171, Ruth 138, Ruth (Hunt) 296, Ruth Ann 335, Ruth Ella (Hunt) 228, 311, 319, 334, 335, Ruth Joan 311, 334, Stephanie Nichole 335, Steven Paul 335, Susan 334, Susanna 190, Theodore Phillip 333, Thomas 334, Thomas Mark 334, Viola 334, Vivian Achor 36, Willard Douglas, 296, 333, 334, 335, William 106, 334, William A. 148, William Douglas 335, William Paul 258, 334, 335, Zelphy 191
WHITECOTTON, Darlene 332
WHITED, Betty 142, Delpha (Hammond) 142, 198, Edward 142, Harry 198, Harry Edward 142, James 142
WHITEHEAD, Bob 97, George Lee 278, Ida (Gehlert) 278, Robert 174, William H. 278
WHITEHOUSE, Dick 23
WHITEMAN, 335, Dale 335, Karen Jo 335, Lisa Kay 336, Mabel (Helton) 335, Ralph Vernon 335, Russell 335
WHITESIDES, Mabel Elizabeth 298
WHITEZEL, J.W. 236
WHITFIELD, Isabella 160
WHITMAN, Florence G. 14, George A. 13, Jacob 51
WHITTAKER, Isaac 31
WHITTED, Rebecca Ann 276
WIBEL, Clarence 292, Elizabeth 33, Essie 292, George 292, Levi 33, Marion 292, Nancy 292, Vern 292, Virginia 292, Harry 75, L. 34
WICKERSHAM 48, 317, Moses 44
WIGENT, Ronald 325
WIKEL, Mike 187
WIKLE, Claude 255, Eva Lenon 145, Flora (Mason) 255
WILCOX, Caroline Josephine 181, Frances Pohl 181, George 190, Madeline 22, 23, Samuel Willis 181
WILCOXON, Helen Lydia 299
WILES, John C. 125, Richard L. 66
WILEY, Richard 158, Richard M. 158
WILKERSON, Mahalla Emmaline 212
WILKINSON, Anna Matilda (Rudy) 329, B.F. 34, Benjamin 245, Benjamin Franklin 329, Bulah (Hilton) 329, Lillis Cook 160, Minnie Mae 329, William Clinton (Clint) 329
WILLETTS, Clarence 41
WILLIAMS 229, A.L. 125, Adam 175, Amanda 298, Ansen J. 33, Arleen Mae 336, Arnold A. 336, Arnold Orlando 336, Arthur 33, Bernice 285, C.C. "Bud" 54, 56, Carl 14, Carol Diana 336, Cecil 336, Constance Sue 336, Daniel 219, 336, Dean Russell 336, Deloris (Knight) 232, Don 21, 23, Dustina Ann 336, Earl 336, Elijah 285, Elizabeth Ann 257, Emma P. (Brown) 285, Ethel S. "Hall" 336, Etwol 247, Florence 336, Floyd 180, Frank 175, Freeborn 336, G.W. 95, Gertrude 336, Glen 269, H. Jerome 336, Henry Milton 245, Herbert E. 132, Herschel 298, Jack 157, 199, 255, Jacque 22, Jeff 157, 199, 255, Jennie 157, 199, 255, Jenny 336, John 12, 336, John H. 80, John L. 336, John N. 336, John Robert 336, Johnnie Margaret 177, Joseph 336, Joseph F. 257, Kathy Jane 182, Leena 322, Lois 21, Loretta 336, Loretty 336, Lynn 302, Madge L. "Decker" 336, Margaret 143, Mark S. 234, Martha Elizabeth "Edgar" 336, Martha Patricia 170, Mary 336, Mary Catherine Lawrence 245, Melissa (LaForge) 285, Mercy 336, Molly 197, Naomi Laura M. 327, Napoleon Bonapart 336, Orlando B. 336, Patience 336, Peleg 336, Providence 336, Richard 175, Richard W. 336, Robert H. 336, Roberta Ann 336, Roger 336, Roger Jr. 336, Ross B. 285, Ross Benjamin 285, Russell Bruce 336, Sarah A. 336, Sarah "Bryant" 336, Sarah Frances 209, Shanna 322, Stella Bell Herron 336, Sue 192, Susan "Fox" 336, Vergil 336, Walter 287, William 336, William A. 336, William G. 336, William H. 336
WILLIAMSON, Adda Elizabeth 199, Charity 155, Edward E. 80, Flora Hyman 199, Janet Gayle 271, Mercelle 199
WILLIS, David 195, Lydia (Coggshall) 195, Sarah J. 211
WILLITS 85, Austin 231, Austin H. 231, C.C. 32, 34, Kate 247, 324, Sarah Ellen (Lindley) 231
WILLITS-KURTZ 32
WILLMAN, Jeanne Schrader 303
WILLOWBY 42
WILLSON, Anna Jane 190, Edward L. 190, Geneva (Agness) 190, Lawrence 190
WILSON 59, Amanda 199, Amaryllis 337, Ambros 15, Ambrose 278, 336, Amelia 337, Ann Ella (Ford) 282, Anna Pearl 151, Arbutus (Bryan) 337, Ardee 337, Asa J. 337, Avonnelle 337, Bashie 337, Ben 72, Bertha 14, Bill 134, Brenda 199, Brian 199, Brian II 199, C. Meredith 288, C.S. 18, Callie 337, Charles 207, Charles S. 19, Cheryl 337, Chester 337, Claude 223, Constance 337, Crystal 174, Dee Ann 337, Diana 337, Donna Sue 282, Dora E. 231, Dorothy 337, Earl 337, Edith 223, Edna 327, Elias 48, Eliza 207, Elizabeth 337, Ellen (Boose) 223, Ellen Jane Longfellow 326, Elroy 174, Elva 174, Elva Rachel 162, Emma 145, Estelle 174, Ethel 223, Eunice 278, Flora 219, Florence 336, Frank 336, Gale 337, Gary 337. George. 270, 336, Glen 337, Glen J. 199, Glen L. 337, Glenn E. 199, Goldie K. (Bausum) 199, Gregory 337, Guy 15, 146, 196, 211, 336, Harriet Stringer 207, Indiana Ann (Baldwin) 151, Inis 337, Irma 223, Isaac 254, James 270, Janet P. 337, Jessie 337, John 19, 146, 337, John C. 151, 336, John M. 145, 151, Kent 337, Kevin 190, Kim (Bowlin) 199, Kris 337, Kylee 337, Laird E. 337 Laura Ann (Crites) 151, 262, Lauren 337, Lelah Loucinda 325, Leonard 201, Lida Laura 278, Lisa 336, Loren D. 337, Lydia 234, Lyndal 196, 336, Madge Freeland 196, Mae Jewel (Evans) 158, Margaret Robinson 270, Marjorie 337, Marjory 337, Mary 72, 196, 253, 337, Mary (McDowell) 151, Mary Elizabeth 205, Mary Helen 337, Mary Jane 270, Mary S. 225, Max 337, McDonald George 336 McDonald "Mack," 336, Michelle 336, Mildred 337, Miriam Elizabeth (Hall) 158, Olivia 337, Orville (Bud) 223, Pearl 145, 174, Peter 270, Phoebe 223, Phoebe Griffith 278, Polly (McDowell) 336, Ron 104, Ronald 337, Roscoe 151, 162, Roscoe Alvin 174, 262, Ross 287, Samuel 207, Scanlon 337, Sharon 196, 336, Shaun 337, Shirlee 337, Simeon 199, Stella 342, Stephen 336, Steve 46, Sylvester 223, 256, 336, Tessa Estelle 262, Thomas 337, Thomas I. 19, Travis 337, Tyler 337, Walter 75, Wayne 337, William 47, 325, 336, William C. 337, William, Jr. 282, William M. 158, Willie James 158
WILSTED, Gertrude (Neal) 313, Harold 313, Myra Patricia 313
WILT, W.B. 27
WILTROUT, Susanne 234
WILTSE, Martha 143
WILTSIN, Ansel R. 19
WIMMER, Mable D. 247, Ruth 172
WINDLOW, Jessie H. 48
WINEGARDNER, M. 36
WINES, Elizabeth 167, Howard 208, John 236, Willie 52, 64
WINGFIELD, Elizabeth 325
WININGAR, Warren 202
WINNIGER, Betty 280
WINSLOW, Doris 186, Edgar A. 186, James Frederick 331, Lester 3, Marjorie Dianne Miller 331, Patricia 257
WINTERODE, J.D. 33
WINTERROWD 28, J.D. 34, M.C. 34
WINTLAND, Fred 300, Kathi 300, Lisa 300
WINTRODE, Candace Kay 320, Herbert Dale 320
WISE, Anna A. Schrader 303, George W. 85, S.P. 34, W. Robert 248, W.A. 34
WISEHART, Absolom 162, Carl 24, 25, Frank 162, Mary (Keisling) 162, Nora 162
WISEMAN, Harold Victor 328, Jennifer Marie 249, Raymond Victor 328
WITHAM, Katherine 108
WITSON, Minervia 323, Sarah 323
WITTIG, Cynthia Jane 182
WITTKAMPER, John W. 85
WOESSNER, Elizabeth 311
WOHLFORD, Paul 29
WOHRER, Ellen (Ella) B. 147
WOLF 86, Francis I. 343, Mikki 281
WOLFE, Arthur 255, Barbara Jean Herron 164, E. Gladys (Rinehart) 255, Howard 255, Linda 255, Phyllis Goodman 219, Rebecca Ellen 245
WOLFORD, Arthur 316, Arthur H. 337, Aruther Henry 293, Chester Arther 337, Daniel 337, David 337, Deborah (Carroll) 337, Della Marie 337, Della May 337, Dollie E. 337, Earnest Harold 337, Edna Pearl 337, Edward E. 337, Ethel 293, Ethel Bowen 316, Everett Arlow 337, Goldie Effie May 337, Harold L. 337, Jesse Melton 337, John H. 337, John Michael 337, Mildred Bell 293, 316, Myrtle Lavana 337, Nathan Emery 337, Oliver Burdett 337, Ralph Eugene 337, Robert James 337, Roy Thomas 337, Sarrah Etta 337, Solmon 337, Walter Kenneth 337, William Raymond 337
WOLTER, Harry 119
WOOD, Ann 336, Annie Mae 186, Arletta 186, Cecil Dale 186, Charles 276, Charles A. 338, Charles Raymond, Jr. 338, Connie Sue 186, Etta 139, George Harley 338, George Philip 337, George William 338, Hannah French Washer 338, Ivah Mae 309, Jennifer 179, John Richard 338, Louisa 139, Mae Belle 227, Mame 139, Mary Elizabeth Hine 337, "Mayme" 338, Raymond 186, Robert Mills 338, Roger 64, William 33, Worley Drinkwater 338
WOODFIELD, Joseph 156
WOODMANS, H. 36
WOODMANSE, F. 36
WOODMANSEE, Maggie 223
WOODRING, Anita Louise 147, Ethel 338, Hannah (Isley) 281, John 281, Mildred 171
WOODRUFF, Amanda Jane (Pierce) 300, Audrey Monica 300, 338, Charles Herbert 338, Edward Charles "E.C." 300, Edward Charles Jr. "Ed" 338, Garland 338, Gordon 338, Helen Jane 338, Herbert R. 338, James Paul 338, Juanita 338, Le Roy 338, Ludica Lucille 338, Mayne 338, Nancy Ellen "Nell" 338, Paul 338, Raymond Charles 338, Robert 338
WOODS 245, Ann Overstreet 322, David 23, 86, 172, Ephraim 59, Ephriam 281, Ephrum 15, Green 89, Hubert 322, John 322, Josiah 59, Malvina 171, Mary Anna Miller 59, Simon P. 16, Simon Peter 59, Thomas 96
WOODWARD, Asa 66, Chelsea 225, Cheryl (Andrews) 225, Donald 225, Elysia 225, Howard 322, Lezlie 225, Matthew 225, Patrick 225, Ron 225, Thomas 225, Westley 225
WOODWORTH, Maria B. 93
WOODY, George 25, George L. 222, H.G. 103, Horace G. 45
WOOLDRIDGE, Col. 169, Marilyn 243, Marilyn Frances (Lambert) 180
WOOLEY, Dorothy 287
WOOLLEY, Anna Francis 338, Ardra Charles 338, Camela Lynn 333, Catharine 217, Catharine Dorcas 338, Charles Claborn 338, Charles Edgar 338, Clora Alice 197, 338, Donald Earl 333, Elizabeth Jane 333, Hubbard Allen 338, James Madison 338, James W. 338, John 305, Laura Lee 338, Mabel Irene Oakes 338, Martha Jane 338, Martin Newell 338, Matthew Kent 333, Milford Franklin 338, Ora Ashton 338, Ostin Lee 338
WOOLVERTON, Sarah 205
WOOTEN, William 60
WORD, Robert Reid 226
WORDYKE, John 33
WORREL, William W. 177
WORTHINGTON, Ivaah 147, Juanita 258, Paul 336
WORTHMAN, Raymond E. 319, Stephanie Kay Taylor 319
WOTRING, Bruce 85
WRIGHT, Alvie 208, Amos 339, Ann 339, Arminda T. 319, Betty 339, Charity 339, Chester G. 339, Chester G. Jr. 339, Chet Jr. 65, Clifford T. 339, Clifton 339, Conrad C. 339, Curtis 339, Daniel 339, David 339, Dewey Charles 339, Dorothy 268, E. 34, Edmund 27, Edward 33, Elizabeth 339, Ella G. 339, Elsie D. 66, Embert 286, Emma 339, Ethel G. 339, Florence 21, 251, Fred 3, George B.M. 339, George Dewey 339, Gulielma 66, Helen Hankins 208, Isaac 339, Isabelle 339, James 339, Jeanne (Beck) 207, John 27, 339, John O. 339, John P. 66, John Prior 46, 47, 339, Jonathan 35, Josiah 33, Judd 97, L. 269, Larry Edward 339, Lavonne 283, Leland "Cinco" 25, Leroy 339, Lillis 160, Lorrie 339, Luna 66, Mark 224, Mary 339, Milton 28, Minnie 286, Nancy Ann 339, Naomi 339, Orville 28, Pearl 339, Rachel 339, Rhoda 339, Richard 339, Sara 224, Sarah 339, Susannah 339, Thomas J. 339, Vashti 339, Wallace Lee 299, Wesley 224, Wilbur 28, William 33, Wm 339
WRIGHTSMAN, Abram 35
WUNDER, Leo "Bud" 52, Michael 293
WYANT, Aaron 239, Alan 239, Bermal Oscar 168, Catherine (Straley) 168, Catherine Kenworthy 340, Charles 180, 340, Chelsea Leo 168, Clay 340, Cleola Catherine 168, Clora Louise 168, Darwin 319, Donald R. 340, Ernest 340, Garnet Mae 168, Hugh Kenneth 168, Kamron

239, Kylie Brooks 319, Kym Coomler 340, Maurice Elvie 168, Ruby Blanch 168, Samuel Luke 340, Treva Irene 168, Velda Lorene 168, Vernida Ann 168, William Franklin 168, William Henry 168, William R. 168, Winifred L. Jones 180, Wm. Thomas 340

WYATT, Clarence Lester 270, Harry 270, John F. 270, Lottie May 270, Lura 270, Maude 270, William 270

WYBREW, Chester 217

WYCKOFF, Mary 216

WYGANT, Patricia 252

WYNN, Zella A. 288

WYRICK, Betty Mullen 206, Carissa 324, Corey 324, Dennis E. 268, Guy 268, Helen 99, Hugh 324, Miriam 206, Nannette 232, Opal 26, Phyllis Kimberly Hayen 214, Roger Kent 268, Sue 324, Wayne 48

WYSONG, Ardell 256, Susie 256

X

XAVER, Adalene C. 266

Y

YAGER 169, Charles Justin 148, Eli 248, Ersie Elizabeth (Grinslade) 205, Esther Yvonne (Vonnie) 148, Fredrick William 148, Ida Belle 248, J.C. 90, J.P. 90, Jesse 222, Jesse C. 90, Jesse Clore 248, L.M. 90, Lawrence 248, Leora K. 90, M. Catherine 90, Marsha Elaine 148, Pamela Jolynn 148, Pressly 248, Sally 247, Sarah 248, William C. 313

YAGER-SMITH 32

YANCEY, Charles Benjamin 188, John 188, Lewis Davis 188, Mary (Layton) 188, Mildred Winefred (Kavanaugh) 188

YARBOROUGH, Sonya (Brown) 157

YARIAN, Aloha 196, J.E. 83

YARLING, Carl G. 213, Carl G. Jr. 213

YASKO, David 74

YATER, Bill 202, 313, Clarence F. 153, Earl 96, Ella Mae 313, Helen 107, Mabel 96, Phoebe 313, Theresa Pearl Elleman 185, 209

YEAGER, C.H. 172, J.C. 34

YEAGY, George 323

YERIGAN, James Manford 286, Loudisa J. (Pierce) 289, Mathias 286, 289, Samuel C. 286

YOCKEY, Doug 80

YODER 29, C.C. 34, Elizabeth 258, Karen 236, Noah 39, 41, Virginia (Wagoner) 255

YODER-HELMUTH 32

YODERS 39

YORK, Blanche 341, Carol (Ashcraft) 170, Edna 341, Emery 170, John 341, John E. "Bud" 341, Lillie 264, Mary Louise 341, Michele 170, Robert 341, Woodrow 341

YOUNG 189, A. 34, Arthur 340, Benjamin B. 341, Betty (Massey) 193, Betty Jane (Massey) 340, Charles 341, Charles Coleman 340, Charles J. 194, Charles Joseph 166, 257, 340, Charles Joseph 166, Charlotte 242, Charlotte Hollingsworth 222, Daisy 340, David H. 340, Dirk 337, Donald R. 340, Donald Richard 341, Douglas DeWayne 340, Douglas Wayne 341, Eli Hendrick 340, Elijah E. 251, Eliza (Weaver) 340, Eliza Emily 231, Eliza Myrtle 251, Elizabeth 257, Elizabeth A. 141, Ellinor 231, Flora Ann (Harrison) 251, George Nelson 251, Harold Raymond 340, Harriet A. 273, Harriet May 340, Helen Louise 340, 341, Henry 231, J. Russell 340, J.H. 125, James 340, James M. 340, Jay 196, Jeff 23, John 74, 340, John Emmett 341, Joseph Le Roy 166, 257, 340, Joseph Wesley 340, Josephus 340, Kathleen 283, Kathy Jo 340, Lafayette E. 340, Larry 196, Laurie 196, Leigh 196, Leonard Fountain 340, Leslie 196, LuAnn 196, Luann 83, Mamie Lunger 341, Margaret Josephine 341, Marvin 340, Marvin Edgar 340, Mary 218, Mary E. 269, Mary Elizabeth C. 291, Mary Ellen 340, Mary Ellen (Bush) 340, Mary Jo 99, Matilda 216, Max Lee 166, 257, 340, Melvin Elmer 340, Nellie Gay (Brewer) 340, Norma 224, Olive Melissa (Gordon) 251, Oliver 44, Peter B. 341, Phillip 340, Reid 196, Rhoda 341, Richard E. 303, Robert L. 340, Rosalene 340, Ruth Rennaker 36, Samuel 340, Spencer 340, Steven Michael 166, 257, 340, Susan Gay 166, 257, 340, Walter 321, William 196, 341, Wilma 230

YOUNGBLOOD, Emma Novella 195

YOUNGJOHNS, Marian Alicia 177, Richard 177

YOUNGMAN, Fred 50, 341, Fredrick 49, Loren 218, Michael 341

YOUNKIN, Emma Jane 266, Gertrude 23, Isaac 266, Jacob 266

YUZZOLIN, J. 180

Z

ZAMBERLAN, Rhonda 188

ZANO, Susan Jane Spindt 276

ZECH, Johann Jakob 342

ZECK, Andreas 342, Bessie 342, Brad 342, Brenda 342, Catherine 342, Clarke 342, Daniel 342, Dawn 342, Deborah 342, Donald 342, Elouise 340, Everett 342, Hans Nickle 342, Johan Daniel 342, Johan Dietrich 342, Johan George 342, Johan Jacob 342, Johan Jacob, Jr. 342, Johan Michael 342, John 26, Jon 342, Jon Dean 342, Melanie 342, Ora 342, Patty 342, Rod 342, Ryan 342, Sara 342, Suzanne 342

ZEHRING, Forest 129

ZEIGLER, Adaline Lavina 342, Christian 342, Claudia 172, Dorothy May 343, James C. 342, Joseph A. 342, Maude Marie 343, Maude Marie 172, Oscar Clayton 342, Raymond George 343, William 172, William Joseph 172, 342

ZELIGMAN, Mollie 195

ZELL, Hilda 14, Sandy 107

ZENOR, Frank Allen 247, Howard 247, Madeleine 247, Walter 247

ZENTMEYER, Roanna 174

ZENTMYER, Israel 52

ZEPPETELLA, Nicholas 179

ZERBE 39, Charles 245, 343, Charles C. 343, Clara 34, Clara T. 343, David 343, George 343, George Washington 343, John 43, John L. 343, John Phillip 343, John Wesley 343, Johnnie 42, Laura Etta 343, Lorentz 343, Mardin 343, Mary Ann (Butcher) 308, 34, Mary E. 343, Mary Elizabeth 343, Maude 343, Nora 343, Robert D. 343, Robert David 343, Roscoe 343, Sarah Ann 343, William 308, 343, William H. 343

ZERING, Olive 59

ZIMMER, Thomas 92

ZIMMERMAN, Bertha L. 203, Casper 194, Elizabeth (Ardner) 194, Lola Belle 194, 308, Paul Warren 194, Robert Frazee 172, 194, Stanley T. 321, William 194, 267

ZIMMERMANN, Rosemary Redding 222

ZIRKLE 55, Beth Ann 224, Betty 172, Brittany 224, Brooklyn 224, Perry 55

ZOLA, LuAnna, (m. Dearinger) 183

ZOLLNER, Bertha 151, Erma 151, Fred 151, Paul 151

ZOOK 39, Charles 212

ZUPPARDO, Joseph 12

Family Tree

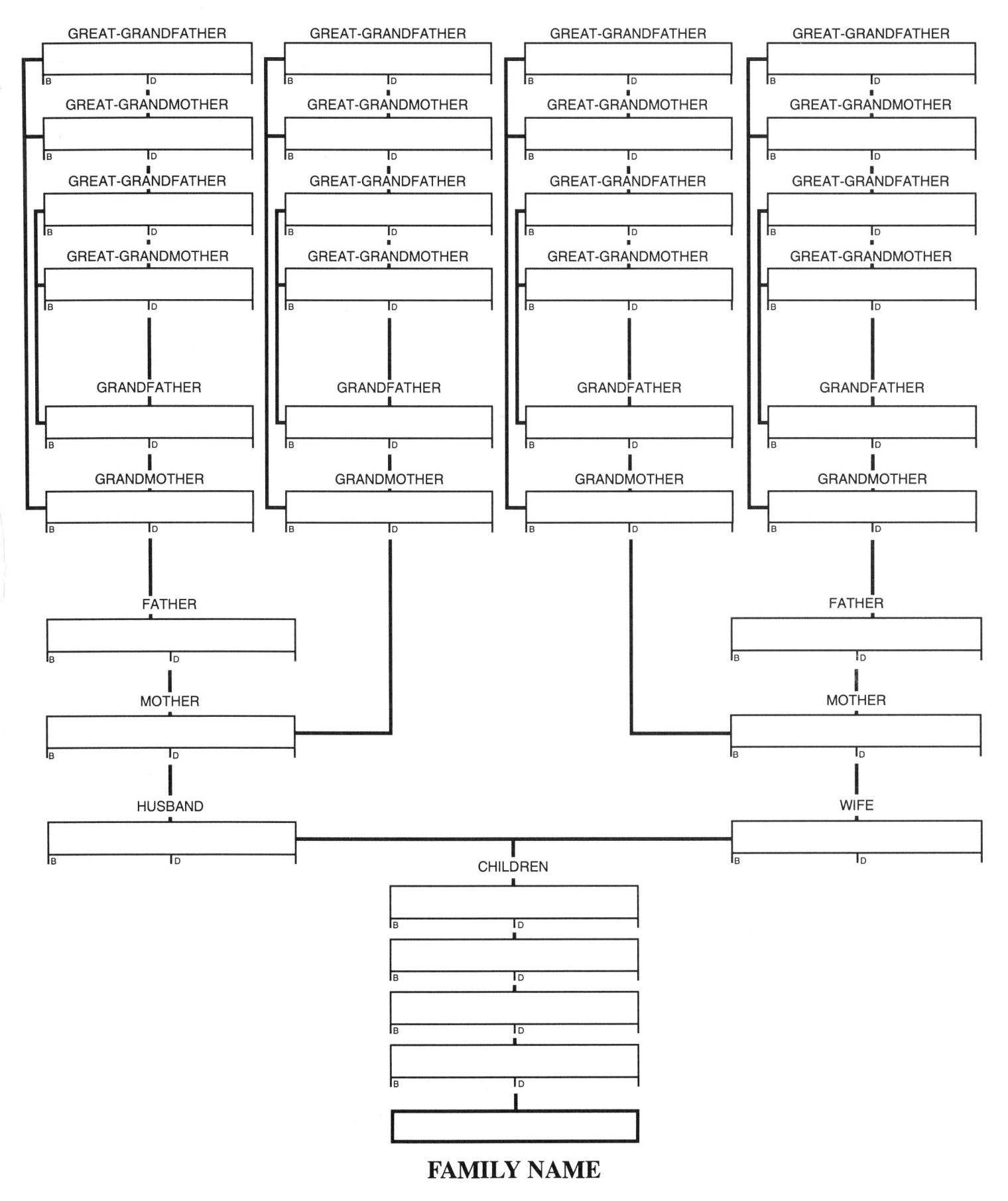

GREAT-GRANDFATHER	GREAT-GRANDFATHER	GREAT-GRANDFATHER	GREAT-GRANDFATHER
B / D	B / D	B / D	B / D
GREAT-GRANDMOTHER	GREAT-GRANDMOTHER	GREAT-GRANDMOTHER	GREAT-GRANDMOTHER
B / D	B / D	B / D	B / D
GREAT-GRANDFATHER	GREAT-GRANDFATHER	GREAT-GRANDFATHER	GREAT-GRANDFATHER
B / D	B / D	B / D	B / D
GREAT-GRANDMOTHER	GREAT-GRANDMOTHER	GREAT-GRANDMOTHER	GREAT-GRANDMOTHER
B / D	B / D	B / D	B / D
GRANDFATHER	GRANDFATHER	GRANDFATHER	GRANDFATHER
B / D	B / D	B / D	B / D
GRANDMOTHER	GRANDMOTHER	GRANDMOTHER	GRANDMOTHER
B / D	B / D	B / D	B / D

FATHER — B / D

MOTHER — B / D

HUSBAND — B / D

FATHER — B / D

MOTHER — B / D

WIFE — B / D

CHILDREN

B / D

B / D

B / D

B / D

FAMILY NAME

Family Record

NAME	BIRTH		DEATH	
	Date	Place	Date	Place